SENECA

STEMS, ETCHINGS, CUTS, AND PATTERNS

Schiffer Publishing Ltd

4880 Lower Valley Road, Atglen, PA 19310 USA

A GUIDE TO CATALOGS AND PRICES

Acknowledgment

We wish to thank Jim and Marjorie Wiley, who graciously
provided the catalogs upon which this work is based.

Copyright © 2000 by Schiffer Publishing Ltd.
Library of Congress Card Number: 00-105921

Designed by Anne Davidsen
Type set in CopprplGoth Bd BT/Humanst521 BT

ISBN: 0-7643-1140-9
Printed in China
1 2 3 4

Published by Schiffer Publishing Ltd.
4880 Lower Valley Road
Atglen, PA 19310
Phone: (610) 593-1777; Fax: (610) 593-2002
E-mail: Schifferbk@aol.com
Please visit our web site catalog at **www.schifferbooks.com**
We are always looking for people to write books on new and related subjects. If you have
an idea for a book please contact us at the above address.

This book may be purchased from the publisher.
Include $3.95 for shipping.
Please try your bookstore first.
You may write for a free catalog.

In Europe, Schiffer books are distributed by
Bushwood Books
6 Marksbury Ave.
Kew Gardens
Surrey TW9 4JF England
Phone: 44 (0) 20 8392-8585; Fax: 44 (0) 20 8392-9876
E-mail: Bushwd@aol.com
Free postage in the U.K., Europe; air mail at cost.

CONTENTS

INTRODUCTION

This is a reference guide to many of the Seneca Glass Company's wares as featured in their own catalogs. The catalogs presented here span the years from the company's early production to their later offerings from the 1960s on through to the early 1980s. While there are decade-spanning gaps in the catalogs that were available, it was felt that the information provided in the catalogs available would prove to be valuable research and identification tools for everyone interested in Seneca Glass and/or the American glass making industry of the twentieth century. Indexes in the back of the book provide quick and easy access to the many glassware forms and decorations found within this volume. They are organized by Series Names, Line Numbers, and Etching/Cut Numbers. Values are included with the catalog pages.

A brief overview of is also provided to familiarize readers with both the Seneca Glass Company and the handmade, blown glasswares produced by the talented artisans of this prolific firm.

Seneca Glass

Immigrant German businessmen and artists knowledgeable in the art of glassmaking first established the Seneca Glass Company in Seneca County, Ohio, in 1891. The staff set up shop in the former Fostoria Glass Factory, naming their company for both a notable regional Indian tribe and for the county in which they had begun their work. However, the business community of up-and-coming Morgantown, West Virginia, made Seneca's management an offer so appealing that they agreed to move their operations to West Virginia in 1896. While the location changed, the Seneca name remained. Over the years, the Seneca Glass Company developed a reputation for creating some of the finest lead crystal glassware available.

More specifically, Seneca produced handmade, mold blown glass, although the company seems to have been reluctant to mention the fact that molds were used to shape the glass. This glassware type was produced by first gathering and shaping a small ball of molten glass (a.k.a. "gather")

on the end of a hollow pipe or rod. The glass blower inserted the gather into an iron mold and blew into the pipe, forcing the hot glass to conform to the interior shape of the mold. Depending on the specific object being produced, several operations could have followed. For example, on stemware, the molding of the stem and foot might have been done with forms and paddles. Once an item was formed, it was annealed (reheated and allowed to cool gradually and uniformly to avoid shattering the glass) as it was passed through a tunnel-like oven called a lehr. The cooled object was then sent on for finishing operations, including the removal of excess glass, grinding, and polishing.

Over some ninety-two years of production—the firm would cease operations in 1983—Seneca produced quality, delicate, lead, blown table and barware in this manner in a wide variety of forms. Specific glassware forms included goblets, sherbets, tall sherbets or champagnes, cocktails, oyster cocktails, sherries, wine glasses, clarets, and cordial glasses, classified as "stemwares;" ice teas, hi-balls, old fashioneds, juices, and water glasses, grouped as "tumblers;" and a variety of "decorative glasswares" or "artwares" included bowls, candleholders, and vases.

The company was best known for their cut glass patterns. Some of the patterns were so complex, they took an experienced cutter twelve hours to complete. In later years, Seneca developed an archives of over one thousand cut glass patterns. All one thousand patterns remained available to customers who needed to replace pieces or expand a set. It did not matter if the pattern was long out of date; cutters would most likely be able to reach back into the archives, retrieving and reproducing the desired pattern.

The Seneca Glass Company also produced wares decorated with needle and plate etchings and sandblasted decorations. Other decorative techniques were also available, including banding and metallic decorations. In addition, the company offered a variety of colored glasswares over the years, mostly from the 1950s onward. Colorful glassware lines from the 1950s forward included Brocado, Cascade, Driftwood Casual, The Fashionables, and Quilt.

Late Nineteenth Century & Twentieth Century Glassware Design

In the early decades of the twentieth century, the Seneca Glass Company emphasized their production of crystal clear glassware decorated with elaborate cut glass patterns. However, many glass companies were following trends toward simplified and more colorful glass forms. Bearing this in mind, Seneca would follow suit and produce some of the simpler and more colorful wares as well. An article from 1934 stated: "Most factories had kept in mind the great popularity of the buffet supper and created many varieties of articles for the convenience—and pride—of the hostess at such a party." (*China, Glass and Lamps* 1934, 11-16)

Blown and pressed art glass would retain its popularity until around the beginning of the first world war. Brilliant and deeply cut glass, popular near the end of the nineteenth century, was continued in the early twentieth century; however, by the 1920s, this expensive glassware would be in lesser demand as economic depression loomed. Cut glass would not return to heightened popularity until the 1940s.

Handmade, mold blown glass and machine made glasswares were in direct competition for the consumer's dollars. By the 1930s, roughly half of all the glass produced in the United States would be entirely machine made.

To survive in the competitive marketplace, glass factories had to appeal to a wide range of tastes. Colored glass drew attention in the 1920s and was much in demand in the 1930s. By 1935, roughly half the glass being produced sported colors. Colored glass during the Depression years was generally bright and cheerful. Art Deco colors and shapes were added to glassware lines in the 1930s as well.

Barware (with the repeal of Prohibition [1920-1933]) and kitchenware were important production items for factories in the 1930s and 1940s, as they could be produced in large quantities at low production costs. Refrigerator storage dishes and oven-proof glass cookware were introduced for the modern kitchen. At times, serving dishes and punch bowls were sold together with metal holders.

After World War II, during the 1940s, cut crystal stemware would return as a popular form, especially as gifts for the bride—a situation that worked well for Seneca Glass. Color, form, and texture be prominent features in post-war era designs. Later examples of Seneca glasswares reflect this trend.

A Short History of the Seneca Glass Company and Its Wares

In 1896, the Seneca Glass Company moved from Seneca County, Ohio, to Morgantown, West Virginia. To convince Seneca's management to move, a Morgantown investment firm offered the glass company a subsidy and free land upon which to build their plant. The property was located along the Monongahela River, providing all the water necessary to run a glass plant, along with direct access to steamboat lines. Additionally, rail transportation to Pittsburgh had just opened in 1894, and the railroad lines ran directly through the proposed factory site. Further sweetening the deal, the Baltimore and Ohio Railroad agreed to transfer all of Seneca's movable equipment from the Ohio factory to the new Morgantown location for free. (Robinson 1955, 95; Six 1991, 71)

Seneca Glass Company's management accepted the offer on June 18, 1896, agreeing to have the Morgantown Building and Investment Company construct the factory and a 14 pot glass furnace, a $20,000 project. The contractors agreed to have the facility ready for production in Morgantown on January 1, 1897.

The Seneca Glass Company, located at Beechurst Avenue and 7th Street, was a success. The company's initial production was also described in the *New Dominion* newspaper in 1897:

> The output with the present working force in tumblers alone is 3,000 dozen per day. If the natural gas was to go off for one short hour while the glass was being tempered the firm would sustain a loss of $2000 . . . their specialties are water pitchers, water bottles, finger bowls, goblets, punch tumblers, sherbet glasses and all kinds of diminutive glasses for cordials. (Core 1982, 220)

Among Seneca's early wares were also bar bottles, covered candy jars, cream and sugar sets, nappies, plates, trays, and vases. A significant portion of the company's early production was dedicated to the manufacture of thin, etched tumblers used both in bars and as advertisements for a wide variety of organizations and products. (Page et al. 1995, viii)

With the initial success of the Seneca Glass Company, Morgantown quickly developed a thriving glass industry. While Seneca was the first glass factory in the city, The Morgantown Glass Works soon followed Seneca's example, opening for business in the city in 1899. By 1910, nine glass plants were located in the city. With the introduction of the glass industry to Morgantown, skilled glass artisans from France, Belgium, and Germany began arriving in significant numbers to fill positions in these firms.

In June 1902, a fire destroyed a large portion of the Seneca factory, leaving behind much of the original 1896 brick construction encompassing the 14 pot furnace and the lehr. After the fire, insurance covered the reconstruction of the plant, directed by Elmer Jacobs, a prominent Morgantown architect.

As the years passed, the Seneca Glass Company factory site would spread out over four acres of ground. In 1913, Seneca built a second factory, Factory B, in nearby Star City, West Virginia. Factory B produced "lime blown" (machine-made) tumblers and undecorated wares. Although shut down for almost a year in 1928-1929, Factory B would continue production into the 1930s. Included among Factory B's Depression era wares were a variety of colored glasswares including cobalt and transparent colors (such as light green and topaz) considered very modern in 1932. (McKenzie 1921; Fleming Associates 1986; Core 1982, 394; Core 1984, 35; Page et al. 1995, ix-x) These wares would have been quite useful to the company as it entered into the Depression years (dating roughly from 1929 to the advent of World War II). During those lean years, expensive cut glass was overlooked in favor of less expensive wares of the type produced at Factory B.

Returning to 1920, the Seneca Glass Company offered a new line of deep etched glassware. So numerous were the firm's offerings in fact that three catalogs were produced. The catalogs were divided by decorating techniques, one featuring lightly cut wares, another deep etched products, and the third contained an assortment of "miscellaneous" wares. (Six 1991, 73)

Following the difficult Depression years (Seneca was forced to close Factory B during the 1930s), elegant and expensive tablewares returned to favor. As the company entered the decade of the 1950s, however, it soon became apparent that the popularity of elegant glassware was to be short-lived. The Seneca Glass Company began producing less costly glassware more appropriate for informal dinners and parties—occasions which had been growing in favor and frequency with the American public since the Depression era.

Seneca's first offering in informal glassware was the Driftwood Casual series, a pattern that was to remain popular for nearly thirty years. Driftwood Casual, initially offered in limited forms and colors, was to be Seneca's best known product line in its time. As the years passed, new items, including beverage glasses, candy dishes, pitchers, and plates, in a wide variety of colors were added to the Driftwood Casual line. (Page et al. 1995, x-xi)

Seneca would enjoy notoriety during the late 1950s and early 1960s. For three years running, 1956-1958, Seneca received the top award for fine quality tableware from B. Altman and Company of New York. Beginning on April 1, 1957, and continuing on throughout that summer, Seneca participated in the 350th anniversary celebration of the establishment of Jamestown, Virginia. Four other Morgantown glass firms joined Seneca in the festivities: Morgantown Glassware Guild, Beaumont Company, Davis-Lynch Glass Company, and Quality Glass Company. In the early 1960s, Seneca returned to the public's attention when they filled an order for Vice President Lyndon Johnson for Seneca glassware from the Epicure line. Mrs. Johnson placed the order and used the glassware, decorated with the Vice President's initials and a Stetson hat, in their home. Epicure was a tulip shaped stemware line featuring a delicate hand-drawn stem. (Aull 1965, 6; Seneca Glass Company 1963)

In 1973, Seneca again received public attention when the factory complex was added to the Historic American Engineering Records/West Virginia Survey. A documentary film about the factory was also produced at this time.

Trouble was afoot for Morgantown's glass companies in the 1970s. The *Morgantown Post* of April 8, 1971, reported that Morgantown's glass companies (Seneca Glass Company, Morgantown Glassware Guild, Gentile Glass Company, and Monongalia Valley Cut Glass Company among them) were threatened with collapse due to foreign competition.

In an attempt to thwart international competitors in the 1970s, Seneca produced a variety of informal glassware lines in eye-catching colors. Many of these lines would last no longer than a year or two. Among the later wares produced by Seneca were pattern molded stemwares, covered candy bowls, stacking Christmas tree containers, and vases. Colors employed during the 1970s included Accent Red, Amber, Black, Buttercup, Cinnamon, Delphine Blue, Lime Green, Moss Green, Peacock Blue, Plum, Ritz Blue, and Sahara.

In 1982, the Seneca Glass Company was sold to a group of Malaysian investors. The firm's name was changed to Seneca Crystal Incorporated. In August 1983, the company filed for bankruptcy. Seneca stock and equipment was then sold and dispersed. In 1984 the Seneca building was purchased by Sanders Floor Covering Incorporated. Then, in 1985, the Seneca factory was added to the National Register of Historic Places. (Core 1984, 487; Page et al. 1995, x-xi; Fleming Associates 1986)

Since that time, the glass factory structure has been transformed through adaptive reuse into a complex of shops and a modest museum displaying many of the tools used to create Seneca's brilliant glassware, photographs of the original factory, its founders, and the surrounding town, and even the factory's original freight elevator. While many of the larger factory areas are now divided, much of the structure's original character remains, along with the massive furnace at the heart of the factory. Also of interest, the walls and corridors are decorated with paintings and murals dedicated to Seneca's past and the past of glassmaking. So, while Seneca no longer produces its varied glasswares that have so captured the attentions of today's collectors, the Seneca factory site may still be visited by all those who are interested in America's fascinating glassmaking past.

Values

The values provided in the book are for items in mint condition. Values vary immensely according to the condition of the piece, the location of the market, and the overall quality of the design and manufacture. Condition is always most important in assigning a value. Prices around the nation will vary, and those at specialty antique shows will vary from those at general shows. Of course, being in the right place at the right time can make all the difference. The prices you see are general values providing a range for the objects *shown*, rather than individual prices for all items *listed* on a catalog page.

All of these factors make it *impossible* to create an absolutely accurate price list; however, a useful *general* pricing guide may be offered. No attempt is being made here to set prices in the secondary market. The values provided reflect what one *might realistically expect to pay* for Seneca glassware in mint condition and are listed in U.S. dollars.

BIBLIOGRAPHY

Aull, William J., Jr. *Sand, fire n' things. Beaumont Company, Davis-Lynch Glass Co., Morgantown Glassware Guild, Seneca Glass Company.* Produced in cooperation with the four companies listed, c. 1965.

China, Glass, and Lamps. "New Wares For 1934 Featured Successful Exhibitions For Trade. Advance in Dinnerware Design and Decoration Received Wide Attention. Attendance and Business in Pittsburgh Well Ahead of 1933. Return of Liquors Helped Glass." 1934.

Core, Earl L. *The Monongalia Story. A Bicentennial History.* Parsons, West Virginia: McClain Printing Company, 1982.

_____. *The Monongalia Story. A Bicentennial History.* Parsons, West Virginia: McClain Printing Company, 1984.

Fleming Associates, Delores A. "Seneca Glass Company. 1891-1983." Pamphlet prepared by Delores A. Fleming Associates, History Contractors, 1986.

McKenzie, L. E. *Morgantown District Industrial and Business Survey.* Morgantown, West Virginia: Morgantown Chamber of Commerce, 1921.

Page, Bob, and Dale Frederiksen. *Seneca Glass Company. 1891-1983. A Stemware Identification Guide.* Greensboro, North Carolina: Page-Frederiksen Publishing Company, 1995.

Robinson, Felix G. "Seneca in its Sixty Seventh Year." *Tableland Trails* II (I), Spring 1955.

Seneca Glass Company. *History of Seneca Glass Company. Beechurst Avenue between 6th and 8th Streets. Morgantown, West Virginia.* "American Craftsmanship at its Best ... since 1891." Company produced material, 1963.

Six, Dean. "Decorating Techniques at Seneca Glass." *Glass Collector's Digest* IV (6), April/May 1991, pp. 71-78.

CATALOG #2

Figure 1.
$10-15 each

Figure 2.

$10-20 each

Our Facilities for this Class of Etching and Enameling are Unsurpassed.

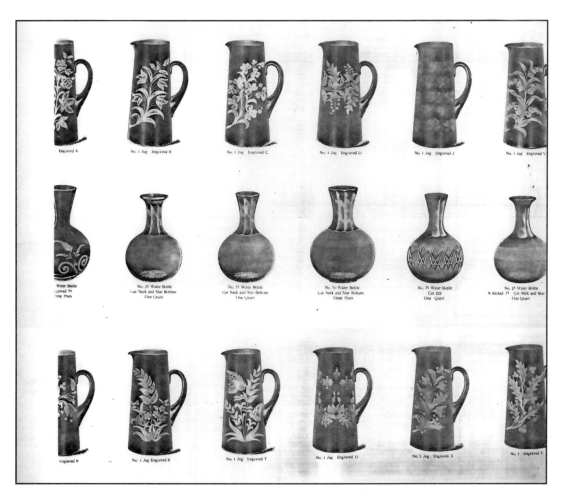

Figure 3.

Top row: $100-150 each
Middle row: $50-75 each
Bottom row: $100-150 each

9

SENECA GLASS COMPANY, MORGANTOWN, W. VA.

The No. 1 Tankard Jugs are made in the following capacity: ½ pt., 1 pt., 2 pt., 3 pt. and 4 pt.

Figure 4.

Top row: $50-75 each
Middle and bottom rows: $100-150 each

These are the Regular Half-Gallon Tankards

Figure 5.
Sets: $200-275 each

Figure 6.

$50-100 each
Sets: $100-150 each

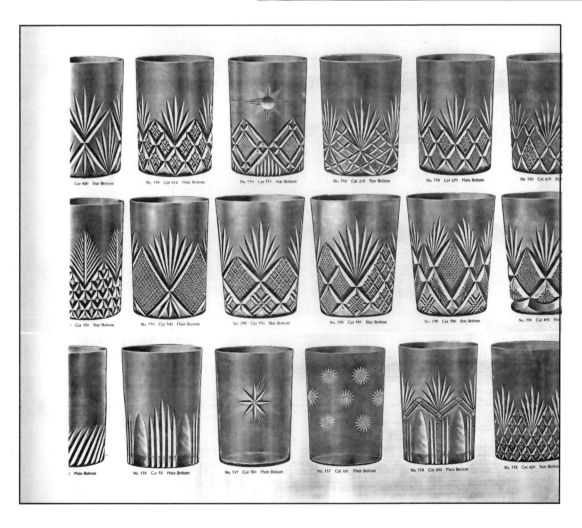

Figure 7.

$10-15 each

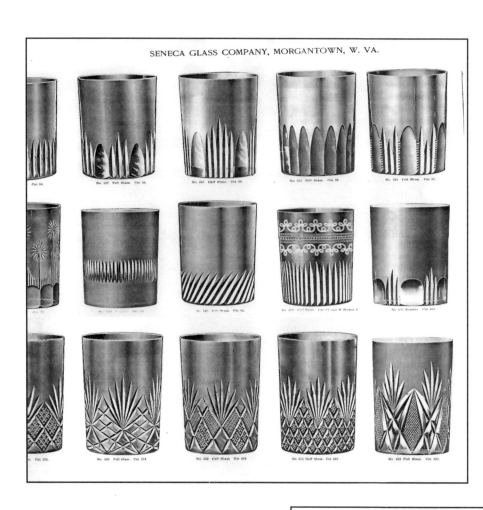

Figure 8.
$10-15 each

Figure 9.
$10-15 each

Figure 10.
$10-15 each

Figure 11.
$10-15 each

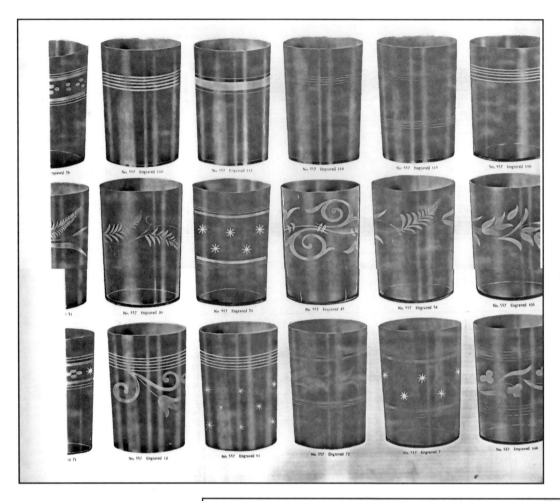

Figure 12.

$10-15 each

Figure 13.

$10-15 each

No. 557 Etched My Regards
No. 557 Etched 449
No. 557 Etched 451
No. 557 Etched 459
No. 557 Etched 462

No. 557 Etched 446
No. 557 Etched 453
No. 557 Etched 441
No. 557 Etched 448
No. 557 Etched 457

No. Etched 440
No. 557 Etched 450
No. 557 Etched 452
No. 557 Etched 445
No. 619 Engraved 61

Figure 14.

$10-20 each

No. 619 Engraved 16
No. 619 Engraved 28
No. 619 N. Etched 75
No. 619 N. Etched 90
No. 619 Cut 101
No. 619 Cut 30

No. 619 Engraved 14
No. 619 Engraved 7
No. 619 Engraved 74
No. 619 Engraved 83
No. 619 Engraved 76
No. 619 Engraved

No. 619 Engraved 47
No. 619 Engraved 55
No. 619 Engraved 50
No. 619 Engraved Star Bottom
No. 619 Engraved 61
No. 619 Engraved

Figure 15.

$10-15 each

CATALOG #3

Page 3. $15-25 each

Page 4. $15-25 each

Page 5.

$20-40 each
Decanter: $60-80

Page 6.

Top row: $25-50 each
Bottom row: $50-70 each

Page 7.

$15-25 each

Page 8.

$20-40 each
Decanter: $60-80 each

Page 9.

Top row: $10-25 each
Bottom row: $50-75 each

Page 10.

Top row: $15-20 each
Bottom row: $15-35 each

Page 11.

Top row: $15-25 each
Bottom row: $15-45 each

Page 12.

Top row: $30-40 each
Bottom row: $50-75 each

Page 13.

$25-50 each
Decanter: $70-90

Page 14.

$20-60 each

Page 15.

$15-25 each

Page 16.

$15-25 each

Catalog #4

Page 1.

$8-12 each

No. 499. GOBLET
Optic, Cut 373

No 499. SAU. CHAMP.
Optic, Cut 373

No. 499. SHERBET
Optic, Cut 373

No. 499. WINE
Optic, Cut 373

No. 499. COCKTAIL
Optic, Cut 373

No. 499. CORDIAL
Optic, Cut 373

No. 499. 2¾ oz. Ftd. TUMBLER
Optic, Cut 373

No. 499. 4 oz. Ftd. TUMBLER
Optic, Cut 373

No. 499. 6 oz. Ftd. TUMBLER
Optic, Cut 373

No. 499. 9 oz. Ftd. TUMBLER
Optic, Cut 373

No. 499. 12 oz. Ftd. TUMBLER
Optic, Cut 373

Page 2.

$15-25 each

No. 150. GOBLET
Optic, Cut 250

No 150. SAU. CHAMP.
Optic, Cut 250

No. 150. SHERBET
Optic, Cut 250

No. 3. CANDLESTICK
Cut 250

No. 150. WINE
Optic, Cut 250

No. 150. COCKTAIL
Optic, Cut 250

No. 150. CORDIAL
Optic, Cut 250

No. 3. 2¾ oz. Ftd. TUMBLER
Optic, Cut 250

No. 3. 4 oz. Ftd. TUMBLER
Optic, Cut 250

No. 3. 6 oz. Ftd. TUMBLER
Optic, Cut 250

No. 3. 9 oz. Ftd. TUMBLER
Optic, Cut 250

No. 3. 12 oz. Ftd. TUMBLER
Optic, Cut 250

SENECA GLASS COMPANY, MORGANTOWN, W. VA.

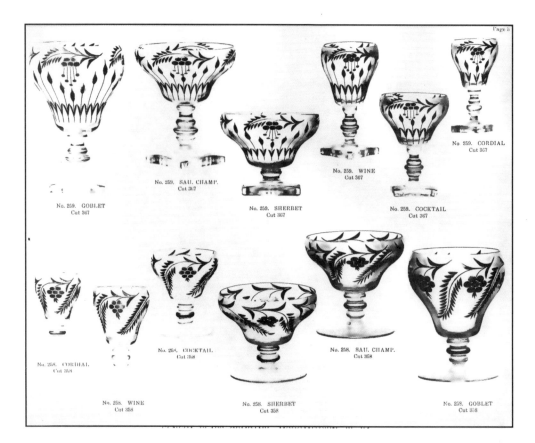

No. 259. GOBLET
Cut 367

No. 259. SAU. CHAMP.
Cut 367

No. 259. SHERBET
Cut 367

No. 259. WINE
Cut 367

No. 259. COCKTAIL
Cut 367

No. 259. CORDIAL
Cut 367

No. 258. CORDIAL
Cut 358

No. 258. WINE
Cut 358

No. 258. COCKTAIL
Cut 358

No. 258. SHERBET
Cut 358

No. 258. SAU. CHAMP.
Cut 358

No. 258. GOBLET
Cut 358

Page 3.

$20-30 each

No. B260. GOBLET
Optic, Cut B 44

No. B260. SAU. CHAMP.
Optic, Cut B 44

No. B260. SHERBET
Optic, Cut B 44

No. B260. WINE
Optic, Cut B 44

No. B260. COCKTAIL
Optic, Cut B 44

No. B260. CORDIAL
Optic, Cut B 44

No. B6. 2½ oz. Ftd. TUMBLER
Optic, Cut B 44

No. B6. 4 oz. Ftd. TUMBLER
Optic, Cut B 44

No. B6. 6 oz. Ftd. TUMBLER
Optic, Cut B 44

No. B6. 9 oz. Ftd. TUMBLER
Optic, Cut B 44

No. B6. 12 oz. Ftd. TUMBLER
Optic, Cut B 44

SENECA GLASS COMPANY MORGANTOWN, W. VA.

Page 4.

$15-25 each

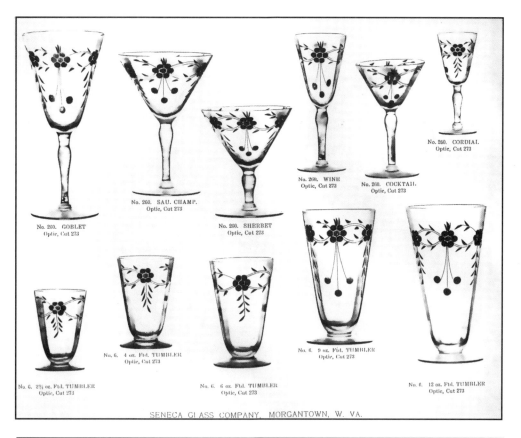

Page 5.

$15-25 each

No. 260. GOBLET
Optic, Cut 273

No. 260. SAU. CHAMP.
Optic, Cut 273

No. 260. SHERBET
Optic, Cut 273

No. 260. WINE
Optic, Cut 273

No. 260. COCKTAIL
Optic, Cut 273

No. 260. CORDIAL.
Optic, Cut 273

No. 6. 2¾ oz. Ftd. TUMBLER
Optic, Cut 273

No. 6. 4 oz. Ftd. TUMBLER
Optic, Cut 273

No. 6. 6 oz. Ftd. TUMBLER
Optic, Cut 273

No. 6. 9 oz. Ftd. TUMBLER
Optic, Cut 273

No. 6. 12 oz. Ftd. TUMBLER
Optic, Cut 273

SENECA GLASS COMPANY, MORGANTOWN, W. VA.

Page 6.

$15-25 each

No. 459. GOBLET
Cut 204

No. 459. SHERBET
Cut 204

No. 459. WINE
Cut 204

No. 459. COCKTAIL.
Cut 204

No. 459. CORDIAL
Cut 204

No. 482. 2¾ oz. Ftd. TUMBLER
Cut 204

No. 482. 4 oz. Ftd. TUMBLER
Cut 204

No. 482. 6 oz. Ftd. TUMBLER
Cut 204

No. 482. 9 oz. Ftd. TUMBLER
Cut 204

No. 482. 12 oz. Ftd. TUMBLER
Cut 204

SENECA GLASS COMPANY, MORGANTOWN, W. VA.

23

No. 465. GOBLET
Optic, Cut 33

No. 465. SAU. CHAMP.
Optic, Cut 33

No. 465. SHERBET
Optic, Cut 33

No. 465. WINE
Optic, Cut 33

No. 465. COCKTAIL
Optic, Cut 33

No. 465. CORDIAL
Optic, Cut 33

No. 465. 2½ oz. Ftd. TUMBLER
Optic, Cut 33

No. 465. 4 oz. Ftd. TUMBLER
Optic, Cut 33

No. 465. 6 oz. Ftd. TUMBLER
Optic, Cut 33

No. 465. 9 oz. Ftd. TUMBLER
Optic, Cut 33

No. 465. 12 oz. Ftd. TUMBLER
Optic, Cut 33

SENECA GLASS COMPANY, MORGANTOWN, W. VA.

Page 7.

$15-25 each

No. 475. GOBLET
Optic, Cut 31

No. 475. SAU. CHAMP.
Optic, Cut 31

No. 475. SHERBET
Optic, Cut 31

No. 475. WINE
Optic, Cut 31

No. 475. COCKTAIL
Optic, Cut 31

No. 475. CORDIAL
Optic, Cut 31

No. 475. 2½ oz. Ftd. TUMBLER
Optic, Cut 31

No. 475. 4 oz. Ftd. TUMBLER
Optic, Cut 31

No. 475. 6 oz. Ftd. TUMBLER
Optic, Cut 31

No. 475. 9 oz. Ftd. TUMBLER
Optic, Cut 31

No. 475. 12 oz. Ftd. TUMBLER
Optic, Cut 31

SENECA GLASS COMPANY, MORGANTOWN, W. VA.

Page 8.

$15-25 each

Page 9.

$15-25 each

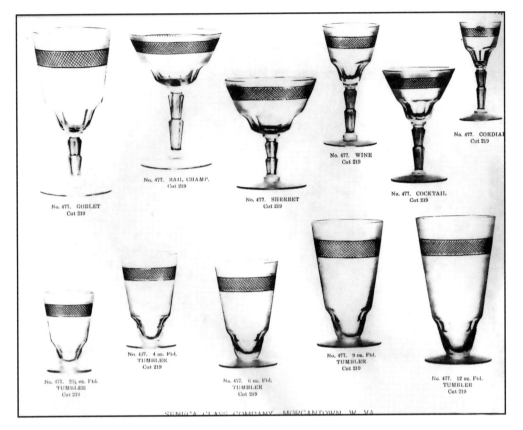

No. 477. GOBLET
Cut 219

No. 477. SAU. CHAMP.
Cut 219

No. 477. SHERBET
Cut 219

No. 477. WINE
Cut 219

No. 477. COCKTAIL
Cut 219

No. 477. CORDIAL
Cut 219

No. 477. 2½ oz. Ftd.
TUMBLER
Cut 219

No. 477. 4 oz. Ftd.
TUMBLER
Cut 219

No. 477. 6 oz. Ftd.
TUMBLER
Cut 219

No. 477. 9 oz. Ftd.
TUMBLER
Cut 219

No. 477. 12 oz. Ftd.
TUMBLER
Cut 219

SENECA GLASS COMPANY, MORGANTOWN, W. VA.

Page 10.

$15-25 each

No. 481. GOBLET
Optic, Cut 370

No. 481. SAU. CHAMP.
Optic, Cut 370

No. 481. SHERBET
Optic, Cut 370

No. 481. WINE
Optic, Cut 370

No. 481. COCKTAIL
Optic, Cut 370

No. 481. CORDIAL
Optic, Cut 370

No. 481. 2½ oz. Ftd. TUMBLER
Cut 370

No. 481. 4 oz. Ftd. TUMBLER
Cut 370

No. 481. 6 oz. Ftd. TUMBLER
Cut 370

No. 481. 9 oz. Ftd. TUMBLER
Cut 370

No. 481. 12 oz. Ftd. TUMBLER
Cut 370

SENECA GLASS COMPANY, MORGANTOWN, W. VA.

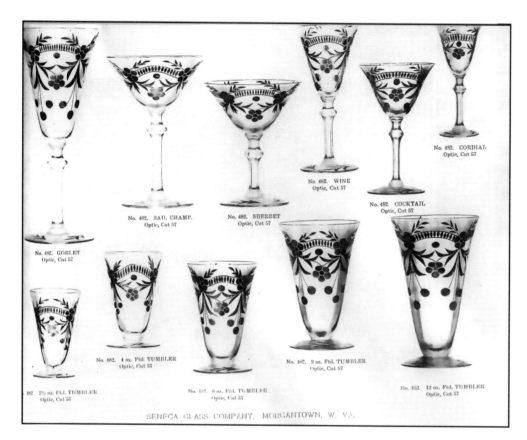

No. 482. GOBLET
Optic, Cut 57

No. 482. SAU. CHAMP.
Optic, Cut 57

No. 482. SHERBET
Optic, Cut 57

No. 482. WINE
Optic, Cut 57

No. 482. COCKTAIL
Optic, Cut 57

No. 482. CORDIAL
Optic, Cut 57

182. 2½ oz. Ftd. TUMBLER
Optic, Cut 57

No. 482. 4 oz. Ftd. TUMBLER
Optic, Cut 57

No. 482. 6 oz. Ftd. TUMBLER
Optic, Cut 57

No. 482. 9 oz. Ftd. TUMBLER
Optic, Cut 57

No. 482. 12 oz. Ftd. TUMBLER
Optic, Cut 57

SENECA GLASS COMPANY, MORGANTOWN, W. VA.

Page 11.

$15-25 each

No. 482. GOBLET
Optic, Cut 61

No. 482. SAU. CHAMP.
Optic, Cut 61

No. 482. SHERBET
Optic, Cut 61

No. 482. WINE
Optic, Cut 61

No. 482. COCKTAIL
Optic, Cut 61

No. 482. CORDIAL
Optic, Cut 61

No. 482. 2½ oz. Ftd. TUMBLER
Optic, Cut 61

No. 482. 4 oz. Ftd. TUMBLER
Optic, Cut 61

No. 482. 6 oz. Ftd. TUMBLER
Optic, Cut 61

No. 482. 9 oz. Ftd. TUMBLER
Optic, Cut 61

No. 482. 12 oz. Ftd. TUMBLER
Optic, Cut 61

SENECA GLASS COMPANY, MORGANTOWN, W. VA.

Page 12.

$15-25 each

Page 13.

$25-35 each

No. 482. GOBLET
Optic, Cut 260

No. 482. SAU. CHAMP.
Optic, Cut 260

No. 482. SHERBET
Optic, Cut 260

No. 482. WINE
Optic, Cut 260

No. 482. COCKTAIL
Optic, Cut 260

No. 482. CORDIAL
Optic, Cut 260

No. 482. 2½ oz. Ftd. TUMBLER
Optic, Cut 260

No. 482. 4 oz. Ftd. TUMBLER
Optic, Cut 260

No. 482. 6 oz. Ftd. TUMBLER
Optic, Cut 260

No. 482. 9 oz. Ftd. TUMBLER
Optic, Cut 260

No. 482. 12 oz. Ftd. TUMBLER
Optic, Cut 260

SENECA GLASS COMPANY, MORGANTOWN, W. VA.

Page 14.

$15-25 each

No. 484. GOBLET
Optic, Cut 369

No. 484. SAU. CHAMP.
Optic, Cut 369

No. 484. SHERBET
Optic, Cut 369

No. 484. WINE
Optic, Cut 369

No. 484. COCKTAIL
Optic, Cut 369

No. 484. CORDIAL
Optic, Cut 369

No. 484. 2½ oz. Ftd. TUMBLER
Optic, Cut 369

No. 484. 4 oz. Ftd. TUMBLER
Optic, Cut 369

No. 484. 6 oz. Ftd. TUMBLER
Optic, Cut 369

No. 484. 9 oz. Ftd. TUMBLER
Optic, Cut 369

No. 484. 12 oz. Ftd. TUMBLER
Optic, Cut 369

SENECA GLASS COMPANY, MORGANTOWN, W. VA.

No. 485. GOBLET
Optic, Cut 58

No. 485. SAU. CHAMP.
Optic, Cut 58

No. 485. SHERBET
Optic, Cut 58

No. 485. WINE
Optic, Cut 58

No. 485. COCKTAIL
Optic, Cut 58

No. 485. CORDIAL
Optic, Cut 58

No. 485. 2½ oz. Ftd.
TUMBLER
Optic, Cut 58

No. 486. 4 oz. Ftd.
TUMBLER
Optic, Cut 58

No. 485. 6 oz. Ftd.
TUMBLER
Optic, Cut 58

No. 485. 9 oz. Ftd.
TUMBLER
Optic, Cut 58

No. 485. 12 oz. Ftd.
TUMBLER
Optic, Cut 58

No. 485. COMPOTE
Optic, Cut 58

SENECA GLASS COMPANY, MORGANTOWN, W. VA.

Page 15.

$15-25 each

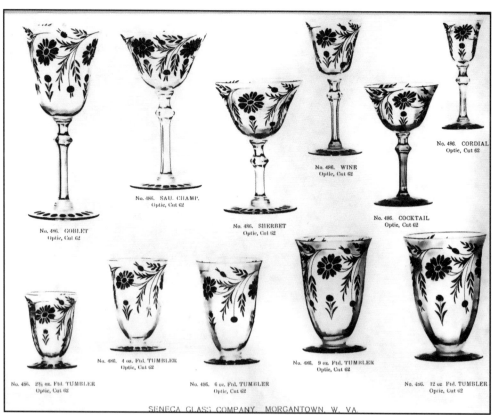

No. 486. GOBLET
Optic, Cut 62

No. 486. SAU. CHAMP.
Optic, Cut 62

No. 486. SHERBET
Optic, Cut 62

No. 486. WINE
Optic, Cut 62

No. 486. COCKTAIL
Optic, Cut 62

No. 486. CORDIAL
Optic, Cut 62

No. 486. 2½ oz. Ftd. TUMBLER
Optic, Cut 62

No. 486. 4 oz. Ftd. TUMBLER
Optic, Cut 62

No. 486. 6 oz. Ftd. TUMBLER
Optic, Cut 62

No. 486. 9 oz. Ftd. TUMBLER
Optic, Cut 62

No. 486. 12 oz. Ftd. TUMBLER
Optic, Cut 62

SENECA GLASS COMPANY, MORGANTOWN, W. VA.

Page 16.

$15-25 each

Page 17.

$15-25 each

No. 492. GOBLET
Optic, Cut 287

No. 492. SAU. CHAMP.
Optic, Cut 287

No. 492. SHERBET
Optic, Cut 287

No. 492. WINE
Optic, Cut 287

No. 492. COCKTAIL
Optic, Cut 287

No. 492. CORDIAL
Optic, Cut 287

No. 492. CANDLESTICK
Optic, Cut 287

No. 492. 2½ oz. Ftd. TUMBLER
Optic, Cut 287

No. 492. 4 oz. Ftd. TUMBLER
Optic, Cut 287

No. 492. 6 oz. Ftd. TUMBLER
Optic, Cut 287

No. 492. 9 oz. Ftd. TUMBLER
Optic, Cut 287

No. 492. 12 oz. Ftd. TUMBLER
Optic, Cut 287

SENECA GLASS COMPANY, MORGANTOWN, W. VA

Page 18.

$15-25 each

No. 492. GOBLET
Optic, Cut 293

No. 492. SAU. CHAMP.
Optic, Cut 293

No. 492. SHERBET
Optic, Cut 293

No. 492. WINE
Optic, Cut 293

No. 492. COCKTAIL
Optic, Cut 293

No. 492. CORDIAL
Optic, Cut 293

No. 492. 2½ oz. Ftd.
TUMBLER
Cut 293

No. 492. 4 oz. Ftd.
TUMBLER
Optic, Cut 287

No. 492. 6 oz. Ftd.
TUMBLER
Cut 293

No. 492. 9 oz. Ftd.
TUMBLER
Optic, Cut 287

No. 492. 12 oz. Ftd.
TUMBLER
Cut 293

SENECA GLASS COMPANY, MORGANTOWN, W. VA

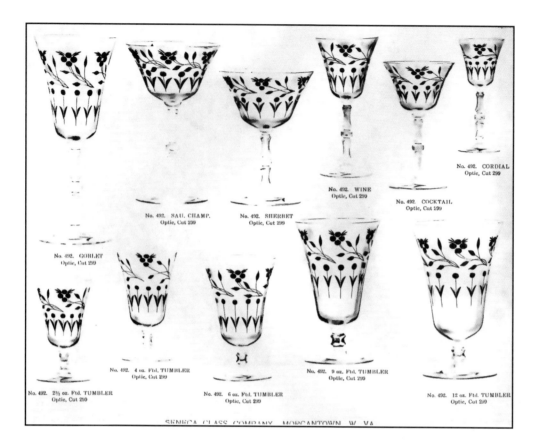

No. 492. GOBLET
Optic, Cut 299

No. 492. SAU. CHAMP.
Optic, Cut 299

No. 492. SHERBET
Optic, Cut 299

No. 492. WINE
Optic, Cut 299

No. 492. COCKTAIL
Optic, Cut 299

No. 492. CORDIAL
Optic, Cut 299

No. 492. 2½ oz. Ftd. TUMBLER
Optic, Cut 299

No. 492. 4 oz. Ftd. TUMBLER
Optic, Cut 299

No. 492. 6 oz. Ftd. TUMBLER
Optic, Cut 299

No. 492. 9 oz. Ftd. TUMBLER
Optic, Cut 299

No. 492. 12 oz. Ftd. TUMBLER
Optic, Cut 299

SENECA GLASS COMPANY, MORGANTOWN, W. VA.

Page 19.

$15-25 each

No. 493. GOBLET
Optic, Cut 262

No. 493. SAU. CHAMP.
Optic, Cut 262

No. 493. SHERBET
Optic, Cut 262

No. 493. WINE
Optic, Cut 262

No. 493. COCKTAIL
Optic, Cut 262

No. 493. CORDIAL
Optic, Cut 262

No. 3. 4 oz. Ftd. TUMBLER
Optic, Cut 262

No. 3. 6 oz. Ftd. TUMBLER
Optic, Cut 262

No. 3. 9 oz. Ftd. TUMBLER
Optic, Cut 262

No. 3. 12 oz. Ftd. TUMBLER
Optic, Cut 262

SENECA GLASS COMPANY, MORGANTOWN, W. VA.

Page 20.

$15-25 each

Page 21.

$25-35 each

No. 499. GOBLET
Optic, Cut 373

No 499. SAU. CHAMP.
Optic, Cut 373

No. 499. SHERBET
Optic, Cut 373

No. 499. WINE
Optic, Cut 373

No. 499. COCKTAIL
Optic, Cut 373

No. 499. CORDIAL
Optic, Cut 373

No. 499. 2¾ oz. Ftd. TUMBLER
Optic, Cut 373

No. 499. 4 oz. Ftd. TUMBLER
Optic, Cut 373

No. 499. 6 oz. Ftd. TUMBLER
Optic, Cut 373

No. 499. 9 oz. Ftd. TUMBLER
Optic, Cut 373

No. 499. 12 oz. Ftd. TUMBLER
Optic, Cut 373

SENECA GLASS COMPANY, MORGANTOWN, W. VA.

Page 22.

$15-25 each

No. 903. GOBLET
Cut 342

No. 903. SAU. CHAMP.
Cut 342

No. 903. SHERBET
Cut 342

No. 903. WINE
Cut 342

No. 903. COCKTAIL
Cut 342

No. 903. CORDIAL
Cut 342

No. 903. 2½ oz. Ftd. TUMBLER
Cut 342

No. 903. 3½ oz. Ftd. TUMBLER
Cut 342

No. 903. 5 oz. Ftd. TUMBLER
Cut 342

No. 903. 9 oz. Ftd. TUMBLER
Cut 342

No. 903. 12 oz. Ftd. TUMBLER
Cut 342

SENECA GLASS COMPANY, MORGANTOWN, W. VA.

31

No. 8000. SAU. CHAMP.
Optic, Cut 121

No. 8000. WINE
Optic, Cut 121

No 8000. CORDI
Optie, Cut 121

No. 8000. GOBLET
Optic, Cut 121

No. 8000. SHERBET
Optie, Cut 121

No. 8000. COCKTAIL
Optic, Cut 57

No. 3. 4 oz. Ftd. TUMBLER
Optie, Cut 121

No. 3. 2½ oz. Ftd. TUMBLER
Optie, Cut 121

No 3. 6 oz. Ftd. TUMBLER
Optie, Cut 121

No. 3. 9 oz. Ftd. TUMBLER
Optic, Cut 121

No. 3. 12 oz. Ftd. TUMBLER
Optie, Cut 121

SENECA GLASS COMPANY, MORGANTOWN, W. VA.

Page 23.

$10-20 each

No. 492. GOBLET
Optic, Cut 2½6

No. 482. GOBLET
Optic, Cut 259

No. 492. GOBLET
Optic, Cut 261

No. 482. GOBLET
Optic, Cut 218

No. 515. GOBLET
Optic, Cut 374

No. 475. GOBLET
Optic, Cut 258

No. 499. GOBLET
Optic, Cut 371

No. 492. GOBLET
Optic, Cut 300

No. 963. GOBLET
Plain, Cut 838

No. 492. GOBLET
Optic, Cut 308

No. 482. GOBLET
Optic, Cut 64

SENECA GLASS COMPANY, MORGANTOWN, W. VA.

Page 24.

$20-30 each

32

Page 25.

$20-30 each
Rose bowl: $40-50
Cut 43 Tumblers: $8-10 each

No. 484. GOBLET, D. E.
Optic, 632

No. 8000. H. S. CHAMP.
Optic, Cut 57

No. 8000. H. S. S. CHAMP.
Optic, Cut 57

No. 16. SUGAR
Optic, Cut 287

No. 16. CREAM
Optic, Cut 287

No. 1. OIL C/N
Optic, Cut 121

MUSTARD
Optic, Cut 57

MARMALADE
Optic, Cut 57

No. 30. R. E. Candlestick
Cut 57

No. 82. 6 oz.
Cut 43

No. 88. 9 oz.
Cut 43

No. 85. 7¾ oz.
Cut 43

No. 903. FINGER BOWL
Cut 367

No. 8000. FINGER BOWL
Optic, Cut 308

No. 465. FINGER BOWL
Optic, Cut 57

No. 1. GRAPE FRUIT
Optic, Cut 56

No. 1. ROSE BOWL
Optic, Cut 57

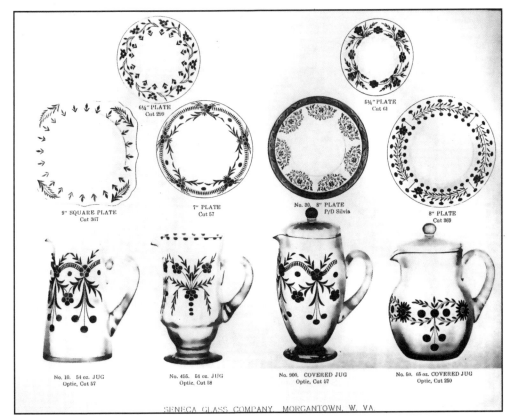

6¼" PLATE
Cut 299

5¼" PLATE
Cut 61

9" SQUARE PLATE
Cut 367

7" PLATE
Cut 57

No. 30. 8" PLATE
P/D Silvia

8" PLATE
Cut 369

Page 26.

Pitchers: $100-150 each
Plates: $20-30 each

No. 16. 54 oz. JUG
Optic, Cut 57

No. 455. 54 oz. JUG
Optic, Cut 58

No. 900. COVERED JUG
Optic, Cut 57

No. 50. 65 oz. COVERED JUG
Optic, Cut 250

SENECA GLASS COMPANY, MORGANTOWN, W. VA.

No. 459. 8½" VASE
Optic, Cut 286

No. 2. ROSE BOWL
Optic, Cut 260

No. 481. COMPOTE
Optic, Cut 57

No. 3. 1 Pt. DECANTER
Optic, Cut 250

No. 455. CANDY JAR
Optic, Cut 31

No. 3. 10" VASE
Optic, Cut 58

No. 3. 2 Pt. DECANTER
Optic, Cut 57

No. 255. COCKTAIL SHAKER
Optic, Cut 121

No. 1. CONSOLE BOWL
Cut 326

No. 30. CONSOLE BOWL
Cut 57

SENECA GLASS COMPANY, MORGANTOWN, W. VA.

Page 27.

$50-90 each
Console: $90-100

No. 499. GOBLET
Optic, P/D Estes

No. 499. SAU. CHAMP.
Optic, P/D Estes

No. 499. FINGER BOWL
Optic, P/D Estes

No. 499. COCKTAIL
Optic, P/D Estes

No. 499. CORDIAL
Optic, P/D Estes

No. 499. 12 oz. Ftd. TUMBLER
Optic, P/D Estes

No. 499. SHERBET
Optic, P/D Estes

No. 499. WINE
Optic, P/D Estes

No. 900. JUG
Optic, P/D Estes

No. 499. PARFAIT
Optic, P/D Estes

No. 30. 8" PLATE
P/D Estes

No. 30. CANDLESTICK
P/D Estes

No. 1. 12" CONSOLE BOWL
P/D Estes

No. 30. CANDLESTICK
P/D Estes

Page 28.

$25-35 each
Console: $80-110
Jug: $70-90

Page 29.

$25-35 each

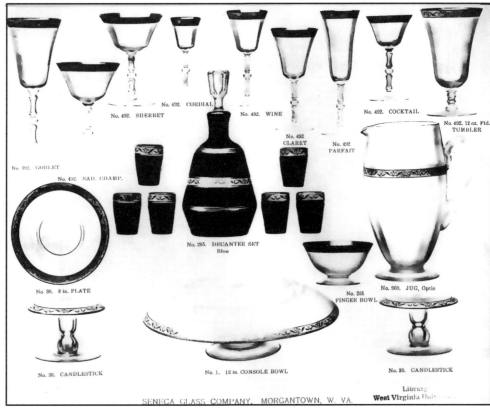

Page 30.

Stems: $15-20 each
Console bowl: $90-110 each
Decanter set: $100-125
Jug: $60-80

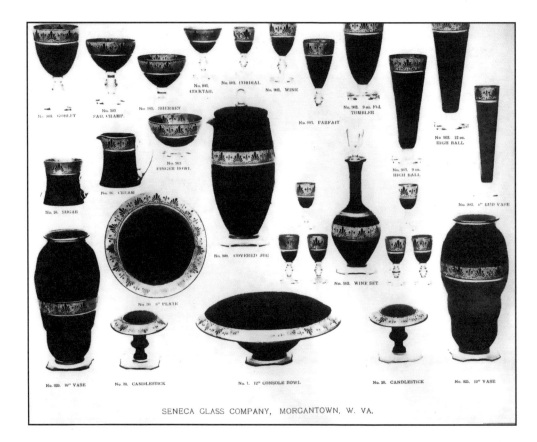

No. 903. GOBLET
No. 903. SAU. CHAMP.
No. 903. SHERBET
No. 903. COCKTAIL
No. 903. CORDIAL
No. 903. WINE
No. 903. 9 oz. Ftd. TUMBLER
No. 903. PARFAIT
No. 903. 12 oz. HIGH BALL
No. 903. FINGER BOWL
No. 16. CREAM
No. 16. SUGAR
No. 903. 9 oz. HIGH BALL
No. 903. 8" BUD VASE
No. 900. COVERED JUG
No. 30. 8" PLATE
No. 903. WINE SET
No. 920. 10" VASE
No. 30. CANDLESTICK
No. 1. 12" CONSOLE BOWL
No. 30. CANDLESTICK
No. 925. 10" VASE

SENECA GLASS COMPANY, MORGANTOWN, W. VA.

Page 31.

$60-90 each
Stems: $20-30 each

No. 260. GOBLET Optic
No. 260. WINE Optic
No. 260. CLARET Optic
No. 260. SAU. CHAMP. Optic
No. 3. Ftd. TUMBLER Made in 2½-3-4-6-9 and 12 oz. Sizes
No. 260. FINGER BOWL Optic
No. 16. 54 oz. JUG Optic
No. 260. SHERBET Optic
No. 260. CORDIAL Optic
No. 260. COCKTAIL Optic
No. 260. PARFAIT Optic
No. 30. 8" PLATE

SENECA GLASS COMPANY, MORGANTOWN, W. VA.

Page 32.

$20-30 each
Jug: $70-90

Page 33.

Stems: $15-25 each

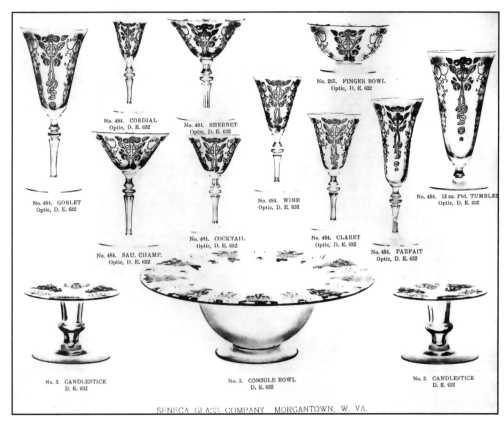

Page 34.

Stems: $15-25 each
Console bowl: $90-110
Candlestick: $40-50 pair

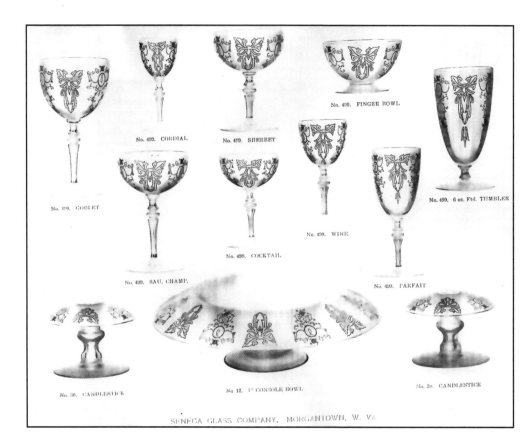

No. 499. CORDIAL

No. 499. SHERBET

No. 499. FINGER BOWL

No. 499. GOBLET

No. 499. WINE

No. 499. 6 oz. Ftd. TUMBLER

No. 499. COCKTAIL

No. 499. SAU. CHAMP.

No. 499. PARFAIT

No. 30. CANDLESTICK

No. 12. 1" CONSOLE BOWL

No. 30. CANDLESTICK

SENECA GLASS COMPANY, MORGANTOWN, W. VA.

Page 35.

Stems: $15-25 each

No. 499. FINGER BOWL
Optie, D. E. 634

No. 499. CORDIAL
Optie, D. E. 634

No. 499. WINE
Optie, D. E. 634

No. 499. 12 oz. Ftd.
TUMBLER
Optie, D. E. 634

No. 499. GOBLET
Optie, D. E. 634

No. 499. SHERBET
Optie, D. E. 634

No. 499. PARFAIT
Optie, D. E. 624

No. 499. COCKTAIL
Optie, D. E. 634

No. 499. SAU. CHAMP.
Optie, D. E. 634

No. 30. CANDLESTICK
D. E. 634

No. 1. 12" CONSOLE BOWL
D. E. 634

No. 30. CANDLESTICK
D. E. 634

SENECA GLASS COMPANY MORGANTOWN, W. VA.

Page 36.

Stems: $15-25 each
Console bowl: $50-60
Candlestick: $40-50 pair

Catalog #5

Page 1.

$10-15 each

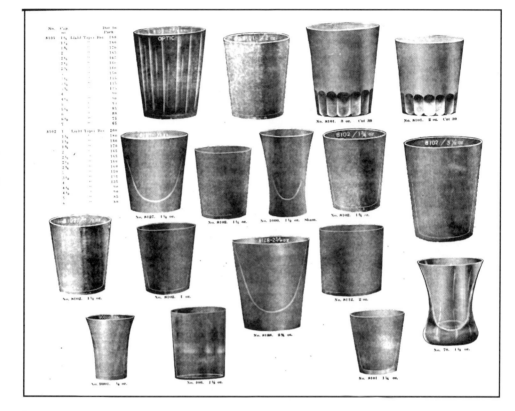

Page 2.

$8-10 each

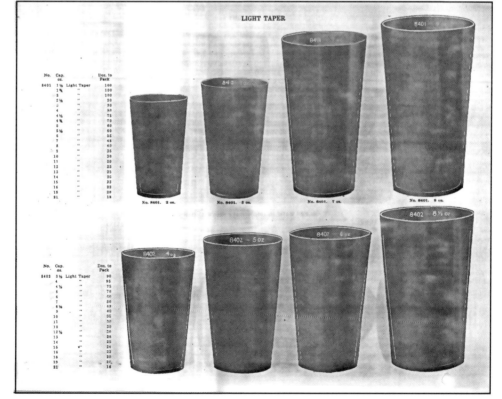

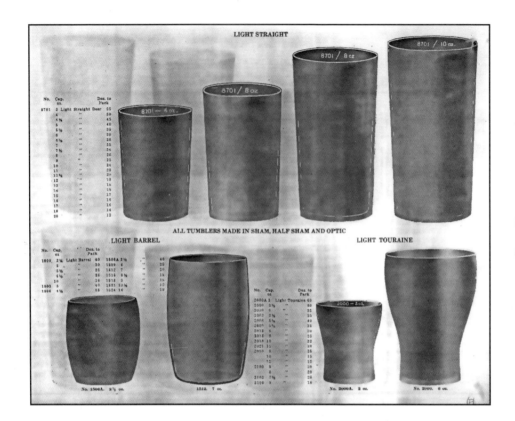

Page 3.

$8-10 each

Page 4.

$10-15 each

No. 100. Goblet. Regular 9 oz.
Doz. to pack 9.

No. 60. Goblet. 6 oz.
Doz. to pack 12.

No. 1207. Champagne. 7½ oz.
Doz. to pack 12.

No. 7000. Champagne. 5 oz.
Doz. to pack 15.

No. 83. Goblet. 9 oz.
Doz. to pack 10.

No. 12. Goblet. 8½ oz. Optic.
Doz. to pack 10.

Page 5.

$10-15 each

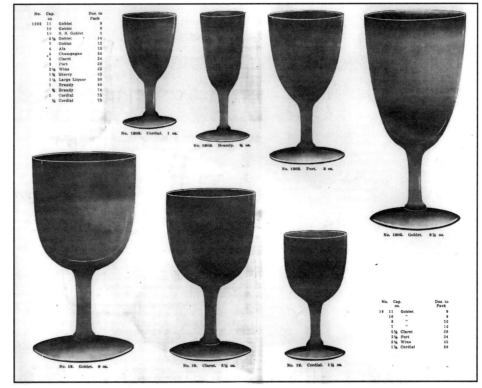

No.	Cap. oz.		Doz. to Pack
1202	11	Goblet	9
	10	Goblet	9
	10	S. S. Goblet	9
	8¼	Goblet	10
	7	Goblet	12
	6	Ale	15
	5	Champagne	24
	4	Claret	24
	3	Port	30
	2½	Wine	35
	1¾	Sherry	35
	1½	Large Liquor	50
	1	Brandy	60
	¾	Brandy	70
	1	Cordial	75
	½	Cordial	75

No. 1202. Cordial. 1 oz.

No. 1202. Brandy. ¾ oz.

No. 1202. Port. 3 oz.

No. 1202. Goblet. 8½ oz.

Page 6.

$10-15 each

No. 19. Goblet. 8 oz.

No. 19. Claret. 5½ oz.

No. 19. Cordial. 1½ oz.

No.	Cap. oz.		Doz. to Pack
19	11	Goblet	9
	10	"	9
	8	"	10
	7	"	15
	5½	Claret	20
	3½	Port	24
	2½	Wine	35
	1½	Cordial	50

41

No.	Cap. oz.		Doz. to Pack
34	11	Goblet	8
	10	"	9
	10	" S. S.	10
	9	"	9
	8	"	10
	6½	"	12
	5½	Champagne	18
	4	Claret	20
	3	Port	25
	2½	Wine	25
	2	Sherry	28
	1½	Cordial	50
	1	Brandy	75
	4½	R. Wine	18
		Rhine Wine 1	18
	4½	Hot Whiskey	20
	4	Cocktail	20
	3	Cre. de Ment.	25
	6	Sau. Champ.	10
	5	H. S. Champ.	10
	5	H. S. S. Ch'p.	10
	7	Fruit	....

No. 34. Cordial. 1½ oz.

No. 34. Wine. 2½ oz.

No. 34. Cocktail. 4 oz.

No. 34. Goblet. 8 oz.

No. 1202. Sherbet Optic. 5 oz.
Doz. to pack 15.

No. 34. Sherbet. 5 oz.
Doz to pack 14.

No. 300. Sherbet. 4½ oz.
Doz to pack 14.

Page 7.

$10-15 each

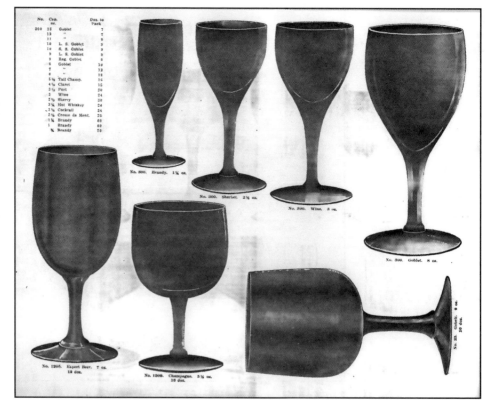

No.	Cap. oz.		Doz. to Pack
300	13	Goblet	7
	13	"	7
	11	"	9
	10	L. S. Goblet	9
	10	S. S. Goblet	9
	9	L. S. Goblet	9
	9	Reg. Goblet	9
	8	Goblet	10
	7	"	12
	6	"	12
	5½	Tall Champ.	16
	4½	Claret	15
	2½	Port	20
	2	Wine	24
	2½	Sherry	28
	3½	Hot Whiskey	24
	3½	Cocktail	24
	2½	Creme de Ment.	25
	1½	Brandy	60
	1	Brandy	60
	¾	Brandy	70

No. 300. Brandy. 1½ oz.

No. 300. Sherbet. 2½ oz.

No. 300. Wine. 3 oz.

No. 300. Goblet. 8 oz.

Page 8.

$10-20 each

No. 1205. Export Beer. 7 oz.
12 doz.

No. 1209. Champagne. 5½ oz.
16 doz.

No. 35. Goblet. 8 oz.
10 doz.

No.	Cap. oz.		Dox. to Pack
8000	11	Goblet	8
	10	"	8
	8	" optic	9
	6	Goblet	15
	6	Tall Claret	15
	5½	Tall Champagne	16
	4	Claret	20
	4	R. Wine optic	20
	4	Cocktail	24
	2½	Creme de Menic.	25
	5	Port, optic	24
	2	Wine	24
	1	Brandy	60
	¾	Brandy	70
	1¼	Cordial	82
	¾	Cordial, optic	40
	7	Lg. Sau. Champ.	19
	6¼	Sau. Champ.	12
	6	H.S.S.Champ. opt.	10
	5¼	H. S. Champ.	15
	4½	Burgundy	19

No. 8000. Cordial Optic. ¾ oz.

No. 8000. Port Optic. 8 oz.

No. 8000. Rhine Wine Optic. 4 oz.

No. 8000. Goblet Optic. 9 oz.

No. 1202. Egg. 4 oz. Doz. to pack 22.

No. 1800. Finger Bowl. Doz. to pack 18.

No. 502. Custard. 6 oz. Doz. to pack 22.

Page 9.

$10-15 each

No.	Cap. oz.		Dox. to Pack
1	3	Cocktail	24
5	3	"	24
6	3	"	24
11	2½	"	24
21	3½	"	24
7	3½	Rhine Wine	15
2	3½	"	12

Page 10.

$10-15 each

No. 1. Cocktail. 3 oz.

No. 5. Cocktail. 3 oz.

No. 6. Cocktail. 3 oz.

No. 7. Rhine Wine. 3½ oz.

No. 2. Rhine Wine. 3½ oz.

No. 11. Cocktail. 2½ oz.

No. 21. Cocktail. 3½ oz.

No. 100. Creme de Menthe. 2 oz.
Doz. to pack 25.

No. 54. Creme de Menthe. 5 oz.
Doz. to pack 25.

No. 7. Sherry. 2 oz.
Doz. to pack 25.

No. 3. Sherry. 2 oz.
Doz. to pack 25.

No. 5. Ale. 8 oz.

No. 7. Hot Whiskey. 8½ oz.

No. 1. Saucer Champagne. 5 oz.
Doz. to pack 10.

No. 54. Hollow Stem Saucer Champagne. 5 oz.
Doz. to pack 10.

Page 11.

$10-15 each

ALL ITEMS SHOWN ON THIS PAGE
ARE MADE OF THE PUREST COLOR
LEAD GLASS.

No. 75. Water Bottle. Capacity
2½ pints.

No. 1. Decanter. Made in 26 oz.
and 32 oz. Capacity.

No. 54. Fruit. 7 oz.

No. 10. Tankard. Made in the following sizes: 8, 10, 15, 21, 31, 42, 54, 65 and 80 oz.

No. 40. Jug. Made in the following sizes: 16, 32, 54 and 72 oz.

No. 15. Jug. Made in the following sizes: 8, 16 and 48 oz.

Page 12.

$25-50 each

44

STAPLE ITEMS WHICH WILL SELL ON SIGHT, AND
SHOULD BE CARRIED IN STOCK ALL THE TIME. YOU
MAY ORDER IN QUANTITIES TO SUIT YOUR NEEDS.

No. 50. 65 oz. Covered Jug.

No. 20. Jug. Made in the following sizes: 8, 16, 32 and 32 oz.

No. 40. Sugar and Cream Set.

Page 13.

$25-35 each
Covered jug: $50-60

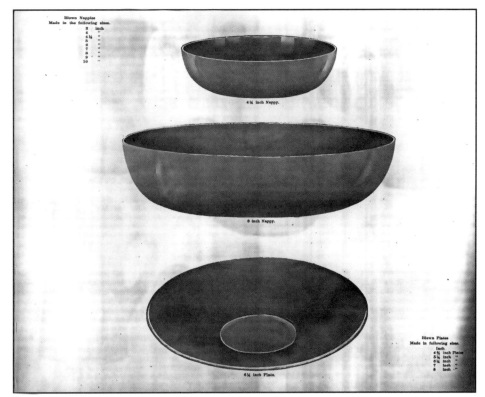

Blown Nappies
Made in the following sizes.

3	inch
4	"
4½	"
5	"
6	"
7	"
8	"
9	"
10	"

4¼ inch Nappy.

8 inch Nappy.

Blown Plates
Made in following sizes.
Inch
4½ inch Plate
5½ inch "
6½ inch "
7 inch "
8 inch "

6¼ inch Plate.

Page 14.

$10-20 each

45

No. 1102. Custard. 6½ oz.
Doz. to pack 20.

No. 769. Custard. 7 oz.
Doz. to pack 20.

No. 1107. Custard. 5 oz.
Doz. to pack 25.

HANDLED ICE TEA OR LEMONADE GLASSES

No. 8401. 10 oz. Handled.

No. 460. 10 oz. Handled.

No. 1. Handled Footed Ice Tea.

Page 15.

$10-15 each

Page 16.

$15-25 each
Tankard Water Set: $100-125

No. 19. Cordial 1½ oz. Engraved 282.

No. 19. Wine 2½ oz. Engraved 283.

No. 19. Claret or Champagne 5½ oz. Engraved 283.

No. 19. Goblet 9 oz. Engraved 283.

No. 1202. Wine 2½ oz. Engraved 412.

No. 1. Tankard Water Set. Engraved 444. 1 Doz. Sets to package.

No. 1202. Wine 2½ oz. Engraved 390.

REFER TO 1902 LINE FOR ITEMS MADE IN THIS ENGRAVING.

REFER TO 1902 LINE FOR ITEMS MADE IN THIS ENGRAVING. SEE PAGE 8.

No.	Cap. oz.		Doz. to pack
19	11	Goblet	9
	10	"	9
	8	"	10
	7	"	15
	5½	Claret	20
	3½	Port	24
	2½	Wine	25
	1½	Cordial	50

Page 17. $15-20 each

Page 18. $8-12 each

Page 19.

Top row: $8-12 each
Water bottle and finger bowl: $40-50 each

1967 Catalog

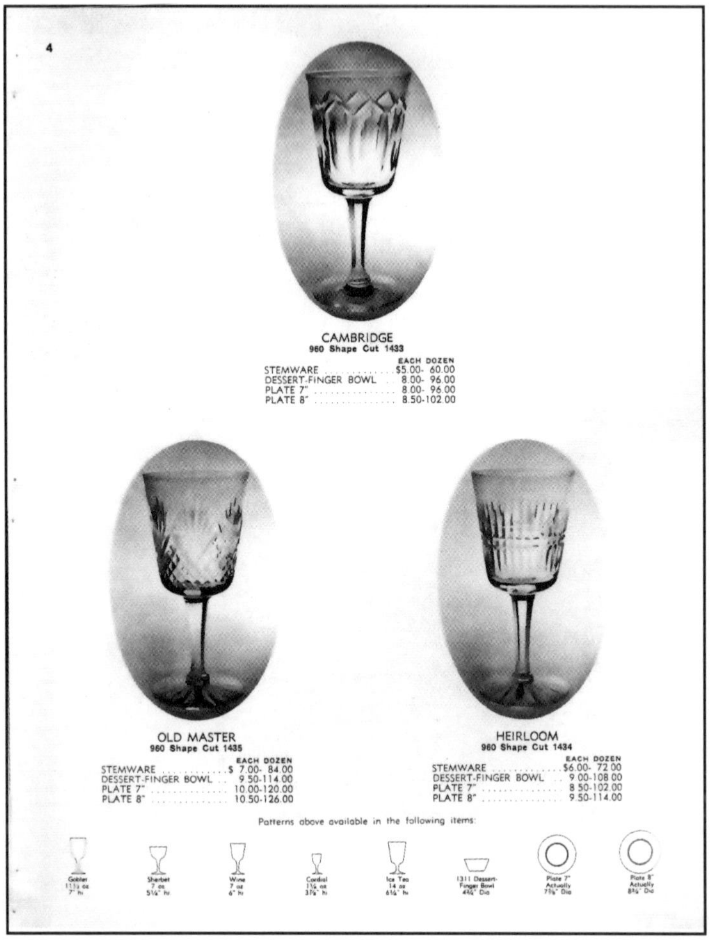

4

CAMBRIDGE
960 Shape Cut 1433

	EACH DOZEN
STEMWARE	$5.00- 60.00
DESSERT-FINGER BOWL	8.00- 96.00
PLATE 7"	8.00- 96.00
PLATE 8"	8.50-102.00

OLD MASTER
960 Shape Cut 1435

	EACH DOZEN
STEMWARE	$ 7.00- 84.00
DESSERT-FINGER BOWL	9.50-114.00
PLATE 7"	10.00-120.00
PLATE 8"	10.50-126.00

HEIRLOOM
960 Shape Cut 1434

	EACH DOZEN
STEMWARE	$6.00- 72.00
DESSERT-FINGER BOWL	9.00-108.00
PLATE 7"	8.50-102.00
PLATE 8"	9.50-114.00

Patterns above available in the following items:

Goblet 11½ oz 7" ht
Sherbet 7 oz 5¼" ht
Wine 7 oz 6" ht
Cordial 1¼ oz 3⅞" ht
Ice Tea 14 oz 6¼" ht
1311 Dessert-Finger Bowl 4¼" Dia
Plate 7" Actually 7⅝" Dia
Plate 8" Actually 8¾" Dia

Page 4. $15-25 each

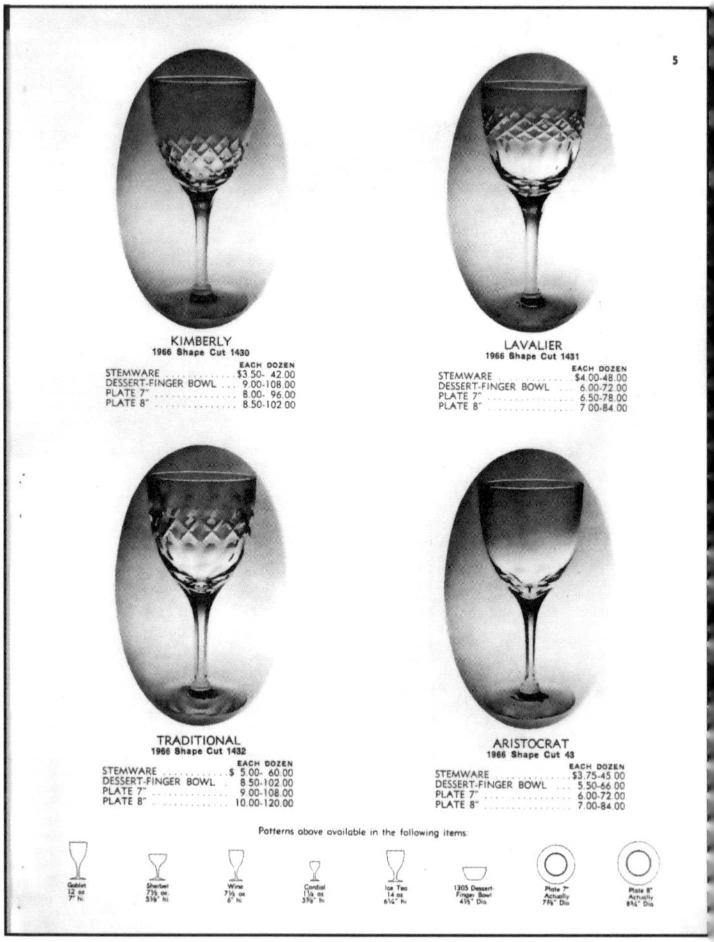

5

KIMBERLY
1966 Shape Cut 1430

	EACH DOZEN
STEMWARE	$3.50- 42.00
DESSERT-FINGER BOWL	9.00-108.00
PLATE 7"	8.00- 96.00
PLATE 8"	8.50-102.00

LAVALIER
1966 Shape Cut 1431

	EACH DOZEN
STEMWARE	$4.00-48.00
DESSERT-FINGER BOWL	6.00-72.00
PLATE 7"	6.50-78.00
PLATE 8"	7.00-84.00

TRADITIONAL
1966 Shape Cut 1432

	EACH DOZEN
STEMWARE	$ 5.00- 60.00
DESSERT-FINGER BOWL	8.50-102.00
PLATE 7"	9.00-108.00
PLATE 8"	10.00-120.00

ARISTOCRAT
1966 Shape Cut 43

	EACH DOZEN
STEMWARE	$3.75-45.00
DESSERT-FINGER BOWL	5.50-66.00
PLATE 7"	6.00-72.00
PLATE 8"	7.00-84.00

Patterns above available in the following items:

Goblet 12 oz 7" ht
Sherbet 7½ oz 5⅛" ht
Wine 7½ oz 6" ht
Cordial 1¼ oz 3⅝" ht
Ice Tea 14 oz 6¼" ht
1305 Dessert-Finger Bowl 4½" Dia
Plate 7" Actually 7⅝" Dia
Plate 8" Actually 8¾" Dia

Page 5. $10-20 each

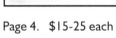

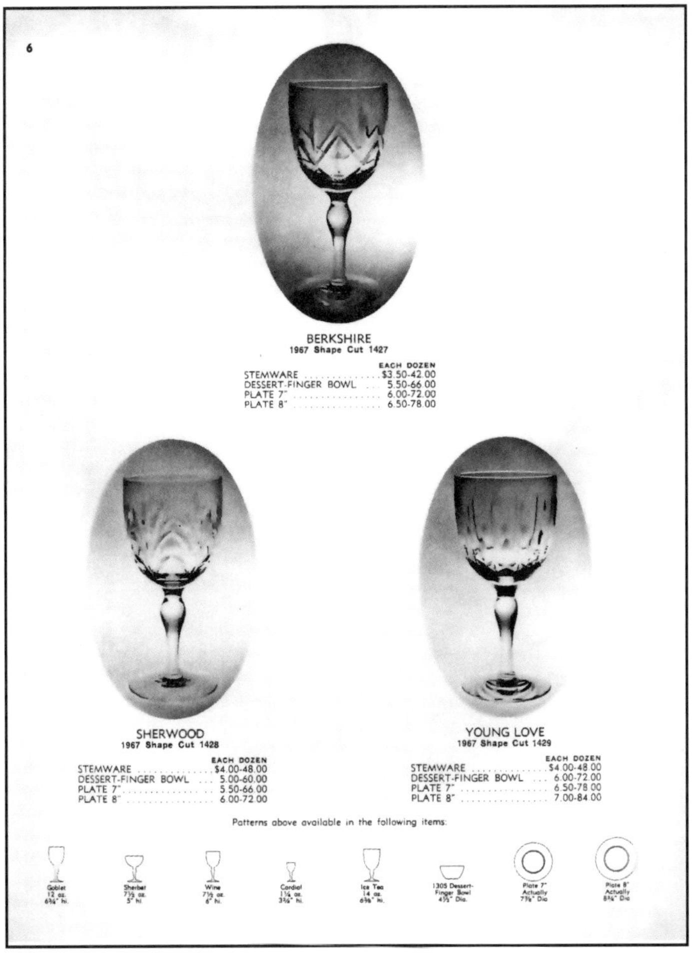

6

BERKSHIRE
1967 Shape Cut 1427

	EACH DOZEN
STEMWARE	$3.50-42.00
DESSERT-FINGER BOWL	5.50-66.00
PLATE 7"	6.00-72.00
PLATE 8"	6.50-78.00

SHERWOOD
1967 Shape Cut 1428

	EACH DOZEN
STEMWARE	$4.00-48.00
DESSERT-FINGER BOWL	5.00-60.00
PLATE 7"	5.50-66.00
PLATE 8"	6.00-72.00

YOUNG LOVE
1967 Shape Cut 1429

	EACH DOZEN
STEMWARE	$4.00-48.00
DESSERT-FINGER BOWL	6.00-72.00
PLATE 7"	6.50-78.00
PLATE 8"	7.00-84.00

Patterns above available in the following items:

Goblet 12 oz. 6¾" hi. · Sherbet 7½ oz. 5" hi. · Wine 7½ oz. 6" hi. · Cordial 1¼ oz. 3⅜" hi. · Ice Tea 14 oz. 6⅜" hi. · 1305 Dessert-Finger Bowl 4½" Dia. · Plate 7" Actually 7⅞" Dia · Plate 8" Actually 8¾" Dia

Page 6. $10-20 each

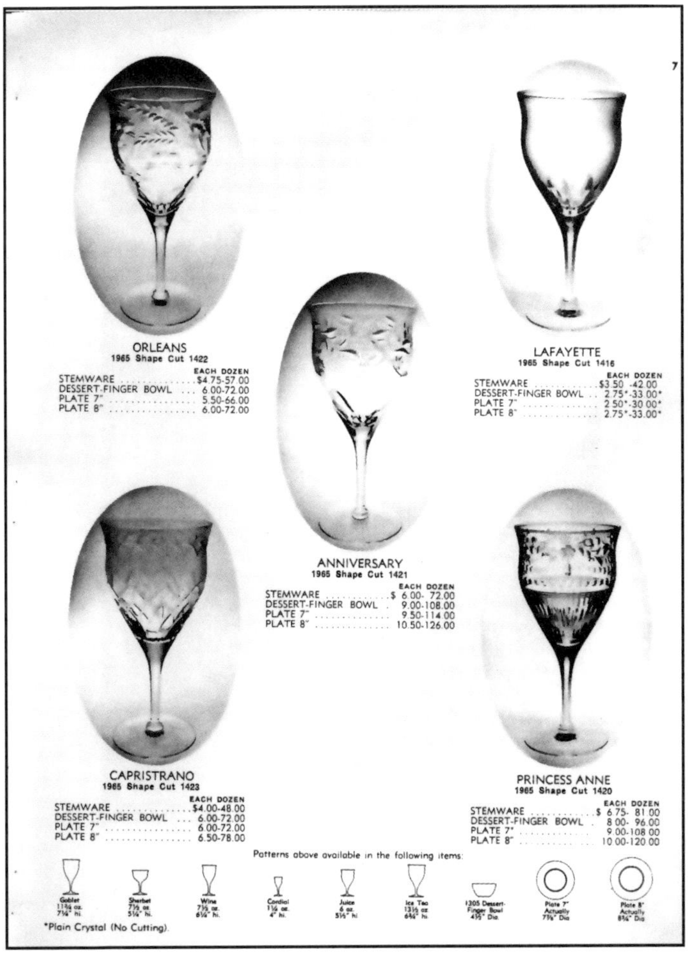

7

ORLEANS
1965 Shape Cut 1422

	EACH DOZEN
STEMWARE	$4.75-57.00
DESSERT-FINGER BOWL	6.00-72.00
PLATE 7"	5.50-66.00
PLATE 8"	6.00-72.00

LAFAYETTE
1965 Shape Cut 1416

	EACH DOZEN
STEMWARE	$3.50 -42.00
DESSERT-FINGER BOWL	2.75*-33.00*
PLATE 7"	2.50*-30.00*
PLATE 8"	2.75*-33.00*

ANNIVERSARY
1965 Shape Cut 1421

	EACH DOZEN
STEMWARE	$ 6.00- 72.00
DESSERT-FINGER BOWL	9.00-108.00
PLATE 7"	9.50-114.00
PLATE 8"	10.50-126.00

CAPRISTRANO
1965 Shape Cut 1423

	EACH DOZEN
STEMWARE	$4.00-48.00
DESSERT-FINGER BOWL	6.00-72.00
PLATE 7"	6.00-72.00
PLATE 8"	6.50-78.00

PRINCESS ANNE
1965 Shape Cut 1420

	EACH DOZEN
STEMWARE	$ 6.75- 81.00
DESSERT-FINGER BOWL	8.00- 96.00
PLATE 7"	9.00-108.00
PLATE 8"	10.00-120.00

Patterns above available in the following items:

Goblet 11¾ oz. 7¼" hi. · Sherbet 7½ oz. 5¼" hi. · Wine 7½ oz. 6¼" hi. · Cordial 1¼ oz. 4" hi. · Juice 6 oz. 5½" hi. · Ice Tea 13½ oz. 6¾" hi. · 1305 Dessert-Finger Bowl 4½" Dia. · Plate 7" Actually 7⅞" Dia · Plate 8" Actually 8¾" Dia

*Plain Crystal (No Cutting).

Page 7. $15-25 each

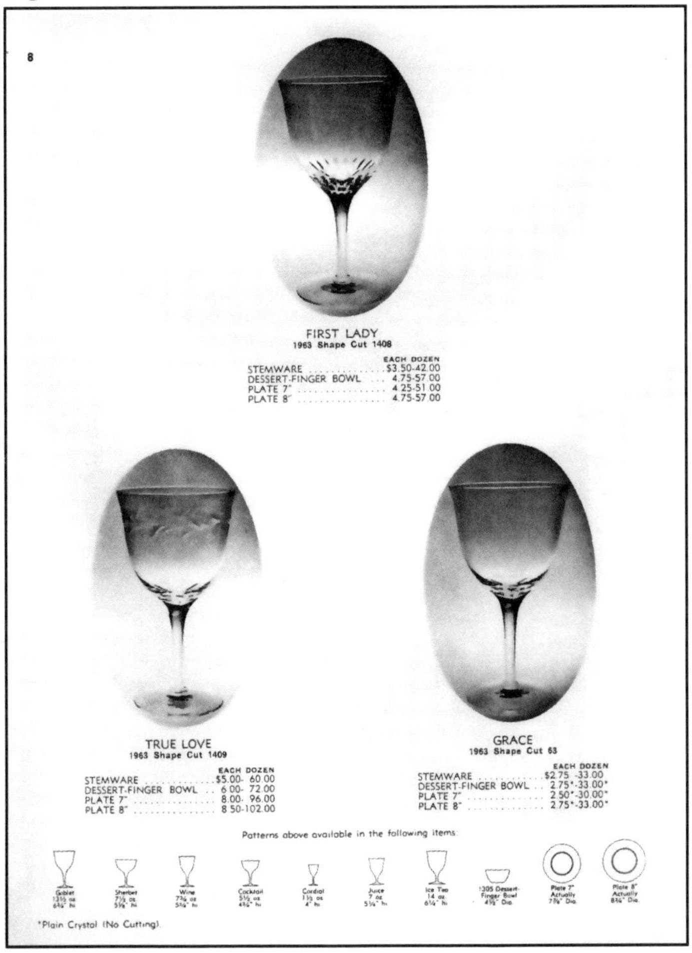

8

FIRST LADY
1963 Shape Cut 1408

	EACH DOZEN
STEMWARE	$3.50-42.00
DESSERT-FINGER BOWL	4.75-57.00
PLATE 7"	4.25-51.00
PLATE 8"	4.75-57.00

TRUE LOVE
1963 Shape Cut 1409

	EACH DOZEN
STEMWARE	$5.00- 60.00
DESSERT-FINGER BOWL	6.00- 72.00
PLATE 7"	8.00- 96.00
PLATE 8"	8.50-102.00

GRACE
1963 Shape Cut 63

	EACH DOZEN
STEMWARE	$2.75 -33.00
DESSERT-FINGER BOWL	2.75*-33.00*
PLATE 7"	2.50*-30.00*
PLATE 8"	2.75*-33.00*

Patterns above available in the following items:

Goblet 13½ oz 6¾" hi · Sherbet 7½ oz. 5⅝" hi · Wine 7¾ oz 5¾" hi · Cocktail 5½ oz 4¾" hi · Cordial 1½ oz 4" hi · Juice 7 oz 5¼" hi · Ice Tea 14 oz. 6¼" hi · 1305 Dessert-Finger Bowl 4½" Dia. · Plate 7" Actually 7⅞" Dia. · Plate 8" Actually 8¾" Dia.

*Plain Crystal (No Cutting).

Page 8. $10-15 each

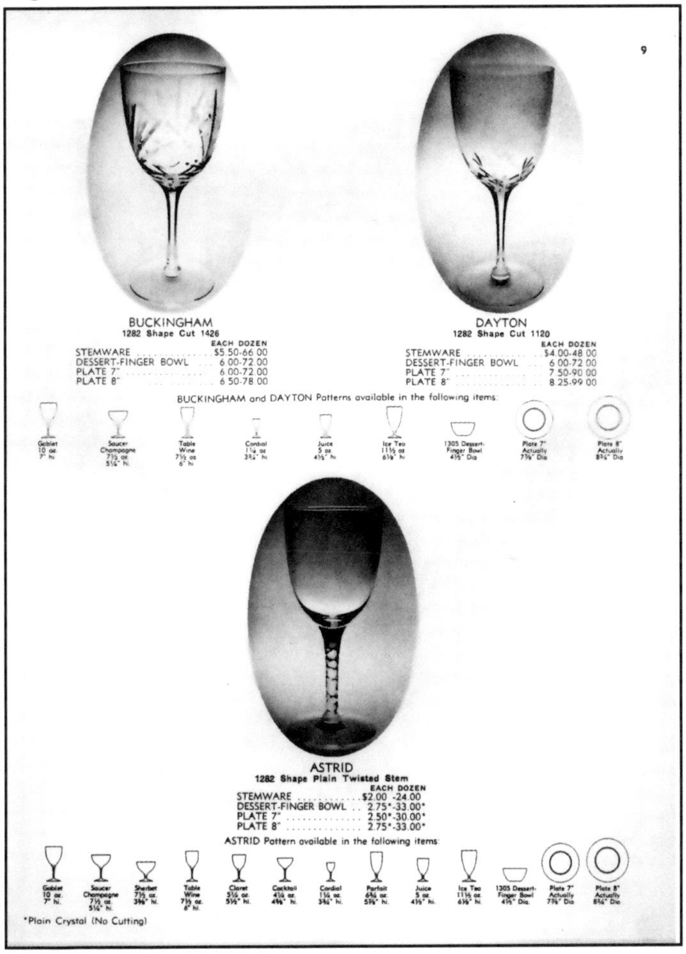

9

BUCKINGHAM
1282 Shape Cut 1426

	EACH DOZEN
STEMWARE	$5.50-66.00
DESSERT-FINGER BOWL	6.00-72.00
PLATE 7"	6.00-72.00
PLATE 8"	6.50-78.00

DAYTON
1282 Shape Cut 1120

	EACH DOZEN
STEMWARE	$4.00-48.00
DESSERT-FINGER BOWL	6.00-72.00
PLATE 7"	7.50-90.00
PLATE 8"	8.25-99.00

BUCKINGHAM and DAYTON Patterns available in the following items:

Goblet 10 oz. 7" hi · Saucer Champagne 7½ oz 5¼" hi. · Table Wine 7½ oz 6" hi · Cordial 1¼ oz 3¾" hi · Juice 5 oz. 4½" hi · Ice Tea 11½ oz 6⅛" hi · 1305 Dessert-Finger Bowl 4½" Dia · Plate 7" Actually 7⅞" Dia · Plate 8" Actually 8¾" Dia

ASTRID
1282 Shape Plain Twisted Stem

	EACH DOZEN
STEMWARE	$2.00 -24.00
DESSERT-FINGER BOWL	2.75*-33.00*
PLATE 7"	2.50*-30.00*
PLATE 8"	2.75*-33.00*

ASTRID Pattern available in the following items:

Goblet 10 oz. 7" hi. · Saucer Champagne 7½ oz. 5¼" hi. · Sherbet 7½ oz. 3⅝" hi. · Table Wine 7½ oz. 6" hi. · Claret 5½ oz. 5½" hi. · Cocktail 4¼ oz. 4⅝" hi. · Cordial 1¼ oz. 3¾" hi. · Parfait 6¾ oz. 5⅞" hi. · Juice 5 oz. 4½" hi. · Ice Tea 11½ oz. 6⅜" hi. · 1305 Dessert-Finger Bowl 4½" Dia. · Plate 7" Actually 7⅞" Dia · Plate 8" Actually 8¾" Dia

*Plain Crystal (No Cutting)

Page 9. $10-15 each

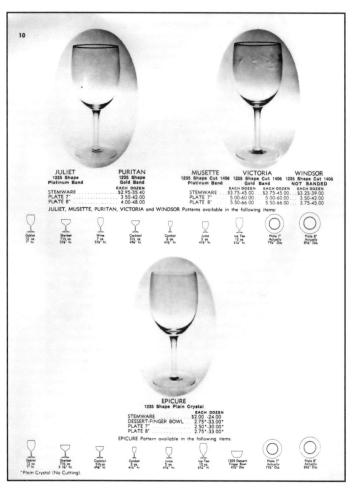

10				

JULIET / PURITAN / MUSETTE / VICTORIA / WINDSOR

	JULIET 1235 Shape Platinum Band	PURITAN 1235 Shape Gold Band	MUSETTE 1235 Shape Cut 1406 Platinum Band	VICTORIA 1235 Shape Cut 1406 Gold Band	WINDSOR 1235 Shape Cut 1406 NOT BANDED
	EACH DOZEN		EACH DOZEN	EACH DOZEN	EACH DOZEN
STEMWARE	$2.95-35.40		$3.75-45.00	$3.75-45.00	$3.25-39.00
PLATE 7"	3.50-42.00		5.00-60.00	5.00-60.00	3.50-42.00
PLATE 8"	4.00-48.00		5.50-66.00	5.50-66.00	3.75-45.00

JULIET, MUSETTE, PURITAN, VICTORIA and WINDSOR Patterns available in the following items:

EPICURE
1235 Shape Plain Crystal

	EACH DOZEN
STEMWARE	$2.00 -24.00
DESSERT-FINGER BOWL	2.75*-33.00*
PLATE 7"	2.50*-30.00*
PLATE 8"	2.75*-33.00*

EPICURE Pattern available in the following items:

*Plain Crystal (No Cutting).

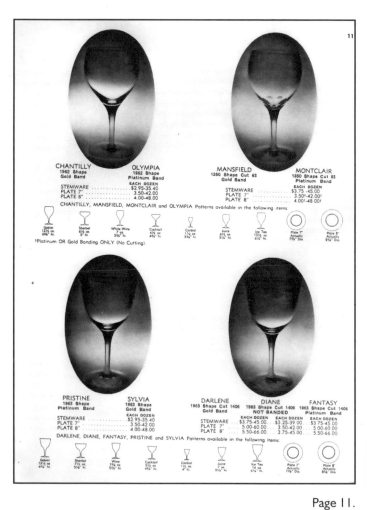

				11

CHANTILLY / OLYMPIA / MANSFIELD / MONTCLAIR

	CHANTILLY 1962 Shape Gold Band	OLYMPIA 1962 Shape Platinum Band	MANSFIELD 1350 Shape Cut 63 Gold Band	MONTCLAIR 1350 Shape Cut 63 Platinum Band
	EACH DOZEN		EACH DOZEN	
STEMWARE	$2.95-35.40		$3.75 -45.00	
PLATE 7"	3.50-42.00		3.50*-42.00†	
PLATE 8"	4.00-48.00		4.00†-48.00†	

CHANTILLY, MANSFIELD, MONTCLAIR and OLYMPIA Patterns available in the following items:

†Platinum OR Gold Banding ONLY (No Cutting).

PRISTINE / SYLVIA / DARLENE / DIANE / FANTASY

	PRISTINE 1963 Shape Platinum Band	SYLVIA 1963 Shape Gold Band	DARLENE 1963 Shape Cut 1406 Gold Band	DIANE 1963 Shape Cut 1406 NOT BANDED	FANTASY 1963 Shape Cut 1406 Platinum Band
	EACH DOZEN		EACH DOZEN	EACH DOZEN	EACH DOZEN
STEMWARE	$2.95-35.40		$3.75-45.00	$3.25-39.00	$3.75-45.00
PLATE 7"	3.50-42.00		5.00-60.00	3.50-42.00	5.00-60.00
PLATE 8"	4.00-48.00		5.50-66.00	3.75-45.00	5.50-66.00

DARLENE, DIANE, FANTASY, PRISTINE and SYLVIA Patterns available in the following items:

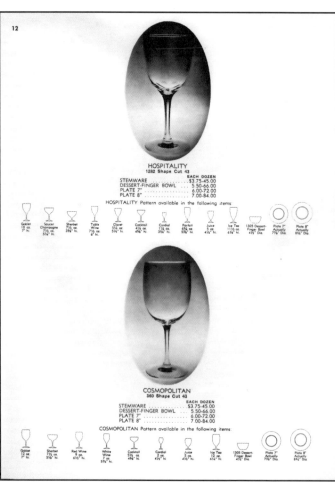

12				

HOSPITALITY
1282 Shape Cut 43

	EACH DOZEN
STEMWARE	$3.75-45.00
DESSERT-FINGER BOWL	5.50-66.00
PLATE 7"	6.00-72.00
PLATE 8"	7.00-84.00

HOSPITALITY Pattern available in the following items:

COSMOPOLITAN
360 Shape Cut 43

	EACH DOZEN
STEMWARE	$3.75-45.00
DESSERT-FINGER BOWL	5.50-66.00
PLATE 7"	6.00-72.00
PLATE 8"	7.00-84.00

COSMOPOLITAN Pattern available in the following items:

Page 10.

$10-12 each

Page 11.

$10-12 each

Page 12.

$10-12 each

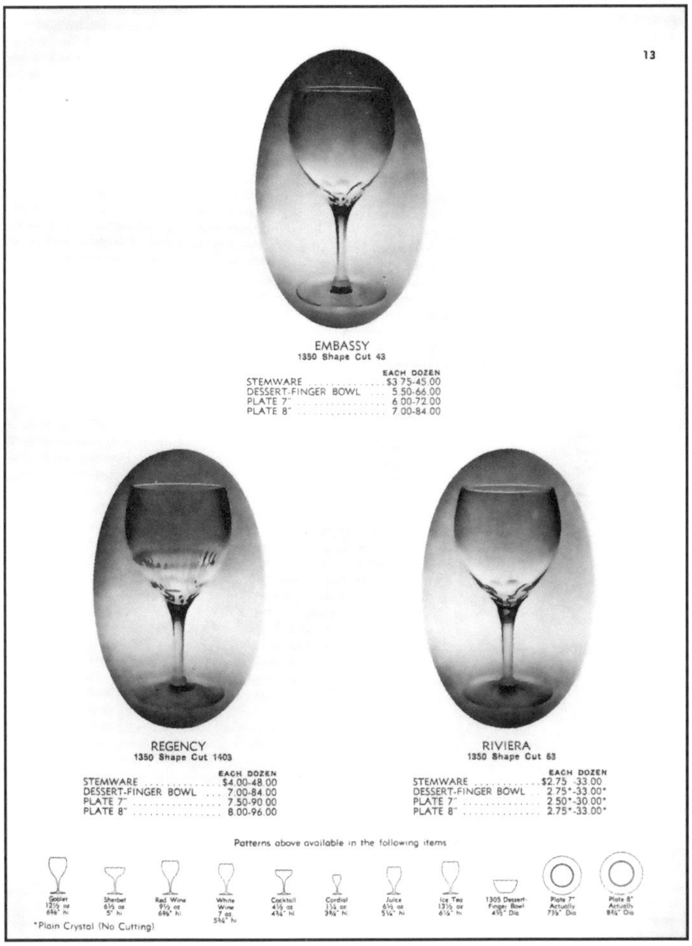

13

EMBASSY
1350 Shape Cut 43

	EACH DOZEN
STEMWARE	$3.75-45.00
DESSERT-FINGER BOWL	5.50-66.00
PLATE 7"	6.00-72.00
PLATE 8"	7.00-84.00

REGENCY
1350 Shape Cut 1403

	EACH DOZEN
STEMWARE	$4.00-48.00
DESSERT-FINGER BOWL	7.00-84.00
PLATE 7"	7.50-90.00
PLATE 8"	8.00-96.00

RIVIERA
1350 Shape Cut 63

	EACH DOZEN
STEMWARE	$2.75 -33.00
DESSERT-FINGER BOWL	2.75*-33.00*
PLATE 7"	2.50*-30.00*
PLATE 8"	2.75*-33.00*

Patterns above available in the following items

Goblet 12½ oz 6⅝" hi · Sherbet 6½ oz 5" hi · Red Wine 9½ oz 6⅝" hi · White Wine 7 oz 5¾" hi · Cocktail 4½ oz 4¾" hi · Cordial 1¼ oz 3¾" hi · Juice 6½ oz 5¼" hi · Ice Tea 13½ oz 6½" hi · 1305 Dessert-Finger Bowl 4½" Dia · Plate 7" Actually 7⅝" Dia · Plate 8" Actually 8¾" Dia

*Plain Crystal (No Cutting)

Page 13.

$10-12 each

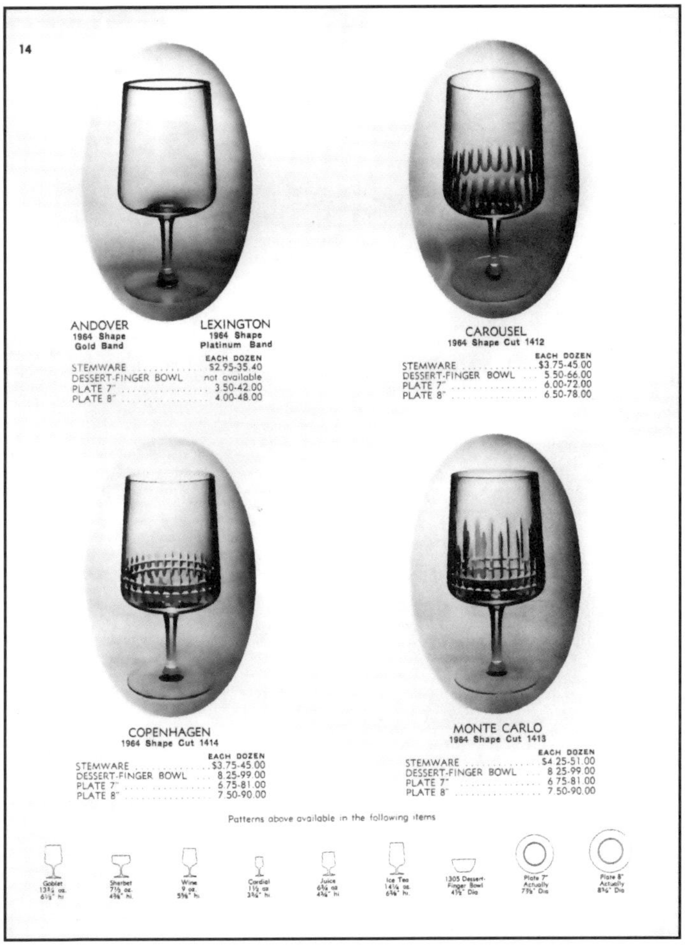

14

ANDOVER
1964 Shape
Gold Band

LEXINGTON
1964 Shape
Platinum Band

	EACH DOZEN
STEMWARE	$2.95-35.40
DESSERT-FINGER BOWL	not available
PLATE 7"	3.50-42.00
PLATE 8"	4.00-48.00

CAROUSEL
1964 Shape Cut 1412

	EACH DOZEN
STEMWARE	$3.75-45.00
DESSERT-FINGER BOWL	5.50-66.00
PLATE 7"	6.00-72.00
PLATE 8"	6.50-78.00

COPENHAGEN
1964 Shape Cut 1414

	EACH DOZEN
STEMWARE	$3.75-45.00
DESSERT-FINGER BOWL	8.25-99.00
PLATE 7"	6.75-81.00
PLATE 8"	7.50-90.00

MONTE CARLO
1964 Shape Cut 1413

	EACH DOZEN
STEMWARE	$4.25-51.00
DESSERT-FINGER BOWL	8.25-99.00
PLATE 7"	6.75-81.00
PLATE 8"	7.50-90.00

Patterns above available in the following items

Goblet 13¾ oz. 6½" hi · Sherbet 7½ oz. 4⅜" hi · Wine 9 oz. 5⅝" hi · Cordial 1½ oz 3¾" hi · Juice 6¾ oz 4¾" hi · Ice Tea 14¼ oz. 6⅜" hi · 1305 Dessert-Finger Bowl 4½" Dia · Plate 7" Actually 7⅝" Dia · Plate 8" Actually 8¾" Dia

Page 14.

Andover: $8-10 each
Others: $10-15 each

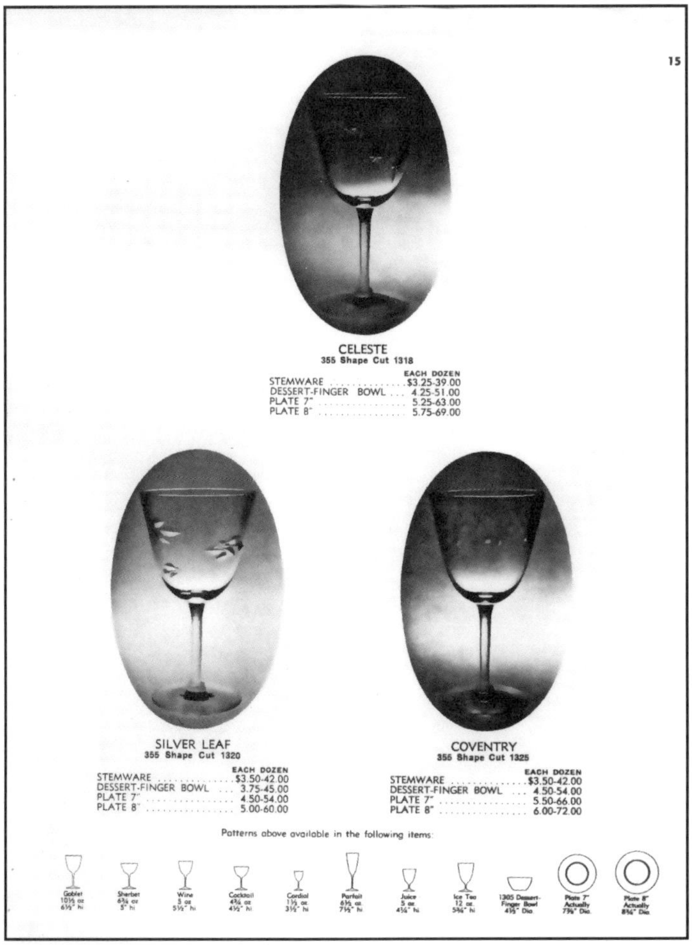

15

CELESTE
355 Shape Cut 1318

	EACH DOZEN
STEMWARE	$3.25-39.00
DESSERT-FINGER BOWL	4.25-51.00
PLATE 7"	5.25-63.00
PLATE 8"	5.75-69.00

SILVER LEAF
355 Shape Cut 1320

	EACH DOZEN
STEMWARE	$3.50-42.00
DESSERT-FINGER BOWL	3.75-45.00
PLATE 7"	4.50-54.00
PLATE 8"	5.00-60.00

COVENTRY
355 Shape Cut 1325

	EACH DOZEN
STEMWARE	$3.50-42.00
DESSERT-FINGER BOWL	4.50-54.00
PLATE 7"	5.50-66.00
PLATE 8"	6.00-72.00

Patterns above available in the following items:

Goblet 10½ oz 6½" hi · Sherbet 6¾ oz 5" hi · Wine 5 oz 5½" hi · Cocktail 4¾ oz 4½" hi · Cordial 1½ oz 3½" hi · Parfait 6½ oz 7½" hi · Juice 5 oz 4¼" hi · Ice Tea 12 oz 5¾" hi · 1305 Dessert-Finger Bowl 4½" Dia · Plate 7" Actually 7⅝" Dia · Plate 8" Actually 8¾" Dia

Page 15.

$10-15 each

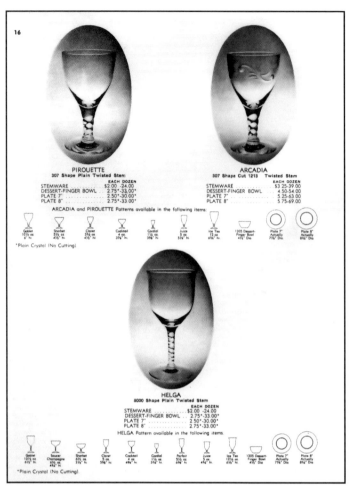

16

PIROUETTE
307 Shape Plain Twisted Stem

	EACH DOZEN
STEMWARE	$2.00 -24.00
DESSERT-FINGER BOWL	2.75*-33.00*
PLATE 7"	2.50*-30.00*
PLATE 8"	2.75*-33.00*

ARCADIA
307 Shape Cut 1213 Twisted Stem

	EACH DOZEN
STEMWARE	$3 25-39.00
DESSERT-FINGER BOWL	4.50-54.00
PLATE 7"	5.25-63.00
PLATE 8"	5.75-69.00

ARCADIA and PIROUETTE Patterns available in the following items:

*Plain Crystal (No Cutting).

HELGA
8000 Shape Plain Twisted Stem

	EACH DOZEN
STEMWARE	$2.00 -24.00
DESSERT-FINGER BOWL	2.75*-33.00*
PLATE 7"	2.50*-30.00*
PLATE 8"	2.75*-33.00*

HELGA Pattern available in the following items:

*Plain Crystal (No Cutting).

Page 16.

$10-15 each

17

LAUREL
912 Shape Cut 121 & 39

	EACH DOZEN
STEMWARE	$5.25-63.00
DESSERT-FINGER BOWL	5.25-63.00
PLATE 7"	5.50-66.00
PLATE 8"	6.00-72.00

RAMONA
912 Shape Cut 1006

	EACH DOZEN
STEMWARE	$4.50-54.00
DESSERT-FINGER BOWL	5.00-60.00
PLATE 7"	5.50-66.00
PLATE 8"	5.75-69.00

DOLLY MADISON — JANE EYRE
912 Shape Cut 189

	EACH DOZEN
STEMWARE	$4.00-48.00
DESSERT-FINGER BOWL	5.50-66.00
PLATE 7"	6.00-72.00
PLATE 8"	7.00-84.00

Patterns above available in the following items:

Page 17.

$15-20 each

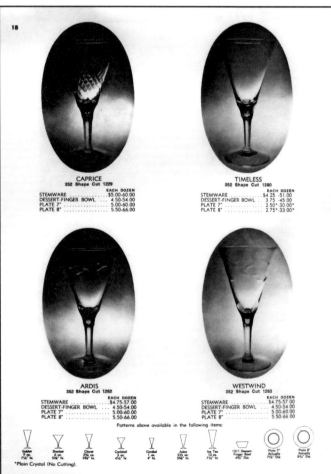

18

CAPRICE
352 Shape Cut 1229

	EACH DOZEN
STEMWARE	$5.00-60.00
DESSERT-FINGER BOWL	4.50-54.00
PLATE 7"	5.00-60.00
PLATE 8"	5.50-66.00

TIMELESS
352 Shape Cut 1380

	EACH DOZEN
STEMWARE	$4.25 -51.00
DESSERT-FINGER BOWL	3.75 -45.00
PLATE 7"	2.50*-30.00*
PLATE 8"	2.75*-33.00*

ARDIS
352 Shape Cut 1262

	EACH DOZEN
STEMWARE	$4.75-57.00
DESSERT-FINGER BOWL	4.50-54.00
PLATE 7"	5.00-60.00
PLATE 8"	5.50-66.00

WESTWIND
352 Shape Cut 1263

	EACH DOZEN
STEMWARE	$4.75-57.00
DESSERT-FINGER BOWL	4.50-54.00
PLATE 7"	5.00-60.00
PLATE 8"	5.50-66.00

Patterns above available in the following items:

*Plain Crystal (No Cutting).

Page 18.

$15-20 each

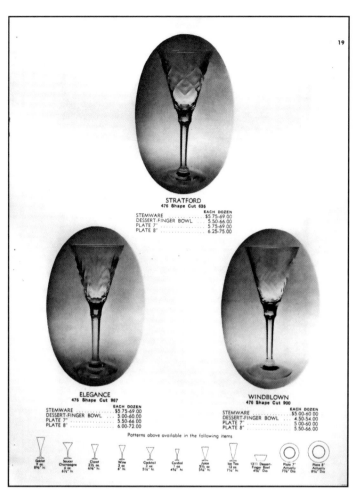

19

STRATFORD
476 Shape Cut 636

STEMWARE	EACH	DOZEN
STEMWARE	$5.75	69.00
DESSERT-FINGER BOWL	5.50	66.00
PLATE 7"	5.75	69.00
PLATE 8"	6.25	75.00

ELEGANCE
476 Shape Cut 967

STEMWARE	EACH	DOZEN
STEMWARE	$5.75	69.00
DESSERT-FINGER BOWL	5.00	60.00
PLATE 7"	5.50	66.00
PLATE 8"	6.00	72.00

WINDBLOWN
476 Shape Cut 900

STEMWARE	EACH	DOZEN
STEMWARE	$5.00	60.00
DESSERT-FINGER BOWL	4.50	54.00
PLATE 7"	5.00	60.00
PLATE 8"	5.50	66.00

Patterns above available in the following items:

20

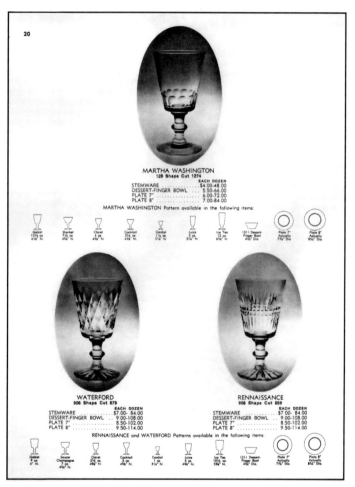

MARTHA WASHINGTON
128 Shape Cut 1274

STEMWARE	EACH	DOZEN
STEMWARE	$4.00	48.00
DESSERT-FINGER BOWL	5.50	66.00
PLATE 7"	6.00	72.00
PLATE 8"	7.00	84.00

MARTHA WASHINGTON Pattern available in the following items:

WATERFORD
908 Shape Cut 879

STEMWARE	EACH	DOZEN
STEMWARE	$7.00	84.00
DESSERT-FINGER BOWL	9.00	108.00
PLATE 7"	8.50	102.00
PLATE 8"	9.50	114.00

RENNAISSANCE
908 Shape Cut 859

STEMWARE	EACH	DOZEN
STEMWARE	$7.00	84.00
DESSERT-FINGER BOWL	9.00	108.00
PLATE 7"	8.50	102.00
PLATE 8"	9.50	114.00

RENNAISSANCE and WATERFORD Patterns available in the following items:

21

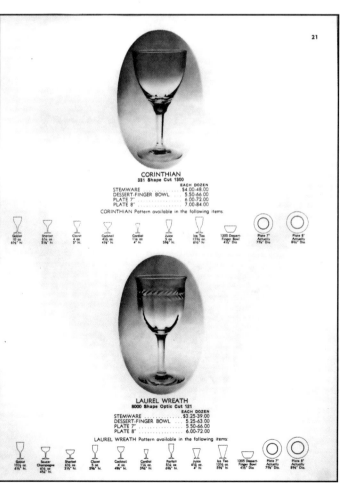

CORINTHIAN
331 Shape Cut 1300

STEMWARE	EACH	DOZEN
STEMWARE	$4.00	48.00
DESSERT-FINGER BOWL	5.50	66.00
PLATE 7"	6.00	72.00
PLATE 8"	7.00	84.00

CORINTHIAN Pattern available in the following items:

LAUREL WREATH
8000 Shape Optic Cut 121

STEMWARE	EACH	DOZEN
STEMWARE	$3.25	39.00
DESSERT-FINGER BOWL	5.25	63.00
PLATE 7"	5.50	66.00
PLATE 8"	6.00	72.00

LAUREL WREATH Pattern available in the following items:

Page 16.

$15-20 each

Page 17.

$15-20 each

Page 18.

$10-15 each

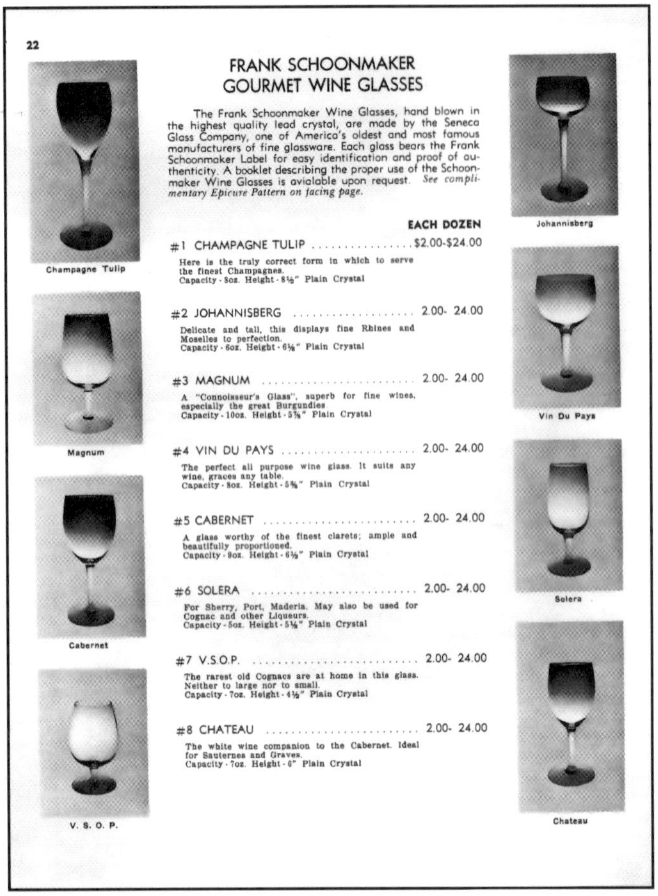

FRANK SCHOONMAKER GOURMET WINE GLASSES

The Frank Schoonmaker Wine Glasses, hand blown in the highest quality lead crystal, are made by the Seneca Glass Company, one of America's oldest and most famous manufacturers of fine glassware. Each glass bears the Frank Schoonmaker Label for easy identification and proof of authenticity. A booklet describing the proper use of the Schoonmaker Wine Glasses is avialable upon request. *See complimentary Epicure Pattern on facing page.*

EACH DOZEN

#1 CHAMPAGNE TULIP .... $2.00-$24.00
Here is the truly correct form in which to serve the finest Champagnes.
Capacity - 8oz. Height - 8½" Plain Crystal

#2 JOHANNISBERG 2.00- 24.00
Delicate and tall, this displays fine Rhines and Moselles to perfection.
Capacity - 6oz. Height - 6⅛" Plain Crystal

#3 MAGNUM 2.00- 24.00
A "Connoisseur's Glass", superb for fine wines, especially the great Burgundies
Capacity - 10oz. Height - 5⅞" Plain Crystal

#4 VIN DU PAYS 2.00- 24.00
The perfect all purpose wine glass. It suits any wine, graces any table.
Capacity - 8oz. Height - 5⅝" Plain Crystal

#5 CABERNET 2.00- 24.00
A glass worthy of the finest clarets; ample and beautifully proportioned.
Capacity - 9oz. Height - 6½" Plain Crystal

#6 SOLERA 2.00- 24.00
For Sherry, Port, Maderia. May also be used for Cognac and other Liqueurs.
Capacity - 5oz. Height - 5⅛" Plain Crystal

#7 V.S.O.P. 2.00- 24.00
The rarest old Cognacs are at home in this glass. Neither to large nor to small.
Capacity - 7oz. Height - 4½" Plain Crystal

#8 CHATEAU 2.00- 24.00
The white wine companion to the Cabernet. Ideal for Sauternes and Graves.
Capacity - 7oz. Height - 6" Plain Crystal

Champagne Tulip · Johannisberg · Magnum · Vin Du Pays · Cabernet · Solera · V. S. O. P. · Chateau

Page 22. $8-12 each

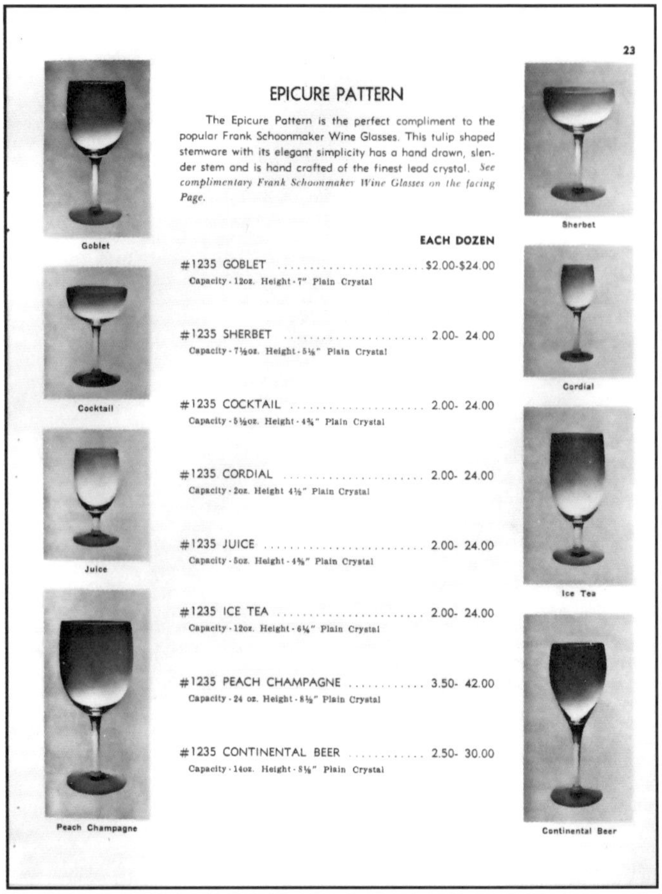

EPICURE PATTERN

The Epicure Pattern is the perfect compliment to the popular Frank Schoonmaker Wine Glasses. This tulip shaped stemware with its elegant simplicity has a hand drawn, slender stem and is hand crafted of the finest lead crystal. *See complimentary Frank Schoonmaker Wine Glasses on the facing Page.*

EACH DOZEN

#1235 GOBLET .... $2.00-$24.00
Capacity - 12oz. Height - 7" Plain Crystal

#1235 SHERBET 2.00- 24.00
Capacity - 7½oz. Height - 5⅛" Plain Crystal

#1235 COCKTAIL 2.00- 24.00
Capacity - 5½oz. Height - 4¾" Plain Crystal

#1235 CORDIAL 2.00- 24.00
Capacity - 2oz. Height 4½" Plain Crystal

#1235 JUICE 2.00- 24.00
Capacity - 5oz. Height - 4⅝" Plain Crystal

#1235 ICE TEA 2.00- 24.00
Capacity - 12oz. Height - 6¼" Plain Crystal

#1235 PEACH CHAMPAGNE 3.50- 42.00
Capacity - 24 oz. Height - 8½" Plain Crystal

#1235 CONTINENTAL BEER 2.50- 30.00
Capacity - 14oz. Height - 8⅛" Plain Crystal

Goblet · Sherbet · Cocktail · Cordial · Juice · Ice Tea · Peach Champagne · Continental Beer

Page 23. $8-12 each

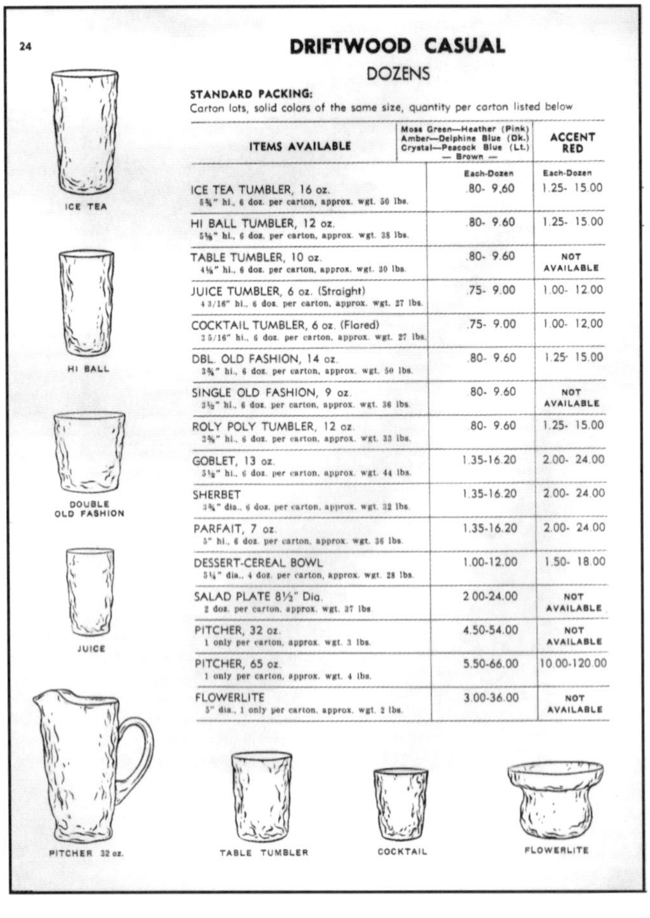

DRIFTWOOD CASUAL

DOZENS

STANDARD PACKING:
Carton lots, solid colors of the same size, quantity per carton listed below

ITEMS AVAILABLE	Moss Green—Heather (Pink) Amber—Delphine Blue (Dk.) Crystal—Peacock Blue (Lt.) — Brown —	ACCENT RED
	Each-Dozen	Each-Dozen
ICE TEA TUMBLER, 16 oz. 5¾" hi., 6 doz. per carton, approx. wgt. 50 lbs.	.80- 9,60	1.25- 15.00
HI BALL TUMBLER, 12 oz. 5⅛" hi., 6 doz. per carton, approx. wgt. 38 lbs.	.80- 9.60	1.25- 15.00
TABLE TUMBLER, 10 oz. 4⅛" hi., 6 doz. per carton, approx. wgt. 30 lbs.	.80- 9.60	NOT AVAILABLE
JUICE TUMBLER, 6 oz. (Straight) 4 3/16" hi., 6 doz. per carton, approx. wgt. 27 lbs.	.75- 9.00	1.00- 12.00
COCKTAIL TUMBLER, 6 oz. (Flared) 3 5/16" hi., 6 doz. per carton, approx. wgt. 27 lbs.	.75- 9.00	1.00- 12,00
DBL. OLD FASHION, 14 oz. 3¾" hi., 6 doz. per carton, approx. wgt. 50 lbs.	.80- 9.60	1.25- 15.00
SINGLE OLD FASHION, 9 oz. 3½" hi., 6 doz. per carton, approx. wgt. 36 lbs.	.80- 9.60	NOT AVAILABLE
ROLY POLY TUMBLER, 12 oz. 3⅝" hi., 6 doz. per carton, approx. wgt. 33 lbs.	.80- 9.60	1.25- 15.00
GOBLET, 13 oz. 5½" hi., 6 doz. per carton, approx. wgt. 44 lbs.	1.35-16.20	2.00- 24.00
SHERBET 3¾" dia., 6 doz. per carton, approx. wgt. 32 lbs.	1.35-16.20	2.00- 24.00
PARFAIT, 7 oz. 5" hi., 6 doz. per carton, approx. wgt. 36 lbs.	1.35-16.20	2.00- 24.00
DESSERT-CEREAL BOWL 5¼" dia., 4 doz. per carton, approx. wgt. 28 lbs.	1.00-12.00	1.50- 18.00
SALAD PLATE 8½" Dia. 2 doz. per carton, approx. wgt. 37 lbs.	2 00-24.00	NOT AVAILABLE
PITCHER, 32 oz. 1 only per carton, approx. wgt. 3 lbs.	4.50-54.00	NOT AVAILABLE
PITCHER, 65 oz. 1 only per carton, approx. wgt. 4 lbs.	5.50-66.00	10.00-120.00
FLOWERLITE 5" dia., 1 only per carton, approx. wgt. 2 lbs.	3.00-36.00	NOT AVAILABLE

ICE TEA · HI BALL · DOUBLE OLD FASHION · JUICE · PITCHER 32 oz. · TABLE TUMBLER · COCKTAIL · FLOWERLITE

Page 24. $8-12 each

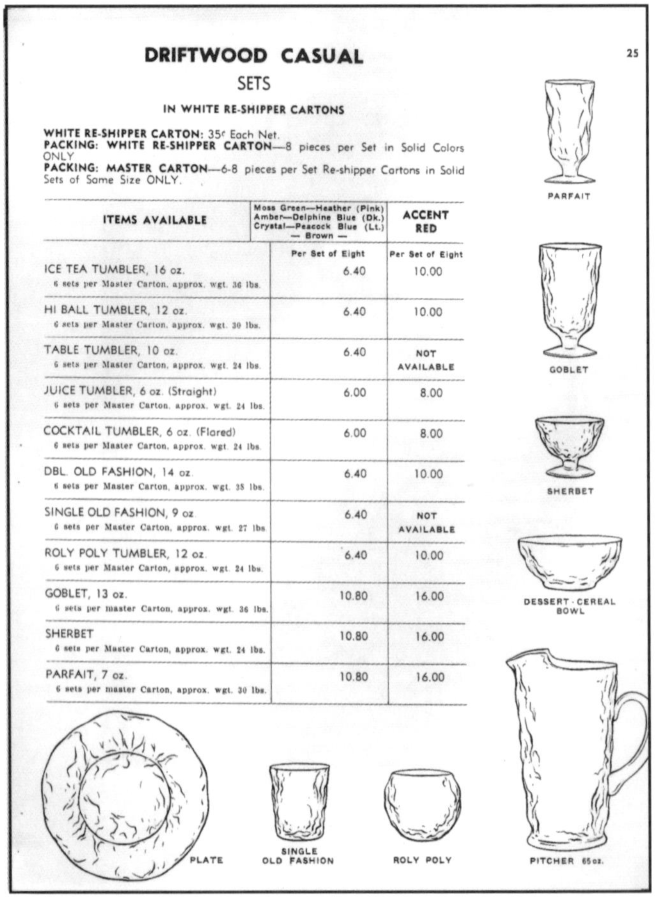

DRIFTWOOD CASUAL

SETS

IN WHITE RE-SHIPPER CARTONS

WHITE RE-SHIPPER CARTON: 35¢ Each Net.
PACKING: WHITE RE-SHIPPER CARTON—8 pieces per Set in Solid Colors ONLY
PACKING: MASTER CARTON—6-8 pieces per Set Re-shipper Cartons in Solid Sets of Same Size ONLY.

ITEMS AVAILABLE	Moss Green—Heather (Pink) Amber—Delphine Blue (Dk.) Crystal—Peacock Blue (Lt.) — Brown —	ACCENT RED
	Per Set of Eight	Per Set of Eight
ICE TEA TUMBLER, 16 oz. 6 sets per Master Carton, approx. wgt. 36 lbs.	6.40	10.00
HI BALL TUMBLER, 12 oz. 6 sets per Master Carton, approx. wgt. 30 lbs.	6.40	10.00
TABLE TUMBLER, 10 oz. 6 sets per Master Carton, approx. wgt. 24 lbs.	6.40	NOT AVAILABLE
JUICE TUMBLER, 6 oz. (Straight) 6 sets per Master Carton, approx. wgt. 24 lbs.	6.00	8.00
COCKTAIL TUMBLER, 6 oz. (Flared) 6 sets per Master Carton, approx. wgt. 24 lbs.	6.00	8.00
DBL. OLD FASHION, 14 oz. 6 sets per Master Carton, approx. wgt. 35 lbs.	6.40	10.00
SINGLE OLD FASHION, 9 oz 6 sets per Master Carton, approx. wgt. 27 lbs	6.40	NOT AVAILABLE
ROLY POLY TUMBLER, 12 oz. 6 sets per Master Carton, approx. wgt. 24 lbs.	6.40	10.00
GOBLET, 13 oz. 6 sets per master Carton, approx. wgt. 36 lbs.	10.80	16.00
SHERBET 6 sets per Master Carton, approx. wgt. 24 lbs.	10.80	16.00
PARFAIT, 7 oz. 6 sets per master Carton, approx. wgt. 30 lbs.	10.80	16.00

PARFAIT · GOBLET · SHERBET · DESSERT-CEREAL BOWL · PLATE · SINGLE OLD FASHION · ROLY POLY · PITCHER 65 oz.

Page 25. $10-15 each

1968 Catalog

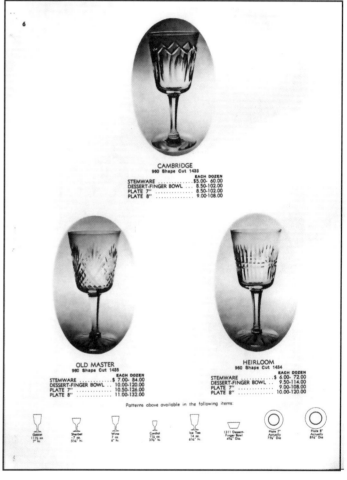

Page 5.

$15-20 each

Page 6.

$15-25 each

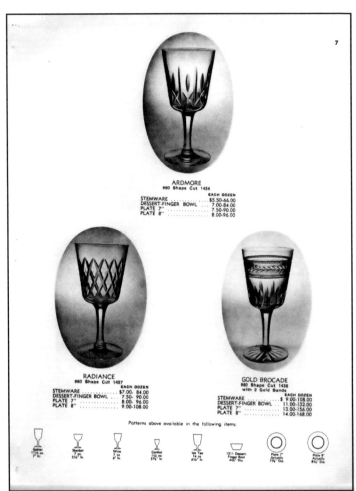

7

ARDMORE
960 Shape Cut 1436

	EACH	DOZEN
STEMWARE	$5.50	66.00
DESSERT-FINGER BOWL	7.00	84.00
PLATE 7"	7.50	90.00
PLATE 8"	8.00	96.00

RADIANCE
960 Shape Cut 1437

	EACH	DOZEN
STEMWARE	$7.00	84.00
DESSERT-FINGER BOWL	7.50	90.00
PLATE 7"	8.00	96.00
PLATE 8"	9.00	108.00

GOLD BROCADE
960 Shape Cut 1438
with 2 Gold Bands

	EACH	DOZEN
STEMWARE	$9.00	108.00
DESSERT-FINGER BOWL	11.00	132.00
PLATE 7"	13.00	156.00
PLATE 8"	14.00	168.00

Patterns above available in the following items.

Page 7.

$15-20 each

8

KIMBERLY
1966 Shape Cut 1430

	EACH	DOZEN
STEMWARE	$3.75	45.00
DESSERT-FINGER BOWL	9.50	114.00
PLATE 7"	8.50	102.00
PLATE 8"	9.00	108.00

LAVALIER
1966 Shape Cut 1431

	EACH	DOZEN
STEMWARE	$4.25	51.00
DESSERT-FINGER BOWL	6.50	78.00
PLATE 7"	7.00	84.00
PLATE 8"	7.50	90.00

BRIDAL TIARA
1966 Shape Cut 1439

	EACH	DOZEN
STEMWARE	$4.00	48.00
DESSERT-FINGER BOWL	5.50	66.00
PLATE 7"	6.00	72.00
PLATE 8"	6.50	78.00

TRADITIONAL
1966 Shape Cut 1432

	EACH	DOZEN
STEMWARE	$5.25	63.00
DESSERT-FINGER BOWL	9.00	108.00
PLATE 7"	9.50	114.00
PLATE 8"	10.50	126.00

ARISTOCRAT
1966 Shape Cut 43

	EACH	DOZEN
STEMWARE	$4.00	48.00
DESSERT-FINGER BOWL	6.00	72.00
PLATE 7"	6.50	78.00
PLATE 8"	7.50	90.00

Patterns above available in the following items:

Page 8.

$15-20 each

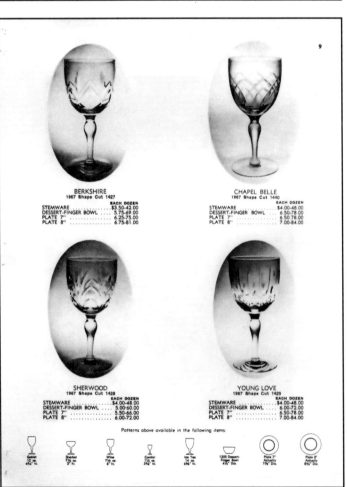

9

BERKSHIRE
1967 Shape Cut 1427

	EACH	DOZEN
STEMWARE	$3.50	42.00
DESSERT-FINGER BOWL	5.75	69.00
PLATE 7"	6.25	75.00
PLATE 8"	6.75	81.00

CHAPEL BELLE
1967 Shape Cut 1440

	EACH	DOZEN
STEMWARE	$4.00	48.00
DESSERT-FINGER BOWL	6.50	78.00
PLATE 7"	6.50	78.00
PLATE 8"	7.00	84.00

SHERWOOD
1967 Shape Cut 1428

	EACH	DOZEN
STEMWARE	$4.00	48.00
DESSERT-FINGER BOWL	5.00	60.00
PLATE 7"	5.50	66.00
PLATE 8"	6.00	72.00

YOUNG LOVE
1967 Shape Cut 1429

	EACH	DOZEN
STEMWARE	$4.00	48.00
DESSERT-FINGER BOWL	6.00	72.00
PLATE 7"	6.50	78.00
PLATE 8"	7.00	84.00

Patterns above available in the following items.

Page 9.

$15-20 each

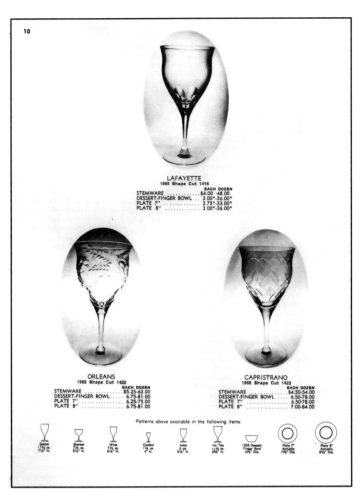

LAFAYETTE
1965 Shape Cut 1416

	EACH	DOZEN
STEMWARE	$4.00	48.00
DESSERT-FINGER BOWL	3.00	36.00*
PLATE 7"	2.75*	33.00*
PLATE 8"	3.00*	36.00*

ORLEANS
1965 Shape Cut 1422

	EACH	DOZEN
STEMWARE	$5.25	63.00
DESSERT-FINGER BOWL	6.75	81.00
PLATE 7"	6.25	75.00
PLATE 8"	6.75	81.00

CAPRISTRANO
1965 Shape Cut 1423

	EACH	DOZEN
STEMWARE	$4.50	54.00
DESSERT-FINGER BOWL	6.50	78.00
PLATE 7"	6.50	78.00
PLATE 8"	7.00	84.00

Patterns above available in the following items:

Goblet 11¾ oz. 7½" h. — Sherbet 7½ oz. 5½" h. — Wine 7½ oz. 6½" h. — Cordial 1½ oz. 4" h. — Juice 6 oz. 5½" h. — Ice Tea 13½ oz. 6½" h. — 1305 Dessert-Finger Bowl 4½" Dia. — Plate 7" Actually 7⅞" Dia. — Plate 8" Actually 8¾" Dia.

Page 10.

Lafayette: $10-15 each
Others: $15-25 each

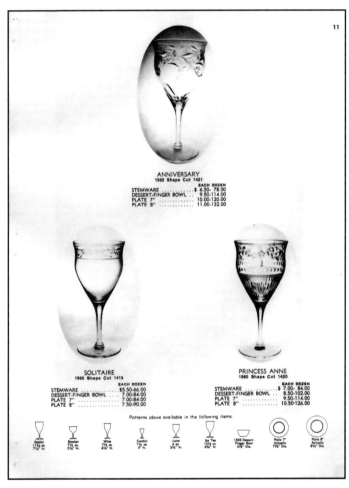

ANNIVERSARY
1965 Shape Cut 1421

	EACH	DOZEN
STEMWARE	$ 6.50	78.00
DESSERT-FINGER BOWL	9.50	114.00
PLATE 7"	10.00	120.00
PLATE 8"	11.00	132.00

SOLITAIRE
1965 Shape Cut 1419

	EACH	DOZEN
STEMWARE	$5.50	66.00
PLATE 7"	7.00	84.00
PLATE 8"	7.50	90.00

PRINCESS ANNE
1965 Shape Cut 1420

	EACH	DOZEN
STEMWARE	$ 7.00	84.00
DESSERT-FINGER BOWL	8.50	102.00
PLATE 7"	9.50	114.00
PLATE 8"	10.50	126.00

Patterns above available in the following items:

Goblet 11¾ oz. 7½" h. — Sherbet 7½ oz. 5½" h. — Wine 7½ oz. 6½" h. — Cordial 1½ oz. 4" h. — Juice 6 oz. 5½" h. — Ice Tea 13½ oz. 6½" h. — 1305 Dessert-Finger Bowl 4½" Dia. — Plate 7" Actually 7⅞" Dia. — Plate 8" Actually 8¾" Dia.

Page 11.

Solitaire: $15-25 each
Others: $25-35 each

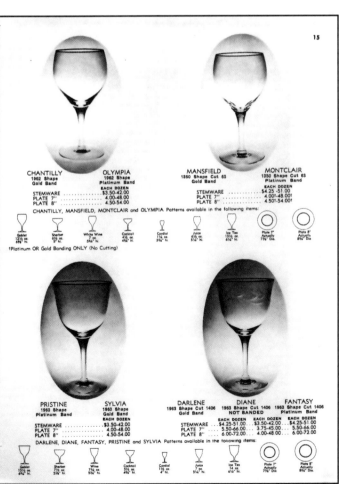

	CHANTILLY 1962 Shape Gold Band / OLYMPIA 1962 Shape Platinum Band		MANSFIELD 1350 Shape Cut 63 Gold Band / MONTCLAIR 1350 Shape Cut 63 Platinum Band	
	EACH	DOZEN	EACH	DOZEN
STEMWARE	$3.50	42.00	$4.25	51.00
PLATE 7"	4.00	48.00	4.00	48.00†
PLATE 8"	4.50	54.00	4.50	54.00†

CHANTILLY, MANSFIELD, MONTCLAIR and OLYMPIA Patterns available in the following items:

Goblet 12½ oz. 6⅝" h. — Sherbet 6½ oz. 5" h. — White Wine 4½ oz. 5½" h. — Cocktail 4½ oz. 4½" h. — Cordial 1½ oz. 3½" h. — Juice 6½ oz. 5½" h. — Ice Tea 13½ oz. 6½" h. — Plate 7" Actually 7⅞" Dia. — Plate 8" Actually 8¾" Dia.

†Platinum OR Gold Banding ONLY (No Cutting)

PRISTINE 1963 Shape Platinum Band / **SYLVIA** 1963 Shape Gold Band

	EACH	DOZEN
STEMWARE	$3.50	42.00
PLATE 7"	4.00	48.00
PLATE 8"	4.50	54.00

	DARLENE 1963 Shape Cut 1406		DIANE 1963 Shape Cut 1406 NOT BANDED		FANTASY 1963 Shape Cut 1406 Platinum Band	
	EACH	DOZEN	EACH	DOZEN	EACH	DOZEN
STEMWARE	$4.25	51.00	$3.50	42.00	$4.25	51.00
PLATE 7"	5.50	66.00	3.75	45.00	5.50	66.00
PLATE 8"	6.00	72.00	4.00	48.00	6.00	72.00

DARLENE, DIANE, FANTASY, PRISTINE and SYLVIA Patterns available in the following items:

Goblet 13½ oz. 6½" h. — Sherbet 7½ oz. 5½" h. — Wine 7½ oz. 5½" h. — Cocktail 4½ oz. 4½" h. — Cordial 1½ oz. 4" h. — Juice 7 oz. 5¼" h. — Ice Tea 14 oz. 6½" h. — Plate 7" Actually 7⅞" Dia. — Plate 8" Actually 8¾" Dia.

Page 15.

$10-15 each

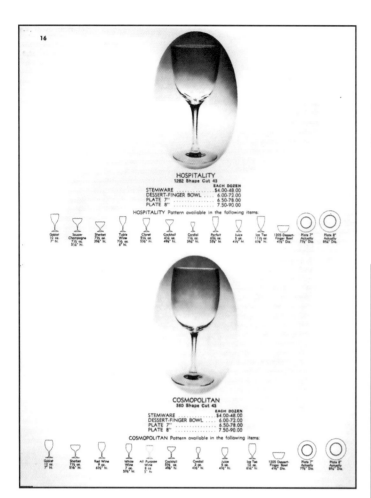

HOSPITALITY
1282 Shape Cut 43

STEMWARE	EACH	DOZEN
STEMWARE	$4.00	48.00
DESSERT-FINGER BOWL	6.00	72.00
PLATE 7"	6.50	78.00
PLATE 8"	7.50	90.00

HOSPITALITY Pattern available in the following items:

COSMOPOLITAN
360 Shape Cut 43

STEMWARE	EACH	DOZEN
STEMWARE	$4.00	48.00
DESSERT-FINGER BOWL	6.00	72.00
PLATE 7"	6.50	78.00
PLATE 8"	7.50	90.00

COSMOPOLITAN Pattern available in the following items:

Page 16.

$10-15 each

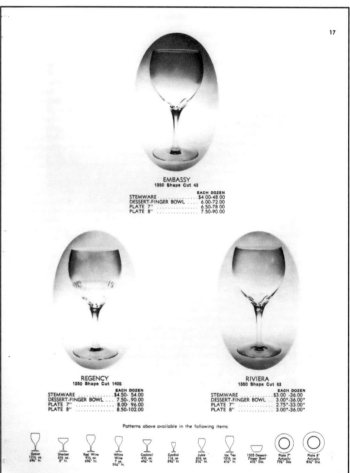

EMBASSY
1350 Shape Cut 43

STEMWARE	EACH	DOZEN
STEMWARE	$4.00	48.00
DESSERT-FINGER BOWL	6.00	72.00
PLATE 7"	6.50	78.00
PLATE 8"	7.50	90.00

REGENCY
1350 Shape Cut 1403

STEMWARE	EACH	DOZEN
STEMWARE	$4.50	54.00
DESSERT-FINGER BOWL	7.50	90.00
PLATE 7"	8.00	96.00
PLATE 8"	8.50	102.00

RIVIERA
1350 Shape Cut 63

STEMWARE	EACH	DOZEN
STEMWARE	$3.00	36.00
DESSERT-FINGER BOWL	3.00	36.00
PLATE 7"	2.75	33.00
PLATE 8"	3.00	36.00

Patterns above available in the following items

Page 17.

$10-15 each

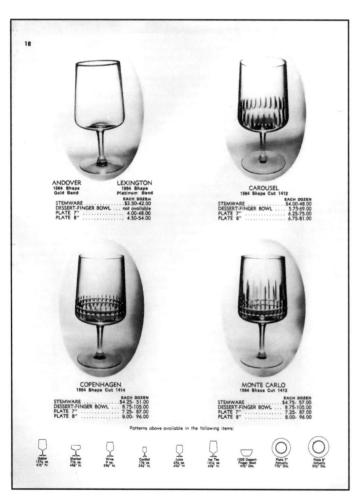

ANDOVER
1964 Shape
Gold Band

LEXINGTON
1964 Shape
Platinum Band

STEMWARE	EACH	DOZEN
STEMWARE	$3.50	42.00
DESSERT-FINGER BOWL	not available	
PLATE 7"	4.00	48.00
PLATE 8"	4.50	54.00

CAROUSEL
1964 Shape Cut 1412

STEMWARE	EACH	DOZEN
STEMWARE	$4.00	48.00
DESSERT-FINGER BOWL	5.75	69.00
PLATE 7"	6.25	75.00
PLATE 8"	6.75	81.00

COPENHAGEN
1964 Shape Cut 1414

STEMWARE	EACH	DOZEN
STEMWARE	$4.25	51.00
DESSERT-FINGER BOWL	8.75	105.00
PLATE 7"	7.25	87.00
PLATE 8"	8.00	96.00

MONTE CARLO
1964 Shape Cut 1413

STEMWARE	EACH	DOZEN
STEMWARE	$4.75	57.00
DESSERT-FINGER BOWL	8.75	105.00
PLATE 7"	7.25	87.00
PLATE 8"	8.00	96.00

Patterns above available in the following items:

Page 18.

$8-15 each

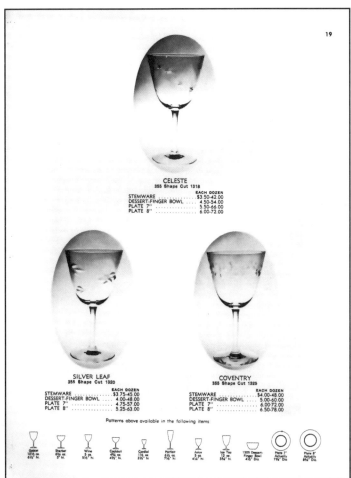

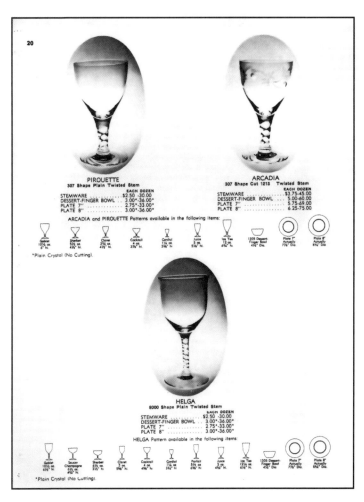

19

CELESTE
355 Shape Cut 1318

	EACH	DOZEN
STEMWARE	$3.50	42.00
DESSERT-FINGER BOWL	4.50	54.00
PLATE 7"	5.50	66.00
PLATE 8"	6.00	72.00

SILVER LEAF
355 Shape Cut 1320

	EACH	DOZEN
STEMWARE	$3.75	45.00
DESSERT-FINGER BOWL	4.00	48.00
PLATE 7"	4.75	57.00
PLATE 8"	5.25	63.00

COVENTRY
355 Shape Cut 1325

	EACH	DOZEN
STEMWARE	$4.00	48.00
DESSERT-FINGER BOWL	5.00	60.00
PLATE 7"	6.00	72.00
PLATE 8"	6.50	78.00

Patterns above available in the following items:

Page 19.

$10-15 each

20

PIROUETTE
307 Shape Plain Twisted Stem

	EACH	DOZEN
STEMWARE	$2.50	30.00
DESSERT-FINGER BOWL	3.00*	36.00*
PLATE 7"	2.75*	33.00*
PLATE 8"	3.00*	36.00*

ARCADIA
307 Shape Cut 1213 Twisted Stem

	EACH	DOZEN
STEMWARE	$3.75	45.00
DESSERT-FINGER BOWL	5.00	60.00
PLATE 7"	5.75	69.00
PLATE 8"	6.25	75.00

ARCADIA and PIROUETTE Patterns available in the following items:

*Plain Crystal (No Cutting).

HELGA
8000 Shape Plain Twisted Stem

	EACH	DOZEN
STEMWARE	$2.50	30.00
DESSERT-FINGER BOWL	3.00*	36.00*
PLATE 7"	2.75*	33.00*
PLATE 8"	3.00*	36.00*

HELGA Pattern available in the following items:

*Plain Crystal (No Cutting).

Page 20.

$10-15 each

21

LAUREL
912 Shape Cut 121 & 39

	EACH	DOZEN
STEMWARE	$5.75	69.00
DESSERT-FINGER BOWL	5.75	69.00
PLATE 7"	6.00	72.00
PLATE 8"	6.50	78.00

RAMONA
912 Shape Cut 1006

	EACH	DOZEN
STEMWARE	$5.00	60.00
DESSERT-FINGER BOWL	5.50	66.00
PLATE 7"	6.00	72.00
PLATE 8"	6.25	75.00

DOLLY MADISON — JANE EYRE
912 Shape Cut 139

	EACH	DOZEN
STEMWARE	$4.50	54.00
DESSERT-FINGER BOWL	6.00	72.00
PLATE 7"	6.50	78.00
PLATE 8"	7.50	90.00

Patterns above available in the following items

Page 21.

$15-20 each

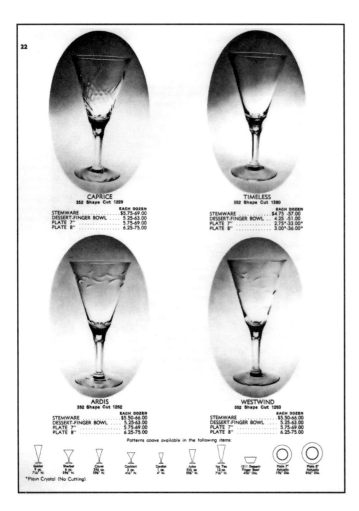

CAPRICE
352 Shape Cut 1229

STEMWARE	EACH	DOZEN
STEMWARE	$5.75	69.00
DESSERT-FINGER BOWL	5.25	63.00
PLATE 7"	5.75	69.00
PLATE 8"	6.25	75.00

TIMELESS
352 Shape Cut 1380

STEMWARE	EACH	DOZEN
STEMWARE	$4.75	57.00
DESSERT-FINGER BOWL	4.25	51.00
PLATE 7"	2.75*-	33.00*
PLATE 8"	3.00*-	36.00*

ARDIS
352 Shape Cut 1262

STEMWARE	EACH	DOZEN
STEMWARE	$5.50	66.00
DESSERT-FINGER BOWL	5.25	63.00
PLATE 7"	5.75	69.00
PLATE 8"	6.25	75.00

WESTWIND
352 Shape Cut 1263

STEMWARE	EACH	DOZEN
STEMWARE	$5.50	66.00
DESSERT-FINGER BOWL	5.25	63.00
PLATE 7"	5.75	69.00
PLATE 8"	6.25	75.00

Patterns above available in the following items:

*Plain Crystal (No Cutting).

Page 22.

$15-20 each

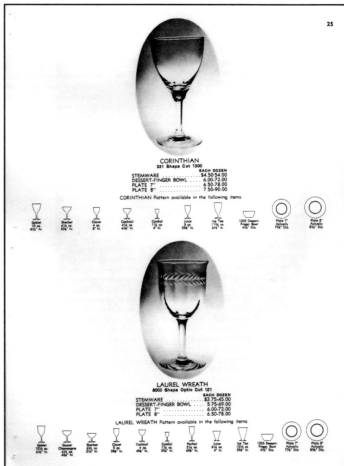

CORINTHIAN
331 Shape Cut 1300

STEMWARE	EACH	DOZEN
STEMWARE	$4.50	54.00
DESSERT-FINGER BOWL	6.00	72.00
PLATE 7"	6.50	78.00
PLATE 8"	7.50	90.00

CORINTHIAN Pattern available in the following items:

LAUREL WREATH
8000 Shape Optic Cut 121

STEMWARE	EACH	DOZEN
STEMWARE	$3.75	45.00
DESSERT-FINGER BOWL	5.75	69.00
PLATE 7"	6.00	72.00
PLATE 8"	6.50	78.00

LAUREL WREATH Pattern available in the following items:

Page 25.

$10-15 each

WOODSTOCK
578 Shape Cut 1370

STEMWARE	EACH	DOZEN
STEMWARE	$4.00	48.00
DESSERT-FINGER BOWL	4.75	57.00
PLATE 7"	5.00	60.00
PLATE 8"	5.50	66.00

WOODSTOCK Pattern Available in the Following Items:

SCROLL
3214 Shape Cut 1309

STEMWARE	EACH	DOZEN
STEMWARE	$5.25	63.00
DESSERT-FINGER BOWL	5.00	60.00
PLATE 7"	5.75	69.00
PLATE 8"	6.25	75.00

REGAL
3214 Shape Cut 1308

STEMWARE	EACH	DOZEN
STEMWARE	$5.25	63.00
DESSERT-FINGER BOWL	6.00	72.00
PLATE 7"	6.50	78.00
PLATE 8"	7.50	90.00

SCROLL and REGAL Pattern Available in the Following Items:

Page 26.

$15-20 each

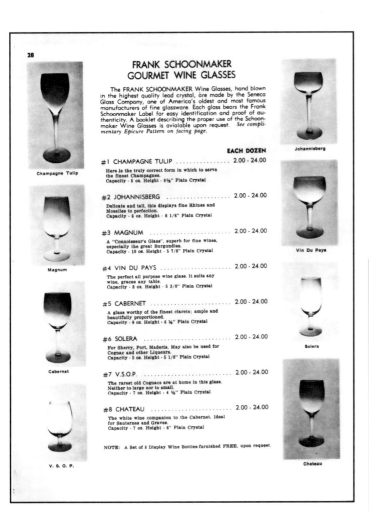

28

FRANK SCHOONMAKER
GOURMET WINE GLASSES

The FRANK SCHOONMAKER Wine Glasses, hand blown in the highest quality lead crystal, are made by the Seneca Glass Company, one of America's oldest and most famous manufacturers of fine glassware. Each glass bears the Frank Schoonmaker Label for easy identification and proof of authenticity. A booklet describing the proper use of the Schoonmaker Wine Glasses is available upon request. *See complimentary Epicure Pattern on facing page.*

	EACH	DOZEN

#1 CHAMPAGNE TULIP .... 2.00 - 24.00

Here is the truly correct form in which to serve the finest Champagnes.
Capacity - 8 oz. Height - 8½" Plain Crystal

#2 JOHANNISBERG .... 2.00 - 24.00

Delicate and tall, this displays fine Rhines and Moselles to perfection.
Capacity - 6 oz. Height - 6 1/8" Plain Crystal

#3 MAGNUM .... 2.00 - 24.00

A "Connoisseur's Glass", superb for fine wines, especially the great Burgundies.
Capacity - 10 oz. Height - 5 7/8" Plain Crystal

#4 VIN DU PAYS .... 2.00 - 24.00

The perfect all purpose wine glass. It suits any wine, graces any table.
Capacity - 8 oz. Height - 5 3/8" Plain Crystal

#5 CABERNET .... 2.00 - 24.00

A glass worthy of the finest clarets; ample and beautifully proportioned.
Capacity - 9 oz. Height - 6 ¼" Plain Crystal

#6 SOLERA .... 2.00 - 24.00

For Sherry, Port, Maderia. May also be used for Cognac and other Liqueurs.
Capacity - 5 oz. Height - 5 1/8" Plain Crystal

#7 V.S.O.P. .... 2.00 - 24.00

The rarest old Cognacs are at home in this glass. Neither to large nor to small.
Capacity - 7 oz. Height - 4 ¼" Plain Crystal

#8 CHATEAU .... 2.00 - 24.00

The white wine companion to the Cabernet. Ideal for Sauternes and Graves.
Capacity - 7 oz. Height - 6" Plain Crystal

NOTE: A Set of 8 Display Wine Bottles furnished FREE, upon request.

Champagne Tulip

Magnum

Cabernet

V. S. O. P.

Johannisberg

Vin Du Pays

Solera

Chateau

Page 28.

$8-12 each

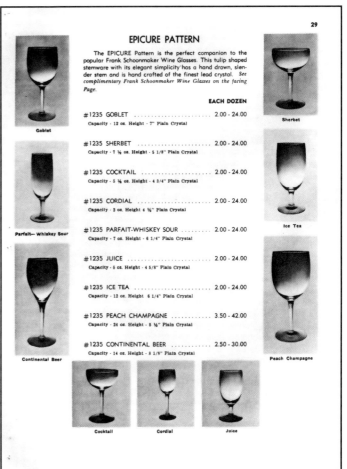

29

EPICURE PATTERN

The EPICURE Pattern is the perfect companion to the popular Frank Schoonmaker Wine Glasses. This tulip shaped stemware with its elegant simplicity has a hand drawn, slender stem and is hand crafted of the finest lead crystal. *See complimentary Frank Schoonmaker Wine Glasses on the facing Page.*

	EACH	DOZEN

#1235 GOBLET .... 2.00 - 24.00
Capacity - 12 oz. Height - 7" Plain Crystal

#1235 SHERBET .... 2.00 - 24.00
Capacity - 7 ¼ oz. Height - 5 1/8" Plain Crystal

#1235 COCKTAIL .... 2.00 - 24.00
Capacity - 5 ¼ oz. Height - 4 3/4" Plain Crystal

#1235 CORDIAL .... 2.00 - 24.00
Capacity - 2 oz. Height 4 ½" Plain Crystal

#1235 PARFAIT-WHISKEY SOUR .... 2.00 - 24.00
Capacity - 7 oz. Height - 6 1/4" Plain Crystal

#1235 JUICE .... 2.00 - 24.00
Capacity - 5 oz. Height - 4 5/8" Plain Crystal

#1235 ICE TEA .... 2.00 - 24.00
Capacity - 12 oz. Height 6 1/4" Plain Crystal

#1235 PEACH CHAMPAGNE .... 3.50 - 42.00
Capacity - 24 oz. Height - 8 ½" Plain Crystal

#1235 CONTINENTAL BEER .... 2.50 - 30.00
Capacity - 14 oz. Height - 8 1/8" Plain Crystal

Goblet

Parfait— Whiskey Sour

Continental Beer

Sherbet

Ice Tea

Peach Champagne

Cocktail

Cordial

Juice

Page 29.

$8-12 each

1969 Catalog

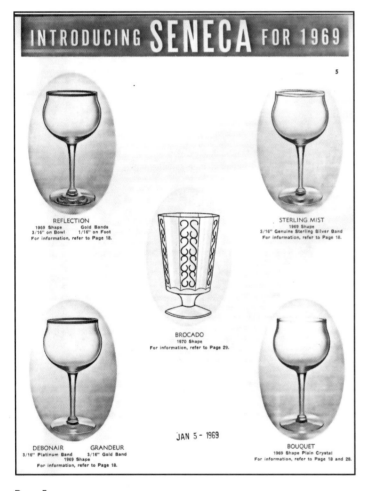

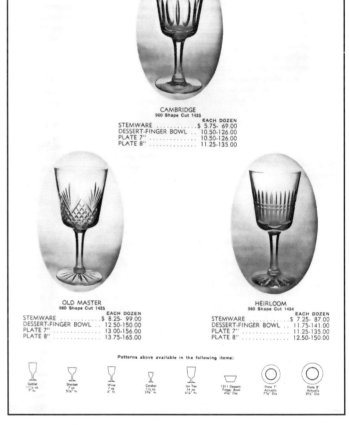

Page 5.

$10-15 each

Page 6.

$15-25 each

ARDMORE
960 Shape Cut 1436

	EACH	DOZEN
STEMWARE	$ 6.50-	78.00
DESSERT-FINGER BOWL	8.75-	105.00
PLATE 7"	9.50-	114.00
PLATE 8"	10.00-	120.00

JAN 5 - 1969

RADIANCE
960 Shape Cut 1437

	EACH	DOZEN
STEMWARE	$ 8.25-	99.00
DESSERT-FINGER BOWL	9.50-	114.00
PLATE 7"	10.00-	120.00
PLATE 8"	11.25-	135.00

GOLD BROCADE
960 Shape Cut 1438
with 2 Gold Bands

	EACH	DOZEN
STEMWARE	$10.50-	126.00
DESSERT-FINGER BOWL	13.75-	165.00
PLATE 7"	16.25-	195.00
PLATE 8"	17.50-	210.00

Patterns above available in the following items:

KIMBERLY
1966 Shape Cut 1430

	EACH	DOZEN
STEMWARE	$ 4.50-	54.00
DESSERT-FINGER BOWL	11.75-	141.00
PLATE 7"	10.50-	126.00
PLATE 8"	11.25-	135.00

BRIDAL TIARA
1966 Shape Cut 1439

	EACH	DOZEN
STEMWARE	$4.75-	57.00
DESSERT-FINGER BOWL	7.00-	84.00
PLATE 7"	7.50-	90.00
PLATE 8"	8.00-	96.00

LAVALIER
1966 Shape Cut 1431

	EACH	DOZEN
STEMWARE	$5.00-	60.00
DESSERT-FINGER BOWL	8.00-	96.00
PLATE 7"	8.75-	105.00
PLATE 8"	9.50-	114.00

Patterns above available in the following items:

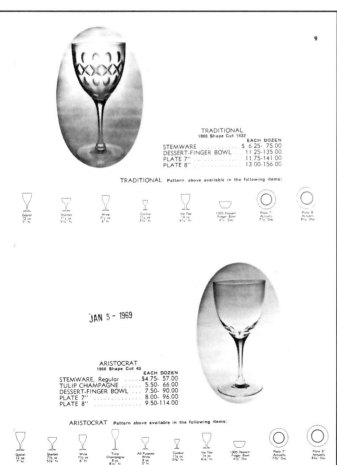

TRADITIONAL
1966 Shape Cut 1432

	EACH	DOZEN
STEMWARE	$ 6.25-	75.00
DESSERT-FINGER BOWL	11.25-	135.00
PLATE 7"	11.75-	141.00
PLATE 8"	13.00-	156.00

TRADITIONAL Pattern above available in the following items:

JAN 5 - 1969

ARISTOCRAT
1966 Shape Cut 43

	EACH	DOZEN
STEMWARE, Regular	$4.75-	57.00
TULIP CHAMPAGNE	5.50-	66.00
DESSERT-FINGER BOWL	7.50-	90.00
PLATE 7"	8.00-	96.00
PLATE 8"	9.50-	114.00

ARISTOCRAT Pattern above available in the following items:

Page 7.

Top: $15-25 each
Bottom row: $25-30 each

Page 8.

$15-20 each

Page 9.

Top: $20-25 each
Bottom: $15-20 each

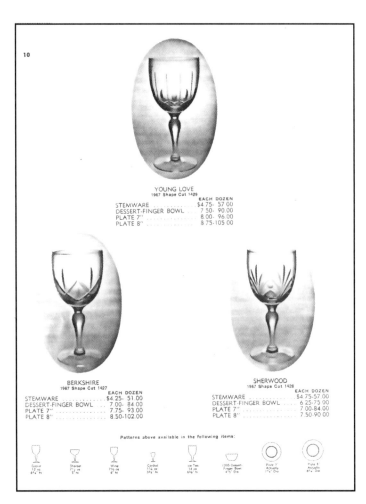

10

YOUNG LOVE
1967 Shape Cut 1429

	EACH	DOZEN
STEMWARE	$4.75-	57.00
DESSERT-FINGER BOWL	7.50-	90.00
PLATE 7"	8.00-	96.00
PLATE 8"	8.75-	105.00

BERKSHIRE
1967 Shape Cut 1427

	EACH	DOZEN
STEMWARE	$4.25-	51.00
DESSERT-FINGER BOWL	7.00-	84.00
PLATE 7"	7.75-	93.00
PLATE 8"	8.50-	102.00

SHERWOOD
1967 Shape Cut 1428

	EACH	DOZEN
STEMWARE	$4.75-	57.00
DESSERT-FINGER BOWL	6.25-	75.00
PLATE 7"	7.00-	84.00
PLATE 8"	7.50-	90.00

Patterns above available in the following items:

Goblet 12 oz 6¾" hi — Sherbet 7½ oz 5" hi — Wine 7½ oz 6" hi — Cordial 1¼ oz 3½" hi — Ice Tea 14 oz 6¾" hi — 1305 Dessert Finger Bowl 4½" Dia — Plate 7" Actually 7⅜" Dia — Plate 8" Actually 8⅜" Dia

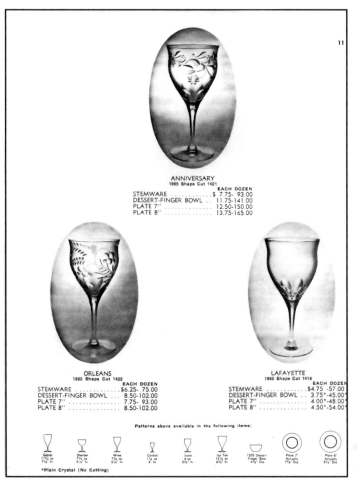

11

ANNIVERSARY
1965 Shape Cut 1421

	EACH	DOZEN
STEMWARE	$7.75-	93.00
DESSERT-FINGER BOWL	11.75-	141.00
PLATE 7"	12.50-	150.00
PLATE 8"	13.75-	165.00

ORLEANS
1965 Shape Cut 1422

	EACH	DOZEN
STEMWARE	$6.25-	75.00
DESSERT-FINGER BOWL	8.50-	102.00
PLATE 7"	7.75-	93.00
PLATE 8"	8.50-	102.00

LAFAYETTE
1965 Shape Cut 1416

	EACH	DOZEN
STEMWARE	$4.75-	57.00
DESSERT-FINGER BOWL	3.75*-	45.00
PLATE 7"	4.00*-	48.00
PLATE 8"	4.50*-	54.00

Patterns above available in the following items:

Goblet 11¾ oz 7½" hi — Sherbet 7½ oz 5¼" hi — Wine 7½ oz 6½" hi — Cordial 1¼ oz 4" hi — Juice 6 oz 5¼" hi — Ice Tea 13½ oz 6½" hi — 1305 Dessert Finger Bowl 4½" Dia — Plate 7" Actually 7⅜" Dia — Plate 8" Actually 8⅜" Dia

*Plain Crystal (No Cutting)

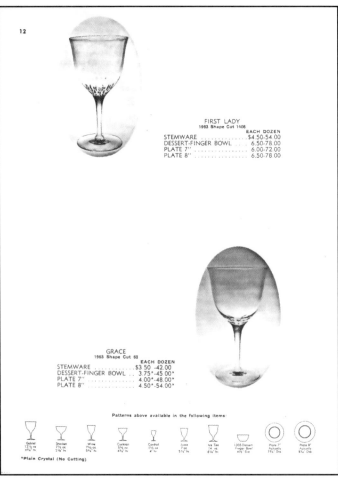

12

FIRST LADY
1963 Shape Cut 1408

	EACH	DOZEN
STEMWARE	$4.50-	54.00
DESSERT-FINGER BOWL	6.50-	78.00
PLATE 7"	6.00-	72.00
PLATE 8"	6.50-	78.00

GRACE
1963 Shape Cut 63

	EACH	DOZEN
STEMWARE	$3.50-	42.00
DESSERT-FINGER BOWL	3.75*-	45.00*
PLATE 7"	4.00*-	48.00*
PLATE 8"	4.50*-	54.00*

Patterns above available in the following items:

Goblet 13½ oz 6¾" hi — Sherbet 7½ oz 5" hi — Wine 7½ oz 5½" hi — Cocktail 5½ oz 4½" hi — Cordial 1½ oz 4" hi — Juice 7 oz 5" hi — Ice Tea 14 oz 6½" hi — 1305 Dessert Finger Bowl 4½" Dia — Plate 7" Actually 7⅜" Dia — Plate 8" Actually 8⅜" Dia

*Plain Crystal (No Cutting)

Page 10.

$15-20 each

Page 11.

Lafayette: $15-20 each
Others: $25-35 each

Page 12.

Top: $15-20 each
Bottom: $10-15 each

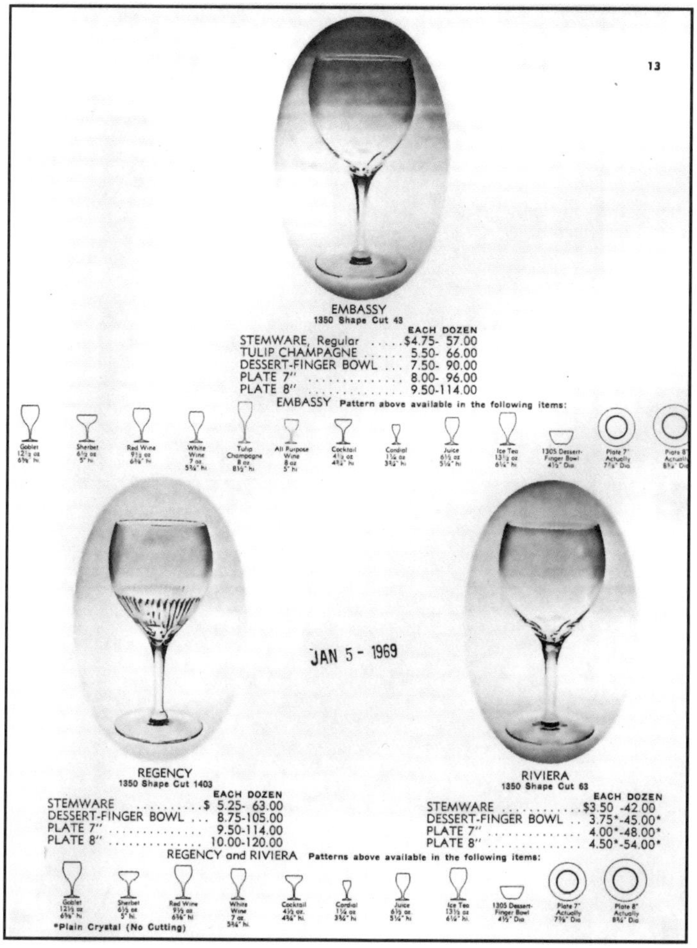

13

EMBASSY
1350 Shape Cut 43

	EACH	DOZEN
STEMWARE, Regular	$4.75-	57.00
TULIP CHAMPAGNE	5.50-	66.00
DESSERT-FINGER BOWL	7.50-	90.00
PLATE 7"	8.00-	96.00
PLATE 8"	9.50-	114.00

EMBASSY Pattern above available in the following items:

Goblet 12½ oz 6⅝" ht · Sherbet 6½ oz 5" ht · Red Wine 9½ oz 6⅝" ht · White Wine 7 oz 5¾" ht · Tulip Champagne 8 oz 8½" ht · All Purpose Wine 8 oz 5" ht · Cocktail 4½ oz 4¾" ht · Cordial 1¼ oz 3¾" ht · Juice 6½ oz 5¼" ht · Ice Tea 13½ oz 6¼" ht · 1305 Dessert-Finger Bowl 4½" Dia · Plate 7" Actually 7⅞" Dia · Plate 8" Actually 8¾" Dia

JAN 5 - 1969

REGENCY
1350 Shape Cut 1403

	EACH	DOZEN
STEMWARE	$ 5.25-	63.00
DESSERT-FINGER BOWL	8.75-	105.00
PLATE 7"	9.50-	114.00
PLATE 8"	10.00-	120.00

RIVIERA
1350 Shape Cut 63

	EACH	DOZEN
STEMWARE	$3.50	-42.00
DESSERT-FINGER BOWL	3.75*	-45.00*
PLATE 7"	4.00*	-48.00*
PLATE 8"	4.50*	-54.00*

REGENCY and RIVIERA Patterns above available in the following items:

Goblet 12½ oz 6⅝" ht · Sherbet 6½ oz 5" ht · Red Wine 9½ oz 6⅝" ht · White Wine 7 oz 5¾" ht · Cocktail 4½ oz 4¾" ht · Cordial 1¼ oz 3¾" ht · Juice 6½ oz 5¼" ht · Ice Tea 13½ oz 6½" ht · 1305 Dessert-Finger Bowl 4½" Dia · Plate 7" Actually 7⅞" Dia · Plate 8" Actually 8¾" Dia

*Plain Crystal (No Cutting)

Page 13.

$15-20 each

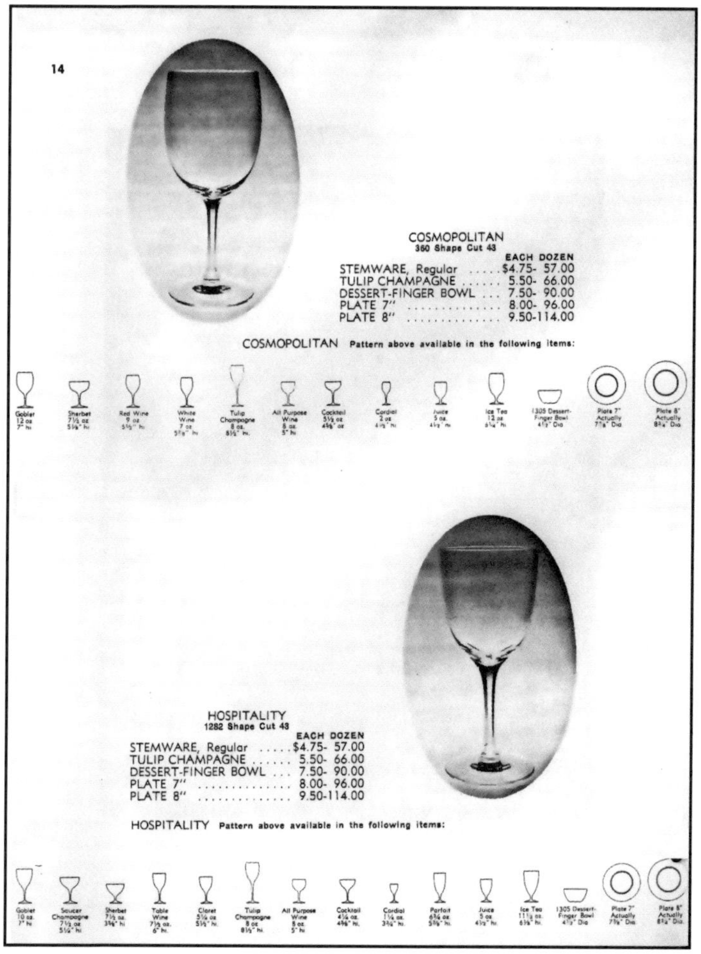

14

COSMOPOLITAN
350 Shape Cut 43

	EACH	DOZEN
STEMWARE, Regular	$4.75-	57.00
TULIP CHAMPAGNE	5.50-	66.00
DESSERT-FINGER BOWL	7.50-	90.00
PLATE 7"	8.00-	96.00
PLATE 8"	9.50-	114.00

COSMOPOLITAN Pattern above available in the following items:

Goblet 12 oz 7" ht · Sherbet 7½ oz 5⅛" ht · Red Wine 9 oz 5½" ht · White Wine 7 oz 5⅞" ht · Tulip Champagne 8 oz 8½" ht · All Purpose Wine 8 oz 5" ht · Cocktail 5½ oz 4⅝" oz · Cordial 2 oz 4½" ht · Juice 5 oz 4½" ht · Ice Tea 12 oz 6¼" ht · 1305 Dessert-Finger Bowl 4½" Dia · Plate 7" Actually 7⅞" Dia · Plate 8" Actually 8¾" Dia

HOSPITALITY
1282 Shape Cut 43

	EACH	DOZEN
STEMWARE, Regular	$4.75-	57.00
TULIP CHAMPAGNE	5.50-	66.00
DESSERT-FINGER BOWL	7.50-	90.00
PLATE 7"	8.00-	96.00
PLATE 8"	9.50-	114.00

HOSPITALITY Pattern above available in the following items:

Goblet 10 oz 7" ht · Saucer Champagne 7½ oz 5¼" ht · Sherbet 7½ oz 3⅝" ht · Table Wine 7½ oz 6" ht · Claret 5¼ oz 5½" ht · Tulip Champagne 8 oz 8½" ht · All Purpose Wine 8 oz 5" ht · Cocktail 4¼ oz 4⅝" ht · Cordial 1¼ oz 3¾" ht · Parfait 6¾ oz 5⅝" ht · Juice 5 oz 4½" ht · Ice Tea 11½ oz 6⅛" ht · 1305 Dessert-Finger Bowl 4½" Dia · Plate 7" Actually 7⅞" Dia · Plate 8" Actually 8¾" Dia

Page 14.

$15-20 each

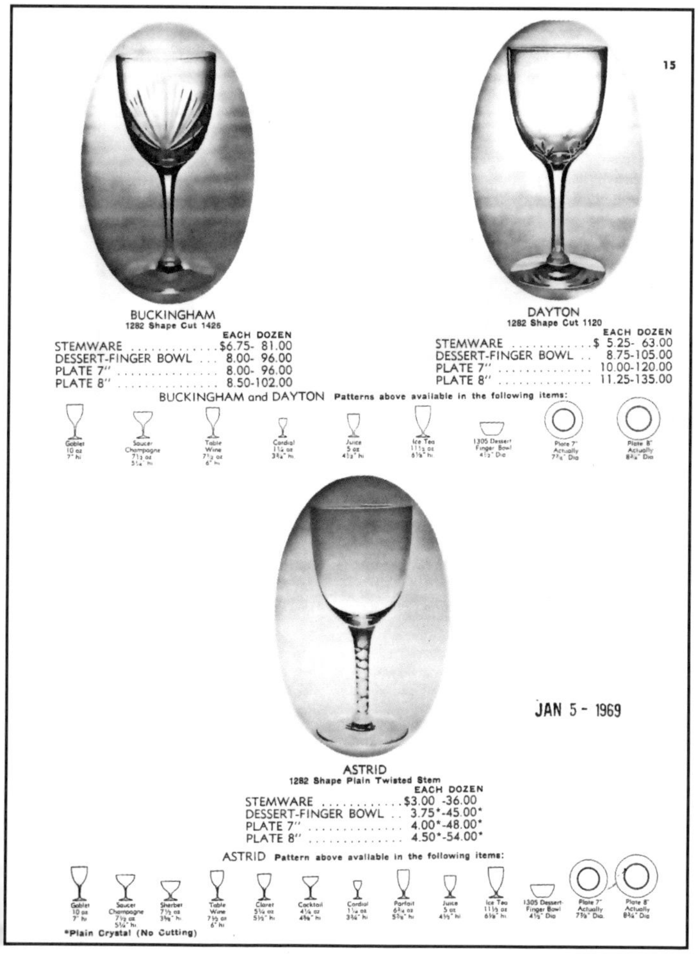

15

BUCKINGHAM
1282 Shape Cut 1426

	EACH	DOZEN
STEMWARE	$6.75-	81.00
DESSERT-FINGER BOWL	8.00-	96.00
PLATE 7"	8.00-	96.00
PLATE 8"	8.50-	102.00

DAYTON
1282 Shape Cut 1120

	EACH	DOZEN
STEMWARE	$ 5.25-	63.00
DESSERT-FINGER BOWL	8.75-	105.00
PLATE 7"	10.00-	120.00
PLATE 8"	11.25-	135.00

BUCKINGHAM and DAYTON Patterns above available in the following items:

Goblet 10 oz 7" ht · Saucer Champagne 7½ oz 5¼" ht · Table Wine 7½ oz 6" ht · Cordial 1¼ oz 3¾" ht · Juice 5 oz 4½" ht · Ice Tea 11½ oz 6⅛" ht · 1305 Dessert Finger Bowl 4½" Dia · Plate 7" Actually 7⅞" Dia · Plate 8" Actually 8¾" Dia

JAN 5 - 1969

ASTRID
1282 Shape Plain Twisted Stem

	EACH	DOZEN
STEMWARE	$3.00	-36.00
DESSERT-FINGER BOWL	3.75*	-45.00*
PLATE 7"	4.00*	-48.00*
PLATE 8"	4.50*	-54.00*

ASTRID Pattern above available in the following items:

Goblet 10 oz 7" ht · Saucer Champagne 7½ oz 5¼" ht · Sherbet 7½ oz 3⅝" ht · Table Wine 7½ oz 6" ht · Claret 5¼ oz 5½" ht · Cocktail 4¼ oz 4⅝" ht · Cordial 1¼ oz 3¾" ht · Parfait 6¾ oz 5⅝" ht · Juice 5 oz 4½" ht · Ice Tea 11½ oz 6⅛" ht · 1305 Dessert-Finger Bowl 4½" Dia · Plate 7" Actually 7⅞" Dia · Plate 8" Actually 8¾" Dia

*Plain Crystal (No Cutting)

Page 15.

Top: $15-20 each
Bottom: $10-15 each

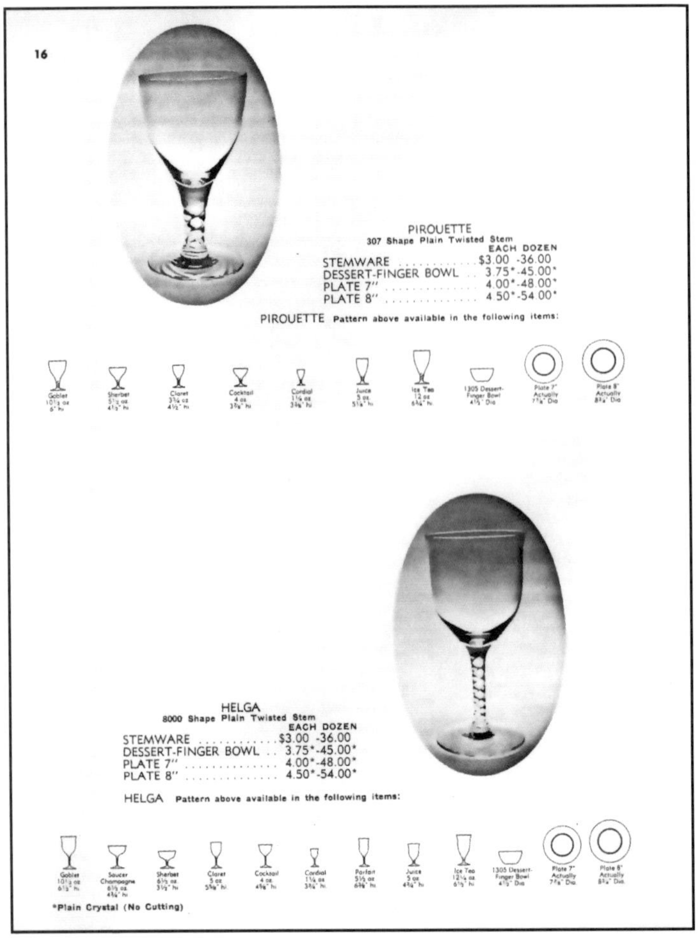

16

PIROUETTE
307 Shape Plain Twisted Stem

	EACH DOZEN
STEMWARE	$3.00 -36.00
DESSERT-FINGER BOWL	3.75*-45.00*
PLATE 7"	4.00*-48.00*
PLATE 8"	4.50*-54.00*

PIROUETTE Pattern above available in the following items:

Goblet 10½ oz 6" hi · Sherbet 5½ oz 4½" hi · Claret 3¾ oz 4½" hi · Cocktail 4 oz 3⅞" hi · Cordial 1¼ oz 3⅝" hi · Juice 5 oz 5⅛" hi · Ice Tea 12 oz 6¾" hi · 1305 Dessert-Finger Bowl 4½" Dia · Plate 7" Actually 7⅞" Dia · Plate 8" Actually 8¾" Dia

HELGA
8000 Shape Plain Twisted Stem

	EACH DOZEN
STEMWARE	$3.00 -36.00
DESSERT-FINGER BOWL	3.75*-45.00*
PLATE 7"	4.00*-48.00*
PLATE 8"	4.50*-54.00*

HELGA Pattern above available in the following items:

Goblet 10½ oz 6½" hi · Saucer Champagne 6½ oz 4¾" hi · Sherbet 6½ oz 3½" hi · Claret 5 oz 5⅝" hi · Cocktail 4 oz 4⅝" hi · Cordial 1¼ oz 3¾" hi · Parfait 5½ oz 6⅝" hi · Juice 5 oz 4¾" hi · Ice Tea 12¼ oz 6½" hi · 1305 Dessert-Finger Bowl 4½" Dia · Plate 7" Actually 7⅞" Dia · Plate 8" Actually 8¾" Dia

*Plain Crystal (No Cutting)

Page 16.

$10-15 each

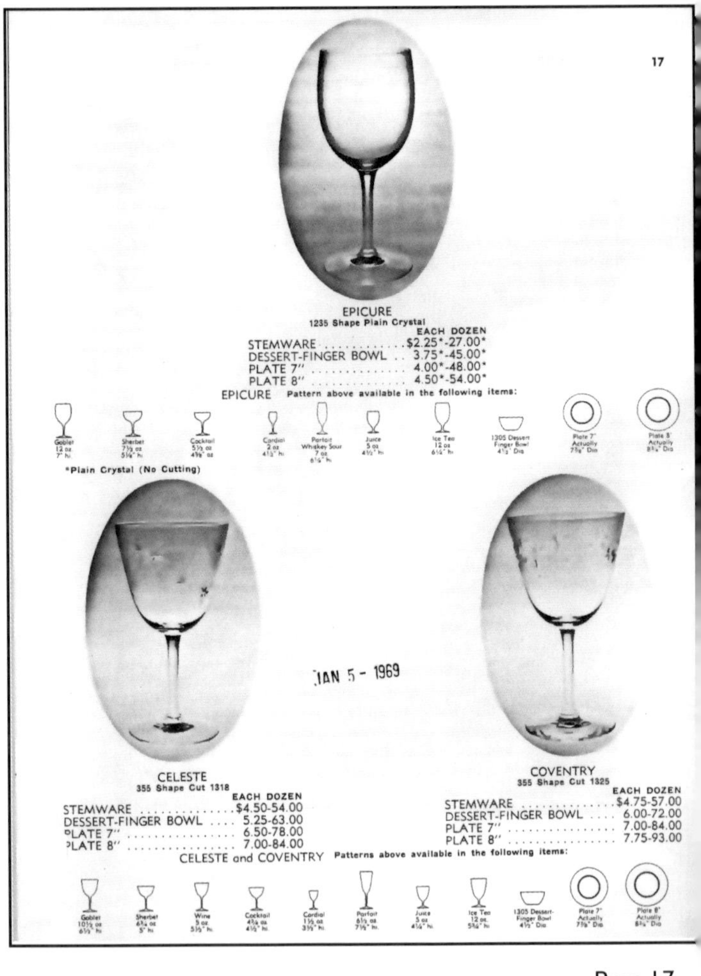

17

EPICURE
1235 Shape Plain Crystal

	EACH DOZEN
STEMWARE	$2.25*-27.00*
DESSERT-FINGER BOWL	3.75*-45.00*
PLATE 7"	4.00*-48.00*
PLATE 8"	4.50*-54.00*

EPICURE Pattern above available in the following items:

Goblet 12 oz 7" hi · Sherbet 7½ oz 5⅛" hi · Cocktail 5½ oz 4⅝" oz · Cordial 2 oz 4½" hi · Parfait Whiskey Sour 7 oz 6¼" hi · Juice 5 oz 4½" hi · Ice Tea 12 oz 6½" hi · 1305 Dessert Finger Bowl 4½" Dia · Plate 7" Actually 7⅞" Dia · Plate 8" Actually 8¾" Dia

*Plain Crystal (No Cutting)

JAN 5 - 1969

CELESTE
355 Shape Cut 1318

	EACH DOZEN
STEMWARE	$4.50-54.00
DESSERT-FINGER BOWL	5.25-63.00
PLATE 7"	6.50-78.00
PLATE 8"	7.00-84.00

COVENTRY
355 Shape Cut 1325

	EACH DOZEN
STEMWARE	$4.75-57.00
DESSERT-FINGER BOWL	6.00-72.00
PLATE 7"	7.00-84.00
PLATE 8"	7.75-93.00

CELESTE and COVENTRY Patterns above available in the following items:

Goblet 10½ oz 6½" hi · Sherbet 6¾ oz 5" hi · Wine 5 oz 5½" hi · Cocktail 4¾ oz 4½" hi · Cordial 1½ oz 3½" hi · Parfait 6½ oz 7½" hi · Juice 5 oz 4¼" hi · Ice Tea 12 oz 5¾" hi · 1305 Dessert-Finger Bowl 4½" Dia · Plate 7" Actually 7⅞" Dia · Plate 8" Actually 8¾" Dia

Page 17.

$8-12 each

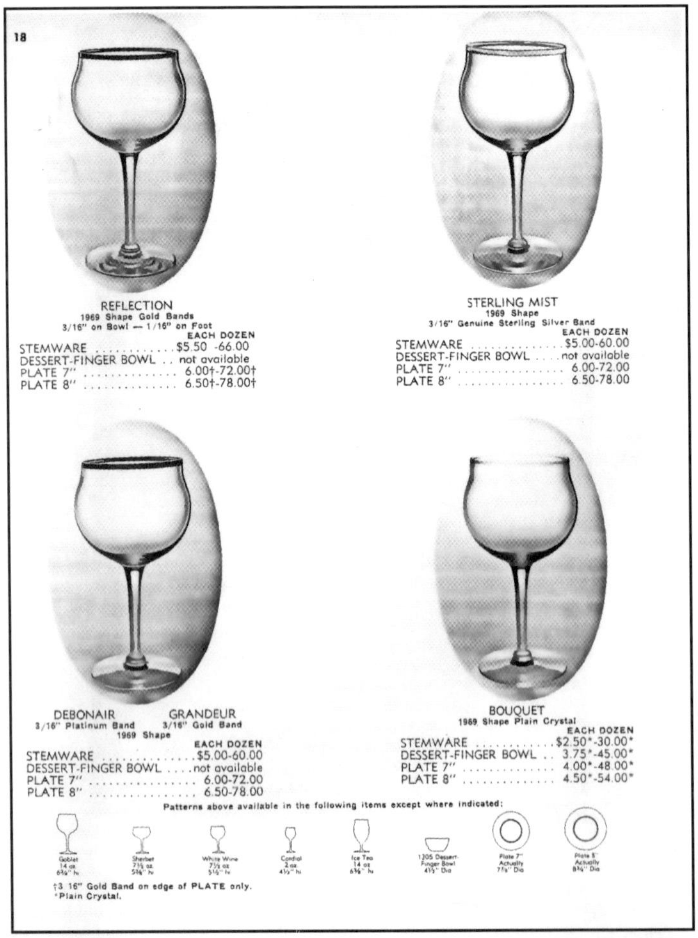

18

REFLECTION
1969 Shape Gold Bands
3/16" on Bowl — 1/16" on Foot

	EACH DOZEN
STEMWARE	$5.50 -66.00
DESSERT-FINGER BOWL	not available
PLATE 7"	6.00†-72.00†
PLATE 8"	6.50†-78.00†

STERLING MIST
1969 Shape
3/16" Genuine Sterling Silver Band

	EACH DOZEN
STEMWARE	$5.00-60.00
DESSERT-FINGER BOWL	not available
PLATE 7"	6.00-72.00
PLATE 8"	6.50-78.00

DEBONAIR — 3/16" Platinum Band
GRANDEUR — 3/16" Gold Band
1969 Shape

	EACH DOZEN
STEMWARE	$5.00-60.00
DESSERT-FINGER BOWL	not available
PLATE 7"	6.00-72.00
PLATE 8"	6.50-78.00

BOUQUET
1969 Shape Plain Crystal

	EACH DOZEN
STEMWARE	$2.50*-30.00*
DESSERT-FINGER BOWL	3.75*-45.00*
PLATE 7"	4.00*-48.00*
PLATE 8"	4.50*-54.00*

Patterns above available in the following items except where indicated:

Goblet 14 oz 6¾" hi · Sherbet 7½ oz 5⅜" hi · White Wine 7½ oz 5½" hi · Cordial 2 oz 4½" hi · Ice Tea 14 oz 6⅜" hi · 1305 Dessert-Finger Bowl 4½" Dia · Plate 7" Actually 7⅞" Dia · Plate 8" Actually 8¾" Dia

†3 16" Gold Band on edge of PLATE only.
*Plain Crystal.

Page 18.

$10-15 each

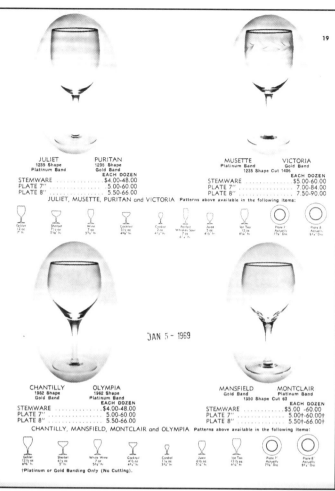

JULIET
1235 Shape
Platinum Band

PURITAN
1235 Shape
Gold Band

	EACH	DOZEN
STEMWARE	$4.00-48.00	
PLATE 7"	5.00-60.00	
PLATE 8"	5.50-66.00	

MUSETTE
Platinum Band

VICTORIA
Gold Band
1235 Shape Cut 1406

	EACH	DOZEN
STEMWARE	$5.00-60.00	
PLATE 7"	7.00-84.00	
PLATE 8"	7.50-90.00	

JULIET, MUSETTE, PURITAN and VICTORIA   Patterns above available in the following items:

JAN 5 - 1969

CHANTILLY
1962 Shape
Gold Band

OLYMPIA
1962 Shape
Platinum Band

	EACH	DOZEN
STEMWARE	$4.00-48.00	
PLATE 7"	5.00-60.00	
PLATE 8"	5.50-66.00	

MANSFIELD
Gold Band

MONTCLAIR
Platinum Band
1350 Shape Cut 63

	EACH	DOZEN
STEMWARE	$5.00 -60.00	
PLATE 7"	5.00†-60.00†	
PLATE 8"	5.50†-66.00†	

CHANTILLY, MANSFIELD, MONTCLAIR and OLYMPIA   Patterns above available in the following items:

†Platinum or Gold Banding Only (No Cutting).

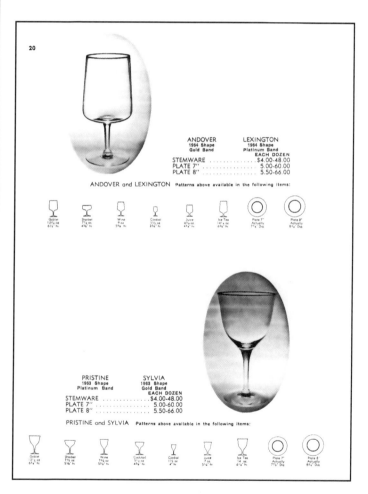

ANDOVER
1964 Shape
Gold Band

LEXINGTON
1964 Shape
Platinum Band

	EACH	DOZEN
STEMWARE	$4.00-48.00	
PLATE 7"	5.00-60.00	
PLATE 8"	5.50-66.00	

ANDOVER and LEXINGTON   Patterns above available in the following items:

PRISTINE
1963 Shape
Platinum Band

SYLVIA
1963 Shape
Gold Band

	EACH	DOZEN
STEMWARE	$4.00-48.00	
PLATE 7"	5.00-60.00	
PLATE 8"	5.50-66.00	

PRISTINE and SYLVIA   Patterns above available in the following items:

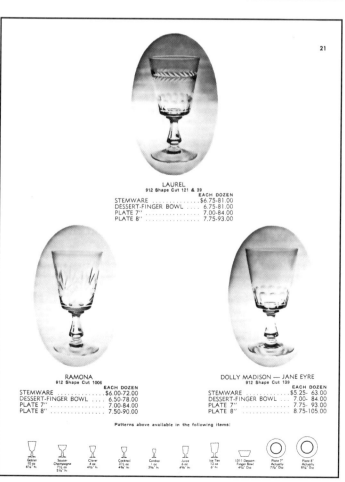

LAUREL
912 Shape Cut 121 & 39

	EACH	DOZEN
STEMWARE	$6.75-81.00	
DESSERT-FINGER BOWL	6.75-81.00	
PLATE 7"	7.00-84.00	
PLATE 8"	7.75-93.00	

RAMONA
912 Shape Cut 1006

	EACH	DOZEN
STEMWARE	$6.00-72.00	
DESSERT-FINGER BOWL	6.50-78.00	
PLATE 7"	7.00-84.00	
PLATE 8"	7.50-90.00	

DOLLY MADISON — JANE EYRE
912 Shape Cut 139

	EACH	DOZEN
STEMWARE	$5 25- 63.00	
DESSERT-FINGER BOWL	7.00- 84.00	
PLATE 7"	7.75- 93.00	
PLATE 8"	8.75-105.00	

Patterns above available in the following items:

Page 19.

$10-15 each

Page 20.

$10-15 each

Page 21.

$15-20 each

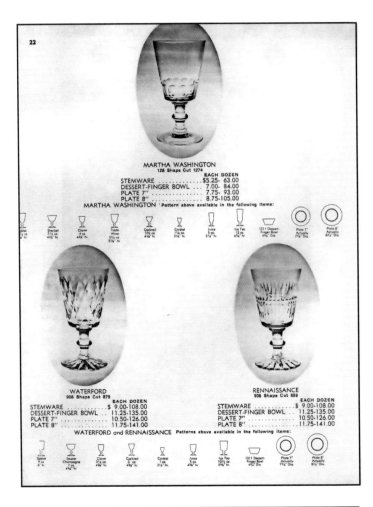

22

MARTHA WASHINGTON
128 Shape Cut 1274

	EACH	DOZEN
STEMWARE	$5.25-	63.00
DESSERT-FINGER BOWL	7.00-	84.00
PLATE 7"	7.75-	93.00
PLATE 8"	8.75-	105.00

MARTHA WASHINGTON Pattern above available in the following items:

WATERFORD
908 Shape Cut 879

	EACH	DOZEN
STEMWARE	$ 9.00-	108.00
DESSERT-FINGER BOWL	11.25-	135.00
PLATE 7"	10.50-	126.00
PLATE 8"	11.75-	141.00

RENNAISSANCE
908 Shape Cut 859

	EACH	DOZEN
STEMWARE	$ 9.00-	108.00
DESSERT-FINGER BOWL	11.25-	135.00
PLATE 7"	10.50-	126.00
PLATE 8"	11.75-	141.00

WATERFORD and RENNAISSANCE Patterns above available in the following items:

Page 22.

Top: $15-20 each
Bottom row: $20-30 each

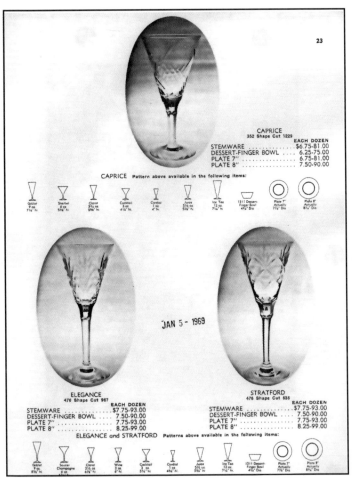

23

CAPRICE
352 Shape Cut 1229

	EACH	DOZEN
STEMWARE	$6.75-	81.00
DESSERT-FINGER BOWL	6.25-	75.00
PLATE 7"	6.75-	81.00
PLATE 8"	7.50-	90.00

CAPRICE Pattern above available in the following items:

JAN 5 - 1969

ELEGANCE
476 Shape Cut 967

	EACH	DOZEN
STEMWARE	$7.75-	93.00
DESSERT-FINGER BOWL	7.50-	90.00
PLATE 7"	7.75-	93.00
PLATE 8"	8.25-	99.00

STRATFORD
476 Shape Cut 836

	EACH	DOZEN
STEMWARE	$7.75-	93.00
DESSERT-FINGER BOWL	7.50-	90.00
PLATE 7"	7.75-	93.00
PLATE 8"	8.25-	99.00

ELEGANCE and STRATFORD Patterns above available in the following items:

Page 23.

$20-30 each

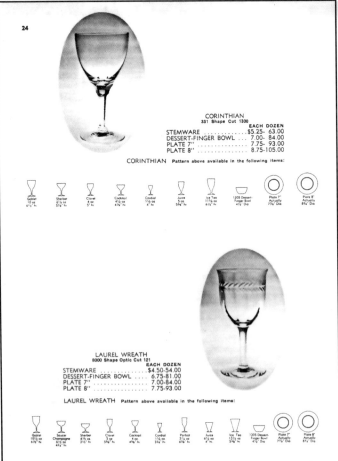

24

CORINTHIAN
331 Shape Cut 1300

	EACH	DOZEN
STEMWARE	$5.25-	63.00
DESSERT-FINGER BOWL	7.00-	84.00
PLATE 7"	7.75-	93.00
PLATE 8"	8.75-	105.00

CORINTHIAN Pattern above available in the following items:

LAUREL WREATH
8000 Shape Optic Cut 121

	EACH	DOZEN
STEMWARE	$4.50-	54.00
DESSERT-FINGER BOWL	6.75-	81.00
PLATE 7"	7.00-	84.00
PLATE 8"	7.75-	93.00

LAUREL WREATH Pattern above available in the following items:

Page 24.

$15-20 each

Page 26.

$8-12 each

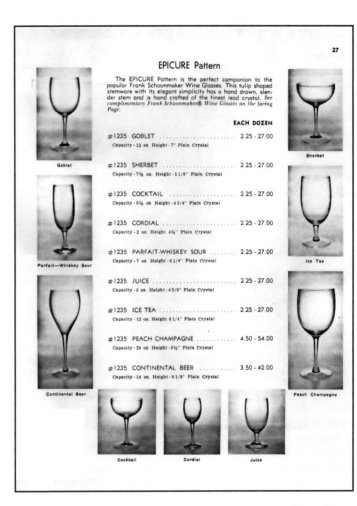
Page 27.

$8-12 each

Page 28.

$8-12 each

BROCADO by SENECA 29

...translates the courtly elegance of a treasured post into a refreshingly new pattern for contemporary tastes and needs. Dramatically contrasts smooth panels and lines with an intricately carved design.

AVOCADO

#1970 Footed SHERBET $2.50-30.00
EACH DOZEN
7½ ounces 3½" height
STANDARD PACKING:
6 doz. Ctn., approx. wt. 40 lbs.

SAHARA

MOROCCO

#1970 Footed JUICE or WINE $2.50-30.00
EACH DOZEN
7½ ounces 4⅝" height
STANDARD PACKING:
6 doz. Ctn., approx. wt. 40 lbs.

#1970 Footed GOBLET $2.50-30.00
EACH DOZEN
14 ounces 5½" height
STANDARD PACKING:
6 doz. Ctn., approx. wt. 47 lbs.

CRISTALINO

TOLEDO

#1970 BEVERAGE $1.25-15.00
EACH DOZEN
16 ounces 5⅞" height
STANDARD PACKING:
6 doz. Ctn., approx. wt. 51 lbs.

#1970 ON THE ROCKS $1.25-15.00
EACH DOZEN
10½ ounces 3⅝" height
STANDARD PACKING:
6 doz. Ctn., approx. wt. 42 lbs.

STANDARD PACKING: Carton lots, solid Colors of the same Item, quantity per Carton listed above.

The BROCADO Items above are available in the following Colors:

AVOCADO	CRISTALINO	MOROCCO	SAHARA	TOLEDO
(Green)	(Crystal)	(Brown)	(Yellow)	(Grey)

Page 29.

$8-10 each

Driftwood Casual by Seneca 31

DRIFTWOOD CASUAL
by SENECA
HAND BLOWN
LOOK FOR THIS SEAL
ON EVERY ITEM

Quality, Design and the Colors of handmade DRIFTWOOD CASUAL are indicative of Seneca's more than 75 years of glassmaking excellence

DRIFTWOOD CASUAL is available in sixteen items and eight colors.

Refer to facing Page 30, for Prices and other information.

ICE TEA
Moss Green

PITCHER
Cinnamon

COCKTAIL
Buttercup

GOBLET
Delphine Blue

DOUBLE OLD FASHION
Accent Red

HI-BALL
Peacock Blue

DESSERT-CEREAL BOWL
Crystal

JUICE
Amber

The above and other Items in DRIFTWOOD CASUAL are available in the following colors:

Accent Red	Amber	Buttercup (Yellow)	Cinnamon (Brown)	Crystal	Delphine Blue	Moss Green	Peacock Blue

Page 31.

$8-15 each
Pitcher: $30-40

1970 Catalog

INTRODUCING **SENECA** FOR 1970

5

BRISTOL
1971 Shape Cut 1441
For information, refer to Page 11.

KINGSLEY
1971 Shape Cut 1442
For information, refer to Page 11.

BOUQUET
1969 Shape
Available in Crystal AND 5 Colors.
For information, refer to Page 19
and 27 and color insert.

CLAREMONT
PLATINUM BAND
and LINE
1971 Shape
For information, refer to Page 11.

REMEMBRANCE
GOLD BAND
and LINE

SEVILLE
1971 Shape
Available in Crystal AND 5 Colors.
For information, refer to Page 11
and color insert.

Page 5.

$15-20 each

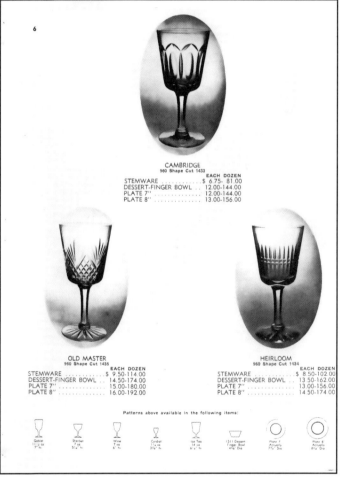

6

CAMBRIDGE
960 Shape Cut 1433

	EACH	DOZEN
STEMWARE	$ 6.75-	81.00
DESSERT-FINGER BOWL	12.00-	144.00
PLATE 7″	12.00-	144.00
PLATE 8″	13.00-	156.00

OLD MASTER
960 Shape Cut 1435

	EACH	DOZEN
STEMWARE	$ 9.50-	114.00
DESSERT-FINGER BOWL	14.50-	174.00
PLATE 7″	15.00-	180.00
PLATE 8″	16.00-	192.00

HEIRLOOM
960 Shape Cut 1434

	EACH	DOZEN
STEMWARE	$ 8.50-	102.00
DESSERT-FINGER BOWL	13.50-	162.00
PLATE 7″	13.00-	156.00
PLATE 8″	14.50-	174.00

Patterns above available in the following items:

Page 6.

$15-25 each

ARDMORE
960 Shape Cut 1436

	EACH	DOZEN
STEMWARE	$ 7.50-	90.00
DESSERT-FINGER BOWL	10.00-	120.00
PLATE 7"	11.00-	132.00
PLATE 8"	11.50-	138.00

RADIANCE
960 Shape Cut 1437

	EACH	DOZEN
STEMWARE	$ 9.50-	114.00
DESSERT-FINGER BOWL	11.00-	132.00
PLATE 7"	11.50-	138.00
PLATE 8"	13.00-	156.00

GOLD BROCADE
960 Shape Cut 1438
with 2 Gold Bands

	EACH	DOZEN
STEMWARE	$12.00-	144.00
DESSERT-FINGER BOWL	16.00-	192.00
PLATE 7"	19.00-	228.00
PLATE 8"	20.00-	240.00

Patterns above available in the following items:

Goblet 11½ oz. 7" h.   Sherbet 7 oz. 5¼" h.   Wine 7 oz. 6" h.   Cordial 1¼ oz. 3⅝" h.   Ice Tea 14 oz. 6¼" h.   1311 Dessert-Finger Bowl 4½" Dia.   Plate 7" Actually 7⅜" Dia.   Plate 8" Actually 8⅛" Dia.

KIMBERLY
1966 Shape Cut 1430

	EACH	DOZEN
STEMWARE	$ 5.25-	63.00
DESSERT-FINGER BOWL	13.50-	162.00
PLATE 7"	12.00-	144.00
PLATE 8"	13.00-	156.00

BRIDAL TIARA
1966 Shape Cut 1439

	EACH	DOZEN
STEMWARE	$ 5.50-	66.00
DESSERT-FINGER BOWL	8.00-	96.00
PLATE 7"	8.75-	105.00
PLATE 8"	9.25-	111.00

LAVALIER
1966 Shape Cut 1431

	EACH	DOZEN
STEMWARE	$ 5.75-	69.00
DESSERT-FINGER BOWL	9.25-	111.00
PLATE 7"	10.00-	120.00
PLATE 8"	11.00-	132.00

Patterns above available in the following items:

Goblet 12 oz. 7" h.   Sherbet 7½ oz. 5¼" h.   Wine 7½ oz. 6" h.   Cordial 1¼ oz. 3⅝" h.   Ice Tea 14 oz. 6¼" h.   1305 Dessert-Finger Bowl 4½" Dia.   Plate 7" Actually 7⅜" Dia.   Plate 8" Actually 8⅛" Dia.

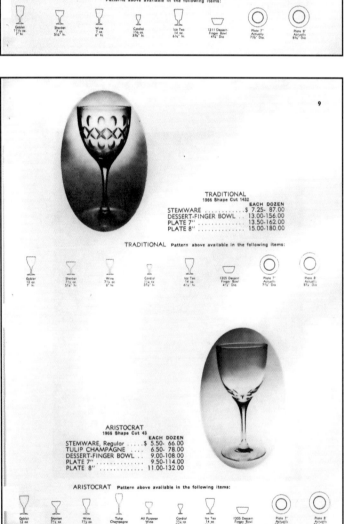

TRADITIONAL
1966 Shape Cut 1432

	EACH	DOZEN
STEMWARE	$ 7.25-	87.00
DESSERT-FINGER BOWL	13.00-	156.00
PLATE 7"	13.50-	162.00
PLATE 8"	15.00-	180.00

TRADITIONAL Pattern above available in the following items:

Goblet 12 oz. 7" h.   Sherbet 7½ oz. 5¼" h.   Wine 7½ oz. 6" h.   Cordial 1¼ oz. 3⅝" h.   Ice Tea 14 oz. 6¼" h.   1305 Dessert-Finger Bowl 4½" Dia.   Plate 7" Actually 7⅜" Dia.   Plate 8" Actually 8⅛" Dia.

ARISTOCRAT
1966 Shape Cut 43

	EACH	DOZEN
STEMWARE, Regular	$ 5.50-	66.00
TULIP CHAMPAGNE	6.50-	78.00
DESSERT-FINGER BOWL	9.00-	108.00
PLATE 7"	9.50-	114.00
PLATE 8"	11.00-	132.00

ARISTOCRAT Pattern above available in the following items:

Goblet 12 oz. 7" h.   Sherbet 7½ oz. 5¼" h.   Wine 7½ oz. 6" h.   Tulip Champagne 8 oz. 8½" h.   All Purpose Wine 8 oz. 5" h.   Cordial 1¼ oz. 3⅝" h.   Ice Tea 14 oz. 6¼" h.   1305 Dessert-Finger Bowl 4½" Dia.   Plate 7" Actually 7⅜" Dia.   Plate 8" Actually 8⅛" Dia.

Page 7.

$20-30 each

Page 8.

$15-20 each

Page 9.

$15-20 each

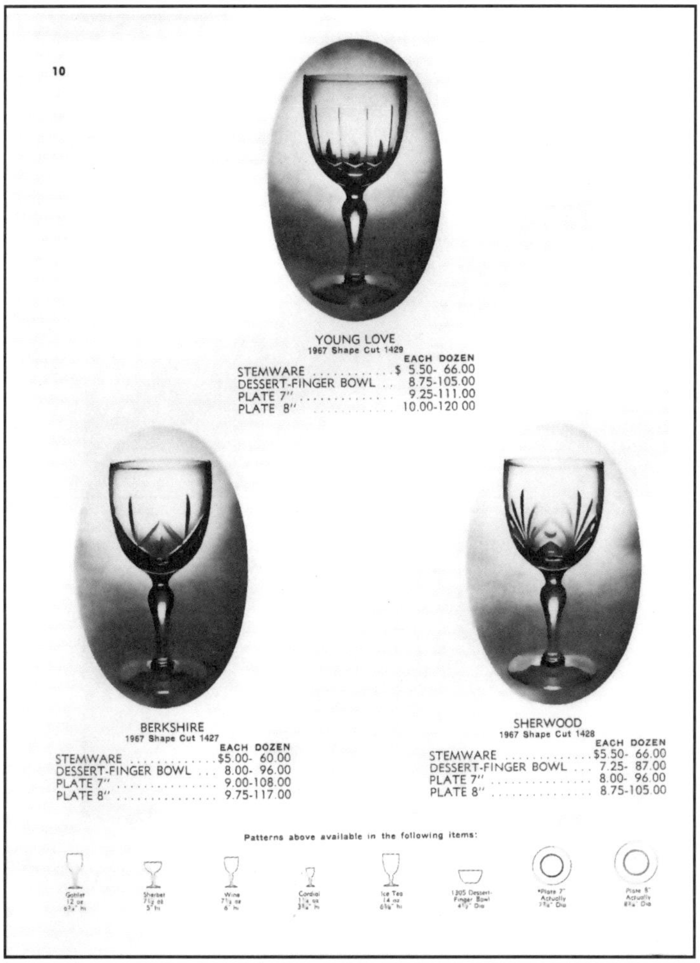

10

YOUNG LOVE
1967 Shape Cut 1429

	EACH	DOZEN
STEMWARE	$ 5.50-	66.00
DESSERT-FINGER BOWL	8.75-	105.00
PLATE 7"	9.25-	111.00
PLATE 8"	10.00-	120.00

BERKSHIRE
1967 Shape Cut 1427

	EACH	DOZEN
STEMWARE	$5.00-	60.00
DESSERT-FINGER BOWL	8.00-	96.00
PLATE 7"	9.00-	108.00
PLATE 8"	9.75-	117.00

SHERWOOD
1967 Shape Cut 1428

	EACH	DOZEN
STEMWARE	$5.50-	66.00
DESSERT-FINGER BOWL	7.25-	87.00
PLATE 7"	8.00-	96.00
PLATE 8"	8.75-	105.00

Patterns above available in the following items:

Goblet 12 oz 6¾" ht · Sherbet 7½ oz 5" ht · Wine 7½ oz 6" ht · Cordial 1¼ oz 3¾" ht · Ice Tea 14 oz 6⅝" ht · 1305 Dessert-Finger Bowl 4½" Dia · *Plate 7" Actually 7⅞" Dia · Plate 8" Actually 8¾" Dia

Page 10.

$15-20 each

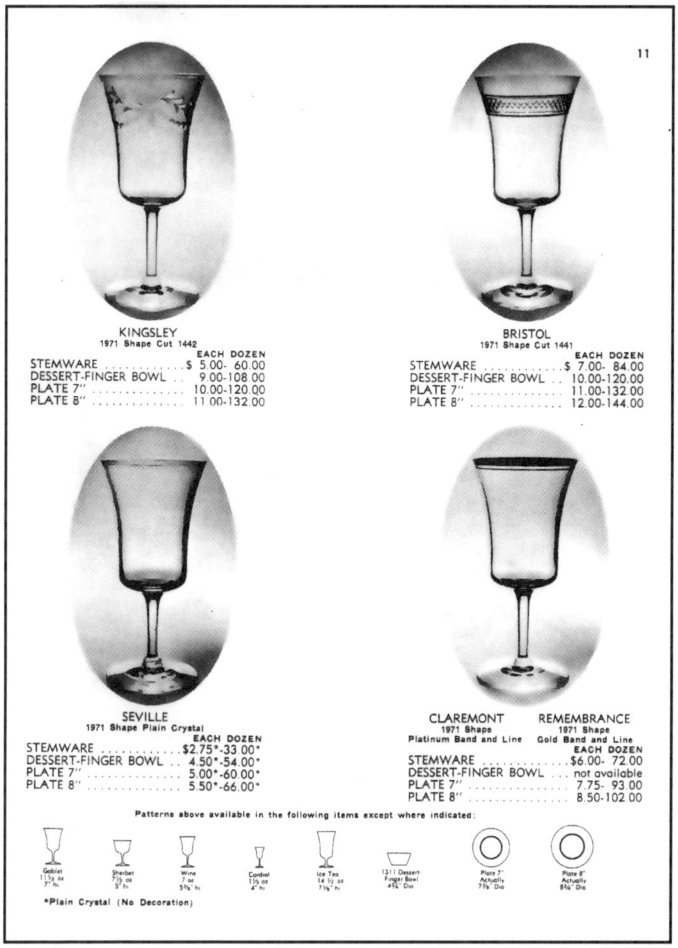

11

KINGSLEY
1971 Shape Cut 1442

	EACH	DOZEN
STEMWARE	$ 5.00-	60.00
DESSERT-FINGER BOWL	9.00-	108.00
PLATE 7"	10.00-	120.00
PLATE 8"	11.00-	132.00

BRISTOL
1971 Shape Cut 1441

	EACH	DOZEN
STEMWARE	$ 7.00-	84.00
DESSERT-FINGER BOWL	10.00-	120.00
PLATE 7"	11.00-	132.00
PLATE 8"	12.00-	144.00

SEVILLE
1971 Shape Plain Crystal

	EACH	DOZEN
STEMWARE	$2.75*-	33.00*
DESSERT-FINGER BOWL	4.50*-	54.00*
PLATE 7"	5.00*-	60.00*
PLATE 8"	5.50*-	66.00*

CLAREMONT
1971 Shape
Platinum Band and Line

REMEMBRANCE
1971 Shape
Gold Band and Line

	EACH	DOZEN
STEMWARE	$6.00-	72.00
DESSERT-FINGER BOWL	not available	
PLATE 7"	7.75-	93.00
PLATE 8"	8.50-	102.00

Patterns above available in the following items except where indicated:

Goblet 11½ oz 7" ht · Sherbet 7½ oz 5" ht · Wine 7 oz 5⅝" ht · Cordial 1½ oz 4" ht · Ice Tea 14½ oz 7⅛" ht · 1311 Dessert-Finger Bowl 4¾" Dia · Plate 7" Actually 7⅞" Dia · Plate 8" Actually 8¾" Dia

*Plain Crystal (No Decoration)

Page 11.

$15-20 each
Bottom left: $8-10 each

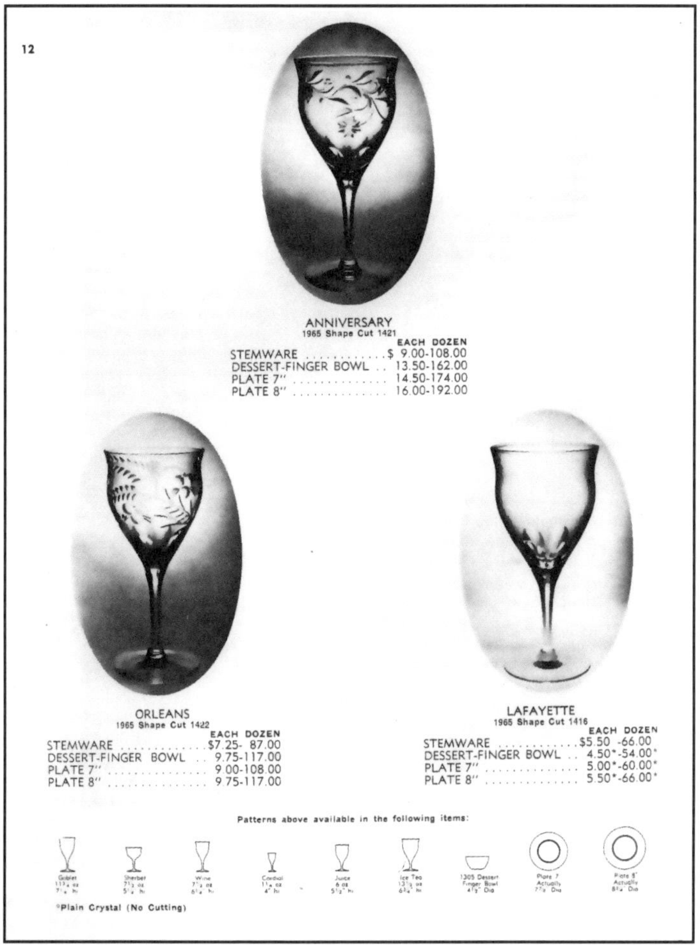

12

ANNIVERSARY
1965 Shape Cut 1421

	EACH	DOZEN
STEMWARE	$ 9.00-	108.00
DESSERT-FINGER BOWL	13.50-	162.00
PLATE 7"	14.50-	174.00
PLATE 8"	16.00-	192.00

ORLEANS
1965 Shape Cut 1422

	EACH	DOZEN
STEMWARE	$7.25-	87.00
DESSERT-FINGER BOWL	9.75-	117.00
PLATE 7"	9.00-	108.00
PLATE 8"	9.75-	117.00

LAFAYETTE
1965 Shape Cut 1416

	EACH	DOZEN
STEMWARE	$5.50 -	66.00
DESSERT-FINGER BOWL	4.50*-	54.00*
PLATE 7"	5.00*-	60.00*
PLATE 8"	5.50*-	66.00*

Patterns above available in the following items:

Goblet 11¾ oz 7¼" ht · Sherbet 7½ oz 5¼" ht · Wine 7½ oz 6¼" ht · Cordial 1¼ oz 4" ht · Juice 6 oz 5½" ht · Ice Tea 13½ oz 6¾" ht · 1305 Dessert Finger Bowl 4½" Dia · Plate 7 Actually 7⅞" Dia · Plate 8" Actually 8¾" Dia

*Plain Crystal (No Cutting)

Page 12.

$25-35 each
Bottom right: $15-25 each

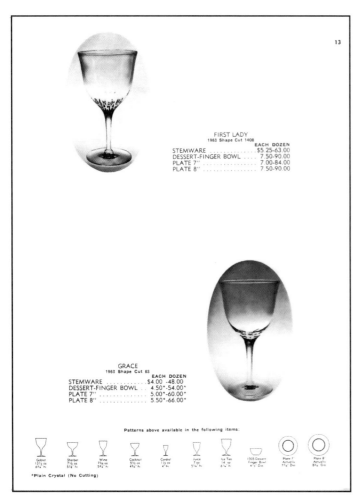

13

FIRST LADY
1963 Shape Cut 1408

	EACH	DOZEN
STEMWARE	$5.25	63.00
DESSERT-FINGER BOWL	7.50	90.00
PLATE 7"	7.00	84.00
PLATE 8"	7.50	90.00

GRACE
1963 Shape Cut 63

	EACH	DOZEN
STEMWARE	$4.00	48.00
DESSERT-FINGER BOWL	4.50*	54.00*
PLATE 7"	5.00*	60.00*
PLATE 8"	5.50*	66.00*

Patterns above available in the following items:

*Plain Crystal (No Cutting)

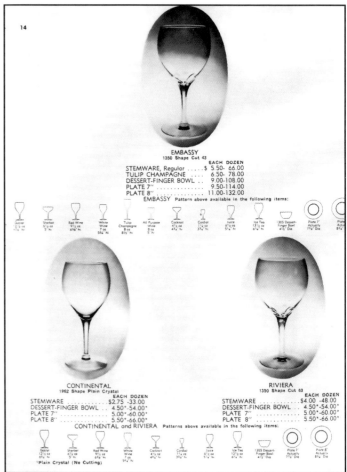

14

EMBASSY
1350 Shape Cut 43

	EACH	DOZEN
STEMWARE, Regular	$ 5.50	66.00
TULIP CHAMPAGNE	6.50	78.00
DESSERT-FINGER BOWL	9.00	108.00
PLATE 7"	9.50	114.00
PLATE 8"	11.00	132.00

EMBASSY Pattern above available in the following items:

CONTINENTAL
1962 Shape Plain Crystal

	EACH	DOZEN
STEMWARE	$2.75	33.00
DESSERT-FINGER BOWL	4.50*	54.00*
PLATE 7"	5.00*	60.00*
PLATE 8"	5.50*	66.00*

RIVIERA
1350 Shape Cut 63

	EACH	DOZEN
STEMWARE	$4.00	48.00
DESSERT-FINGER BOWL	4.50*	54.00*
PLATE 7"	5.00*	60.00*
PLATE 8"	5.50*	66.00*

CONTINENTAL and RIVIERA Patterns above available in the following items:

*Plain Crystal (No Cutting)

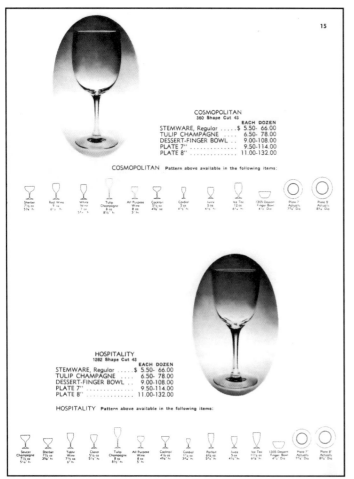

15

COSMOPOLITAN
360 Shape Cut 43

	EACH	DOZEN
STEMWARE, Regular	$ 5.50	66.00
TULIP CHAMPAGNE	6.50	78.00
DESSERT-FINGER BOWL	9.00	108.00
PLATE 7"	9.50	114.00
PLATE 8"	11.00	132.00

COSMOPOLITAN Pattern above available in the following items:

HOSPITALITY
1202 Shape Cut 43

	EACH	DOZEN
STEMWARE, Regular	$ 5.50	66.00
TULIP CHAMPAGNE	6.50	78.00
DESSERT-FINGER BOWL	9.00	108.00
PLATE 7"	9.50	114.00
PLATE 8"	11.00	132.00

HOSPITALITY Pattern above available in the following items:

Page 13.

$15-20 each

Page 14.

$10-15 each

Page 15.

$15-20 each

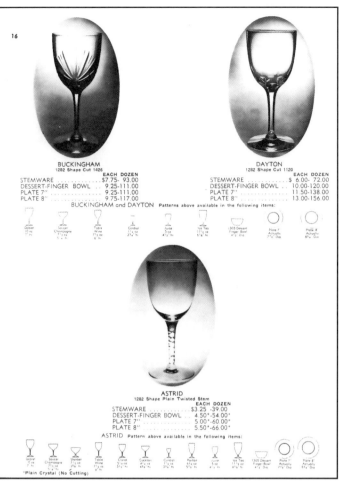

BUCKINGHAM
1282 Shape Cut 1426

	EACH DOZEN
STEMWARE	$7.75- 93.00
DESSERT-FINGER BOWL	9.25-111.00
PLATE 7''	9.25-111.00
PLATE 8''	9.75-117.00

DAYTON
1282 Shape Cut 1120

	EACH DOZEN
STEMWARE	$ 6.00- 72.00
DESSERT-FINGER BOWL	10.00-120.00
PLATE 7''	11.50-138.00
PLATE 8''	13.00-156.00

BUCKINGHAM and DAYTON Patterns above available in the following items:

ASTRID
1282 Shape Plain Twisted Stem

	EACH DOZEN
STEMWARE	$3.25 -39.00
DESSERT-FINGER BOWL	4.50*-54.00*
PLATE 7''	5.00*-60.00*
PLATE 8''	5.50*-66.00*

ASTRID Pattern above available in the following items:

*Plain Crystal (No Cutting)

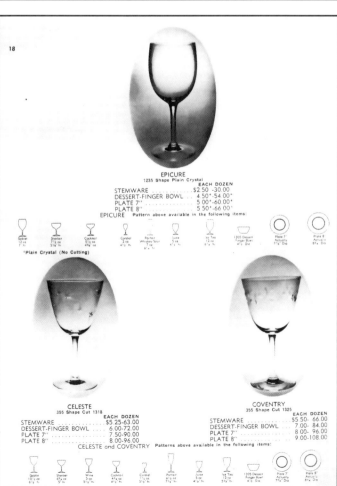

EPICURE
1235 Shape Plain Crystal

	EACH DOZEN
STEMWARE	$2.50 -30.00
DESSERT-FINGER BOWL	4.50*-54.00*
PLATE 7''	5.00*-60.00*
PLATE 8''	5.50*-66.00*

EPICURE Pattern above available in the following items:

*Plain Crystal (No Cutting)

CELESTE
355 Shape Cut 1318

	EACH DOZEN
STEMWARE	$5.25-63.00
DESSERT-FINGER BOWL	6.00-72.00
PLATE 7''	7.50-90.00
PLATE 8''	8.00-96.00

COVENTRY
355 Shape Cut 1325

	EACH DOZEN
STEMWARE	$5.50- 66.00
DESSERT-FINGER BOWL	7.00- 84.00
PLATE 7''	8.00- 96.00
PLATE 8''	9.00-108.00

CELESTE and COVENTRY Patterns above available in the following items:

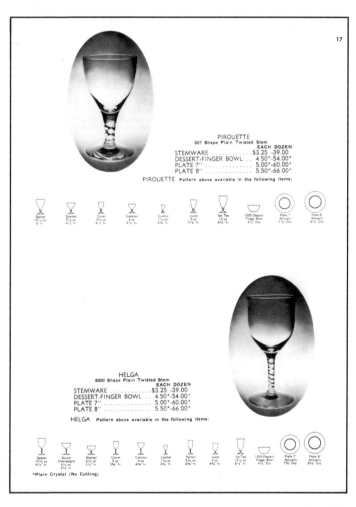

PIROUETTE
307 Shape Plain Twisted Stem

	EACH DOZEN
STEMWARE	$3.25 -39.00
DESSERT-FINGER BOWL	4.50*-54.00*
PLATE 7''	5.00*-60.00*
PLATE 8''	5.50*-66.00*

PIROUETTE Pattern above available in the following items:

HELGA
8000 Shape Plain Twisted Stem

	EACH DOZEN
STEMWARE	$3.25 -39.00
DESSERT-FINGER BOWL	4.50*-54.00*
PLATE 7''	5.00*-60.00*
PLATE 8''	5.50*-66.00*

HELGA Pattern above available in the following items:

*Plain Crystal (No Cutting)

Page 16.

Top row: $15-20 each
Bottom: $8-10 each

Page 17.

$8-12 each

Page 18.

Top: $8-10 each
Bottom row: $12-15

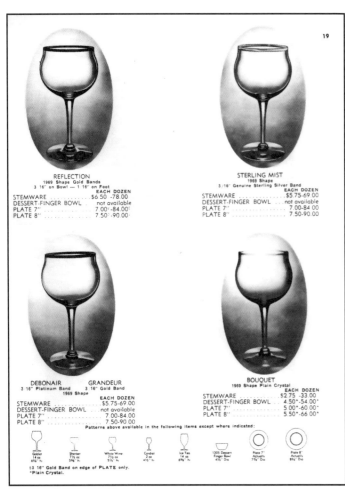

REFLECTION
1969 Shape Gold Bands
3 16" on Bowl — 1 16" on Foot

	EACH	DOZEN
STEMWARE	$6.50	-78.00
DESSERT-FINGER BOWL	not available	
PLATE 7"	7.00	-84.00
PLATE 8"	7.50	-90.00

STERLING MIST
1969 Shape
3/16" Genuine Sterling Silver Band

	EACH	DOZEN
STEMWARE	$5.75	-69.00
DESSERT-FINGER BOWL	not available	
PLATE 7"	7.00	-84.00
PLATE 8"	7.50	-90.00

DEBONAIR **GRANDEUR**
3 16" Platinum Band   3 16" Gold Band
1969 Shape

	EACH	DOZEN
STEMWARE	$5.75	-69.00
DESSERT-FINGER BOWL	not available	
PLATE 7"	7.00	-84.00
PLATE 8"	7.50	-90.00

BOUQUET
1969 Shape Plain Crystal

	EACH	DOZEN
STEMWARE	$2.75	-33.00
DESSERT-FINGER BOWL	4.50*	-54.00*
PLATE 7"	5.00*	-60.00*
PLATE 8"	5.50*	-66.00*

Patterns above available in the following items except where indicated:

Goblet 14 oz 6⅝" h • Sherbet 7½ oz 5⅝" h • White Wine 7½ oz 5½" h • Cordial 2 oz 4½" h • Ice Tea 14 oz 6¾" h • 1305 Dessert Finger Bowl 4½" Dia • Plate 7" Actually 7½" Dia • Plate 8" Actually 8½" Dia

†3 16" Gold Band on edge of PLATE only.
*Plain Crystal.

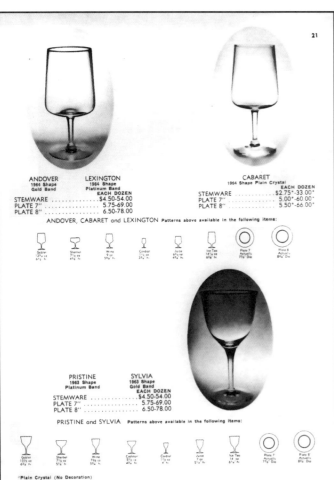

ANDOVER **LEXINGTON**
1964 Shape   1964 Shape
Gold Band   Platinum Band

	EACH	DOZEN
STEMWARE	$4.50	-54.00
PLATE 7"	5.75	-69.00
PLATE 8"	6.50	-78.00

CABARET
1964 Shape Plain Crystal

	EACH	DOZEN
STEMWARE	$2.75	-33.00*
PLATE 7"	5.00*	-60.00*
PLATE 8"	5.50*	-66.00*

ANDOVER, CABARET and LEXINGTON Patterns above available in the following items:

Goblet 13½ oz 6½" h • Sherbet 7½ oz 5⅛" h • Wine 9 oz 5¾" h • Cordial 2 oz 3½" h • Juice 6½ oz 4¾" h • Ice Tea 14½ oz 6½" h • Plate 7 Actually 7½" Dia • Plate 8 Actually 8½" Dia

PRISTINE **SYLVIA**
1963 Shape   1963 Shape
Platinum Band   Gold Band

	EACH	DOZEN
STEMWARE	$4.50	-54.00
PLATE 7"	5.75	-69.00
PLATE 8"	6.50	-78.00

PRISTINE and SYLVIA Patterns above available in the following items:

Goblet 13½ oz 6½" h • Sherbet 7½ oz 5⅛" h • Wine 9 oz 5¾" h • Cocktail 4½ oz 4½" h • Cordial 2 oz 4" h • Juice 7 oz 5½" h • Ice Tea 14 oz 6½" h • Plate 7 Actually 7½" Dia • Plate 8 Actually 8½" Dia

*Plain Crystal (No Decoration)

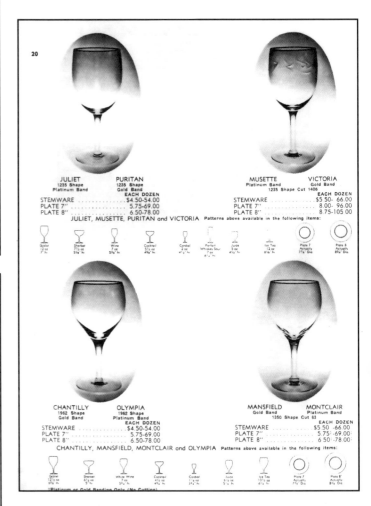

JULIET **PURITAN**
1235 Shape   1235 Shape
Platinum Band   Gold Band

	EACH	DOZEN
STEMWARE	$4.50	-54.00
PLATE 7"	5.75	-69.00
PLATE 8"	6.50	-78.00

MUSETTE **VICTORIA**
Platinum Band   Gold Band
1235 Shape Cut 1406

	EACH	DOZEN
STEMWARE	$5.50	-66.00
PLATE 7"	8.00	-96.00
PLATE 8"	8.75	-105.00

JULIET, MUSETTE, PURITAN and VICTORIA Patterns above available in the following items:

Goblet 12 oz 7" h • Sherbet 6½ oz 5½" h • Wine 7 oz 5⅝" h • Cocktail 5½ oz 4⅝" h • Cordial 2 oz 4½" h • Perfect Whiskey Sour 7 oz 4¾" h • Juice 5 oz 4½" h • Ice Tea 12 oz 6½" h • Plate 7 Actually 7½" Dia • Plate 8 Actually 8½" Dia

CHANTILLY **OLYMPIA**
1962 Shape   1962 Shape
Gold Band   Platinum Band

	EACH	DOZEN
STEMWARE	$4.50	-54.00
PLATE 7"	5.75	-69.00
PLATE 8"	6.50	-78.00

MANSFIELD **MONTCLAIR**
Gold Band   Platinum Band
1350 Shape Cut 63

	EACH	DOZEN
STEMWARE	$5.50	-66.00
PLATE 7"	5.75	-69.00
PLATE 8"	6.50	-78.00

CHANTILLY, MANSFIELD, MONTCLAIR and OLYMPIA Patterns above available in the following items:

Goblet 12 oz 6½" h • Sherbet 6½ oz 5" h • White Wine 7 oz 5¾" h • Cocktail 4½ oz 4½" h • Cordial 1 oz 4" h • Juice 5½ oz 4½" h • Ice Tea 13½ oz 6½" h • Plate 7 Actually 7½" Dia • Plate 8 Actually 8½" Dia

*Platinum or Gold Banding Only (No Cutting)

Page 19.

$15-10 each
Bottom right: $8-10 each

Page 20.

$5-20 each

Page 21.

Top right: $8-10 each
$10-15 each

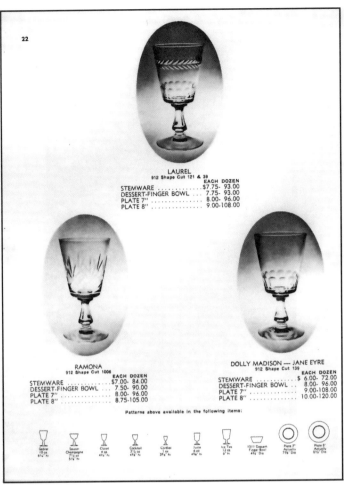

22

LAUREL
912 Shape Cut 121 & 39

	EACH	DOZEN
STEMWARE	$7.75-	93.00
DESSERT-FINGER BOWL	7.75-	93.00
PLATE 7"	8.00-	96.00
PLATE 8"	9.00-	108.00

RAMONA
912 Shape Cut 1006

	EACH	DOZEN
STEMWARE	$7.00-	84.00
DESSERT-FINGER BOWL	7.50-	90.00
PLATE 7"	8.00-	96.00
PLATE 8"	8.75-	105.00

DOLLY MADISON — JANE EYRE
912 Shape Cut 139

	EACH	DOZEN
STEMWARE	$ 6.00-	72.00
DESSERT-FINGER BOWL	8.00-	96.00
PLATE 7"	9.00-	108.00
PLATE 8"	10.00-	120.00

Patterns above available in the following items:

23

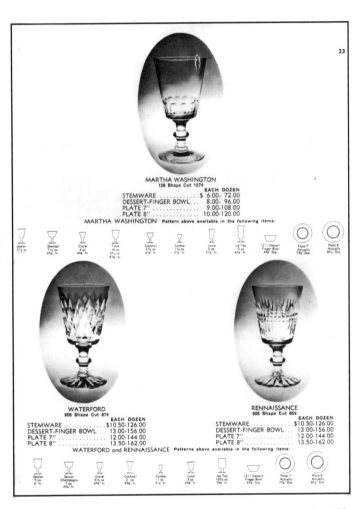

MARTHA WASHINGTON
128 Shape Cut 1274

	EACH	DOZEN
STEMWARE	$ 6.00-	72.00
DESSERT-FINGER BOWL	8.00-	96.00
PLATE 7"	9.00-	108.00
PLATE 8"	10.00-	120.00

MARTHA WASHINGTON Pattern above available in the following items:

WATERFORD
908 Shape Cut 879

	EACH	DOZEN
STEMWARE	$10.50-	126.00
DESSERT-FINGER BOWL	13.00-	156.00
PLATE 7"	12.00-	144.00
PLATE 8"	13.50-	162.00

RENNAISSANCE
908 Shape Cut 859

	EACH	DOZEN
STEMWARE	$10.50-	126.00
DESSERT-FINGER BOWL	13.00-	156.00
PLATE 7"	12.00-	144.00
PLATE 8"	13.50-	162.00

WATERFORD and RENNAISSANCE Patterns above available in the following items:

24

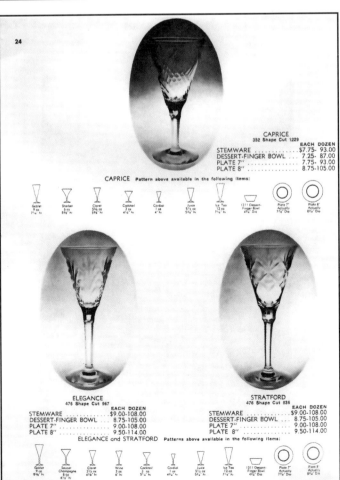

CAPRICE
352 Shape Cut 1229

	EACH	DOZEN
STEMWARE	$7.75-	93.00
DESSERT-FINGER BOWL	7.25-	87.00
PLATE 7"	7.75-	93.00
PLATE 8"	8.75-	105.00

CAPRICE Pattern above available in the following items:

ELEGANCE
476 Shape Cut 967

	EACH	DOZEN
STEMWARE	$9.00-	108.00
DESSERT-FINGER BOWL	8.75-	105.00
PLATE 7"	9.00-	108.00
PLATE 8"	9.50-	114.00

STRATFORD
476 Shape Cut 838

	EACH	DOZEN
STEMWARE	$9.00-	108.00
DESSERT-FINGER BOWL	8.75-	105.00
PLATE 7"	9.00-	108.00
PLATE 8"	9.50-	114.00

ELEGANCE and STRATFORD Patterns above available in the following items:

Page 22.

Top: $20-30 each
Bottom row: $15-25 each

Page 23.

Top: $15-20 each
Bottom row: $20-30 each

Page 24.

$20-30 each

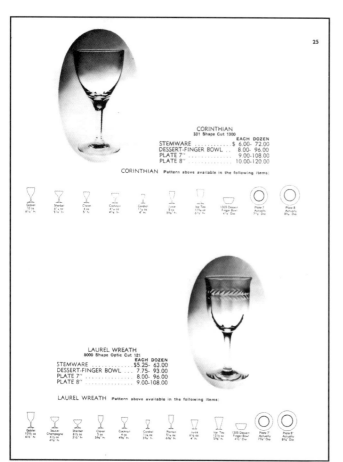

CORINTHIAN
331 Shape Cut 1300

	EACH	DOZEN
STEMWARE	$ 6.00	72.00
DESSERT-FINGER BOWL	8.00	96.00
PLATE 7"	9.00	108.00
PLATE 8"	10.00	120.00

CORINTHIAN Pattern above available in the following items:

LAUREL WREATH
8000 Shape Optic Cut 121

	EACH	DOZEN
STEMWARE	$5.25	63.00
DESSERT-FINGER BOWL	7.75	93.00
PLATE 7"	8.00	96.00
PLATE 8"	9.00	108.00

LAUREL WREATH Pattern above available in the following items:

Bouquet

by **SENECA**

BOUQUET
1969 Shape Plain Crystal

	EACH	DOZEN
STEMWARE	$2.75	33.00

BOUQUET, designed and generously proportioned as a beautiful gourmet wine Pattern, is hand crafted of the finest lead crystal. Every item bears a Label identifying and describing the recommended usage of each glass.
The BOUQUET gourmet wine Pattern is available in the items featured below.

Goblet 14 oz. 6¾" hi. · Sherbet 7½ oz. 5⅜" hi. · Red Wine 9½ oz. 6" hi. · White Wine 7½ oz. 5½" hi. · Cordial 2 oz. 4½" hi. · Sherry/Port 5 oz. 5¼" hi. · Tulip Champagne 8 oz. 8⅛" hi.

Page 25. $15-20 each

Page 27. $8-12 each

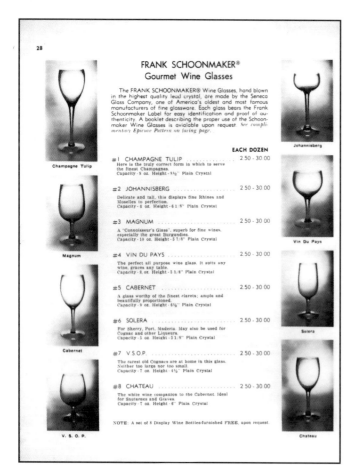

FRANK SCHOONMAKER® Gourmet Wine Glasses

The FRANK SCHOONMAKER® Wine Glasses, hand blown in the highest quality lead crystal, are made by the Seneca Glass Company, one of America's oldest and most famous manufacturers of fine glassware. Each glass bears the Frank Schoonmaker Label for easy identification and proof of authenticity. A booklet describing the proper use of the Schoonmaker Wine Glasses is available upon request. *See complimentary Epicure Pattern on facing page.*

	EACH	DOZEN
#1 CHAMPAGNE TULIP	2.50	30.00

Here is the truly correct form in which to serve the finest Champagnes.
Capacity · 8 oz. Height · 8½" Plain Crystal

	EACH	DOZEN
#2 JOHANNISBERG	2.50	30.00

Delicate and tall, this displays fine Rhines and Moselles to perfection.
Capacity · 6 oz. Height · 6 1/8" Plain Crystal

	EACH	DOZEN
#3 MAGNUM	2.50	30.00

A "Connoisseur's Glass", superb for fine wines, especially the great Burgundies.
Capacity · 10 oz. Height · 5 7/8" Plain Crystal

	EACH	DOZEN
#4 VIN DU PAYS	2.50	30.00

The perfect all purpose wine glass. It suits any wine, graces any table.
Capacity · 8 oz. Height · 5 3/8" Plain Crystal

	EACH	DOZEN
#5 CABERNET	2.50	30.00

A glass worthy of the finest clarets; ample and beautifully proportioned.
Capacity · 8 oz. Height · 6½" Plain Crystal

	EACH	DOZEN
#6 SOLERA	2.50	30.00

For Sherry, Port, Madeira. May also be used for Cognac and other Liqueurs.
Capacity · 5 oz. Height · 5 1/8" Plain Crystal

	EACH	DOZEN
#7 V.S.O.P.	2.50	30.00

The rarest old Cognacs are at home in this glass. Neither too large nor too small.
Capacity · 7 oz. Height · 4½" Plain Crystal

	EACH	DOZEN
#8 CHATEAU	2.50	30.00

The white wine companion to the Cabernet. Ideal for Sauternes and Graves.
Capacity · 7 oz. Height · 6" Plain Crystal

NOTE: A set of 8 Display Wine Bottles furnished FREE upon request.

Champagne Tulip · Magnum · Cabernet · V.S.O.P. · Johannisberg · Vin Du Pays · Solera · Chateau

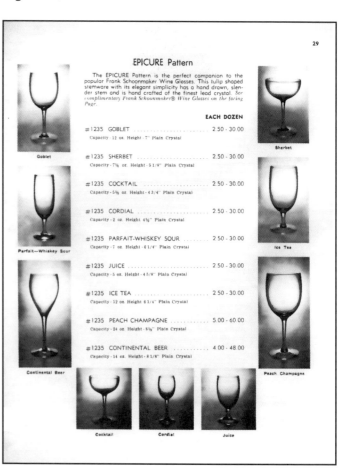

EPICURE Pattern

The EPICURE Pattern is the perfect companion to the popular Frank Schoonmaker Wine Glasses. This tulip shaped stemware with its elegant simplicity has a hand drawn, slender stem and is hand crafted of the finest lead crystal. *See complimentary Frank Schoonmaker® Wine Glasses on the facing Page.*

	EACH	DOZEN
#1235 GOBLET	2.50	30.00

Capacity · 12 oz. Height · 7" Plain Crystal

	EACH	DOZEN
#1235 SHERBET	2.50	30.00

Capacity · 7½ oz. Height · 5 1/8" Plain Crystal

	EACH	DOZEN
#1235 COCKTAIL	2.50	30.00

Capacity · 5¼ oz. Height · 4 3/4" Plain Crystal

	EACH	DOZEN
#1235 CORDIAL	2.50	30.00

Capacity · 2 oz. Height · 4½" Plain Crystal

	EACH	DOZEN
#1235 PARFAIT-WHISKEY SOUR	2.50	30.00

Capacity · 7 oz. Height · 6 1/4" Plain Crystal

	EACH	DOZEN
#1235 JUICE	2.50	30.00

Capacity · 5 oz. Height · 4 5/8" Plain Crystal

	EACH	DOZEN
#1235 ICE TEA	2.50	30.00

Capacity · 12 oz. Height · 6 1/4" Plain Crystal

	EACH	DOZEN
#1235 PEACH CHAMPAGNE	5.00	60.00

Capacity · 24 oz. Height · 8½" Plain Crystal

	EACH	DOZEN
#1235 CONTINENTAL BEER	4.00	48.00

Capacity · 14 oz. Height · 8 1/8" Plain Crystal

Goblet · Parfait—Whiskey Sour · Continental Beer · Sherbet · Ice Tea · Peach Champagne · Cocktail · Cordial · Juice

Page 28. $8-12 each

Page 29. $8-12 each

1971 Catalog

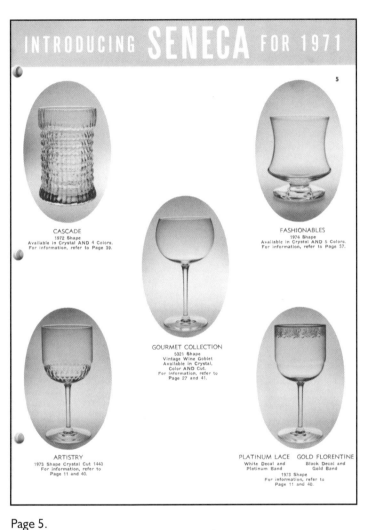

Page 5.

$10-15 each

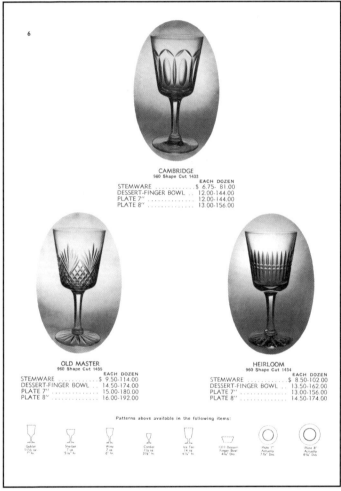

Page 6.

$15-25 each

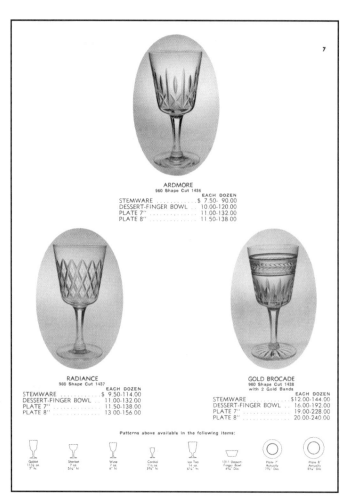

ARDMORE
960 Shape Cut 1436

	EACH	DOZEN
STEMWARE	$ 7.50	90.00
DESSERT-FINGER BOWL	10.00	120.00
PLATE 7"	11.00	132.00
PLATE 8"	11.50	138.00

RADIANCE
960 Shape Cut 1437

	EACH	DOZEN
STEMWARE	$ 9.50	114.00
DESSERT-FINGER BOWL	11.00	132.00
PLATE 7"	11.50	138.00
PLATE 8"	13.00	156.00

GOLD BROCADE
960 Shape Cut 1438
with 2 Gold Bands

	EACH	DOZEN
STEMWARE	$12.00	144.00
DESSERT-FINGER BOWL	16.00	192.00
PLATE 7"	19.00	228.00
PLATE 8"	20.00	240.00

Patterns above available in the following items:

Goblet 11½ oz. 7" hi. — Sherbet 7 oz. 5¼" hi. — Wine 7 oz. 6" hi. — Cordial 1¼ oz. 3¾" hi. — Ice Tea 14 oz. 6¼" hi. — 1311 Dessert-Finger Bowl 4½" Dia. — Plate 7" Actually 7¾" Dia. — Plate 8" Actually 8¼" Dia.

Page 7.

$15-25 each

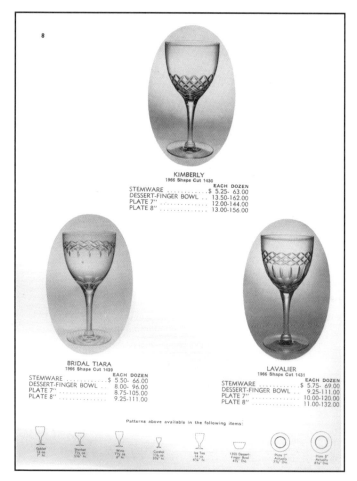

KIMBERLY
1966 Shape Cut 1430

	EACH	DOZEN
STEMWARE	$ 5.25	63.00
DESSERT-FINGER BOWL	13.50	162.00
PLATE 7"	12.00	144.00
PLATE 8"	13.00	156.00

BRIDAL TIARA
1966 Shape Cut 1439

	EACH	DOZEN
STEMWARE	$ 5.50	66.00
DESSERT-FINGER BOWL	8.00	96.00
PLATE 7"	8.75	105.00
PLATE 8"	9.25	111.00

LAVALIER
1966 Shape Cut 1431

	EACH	DOZEN
STEMWARE	$ 5.75	69.00
DESSERT-FINGER BOWL	9.25	111.00
PLATE 7"	10.00	120.00
PLATE 8"	11.00	132.00

Patterns above available in the following items:

Goblet 12 oz. 7" hi. — Sherbet 7½ oz. 5¼" hi. — Wine 7½ oz. 6" hi. — Cordial 1¼ oz. 3¾" hi. — Ice Tea 14 oz. 6¼" hi. — 1305 Dessert-Finger Bowl 4½" Dia. — Plate 7" Actually 7¾" Dia. — Plate 8" Actually 8¼" Dia.

Page 8.

$15-20 each

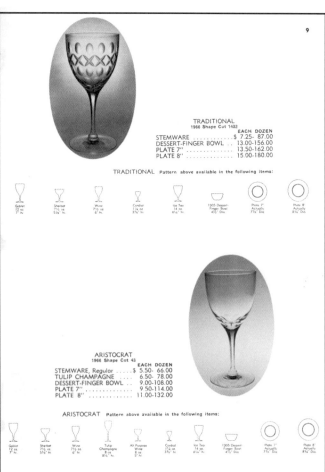

TRADITIONAL
1966 Shape Cut 1432

	EACH	DOZEN
STEMWARE	$ 7.25	87.00
DESSERT-FINGER BOWL	13.00	156.00
PLATE 7"	13.50	162.00
PLATE 8"	15.00	180.00

TRADITIONAL Pattern above available in the following items:

Goblet 12 oz. 7" hi. — Sherbet 7½ oz. 5¼" hi. — Wine 7½ oz. 6" hi. — Cordial 1¼ oz. 3¾" hi. — Ice Tea 14 oz. 6¼" hi. — 1305 Dessert-Finger Bowl 4½" Dia. — Plate 7" Actually 7¾" Dia. — Plate 8" Actually 8¼" Dia.

ARISTOCRAT
1966 Shape Cut 43

	EACH	DOZEN
STEMWARE, Regular	$ 5.50	66.00
TULIP CHAMPAGNE	6.50	78.00
DESSERT-FINGER BOWL	9.00	108.00
PLATE 7"	9.50	114.00
PLATE 8"	11.00	132.00

ARISTOCRAT Pattern above available in the following items:

Goblet 12 oz. 7" hi. — Sherbet 7½ oz. 5¼" hi. — Wine 7½ oz. 6" hi. — Tulip Champagne 8 oz. 6½" hi. — All Purpose Wine 8 oz. 5" hi. — Cordial 1¼ oz. 3¾" hi. — Ice Tea 14 oz. 6¼" hi. — 1305 Dessert-Finger Bowl 4½" Dia. — Plate 7" Actually 7¾" Dia. — Plate 8" Actually 8¼" Dia.

Page 9.

$15-20 each

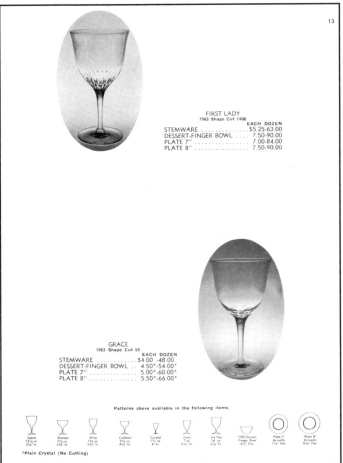

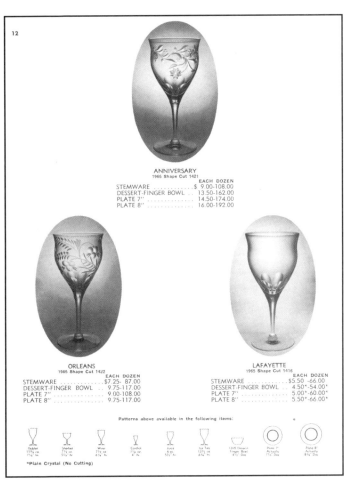

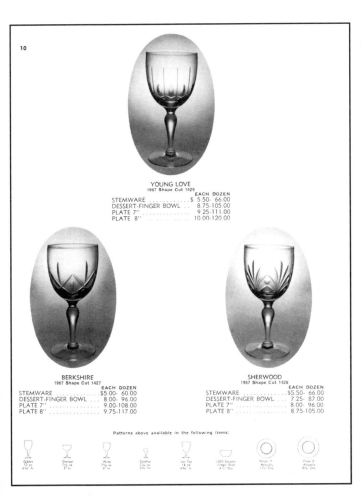

10

YOUNG LOVE
1967 Shape Cut 1429

	EACH	DOZEN
STEMWARE	$ 5.50-	66.00
DESSERT-FINGER BOWL	8.75-	105.00
PLATE 7"	9.25-	111.00
PLATE 8"	10.00-	120.00

BERKSHIRE
1967 Shape Cut 1427

	EACH	DOZEN
STEMWARE	$5.00-	60.00
DESSERT-FINGER BOWL	8.00-	96.00
PLATE 7"	9.00-	108.00
PLATE 8"	9.75-	117.00

SHERWOOD
1967 Shape Cut 1428

	EACH	DOZEN
STEMWARE	$5.50-	66.00
DESSERT-FINGER BOWL	7.25-	87.00
PLATE 7"	8.00-	96.00
PLATE 8"	8.75-	105.00

Patterns above available in the following items:

13

FIRST LADY
1963 Shape Cut 1408

	EACH	DOZEN
STEMWARE	$5.25-	63.00
DESSERT-FINGER BOWL	7.50-	90.00
PLATE 7"	7.00-	84.00
PLATE 8"	7.50-	90.00

GRACE
1963 Shape Cut 63

	EACH	DOZEN
STEMWARE	$4.00-	48.00
DESSERT-FINGER BOWL	4.50*-	54.00*
PLATE 7"	5.00*-	60.00*
PLATE 8"	5.50*-	66.00*

Patterns above available in the following items:

*Plain Crystal (No Cutting)

12

ANNIVERSARY
1965 Shape Cut 1421

	EACH	DOZEN
STEMWARE	$ 9.00-	108.00
DESSERT-FINGER BOWL	13.50-	162.00
PLATE 7"	14.50-	174.00
PLATE 8"	16.00-	192.00

ORLEANS
1965 Shape Cut 1422

	EACH	DOZEN
STEMWARE	$7.25-	87.00
DESSERT-FINGER BOWL	9.75-	117.00
PLATE 7"	9.00-	108.00
PLATE 8"	9.75-	117.00

LAFAYETTE
1965 Shape Cut 1416

	EACH	DOZEN
STEMWARE	$5.50-	66.00
DESSERT-FINGER BOWL	4.50*-	54.00*
PLATE 7"	5.00*-	60.00*
PLATE 8"	5.50*-	66.00*

Patterns above available in the following items:

*Plain Crystal (No Cutting)

Page 10.

$15-20 each

Page 11.

$25-35 each
Bottom right: $15-20 each

Page 12.

$15-20 each

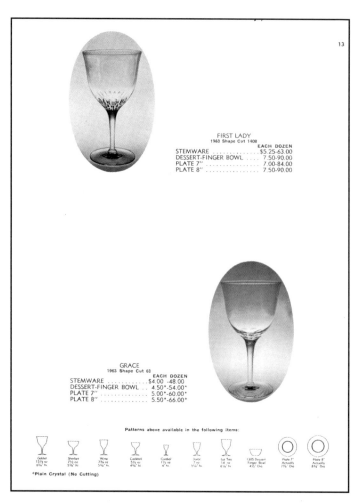

FIRST LADY
1963 Shape Cut 1408

	EACH	DOZEN
STEMWARE	$5.25	63.00
DESSERT-FINGER BOWL	7.50	90.00
PLATE 7"	7.00	84.00
PLATE 8"	7.50	90.00

13

Page 13.

$10-15 each

GRACE
1963 Shape Cut 63

	EACH	DOZEN
STEMWARE	$4.00	-48.00
DESSERT-FINGER BOWL	4.50*	-54.00*
PLATE 7"	5.00*	-60.00*
PLATE 8"	5.50*	-66.00*

Patterns above available in the following items:

*Plain Crystal (No Cutting)

14

EMBASSY
1350 Shape Cut 43

	EACH	DOZEN
STEMWARE, Regular	$ 5.50	66.00
TULIP CHAMPAGNE	6.50	78.00
DESSERT-FINGER BOWL	9.00	108.00
PLATE 7"	9.50	114.00
PLATE 8"	11.00	132.00

EMBASSY Pattern above available in the following items:

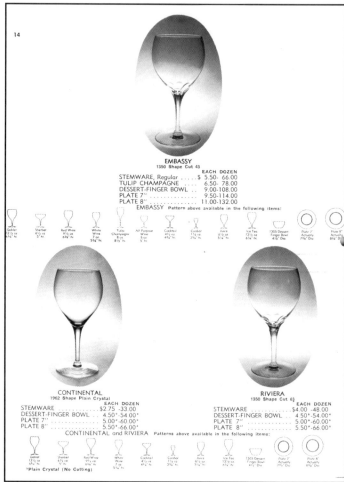

CONTINENTAL
1962 Shape Plain Crystal

	EACH	DOZEN
STEMWARE	$2.75	-33.00
DESSERT-FINGER BOWL	4.50*	-54.00*
PLATE 7"	5.00*	-60.00*
PLATE 8"	5.50*	-66.00*

RIVIERA
1350 Shape Cut 63

	EACH	DOZEN
STEMWARE	$4.00	-48.00
DESSERT-FINGER BOWL	4.50*	-54.00*
PLATE 7"	5.00*	-60.00*
PLATE 8"	5.50*	-66.00*

CONTINENTAL and RIVIERA Patterns available in the following items:

*Plain Crystal (No Cutting)

Page 14.

$10-15 each

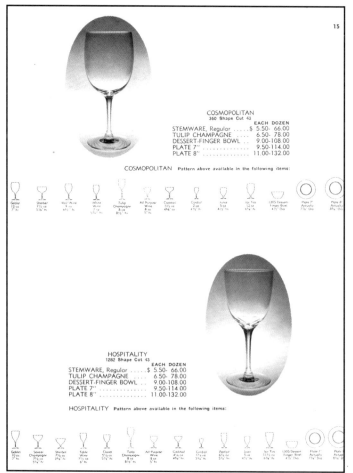

15

COSMOPOLITAN
360 Shape Cut 43

	EACH	DOZEN
STEMWARE, Regular	$ 5.50	66.00
TULIP CHAMPAGNE	6.50	78.00
DESSERT-FINGER BOWL	9.00	108.00
PLATE 7"	9.50	114.00
PLATE 8"	11.00	132.00

COSMOPOLITAN Pattern above available in the following items:

HOSPITALITY
1282 Shape Cut 43

	EACH	DOZEN
STEMWARE, Regular	$ 5.50	66.00
TULIP CHAMPAGNE	6.50	78.00
DESSERT-FINGER BOWL	9.00	108.00
PLATE 7"	9.50	114.00
PLATE 8"	11.00	132.00

HOSPITALITY Pattern above available in the following items:

Page 15.

$10-15 each

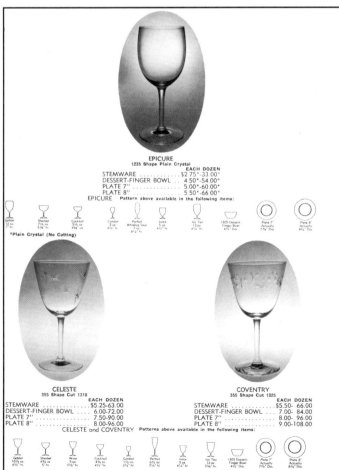

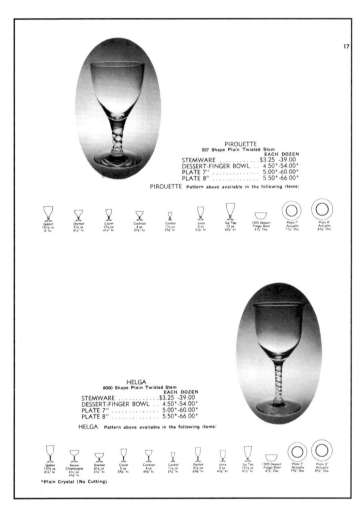

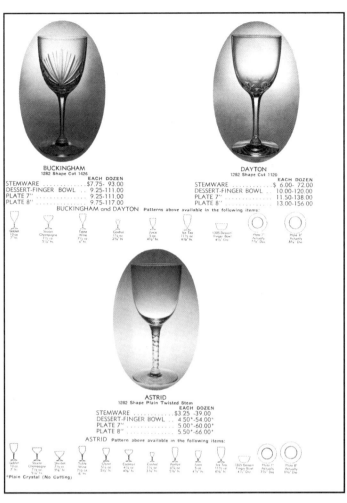

BUCKINGHAM
1282 Shape Cut 1426

	EACH	DOZEN
STEMWARE	$7.75	93.00
DESSERT-FINGER BOWL	9.25	111.00
PLATE 7"	9.25	111.00
PLATE 8"	9.75	117.00

BUCKINGHAM and DAYTON Patterns above available in the following items:

DAYTON
1282 Shape Cut 1120

	EACH	DOZEN
STEMWARE	$ 6.00	72.00
DESSERT-FINGER BOWL	10.00	120.00
PLATE 7"	11.50	138.00
PLATE 8"	13.00	156.00

ASTRID
1282 Shape Plain Twisted Stem

	EACH	DOZEN
STEMWARE	$3.25	-39.00
DESSERT-FINGER BOWL	4.50*	-54.00*
PLATE 7"	5.00*	-60.00*
PLATE 8"	5.50*	-66.00*

ASTRID Pattern above available in the following items:

*Plain Crystal (No Cutting)

PIROUETTE
307 Shape Plain Twisted Stem

	EACH	DOZEN
STEMWARE	$3.25	-39.00
DESSERT-FINGER BOWL	4.50*	-54.00*
PLATE 7"	5.00*	-60.00*
PLATE 8"	5.50*	-66.00*

PIROUETTE Pattern above available in the following items:

HELGA
8000 Shape Plain Twisted Stem

	EACH	DOZEN
STEMWARE	$3.25	-39.00
DESSERT-FINGER BOWL	4.50*	-54.00*
PLATE 7"	5.00*	-60.00*
PLATE 8"	5.50*	-66.00*

HELGA Pattern above available in the following items:

*Plain Crystal (No Cutting)

EPICURE
1235 Shape Plain Crystal

	EACH	DOZEN
STEMWARE	$2.75*	-33.00*
DESSERT-FINGER BOWL	4.50*	-54.00*
PLATE 7"	5.00*	-60.00*
PLATE 8"	5.50*	-66.00*

EPICURE Pattern above available in the following items:

*Plain Crystal (No Cutting)

CELESTE
355 Shape Cut 1318

	EACH	DOZEN
STEMWARE	$5.25	-63.00
DESSERT-FINGER BOWL	6.00	-72.00
PLATE 7"	7.50	-90.00
PLATE 8"	8.00	-96.00

COVENTRY
355 Shape Cut 1325

	EACH	DOZEN
STEMWARE	$5.50	-66.00
DESSERT-FINGER BOWL	7.00	-84.00
PLATE 7"	8.00	-96.00
PLATE 8"	9.00	-108.00

CELESTE and COVENTRY Patterns above available in the following items:

17

Page 16.

Top row: $15-20 each
Bottom: $8-12 each

Page 17.

$8-12 each

Page 18.

Top: $8-12 each
Bottom row: $15-20 each

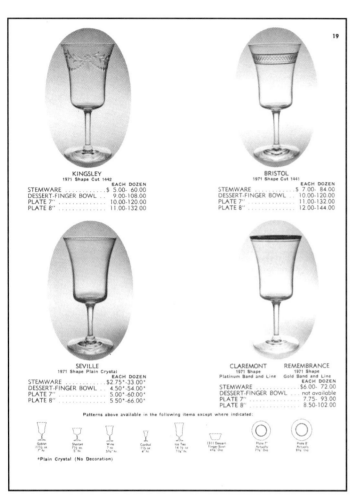

19

KINGSLEY
1971 Shape Cut 1442

	EACH	DOZEN
STEMWARE	$ 5.00-	60.00
DESSERT-FINGER BOWL	9.00-108.00	
PLATE 7″	10.00-120.00	
PLATE 8″	11.00-132.00	

BRISTOL
1971 Shape Cut 1441

	EACH	DOZEN
STEMWARE	$ 7.00-	84.00
DESSERT-FINGER BOWL	10.00-120.00	
PLATE 7″	11.00-132.00	
PLATE 8″	12.00-144.00	

SEVILLE
1971 Shape Plain Crystal

	EACH	DOZEN
STEMWARE	$2.75*-33.00*	
DESSERT-FINGER BOWL	4.50*-54.00*	
PLATE 7″	5.00*-60.00*	
PLATE 8″	5.50*-66.00*	

CLAREMONT **REMEMBRANCE**
1971 Shape / 1971 Shape
Platinum Band and Line / Gold Band and Line

	EACH	DOZEN
STEMWARE	$6.00-	72.00
DESSERT-FINGER BOWL	not available	
PLATE 7″	7.75- 93.00	
PLATE 8″	8.50-102.00	

Patterns above available in the following items except where indicated:

*Plain Crystal (No Decoration)

Page 19.

$15-20 each
Bottom left: $8-12 each

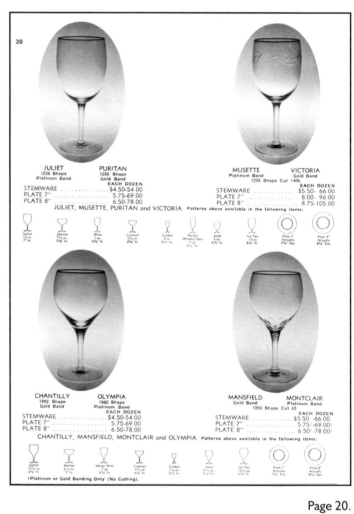

20

JULIET **PURITAN**
1235 Shape / 1235 Shape
Platinum Band / Gold Band

	EACH	DOZEN
STEMWARE	$4.50-54.00	
PLATE 7″	5.75-69.00	
PLATE 8″	6.50-78.00	

MUSETTE **VICTORIA**
Platinum Band / 1235 Shape Cut 1406

	EACH	DOZEN
STEMWARE	$5.50- 66.00	
PLATE 7″	8.00- 96.00	
PLATE 8″	8.75-105.00	

JULIET, MUSETTE, PURITAN and VICTORIA Patterns above available in the following items:

CHANTILLY **OLYMPIA**
1962 Shape / 1962 Shape
Gold Band / Platinum Band

	EACH	DOZEN
STEMWARE	$4.50-54.00	
PLATE 7″	5.75-69.00	
PLATE 8″	6.50-78.00	

MANSFIELD **MONTCLAIR**
Gold Band / Platinum Band
| / 1350 Shape Cut 63

	EACH	DOZEN
STEMWARE	$5.50- 66.00	
PLATE 7″	5.75- 69.00	
PLATE 8″	6.50- 78.00	

CHANTILLY, MANSFIELD, MONTCLAIR and OLYMPIA Patterns above available in the following items:

†Platinum or Gold Banding Only (No Cutting).

Page 20.

$10-15 each

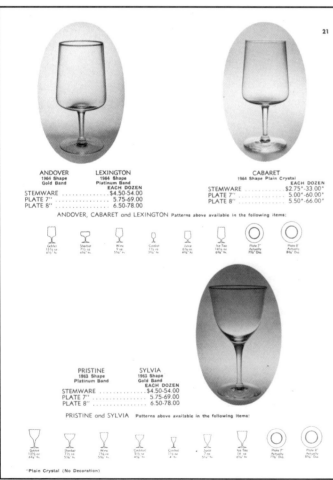

21

ANDOVER **LEXINGTON**
1964 Shape / 1964 Shape
Gold Band / Platinum Band

	EACH	DOZEN
STEMWARE	$4.50-54.00	
PLATE 7″	5.75-69.00	
PLATE 8″	6.50-78.00	

CABARET
1964 Shape Plain Crystal

	EACH	DOZEN
STEMWARE	$2.75*-33.00*	
PLATE 7″	5.00*-60.00*	
PLATE 8″	5.50*-66.00*	

ANDOVER, CABARET and LEXINGTON Patterns above available in the following items:

PRISTINE **SYLVIA**
1963 Shape / 1963 Shape
Platinum Band / Gold Band

	EACH	DOZEN
STEMWARE	$4.50-54.00	
PLATE 7″	5.75-69.00	
PLATE 8″	6.50-78.00	

PRISTINE and SYLVIA Patterns above available in the following items:

*Plain Crystal (No Decoration)

Page 21.

$10-15 each
Top right: $8-12 each

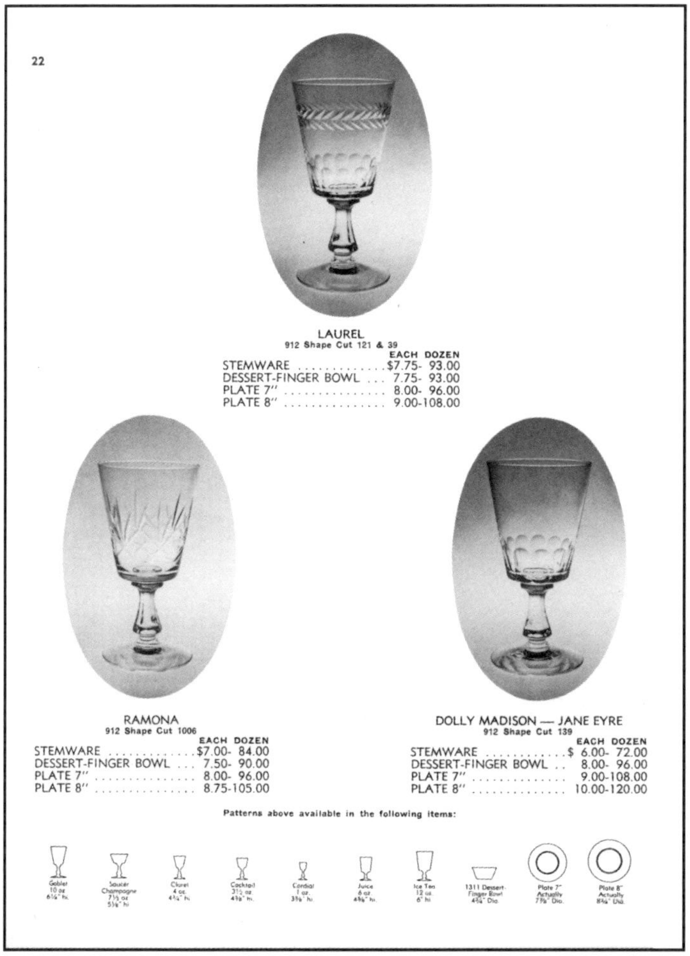

22

LAUREL
912 Shape Cut 121 & 39

	EACH DOZEN
STEMWARE	$7.75- 93.00
DESSERT-FINGER BOWL	7.75- 93.00
PLATE 7"	8.00- 96.00
PLATE 8"	9.00-108.00

RAMONA
912 Shape Cut 1006

	EACH DOZEN
STEMWARE	$7.00- 84.00
DESSERT-FINGER BOWL	7.50- 90.00
PLATE 7"	8.00- 96.00
PLATE 8"	8.75-105.00

DOLLY MADISON — JANE EYRE
912 Shape Cut 139

	EACH DOZEN
STEMWARE	$ 6.00- 72.00
DESSERT-FINGER BOWL	8.00- 96.00
PLATE 7"	9.00-108.00
PLATE 8"	10.00-120.00

Patterns above available in the following items:

Goblet 10 oz 6 1/8" hi. · Saucer Champagne 7 1/2 oz 5 1/8" hi · Claret 4 oz. 4 3/4" hi · Cocktail 3 1/2 oz. 4 3/8" hi. · Cordial 1 oz. 3 5/8" hi. · Juice 6 oz. 4 5/8" hi. · Ice Tea 12 oz. 6" hi. · 1311 Dessert-Finger Bowl 4 3/4" Dia. · Plate 7" Actually 7 3/8" Dia. · Plate 8" Actually 8 3/4" Dia.

Page 22.

$15-25 each

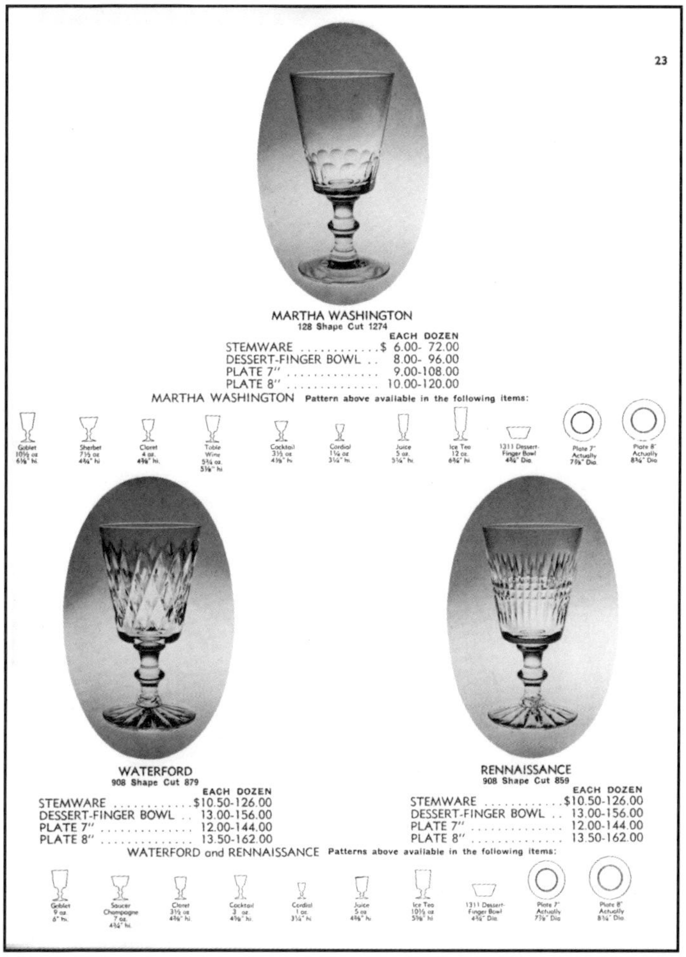

23

MARTHA WASHINGTON
128 Shape Cut 1274

	EACH DOZEN
STEMWARE	$ 6.00- 72.00
DESSERT-FINGER BOWL	8.00- 96.00
PLATE 7"	9.00-108.00
PLATE 8"	10.00-120.00

MARTHA WASHINGTON Pattern above available in the following items:

Goblet 10 1/2 oz 6 1/8" hi. · Sherbet 7 1/2 oz 4 3/4" hi · Claret 4 oz. 4 3/8" hi. · Table Wine 5 3/4 oz. 5 1/8" hi · Cocktail 3 1/2 oz 4 1/8" hi · Cordial 1 1/4 oz 3 1/4" hi. · Juice 5 oz. 5 1/4" hi. · Ice Tea 12 oz. 6 3/4" hi. · 1311 Dessert-Finger Bowl 4 3/4" Dia. · Plate 7" Actually 7 5/8" Dia. · Plate 8" Actually 8 3/4" Dia.

WATERFORD
908 Shape Cut 879

	EACH DOZEN
STEMWARE	$10.50-126.00
DESSERT-FINGER BOWL	13.00-156.00
PLATE 7"	12.00-144.00
PLATE 8"	13.50-162.00

RENNAISSANCE
908 Shape Cut 859

	EACH DOZEN
STEMWARE	$10.50-126.00
DESSERT-FINGER BOWL	13.00-156.00
PLATE 7"	12.00-144.00
PLATE 8"	13.50-162.00

WATERFORD and RENNAISSANCE Patterns above available in the following items:

Goblet 9 oz. 6" hi. · Saucer Champagne 7 oz. 4 3/4" hi. · Claret 3 1/2 oz 4 3/8" hi. · Cocktail 3 oz. 4 1/8" hi. · Cordial 1 oz. 3 1/4" hi · Juice 5 oz 4 5/8" hi · Ice Tea 10 1/2 oz 5 5/8" hi · 1311 Dessert-Finger Bowl 4 3/4" Dia. · Plate 7" Actually 7 5/8" Dia · Plate 8" Actually 8 3/4" Dia.

Page 23.

Top: $15-20 each
Bottom row: $20-30 each

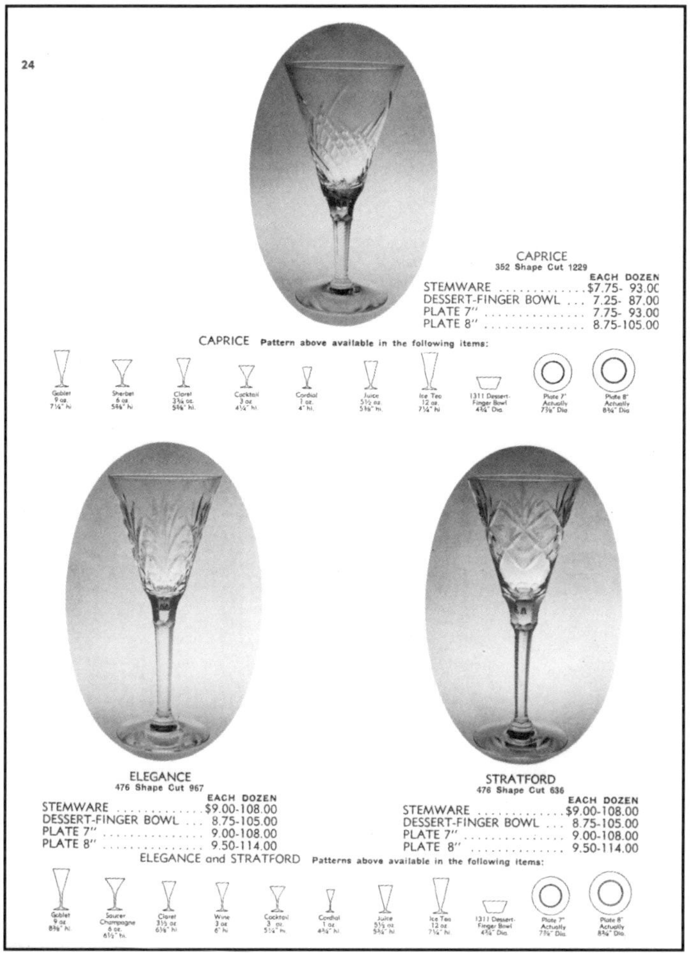

24

CAPRICE
352 Shape Cut 1229

	EACH DOZEN
STEMWARE	$7.75- 93.0C
DESSERT-FINGER BOWL	7.25- 87.00
PLATE 7"	7.75- 93.00
PLATE 8"	8.75-105.00

CAPRICE Pattern above available in the following items:

Goblet 9 oz. 7 1/4" hi · Sherbet 6 oz. 5 5/8" hi · Claret 3 3/4 oz. 5 5/8" hi. · Cocktail 3 oz 4 1/4" hi. · Cordial 1 oz. 4" hi. · Juice 5 1/2 oz. 5 3/8" hi. · Ice Tea 12 oz. 7 1/4" hi · 1311 Dessert-Finger Bowl 4 3/4" Dia. · Plate 7" Actually 7 5/8" Dia · Plate 8" Actually 8 3/4" Dia

ELEGANCE
476 Shape Cut 967

	EACH DOZEN
STEMWARE	$9.00-108.00
DESSERT-FINGER BOWL	8.75-105.00
PLATE 7"	9.00-108.00
PLATE 8"	9.50-114.00

STRATFORD
476 Shape Cut 636

	EACH DOZEN
STEMWARE	$9.00-108.00
DESSERT-FINGER BOWL	8.75-105.00
PLATE 7"	9.00-108.00
PLATE 8"	9.50-114.00

ELEGANCE and STRATFORD Patterns above available in the following items:

Goblet 9 oz 8 3/8" hi. · Saucer Champagne 6 oz. 6 1/2" hi. · Claret 3 1/2 oz 6 1/8" hi · Wine 3 oz 6" hi · Cocktail 3 oz. 5 1/4" hi. · Cordial 1 oz 4 3/4" hi. · Juice 5 1/2 oz 5 3/4" hi. · Ice Tea 12 oz 7 1/4" hi. · 1311 Dessert-Finger Bowl 4 3/4" Dia. · Plate 7" Actually 7 5/8" Dia. · Plate 8" Actually 8 3/4" Dia.

Page 24.

$20-30 each

25

CORINTHIAN
331 Shape Cut 1300

	EACH	DOZEN
STEMWARE	$ 6.00	72.00
DESSERT-FINGER BOWL	8.00	96.00
PLATE 7"	9.00	108.00
PLATE 8"	10.00	120.00

CORINTHIAN Pattern above available in the following items:

LAUREL WREATH
8000 Shape Optic Cut 121

	EACH	DOZEN
STEMWARE	$5.25	63.00
DESSERT-FINGER BOWL	7.75	93.00
PLATE 7"	8.00	96.00
PLATE 8"	9.00	108.00

LAUREL WREATH Pattern above available in the following items:

Page 25.

$15-20 each

27

GOURMET COLLECTION
featuring
Vintage Wine Goblet
#5321 Shape Plain Crystal

	EACH	DOZEN
STEMWARE	$3.00	36.00

Gourmet Collection

by
SENECA

The GOURMET COLLECTION, bubble shaped, thin-stemmed and generously proportioned, is handcrafted of the finest lead crystal.
Each Glass bears a Label identifying and describing its recommended usage.
The GOURMET COLLECTION is available in the Items featured below.

Magnum Wine Goblet 18 oz. 7⅜" hi. — Vintage Wine Goblet 14 oz. 7" hi. — Red Wine 10½ oz. 6⅞" hi — White Wine 8½ oz. 6⅜" hi — Champagne 9½ oz. 8" hi — Sherry and Port 5 oz. 6" hi — Dessert-Champagne 11 oz. 4⅞" hi — Brandy and Liqueur 2½ oz. 4½" hi

Page 27.

$8-12 each

28

FRANK SCHOONMAKER®
Wine Glasses

THE FRANK SCHOONMAKER® Wine Glasses, hand blown in the highest quality lead crystal, are made by the Seneca Glass Company, one of America's oldest and most famous manufacturers of fine glassware. Each glass bears the Frank Schoonmaker Label for easy identification and proof of authenticity. A booklet describing the proper use of the Schoonmaker Wine Glasses is available upon request. *See complimentary Epicure Pattern on facing page.*

EACH DOZEN

#1 CHAMPAGNE TULIP 2.75-33.00
Here is the truly correct form in which to serve the finest Champagnes.
Capacity - 8 oz. Height - 8½" Plain Crystal

#2 JOHANNISBERG 2.75-33.00
Delicate and tall, this displays fine Rhines and Moselles to perfection.
Capacity - 6 oz. Height - 6 1/8" Plain Crystal

#3 MAGNUM 2.75-33.00
A "Connoisseur's Glass", superb for fine wines, especially the great Burgundies.
Capacity - 10 oz. Height - 5 7/8" Plain Crystal

#4 VIN DU PAYS 2.75-33.00
The perfect all purpose wine glass. It suits any wine, graces any table.
Capacity - 8 oz. Height - 5 3/8" Plain Crystal

#5 CABERNET 2.75-33.00
A glass worthy of the finest clarets; ample and beautifully proportioned.
Capacity - 9 oz. Height - 6½" Plain Crystal

#6 SOLERA 2.75-33.00
For Sherry, Port, Madeira. May also be used for Cognac and other Liqueurs.
Capacity - 5 oz. Height - 5 1/8" Plain Crystal

#7 V.S.O.P. 2.75-33.00
The rarest old Cognacs are at home in this glass. Neither too large nor too small.
Capacity - 7 oz. Height - 4½" Plain Crystal

#8 CHATEAU 2.75-33.00
The white wine companion to the Cabernet. Ideal for Sauternes and Graves.
Capacity - 7 oz. Height - 6" Plain Crystal

NOTE: A set of 8 Display Wine Bottles furnished FREE, upon request.

Champagne Tulip

Magnum

Cabernet

V. S. O. P.

Johannisberg

Vin Du Pays

Solera

Chateau

Page 28.

$8-12 each

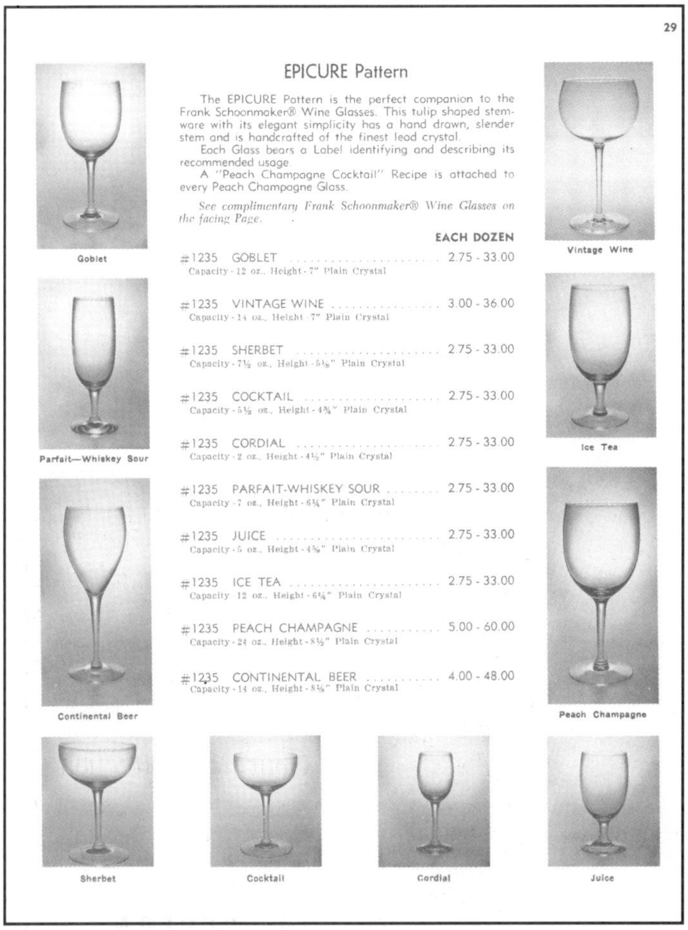

29

EPICURE Pattern

The EPICURE Pattern is the perfect companion to the Frank Schoonmaker® Wine Glasses. This tulip shaped stemware with its elegant simplicity has a hand drawn, slender stem and is handcrafted of the finest lead crystal.

Each Glass bears a Label identifying and describing its recommended usage.

A "Peach Champagne Cocktail" Recipe is attached to every Peach Champagne Glass.

See complimentary Frank Schoonmaker® Wine Glasses on the facing Page.

	EACH DOZEN
#1235 GOBLET — Capacity - 12 oz., Height - 7" Plain Crystal	2.75 - 33.00
#1235 VINTAGE WINE — Capacity - 14 oz., Height - 7" Plain Crystal	3.00 - 36.00
#1235 SHERBET — Capacity - 7½ oz., Height - 5⅛" Plain Crystal	2.75 - 33.00
#1235 COCKTAIL — Capacity - 5½ oz., Height - 4¾" Plain Crystal	2.75 - 33.00
#1235 CORDIAL — Capacity - 2 oz., Height - 4½" Plain Crystal	2.75 - 33.00
#1235 PARFAIT-WHISKEY SOUR — Capacity - 7 oz., Height - 6¼" Plain Crystal	2.75 - 33.00
#1235 JUICE — Capacity - 5 oz., Height - 4⅝" Plain Crystal	2.75 - 33.00
#1235 ICE TEA — Capacity 12 oz., Height - 6¼" Plain Crystal	2.75 - 33.00
#1235 PEACH CHAMPAGNE — Capacity - 24 oz., Height - 8½" Plain Crystal	5.00 - 60.00
#1235 CONTINENTAL BEER — Capacity - 14 oz., Height - 8⅛" Plain Crystal	4.00 - 48.00

Goblet · Vintage Wine · Parfait—Whiskey Sour · Ice Tea · Continental Beer · Peach Champagne · Sherbet · Cocktail · Cordial · Juice

Page 29.

$8-12 each

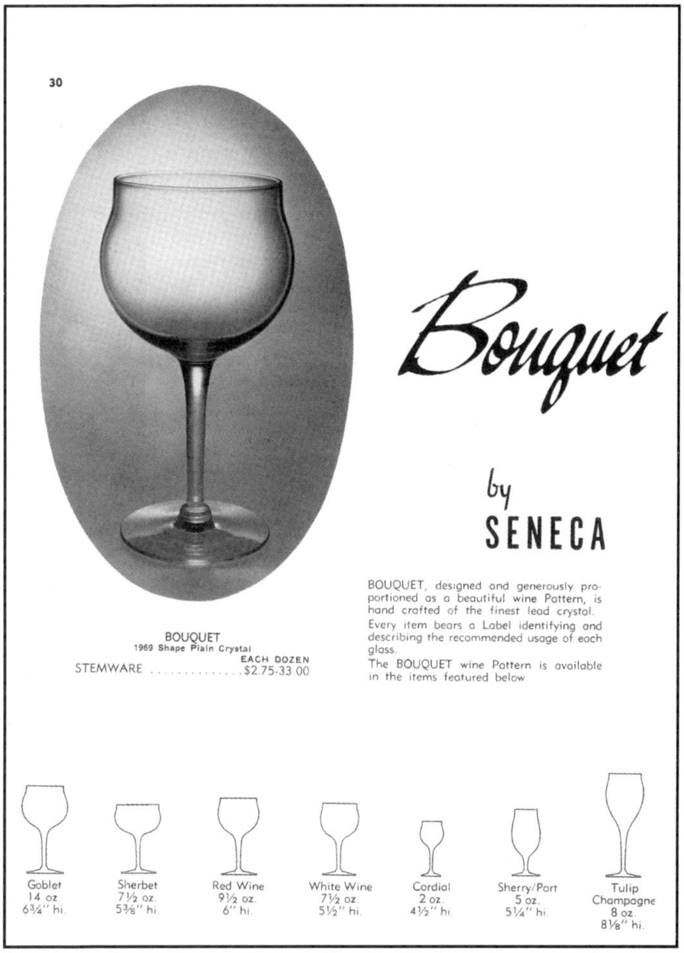

30

Bouquet
by
SENECA

BOUQUET
1969 Shape Plain Crystal

STEMWARE .... EACH DOZEN $2.75-33.00

BOUQUET, designed and generously proportioned as a beautiful wine Pattern, is hand crafted of the finest lead crystal. Every item bears a Label identifying and describing the recommended usage of each glass.
The BOUQUET wine Pattern is available in the items featured below.

Goblet	Sherbet	Red Wine	White Wine	Cordial	Sherry/Port	Tulip Champagne
14 oz.	7½ oz.	9½ oz.	7½ oz.	2 oz.	5 oz.	8 oz.
6¾" hi.	5⅜" hi.	6" hi.	5½" hi.	4½" hi.	5¼" hi.	8⅛" hi.

Page 30.

$8-12 each

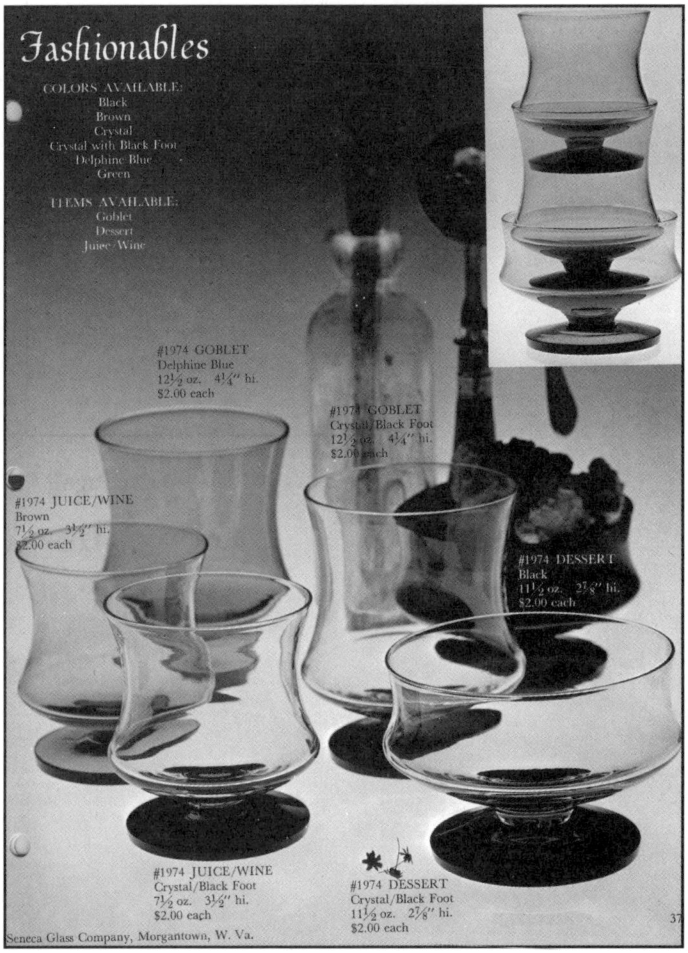

Fashionables
COLORS AVAILABLE:
Black
Brown
Crystal
Crystal with Black Foot
Delphine Blue
Green
ITEMS AVAILABLE:
Goblet
Dessert
Juice/Wine
#1974 GOBLET Delphine Blue 12½ oz. 4¼" hi. $2.00 each
#1974 GOBLET Crystal/Black Foot 12½ oz. 4¼" hi. $2.00 each
#1974 JUICE/WINE Brown 7½ oz. 3½" hi. $2.00 each
#1974 DESSERT Black 11½ oz. 2⅞" hi. $2.00 each
#1974 JUICE/WINE Crystal/Black Foot 7½ oz. 3½" hi. $2.00 each
#1974 DESSERT Crystal/Black Foot 11½ oz. 2⅞" hi. $2.00 each
Seneca Glass Company, Morgantown, W. Va.
37

Page 37.

$10-15 each

Driftwood Casual

COLORS AVAILABLE:
Amber
Buttercup (Yellow)
Cinnamon (Brown)
Crystal
Delphine Blue
Grey
Moss Green
Peacock Blue
Accent Red

PRICES EACH

ITEMS AVAILABLE	Standard Colors	Accent Red
Ice Tea	$1.00	$ 1.95
Hi Ball	1.00	1.95
Old Fashion	1.00	1.95
Roly Poly	1.00	1.95
Juice	1.00	1.95
Cocktail	1.00	1.95
Goblet	1.95	3.25
Sherbet	1.95	3.25
Dessert-Cereal Bowl	1.35	2.25
Plate	3.00	
Pitcher 32 oz.	5.50	
Pitcher 65 oz.	6.50	10.50
Flowerlite	5.00	
Bud Vase	2.00	
Covered Dish	5.00	

#1980 PITCHER
Accent Red
65 oz.
$10.50 each

#1980 ROLY POLY
Moss Green
12 oz.
$1.00 each

#1980 GOBLET
Buttercup (Yellow)
18 oz.   5¾" hi.
$1.95 each

#1980 ICE TEA
Delphine Blue
16 oz.   5¾" hi.
$1.00 each

#1980 SHERBET
Cinnamon (Brown)
6 oz.   3" hi.
$1.95 each

#1980 OLD FASHION
Amber
14 oz.   3¾" hi.
$1.00 each

38 Seneca Glass Company, Morgantown, W. Va.

Page 38.

$10-15 each

Cascade

COLORS AVAILABLE:
Crystal
Green
Grey
Peacock Blue
Yellow

ITEMS AVAILABLE:
Beverage
Old Fashion

#1972 BEVERAGE
Yellow
15½ oz.   5" hi.
$1.50 each

#1972 OLD FASHION
Green
11½ oz.   3¾" hi.
$1.50 each

#1972 OLD FASHION
Grey
11½ oz.   3¾" hi.
$1.50 each

#1972 OLD FASHION
Crystal
11½ oz.   3¾" hi.
$1.50 each

#1972 BEVERAGE
Peacock Blue
15½ oz.   5" hi.
$1.50 each

#1972 OLD FASHION
Yellow
11½ oz.   3¾" hi.
$1.50 each

Seneca Glass Company, Morgantown, W. Va.

Page 39.

$10-15 each

COLORS and DESIGNS
AVAILABLE:
Blue Crystal Foot
Pink Crystal Foot
Blue Crystal Foot Cut 1443
Pink Crystal Foot Cut 1443
Black Decal
and Gold Band
White Decal
and Platinum Band

ITEMS AVAILABLE:
Goblet
Sherbet
Wine
Cordial
Ice Tea

INTRIGUE
#1973 WINE
Blue Crystal Foot Cut 1443
8½ oz.   6½" hi.
$5.00 each

GALAXY (Blue)
#1973 ICE TEA
Blue Crystal Foot
17½ oz.   7½" hi.
$3.50 each

GOLD FLORENTINE
#1973 GOBLET
Black Decal/Gold Band
13 oz.   7" hi.
$4.50 each

ENCHANTMENT
#1973 SHERBET
Pink/Crystal Foot Cut 1443
7½ oz.   5⅛" hi.
$5.00 each

PLATINUM LACE
#1973 GOBLET
White Decal/Platinum Band
13 oz.   7" hi.
$4.50 each

GALAXY (Pink)
#1973 CORDIAL
Pink/Crystal Foot
1½ oz.   4" hi.
$3.50 each

40 Seneca Glass Company, Morgantown, W. Va.

Page 40.

$15-20 each

ILLUSION
#5321 GOBLET
Pink/Crystal Foot Cut 1443
14 oz.   7" hi.
$5.00 each

ROYALTY
#5321 WHITE WINE
Crystal Cut 1443
8½ oz.   6⅝" hi.
$5.00 each

ILLUSION
#5321 WHITE WINE
Pink/Crystal Foot Cut 1443
8½ oz.   6⅝" hi.
$5.00 each

CLASSIC
#5321 DESSERT-
CHAMPAGNE
Blue/Crystal Foot
Cut 1443
11 oz.   4⅞" hi.
$5.00 each

CHALET (Pink)
#5321 GOBLET
Pink/Crystal Foot
14 oz.   7" hi.
$3.50 each

CHALET (Pink)
#5321 WHITE WINE
Pink/Crystal Foot
8½ oz.   6¾" hi.
$3.50 each

CHALET (Pink)
#5321 DESSERT-CHAMPAGNE
Pink/Crystal Foot
11 oz.   4⅞" hi.
$3.50 each

Seneca Glass Company,
Morgantown, W. Va.   41

Page 41. $8-15 each

Seville

#1971 ICE TEA
Green
14½ oz.   7½" hi.
$3.50 each

#1971 WINE
Delphine Blue
7 oz.   5⅞" hi.
$3.50 each

#1971 SHERBET
Grey
7½ oz.   5" hi.
$3.50 each

#1971 GOBLET
Yellow
11½ oz.   7" hi.
$3.50 each

#1971 CORDIAL
Brown
1½ oz.   4" hi.
$3.50 each

42 Seneca Glass Company, Morgantown, W. Va.

Page 42. $8-15 each

Bouquet

#1969 ICE TEA
Grey
14 oz.   6⅜" hi.
$3.50 each

#1969 WINE
Brown
7½ oz.   5¾" hi.
$3.50 each

#1969 CORDIAL
Yellow
2 oz.   4½" hi.
$3.50 each

#1969 GOBLET
Delphine Blue
14 oz.   6¾" hi.
$3.50 each

#1969 SHERBET
Green
7½ oz.   5⅜" hi.
$3.50 each

Seneca Glass Company, Morgantown, W. Va.   43

Page 43. $8-15 each

Cabaret

#1964 ICE TEA
Brown/Crystal Foot
14½ oz.   6⅞" hi.
$3.50 each

#1964 WINE
Green/Crystal Foot
9 oz.   5⅝" hi.
$3.50 each

#1964 SHERBET
Grey/Crystal Foot
7½ oz.   4⅞" hi.
$3.50 each

#1964 GOBLET
Delphine Blue/Crystal Foot
13¾ oz.   6½" hi.
$3.50 each

#1964 CORDIAL
Yellow/Crystal Foot
1½ oz.   3⅜" hi.
$3.50 each

44 Seneca Glass Company, Morgantown, W. Va.

Photography and Lithography by Papure Brothers, Parkersburg, W. Va.

Page 44. $8-15 each

1972 CATALOG

The Fashionables

Colors Available:
Black
Brown
Crystal
Crystal with Black Foot
Delphine Blue
Green
Plum

Items Available:
Goblet
Dessert
Juice/Wine
Beverage
Old Fashion
6-piece Cocktail/
Juice Set

1974 6-pc.
Cocktail/Juice Set
Crystal with Black Foot
Mixer 40 oz. Glasses 7½ oz.

1974 Old Fashion
Delphine Blue
9½ oz. 4" hi.

1974 Goblet
Black
12½ oz. 4¼" hi.

1974 Beverage
Crystal
14 oz. 5" hi.

1974 Dessert
Plum
11½ oz. 2⅞" hi.

1974 Juice/Wine
Brown
7½ oz. 3½" hi.

Seneca Glass Company, Morgantown, W. Va.

Page 3. $10-15 each

Driftwood Casual

Items Available:
Ice Tea
Hi Ball
Old Fashion
Roly Poly
Juice
Cocktail
Goblet
Sherbet
Dessert-Cereal Bowl
Plate
Pitcher 32 oz.
Pitcher 65 oz.
Flowerlite
Bud Vase
Covered Dish

Colors Available:
Amber
Buttercup (Yellow)
Cinnamon (Brown)
Crystal
Delphine Blue
Grey
Moss Green
Peacock Blue
Accent Red

1980 Pitcher
Accent Red
65 oz. 9½" hi.

1980 Goblet
Buttercup (Yellow)
5½" hi.

1980 Ice Tea
Delphine Blue
16 oz. 5¾" hi.

1980 Roly Poly

1980 Old Fashion
Amber
14 oz. 3¾" hi.

1980 Sherbet
Cinnamon (Brown)
6 oz. 3" hi.

Page 4. $10-15 each

Page 5.

$10-15 each

Page 6.

Two Tone, top left: $15-20 each
$10-15 each

Page 7.

$10-15 each

Nocturne

Colors Available:
...

Items Available:
...

1975 Ice Tea
...

1975 Old Fashion
Black
12½ oz. 3¾" hi.

1975 Wine
Brown
8½ oz. 6½" hi.

1975 Sherbet
Plum
7 oz. 4⅝" hi.

1975 Cordial
Crystal
1½ oz. 4⅝" hi.

1975 Beverage
Brown
16 oz. 5¾" hi.

1975 Goblet
Plum
11 oz. 7½" hi.

Seneca Glass Company, Morgantown, W. Va.

Page 8.

$15-20 each

Colors Available:
Brown
Delphine Blue
Green
Grey
Yellow

Items Available:
Goblet
Sherbet
Wine
Cordial
Ice Tea

Bouquet

1969 Wine
Brown
7½ oz. 5½" hi.

1969 Ice Tea
Grey
14 oz. 6⅜" hi.

1969 Cordial
Yellow
2 oz. 4½" hi.

1969 Goblet
Delphine Blue
14 oz. 6¾" hi.

1969 Sherbet
Green
7½ oz. 5⅜" hi.

Seneca Glass Company, Morgantown, W. Va.

Page 9.

$10-15 each

Seville

Colors Available:
Brown
Delphine Blue
Green
Grey
Yellow

Items Available:
Goblet
Sherbet
Wine
Cordial
Ice Tea

1971 Ice Tea
Green
14½ oz. 7⅛" hi.

1971 Wine
Delphine Blue
7 oz. 5⅞" hi.

1971 Sherbet
Grey
7½ oz. 5" hi.

1971 Goblet
Yellow
11½ oz. 7" hi.

1971 Cordial
Brown
1½ oz. 4" hi.

O Seneca Glass Company, Morgantown, W. Va.

Page 10.

$10-15 each

Gourmet Collection

by

SENECA

GOURMET COLLECTION
featuring
Vintage Wine Goblet

5321 Shape Plain Crystal

The GOURMET COLLECTION, bubble shaped, thin-stemmed and generously proportioned, is handcrafted of the finest lead crystal.

Each Glass bears a Label identifying and describing its recommended usage.

The GOURMET COLLECTION is available in the Items featured below.

Magnum Wine Goblet
18 oz
7⅞" hi.

Vintage Wine Goblet
14 oz
7" hi.

Red Wine
10½ oz
6⅞" hi.

White Wine
8½ oz
6⅝" hi.

Champagne
9½ oz
8" hi.

Sherry and Port
5 oz
6" hi.

Dessert-Champagne
11 oz
4⅞" hi.

Brandy and Liqueur
2½ oz
4½" hi.

EPICURE Pattern

The EPICURE Pattern is the perfect companion to the Frank Schoonmaker® Wine Glasses. This tulip shaped stemware with its elegant simplicity has a hand drawn, slender stem and is handcrafted of the finest lead crystal.

Each Glass bears a Label identifying and describing its recommended usage.

A "Peach Champagne Cocktail" Recipe is attached to every Peach Champagne Glass.

See complimentary Frank Schoonmaker® Wine Glasses on the facing Page.

1235 Goblet
12 oz. 7" hi.

1235 Vintage Wine
14 oz. 7" hi.

1235 Continental Beer
14 oz. 8⅛" hi.

1235 Dessert-Champagne
7½ oz. 5⅛" hi.

1235 Peach Champagne
24 oz. 8½" hi.

1235 Beverage
15 oz. 5" hi.

1235 (463) Brandy Inhaler
22 oz. 6" hi.

1235 Parfait-Whiskey Sour
7 oz. 6¼" hi.

1235 Ice Tea
12 oz. 6¼" hi.

1235 Old Fashion
11½ oz. 3¾" hi.

1235 Cocktail
5½ oz. 4⅜" hi.

1235 Cordial
2 oz. 4½" hi.

1235 Juice
5 oz. 4⅝" hi.

12

Champagne Tulip

Magnum

Cabernet

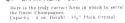

V. S. O. P.

FRANK SCHOONMAKER®
Wine Glasses

The FRANK SCHOONMAKER® Wine Glasses, hand blown in the highest quality lead crystal, are made by the Seneca Glass Company, one of America's oldest and most famous manufacturers of fine glassware. Each glass bears the Frank Schoonmaker Label for easy identification and proof of authenticity. A booklet describing the proper use of the Schoonmaker Wine Glasses is available upon request. *See complimentary Epicure Pattern on facing page.*

#1 CHAMPAGNE TULIP
Here is the truly correct form in which to serve the finest Champagnes.
Capacity - 8 oz. Height - 8½" Plain Crystal

#2 JOHANNISBERG
Delicate and tall, this displays fine Rhines and Moselles to perfection.
Capacity - 8 oz. Height - 6¼" Plain Crystal

#3 MAGNUM
A "Connoisseur's Glass", superb for fine wines, especially the great Burgundies.
Capacity - 18 oz. Height - 5¾" Plain Crystal

#4 VIN DU PAYS
The perfect all purpose wine glass. It suits any wine, graces any table.
Capacity - 8 oz. Height - 5¾" Plain Crystal

#5 CABERNET
A glass worthy of the finest clarets; ample and beautifully proportioned.
Capacity - 9 oz. Height - 6½" Plain Crystal

#6 SOLERA
For Sherry, Port, Madeira. May also be used for Cognac and other Liqueurs.
Capacity - 5 oz. Height - 5½" Plain Crystal

#7 V.S.O.P
The rarest old Cognacs are at home in this glass. Neither too large nor too small.
Capacity - 7 oz. Height - 4½" Plain Crystal

#8 CHATEAU
The white wine companion to the Cabernet. Ideal for Sauternes and Graves.
Capacity - 7 oz. Height - 6" Plain Crystal

NOTE: A set of 8 Display Wine Bottles furnished FREE, upon request.

Johannisberg

Vin Du Pays

Solera

Chateau

Page 11.

$8-12 each

Page 12.

$8-12 each

Page 13.

$8-12 each

Bouquet
by SENECA

BOUQUET, designed and generously proportioned as a beautiful wine Pattern, is hand crafted of the finest lead crystal.
Every item bears a Label identifying and describing the recommended usage of each glass.
The BOUQUET wine Pattern is available in the items featured below

BOUQUET
1969 Shape Plain Crystal

| Goblet 14 oz 6¾" hi | Sherbet 7½ oz 5⅜" hi | Red Wine 9½ oz 6" hi | White Wine 7½ oz 5½" hi | Cordial 2 oz 4½" hi | Sherry Port 5 oz 5¼" hi | Tulip Champagne 8 oz 8⅛" hi |

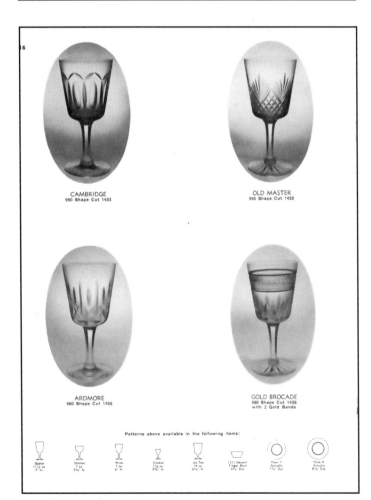

CAMBRIDGE
960 Shape Cut 1433

OLD MASTER
960 Shape Cut 1435

ARDMORE
960 Shape Cut 1436

GOLD BROCADE
960 Shape Cut 1438 with 2 Gold Bands

Patterns above available in the following items:

| Goblet 11½ oz 7" hi | Sherbet 7 oz 5¼" hi | Wine 7 oz 6" hi | Cordial 1¼ oz 3¾" hi | Ice Tea 14 oz 6¼" hi | 1311 Dessert Finger Bowl 4¾" Dia | Plate 7 Actually 7¾" Dia | Plate 8 Actually 8¼" Dia |

Page 14.

$8-12 each

#1235 Cordials
EPICURE Pattern.
Reference—Page 13.

#1 Carafe Plain Crystal
20 oz. 7½" hi

#5321 Brandy Liqueur
GOURMET COLLECTION.
Reference—Page 11.

#8 Chateau and #5 Cabernet
FRANK SCHOONMAKER WINES.
Reference—Page 12.

#1 Carafe Plain Crystal
32 oz. 8½" hi.

#5321 Red Wine and White Wine
GOURMET COLLECTION
Reference—Page 11.

Page 15.

$8-12 each
Bottom center: $25-35 each

Page 16.

$15-25 each

94

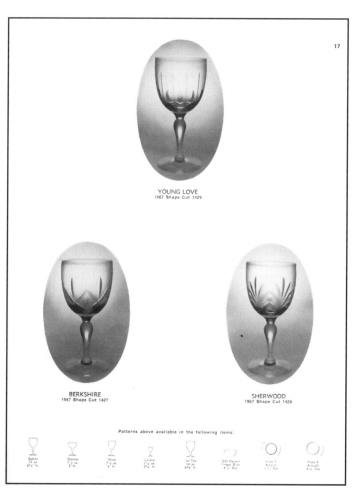

YOUNG LOVE
1967 Shape Cut 1429

BERKSHIRE
1967 Shape Cut 1427

SHERWOOD
1967 Shape Cut 1426

Patterns above available in the following items:

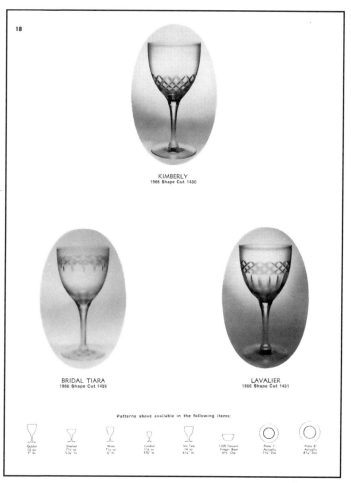

KIMBERLY
1966 Shape Cut 1430

BRIDAL TIARA
1966 Shape Cut 1439

LAVALIER
1966 Shape Cut 1431

Patterns above available in the following items:

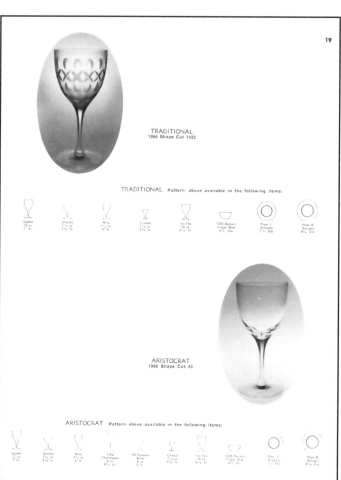

TRADITIONAL
1966 Shape Cut 1432

TRADITIONAL   Pattern above available in the following items:

ARISTOCRAT
1966 Shape Cut 43

ARISTOCRAT   Pattern above available in the following items:

Page 17.

$15-20 each

Page 18.

$15-20 each

Page 19.

$15-20 each

95

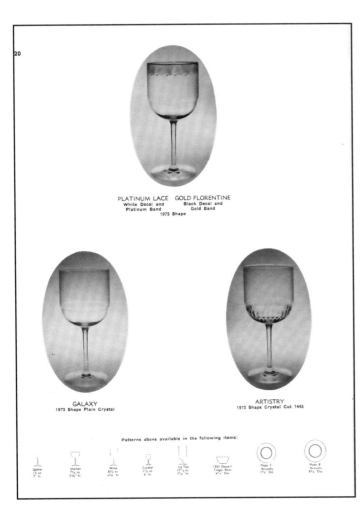

PLATINUM LACE
White Decal and
Platinum Band
1973 Shape

GOLD FLORENTINE
Black Decal and
Gold Band

GALAXY
1973 Shape Plain Crystal

ARTISTRY
1973 Shape Crystal Cut 1443

Patterns above available in the following items:

Page 20.

$15-20 each

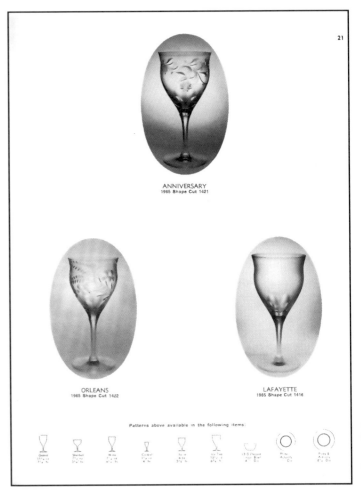

ANNIVERSARY
1965 Shape Cut 1421

ORLEANS
1965 Shape Cut 1422

LAFAYETTE
1965 Shape Cut 1416

Patterns above available in the following items:

Page 21.

$25-35 each
Bottom right: $15-20 each

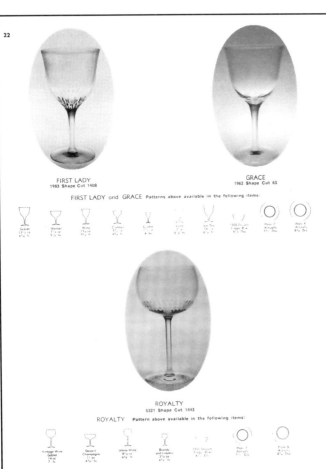

FIRST LADY
1963 Shape Cut 1408

GRACE
1963 Shape Cut 63

FIRST LADY and GRACE Patterns above available in the following items:

ROYALTY
5321 Shape Cut 1443

ROYALTY Pattern above available in the following items:

Page 22.

$10-20 each

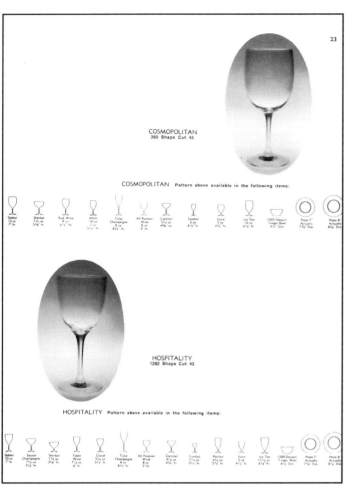

COSMOPOLITAN
360 Shape Cut 43

COSMOPOLITAN   Pattern above available in the following items:

Page 23.

$10-20 each

HOSPITALITY
1282 Shape Cut 43

HOSPITALITY   Pattern above available in the following items:

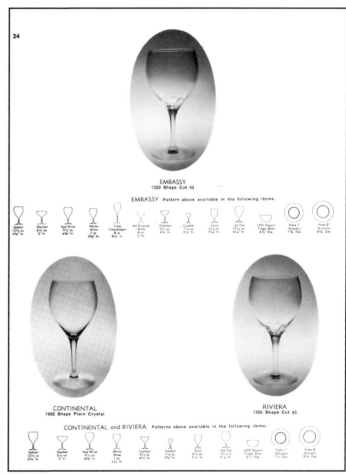

EMBASSY
1350 Shape Cut 43

EMBASSY   Pattern above available in the following items:

CONTINENTAL
1962 Shape Plain Crystal

RIVIERA
1350 Shape Cut 63

CONTINENTAL and RIVIERA   Patterns above available in the following items:

Page 24.

$10-20 each

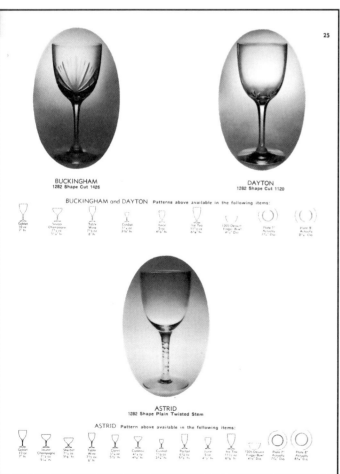

BUCKINGHAM
1282 Shape Cut 1426

DAYTON
1282 Shape Cut 1120

BUCKINGHAM and DAYTON   Patterns above available in the following items:

ASTRID
1282 Shape Plain Twisted Stem

ASTRID   Pattern above available in the following items:

Page 25.

$10-20 each

97

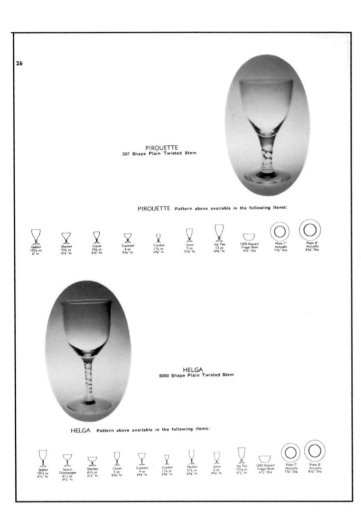

PIROUETTE
307 Shape Plain Twisted Stem

PIROUETTE Pattern above available in the following items:

Goblet 10½ oz 6" hi | Sherbet 5½ oz 4½" hi | Claret 3¼ oz 4½" hi | Cocktail 4 oz 3¾" hi | Cordial 1¼ oz 3¾" hi | Juice 5 oz 5½" hi | Ice Tea 12 oz 6¼" hi | 1305 Dessert Finger Bowl 4½" Dia | Plate 7" Actually 7½" Dia | Plate 8" Actually 8¼" Dia

HELGA
8000 Shape Plain Twisted Stem

HELGA Pattern above available in the following items:

Goblet 10½ oz 6½" hi | Saucer Champagne 6½ oz 4½" hi | Sherbet 6½ oz 3½" hi | Claret 5 oz 5¾" hi | Cocktail 4 oz 4½" hi | Cordial 1¼ oz 3¾" hi | Parfait 5½ oz 6¾" hi | Juice 5 oz 4½" hi | Ice Tea 12½ oz 6½" hi | 1305 Dessert Finger Bowl 4½" Dia | Plate 7" Actually 7½" Dia | Plate 8" Actually 8¼" Dia

Page 26.

$10-15 each

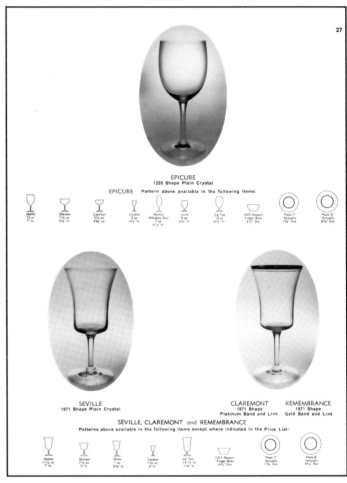

EPICURE
1235 Shape Plain Crystal

EPICURE Pattern above available in the following items:

Goblet 12 oz 7" hi | Sherbet 7½ oz 5½" hi | Cocktail 5½ oz 4½" hi | Cordial 2 oz 4½" hi | Parfait Whiskey Sour 7 oz 6¼" hi | Juice 5 oz 4½" hi | Ice Tea 12 oz 6¼" hi | 1305 Dessert Finger Bowl 4½" Dia | Plate 7" Actually 7½" Dia | Plate 8" Actually 8¼" Dia

SEVILLE
1971 Shape Plain Crystal

CLAREMONT
1971 Shape
Platinum Band and Line

REMEMBRANCE
1971 Shape
Gold Band and Line

SEVILLE, CLAREMONT and REMEMBRANCE
Patterns above available in the following items except where indicated in the Price List:

Goblet 11½ oz 7" hi | Sherbet 7½ oz 5" hi | Wine 7 oz 5¾" hi | Cordial 1½ oz 4" hi | Ice Tea 14½ oz 7¼" hi | 1311 Dessert Finger Bowl 4½" Dia | Plate 7" Actually 7½" Dia | Plate 8" Actually 8¼" Dia

Page 27.

$10-15 each

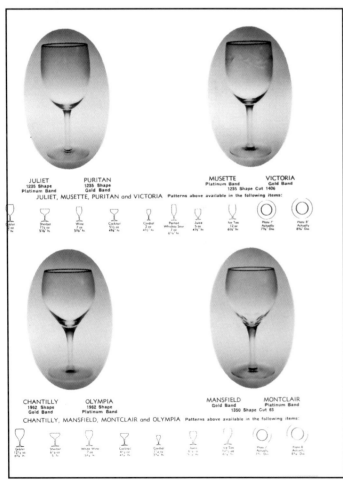

JULIET
1235 Shape
Platinum Band

PURITAN
1235 Shape
Gold Band

MUSETTE
Platinum Band

VICTORIA
Gold Band
1235 Shape Cut 1406

JULIET, MUSETTE, PURITAN and VICTORIA Patterns above available in the following items:

Goblet 12 oz 7" hi | Sherbet 7½ oz 5½" hi | Wine 5 oz 5¾" hi | Cocktail 5½ oz 4½" hi | Cordial 2 oz 4½" hi | Parfait Whiskey Sour 7 oz 6¼" hi | Juice 5 oz 4½" hi | Ice Tea 12 oz 6¼" hi | Plate 7" Actually 7½" Dia | Plate 8" Actually 8¼" Dia

CHANTILLY
1962 Shape
Gold Band

OLYMPIA
1962 Shape
Platinum Band

MANSFIELD
Gold Band

MONTCLAIR
Platinum Band
1350 Shape Cut 63

CHANTILLY, MANSFIELD, MONTCLAIR and OLYMPIA Patterns above available in the following items:

Goblet 12½ oz 6¾" hi | Sherbet 6½ oz 5" hi | White Wine 5½ oz 5¾" hi | Cocktail 4½ oz 4½" hi | Cordial 1½ oz 3½" hi | Juice 5½ oz 4½" hi | Ice Tea 12½ oz 6¼" hi | Plate 7" Actually 7½" Dia | Plate 8" Actually 8¼" Dia

Page 28.

$10-15 each

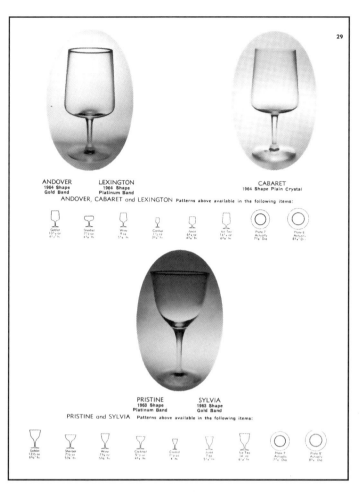

ANDOVER
1964 Shape
Gold Band
LEXINGTON
1964 Shape
Platinum Band

CABARET
1964 Shape Plain Crystal

ANDOVER, CABARET and LEXINGTON Patterns above available in the following items:

Goblet
13½ oz
6½" hi.
Sherbet
7½ oz
4½" hi.
Wine
9 oz
5¼" hi.
Cordial
1½ oz
3½" hi.
Juice
5¾ oz
4¾" hi.
Ice Tea
14½ oz
6¾" hi.
Plate 7
Actually
7¼" Dia.
Plate 8
Actually
8¼" D.

PRISTINE
1963 Shape
Platinum Band
SYLVIA
1963 Shape
Gold Band

PRISTINE and SYLVIA   Patterns above available in the following items:

Goblet
13½ oz
6½" hi.
Sherbet
7½ oz
5½" hi.
Wine
7½ oz
5¼" hi.
Cocktail
5½ oz
4½" hi.
Cordial
1½ oz
4" hi.
Juice
7 oz
5¼" hi.
Ice Tea
14 oz
6¾" hi.
Plate 7
Actually
7¼" Dia.
Plate 8
Actually
8¼" Dia.

Page 29.

$10-12 each

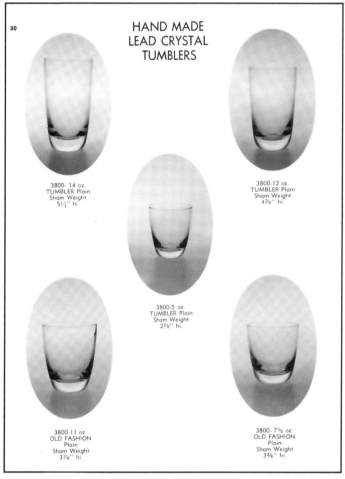

HAND MADE LEAD CRYSTAL TUMBLERS

3800- 14 oz.
TUMBLER Plain
Sham Weight
5½" hi.

3800- 12 oz.
TUMBLER Plain
Sham Weight
4⅞" hi.

3800- 5 oz.
TUMBLER Plain
Sham Weight
2⅞" hi.

3800- 11 oz.
OLD FASHION
Plain
Sham Weight
3⅞" hi.

3800- 7½ oz.
OLD FASHION
Plain
Sham Weight
3⅜" hi.

Page 30.

$8-10 each

CUT 39 TUMBLERS

Cut #39 indicates the Flutes at the base of the Tumblers are 1¼" high and ½" wide. Tumblers Cut #39 have a flat unpolished base.

#8701-14 oz.
TUMBLER
Regular Weight
CUT 39 5½" hi.
#8701-12 oz.
TUMBLER
Regular Weight
CUT 39 5" hi.
#8701-10 oz.
TUMBLER
Regular Weight
CUT 39 4½" hi.
#636-10 oz.
TABLE TUMBLER
Regular Weight
CUT 39 3½" hi.
#65-7½ oz.
OLD FASHION
Sham Weight
CUT 39 3¾" hi.
#88-9 oz.
OLD FASHION
Sham Weight
CUT 39 3½" hi.

CUT 45 TUMBLERS

Cut #45 indicates the Flutes at the base of the Tumblers are 1½" high and ¾" wide. Tumblers Cut #45 have a flat unpolished base.

#8701-14 oz.
TUMBLER
Sham Weight
CUT 45 5½" hi.
#8701-12 oz.
TUMBLER
Sham Weight
CUT 45 5" hi.
#8701-10 oz.
TUMBLER
Sham Weight
CUT 45 4½" hi.
#636-10 oz.
TABLE TUMBLER
Sham Weight
CUT 45 3½" hi.
#65-7½ oz.
OLD FASHION
Sham Weight
CUT 45 3¾" hi.
#88-9 oz.
OLD FASHION
Sham Weight
CUT 45 3½" hi.
#1450-12 oz.
OLD FASHION
Sham Weight
CUT 45 3½" hi.

CUT 43 TUMBLERS

Cut #43 indicates the Flutes at the base of the Tumblers are 1¾" high and ¾" wide. Tumblers Cut #43 have a hand cut and hand polished (punty) base.

#8701-14 oz.
TUMBLER
Sham Weight
CUT 43 5½" hi.
#8701-12 oz.
TUMBLER
Sham Weight
CUT 43 5" hi.
#8701-10 oz.
TUMBLER
Sham Weight
#636-10 oz.
TABLE TUMBLER
Sham Weight
#65-7½ oz.
OLD FASHION
Sham Weight
#88-9 oz.
OLD FASHION
Sham Weight
#1450-12 oz.
OLD FASHION
Sham Weight

Page 31.

$8-10 each

1973 CATALOG

Page 2.

$8-12 each

Page 3.

$8-12 each

Frank Schoonmaker®
Wine Glasses by SENECA
"THE GLASSES FOR GREAT WINES"
The FRANK SCHOONMAKER® Wine Glasses hand made in the highest quality lead crystal, are made by the Seneca Glass Company, one of America's oldest and most famous manufacturers of fine glassware. Each glass, a signed original, bears the Frank Schoonmaker® Label for easy identification and proof of authenticity.
FRANK SCHOONMAKER® WINE GLASSES
Plain Crystal
Each
1 Champagne Tulip $ 3.25
2 Johannisberg 3.25
3 Magnum 3.25
4 Vin Du Pays 3.25
5 Cabernet 3.25
6 Solera 3.25
7 V.S.O.P. 3.25
8 Chateau 3.25
Champagne Tulip
Johannisberg
Magnum
Cabernet
Chateau
V. S. O. P.
Vin Du Pays
Solera
Seneca Oval featured in background. Refer to Seneca's Price List #73 for details.
NOTE: A set of 8 Display Wine Bottles — furnished FREE, upon request.
FRANK SCHOONMAKER® Wine Glasses Plain Lead Crystal available in the following items:
Champagne Tulip 8 oz. 8½" hi.
Johannisberg 6 oz. 6⅛" hi.
Magnum 10 oz. 5⅞" hi.
Vin Du Pays 8 oz. 5⅜" hi.
Cabernet 9 oz. 6½" hi.
Solera 5 oz. 5⅛" hi.
V. S. O. P. 7 oz. 4½" hi.
Chateau 7 oz. 6" hi.
4

Page 4.

$8-15 each

Epicure Collection
by SENECA
Designed by seasoned craftsmen at Seneca, EPICURE compliments the Frank Schoonmaker® Wine Glasses to complete that "Total" Glass Service. Each glass, a signed original, is labeled identifying and describing its recommended usage.
EPICURE COLLECTION
1235 Shape Plain Crystal
Each
1235 Goblet $ 3.25
1235 Dessert-Champagne 3.25
1235 Cocktail 3.25
1235 Cordial 3.25
1235 Parfait-Whiskey Sour 3.25
1235 Juice 3.25
1235 Ice Tea 3.25
1235 Vintage Wine 3.75
1235 Peach Champagne 5.50
1235 Continental Beer 4.50
1235 (463) Brandy Inhaler 4.50
1235 Beverage 2.50
1235 Old Fashion 2.50
Peach Champagne
Dessert-Champagne
Continental Beer
Vintage Wine
Wine Goblet
Cordial
Brandy Inhaler
The Seneca Oval with chain featured in the background is an excellent display prop. For details consult Seneca's Price List #73 Index
#1235 EPICURE COLLECTION Plain Lead Crystal available in the following items:
Goblet 12 oz. 7" hi.
Vintage Wine 14 oz. 7" hi.
Dessert-Champagne 7½ oz. 5⅛" hi.
Cocktail 5½ oz. 4¾" hi.
Cordial 2 oz. 4½" hi.
Parfait-Whiskey Sour 7 oz. 6¼" hi.
Juice 5 oz. 4⅜" hi.
Ice Tea 12 oz. 6¼" hi.
Peach Champagne 24 oz. 8½" hi.
Continental Beer 14 oz. 8⅛" hi.
Brandy Inhaler 22 oz. 6" hi.
Beverage 15 oz. 5" hi.
Old Fashion 11½ oz. 3¾" hi.

Page 5.

$8-15 each

Le Chateau Series
by SENECA
The Shape favored by many "Continentals" to enhance the "Chateau Class" wines. Made with the same expertise as all Seneca glasses, LE CHATEAU SERIES carries its own label for easy identification and recommended usage.
LE CHATEAU SERIES
1977 Shape Plain Crystal
Each
1977 Cabinet Wine $ 3.75
1977 Sparkling Wine 3.75
1977 Red Wine 3.75
1977 White Wine 3.75
1977 Dessert-Champagne 3.75
1977 Sherry and Port 3.75
1977 Brandy and Liqueur 3.75
Cabinet Wine
White Wine
Red Wine
Sherry and Port
#1977 LE CHATEAU SERIES Plain Lead Crystal available in the following items:
Cabinet Wine 15½ oz. 9⅛" hi.
Red Wine 12½ oz. 8⅝" hi.
Sparkling Wine 9 oz. 8" hi.
White Wine 7 oz. 7⅜" hi.
Sherry and Port 5 oz. 7" hi.
Dessert-Champagne 7½ oz. 6⅛" hi.
Brandy and Liqueur 2½ oz. 6" hi.
6

Page 6.

$8-15 each

Falerno
(Fal-lair-no)
by SENECA

The most celebrated wine (Falernian) of ancient Rome, praised in the most extravagant fashion by Pliny and Horace, and considered "immortal," certain vintages having been opened and found good after over a century. FALERNO Glasses lend charisma to the best vintage wines of today. Handmade in Seneca's lead crystal with hand cut paneled stem to make it the peer of the world's finest crystal stemware. Each glass is a signed original.

FALERNO 1977 Shape Cut 43	
	Each
Stemware	$ 7.00
Dessert-Finger Bowl	9.75
Plate 7"	10.50
Plate 8"	12.00

Sparkling Wine

Cabinet Wine

White Wine

Red Wine

Dessert-Champagne

Brandy and Liqueur

Sherry and Port

Seneca Oval featured in background. Refer to Seneca's Price List #73 for details.

The FALERNO Pattern #1977 Shape Cut #43 available in the following items:

Cabinet Wine 15½ oz. 9⅜" hi.	Red Wine 12½ oz. 8⅜" hi.	Sparkling Wine 9 oz. 8" hi.	White Wine 7 oz. 7⅝" hi.	Sherry and Port 5 oz. 7" hi.	Dessert-Champagne 7½ oz. 6⅜" hi.	Brandy and Liqueur 2½ oz. 6" hi.

Page 7.

$8-15 each

Connoisseur Collection
by SENECA

Handmade in Seneca's lead crystal with hand cut paneled stem to make it the peer of the world's finest crystal stemware. Each glass is a signed original.

CONNOISSEUR COLLECTION 5321 Shape Cut 43		
		Each
5321	Magnum Wine Goblet	$ 7.00
5321	Vintage Wine Goblet	7.00
5321	Red Wine	7.00
5321	White Wine	7.00
5321	Dessert-Champagne	7.00
5321	Champagne	7.00
5321	Sherry and Port	7.00
5321	Brandy and Liqueur	7.00

Magnum Wine Goblet

Vintage Wine Goblet

Red Wine

Sherry and Port

Champagne

White Wine

Brandy and Liqueur

Dessert-Champagne

The Seneca Oval with chain featured in background is an excellent display prop. For details consult Seneca's Price List #73.

The CONNOISSEUR COLLECTION #5321 Shape Cut #43 available in the following items:

Magnum Wine Goblet 18 oz. 7⅜" hi.	Vintage Wine Goblet 14 oz. 7" hi.	Red Wine 10½ oz. 6⅞" hi.	White Wine 8½ oz. 6⅝" hi.	Champagne 9½ oz. 8" hi.	Sherry and Port 5 oz. 6" hi.	Dessert-Champagne 11 oz. 4⅜" hi.	Brandy and Liqueur 2½ oz. 4½" hi.

8

Page 8.

$8-15 each

Cosmopolitan
by SENECA

COSMOPOLITAN 360 Shape Cut 43	
	Each
Stemware, regular	$ 6.00
Tulip Champagne	7.00
Dessert-Finger Bowl	9.75
Plate 7"	10.50
Plate 8"	12.00

Goblet

White Wine

Sherbet

All Purpose Wine

Cordial

Red Wine

Handmade in Seneca's lead crystal with hand cut paneled stem to make it the peer of the world's finest crystal stemware. Each glass is a signed original.

The Seneca Ovals with chain featured in the background is an excellent display prop. For details consult Seneca's Price List #73 Index.

The COSMOPOLITAN Pattern #360 Shape Cut #43 available in the following items:

Goblet 12 oz. 7" hi.	Sherbet 7½ oz. 5½" hi.	Red Wine 9 oz. 6½" hi.	White Wine 7 oz. 5⅜" hi.	Tulip Champagne 8 oz. 8½" hi.	All Purpose Wine 8 oz. 5" hi.	Cocktail 5½ oz. 4⅝" hi.	Cordial 2 oz. 4½" hi.	Juice 5 oz. 4½" hi.	Ice Tea 12 oz. 6¼" hi.

Page 9.

$8-15 each

102

Lead Crystal *Carafes*

by SENECA

Seneca's Carafes are available individually and in packed Carafe-Wine Sets. The Carafe-Wine Sets are pre-packed in the following combinations: 7-piece Set consisting of 1 Carafe and 6 wine glasses and a 5 piece Set consisting of 1 Carafe and 4 wine glasses. Refer to Seneca's Price List #73 for details.

The Gourmet Collection, Le Chateau Series and Frank Schoonmaker® Wine Glasses as well as Seneca's Display Oval are featured in the background. For details refer to Seneca's Price List #73 Index.

LEAD CRYSTAL CARAFES

	Each
120-20 ounce Carafe Plain Crystal	$ 6.50
132-32 ounce Carafe Plain Crystal	6.50

INFORMATION ON SENECA'S CARAFE-WINE SET and CARAFE-CORDIAL SET

Seneca's Lead Crystal Carafes are available individually and in boxed Sets. The Carafe-Wine and Carafe-Cordial Sets are pre-packed in the following combinations: 7 piece Set and 5 piece Set. The 7 piece Set consists of 1 large or small Carafe and 6 glasses. The 5 piece Set consists of 1 large or small Carafe and 4 glasses.

Please specify- quantity in Set, Carafe size, glasses and pattern.

The Retail Price of a Carafe-Wine and Carafe-Cordial Set is determined by deciding on the number of glasses in the Set (4 or 6). Multiply that number (4 or 6) by the price of the wine or cordial glasses. Then add the price of the Carafe.

NOTE: The white re-shipper (5 or 7 piece Set) carton cost is 75¢ Net each.

EXAMPLE: The Retail price of a 7 piece Carafe-Wine Set consisting of 6 Red Wines in the "Gourmet Collection" Pattern and 1-32 ounce Carafe is $29.00 plus the carton cost of 75¢ Net. Price determined: 6 Red Wines @ $3.75 = $22.50 + 1 Carafe @ $6.50 = $29.00.

#120 Carafe
20 ounce

#132 Carafe
32 ounce

10

Page 10.

$25-35 each

Driftwood Casual

by SENECA

Items Available:
Ice Tea
Hi Ball
Old Fashion
Roly Poly
Juice
Cocktail
Goblet
Sherbet
Dessert-Cereal Bowl
Plate
Pitcher 32 oz.
Pitcher 65 oz.
Flowerlite
Bud Vase
Covered Dish

Colors Available:
Accent Red
Amber
Buttercup (Yellow)
Cinnamon (Brown)
Crystal
Delphine Blue
Grey
Moss Green
Peacock Blue
Plum

DRIFTWOOD CASUAL

	Standard Colors Each	Accent Red Each
1980 Ice Tea Tumbler	$ 1.25	$ 2.35
1980 Hi Ball Tumbler	1.25	2.35
1980 Old Fashion Tumbler	1.25	2.35
1980 Roly Poly Tumbler	1.25	2.35
1980 Juice Tumbler	1.25	2.35
1980 Cocktail Tumbler	1.25	2.35
1980 Goblet	2.50	3.75
1980 Sherbet	2.50	3.75
1980 Dessert-Cereal Bowl	1.60	2.55
1980 Plate	3.50	Not Available
1980 Pitcher 32 oz.	6.00	Not Available
1980 Pitcher 65 oz.	7.00	11.00
1980 Flowerlite	5.50	Not Available
1980 Bud Vase	2.25	Not Available
1980 Covered Dish	5.50	Not Available

1980 Ice Tea
Delphine Blue
16 oz. 5¼" hi.

1980 Goblet
Buttercup (Yellow) 5¼" hi.

1980 Sherbet
Cinnamon (Brown)
6 oz. 3" hi.

1980 Old Fashion
Amber
14 oz. 3¾" hi.

11

Page 11.

$8-15 each

The Fashionables

by SENECA

THE FASHIONABLES

	Each
1974H High Stemmed Goblet	$ 3.75
1974H High Stemmed Dessert	3.75
1974H High Stemmed Juice Wine	3.75
1974L Low Stemmed Goblet	2.75
1974L Low Stemmed Dessert	2.75
1974L Low Stemmed Juice Wine	2.75
1974 Beverage	2.50
1974 Old Fashion	2.50
1974-6 piece Cocktail Juice Set	16.00

NOTE: The 1974H High Stemmed Goblet, Dessert and Juice Wine available in all The Fashionables Colors EXCEPT Brown and Crystal with Black Foot.

Colors available:
Black
Brown
Crystal
Crystal with Black Foot
Delphine Blue
Green
Plum
Yellow

1974 Beverage
14 oz. 5" hi.

1974 Old Fashion
Plum
5¼ oz. 4" hi.

1974H Goblet
Black
12½ oz. 6¼" hi.

1974L Goblet
Crystal
12½ oz. 4¼" hi.

1974L Juice/Wine
Plum
5½ oz. 2½" hi.

1974L Dessert
Delphine Blue

12

Page 12.

$10-15 each

103

GREEN

1974 6-piece
Cocktail/Juice Set
Crystal with Black Foot
Mixer 40 oz.   Glasses 7½ oz.

1974H Juice/Wine
Yellow
7½ oz.   5¾" hi.

1974H Dessert
Yellow

13

Page 13.

$10-15 each

CASCADE		Each
1972 Beverage		$ 1.50
1972 Old Fashion		1.50
1972 Cocktail Juice		1.50
1972 - 6 pc. Cocktail Juice Set		10.00

Items Available:
Beverage
Old Fashion
Cocktail/Juice
6-pc. Cocktail
Juice Set

Cascade
by *SENECA*

Colors Available:
Crystal
Green
Grey
Peacock Blue
Yellow

1972 6-pc.
Cocktail Juice Set
Peacock Blue
Mixer 40 oz.   Glasses 7½ oz.

1972 Old Fashion
Green
11½ oz.   3¾" hi.

1972
Cocktail/Juice
Crystal
7½ oz.   3¼" hi.

1972 Beverage
Grey
15½ oz.   5" hi.

1972 Beverage
Yellow
15½ oz.   5" hi.

14

Page 14.

$10-15 each
Pitcher: $40-50 each

Colors Available:
Black
Crystal
Crystal with Black Foot

Today

TODAY		Each
1976 Goblet		$ 3.00
1976 Dessert		3.00
1976 Juice/Wine		3.00

Items Available:
Goblet
Dessert
Juice/Wine

1976 Dessert
Crystal with Black Foot
10½ oz.   2⅝" hi.

1976 Goblet
Black
17½ oz.   4⅛" hi.

1976 Juice/Wine
Crystal
9½ oz.   3⅝" hi.

SOCIABLES		Each
3875 Goblet		$ 2.50
3875 Dessert		2.50
3875 Juice Cocktail		2.50
3875 Beverage		2.50

Colors Available:
Crystal
Delphine Blue
Green
Grey
Plum

Sociables

3875 Goblet
Delphine Blue
12½ oz.   3⅞" hi.

3875 Beverage
Plum
16 oz.   5⅛" hi.

3875
Juice/Cocktail
Crystal
9 oz.   3¼" hi.

3875 Dessert
Grey
11½ oz.   2¾" hi.

3875 Beverage
Green
16 oz.   5⅛" hi.

Items Available:
Goblet
Dessert
Juice/Cocktail
Beverage

15

Page 15.

$10-15 each

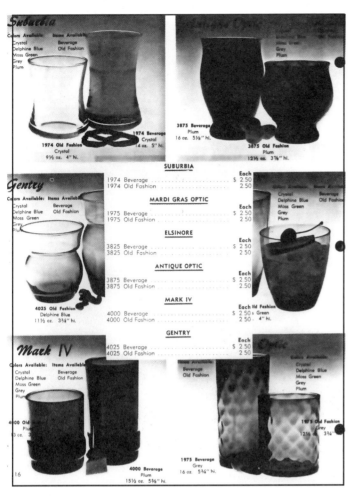

Suburbia

Colors Available:
Crystal
Delphine Blue
Moss Green
Grey
Plum

Items Available:
Beverage
Old Fashion

1974 Old Fashion
Crystal
9½ oz. 4" hi.

1974 Beverage
Crystal
14 oz. 5" hi.

3875 Beverage
Plum
16 oz. 5½" hi.

3875 Old Fashion
Plum
12½ oz. 3⅜" hi.

Gentry

Colors Available:
Crystal
Delphine Blue
Moss Green
Grey
Plum

Items Available:
Beverage
Old Fashion

4025 Old Fashion
Delphine Blue
11½ oz. 3¾" hi.

SUBURBIA		Each
1974 Beverage		$ 2.50
1974 Old Fashion		2.50
MARDI GRAS OPTIC		Each
1975 Beverage		$ 2.50
1975 Old Fashion		2.50
ELSINORE		Each
3825 Beverage		$ 2.50
3825 Old Fashion		2.50
ANTIQUE OPTIC		Each
3875 Beverage		$ 2.50
3875 Old Fashion		2.50
MARK IV		Each
4000 Beverage		$ 2.50
4000 Old Fashion		2.50
GENTRY		Each
4025 Beverage		$ 2.50
4025 Old Fashion		2.50

Mark IV

Colors Available:
Crystal
Delphine Blue
Moss Green
Grey
Plum

Items Available:
Beverage
Old Fashion

4000 Old Fashion
Plum
13 oz.

4000 Beverage
Plum
15½ oz. 5⅜" hi.

1975 Beverage
Grey
16 oz. 5¾" hi.

1975 Old Fashion
Grey
12¼ oz. 3¾" hi.

Colors Available:
Crystal
Delphine Blue
Moss Green
Grey
Plum

16

Page 16.

$8-15 each

Seville by SENECA

SEVILLE (Color)		Each
1971 Goblet		$ 4.25
1971 Sherbet		4.25
1971 Wine		4.25
1971 Cordial		4.25
1971 Ice Tea		4.25

Colors Available:
Brown
Delphine Blue
Green
Grey
Yellow

Items Available:
Goblet
Sherbet
Wine
Cordial
Ice Tea

1971 Ice Tea
Green
14½ oz. 7⅛" hi.

1971 Wine
Delphine Blue
7 oz. 5⅞" hi.

1971 Sherbet
Grey
7½ oz. 5" hi.

1971 Goblet
Yellow
11½ oz. 7" hi.

1971 Cordial
Brown
1½ oz. 4" hi.

8

Nocturne by SENECA

NOCTURNE		Each
1975 Goblet		$ 4.25
1975 Sherbet		4.25
1975 Wine		4.25
1975 Cordial		4.25
1975 Ice Tea		4.25
1975 Beverage		2.50
1975 Old Fashion		2.50

Ice Tea
Yellow

Goblet
Yellow

1975 Old Fashion
Black
12½ oz. 3¾" hi.

1975 Wine
Brown
8½ oz. 6½" hi.

1975 Sherbet
Plum
7 oz. 4⅝" hi.

1975 Cordial
Crystal
1½ oz. 4⅝" hi.

1975 Beverage
Brown
16 oz. 5¾" hi.

1975 Goblet
Plum
11 oz. 7½" hi.

17

Page 17.

$8-15 each

Page 18.

$8-15 each

Continuing...SENECA the most beautiful Crystal in the world...Since 1891

First Lady Sherbet

Astrid Table Wine

Page 19. $15-25 each

NEWPORT 960 Shape Cut 43	Each
Stemware $4.00	$ 7.00
Dessert-Finger Bowl ...	9.75
Plate 7''	10.50
Plate 8''	12.00

Newport

by SENECA

Ice Tea

Goblet

Wine

Cordial

Sherbet

The Seneca Oval with items featured in the background is an excellent display piece. For details consult Seneca's Price List 21, Index

The NEWPORT Pattern #960 Shape Cut #43 available in the following items

| Goblet 11½ oz. 7'' hi. | Sherbet 7 oz. 5¼'' hi. | Wine 7 oz. 6'' hi. | Cordial 1½ oz. 3⅜'' hi. | Ice Tea 14 oz. 6¼'' hi. | 1311 Dessert-Finger Bowl 4½'' Dia. | Plate 7'' Actually 7⅛'' Dia. | Plate 8'' Actually 8¾'' Dia. |

20

Page 20. $15-25 each

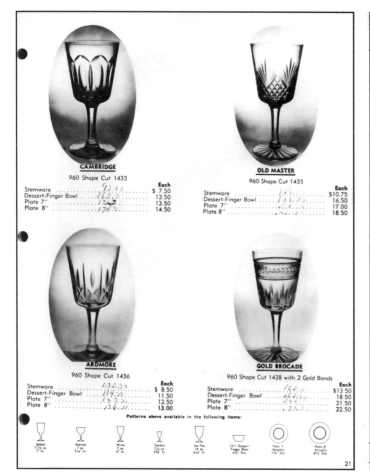

CAMBRIDGE
960 Shape Cut 1433

	Each
Stemware	$ 7.50
Dessert-Finger Bowl ...	13.50
Plate 7''	13.50
Plate 8''	14.50

OLD MASTER
960 Shape Cut 1435

	Each
Stemware	$10.75
Dessert-Finger Bowl ...	16.50
Plate 7''	17.00
Plate 8''	18.50

ARDMORE
960 Shape Cut 1436

	Each
Stemware	$ 8.50
Dessert-Finger Bowl ...	11.50
Plate 7''	12.50
Plate 8''	13.00

GOLD BROCADE
960 Shape Cut 1438 with 2 Gold Bands

	Each
Stemware	$13.50
Dessert-Finger Bowl ...	18.50
Plate 7''	21.50
Plate 8''	22.50

Patterns above available in the following items:

Goblet 11½ oz 7'' hi.

Sherbet 7 oz 5¼'' hi.

Wine 7 oz 6'' hi.

Cordial 1½ oz 3⅜'' hi.

Ice Tea 14 oz 6¼'' hi.

1311 Dessert-Finger Bowl 4½'' Dia.

Plate 7'' Actually 7⅛'' Dia.

Plate 8'' Actually 8¾'' Dia.

21

Page 21. $15-25 each

YOUNG LOVE
1967 Shape Cut 1429

	Each
Stemware	$ 6.25
Dessert-Finger Bowl ...	9.75
Plate 7''	10.50
Plate 8''	11.50

BERKSHIRE
1967 Shape Cut 1427

	Each
Stemware	$ 5.75
Dessert-Finger Bowl ...	9.00
Plate 7''	10.00
Plate 8''	10.75

SHERWOOD
1967 Shape Cut 1428

	Each
Stemware	$ 6.25
Dessert-Finger Bowl ...	8.25
Plate 7''	9.00
Plate 8''	9.75

Patterns above available in the following items:

Goblet 12 oz. 6½'' hi.

Sherbet 7½ oz 5'' hi.

Wine 7½ oz. 6'' hi.

Cordial 1½ oz. 3⅝'' hi.

Ice Tea 14 oz. 6¼'' hi.

1305 Dessert-Finger Bowl 4½'' Dia.

Plate 7'' Actually 7⅛'' Dia.

Plate 8'' Actually 8¾'' Dia.

Page 22. $15-25 each

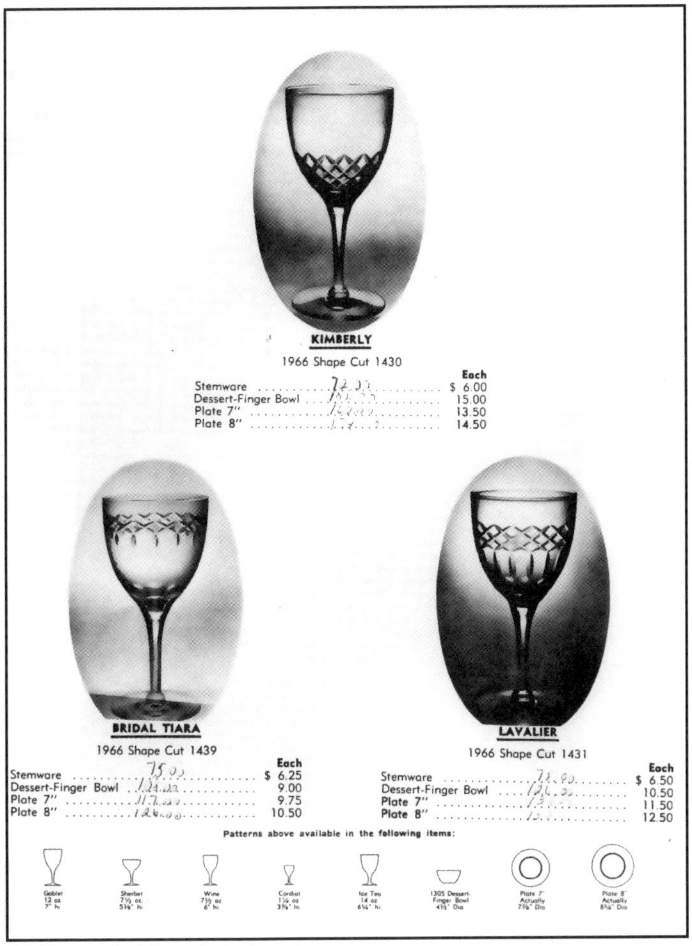

KIMBERLY
1966 Shape Cut 1430

	Each
Stemware	$ 6.00
Dessert-Finger Bowl	15.00
Plate 7"	13.50
Plate 8"	14.50

BRIDAL TIARA
1966 Shape Cut 1439

	Each
Stemware	$ 6.25
Dessert-Finger Bowl	9.00
Plate 7"	9.75
Plate 8"	10.50

LAVALIER
1966 Shape Cut 1431

	Each
Stemware	$ 6.50
Dessert-Finger Bowl	10.50
Plate 7"	11.50
Plate 8"	12.50

Patterns above available in the following items:

Goblet 12 oz 7" ht · Sherbet 7½ oz 5⅛" ht · Wine 7½ oz 6" ht · Cordial 1¼ oz 3⅝" ht · Ice Tea 14 oz 6¼" ht · 1305 Dessert-Finger Bowl 4½" Dia · Plate 7" Actually 7⅞" Dia · Plate 8" Actually 8¾" Dia

Page 23.

$15-20 each

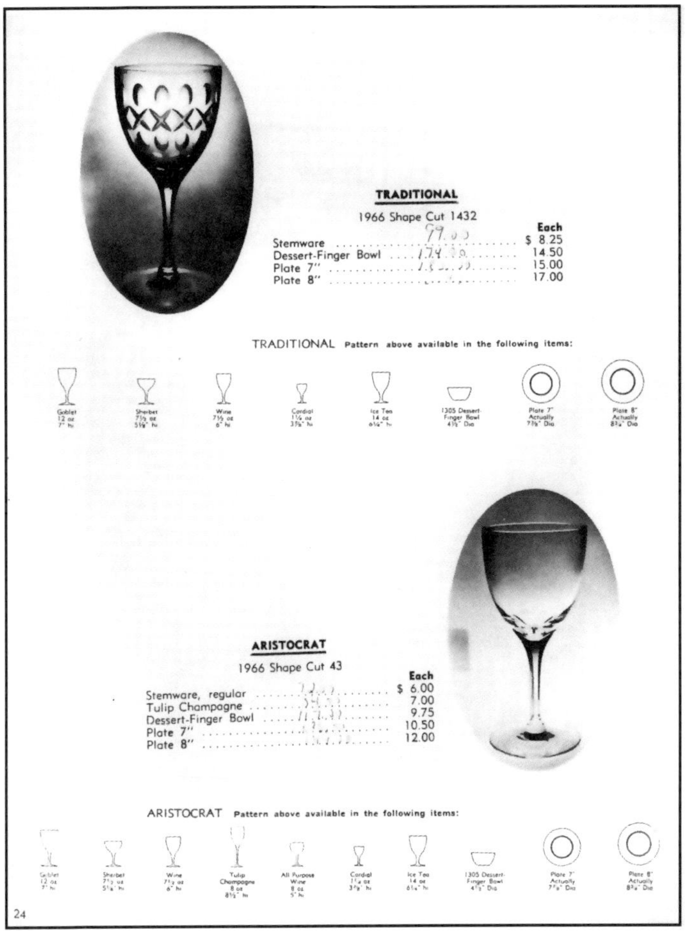

TRADITIONAL
1966 Shape Cut 1432

	Each
Stemware	$ 8.25
Dessert-Finger Bowl	14.50
Plate 7"	15.00
Plate 8"	17.00

TRADITIONAL **Pattern above available in the following items:**

Goblet 12 oz 7" ht · Sherbet 7½ oz 5⅛" ht · Wine 7½ oz 6" ht · Cordial 1¼ oz 3⅞" ht · Ice Tea 14 oz 6¼" ht · 1305 Dessert Finger Bowl 4½" Dia · Plate 7" Actually 7⅞" Dia · Plate 8" Actually 8¾" Dia

ARISTOCRAT
1966 Shape Cut 43

	Each
Stemware, regular	$ 6.00
Tulip Champagne	7.00
Dessert-Finger Bowl	9.75
Plate 7"	10.50
Plate 8"	12.00

ARISTOCRAT **Pattern above available in the following items:**

Goblet 12 oz 7" ht · Sherbet 7½ oz 5⅛" ht · Wine 7½ oz 6" ht · Tulip Champagne 8 oz 8½" ht · All Purpose Wine 8 oz 5" ht · Cordial 1¼ oz 3⅞" ht · Ice Tea 14 oz 6¼" ht · 1305 Dessert-Finger Bowl 4½" Dia · Plate 7" Actually 7⅞" Dia · Plate 8" Actually 8¾" Dia

24

Page 24.

$15-20 each

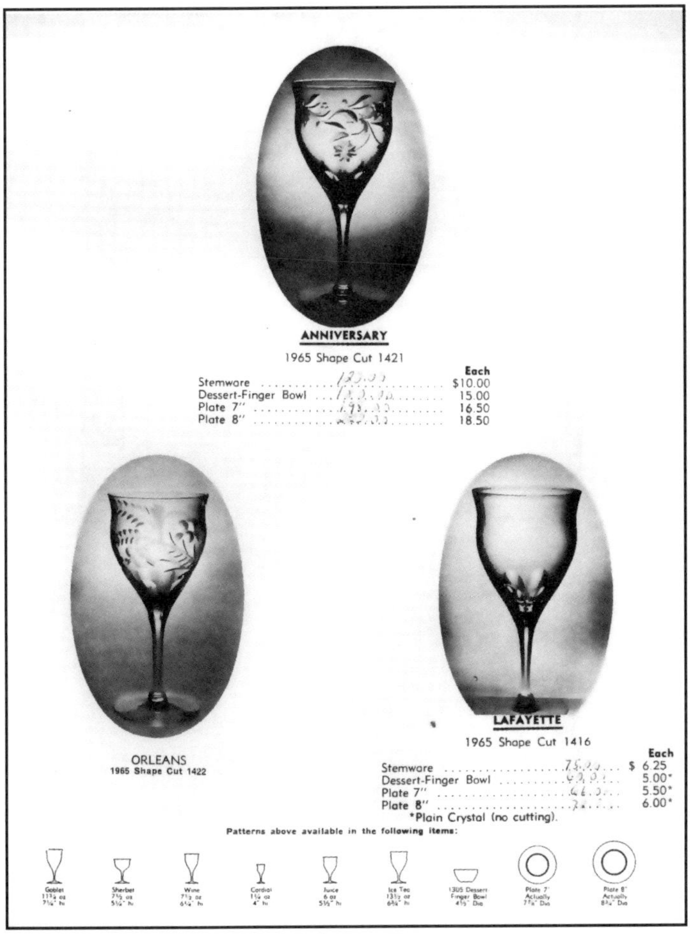

ANNIVERSARY
1965 Shape Cut 1421

	Each
Stemware	$10.00
Dessert-Finger Bowl	15.00
Plate 7"	16.50
Plate 8"	18.50

ORLEANS
1965 Shape Cut 1422

LAFAYETTE
1965 Shape Cut 1416

	Each
Stemware	$ 6.25
Dessert-Finger Bowl	5.00*
Plate 7"	5.50*
Plate 8"	6.00*

*Plain Crystal (no cutting).

Patterns above available in the following items:

Goblet 11¾ oz 7¼" ht · Sherbet 7½ oz 5½" ht · Wine 7½ oz 6½" ht · Cordial 1¼ oz 4" ht · Juice 6 oz 5½" ht · Ice Tea 13½ oz 6¾" ht · 1305 Dessert Finger Bowl 4½" Dia · Plate 7" Actually 7⅞" Dia · Plate 8" Actually 8¾" Dia

Page 25.

$25-35 each
Bottom right: $15-20 each

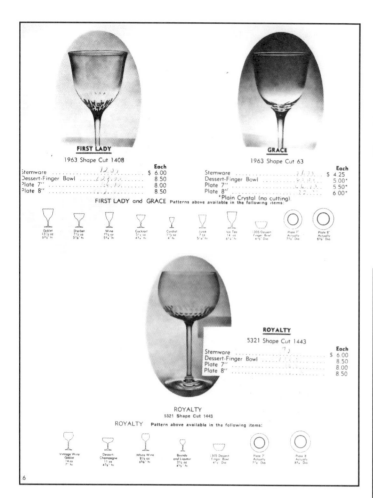

FIRST LADY
1963 Shape Cut 1408

	Each
Stemware	$ 6.00
Dessert-Finger Bowl	8.50
Plate 7"	8.00
Plate 8"	8.50

GRACE
1963 Shape Cut 63

	Each
Stemware	$ 4.25
Dessert-Finger Bowl	5.00*
Plate 7"	5.50*
Plate 8"	6.00*
*Plain Crystal (no cutting).	

FIRST LADY and GRACE Patterns above available in the following items:

ROYALTY
5321 Shape Cut 1443

	Each
Stemware	$ 6.00
Dessert-Finger Bowl	8.50
Plate 7"	8.00
Plate 8"	8.50

ROYALTY
5321 Shape Cut 1443

ROYALTY Pattern above available in the following items:

6

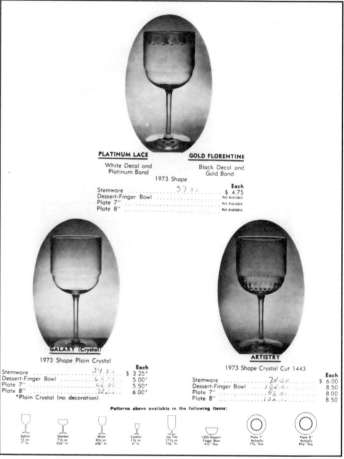

PLATINUM LACE
White Decal and
Platinum Band

GOLD FLORENTINE
Black Decal and
Gold Band

1973 Shape

	Each
Stemware	$ 4.75
Dessert-Finger Bowl	Not Available
Plate 7"	Not Available
Plate 8"	Not Available

GALAXY (Crystal)
1973 Shape Plain Crystal

	Each
Stemware	$ 3.25
Dessert-Finger Bowl	5.00*
Plate 7"	5.50*
Plate 8"	6.00*
*Plain Crystal (no decoration).	

ARTISTRY
1973 Shape Crystal Cut 1443

	Each
Stemware	$ 6.00
Dessert-Finger Bowl	8.50
Plate 7"	8.00
Plate 8"	8.50

Patterns above available in the following items:

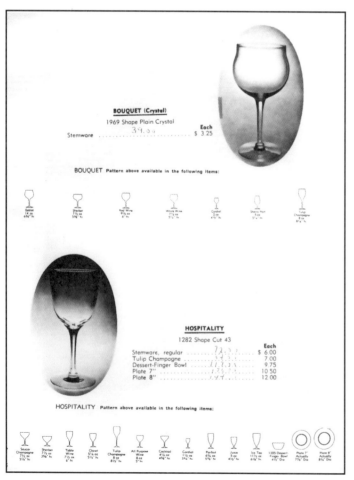

BOUQUET (Crystal)
1969 Shape Plain Crystal

	Each
Stemware	$ 3.25

BOUQUET Pattern available in the following items:

HOSPITALITY
1282 Shape Cut 43

	Each
Stemware, regular	$ 6.00
Tulip Champagne	7.00
Dessert-Finger Bowl	9.75
Plate 7"	10.50
Plate 8"	12.00

HOSPITALITY Pattern above available in the following items:

Page 26.

$10-20 each

Page 27.

$15-20 each
Bottom left: $10-12 each

Page 28.

Top: $8-12 each
Bottom: $10-15 each

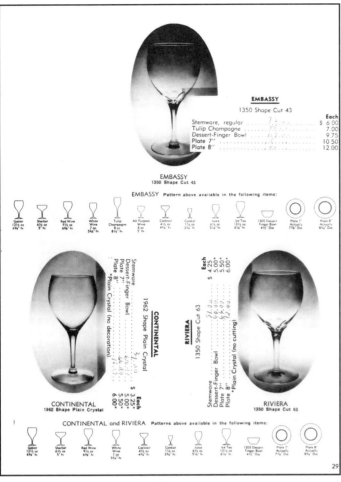

EMBASSY
1350 Shape Cut 43

	Each
Stemware, regular	$ 6.00
Tulip Champagne	7.00
Dessert-Finger Bowl	9.75
Plate 7''	10.50
Plate 8''	12.00

EMBASSY
1350 Shape Cut 43

EMBASSY Pattern above available in the following items:

CONTINENTAL
1962 Shape Plain Crystal

	Each
Stemware	$ 3.25
Dessert-Finger Bowl	5.00*
Plate 7''	5.50*
Plate 8''	6.00*
*Plain Crystal (no decoration).	

RIVIERA
1350 Shape Cut 63

	Each
Stemware	$ 4.25
Dessert-Finger Bowl	5.50*
Plate 7''	5.50*
Plate 8''	6.00*
*Plain Crystal (no cutting).	

CONTINENTAL
1962 Shape Plain Crystal

RIVIERA
1350 Shape Cut 63

CONTINENTAL and RIVIERA Patterns above available in the following items:

29

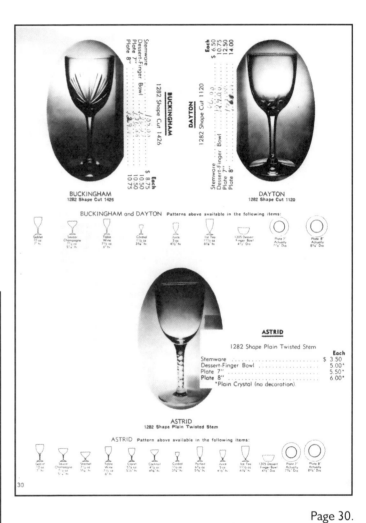

BUCKINGHAM
1282 Shape Cut 1426

	Each
Stemware	$ 8.75
Dessert-Finger Bowl	10.50
Plate 7''	10.50
Plate 8''	10.75

DAYTON
1282 Shape Cut 1120

	Each
Stemware	$ 6.50
Dessert-Finger Bowl	10.75
Plate 7''	12.50
Plate 8''	14.00

BUCKINGHAM
1282 Shape Cut 1426

DAYTON
1282 Shape Cut 1120

BUCKINGHAM and DAYTON Patterns above available in the following items:

ASTRID
1282 Shape Plain Twisted Stem

	Each
Stemware	$ 3.50
Dessert-Finger Bowl	5.00*
Plate 7''	5.50*
Plate 8''	6.00*
*Plain Crystal (no decoration).	

ASTRID
1282 Shape Plain Twisted Stem

ASTRID Pattern above available in the following items:

30

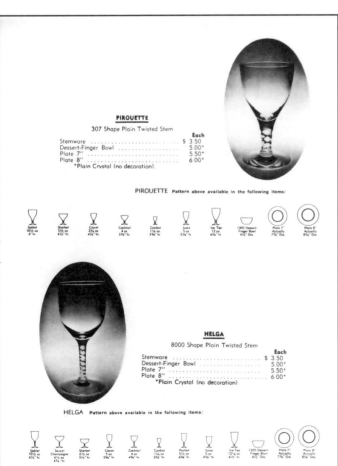

PIROUETTE
307 Shape Plain Twisted Stem

	Each
Stemware	$ 3.50
Dessert-Finger Bowl	5.00*
Plate 7''	5.50*
Plate 8''	6.00*
*Plain Crystal (no decoration).	

PIROUETTE Pattern above available in the following items:

HELGA
8000 Shape Plain Twisted Stem

	Each
Stemware	$ 3.50
Dessert-Finger Bowl	5.00*
Plate 7''	5.50*
Plate 8''	6.00*
*Plain Crystal (no decoration).	

HELGA Pattern above available in the following items:

31

Page 29.

$10-15 each
Bottom left: $8-12 each

Page 30.

$10-15 each

Page 31.

$10-12 each

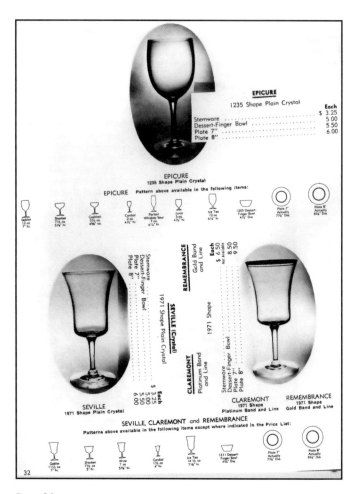

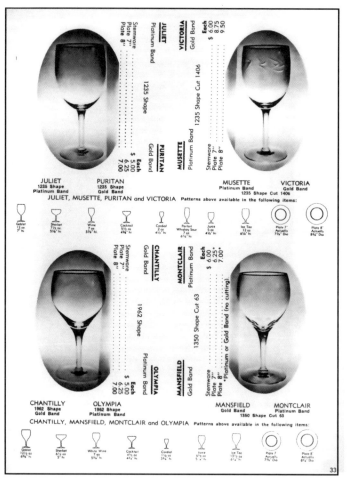

Page 32.

$10-15 each

Page 33.

$10-15 each

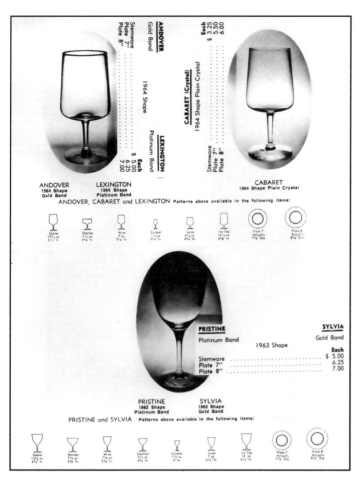

ANDOVER
1964 Shape
Gold Band

LEXINGTON
1964 Shape
Platinum Band

CABARET
1964 Shape Plain Crystal

ANDOVER, CABARET and LEXINGTON Patterns above available in the following items:

PRISTINE
1963 Shape
Platinum Band

SYLVIA
1963 Shape
Gold Band

	Each
Stemware	$ 5.00
Plate 7''	6.25
Plate 8''	7.00

PRISTINE and SYLVIA Patterns above available in the following items:

Page 34.

$8-12 each

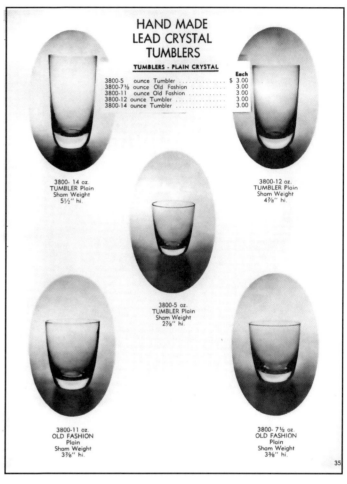

HAND MADE LEAD CRYSTAL TUMBLERS

TUMBLERS - PLAIN CRYSTAL

	Each
3800-5 ounce Tumbler	$ 3.00
3800-7½ ounce Old Fashion	3.00
3800-11 ounce Old Fashion	3.00
3800-12 ounce Tumbler	3.00
3800-14 ounce Tumbler	3.00

3800- 14 oz.
TUMBLER Plain
Sham Weight
5½'' hi.

3800-12 oz.
TUMBLER Plain
Sham Weight
4⅞'' hi.

3800-5 oz.
TUMBLER Plain
Sham Weight
2⅞'' hi.

3800-11 oz.
OLD FASHION
Plain
Sham Weight
3⅞'' hi.

3800- 7½ oz.
OLD FASHION
Plain
Sham Weight
3⅜'' hi.

35

Page 35.

$8-12 each

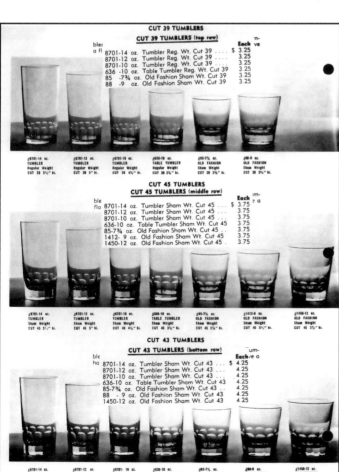

CUT 39 TUMBLERS

CUT 39 TUMBLERS (top row)

	Each
8701-14 oz. Tumbler Reg. Wt. Cut 39	$ 3.25
8701-12 oz. Tumbler Reg. Wt. Cut 39	3.25
8701-10 oz. Tumbler Reg. Wt. Cut 39	3.25
636 -10 oz. Table Tumbler Reg. Wt. Cut 39	3.25
85 -7¾ oz. Old Fashion Sham Wt. Cut 39	3.25
88 -9 oz. Old Fashion Sham Wt. Cut 39	3.25

CUT 45 TUMBLERS

CUT 45 TUMBLERS (middle row)

	Each
8701-14 oz. Tumbler Sham Wt. Cut 45	$ 3.75
8701-12 oz. Tumbler Sham Wt. Cut 45	3.75
8701-10 oz. Tumbler Sham Wt. Cut 45	3.75
636-10 oz. Table Tumbler Sham Wt. Cut 45	3.75
85-7¾ oz. Old Fashion Sham Wt. Cut 45	3.75
1412- 9 oz. Old Fashion Sham Wt. Cut 45	3.75
1450-12 oz. Old Fashion Sham Wt. Cut 45	3.75

CUT 43 TUMBLERS

CUT 43 TUMBLERS (bottom row)

	Each
8701-14 oz. Tumbler Sham Wt. Cut 43	$ 4.25
8701-12 oz. Tumbler Sham Wt. Cut 43	4.25
8701-10 oz. Tumbler Sham Wt. Cut 43	4.25
636-10 oz. Table Tumbler Sham Wt. Cut 43	4.25
85-7¾ oz. Old Fashion Sham Wt. Cut 43	4.25
88 - 9 oz. Old Fashion Sham Wt. Cut 43	4.25
1450-12 oz. Old Fashion Sham Wt. Cut 43	4.25

36

Page 36.

$8-12 each

1975 Catalog

Page 2.

$8-15 each

Page 3.

$8-15 each

Frank Schoonmaker®
Wine Glasses by SENECA
"THE GLASSES FOR GREAT WINES"

The FRANK SCHOONMAKER'S Wine Glasses, hand-made in the highest quality lead crystal, are made by the Seneca Glass Company, one of America's oldest and most famous manufacturers of fine glassware. Each glass, a signed original, bears the Frank Schoon-maker® Label for easy identification and proof of authenticity.

Champagne Tulip

Johannisberg

Cabernet

Chateau

Vin Du Pays

Magnum

Solera

V. S. O. P.

Seneca Oval featured in background. Refer to Seneca's Price List #75 for details.

NOTE: A set of 8 Display Wine Bottles — furnished FREE, upon request.

FRANK SCHOONMAKER® Wine Glasses Plain Lead Crystal available in the following items:

| Champagne Tulip 8 oz. 8½" hi. | Johannisberg 6 oz. 6⅛" hi. | Magnum 10 oz. 5⅝" hi. | Vin Du Pays 8 oz. 5⅜" hi. | Cabernet 9 oz. 6½" hi. | Solera 5 oz. 5⅜" hi. | V. S. O. P. 7 oz. 4½" hi. | Chateau 7 oz. 6" hi. |

Page 4.

$8-15 each

Epicure Collection
by SENECA

Designed by seasoned craftsmen of Seneca, EPICURE complements the Frank Schoonmaker® Wine Glasses to complete that "Total" Glass Service. Each glass, a signed original, is labeled identifying and describing its recommended usage.

Peach Champagne

Vintage Wine

Dessert-Champagne

Cordial

Brandy Inhaler

Continental Beer

Wine Goblet

The Seneca Oval with chain featured in the background is an excellent display prop. For details consult Seneca's Price List #75.

#1235 EPICURE COLLECTION Plain Lead Crystal available in the following items:

| Goblet 12 oz. 7" hi. | Vintage Wine 14 oz. 7" hi. | Dessert-Champagne 7½ oz. 5⅜" hi. | Cocktail 5½ oz. 4¾" hi. | Cordial 2 oz. 4½" hi. | Ice Tea 12 oz. 6¼" hi. | Peach Champagne 24 oz. 8½" hi. | Continental Beer 14 oz. 8½" hi. | Brandy Inhaler 22 oz. 6" hi. |

Page 5.

$8-15 each

Le Chateau Series
by SENECA

The Shape favored by many "Continentals" to enhance the "Chateau Class" wines. Made with the same expertise as all Seneca glasses, LE CHATEAU SERIES carries its own label for easy identification and recommended usage.

Cabinet Wine

White Wine

Red Wine

Sherry and Port

Dessert Champagne

Brandy and Liqueur

#1977 LE CHATEAU SERIES Plain Lead Crystal available in the following items:

| Cabinet Wine 15½ oz. 9½" hi. | Red Wine 12½ oz. 8½" hi. | Sparkling Wine 9 oz. 8" hi. | White Wine 7 oz. 7⅝" hi. | Sherry and Port 5 oz. 7" hi. | Dessert-Champagne 7½ oz. 6⅛" hi. | Brandy and Liqueur 2½ oz. 6" hi. |

Page 6.

$8-15 each

Page 7. $8-15 each

Page 8. $8-15 each

Page 9. $8-15 each

Page 10. $8-15 each, Bottom center right: $30-40 each

Page 11.

$10-15 each

Page 12.

$20-25 each

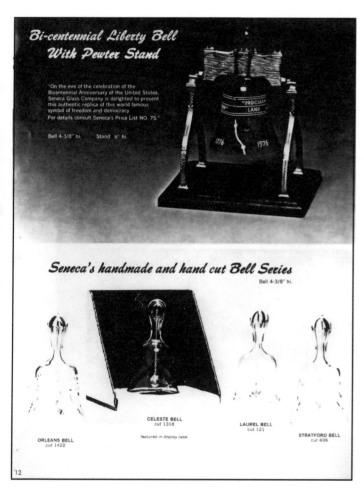

Page 13.

$20-25 each

The Fashionables
Plain Crystal and Colors
by SENECA

High Stem Goblet
Ritz Blue

High Stem Dessert
Crystal

High Stem Juice/Wine
Yellow

High Stem Ice Tea
Black

Low Stem Goblet
Accent Red

Low Stem Dessert
Delphina Blue

Low Stem Juice/Wine
Moss Green

Old Fashion
Brown

Beverage
Black

THE FASHIONABLES #1974 Plain Crystal and Colors available in the following items:

High Stem Goblet 12-1/2 oz. 6-1/4" hi.	High Stem Dessert 11-1/2 oz. 4-5/8" hi.	High Stem Juice/Wine 7-1/2 oz. 5-3/8" hi.	High Stem Ice Tea 15 oz. 6-5/8" hi.	Low Stem Goblet 12-1/2 oz. 4-1/4" hi.	Low Stem Dessert 11-1/2 oz. 2-7/8" hi.	Low Stem Juice/Wine 7-1/2 oz. 3-1/2" hi.	Old Fashion 9-1/2 oz. 4" hi.	Beverage 14 oz. 5" hi.

14

Page 14.

$10-15 each

The Fashionables
Hourglass Optic and Colors
by SENECA

High Stem Goblet
Hourglass Optic
Brown

High Stem Dessert
Hourglass Optic
Moss Green

High Stem Juice/Wine
Hourglass Optic
Delphine Blue

High Stem Ice Tea
Hourglass Optic
Crystal

Low Stem Goblet
Hourglass Optic
Yellow

Low Stem Dessert
Hourglass Optic
Ritz Blue

Low Stem Juice/Wine
Hourglass Optic
Accent Red

"THE FASHIONABLES #1974 Hourglass Optic and Colors available in the following items:"

High Stem Goblet 12-1/2 oz. 6-1/4" high	High Stem Dessert 11-1/2 oz. 4-5/8" hi.	High Stem Juice/Wine 7-1/2 oz. 5-3/8" hi.	High Stem Ice Tea 15 oz. 6-5/8" hi.	Low Stem Goblet 12-1/2 oz. 4-1/4" hi.	Low Stem Dessert 11-1/2 oz. 2-7/8" hi.	Low Stem Juice/Wine 7-1/2 oz. 3-1/2" hi.

15

Page 15.

$8-15 each

Driftwood Casual
by SENECA

#1980 Ice Tea
Moss Green
16 oz. 5-3/4" hi.

#1980 Pitcher 32 oz.
Ritz Blue

#1980 Hi Ball
Brown
12 oz., 5-1/8" hi.

#1980 Roly Poly
Amber
12 oz., 3-1/2" hi.

#1980 On The Rocks
Yellow
9-3/4 oz., 3-7/8" hi.

#1980 Footed Juice/Wine
Crystal
10 oz., 3-7/8" hi.

#1980 Dessert-Cereal Bowl
Yellow
13-1/2 oz., 5-1/4" dia.

Page 16.

$8-15 each

Page 17.

$10-15 each

Page 18.

$10-15 each
Pitcher: $50-60 each

Page 19.

$10-15 each

Page 20.

$15-25 each

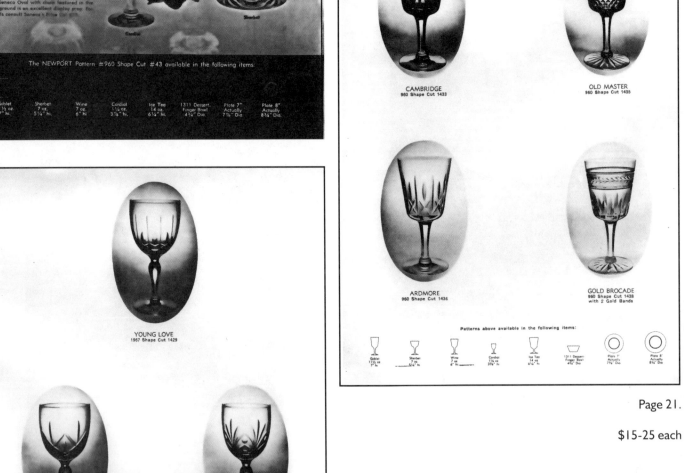

Page 21.

$15-25 each

Page 22.

$15-25 each

KIMBERLY
1966 Shape Cut 1430

BRIDAL TIARA
1966 Shape Cut 1439

LAVALIER
1966 Shape Cut 1431

Patterns above available in the following items:

Page 23.

$15-20 each

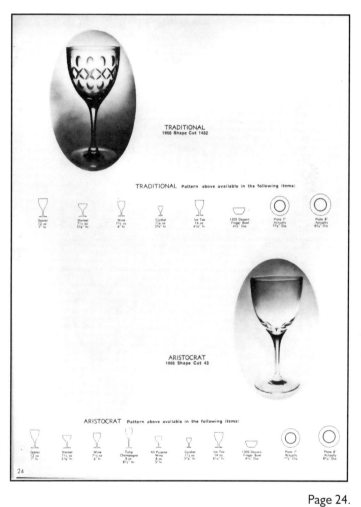

TRADITIONAL
1966 Shape Cut 1432

TRADITIONAL Pattern above available in the following items:

ARISTOCRAT
1966 Shape Cut 43

ARISTOCRAT Pattern above available in the following items:

Page 24.

$15-20 each

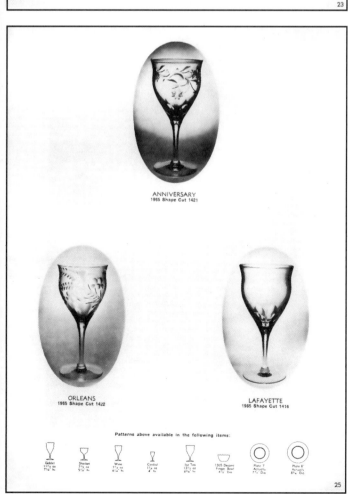

ANNIVERSARY
1965 Shape Cut 1421

ORLEANS
1965 Shape Cut 1422

LAFAYETTE
1965 Shape Cut 1416

Patterns above available in the following items:

Page 25.

$25-35 each

FIRST LADY
1963 Shape Cut 1408

GRACE
1963 Shape Cut 63

FIRST LADY and GRACE Patterns above available in the following items:

HOSPITALITY
1282 Shape Cut 43

HOSPITALITY Pattern above available in the following items:

Page 26.

$10-20 each

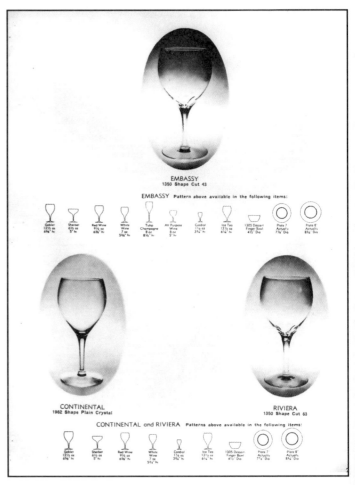

EMBASSY
1350 Shape Cut 43

EMBASSY Pattern above available in the following items:

CONTINENTAL
1962 Shape Plain Crystal

RIVIERA
1350 Shape Cut 63

CONTINENTAL and RIVIERA Patterns above available in the following items:

Page 27.

$10-20 each

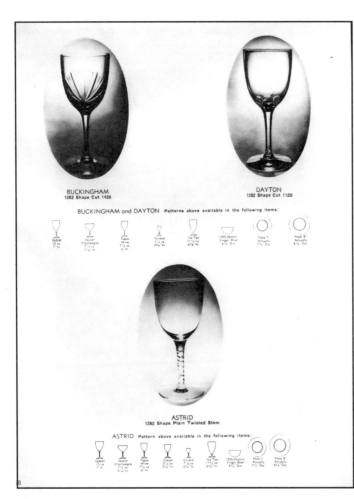

BUCKINGHAM
1282 Shape Cut 1426

DAYTON
1282 Shape Cut 1120

BUCKINGHAM and DAYTON Patterns above available in the following items:

ASTRID
1282 Shape Plain Twisted Stem

ASTRID Pattern above available in the following items:

Page 28.

$10-20 each

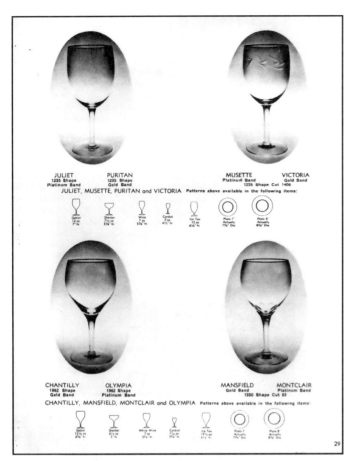

JULIET
1235 Shape
Platinum Band

PURITAN
1235 Shape
Gold Band

MUSETTE
Platinum Band
1235 Shape Cut 1406

VICTORIA
Gold Band

JULIET, MUSETTE, PURITAN and VICTORIA Patterns above available in the following items:

CHANTILLY
1962 Shape
Gold Band

OLYMPIA
1962 Shape
Platinum Band

MANSFIELD
Gold Band
1350 Shape Cut 63

MONTCLAIR
Platinum Band

CHANTILLY, MANSFIELD, MONTCLAIR and OLYMPIA Patterns above available in the following items:

Page 29. $10-20 each

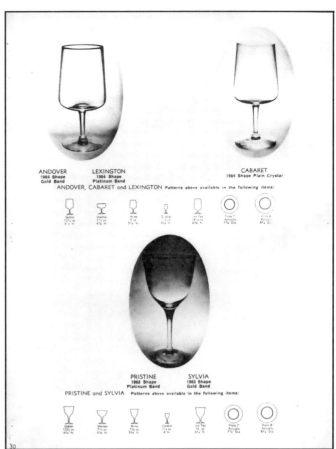

ANDOVER
1964 Shape
Gold Band

LEXINGTON
1964 Shape
Platinum Band

CABARET
1964 Shape Plain Crystal

ANDOVER, CABARET and LEXINGTON Patterns above available in the following items:

PRISTINE
1963 Shape
Platinum Band

SYLVIA
1963 Shape
Gold Band

PRISTINE and SYLVIA Patterns above available in the following items:

Page 30. $10-20 each

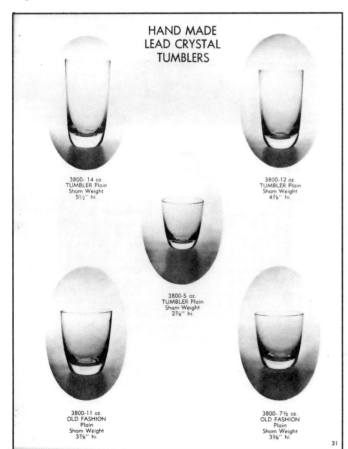

HAND MADE
LEAD CRYSTAL
TUMBLERS

3800- 14 oz.
TUMBLER Plain
Sham Weight
5½" hi.

3800-12 oz.
TUMBLER Plain
Sham Weight
4⅞" hi.

3800-5 oz.
TUMBLER Plain
Sham Weight
2⅞" hi.

3800-11 oz.
OLD FASHION
Plain
Sham Weight
3⅞" hi.

3800- 7½ oz.
OLD FASHION
Plain
Sham Weight
3⅜" hi

Page 31. $8-12 each

CUT 39 TUMBLERS

Cut #39 indicates the Flutes at the base of the Tumblers are 1¼" high and ½" wide. Tumblers Cut #39 have a flat unpolished base.

CUT 45 TUMBLERS

Cut #45 indicates the Flutes at the base of the Tumblers are 1⅛" high and ¾" wide. Tumblers Cut #45 have a flat unpolished base

CUT 43 TUMBLERS

Cut #43 indicates the Flutes at the base of the Tumblers are 1¾" high and ¾" wide. Tumblers Cut #43 have a hand cut and hand polished (punty) base.

Page 32. $8-12 each

121

1976 CATALOG

Elite Collection

SUNBURST and WICKER Patterns, part of Seneca's Elite Collection, are totally mouth blown, hand made and hand cut in very high Lead Crystal.

WICKER
970 Shape Cut 1446

SUNBURST
970 Shape Cut 1447

Patterns above available in the following items:

Goblet	Sherbet	Wine	Cordial
9½ oz.	7½ oz.	5 oz.	2 oz.
8½" hi.	6½" hi.	7¼" hi.	5¼" hi.

Page 3

Page 3.

$20-30 each

Elite Collection

CHALICE and TAPESTRY Patterns, part of Seneca's Elite Collection, are totally mouth blown, hand made and hand cut in very high Lead Crystal.

CHALICE
972 Shape Cut 1448

TAPESTRY
972 Shape Cut 1449

Patterns above available in the following items:

Goblet	Sherbet	Wine	Cordial
13 oz.	9 oz.	7½ oz.	3 oz.
7½" hi.	6" hi.	6½" hi.	5-5/8" hi.

Page 4

Page 4.

$15-25 each

Elite Collection

BRITTANY and CLASSIC Patterns, part of Seneca's Elite Collection, are totally mouth blown, hand made and hand cut in very high Lead Crystal.

BRITTANY
974 Shape Cut 1451

CLASSIC
974 Shape Cut 1450

Patterns above available in the following items:

Goblet	Sherbet	Wine	Cordial
10 oz.	6-1/2 oz.	6 oz.	2-1/4 oz.
7-1/2" hi.	5-1/2" hi.	6-5/8" hi.	5-1/4" hi.

Page 5

Page 5.

$15-25 each

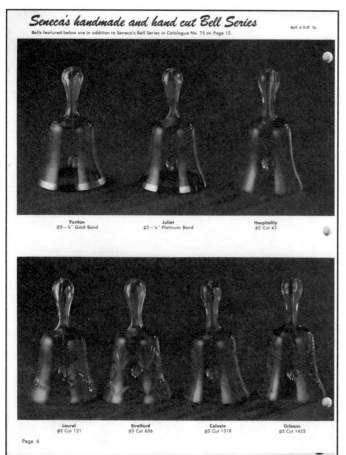

Bells featured below are in addition to Seneca's Bell Series in Catalogue No. 75 on Page 12.

Bell 4-3/8" hi.

Puriton
#3 — ¼" Gold Band

Juliet
#3 — ¼" Platinum Band

Hospitality
#3 Cut 43

Laurel
#3 Cut 121

Stratford
#3 Cut 636

Celeste
#3 Cut 1318

Orleans
#3 Cut 1422

Page 6

Page 6. $10-20 each

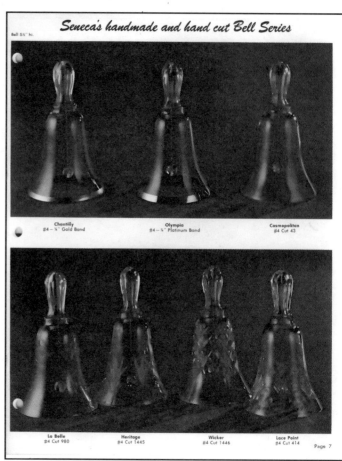

Bell 5½" hi.

Chantilly
#4 — ¼" Gold Band

Olympia
#4 — ¼" Platinum Band

Cosmopolitan
#4 Cut 43

La Belle
#4 Cut 980

Heritage
#4 Cut 1445

Wicker
#4 Cut 1446

Lace Point
#4 Cut 414

Page 7

Page 7. $10-20 each

Reflection by SENECA

The REFLECTION Pattern #976 Shape Crystal Optic available in the following items:

Goblet	Sherbet	Wine	Cordial
13 oz.	9 oz.	5-3/4 oz.	2-1/4 oz.
7-3/4 hi.	5-3/8 hi.	6-5/8 hi.	5-1/4 hi.

Goblet

Page 8

Page 8. $10-15 each

MODERNE by SENECA

The MODERNE Pattern #971 Shape Crystal Optic available in the following items:

Goblet	Sherbet	Wine	Cordial
9¾ oz.	7½ oz.	5 oz.	2 oz.
8½ hi.	6½ hi.	7¼ hi.	5¼ hi.

Goblet

Page 9

Page 9. $15-25 each

Fascination by SENECA

Goblet

The FASCINATION Pattern #978 Shape Crystal Optic available in the following items:

Goblet	Sherbet	Wine	Cordial
14 oz.	9 oz.	5-3/4 oz.	3 oz.
7-7/8" hi.	5¼" hi.	6½" hi.	5-5/8" hi.

Page 10

Page 10.

$10-15 each

Seneca's ON THE ROCKS *Series*

15½ oz. 4½" hi.

Brittany	Sunburst	Chalice
#1978 Cut 1451	#1978 Cut 1447	#1978 Cut 1448

Wicker	America	Ultra
#1978 Cut 1446	#1978 Cut 1444	#1978 Cut 43

Page 11

Page 11.

$8-12 each

Sculpture by SENECA

Colors Available:
Crystal
Delphine Blue
Lime Green
Sahara

Goblet
Crystal

Goblet
Lime Green

Goblet
Sahara

Goblet
Delphine
Blue

The SCULPTURE Pattern #975 available in the following items:

Ice Tea	Hi Ball	Double Old Fashion	Juice	Footed Goblet	Bowl
17 oz.	12½ oz.	12 oz.	6 oz.	14 oz.	13 oz.
5-3/4" hi.	5¼" hi.	3-7/8" hi.	4-1/8" hi.	5½" hi.	4½" dia.

Page 12

Page 12.

$8-12 each

125

1977 Catalog

Gourmet Collection
by SENECA

The GOURMET COLLECTION, bubble shaped, thin stemmed and generously proportioned is handcrafted of the finest lead crystal. These contemporary shaped glasses have been designed to enhance the enjoyment of that favorite beverage. Each glass is a signed original and bears a label identifying and describing its recommended usage.

Dessert-Champagne

Vintage Wine Goblet

Red Wine

Champagne

#5321 GOURMET COLLECTION Plain Lead

Grande Bordeaux 24 oz. 7⅝" hi.

Magnum Wine Goblet 18 oz. 7⅜" hi.

Vintage Wine Goblet 14 oz. 7" hi.

Red Wine 10½ oz. 6⅞" hi.

White Wine 8½ oz. 6⅝" hi.

Magnum Wine Goblet

Grande Bordeaux

Brandy and Liqueur

Sherry and Port

White Wine

The #120 and #132 Carafes are featured above. For details refer to Seneca's Price List #77 index.

Crystal available in the following items:

Champagne 9½ oz. 8" hi.

Sherry and Port 5 oz. 6" hi.

Dessert-Champagne 11 oz. 4⅞" hi.

Brandy and Liqueur 2½ oz. 4½" hi.

Page 2.

$8-15 each

Page 3.

$8-15 each

Frank Schoonmaker®
Wine Glasses by SENECA
"THE GLASSES FOR GREAT WINES"
he FRANK SCHOONMAKER® Wine Glasses, hand-
ade in the highest quality lead crystal, are made by
e Seneca Glass Company, one of America's oldest
nd most famous manufacturers of fine glassware.
ach glass, a signed original, bears the Frank Schoon-
aker® Label for easy identification and proof of
thenticity.
Champagne Tulip
Johannisberg
Magnum
Cabernet
Chateau
Vin Du Pays
Solero
V. S. O. P.
FRANK SCHOONMAKER® Wine Glasses Plain Lead Crystal available in the following items:
Champagne Tulip 8 oz. 8½" hi.
Johannisberg 6 oz. 6⅛" hi.
Magnum 10 oz. 5⅞" hi.
Vin Du Pays 8 oz. 5⅜" hi.
Cabernet 9 oz. 6½" hi.
Solero 5 oz. 5⅛" hi.
V. S. O. P. 7 oz. 4½" hi.
Chateau 7 oz. 6" hi.

Page 4.

$8-15 each

Epicure Collection
by SENECA
Designed by seasoned craftsmen at Seneca, EPICURE compliments the Frank Schoonmaker® Wine Glasses to complete that "Total" Glass Service. Each glass, a signed original, is labeled identifying and describing its recommended usage.
Peach Champagne
Dessert-Champagne
Continental Beer
Vintage Wine
Wine Goblet
Cordial
Brandy Inhaler
#1235 EPICURE COLLECTION Plain Lead Crystal available in the following items:
Goblet 12 oz. 7" hi.
Vintage Wine 14 oz. 7" hi.
Dessert-Champagne 7½ oz. 5⅛" hi.
Cocktail 5½ oz. 4¾" hi.
Cordial 2 oz. 4½" hi.
Ice Tea 12 oz. 6¼" hi.
Peach Champagne 24 oz. 8½" hi.
Continental Beer 14 oz. 8⅛" hi.
Brandy Inhaler 22 oz. 6" hi.

Page 5.

$8-15 each

Le Chateau Series
by SENECA
The Shape favored by many "Continentals" to enhance the "Chateau Class" wines. Made with the same expertise as all Seneca glasses, LE CHATEAU SERIES carries its own label for easy identification and recommended usage.
Cabinet Wine
Sparkling Wine
White Wine
Red Wine
Brandy and Liqueur
Dessert-Champagne
#1977 LE CHATEAU SERIES Plain Lead Crystal available in the following items:
Cabinet Wine 15½ oz. 9⅛" hi.
Red Wine 12½ oz. 8⅜" hi.
Sparkling Wine 9 oz. 8" hi.
White Wine 7 oz. 7⅝" hi.
Sherry and Port 5 oz. 7" hi.
Dessert-Champagne 7½ oz. 6⅛" hi.
Brandy and Liqueur 2½ oz. 6" hi.

Page 6.

$8-15 each

Falerno
(Fal-lair-no)
by SENECA
The most celebrated wine (Falernian) of ancient Rome, praised in the most extravagant fashion by Pliny and Horace, and considered "immortal," certain vintages having been opened and found good after over a century. FALERNO Glasses lend charisma to the best vintage wines of today. Handmade in Seneca's lead crystal with hand cut paneled stem to make it the peer of the world's finest crystal stemware. Each glass is a signed original.
Sparkling Wine
Cabinet Wine
White Wine
Red Wine
Dessert-Champagne
Brandy and Liqueur
Sherry and Port
The FALERNO Pattern #1977 Shape Cut #43 available in the following items:
Cabinet Wine 15½ oz. 9⅛" hi.
Red Wine 12½ oz. 8⅝" hi.
Sparkling Wine 9 oz. 8" hi.
White Wine 7 oz. 7⅝" hi.
Sherry and Port 5 oz. 7" hi.
Dessert-Champagne 7½ oz. 6⅛" hi.
Brandy and Liqueur 2½ oz. 6" hi.

Page 7.

$8-15 each

Connoisseur Collection
by SENECA
Handmade in Seneca's lead crystal with hand cut paneled stem to make it the peer of the world's finest crystal stemware. Each glass is a signed original.
Magnum Wine Goblet
Vintage Wine Goblet
Champagne
Red Wine
Sherry and Port
White Wine
Brandy and Liqueur
Dessert- Champagne
The CONNOISSEUR COLLECTION #5321 Shape Cut #43 available in the following items:
Magnum Wine Goblet 18 oz. 7⅜" hi.
Vintage Wine Goblet 14 oz. 7" hi.
Red Wine 10½ oz. 6⅞" hi.
White Wine 8½ oz. 6⅝" hi.
Champagne 8 oz. 8½" hi.
Sherry and Port 5 oz. 6" hi.
Dessert-Champagne 11 oz. 4⅞" hi.
Brandy and Liqueur 2½ oz. 4½" hi.
8

Page 8.

$8-15 each

Cosmopolitan
by SENECA
Tulip Champagne
Goblet
Sherbet
White Wine
All Purpose Wine
Cordial
Red Wine
ndmade in Seneca's lead crystal with hand cut paneled stem
make it the peer of the world's finest crystal stemware.
h glass is a signed original.
The COSMOPOLITAN Pattern #360 Shape Cut #43 available in the following items:
Goblet 12 oz. 7" hi.
Sherbet 7½ oz. 5⅛" hi.
Red Wine 9 oz. 6½" hi.
White Wine 7 oz. 5⅞" hi.
Tulip Champagne 8 oz. 8½" hi.
All Purpose Wine 8 oz. 5" hi.
Cocktail 5½ oz. 4⅝" hi.
Cordial 2 oz. 4½" hi.
Ice Tea 12 oz. 6¼" hi.
9

Page 9.
$8-15 each

Page 10. $8-15 each, Bottom center right: $30-40 each

Page 11. $8-15 each

Page 12. $8-15 each, Pitcher: $40-50 each

Page 13. $ 8-15 each, Pitcher: $40-50 each

Page 14. $10-15 each

Page 15. $10-15 each, Pitcher: $50-60 each

Page 16. $10-15 each

Page 17. $20-25 each

Page 18.

$15-20 each

Reflection by SENECA

The REFLECTION Pattern #976 Shape Crystal Optic available in the following items:

Goblet 13 oz. 7-3/4" hi.	Sherbet 9 oz. 5-3/8" hi.	Wine 7 oz. 6-5/8" hi.	Cordial 2-1/4 oz. 5-1/4" hi.

18

MODERNE by SENECA

Goblet

The MODERNE Pattern #971 Shape Crystal Optic available in the following items:

Goblet 9½ oz. 8⅝" hi.	Sherbet 7⅝ oz. 6⅛" hi.	Wine 5 oz. 7¼" hi.	Cordial 2 oz. 5¼" hi.

19

Page 19.

$15-20 each

Fascination by SENECA

Goblet

Page 20.

$15-20 each

The FASCINATION Pattern #978 Shape Crystal Optic available in the following items:

Goblet 14 oz. 7-7/8" hi.	Sherbet 9 oz. 5½" hi.	Wine 5-3/4 oz. 6½" hi.	Cordial 3 oz. 5-5/8" hi.

20

Limited Edition
LIBERTY BELL
with
Pewter Stand and Solid Black Walnut Base

Photographed Actual Size 6" high.   Bell 4-3/8" high.

History in the Making . . .

Truly a bell collector's dream.

Seneca's 5,000 Bicentennial Liberty Bells, dated 1776-1976, have been sold. This original will never be made again and Collectors are asking substantially more than the purchased price.

Now, Seneca introduces another limited-edition Liberty Bell. Complete with pewter stand as shown, this authentic replica of our country's freedom symbol will be dated 1977, and limited to a quantity of just 5,000.

Another Seneca original in a set that will continue in 1978 and many years to come.

Note: Additional Collectors' Bells on pages 22 and 23.

21

Page 21.

$45-55 each

Page 22.

$25-50 each

Page 23.

$25-50 each

Page 24. $10-15 each

Page 25. $10-15 each

Page 26. $20-30 each

Page 27. $20-30 each

Elite Collection

SUNBURST and WICKER Patterns, part of Seneca's Elite Collection, are totally mouth blown, hand made and hand cut in very high Lead Crystal.

WICKER
970 Shape Cut 1446

SUNBURST
970 Shape Cut 1447

Patterns above available in the following items:

Goblet	Sherbet	Wine	Cordial
9½ oz.	7½ oz.	5 oz.	2 oz.
8½" hi.	6½" hi.	7¼" hi.	5¼" hi.

28

Page 28. $15-25 each

Elite Collection

CHALICE and TAPESTRY Patterns, part of Seneca's Elite Collection, are totally mouth blown, hand made and hand cut in very high Lead Crystal.

CHALICE
972 Shape Cut 1448

TAPESTRY
972 Shape Cut 1449

Patterns above available in the following items:

Goblet	Sherbet	Wine	Cordial
13 oz.	9 oz.	7½ oz.	3 oz.
7½" hi.	6" hi.	6½" hi.	5-5/8" hi.

29

Page 29. $15-25 each

Elite Collection

BRITTANY and CLASSIC Patterns, part of Seneca's Elite Collection, are totally mouth blown, hand made and hand cut in very high Lead Crystal.

BRITTANY
974 Shape Cut 1451

CLASSIC
974 Shape Cut 1450

Patterns above available in the following items:

Goblet	Sherbet	Wine	Cordial
10 oz.	6-1/2 oz.	6 oz.	2-1/4 oz.
7-1/2" hi.	5-1/2" hi.	6-5/8" hi.	5-1/4" hi.

30

Page 30. $15-25 each

Newport
by *SENECA*

Wine

Ice Tea

Goblet

Cordial

Sherbet

The NEWPORT Pattern #960 Shape Cut #43 available in the following items:

Goblet	Sherbet	Wine	Cordial	Ice Tea	1311 Dessert. Finger Bowl	Plate 7"	Plate 8"
11½ oz.	7 oz.	7 oz.	1¼ oz.	14 oz.		Actually	Actually
7" hi.	5¼" hi.	6" hi.	3⅜" hi.	6¼" hi.	4½" Dia.	7⅞" Dia.	8¾" Dia.

31

Page 31. $10-15 each

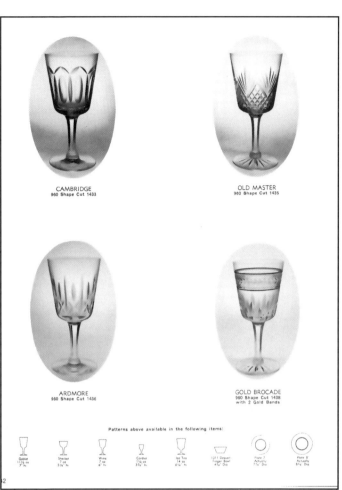

CAMBRIDGE
960 Shape Cut 1433

OLD MASTER
960 Shape Cut 1435

ARDMORE
960 Shape Cut 1436

GOLD BROCADE
960 Shape Cut 1438
with 2 Gold Bands

Patterns above available in the following items:

Page 32.

$15-25 each

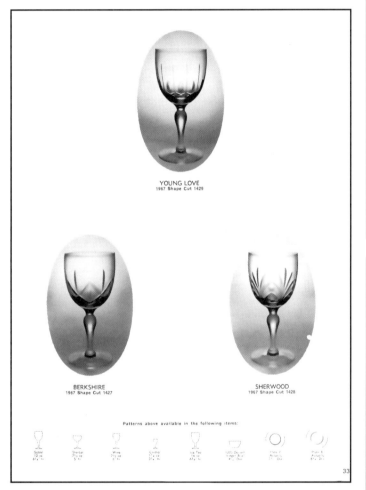

YOUNG LOVE
1967 Shape Cut 1429

BERKSHIRE
1967 Shape Cut 1427

SHERWOOD
1967 Shape Cut 1428

Patterns above available in the following items:

Page 33.

$15-25 each

KIMBERLY
1966 Shape Cut 1430

BRIDAL TIARA
1966 Shape Cut 1439

LAVALIER
1966 Shape Cut 1431

Patterns above available in the following items:

Page 34.

$15-25 each

135

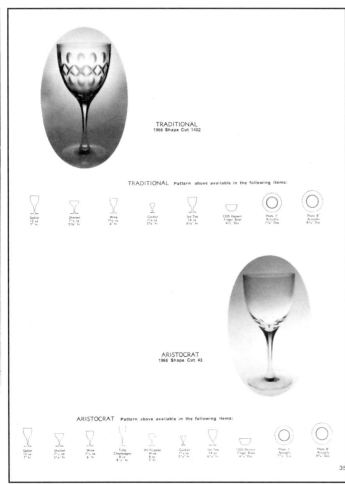

TRADITIONAL
1966 Shape Cut 1432

Page 35.

$10-20 each

TRADITIONAL Pattern above available in the following items:

ARISTOCRAT
1966 Shape Cut 43

ARISTOCRAT Pattern above available in the following items:

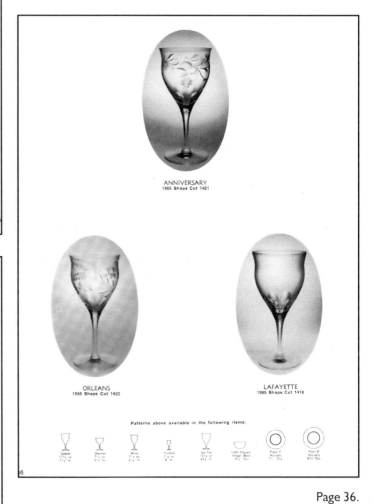

ANNIVERSARY
1965 Shape Cut 1421

ORLEANS
1965 Shape Cut 1422

LAFAYETTE
1965 Shape Cut 1416

Patterns above available in the following items:

Page 36.

$25-35 each

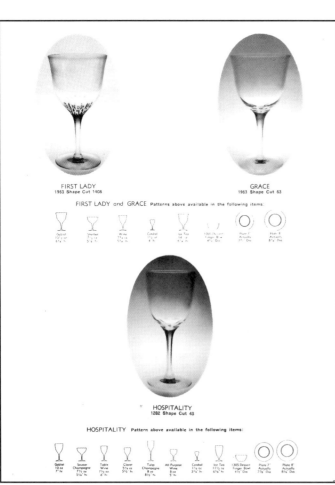

FIRST LADY
1963 Shape Cut 1408

GRACE
1963 Shape Cut 63

FIRST LADY and GRACE Patterns above available in the following items:

HOSPITALITY
1282 Shape Cut 43

HOSPITALITY Pattern above available in the following items:

Page 37.

$10-15 each

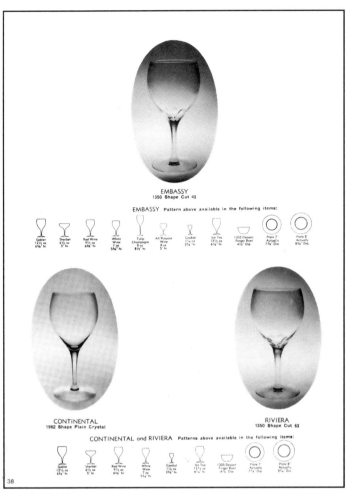

EMBASSY
1350 Shape Cut 43

EMBASSY Pattern above available in the following items:

| Goblet 12½ oz 6⅝" hi | Sherbet 6½ oz 5" hi | Red Wine 9½ oz 6⅛" hi | White Wine 7 oz 5¾" hi | Tulip Champagne 8 oz 8½" hi | All Purpose 8 oz 5" hi | Cordial 1¼ oz 3¾" hi | Ice Tea 13½ oz 6½" hi | 1305 Dessert Finger Bowl 4½" Dia | Plate 7 Actually 7⅝" Dia | Plate 8 Actually 8¼" Dia |

CONTINENTAL
1962 Shape Plain Crystal

RIVIERA
1350 Shape Cut 63

CONTINENTAL and RIVIERA Patterns above available in the following items:

| Goblet 12½ oz 6⅝" hi | Sherbet 6½ oz 5" hi | Red Wine 9½ oz 6⅛" hi | White Wine 7 oz 5¾" hi | Cordial 1¼ oz 3¾" hi | Ice Tea 13½ oz 6½" hi | 1305 Dessert Finger Bowl 4½" Dia | Plate 7 Actually 7⅝" Dia | Plate 8 Actually 8¼" Dia |

38

Page 38.

$10-20 each

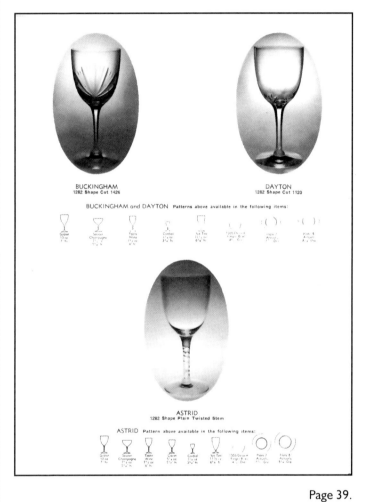

BUCKINGHAM
1282 Shape Cut 1426

DAYTON
1282 Shape Cut 1120

BUCKINGHAM and DAYTON Patterns above available in the following items:

| Goblet 10 oz 7" hi | Saucer Champagne 7½ oz 5½" hi | Table Wine 4½ oz 6" hi | Cordial 1¼ oz 3½" hi | Ice Tea 11½ oz 6½" hi | 1305 Dessert Finger Bowl 4½" Dia | Plate 7 Actually 7⅝" Dia | Plate 8 Actually 8¼" Dia |

ASTRID
1282 Shape Plain Twisted Stem

ASTRID Pattern above available in the following items:

| Goblet 10 oz 7" hi | Saucer Champagne 7½ oz 5½" hi | Table Wine 5½ oz 6" hi | Claret 5½ oz 5½" hi | Cordial 1¼ oz 3½" hi | Ice Tea 11½ oz 6½" hi | 1305 Dessert Finger Bowl 4½" Dia | Plate 7 Actually 7⅝" Dia | Plate 8 Actually 8¼" Dia |

Page 39.

$10-20 each

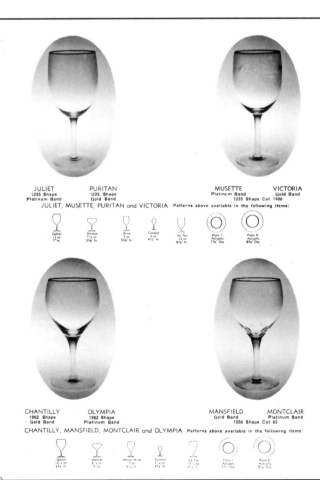

JULIET
1235 Shape
Platinum Band

PURITAN
1235 Shape
Gold Band

MUSETTE
Platinum Band

VICTORIA
Gold Band
1235 Shape Cut 1406

JULIET, MUSETTE, PURITAN and VICTORIA Patterns above available in the following items:

| Goblet 12 oz 7" hi | Sherbet 7½ oz 5⅜" hi | Wine 7 oz 5⅜" hi | Cordial 2 oz 4½" hi | Ice Tea 12 oz 6½" hi | Plate 7 Actually 7⅝" Dia | Plate 8 Actually 8¼" Dia |

CHANTILLY
1962 Shape
Gold Band

OLYMPIA
1962 Shape
Platinum Band

MANSFIELD
Gold Band

MONTCLAIR
Platinum Band
1350 Shape Cut 63

CHANTILLY, MANSFIELD, MONTCLAIR and OLYMPIA Patterns above available in the following items:

| Goblet 12½ oz 6⅝" hi | Sherbet 6 oz 5" hi | White Wine 7 oz 5" hi | Cordial 1 oz 3¼" hi | Ice Tea 13½ oz 6½" hi | Plate 7 Actually 7⅝" Dia | Plate 8 Actually 8¼" Dia |

Page 40.

$10-20 each

Page 38.

$8-12 each

ANDOVER
1964 Shape
Gold Band

LEXINGTON
1964 Shape
Platinum Band

CABARET
1964 Shape Plain Crystal

ANDOVER, CABARET and LEXINGTON Patterns above available in the following items:

PRISTINE
1963 Shape
Platinum Band

SYLVIA
1963 Shape Gold Band

PRISTINE and SYLVIA Patterns above available in the following items:

41

HAND MADE LEAD CRYSTAL TUMBLERS

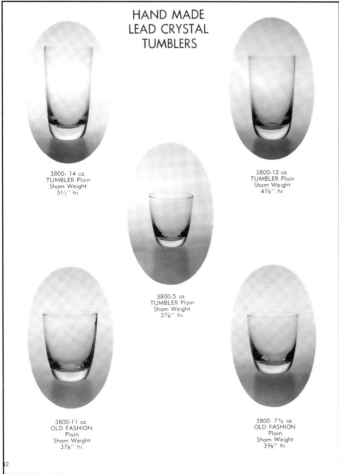

3800- 14 oz.
TUMBLER Plain
Sham Weight
5½" hi.

3800-12 oz.
TUMBLER Plain
Sham Weight
4⅞" hi.

3800-5 oz.
TUMBLER Plain
Sham Weight
2⅞" hi.

3800-11 oz.
OLD FASHION
Plain
Sham Weight
3⅞" hi.

3800- 7½ oz.
OLD FASHION
Plain
Sham Weight
3⅜" hi.

Page 39.

$8-12 each

CUT 39 TUMBLERS

Cut #39 indicates the Flutes at the base of the Tumblers are 1¼" high and ½" wide. Tumblers Cut #39 have a flat unpolished base

CUT 45 TUMBLERS

Cut #45 indicates the Flutes at the base of the Tumblers are 1½" high and ¾" wide. Tumblers Cut #45 have a flat unpolished base

CUT 43 TUMBLERS

Cut #43 indicates the Flutes at the base of the Tumblers are 1¾" high and ¾" wide. Tumblers Cut #43 have a hand cut and hand polished (punty) base

Page 40.

$8-12 each

43

1978 Catalog

Page 1.

$25-35 each

Page 2.

$25-35 each

Page 3.

$15-20 each

Page 4.

$25+ each
Christmas: $15-20

Page 5.

$25+ each

Page 6. $8-15 each

Page 7. $8-12 each

Page 8. $10-15 each

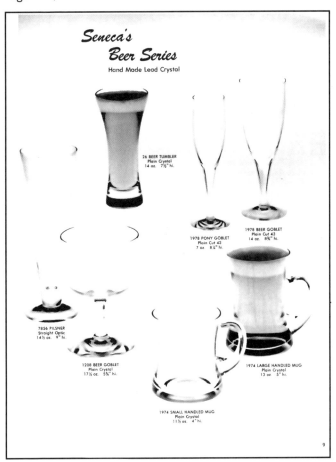

Page 9. $10-15 each

Seneca's Bloody Mary Set

The Fashionables

6 piece Mixer Set
HAND MADE LEAD CRYSTAL
with Black Foot

1974 MIXER
Lead Crystal w/Black Foot
with stir rod
40 oz.

1974 BLOODY MARY
Lead Crystal w/Black Foot
15½ oz.   6¾" hi.

Mixer set individually boxed

10

Page 10.

$15-35 each

Seneca's Bloody Mary Set

Cascade

6 piece Mixer Set
HAND MADE LEAD CRYSTAL

1972 MIXER
Lead Crystal
with stir rod
40 oz.

1972 BLOODY MARY
Lead Crystal
14½ oz   5⅝" hi.

Mixer set individually boxed

11

Page 11.

$15-35 each

The Tree by SENECA

The Artisans of Seneca Glass introduce The Tree—hand-made lead-crystal, multi-use stack jars that, in their basic configuration, are shaped like the old-favorite Christmas Tree.

Available in Accent Red, Crystal and Moss Green, additional year-round uses are limited only by your imagination.

50 THE TREE
Accent Red
with drape optic
10⅝" hi.

50 THE TREE
Lead Crystal
10⅝" hi.

50 THE TREE
Moss Green
10⅝" hi.

The 4 piece TREE is individually Boxed

Page 12.

$15-35 each

Page 13. $45-60 each

Page 14. $15-25 each

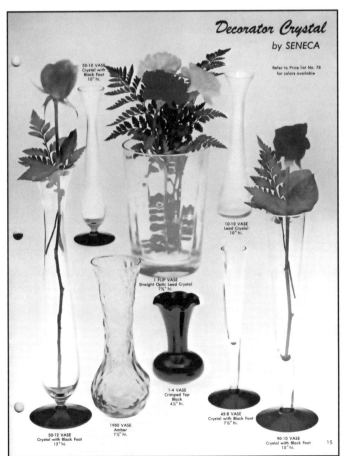

Page 15. $10-20 each

Page 16. $10-15 each

1979 CATALOG

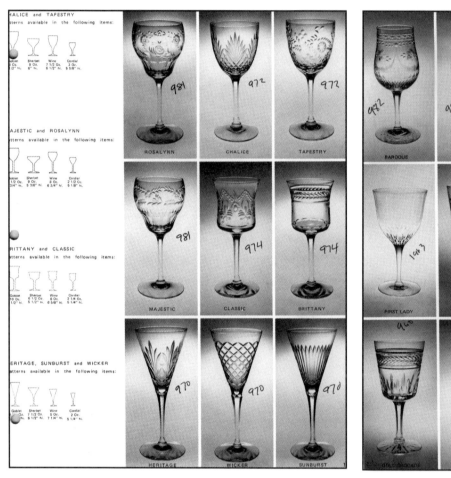

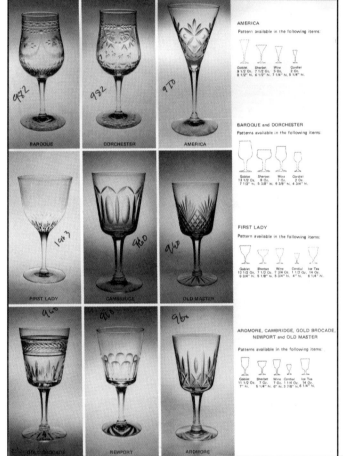

Page 1.

$15-30 each

Page 2.

$15-30 each

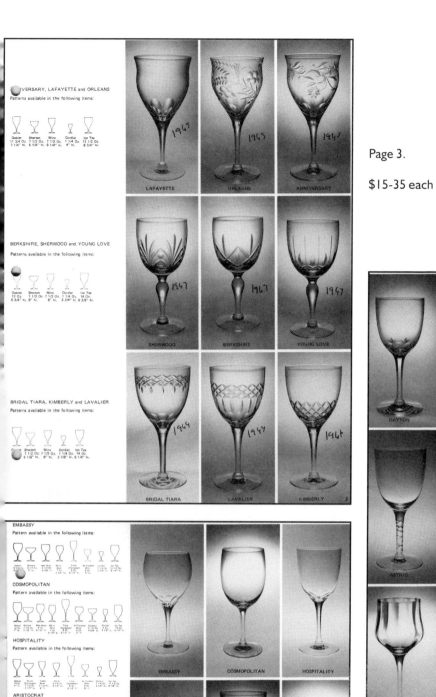

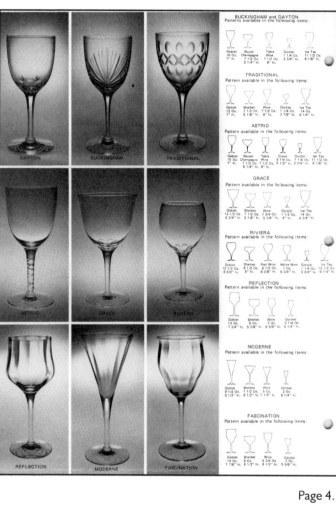

Page 3.

$15-35 each

Page 4.

$10-20 each

Page 5.

$10-15 each

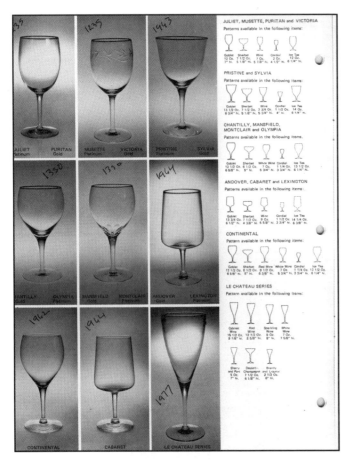

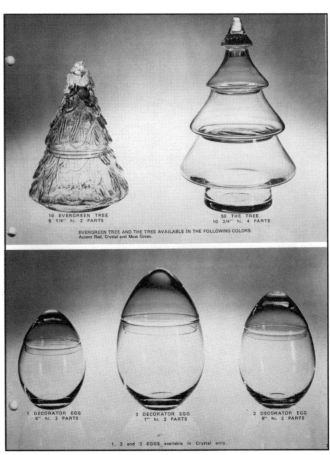

Page 6. $8-15 each

Page 7.   Eggs: $45-60 each; Left tree: $30-35; Right tree: $75+

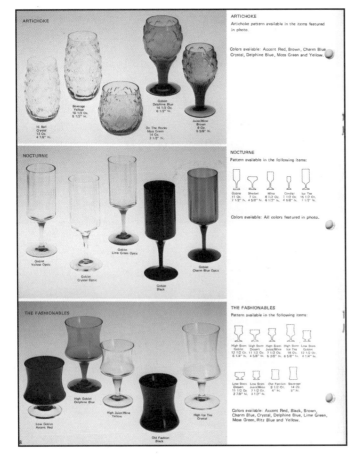

Page 8. $10-15 each

Page 9. $8-15 each; Pitcher: $75+

GOURMET COLLECTION
Available in the following items:

FRANK SCHOONMAKER® WINES
Available in the following items:

EPICURE COLLECTION
Available in the following items:

Page 10.

$10-20 each

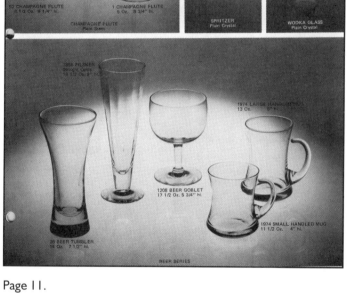

Page 11.

$10-20 each

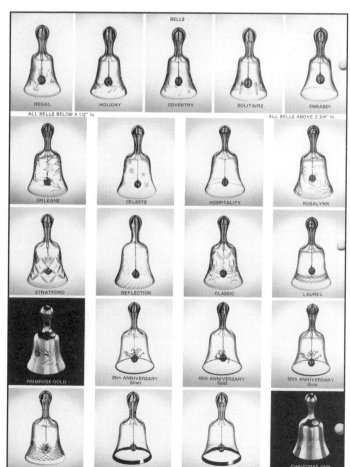

Page 12.

$25+each

147

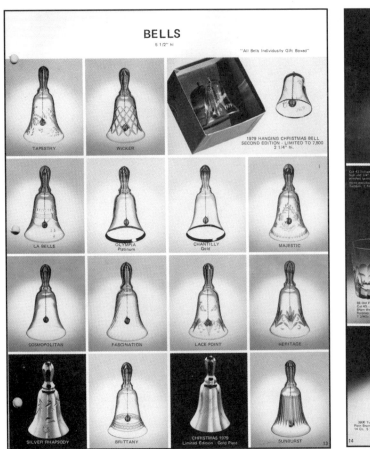

Page 13. $25+ each

Page 14. $15-25 each

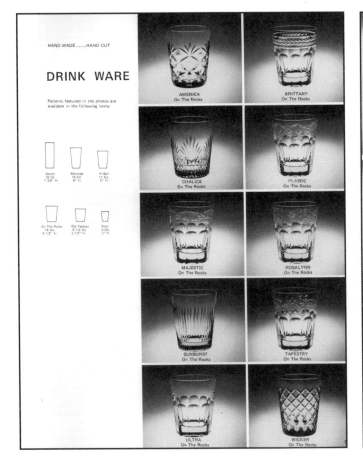

Page 15. $10-15 each

Page 16. $8-12 each

1980 CATALOG

Page 1.

$8-15 each

Page 2.

$8-15 each
Pitcher: $75+

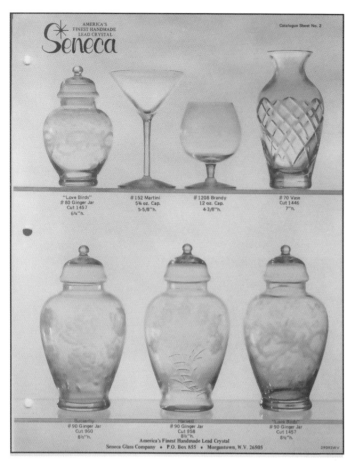

Page 3. Ginger Jars: $110+ each; $24-45 each

Page 4. $20-30 each; Ginger Jars: $110+ each; Bells: $25+ each

Page 5. $10-15 each

Page 6.

$10-15 each

1981 CATALOG

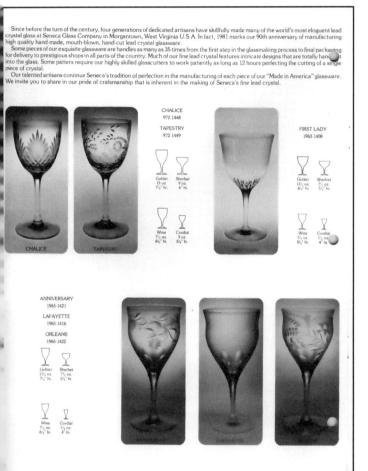

Page 1.

$15-30 each

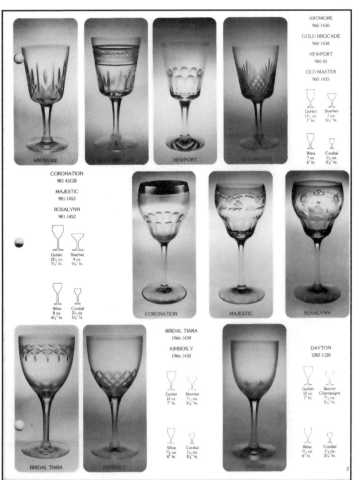

Page 2.

$15-30 each

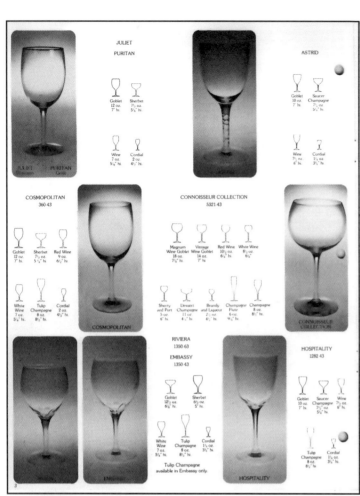

JULIET PURITAN

Goblet 12 oz. 7" hi.
Sherbet 7½ oz. 5½" hi.
Wine 7 oz. 5¼" hi.
Cordial 2 oz. 4½" hi.

JULIET · PURITAN · Cordial

ASTRID

Goblet 10 oz. 7" hi.
Saucer Champagne 7½ oz. 5½" hi.
Wine 7 oz. 6" hi.
Cordial 1½ oz. 3½" hi.

COSMOPOLITAN 360-43

Goblet 12 oz. 7" hi.
Sherbet 7½ oz. 5½" hi.
Red Wine 9 oz. 6½" hi.
White Wine 7 oz. 5½" hi.
Tulip Champagne 8 oz. 8½" hi.
Cordial 2 oz. 4½" hi.

COSMOPOLITAN

CONNOISSEUR COLLECTION 5321 43

Magnum Wine Goblet 18 oz. 7½" hi.
Vintage Wine Goblet 14 oz. 7" hi.
Red Wine 10½ oz. 6½" hi.
White Wine 8½ oz. 6½" hi.

Sherry and Port 5 oz. 6½" hi.
Dessert Champagne 11 oz. 4¼" hi.
Brandy and Liqueur 6 oz. 4½" hi.
Champagne Flute 6 oz. 9½" hi.
Champagne 8 oz. 8½" hi.

CONNOISSEUR COLLECTION

RIVIERA 1350·63
EMBASSY 1350·43

Goblet 12½ oz. 6½" hi.
Sherbet 6½ oz. 5" hi.
White Wine 7 oz. 5½" hi.
Tulip Champagne 8 oz. 8½" hi.
Cordial 1½ oz. 3½" hi.

Tulip Champagne available in Embassy only.

EMBASSY

HOSPITALITY 1282 43

Goblet 10 oz. 7" hi.
Saucer Champagne 7½ oz. 5½" hi.
Wine 7 oz. 6" hi.
Tulip Champagne 8 oz. 8½" hi.
Cordial 1½ oz. 3½" hi.

HOSPITALITY

Page 3.

$10-15 each

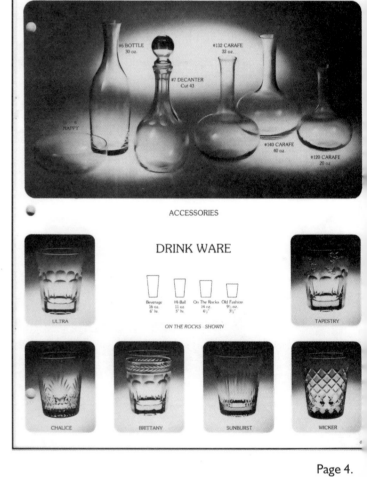

#6 BOTTLE 30 oz.
#7 DECANTER Cut 43
#132 CARAFE 32 oz.
#140 CARAFE 40 oz.
#120 CARAFE 20 oz.
NAPPY

ACCESSORIES

DRINK WARE

Beverage 16 oz. 6" hi.
Hi-Ball 11 oz. 5" hi.
On The Rocks 14 oz. 4½"
Old Fashion 9½ oz. 3½"

ON THE ROCKS · SHOWN

ULTRA

TAPESTRY

CHALICE

BRITTANY

SUNBURST

WICKER

Page 4.

$10-15 each
Decanter: $80+
Carafes: $20+ each.

IMAGES

(A) Goblet (Brown) 14½ oz.
(B) Wine (Yellow) 9 oz.
(C) On The Rocks (Lime Green) 10½ oz.
(D) Double Old Fashion (Crystal) 13½ oz.
(E) Bowl (Lime Green) 4½ dia.
(F) Cooler (Yellow) 19 oz.
(G) Juice (Moss Green) 7½ oz.
(H) Hi Ball (Crystal) 13½ oz.
(I) Ice Tea (Charm Blue) 15½ oz.

Items in IMAGES are available in the following colors:
Brown, Charm Blue, Crystal, Lime Green, Moss Green, Yellow.

DRIFTWOOD CASUAL

(A) Ice Tea (Brown) 16 oz.
(B) Hi Ball (Charm Blue) 12 oz.
(C) Bowl (Crystal) 5¼ dia.
(D) Goblet (Accent Red) 13 oz.
(E) Pitcher (Crystal) 65 oz.
(F) Juice (Delphine Blue) 6 oz.
(G) Sherbet (Yellow) 5 oz.
(H) Cocktail (Moss Green) 6 oz.
(I) Cooler (Amber) 22 oz.
(J) Double Old Fashion (Lime Green) 14 oz.

Items in DRIFTWOOD CASUAL are available in the following colors:
Accent Red, Amber, Brown, Charm Blue, Crystal, Delphine Blue,
Lime Green, Moss Green, Yellow.

Page 5.

$8-15 each
Pitcher: $50-60

REFLECTION

Goblet
13 oz.
7¾" hi.

Sherbet
9 oz.
5½" hi.

Wine
7 oz.
6¼" hi.

Cordial
2½ oz.
3½" hi.

Items in REFLECTION are available in the following colors:
Brown, Charm Blue, Crystal, Lime Green, Yellow.

CASCADE

(A) Cooler 18½ oz.
(B) Beverage 15½ oz.

(C) Old Fashion 11½ oz.
(D) Cocktail/Juice 7½ oz.

CASCADE available in crystal only.

6

Page 6.

$10-15 each

GOURMET COLLECTION

| Grande Bordeaux 24 oz. 7¾" hi. | Magnum Wine Goblet 18 oz. 7⅛" hi. | Vintage Wine Goblet 14 oz. 7" | Red Wine 10½ oz. 6½" hi. | White Wine 8½ oz. 6¼" hi. | Champagne 9½ oz. 8" hi. | Champagne Flute 6 oz. 9½" hi. | Dessert Champagne 11 oz. 4½" hi. | Brandy and Liqueur 2½ oz. 4½" hi. | Sherry and Port 5 oz. |

7

Page 7.

$10-15 each

FRANK SCHOONMAKER® WINES

| Champagne Tulip 8 oz. 8½" hi. | Johannisberg 6 oz. 6½" hi. | Magnum 10 oz. 5½" hi. | Vin Du Pays 8 oz. 5½" hi. | Cabernet 9 oz. 6½" hi. | Solera 5 oz. 5½" hi. | V.S.O.P. 7 oz. 4½" hi. | Chateau 7 oz. 6" hi. |

8

Page 8.

$10-15 each

EPICURE COLLECTION

Page 10.

$10-15 each

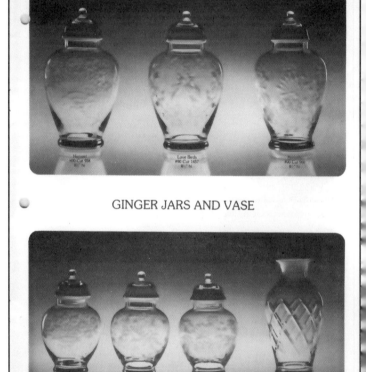

GINGER JARS AND VASE

Page 11.

Vase: $20-40 each
Ginger Jars: $110+ each

1981 HANGING CHRISTMAS BELL

AMERICA'S
FINEST HANDMADE
LEAD CRYSTAL
Seneca
Glass Company

709 BEECHURST AVENUE, MORGANTOWN, WEST VIRGINIA 26505   304/292-7121

Page 12.

$25+ each
Christmas: $15-20

1982 Catalog

Page 1.

$10-15 each

Page 1P.

$8-15 each
Pitcher: $50-60

FRANK SCHOONMAKER® COLLECTION

Page 2. $8-15 each

GOURMET COLLECTION

Page 2P. $8-15 each

EPICURE COLLECTION

Page 3. $8-15 each

FRANK SCHOONMAKER® WINES

Page 3P. $8-15 each

FLUTE

Page 4. $8-12 each

EPICURE COLLECTION

Page 4P. $8-12 each

CUT 43 STEMWARE

Page 4. $8-12 each

WINE ACCESSORIES

AMERICA'S
FINEST HANDMADE
LEAD CRYSTAL
Seneca
Glass Company

709 BEECHURST AVENUE, MORGANTOWN, WEST VIRGINIA 26505 304/292-7121

Page 4P. $20-30 each; Decanter: $80+

Page 5. $8-12 each

WINE ACCESSORIES

Page 5P. $20-30 each; Decanter: $80+

Page 6. $8-10 each

Page 7. $8-10 each

RIVIERA

| Goblet 12½ oz. 6¼" hi. | Sherbet 6½ oz. 5" hi. | White Wine 7 oz. 5¼" hi. | Tulip Champagne 8 oz. 8½" hi. | Cordial 1¼ oz. 3¼" hi. |

Page 8.

$10-15 each

PALM OPTIC
STEMWARE

| #1235 Martini 5½ oz. 6" hi. | #7780 Wine Goblet 9½ oz. 6¼" hi. | #7197 Wine Goblet 8 oz. 5¼" hi. | | | | | #1235 Parfait Whiskey Sour 6½ oz. 6¼" hi. | #7 Sherry 3 oz. 5¼" hi. | #1235 Brandy Inhaler 12 oz. 4¾" hi. |
| #1235 Juice 5 oz. 4½" hi. | #1235 Goblet 12 oz. 7" hi. | #1235 Vintage Wine 14 oz. 7" hi. | #1235 Dessert Champagne 5½" hi. | #1235 Cocktail 3½ oz. 4¼" hi. | #1235 Cordial 2 oz. 4½" hi. | #1235 Brandy Inhaler 22 oz. 6" hi. | #1235 Ice Tea 12 oz. 6¼" hi. | #1235 Peach Champagne 24 oz. 8½" hi. | #1235 Continental Beer 14 oz. 8¼" hi. |

Page 9.

$10-15 each

PALM & PEACOCK
OPTIC TUMBLERS

Page 10.

$8-10 each

SENECA™
CRYSTAL INC.
PEACOCK OPTIC
STEMWARE
Grande Bordeaux 24 oz. 7⅝" hi.
Magnum Wine Goblet 18 oz. 7⅝" hi.
Vintage Wine Goblet 14 oz. 7" hi.
Red Wine 10½ oz. 6⅞" hi.
White Wine 8½ oz. 6⅜" hi.
Champagne 9½ oz. 8" hi.
Flute 6 oz. 9¼" hi.
Dessert Champagne 11 oz. 4⅞" hi.
Brandy and Liqueur 2½ oz. 4½" hi.
Sherry and Port 5 oz. 6" hi.

Page 11.

$10-15 each

SENECA™
CRYSTAL INC.
STRAIGHT OPTIC TUMBLERS
#9823 Tumbler Straight 10 Optic Regular Weight 5⅛" hi. 11 oz.
#9823 (2825) Tumbler Straight 12 Optic Sham Weight 4¾" hi. 9 oz.
#636 Tumbler Straight 16 Optic Regular Weight 4" hi. 9 oz.
#9491 Tumbler Sham Weight 7" hi. 12 oz.
#2828 Tumbler Regular Weight 4⅝" hi. 9½ oz.
#8701-14 oz. Tumbler Sham Weight 5½" hi.
#8701 Tumbler Sham Weight 5⅛" hi. 10 oz.
#8701 Tumbler Sham Weight 9 oz. 5" hi.
#8701 Tumbler Sham Weight 4¼" hi. 9 oz.
#85 Old Fashion Sham Weight 3⅜" hi. 8 oz.
#8127 Old Fashion Sham Weight 3" hi. 5½ oz.

Page 12.

$8-10 each

SENECA™
CRYSTAL INC.
GOBLET
WINE
KIMBERLY
Goblet 12 oz. 7" hi.
Sherbet 7½ oz. 5¼" hi.
Ice Tea 13 oz. 6¾" hi.
Wine 7½ oz. 6" hi.
Cordial 1¼ oz. 4" hi.

Page 13.

$10-15 each

CHALICE

| Beverage 16 oz. 6" hi. | Hi-Ball 11 oz. 5" hi. | On The Rocks 14 oz. 4½" hi. | Old Fashion 9½ oz. 3½" hi. | Goblet 11 oz. 7½" hi. | Sherbet 9 oz. 6" hi. | Wine 7½ oz. 6½" hi. | Cordial 3 oz. 5¾" hi. | Ice Tea 15½ oz. 6¼" hi. | Flute 6 oz. 9¼" hi. |

Page 14.

$10-15 each

ARDMORE GOBLET

ARDMORE SHERBET

JULIET CORDIAL PLATINUM BAND

PURITAN WINE GOLD BAND

ARDMORE, JULIET & PURITAN

ARDMORE					JULIET & PURITAN				
Ice Tea 14 oz. 6¼" hi.	Goblet 10½ oz. 7" hi.	Sherbet 7 oz. 5¾" hi.	Wine 7 oz. 6" hi.	Cordial 1½ oz. 4¼" hi.	Goblet 12 oz. 7" hi.	Sherbet 7½ oz. 5¼" hi.	Wine 7 oz. 5¾" hi.	Cordial 2 oz. 4½" hi.	Ice Tea 12 oz. 6½" hi.

Page 15.

$10-15 each

IMAGES IN DRIFTWOOD CASUAL D.C.

QUILT

IMAGES, DRIFTWOOD CASUAL & QUILT

IMAGES
| a. Goblet 14½ oz. 6¼" hi. | b. Wine 9 oz. 4¾" hi. | c. On The Rocks 10½ oz. 3½" hi. | d. Double Old Fashion 13½ oz. 4½" hi. | e. Bowl 4½ dia. |

DRIFTWOOD CASUAL
| a. Ice Tea 16 oz. 5¼" hi. | b. Hi-Ball 12 oz. 5¼" hi. | c. Bowl 5¼ dia. | d. Goblet 13 oz. | e. Pitcher 65 oz. |

| f. Cooler 19 oz. 6½" hi. | g. Juice 7½ oz. 4¼" hi. | h. Hi-Ball 13¾ oz. 5¼" hi. | i. Ice Tea 15½ oz. 6¼" hi. |

| f. Juice 6 oz. 4¼" hi. | g. Sherbet 3½ dia. 3" hi. | h. Cocktail 6 oz. 3½" hi. | i. Cooler 22 oz. 6½" hi. | j. Double Old Fashion 14 oz. 4¼" hi. |

IMAGES available in the following colors:
Brown, Charm Blue, Crystal, Lime Green, Moss Green, Yellow.

DRIFTWOOD CASUAL available in the following colors: Accent Red, Amber, Brown, Charm Blue, Crystal, Delphine Blue, Lime Green, Moss Green, Yellow.

QUILT PATTERN available in the following colors: Brown, Charm Blue, Crystal, Yellow.

| a. Cooler 22 oz. 6½" hi. | b. Beverage 18 oz. 6½" hi. | c. Hi-Ball 12 oz. 5¼" hi. | d. Old Fashion 13 oz. 4½" hi. | e. Juice 7 oz. 4½" hi. |

Page 16.

$8-15 each
Pitcher: $50-60

1983 CATALOG

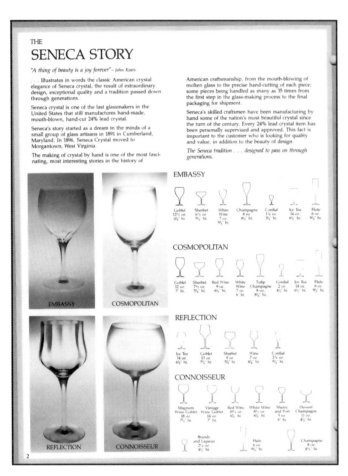

Page 2.

$10-15 each

Page 3.

$15-25 each

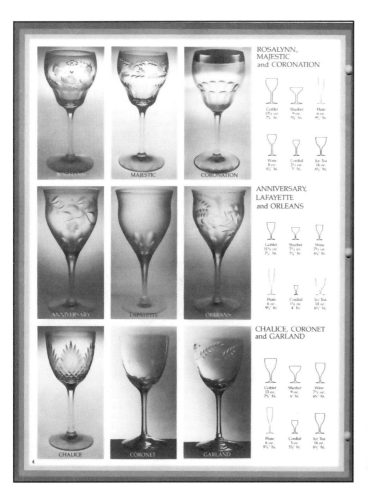

ROSALYNN, MAJESTIC and CORONATION

ANNIVERSARY, LAFAYETTE and ORLEANS

CHALICE, CORONET and GARLAND

Page 4.

$15-35 each

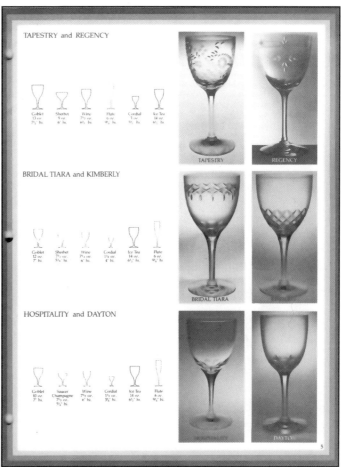

TAPESTRY and REGENCY

BRIDAL TIARA and KIMBERLY

HOSPITALITY and DAYTON

Page 5.

$15-20 each

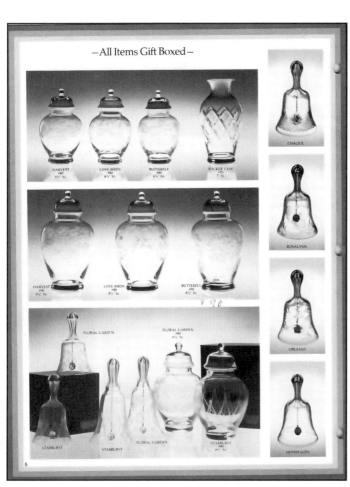

—All Items Gift Boxed—

Page 6.

$20-40 each
Ginger Jars: $110+ each

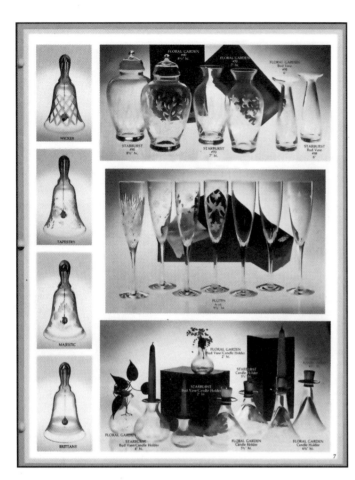

Page 7.

$8-12 each
Bells: $25+ each
Ginger Jars: $110+ each

Gourmet Collection

Page 8.

$8-12 each

Frank Schoonmaker® Wines

Page 9.

$8-12 each

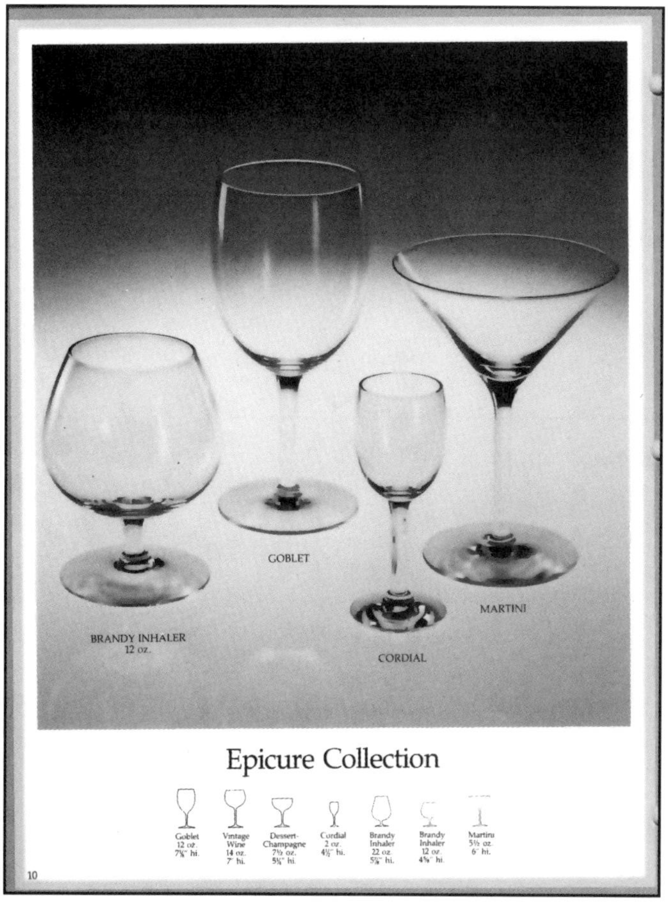
GOBLET
MARTINI
BRANDY INHALER
12 oz.
CORDIAL
Epicure Collection
Goblet 12 oz. 7⅞" hi.
Vintage Wine 14 oz. 7" hi.
Dessert-Champagne 7½ oz. 5¾" hi.
Cordial 2 oz. 4½" hi.
Brandy Inhaler 22 oz. 5⅝" hi.
Brandy Inhaler 12 oz. 4⅝" hi.
Martini 5½ oz. 6" hi.
10

Page 10.

$10-15 each

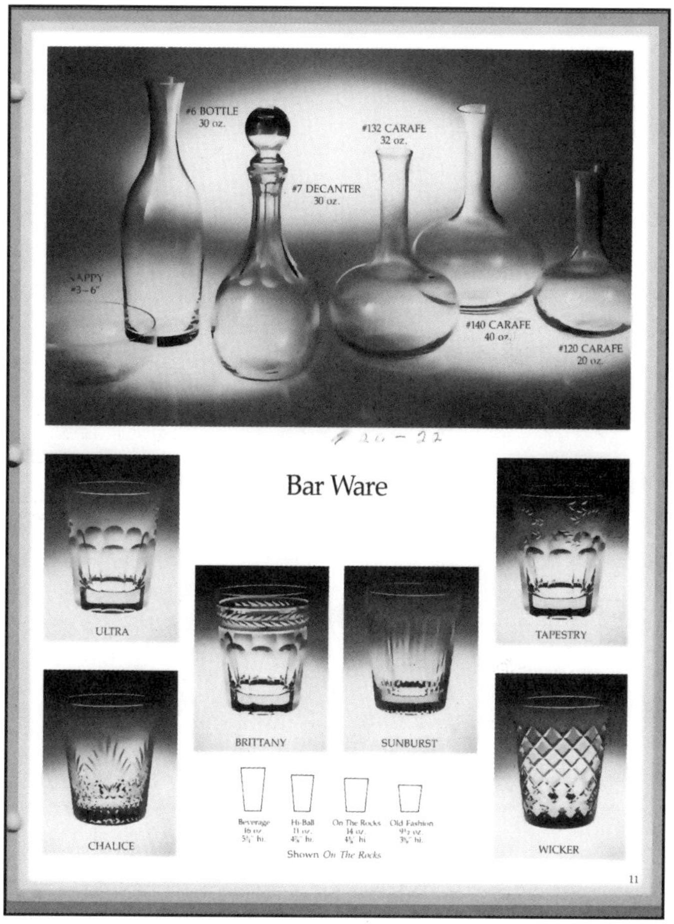
#6 BOTTLE
30 oz.
#132 CARAFE
32 oz.
#7 DECANTER
30 oz.
#140 CARAFE
40 oz.
#120 CARAFE
20 oz.
Bar Ware
ULTRA
TAPESTRY
BRITTANY
SUNBURST
CHALICE
WICKER
Beverage 16 oz. 5¾" hi.
Hi-Ball 11 oz. 4⅞" hi.
On The Rocks 14 oz. 4⅜" hi.
Old Fashion 9½ oz. 3⅞" hi.
Shown On The Rocks
11

Page11.

$10-15 each
Decanter: $80+
Carafes: $20+ each

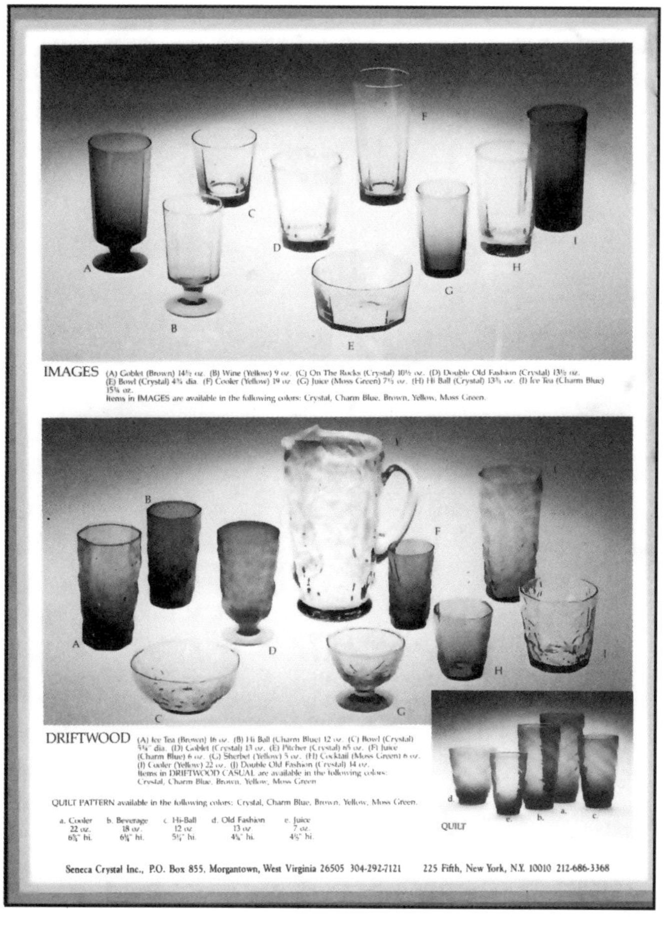
IMAGES (A) Goblet (Brown) 14½ oz. (B) Wine (Yellow) 9 oz. (C) On The Rocks (Crystal) 10½ oz. (D) Double Old Fashion (Crystal) 13½ oz. (E) Bowl (Crystal) 4¾ dia. (F) Cooler (Yellow) 19 oz. (G) Juice (Moss Green) 7½ oz. (H) Hi Ball (Crystal) 13¾ oz. (I) Ice Tea (Charm Blue) 15¾ oz.
Items in IMAGES are available in the following colors: Crystal, Charm Blue, Brown, Yellow, Moss Green.
DRIFTWOOD (A) Ice Tea (Brown) 16 oz. (B) Hi Ball (Charm Blue) 12 oz. (C) Bowl (Crystal) 5¾" dia. (D) Goblet (Crystal) 13 oz. (E) Pitcher (Crystal) 65 oz. (F) Juice (Charm Blue) 6 oz. (G) Sherbet (Yellow) 5 oz. (H) Cocktail (Moss Green) 6 oz. (I) Cooler (Yellow) 22 oz. (J) Double Old Fashion (Crystal) 14 oz.
Items in DRIFTWOOD CASUAL are available in the following colors: Crystal, Charm Blue, Brown, Yellow, Moss Green
QUILT PATTERN available in the following colors: Crystal, Charm Blue, Brown, Yellow, Moss Green.
a. Cooler 22 oz. 6¾" hi.
b. Beverage 18 oz. 6¼" hi.
c. Hi-Ball 12 oz. 5¼" hi.
d. Old Fashion 13 oz. 4⅝" hi.
e. Juice 7 oz. 4½" hi.
QUILT
Seneca Crystal Inc., P.O. Box 855, Morgantown, West Virginia 26505 304-292-7121
225 Fifth, New York, N.Y. 10010 212-686-3368

Page 12.

$8-15 each
Pitcher: $50-60

1967 Advertisements

WHITEBROOK MAR 14 1967

SENECA GLASS COMPANY

American Craftsmanship at its Best...since 1891

CAMELOT MAR 14 1967

SENECA GLASS COMPANY

American Craftsmanship at its Best...since 1891

CAROUSEL MAR 14 1967

SENECA GLASS COMPANY

American Craftsmanship at its Best...since 1891

MAR 14 1967

CHANTILLY and OLYMPIA

SENECA GLASS COMPANY

American Craftsmanship at its Best...since 1891

SENECA GLASS COMPANY. Highlight of this firm's offerings in fine crystal are three new stemware colors, heather, peacock blue, and amber, offered in three shapes, with seven items in each shape. Priced to retail for $1.50 a stem.

EPICURE MAR 14 1967

SENECA GLASS COMPANY

American Craftsmanship at its Best...since 1891

MAR 14 1967

MUSETTE, VICTORIA and WINDSOR

SENECA GLASS COMPANY

American Craftsmanship at its Best...since 1891

LAFAYETTE MAR 14 1967

SENECA GLASS COMPANY

American Craftsmanship at its Best...since 1891

HELGA MAR 14 1967

SENECA GLASS COMPANY

American Craftsmanship at its Best...since 1891

$10-20 each

1970 ADVERTISEMENTS

BROCADO
ADVERTISEMENTS

$8-15 each

$8-15 each

CATALOG SHEETS

Catalog sheet No. 2

AMERICA'S
FINEST HANDMADE
LEAD CRYSTAL

Seneca

| No. 80 Ginger Jar Cut 958 | No. 80 Ginger Jar Cut 960 | 1980 Christmas Hanging Bell | Morning Star Handcut Hanging Bell |

| No. 6 Bottle 24 Oz. | No. 7 Bottle Cut 43 32 Oz. | No. 140 40 Oz. Carafe | No. 3 - 6" Nappy |

America's Finest Handmade Lead Crystal

Seneca Glass Company   P.O. Box 855   Morgantown, WV 26505

1972.

$30-50 each
Ginger Jars: $110+ each
Christmas Bells: $15-20 each

CRINKLE GLASS

$8-15 each
Pitcher: $30-40 each

DRIFTWOOD

$8-15 each

$8-15 each

$8-15 each
Pitcher: $50-60

$8-15 each
Pitchers: $50-60 each

$8-15 each
Pitcher: $50-60

$8-15 each
Pitcher: $50-60

"Driftwood Casual"

by Seneca Glass Co. Morgantown, W. Va.

The origination of the artful design of Driftwood Casual is created from the floating pieces of driftwood which are captured in the glass and the exquisite frosting effect by fine mold work.

Professionally skilled employees and production methods provide us with the ability to produce the Casual Line in fourteen different items and eight beautiful colors.

Without recourse Driftwood Casual will be a favorite of young brides as well as the modern homemaker.

(SEE REVERSE SIDE FOR NEW ADDITIONS)

$8-15 each
Pitcher: $50-60

Candy Jar and Cover

Roly Poly Hi-Ball 12 oz.

Roly Poly Old Fashioned 9 oz.

Roly Poly Cocktail 5 oz.

Handled Ice Tea or Beer Mug 16 oz.

Juice Pitcher 32 oz.

Ash Tray

Salad or Fruit Bowl

$8-15 each, Top left, top right, bottom left and bottom right: $30-40 each

GOURMET COLLECTION

Gourmet Collection by **SENECA**

SENECA GLASS CO. MORGANTOWN. W.Va. 26505

When wine is served there should be an aura of elegance in dining. Seneca Glass Company, foremost manufacturer of lead crystal glassware since 1891 now presents its newest creation the GOURMET COLLECTION of fine wine glasses to compliment this special occasion. Bubble shaped, thin-stemmed and generously proportioned they are handcrafted of the finest lead crystal. A more detailed description of the Glasses in the GOURMET COLLECTION follows throughout this brochure. The 32 ounce and 20 ounce Carafes featured above are excellent companions and proper for dispensing wine.

These two glasses are especially designed and wonderfully suited for use before that special dinner or after small. The Sherry Port Glass is ideal for serving dry cocktail or aperitif sherry and dessert wines such as port madeira and sweet sherry. The Brandy Liqueur Glass, of course, is a delight to true lovers of fine cognacs, armagnacs and liqueurs.

Vintage Wine Goblet 14 ounces

Magnum Wine Goblet 18 ounces

Grande Bordeaux 24 ounces

The Grande Bordeaux, Magnum Wine Goblet and Vintage Wine Goblet lend themselves to the serving of most dry table wines such as red, white and rosé. Properly filled 1/3 to 1/2 capacity they are the ideal glasses for relishing the bouquet and exquisite taste of great wines. Anyone of these elegant handmade glasses would be more than acceptable for any fine table wine and could do double duty as a stemmed on the rocks glass or water goblet.

White Wine 9 ounces

Red Wine 11 ounces

The GOURMET COLLECTION Red Wine and White Wine Glasses were created for the more conservative hostess who prefers to maintain distinct serving and pouring style for each wine. The smaller White Wine Glass is perfect. The larger Red Wine Glass is used with meat or game.

Dessert Champagne 8 ounces

Champagne 9 ounces

Seneca's GOURMET COLLECTION features two beautiful glasses for serving champagne and dessert. The tulip-shaped Champagne was designed in the French tradition for serving champagne. Cold Duck and sparkling wines. Tall and elegant it is styled to suit a great occasion. The Dessert Champagne is traditionally American doubling as a glass for desserts and champagne.

$8-15 each

174

GREAT WINES

$8-15 each

The Vin du Pays
8 ounces

The Champagne Tulip
8 ounces

The Vin du Pays is a functionally sturdy and generous glass that will suit any wine — grace even a connoisseur's table. It is everything that a good, simple, all-purpose wine glass should be.

All sorts of glasses have been used for Champagne. The flat saucer-glass (in which the wine loses its sparkle, almost at once). The hollow-stem (which is pretty, but almost impossible to wash). The flute (nice, especially for beer). And, finally this Champagne Tulip . . . tall, elegant, perhaps a bit fragile, equal to a great occasion . . . like Champagne. All experts prefer it.

The Chateau
7 ounce White Wine

The Cabernet
9 ounce Red Wine

When two wines are served, the white wine, whether a dry white wine (served before the red) or a sweet white wine (served with dessert), or even a sparkling wine, gets the small glass. The red wine gets the big one. Filled one-third full (never more than half) these glasses will make any fine wine taste immeasurably better, and give you an idea of just how good it really can be.

The Solera
3 ounce

The VSOP
7 ounce

Here are two glasses wonderfully suited for use before a special dinner or at its end. The Solera (and not the little 2 ounce inverted cone, commonly called a "Sherry glass" in this country) is the right and proper glass for Sherry, Port, Madeira. It can also be used for cocktails, and many experts prefer it to all others for brandy and liqueurs. The VSOP is a snifter, but an unostentatious and graceful one, fitting snugly in the palm of the hand. A glass to delight your true lover of fine Cognacs, Armagnacs and other brandies.

The Johannisberg
6 ounce. For Rhine, Moselle, Riesling, etc.

The Magnum
10 ounce. For great red Burgundies, etc.

These two glasses aren't for everybody. You will want them only if you serve or plan to serve great wine. They are no better than their companion pieces in this group, but they are wholly traditional. To use them is to pay a well-deserved tribute to the skill and care and love that the vintners have given to the wines you drink. Both say, to your guests, "here is something extraordinary," and you should never use them unless the wine is worthy of its glass.

$8-15 each

DATE UNKNOWN

$10-20 each

$10-20 each

$10-20 each

$10-20 each

■ STRIPES, AND CIRCLES, in contrast, but not lacking harmony, keynote this table at the recent Tables of the Nation's exhibit at Rockefeller Center, New York. A modern American setting, it was arranged by Marguerita Morgantime who also designed the linen and the Centerpiece. Glass by Seneca.

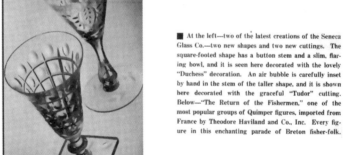

$25-35 each

■ At the left—two of the latest creations of the Seneca Glass Co.—two new shapes and two new cuttings. The square-footed shape has a button stem and a slim, flaring bowl, and it is seen here decorated with the lovely "Duchess" decoration. An air bubble is carefully inset by hand in the stem of the taller shape, and it is shown here decorated with the graceful "Tudor" cutting. Below—"The Return of the Fishermen," one of the most popular groups of Quimper figures, imported from France by Theodore Haviland and Co., Inc. Every figure in this enchanting parade of Breton fisher-folk.

MUSETTE, VICTORIA and WINDSOR

SENECA GLASS COMPANY

American Craftsmanship at its Best...since 1891

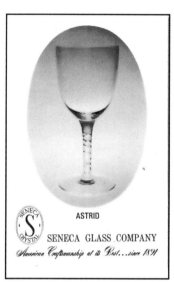

ASTRID

SENECA GLASS COMPANY

American Craftsmanship at its Best...since 1891

● Illustrated at the left is a new stemware shape just introduced by the Seneca Glass Co. It is No. 1025, and it is characterized by a fine simplicity. Notice the unusual combination of tall, slim lines in the bowl and a repetition of spherical curves in the ball stem. The design appears in a complete line of stemware.

★ Tall and slim, these 16-ounce glasses for long, Summer drinks can be retailed for $5.00 for six. They are made by the Seneca Glass Co., and come in six different colors — ruby, Florentine green, royal blue, ocean blue, burgundy and amber—with square, crystal feet.

$10-20 each

SENECA CRYSTAL

... OLYMPIA, CHANTILLY and CONTINENTAL

SEP 9 1964

"American Craftsmanship at its Best"
... since 1891

SENECA GLASS COMPANY. "Lafayette" in fine handmade American crystal features a petal cutting; it decorates a sherbet, wine, cordial, ice tea and juice in addition to the goblet shown. Retail price, $3.50 a stem.

Beautiful,
elegant styling...

Her pride and joy

EPICURE...
A tulip-shaped stemware pattern with a hand drawn, slender stem . . . hand crafted of the finest lead crystal. A fine new shape to compliment the popular Frank Schoonmaker wine glasses.

Selection of stemware for your table setting is an art—and you are the artist most highly qualified to make this important choice.

SENECA CRYSTAL — famous since 1891— offers you the superb brilliance of its full lead crystal, flawless craftsmanship and on unusually wide range of shapes and cuttings.

Compare these illustrations with the china, sterling and stainless flatware you already have or intend to purchase. Whether you prefer modern simplicity or traditional elegance, there is a Seneca design to perfectly blend with a table setting of your own creation.

Seneca Glass Company MORGANTOWN, WEST VIRGINIA

American Craftsmanship at its Best ... since 1891

"RENAISSANCE"
This reproduction of a famous French design will be cherished forever as a tableware heirloom.

"TIMELESS"
A design of modern character, yet its classic grace is adaptable to formal entertaining regardless of the period of your table setting.

"COVENTRY"
A delicate vine of berries and leaves gracefully encircles this modern-classic stemware . . . creating a distinctive beauty all its own.

"LYRIC"
The enchantment of wind swept branches against a star studded sky is perpetuated in glistening crystal with Seneca skill and craftsmanship.

"JULIET"
Tulip-shaped with a hand drawn, slender stem . . . wears a band of purest platinum; PURITAN (same shape) with gold.

"CELESTE"
The captivating beauty of shimmering stars is stylized with crisp elegance on a simple, modern shape.

"WATERFORD"
Diamond-like brilliance is achieved by deep, hand cutting on heavy lead crystal; inspired by antique treasures of the past for today's table settings.

"EMBASSY"
A full-cut stem, continued into the base of the bowl, forms a charming rosette. Truly a design for the discriminating hostesses.

"CAPRICE"
A new, modern design of matchless beauty in clearest crystal achieves excellence in contemporary table appointments.

"CHAMPAGNE"
Beautifully hand cut, superbly handmade in clear crystal . . . its perfect proportions sparkling amid any table setting.

"MARTHA WASHINGTON"
Americana at its grandest in hand cut crystal that beautifully blends with period, colonial or contemporary moods in table settings.

"SUNRISE"
Handcuttings simulating rays of sunlight contrast with the otherwise utter simplicity of this beguiling pattern.

$15-25 each

"LAUREL"
Hand cut with the ageless symbol of classicism—the laurel wreath—perfect for table settings in any period.

"SONATA"
Exquisite delicacy and rhythm is personified in this outstanding example of superb craftsmanship.

"WESTWIND"
Slender, buoyant leaves tossed by the wind create a unique stemware theme that delights the eye and enriches your table setting.

"HOSPITALITY"
The graceful beauty of shape, enhanced by a handcut stem, makes this design the choice of the discriminating hostesses.

"SCROLL"
Combining a tapered bowl with hand cut scrollwork, gives a subtly romantic touch to contemporary settings.

"REGENCY"
A stately pattern, combining the cool look of purity of design with the precise handcuttings flaring out from the fluted base of the bowl.

"BILLINGSLEY ROSE"
A floral spray with realistic grace and detail is engraved on stemware destined as a treasured family heirloom.

"SERENADE"
A melody of classic beauty, uniting the softly curving contours of the bowl with a perfectly proportioned stem and foot.

"ARDIS"
A modern version of the classic wreath on a dramatically tapered shape . . . a fascinating blend of the traditional with the contemporary.

"RAMONA"
Strikingly brilliant . . . with deep, mitre handcutting on a chalice bowl held by a handsome baluster stem. A bold statement of beauty for the well appointed table.

"COSMOPOLITAN"
The graceful beauty of a mouth-blown bowl, enhanced by a handmade and hand cut stem, makes this design the choice of the discriminating hostesses.

"ASTRAL"
Interlacing stars and leaves create an unusual border that harmonize perfectly with many dinnerware patterns of contemporary design.

$15-25 each

"MUSETTE"
Interlacing leaves create an unusual border that harmonizes perfectly with a rim of Platinum; VICTORIA (same shape and cutting) with gold.

"GOURMET"
Delicate in appearance; yet, sturdy . . . because it is hand blown in the finest lead crystal—especially preferred by wine lovers.

"CHANTILLY"
Superbly handmade in clear lead crystal . . . wears a band of gold gracing its rim with dignity and beauty; OLYMPIA (same shape) with platinum.

"FLAIR"
A modern stemware pattern with a hand-drawn, slender stem . . . hand crafted of the finest quality crystal.

"ASTRID"
Grace, simplicity and perfect proportion are accented by a slender, hand twisted stem . . . true beauty and fine quality at a moderate cost.

"MANSFIELD"
The simplicity of the bowl is enriched by a handcut rosette at the base and a handpainted band of gold at the rim . . . MONTCLAIR (same shape and cutting) with platinum.

"PIROUETTE"
The shape of tomorrow for table settings of today . . . a swirl of loveliness for table settings with a flair.

"RIVIERA"
The elegant simplicity of the bowl is enriched by a handcut rosette at its base. A homemaker's dream.

"CONTINENTAL"
A hand fashioned stem and foot with a mouth blown bowl creates this modern tulip shaped stemware pattern.

"CONNOISSEUR"
American craftsmanship at its finest—in elegant, thin blown crystal . . . loveliness in crystal that every discerning homemaker dreams of owning.

"HELGA"
Line and rhythm are both personified in the unity of the flared bowl and twisted stem . . . . created for table settings of subtle moods.

"HOSTESS BELL"
Available in most patterns . . . conversational and decorative as well as useful . . . the Bell is 4½" in height and 2¾" base diameter.

$15-25 each

Series Name Index

This index is organized by Series Names, as they were used in the various catalogs. Secondarily it is organized by Line Numbers and Etching Cut Numbers, when they were used, in that order. This will help the reader use this index as a cross-reference with the other indexes in the book. Shapes, dimensions and volume, color, and other information are also provided whenever available.

Each entry has References to the catalogs and other illustrations in the book, by number or date. The first number identifies the catalog; the second number is the page of the catalog where the item can be found; and the bracketed number is the position of the item on the catalog page. The first position number is the row, and the second is the placement, counting from the left. If the item appears in multiple catalogs, each appearence will be referenced.

This indexing was dependent upon Seneca's own identification of items. At times there may be multiple entries, because of some slightly different way of identifying a product.

While we recognize some of the shortcomings of these indexes, it is hoped that, in the main, they will be useful to the collector in finding a particular item of interest.

Ardis. Line: 352. Cut: 1262. Ice Tea. 12 oz. 7-1/4 inches tall. **References:** 1967, page 18 [2-7]; 1968, page 22 [2-7]

Ardis. Line: 352. Cut: 1262. Juice. 5-1/2 oz. 5-3/8 inches tall. **References:** 1967, page 18 [2-6]; 1968, page 22 [2-6]

Ardis. Line: 352. Cut: 1262. Plate. 7 inches diam. Actually 7-7/8" Dia. **References:** 1967, page 18 [2-9]; 1968, page 22 [2-9]

Ardis. Line: 352. Cut: 1262. Plate. 8 inches diam. Actually 8-3/4" Dia. **References:** 1967, page 18 [2-10]; 1968, page 22 [2-10]

Ardis. Line: 352. Cut: 1262. Sherbet. 6 oz. 5-3/8 inches tall. **References:** 1967, page 18 [2-2]; 1968, page 22 [2-2]

Ardmore. Champagne Flute. 6 oz. 9-1/4 inches tall. **References:** 1983, page 3 [1-3]

Ardmore. Cordial. 1-1/2 oz. 4 inches tall. **References:** 1979, page 2 [3-14]; 1983, page 3 [1-5]

Ardmore. Cordial. 1-1/4 oz. 3-7/8 inches tall. **References:** 1982, page 15 [1-5]

Ardmore. Goblet. 11-1/2 oz. 7 inches tall. **References:** 1979, page 2 [3-11]; 1982, page 15 [1-2]; 1983, page 3 [1-1]

Ardmore. Ice Tea. 14 oz. 6-1/4 inches tall. **References:** 1979, page 2 [3-15]; 1982, page 15 [1-1]; 1983, page 3 [1-6]

Ardmore. Sherbet. 7 oz. 5-1/4 inches tall. **References:** 1979, page 2 [3-12]; 1982, page 15 [1-3]; 1983, page 3 [1-2]

Ardmore. Wine. 7 oz. 6 inches tall. **References:** 1979, page 2 [3-13]; 1982, page 15 [1-4]; 1983, page 3 [1-4]

Ardmore. Line: 960. Cut: 1436. 1311 Dessert-Finger Bowl. 4-3/4 inches diam. **References:** 1968, page 7 [1-6]; 1969, page 7 [1-6]; 1970, page 7 [1-6]; 1971, page 7 [1-6]; 1972, page 16 [2-6]; 1973, page 21 [2-6]; 1975, page 21 [2-6]; 1977, page 32 [2-6]

Ardmore. Line: 960. Cut: 1436. Cordial. 1-1/4 oz. 3-7/8 inches tall. **References:** 1968, page 7 [1-4]; 1969, page 7 [1-4]; 1970, page 7 [1-4]; 1971, page 7 [1-4]; 1972, page 16 [2-4]; 1973, page 21 [2-4]; 1975, page 21 [2-4]; 1977, page 32 [2-4]; 1981, page 2 [1-4]

Ardmore. Line: 960. Cut: 1436. Goblet. 11-1/2 oz. 7 inches tall. **References:** 1968, page 7 [1-1]; 1969, page 7 [1-1]

Ardmore. Line: 960. Cut: 1436. Goblet. 11-1/2 oz. 7 inches tall. **References:** 1970, page 7 [1-1]; 1971, page 7 [1-1]; 1972, page 16 [2-1]; 1973, page 21 [2-1]; 1975, page 21 [2-1]; 1977, page 32 [2-1]; 1981, page 2 [1-1]

Ardmore. Line: 960. Cut: 1436. Ice Tea. 14 oz. 6-1/4 inches tall. **References:** 1968, page 7 [1-5]; 1969, page 7 [1-5]; 1970, page 7 [1-5]; 1971, page 7 [1-5]; 1972, page 16 [2-5]; 1973, page 21 [2-5]; 1975, page 21 [2-5]; 1977, page 32 [2-5]

Ardmore. Line: 960. Cut: 1436. Plate. 7 inches diam. Actually 7-7/8" Dia. **References:** 1968, page 7 [1-7]; 1969, page 7 [1-7]; 1970, page 7 [1-7]; 1971, page 7 [1-7]; 1972, page 16 [2-7]; 1973, page 21 [2-7]; 1975, page 21 [2-7]; 1977, page 32 [2-7]

Ardmore. Line: 960. Cut: 1436. Plate. 8 inches diam. Actually 8-3/4" Dia. **References:** 1968, page 7 [1-8]; 1969, page 7 [1-8]; 1970, page 7 [1-8]; 1971, page 7 [1-8]; 1972, page 16 [2-8]; 1973, page 21 [2-8]; 1975, page 21 [2-8]; 1977, page 32 [2-8]

Ardmore. Line: 960. Cut: 1436. Sherbet. 7 oz. 5-1/4 inches tall. **References:** 1968, page 7 [1-2]; 1969, page 7 [1-2]; 1970, page 7 [1-2]; 1971, page 7 [1-2]; 1972, page 16 [2-2]; 1973, page 21 [2-2]; 1975, page 21 [2-2]; 1977, page 32 [2-2]; 1981, page 2 [1-2]

Ardmore. Line: 960. Cut: 1436. Wine. 7 oz. 6 inches tall. **References:** 1968, page 7 [1-3]; 1969, page 7 [1-3]; 1970, page 7 [1-3]; 1971, page 7 [1-3]; 1972, page 16 [2-3]; 1973, page 21 [2-3]; 1975, page 21 [2-3]; 1977, page 32 [2-3]; 1981, page 2 [1-3]

Aristocrat. All Purpose Wine Goblet. 8 oz. 5 inches tall. **References:** 1979, page 5 [2-5]

Aristocrat. Cordial. 1-1/4 oz. 3-7/8 inches tall. **References:** 1979, page 5 [2-6]

Aristocrat. Goblet. 12 oz. 7 inches tall. **References:** 1979, page 5 [2-1]

Aristocrat. Ice Tea. 14 oz. 6-1/4 inches tall. **References:** 1979, page 5 [2-7]

Aristocrat. Sherbet. 7-1/2 oz. 5-1/8 inches tall. **References:** 1979, page 5 [2-2]

Aristocrat. Tulip Champagne. 8 oz. 8-1/2 inches tall. **References:** 1979, page 5 [2-4]

Aristocrat. Wine. 7-1/2 oz. 6 inches tall. **References:** 1979, page 5 [2-3]

Aristocrat. Line: 1966. Cut: 43. 1305 Dessert-Finger Bowl. 4-1/2 inches diam. **References:** 1972, page 19 [2-8]; 1973, page 24 [2-8]; 1967, page 5 [2-14]; 1968, page 8 [3-14]; 1969, page 9 [2-8]; 1970, page 9 [2-8]; 1971, page 9 [2-8]; 1975, page 24 [2-8]; 1977, page 35 [2-8]

Aristocrat. Line: 1966. Cut: 43. All Purpose Wine Goblet. 8 oz. 5 inches tall. **References:** 1969, page 9 [2-5]; 1970, page 9 [2-5]; 1971, page 9 [2-5]; 1972, page 19 [2-5]; 1973, page 24 [2-5]; 1975, page 24 [2-5]; 1977, page 35 [2-5]

Aristocrat. Line: 1966. Cut: 43. Cordial. 1-1/4 oz. / 3-7/8" hi. **References:** 1967, page 5 [2-12]; 1968, page 8 [3-12]; 1969, page 9 [2-6]; 1970, page 9 [2-6]; 1971, page 9 [2-6]; 1972, page 19 [2-6]; 1973, page 24 [2-6]; 1975, page 24 [2-6]; 1977, page 35 [2-6]

Aristocrat. Line: 1966. Cut: 43. Goblet. 12 oz. / 7" hi. **References:** 1967, page 5 [2-9]; 1968, page 8 [3-9]; 1969, page 9 [2-1]; 1970, page 9 [2-1]; 1971, page 9 [2-1]; 1972, page 19 [2-1]; 1973, page 24 [2-1]; 1975, page 24 [2-1]; 1977, page 35 [2-1]

Aristocrat. Line: 1966. Cut: 43. Ice Tea. 14 oz. / 6-1/4" hi. **References:** 1967, page 5 [2-13]; 1968, page 8 [3-13]; 1969, page 9 [2-7]; 1970, page 9 [2-7]; 1971, page 9 [2-7]; 1972, page 19 [2-7]; 1973, page 24 [2-7]; 1975, page 24 [2-7]; 1977, page 35 [2-7]

Aristocrat. Line: 1966. Cut: 43. Plate. 7" / Actually 7-7/8" Dia. **References:** 1967, page 5 [2-15]; 1968, page 8 [3-15]; 1969, page 9 [2-9]; 1970, page 9 [2-9]; 1971, page 9 [2-9]; 1972, page 19 [2-9]; 1973, page 24 [2-9]; 1975, page 24 [2-9]; 1977, page 35 [2-9]

Aristocrat. Line: 1966. Cut: 43. Plate. 8" / Actually 8-3/4" Dia. **References:** 1967, page 5 [2-16]; 1968, page 8 [3-16]; 1969, page 9 [2-10]; 1970, page 9 [2-10]; 1971, page 9 [2-10]; 1972, page 19 [2-10]; 1973, page 24 [2-10]; 1975, page 24 [2-10]; 1977, page 35 [2-10]

Aristocrat. Line: 1966. Cut: 43. Sherbet. 7-1/2 oz. / 5-1/8" hi. **References:** 1967, page 5 [2-10]; 1968, page 8 [3-10]; 1969, page 9 [2-2]; 1970, page 9 [2-2]; 1971, page 9 [2-2]; 1972, page 19 [2-2]; 1973, page 24 [2-2]; 1975, page 24 [2-2]; 1977, page 35 [2-2]

Aristocrat. Line: 1966. Cut: 43. Tulip Champagne. 8 oz. 8-1/2 inches tall. **References:** 1969, page 9 [2-4]; 1970, page 9 [2-4]; 1971, page 9 [2-4]; 1972, page 19 [2-4]; 1973, page 24 [2-4]; 1975, page 24 [2-4]; 1977, page 35 [2-4]

Aristocrat. Line: 1966. Cut: 43. Wine. 7-1/2 oz. / 6" hi. **References:** 1967, page 5 [2-11]; 1968, page 8 [3-11]; 1969, page 9 [2-3]; 1970, page 9 [2-3]; 1971, page 9 [2-3]; 1972, page 19 [2-3]; 1973, page 24 [2-3]; 1975, page 24 [2-3]; 1977, page 35 [2-3]

Artichoke. Beverage. 18-1/2 oz. 5-1/2 inches tall. Yellow. Colors: Accent Red, Brown, Charm Blue, Crystal, Delphine Blue, Moss Green, Yellow. **References:** 1979, page 8 [1-2]

Artichoke. Goblet. 14-1/2 oz. 6-1/2 inches tall. Delphine Blue. Colors: Accent Red, Brown, Charm Blue, Crystal, Delphine Blue, Moss Green, Yellow. **References:** 1979, page 8 [1-4]

Artichoke. Hi Ball. 13 oz. 4-7/8 inches tall. Crystal. Colors: Accent Red, Brown, Charm Blue, Crystal, Delphine Blue, Moss Green, Yellow. **References:** 1979, page 8 [1-1]

Artichoke. Juice/Wine. 9 oz. 5-5/8 inches tall. Brown. Colors: Accent Red, Brown, Charm Blue, Crystal, Delphine Blue, Moss Green, Yellow. **References:** 1979, page 8 [1-5]

Artichoke. On The Rocks. 14 oz. 3-1/2 inches tall. Moss Green. Colors: Accent Red, Brown, Charm Blue, Crystal, Delphine Blue, Moss Green, Yellow. **References:** 1979, page 8 [1-3]

Artichoke. Line: 1985. Beverage. Mouth blown, hand made and hand finished. Colors: Brown, Crystal, Crystal w/Black Foot, Delphine Blue, Moss Green, Yellow. **References:** 1978, page 3 [1-3]

Artichoke. Line: 1985. Goblet. 6-3/8 inches tall. Mouth blown, hand made and hand finished. Colors: Brown, Crystal, Crystal w/Black Foot, Delphine Blue, Moss Green, Yellow. **References:** 1978, page 3 [1-1]

Artichoke. Line: 1985. Hi Ball. Mouth blown, hand made and hand finished. Colors: Brown, Crystal, Crystal w/Black Foot, Delphine Blue, Moss Green, Yellow. **References:** 1978, page 3 [1-4]

Artichoke. Line: 1985. Juice/Wine. Mouth blown, hand made and hand finished. Colors: Brown, Crystal, Crystal w/Black Foot, Delphine Blue, Moss Green, Yellow. **References:** 1978, page 3 [1-2]

Artichoke. Line: 1985. On The Rocks. Mouth blown, hand made and hand finished. Colors: Brown, Crystal, Crystal w/Black Foot, Delphine Blue, Moss Green, Yellow. **References:** 1978, page 3 [1-5]

Artichoke. Line: 1985. Plate. Mouth blown, hand made and hand finished. Colors: Brown, Crystal, Crystal w/Black Foot, Delphine Blue, Moss Green, Yellow. **References:** 1978, page 3 [1-6]

Artistry. Line: 1973. Cut: 1443. 1305 Dessert-Finger Bowl. 4-1/2 inches diam. Crystal. **References:** 1972, page 20 [2-14]; 1973, page 27 [2-14]

Artistry. Line: 1973. Cut: 1443. Cordial. 1-1/2 oz. 4 inches tall. Crystal. **References:** 1972, page 20 [2-12]; 1973, page 27 [2-12]

Artistry. Line: 1973. Cut: 1443. Goblet. 13 oz. 7 inches tall. Crystal. **References:** 1972, page 20 [2-9]; 1973, page 27 [2-9]

Artistry. Line: 1973. Cut: 1443. Ice Tea. 17-1/2 oz. 7-1/8 inches tall. Crystal. **References:** 1972, page 20 [2-13]; 1973, page 27 [2-13]

Artistry. Line: 1973. Cut: 1443. Plate. 7 inches diam. Crystal, Actually 7-7/8" Dia. **References:** 1972, page 20 [2-15]; 1973, page 27 [2-15]

Artistry. Line: 1973. Cut: 1443. Plate. 8 inches diam. Crystal, Actually 8-3/4" Dia. **References:** 1972, page 20 [2-16]; 1973, page 27 [2-16]

Artistry. Line: 1973. Cut: 1443. Sherbet. 7-1/2 oz. 5-1/8 inches tall. Crystal. **References:** 1972, page 20 [2-10]; 1973, page 27 [2-10]

Artistry. Line: 1973. Cut: 1443. Wine. 8-1/2 oz. 6-3/8 inches tall. Crystal. **References:** 1972, page 20 [2-11]; 1973, page 27 [2-11]

Astrid. Claret. 5-1/4 oz. 5-1/2 inches tall. **References:** 1979, page 4 [2-4]

Astrid. Cordial. 1-1/4 oz. 3-3/4 inches tall. **References:** 1979, page 4 [2-5]; 1981, page 3 [1-12]

Astrid. Goblet. 10 oz. 7 inches tall. **References:** 1979, page 4 [2-1]; 1981, page 3 [1-9]

Astrid. Ice Tea. 11-1/2 oz. 6-1/8 inches tall. **References:** 1979, page 4 [2-6]

Astrid. Saucer Champagne. 7-1/2 oz. 5-1/4 inches tall. **References:** 1979, page 4 [2-2]; 1981, page 3 [1-10]

Astrid. Table Wine Goblet. 7-1/2 oz. 6 inches tall. **References:** 1979, page 4 [2-3]; 1981, page 3 [1-11]

Astrid. Line: 1282. 1305 Dessert-Finger Bowl. 4-1/2" Dia. **References:** 1967, page 9 [2-11]; 1969, page 15 [2-11]; 1970, page 16 [2-11]; 1971, page 16 [2-11]; 1972, page 25 [2-11]; 1973, page 30 [2-11]; 1975, page 28 [2-7]; 1977, page 39 [2-7]

Astrid. Line: 1282. Claret. 5-1/4 oz. / 5-1/2" hi. **References:** 1967, page 9 [2-5]

Astrid. Line: 1282. Claret. 5-1/4 oz. 5-1/2 inches tall. Plain Twisted Stem. **References:** 1969, page 15 [2-5]; 1970, page 16 [2-5]; 1971, page 16 [2-5]; 1972, page 25 [2-5]; 1973, page 30 [2-5]; 1975, page 28 [2-4]; 1977, page 39 [2-4]

Astrid. Line: 1282. Cocktail. 4-1/4 oz. / 4-5/8" hi. **References:** 1967, page 9 [2-6]; 1969, page 15 [2-6]; 1970, page 16 [2-6]

Astrid. Line: 1282. Cocktail. 4-1/4 oz. 4-5/8 inches tall. Plain Twisted Stem. **References:** 1971, page 16 [2-6]; 1972, page 25 [2-6]; 1973, page 30 [2-6]

Astrid. Line: 1282. Cordial. 1-1/4 oz. / 3-3/4" hi. **References:** 1967, page 9 [2-7]; 1969, page 15 [2-7]; 1970, page 16 [2-7]; 1971, page 16 [2-7]; 1972, page 25 [2-7]; 1973, page 30 [2-7]; 1975, page 28 [2-5]; 1977, page 39 [2-5]

Astrid. Line: 1282. Goblet. 10 oz. / 7" hi. Plain Twisted Stem. **References:** 1967, page 9 [2-1]; 1969, page 15 [2-1]; 1970, page 16 [2-1]; 1971, page 16 [2-1]; 1972, page 25 [2-1]; 1973, page 30 [2-1]; 1975, page 28 [2-1]; 1977, page 39 [2-1]

Astrid. Line: 1282. Ice Tea. 11-1/2 oz. / 6-1/8" hi. **References:** 1967, page 9 [2-10]; 1969, page 15 [2-10]; 1970, page 16 [2-10]; 1971, page 16 [2-10]; 1972, page 25 [2-10]; 1973, page 30 [2-10]; 1975, page 28 [2-6]; 1977, page 39 [2-6]

Astrid. Line: 1282. Juice. 5 oz. / 4-1/2" hi. **References:** 1967, page 9 [2-9]

Astrid. Line: 1282. Juice. 5 oz. 4-1/2 inches tall. Plain Twisted Stem. **References:** 1969, page 15 [2-9]; 1970, page 16 [2-9]; 1971, page 16 [2-9]; 1972, page 25 [2-9]; 1973, page 30 [2-9]

Astrid. Line: 1282. Parfait. 6-3/4 oz. / 5-7/8" hi. **References:** 1967, page 9 [2-8]

Astrid. Line: 1282. Parfait. 6-3/4 oz. 5-7/8 inches tall. Plain Twisted Stem. **References:** 1969, page 15 [2-8]; 1970, page 16 [2-8]; 1971, page 16 [2-8]; 1972, page 25 [2-8]; 1973, page 30 [2-8]

Astrid. Line: 1282. Plate. 7" / Actually 7-7/8" Dia. **References:** 1967, page 9 [2-12]; 1969, page 15 [2-12]; 1970, page 16 [2-12]; 1971, page 16 [2-12]; 1972, page 25 [2-12]; 1973, page 30 [2-12]; 1975, page 28 [2-8]; 1977, page 39 [2-8]

Astrid. Line: 1282. Plate. 8" / Actually 8-3/4" Dia. **References:** 1967, page 9 [2-13]; 1969, page 15 [2-13]; 1970, page 16 [2-13]; 1971, page 16 [2-13]; 1972, page 25 [2-13]; 1973, page 30 [2-13]; 1975, page 28 [2-9]; 1977, page 39 [2-9]

Astrid. Line: 1282. Saucer Champagne. 7-1/2 oz. / 5-1/4" hi. **References:** 1967, page 9 [2-2]; 1969, page 15 [2-2]; 1970, page 16 [2-2]; 1971, page 16 [2-2]; 1972, page 25 [2-2]; 1973, page 30 [2-2]; 1975, page 28 [2-2]; 1977, page 39 [2-2]

Astrid. Line: 1282. Sherbet. 7-1/2 oz. / 3-5/8" hi. **References:** 1967, page 9 [2-3]

Astrid. Line: 1282. Sherbet. 7-1/2 oz. 3-5/8 inches tall. Plain Twisted Stem. **References:** 1969, page 15 [2-3]; 1970, page 16 [2-3]; 1971, page 16 [2-3]; 1972, page 25 [2-3]; 1973, page 30 [2-3]

Astrid. Line: 1282. Table Wine Goblet. 7-1/2 oz. / 6" hi. **References:** 1967, page 9 [2-4]

Astrid. Line: 1282. Table Wine Goblet. 7-1/2 oz. 6 inches tall. Plain Twisted Stem. **References:** 1969, page 15 [2-4]; 1970, page 16 [2-4]; 1971, page 16 [2-4]; 1972, page 25 [2-4]; 1973, page 30 [2-4]; 1975, page 28 [2-3]; 1977, page 39 [2-3]

Baroque. Cordial. 2 oz. 4-3/4 inches tall. **References:** 1979, page 2 [1-4]

Baroque. Goblet. 13-1/2 oz. 7-1/2 inches tall. **References:** 1979, page 2 [1-1]

Baroque. Sherbet. 8 oz. 5-3/8 inches tall. **References:** 1979, page 2 [1-2]

Baroque. Sherbet. 7-1/2 oz. 6-1/2 inches tall. **References:** 1979, page 2 [1-6]

Baroque. Wine. 7 oz. 6-3/8 inches tall. **References:** 1979, page 2 [1-3]

Beer Series. Line: 26. Beer Goblet. 14 oz. 7-1/2 inches tall. Plain Crystal. **References:** 1978, page 9 [1-1]

Beer Series. Line: 26. Beer Tumbler. 14 oz. 7-1/2 inches tall. **References:** 1979, page 11 [2-1]

Beer Series. Line: 1208. Beer Goblet. 17-1/2 oz. 5-3/4 inches tall. Plain Crystal. **References:** 1978, page 9 [2-2]; 1979, page 11 [2-3]

Beer Series. Line: 1974. Large Handled Mug. 13 oz. 5 inches tall. Plain Crystal. **References:** 1978, page 9 [2-4]; 1979, page 11 [2-5]

Beer Series. Line: 1974. Small Handled Mug. 11-1/2 oz. 4 inches tall. Plain Crystal. **References:** 1978, page 9 [2-3]; 1979, page 11 [2-4]

Beer Series. Line: 1978. Cut: 43. Beer Goblet. 14 oz. 8-3/4 inches tall. Plain. **References:** 1978, page 9 [1-3]

Beer Series. Line: 1978. Cut: 43. Pony Goblet. 7 oz. 8-1/4 inches tall. Plain. **References:** 1978, page 9 [1-2]

Beer Series. Line: 7856. Pilsner. 14-1/2 oz. 9 inches tall. Straight Optic. **References:** 1978, page 9 [2-1]; 1979, page 11 [2-2]

Bellaire. Line: 1974. Beverage. 12-1/2 oz. 5 inches tall. Crystal Full Sham. **References:** 1978, page 7 [2-4]; 1979, page 16 [2-4]

Bellaire. Line: 1974. Old Fashion. 10 oz. 4 inches tall. Crystal Full Sham. **References:** 1978, page 7 [2-5]; 1979, page 16 [2-5]

Berkshire. Cordial. 1-1/4 oz. 3-3/4 inches tall. **References:** 1979, page 3 [2-9]

Berkshire. Goblet. 12 oz. 6-3/4 inches tall. **References:** 1979, page 3 [2-6]

Berkshire. Ice Tea. 14 oz. 6-3/8 inches tall. **References:** 1979, page 3 [2-10]

Berkshire. Sherbet. 7-1/2 oz. 5 inches tall. **References:** 1979, page 3 [2-7]

Berkshire. Wine. 7-1/2 oz. 6 inches tall. **References:** 1979, page 3 [2-8]

Berkshire. Line: 1967. Cut: 1427. 1305 Dessert-Finger Bowl. 4-1/2" Dia. **References:** 1967, page 6 [1-6]; 1968, page 9 [1-6]; 1969, page 10 [2-6]; 1970, page 10 [2-6]; 1971, page 10 [2-6]; 1972, page 17 [2-6]; 1973, page 22 [2-6]; 1975, page 22 [2-6]; 1977, page 33 [2-6]

Berkshire. Line: 1967. Cut: 1427. Cordial. 1-1/4 oz. / 3-3/4" hi. **References:** 1967, page 6 [1-4]; 1968, page 9 [1-4]; 1969, page 10 [2-4]; 1970,

page 10 [2-4]; 1971, page 10 [2-4]; 1972, page 17 [2-4]; 1973, page 22 [2-4]; 1975, page 22 [2-4]; 1977, page 33 [2-4]

Berkshire. Line: 1967. Cut: 1427. Goblet. 12 oz. / 6-3/4" hi. **References:** 1967, page 6 [1-1]; 1968, page 9 [1-1]; 1969, page 10 [2-1]; 1970, page 10 [2-1]; 1971, page 10 [2-1]; 1972, page 17 [2-1]; 1973, page 22 [2-1]; 1975, page 22 [2-1]; 1977, page 33 [2-1]

Berkshire. Line: 1967. Cut: 1427. Ice Tea. 14 oz. / 6-3/8" hi. **References:** 1967, page 6 [1-5]; 1968, page 9 [1-5]; 1969, page 10 [2-5]; 1970, page 10 [2-5]; 1971, page 10 [2-5]; 1972, page 17 [2-5]; 1973, page 22 [2-5]; 1975, page 22 [2-5]; 1977, page 33 [2-5]

Berkshire. Line: 1967. Cut: 1427. Plate. 7" / Actually 7-7/8" Dia. **References:** 1967, page 6 [1-7]; 1968, page 9 [1-7]; 1969, page 10 [2-7]; 1970, page 10 [2-7]; 1971, page 10 [2-7]; 1972, page 17 [2-7]; 1973, page 22 [2-7]; 1975, page 22 [2-7]; 1977, page 33 [2-7]

Berkshire. Line: 1967. Cut: 1427. Plate. 8" / Actually 8-3/4" Dia. **References:** 1967, page 6 [1-8]; 1968, page 9 [1-8]; 1969, page 10 [2-8]; 1970, page 10 [2-8]; 1971, page 10 [2-8]; 1972, page 17 [2-8]; 1973, page 22 [2-8]; 1975, page 22 [2-8]; 1977, page 33 [2-8]

Berkshire. Line: 1967. Cut: 1427. Sherbet. 7-1/2 oz. / 5" hi. **References:** 1967, page 6 [1-2]; 1968, page 9 [1-2]; 1969, page 10 [2-2]; 1970, page 10 [2-2]; 1971, page 10 [2-2]; 1972, page 17 [2-2]; 1973, page 22 [2-2]; 1975, page 22 [2-2]; 1977, page 33 [2-2]

Berkshire. Line: 1967. Cut: 1427. Wine. 7-1/2 oz. / 6" hi. **References:** 1967, page 6 [1-3]; 1968, page 9 [1-3]; 1969, page 10 [2-3]; 1970, page 10 [2-3]; 1971, page 10 [2-3]; 1972, page 17 [2-3]; 1973, page 22 [2-3]; 1975, page 22 [2-3]; 1977, page 33 [2-3]

Bouquet. Champagne Flute. 6 oz. 9-1/4 inches tall. **References:** 1983, page 3 [2-4]

Bouquet. Cordial. 1-1/2 oz. 4 inches tall. **References:** 1983, page 3 [2-5]

Bouquet. Goblet. 13-1/2 oz. 6-3/4 inches tall. **References:** 1983, page 3 [2-1]

Bouquet. Ice Tea. 14 oz. 6-1/4 inches tall. **References:** 1983, page 3 [2-6]

Bouquet. Sherbet. 7-1/2 oz. 5-1/4 inches tall. **References:** 1983, page 3 [2-2]

Bouquet. Wine. 7-3/4 oz. 5-7/8 inches tall. **References:** 1983, page 3 [2-3]

Bouquet. Line: 1963. Cut: 1458. Cordial. 1-1/2 oz. 4 inches tall. **References:** 1982, page 1 [2-4]

Bouquet. Line: 1963. Cut: 1458. Goblet. 13-1/2 oz. 6-3/4 inches tall. **References:** 1982, page 1 [2-1]

Bouquet. Line: 1963. Cut: 1458. Ice Tea. 14 oz. 6-1/4 inches tall. **References:** 1982, page 1 [2-5]

Bouquet. Line: 1963. Cut: 1458. Sherbet. 7-1/2 oz. 5-1/8 inches tall. **References:** 1982, page 1 [2-2]

Bouquet. Line: 1963. Cut: 1458. Wine. 7-3/4 oz. 5-3/4 inches tall. **References:** 1982, page 1 [2-3]

Bouquet. Line: 1969. 1305 Dessert-Finger Bowl. 4-1/2 inches diam. Plain Crystal. **References:** 1969, page 18 [2-22]; 1970, page 19 [2-22]

Bouquet. Line: 1969. Cordial. 2 oz. 4-1/2 inches tall. Plain Crystal. **References:** 1969, page 18 [2-20]; 1969, page 28 [1-5]; 1970, page 19 [2-20]; 1971, page 30 [1-5]; 1972, page 14 [1-5]; 1973, page 28 [1-5]

Bouquet. Line: 1969. Cordial. 2 oz. 4-1/2 inches tall. Yellow. **References:** 1970, page 1 [1-4]

Bouquet. Line: 1969. Cordial. 2 oz. 4-1/2 inches tall. Yellow
Colors Available: Brown, Delphine Blue, Green, Grey, Yellow. **References:** 1971, page 43 [2-1]; 1972, page 9 [2-1]

Bouquet. Line: 1969. Goblet. 14 oz. 6-3/4 inches tall. Plain Crystal. **References:** 1969, page 18 [2-17]; 1969, page 28 [1-1]; 1970, page 19 [2-17]; 1971, page 30 [1-1]; 1972, page 14 [1-1]; 1973, page 28 [1-1]

Bouquet. Line: 1969. Goblet. 14 oz. 6-3/4 inches tall. Delphine Blue. **References:** 1970, page 1 [1-1]

Bouquet. Line: 1969. Goblet. 14 oz. 6-3/4 inches tall. Delphine Blue
Colors Available: Brown, Delphine Blue, Green, Grey, Yellow. **References:** 1971, page 43 [2-2]; 1972, page 9 [2-2]

Bouquet. Line: 1969. Ice Tea. 14 oz. 6-3/8 inches tall. Plain Crystal. **References:** 1969, page 18 [2-21]; 1970, page 19 [2-21]

Bouquet. Line: 1969. Ice Tea. 14 oz. 6-3/8 inches tall. Grey. **References:** 1970, page 1 [1-5]

Bouquet. Line: 1969. Ice Tea. 14 oz. 6-/38 inches tall. Grey
Colors Available: Brown, Delphine Blue, Green, Grey, Yellow. **References:** 1971, page 43 [1-2]; 1972, page 9 [1-2]

Bouquet. Line: 1969. Plate. 7 inches diam. Plain Crystal. **References:** 1969, page 18 [2-23]; 1970, page 19 [2-23]

Bouquet. Line: 1969. Plate. 8 inches diam. Plain Crystal. **References:** 1969, page 18 [2-24]; 1970, page 19 [2-24]

Bouquet. Line: 1969. Red Wine Goblet. 9-1/2 oz. 6 inches tall. Plain Crystal. **References:** 1969, page 28 [1-3]; 1971, page 30 [1-3]; 1972, page 14 [1-3]; 1973, page 28 [1-3]

Bouquet. Line: 1969. Sherbet. 7-1/2 oz. 5-3/8 inches tall. Plain Crystal. **References:** 1969, page 18 [2-18]; 1969, page 28 [1-2]; 1970, page 19 [2-18]; 1971, page 30 [1-2]; 1972, page 14 [1-2]; 1973, page 28 [1-2]

Bouquet. Line: 1969. Sherbet. 7-1/2 oz. 5-3/8 inches tall. Green. **References:** 1970, page 1 [1-2]

Bouquet. Line: 1969. Sherbet. 7-1/2 oz. 5-3/8 inches tall. Green
Colors Available: Brown, Delphine Blue, Green, Grey, Yellow. **References:** 1971, page 43 [2-3]; 1972, page 9 [2-3]

Bouquet. Line: 1969. Sherry/Port. 5 oz. 5-1/4 inches tall. Plain Crystal. **References:** 1969, page 28 [1-6]; 1971, page 30 [1-6]; 1972, page 14 [1-6]; 1973, page 28 [1-6]

Bouquet. Line: 1969. Tulip Champagne. 8 oz. 8-1/8 inches tall. Plain Crystal. 1971, page 30 [1-7]; 1972, page 14 [1-7]; 1973, page 28 [1-7]

Bouquet. Line: 1969. White Wine Goblet. 7-1/2 oz. 5-1/2 inches tall. Plain Crystal. **References:** 1969, page 18 [2-19]; 1969, page 28 [1-4]; 1970, page 19 [2-19]; 1971, page 30 [1-4]; 1972, page 14 [1-4]; 1973, page 28 [1-4]

Bouquet. Line: 1969. Wine. 7-1/2 oz. 5-1/2 inches tall. Brown. **References:** 1970, page 1 [1-3]

Bouquet. Line: 1969. Wine. 7-1/2 oz. 5-1/2 inches tall. Brown
Colors Available: Brown, Delphine Blue, Green, Grey, Yellow. **References:** 1971, page 43 [1-1]; 1972, page 9 [1-1]

Bridal Tiara. Champagne Flute. 6 oz. 9-1/4 inches tall. **References:** 1983, page 5 [2-6]

Bridal Tiara. Cordial. 1-1/4 oz. 3-7/8 inches tall. **References:** 1979, page 3 [3-4]; 1983, page 5 [2-4]

Bridal Tiara. Goblet. 12 oz. 7 inches tall. **References:** 1979, page 3 [3-1]; 1983, page 5 [2-1]

Bridal Tiara. Ice Tea. 14 oz. 6-1/4 inches tall. **References:** 1979, page 3 [3-5]; 1983, page 5 [2-5]

Bridal Tiara. Sherbet. 7-1/2 oz. 5-1/8 inches tall. **References:** 1979, page 3 [3-2]; 1983, page 5 [2-2]

Bridal Tiara. Wine. 7-1/2 oz. 6 inches tall. **References:** 1979, page 3 [3-3]; 1983, page 5 [2-3]

Bridal Tiara. Line: 1966. Cut: 1439. 1305 Dessert-Finger Bowl. 4-1/2 inches diam. **References:** 1968, page 8 [2-6]; 1969, page 8 [2-6]; 1970, page 8 [2-6]; 1971, page 8 [2-6]; 1972, page 18 [2-6]; 1973, page 23 [2-6]; 1975, page 23 [2-6]; 1977, page 34 [2-6]

Bridal Tiara. Line: 1966. Cut: 1439. Cordial. 1-1/4 oz. 3-7/8 inches tall. **References:** 1968, page 8 [2-4]; 1969, page 8 [2-4]; 1970, page 8 [2-4]; 1971, page 8 [2-4]; 1972, page 18 [2-4]; 1973, page 23 [2-4]; 1975, page 23 [2-4]; 1977, page 34 [2-4]; 1981, page 2 [3-4]

Bridal Tiara. Line: 1966. Cut: 1439. Goblet. 12 oz. 7 inches tall. **References:** 1968, page 8 [2-1]; 1969, page 8 [2-1]; 1970, page 8 [2-1]; 1971, page 8 [2-1]; 1972, page 18 [2-1]; 1973, page 23 [2-1]; 1975, page 23 [2-1]; 1977, page 34 [2-1]; 1981, page 2 [3-1]

Bridal Tiara. Line: 1966. Cut: 1439. Ice Tea. 14 oz. 6-/14 inches tall. **References:** 1968, page 8 [2-5]; 1969, page 8 [2-5]; 1970, page 8 [2-5]; 1971, page 8 [2-5]; 1972, page 18 [2-5]; 1973, page 23 [2-5]; 1975, page 23 [2-5]; 1977, page 34 [2-5]

Bridal Tiara. Line: 1966. Cut: 1439. Plate. 7 inches diam. Actually 7-7/8" Dia. **References:** 1968, page 8 [2-7]; 1969, page 8 [2-7]; 1970, page 8 [2-7]; 1971, page 8 [2-7]; 1972, page 18 [2-7]; 1973, page 23 [2-7]; 1975, page 23 [2-7]; 1977, page 34 [2-7]

Bridal Tiara. Line: 1966. Cut: 1439. Plate. 8 inches diam. Actually 8-3/4" Dia. **References:** 1968, page 8 [2-8]; 1969, page 8 [2-8]; 1970, page 8 [2-8]; 1971, page 8 [2-8]; 1972, page 18 [2-8]; 1973, page 23 [2-8]; 1975, page 23 [2-8]; 1977, page 34 [2-8]

Bridal Tiara. Line: 1966. Cut: 1439. Sherbet. 7-1/2 oz. 5-1/8 inches tall. **References:** 1968, page 8 [2-2]; 1969, page 8 [2-2]; x1970, page 8 [2-2]; x1971, page 8 [2-2]; 1972, page 18 [2-2]; 1973, page 23 [2-2]; 1975, page 23 [2-2]; 1977, page 34 [2-2]; 1981, page 2 [3-2]

Bridal Tiara. Line: 1966. Cut: 1439. Wine. 7-1/2 oz. 6 inches tall. **References:** 1968, page 8 [2-3]; 1969, page 8 [2-3]; 1970, page 8 [2-3]; 1971, page 8 [2-3]; 1972, page 18 [2-3]; 1973, page 23 [2-3]; 1975, page 23 [2-3]; 1977, page 34 [2-3]; 1981, page 2 [3-3]

Bristol. Line: 1971. Cut: 1441. 1311 Dessert-Finger Bowl. 4-3/4 inches diam. **References:** 1971, page 19 [1-14]

Bristol. Line: 1971. Cut: 1441. Cordial. 1-1/2 oz. 4 inches tall. **References:** 1971, page 19 [1-12]

Bristol. Line: 1971. Cut: 1441. Goblet. 11-1/2 oz. 7 inches tall. **References:** 1971, page 19 [1-9]

Bristol. Line: 1971. Cut: 1441. Ice Tea. 14-1/2 oz. 7-1/8 inches tall. **References:** 1971, page 19 [1-13]

Bristol. Line: 1971. Cut: 1441. Plate. 7 inches diam. Actually 7-7/8" Dia. **References:** 1971, page 19 [1-15]

Bristol. Line: 1971. Cut: 1441. Plate. 8 inches diam. Actually 8-3/4" Dia. **References:** 1971, page 19 [1-16]

Bristol. Line: 1971. Cut: 1441. Sherbet. 7-1/2 oz. 5 inches tall. **References:** 1971, page 19 [1-10]

Bristol. Line: 1971. Cut: 1441. Wine. 7 oz. 5-7/8 inches tall. **References:** 1971, page 19 [1-11]

Brittany. Bell. **References:** 1981, page 11 [3-4]; 1983, page 7 [1-4L]

Brittany. Beverage. 16 oz. 6 inches tall. Hand Made....Hand Cut. **References:** 1979, page 15 [1-8]; 1981, page 4 [3-5]

Brittany. Beverage. 16 oz. 5-3/4 inches tall. **References:** 1983, page 11 [M-1L]

Brittany. Cooler. 16 oz. 7-3/8 inches tall. Hand Made....Hand Cut. **References:** 1979, page 15 [1-7]

Brittany. Cordial. 2-1/4 oz. 5-1/4 inches tall. **References:** 1979, page 1 [2-12]

Brittany. Goblet. 10 oz. 7-1/2 inches tall. **References:** 1979, page 1 [2-9]

Brittany. Hi Ball. 11 oz. 5 inches tall. Hand Made....Hand Cut. **References:** 1979, page 15 [1-9]; 1981, page 4 [3-6]

Brittany. Hi Ball. 11 oz. 4-7/8 inches tall. **References:** 1983, page 11 [M-2L]

Brittany. Old Fashion. 9-1/2 oz. 3-1/2 inches tall. Hand Made....Hand Cut. **References:** 1979, page 15 [1-11]; 1981, page 4 [3-8]

Brittany. Old Fashion. 9-1/2 oz. 3-5/8 inches tall. **References:** 1983, page 11 [M-4L]

Brittany. On The Rocks. 14 oz. 4-1/2 inches tall. Hand Made, Hand Cut. **References:** 1979, page 15 [1-10]; 1981, page 4 [3-7]

Brittany. On The Rocks. 14 oz. 4-3/8 inches tall. **References:** 1983, page 11 [M-3L]

Brittany. Pony. 3 oz. 3 inches tall. Hand Made....Hand Cut. **References:** 1979, page 15 [1-12]

Brittany. Sherbet. 6-1/2 oz. 5-1/2 inches tall. **References:** 1979, page 1 [2-10]

Brittany. Wine. 6 oz. 6-5/8 inches tall. **References:** 1979, page 1 [2-11]

Brittany. Cut: 1451. Ice Server. 7-3/4 inches tall. **References:** 1978, page 6 [1-2]

Brittany. Line: 4. Bell. 5-1/2 inches tall. All Bells Individually Gift Boxed. **References:** 1979, page 13 [4-2]

Brittany. Line: 4. Cut: 1451. Bell. 5-1/2 inches tall. **References:** 1977, page 23 [3-2]

Brittany. Line: 974. Cut: 1451. Cordial. 2-1/4 oz. 5-1/4 inches tall. **References:** 1976, page 5 [1-4]; 1977, page 30 [1-4]

Brittany. Line: 974. Cut: 1451. Goblet. 10 oz. 7-1/2 inches tall. **References:** 1976, page 5 [1-1]; 1977, page 30 [1-1]

Brittany. Line: 974. Cut: 1451. Sherbet. 6-1/2 oz. 5-1/2 inches tall. **References:** 1976, page 5 [1-2]; 1977, page 30 [1-2]

Brittany. Line: 974. Cut: 1451. Wine. 6 oz. 6-5/8 inches tall. **References:** 1976, page 5 [1-3]; 1977, page 30 [1-3]

Brittany. Line: 1978. Cut: 1451. Beverage. 16-1/2 oz. 5-7/8 inches tall. **References:** 1977, page 25 [1-1]

Brittany. Line: 1978. Cut: 1451. Old Fashion. 9-1/2 oz. 3-1/2 inches tall. **References:** 1977, page 25 [1-3]

Brittany. Line: 1978. Cut: 1451. On the Rocks. 15-1/2 oz. 4-1/2 inches tall. **References:** 1976, page 11 [1-1]; 1977, page 25 [1-2]

Brocado. Line: 1970 Footed. Beverage. 16 oz. 5-7/8 inches tall. Color: Cristalino (Crystal). **References:** 1969, page 29 [2-1]

Brocado. Line: 1970. Beverage. 16 oz. 5-7/8 inches tall. Toledo. **References:** 1970, page 6 [1-5]

Brocado. Line: 1970 Footed. Goblet. 14 oz. 5-1/2 inches tall. Color: Sahara (Yellow). **References:** 1969, page 29 [1-2]

Brocado. Line: 1970. Goblet. 14 oz. 5-1/2 inches tall. Cristalino. **References:** 1970, page 6 [1-1]

Brocado. Line: 1970 Footed. Juice or Wine Goblet. 7-1/2 oz. 4-3/8 inches tall. Color: Morocco (Brown). **References:** 1969, page 29 [1-3]

Brocado. Line: 1970. Old Fashion. 14 oz. 4 inches tall. Avocado. **References:** 1970, page 6 [1-4]

Brocado. Line: 1970. On The Rocks. 10-1/2 oz. 3-5/8 inches tall. Footed. Colors: Toledo (Grey). **References:** 1969, page 29 [2-2]

Brocado. Line: 1970. Roly Poly. 13 oz. 3-1/4 inches tall. Sahara. **References:** 1970, page 6 [1-3]

Brocado. Line: 1970 Footed. Sherbet. 7-1/2 oz. 3-1/2 inches tall. Color: Avocado (Green). **References:** 1969, page 29 [1-1]

Brocado. Line: 1970. Sherbet. 7-1/2 oz. 3-1/2 inches tall. Morocco. **References:** 1970, page 6 [1-2]

Buckingham. Cordial. 1-1/4 oz. 3-3/4 inches tall. **References:** 1979, page 4 [1-9]

Buckingham. Goblet. 10 oz. 7 inches tall. **References:** 1979, page 4 [1-6]

Buckingham. Ice Tea. 11-1/2 oz. 6-1/8 inches tall. **References:** 1979, page 4 [1-10]

Buckingham. Saucer Champagne. 7-1/2 oz. 5-1/4 inches tall. **References:** 1979, page 4 [1-7]

Buckingham. Table Wine Goblet. 7-1/2 oz. 6 inches tall. **References:** 1979, page 4 [1-8]

Buckingham. Line: 1282. Cut: 1426. 1305 Dessert-Finger Bowl. 4-1/2" Dia. **References:** 1967, page 9 [1-7]; 1969, page 15 [1-7]; 1970, page 16 [1-7]; 1971, page 16 [1-7]; 1972, page 25 [1-7]; 1973, page 30 [1-7]; 1975, page 28 [1-6]; 1977, page 39 [1-6]

Buckingham. Line: 1282. Cut: 1426. Cordial. 1-1/4 oz. / 3-3/4" hi. **References:** 1967, page 9 [1-4]; 1969, page 15 [1-4]; 1970, page 16 [1-4]; 1971, page 16 [1-4]; 1972, page 25 [1-4]; 1973, page 30 [1-4]; 1975, page 28 [1-4]; 1977, page 39 [1-4]

Buckingham. Line: 1282. Cut: 1426. Goblet. 10 oz. / 7" hi. **References:** 1967, page 9 [1-1]; 1969, page 15 [1-1]; 1970, page 16 [1-1]; 1971, page 16 [1-1]; 1972, page 25 [1-1]; 1973, page 30 [1-1]; 1975, page 28 [1-1]; 1977, page 39 [1-1]

Buckingham. Line: 1282. Cut: 1426. Ice Tea. 11-1/2 oz. / 6-1/8" hi. **References:** 1967, page 9 [1-6]; 1969, page 15 [1-6]; 1970, page 16 [1-6]; 1971, page 16 [1-6]; 1972, page 25 [1-6]; 1973, page 30 [1-6]; 1975, page 28 [1-5]; 1977, page 39 [1-5]

Buckingham. Line: 1282. Cut: 1426. Juice. 5 oz. / 4-1/2" hi. **References:** 1967, page 9 [1-5]; 1969, page 15 [1-5]; 1970, page 16 [1-5]; 1971, page 16 [1-5]; 1972, page 25 [1-5]; 1973, page 30 [1-5]

Buckingham. Line: 1282. Cut: 1426. Plate. 7" / Actually 7-7/8" Dia. **References:** 1967, page 9 [1-8]; 1969, page 15 [1-8]; 1970, page 16 [1-8]; 1971, page 16 [1-8]; 1972, page 25 [1-8]; 1973, page 30 [1-8]; 1975, page 28 [1-7]; 1977, page 39 [1-7]

Buckingham. Line: 1282. Cut: 1426. Plate. 8" / Actually 8-3/4" Dia. **References:** 1967, page 9 [1-9]; 1969, page 15 [1-9]; 1970, page 16 [1-9]; 1971, page 16 [1-9]; 1972, page 25 [1-9]; 1973, page 30 [1-9]; 1975, page 28 [1-8]; 1977, page 39 [1-8]

Buckingham. Line: 1282. Cut: 1426. Saucer Champagne. 7-1/2 oz. / 5-1/4" hi. **References:** 1967, page 9 [1-2]; 1969, page 15 [1-2]; 1970, page 16 [1-2]; 1971, page 16 [1-2]; 1972, page 25 [1-2]; 1973, page 30 [1-2]; 1975, page 28 [1-2]; 1977, page 39 [1-2]

Buckingham. Line: 1282. Cut: 1426. Table Wine Goblet. 7-1/2 oz. / 6" hi. **References:** 1967, page 9 [1-3]; 1969, page 15 [1-3]; 1970, page 16 [1-3]; 1971, page 16 [1-3]; 1972, page 25 [1-3];

1973, page 30 [1-3]; 1975, page 28 [1-3]; 1977, page 39 [1-3]

Butterfly. Line: 80. Ginger Jar. 6-1/4 inches tall. All Items Gift Boxed. **References:** 1983, page 6 [1-3L]

Butterfly. Line: 80. Cut: 960. Ginger Jar. 6-1/4 inches tall. **References:** 1981, page 10 [2-3]

Butterfly. Line: 90. Ginger Jar. 8-1/2 inches tall. **References:** 1983, page 6 [2-3L]

Butterfly. Line: 90. Cut: 960. Ginger Jar. 8-1/2 inches tall. **References:** 1980, page 3 [2-1]; 1981, page 10 [1-3]

Cabaret. Cordial. 1-1/2 oz. 3-3/4 inches tall. **References:** 1979, page 6 [3-10]

Cabaret. Goblet. 13-3/4 oz. 6-1/2 inches tall. **References:** 1979, page 6 [3-7]

Cabaret. Ice Tea. 14-1/4 oz. 6-3/8 inches tall. **References:** 1979, page 6 [3-11]

Cabaret. Sherbet. 7-1/2 oz. 4-3/8 inches tall. **References:** 1979, page 6 [3-8]

Cabaret. Wine. 9 oz. 5-5/8 inches tall. **References:** 1979, page 6 [3-9]

Cabaret. Line: 1964. Cordial. 1-1/2 oz. 3-3/4 inches tall. Yellow, Crystal Foot. **References:** 1970, page 3 [1-4]

Cabaret. Line: 1964. Cordial. 1-1/2 oz. 3-3/4 inches tall. Greenbrier, Platinum Band, Crystal Foot. **References:** 1970, page 4 [1-4]

Cabaret. Line: 1964. Cordial. 1-1/2 oz. 3-3/4 inches tall. Plain Crystal. **References:** 1970, page 21 [1-20]; 1971, page 21 [1-20]; 1972, page 29 [1-20]; 1973, page 34 [1-20]; 1975, page 30 [1-18]; 1977, page 41 [1-18]

Cabaret. Line: 1964. Cordial. 1-1/2 oz. 3-3/4 inches tall. Yellow/Crystal Foot. Colors Available: Brown/Crystal Foot, Delphine Blue/Crystal Foot, Green/Crystal Foot, Grey/Crystal Foot, Yellow/Crystal Foot. **References:** 1971, page 44 [2-3]

Cabaret. Line: 1964. Goblet. 13-3/4 oz. 6-1/2 inches tall. Delphine Blue, Crystal Foot. **References:** 1970, page 3 [1-1]

Cabaret. Line: 1964. Goblet. 13-3/4 oz. 6-1/2 inches tall. Silver Dawn, Platinum Band, Crystal Foot. **References:** 1970, page 4 [1-1]

Cabaret. Line: 1964. Goblet. 13-3/4 oz. 6-1/2 inches tall. Plain Crystal. **References:** 1970, page 21 [1-17]; 1971, page 21 [1-17]; 1972, page 29 [1-17]; 1973, page 34 [1-17]; 1975, page 30 [1-15]; 1977, page 41 [1-15]

Cabaret. Line: 1964. Goblet. 13-3/4 oz. 6-1/2 inches tall. Delphine Blue/Crystal Foot. Colors Available: Brown/Crystal Foot, Delphine Blue/Crystal Foot, Green/Crystal Foot, Grey/Crystal Foot, Yellow/Crystal Foot. **References:** 1971, page 44 [2-2]

Cabaret. Line: 1964. Ice Tea. 14-1/4 oz. 6-3/8 inches tall. Brown, Crystal Foot. **References:** 1970, page 3 [1-5]

Cabaret. Line: 1964. Ice Tea. 14-1/4 oz. 6-3/8 inches tall. Sunset Gold, Gold Band, Crystal Foot. **References:** 1970, page 4 [1-5]

Cabaret. Line: 1964. Ice Tea. 14-1/4 oz. 6-3/8 inches tall. Plain Crystal. **References:** 1970, page 21 [1-22]; 1971, page 21 [1-22]; 1972, page 29 [1-22]; 1973, page 34 [1-22]; 1975, page 30 [1-19]; 1977, page 41 [1-19]

Cabaret. Line: 1964. Ice Tea. 14-1/4 oz. 6-3/8 inches tall. Brown/Crystal Foot. Colors Available: Brown/Crystal Foot, Delphine Blue/Crystal Foot, Green/Crystal Foot, Grey/Crystal Foot, Yellow/Crystal Foot. **References:** 1971, page 44 [1-1]

Cabaret. Line: 1964. Juice. 6-3/4 oz. 4-3/4 inches tall. Plain Crystal. **References:** 1970, page 21 [1-21]; 1971, page 21 [1-21]; 1972, page 29 [1-21]; 1973, page 34 [1-21]

Cabaret. Line: 1964. Plate. 7 inches diam. Plain Crystal, Actually 7-7/8" Dia. **References:** 1970, page 21 [1-23]; 1971, page 21 [1-23]; 1972, page 29 [1-23]; 1973, page 34 [1-23]; 1975, page 30 [1-20]; 1977, page 41 [1-20]

Cabaret. Line: 1964. Plate. 8 inches diam. Plain Crystal, Actually 8-3/4" Dia. **References:** 1970, page 21 [1-24]; 1971, page 21 [1-24]; 1972, page 29 [1-24]; 1973, page 34 [1-24]; 1975, page 30 [1-21]; 1977, page 41 [1-21]

Cabaret. Line: 1964. Sherbet. 7-1/2 oz. 4-3/8 inches tall. Grey, Crystal Foot. **References:** 1970, page 3 [1-2]

Cabaret. Line: 1964. Sherbet. 7-1/2 oz. 4-3/8 inches tall. Blue Mist, Delphine Blue, Platinum Band, Crystal Foot. **References:** 1970, page 4 [1-2]

Cabaret. Line: 1964. Sherbet. 7-1/2 oz. 4-3/8 inches tall. Plain Crystal. **References:** 1970, page 21 [1-18]; 1971, page 21 [1-18]; 1972, page 29 [1-18]; 1973, page 34 [1-18]; 1975, page 30 [1-16]; 1977, page 41 [1-16]

Cabaret. Line: 1964. Sherbet. 7-1/2 oz. 4-3/8 inches tall. Grey/Crystal Foot. Colors Available: Brown/Crystal Foot, Delphine Blue/Crystal Foot, Green/Crystal Foot, Grey/Crystal Foot, Yellow/Crystal Foot. **References:** 1971, page 44 [2-1]

Cabaret. Line: 1964. Wine. 9 oz. 5-5/8 inches tall. Green, Crystal Foot. **References:** 1970, page 3 [1-3]

Cabaret. Line: 1964. Wine. 9 oz. 5-5/8 inches tall. Desert Gold, Gold Band, Crystal Foot. **References:** 1970, page 4 [1-3]

Cabaret. Line: 1964. Wine. 9 oz. 5-5/8 inches tall. Plain Crystal. **References:** 1970, page 21 [1-19]; 1971, page 21 [1-19]; 1972, page 29 [1-19]; 1973, page 34 [1-19]; 1975, page 30 [1-17]; 1977, page 41 [1-17]

Cabaret. Line: 1964. Wine. 9 oz. 5-5/8 inches tall. Green/Crystal Foot. Colors Available: Brown/Crystal Foot, Delphine Blue/Crystal Foot, Green/Crystal Foot, Grey/Crystal Foot, Yellow/Crystal Foot. **References:** 1971, page 44 [1-2]

Cambridge. Cordial. 1-1/2 oz. 4 inches tall. **References:** 1979, page 2 [2-9]

Cambridge. Goblet. 11-1/2 oz. 7 inches tall. **References:** 1979, page 2 [2-6]

Cambridge. Ice Tea. 14 oz. 6-1/4 inches tall. **References:** 1979, page 2 [2-10]

Cambridge. Sherbet. 7 oz. 5-1/4 inches tall. **References:** 1979, page 2 [2-7]

Cambridge. Wine. 7 oz. 6 inches tall. **References:** 1979, page 2 [2-8]

Cambridge. Line: 960. Cut: 1433. 1311 Dessert-Finger Bowl. 4-3/4" Dia. **References:** 1967, page 4 [1-6]; 1968, page 4 [1-6]; 1969, page 6 [1-6]; 1970, page 6 [1-6]; 1971, page 6 [1-6]; 1972, page 16 [1-6]; 1973, page 21 [1-6]; 1975, page 21 [1-6]; 1977, page 32 [1-6]

Cambridge. Line: 960. Cut: 1433. Cordial. 1-1/4 oz. / 3-7/8" hi. **References:** 1967, page 4 [1-4]; 1968, page 6 [1-4]; 1969, page 6 [1-4]; 1970, page 6 [1-4]; 1971, page 6 [1-4]; 1972, page 16 [1-4]; 1973, page 21 [1-4]; 1975, page 21 [1-4]; 1977, page 32 [1-4]

Cambridge. Line: 960. Cut: 1433. Goblet. 11-1/2 oz. / 7" hi. **References:** 1967, page 4 [1-1]; 1968, page 6 [1-1]; 1969, page 6 [1-1]; 1970, page 6 [1-1]; 1971, page 6 [1-1]; 1972, page 16 [1-1]; 1973, page 21 [1-1]; 1975, page 21 [1-1]; 1977, page 32 [1-1]

Cambridge. Line: 960. Cut: 1433. Ice Tea. 14 oz. / 6-1/4" hi. **References:** 1967, page 4 [1-5]; 1968, page 6 [1-5]; 1969, page 6 [1-5]; 1970, page 6 [1-5]; 1971, page 6 [1-5]; 1972, page 16 [1-5]; 1973, page 21 [1-5]; 1975, page 21 [1-5]; 1977, page 32 [1-5]

Cambridge. Line: 960. Cut: 1433. Plate. 7" / Actually 7-7/8 inch. **References:** 1967, page 4 [1-7]; 1968, page 4 [1-7]; 1969, page 6 [1-7]; 1970, page 6 [1-7]; 1971, page 6 [1-7]; 1972, page 16 [1-7]; 1973, page 21 [1-7]; 1975, page 21 [1-7]; 1977, page 32 [1-7]

Cambridge. Line: 960. Cut: 1433. Plate. 8" / Actually 8-3/4 inch. **References:** 1967, page 4 [1-8]; 1968, page 6 [1-8]; 1969, page 6 [1-8]; 1970, page 6 [1-8]; 1971, page 6 [1-8]; 1972, page 16 [1-8]; 1973, page 21 [1-8]; 1975, page 21 [1-8]; 1977, page 32 [1-8]

Cambridge. Line: 960. Cut: 1433. Sherbet. 7 oz. / 5-1/4" hi. **References:** 1967, page 4 [1-2]; 1968, page 46 [1-2]; 1969, page 6 [1-2]; 1970, page 6 [1-2]; 1971, page 6 [1-2]; 1972, page 16 [1-2]; 1973, page 21 [1-2]; 1975, page 21 [1-2]; 1977, page 32 [1-2]

Cambridge. Line: 960. Cut: 1433. Wine. 7 oz. / 6" hi. **References:** 1967, page 4 [1-3]; 1968, page 6 [1-3]; 1969, page 6 [1-3]; 1970, page 6 [1-3]; 1971, page 6 [1-3]; 1972, page 16 [1-3]; 1973, page 21 [1-3]; 1975, page 21 [1-3]; 1977, page 32 [1-3]

Camelot. Cordial. 1-1/4 oz. **References:** 1967, page [Advertisement]

Camelot. Footed Ice Tea. 13-1/2 oz. **References:** 1967, page [Advertisement]

Camelot. Footed Juice. 6 oz. **References:** 1967, page [Advertisement]

Camelot. Goblet. 11-3/4 oz. **References:** 1967, page [Advertisement]

Camelot. Sherbet. 7-1/2 oz. **References:** 1967, page [Advertisement]

Camelot. Wine. 7-1/2 oz. **References:** 1967, page [Advertisement]

Caprice. Line: 352. Cut: 1229. 1311 Dessert-Finger Bowl. 4-3/4 inches diam. **References:** 1967, page 18 [1-8]; 1968, page 22 [1-8]; 1969, page 23 [1-8]; 1970, page 24 [1-8]; 1971, page 24 [1-8]

Caprice. Line: 352. Cut: 1229. Claret. 3-3/4 oz. 5-5/8 inches tall. **References:** 1967, page 18 [1-3]; 1968, page 22 [1-3]; 1969, page 23 [1-3]; 1970, page 24 [1-3]; 1971, page 24 [1-3]

Caprice. Line: 352. Cut: 1229. Cocktail. 3 oz. 4-1/4 inches tall. **References:** 1967, page 18 [1-4]; 1968, page 22 [1-4]; 1969, page 23 [1-4]; 1970, page 24 [1-4]; 1971, page 24 [1-4]

Caprice. Line: 352. Cut: 1229. Cordial. 1 oz. 4 inches tall. **References:** 1967, page 18 [1-5]; 1968, page 22 [1-5]; 1969, page 23 [1-5]; 1970, page 24 [1-5]; 1971, page 24 [1-5]

Caprice. Line: 352. Cut: 1229. Goblet. 9 oz. 7-1/4 inches tall. **References:** 1967, page 18 [1-1]; 1968, page 22 [1-1]; 1969, page 23 [1-1]; 1970, page 24 [1-1]; 1971, page 24 [1-1]

Caprice. Line: 352. Cut: 1229. Ice Tea. 12 oz. 7-1/4 inches tall. **References:** 1967, page 18 [1-7]; 1968, page 22 [1-7]; 1969, page 23 [1-7]; 1970, page 24 [1-7]; 1971, page 24 [1-7]

Caprice. Line: 352. Cut: 1229. Juice. 5-1/2 oz. 5-3/8 inches tall. **References:** 1967, page 18 [1-6]; 1968, page 22 [1-6]; 1969, page 23 [1-6]; 1970, page 24 [1-6]; 1971, page 24 [1-6]

Caprice. Line: 352. Cut: 1229. Plate. 7 inches diam. Actually 7-7/8" Dia. **References:** 1967, page 18 [1-9]; 1968, page 22 [1-9]; 1969, page 23 [1-9]; 1970, page 24 [1-9]; 1971, page 24 [1-9]

Caprice. Line: 352. Cut: 1229. Plate. 8 inches diam. Actually 8-3/4" Dia. **References:** 1967, page 18 [1-10]; 1968, page 22 [1-10]; 1969, page 23 [1-10]; 1970, page 24 [1-10]; 1971, page 24 [1-10]

Caprice. Line: 352. Cut: 1229. Sherbet. 6 oz. 5-3/8 inches tall. **References:** 1967, page 18 [1-2]; 1968, page 22 [1-2]; 1969, page 23 [1-2]; 1970, page 24 [1-2]; 1971, page 24 [1-2]

Capristrano. Line: 1965. Cut: 1423. 1305 Dessert-Finger Bowl. 4-1/2" Dia. **References:** 1967, page 7 [3-7]; 1968, page 10 [2-16]

Capristrano. Line: 1965. Cut: 1423. Cordial. 1-1/4 oz. - 4" hi. **References:** 1967, page 7 [3-4]; 1968, page 10 [2-13]

Capristrano. Line: 1965. Cut: 1423. Goblet. 11-3/4 oz. / 7-1/4" hi. **References:** 1967, page 7 [3-1]; 1968, page 10 [2-10]

Capristrano. Line: 1965. Cut: 1423. Ice Tea. 13-1/2 oz. / 6-3/4" hi. **References:** 1967, page 7 [3-6]; 1968, page 10 [2-15]

Capristrano. Line: 1965. Cut: 1423. Juice. 6 oz. / 5-1/2" hi. **References:** 1967, page 7 [3-5]; 1968, page 10 [2-14]

Capristrano. Line: 1965. Cut: 1423. Plate. 7" / Actually 7-7/8" Dia. **References:** 1967, page 7 [3-8]; 1968, page 10 [2-17]

Capristrano. Line: 1965. Cut: 1423. Plate. 8" / Actually 8-3/4" Dia. **References:** 1967, page 7 [3-9]; 1968, page 10 [2-18]

Capristrano. Line: 1965. Cut: 1423. Sherbet. 7-1/2 oz. / 5-1/4" hi. **References:** 1967, page 7 [3-2]; 1968, page 10 [2-11]

Capristrano. Line: 1965. Cut: 1423. Wine. 1-1/4 oz. / 4" hi. **References:** 1967, page 7 [3-3]; 1968, page 10 [2-12]

Carousel. Line: 1964. Cut: 1412. 1305 Dessert-Finger Bowl. 4-1/2 inches diam. **References:** 1967, page 14 [1-25]; 1968, page 18 [1-25]; 1968, page 18 [1-25]

Carousel. Line: 1964. Cut: 1412. Cordial. 1-1/2 oz. 3-3/4 inches tall. **References:** 1967, page 14 [1-22]; 1968, page 18 [1-22]; 1968, page 18 [1-22]

Carousel. Line: 1964. Cut: 1412. Goblet. 13-3/4 oz. / 6-1/2" hi. **References:** 1967, page 14 [1-19]; 1968, page 18 [1-19]; 1968, page 18 [1-19]

Carousel. Line: 1964. Cut: 1412. Ice Tea. 14-1/4 oz. 6-3/8 inches tall. **References:** 1967, page 14 [1-24]; 1968, page 18 [1-24]; 1968, page 18 [1-24]

Carousel. Line: 1964. Cut: 1412. Juice. 6-3/4 oz. 4-3/4 inches tall. **References:** 1967, page 14 [1-23]; 1968, page 18 [1-23]; 1968, page 18 [1-23]

Carousel. Line: 1964. Cut: 1412. Plate. 7 inches diam. Actually 7-7/8" Dia. **References:** 1967, page 14 [1-26]; 1968, page 18 [1-26]; 1968, page 18 [1-26]

Carousel. Line: 1964. Cut: 1412. Plate. 8 inches diam. Actually 8-3/4" Dia. **References:** 1967, page 14 [1-27]; 1968, page 18 [1-27]; 1968, page 18 [1-27]

Carousel. Line: 1964. Cut: 1412. Sherbet. 7-1/2 oz. / 4-3/8" hi. **References:** 1967, page 14 [1-20]; 1968, page 18 [1-20]; 1968, page 18 [1-20]

Carousel. Line: 1964. Cut: 1412. Wine. 9 oz. / 5-5/8" hi. **References:** 1967, page 14 [1-21]; 1968, page 18 [1-21]; 1968, page 18 [1-21]

Cascade. Bar Pitcher. 40 oz. Crystal. Colors: Accent Red, Brown, Charm Blue, Crystal, Lime Green, Moss Green, Ritz Blue, Yellow. **References:** 1979, page 9 [2-2]

Cascade. Beverage. 15-1/2 oz. 5 inches tall. Lime Green. Colors: Accent Red, Brown, Charm Blue, Crystal, Lime Green, Moss Green, Ritz Blue, Yellow. **References:** 1979, page 9 [2-3]; 1981, page 6 [2-2]

Cascade. Bowl. 4-1/2 inches diam. Ritz Blue. Colors: Accent Red, Brown, Charm Blue, Crystal, Lime Green, Moss Green, Ritz Blue, Yellow. **References:** 1979, page 9 [3-2]

Cascade. Cocktail/Juice. 7-1/2 oz. 3-1/4 inches tall. Brown. Colors: Accent Red, Brown, Charm Blue, Crystal, Lime Green, Moss Green, Ritz Blue, Yellow. **References:** 1979, page 9 [3-1]; 1981, page 6 [2-4]

Cascade. Cooler. 18-1/2 oz. 6-3/4 inches tall. Charm Blue. Colors: Accent Red, Brown, Charm Blue, Crystal, Lime Green, Moss Green, Ritz Blue, Yellow. **References:** 1979, page 9 [1-1]; 1981, page 6 [2-1]

Cascade. Footed Goblet. 15-1/2 oz. 6 inches tall. Moss Green. Colors: Accent Red, Brown, Charm Blue, Crystal, Lime Green, Moss Green, Ritz Blue, Yellow. **References:** 1979, page 9 [1-3]

Cascade. Footed Juice/ Wine Goblet. 9 oz. 4-3/8 inches tall. Accent Red. Colors: Accent Red, Brown, Charm Blue, Crystal, Lime Green, Moss Green, Ritz Blue, Yellow. **References:** 1979, page 9 [2-1]

Cascade. Old Fashion. 11-1/2 oz. 3-3/4 inches tall. Yellow. Colors: Accent Red, Brown, Charm Blue, Crystal, Lime Green, Moss Green, Ritz Blue, Yellow. **References:** 1979, page 9 [1-2]; 1981, page 6 [2-3]

Cascade. Line: 1972. Bar Pitcher w/Stir Rod. 40 oz. Crystal. Colors: Accent Red, Brown, Crystal, Lime Green, Moss Green, Ritz Blue, Yellow. **References:** 1977, page 14-15 [1-6]

Cascade. Line: 1972. Beverage. 15-1/2 oz. 5 inches tall. Yellow, Peacock Blue. Colors Available: Crystal, Green, Grey. **References:** 1971, page 39 [1-1 & 3-1]; 1972, page 5 [2-3, 2-4]; 1973, page 14 [2-3, 2-4]

Cascade. Line: 1972. Beverage. 15-1/2 oz. 5 inches tall. Moss Green. Colors: Accent Red, Brown, Crystal, Lime Green, Moss Green, Ritz Blue, Yellow. **References:** 1977, page 14-15 [1-2]

Cascade. Line: 1972. Bowl. 13 oz. 4-1/2 inches diam. Crystal. Colors: Accent Red, Brown, Crystal, Lime Green, Moss Green, Ritz Blue, Yellow. **References:** 1977, page 14-15 [1-5]

Cascade. Line: 1972. Cocktail/Juice. 7-1/2 oz. 3-1/4 inches tall. Crystal. Colors: Crystal, Green, Grey, Peacock Blue, Yellow. **References:** 1972, page 5 [2-2]; 1973, page 14 [2-2]

Cascade. Line: 1972. Cocktail/Juice. 7-1/2 oz. 3-1/4 inches tall. Brown. Colors: Accent Red, Brown, Crystal, Lime Green, Moss Green, Ritz Blue, Yellow. **References:** 1977, page 14-15 [1-7]

Cascade. Line: 1972. Cocktail/Juice Set. Peacock Blue, Mixer 40oz., Glasses 7-1/2oz. Colors: Crystal, Green, Grey, Peacock Blue, Yellow. **References:** 1972, page 5 [2-3]; 1973, page 14 [2-3]. **References:** 1972, page 5 [1-1]; 1973, page 14 [1-1]

Cascade. Line: 1972. Cooler. 18-1/2 oz. 6-3/4 inches tall. Colors: Crystal. **References:** 1978, page 16 [1-2]

Cascade. Line: 1972. Footed Goblet. 15-1/2 oz. 6 inches tall. Ritz Blue. Colors: Accent Red, Brown, Crystal, Lime Green, Moss Green, Ritz Blue, Yellow. **References:** 1977, page 14-15 [1-1]

Cascade. Line: 1972. Footed Juice/Wine. 9 oz. 4-3/8 inches tall. Accent Red. Colors: Accent Red, Brown, Crystal, Lime Green, Moss Green, Ritz Blue, Yellow. **References:** 1977, page 14-15 [1-3]

Cascade. Line: 1972. Goblet, Bloody Mary Set. 14-1/2 oz. 5-3/4 inches tall. Lead Crystal. **References:** 1978, page 11 [1-2]

Cascade. Line: 1972. Mixer, Bloody Mary Set. 40 oz. Lead Crystal w/Stir Rod. **References:** 1978, page 11 [1-1]

Cascade. Line: 1972. Old Fashion. 11-1/2 oz. 3-3/4 inches tall. Grey, Green, Crystal, Yellow. Colors Available: Peacock Blue. **References:** 1971, page 39 [2-1,2,3 & 3-2]; 1972, page 5 [2-1];

1973, page 14 [2-1]; 1977, page 14-15 [1-4]

Celeste. Bell. 4-1/2 inches tall. **References:** 1979, page 12 [2-2]

Celeste. Line: 3. Cut: 1318. Bell. 4-3/8 inches tall. Handmade and Hand Cut / Featured in display case. **References:** 1975, page 12 [2-2]; 1976, page 6 [2-3]; 1977, page 22 [5-2]

Celeste. Line: 355. Cut: 1318. 1305 Dessert-Finger Bowl. 4-1/2 inches diam. **References:** 1967, page 15 [1-9]; 1968, page 19 [1-9]; 1969, page 17 [2-9]; 1970, page 18 [2-9]; 1971, page 18 [2-9]

Celeste. Line: 355. Cut: 1318. Cocktail. 4-3/4 oz. 4-1/2 inches tall. **References:** 1967, page 15 [1-4]; 1968, page 19 [1-4]; 1969, page 17 [2-4]; 1970, page 18 [2-4]; 1971, page 18 [2-4]

Celeste. Line: 355. Cut: 1318. Cordial. 1-1/2 oz. 3-1/2 inches tall. **References:** 1967, page 15 [1-5]; 1968, page 19 [1-5]; 1969, page 17 [2-5]; 1970, page 18 [2-5]; 1971, page 18 [2-5]

Celeste. Line: 355. Cut: 1318. Goblet. 10-1/2 oz. 6-1/2 inches tall. **References:** 1967, page 15 [1-1]; 1968, page 19 [1-1]; 1969, page 17 [2-1]; 1970, page 18 [2-1]; 1971, page 18 [2-1]

Celeste. Line: 355. Cut: 1318. Ice Tea. 12 oz. 5-3/4 inches tall. **References:** 1967, page 15 [1-8]; 1968, page 19 [1-8]; 1969, page 17 [2-8]; 1970, page 18 [2-8]; 1971, page 18 [2-8]

Celeste. Line: 355. Cut: 1318. Juice. 5 oz. 4-1/4 inches tall. **References:** 1967, page 15 [1-7]; 1968, page 19 [1-7]; 1969, page 17 [2-7]; 1970, page 18 [2-7]; 1971, page 18 [2-7]

Celeste. Line: 355. Cut: 1318. Parfait. 6-1/2 oz. 7-1/2 inches tall. **References:** 1967, page 15 [1-6]; 1968, page 19 [1-6]; 1969, page 17 [2-6]; 1970, page 18 [2-6]; 1971, page 18 [2-6]

Celeste. Line: 355. Cut: 1318. Plate. 7 inches diam. Actually 7-7/8" Dia. **References:** 1967, page 15 [1-10]; 1968, page 19 [1-10]; 1969, page 17 [2-10]; 1970, page 18 [2-10]; 1971, page 18 [2-10]

Celeste. Line: 355. Cut: 1318. Plate. 8 inches diam. Actually 8-3/4" Dia. **References:** 1967, page 15 [1-11]; 1968, page 19 [1-11]; 1969, page 17 [2-11]; 1970, page 18 [2-11]; 1971, page 18 [2-11]

Celeste. Line: 355. Cut: 1318. Sherbet. 6-3/4 oz. 5 inches tall. **References:** 1967, page 15 [1-2]; 1968, page 19 [1-2]; 1969, page 17 [2-2]; 1970, page 18 [2-2]; 1971, page 18 [2-2]

Celeste. Line: 355. Cut: 1318. Wine. 5 oz. 5-1/2 inches tall. **References:** 1967, page 15 [1-3]; 1968, page 19 [1-3]; 1969, page 17 [2-3]; 1970, page 18 [2-3]; 1971, page 18 [2-3]

Century. Cocktail. **References:** 1964 Advertisement

Century. Cordial. **References:** 1964 Advertisement

Century. Footed Ice Tea. **References:** 1964 Advertisement

Century. Footed Juice. **References:** 1964 Advertisement

Century. Goblet. **References:** 1964 Advertisement

Century. Saucer Champagne. **References:** 1964 Advertisement

Century. White Wine Goblet. **References:** 1964 Advertisement

Chalet. Line: 5321. Dessert-Champagne. 11 oz. 4-7/8 inches tall. Pink/Crystal Foot. Colors Available: Blue/Crystal Foot, Pink/Crystal Foot, Crystal Cut 1443, Blue/Crystal Foot Cut 1443, Pink/Crystal Foot Cut 1443. Item Available: Goblet, Dessert-Champagne, White Wine. **References:** 1971, page 41 [3-2]

Chalet. Line: 5321. Goblet. 14 oz. 7 inches tall. Pink/Crystal Foot. Colors Available: Blue/Crystal Foot, Pink/Crystal Foot, Crystal Cut 1443, Blue/Crystal Foot Cut 1443, Pink/Crystal Foot Cut 1443. Item Available: Goblet, Dessert-Champagne, White Wine. **References:** 1971, page 41 [3-1]

Chalet. Line: 5321. White Wine Goblet. 8-1/2 oz. 6-5/8 inches tall. Pink/Crystal Foot. Colors Available: Blue/Crystal Foot, Pink/Crystal Foot, Crystal Cut 1443, Blue/Crystal Foot Cut 1443, Pink/Crystal Foot Cut 1443. Item Available: Goblet, Dessert-Champagne, White Wine. **References:** 1971, page 41 [3-3]

Chalice. Bell. 4-1/2 inches tall. **References:** 1979, page 12 [5-1]; 1981, page 11 [2-4]; 1983, page 6 [1-1R]

Chalice. Beverage. 16 oz. 6 inches tall. Hand Made....Hand Cut. **References:** 1979, page 15 [2-2]; 1981, page 4 [3-1]; 1982, page 14 [1-1]; 1983, page 11 [3-1L]

Chalice. Champagne Flute. 6 oz. 9-1/4 inches tall. **References:** 1982, page 14 [1-10]; 1983, page 4 [3-4]

Chalice. Cooler. 16 oz. 7-3/8 inches tall. Hand Made....Hand Cut. **References:** 1979, page 15 [2-1]

Chalice. Cordial. 3 oz. 5-5/8 inches tall. **References:** 1979, page 1 [1-8]; 1982, page 14 [1-8]; 1983, page 4 [3-5]

Chalice. Goblet. 13 oz. 7-1/2 inches tall. **References:** 1979, page 1 [1-5]; 1982, page 14 [1-5]; 1983, page 4 [3-1]

Chalice. Hi Ball. 11 oz. 5 inches tall. Hand Made....Hand Cut. **References:** 1979, page 15 [2-3]; 981, page 4 [3-2]; 1982, page 14 [1-2]; 1983, page 11 [3-2L]

Chalice. Ice Tea. 15-1/2 oz. 6-7/8 inches tall. **References:** 1982, page 14 [1-9]; 1983, page 4 [3-6]

Chalice. Old Fashion. 9-1/2 oz. 3-1/2 inches tall. Hand Made....Hand Cut. **References:** 1979, page 15 [2-5]; 1981, page 4 [3-4]; 1982, page 14 [1-4]; 1983, page 11 [3-4L]

Chalice. On The Rocks. 14 oz. 4-1/2 inches tall. Hand Made, Hand Cut. **References:** 1979, page 15 [2-4]; 1981, page 4 [3-3]; 1982, page 14 [1-3]; 1983, page 11 [3-3L]

Chalice. Pony. 3 oz. 3 inches tall. Hand Made....Hand Cut. **References:** 1979, page 15 [2-6]

Chalice. Sherbet. 9 oz. 6 inches tall. **References:** 1979, page 1 [1-6]; 1982, page 14 [1-6]; 1983, page 4 [3-2]

Chalice. Wine. 7-1/2 oz. 6-1/2 inches tall. **References:** 1979, page 1 [1-7]; 1982, page 14 [1-7]; 1983, page 4 [3-3]

Chalice. Line: 3. Cut: 1448. Bell. 4-3/8 inches tall. **References:** 1977, page 22 [4-1]

Chalice. Line: 972. Cut: 1448. Cordial. 3 oz. 5-5/8 inches tall. **References:** 1976, page 4 [1-4]; 1977, page 29 [1-4]; 1981, page 1 [1-4]

Chalice. Line: 972. Cut: 1448. Goblet. 13 oz. 7-1/2 inches tall. **References:** 1976, page 4 [1-1]; 1977, page 29 [1-1]; 1981, page 1 [1-1]

Chalice. Line: 972. Cut: 1448. Sherbet. 9 oz. 6 inches tall. **References:** 1976, page 4 [1-2]; 1977, page 29 [1-2]; 1981, page 1 [1-2]

Chalice. Line: 972. Cut: 1448. Wine. 7-1/2 oz. 6-1/2 inches tall. **References:** 1976, page 4 [1-3]; 1977, page 29 [1-3]; 1981, page 1 [1-3]

Chalice. Line: 1978. Cut: 1448. Beverage. **References:** 1977, page 24 [1-2]

Chalice. Line: 1978. Cut: 1448. On the Rocks. 15-1/2 oz. 4-1/2 inches tall. **References:** 1976, page 11 [1-3]

Chantilly. Cordial. 1-1/4 oz. 3-3/4 inches tall. Gold Band. **References:** 1979, page 6 [2-5]

Chantilly. Goblet. 12-1/2 oz. 6-5/8 inches tall. Gold Band. **References:** 1979, page 6 [2-1]

Chantilly. Ice Tea. 13-1/2 oz. 6-1/4 inches tall. Gold Band. **References:** 1979, page 6 [2-7]

Chantilly. Sherbet. 6-1/2 oz. 5 inches tall. Gold Band. **References:** 1979, page 6 [2-2]

Chantilly. White Wine Goblet. 7 oz. 5-3/4 inches tall. Gold Band. **References:** 1979, page 6 [2-3]

Chantilly. Line: 4. Bell. 5-1/2 inches tall. 1/4" Gold Band. All Bells Individually Gift Boxed. **References:** 1976, page 7 [1-1]; 1977, page 23 [2-1]; 1979, page 13 [2-3]

Chantilly. Line: 1962. Cocktail. 4-1/2 oz. / 4-3/4" hi. Gold Band. **References:** 1967, page 11 [1-4]; 1968, page 15 [1-4]; 1969, page 19 [2-4]; 1970, page 20 [2-4]; 1971, page 20 [2-4]; 1972, page 28 [2-4]; 1973, page 33 [2-4]

Chantilly. Line: 1962. Cordial. 1-1/4 oz. / 3-3/4" hi. Gold Band. **References:** 1967, page 11 [1-5]; 1968, page 15 [1-5]; 1969, page 19 [2-5]; 1970, page 20 [2-5]; 1971, page 20 [2-5]; 1972, page 28 [2-5]; 1973, page 33 [2-5]; 1975, page 29 [2-5]; 1977, page 40 [2-5]

Chantilly. Line: 1962. Goblet. 12-1/2 oz. / 6-5/8" hi. Gold Band. **References:** 1967, page 11 [1-1]; 1968, page 15 [1-1]; 1969, page 19 [2-1]; 1970, page 20 [2-1]; 1971, page 20 [2-1]; 1972, page 28 [2-1]; 1973, page 33 [2-1]; 1975, page 29 [2-1]; 1977, page 40 [2-1]

Chantilly. Line: 1962. Ice Tea. 13-1/2 oz. / 6-1/4" hi. Gold Band. **References:** 1967, page 11 [1-7]; 1968, page 15 [1-7]; 1969, page 19 [2-7]; 1970, page 20 [2-7]; 1971, page 20 [2-7]; 1972, page 28 [2-7]; 1973, page 33 [2-7]; 1975, page 29 [2-7]; 1977, page 40 [2-7]

Chantilly. Line: 1962. Juice. 6-1/2 oz. / 5-1/4" hi. Gold Band. **References:** 1967, page 11 [1-6]; 1968, page 15 [1-6]; 1969, page 19 [2-6]; 1970, page 20 [2-6]; 1971, page 20 [2-6]; 1972, page 28 [2-6]; 1973, page 33 [2-6]

Chantilly. Line: 1962. Plate. 7" / Actually 7-7/8" Dia. Gold Band. **References:** 1967, page 11 [1-8]; 1968, page 15 [1-8]; 1969, page 19 [2-8]; 1970, page 20 [2-8]; 1971, page 20 [2-8]; 1972, page 28 [2-8]; 1973, page 33 [2-8]; 1975, page 29 [2-8]; 1977, page 40 [2-8]

Chantilly. Line: 1962. Plate. 8" / Actually 8-3/4" Dia. Gold Band. **References:** 1967, page 11 [1-9]; 1968, page 15 [1-9]; 1969, page 19 [2-9]; 1970, page 20 [2-9]; 1971, page 20 [2-9]; 1972, page 28 [2-9]; 1973, page 33 [2-9]; 1975, page 29 [2-9]; 1977, page 40 [2-9]

Chantilly. Line: 1962. Sherbet. 6-1/2 oz. / 5" hi. Gold Band. **References:** 1967, page 11 [1-2]; 1968, page 15 [1-2]; 1969, page 19 [2-2]; 1970, page 20 [2-2]; 1971, page 20 [2-2]; 1972, page 28 [2-2]; 1973, page 33 [2-2]; 1975, page 29 [2-2]; 1977, page 40 [2-2]

Chantilly. Line: 1962. White Wine. 7 oz. 5-3/4 inches tall. Gold Band. **References:** 1975, page 29 [2-3]; 1977, page 40 [2-3]; x1967, page 11 [1-3]; 1968, page 15 [1-3]; 1969, page 19 [2-3]; 1970, page 20 [2-3]; 1971, page 20 [2-3]; 1972, page 28 [2-3]; 1973, page 33 [2-3]

Chapel Belle. Line: 1967. Cut: 1440. 1305 Dessert-Finger Bowl. 4-1/2 inches diam. **References:** 1968, page 9 [1-14]

Chapel Belle. Line: 1967. Cut: 1440. Cordial. 1-1/4 oz. 3-3/4 inches tall. **References:** 1968, page 9 [1-12]

Chapel Belle. Line: 1967. Cut: 1440. Goblet. 12 oz. 6-3/4 inches tall. **References:** 1968, page 9 [1-9]

Chapel Belle. Line: 1967. Cut: 1440. Ice Tea. 14 oz. 6-3/8 inches tall. **References:** 1968, page 9 [1-13]

Chapel Belle. Line: 1967. Cut: 1440. Plate. 7 inches diam. Actually 7-7/8" Dia. **References:** 1968, page 9 [1-15]

Chapel Belle. Line: 1967. Cut: 1440. Plate. 8 inches diam. Actually 8-3/4" Dia. **References:** 1968, page 9 [1-16]

Chapel Belle. Line: 1967. Cut: 1440. Sherbet. 7-1/2 oz. 5 inches tall. **References:** 1968, page 9 [1-10]

Chapel Belle. Line: 1967. Cut: 1440. Wine. 7-1/2 oz. 6 inches tall. **References:** 1968, page 9 [1-11]

Christmas. Bell Gift Box. **References:** 1978, page 16 [3-2]

Christmas. Hanging Bell. **References:** 1980, page 4 [1-3]; 1981, page 11 [1-1]

Claremont. Line: 1971. 1311 Dessert-Finger. 4-3/4 inches diam. Platinum Band and Line. **References:** 1970, page 11 [2-14]; 1971, page 19 [2-14]; 1972, page 27 [2-14]; 1973, page 32 [2-14]

Claremont. Line: 1971. Cordial. 1-1/2 oz. 4 inches tall. Platinum Band and Line. **References:** 1970, page 11 [2-12]; 1971, page 19 [2-12]; 1972, page 27 [2-12]; 1973, page 32 [2-12]

Claremont. Line: 1971. Goblet. 11-1/2 oz. 7 inches tall. Platinum Band and Line. **References:** 1970, page 11 [2-9]; 1971, page 19 [2-9]; 1972, page 27 [2-9]; 1973, page 32 [2-9]

Claremont. Line: 1971. Ice Tea. 14-1/2 oz. 7-1/8 inches tall. Platinum Band and Line. **References:** 1970, page 11 [2-13]; 1971, page 19 [2-13]; 1972, page 27 [2-13]; 1973, page 32 [2-13]

Claremont. Line: 1971. Plate. 7 inches diam. Platinum Band and Line, Actually 7-7/8" Dia. **References:** 1970, page 11 [2-15]; 1971, page 19 [2-15]; 1972, page 27 [2-15]; 1973, page 32 [2-15]

Claremont. Line: 1971. Plate. 8 inches diam. Platinum Band and Line, Actually 8-3/4" Dia. **References:** 1970, page 11 [2-16]; 1971, page 19 [2-16]; 1972, page 27 [2-16]; 1973, page 32 [2-16]

Claremont. Line: 1971. Sherbet. 7-1/2 oz. 5 inches tall. Platinum Band and Line. **References:** 1970, page 11 [2-10]; 1971, page 19 [2-10]; 1972, page 27 [2-10]; 1973, page 32 [2-10]

Claremont. Line: 1971. Wine. 7 oz. 5-7/8 inches tall. Platinum Band and Line. **References:** 1970, page 11 [2-11]; 1971, page 19 [2-11]; 1972, page 27 [2-11]; 1973, page 32 [2-11]

Classic. Bell. 4-1/2 inches tall. **References:** 1979, page 12 [3-3]

Classic. Beverage. 16 oz. 6 inches tall. Hand Made....Hand Cut. **References:** 1979, page 15 [2-8]

Classic. Cooler. 16 oz. 7-3/8 inches tall. Hand Made....Hand Cut. **References:** 1979, page 15 [2-7]

Classic. Cordial. 2-1/4 oz. 5-1/4 inches tall. **References:** 1979, page 1 [2-8]

Classic. Goblet. 10 oz. 7-1/2 inches tall. **References:** 1979, page 1 [2-5]

Classic. Hi Ball. 11 oz. 5 inches tall. Hand Made....Hand Cut. **References:** 1979, page 15 [2-9]

Classic. Old Fashion. 9-1/2 oz. 3-1/2 inches tall. Hand Made....Hand Cut. **References:** 1979, page 15 [2-11]

Classic. On The Rocks. 14 oz. 4-1/2 inches tall. Hand Made, Hand Cut. **References:** 1979, page 15 [2-10]

Classic. Pony. 3 oz. 3 inches tall. Hand Made....Hand Cut. **References:** 1979, page 15 [2-12]

Classic. Sherbet. 6-1/2 oz. 5-1/2 inches tall. **References:** 1979, page 1 [2-6]

Classic. Wine. 6 oz. 6-5/8 inches tall. **References:** 1979, page 1 [2-7]

Classic. Line: 3. Cut: 1450. Bell. 4-3/8 inches tall. **References:** 1977, page 22 [2-1]

Classic. Line: 974. Cut: 1450. Cordial. 2-1/4 oz. 5-1/4 inches tall. **References:** 1976, page 5 [1-8]; 1977, page 30 [1-8]

Classic. Line: 974. Cut: 1450. Goblet. 10 oz. 7-1/2 inches tall. **References:** 1976, page 5 [1-5]; 1977, page 30 [1-5]

Classic. Line: 974. Cut: 1450. Sherbet. 6-1/2 oz. 5-1/2 inches tall. **References:** 1976, page 5 [1-6]; 1977, page 30 [1-6]

Classic. Line: 974. Cut: 1450. Wine. 6 oz. 6-5/8 inches tall. **References:** 1976, page 5 [1-7]; 1977, page 30 [1-7]

Classic. Line: 1978. Cut: 1450S. On The Rocks. **References:** 1977, page 24 [2-2]

Classic. Line: 5321. Cut: 1443. Dessert-Champagne. 11 oz. 4-7/8 inches tall. Blue/Crystal Foot. Colors Available: Blue/Crystal Foot, Pink/Crystal Foot, Crystal Cut 1443, Blue/Crystal Foot Cut 1443, Pink/Crystal Foot Cut 1443. Item Available: Goblet, Dessert-Champagne, White Wine. **References:** 1971, page 41 [3-4]

Connoisseur Collection. Brandy and Liqueur. 2-1/2 oz. 4-1/2 inches tall. **References:** 1979, page 5 [2-22]; 1983, page 2 [2-12]

Connoisseur Collection. Champagne. 8 oz. 8-1/2 inches tall. **References:** 1979, page 5 [2-19]; 1983, page 2 [2-14]

Connoisseur Collection. Champagne Flute. 6 oz. 9-1/4 inches tall. **References:** 1983, page 2 [2-13]

Connoisseur Collection. Dessert-Champagne. 11 oz. 4-7/8 inches tall. **References:** 1979, page 5 [2-21]; 1983, page 2 [2-11]

Connoisseur Collection. Magnum Wine Goblet. 18 oz. 7-3/8 inches tall. **References:** 1979, page 5 [2-15]; 1983, page 2 [2-6]

Connoisseur Collection. Red Wine Goblet. 10-1/2 oz. 6-7/8 inches tall. **References:** 1979, page 5 [2-17]; 1983, page 2 [2-8]

Connoisseur Collection. Sherry and Port. 5 oz. 6 inches tall. **References:** 1979, page 5 [2-20]; 1983, page 2 [2-10]

Connoisseur Collection. Vintage Wine Goblet. 14 oz. 7 inches tall. **References:** 1979, page 5 [2-16]; 1983, page 2 [2-7]

Connoisseur Collection. White Wine Goblet. 8-1/2 oz. 6-5/8 inches tall. **References:** 1979, page 5 [2-18]; 1983, page 2 [2-9]

Connoisseur Collection. Cut: 43. Brandy and Liqueur. 2-1/2 oz. 4-1/2 inches tall. **References:** 1982, page 5 [3-7]

Connoisseur Collection. Cut: 43. Champagne Flute. 6 oz. 9-1/4 inches tall. **References:** 1982, page 5 [3-8]

Connoisseur Collection. Cut: 43. Dessert-Champagne. 11 oz. 4-7/8 inches tall. **References:** 1982, page 5 [3-6]

Connoisseur Collection. Cut: 43. Magnum Wine Goblet. 18 oz. 7-3/8 inches tall. **References:** 1982, page 5 [3-1]

Connoisseur Collection. Cut: 43. Red Wine Goblet. 10-1/2 oz. 6-7/8 inches tall. **References:** 1982, page 5 [3-3]

Connoisseur Collection. Cut: 43. Sherry and Port. 5 oz. 6 inches tall. **References:** 1982, page 5 [3-5]

Connoisseur Collection. Cut: 43. Tulip Champagne. 8 oz. 8-1/2 inches tall. **References:** 1982, page 5 [3-9]

Connoisseur Collection. Cut: 43. Vintage Wine Goblet. 14 oz. 7 inches tall. **References:** 1982, page 5 [3-2]

Connoisseur Collection. Cut: 43. White Wine Goblet. 8-1/2 oz. 6-5/8 inches tall. **References:**

4-1/2 inches tall. **References:** 1967, page 15 [2-15]; 1968, page 19 [2-15]; 1969, page 17 [2-15]; 1970, page 18 [2-15]; 1971, page 18 [2-15]

Coventry. Line: 355. Cut: 1325. Cordial. 1-1/2 oz. 3-1/2 inches tall. **References:** 1967, page 15 [2-16]; 1968, page 19 [2-16]; 1969, page 17 [2-16]; 1970, page 18 [2-16]; 1971, page 18 [2-16]

Coventry. Line: 355. Cut: 1325. Goblet. 10-1/2 oz. 6-1/2 inches tall. **References:** 1967, page 15 [2-12]; 1968, page 19 [2-12]; 1969, page 17 [2-12]; 1970, page 18 [2-12]; 1971, page 18 [2-12]

Coventry. Line: 355. Cut: 1325. Ice Tea. 12 oz. 5-3/4 inches tall. **References:** 1967, page 15 [2-19]; 1968, page 19 [2-19]; 1969, page 17 [2-19]; 1970, page 18 [2-19]; 1971, page 18 [2-19]

Coventry. Line: 355. Cut: 1325. Juice. 5 oz. 4-1/4 inches tall. **References:** 1967, page 15 [2-18]; 1968, page 19 [2-18]; 1969, page 17 [2-18]; 1970, page 18 [2-18]; 1971, page 18 [2-18]

Coventry. Line: 355. Cut: 1325. Parfait. 6-1/2 oz. 7-1/2 inches tall. **References:** 1967, page 15 [2-17]; 1968, page 19 [2-17]; 1969, page 17 [2-17]; 1970, page 18 [2-17]; 1971, page 18 [2-17]

Coventry. Line: 355. Cut: 1325. Plate. 7 inches diam. Actually 7-7/8" Dia. **References:** 1967, page 15 [2-21]; 1968, page 19 [2-21]; 1969, page 17 [2-21]; 1970, page 18 [2-21]; 1971, page 18 [2-21]

Coventry. Line: 355. Cut: 1325. Plate. 8 inches diam. Actually 8-3/4" Dia. **References:** 1967, page 15 [2-22]; 1968, page 19 [2-22]; 1969, page 17 [2-22]; 1970, page 18 [2-22]; 1971, page 18 [2-22]

Coventry. Line: 355. Cut: 1325. Sherbet. 6-3/4 oz. 5 inches tall. **References:** 1967, page 15 [2-13]; 1968, page 19 [2-13]; 1969, page 17 [2-13]; 1970, page 18 [2-13]; 1971, page 18 [2-13]

Coventry. Line: 355. Cut: 1325. Wine. 5 oz. 5-1/2 inches tall. **References:** 1967, page 15 [2-14]; 1968, page 19 [2-14]; 1969, page 17 [2-14]; 1970, page 18 [2-14]; 1971, page 18 [2-14]

Crinkle Glass. Line: 1820. Beverage. 14 oz. 5-5/8 inches tall. 5W. Colors: Accent Red. **References:** Advertisement

Crinkle Glass. Line: 1820. Bowl. 5 inches diam. 5B. Colors: Topaz. **References:** Advertisement

Crinkle Glass. Line: 1820. Cooler. 20 oz. 6-3/4 inches tall. 5W/2. Colors: Delphine Blue. **References:** Advertisement

Crinkle Glass. Line: 1820. Double Old Fashion. 12 oz. 3-1/2 inches tall. 5R/2. Colors: Moss Green. **References:** Advertisement

Crinkle Glass. Line: 1820. Footed Goblet. 13 oz. 5-1/4 inches tall. 5T. Colors: Moss Green. **References:** Advertisement

Crinkle Glass. Line: 1820. Footed Sherbet. 6 oz. 2-7/8 inches tall. 5S. Colors: Crystal. **References:** Advertisement

Crinkle Glass. Line: 1820. Juice. 6 oz. 4 inches tall. 5W-1/4. Colors: Lime Green. **References:** Advertisement

Crinkle Glass. Line: 1820. Pitcher. 50 oz. 8 inches tall. 5PT. Colors: Moss Green. **References:** Advertisement

Darlene. Line: 1963. Cut: 1406. Cocktail. 5-1/2 oz. / 4-3/4" hi. Gold Band. **References:** 1967, page 11 [2-22]; 1968, page 15 [2-22]

Darlene. Line: 1963. Cut: 1406. Cordial. 1-1/2 oz. / 4" hi. Gold Band. **References:** 1967, page 11 [2-23]; 1968, page 15 [2-23]

Darlene. Line: 1963. Cut: 1406. Goblet. 13-1/2 oz. / 6-3/4" hi. Gold Band. **References:** 1967, page 11 [2-19]; 1968, page 15 [2-19]

Darlene. Line: 1963. Cut: 1406. Ice Tea. 14 oz. / 6-1/4" hi. Gold Band. **References:** 1967, page 11 [2-25]; 1968, page 15 [2-25]

Darlene. Line: 1963. Cut: 1406. Juice. 7 oz. / 5-1/4" hi. Gold Band. **References:** 1967, page 11 [2-24]; 1968, page 15 [2-24]

Darlene. Line: 1963. Cut: 1406. Plate. 7" / Actually 7-7/8" Dia. Gold Band. **References:** 1967, page 11 [2-26]; 1968, page 15 [2-26]

Darlene. Line: 1963. Cut: 1406. Plate. 8" / Actually 8-3/4" Dia. Gold Band. **References:** 1967, page 11 [2-27]; page 15 [2-27]

Darlene. Line: 1963. Cut: 1406. Sherbet. 7-1/2 oz. / 5-1/8" hi. Gold Band. **References:** 1967, page 11 [2-20]; 1968, page 15 [2-20]

Darlene. Line: 1963. Cut: 1406. Wine. 7-3/4 oz. / 5-3/4" hi. Gold Band. **References:** 1967, page 11 [2-21]; 1968, page 15 [2-21]

Dayton. Champagne Flute. 6 oz. 9-1/4 inches tall. **References:** 1983, page 5 [3-12]

Dayton. Cordial. 1-1/4 oz. 3-3/4 inches tall. **References:** 1979, page 4 [1-4]; 1983, page 5 [3-10]

Dayton. Goblet. 10 oz. 7 inches tall. **References:** 1979, page 4 [1-1]; 1983, page 5 [3-7]

Dayton. Ice Tea. 11-1/2 oz. 6-1/8 inches tall. **References:** 1979, page 4 [1-5]; 1983, page 5 [3-11]

Dayton. Saucer Champagne. 7-1/2 oz. 5-1/4 inches tall. **References:** 1979, page 4 [1-2]; 1983, page 5 [3-8]

Dayton. Table Wine Goblet. 7-1/2 oz. 6 inches tall. **References:** 1979, page 4 [1-3]; 1983, page 5 [3-9]

Dayton. Line: 1282. Cut: 1120. 1305 Dessert-Finger Bowl. 4-1/2" Dia. **References:** 1967, page 9 [1-16]; 1969, page 15 [1-16]; 1970, page 16 [1-16]; 1971, page 16 [1-16]; 1972, page 25 [1-16]; 1973, page 30 [1-16]; 1975, page 28 [1-14]; 1977, page 39 [1-14]

Dayton. Line: 1282. Cut: 1120. Cordial. 1-1/4 oz. / 3-3/4" hi. **References:** 1967, page 9 [1-13]; 1969, page 15 [1-13]; 1970, page 16 [1-13]; 1971, page 16 [1-13]; 1972, page 25 [1-13]; 1973, page 30 [1-13]; 1975, page 28 [1-12]; 1977, page 39 [1-12]; 1981, page 2 [3-12]

Dayton. Line: 1282. Cut: 1120. Goblet. 10 oz. / 7" hi. **References:** 1967, page 9 [1-10]; 1969, page 15 [1-10]; 1970, page 16 [1-10]; 1971, page 16 [1-10]; 1972, page 25 [1-10]; 1973, page 30 [1-10]; 1975, page 28 [1-9]; 1977, page 39 [1-9]; 1981, page 2 [3-9]

Dayton. Line: 1282. Cut: 1120. Ice Tea. 11-1/2 oz. / 6-1/8" hi. **References:** 1967, page 9 [1-15]; 1969, page 15 [1-15]; 1970, page 16 [1-15]; 1971, page 16 [1-15]; 1972, page 25 [1-15]; 1973, page 30 [1-15]; 1975, page 28 [1-13]; 1977, page 39 [1-13]

Dayton. Line: 1282. Cut: 1120. Juice. 5 oz. / 4-1/2 hi. **References:** 1967, page 9 [1-14]; 1969, page 15 [1-14]; 1970, page 16 [1-14]; 1971, page 16 [1-14]; 1972, page 25 [1-14]; 1973, page 30 [1-14]

Dayton. Line: 1282. Cut: 1120. Plate. 7" / Actually 7-7/8" Dia. **References:** 1967, page 9 [1-17]; 1969, page 15 [1-17]; 1970, page 16 [1-17]; 1971, page 16 [1-17]; 1972, page 25 [1-17]; 1973, page 30 [1-17]; 1975, page 28 [1-15]; 1977, page 39 [1-15]

Dayton. Line: 1282. Cut: 1120. Plate. 8" / Actually 8-3/4" Dia. **References:** 1967, page 9 [1-18]; 1969, page 15 [1-18]; 1970, page 16 [1-18]; 1971, page 16 [1-18]; 1972, page 25 [1-18]; 1973, page 30 [1-18]; 1975, page 28 [1-16]; 1977, page 39 [1-16]

Dayton. Line: 1282. Cut: 1120. Saucer Champagne. 7-1/2 oz. / 5-1/4" hi. **References:** 1967, page 9 [1-11]; 1969, page 15 [1-11]; 1970, page 16 [1-11]; 1971, page 16 [1-11]; 1972, page 25 [1-11]; 1973, page 30 [1-11]; 1975, page 28 [1-10]; 1977, page 39 [1-10]; 1981, page 2 [3-10]

Dayton. Line: 1282. Cut: 1120. Table Wine Goblet. 7-1/2 oz. / 6" hi. **References:** 1967, page 9 [1-12]; 1969, page 15 [1-12]; 1970, page 16 [1-12]; 1971, page 16 [1-12]; 1972, page 25 [1-12]; 1973, page 30 [1-12]; 1975, page 28 [1-11]; 1977, page 39 [1-11]; 1981, page 2 [3-11]

Debonair. Line: 1969. 1305 Dessert-Finger Bowl. 4-1/2 inches diam. 3/16" Platinum Band. **References:** 1969, page 18 [2-6]; 1970, page 19 [2-6]

Debonair. Line: 1969. Cordial. 2 oz. 4-1/2 inches tall. 3/16" Platinum Band. **References:** 1969, page 18 [2-4]; 1970, page 19 [2-4]

Debonair. Line: 1969. Goblet. 14 oz. 6-3/4 inches tall. 3/16" Platinum Band. **References:** 1969, page 18 [2-1]; 1970, page 19 [2-1]

Debonair. Line: 1969. Ice Tea. 14 oz. 6-3/8 inches tall. 3/16" Platinum Band. **References:** 1969, page 18 [2-5]; 1970, page 19 [2-5]

Debonair. Line: 1969. Plate. 7 inches diam. 3/16" Platinum Band, Actually 7-7/8" Dia. **References:** 1969, page 18 [2-7]; 1970, page 19 [2-7]

Debonair. Line: 1969. Plate. 8 inches diam. 3/16" Platinum Band, Actually 8-3/4" Dia. **References:** 1969, page 18 [2-8]; 1970, page 19 [2-8]

Debonair. Line: 1969. Sherbet. 7-1/2 oz. 5-3/8 inches tall. 3/16" Platinum Band. **References:** 1969, page 18 [2-2]; 1970, page 19 [2-2]

Debonair. Line: 1969. White Wine Goblet. 7-1/2 oz. 5-1/2 inches tall. 3/16" Platinum Band. **References:** 1969, page 18 [2-3]; 1970, page 19 [2-3]

Diane. Line: 1963. Cut: 1406. Cocktail. 5-1/2 oz. / 4-3/4" hi. NOT BANDED. **References:** 1967, page 11 [2-31]; 1968, page 15 [2-31]

Diane. Line: 1963. Cut: 1406. Cordial. 1-1/2 oz. / 4" hi. NOT BANDED. **References:** 1967, page 11 [2-32]; 1968, page 15 [2-32]

Diane. Line: 1963. Cut: 1406. Goblet. 13-1/2 oz. / 6-3/4" hi. NOT BANDED. **References:** 1967, page 11 [2-28]; 1968, page 15 [2-28]

Diane. Line: 1963. Cut: 1406. Ice Tea. 14 oz. / 6-1/4" hi. NOT BANDED. **References:** 1967, page 11 [2-34]; 1968, page 15 [2-34]

Diane. Line: 1963. Cut: 1406. Juice. 7 oz. / 5-1/4" hi. NOT BANDED. **References:** 1967, page 11 [2-33]; 1968, page 15 [2-33]

Diane. Line: 1963. Cut: 1406. Plate. 7" / Actually 7-7/8" Dia. NOT BANDED. **References:** 1967, page 11 [2-35]; 1968, page 15 [2-35]

Diane. Line: 1963. Cut: 1406. Plate. 8" / Actually 8-3/4" Dia. NOT BANDED. **References:** 1967, page 11 [2-36]; 1968, page 15 [2-36]

Diane. Line: 1963. Cut: 1406. Sherbet. 7-1/2 oz. / 5-1/8" hi. NOT BANDED. **References:** 1967, page 11 [2-29]; 1968, page 15 [2-29]

Diane. Line: 1963. Cut: 1406. Wine. 7-3/4 oz. / 5-3/4" hi. NOT BANDED. **References:** 1967, page 11 [2-30]; 1968, page 15 [2-30]

Dolly Madison-Jane Eyre. Line: 912. Cut: 139. 1311 Dessert-Finger Bowl. 4-3/4 inches diam. **References:** 1967, page 17 [2-18]; 1968, page 21 [2-18]; 1969, page 21 [2-18]; 1970, page 22 [2-18]; 1971, page 22 [2-18]

Dolly Madison-Jane Eyre. Line: 912. Cut: 139. Claret. 4 oz. 4-3/4 inches tall. **References:** 1967, page 17 [2-13]; 1968, page 21 [2-13]; 1969, page 21 [2-13]; 1970, page 22 [2-13]; 1971, page 22 [2-13]

Dolly Madison-Jane Eyre. Line: 912. Cut: 139. Cocktail. 3-1/2 oz. 4-3/8 inches tall. **References:** 1967, page 17 [2-14]; 1968, page 21 [2-14]; 1969, page 21 [2-14]; 1970, page 22 [2-14]; 1971, page 22 [2-14]

Dolly Madison-Jane Eyre. Line: 912. Cut: 139. Cordial. 1 oz. 3-5/8 inches tall. **References:** 1967, page 17 [2-15]; 1968, page 21 [2-15]; 1969, page 21 [2-15]; 1970, page 22 [2-15]; 1971, page 22 [2-15]

Dolly Madison-Jane Eyre. Line: 912. Cut: 139. Goblet. 10 oz. 6-1/4 inches tall. **References:** 1967, page 17 [2-11]; 1968, page 21 [2-11]; 1969, page 21 [2-11]; 1970, page 22 [2-11]; 1971, page 22 [2-11]

Dolly Madison-Jane Eyre. Line: 912. Cut: 139. Ice Tea. 12 oz. 6 inches tall. **References:** 1967, page 17 [2-17]; 1968, page 21 [2-17]; 1969, page 21 [2-17]; 1970, page 22 [2-17]; 1971, page 22 [2-17]

Dolly Madison-Jane Eyre. Line: 912. Cut: 139. Juice. 6 oz. 4-5/8 inches tall. **References:** 1967, page 17 [2-16]; 1968, page 21 [2-16]; 1969, page 21 [2-16]; 1970, page 22 [2-16]; 1971, page 22 [2-16]

Dolly Madison-Jane Eyre. Line: 912. Cut: 139. Plate. 7 inches diam. Actually 7-7/8" Dia. **References:** 1967, page 17 [2-19]; 1968, page 21 [2-19]; 1969, page 21 [2-19]; 1970, page 22 [2-19]; 1971, page 22 [2-19]

Dolly Madison-Jane Eyre. Line: 912. Cut: 139. Plate. 8 inches diam. Actually 8-3/4" Dia. **References:** 1967, page 17 [2-20]; 1968, page 21 [2-20]; 1969, page 21 [2-20]; 1970, page 22 [2-20]; 1971, page 22 [2-20]

Dolly Madison-Jane Eyre. Line: 912. Cut: 139. Saucer Champagne. 7-1/2 oz. 5-1/8 inches tall. **References:** 1967, page 17 [2-12]; 1968, page 21 [2-12]; 1969, page 21 [2-12]; 1970, page 22 [2-12]; 1971, page 22 [2-12]

Dorchester. Cordial. 2 oz. 4-3/4 inches tall. **References:** 1979, page 2 [1-8]

Dorchester. Goblet. 13-1/2 oz. 7-1/2 inches tall. **References:** 1979, page 2 [1-5]

Dorchester. Sherbet. 8 oz. 5-3/8 inches tall. **References:** 1979, page 2 [1-6]

Dorchester. Wine. 7 oz. 6-3/8 inches tall. **References:** 1979, page 2 [1-7]

Driftwood Casual. Ash Tray. **References:** Advertisement

Driftwood Casual. Ash Tray. 6 inches diam. Moss Green-Buttercup (Yellow), Amber-Delphine Blue (Dk.), Crystal-Peacock Blue (Lt.), Cinnamon (Brown). **References:** 1969, page 30 [Not Shown]

Driftwood Casual. Bowl. Colors: Accent Red, Amber, Brown, Charm Blue, Delphine Blue, Lime Green, Moss Green, Yellow. **References:** 1980, page 2 [2-3]

Driftwood Casual. Bowl. 5-1/2 inches diam. Crystal. Colors: Accent Red, Amber, Brown, Charm Blue, Crystal, Delphine Blue, Lime Green, Moss Green, Yellow. **References:** 1981, page 5 [2-3]; 1982, page 2 [2-3]; 1982, page 16 [1-12]; 1983, page 12 [2-3]

Driftwood Casual. Bud Vase. 7-1/4 inches tall. Moss Green-Buttercup (Yellow), Amber-Delphine Blue (Dk.), Crystal-Peacock Blue (Lt.), Cinnamon (Brown). **References:** 1969, page 30 [Not Shown]

Driftwood Casual. Candy Jar and Cover. **References:** Advertisement

Driftwood Casual. Cocktail. 5 oz. **References:** Advertisement

Driftwood Casual. Cocktail. **References:** 1964 Advertisement

Driftwood Casual. Cocktail. 6 oz. 3-5/16 inches tall. Colors: Moss Green, Heather (Pink), Amber, Delphine Blue (Dk.), Crystal, Peacock Blue (Lt.), Brown / Accent Red. **References:** 1967, page 24 [Bottom]; 1968, page 30 [Not Shown]; 1969, page 30 [Not Shown]; 1979, page 9 [3-3]

Driftwood Casual. Cocktail. Colors: Accent Red, Amber, Brown, Charm Blue, Delphine Blue, Lime Green, Moss Green, Yellow. **References:** 1980, page 2 [1-6]

Driftwood Casual. Cocktail. 6 oz. Colors: Accent Red, Amber, Brown, Charm Blue, Crystal, Delphine Blue, Lime Green, Moss Green, Yellow. **References:** 1981, page 5 [2-8]; 1982, page 2 [2-8]

Driftwood Casual. Cocktail. 6 oz. 3-3/8 inches tall. Colors: Accent Red, Amber, Brown, Charm Blue, Crystal, Delphine Blue, Lime Green, Moss Green, Yellow. **References:** 1982, page 16 [1-17]

Driftwood Casual. Cocktail. 6 oz. Colors: Crystal, Charm Blue, Brown, Yellow, Moss Green. **References:** 1983, page 12 [2-8]

Driftwood Casual. Compote. Charm Blue. Colors: Accent Red, Amber, Brown, Charm Blue, Crystal, Delphine Blue, Lime Green, Moss Green, Ritz Blue, Yellow. **References:** 1979, page 9 [3-1]

Driftwood Casual. Cooler. Lime Green. Colors: Accent Red, Amber, Brown, Charm Blue, Crystal, Delphine Blue, Lime Green, Moss Green, Ritz Blue, Yellow. **References:** 1979, page 9 [1-1]

Driftwood Casual. Cooler. Colors: Accent Red, Amber, Brown, Charm Blue, Delphine Blue, Lime Green, Moss Green, Yellow. **References:** 1980, page 2 [1-1]

Driftwood Casual. Cooler. 22 oz. Amber. Colors: Accent Red, Amber, Brown, Charm Blue, Crystal, Delphine Blue, Lime Green, Moss Green, Yellow. **References:** 1981, page 5 [2-9]; 1982, page 2 [2-9]; 1982, page 16 [1-18]; 1983, page 12 [2-9]

Driftwood Casual. Covered Dish. 5 inches tall. Moss Green-Buttercup (Yellow), Amber-Delphine Blue (Dk.), Crystal-Peacock Blue (Lt.), Cinnamon (Brown). **References:** 1969, page 30 [Not Shown]

Driftwood Casual. Dessert Cereal. Yellow. Colors: Accent Red, Amber, Brown, Charm Blue, Crystal, Delphine Blue, Lime Green, Moss Green, Ritz Blue, Yellow. **References:** 1979, page 9 [4-1]

Driftwood Casual. Dessert-Cereal Bowl. 5-1/4 inches diam. Colors: Moss Green, Heather (Pink), Amber, Delphine Blue (Dk.), Crystal, Peacock Blue (Lt.), Brown / Accent Red. **References:** 1967, page 24 [Not Shown]; 1968, page 30 [Not Shown]

Driftwood Casual. Dessert-Cereal Bowl. 5-1/4 inches diam. Moss Green-Buttercup (Yellow), Amber-Delphine Blue (Dk.), Crystal-Peacock Blue (Lt.), Cinnamon (Brown), Accent Red. **References:** 1969, page 30 [Not Shown]

Driftwood Casual. Double Old Fashion. **References:** 1964 Advertisement

Driftwood Casual. Double Old Fashion. 14 oz. 3-3/4 inches tall. Colors: Moss Green, Heather (Pink), Amber, Delphine Blue (Dk.), Crystal, Peacock Blue (Lt.), Brown / Accent Red. **References:** 1967, page 24 [L-3]; 1968, page 30 [Not Shown]

Driftwood Casual. Double Old Fashion. 14 oz. 3-3/4 inches tall. Moss Green-Buttercup (Yellow), Amber-Delphine Blue (Dk.), Crystal-Peacock Blue (Lt.), Cinnamon (Brown), Accent Red. **References:** 1969, page 30 [Not Shown]

Driftwood Casual. Double Old Fashion. Colors: Accent Red, Amber, Brown, Charm Blue, Crystal, Delphine Blue, Lime Green, Moss Green, Ritz Blue, Yellow. **References:** 1979, page 9 [4-2]

Driftwood Casual. Double Old Fashion. Colors: Accent Red, Amber, Brown, Charm Blue, Delphine Blue, Lime Green, Moss Green, Yellow. **References:** 1980, page 2 [1-5]

Driftwood Casual. Double Old Fashion. 14 oz. Lime Green. Colors: Accent Red, Amber, Brown, Charm Blue, Crystal, Delphine Blue, Lime Green, Moss Green, Yellow. **References:** 1981, page 5 [2-10]; 1982, page 2 [2-10]

Driftwood Casual. Double Old Fashion. 14 oz. 3-7/8 inches tall. Colors: Accent Red, Amber, Brown, Charm Blue, Crystal, Delphine Blue, Lime Green, Moss Green, Yellow. **References:** 1982, page 16 [1-19]; 1983, page 12 [2-10]

Driftwood Casual. Double Old-Fashion. **References:** 1964 Advertisement

Driftwood Casual. Flowerlite. 5 inches diam. Colors: Moss Green, Heather (Pink), Amber, Delphine Blue (Dk.), Crystal, Peacock Blue (Lt.), Brown. **References:** 1967, page 24 [Not Shown]; 1968, page 30 [Not Shown]

Driftwood Casual. Flowerlite. 5 inches diam. Moss Green-Buttercup (Yellow), Amber-Delphine Blue (Dk.), Crystal-Peacock Blue (Lt.), Cinnamon (Brown). **References:** 1969, page 30 [Not Shown]

Driftwood Casual. Goblet. 13 oz. 5-1/2 inches tall. Colors: Moss Green, Heather (Pink), Amber, Delphine Blue (Dk.), Crystal, Peacock Blue (Lt.), Brown / Accent Red. **References:** 1967, page 24 [Not Shown]; 1968, page 30 [Not Shown]

Driftwood Casual. Goblet. 13 oz. 5-1/2 inches tall. Colors: Moss Green-Buttercup (Yellow), Amber-Delphine Blue (Dk.), Crystal-Peacock Blue (Lt.), Cinnamon (Brown), Accent Red. **References:** 1969, page 30 [Not Shown]

Driftwood Casual. Goblet. Colors: Accent Red, Amber, Brown, Charm Blue, Crystal, Delphine Blue, Lime Green, Moss Green, Ritz Blue, Yellow. **References:** 1979, page 9 [2-1]; 1980, page 2 [2-1]; 1981, page 5 [2-4]; 1982, page 2 [2-4]; 1982, page 16 [1-13]

Driftwood Casual. Goblet. 13 oz. Colors: Crystal, Charm Blue, Brown, Yellow, Moss Green. **References:** 1983, page 12 [2-4]

Driftwood Casual. Handled Ice Tea or Beer Mug. 16 oz. **References:** Advertisement

Driftwood Casual. Hi Ball. 12 oz. **References:** Advertisement; 1964 Advertisement; 1964 Advertisement

Driftwood Casual. Hi Ball. 12 oz. 5-1/8 inches tall. Colors: Moss Green, Heather (Pink), Amber, Delphine Blue (Dk.), Crystal, Peacock Blue (Lt.), Brown / Accent Red. **References:** 1967, page 24 [L-2]; 1968, page 30 [Not Shown]

Driftwood Casual. Hi Ball. 12 oz. 5-1/8 inches tall. Moss Green-Buttercup (Yellow), Amber-Delphine Blue (Dk.), Crystal-Peacock Blue (Lt.), Cinnamon (Brown), Accent Red. **References:** 1969, page 30 [Not Shown]

Driftwood Casual. Hi Ball. Brown. Colors: Accent Red, Amber, Brown, Charm Blue, Crystal, Delphine Blue, Lime Green, Moss Green, Ritz Blue, Yellow. **References:** 1979, page 9 [2-3]

Driftwood Casual. Hi Ball. Colors: Accent Red, Amber, Brown, Charm Blue, Delphine Blue, Lime Green, Moss Green, Yellow. **References:** 1980, page 2 [1-3]

Driftwood Casual. Hi Ball. 12 oz. Charm Blue. Colors: Accent Red, Amber, Brown, Charm Blue, Crystal, Delphine Blue, Lime Green, Moss Green, Yellow. **References:** 1981, page 5 [2-2]; 1982, page 2 [2-2]

Driftwood Casual. Hi Ball. 12 oz. 5-1/8 inches tall. Colors: Accent Red, Amber, Brown, Charm Blue, Crystal, Delphine Blue, Lime Green, Moss Green, Yellow. **References:** 1982, page 16 [1-11]

Driftwood Casual. Hi Ball. 12 oz. Colors: Crystal, Charm Blue, Brown, Yellow, Moss Green. **References:** 1983, page 12 [2-2]

Driftwood Casual. Ice Tea. 16 oz. 5-3/4 inches tall. Colors: Moss Green, Heather (Pink), Amber, Delphine Blue (Dk.), Crystal, Peacock Blue (Lt.), Brown / Accent Red. **References:** 1967, page 24 [L-1]; 1968, page 30 [Not Shown]

Driftwood Casual. Ice Tea. 16 oz. 5-3/4 inches tall. Moss Green-Buttercup (Yellow), Amber-Delphine Blue (Dk.), Crystal-Peacock Blue (Lt.), Cinnamon (Brown), Accent Red. **References:** 1969, page 30 [Not Shown]

Driftwood Casual. Ice Tea. Colors: Accent Red, Amber, Brown, Charm Blue, Delphine Blue, Lime Green, Moss Green, Yellow. **References:** 1980, page 2 [1-2]

Driftwood Casual. Ice Tea. 16 oz. Brown. Colors: Accent Red, Amber, Brown, Charm Blue, Crystal, Delphine Blue, Lime Green, Moss Green, Yellow. **References:** 1981, page 5 [2-1]; 1982, page 2 [2-1]

Driftwood Casual. Ice Tea. 16 oz. 5-3/4 inches tall. Yellow. Colors: Accent Red, Amber, Brown, Charm Blue, Crystal, Delphine Blue, Lime Green, Moss Green, Yellow. **References:** 1982, page 16 [1-10]

Driftwood Casual. Ice Tea. 16 oz. Colors: Crystal, Charm Blue, Brown, Yellow, Moss Green. **References:** 1983, page 12 [2-1]

Driftwood Casual. Juice. 6 oz. **References:** 1964 Advertisement; 1964 Advertisement

Driftwood Casual. Juice. 6 oz. 4-3/16 inches tall. Colors: Moss Green, Heather (Pink), Amber, Delphine Blue (Dk.), Crystal, Peacock Blue (Lt.), Brown / Accent Red. **References:** 1967, page 24 [L-4]; 1968, page 30 [Not Shown]

Driftwood Casual. Juice. 6 oz. 4-1/4 inches tall. Moss Green-Buttercup (Yellow), Amber-Delphine Blue (Dk.), Crystal-Peacock Blue (Lt.), Cinnamon (Brown), Accent Red. **References:** 1969, page 30 [Not Shown]

Driftwood Casual. Juice. Delphine Blue. Colors: Accent Red, Amber, Brown, Charm Blue, Crystal, Delphine Blue, Lime Green, Moss Green, Ritz Blue, Yellow. **References:** 1979, page 9 [3-4]

Driftwood Casual. Juice. Colors: Accent Red, Amber, Brown, Charm Blue, Delphine Blue, Lime Green, Moss Green, Yellow. **References:** 1980, page 2 [1-4]

Driftwood Casual. Juice. 6 oz. Delphine Blue. Colors: Accent Red, Amber, Brown, Charm Blue, Crystal, Delphine Blue, Lime Green, Moss Green, Yellow. **References:** 1981, page 5 [2-6]; 1982, page 2 [2-6]

Driftwood Casual. Juice. 6 oz. 4-1/8 inches tall. Colors: Accent Red, Amber, Brown, Charm Blue, Crystal, Delphine Blue, Lime Green, Moss Green, Yellow. **References:** 1982, page 16 [1-15]

Driftwood Casual. Juice. 6 oz. Colors: Crystal, Charm Blue, Brown, Yellow, Moss Green. **References:** 1983, page 12 [2-6]

Driftwood Casual. Juice Pitcher. 32 oz. **References:** Advertisement

Driftwood Casual. Juice/Wine. Lime Green. Colors: Accent Red, Amber, Brown, Charm Blue, Crystal, Delphine Blue, Lime Green, Moss Green, Ritz Blue, Yellow. **References:** 1979, page 9 [3-2]

Driftwood Casual. Old Fashion. 9 oz. **References:** Advertisement

Driftwood Casual. Old Fashion. **References:** 1964 Advertisement; 1964 Advertisement

Driftwood Casual. On The Rocks. Ritz Blue. Colors: Accent Red, Amber, Brown, Charm Blue, Crystal, Delphine Blue, Lime Green, Moss Green, Ritz Blue, Yellow. **References:** 1979, page 9 [2-2]

Driftwood Casual. Parfait. 7 oz. 5 inches tall. Colors: Moss Green, Heather (Pink), Amber, Delphine Blue (Dk.), Crystal, Peacock Blue (Lt.), Brown / Accent Red. **References:** 1967, page 24 [Not Shown]; 1968, page 30 [Not Shown]

Driftwood Casual. Pitcher. 65 oz. **References:** 1964 Advertisement; 1964 Advertisement

Driftwood Casual. Pitcher. 65 oz. Colors: Moss Green, Heather (Pink), Amber, Delphine Blue (Dk.), Crystal, Peacock Blue (Lt.), Brown / Accent Red. **References:** 1967, page 24 [Not Shown]; 1968, page 30 [Not Shown]

Driftwood Casual. Pitcher. 65 oz. Colors: Moss Green-Buttercup (Yellow), Amber-Delphine Blue (Dk.), Crystal-Peacock Blue (Lt.), Cinnamon (Brown), Accent Red. **References:** 1969, page 30 [Not Shown]

Driftwood Casual. Pitcher. 65 oz. Accent Red. Colors: Accent Red, Amber, Brown, Charm Blue, Crystal, Delphine Blue, Lime Green, Moss Green, Ritz Blue, Yellow. **References:** 1979, page 9 [1-3]

Driftwood Casual. Pitcher. 65 oz. Colors: Moss Green, Heather (Pink), Amber, Delphine Blue (Dk.), Crystal, Peacock Blue (Lt.), Brown / Accent Red. **References:**

Driftwood Casual. Pitcher. 65 oz. Crystal. Colors: Accent Red, Amber, Brown, Charm Blue, Crystal, Delphine Blue, Lime Green, Moss Green, Yellow. **References:** 1981, page 5 [2-5]; 1982, page 2 [2-5]

Driftwood Casual. Pitcher. 65 oz. Yellow. Colors: Accent Red, Amber, Brown, Charm Blue, Crystal, Delphine Blue, Lime Green, Moss Green, Yellow. **References:** 1982, page 16 [1-14]

Driftwood Casual. Pitcher. 65 oz. Colors: Crystal, Charm Blue, Brown, Yellow, Moss Green. **References:** 1983, page 12 [2-5]

Driftwood Casual. Pitcher. 32 oz. Colors: Moss Green, Heather (Pink), Amber, Delphine Blue (Dk.), Crystal, Peacock Blue (Lt.), Brown. **References:** 1967, page 24 [L-5]; 1968, page 30 [Not Shown]

Driftwood Casual. Pitcher. 32 oz. Colors: Moss Green-Buttercup (Yellow), Amber-Delphine Blue (Dk.), Crystal-Peacock Blue (Lt.), Cinnamon (Brown). **References:** 1969, page 30 [Not Shown]

Driftwood Casual. Pitcher. 32 oz. Charm Blue. Colors: Accent Red, Amber, Brown, Charm Blue, Crystal, Delphine Blue, Lime Green, Moss Green, Ritz Blue, Yellow. **References:** 1979, page 9 [1-4]

Driftwood Casual. Pitcher. Colors: Accent Red, Amber, Brown, Charm Blue, Delphine Blue, Lime Green, Moss Green, Yellow. **References:** 1980, page 2 [2-4]

Driftwood Casual. Plate. 8 inches diam. **References:** 1964 Advertisement; 1964 Advertisement

Driftwood Casual. Plate. Crystal. Colors: Accent Red, Amber, Brown, Charm Blue, Crystal, Delphine Blue, Lime Green, Moss Green, Ritz Blue, Yellow. **References:** 1979, page 9 [1-2]

Driftwood Casual. Roly Poly. 12 oz. 3-3/8 inches tall. Colors: Moss Green, Heather (Pink), Amber, Delphine Blue (Dk.), Crystal, Peacock Blue (Lt.), Brown / Accent Red. **References:** 1967, page 24 [Not Shown]; 1968, page 30 [Not Shown]

Driftwood Casual. Roly Poly. 12 oz. 3-3/8 inches tall. Colors: Moss Green-Buttercup (Yellow), Amber-Delphine Blue (Dk.), Crystal-Peacock Blue (Lt.), Cinnamon (Brown), Accent Red. **References:** 1969, page 30 [Not Shown]

Driftwood Casual. Roly Poly. Amber. Colors: Accent Red, Amber, Brown, Charm Blue, Crystal, Delphine Blue, Lime Green, Moss Green, Ritz Blue, Yellow. **References:** 1979, page 9 [4-3]

Driftwood Casual. Salad or Fruit Bowl. **References:** Advertisement

Driftwood Casual. Salad Plate. 8-1/2 inches diam. Colors: Amber, Buttercup, Cinnamon, Crystal, Delphine Blue, Moss Green, Peacock Blue. **References:** Advertisement

Driftwood Casual. Salad Plate. 8-1/2 inches diam. Colors: Moss Green, Heather (Pink), Amber, Delphine Blue (Dk.), Crystal, Peacock Blue (Lt.), Brown. **References:** 1967, page 24 [Not Shown]; 1968, page 30 [Not Shown]

Driftwood Casual. Salad Plate. 8-1/2 inches diam. Colors: Moss Green-Buttercup (Yellow), Amber-Delphine Blue (Dk.), Crystal-Peacock Blue (Lt.), Cinnamon (Brown). **References:** 1969, page 30 [Not Shown]

Driftwood Casual. Sherbet. 3-3/4 inches diam. Colors: Moss Green, Heather (Pink), Amber, Delphine Blue (Dk.), Crystal, Peacock Blue (Lt.), Brown / Accent Red. **References:** 1967, page 24 [Not Shown]; 1968, page 30 [Not Shown]; 1969, page 30 [Not Shown]

Driftwood Casual. Sherbet. Colors: Accent Red, Amber, Brown, Charm Blue, Delphine Blue, Lime Green, Moss Green, Yellow. **References:** 1980, page 2 [2-2]

Driftwood Casual. Sherbet. 5 oz. Yellow. Colors: Accent Red, Amber, Brown, Charm Blue, Crystal, Delphine Blue, Lime Green, Moss Green, Yellow. **References:** 1981, page 5 [2-7]; 1982, page 2 [2-7]

Driftwood Casual. Sherbet. 3-3/4 oz. 3 inches tall. Brown. Colors: Accent Red, Amber, Brown, Charm Blue, Crystal, Delphine Blue, Lime Green, Moss Green, Yellow. **References:** 1982, page 16 [1-16]

Driftwood Casual. Sherbet. 5 oz. Colors: Crystal, Charm Blue, Brown, Yellow, Moss Green. **References:** 1983, page 12 [2-7]

Driftwood Casual. Sherbet, Footed. **References:** 1964 Advertisement; 1964 Advertisement

Driftwood Casual. Single Old Fashion. 9 oz. 3-1/2 inches tall. Colors: Moss Green, Heather (Pink), Amber, Delphine Blue (Dk.), Crystal, Peacock Blue (Lt.), Brown. **References:** 1967, page 24 [Not Shown]; 1968, page 30 [Not Shown]

Driftwood Casual. Table Tumbler. 10 oz. 4-1/8 inches tall. Colors: Moss Green, Heather (Pink), Amber, Delphine Blue (Dk.), Crystal, Peacock Blue (Lt.), Brown. **References:** 1967, page 24 [Bottom]; 1968, page 30 [Not Shown]

Driftwood Casual. Water Tumbler. 10 oz. **References:** 1964 Advertisement; 1964 Advertisement

Driftwood Casual. Line: 1980. Cooler. 22 oz. 6-3/4 inches tall. Colors: Moss Green. **References:** 1978, page 16 [1-1]

Driftwood Casual. Line: 1980. Cooler (Not Featured). Colors: Accent Red, Amber, Brown, Crystal, Delphine Blue, Lime Green, Moss Green, Ritz Blue, Yellow. **References:** 1977, page 12-13 [2-7]

Driftwood Casual. Line: 1980. Dessert-Cereal Bowl. 13-1/2 oz. 5-1/4 inches diam. Yellow. Colors: Accent Red, Amber, Brown, Crystal, Delphine Blue, Lime Green, Moss Green, Ritz Blue, Yellow. **References:** 1975, page 16-17 [2-3]; 1977, page 12-13 [2-3]

Driftwood Casual. Line: 1980. Double Old Fashion. 14 oz. 3-7/8 inches tall. Ritz Blue. Colors: Accent Red, Amber, Brown, Crystal, Delphine Blue, Lime Green, Moss Green, Ritz Blue, Yellow. **References:** 1975, page 16-17 [1-5]; 1977, page 12-13 [1-5]

Driftwood Casual. Line: 1980. Footed Compote. 13 oz. 4-3/4 inches tall. Accent Red. Colors: Accent Red, Amber, Brown, Crystal, Delphine Blue, Lime Green, Moss Green, Ritz Blue, Yellow. **References:** 1975, page 16-17 [2-5]; 1977, page 12-13 [2-5]

Driftwood Casual. Line: 1980. Footed Goblet. 13 oz. 5-3/8 inches tall. Accent Red. Colors: Accent Red, Amber, Brown, Crystal, Delphine Blue, Lime Green, Moss Green, Ritz Blue, Yellow. **References:** 1975, page 16-17 [1-6]; 1977, page 12-13 [1-6]

Driftwood Casual. Line: 1980. Footed Juice/Wine. 10 oz. 3-7/8 inches tall. Crystal. Colors: Accent Red, Amber, Brown, Crystal, Delphine Blue, Lime Green, Moss Green, Ritz Blue, Yellow. **References:** 1975, page 16-17 [2-2]; 1977, page 12-13 [2-2]

Driftwood Casual. Line: 1980. Goblet. 13 oz. 5-1/2 inches tall. Buttercup (Yellow). Colors Available: Amber, Cinnamon (Brown), Crystal, Delphine Blue, Grey, Moss Green, Peacock Blue, Accent Red. **References:** 1970, page 5 [1-1]; 1971, page 38 [2-3]; 1972, page 4 [2-3]

Driftwood Casual. Line: 1980. Goblet. 13 oz. 5-1/2 inches tall. Colors: Amber, Buttercup (Yellow), Cinnamon (Brown), Crystal, Delphine Blue, Grey, Moss Green, Peacock Blue, Accent Red, Plum. **References:** 1973, page 11 [1-1]

Driftwood Casual. Line: 1980. Hi Ball. 12 oz. 5-1/8 inches tall. Brown. Colors: Accent Red, Amber, Brown, Crystal, Delphine Blue, Lime Green, Moss Green, Ritz Blue, Yellow. **References:** 1975, page 16-17 [1-2]; 1977, page 12-13 [1-2]

Driftwood Casual. Line: 1980. Ice Tea. 16 oz. 5-3/4 inches tall. Delphine Blue. **References:** 1970, page 5 [1-5]

Driftwood Casual. Line: 1980. Ice Tea. 16 oz. 5-3/4 inches tall. Delphine Blue. Colors Available: Amber, Buttercup (Yellow), Cinnamon (Brown), Crystal, Delphine Blue, Grey, Moss Green, Peacock Blue, Accent Red. **References:** 1971, page 38 [2-1]

Driftwood Casual. Line: 1980. Ice Tea. 16 oz. 5-3/4 inches tall. Colors: Amber, Buttercup (Yellow), Cinnamon (Brown), Crystal, Delphine Blue, Grey, Moss Green, Peacock Blue, Accent Red. **References:** 1972, page 4 [2-1]; 1973, page 11 [2-1]; 1975, page 16-17 [1-1]; 1977, page 12-13 [1-1]

Driftwood Casual. Line: 1980. Juice. 6 oz. 4-1/8 inches tall. Delphine Blue. Colors: Accent Red, Amber, Brown, Crystal, Delphine Blue, Lime Green, Moss Green, Ritz Blue, Yellow. **References:** 1975, page 16-17 [2-6]; 1977, page 12-13 [2-6]

Driftwood Casual. Line: 1980. Old Fashion. 14 oz. 3-3/4 inches tall. Amber. **References:** 1970, page 5 [1-4]

Driftwood Casual. Line: 1980. Old Fashion. 14 oz. 3-3/4 inches tall. Amber. Colors Available: Buttercup (Yellow), Cinnamon (Brown), Crystal, Delphine Blue, Grey, Moss Green, Peacock Blue, Accent Red. **References:** 1971, page 38 [3-1]; 1972, page 4 [3-1]

Driftwood Casual. Line: 1980. Old Fashion. 14 oz. 3-3/4 inches tall. Colors: Amber, Buttercup (Yellow), Cinnamon (Brown), Crystal, Delphine Blue, Grey, Moss Green, Peacock Blue, Accent Red, Plum. **References:** 1973, page 11 [2-2]

Driftwood Casual. Line: 1980. On The Rocks. 9-3/4

oz. 3-7/8 inches tall. Yellow. Colors: Accent Red, Amber, Brown, Crystal, Delphine Blue, Lime Green, Moss Green, Ritz Blue, Yellow. **References:** 1975, page 16-17 [2-1]; 1977, page 12-13 [2-1]

Driftwood Casual. Line: 1980. Pitcher. 65 oz. 9-1/2 inches tall. Accent Red. Colors Available: Amber, Buttercup (Yellow), Cinnamon (Brown), Crystal, Delphine Blue, Grey, Moss Green, Peacock Blue, Accent Red. **References:** 1971, page 38 [1-1]; 1972, page 4 [1-1]

Driftwood Casual. Line: 1980. Pitcher. 32 oz. Ritz Blue. Colors: Accent Red, Amber, Brown, Crystal, Delphine Blue, Lime Green, Moss Green, Ritz Blue, Yellow. **References:** 1975, page 16-17 [1-3]

Driftwood Casual. Line: 1980. Pitcher. 65 oz. Accent Red. Colors: Accent Red, Amber, Brown, Crystal, Delphine Blue, Lime Green, Moss Green, Ritz Blue, Yellow. **References:** 1975, page 16-17 [1-7]

Driftwood Casual. Line: 1980. Pitcher. 32 oz. Ritz Blue. Colors: Accent Red, Amber, Brown, Crystal, Delphine Blue, Lime Green, Moss Green, Ritz Blue, Yellow. **References:** 1977, page 12-13 [1-3]

Driftwood Casual. Line: 1980. Pitcher. 65 oz. Accent Red. Colors: Accent Red, Amber, Brown, Crystal, Delphine Blue, Lime Green, Moss Green, Ritz Blue, Yellow. **References:** 1977, page 12-13 [1-7]

Driftwood Casual. Line: 1980. Roly Poly. 12 oz. 3-3/8 inches tall. Moss Green. **References:** 1970, page 5 [1-3]

Driftwood Casual. Line: 1980. Roly Poly. 12 oz. 3-3/8 inches tall. Moss Green. Colors Available: Amber, Buttercup (Yellow), Cinnamon (Brown), Crystal, Delphine Blue, Grey, Peacock Blue, Accent Red. **References:** 1971, page 38 [2-2]; 1972, page 4 [2-2]

Driftwood Casual. Line: 1980. Roly Poly. 12 oz. 3-1/2 inches tall. Amber. Colors: Accent Red, Amber, Brown, Crystal, Delphine Blue, Lime Green, Moss Green, Ritz Blue, Yellow. **References:** 1975, page 16-17 [1-4]; 1977, page 12-13 [1-4]

Driftwood Casual. Line: 1980. Salad Plate. 8-1/2 inches diam. Crystal. Colors: Accent Red, Amber, Brown, Crystal, Delphine Blue, Lime Green, Moss Green, Ritz Blue, Yellow. **References:** 1975, page 16-17 [2-4]; 1977, page 12-13 [2-4]

Driftwood Casual. Line: 1980. Sherbet. 6 oz. 3 inches tall. Cinnamon. **References:** 1970, page 5 [1-2]

Driftwood Casual. Line: 1980. Sherbet. 6 oz. 3 inches tall. Cinnamon (Brown). Colors Available: Amber, Buttercup (Yellow), Crystal, Delphine Blue, Grey, Moss Green, Peacock Blue, Accent Red. **References:** 1971, page 38 [3-2]; 1972, page 4 [3-2]

Driftwood Casual. Line: 1980. Sherbet. 6 oz. 3 inches tall. Colors: Amber, Buttercup (Yellow), Cinnamon (Brown), Crystal, Delphine Blue, Grey, Moss Green, Peacock Blue, Accent Red, Plum. **References:** 1973, page 11 [2-3]

Dundee. Line: 1235. Beverage. 13 oz. 5 inches tall. Crystal Full Sham. **References:** 1978, page 7 [3-3]; 1979, page 16 [3-3]

Dundee. Line: 1235. Old Fashion. 10 oz. 4 inches tall. Crystal Full Sham. **References:** 1978, page 7 [3-4]; 1979, page 16 [3-4]

Elegance. Line: 476. Cut: 967. 1311 Dessert-Finger Bowl. 4-3/4 inches diam. **References:** 1967, page 19 [2-9]; 1969, page 23 [2-9]; 1970, page 24 [2-9]; 1971, page 24 [2-9]

Elegance. Line: 476. Cut: 967. Claret. 3-1/2 oz. 6-1/8 inches tall. **References:** 1967, page 19 [2-3]; 1969, page 23 [2-3]; 1970, page 24 [2-3]; 1971, page 24 [2-3]

Elegance. Line: 476. Cut: 967. Cocktail. 3 oz. 5-1/4 inches tall. **References:** 1967, page 19 [2-5]; 1969, page 23 [2-5]; 1970, page 24 [2-5]; 1971, page 24 [2-5]

Elegance. Line: 476. Cut: 967. Cordial. 1 oz. 4-3/4 inches tall. **References:** 1967, page 19 [2-6]; 1969, page 23 [2-6]; 1970, page 24 [2-6]; 1971, page 24 [2-6]

Elegance. Line: 476. Cut: 967. Goblet. 9 oz. 8-3/8 inches tall. **References:** 1967, page 19 [2-1]; 1969, page 23 [2-1]; 1970, page 24 [2-1]; 1971, page 24 [2-1]

Elegance. Line: 476. Cut: 967. Ice Tea. 12 oz. 7-1/4 inches tall. **References:** 1967, page 19 [2-8]; 1969, page 23 [2-8]; 1970, page 24 [2-8]; 1971, page 24 [2-8]

Elegance. Line: 476. Cut: 967. Juice. 5-1/2 oz. 5-3/4 inches tall. **References:** 1967, page 19 [2-7]; 1969, page 23 [2-7]; 1970, page 24 [2-7]; 1971, page 24 [2-7]

Elegance. Line: 476. Cut: 967. Plate. 7 inches diam. Actually 7-7/8" Dia. **References:** 1967, page 19 [2-10]; 1969, page 23 [2-10]; 1970, page 24 [2-10]; 1971, page 24 [2-10]

Elegance. Line: 476. Cut: 967. Plate. 8 inches diam. Actually 8-3/4" Dia. **References:** 1967, page 19 [2-11]; 1969, page 23 [2-11]; 1970, page 24 [2-11]; 1971, page 24 [2-11]

Elegance. Line: 476. Cut: 967. Saucer Champagne. 6 oz. 6-1/2 inches tall. **References:** 1967, page 19 [2-2]; 1969, page 23 [2-2]; 1970, page 24 [2-2]; 1971, page 24 [2-2]

Elegance. Line: 476. Cut: 967. Wine. 3 oz. 6 inches tall. **References:** 1967, page 19 [2-4]; 1969, page 23 [2-4]; 1970, page 24 [2-4]; 1971, page 24 [2-4]

Elite Collection. Line: 982. Cut: 1445. Cordial. 2 oz. 4-3/4 inches tall. **References:** 1978, page 2 [1-4]

Elite Collection. Line: 982. Cut: 1445. Goblet. 13-1/2 oz. 7-1/2 inches tall. **References:** 1978, page 2 [1-1]

Elite Collection. Line: 982. Cut: 1445. Sherbet. 8 oz. 5-3/8 inches tall. **References:** 1978, page 2 [1-2]

Elite Collection. Line: 982. Cut: 1445. Wine. 7 oz. 6-3/8 inches tall. **References:** 1978, page 2 [1-3]

Elite Collection. Line: 982. Cut: 1454. Cordial. 2 oz. 4-3/4 inches tall. **References:** 1978, page 2 [1-8]

Elite Collection. Line: 982. Cut: 1454. Goblet. 13-1/2 oz. 7-1/2 inches tall. **References:** 1978, page 2 [1-5]

Elite Collection. Line: 982. Cut: 1454. Sherbet. 8 oz. 5-3/8 inches tall. **References:** 1978, page 2 [1-6]

Elite Collection. Line: 982. Cut: 1454. Wine. 7 oz. 6-3/8 inches tall. **References:** 1978, page 2 [1-7]

Elsinore. Line: 1975. Beverage. 16 oz. 5-3/4 inches tall. Grey. Colors: Crystal, Delphine Blue, Moss Green, Grey, Plum. **References:** 1972, page 7 [BR-1]

Elsinore. Line: 1975. Old Fashion. 12-1/2 oz. 3-3/4 inches tall. Grey. Colors: Crystal, Delphine Blue, Moss Green, Grey, Plum. **References:** 1972, page 7 [BR-2]

Elsinore. Line: 3825. Beverage. 17-1/2 oz. 5-1/2 inches tall. Moss Green. Colors: Crystal, Delphine Blue, Moss Green, Grey, Plum. **References:** 1972, page 7 [MR-1]; 1973, page 16 [MR-1]

Elsinore. Line: 3825. Old Fashion. 13 oz. 4 inches tall. Moss Green. Colors: Crystal, Delphine Blue, Moss Green, Grey, Plum. **References:** 1972, page 7 [MR-2]; 1973, page 16 [MR-2]

Embassy. All Purpose Wine Goblet. 8 oz. 5 inches tall. **References:** 1979, page 5 [1-6]

Embassy. Bell. 3-3/4 inches tall. **References:** 1979, page 12 [1-5]

Embassy. Champagne. 8 oz. 8-1/4 inches tall. **References:** 1983, page 2 [1-4]

Embassy. Champagne Flute. 6 oz. 9-1/4 inches tall. **References:** 1983, page 2 [1-7]

Embassy. Cordial. 1-1/4 oz. 3-3/4 inches tall. **References:** 1979, page 5 [1-7]; 1983, page 2 [1-5]

Embassy. Goblet. 12-1/2 oz. 6-5/8 inches tall. **References:** 1979, page 5 [1-1]; 1983, page 2 [1-1]

Embassy. Ice Tea. 13-1/2 oz. 6-1/4 inches tall. **References:** 1979, page 5 [1-8]; 1983, page 2 [1-6]

Embassy. Red Wine Goblet. 9-1/2 oz. 6-3/8 inches tall. **References:** 1979, page 5 [1-3]

Embassy. Sherbet. 6-1/2 oz. 5 inches tall. **References:** 1979, page 5 [1-2]; 1983, page 2 [1-2]

Embassy. Tulip Champagne. 8 oz. 8-1/2 inches tall. **References:** 1979, page 5 [1-5]

Embassy. White Wine Goblet. 7 oz. 5-3/4 inches tall. **References:** 1979, page 5 [1-4]; 1983, page 2 [1-3]

Embassy. Cut: 43. Cordial. 1-1/4 oz. 3-3/4 inches tall. **References:** 1982, page 5 [2-11]

Embassy. Cut: 43. Goblet. 12-1/2 oz. 6-5/8 inches tall. **References:** 1982, page 5 [2-7]

Embassy. Cut: 43. Sherbet. 6-1/2 oz. 5 inches tall. **References:** 1982, page 5 [2-8]

Embassy. Cut: 43. Tulip Champagne. 8 oz. 8-1/2 inches tall. **References:** 1982, page 5 [2-10]

Embassy. Cut: 43. White Wine Goblet. 7 oz. 5-3/4 inches tall. **References:** 1982, page 5 [2-9]

Embassy. Line: 1350. Cut: 43. 1305 Dessert-Finger Bowl. 4-1/2 inches diam. **References:** 1972, page 24 [1-11]; 1973, page 29 [1-11]; 1967, page 13 [1-9]; 1968, page 17 [1-9]; 1969, page 13 [1-11]; 1970, page 14 [1-11]; 1971, page 14 [1-11]; 1975, page 27 [1-9]; 1977, page 38 [1-9]

Embassy. Line: 1350. Cut: 43. All Purpose Wine Goblet. 8 oz. 5 inches tall. **References:** 1969, page 13 [1-6]; 1970, page 14 [1-6]; 1971, page 14 [1-6]; 1972, page 24 [1-6]; 1973, page 29 [1-6]; 1975, page 27 [1-6]; 1977, page 38 [1-6]

Embassy. Line: 1350. Cut: 43. Cocktail. 4-1/2 oz. / 4-3/4" hi. **References:** 1967, page 13 [1-5]; 1968, page 17 [1-5]; 1969, page 13 [1-7]; 1970, page 14 [1-7]; 1971, page 14 [1-7]; 1972, page 24 [1-7]; 1973, page 29 [1-7]

Embassy. Line: 1350. Cut: 43. Cordial. 1-1/4 oz. / 3-3/4" hi. **References:** 1967, page 13 [1-6]; 1968, page 17 [1-6]; 1969, page 13 [1-8]; 1970, page 14 [1-8]; 1971, page 14 [1-8]; 1972, page 24 [1-8]; 1973, page 29 [1-8]; 1975, page 27 [1-7]; 1977, page 38 [1-7]; 1981, page 3 [3-10]

Embassy. Line: 1350. Cut: 43. Goblet. 12-1/2oz. / 6-5/8" hi. **References:** 1967, page 13 [1-1]; 1968, page 17 [1-1]; 1969, page 13 [1-1]; 1970, page 14 [1-1]; 1971, page 14 [1-1]; 1972, page 24 [1-1]; 1973, page 29 [1-1]; 1975, page 27 [1-1]; 1977, page 38 [1-1]; 1981, page 3 [3-6]

Embassy. Line: 1350. Cut: 43. Ice Tea. 13-1/2 oz. / 6-1/4" hi. **References:** 1967, page 13 [1-8]; 1968, page 17 [1-8]; 1969, page 13 [1-10]; 1970, page 14 [1-10]; 1971, page 14 [1-10]; 1972, page 24 [1-10]; 1973, page 29 [1-10]; 1975, page 27 [1-8]; 1977, page 38 [1-8]

Embassy. Line: 1350. Cut: 43. Juice. 6-1/2 oz. / 5-1/4" hi. **References:** 1967, page 13 [1-7]; 1968, page 17 [1-7]; 1969, page 13 [1-9]; 1970, page 14 [1-9]; 1971, page 14 [1-9]; 1972, page 24 [1-9]; 1973, page 29 [1-9]

Embassy. Line: 1350. Cut: 43. Plate. 7" / Actually 7-7/8" Dia. **References:** 1967, page 13 [1-10]; 1968, page 17 [1-10]; 1969, page 13 [1-11]; 1970, page 14 [1-11]; 1971, page 14 [1-11]; 1972, page 24 [1-12]; 1973, page 29 [1-12]; 1975, page 27 [1-10]; 1977, page 38 [1-10]

Embassy. Line: 1350. Cut: 43. Plate. 8" / Actually 8-3/4" Dia. **References:** 1967, page 13 [1-11]; 1968, page 17 [1-11]; 1969, page 13 [1-13]; 1970, page 14 [1-13]; 1971, page 14 [1-13]; 1972, page 24 [1-13]; 1973, page 29 [1-13]; 1975, page 27 [1-11]; 1977, page 38 [1-11]

Embassy. Line: 1350. Cut: 43. Red Wine Goblet. 9-1/2 oz. / 6-3/8" hi. **References:** 1967, page 13 [1-3]; 1968, page 17 [1-3]; 1969, page 13 [1-3]; 1970, page 14 [1-3]; 1971, page 14 [1-3]; 1972, page 24 [1-3]; 1973, page 29 [1-3]; 1975, page 27 [1-3]; 1977, page 38 [1-3]

Embassy. Line: 1350. Cut: 43. Sherbet. 6-1/2 oz. / 5" hi. **References:** 1967, page 13 [1-2]; 1968, page 17 [1-2]; 1969, page 13 [1-2]; 1970, page 14 [1-2]; 1971, page 14 [1-2]; 1972, page 24 [1-2]; 1973, page 29 [1-2]; 1975, page 27 [1-2]; 1977, page 38 [1-2]; 1981, page 3 [3-7]

Embassy. Line: 1350. Cut: 43. Tulip Champagne. 8 oz. 8-1/2 inches tall. **References:** 1969, page 13 [1-5]; 1970, page 14 [1-5]; 1971, page 14 [1-5]; 1972, page 24 [1-5]; 1973, page 29 [1-5]; 1975, page 27 [1-5]; 1977, page 38 [1-5]; 1981, page 3 [3-9]

Embassy. Line: 1350. Cut: 43. White Wine. 7 oz. 5-3/4 inches tall. **References:** 1975, page 27 [1-4]; 1967, page 13 [1-4]; 1968, page 17 [1-4]; 1969, page 13 [1-4]; 1970, page 14 [1-4]; 1971, page 14 [1-4]; 1972, page 24 [1-4]; 1973, page 29 [1-4]; 1977, page 38 [1-4]; 1981, page 3 [3-8]

Empire. Line: 1975. Beverage. 13 oz. 5-3/4 inches tall. Crystal Full Sham. **References:** 1978, page 7 [2-2]; 1979, page 16 [2-2]

Empire. Line: 1975. Cooler. 16 oz. 7-3/8 inches tall. Crystal Full Sham. **References:** 1979, page 16 [2-1]

Empire. Line: 1975. Old Fashion. 10 oz. 4 inches tall. Crystal Full Sham. **References:** 1978, page 7 [2-3]; 1979, page 16 [2-3]

Empire. Line: 1975. Zombie Tumbler. 16 oz. 7-3/8 inches tall. Crystal Full Sham. **References:** 1978, page 7 [2-1]

Enchantment. Line: 1973. Cut: 1443. Sherbet. 7-1/2 oz. 5-1/8 inches tall. Pink/Crystal Foot. Colors & Designs Available: Blue/Crystal Foot, Pink/Crystal Foot, Blue/Crystal Foot/Cut 1443, Pink/Crystal Foot/Cut 1443, Black Decal and Gold Band, White Decal and Platinum Band. No price. **References:** 1971, page 40 [2-2]

Epicure Collection. Brandy Inhaler. 22 oz. 6 inches tall. **References:** 1979, page 10 [3-9]; 1981, page 9 [1-5]; 1981, page 9 [1-6]; 1982, page 6 [1-5]; 1982, page 6 [1-6]; 1982, page 3 [1-4]; 1982, page 3 [2-6]; 1983, page 10 [1-5]; 1983, page 10 [1-6]

Epicure Collection. Cocktail. 5-1/2 oz. 4-3/4 inches tall. **References:** 1979, page 10 [3-4]; 1982, page 3 [2-4]

Epicure Collection. Continental Beer. 14 oz. 8-1/8 inches tall. **References:** 1979, page 10 [3-8]; 1982, page 3 [2-9]

Epicure Collection. Cordial. 2 oz. 4-1/2 inches tall. **References:** 1979, page 10 [3-5]; 1981, page 9 [1-4]; 1982, page 6 [1-4]; 1982, page 3 [2-5]; 1983, page 10 [1-4]

Epicure Collection. Dessert-Champagne. 7-1/2 oz. 5-1/8 inches tall. **References:** 1979, page 10 [3-3]; 1981, page 9 [1-3]; 1982, page 6 [1-3]; 1982, page 3 [2-3]; 1983, page 10 [1-3]

Epicure Collection. Goblet. 12 oz. 7 inches tall. **References:** 1979, page 10 [3-1]; 1981, page 9 [1-1]; 1982, page 6 [1-1]; 1982, page 3 [2-1]; 1983, page 10 [1-1]

Epicure Collection. Ice Tea. 12 oz. 6-1/4 inches tall. **References:** 1979, page 10 [3-6]; 1982, page 3 [2-7]

Epicure Collection. Juice. 5 oz. 4-5/8 inches tall. **References:** 1982, page 3 [1-1]

Epicure Collection. Martini. 5-1/2 oz. 6 inches tall. **References:** 1981, page 9 [1-7]; 1982, page 6 [1-7]; 1982, page 3 [1-3]; 1983, page 10 [1-7]

Epicure Collection. Parfait-Whiskey Sour. 6-1/2 oz. 6-1/4 inches tall. **References:** 1982, page 3 [1-2]

Epicure Collection. Peach Champagne. 24 oz. 8-1/2 inches tall. **References:** 1979, page 10 [3-7]; 1982, page 3 [2-8]

Epicure Collection. Vintage Wine Goblet. 14 oz. 7 inches tall. **References:** 1979, page 10 [3-2]; 1981, page 9 [1-2]; 1982, page 6 [1-2]; 1982, page 3 [2-2]; 1983, page 10 [1-2]

Epicure Collection. Line: 1235. 1305 Dessert-Finger Bowl. 4-1/2" Dia. Plain Crystal, (No Cutting). **References:** 1967, page 10 [2-7]; 1969, page 17 [1-8]; 1970, page 18 [1-8]; 1971, page 18 [1-8]; 1972, page 27 [1-8]; 1973, page 32 [1-8]

Epicure Collection. Line: 1235. Beverage. 15 oz. 5 inches tall. **References:** 1972, page 13 [L-3]; 1975/I-75, page 10 [3-1]

Epicure Collection. Line: 1235. Beverage. 15 oz. 5 inches tall. Plain Lead Crystal. **References:** 1973, page 5 [1-12]

Epicure Collection. Line: 1235. Brandy Inhaler. 22 oz. 6 inches tall. **References:** 1972, page 13 [ML]; 1972, page 13 [ML]; 1975, page 5 [1-9]; 1977, page 5 [1-9]

Epicure Collection. Line: 1235. Brandy Inhaler. 22 oz. 6 inches tall. Plain Lead Crystal. **References:** 1973, page 5 [1-11]

Epicure Collection. Line: 1235. Cocktail. 5-1/2 oz. / 4-5/8" hi. Plain Crystal. **References:** 1967, page 10 [2-3]; 1969, page 17 [1-3]; 1970, page 18 [1-3]; 1971, page 18 [1-3]; 1972, page 27 [1-3]; 1973, page 5 [1-4]; 1973, page 32 [1-3]

Epicure Collection. Line: 1235. Cocktail. 5-1/2 oz. 4-3/4 inches tall. **References:** 1967, page 23 [L-2]; 1968, page 29 [L-2]; 1969, page 27 [L-2]; 1970, page 29 [BL]; 1971, page 29 [BL]; 1972, page 13 [BL]; 1975, page 5 [1-4]; 1977, page 5 [1-4]; 1975/I-75, page 10 [4-2]

Epicure Collection. Line: 1235. Continental Beer. 14 oz. 8-1/8 inches tall. **References:** 1967, page 23 [R-4]; 1968, page 29 [R-4]; 1969, page 27 [R-4]; 1970, page 29 [L-3]; 1971, page 29 [L-3]; 1972, page 13 [L-2]; 1975, page 5 [1-8]; 1977, page 5 [1-8]; 1975/I-75, page 10 [2-1]

Epicure Collection. Line: 1235. Continental Beer. 14 oz. 8-1/8 inches tall. Plain Lead Crystal. **References:** 1973, page 5 [1-10]

Epicure Collection. Line: 1235. Cordial. 2 oz. / 4-1/2" hi. Plain Crystal. **References:** 1967, page 10 [2-4]; 1969, page 17 [1-4]; 1970, page 18 [1-4]; 1971, page 18 [1-4]; 1972, page 27 [1-4]; 1973, page 5 [1-5]; 1973, page 32 [1-4]

Epicure Collection. Line: 1235. Cordial. 2 oz. 4-1/2 inches tall. **References:** 1967, page 23 [R-2]; 1968, page 29 [R-2]; 1969, page 27 [R-2]; 1970, page 29 [BM]; 1971, page 29 [BR]; 1972, page 13 [BR]; 1975, page 5 [1-5]; 1977, page 5 [1-5]; 1975/I-75, page 10 [4-3]

Epicure Collection. Line: 1235. Dessert-Champagne. 7-1/2 oz. 5-1/8 inches tall. **References:** 1972, page 13 [M]

Epicure Collection. Line: 1235. Dessert-Champagne. 7-1/2 oz. 5-1/8 inches tall. Plain Lead Crystal. **References:** 1973, page 5 [1-3]

Epicure Collection. Line: 1235. Dessert-Champagne. 7-1/2 oz. 5-1/8 inches tall. **References:** 1975, page 5 [1-3]; 1977, page 5 [1-3]; 1975/I-75, page 10 [2-2]

Epicure Collection. Line: 1235. Goblet. 12 oz. / 7" hi. Plain Crystal. **References:** 1967, page 10 [2-1]; 1969, page 17 [1-1]; 1970, page 18 [1-1]; 1971, page 18 [1-1]; 1972, page 27 [1-1]; 1973, page 5 [1-1]; 1973, page 32 [1-1]

Epicure Collection. Line: 1235. Goblet. 12 oz. 7 inches tall. **References:** 1967, page 23 [L-1]; 1968, page 29 [L-1]; 1969, page 27 [L-1]; 1970, page 29 [L-1]; 1971, page 29 [L-1]; 1972, page 13 [L-1]; 1975, page 5 [1-1]; 1977, page 5 [1-1]; 1975/I-75, page 10 [1-1]

Epicure Collection. Line: 1235. Ice Tea. 12 oz. / 6-1/4" hi. Plain Crystal. **References:** 1967, page 10 [2-6]; 1969, page 17 [1-7]; 1970, page 18 [1-7]; 1971, page 18 [1-7]; 1972, page 27 [1-7]; 1973, page 5 [1-8]; 1973, page 32 [1-7]

Epicure Collection. Line: 1235. Ice Tea. 12 oz. 6-1/4 inches tall. **References:** 1967, page 23 [R-3]; 1968, page 29 [R-3]; 1969, page 27 [R-3]; 1970, page 29 [R-2]; 1971, page 29 [R-2]; 1972, page 13 [R-3]; 1975, page 5 [1-6]; 1977, page 5 [1-6]; 1975/I-75, page 10 [3-4]

Epicure Collection. Line: 1235. Juice. 5 oz. / 4-1/2" hi. Plain Crystal. **References:** 1967, page 10 [2-5]; 1969, page 17 [1-6]; 1970, page 18 [1-6]; 1971, page 18 [1-6]; 1972, page 27 [1-6]; 1973, page 5 [1-7]; 1973, page 32 [1-6]

Epicure Collection. Line: 1235. Juice. 5 oz. 4-5/8 inches tall. **References:** 1967, page 23 [L-3]; 1968, page 29 [L-3]; 1969, page 27 [L-3]; 1970, page 29 [BR]; 1971, page 29 [R-4]; 1972, page 13 [R-4]; 1975/I-75, page 10 [4-4]

Epicure Collection. Line: 1235. Old Fashion. 11-1/2 oz. 3-3/4 inches tall. **References:** 1972, page 13 [L-4]; 1975/I-75, page 10 [4-1]

Epicure Collection. Line: 1235. Old Fashion. 11-1/2 oz. 3-3/4 inches tall. Plain Lead Crystal. **References:** 1973, page 5 [1-13]

Epicure Collection. Line: 1235. Parfait Whiskey Sour. 7 oz. 6-1/4 inches tall. Plain Crystal. **References:** 1969, page 17 [1-5]; 1970, page 18 [1-5]; 1971, page 18 [1-5]; 1972, page 27 [1-5]; 1973, page 32 [1-5]

Epicure Collection. Line: 1235. Parfait-Whiskey Sour. 7 oz. 6-1/4 inches tall. **References:** 1968, page 29 [L-2]; 1970, page 29 [L-2]; 1970, page 29 [L-2]; 1971, page 29 [L-2]; 1972, page 13 [MR]; 1975/I-75, page 10 [3-3]

Epicure Collection. Line: 1235. Parfait-Whiskey Sour. 7 oz. 6-1/4 inches tall. Plain Lead Crystal. **References:** 1973, page 5 [1-6]

Epicure Collection. Line: 1235. Peach Champagne. 24 oz. 8-1/2 inches tall. **References:** 1967, page 23 [L-4]; 1968, page 29 [L-4]; 1969, page 27 [L-4]; 1970, page 29 [L-3]; 1971, page 29 [R-3]; 1972, page 13 [R-2]; 1975, page 5 [1-7]; 1977, page 5 [1-7]; 1975/I-75, page 10 [2-3]

Epicure Collection. Line: 1235. Peach Champagne. 24 oz. 8-1/2 inches tall. Plain Lead Crystal. **References:** 1973, page 5 [1-9]

Epicure Collection. Line: 1235. Plate. 7" / 7-7/8" Dia. Plain Crystal, (No Cutting). **References:** 1967, page 10 [2-8]; 1969, page 17 [1-9]; 1970, page 18 [1-9]; 1971, page 18 [1-9]; 1972, page 27 [1-9]; 1973, page 32 [1-9]

Epicure Collection. Line: 1235. Plate. 8" / 8-3/4" Dia. Plain Crystal, (No Cutting). **References:** 1967, page 10 [2-9]; 1969, page 17 [1-10]; 1970, page 18 [1-10]; 1971, page 18 [1-10]; 1972, page 27 [1-10]; 1973, page 32 [1-10]

Epicure Collection. Line: 1235. Sherbet. 7-1/2 oz. / 5-1/8" hi. Plain Crystal. **References:** 1967, page 10 [2-2]; 1969, page 17 [1-2]; 1970, page 18 [1-2]; 1971, page 18 [1-2]; 1972, page 27 [1-2]; 1973, page 32 [1-2]

Epicure Collection. Line: 1235. Sherbet. 7-1/2 oz. 5-1/8 inches tall. **References:** 1967, page 23 [R-1]; 1968, page 29 [R-1]; 1969, page 27 [R-1]; 1970, page 29 [R-1]; 1971, page 29 [L-4]

Epicure Collection. Line: 1235. Vintage Wine Goblet. 14 oz. 7 inches tall. **References:** 1971, page 29 [R-1]; 1972, page 13 [R-1]; 1975, page 5 [1-2]; 1977, page 5 [1-2]; 1977, page 5 [1-2]; 1975/I-75, page 10 [1-2]

Epicure Collection. Line: 1235. Vintage Wine Goblet. 14 oz. 7 inches tall. Plain Lead Crystal. **References:** 1973, page 5 [1-2]

Epicure Collection. Line: 1235 (463). Brandy Inhaler. 23 oz. 5-3/4 inches tall. **References:** 1975/I-75, page 10 [3-2]

Falerno. Brandy and Liqueur. 2-1/2 oz. 6 inches tall. **References:** 1979, page 5 [2-14]

Falerno. Cabinet Wine Goblet. 15-1/2 oz. 9-1/8 inches tall. **References:** 1979, page 5 [2-8]

Falerno. Dessert-Champagne. 7-1/2 oz. 6-1/8 inches tall. **References:** 1979, page 5 [2-13]

Falerno. Red Wine Goblet. 12-1/2 oz. 8-5/8 inches tall. **References:** 1979, page 5 [2-9]

Falerno. Sherry and Port. 5 oz. 7 inches tall. **References:** 1979, page 5 [2-12]

Falerno. Sparkling Wine Goblet. 9 oz. 8 inches tall. **References:** 1979, page 5 [2-10]

Falerno. White Wine Goblet. 7 oz. 7-5/8 inches tall. **References:** 1979, page 5 [2-11]

Falerno. Line: 1977. Cut: 43. Brandy and Liqueur. 2-1/2 oz. 6 inches tall. **References:** 1973, page 7 [1-7]; 1975, page 7 [1-7]; 1977, page 7 [1-7]

Falerno. Line: 1977. Cut: 43. Cabinet Wine Goblet. 15-1/2 oz. 9-1/8 inches tall. **References:** 1973, page 7 [1-1]; 1975, page 7 [1-1]; 1977, page 7 [1-1]

Falerno. Line: 1977. Cut: 43. Dessert-Champagne. 7-1/2 oz. 6-1/8 inches tall. **References:** 1973, page 7 [1-6]; 1975, page 7 [1-6]; 1977, page 7 [1-6]

Falerno. Line: 1977. Cut: 43. Red Wine Goblet. 12-1/2 oz. 8-5/8 inches tall. **References:** 1973, page 7 [1-2]; 1975, page 7 [1-2]; 1977, page 7 [1-2]

Falerno. Line: 1977. Cut: 43. Sherry and Port. 5 oz. 7 inches tall. **References:** 1973, page 7 [1-5]; 1975, page 7 [1-5]; 1977, page 7 [1-5]

Falerno. Line: 1977. Cut: 43. Sparkling Wine Goblet. 9 oz. 8 inches tall. **References:** 1973, page 7 [1-3]; 1975, page 7 [1-3]; 1977, page 7 [1-3]

Falerno. Line: 1977. Cut: 43. White Wine. 7 oz. 7-5/8 inches tall. **References:** 1975, page 7 [1-4]; 1973, page 7 [1-4]; 1977, page 7 [1-4]

Fantasy. Line: 1963. Cut: 1406. Cocktail. 5-1/2 oz. / 4-3/4" hi. Platinum Band. **References:** 1967, page 11 [2-40]; 1968, page 15 [2-40]; 1967, page 11 [2-41]

Fantasy. Line: 1963. Cut: 1406. Cordial. 1-1/2 oz. / 4" hi. Platinum Band. **References:** 1968, page 15 [2-41]; 1967, page 11 [2-37]; 1968, page 15 [2-37]

Fantasy. Line: 1963. Cut: 1406. Ice Tea. 14 oz. / 6-1/4" hi. Platinum Band. **References:** 1967, page 11 [2-43]; 1968, page 15 [2-43]

Fantasy. Line: 1963. Cut: 1406. Juice. 7 oz. / 5-1/4" hi. Platinum Band. **References:** 1967, page 11 [2-42]; 1968, page 15 [2-42]

Fantasy. Line: 1963. Cut: 1406. Plate. 7" / Actually 7-7/8" Dia. Platinum Band. **References:** 1967, page 11 [2-44]; 1968, page 15 [2-44]

Fantasy. Line: 1963. Cut: 1406. Plate. 8" / Actually 8-3/4" Dia. Platinum Band. **References:** 1967, page 11 [2-45]; 1968, page 15 [2-45]

Fantasy. Line: 1963. Cut: 1406. Sherbet. 7-1/2 oz. / 5-1/8" hi. Platinum Band. **References:** 1967, page 11 [2-38]; 1968, page 15 [2-38]

Fantasy. Line: 1963. Cut: 1406. Wine. 7-3/4 oz. / 5-3/4" hi. Platinum Band. **References:** 1967, page 11 [2 39]; 1968, page 15 [2-39]

Fascination. Cordial. 3 oz. 5-5/8 inches tall. **References:** 1979, page 4 [3-12]

Fascination. Goblet. 14 oz. 7-7/8 inches tall. **References:** 1979, page 4 [3-9]

Fascination. Sherbet. 9 oz. 5-1/2 inches tall. **References:** 1979, page 4 [3-10]

Fascination. Wine. 5-3/4 oz. 6-1/2 inches tall. **References:** 1979, page 4 [3-11]

Fascination. Line: 4. Bell. 5-1/2 inches tall. Optic. **References:** 1977, page 23 [1-1]

Fascination. Line: 4. Bell. 5-1/2 inches tall. All Bells Individually Gift Boxed. **References:** 1979, page 13 [3-2]

Fascination. Line: 978. Cordial. 3 oz. 5-5/8 inches tall. **References:** 1976, page 10 [1-4]

Fascination. Line: 978. Cordial. 3 oz. 5-5/8 inches tall. Crystal Optic. **References:** 1977, page 20 [1-4]

Fascination. Line: 978. Goblet. 14 oz. 7-7/8 inches tall. **References:** 1976, page 10 [1-1]

Fascination. Line: 978. Goblet. 14 oz. 7-7/8 inches tall. Crystal Optic. **References:** 1977, page 20 [1-1]

Fascination. Line: 978. Sherbet. 9 oz. 5-1/2 inches tall. **References:** 1976, page 10 [1-2]

Fascination. Line: 978. Sherbet. 9 oz. 5-1/2 inches tall. Crystal Optic. **References:** 1977, page 20 [1-2]

Fascination. Line: 978. Wine. 5-3/4 oz. 6-1/2 inches tall. **References:** 1976, page 10 [1-3]

Fascination. Line: 978. Wine. 5-3/4 oz. 6-1/2 inches tall. Crystal Optic. **References:** 1977, page 20 [1-3]

Fashionables, The. High Stem Dessert. 11-1/2 oz. 4-5/8 inches tall. Colors: Accent Red, Black, Brown, Charm Blue, Crystal, Delphine Blue, Lime Green, Moss Green, Rtiz Blue, Yellow. **References:** 1979, page 8 [3-2]

Fashionables, The. High Stem Goblet. 12-1/2 oz. 6-1/4 inches tall. Colors: Accent Red, Black, Brown, Charm Blue, Crystal, Delphine Blue, Lime Green, Moss Green, Rtiz Blue, Yellow. **References:** 1979, page 8 [3-1]

Fashionables, The. High Stem Ice Tea. 15 oz. 6-5/8 inches tall. Colors: Accent Red, Black, Brown, Charm Blue, Crystal, Delphine Blue, Lime Green, Moss Green, Rtiz Blue, Yellow. **References:** 1979, page 8 [3-4]

Fashionables, The. High Stem Juice/Wine. 7-1/2 oz. 5-3/8 inches tall. Colors: Accent Red, Black, Brown, Charm Blue, Crystal, Delphine Blue, Lime Green, Moss Green, Rtiz Blue, Yellow. **References:** 1979, page 8 [3-3]

Fashionables, The. Low Stem Beverage. 14 oz. 5 inches tall. Colors: Accent Red, Black, Brown, Charm Blue, Crystal, Delphine Blue, Lime Green, Moss Green, Rtiz Blue, Yellow. **References:** 1979, page 8 [3-9]

Fashionables, The. Low Stem Dessert. 11-1/2 oz. 2-7/8 inches tall. Colors: Accent Red, Black, Brown, Charm Blue, Crystal, Delphine Blue, Lime Green, Moss Green, Rtiz Blue, Yellow. **References:** 1979, page 8 [3-6]

Fashionables, The. Low Stem Goblet. 12-1/2 oz. 4-1/4 inches tall. Colors: Accent Red, Black, Brown, Charm Blue, Crystal, Delphine Blue, Lime Green, Moss Green, Rtiz Blue, Yellow. **References:** 1979, page 8 [3-5]

Fashionables, The. Low Stem Juice/Wine. 7-1/2 oz. 3-1/2 inches tall. Colors: Accent Red, Black, Brown, Charm Blue, Crystal, Delphine Blue, Lime Green, Moss Green, Rtiz Blue, Yellow. **References:** 1979, page 8 [3-7]

Fashionables, The. Low Stem Old Fashion. 9-1/2 oz. 4 inches tall. Colors: Accent Red, Black, Brown, Charm Blue, Crystal, Delphine Blue, Lime Green, Moss Green, Rtiz Blue, Yellow. **References:** 1979, page 8 [3-8]

Fashionables, The. Line: 1974. Set. Beverage. 14 oz. 5 inches tall. Crystal with Black Foot, Mixer 40oz./Glasses 7-1/2oz. Colors: Black, Brown, Crystal, Crystal with Black Foot, Delphine Blue, Green, Plum. **References:** 1972, page 3 [2-3]

Fashionables, The. Line: 1974. Beverage. 14 oz. 5 inches tall. Colors: Black, Brown, Crystal, Crystal w/Black Foot, Delphine Blue, Green, Plum, Yellow. **References:** 1973, page 12 [1-2]

Fashionables, The. Line: 1974. Beverage. 14 oz. 5 inches tall. Black, Plain Crystal. Colors: Accent Red, Black, Brown, Crystal, Delphine Blue, Moss Green, Ritz Blue, Yellow. **References:** 1975, page 14 [2-5]

Fashionables, The. Line: 1974. Beverage. 14 oz. 5 inches tall. Black. Colors: Accent Red, Black, Brown, Crystal, Delphine Blue, Lime Green, Moss Green, Ritz Blue, Yellow. **References:** 1977, page 16 [2-5]

Fashionables, The. Line: 1974. Cocktail/Juice 6 pc. Set. Mixer 40 oz., Glasses 7-1/2 oz. Colors: Black, Brown, Crystal, Crystal w/Black Foot, Delphine Blue, Green, Plum, Yellow. **References:** 1973, page 13 [1-1]

Fashionables, The. Line: 1974. Cocktail/Juice Set. Crystal with Black Foot, Mixer 40oz./Glasses 7-1/2oz. Colors: Black, Brown, Crystal, Crystal with Black Foot, Delphine blue, Green, Plum. **References:** 1972, page 3 [1-1]

Fashionables, The. Line: 1974. Dessert. 11-1/2 oz. 2-7/8 inches tall. Crystal/Black Foot. Colors Available: Black, Brown, Crystal, Crystal with Black Foot, Delphine Blue, Green. **References:** 1971, page 37 [3-2]

Fashionables, The. Line: 1974. Set. Dessert. 11-1/2 oz. 2-7/8 inches tall. Crystal with Black Foot, Mixer 40oz./Glasses 7-1/2oz. Colors: Black, Brown, Crystal, Crystal with Black Foot, Delphine blue, Green, Plum. **References:** 1972, page 3 [3-1]

Fashionables, The. Line: 1974L. Dessert. 11-1/2 oz. 2-7/8 inches tall. Colors: Black, Crystal, Delphine Blue, Green, Plum, Yellow. **References:** 1973, page 12 [3-1]; 1973, page 13 [2-1]

Fashionables, The. Line: 1974. Goblet. 12-1/2 oz. 4-1/4 inches tall. Delphine Blue. Colors Available: Black, Brown, Crystal, Crystal with Black Foot, Delphine Blue, Green. **References:** 1971, page 37 [1-1]

Fashionables, The. Line: 1974. Goblet. 12-1/2 oz. 4-1/4 inches tall. Crystal/Black Foot. Colors Available: Black, Brown, Crystal, Crystal with Black Foot, Delphine Blue, Green. **References:** 1971, page 37 [2-2]

Fashionables, The. Line: 1974. Set. Goblet. 12-1/2 oz. 4-1/4 inches tall. Crystal with Black Foot, Mixer 40oz./Glasses 7-1/2oz. Colors: Black, Brown, Crystal, Crystal with Black Foot, Delphine blue, Green, Plum. **References:** 1972, page 3 [2-2]

Fashionables, The. Line: 1974H. Goblet. 12-1/2 oz. 6-1/4 inches tall. Colors: Black, Crystal, Delphine Blue, Green, Plum, Yellow. **References:** 1973, page 12 [2-1]; 1973, page 12 [2-2]

Fashionables, The. Line: 1974. Goblet, Bloody Mary Set. 15-1/2 oz. 6-3/4 inches tall. Lead Crystal w/ Black Foot. **References:** 1978, page 10 [1-2]

Fashionables, The. Line: 1974. High Stem Dessert. 11-1/2 oz. 4-5/8 inches tall. Crystal, Plain Crystal. Colors: Accent Red, Black, Brown, Crystal, Delphine Blue, Moss Green, Ritz Blue, Yellow. **References:** 1975, page 14 [1-2]

Fashionables, The. Line: 1974. High Stem Dessert. 11-1/2 oz. 4-5/8 inches tall. Crystal, Hourglass Optic. Colors: Accent Red, Black, Brown, Crystal, Delphine Blue, Moss Green, Ritz Blue, Yellow. **References:** 1975, page 15 [1-2]

Fashionables, The. Line: 1974. High Stem Dessert. 11-1/2 oz. 4-5/8 inches tall. Crystal. Colors: Accent Red, Black, Brown, Crystal, Delphine Blue, Lime Green, Moss Green, Ritz Blue, Yellow. **References:** 1977, page 16 [1-2]

Fashionables, The. Line: 1974. High Stem Goblet. 12-1/2 oz. 6-1/4 inches tall. Ritz Blue, Plain Crystal. Colors: Accent Red, Black, Brown, Crystal, Delphine Blue, Moss Green, Ritz Blue, Yellow. **References:** 1975, page 14 [1-1]

Fashionables, The. Line: 1974. High Stem Goblet. 12-1/2 oz. 6-1/4 inches tall. Ritz Blue, Hourglass Optic. Colors: Accent Red, Black, Brown, Crystal, Delphine Blue, Moss Green, Ritz Blue, Yellow. **References:** 1975, page 15 [1-1]

Fashionables, The. Line: 1974. High Stem Goblet. 12-1/2 oz. 6-1/4 inches tall. Ritz Blue. Colors: Accent Red, Black, Brown, Crystal, Delphine Blue, Lime Green, Moss Green, Ritz Blue, Yellow. **References:** 1977, page 16 [1-1]

Fashionables, The. Line: 1974. High Stem Ice Tea. 15 oz. 6-5/8 inches tall. Black, Plain Crystal. Colors: Accent Red, Black, Brown, Crystal, Delphine Blue, Moss Green, Ritz Blue, Yellow. **References:** 1975, page 14 [1-4]

Fashionables, The. Line: 1974. High Stem Ice Tea. 15 oz. 6-5/8 inches tall. Black, Hourglass Optic. Colors: Accent Red, Black, Brown, Crystal, Delphine Blue, Moss Green, Ritz Blue, Yellow. **References:** 1975, page 15 [1-4]

Fashionables, The. Line: 1974. High Stem Ice Tea. 15 oz. 6 5/8 inches tall. Black. Colors: Accent Red, Black, Brown, Crystal, Delphine Blue, Lime Green, Moss Green, Ritz Blue, Yellow. **References:** 1977, page 16 [1-4]

Fashionables, The. Line: 1974. High Stem Juice/Wine. 7-1/2 oz. 5-3/8 inches tall. Yellow, Plain Crystal. Colors: Accent Red, Black, Brown, Crystal, Delphine Blue, Moss Green, Ritz Blue, Yellow. **References:** 1975, page 14 [1-3]

Fashionables, The. Line: 1974. High Stem Juice/Wine. 7-1/2 oz. 5-3/8 inches tall. Yellow, Hourglass Optic. Colors: Accent Red, Black, Brown, Crystal, Delphine Blue, Moss Green, Ritz Blue, Yellow. **References:** 1975, page 15 [1-3]

Fashionables, The. Line: 1974. High Stem Juice/Wine. 7-1/2 oz. 5-3/8 inches tall. Yellow. Colors: Accent Red, Black, Brown, Crystal, Delphine Blue, Lime Green, Moss Green, Ritz Blue, Yellow. **References:** 1977, page 16 [1-3]

Fashionables, The. Line: 1974. Juice/Wine. 7-1/2 oz. 3-1/2 inches tall. Colors Available: Black, Brown, Crystal, Crystal with Black Foot, Delphine Blue, Green. **References:** 1971, page 37 [2-1]; 1971, page 37 [3-1]

Fashionables, The. Line: 1974. Set. Juice/Wine. 7-1/2 oz. 3-1/2 inches tall. Crystal with Black Foot, Mixer 40oz./Glasses 7-1/2oz. Colors: Black, Brown, Crystal, Crystal with Black Foot, Delphine blue, Green, Plum. **References:** 1972, page 3 [3-2]

Fashionables, The. Line: 1974L. Juice/Wine. 7-1/2 oz. 3-1/2 inches tall. Colors: Black, Crystal, Delphine Blue, Green, Plum, Yellow. **References:** 1973, page 12 [3-2]

Fashionables, The. Line: 1974H. Juice/Wine. 7-1/2 oz. 5-3/8 inches tall. Colors: Black, Crystal, Delphine Blue, Green, Plum, Yellow. **References:** 1973, page 13 [1-2]

Fashionables, The. Line: 1974. Low Stem Dessert. 11-1/2 oz. 2-7/8 inches tall. Colors: Accent Red, Black, Brown, Crystal, Delphine Blue, Moss Green, Ritz Blue, Yellow. **References:** 1975, page 14 [2-2]; 1977, page 16 [2-2]

Fashionables, The. Line: 1974. Low Stem Dessert. 11-1/2 oz. 2-7/8 inches tall. Delphine Blue, Hourglass Optic. Colors: Accent Red, Black, Brown, Crystal, Delphine Blue, Moss Green, Ritz Blue, Yellow. **References:** 1975, page 15 [2-2]

Fashionables, The. Line: 1974. Low Stem Goblet. 12-1/2 oz. 4-1/4 inches tall. Accent Red, Plain Crystal. Colors: Accent Red, Black, Brown, Crystal, Delphine Blue, Moss Green, Ritz Blue, Yellow. **References:** 1975, page 14 [2-1]; 1977, page 16 [2-1]

Fashionables, The. Line: 1974. Low Stem Goblet. 12-1/2 oz. 4-1/4 inches tall. Hourglass Optic. Colors: Accent Red, Black, Brown, Crystal, Delphine Blue, Moss Green, Ritz Blue, Yellow. **References:** 1975, page 15 [2-1]

Fashionables, The. Line: 1974. Low Stem Juice/ Wine. 7-1/2 oz. 3-1/2 inches tall. Plain Crystal. Colors: Accent Red, Black, Brown, Crystal, Delphine Blue, Moss Green, Ritz Blue, Yellow. **References:** 1975, page 14 [2-3]

Fashionables, The. Line: 1974. Low Stem Juice/ Wine. 7-1/2 oz. 3-1/2 inches tall. Hourglass Optic. Colors: Accent Red, Black, Brown, Crystal, Delphine Blue, Moss Green, Ritz Blue, Yellow. **References:** 1975, page 15 [2-3]

Fashionables, The. Line: 1974. Low Stem Juice/ Wine. 7-1/2 oz. 3-1/2 inches tall. Colors: Accent Red, Black, Brown, Crystal, Delphine Blue, Lime Green, Moss Green, Ritz Blue, Yellow. **References:** 1977, page 16 [2-3]

Fashionables, The. Line: 1974. Mixer, Bloody Mary Set. 40 oz. Lead Crystal w/Black Foot With Stir Rod. **References:** 1978, page 10 [1-1]

Fashionables, The. Line: 1974. Set. Old Fashion. 9-1/2 oz. 4 inches tall. Crystal with Black Foot, Mixer 40oz./Glasses 7-1/2oz. Colors: Black, Brown, Crystal, Crystal with Black Foot, Delphine blue, Green, Plum. **References:** 1972, page 3 [2-1]

Fashionables, The. Line: 1974. Old Fashion. 9-1/2 oz. 4 inches tall. Colors: Black, Brown, Crystal, Crystal w/Black Foot, Delphine Blue, Green, Plum, Yellow. **References:** 1973, page 12 [1-1]

Fashionables, The. Line: 1974. Old Fashion. 9-1/2 oz. 4 inches tall. Brown, Plain Crystal. Colors: Accent Red, Black, Brown, Crystal, Delphine Blue, Moss Green, Ritz Blue, Yellow. **References:** 1975, page 14 [2-4]

Fashionables, The. Line: 1974. Old Fashion. 9-1/2 oz. 4 inches tall. Brown. Colors: Accent Red, Black, Brown, Crystal, Delphine Blue, Lime Green, Moss Green, Ritz Blue, Yellow. **References:** 1977, page 16 [2-4]

First Lady. Champagne Flute. 6 oz. 9-1/4 inches tall. **References:** 1983, page 3 [2-16]

First Lady. Cocktail. **References:** 1964 Advertisement

First Lady. Cordial. **References:** 1964 Advertisement

First Lady. Cordial. 1-1/2 oz. 4 inches tall. **References:** 1979, page 2 [2-4]; 1983, page 3 [2-17]

First Lady. Footed Ice Tea. **References:** 1964 Advertisement

First Lady. Footed Juice. **References:** 1964 Advertisement

First Lady. Goblet. **References:** 1964 Advertise-ment; 1964 Advertisement

First Lady. Goblet. 13-1/2 oz. 6-3/4 inches tall. **References:** 1979, page 2 [2-1]; 1983, page 3 [2-13]

First Lady. Ice Tea. 14 oz. 6-1/4 inches tall. **References:** 1979, page 2 [2-5]; 1983, page 3 [2-18]

First Lady. Saucer Champagne. **References:** 1964 Advertisement; 1964 Advertisement

First Lady. Sherbet. 7-1/2 oz. 5-1/8 inches tall. **References:** 1979, page 2 [2-2]; 1983, page 3 [2-14]

First Lady. Water Goblet. **References:** 1964 Advertisement

First Lady. White Wine Goblet. **References:** 1964 Advertisement

First Lady. Wine. **References:** 1964 Advertisement

First Lady. Wine. 7-3/4 oz. 5-3/4 inches tall. **References:** 1979, page 2 [2-3]; 1983, page 3 [2-15]

First Lady. Line: 1963. Cut: 1408. 1305 Dessert-Finger Bowl. 4-1/4 inches diam. **References:** 1970, page 13 [1-8]; 1976, page 26 [1-6]; 1977, page 37 [1-6]

First Lady. Line: 1963. Cut: 1408. Cocktail. 5-1/2 oz. 4-3/4 inches tall. **References:** 1970, page 13 [1-4]

First Lady. Line: 1963. Cut: 1408. Cordial. 1-1/2 oz. 4 inches tall. **References:** 1970, page 13 [1-5]; 1975, page 26 [1-4]; 1977, page 37 [1-4]; 1981, page 1 [1-12]

First Lady. Line: 1963. Cut: 1408. Goblet. 13-1/2 oz. 6-3/4 inches tall. **References:** 1970, page 13 [1-1]; 1975, page 26 [1-1]; 1977, page 37 [1-1]; 1981, page 1 [1-9]

First Lady. Line: 1963. Cut: 1408. Ice Tea. 14 oz. 6-1/4 inches tall. **References:** 1970, page 13 [1-7]; 1975, page 26 [1-5]; 1977, page 37 [1-5]

First Lady. Line: 1963. Cut: 1408. Juice. 7 oz. 5-1/4 inches tall. **References:** 1970, page 13 [1-6]

First Lady. Line: 1963. Cut: 1408. Plate. 7 inches diam. Actually 7-7/8" Dia. **References:** 1970, page 13 [1-9]; 1975, page 26 [1-7]; 1977, page 37 [1-7]

First Lady. Line: 1963. Cut: 1408. Plate. 8 inches diam. Actually 8-3/4" Dia. **References:** 1970, page 13 [1-10]; 1975, page 26 [1-8]; 1977, page 37 [1-8]

First Lady. Line: 1963. Cut: 1408. Sherbet. 7-1/2 oz. 5-1/8 inches tall. **References:** 1970, page 13 [1-2]; 1975, page 26 [1-2]; 1977, page 37 [1-2]; 1981, page 1 [1-10]

First Lady. Line: 1963. Cut: 1408. Wine. 7-3/4 oz. 5-3/4 inches tall. **References:** 1970, page 13 [1-3]; 1975, page 26 [1-3]; 1977, page 37 [1-3]; 1981, page 1 [1-11]

First Lady. Line: 1963. Cut: 1409. 1305 Dessert-Finger Bowl. 4-1/4" Dia. **References:** 1967, page 8 [1-8]; 1968, page 12 [1-8]; 1969, page 12 [1-8]; 1971, page 13 [1-8]; 1972, page 22 [1-8]; 1973, page 26 [1-8]

First Lady. Line: 1963. Cut: 1409. Cocktail. 5-1/2 oz. / 4-3/4" hi. **References:** 1967, page 8 [1-4]; 1968, page 12 [1-4]; 1969, page 12 [1-4]; 1971, page 13 [1-4]; 1972, page 22 [1-4]; 1973, page 26 [1-4]

First Lady. Line: 1963. Cut: 1409. Cordial. 1-1/2 oz. / 4" hi. **References:** 1967, page 8 [1-5]; 1968, page 12 [1-5]; 1969, page 12 [1-5]; 1971, page 13 [1-5]; 1972, page 22 [1-5]; 1973, page 26 [1-5]

First Lady. Line: 1963. Cut: 1409. Goblet. 13-1/2 oz. / 6-3/4" hi. **References:** 1967, page 8 [1-1]; 1968, page 12 [1-1]; 1969, page 12 [1-1]; 1971, page 13 [1-1]; 1972, page 22 [1-1]; 1973, page 26 [1-1]

First Lady. Line: 1963. Cut: 1409. Ice Tea. 14 oz. / 6-1/4" hi. **References:** 1967, page 8 [1-7]; 1968, page 12 [1-7]; 1969, page 12 [1-7]; 1971, page 13 [1-7]; 1972, page 22 [1-7]; 1973, page 26 [1-7]

First Lady. Line: 1963. Cut: 1409. Juice. 7 oz. / 5-1/4" hi. **References:** 1967, page 8 [1-6]; 1968, page 12 [1-6]; 1969, page 12 [1-6]; 1971, page 13 [1-6]; 1972, page 22 [1-6]; 1973, page 26 [1-6]

First Lady. Line: 1963. Cut: 1409. Plate. 7" / Actually 7-7/8" Dia. **References:** 1967, page 8 [1-9]; 1968, page 12 [1-9]; 1969, page 12 [1-9]; 1971, page 13 [1-9]; 1972, page 22 [1-9]; 1973, page 26 [1-9]

First Lady. Line: 1963. Cut: 1409. Plate. 8" / Actually 8-3/4" Dia. **References:** 1967, page 8 [1-10]; 1968, page 12 [1-10]; 1969, page 12 [1-10]; 1971, page 13 [1-10]; 1972, page 22 [1-10]; 1973, page 26 [1-10]

First Lady. Line: 1963. Cut: 1409. Sherbet. 7-1/2 oz. / 5-1/8" hi. **References:** 1967, page 8 [1-2]; 1968, page 11 [1-2]; 1969, page 11 [1-2]; 1971, page 13 [1-2]; 1972, page 22 [1-2]; 1973, page 26 [1-2]

First Lady. Line: 1963. Cut: 1409. Wine. 7-3/4 oz. / 5-3/4" hi. **References:** 1967, page 8 [1-3]; 1968, page 12 [1-3]; 1969, page 12 [1-3]; 1971, page 13 [1-3]; 1972, page 22 [1-3]; 1973, page 26 [1-3]

Floral Garden. Bell. **References:** 1983, page 6 [3-1L]

Floral Garden. Bud Vase/Candle Holder. 4 inches tall. **References:** 1983, page 7 [3-1R]

Floral Garden. Bud Vase/Candle Holder. 2 inches tall. **References:** 1983, page 7 [3-4R]

Floral Garden. Candle Holder. 5-1/2 inches tall. **References:** 1983, page 7 [3-5R]

Floral Garden. Candle Holder. 6-1/2 inches tall. **References:** 1983, page 7 [3-7R]

Floral Garden. Line: 70. Vase. 7 inches tall. **References:** 1983, page 7 [1-4R]

Floral Garden. Line: 90. Ginger Jar. 8-1/2 inches tall. **References:** 1983, page 7 [1-2R]

Floral Garden. Line: 98. Bud Vase. 6 inches tall. **References:** 1983, page 7 [1-5R]

Frank Schoonmaker Collection. Cabernet. 9 oz. 6-1/2 inches tall. **References:** 1967, page 22 [L-3]; 1968, page 28 [L-3]; 1969, page 26 [L-3]; 1970, page 28 [L-3]; 1971, page 28 [L-3]; 1972, page 12 [L-3]; 1973, page 4 [1-5]; 1975, page 4 [1-5]; 1977, page 4 [1-5]; 1979, page 10 [2-5]; 1981, page 8 [1-5]; 1982, page 5 [1-5]; 1982, page 2 [1-5]; 1983, page 9 [1-5]; 1975/I-75, page 9 [3-1]

Frank Schoonmaker Collection. Champagne Tulip. 8 oz. 8-1/2 inches tall. **References:** 1967, page 22 [L-1]; 1968, page 28 [L-1]; 1969, page 26 [L-1]; 1970, page 28 [L-1]; 1971, page 28 [L-1]; 1972, page 12 [L-1]; 1973, page 4 [1-1]; 1975, page 4 [1-1]; 1977, page 4 [1-1]; 1979, page 10 [2-1]; 1981, page 8 [1-1]; 1982, page 5 [1-1]; 1982, page 2 [1-1]; 1983, page 9 [1-1]

Frank Schoonmaker Collection. Champagne Tulip. 8-1/2 oz. 8-1/4 inches tall. Plain Crystal. **References:** 1975/I-75, page 9 [1-1]

Frank Schoonmaker Collection. Chateau. 7 oz. 6 inches tall. **References:** 1967, page 22 [R-4]; 1968, page 28 [R-4]; 1969, page 26 [R-4]; 1970, page 28 [R-4]; 1971, page 28 [R-4]; 1972, page 12 [R-4]; 1973, page 4 [1-8]; 1975, page 4 [1-8]; 1977, page 4 [1-8]; 1979, page 10 [2-8]; 1981, page 8 [1-8]; 1982, page 5 [1-8]; 1982, page 2 [1-8]; 1983, page 9 [1-8]; 1975/I-75, page 9 [4-2]

Frank Schoonmaker Collection. Johannisberg. 6 oz. 6-1/8 inches tall. **References:** 1967, page 22 [R-1]; 1968, page 28 [R-1]; 1969, page 26 [R-1]; 1970, page 28 [R-1]; 1971, page 28 [R-1]; 1972, page 12 [R-1]; 1973, page 4 [1-2]; 1975, page 4 [1-2]; 1977, page 4 [1-2]; 1979, page 10 [2-2]; 1981, page 8 [1-2]; 1982, page 5 [1-2]; 1982, page 2 [1-2]; 1983, page 9 [1-2]

Frank Schoonmaker Collection. Johannisberg. 6 oz. 6-1/8 inches tall. Plain Crystal. **References:** 1975/I-75, page 9 [1-2]

Frank Schoonmaker Collection. Magnum. 10 oz. 5-7/8 inches tall. **References:** 1967, page 22 [L-2]; 1968, page 28 [L-2]; 1969, page 26 [L-2]; 1970, page 28 [L-2]; 1971, page 28 [L-2]; 1972, page 12 [L-2]; 1973, page 4 [1-3]; 1975, page 4 [1-3]; 1977, page 4 [1-3]; 1979, page 10 [2-3]; 1981, page 8 [1-3]; 1982, page 5 [1-3]; 1982, page 2 [1-3]; 1983, page 9 [1-3]

Frank Schoonmaker Collection. Magnum. 10 oz. 5-7/8 inches tall. Plain Crystal. **References:** 1975/I-75, page 9 [2-1]

Frank Schoonmaker Collection. Solera. 5 oz. 5-1/8 inches tall. **References:** 1967, page 22 [R-3]; 1968, page 28 [R-3]; 1969, page 26 [R-3]; 1970, page 28 [R-3]; 1971, page 28 [R-3]; 1972, page 12 [R-3]; 1973, page 4 [1-6]; 1975, page 4 [1-5]; 1977, page 4 [1-5]; 1979, page 10 [2-6]; 1981, page 8 [1-6]; 1982, page 5 [1-6]; 1982, page 2 [1-6]; 1983, page 9 [1-6]; 1975/I-75, page 9 [3-2]

Frank Schoonmaker Collection. V.S.O.P. 7 oz. 4-1/2 inches tall. **References:** 1967, page 22 [L-4]; 1968, page 28 [L-4]; 1969, page 26 [L-4]; 1970, page 28 [L-4]; 1971, page 28 [L-4]; 1972, page 12 [L-4]; 1973, page 4 [1-7]; 1975, page 4 [1-7]; 1977, page 4 [1-7]; 1979, page 10 [2-7]; 1981, page 8 [1-7]; 1982, page 5 [1-7]; 1982, page 2 [1-7]; 1983, page 9 [1-7]; 1975/I-75, page 9 [4-1]

Frank Schoonmaker Collection. Vin Du Pays. 8 oz. 5-3/8 inches tall. **References:** 1967, page 22 [R-2]; 1968, page 28 [R-2]; 1969, page 26 [R-2]; 1970, page 28 [R-2]; 1971, page 28 [R-2]; 1972, page 12 [R-2]; 1973, page 4 [1-4]; 1975, page 4 [1-4]; 1977, page 4 [1-4]; 1979, page 10 [2-4]; 1981, page 8 [1-4]; 1982, page 5 [1-4]; 1982, page 2 [1-4]; 1983, page 9 [1-4]; 1975/I-75, page 9 [2-2]

Galaxy. Line: 1973. 1305 Dessert-Finger Bowl. 4-1/2 inches diam. Plain Crystal. **References:** 1971, page 11 [2-6]; 1972, page 20 [2-6]; 1973, page 27 [2-6]; 1971, page 11 [2-4]

Galaxy. Line: 1973. Cordial. 1-1/2 oz. 4 inches tall. Pink/Crystal Foot. Colors & Designs Available: Blue/Crystal Foot, Pink/Crystal Foot, Blue/ Crystal Foot/Cut 1443, Pink/Crystal Foot/Cut 1443, Black Decal and Gold Band, White Decal and Platinum Band. **References:** 1971, page 40 [2-4]

Galaxy. Line: 1973. Cordial. 1-1/2 oz. 4 inches tall. Plain Crystal. **References:** 1972, page 20 [2-4]; 1973, page 27 [2-4]

Galaxy. Line: 1973. Goblet. 13 oz. 7 inches tall. Plain Crystal. **References:** 1971, page 11 [2-1]; 1972, page 20 [2-1]; 1973, page 27 [2-1]

Galaxy. Line: 1973. Ice Tea. 17-1/2 oz. 7-1/8 inches tall. Plain Crystal. **References:** 1971, page 11 [2-5]

Galaxy. Line: 1973. Ice Tea. 17-1/2 oz. 7-1/8 inches tall. Blue/Crystal Foot. Colors & Designs Available: Blue/Crystal Foot, Pink/Crystal Foot, Blue/Crystal Foot/Cut 1443, Pink/Crystal Foot/ Cut 1443, Black Decal and Gold Band, White Decal and Platinum Band. **References:** 1971, page 40 [1-2]

Galaxy. Line: 1973. Ice Tea. 17-1/2 oz. 7-1/8 inches tall. Plain Crystal. **References:** 1972, page 20 [2-5]; 1973, page 27 [2-5]

Galaxy. Line: 1973. Plate. 7 inches diam. Plain Crystal, Actually 7-7/8" Dia. **References:** 1971, page 11 [2-7]; 1972, page 20 [2-7]; 1973, page 27 [2-7]

Galaxy. Line: 1973. Plate. 8 inches diam. Plain Crystal, Actually 8-3/4" Dia. **References:** 1971, page 11 [2-8]; 1972, page 20 [2-8]; 1973, page 27 [2-8]

Galaxy. Line: 1973. Sherbet. 7-1/2 oz. 5-1/8 inches tall. Plain Crystal. **References:** 1971, page 11 [2-2]; 1972, page 20 [2-2]; 1973, page 27 [2-2]

Galaxy. Line: 1973. Wine. 8-1/2 oz. 6-3/8 inches tall. Plain Crystal. **References:** 1971, page 11 [2-3]; 1972, page 20 [2-3]; 1973, page 27 [2-3]

Garland. Champagne Flute. 6 oz. 9-1/4 inches tall. **References:** 1983, page 4 [3-16]

Garland. Cordial. 3 oz. 5-1/2 inches tall. **References:** 1983, page 4 [3-17]

Garland. Goblet. 13 oz. 7-1/2 inches tall. **References:** 1983, page 4 [3-13]

Garland. Ice Tea. 14 oz. 6-1/2 inches tall. **References:** 1983, page 4 [3-18]

Garland. Sherbet. 9 oz. 6 inches tall. **References:** 1983, page 4 [3-14]

Garland. Wine. 7-1/2 oz. 6-1/2 inches tall. **References:** 1983, page 4 [3-15]

Garland. Line: 972. Cut: 1463. Cordial. 3 oz. 5-5/8 inches tall. **References:** 1982, page 2 [2-4]

Garland. Line: 972. Cut: 1463. Goblet. 13 oz. 7-1/2 inches tall. **References:** 1982, page 2 [2-1]

Garland. Line: 972. Cut: 1463. Ice Tea. 14 oz. 6-1/2 inches tall. **References:** 1982, page 2 [2-5]

Garland. Line: 972. Cut: 1463. Sherbet. 9 oz. 6 inches tall. **References:** 1982, page 2 [2-2]

Garland. Line: 972. Cut: 1463. Wine. 7-1/2 oz. 6-1/2 inches tall. **References:** 1982, page 2 [2-3]

Gentry. Line: 4025. Beverage. 17 oz. 5-1/4 inches tall. Delphine Blue. Colors: Crystal, Delphine Blue, Moss Green, Grey, Plum. **References:** 1972, page 7 [ML-2]; 1973, page 16 [ML-2]

Gentry. Line: 4025. Old Fashion. 11-1/2 oz. 3-3/4 inches tall. Delphine Blue. Colors: Crystal, Delphine Blue, Moss Green, Grey, Plum. **References:** 1972, page 7 [ML-1]; 1973, page 16 [ML-1]

Gold Brocade. Champagne Flute. 6 oz. 9-1/4 inches tall. **References:** 1983, page 3 [1-15]

Gold Brocade. Cordial. 1-1/2 oz. 4 inches tall. **References:** 1979, page 2 [3-4]; 1983, page 3 [1-17]

Gold Brocade. Goblet. 11-1/2 oz. 7 inches tall. **References:** 1979, page 2 [3-1]; 1983, page 3 [1-13]

Gold Brocade. Ice Tea. 14 oz. 6-1/4 inches tall. **References:** 1979, page 2 [3-5]; 1983, page 3 [1-18]

Gold Brocade. Sherbet. 7 oz. 5-1/4 inches tall. **References:** 1979, page 2 [3-2]; 1983, page 3 [1-14]

Gold Brocade. Wine. 7 oz. 6 inches tall. **References:** 1979, page 2 [3-3]; 1983, page 3 [1-16]

Gold Brocade. Line: 960. Cut: 1436. Plate. 8 inches diam. Actually 8-3/4" Dia., 2 Gold Bands. **References:** 1975, page 21 [2-16]; 1977, page 32 [2-16]

Gold Brocade. Line: 960. Cut: 1438. 1311 Dessert-Finger Bowlr. 4-3/4 inches diam. With 2 Gold Bands. **References:** 1970, page 7 [2-14]; 1971, page 7 [2-14]; 1972, page 16 [2-14]; 1973, page 21 [2-14]; 1975, page 21 [2-14]; 1977, page 32 [2-14]

Gold Brocade. Line: 960. Cut: 1438. Cordial. 1-1/4 oz. 3-7/8 inches tall. With 2 Gold Bands. **References:** 1970, page 7 [2-12]; 1971, page 7 [2-12]; 1972, page 16 [2-12]; 1973, page 21 [2-12]; 1975, page 21 [2-12]; 1977, page 32 [2-12]; 1981, page 2 [1-8]

Gold Brocade. Line: 960. Cut: 1438. Goblet. 11-1/2 oz. 7 inches tall. With 2 Gold Bands. **References:** 1970, page 7 [2-9]; 1971, page 7 [2-9]; 1972, page 16 [2-9]; 1973, page 21 [2-9]; 1975, page 21 [2-9]; 1977, page 32 [2-9]

Gold Brocade. Line: 960. Cut: 1438. Goblet. 11-1/2 oz. 7 inches tall. **References:** 1981, page 2 [1-5]

Gold Brocade. Line: 960. Cut: 1438. Ice Tea. 14 oz. 6-1/4 inches tall. With 2 Gold Bands. **References:** 1970, page 7 [2-13]; 1971, page 7 [2-13]; 1972, page 16 [2-13]; 1973, page 21 [2-13]; 1975, page 21 [2-13]; 1977, page 32 [2-13]

Gold Brocade. Line: 960. Cut: 1438. Plate. 7 inches diam. With 2 Gold Bands, Actually 7-7/8" Dia. **References:** 1970, page 7 [2-15]; 1971, page 7 [2-15]; 1972, page 16 [2-15]; 1973, page 21 [2-15]; 1975, page 21 [2-15]

Gold Brocade. Line: 960. Cut: 1438. Plate. 8 inches diam. With 2 Gold Bands, Actually 8-3/4" Dia. **References:** 1970, page 7 [2-16]; 1971, page 7 [2-16]; 1972, page 16 [2-16]; 1973, page 21 [2-16]; 1977, page 32 [2-15]

Gold Brocade. Line: 960. Cut: 1438. Sherbet. 7 oz. 5-1/4 inches tall. With 2 Gold Bands. **References:** 1970, page 7 [2-10]; 1971, page 7 [2-10]; 1972, page 16 [2-10]; 1973, page 21 [2-10]; 1975, page 21 [2-10]; 1977, page 32 [2-10]; 1981, page 2 [1-6]

Gold Brocade. Line: 960. Cut: 1438. Wine. 7 oz. 6 inches tall. With 2 Gold Bands. **References:** 1970, page 7 [2-11]; 1971, page 7 [2-11]; 1972, page 16 [2-11]; 1973, page 21 [2-11]; 1975, page 21 [2-11]; 1977, page 32 [2-11]; 1981, page 2 [1-7]

Gold Florentine. Line: 1973. 1305 Dessert-Finger Bowl. 4-1/2 inches diam. Black Decal and Gold Band. **References:** 1971, page 11 [1-14]; 1972, page 20 [1-14]; 1973, page 27 [1-14]

Gold Florentine. Line: 1973. Cordial. 1-1/2 oz. 4 inches tall. Black Decal and Gold Band. **References:** 1971, page 11 [1-12]; 1972, page 20 [1-12]; 1973, page 27 [1-12]

Gold Florentine. Line: 1973. Goblet. 13 oz. 7 inches tall. Black Decal and Gold Band. **References:** 1971, page 11 [1-9]

Gold Florentine. Line: 1973. Goblet. 13 oz. 7 inches tall. Black Decal/ Gold Band. Colors & Designs Available: Blue/Crystal Foot, Pink/Crystal Foot, Blue/Crystal Foot/Cut 1443, Pink/Crystal Foot/ Cut 1443, Black Decal and Gold Band, White Decal and Platinum Band. **References:** 1971, page 40 [2-1]

Gold Florentine. Line: 1973. Goblet. 13 oz. 7 inches tall. Black Decal and Gold Band. **References:** 1972, page 20 [1-9]; 1973, page 27 [1-9]

Gold Florentine. Line: 1973. Ice Tea. 17-1/2 oz. 7-1/8 inches tall. Black Decal and Gold Band. **References:** 1971, page 11 [1-13]; 1972, page 20 [1-13]; 1973, page 27 [1-13]

Gold Florentine. Line: 1973. Plate. 7 inches diam. Black Decal and Gold Band, Actually 7-7/8" Dia. **References:** 1971, page 11 [1-15]; 1972, page 20 [1-15]; 1973, page 27 [1-15]

Gold Florentine. Line: 1973. Plate. 8 inches diam. Black Decal and Gold Band, Actually 8-3/4" Dia. **References:** 1971, page 11 [1-16]; 1972, page 20 [1-16]; 1973, page 27 [1-16]

Gold Florentine. Line: 1973. Sherbet. 7-1/2 oz. 5-1/8 inches tall. Black Decal and Gold Band. **References:** 1971, page 11 [1-10]; 1972, page 20 [1-10]; 1973, page 27 [1-10]

Gold Florentine. Line: 1973. Wine. 8-1/2 oz. 6-3/8 inches tall. Black Decal and Gold Band. **References:** 1971, page 11 [1-11]; 1972, page 20 [1-11]; 1973, page 27 [1-11]

Gourmet Collection. Brandy and Liqueur. 2-1/2 oz. 4-1/2 inches tall. **References:** 1979, page 10 [1-8]; 1981, page 7 [1-9]; 1982, page 4 [1-9]; 1982, page 1 [1-9]; 1983, page 8 [1-9]; 1975/I-75, page 8 [1-2]

Gourmet Collection. Brandy-Liqueur. 2-1/2 oz. **References:** 1980, page 6 [2-2]

Gourmet Collection. Champagne. 9-1/2 oz. 8 inches tall. **References:** 1979, page 10 [1-6]

Gourmet Collection. Champagne. 9-1/2 oz. **References:** 1980, page 6 [2-3]

Gourmet Collection. Champagne. 9-1/2 oz. 8 inches tall. **References:** 1981, page 7 [1-6]; 1982, page 4 [1-6]; 1982, page 1 [1-6]; 1975/I-75, page 8 [1-7]

Gourmet Collection. Champagne. 9-1/2 oz. 8-1/4 inches tall. **References:** 1983, page 8 [1-6]

Gourmet Collection. Champagne Flute. 6 oz. 9-1/4 inches tall. **References:** 1981, page 7 [1-7]; 1982, page 4 [1-7]; 1982, page 1 [1-7]; 1983, page 8 [1-7]

Gourmet Collection. Dessert-Champagne. 11 oz. 4-7/8 inches tall. **References:** 1979, page 10 [1-7]; 1981, page 7 [1-8]; 1982, page 4 [1-8]; 1982, page 1 [1-8]; 1983, page 8 [1-8]; 1975/I-75, page 8 [1-4]

Gourmet Collection. Dessert-Champagne. 11 oz. **References:** 1980, page 6 [3-2]

Gourmet Collection. Grande Bordeaux. 24 oz. 7-5/8 inches tall. **References:** 1979, page 10 [1-1]; 1981, page 7 [1-1]; 1982, page 4 [1-1]; 1982, page 1 [1-1]

Gourmet Collection. Grande Bordeaux. 24 oz. 7-1/2 inches tall. **References:** 1980, page 6 [3-4]; 1983, page 8 [1-1]

Gourmet Collection. Magnum Wine Goblet. 18 oz. 7-3/8 inches tall. **References:** 1980, page 6 [1-6]; 1979, page 10 [1-2]; 1981, page 7 [1-2]; 1982, page 4 [1-2]; 1982, page 1 [1-2]; 1983, page 8 [1-2]; 1975/I-75, page 8 [1-1]

Gourmet Collection. Red Wine Goblet. 10-1/2 oz. 6-7/8 inches tall. **References:** 1979, page 10 [1-4]; 1980, page 6 [2-1]; 1981, page 7 [1-4]; 1982, page 4 [1-4]; 1982, page 1 [1-4]; 1983, page 8 [1-4]; 1975/I-75, page 8 [1-3]

Gourmet Collection. Sherry and Port. 5 oz. 6 inches tall. **References:** 1979, page 10 [1-9]; 1981, page 7 [1-10]; 1982, page 4 [1-10]; 1982, page 1 [1-10]; 1983, page 8 [1-10]; 1975/I-75, page 8 [1-8]; 1980, page 6 [3-3]

Gourmet Collection. Vintage Wine Goblet. 14 oz. 7 inches tall. **References:** 1979, page 10 [1-3]; 1980, page 6 [1-5]; 1981, page 7 [1-3]; 1982, page 4 [1-3]; 1982, page 1 [1-3]; 1983, page 8 [1-3]; 1975/I-75, page 8 [1-5]

Gourmet Collection. White Wine. 8-1/2 oz. 6-5/8 inches tall. **References:** 1975/I-75, page 8 [1-6]; 1979, page 10 [1-5]; 1980, page 6 [3-1]; 1981, page 7 [1-5]; 1982, page 4 [1-5]; 1982, page 1 [1-5]; 1983, page 8 [1-5]

Gourmet Collection. Line: 6. Bottle. 30 oz. **References:** 1980, page 6 [1-4]

Gourmet Collection. Line: 120. Carafe. 20 oz. **References:** 1980, page 6 [1-3]

Gourmet Collection. Line: 132. Carafe. 32 oz. **References:** 1980, page 6 [1-2]

Gourmet Collection. Line: 140. Carafe. 40 oz. **References:** 1980, page 6 [1-1]

Gourmet Collection. Line: 5321. Brandy and Liqueur. 2-1/2 oz. 4-1/2 inches tall. Plain Crystal. **References:** 1971, page 27 [1-8]; 1972, page 11 [1-8]; 1973, page 3 [1-9]; 1975, page 2-3 [1-9]; 1977, page 2-3 [1-9]

Gourmet Collection. Line: 5321. Champagne. 9-1/2 oz. 8 inches tall. Plain Crystal. **References:** 1971, page 27 [1-5]; 1972, page 11 [1-5]; 1973, page 3 [1-6]; 1975, page 2-3 [1-6]; 1977, page 2-3 [1-6]

Gourmet Collection. Line: 5321. Dessert-Champagne. 11 oz. 4-7/8 inches tall. Plain Crystal. **References:** 1971, page 27 [1-7]; 1972, page 11 [1-7]; 1973, page 3 [1-8]; 1975, page 2-3 [1-8]; 1977, page 2-3 [1-8]

Gourmet Collection. Line: 5321. Grande Bordeaux. 24 oz. 7-5/8 inches tall. Plain Crystal. **References:** 1973, page 2 [1-1]; 1975, page 2-3 [1-1]; 1977, page 2-3 [1-1]

Gourmet Collection. Line: 5321. Magnum Wine Goblet. 18 oz. 7-3/8 inches tall. Plain Crystal. **References:** 1971, page 27 [1-1]; 1972, page 11 [1-1]; 1973, page 2 [1-2]; 1975, page 2-3 [1-2]; 1977, page 2-3 [1-2]

Gourmet Collection. Line: 5321. Red Wine Goblet. 10-1/2 oz. 6-7/8 inches tall. Plain Crystal. **References:** 1971, page 27 [1-3]; 1972, page 11 [1-3]; 1973, page 2 [1-4]; 1975, page 2-3 [1-4]; 1977, page 2-3 [1-4]

Gourmet Collection. Line: 5321. Sherry and Port. 5 oz. 6 inches tall. Plain Crystal. **References:** 1971, page 27 [1-6]; 1972, page 11 [1-6]; 1973, page 3 [1-7]; 1975, page 2-3 [1-7]; 1977, page 2-3 [1-7]

Gourmet Collection. Line: 5321. Vintage Wine Goblet. 14 oz. 7 inches tall. Plain Crystal. **References:** 1971, page 27 [1-2]; 1972, page 11 [1-2]; 1973, page 2 [1-3]; 1975, page 2-3 [1-3]; 1977, page 2-3 [1-3]

Gourmet Collection. Line: 5321. White Wine. 8-1/2 oz. 6-5/8 inches tall. Plain Lead. **References:** 1975, page 2-3 [1-5]; 1971, page 27 [1-4]; 1972, page 11 [1-4]; 1973, page 2 [1-5]; 1977, page 2-3 [1-5]

Grace. Cordial. 1-1/2 oz. 4 inches tall. **References:** 1979, page 4 [2-10]

Grace. Goblet. 13-1/2 oz. 6-3/4 inches tall. **References:** 1979, page 4 [2-7]

Grace. Ice Tea. 14 oz. 6-3/4 inches tall. **References:** 1979, page 4 [2-11]

Grace. Sherbet. 7-1/2 oz. 5-1/8 inches tall. **References:** 1979, page 4 [2-8]

Grace. Wine. 7-3/4 oz. 5-3/4 inches tall. **References:** 1979, page 4 [2-9]

Grace. Line: 1963. Cut: 63. 1305 Dessert-Finger Bowl. 4-1/2" Dia. **References:** 1967, page 8 [2-18]; 1968, page 12 [2-18]; 1969, page 12 [2-8]; 1970, page 13 [2-8]; 1971, page 13 [2-8]; 1972, page 22 [1-18]; 1973, page 26 [1-18]; 1975, page 26 [1-14]; 1977, page 37 [1-14]

Grace. Line: 1963. Cut: 63. Cocktail. 5-1/2 oz. / 4-3/4" hi. **References:** 1967, page 8 [2-14]; 1968, page 12 [2-14]; 1969, page 12 [2-4]; 1970, page 13 [2-4]; 1971, page 13 [2-4]; 1972, page 22 [1-14]; 1973, page 26 [1-14]

Grace. Line: 1963. Cut: 63. Cordial. 1-1/2 oz. / 4" hi. **References:** 1967, page 8 [2-15]; 1968, page 12 [2-15]; 1969, page 12 [2-5]; 1970, page 13 [2-5]; 1971, page 13 [2-5]; 1972, page 22 [1-15]; 1973, page 26 [1-15]; 1975, page 26 [1-12]; 1977, page 37 [1-12]

Grace. Line: 1963. Cut: 63. Goblet. 13-1/2 oz. / 6-3/4" hi. **References:** 1967, page 8 [2-11]; 1968, page 12 [2-11]; 1969, page 12 [2-1]; 1970, page 13 [2-1]; 1971, page 13 [2-1]; 1972, page 22 [1-11]; 1973, page 26 [1-11]; 1975, page 26 [1-9]; 1977, page 37 [1-9]

Grace. Line: 1963. Cut: 63. Ice Tea. 14 oz. / 6-1/4" hi. **References:** 1967, page 8 [2-17]; 1968, page 12 [2-17]; 1969, page 12 [2-7]; 1970, page 13 [2-7]; 1971, page 13 [2-7]; 1972, page 22 [1-17]; 1973, page 26 [1-17]; 1975, page 26 [1-13]; 1977, page 37 [1-13]

Grace. Line: 1963. Cut: 63. Juice. 7 oz. / 5-1/4" hi. **References:** 1967, page 8 [2-16]; 1968, page 12 [2-16]; 1969, page 12 [2-6]; 1970, page 13 [2-6]; 1971, page 13 [2-6]; 1972, page 22 [1-16]; 1973, page 26 [1-16]

Grace. Line: 1963. Cut: 63. Plate. 7" / Actually 7-7/8" Dia. **References:** 1967, page 8 [2-19]; 1968, page 12 [2-19]; 1969, page 12 [2-9]; 1970, page 13 [2-9]; 1971, page 13 [2-9]; 1972, page 22 [1-19]; 1973, page 26 [1-19]; 1975, page 26 [1-15]; 1977, page 37 [1-15]

Grace. Line: 1963. Cut: 63. Plate. 8" / Actually 8-3/4" Dia. **References:** 1967, page 8 [2-20]; 1968, page 12 [2-20]; 1969, page 12 [2-10]; 1970, page 13 [2-10]; 1971, page 13 [2-10]; 1972, page 22 [1-20]; 1973, page 26 [1-20]; 1975, page 26 [1-16]; 1977, page 37 [1-16]

Grace. Line: 1963. Cut: 63. Sherbet. 7-1/2 oz. / 5-1/8" hi. **References:** 1967, page 8 [2-12]; 1968, page 12 [2-12]; 1969, page 12 [2-2]; 1970, page 13 [2-2]; 1971, page 13 [2-2]; 1972, page 22 [1-12]; 1973, page 26 [1-12]; 1975, page 26 [1-10]; 1977, page 37 [1-10]

Grace. Line: 1963. Cut: 63. Wine. 7-3/4 oz. / 5-3/4" hi. **References:** 1967, page 8 [2-13]; 1968, page 12 [2-13]; 1969, page 12 [2-3]; 1970, page 13 [2-3]; 1971, page 13 [2-3]; 1972, page 22 [1-13]; 1973, page 26 [1-13]; 1975, page 26 [1-11]; 1977, page 37 [1-11]

Grandeur. Line: 1969. 1305 Dessert-Finger Bowl. 4-1/2 inches diam. 3/16" Gold Band on edge of PLATE only. **References:** 1969, page 18 [2-14]; 1970, page 19 [2-14]

Grandeur. Line: 1969. Cordial. 2 oz. 4-1/2 inches tall. 3/16" Gold Band on edge of PLATE only. **References:** 1969, page 18 [2-12]; 1970, page 19 [2-12]

Grandeur. Line: 1969. Goblet. 14 oz. 6-3/4 inches tall. 3/16" Gold Band on edge of PLATE only. **References:** 1969, page 18 [2-9]; 1970, page 19 [2-9]

Grandeur. Line: 1969. Ice Tea. 14 oz. 6-3/8 inches tall. 3/16" Gold Band on edge of PLATE only. **References:** 1969, page 18 [2-13]; 1970, page 19 [2-13]

Grandeur. Line: 1969. Plate. 7 inches diam. 3/16" Gold Band on edge of PLATE only, Actually 7-7/8" Dia. **References:** 1969, page 18 [2-15]; 1970, page 19 [2-15]

Grandeur. Line: 1969. Plate. 8 inches diam. 3/16" Gold Band on edge of PLATE only, Actually 8-3/4" Dia. **References:** 1969, page 18 [2-16]; 1970, page 19 [2-16]

Grandeur. Line: 1969. Sherbet. 7-1/2 oz. 5-3/8 inches tall. 3/16" Gold Band on edge of PLATE only. **References:** 1969, page 18 [2-10]; 1970, page 19 [2-10]

Grandeur. Line: 1969. White Wine Goblet. 7-1/2 oz. 5-1/2 inches tall. 3/16" Gold Band on edge of PLATE only. **References:** 1969, page 18 [2-11]; 1970, page 19 [2-11]

Grape Design. Etching: 608. Plate. 6-1/2 inch. **References:** 3, page 8 [2-1]

Grape Design. Line: 1. Etching: 608. Decanter. 2 Pint. Cut Neck and Star. **References:** 3, page 8 [2-2]

Grape Design. Line: 1. Etching: 608. Grape Fruit. **References:** 3, page 8 [1-1]

Grape Design. Line: 1. Etching: 608. Nappy. 8 inch. **References:** 3, page 9 [1-1]

Grape Design. Line: 1. Etching: 608. Nappy. 4-1/2 inch. **References:** 3, page 9 [1-3]

Grape Design. Line: 1. Etching: 608. Oil. Cut Neck. **References:** 3, page 8 [2-5]

Grape Design. Line: 3. Etching: 608. Comport. **References:** 3, page 8 [1-3]

Grape Design. Line: 4. Etching: 608. Oil. Cut Neck and Star Bottom. **References:** 3, page 9 [3-4]

Grape Design. Line: 10. Etching: 608. Jug. 54 oz. Optic. **References:** 3, page 9 [3-2]

Grape Design. Line: 20. Etching: 608. Jug. 52 oz. **References:** 3, page 9 [3-1]

Grape Design. Line: 34. Etching: 608. Fruit. **References:** 3, page 8 [2-4]

Grape Design. Line: 40. Etching: 608. Cream. **References:** 3, page 9 [2-1]

Grape Design. Line: 40. Etching: 608. Jug. 54 oz. **References:** 3, page 9 [3-3]

Grape Design. Line: 40. Etching: 608. Sugar Bowl. **References:** 3, page 8 [1-6]

Grape Design. Line: 50. Etching: 608. Water Bottle. Cut Neck. **References:** 3, page 8 [2-3]

Grape Design. Line: 300. Etching: 608. Ale. **References:** 3, page 7 [2-3]

Grape Design. Line: 300. Etching: 608. Brandy. **References:** 3, page 7 [2-8]

Grape Design. Line: 300. Etching: 608. Claret. **References:** 3, page 7 [2-5]

Grape Design. Line: 300. Etching: 608. Cocktail. **References:** 3, page 7 [1-3]

Grape Design. Line: 300. Etching: 608. Cordial. **References:** 3, page 7 [2-9]

Grape Design. Line: 300. Etching: 608. Deminth. **References:** 3, page 7 [1-4]

Grape Design. Line: 300. Etching: 608. Goblet. 6 oz. **References:** 3, page 7 [2-4]

Grape Design. Line: 300. Etching: 608. Goblet. 8 oz. **References:** 3, page 7 [1-7]

Grape Design. Line: 300. Etching: 608. Goblet. 9 oz. **References:** 3, page 7 [2-2]

Grape Design. Line: 300. Etching: 608. Goblet. 10 oz. **References:** 3, page 7 [2-1]

Grape Design. Line: 300. Etching: 608. Handled Custard. **References:** 3, page 9 [1-2]

Grape Design. Line: 300. Etching: 608. Individual Almond. **References:** 3, page 7 [1-2]

Grape Design. Line: 300. Etching: 608. Port. **References:** 3, page 7 [2-6]

Grape Design. Line: 300. Etching: 608. Rhine Wine Goblet. **References:** 3, page 7 [1-5]

Grape Design. Line: 300. Etching: 608. Saucer Champ. **References:** 3, page 7 [1-6]

Grape Design. Line: 300. Etching: 608. Sherbert. **References:** 3, page 7 [1-1]

Grape Design. Line: 300. Etching: 608. Tall Goblet. 9 oz. **References:** 3, page 7 [1-8]

Grape Design. Line: 300. Etching: 608. Wine. **References:** 3, page 7 [2-7]

Grape Design. Line: 300. Cut: 43. Etching: 608. Champagne. Hollow Stem. **References:** 3, page 8 [1-2]

Grape Design. Line: 300. Cut: 43. Etching: 608. Saucer Champ. Hollow Stem. **References:** 3, page 8 [1-4]

Grape Design. Line: 630. Etching: 608. Tumbler. 9-1/2 oz. **References:** 3, page 7 [2-3]

Grape Design. Line: 1302. Etching: 608. Finger Bowl. **References:** 3, page 8 [1-5]

Grape Design. Line: 8127. Cut: 39. Etching: 608. Tumbler. 2-1/2 oz. **References:** 3, page 7 [2-2]

Grape Design. Line: 9001. Etching: 608. Tumbler. 8 oz. **References:** 3, page 7 [2-4]

Harvest. Champagne Flute. 6 oz. 9-1/4 inches tall. **References:** 1983, page 3 [2-22]

Harvest. Cordial. 1-1/2 oz. 4 inches tall.

Green, Yellow. **References:** 1981, page 5 [1-9]; 1982, page 2 [1-9]

Images. Ice Tea. 15-1/4 oz. 6 inches tall. Colors: Brown, Charm Blue, Crystal, Lime Green, Moss Green, Yellow. **References:** 1982, page 16 [1-9]

Images. Ice Tea. 15-1/4 oz. Colors: Crystal, Charm Blue, Brown, Yellow, Moss Green. **References:** 1983, page 12 [1-9]

Images. Juice. Colors: Charm Blue, Lime Green, Brown, Yellow, Moss Green. **References:** 1980 Fall/Winter, page 1 [1-4]

Images. Juice. 7-1/2 oz. Moss Green. Colors: Brown, Charm Blue, Crystal, Lime Green, Moss Green, Yellow. **References:** 1981, page 5 [1-7]; 1982, page 2 [1-7]

Images. Juice. 7-1/2 oz. 4-1/4 inches tall. Colors: Brown, Charm Blue, Crystal, Lime Green, Moss Green, Yellow. **References:** 1982, page 16 [1-7]

Images. Juice. 7-1/2 oz. Colors: Crystal, Charm Blue, Brown, Yellow, Moss Green. **References:** 1983, page 12 [1-7]

Images. On The Rocks. Colors: Charm Blue, Lime Green, Brown, Yellow, Moss Green. **References:** 1980 Fall/Winter, page 1 [2-5]

Images. On The Rocks. 10-1/2 oz. Lime Green. Colors: Brown, Charm Blue, Crystal, Lime Green, Moss Green, Yellow. **References:** 1981, page 5 [1-3]; 1982, page 2 [1-3]

Images. On The Rocks. 10-1/2 oz. 3-1/2 inches tall. Colors: Brown, Charm Blue, Crystal, Lime Green, Moss Green, Yellow. **References:** 1982, page 16 [1-3]

Images. On The Rocks. 10-1/2 oz. Colors: Crystal, Charm Blue, Brown, Yellow, Moss Green. **References:** 1983, page 12 [1-3]

Images. Wine. 9 oz. Yellow. Colors: Brown, Charm Blue, Crystal, Lime Green, Moss Green, Yellow. **References:** 1981, page 5 [1-2]; 1982, page 2 [1-2]

Images. Wine. 9 oz. 4-7/8 inches tall. Yellow. Colors: Brown, Charm Blue, Crystal, Lime Green, Moss Green, Yellow. **References:** 1982, page 16 [1-2]

Images. Wine. 9 oz. Colors: Crystal, Charm Blue, Brown, Yellow, Moss Green. **References:** 1983, page 12 [1-2]

Independence Collection. Hi Ball. 13 oz. 5-3/16 inches tall. Colors: Brown, Charm Blue, Crystal, Lime Green, Yellow. **References:** 1979, page 14 [1-2]

Independence Collection. Juice/Wine. 9 oz. 4-1/4 inches tall. Colors: Brown, Charm Blue, Crystal, Lime Green, Yellow. **References:** 1979, page 14 [1-4]

Independence Collection. Luncheon Goblet. 15 oz. 5-1/4 inches tall. Colors: Brown, Charm Blue, Crystal, Lime Green, Yellow. **References:** 1979, page 14 [1-3]

Independence Collection. On The Rocks. 10-1/2 oz. 3-5/8 inches tall. Colors: Brown, Charm Blue, Crystal, Lime Green, Yellow. **References:** 1979, page 14 [1-1]

Intrigue. Line: 1973. Cut: 1443. Wine. 8-1/2 oz. 6-3/8 inches tall. Blue, Crystal Foot. Colors & Designs Available: Blue/Crystal Foot, Pink/Crystal Foot, Blue/Crystal Foot/Cut 1443, Pink/Crystal Foot/Cut 1443, Black Decal and Gold Band, White Decal and Platinum Band. **References:** 1971, page 40 [1-1]

Juliet. Bell. 4-1/2 inches tall. Platinum. **References:** 1979, page 12 [5-2]

Juliet. Cocktail. **References:** 1963 Advertisement; 1964 Advertisement

Juliet. Cordial. **References:** 1963 Advertisement; 1964 Advertisement

Juliet. Cordial. 2 oz. 4-1/2 inches tall. Platinum Band. **References:** 1979, page 6 [1-4]; 1981, page 3 [1-4]

Juliet. Cordial. 2 oz. 4-1/2 inches tall. **References:** 1982, page 15 [1-9]

Juliet. Footed Ice Tea. **References:** 1964 Advertisement

Juliet. Goblet. **References:** 1963 Advertisement; 1964 Advertisement

Juliet. Goblet. 12 oz. 7 inches tall. Platinum Band. **References:** 1979, page 6 [1-1]; 1981, page 3 [1-1]

Juliet. Goblet. 12 oz. 7 inches tall. **References:** 1982, page 15 [1-6]

Juliet. Ice Tea. 12 oz. 6-1/4 inches tall. Platinum Band. **References:** 1979, page 6 [1-5]

Juliet. Ice Tea. 12 oz. 6-1/4 inches tall. **References:** 1982, page 15 [1-10]

Juliet. Juice. **References:** 1963 Advertisement

Juliet. Red Wine Goblet. **References:** 1963 Advertisement; 1964 Advertisement

Juliet. Saucer Champagne. **References:** 1964 Advertisement

Juliet. Sherbet. **References:** 1963 Advertisement

Juliet. Sherbet. 7-1/2 oz. 5-1/8 inches tall. Platinum Band. **References:** 1979, page 6 [1-2]; 1981, page 3 [1-2]

Juliet. Sherbet. 7-1/2 oz. 5-1/8 inches tall. **References:** 1982, page 15 [1-7]

Juliet. Tea. **References:** 1963 Advertisement

Juliet. White Wine Goblet. **References:** 1963 Advertisement; 1964 Advertisement

Juliet. Wine. 7 oz. 5-7/8 inches tall. Platinum Band. **References:** 1979, page 6 [1-3]; 1981, page 3 [1-3]

Juliet. Wine. 7 oz. 5-7/8 inches tall. **References:** 1982, page 15 [1-8]

Juliet. Line: 3. Bell. 4-3/8 inches tall. 1/4" Platinum Band. **References:** 1976, page 6 [1-2]; 1977, page 22 [1-1]

Juliet. Line: 1235. Cocktail. 5-1/2 oz. / 4-5/8" hi. Platinum Band. **References:** 1967, page 10 [1-4]; 1969, page 19 [1-4]; 1970, page 20 [1-4]; 1971, page 20 [1-4]; 1972, page 28 [1-4]; 1973, page 33 [1-4]

Juliet. Line: 1235. Cordial. 2 oz. / 4-1/2" hi. Platinum Band. **References:** 1967, page 10 [1-5]; 1969, page 19 [1-5]; 1970, page 20 [1-5]; 1971, page 20 [1-5]; 1972, page 28 [1-5]; 1973, page 33 [1-5]; 1975, page 29 [1-4]; 1977, page 40 [1-4]

Juliet. Line: 1235. Goblet. 12 oz. / 7" hi. Platinum Band. **References:** 1967, page 10 [1-1]; 1969, page 19 [1-1]; 1970, page 20 [1-1]; 1971, page 20 [1-1]; 1972, page 28 [1-1]; 1973, page 33 [1-1]; 1975, page 29 [1-1]; 1977, page 40 [1-1]

Juliet. Line: 1235. Ice Tea. 12 oz. / 6-1/4" hi. Platinum Band. **References:** 1967, page 10 [1-7]; 1969, page 19 [1-8]; 1970, page 20 [1-8]; 1971, page 20 [1-8]; 1972, page 28 [1-8]; 1973, page 33 [1-8]; 1975, page 29 [1-5]; 1977, page 40 [1-5]

Juliet. Line: 1235. Juice. 5 oz. / 4-1/2" hi. Platinum Band. **References:** 1967, page 10 [1-6]; 1969, page 19 [1-7]
1970, page 20 [1-7]; 1971, page 20 [1-7]; 1972, page 28 [1-7]; 1973, page 33 [1-7]

Juliet. Line: 1235. Parfait Whiskey Sour. 7 oz. 6-1/4 inches tall. Platinum Band. **References:** 1969, page 19 [1-6]; 1970, page 20 [1-6]; 1971, page 20 [1-6]; 1972, page 28 [1-6]; 1973, page 33 [1-6]

Juliet. Line: 1235. Plate. 7" / Actually 7-7/8" Dia. Platinum Band. **References:** 1967, page 10 [1-8]; 1969, page 19 [1-9]; 1970, page 20 [1-9]; 1971, page 20 [1-9]; 1972, page 28 [1-9]; 1973, page 33 [1-9]; 1975, page 29 [1-6]; 1977, page 40 [1-6]

Juliet. Line: 1235. Plate. 8" / Actually 8-3/4" Dia. Platinum Band.
Refere 1971, page 20 [1-10]; 1972, page 28 [1-10]
1973, page 33 [1-10]; 1975, page 29 [1-7]; 1977, page 40 [1-7]

Juliet. Line: 1235. Sherbet. 7-1/2 oz. / 5-1/8" hi Platinum Band. **References:** 1967, page 10 [1-2]; 1969, page 19 [1-2]; 1970, page 20 [1-2]; 1971, page 20 [1-2]; 1972, page 28 [1-2]; 1973, page 33 [1-2]; 1975, page 29 [1-2]; 1977, page 40 [1-2]

Juliet. Line: 1235. Wine. 7 oz. / 5-7/8" hi. Platinum Band. **References:** 1967, page 10 [1-3]; 1969, page 19 [1-3]; 1970, page 20 [1-3]; 1971, page 20 [1-3]; 1972, page 28 [1-3]; 1973, page 33 [1-3]; 1975, page 29 [1-3]; 1977, page 40 [1-3]

Kimberly. Champagne Flute. 6 oz. 9-1/4 inches tall. **References:** 1983, page 5 [2-12]

Kimberly. Cordial. 1-1/4 oz. 3-7/8 inches tall. **References:** 1979, page 3 [3-14]

Kimberly. Cordial. 1-1/4 oz. 4 inches tall. **References:** 1982, page 13 [1-5]; 1983, page 5 [2-10]

Kimberly. Goblet. 12 oz. 7 inches tall. **References:** 1979, page 3 [3-11]; 1982, page 13 [1-1]; 1983, page 5 [2-7]

Kimberly. Ice Tea. 14 oz. 6-1/4 inches tall. **References:** 1979, page 3 [3-15]; 1982, page 13 [1-3]

Kimberly. Ice Tea. 14 oz. 6-1/2 inches tall. **References:** 1983, page 5 [2-11]

Kimberly. Sherbet. 7-1/2 oz. 5-1/8 inches tall. **References:** 1979, page 3 [3-12]

Kimberly. Sherbet. 7-1/2 oz. 5-1/4 inches tall. **References:** 1982, page 13 [1-2]; 1983, page 5 [2-8]

Kimberly. Wine. 7-1/2 oz. 6 inches tall. **References:** 1979, page 3 [3-13]; 1982, page 13 [1-4]; 1983, page 5 [2-9]

Kimberly. Line: 1966. Cut: 1430. 1305 Dessert-Finger Bowl. 4-1/2" Dia. **References:** 1967, page 5 [1-6]; 1968, page 8 [1-6]; 1969, page 8 [1-6]; 1970, page 8 [1-6]; 1971, page 8 [1-6]; 1972, page 18 [1-6]; 1973, page 23 [1-6]; 1975, page 23 [1-6]; 1977, page 34 [1-6]

Kimberly. Line: 1966. Cut: 1430. Cordial. 1-1/4 oz. / 3-7/8" hi. **References:** 1967, page 5 [1-4]; 1968, page 8 [1-4]; 1969, page 8 [1-4]; 1970, page 8 [1-4]; 1971, page 8 [1-4]; 1972, page 18 [1-4]; 1973, page 23 [1-4]; 1975, page 23 [1-4]; 1977, page 34 [1-4]; 1981, page 2 [3-8]; 1975/I-75, page 1 [3-2]

Kimberly. Line: 1966. Cut: 1430. Goblet. 12 oz. / 7" hi. **References:** 1967, page 5 [1-1]; 1968, page 8 [1-1]; 1969, page 8 [1-1]; 1970, page 8 [1-1]; 1971, page 8 [1-1]; 1972, page 18 [1-1]; 1973, page 23 [1-1]; 1975, page 23 [1-1]; 1977, page 34 [1-1]; 1981, page 2 [3-5]; 1975/I-75, page 1 [2-1]

Kimberly. Line: 1966. Cut: 1430. Ice Tea. 14 oz. / 6-1/4" hi. **References:** 1967, page 5 [1-5]; 1968, page 8 [1-5]; 1969, page 8 [1-5]; 1970, page 8 [1-5]; 1971, page 8 [1-5]; 1972, page 18 [1-5]; 1973, page 23 [1-5]; 1975, page 23 [1-5]; 1977, page 34 [1-5]; 1975/I-75, page 1 [3-1]

Kimberly. Line: 1966. Cut: 1430. Plate. 7" / Actually 7-7/8" Dia. **References:** 1967, page 5 [1-7]; 1967, page 5 [1-7]; 1968, page 8 [1-7]; 1969, page 8 [1-7]; 1970, page 8 [1-7]; 1971, page 8 [1-7]; 1972, page 18 [1-7]; 1973, page 23 [1-7]; 1975, page 23 [1-7]; 1977, page 34 [1-7]

Kimberly. Line: 1966. Cut: 1430. Plate. 8" / Actually 8-3/4" Dia. **References:** 1967, page 5 [1-8]; 1968, page 8 [1-8]; 1969, page 8 [1-8]; 1970, page 8 [1-8]; 1971, page 8 [1-8]; 1972, page 18 [1-8]; 1973, page 23 [1-8]; 1975, page 23 [1-8]; 1977, page 34 [1-8]

Kimberly. Line: 1966. Cut: 1430. Sherbet. 7-1/2 oz. / 5-1/8" hi. **References:** 1967, page 5 [1-2]; 1968, page 8 [1-2]; 1969, page 8 [1-2]; 1970, page 8 [1-2]; 1971, page 8 [1-2]; 1972, page 18 [1-2]; 1973, page 23 [1-2]; 1975, page 23 [1-2]; 1977, page 34 [1-2]; 1981, page 2 [3-6]; 1975/I-75, page 1 [1-2]

Kimberly. Line: 1966. Cut: 1430. Wine. 7-1/2 oz. / 6" hi. **References:** 1967, page 5 [1-3]; 1968, page 8 [1-3]; 1969, page 8 [1-3]; 1970, page 8 [1-3]; 1971, page 8 [1-3]; 1972, page 18 [1-3]; 1973, page 23 [1-3]; 1975, page 23 [1-3]; 1977, page 34 [1-3]; 1981, page 2 [3-7]; 1975/I-75, page 1 [1-1]

Kingsley. Line: 1971. Cut: 1441. 1311 Dessert-Finger Bowlr. 4-3/4 inches diam. **References:** 1970, page 11 [1-14]

Kingsley. Line: 1971. Cut: 1441. Cordial. 1-1/2 oz. 4 inches tall. **References:** 1970, page 11 [1-12]

Kingsley. Line: 1971. Cut: 1441. Goblet. 11-1/2 oz. 7 inches tall. **References:** 1970, page 11 [1-9]

Kingsley. Line: 1971. Cut: 1441. Ice Tea. 14-1/2 oz. 7-1/8 inches tall. **References:** 1970, page 11 [1-13]

Kingsley. Line: 1971. Cut: 1441. Plate. 7 inches diam. Actually 7-7/8" Dia. **References:** 1970, page 11 [1-15]

Kingsley. Line: 1971. Cut: 1441. Plate. 8 inches diam. Actually 8-3/4" Dia. **References:** 1970, page 11 [1-16]

Kingsley. Line: 1971. Cut: 1441. Sherbet. 7-1/2 oz. 5 inches tall. **References:** 1970, page 11 [1-10]

Kingsley. Line: 1971. Cut: 1441. Wine. 7 oz. 5-7/8 inches tall. **References:** 1970, page 11 [1-11]

Kingsley. Line: 1971. Cut: 1442. 1311 Dessert-Finger Bowl. 4-3/4 inches diam. **References:** 1970, page 11 [1-6]; 1971, page 19 [1-6]

Kingsley. Line: 1971. Cut: 1442. Cordial. 1-1/2 oz. 4 inches tall. **References:** 1970, page 11 [1-4]; 1971, page 19 [1-4]

Kingsley. Line: 1971. Cut: 1442. Goblet. 11-1/2 oz. 7 inches tall. **References:** 1970, page 11 [1-1]; 1971, page 19 [1-1]

Kingsley. Line: 1971. Cut: 1442. Ice Tea. 14-1/2 oz. 7-1/8 inches tall. **References:** 1970, page 11 [1-5]; 1971. Cut: 1442. Ice Tea. 14-1/2 oz. 7-1/8 inches tall. **References:** 1971, page 19 [1-5]

Kingsley. Line: 1971. Cut: 1442. Plate. 7 inches diam. Actually 7-7/8" Dia. **References:** 1970, page 11 [1-7]; 1971, page 19 [1-7]

Kingsley. Line: 1971. Cut: 1442. Plate. 8 inches diam. Actually 8-3/4" Dia. **References:** 1970, page 11 [1-8]; 1971, page 19 [1-8]

Kingsley. Line: 1971. Cut: 1442. Sherbet. 7-1/2 oz. 5 inches tall. **References:** 1970, page 11 [1-2]; 1971, page 19 [1-2]

Kingsley. Line: 1971. Cut: 1442. Wine. 7 oz. 5-7/8 inches tall. **References:** 1970, page 11 [1-3]; 1971, page 19 [1-3]

La Belle. Line: 4. Cut: 980. Bell. 5-1/2 inches tall. All Bells Individually Gift Boxed. **References:** 1976, page 7 [2-1]; 1977, page 23 [5-1]; 1979, page 13 [2-1]

La Chateau. Line: 1977. Brandy and Liqueur. 2-1/2 oz. 6 inches tall. Plain Lead Crystal. **References:** 1973, page 6 [1-7]

La Chateau. Line: 1977. Cabinet Wine Goblet. 15-1/2 oz. 9-1/8 inches tall. Plain Lead Crystal. **References:** 1973, page 6 [1-1]

La Chateau. Line: 1977. Dessert-Champagne. 7-1/2 oz. 6-1/8 inches tall. Plain Lead Crystal. **References:** 1973, page 6 [1-6]

La Chateau. Line: 1977. Red Wine Goblet. 12-1/2 oz. 8-5/8 inches tall. Plain Lead Crystal. **References:** 1973, page 6 [1-2]

La Chateau. Line: 1977. Sherry and Port. 5 oz. 7 inches tall. Plain Lead Crystal. **References:** 1973, page 6 [1-5]

La Chateau. Line: 1977. Sparkling Wine Goblet. 9 oz. 8 inches tall. Plain Lead Crystal. **References:** 1973, page 6 [1-3]

La Chateau. Line: 1977. White Wine Goblet. 7 oz. 7-5/8 inches tall. Plain Lead Crystal. **References:** 1973, page 6 [1-4]

Lace Point. Line: 4. Cut: 414. Bell. 5-1/2 inches tall. All Bells Individually Gift Boxed. **References:** 1976, page 7 [2-4]; 1977, page 23 [4-1]; 1979, page 13 [3-3]

Lafayette. Champagne Flute. 6 oz. 9-1/4 inches tall. **References:** 1983, page 4 [2-10]

Lafayette. Cordial. 1-1/4 oz. 4 inches tall. **References:** 1979, page 3 [1-4]; 1983, page 4 [2-11]

Lafayette. Goblet. 11-3/4 oz. 7-1/4 inches tall. **References:** 1979, page 3 [1-1]; 1983, page 4 [2-7]

Lafayette. Ice Tea. 13-1/2 oz. 6-3/4 inches tall. **References:** 1979, page 3 [1-5]

Lafayette. Ice Tea. 14 oz. 6-1/2 inches tall. **References:** 1983, page 4 [2-12]

Lafayette. Sherbet. 7-1/2 oz. 5-1/4 inches tall. **References:** 1979, page 3 [1-2]; 1983, page 4 [2-8]

Lafayette. Wine. 7-1/2 oz. 6-1/4 inches tall. **References:** 1979, page 3 [1-3]

Lafayette. Wine. 7-1/2 oz. 6-1/8 inches tall. **References:** 1983, page 4 [2-9]

Lafayette. Line: 1965. Cut: 1416. 1305 Dessert-Finger Bowl. 4-1/2 Dia. **References:** 1967, page 7 [1-16]; 1968, page 10 [1-7]; 1969, page 11 [2-16]; 1970, page 12 [2-16]; 1971, page 12 [2-16]; 1972, page 21 [2-16]; 1973, page 25 [2-16]; 1975, page 25 [2-14]; 1977, page 36 [2-14]

Lafayette. Line: 1965. Cut: 1416. Cordial. 1-1/4 oz. / 4" hi. **References:** 1967, page 7 [1-13]; 1968, page 10 [1-4]; 1969, page 11 [2-13]; 1970, page 12 [2-13]; 1971, page 12 [2-13]; 1972, page 21 [2-13]; 1973, page 25 [2-13]; 1975, page 25 [2-12]; 1977, page 36 [2-12]; 1981, page 1 [2-8]

Lafayette. Line: 1965. Cut: 1416. Goblet. 11-3/4 oz. / 7-1/4" hi. **References:** 1967, page 7 [1-10]; 1968, page 10 [1-1]; 1969, page 11 [2-10]; 1970, page 12 [2-10]; 1971, page 12 [2-10]; 1972, page 21 [2-10]; 1973, page 25 [2-10]; 1975, page 25 [2-9]; 1977, page 36 [2-9]; 1981, page 1 [2-5]

Lafayette. Line: 1965. Cut: 1416. Ice Tea. 13-1/2 oz. / 6-3/4" hi. **References:** 1967, page 7 [1-15]; 1968, page 10 [1-6]; 1969, page 11 [2-15]; 1970, page 12 [2-15]; 1971, page 12 [2-15]; 1972, page 21 [2-15]; 1973, page 25 [2-15]; 1975, page 25 [2-13]; 1977, page 36 [2-13]

Lafayette. Line: 1965. Cut: 1416. Juice. 6 oz. / 5-1/2" hi. **References:** 1967, page 7 [1-14]; 1968, page 10 [1-5]; 1969, page 11 [2-14]; 1970, page 12 [2-14]; 1971, page 12 [2-14]; 1972, page 21 [2-14]; 1973, page 25 [2-14]

Lafayette. Line: 1965. Cut: 1416. Plate. 7" / Actually 7-7/8" Dia. **References:** 1967, page 7 [1-17]; 1968, page 10 [1-8]; 1969, page 11 [2-17]; 1970, page 12 [2-17]; 1971, page 12 [2-17]; 1972, page 21 [2-17]; 1973, page 25 [2-17]; 1975, page 25 [2-15]; 1977, page 36 [2-15]

Lafayette. Line: 1965. Cut: 1416. Plate. 8 inches diam. Actually 8-3/4" Dia. **References:** 1967, page 7 [1-18]; 1968, page 10 [1-9]; 1969, page 11 [2-18]; 1970, page 12 [2-18]; 1971, page 12 [2-18]; 1972, page 21 [2-18]; 1973, page 25 [2-18]; 1975, page 25 [2-16]; 1977, page 36 [2-16]

Lafayette. Line: 1965. Cut: 1416. Sherbet. 7-1/2 oz. / 5-1/4" hi. **References:** 1967, page 7 [1-11]; 1968, page 10 [1-2]; 1969, page 11 [2-11]; 1970, page 12 [2-11]; 1971, page 12 [2-11]; 1972, page 21 [2-11]; 1973, page 25 [2-11]; 1975, page 25 [2-10]; 1977, page 36 [2-10]; 1981, page 1 [2-6]

Lafayette. Line: 1965. Cut: 1416. Wine. 7-1/2 oz. / 6-1/4" hi. **References:** 1967, page 7 [1-12]; 1968, page 10 [1-3]; 1969, page 11 [2-12]; 1970, page 12 [2-12]; 1971, page 12 [2-12]; 1972, page 21 [2-12]; 1973, page 25 [2-12]; 1975, page 25 [2-11]; 1977, page 36 [2-11]; 1981, page 1 [2-7]

Laurel. Cut: 121. Bell. 4-1/2 inches tall. **References:** 1979, page 12 [3-4]

Laurel. Line: 3. Cut: 121. Bell. 4-3/8 inches tall. Handmade and Hand Cut. **References:** 1975, page 12 [2-3]; 1976, page 6 [2-1]; 1977, page 22 [5-3]; 1977, page 22 [5-3]

Laurel. Line: 912. Cuts: 121 and 39. 1311 Dessert-Finger Bowl. 4-3/4 inches diam. **References:** 1967, page 17 [1-8]; 1968, page 21 [1-8]; 1969, page 21 [1-8]; 1970, page 22 [1-8]; 1971, page 22 [1-8]

Laurel. Line: 912. Cuts: 121 and 39. Claret. 4 oz. 4-3/4 inches tall. **References:** 1967, page 17 [1-3]; 1968, page 21 [1-3]; 1969, page 21 [1-3]; 1970, page 22 [1-3]; 1971, page 22 [1-3]

Laurel. Line: 912. Cuts: 121 and 39. Cocktail. 3-1/2 oz. 4-3/8 inches tall. **References:** 1967, page 17 [1-4]; 1968, page 21 [1-4]; 1969, page 21 [1-4]; 1970, page 22 [1-4]; 1971, page 22 [1-4]

Laurel. Line: 912. Cuts: 121 and 39. Cordial. 1 oz. 3-5/8 inches tall. **References:** 1967, page 17 [1-5]; 1968, page 21 [1-5]; 1969, page 21 [1-5]; 1970, page 22 [1-5]; 1971, page 22 [1-5]

Laurel. Line: 912. Cuts: 121 and 39. Goblet. 10 oz. 6-1/4 inches tall. **References:** 1967, page 17 [1-1]; 1968, page 21 [1-1]; 1969, page 21 [1-1]; 1970, page 22 [1-1]; 1971, page 22 [1-1]

Laurel. Line: 912. Cuts: 121 and 39. Ice Tea. 12 oz. 6 inches tall. **References:** 1967, page 17 [1-7]; 1968, page 21 [1-7]; 1969, page 21 [1-7]; 1970, page 22 [1-7]; 1971, page 22 [1-7]

Laurel. Line: 912. Cuts: 121 and 39. Juice. 6 oz. 4-5/8 inches tall. **References:** 1967, page 17 [1-6]; 1968, page 21 [1-6]; 1969, page 21 [1-6]; 1970, page 22 [1-6]; 1971, page 22 [1-6]

Laurel. Line: 912. Cuts: 121 and 39. Plate. 7 inches diam. Actually 7-7/8" Dia. **References:** 1967, page 17 [1-9]; 1968, page 21 [1-9]; 1969, page 21 [1-9]; 1970, page 22 [1-9]; 1971, page 22 [1-9]

Laurel. Line: 912. Cuts: 121 and 39. Plate. 8 inches diam. Actually 8-3/4" Dia. **References:** 1967, page 17 [1-10]; 1968, page 21 [1-10]; 1969, page 21 [1-10]; 1970, page 22 [1-10]; 1971, page 22 [1-10]

Laurel. Line: 912. Cuts: 121 and 39. Saucer Champagne. 7-1/2 oz. 5-1/8 inches tall. **References:** 1967, page 17 [1-2]; 1968, page 21 [1-2]; 1969, page 21 [1-2]; 1970, page 22 [1-2]; 1971, page 22 [1-2]

Laurel Wreath. Line: 8000. Cut: 121. 1305 Dessert-Finger Bowl. 4-1/2 inches diam. Optic. **References:** 1967, page 21 1971, page 25 [2-10]

Laurel Wreath. Line: 8000. Cut: 121. Claret. 5 oz. 5-5/8 inches tall. Optic. **References:** 1967, page 21 [2-4]; 1969, page 24 [2-4]; 1970, page 25 [2-4]; 1971, page 25 [2-4]

Laurel Wreath. Line: 8000. Cut: 121. Cocktail. 4 oz. 4-5/8 inches tall. Optic. **References:** 1967, page 21 [2-5]; 1968, page 25 [2-5]; 1969, page 24 [2-5]; 1970, page 25 [2-5]; 1971, page 25 [2-5]

Laurel Wreath. Line: 8000. Cut: 121. Cordial. 1-1/4 oz. 3-3/4 inches tall. Optic. **References:** 1967, page 21 [2-6]; 1968, page 25 [2-6]; 1969, page 24 [2-6]; 1970, page 25 [2-6]; 1971, page 25 [2-6]

Laurel Wreath. Line: 8000. Cut: 121. Goblet. 10-1/2 oz. 6-1/2 inches tall. Optic. **References:** 1967, page 21 [2-1]; 1968, page 25 [2-1]; 1969, page 24 [2-1]; 1970, page 25 [2-1]; 1971, page 25 [2-1]

Laurel Wreath. Line: 8000. Cut: 121. Ice Tea. 13-1/2 oz. 5-3/8 inches tall. Optic. **References:** 1967, page 21 [2-9]; 1968, page 25 [2-9]; 1969, page 24 [2-9]; 1970, page 25 [2-9]; 1971, page 25 [2-9]

Laurel Wreath. Line: 8000. Cut: 121. Juice. 6-1/4 oz. 4 inches tall. Optic. **References:** 1967, page 21 [2-8]; 1968, page 25 [2-8]; 1969, page 24 [2-8]; 1970, page 25 [2-8]; 1971, page 25 [2-8]

Laurel Wreath. Line: 8000. Cut: 121. Parfait. 5-1/4 oz. 6-3/8 inches tall. Optic. **References:** 1967, page 21 [2-7]; 1968, page 25 [2-7]; 1969, page 24 [2-7]; 1970, page 25 [2-7]; 1971, page 25 [2-7]

Laurel Wreath. Line: 8000. Cut: 121. Plate. 7 inches diam. Optic, Actually 7-7/8" Dia. **References:** 1967, page 21 [2-11]; 1968, page 25 [2-11]; 1969, page 24 [2-11]; 1970, page 25 [2-11]; 1971, page 25 [2-11]

Laurel Wreath. Line: 8000. Cut: 121. Plate. 8 inches diam. Optic, Actually 8-3/8" Dia. **References:** 1967, page 21 [2-12]; 1968, page 25 [2-12]; 1969, page 24 [2-12]; 1970, page 25 [2-12]; 1971, page 25 [2-12]

Laurel Wreath. Line: 8000. Cut: 121. Saucer Champagne. 6-1/2 oz. 4-3/4 inches tall. Optic. **References:** 1967, page 21 [2-2]; 1968, page 25 [2-2]; 1969, page 24 [2-2]; 1970, page 25 [2-2]; 1971, page 25 [2-2]

Laurel Wreath. Line: 8000. Cut: 121. Sherbet. 6-1/2 oz. 3-1/2 inches tall. Optic. **References:** 1967, page 21 [2-3]; 1968, page 25 [2-3]; 1969, page 24 [2-3]; 1970, page 25 [2-3]; 1971, page 25 [2-3]

Lavalier. Cordial. 1-1/4 oz. 3-7/8 inches tall. **References:** 1979, page 3 [3-9]

Lavalier. Goblet. 12 oz. 7 inches tall. **References:** 1979, page 3 [3-6]

Lavalier. Ice Tea. 14 oz. 6-1/4 inches tall. **References:** 1979, page 3 [3-10]

Lavalier. Sherbet. 7-1/2 oz. 5-1/8 inches tall. **References:** 1979, page 3 [3-7]

Lavalier. Wine. 7-1/2 oz. 6 inches tall. **References:** 1979, page 3 [3-8]

Lavalier. Line: 1966. Cut: 1431. 1305 Dessert-Finger Bowl. 4-1/2" Dia. **References:** 1967, page 5 [1-14]; 1968, page 8 [1-14]; 1969, page 8 [2-14]; 1970, page 8 [2-14]; 1971, page 8 [2-14]; 1972, page 18 [2-14]; 1973, page 23 [2-14]; 1975, page 23 [2-14]; 1977, page 34 [2-14]

Lavalier. Line: 1966. Cut: 1431. Cordial. 1-1/4 oz. / 3-7/8" hi. **References:** 1967, page 5 [1-12]; 1968, page 8 [1-12]; 1969, page 8 [2-12]; 1970, page 8 [2-12]; 1971, page 8 [2-12]; 1972, page 18 [2-12]; 1973, page 23 [2-12]; 1975, page 23 [2-12]; 1977, page 34 [2-12]

Lavalier. Line: 1966. Cut: 1431. Goblet. 12 oz. / 7" hi. **References:** 1967, page 5 [1-9]; 1968, page 8 [1-9]; 1969, page 8 [2-9]; 1970, page 8 [2-9]; 1971, page 8 [2-9]; 1972, page 18 [2-9]; 1973, page 23 [2-9]; 1975, page 23 [2-9]; 1977, page 34 [2-9]

Lavalier. Line: 1966. Cut: 1431. Ice Tea. 14 oz. / 6-1/4" hi. **References:** 1967, page 5 [1-13]; 1968, page 8 [1-13]; 1969, page 8 [2-13]; 1970, page 8 [2-13]; 1971, page 8 [2-13]; 1972, page 18 [2-13]; 1973, page 23 [2-13]; 1975, page 23 [2-13]; 1977, page 34 [2-13]

Lavalier. Line: 1966. Cut: 1431. Plate. 7" / Actually 7-7/8" Dia. **References:** 1967, page 5 [1-15]; 1968, page 8 [1-15]; 1969, page 8 [2-15]; 1970, page 8 [2-15]; 1971, page 8 [2-15]; 1972, page 18 [2-15]; 1973, page 23 [2-15]; 1975, page 23 [2-15]; 1977, page 34 [2-15]

Lavalier. Line: 1966. Cut: 1431. Plate. 8" / Actually 8-3/4" Dia. **References:** 1967, page 5 [1-16]; 1968, page 8 [1-16]; 1969, page 8 [2-16]; 1970, page 8 [2-16]; 1971, page 8 [2-16]; 1972, page 18 [2-16]; 1973, page 23 [2-16]; 1975, page 23 [2-16]; 1977, page 34 [2-16]

Lavalier. Line: 1966. Cut: 1431. Sherbet. 7-1/2 oz. / 5-1/8" hi. **References:** 1967, page 5 [1-10]; 1968, page 8 [1-10]; 1969, page 8 [2-10]; 1970, page 8 [2-10]; 1971, page 8 [2-10]; 1972, page 18 [2-10]; 1973, page 23 [2-10]; 1975, page 23 [2-10]; 1977, page 34 [2-10]

Lavalier. Line: 1966. Cut: 1431. Wine. 7-1/2 oz. / 6" hi. **References:** 1967, page 5 [1-11]; 1968, page 8 [1-11]; 1969, page 8 [2-11]; 1970, page 8 [2-11]; 1971, page 8 [2-11]; 1972, page 18 [2-11]; 1973, page 23 [2-11]; 1975, page 23 [2-11]; 1977, page 34 [2-11]

Le Chateau. Brandy and Liqueur. 2-1/2 oz. 6 inches tall. **References:** 1977, page 6 [1-7]; 1979, page 6 [3-18]

Le Chateau. Cabinet Wine Goblet. 15-1/2 oz. 9-1/8 inches tall. **References:** 1977, page 6 [1-1]; 1979, page 6 [3-12]

Le Chateau. Dessert-Champagne. 7-1/2 oz. 6-1/8 inches tall. **References:** 1977, page 6 [1-6]; 1979, page 6 [3-17]

Le Chateau. Red Wine Goblet. 12-1/2 oz. 8-5/8 inches tall. **References:** 1977, page 6 [1-2]; 1979, page 6 [3-13]

Le Chateau. Sherry and Port. 5 oz. 7 inches tall. **References:** 1977, page 6 [1-5]; 1979, page 6 [3-16]

Le Chateau. Sparkling Wine Goblet. 9 oz. 8 inches tall. **References:** 1977, page 6 [1-3]; 1979, page 6 [3-14]

Le Chateau. White Wine Goblet. 7 oz. 7-5/8 inches tall. **References:** 1977, page 6 [1-4]; 1979, page 6 [3-15]

Le Chateau. Line: 1977. Brandy and Liqueur. 2-1/2 oz. 6 inches tall. **References:** 1975, page 6 [1-7]

Le Chateau. Line: 1977. Cabinet Wine Goblet. 15-1/2 oz. 9-1/8 inches tall. **References:** 1975, page 6 [1-1]

Le Chateau. Line: 1977. Dessert-Champagne. 7-1/2 oz. 6-1/8 inches tall. **References:** 1975, page 6 [1-6]

Le Chateau. Line: 1977. Red Wine Goblet. 12-1/2 oz. 8-5/8 inches tall. **References:** 1975, page 6 [1-2]

Le Chateau. Line: 1977. Sherry and Port. 5 oz. 7 inches tall. **References:** 1975, page 6 [1-5]

Le Chateau. Line: 1977. Sparkling Wine Goblet. 9 oz. 8 inches tall. **References:** 1975, page 6 [1-3]

Le Chateau. Line: 1977. White Wine. 7 oz. 7-5/8 inches tall. **References:** 1975, page 6 [1-4]

Lexington. Cordial. 1-1/2 oz. 3-3/4 inches tall. Platinum Band. **References:** 1979, page 6 [2-29]

Lexington. Goblet. 13-3/4 oz. 6-1/2 inches tall. Platinum Band. **References:** 1979, page 6 [2-26]

Lexington. Ice Tea. 14-1/4 oz. 6-3/8 inches tall. Platinum Band. **References:** 1979, page 6 [2-30]

Lexington. Sherbet. 7-1/2 oz. 4-3/8 inches tall. Platinum Band. **References:** 1979, page 6 [2-27]

Lexington. Wine. 9 oz. 5-5/8 inches tall. Platinum Band. **References:** 1979, page 6 [2-28]

Lexington. Line: 1964. 1305 Dessert-Finger Bowl. 4-1/2" Dia. Platinum Band. **References:** 1967, page 14 [1-16]; 1968, page 18 [1-16]

Lexington. Line: 1964. Cordial. 1-1/2 oz. / 3-3/4" hi. Platinum Band. **References:** 1967, page 14 [1-13]; 1968, page 18 [1-13]; 1969, page 20 [1-12]; 1970, page 21 [1-12]; 1971, page 21 [1-12]; 1972, page 29 [1-12]; 1973, page 34 [1-12]; 1975, page 30 [1-11]; 1977, page 41 [1-11]

Lexington. Line: 1964. Goblet. 13-3/4 oz. / 6-1/2" hi. Platinum Band. **References:** 1967, page 14 [1-10]; 1968, page 18 [1-10]; 1969, page 20 [1-9]; 1970, page 21 [1-9]; 1971, page 21 [1-9]; 1972, page 29 [1-9]; 1973, page 34 [1-9]; 1975, page 30 [1-8]; 1977, page 41 [1-8]

Lexington. Line: 1964. Ice Tea. 14-1/4 oz. / 6-3/8" hi. Platinum Band. **References:** 1967, page 14 [1-15]; 1968, page 18 [1-15]; 1969, page 20 [1-14]; 1970, page 21 [1-14]; 1971, page 21 [1-14]; 1972, page 29 [1-14]; 1973, page 34 [1-14]; 1975, page 30 [1-12]; 1977, page 41 [1-12]

Lexington. Line: 1964. Juice. 6-3/4 oz. / 4-3/4" hi. Platinum Band. **References:** 1967, page 14 [1-14]; 1968, page 18 [1-14]; 1969, page 20 [1-13]; 1970, page 21 [1-13]; 1971, page 21 [1-13]; 1972, page 29 [1-13]; 1973, page 34 [1-13]

Lexington. Line: 1964. Plate. 7" / Actually 7-7/8" Dia. Platinum Band. **References:** 1967, page 14 [1-17]; 1968, page 18 [1-17]; 1969, page 20 [1-15]; 1970, page 21 [1-15]; 1971, page 21 [1-15]; 1972, page 29 [1-15]; 1973, page 34 [1-15]; 1975, page 30 [1-13]; 1977, page 41 [1-13]

Lexington. Line: 1964. Plate. 8" / Actually 8-3/4" Dia. Platinum Band. **References:** 1967, page 14 [1-18]; 1968, page 18 [1-18]; 1969, page 20 [1-16]; 1970, page 21 [1-16]; 1971, page 21 [1-16]; 1972, page 29 [1-16]; 1973, page 34 [1-16]; 1975, page 30 [1-14]; 1977, page 41 [1-14]

Lexington. Line: 1964. Sherbet. 7-1/2 oz. / 4-3/8" hi. Platinum Band. **References:** 1967, page 14 [1-11]; 1968, page 18 [1-11]; 1969, page 20 [1-10]; 1970, page 21 [1-10]; 1971, page 21 [1-10]; 1972, page 29 [1-10]; 1973, page 34 [1-10]; 1975, page 30 [1-9]; 1977, page 41 [1-9]

Lexington. Line: 1964. Wine. 9 oz. / 5-5/8" hi. Platinum Band. **References:** 1967, page 14 [1-12]; 1968, page 18 [1-12]; 1969, page 20 [1-11]; 1970, page 21 [1-11]; 1971, page 21 [1-11]; 1972, page 29 [1-11]; 1973, page 34 [1-11]; 1975, page 30 [1-10]; 1977, page 41 [1-10]

Love Birds. Line: 80. Ginger Jar. 6-1/4 inches tall. All Items Gift Boxed. $110-125. **References:** 1983, page 6 [1-2L]

Love Birds. Line: 80. Cut: 1457. Ginger Jar. 6-1/4 inches tall. $110-125. **References:** 1980, page 3 [1-1]; 1981, page 10 [2-2]

Love Birds. Line: 90. Ginger Jar. 8-1/2 inches tall. $135-150. **References:** 1983, page 6 [2-2L]

Love Birds. Line: 90. Cut: 1457. Ginger Jar. 8-1/2 inches tall. $135-150. **References:** 1980, page 3 [2-3]; 1981, page 10 [1-2]

Madison. Line: 1978. Beverage. 16 oz. 6 inches tall. Crystal Full Sham. **References:** 1978, page 7 [1-1]; 1979, page 16 [1-1]

Madison. Line: 1978. Old Fashion. 14 oz. 4-1/2 inches tall. Crystal Full Sham. **References:** 1978, page 7 [1-2]; 1979, page 16 [1-2]

Majestic. Bell. **References:** 1981, page 11 [3-3]

Majestic. Bell. **References:** 1983, page 7 [1-3L]

Majestic. Beverage. 16 oz. 6 inches tall. Hand Made....Hand Cut. **References:** 1979, page 15 [3-2]

Majestic. Champagne Flute. 6 oz. 9-1/4 inches tall. **References:** 1983, page 4 [1-9]

Majestic. Cooler. 16 oz. 7-3/8 inches tall. Hand Made....Hand Cut. **References:** 1979, page 15 [3-1]

Majestic. Cordial. 2-1/2 oz. 5-1/8 inches tall. **References:** 1979, page 1 [2-4]

Majestic. Cordial. 2-1/2 oz. 5 inches tall. **References:** 1983, page 4 [1-11]

Majestic. Goblet. 13-1/2 oz. 7-3/4 inches tall. **References:** 1979, page 1 [2-1]

Majestic. Goblet. 13-1/2 oz. 7-5/8 inches tall. **References:** 1983, page 4 [1-7]

Majestic. Hi Ball. 11 oz. 5 inches tall. Hand Made....Hand Cut. **References:** 1979, page 15 [3-3]

Majestic. Ice Tea. 14 oz. 6-1/2 inches tall. **References:** 1983, page 4 [1-12]

Majestic. Old Fashion. 9-1/2 oz. 3-1/2 inches tall. Hand Made....Hand Cut. **References:** 1979, page 15 [3-5]

Majestic. On The Rocks. 14 oz. 4-1/2 inches tall. Hand Made, Hand Cut. **References:** 1979, page 15 [3-4]

Majestic. Pony. 3 oz. 3 inches tall. Hand Made....Hand Cut. **References:** 1979, page 15 [3-6]

Majestic. Sherbet. 9 oz. 5-3/8 inches tall. $30-35. **References:** 1979, page 1 [2-2]; 1983, page 4 [1-8]

Majestic. Wine. 8 oz. 6-3/4 inches tall. $30-35. **References:** 1979, page 1 [2-3]; 1983, page 4 [1-10]

Majestic. Line: 4. Bell. 5-1/2 inches tall. All Bells Individually Gift Boxed. **References:** 1979, page 13 [2-4]

Majestic. Line: 981. Cut: 1453. Cordial. 2-1/2 oz. 5-1/8 inches tall. **References:** 1977, page 26 [1-8]; 1981, page 2 [2-8]

Majestic. Line: 981. Cut: 1453. Goblet. 13-1/2 oz. 7-3/4 inches tall. **References:** 1977, page 26 [1-5]; 1981, page 2 [2-5]

Majestic. Line: 981. Cut: 1453. Sherbet. 9 oz. 5-3/8 inches tall. $30-35. **References:** 1977, page 26 [1-6]; 1981, page 2 [2-6]

Majestic. Line: 981. Cut: 1453. Wine. 8 oz. 6-3/4 inches tall. **References:** 1977, page 26 [1-7]; 1981, page 2 [2-7]

Majestic. Line: 1978. Cut: 1453S. On The Rocks. **References:** 1977, page 25 [2-2]

Mansfield. Cordial. 1-1/4 oz. 3-3/4 inches tall. Gold Band. **References:** 1979, page 6 [2-14]

Mansfield. Goblet. 12-1/2 oz. 6-5/8 inches tall. Gold Band. **References:** 1979, page 6 [2-11]

Mansfield. Ice Tea. 13-1/2 oz. 6-1/4 inches tall. Gold Band. **References:** 1979, page 6 [2-15]

Mansfield. Sherbet. 6-1/2 oz. 5 inches tall. Gold Band. **References:** 1979, page 6 [2-12]

Mansfield. White Wine Goblet. 7 oz. 5-3/4 inches tall. Gold Band. **References:** 1979, page 6 [2-13]

Mansfield. Line: 1350. Cut: 63. Cocktail. 4-1/2 oz. / 4-3/4" hi. Gold Band. **References:** 1967, page 11 [1-22]; 1968, page 15 [1-22]; 1969, page 19 [2-22]; 1970, page 20 [2-22]; 1971, page 20 [2-22]; 1972, page 28 [2-22]; 1973, page 33 [2-22]

Mansfield. Line: 1350. Cut: 63. Cordial. 1-1/4 oz. / 3-3/4" hi. Gold Band. **References:** 1967, page 11 [1-23]; 1968, page 15 [1-23]; 1969, page 19 [2-23]; 1970, page 20 [2-23]; 1971, page 20 [2-23]; 1972, page 28 [2-23]; 1973, page 33 [2-23]; 1975, page 29 [2-18]; 1977, page 40 [2-18]

Mansfield. Line: 1350. Cut: 63. Goblet. 12-1/2 oz. / 6-5/8" hi. Gold Band. **References:** 1967, page 11 [1-19]; 1968, page 15 [1-19]; 1969, page 19 [2-19]; 1970, page 20 [2-19]; 1971, page 20 [2-19]; 1972, page 28 [2-19]; 1973, page 33 [2-19]; 1975, page 29 [2-15]; 1977, page 40 [2-15]

Mansfield. Line: 1350. Cut: 63. Ice Tea. 13-1/2 oz. / 6-1/4" hi. Gold Band. **References:** 1967, page 11 [1-25]; 1968, page 15 [1-25]; 1969, page 19 [2-25]; 1970, page 20 [2-25]; 1971, page 20 [2-25]; 1972, page 28 [2-25]; 1973, page 33 [2-25]; 1975, page 29 [2-19]; 1977, page 40 [2-19]

Mansfield. Line: 1350. Cut: 63. Juice. 6-1/2 oz. / 5-1/4" hi. Gold Band. **References:** 1967, page 11 [1-24]; 1968, page 15 [1-24]; 1969, page 19 [2-24]; 1970, page 20 [2-24]; 1971, page 20 [2-24]; 1972, page 28 [2-24]; 1973, page 33 [2-24]

Mansfield. Line: 1350. Cut: 63. Plate. 7" / Actually 7-7/8" Dia. Gold Band. **References:** 1967, page 11 [1-26]; 1968, page 15 [1-26]; 1975, page 29 [2-20]; 1977, page 40 [2-20]

Mansfield. Line: 1350. Cut: 63. Plate. 8" / Actually 8-3/4" Dia. Gold Band. **References:** 1967, page 11 [1-27]; 1968, page 15 [1-27]; 1975, page 29 [2-21]; 1977, page 40 [2-21]

Mansfield. Line: 1350. Cut: 63. Plate. 7 inches diam. Gold Band, Platinum or Gold Banding (No Cutting), Actually 7-7/8" Dia. **References:** 1969, page 19 [2-26]; 1970, page 20 [2-26]; 1971, page 20 [2-26]; 1972, page 28 [2-26]; 1973, page 33 [2-26]

Mansfield. Line: 1350. Cut: 63. Plate. 8 inches diam. Gold Band, Platinum or Gold Banding (No Cutting), Actually 8-3/4" Dia. **References:** 1969, page 19 [2-27]; 1970, page 20 [2-27]; 1971, page 20 [2-27]; 1972, page 28 [2-27]; 1973, page 33 [2-27]

Mansfield. Line: 1350. Cut: 63. Sherbet. 6-1/2 oz. / 5" hi. Gold Band. **References:** 1967, page 11 [1-20]; 1968, page 15 [1-20]; 1969, page 19 [2-20]; 1970, page 20 [2-20]; 1971, page 20 [2-20]; <st1>Mansfield. Line: 1350. Cut: 63. Sherbet. 6-1/2 oz. 5 inches tall. Gold Band. **References:** 1973, page 33 [2-20]; 1975, page 29 [2-16]; 1977, page 40 [2-16]

Mansfield. Line: 1350. Cut: 63. White Wine. 7 oz. 5-3/4 inches tall. Gold Band. **References:** 1975, page 29 [2-17]; 1967, page 11 [1-21]; 1968, page 15 [1-21]; 1969, page 19 [2-21]; 1970, page 20 [2-21]; 1971, page 20 [2-21]; 1972, page 28 [2-21]; 1973, page 33 [2-21]; 1977, page 40 [2-17]

Mardi Gras Optic. Line: 1975. Beverage. 16 oz. 5-3/4 inches tall. Colors: Crystal, Delphine Blue, Moss Green, Grey, Plum. **References:** 1973, page 16 [BR-1]

Mardi Gras Optic. Line: 1975. Old Fashion. 12-1/2 oz. 3-3/4 inches tall. Colors: Crystal, Delphine Blue, Moss Green, Grey, Plum. **References:** 1973, page 16 [BR-2]

Mark IV. Line: 4000. Beverage. 15-1/2 oz. 5-3/8 inches tall. Plum. Colors: Crystal, Delphine Blue, Moss Green, Grey, Plum. **References:** 1972, page 7 [BL-2]; 1973, page 16 [BL-2]

Mark IV. Line: 4000. Old Fashion. 3-7/8 inches tall. Plum. Colors: Crystal, Delphine Blue, Moss Green, Grey, Plum. **References:** 1972, page 7 [BL-1]; 1973, page 16 [BL-1]

Marlboro. Line: 1960. Beverage. 16-1/2 oz. 5 inches tall. Crystal Full Sham. $5-8. **References:** 1978, page 7 [3-1]; 1979, page 16 [3-1]

Marlboro. Line: 1960. Old Fashion. 9 oz. 4 inches tall. Crystal Full Sham. $5-8. **References:** 1978, page 7 [3-2]; 1979, page 16 [3-2]

Martha Washington. Line: 128. Cut: 1274. 1311 Dessert-Finger Bowl. 4-3/4 inches diam. **References:** 1967, page 20 [1-8]; 1969, page 22 [1-9]; 1970, page 23 [1-9]; 1971, page 23 [1-9]

Martha Washington. Line: 128. Cut: 1274. Claret. 4 oz. 4-3/8 inches tall. **References:** 1967, page 20 [1-3]; 1969, page 22 [1-3]; 1970, page 23 [1-3]; 1971, page 23 [1-3]

Martha Washington. Line: 128. Cut: 1274. Cocktail. 3-1/2 oz. 4-1/8 inches tall. **References:** 1967, page 20 [1-4]; 1969, page 22 [1-5]; 1970, page 23 [1-5]; 1971, page 23 [1-5]

Martha Washington. Line: 128. Cut: 1274. Cordial. 1-1/4 oz. 3-1/4 inches tall. **References:** 1967, page 20 [1-5]; 1969, page 22 [1-6]; 1970, page 23 [1-6]; 1971, page 23 [1-6]

Martha Washington. Line: 128. Cut: 1274. Goblet. 10-1/2 oz. 6-1/8 inches tall. **References:** 1967, page 20 [1-1]; 1969, page 22 [1-1]; 1970, page 23 [1-1]; 1971, page 23 [1-1]

Martha Washington. Line: 128. Cut: 1274. Ice Tea. 12 oz. 6-3/4 inches tall. **References:** 1967, page 20 [1-7]; 1969, page 22 [1-8]; 1970, page 23 [1-8]; 1971, page 23 [1-8]

Martha Washington. Line: 128. Cut: 1274. Juice. 5 oz. 5-1/4 inches tall. **References:** 1967, page 20 [1-6]; 1969, page 22 [1-7]; 1970, page 23 [1-7]; 1971, page 23 [1-7]

Martha Washington. Line: 128. Cut: 1274. Plate. 7 inches diam. Actually 7-7/8" Dia. **References:** 1967, page 20 [1-9]; 1969, page 22 [1-10]; 1970, page 23 [1-10]; 1971, page 23 [1-10]

Martha Washington. Line: 128. Cut: 1274. Plate. 8 inches diam. Actually 8-3/4" Dia. **References:** 1967, page 20 [1-10]; 1969, page 22 [1-11]; 1970, page 23 [1-11]; 1971, page 23 [1-11]

Martha Washington. Line: 128. Cut: 1274. Sherbet. 7-1/2 oz. 4-3/4 inches tall. **References:** 1967, page 20 [1-2]; 1969, page 22 [1-2]; 1970, page 23 [1-2]; 1971, page 23 [1-2]

Martha Washington. Line: 128. Cut: 1274. Table Wine Goblet. 5-3/4 oz. 5-1/8 inches tall. **References:** 1969, page 22 [1-4]; 1970, page 23 [1-4]; 1971, page 23 [1-4]

Melodie. Cocktail. **References:** 1964 Advertisement

Melodie. Cordial. **References:** 1964 Advertisement

Melodie. Footed Ice Tea. **References:** 1964 Advertisement

Melodie. Footed Juice. **References:** 1964 Advertisement

Melodie. Goblet. **References:** 1964 Advertisement

Melodie. Saucer Champagne. **References:** 1964 Advertisement

Melodie. White Wine Goblet. **References:** 1964 Advertisement

Moderne. Cordial. 2 oz. 5-1/4 inches tall. **References:** 1979, page 4 [3-8]

Moderne. Goblet. 9-1/2 oz. 8-1/2 inches tall. **References:** 1979, page 4 [3-5]

Moderne. Sherbet. 7-1/2 oz. 6-1/4 inches tall. **References:** 1979, page 4 [3-6]

Moderne. Wine. 6 oz. 7-1/4 inches tall. **References:** 1979, page 4 [3-7]

Moderne. Line: 971. Cordial. 2 oz. 5-1/4 inches tall. **References:** 1976, page 9 [1-4]

Moderne. Line: 971. Cordial. 2 oz. 5-1/4 inches tall. Crystal Optic. **References:** 1977, page 19 [1-4]

Moderne. Line: 971. Goblet. 9-1/2 oz. 8-1/2 inches tall. **References:** 1976, page 9 [1-1]

Moderne. Line: 971. Goblet. 9-1/2 oz. 8-1/2 inches tall. Crystal Optic. **References:** 1977, page 19 [1-1]

Moderne. Line: 971. Sherbet. 7-1/2 oz. 6-1/2 inches tall. **References:** 1976, page 9 [1-2]

Moderne. Line: 971. Sherbet. 7-1/2 oz. 6-1/2 inches tall. Crystal Optic. **References:** 1977, page 19 [1-2]

Moderne. Line: 971. Wine. 5 oz. 7-1/4 inches tall. **References:** 1976, page 9 [1-3]

Moderne. Line: 971. Wine. 5 oz. 7-1/4 inches tall. Crystal Optic. **References:** 1977, page 19 [1-3]

Montclair. Cordial. 1-1/4 oz. 3-3/4 inches tall. Platinum Band. **References:** 1979, page 6 [2-19]

Montclair. Goblet. 12-1/2 oz. 6-5/8 inches tall. Platinum Band. **References:** 1979, page 6 [2-16]

Montclair. Ice Tea. 13-1/2 oz. 6-1/4 inches tall. Platinum Band. **References:** 1979, page 6 [2-20]

Montclair. Sherbet. 6-1/2 oz. 5 inches tall. Platinum Band. **References:** 1979, page 6 [2-17]

Montclair. White Wine Goblet. 7 oz. 5-3/4 inches tall. Platinum Band. **References:** 1979, page 6 [2-18]

Montclair. Line: 1350. Cut: 63. Cocktail. 4-1/2 oz. / 4-3/4" hi. Platinum Band. **References:** 1967, page 11 [1-31]; 1968, page 15 [1-31]; 1969, page 19 [2-31]; 1970, page 20 [2-31]; 1971, page 20 [2-31]; 1972, page 28 [2-31]; 1973, page 33 [2-31]

Montclair. Line: 1350. Cut: 63. Cordial. 1-1/4 oz. / 3-3/4" hi. Platinum Band. **References:** 1967, page 11 [1-32]; 1968, page 15 [1-32] 1969, page 19 [2-32]; 1970, page 20 [2-32]; 1971, page 20 [2-32]; 1972, page 28 [2-32]; 1973, page 33 [2-32]; 1975, page 29 [2-25]; 1977, page 40 [2-25]

Montclair. Line: 1350. Cut: 63. Goblet. 12-1/2 oz. / 6-5/8" hi. Platinum Band. **References:** 1967, page 11 [1-28]; 1968, page 15 [1-28]; 1969, page 19 [2-28]; 1970, page 20 [2-28]; 1971, page 20 [2-28]; 1972, page 28 [2-28]; 1973, page 33 [2-28]; 1975, page 29 [2-22]; 1977, page 40 [2-22]

Montclair. Line: 1350. Cut: 63. Ice Tea. 13-1/2 oz. / 6-1/4" hi. Platinum Band. **References:** 1967, page 11 [1-34]; 1968, page 15 [1-34]; 1969, page 19 [2-34]; 1970, page 20 [2-34]; 1971, page 20 [2-34]; 1972, page 28 [2-34]; 1973, page 33 [2-34]; 1975, page 29 [2-26]; 1977, page 40 [2-26]

Montclair. Line: 1350. Cut: 63. Juice. 6-1/2 oz. / 5-1/4" hi. Platinum Band. **References:** 1967, page 11 [1-33]; 1968, page 15 [1-33]; 1969, page 19 [2-33]; 1970, page 20 [2-33]; 1971, page 20 [2-33]; 1972, page 28 [2-33]; 1973, page 33 [2-33]

Montclair. Line: 1350. Cut: 63. Plate. 7 oz. / Actually 7-7/8" Dia. Platinum Band. **References:** 1967, page 11 [1-35]; 1968, page 15 [1-35]; 1975, page 29 [2-27]; 1977, page 40 [2-27]

Montclair. Line: 1350. Cut: 63. Plate. 8 oz. / Actually 8-3/4" Dia. Platinum Band. **References:** 1967, page 11 [1-36]; 1968, page 15 [1-36]; 1975, page 29 [2-28]; 1977, page 40 [2-28]

Montclair. Line: 1350. Cut: 63. Plate. 7 inches diam. Platinum Band, Platinum or Gold Banding (No Cutting), Actually 7-7/8" Dia. **References:** 1969, page 19 [2-35]; 1970, page 20 [2-35]; 1971, page 20 [2-35]; 1972, page 28 [2-35]; 1973, page 33 [2-35]

Montclair. Line: 1350. Cut: 63. Plate. 8 inches diam. Platinum Band, Platinum or Gold Banding (No Cutting), Actually 8-3/4" Dia. **References:** 1969, page 19 [2-36]; 1970, page 20 [2-36]; 1971, page 20 [2-36]; 1972, page 28 [2-36]; 1973, page 33 [2-36]

Montclair. Line: 1350. Cut: 63. Sherbet. 6-1/2 oz. / 5" hi. Platinum Band. **References:** 1967, page 11 [1-29]; 1968, page 15 [1-29]; 1969, page 19 [2-29]; 1970, page 20 [2-29]; 1971, page 20 [2-29]; 1972, page 28 [2-29]; 1973, page 33 [2-29]; 1975, page 29 [2-23]; 1977, page 40 [2-23]

Montclair. Line: 1350. Cut: 63. White Wine. 7 oz. 5-3/4 inches tall. Platinum Band. **References:** 1975, page 29 [2-24]; 1977, page 40 [2-24]; 1967, page 11 [1-30]; 1968, page 15 [1-30]; 1969, page 19 [2-30]; 1970, page 20 [2-30]; 1971, page 20 [2-30]; 1972, page 28 [2-30]; 1973, page 33 [2-30]

Monte Carlo. Line: 1964. Cut: 1413. 1305 Dessert-Finger Bowl. 4-1/2 inches diam. **References:** 1967, page 14 [2-16]; 1968, page 18 [2-16]

Monte Carlo. Line: 1964. Cut: 1413. Cordial. 1-1/2 oz. 3-3/4 inches tall. **References:** 1967, page 14 [2-13]; 1968, page 18 [2-13]

Monte Carlo. Line: 1964. Cut: 1413. Goblet. 13-3/4 oz. 6-1/2 inches tall. **References:** 1967, page 14 [2-10]; 1968, page 18 [2-10]

Monte Carlo. Line: 1964. Cut: 1413. Ice Tea. 14-1/4 oz. 6-3/8 inches tall. **References:** 1967, page 14 [2-15]; 1968, page 18 [2-15]

Monte Carlo. Line: 1964. Cut: 1413. Juice. 6-3/4 oz. 4-3/4 inches tall. **References:** 1967, page 14 [2-14]; 1968, page 18 [2-14]

Monte Carlo. Line: 1964. Cut: 1413. Plate. 7 inches diam. Actually 7-7/8" Dia. **References:** 1967, page 14 [2-17]; 1968, page 18 [2-17]

Monte Carlo. Line: 1964. Cut: 1413. Plate. 8 inches diam. Actually 8-3/4" Dia. **References:** 1967, page 14 [2-18]; 1968, page 18 [2-18]

Monte Carlo. Line: 1964. Cut: 1413. Sherbet. 7-1/2 oz. 4-3/8 inches tall. **References:** 1967, page 14 [2-11]; 1968, page 18 [2-11]

Monte Carlo. Line: 1964. Cut: 1413. Wine. 9 oz. 5-5/8 inches tall. **References:** 1967, page 14 [2-12]; 1968, page 18 [2-12]

Musette. Cordial. 2 oz. 4-1/2 inches tall. Platinum Band. **References:** 1979, page 6 [1-14]

Musette. Goblet. 12 oz. 7 inches tall. Platinum Band. **References:** 1979, page 6 [1-11]

Musette. Ice Tea. 12 oz. 6-1/4 inches tall. Platinum Band. **References:** 1979, page 6 [1-15]

Musette. Sherbet. 7-1/2 oz. 5-1/8 inches tall. Platinum Band. **References:** 1979, page 6 [1-12]

Musette. Wine. 7 oz. 5-7/8 inches tall. Platinum Band. **References:** 1979, page 6 [1-13]

Musette. Line: 1235. Cordial. 2 oz. 4-1/2 inches tall. Platinum Band. **References:** 1975, page 29 [1-18]; 1977, page 40 [1-18]

Musette. Line: 1235. Goblet. 12 oz. 7 inches tall. Platinum Band. **References:** 1975, page 29 [1-15]; 1977, page 40 [1-15]

Musette. Line: 1235. Ice Tea. 12 oz. 6-1/4 inches tall. Platinum Band. **References:** 1975, page 29 [1-19]; 1977, page 40 [1-19]

Musette. Line: 1235. Plate. 7 inches diam. Platinum Band, Actually 7-7/8" Dia. **References:** 1975, page 29 [1-20]; 1977, page 40 [1-20]

Musette. Line: 1235. Plate. 8 inches diam. Platinum Band, Actually 8-3/4" Dia. **References:** 1975, page 29 [1-21]; 1977, page 40 [1-21]

Musette. Line: 1235. Sherbet. 7-1/2 oz. 5-1/8 inches tall. Platinum Band. **References:** 1975, page 29 [1-16]; 1977, page 40 [1-16]

Musette. Line: 1235. Wine. 7 oz. 5-7/8 inches tall. Platinum Band. **References:** 1975, page 29 [1-17]; 1977, page 40 [1-17]

Musette. Line: 1235. Cut: 1406. Cocktail. 5-1/2 oz. / 4-5/8" hi. Platinum Band. **References:** 1967, page 10 [1-22]; 1969, page 19 [1-24]; 1970, page 20 [1-24]; 1971, page 20 [1-24]; 1972, page 28 [1-24]; 1973, page 33 [1-24]

Musette. Line: 1235. Cut: 1406. Cordial. 2 oz. / 4-1/2" hi. Platinum Band. **References:** 1967, page 10 [1-23]; 1969, page 19 [1-25]; 1970, page 20 [1-25]; 1971, page 20 [1-25]; 1972, page 28 [1-25]; 1973, page 33 [1-25]

Musette. Line: 1235. Cut: 1406. Goblet. 12 oz. / 7" hi. Platinum Band. **References:** 1967, page 10 [1-19]; 1969, page 19 [1-21]; 1970, page 20 [1-21]; 1971, page 20 [1-21]; 1972, page 28 [1-21]; 1973, page 33 [1-21]

Musette. Line: 1235. Cut: 1406. Ice Tea. 12 oz. / 6-1/4" hi. Platinum Band. **References:** 1967, page 10 [1-25]; 1969, page 19 [1-28]; 1970, page 20 [1-28]; 1971, page 20 [1-28]; 1972, page 28 [1-28]; 1973, page 33 [1-28]

Musette. Line: 1235. Cut: 1406. Juice. 5 oz. / 4-1/2" hi. Platinum Band. **References:** 1967, page 10 [1-24]; 1969, page 19 [1-27]; 1970, page 20 [1-27]; 1971, page 20 [1-27]; 1972, page 28 [1-27]; 1973, page 33 [1-27]

Musette. Line: 1235. Cut: 1406. Parfait Whiskey Sour. 7 oz. 6-1/4 inches tall. Platinum Band. **References:** 1969, page 19 [1-26]; 1970, page 20 [1-26]; 1971, page 20 [1-26]; 1972, page 28 [1-26]; 1973, page 33 [1-26]

Musette. Line: 1235. Cut: 1406. Plate. 7" / Actually 7-7/8" hi. Platinum Band. **References:** 1967, page 10 [1-26]; 1969, page 19 [1-29]; 1970, page 20 [1-29]; 1971, page 20 [1-29]; 1972, page 28 [1-29]; 1973, page 33 [1-29]

Musette. Line: 1235. Cut: 1406. Plate. 8" / Actually 8-3/4" hi. Platinum Band. **References:** 1967, page 10 [1-27]; 1969, page 19 [1-30]; 1970, page 20 [1-30]; 1971, page 20 [1-30]; 1972, page 28 [1-30]; 1973, page 33 [1-30]

Musette. Line: 1235. Cut: 1406. Sherbet. 7-1/2 oz. / 5-1/8" hi. Platinum Band. **References:** 1967, page 10 [1-20]; 1969, page 19 [1-22]; 1970, page 20 [1-22]; 1971, page 20 [1-22]; 1972, page 28 [1-22]; 1973, page 33 [1-22]

Musette. Line: 1235. Cut: 1406. Wine. 7 oz. / 5-7/8 hi. Platinum Band. **References:** 1967, page 10 [1-21]; 1969, page 19 [1-23]; 1970, page 20 [1-23]; 1971, page 20 [1-23]; 1972, page 28 [1-23]; 1973, page 33 [1-23]

Newport. Champagne Flute. 6 oz. 9-1/4 inches tall. **References:** 1983, page 3 [1-9]

Newport. Cordial. 1-1/2 oz. 4 inches tall. **References:** 1979, page 2 [3-9]; 1983, page 3 [1-11]

Newport. Goblet. 11-1/2 oz. 7 inches tall. **References:** 1979, page 2 [3-6]; 1983, page 3 [1-7]

Newport. Ice Tea. 14 oz. 6-1/4 inches tall. **References:** 1979, page 2 [3-10]; 1983, page 3 [1-12]

Newport. Sherbet. 7 oz. 5-1/4 inches tall. **References:** 1979, page 2 [3-7]; 1983, page 3 [1-8]

Newport. Wine. 7 oz. 6 inches tall. **References:** 1979, page 2 [3-8]; 1983, page 3 [1-10]

Newport. Line: 960. Cut: 43. 1311 Dessert-Finger Bowl. 4-3/4 inches diam. **References:** 1973, page 20 [1-6]; 1975, page 20 [1-6]; 1977, page 31 [1-6]

Newport. Line: 960. Cut: 43. Cordial. 1-1/4 oz. 3-7/8 inches tall. **References:** 1973, page 20 [1-4]; 1975, page 20 [1-4]; 1977, page 31 [1-4]; 1981, page 2 [1-12]

Newport. Line: 960. Cut: 43. Goblet. 11-1/2 oz. 7 inches tall. **References:** 1973, page 20 [1-1]; 1975, page 20 [1-1]; 1977, page 31 [1-1]; 1981, page 2 [1-9]

Newport. Line: 960. Cut: 43. Ice Tea. 14 oz. 6-1/4 inches tall. **References:** 1973, page 20 [1-5]; 1975, page 20 [1-5]; 1977, page 31 [1-5]

Newport. Line: 960. Cut: 43. Plate. 7 inches diam. Actually 7-7/8" Dia. **References:** 1973, page 20 [1-7]; 1975, page 20 [1-7]; 1977, page 31 [1-7]

Newport. Line: 960. Cut: 43. Plate. 8 inches diam. Actually 8-3/4" Dia. **References:** 1973, page 20 [1-8]; 1975, page 20 [1-8]; 1977, page 31 [1-8]

Newport. Line: 960. Cut: 43. Sherbet. 7 oz. 5-1/4 inches tall. **References:** 1973, page 20 [1-2]; 1975, page 20 [1-2]; 1977, page 31 [1-2]; 1981, page 2 [1-10]

Newport. Line: 960. Cut: 43. Wine. 7 oz. 6 inches tall. **References:** 1973, page 20 [1-3]; 1975, page 20 [1-3]; 1977, page 31 [1-3]; 1981, page 2 [1-11]

Nocturne. Cordial. 1-1/2 oz. 4-5/8 inches tall. Colors: Yellow Optic, Crystal Optic, Lime Green Optic, Black, Charm Blue Optic. **References:** 1979, page 8 [2-4]

Nocturne. Goblet. 11 oz. 7-1/2 inches tall. Colors: Yellow Optic, Crystal Optic, Lime Green Optic, Black, Charm Blue Optic. **References:** 1979, page 8 [2-1]

Nocturne. Ice Tea. 15-1/2 oz. 7-1/2 inches tall. Colors: Yellow Optic, Crystal Optic, Lime Green Optic, Black, Charm Blue Optic. **References:** 1979, page 8 [2-5]

Nocturne. Sherbet. 7 oz. 4-5/8 inches tall. Colors: Yellow Optic, Crystal Optic, Lime Green Optic, Black, Charm Blue Optic. **References:** 1979, page 8 [2-2]

Nocturne. Wine. 8-1/2 oz. 6-1/2 inches tall. Colors: Yellow Optic, Crystal Optic, Lime Green Optic, Black, Charm Blue Optic. **References:** 1979, page 8 [2-3]

Nocturne. Line: 1975. Beverage. 16 oz. 5-3/4 inches tall. Brown. Colors: Black, Brown, Crystal, Lime Green, Plum. **References:** 1972, page 8 [2-4]; 1973, page 17 [2-4]

Nocturne. Line: 1975. Cordial. 1-1/2 oz. 4-5/8 inches tall. Crystal. Colors: Black, Brown, Crystal, Lime Green, Plum. **References:** 1972, page 8 [2-3]; 1973, page 17 [2-3]

Nocturne. Line: 1975. Cordial. 1-1/2 oz. 4-5/8 inches tall. Colors: Black. **References:** 1975, page 17 [4-1]

Nocturne. Line: 1975. Cordial. 1-1/2 oz. 4-5/8 inches tall. Colors: Black. **References:** 1977, page 17 [4-1]

Nocturne. Line: 1975. Goblet. 11 oz. 7-1/2 inches tall. Plum. Colors: Black, Brown, Crystal, Lime Green, Plum. **References:** 1972, page 8 [2-5]; 1973, page 17 [2-5]

Nocturne. Line: 1975. Goblet. 11 oz. 7-1/2 inches tall. Colors: Black. **References:** 1975, page 17 [3-2]; 1977, page 17 [3-2]

Nocturne. Line: 1975. Ice Tea. 15-1/2 oz. 7-1/2 inches tall. Lime Green. Colors: Black, Brown, Crystal, Lime Green, Plum. **References:** 1972, page 8 [1-2]; 1973, page 17 [1-2]

Nocturne. Line: 1975. Ice Tea. 15-1/2 oz. 7-1/2 inches tall. Colors: Black. **References:** 1975, page 13 [1-1]; 1977, page 17 [1-1]

Nocturne. Line: 1975. Old Fashion. 12-1/2 oz. 3-3/4 inches tall. Black. Colors: Black, Brown, Crystal, Lime Green, Plum. 1973, page 17 [1-1]

Nocturne. Line: 1975. Sherbet. 7 oz. 4-5/8 inches tall. Plum. Colors: Black, Brown, Crystal, Lime Green, Plum. **References:** 1972, page 8 [2-2]; 1973, page 17 [2-2]

Nocturne. Line: 1975. Sherbet. 7 oz. 4-5/8 inches tall. Colors: Black. **References:** 1975, page 13 [3-1]; 1977, page 17 [3-1]

Nocturne. Line: 1975. Wine. 8-1/2 oz. 6-1/2 inches tall. Brown. Colors: Black, Brown, Crystal, Lime Green, Plum. **References:** 1972, page 8 [2-1]; 1973, page 17 [2-1]

Nocturne. Line: 1975. Wine. 8-1/2 oz. 6-1/2 inches tall. Colors: Black. **References:** 1975, page 13 [2-1]; 1977, page 17 [2-1]

Old Master. Champagne Flute. 6 oz. 9-1/4 inches tall. **References:** 1983, page 3 [1-21]

Old Master. Cordial. 1-1/2 oz. 4 inches tall. **References:** 1979, page 2 [2-14]; 1983, page 3 [1-23]

Old Master. Goblet. 11-1/2 oz. 7 inches tall. **References:** 1979, page 2 [2-11]; 1983, page 3 [1-19]

Old Master. Ice Tea. 14 oz. 6-1/4 inches tall. **References:** 1979, page 2 [2-15]; 1983, page 3 [1-24]

Old Master. Sherbet. 7 oz. 5-1/4 inches tall. **References:** 1979, page 2 [2-12]; 1983, page 3 [1-20]

Old Master. Wine. 7 oz. 6 inches tall. **References:** 1979, page 2 [2-13]; 1983, page 3 [1-22]

Old Master. Line: 960. Cut: 1435. 1311 Dessert-Finger Bowl. 4-3/4" Dia. **References:** 1967, page 4 [2-6]; 1968, page 6 [2-6]; 1969, page 6 [2-6]; 1970, page 6 [2-6]; 1971, page 6 [2-6]; 1972, page 16 [1-14]; 1973, page 21 [1-14]; 1975, page 21 [1-14]; 1977, page 32 [1-14]

Old Master. Line: 960. Cut: 1435. Cordial. 1-1/4 oz. / 3-7/8" hi. **References:** 1967, page 4 [2-4]; 1968, page 6 [2-4]; 1969, page 6 [2-4]; 1970, page 6 [2-4]; 1971, page 6 [2-4]; 1972, page 16 [1-12]; 1973, page 21 [1-12]; 1975, page 21 [1-12]; 1977, page 32 [1-12]; 1981, page 2 [1-16]

Old Master. Line: 960. Cut: 1435. Goblet. 11-1/2 oz. / 7" hi. **References:** 1967, page 4 [2-1]; 1968, page 6 [2-1]; 1969, page 6 [2-1]; 1970, page 6 [2-1]; 1971, page 6 [2-1]; 1972, page 16 [1-9]; 1973, page 21 [1-9]; 1975, page 21 [1-9]; 1977, page 32 [1-9]; 1981, page 2 [1-13]

Old Master. Line: 960. Cut: 1435. Ice Tea. 14 oz. / 6-1/4" hi. **References:** 1967, page 4 [2-5]; 1968, page 6 [2-5]; 1969, page 6 [2-5]; 1970, page 6 [2-5]; 1971, page 6 [2-5]; 1972, page 16 [1-13]; 1973, page 21 [1-13]; 1975, page 21 [1-13]; 1977, page 32 [1-13]

Old Master. Line: 960. Cut: 1435. Plate. 7 inch / Actually 7-7/8 inch. **References:** 1967, page 4 [2-7]; 1968, page 6 [2-7]; 1969, page 6 [2-7]; 1970, page 6 [2-7]; 1971, page 6 [2-7]; 1972, page 16 [1-15]; 1973, page 21 [1-15]; 1975, page 21 [1-15]; 1977, page 32 [1-15]

Old Master. Line: 960. Cut: 1435. Plate. 8 inch / Actually 8-3/4 inch. **References:** 1967, page 4 [2-8]; 1968, page 6 [2-8]; 1969, page 6 [2-8]; 1970, page 6 [2-8]; 1971, page 6 [2-8]; 1972, page 16 [1-16]; 1973, page 21 [1-16]; 1975, page 21 [1-16]; 1977, page 32 [1-16]

Old Master. Line: 960. Cut: 1435. Sherbet. 7 oz. / 5-1/4" hi. **References:** 1967, page 4 [2-2]; 1968, page 6 [2-2]; 1969, page 6 [2-2]; 1970, page 6 [2-2]; 1971, page 6 [2-2]; 1972, page 16 [1-10]; 1973, page 21 [1-10]; 1975, page 21 [1-10]; 1977, page 32 [1-10]; 1981, page 2 [1-14]

Old Master. Line: 960. Cut: 1435. Wine. 4 oz. / 6" hi. **References:** 1967, page 4 [2-3]; 1968, page 6 [2-3]; 1969, page 6 [2-3]; 1970, page 6 [2-3]; 1971, page 6 [2-3]; 1972, page 16 [1-11]; 1973, page 21 [1-11]; 1975, page 21 [1-11]; 1977, page 32 [1-11]; 1981, page 2 [1-15]

Olympia. Cordial. 1-1/4 oz. 3-3/4 inches tall. Platinum Band. **References:** 1979, page 6 [2-9]

Olympia. Goblet. 12-1/2 oz. 6-5/8 inches tall. Platinum Band. **References:** 1979, page 6 [2-6]

Olympia. Ice Tea. 13-1/2 oz. 6-1/4 inches tall. Platinum Band. **References:** 1979, page 6 [2-10]

Olympia. Sherbet. 6-1/2 oz. 5 inches tall. Platinum Band. **References:** 1979, page 6 [2-7]

Olympia. White Wine Goblet. 7 oz. 5-3/4 inches tall. Platinum Band. **References:** 1979, page 6 [2-8]

Olympia. Line: 4. Bell. 5-1/2 inches tall. 1/4" Platinum Band. All Bells Individually Gift Boxed. **References:** 1976, page 7 [1-2]; 1977, page 23 [2-2]; 1979, page 13 [2-2]

Olympia. Line: 1962. Cocktail. 4-1/2 oz. / 4-3/4" hi. Platinum Band. **References:** 1967, page 11 [1-13]; 1968, page 15 [1-13]; 1969, page 19 [2-13]; 1970, page 20 [2-13]; 1971, page 20 [2-13]; 1972, page 28 [2-13]; 1973, page 33 [2-13]

Olympia. Line: 1962. Cordial. 1-1/4 oz. / 3-3/4" hi. Platinum Band. **References:** 1967, page 11 [1-14]; 1968, page 15 [1-14]; 1969, page 19 [2-14]; 1970, page 20 [2-14]; 1971, page 20 [2-14]; 1972, page 28 [2-14]; 1973, page 33 [2-14]; 1975, page 29 [2-11]; 1977, page 40 [2-11]

Olympia. Line: 1962. Goblet. 12-1/2 oz. 6-5/8" hi. Platinum Band. **References:** 1967, page 11 [1-10]; 1968, page 15 [1-10]; 1969, page 19 [2-10]; 1970, page 20 [2-10]; 1971, page 20 [2-10] 1972, page 28 [2-10]; 1973, page 33 [2-10]; 1975, page 29 [2-8]; 1977, page 40 [2-8]

Olympia. Line: 1962. Ice Tea. 13-1/2 oz. / 6-1/4" hi. Platinum Band. **References:** 1967, page 11 [1-16]; 1968, page 15 [1-16]; 1969, page 19 [2-16]; 1970, page 20 [2-16]; 1971, page 20 [2-16]; 1972, page 28 [2-16]; 1973, page 33 [2-16]; 1975, page 29 [2-12]; 1977, page 40 [2-12]

Olympia. Line: 1962. Juice. 6-1/2 oz. / 5-1/4" hi. Platinum Band. **References:** 1967, page 11 [1-15]; 1968, page 15 [1-15]; 1969, page 19 [2-15]; 1970, page 20 [2-15]; 1971, page 20 [2-15]; 1972, page 28 [2-15]; 1973, page 33 [2-15]

Olympia. Line: 1962. Plate. 7" / Actually 7-7/8" Dia. Platinum Band. **References:** 1967, page 11 [1-17]; 1968, page 15 [1-17]; 1969, page 19 [2-17]; 1970, page 20 [2-17]; 1971, page 20 [2-17]; 1972, page 28 [2-17]; 1973, page 33 [2-17]; 1975, page 29 [2-13]; 1977, page 40 [2-13]

Olympia. Line: 1962. Plate. 8" / Actually 8-3/4" Dia. Platinum Band. **References:** 1967, page 11 [1-18]; 1968, page 15 [1-18]; 1969, page 19 [2-18]; 1970, page 20 [2-18]; 1971, page 20 [2-18]; 1972, page 28 [2-18]; 1973, page 33 [2-18]; 1975, page 29 [2-14]; 1977, page 40 [2-14]

Olympia. Line: 1962. Sherbet. 6-1/2 oz. / 5" hi. Platinum Band. **References:** 1967, page 11 [1-11]; 1968, page 15 [1-11]; 1969, page 19 [2-11]; 1970, page 20 [2-11]; 1971, page 20 [2-11]; 1972, page 28 [2-11]; 1973, page 33 [2-11]; 1975, page 29 [2-9]; 1977, page 40 [2-9]

Olympia. Line: 1962. White Wine. 7 oz. 5-3/4 inches tall. Platinum Band. **References:** 1975, page 29 [2-10]; 1977, page 40 [2-10]; 1967, page 11 [1-12]; 1968, page 15 [1-12]; 1969, page 19 [2-12]; 1970, page 20 [2-12]; 1971, page 20 [2-12]; 1972, page 28 [2-12]; 1973, page 33 [2-12]

Orleans. Champagne Flute. 6 oz. 9-1/4 inches tall. **References:** 1983, page 4 [2-16]

Orleans. Cordial. 1-1/4 oz. 4 inches tall. **References:** 1979, page 3 [1-9]; 1983, page 4 [2-17]

Orleans. Goblet. 11-3/4 oz. 7-1/4 inches tall. **References:** 1979, page 3 [1-6]; 1983, page 4 [2-13]

Orleans. Ice Tea. 13-1/2 oz. 6-3/4 inches tall. **References:** 1979, page 3 [1-10]; 1983, page 4 [2-18]

Orleans. Sherbet. 7-1/2 oz. 5-1/4 inches tall. **References:** 1979, page 3 [1-7]; 1983, page 4 [2-14]

Orleans. Wine. 7-1/2 oz. 6-1/4 inches tall. **References:** 1979, page 3 [1-8]; 1983, page 4 [2-15]

Orleans. Cut: 1422. Bell. 4-1/2 inches tall. **References:** 1979, page 12 [2-1]

Orleans. Cut: 1422. Bell. **References:** 1981, page 11 [2-2]; 1983, page 6 [1-3R]

Orleans. Line: 3. Cut: 1422. Bell. 4-3/8 inches tall. Handmade and Hand Cut. **References:** 1975, page 12 [2-1]; 1976, page 6 [2-4]; 1977, page 22 [5-1]

Orleans. Line: 1965. Cut: 1422. 1305 Dessert-Finger Bowl. 4-1/2" Dia. **References:** 1967, page 7 [1-7]; 1968, page 10 [2-7]; 1969, page 10 [2-7]; 1970, page 12 [2-7]; 1971, page 12 [2-7]; 1972, page 21 [2-7]; 1973, page 25 [2-7]; 1975, page 25 [2-6]; 1977, page 36 [2-6]

Orleans. Line: 1965. Cut: 1422. Cordial. 1-1/4 oz. / 4" hi. **References:** 1967, page 7 [1-4]; 1968, page 10 [2-4]; 1969, page 10 [2-4]; 1970, page 12 [2-4]; 1971, page 12 [2-4]; 1972, page 21 [2-4]; 1973, page 25 [2-4]; 1975, page 25 [2-4]; 1977, page 36 [2-4]; 1981, page 1 [2-12]

Orleans. Line: 1965. Cut: 1422. Goblet. 11-3/4 oz. / 7-1/4" hi. **References:** 1967, page 7 [1-1]; 1968, page 10 [2-1]; 1969, page 10 [2-1]; 1970, page 12 [2-1]; 1971, page 12 [2-1]; 1972, page 21 [2-1]; 1973, page 25 [2-1]; 1975, page 25 [2-1]; 1977, page 36 [2-1]; 1981, page 1 [2-9]

Orleans. Line: 1965. Cut: 1422. Ice Tea. 13-1/2 oz. / 6-3/4" hi. **References:** 1967, page 7 [1-6]; 1968, page 10 [2-6]; 1969, page 10 [2-6]; 1970, page 12 [2-6]; 1971, page 12 [2-6]; 1972, page 21 [2-6]; 1973, page 25 [2-6]; 1975, page 25 [2-5]; 1977, page 36 [2-5]

Orleans. Line: 1965. Cut: 1422. Juice. 6 oz. / 5-1/2" hi. **References:** 1967, page 7 [1-5]; 1968, page 10 [2-5]; 1969, page 10 [2-5]; 1970, page 12 [2-5]; 1971, page 12 [2-5]; 1972, page 21 [2-5]; 1973, page 25 [2-5]

Orleans. Line: 1965. Cut: 1422. Plate. 7" / Actually 7-7/8" Dia. **References:** 1967, page 7 [1-8]; 1968, page 10 [2-8]; 1969, page 10 [2-8]; 1970, page 12 [2-8]; 1971, page 12 [2-8]; 1972, page 21 [2-8]; 1973, page 25 [2-8]; 1975, page 25 [2-7]; 1977, page 36 [2-7]

Orleans. Line: 1965. Cut: 1422. Plate. 8" / Actually 8-3/4" Dia. **References:** 1967, page 7 [1-9]; 1968, page 10 [2-9]; 1969, page 10 [2-9]; 1970, page 12 [2-9]; 1971, page 12 [2-9]; 1972, page 21 [2-9]; 1973, page 25 [2-9]; 1975, page 25 [2-8]
1977, page 36 [2-8]

Orleans. Line: 1965. Cut: 1422. Sherbet. 7-1/2 oz. / 5-1/4" hi. **References:** 1967, page 7 [1-2]; 1968, page 10 [2-2]; 1969, page 10 [2-2]; 1970, page 12 [2-2]; 1971, page 12 [2-2]; 1972, page 21 [2-2]; 1973, page 25 [2-2]; 1975, page 25 [2-2]; 1977, page 36 [2-2]; 1981, page 1 [2-10]

Orleans. Line: 1965. Cut: 1422. Wine. 7-1/2 oz. / 6-1/4" hi. **References:** 1967, page 7 [1-3]; 1968, page 10 [2-3]; 1969, page 10 [2-3]; 1970, page 12 [2-3]; 1971, page 12 [2-3]; 1972, page 21 [2-3]; 1973, page 25 [2-3]; 1975, page 25 [2-3]; 1977, page 36 [2-3]; 1981, page 1 [2-11]

Palm Optic. Line: 7. Sherry. 3 oz. 5-1/8 inches tall. **References:** 1982, page 9 [1-5]; 1975/I-75, page 2 [3-1]

Palm Optic. Line: 85. Old Fashion. 7-3/4 oz. 3-3/8 inches tall. Sham Weight. **References:** 1982, page 10 [2-1]

Palm Optic. Line: 463. Brandy Inhaler. 23 oz. 5-3/4 inches tall. **References:** 1975/I-75, page 2 [2-1]

Palm Optic. Line: 1235. Brandy Inhaler. 12 oz. 4-5/8 inches tall. **References:** 1982, page 9 [1-6]

Palm Optic. Line: 1235. Brandy Inhaler. 22 oz. 6 inches tall. **References:** 1982, page 9 [2-7]

Palm Optic. Line: 1235. Cocktail. 5-1/2 oz. 4-3/4 inches tall. **References:** 1982, page 9 [2-5]

Palm Optic. Line: 1235. Continental Beer. 14 oz. 8-1/8 inches tall. **References:** 1982, page 9 [2-10]; 1982, page 9 [2-10]

Palm Optic. Line: 1235. Cordial. 2 oz. 4-1/2 inches tall. **References:** 1982, page 9 [2-6]; 1975/I-75, page 2 [3-2]

Palm Optic. Line: 1235. Dessert-Champagne. 7-1/2 oz. 5-1/8 inches tall. **References:** 1982, page 9 [2-4]

Palm Optic. Line: 1235. Goblet. 12 oz. 7 inches tall. **References:** 1982, page 9 [2-2]

Palm Optic. Line: 1235. Ice Tea. 12 oz. 6-1/4 inches tall. **References:** 1982, page 9 [2-8]

Palm Optic. Line: 1235. Juice. 5 oz. 4-5/8 inches tall. **References:** 1982, page 9 [2-1]

Palm Optic. Line: 1235. Martini. 5-1/2 oz. 6 inches tall. **References:** 1982, page 9 [1-1]

Palm Optic. Line: 1235. Parfait Whiskey Sour. 6-1/2 oz. 6-1/4 inches tall. **References:** 1982, page 9 [1-4]; 1975/I-75, page 2 [2-2]

Palm Optic. Line: 1235. Peach Champagne. 24 oz. 8-1/2 inches tall. **References:** 1982, page 9 [2-9]

Palm Optic. Line: 1235. Vintage Wine Goblet. 14 oz. 7 inches tall. **References:** 1982, page 9 [2-3]

Palm Optic. Line: 2828. Tumbler. 9-1/2 oz. 4-7/8 inches tall. Regular Weight. **References:** 1982, page 10 [1-2]

Palm Optic. Line: 7197. Wine Goblet. 8 oz. 5-1/4 inches tall. **References:** 1982, page 9 [1-3]; 1975/I-75, page 2 [1-2]

Palm Optic. Line: 7780. Wine Goblet. 9-1/2 oz. 6-3/8 inches tall. **References:** 1982, page 9 [1-2]; 1975/I-75, page 2 [1-1]

Palm Optic. Line: 8127. Old Fashion. 5-1/2 oz. 3 inches tall. Sham Weight. **References:** 1982, page 10 [2-2]

Palm Optic. Line: 8701. Tumbler. 14 oz. 5-1/2 inches tall. Sham Weight. **References:** 1982, page 10 [2-3]

Palm Optic. Line: 8701. Tumbler. 12 oz. 5 inches tall. Sham Weight. **References:** 1982, page 10 [2-5]

Palm Optic. Line: 8701. Tumbler. 10 oz. 5-1/8 inches tall. Sham Weight. **References:** 1982, page 10 [2-4]

Palm Optic. Line: 8701. Tumbler. 10 oz. 5-1/8 inches tall. Plain & Palm Optic, Sham Weight. **References:** 1975/I-75, page 7 [3-3]

Palm Optic. Line: 8701. Tumbler. 9 oz. 4-3/4 inches tall. Sham Weight. **References:** 1982, page 10 [2-6]; 1975/I-75, page 7 [3-2]

Palm Optic. Line: 9491. Tumbler. 12 oz. 6 inches tall. Regular Weight. **References:** 1982, page 10 [1-1]

Palm Optic. Line: 9491. Tumbler. 12 oz. 7 inches tall. Plain & Palm Optic, Sham Weight. **References:** 1975/I-75, page 7 [3-1]

Pansy Design. Line: 300. Etching: 610. Ale. **References:** 3, page 16 [1-1]

Pansy Design. Line: 300. Etching: 610. Brandy. **References:** 3, page16 [1-2]

Pansy Design. Line: 300. Etching: 610. Claret. **References:** 3, page 16 [2-5]

Pansy Design. Line: 300. Etching: 610. Cocktail. **References:** 3, page 16 [1-4]

Pansy Design. Line: 300. Etching: 610. Cordial. **References:** 3, page 16 [2-1]

Pansy Design. Line: 300. Etching: 610. Custard. **References:** 3, page 15 [1-1]

Pansy Design. Line: 300. Etching: 610. Deminth. **References:** 3, page 16 [1-5]

Pansy Design. Line: 300. Etching: 610. Goblet. 10 oz. **References:** 3, page 15 [2-1]

Pansy Design. Line: 300. Etching: 610. Goblet. 9 oz. **References:** 3, page 15 [2-2], [2-3]

Pansy Design. Line: 300. Etching: 610. Goblet. 8 oz. **References:** 3, page 15 [2-4]

Pansy Design. Line: 300. Etching: 610. Goblet. 7 oz. **References:** 3, page 15 [2-5]

Pansy Design. Line: 300. Etching: 610. Goblet. 6 oz. **References:** 3, page 15 [2-6]

Pansy Design. Line: 300. Etching: 610. Port. **References:** 3, page 16 [2-4]

Pansy Design. Line: 300. Etching: 610. Rhine Wine Goblet. **References:** 3, page 16 [1-3]

Pansy Design. Line: 300. Etching: 610. Saucer Champ. **References:** 3, page 16 [1-6]

Pansy Design. Line: 300. Etching: 610. Sherbert. **References:** 3, page 15 [3-1]

Pansy Design. Line: 300. Etching: 610. Sherry. **References:** 3, page 16 [2-2]

Pansy Design. Line: 300. Etching: 610. Wine. **References:** 3, page 16 [2-3]

Pansy Design. Line: 300. Cut: 43. Etching: 610. Champagne. Hollow Stem. **References:** 3, page 16 [2-6]

Pansy Design. Line: 300. Cut: 43. Etching: 610. Saucer Champ. Hollow Stem. **References:** 3, page 16 [2-7]

Peacock Optic. Brandy and Liqueur. 2-1/2 oz. 4-1/2 inches tall. **References:** 1982, page 11 [1-9]

Peacock Optic. Champagne. 9-1/2 oz. 8 inches tall. **References:** 1982, page 11 [1-6]

Peacock Optic. Champagne Flute. 6 oz. 9-1/4 inches tall. **References:** 1982, page 11 [1-7]

Peacock Optic. Dessert-Champagne. 11 oz. 4-7/8 inches tall. **References:** 1982, page 11 [1-8]

Peacock Optic. Grande Bordeaux. 24 oz. 7-5/8 inches tall. **References:** 1982, page 11 [1-1]

Peacock Optic. Magnum Wine Goblet. 18 oz. 7-3/8 inches tall. **References:** 1982, page 11 [1-2]

Peacock Optic. Red Wine Goblet. 10-1/2 oz. 6-7/8 inches tall. **References:** 1982, page 11 [1-4]

Peacock Optic. Sherry and Port. 5 oz. 6 inches tall. **References:** 1982, page 11 [1-10]

Peacock Optic. Vintage Wine Goblet. 14 oz. 7 inches tall. **References:** 1982, page 11 [1-3]

Peacock Optic. White Wine Goblet. 8-1/2 oz. 6-5/8 inches tall. **References:** 1982, page 11 [1-5]

Peacock Optic. Line: 1-A. Sherry. 2 oz. 4-3/8 inches tall. **References:** 1975/I-75, page 4 [3-2]

Peacock Optic. Line: 82. Wine Goblet. 11 oz. 5-3/4 inches tall. **References:** 1975/I-75, page 3 [1-2]

Peacock Optic. Line: 85. Old Fashion. 7-3/4 oz. 3-3/8 inches tall. Sham Weight. **References:** 1982, page 10 [2-1]

Peacock Optic. Line: 85. Old Fashion. 8 oz. 3-3/8 inches tall. Sham Weight. **References:** 1975/I-75, page 6 [2-1]

Peacock Optic. Line: 113. Whiskey. 2 oz. 2-1/2 inches tall. Sham Weight, 1/2 oz. 1st Line, 1-1/4 Oz. 2nd Line. **References:** 1975/I-75, page 6 [3-2]

Peacock Optic. Line: 300. Saucer Champagne. 5 oz. 4-1/2 inches tall. **References:** 1975/I-75, page 4 [2-1]

Peacock Optic. Line: 309. Parfait Whiskey Sour. 6-1/2 oz. 6-1/4 inches tall. **References:** 1975/I-75, page 3 [2-1]

Peacock Optic. Line: 1211. Brandy w/Capacity Line. 2 oz. 3-3/4 inches tall. 3/4 Oz. to line. **References:** 1975/I-75, page 3 [3-1]

Peacock Optic. Line: 1211. Cordial. 2 oz. 4 inches tall. **References:** 1975/I-75, page 4 [3-1]

Peacock Optic. Line: 1235. Tulip Champagne. 8-1/2 oz. 8-1/4 inches tall. **References:** 1975/I-75, page 3 [1-2]

Peacock Optic. Line: 1235. Tulip Champagne. 8-1/2 oz. 8-1/4 inches tall. **References:** 1975/I-75, page 3 [1-1]

Peacock Optic. Line: 1235. Wine Goblet. 10-1/2 oz. 6-5/8 inches tall. **References:** 1975/I-75, page 4 [1-2]

Peacock Optic. Line: 2828. Tumbler. 9-1/2 oz. 4-7/8 inches tall. Regular Weight. **References:** 1982, page 10 [1-2]; 1975/I-75, page 6 [1-2]

Peacock Optic. Line: 3000. Whiskey Sour. 5 oz. 5-5/8 inches tall. **References:** 1975/I-75, page 3 [2-2]

Peacock Optic. Line: 6000. Wine Goblet. 10-1/2 oz. 6 inches tall. Short Stem. **References:** 1975/I-75, page 4 [1-1]

Peacock Optic. Line: 7101. All Purpose Wine Goblet. 11 oz. 6 inches tall. **References:** 1975/I-75, page 4 [2-2]

Peacock Optic. Line: 8127. Old Fashion. 5-1/2 oz. 3 inches tall. Sham Weight. **References:** 1982, page 10 [2-2]; 1975/I-75, page 6 [3-1]

Peacock Optic. Line: 8701. Tumbler. 14 oz. 5-1/2 inches tall. Sham Weight. **References:** 1982, page 10 [2-3]

Peacock Optic. Line: 8701. Tumbler. 12 oz. 5 inches tall. Sham Weight. **References:** 1982, page 10 [2-5]

Peacock Optic. Line: 8701. Tumbler. 10 oz. 5-1/8 inches tall. Sham Weight. **References:** 1982, page 10 [2-4]

Peacock Optic. Line: 8701. Tumbler. 9 oz. 4-3/4 inches tall. Sham Weight. **References:** 1982, page 10 [2-6]

Peacock Optic. Line: 9491. Tumbler. 12 oz. 6 inches tall. Regular Weight. **References:** 1982, page 10 [1-1]

Peacock Optic. Line: 9491. Tumbler. 12 oz. 6-3/8 inches tall. Regular Weight. **References:** 1975/I-75, page 6 [2-2]

Peacock Optic. Line: 7199 (1962). Brandy. 7 oz. 4-1/8 inches tall. **References:** 1975/I-75, page 3 [3-2]

Peacock Optic. Line: 8701-11-1/2. Tumbler. 9 oz. 5 inches tall. Sham Weight. **References:** 1975/I-75, page 6 [1-1]

Pirouette. Claret. 3-3/4 oz. **References:** 1963 Advertisement

Pirouette. Cocktail. 4 oz. **References:** 1963 Advertisement

Pirouette. Cordial. 1-1/4 oz. **References:** 1963 Advertisement

Pirouette. Footed Ice Tea. 12 oz. **References:** 1963 Advertisement

Pirouette. Footed Juice. 5 oz. **References:** 1963 Advertisement

Pirouette. Goblet. 10-1/2 oz. **References:** 1963 Advertisement

Pirouette. Sherbet. 5-1/2 oz. **References:** 1963 Advertisement

Pirouette. Line: 307. 1305 Dessert-Finger Bowl. 4-1/2 inches diam. Shape Plain Twisted Stem. **References:** 1967, page 16 [1-8]; 1968, page 20 [1-8]; 1969, page 16 [1-8]; 1970, page 17 [1-8]; 1971, page 17 [1-8]; 1972, page 26 [1-8]; 1973, page 29 [1-8]

Pirouette. Line: 307. Claret. 3-3/4 oz. 4-1/2 inches tall. Shape Plain Twisted Stem. **References:** 1967, page 16 [1-3]; 1968, page 20 [1-3]; 1969, page 16 [1-3]; 1970, page 17 [1-3]; 1971, page 17 [1-3]; 1972, page 26 [1-3]; 1973, page 29 [1-3]

Pirouette. Line: 307. Cocktail. 4 oz. 3-7/8 inches tall. Shape Plain Twisted Stem. **References:** 1967, page 16 [1-4]; 1968, page 20 [1-4]; 1969, page 16 [1-4]; 1970, page 17 [1-4]; 1971, page 17 [1-4]; 1972, page 26 [1-4]; 1973, page 29 [1-4]

Pirouette. Line: 307. Cordial. 1-1/4 oz. 3-3/8 inches tall. Shape Plain Twisted Stem. **References:** 1967, page 16 [1-5]; 1968, page 20 [1-5]; 1969, page 16 [1-5]; 1970, page 17 [1-5]; 1971, page 17 [1-5]; 1972, page 26 [1-5]; 1973, page 29 [1-5]

Pirouette. Line: 307. Goblet. 10-1/2 oz. 6 inches tall. Shape Plain Twisted Stem. **References:** 1967, page 16 [1-1]; 1968, page 20 [1-1]; 1969, page 16 [1-1]; 1970, page 17 [1-1]; 1971, page 17 [1-1]; 1972, page 26 [1-1]; 1973, page 29 [1-1]

Pirouette. Line: 307. Ice Tea. 12 oz. 6-3/4 inches tall. Shape Plain Twisted Stem. **References:** 1967, page 16 [1-7]; 1968, page 20 [1-7]; 1969, page 16 [1-7]; 1970, page 17 [1-7]; 1971, page 17 [1-7]; 1972, page 26 [1-7]; 1973, page 29 [1-7]

Pirouette. Line: 307. Juice. 5 oz. 5-1/8 inches tall. Shape Plain Twisted Stem. **References:** 1967, page 16 [1-6]; 1968, page 20 [1-6]; 1969, page 16 [1-6]; 1970, page 17 [1-6]; 1971, page 17 [1-6]; 1972, page 26 [1-6]; 1973, page 29 [1-6]

Pirouette. Line: 307. Plate. 7 inches diam. Shape Plain Twisted Stem, Actually 7-7/8" Dia. **References:** 1967, page 16 [1-9]; 1968, page 20 [1-9]; 1969, page 16 [1-9]; 1970, page 17 [1-9]; 1971, page 17 [1-9]; 1972, page 26 [1-9]; 1973, page 29 [1-9]

Pirouette. Line: 307. Plate. 8 inches diam. Shape Plain Twisted Stem, Actually 8-3/4" Dia. **References:** 1967, page 16 [1-10]; 1968, page 20 [1-10]
1969, page 16 [1-10]; 1970, page 17 [1-10]; 1971, page 17 [1-10]; 1972, page 26 [1-10]; 1973, page 29 [1-10]

Pirouette. Line: 307. Sherbet. 5-1/2 oz. 4-1/2 inches tall. Shape Plain Twisted Stem. **References:** 1967, page 16 [1-2]; 1968, page 20 [1-2]; 1969, page 16 [1-2]; 1970, page 17 [1-2]; 1971, page 17 [1-2]; 1972, page 26 [1-2]; 1973, page 29 [1-2]

Platinum Lace. Line: 1973. 1305 Dessert-Finger Bowl. 4-1/2 inches diam. White Decal and Platinum Band. **References:** 1971, page 11 [1-6]; 1972, page 20 [1-6]; 1973, page 27 [1-6]

Platinum Lace. Line: 1973. Cordial. 1-1/2 oz. 4 inches tall. White Decal and Platinum Band. **References:** 1971, page 11 [1-4]; 1972, page 20 [1-4]; 1973, page 27 [1-4]

Platinum Lace. Line: 1973. Goblet. 13 oz. 7 inches tall. White Decal and Platinum Band. **References:** 1971, page 11 [1-1]; 1972, page 20 [1-1]; 1973, page 27 [1-1]

Platinum Lace. Line: 1973. Goblet. 13 oz. 7 inches tall. White Decal/Platinum Band. Colors & Designs Available: Blue/Crystal Foot, Pink/Crystal Foot, Blue/Crystal Foot/Cut 1443, Pink/Crystal Foot/Cut 1443, Black Decal and Gold Band, White Decal and Platinum Band. **References:** 1971, page 40 [2-3]

Platinum Lace. Line: 1973. Ice Tea. 17-1/2 oz. 7-1/8 inches tall. White Decal and Platinum Band. **References:** 1971, page 11 [1-5]; 1972, page 20 [1-5]; 1973, page 27 [1-5]

Platinum Lace. Line: 1973. Plate. 7 inches diam. White Decal and Platinum Band, Actually 7-7/8" Dia. **References:** 1971, page 11 [1-7]; 1972, page 20 [1-7]; 1973, page 27 [1-7]

Platinum Lace. Line: 1973. Plate. 8 inches diam. White Decal and Platinum Band, Actually 8-3/4" Dia. **References:** 1971, page 11 [1-8]; 1972, page 20 [1-8]; 1973, page 27 [1-8]

Platinum Lace. Line: 1973. Sherbet. 7-1/2 oz. 5-1/8 inches tall. White Decal and Platinum Band. **References:** 1971, page 11 [1-2]; 1972, page 20 [1-2]; 1973, page 27 [1-2]

Platinum Lace. Line: 1973. Wine. 8-1/2 oz. 6-3/8 inches tall. White Decal and Platinum Band. **References:** 1971, page 11 [1-3]; 1972, page 20 [1-3]; 1973, page 27 [1-3]

Primrose. Bell. 4-1/2 inches tall. Gold. **References:** 1979, page 12 [4-1]

Princess Anne. Line: 1965. Cut: 1420. 1305 Dessert-Finger Bowl. 4-1/2" Dia. **References:** 1967, page 7 [3-16]; 1968, page 11 [2-16]

Princess Anne. Line: 1965. Cut: 1420. Cordial. 1-1/4 oz. / 4 hi. **References:** 1967, page 7 [3-13]; 1968, page 11 [2-13]

Princess Anne. Line: 1965. Cut: 1420. Goblet. 11-3/4 oz. / 7-1/4" hi. **References:** 1967, page 7 [3-10]; 1968, page 11 [2-10]

Princess Anne. Line: 1965. Cut: 1420. Ice Tea. 13-1/2 oz. / 6-3/4" hi. **References:** 1967, page 7 [3-15]; 1968, page 11 [2-15]

Princess Anne. Line: 1965. Cut: 1420. Juice. 6 oz. / 5-1/2" hi. **References:** 1967, page 7 [3-14]; 1968, page 11 [2-14]

Princess Anne. Line: 1965. Cut: 1420. Plate. 7" / Actually 7-7/8" Dia. **References:** 1967, page 7 [3-17]; 1968, page 11 [2-17]

Princess Anne. Line: 1965. Cut: 1420. Plate. 8" / Actually 8-3/4" Dia. **References:** 1967, page 7 [3-18]; 1968, page 11 [2-18]

Princess Anne. Line: 1965. Cut: 1420. Sherbet. 7-1/2 oz. / 5-1/4" hi. **References:** 1967, page 7 [3-11]; 1968, page 11 [2-11]

Princess Anne. Line: 1965. Cut: 1420. Wine. 7-1/2 oz. / 6-1/4" hi. **References:** 1967, page 7 [3-12]; 1968, page 11 [2-12]

Pristine. Cocktail. **References:** 1964 Advertisement

Pristine. Cordial. **References:** 1964 Advertisement

Pristine. Footed Ice Tea. **References:** 1964 Advertisement

Pristine. Footed Juice. **References:** 1964 Advertisement

Pristine. Goblet. **References:** 1964 Advertisement

Pristine. Goblet. 13-1/2 oz. 6-3/4 inches tall. Platinum Band. **References:** 1979, page 6 [1-21]

Pristine. Ice Tea. 14 oz. 6-1/4 inches tall. Platinum Band. **References:** 1979, page 6 [1-25]; 1979, page 6 [1-30]

Pristine. Saucer Champagne. **References:** 1964 Advertisement

Pristine. Sherbet. 7-1/2 oz. 5-1/8 inches tall. Platinum Band. **References:** 1979, page 6 [1-22]

Pristine. White Wine Goblet. **References:** 1964 Advertisement

Pristine. Wine. 7-3/4 oz. 5-3/4 inches tall. Platinum Band. **References:** 1979, page 6 [1-23]

Pristine. Line: 1963. Cocktail. 5-1/2 oz. / 4-3/4" hi. Platinum Band. **References:** 1967, page 11 [2-4]; 1968, page 15 [2-4]; 1969, page 20 [2-4]; 1970, page 21 [2-4]; 1971, page 21 [2-4]; 1972, page 29 [2-4]; 1973, page 34 [2-4]

Pristine. Line: 1963. Cordial. 1-1/2 oz. / 4" hi. Platinum Band. **References:** 1967, page 11 [2-5]; 1968, page 15 [2-5]; 1969, page 20 [2-5]; 1970, page 21 [2-5]; 1971, page 21 [2-5]; 1972, page 29 [2-5]; 1973, page 34 [2-5]; 1975, page 30 [2-4]; 1977, page 41 [2-4]; 1979, page 6 [1-24]

Pristine. Line: 1963. Goblet. 13-1/2 oz. / 6-3/4" hi. Platinum Band. **References:** 1967, page 11 [2-1]; 1968, page 15 [2-1]; 1969, page 20 [2-1]; 1970, page 21 [2-1]; 1971, page 21 [2-1]; 1972, page 29 [2-1]; 1973, page 34 [2-1]; 1975, page 30 [2-1]; 1977, page 41 [2-1]

Pristine. Line: 1963. Ice Tea. 14 oz. / 6-1/4" hi. Platinum Band. **References:** 1967, page 11 [2-7]; 1968, page 15 [2-7]; 1969, page 20 [2-7]; 1970, page 21 [2-7]; 1971, page 21 [2-7]; 1972, page 29 [2-7]; 1973, page 34 [2-7]; 1975, page 30 [2-5]; 1977, page 41 [2-5]

Pristine. Line: 1963. Juice. 7 oz. / 5-1/4" hi. Platinum Band. **References:** 1967, page 11 [2-6]; 1968, page 15 [2-6]; 1969, page 20 [2-6]; 1970, page 21 [2-6]; 1971, page 21 [2-6]; 1972, page 29 [2-6]; 1973, page 34 [2-6]

Pristine. Line: 1963. Plate. 7" / Actually 7-7/8" Dia. Platinum Band. **References:** 1967, page 11 [2-8]; 1968, page 15 [2-8]; 1969, page 20 [2-8]; 1970, page 21 [2-8]; 1971, page 21 [2-8]; 1972, page 29 [2-8]; 1973, page 34 [2-8]; 1977, page 41 [2-6]

Pristine. Line: 1963. Plate. 8" / Actually 8-3/4" Dia. Platinum Band. **References:** 1967, page 11 [2-9]; 1968, page 15 [2-9]; 1969, page 20 [2-9]; 1970, page 21 [2-9]; 1971, page 21 [2-9]; 1972, page 29 [2-9]; 1973, page 34 [2-9]; 1975, page 30 [2-7]; 1977, page 41 [2-7]

Pristine. Line: 1963. Sherbet. 7-1/2 oz. / 5-1/8" hi. Platinum Band. **References:** 1967, page 11 [2-2]; 1968, page 15 [2-2]; 1969, page 20 [2-2]; 1970, page 21 [2-2]; 1971, page 21 [2-2]; 1972, page 29 [2-2]; 1973, page 34 [2-2]; 1975, page 30 [2-2]; 1977, page 41 [2-2]

Pristine. Line: 1963. Wine. 7-3/4 oz. / 5-3/4" hi. Platinum Band. **References:** 1967, page 11 [2-3]; 1968, page 15 [2-3]; 1969, page 20 [2-3]; 1970, page 21 [2-3]; 1971, page 21 [2-3]; 1972, page 29 [2-3]; 1973, page 34 [2-3]; 1975, page 30 [2-3]; 1977, page 41 [2-3]

Puritan. Bell. 4-1/2 inches tall. Gold. **References:** 1979, page 12 [5-3]

Puritan. Cocktail. **References:** 1964 Advertisement

Puritan. Cordial. **References:** 1964 Advertisement

Puritan. Cordial. 2 oz. 4-1/2 inches tall. Gold Band. **References:** 1979, page 6 [1-9]; 1981, page 3 [1-8]

Puritan. Cordial. 2 oz. 4-1/2 inches tall. **References:** 1982, page 15 [1-14]

Puritan. Footed Ice Tea. **References:** 1964 Advertisement

Puritan. Footed Juice. **References:** 1964 Advertisement

Puritan. Goblet. **References:** 1964 Advertisement

Puritan. Goblet. 12 oz. 7 inches tall. Gold Band. **References:** 1979, page 6 [1-6]; 1981, page 3 [1-5]

Puritan. Goblet. 12 oz. 7 inches tall. **References:** 1982, page 15 [1-11]

Puritan. Ice Tea. 12 oz. 6-1/4 inches tall. Gold Band. **References:** 1979, page 6 [1-10]

Puritan. Ice Tea. 12 oz. 6-1/4 inches tall. **References:** 1982, page 15 [1-15]

Puritan. Red Wine Goblet. **References:** 1964 Advertisement

Puritan. Saucer Champagne. **References:** 1964 Advertisement

Puritan. Sherbet. 7-1/2 oz. 5-1/8 inches tall. Gold Band. **References:** 1979, page 6 [1-7]; 1981, page 3 [1-6]

Puritan. Sherbet. 7-1/2 oz. 5-1/8 inches tall. **References:** 1982, page 15 [1-12]

Puritan. White Wine Goblet. **References:** 1964 Advertisement

Puritan. Wine. 7 oz. 5-7/8 inches tall. Gold Band. **References:** 1979, page 6 [1-8]; 1981, page 3 [1-7]

Puritan. Wine. 7 oz. 5-7/8 inches tall. **References:** 1982, page 15 [1-13]

Puritan. Line: 3. Bell. 4-3/8 inches tall. 1/4" Gold Band. **References:** 1976, page 6 [1-1]; 1977, page 22 [1-2]

Puritan. Line: 1235. Cocktail. 5-1/2 oz. / 4-5/8" hi. Gold Band. **References:** 1967, page 10 [1-13]; 1969, page 19 [1-14]; 1970, page 20 [1-14]; 1971, page 20 [1-14]; 1972, page 28 [1-14]; 1973, page 33 [1-14]

Puritan. Line: 1235. Cordial. 2 oz. / 4-1/2" hi. Gold Band. **References:** 1967, page 10 [1-14]; 1969, page 19 [1-15]; 1970, page 20 [1-15]; 1971, page 20 [1-15]; 1972, page 28 [1-15]; 1973, page 33 [1-15]; 1975, page 29 [1-11]; 1977, page 40 [1-11]

Puritan. Line: 1235. Goblet. 12 oz. / 7" hi. Gold Band. **References:** 1967, page 10 [1-10]; 1969, page 19 [1-11]; 1970, page 20 [1-11]; 1971, page 20 [1-11]; 1972, page 28 [1-11]; 1973, page 33 [1-11]; 1975, page 29 [1-8]; 1977, page 40 [1-8]

Puritan. Line: 1235. Ice Tea. 12 oz. / 6-1/4" hi. Gold Band. **References:** 1967, page 10 [1-16]; 1969, page 19 [1-18]; 1970, page 20 [1-18]; 1971, page 20 [1-18]; 1972, page 28 [1-18]; 1973, page 33 [1-18]; 1975, page 29 [1-12]; 1977, page 40 [1-12]

Puritan. Line: 1235. Juice. 5 oz. / 4-1/2" hi. Gold Band. **References:** 1967, page 10 [1-15]; 1967, page 10 [1-17]; 1970, page 20 [1-17]; 1971, page 20 [1-17]; 1972, page 28 [1-17]; 1973, page 33 [1-17]

Puritan. Line: 1235. Parfait Whiskey Sour. 7 oz. 6-1/4 inches tall. Gold Band. **References:** 1969, page 19 [1-16]; 1970, page 20 [1-16]; 1971, page 20 [1-16]; 1972, page 28 [1-16]; 1973, page 33 [1-16]

Puritan. Line: 1235. Plate. 7" / Actually 7-7/8" Dia. Gold Band. **References:** 1967, page 10 [1-17]; 1967, page 10 [1-19]; 1970, page 20 [1-19]; 1971, page 20 [1-19]; 1972, page 28 [1-19]; 1973, page 33 [1-19]; 1975, page 29 [1-13]; 1977, page 40 [1-13]

Puritan. Line: 1235. Plate. 8" / Actually 8-3/4" Dia. Gold Band. **References:** 1967, page 10 [1-18]; 1969, page 19 [1-20]; 1970, page 20 [1-20]; 1971, page 20 [1-20]; 1972, page 28 [1-20]; 1973, page 33 [1-20]; 1975, page 29 [1-14]; 1977, page 40 [1-14]

Puritan. Line: 1235. Sherbet. 7-1/2 oz. / 5-1/8" hi. Gold Band. **References:** 1967, page 10 [1-11]; 1969, page 19 [1-12]; 1970, page 20 [1-12]; 1971, page 20 [1-12]; 1972, page 28 [1-12]; 1973, page 33 [1-12]; 1975, page 29 [1-9]; 1977, page 40 [1-9]

Puritan. Line: 1235. Wine. 7 oz. / 5-7/8" hi. Gold Band. **References:** 1967, page 10 [1-12]; 1969, page 19 [1-13]; 1970, page 20 [1-13]; 1971, page 20 [1-13]; 1972, page 28 [1-13]; 1973, page 33 [1-13]; 1975, page 29 [1-10]; 1977, page 40 [1-10]

Quilt. Beverage. 18 oz. 6-1/4 inches tall. Brown. Colors: Brown, Charm Blue, Crystal, Yellow. **References:** 1982, page 16 [2-2]; 1983, page 12 [2-2]

Quilt. Cooler. 22 oz. 6-3/4 inches tall. Brown. Colors: Brown, Charm Blue, Crystal, Yellow. **References:** 1982, page 16 [2-1]; 1983, page 12 [2-1]

Quilt. Hi Ball. 12 oz. 5-1/4 inches tall. Brown. Colors: Brown, Charm Blue, Crystal, Yellow. **References:** 1982, page 16 [2-3]; 1983, page 12 [2-3]

Quilt. Juice. 7 oz. 4-1/2 inches tall. Brown. Colors: Brown, Charm Blue, Crystal, Yellow. **References:** 1982, page 16 [2-5]; 1983, page 12 [2-5]

Quilt. Old Fashion. 13 oz. 4-1/8 inches tall. Brown. Colors: Brown, Charm Blue, Crystal, Yellow. **References:** 1982, page 16 [2-4]; 1983, page 12 [2-4]

Radiance. Line: 960. Cut: 1437. 1311 Dessert-Finger Bowl. 4-3/4 inches diam. **References:** 1968, page 7 [2-6]; 1969, page 7 [2-6]; 1970, page 7 [2-6]; 1971, page 7 [2-6]

Radiance. Line: 960. Cut: 1437. Cordial. 1-1/4 oz. 3-7/8 inches tall. **References:** 1968, page 7 [2-4]; 1969, page 7 [2-4]; 1970, page 7 [2-4]; 1971, page 7 [2-4]

Radiance. Line: 960. Cut: 1437. Goblet. 11-1/2 oz. 7 inches tall. **References:** 1968, page 7 [2-1]; 1969, page 7 [2-1]; 1970, page 7 [2-1]; 1971, page 7 [2-1]

Radiance. Line: 960. Cut: 1437. Ice Tea. 14 oz. 6-1/4 inches tall. **References:** 1968, page 7 [2-5]; 1969, page 7 [2-5]; 1970, page 7 [2-5]; 1971, page 7 [2-5]

Radiance. Line: 960. Cut: 1437. Plate. 7 inches diam. Actually 7-7/8" Dia. **References:** 1968, page 7 [2-7]; 1969, page 7 [2-7]; 1970, page 7 [2-7]; 1971, page 7 [2-7]

Radiance. Line: 960. Cut: 1437. Plate. 8 inches diam. Actually 8-3/4" Dia. **References:** 1968, page 7 [2-8]; 1969, page 7 [2-8]; 1970, page 7 [2-8]; 1971, page 7 [2-8]

Radiance. Line: 960. Cut: 1437. Sherbet. 7 oz. 5-1/4 inches tall. **References:** 1968, page 7 [2-2]; 1969, page 7 [2-2]; 1970, page 7 [2-2]; 1971, page 7 [2-2]

Radiance. Line: 960. Cut: 1437. Wine. 7 oz. 6 inches tall. **References:** 1968, page 7 [2-3]; 1969, page 7 [2-3]; 1970, page 7 [2-3]; 1971, page 7 [2-3]

Radiance. Line: 960. Cut: 1438. 1311 Dessert-Finger Bowl. 4-3/4 inches diam. With 2 Gold Bands. **References:** 1969, page 7 [2-14]

Radiance. Line: 960. Cut: 1438. Cordial. 1-1/4 oz. 3-7/8 inches tall. With 2 Gold Bands. **References:** 1969, page 7 [2-12]

Radiance. Line: 960. Cut: 1438. Goblet. 11-1/2 oz. 7 inches tall. With 2 Gold Bands. **References:** 1969, page 7 [2-9]

Radiance. Line: 960. Cut: 1438. Ice Tea. 14 oz. 6-1/4 inches tall. With 2 Gold Bands. **References:** 1969, page 7 [2-13]

Radiance. Line: 960. Cut: 1438. Plate. 7 inches diam. With 2 Gold Bands, Actually 7-7/8" Dia. **References:** 1969, page 7 [2-15]

Radiance. Line: 960. Cut: 1438. Plate. 8 inches diam. With 2 Gold Bands, Actually 8-3/4" Dia. **References:** 1969, page 7 [2-16]

Radiance. Line: 960. Cut: 1438. Sherbet. 7 oz. 5-1/4 inches tall. With 2 Gold Bands. **References:** 1969, page 7 [2-10]

Radiance. Line: 960. Cut: 1438. Wine. 7 oz. 6 inches tall. With 2 Gold Bands. **References:** 1969, page 7 [2-11]

Ramona. Line: 912. Cut: 1006. 1311 Dessert-Finger Bowl. 4-3/4 inches diam. **References:** 1967, page 17 [2-8]; 1968, page 21 [2-8]; 1969, page 21 [2-8]; 1970, page 22 [2-8]; 1971, page 22 [2-8]

Ramona. Line: 912. Cut: 1006. Claret. 4 oz. 4-3/4 inches tall. **References:** 1967, page 17 [2-3]; 1968, page 21 [2-3]; 1969, page 21 [2-3]; 1970, page 22 [2-3]; 1971, page 22 [2-3]

Ramona. Line: 912. Cut: 1006. Cocktail. 3-1/2 oz. 4-3/8 inches tall. **References:** 1967, page 17 [2-4]; 1968, page 21 [2-4]; 1969, page 21 [2-4]; 1970, page 22 [2-4]; 1971, page 22 [2-4]

Ramona. Line: 912. Cut: 1006. Cordial. 1 oz. 3-5/8 inches tall. **References:** 1967, page 17 [2-5]; 1968, page 21 [2-5]; 1969, page 21 [2-5]; 1970, page 22 [2-5]; 1971, page 22 [2-5]

Ramona. Line: 912. Cut: 1006. Goblet. 10 oz. 6-1/4 inches tall. **References:** 1967, page 17 [2-1]; 1968, page 21 [2-1]; 1969, page 21 [2-1]; 1970, page 22 [2-1]; 1971, page 22 [2-1]

Ramona. Line: 912. Cut: 1006. Ice Tea. 12 oz. 6 inches tall. **References:** 1967, page 17 [2-7]; 1968, page 21 [2-7]; 1969, page 21 [2-7]; 1970, page 22 [2-7]; 1971, page 22 [2-7]

Ramona. Line: 912. Cut: 1006. Juice. 6 oz. 4-5/8 inches tall. **References:** 1967, page 17 [2-6]; 1968, page 21 [2-6]; 1969, page 21 [2-6]; 1970, page 22 [2-6]; 1971, page 22 [2-6]

Ramona. Line: 912. Cut: 1006. Plate. 7 inches diam. Actually 7-7/8" Dia. **References:** 1967, page 17 [2-9]; 1968, page 21 [2-9]; 1969, page 21 [2-9]; 1970, page 22 [2-9]; 1971, page 22 [2-9]

Ramona. Line: 912. Cut: 1006. Plate. 8 inches diam. Actually 8-3/4" Dia. **References:** 1967, page 17 [2-10]; 1968, page 21 [2-10]; 1969, page 21 [2-10]; 1970, page 22 [2-10]; 1971, page 22 [2-10]

Ramona. Line: 912. Cut: 1006. Saucer Champagne. 7-1/2 oz. 5-1/8 inches tall. **References:** 1967, page 17 [2-2]; 1968, page 21 [2-2]; 1969, page 21 [2-2]; 1970, page 22 [2-2]; 1971, page 22 [2-2]

Reflection. Bell. 4-1/2 inches tall. **References:** 1979, page 12 [3-2]

Reflection. Cordial. 2-1/4 oz. 5-1/4 inches tall. **References:** 1979, page 4 [3-4]; 1983, page 2 [2-5]

Reflection. Cordial. 2-1/4 oz. 5-1/4 inches tall. Colors: Brown, Charm Blue, Crystal, Lime Green, Yellow. **References:** 1981, page 6 [1-4]

Reflection. Goblet. 13 oz. 7-3/4 inches tall. **References:** 1979, page 4 [3-1]; 1983, page 2 [2-2]

Reflection. Goblet. 13 oz. 7-1/2 inches tall. Colors: Brown, Charm Blue, Crystal, Lime Green, Yellow. **References:** 1981, page 6 [1-1]

Reflection. Ice Tea. 14 oz. 6-1/2 inches tall. **References:** 1983, page 2 [2-1]

Reflection. Sherbet. 9 oz. 5-3/8 inches tall. **References:** 1979, page 4 [3-2]; 1983, page 2 [2-3]

Reflection. Sherbet. 9 oz. 5-3/8 inches tall. Colors: Brown, Charm Blue, Crystal, Lime Green, Yellow. **References:** 1981, page 6 [1-2]

Reflection. Wine. 7 oz. 6-5/8 inches tall. **References:** 1979, page 4 [3-3]; 1983, page 2 [2-4]

Reflection. Wine. 7 oz. 6-5/8 inches tall. Colors: Brown, Charm Blue, Crystal, Lime Green,

Yellow. **References:** 1981, page 6 [1-3]

Reflection. Line: 3. Bell. 4-3/8 inches tall. Optic. **References:** 1977, page 22 [4-2]

Reflection. Line: 976. Cordial. 2-1/4 oz. 5-1/4 inches tall. **References:** 1976, page 8 [1-4]

Reflection. Line: 976. Cordial. 2-1/4 oz. 5-1/4 inches tall. Crystal Optic. **References:** 1977, page 18 [1-4]

Reflection. Line: 976. Cordial. Colors: Yellow, Charm Blue, Lime, Crystal, Brown. **References:** 1980, page 5 [1-4]

Reflection. Line: 976. Goblet. 13 oz. 7-3/4 inches tall. **References:** 1976, page 8 [1-1]

Reflection. Line: 976. Goblet. 13 oz. 7-3/4 inches tall. Crystal Optic. **References:** 1977, page 18 [1-1]

Reflection. Line: 976. Goblet. Colors: Yellow, Charm Blue, Lime, Crystal, Brown. **References:** 1980, page 5 [1-1]

Reflection. Line: 976. Sherbet. 9 oz. 5-3/8 inches tall. **References:** 1976, page 8 [1-2]

Reflection. Line: 976. Sherbet. 9 oz. 5-3/8 inches tall. Crystal Optic. **References:** 1977, page 18 [1-2]

Reflection. Line: 976. Sherbet. Colors: Yellow, Charm Blue, Lime, Crystal, Brown. **References:** 1980, page 5 [1-2]

Reflection. Line: 976. Wine. 5-3/4 oz. 6-5/8 inches tall. **References:** 1976, page 8 [1-3]

Reflection. Line: 976. Wine. 7 oz. 6-5/8 inches tall. Crystal Optic. **References:** 1977, page 18 [1-3]

Reflection. Line: 976. Wine. Colors: Yellow, Charm Blue, Lime, Crystal, Brown. **References:** 1980, page 5 [1-3]

Reflection. Line: 1969. 1305 Dessert-Finger Bowl. 4-1/2 inches diam. Gold Bands, 3/16" on Bowl-1/16" on Foot. **References:** 1969, page 18 [1-6]; 1970, page 19 [1-6]

Reflection. Line: 1969. Cordial. 2 oz. 4-1/2 inches tall. Gold Bands, 3/16" on Bowl-1/16" on Foot. **References:** 1969, page 18 [1-4]; 1970, page 19 [1-4]

Reflection. Line: 1969. Goblet. 14 oz. 6-3/4 inches tall. Gold Bands, 3/16" on Bowl-1/16" on Foot. **References:** 1969, page 18 [1-1]; 1970, page 19 [1-1]

Reflection. Line: 1969. Ice Tea. 14 oz. 6-3/8 inches tall. Gold Bands, 3/16" on Bowl-1/16" on Foot. **References:** 1969, page 18 [1-5]; 1970, page 19 [1-5]

Reflection. Line: 1969. Plate. 7 inches diam. Gold Bands, 3/16" on Bowl-1/16" on Foot, Actually 7-7/8" Dia. **References:** 1969, page 18 [1-7]; 1970, page 19 [1-7]

Reflection. Line: 1969. Plate. 8 inches diam. Gold Bands, 3/16" on Bowl-1/16" on Foot, Actually 8-3/4" Dia. **References:** 1969, page 18 [1-8]; 1970, page 19 [1-8]

Reflection. Line: 1969. Sherbet. 7-1/2 oz. 5-3/8 inches tall. Gold Bands, 3/16" on Bowl-1/16" on Foot. **References:** 1969, page 18 [1-2]; 1970, page 19 [1-2]

Reflection. Line: 1969. White Wine Goblet. 7-1/2 oz. 5-1/2 inches tall. Gold Bands, 3/16" on Bowl-1/16" on Foot. **References:** 1969, page 18 [1-3]; 1970, page 19 [1-3]

Regal. Bell. 3-3/4 inches tall. **References:** 1979, page 12 [1-1]

Regal. Line: 3214. Cut: 1308. 1305 Dessert-Finger Bowl. 4-1/2 inches diam. **References:** 1968, page 26 [2-18]

Regal. Line: 3214. Cut: 1308. Cocktail. 4-1/4 oz. 4 inches tall. **References:** 1968, page 26 [2-14]

Regal. Line: 3214. Cut: 1308. Cordial. 1-1/2 oz. 3-3/4 inches tall. **References:** 1968, page 26 [2-15]

Regal. Line: 3214. Cut: 1308. Goblet. 10-1/4 oz. 6-1/8 inches tall. **References:** 1968, page 26 [2-11]

Regal. Line: 3214. Cut: 1308. Ice Tea. 12 oz. 6-3/4 inches tall. **References:** 1968, page 26 [2-17]

Regal. Line: 3214. Cut: 1308. Juice. 5-1/4 oz. 4-7/8 inches tall. **References:** 1968, page 26 [2-16]

Regal. Line: 3214. Cut: 1308. Plate. 7 inches diam. Actually 7-7/8" Dia. **References:** 1968, page 26 [2-19]

Regal. Line: 3214. Cut: 1308. Plate. 8 inches diam. Actually 8-3/4" Dia. **References:** 1968, page 26 [2-20]

Regal. Line: 3214. Cut: 1308. Sherbet. 6-1/2 oz. 4-1/2 inches tall. **References:** 1968, page 26 [2-12]

Regal. Line: 3214. Cut: 1308. Wine. 3-3/4 oz. 5 inches tall. **References:** 1968, page 26 [2-13]

Regency. Champagne Flute. 6 oz. 9-1/4 inches tall.

References: 1983, page 5 [1-10]

Regency. Cordial. 3 oz. 5-1/2 inches tall. **References:** 1983, page 5 [1-11]

Regency. Goblet. 13 oz. 7-1/2 inches tall. **References:** 1983, page 5 [1-7]

Regency. Ice Tea. 14 oz. 6-1/2 inches tall. **References:** 1983, page 5 [1-12]

Regency. Sherbet. 9 oz. 6 inches tall. **References:** 1983, page 5 [1-8]

Regency. Wine. 7-1/2 oz. 6-1/2 inches tall. **References:** 1983, page 5 [1-9]

Regency. Line: 972. Cut: 1463. Cordial. 3 oz. 5-5/8 inches tall. **References:** 1982, page 2 [2-9]

Regency. Line: 972. Cut: 1463. Goblet. 13 oz. 7-1/2 inches tall. **References:** 1982, page 2 [2-6]

Regency. Line: 972. Cut: 1463. Ice Tea. 14 oz. 6-1/2 inches tall. **References:** 1982, page 2 [2-10]

Regency. Line: 972. Cut: 1463. Sherbet. 9 oz. 6 inches tall. **References:** 1982, page 2 [2-7]

Regency. Line: 972. Cut: 1463. Wine. 7-1/2 oz. 6-1/2 inches tall. **References:** 1982, page 2 [2-8]

Regency. Line: 1350. Cut: 1403. 1305 Dessert-Finger Bowl. 4-1/2" Dia. **References:** 1967, page 13 [2-9]; 1968, page 17 [2-9]; 1969, page 13 [2-9]

Regency. Line: 1350. Cut: 1403. Cocktail. 4-1/2 oz. / 4-3/4" hi. **References:** 1967, page 13 [2-5]; 1968, page 17 [2-5]; 1969, page 13 [2-5]

Regency. Line: 1350. Cut: 1403. Cordial. 1-1/4 oz. / 3-3/4" hi. **References:** 1967, page 13 [2-6]; 1968, page 17 [2-6]; 1969, page 13 [2-6]

Regency. Line: 1350. Cut: 1403. Goblet. 12-1/2 oz. / 6-5/8" hi. **References:** 1967, page 13 [2-1]; 1968, page 17 [2-1]; 1969, page 13 [2-1]

Regency. Line: 1350. Cut: 1403. Ice Tea. 13-1/2 oz. / 6-1/4" hi. **References:** 1967, page 13 [2-8]; 1968, page 17 [2-8]; 1969, page 13 [2-8]

Regency. Line: 1350. Cut: 1403. Juice. 6-1/2 oz. / 5-1/4" hi. **References:** 1967, page 13 [2-7]; 1968, page 17 [2-7]; 1969, page 13 [2-7]

Regency. Line: 1350. Cut: 1403. Plate. 7" / Actually 7-7/8" Dia. **References:** 1967, page 13 [2-10]; 1968, page 17 [2-10]; 1969, page 13 [2-10]

Regency. Line: 1350. Cut: 1403. Plate. 8" / Actually 8-3/4" Dia. **References:** 1967, page 13 [2-11]; 1968, page 17 [2-11]; 1969, page 13 [2-11]

Regency. Line: 1350. Cut: 1403. Red Wine Goblet. 9-1/2 oz. / 6-3/8" hi. **References:** 1967, page 13 [2-3]; 1968, page 17 [2-3]; 1969, page 13 [2-3]

Regency. Line: 1350. Cut: 1403. Sherbet. 6-1/2 oz. / 5" hi. **References:** 1967, page 13 [2-2]; 1968, page 17 [2-2]; 1969, page 13 [2-2]

Regency. Line: 1350. Cut: 1403. White Wine Goblet. 7 oz. / 5-3/4" hi. **References:** 1967, page 13 [2-4]; 1968, page 17 [2-4]; 1969, page 13 [2-4]

Remembrance. Line: 1971. 1311 Dessert-Finger. 4-3/4 inches diam. Gold Band and Line. **References:** 1970, page 11 [2-22]; 1971, page 19 [2-22]; 1972, page 27 [2-22]; 1973, page 32 [2-22]

Remembrance. Line: 1971. Cordial. 1-1/2 oz. 4 inches tall. Gold Band and Line. **References:** 1970, page 11 [2-20]; 1971, page 19 [2-20]; 1972, page 27 [2-20]; 1973, page 32 [2-20]

Remembrance. Line: 1971. Goblet. 11-1/2 oz. 7 inches tall. Gold Band and Line. **References:** 1970, page 11 [2-17]; 1971, page 19 [2-17]; 1972, page 27 [2-17]; 1973, page 32 [2-17]

Remembrance. Line: 1971. Ice Tea. 14-1/2 oz. 7-1/8 inches tall. Gold Band and Line. **References:** 1970, page 11 [2-21]; 1971, page 19 [2-21]; 1972, page 27 [2-21]; 1973, page 32 [2-21]

Remembrance. Line: 1971. Plate. 7 inches diam. Gold Band and Line, Actually 7-7/8" Dia. **References:** 1970, page 11 [2-23]; 1971, page 19 [2-23]; 1972, page 27 [2-23]; 1973, page 32 [2-23]

Remembrance. Line: 1971. Plate. 8 inches diam. Gold Band and Line, Actually 8-3/4" Dia. **References:** 1970, page 11 [2-24]; 1971, page 19 [2-24]; 1972, page 27 [2-24]; 1973, page 32 [2-24]

Remembrance. Line: 1971. Sherbet. 7-1/2 oz. 5 inches tall. Gold Band and Line. **References:** 1970, page 11 [2-18]; 1971, page 19 [2-18]; 1972, page 27 [2-18]; 1973, page 32 [2-18]

Remembrance. Line: 1971. Wine. 7 oz. 5-7/8 inches tall. Gold Band and Line. **References:** 1970, page 11 [2-19]; 1971, page 19 [2-19]; 1972, page 27 [2-19]; 1973, page 32 [2-19]

Rennaissance. Line: 908. Cut: 859. 1311 Dessert-Finger Bowlr Bowl. 4-3/4 inches diam. **References:** 1967, page 20 [2-18]; 1969, page

22 [2-18]; 1970, page 23 [2-18]; 1971, page 23 [2-18]

Rennaissance. Line: 908. Cut: 859. Claret. 3-1/2 oz. 4-3/8 inches tall. **References:** 1967, page 20 [2-13]; 1969, page 22 [2-13]; 1970, page 23 [2-13]; 1971, page 23 [2-13]

Rennaissance. Line: 908. Cut: 859. Cocktail. 3 oz. 4-5/8 inches tall. **References:** 1967, page 20 [2-14]; 1969, page 22 [2-14]; 1970, page 23 [2-14]; 1971, page 23 [2-14]

Rennaissance. Line: 908. Cut: 859. Cordial. 1 oz. 3-1/4 inches tall. **References:** 1967, page 20 [2-15]; 1969, page 22 [2-15]; 1970, page 23 [2-15]; 1971, page 23 [2-15]

Rennaissance. Line: 908. Cut: 859. Goblet. 9 oz. 6 inches tall. **References:** 1967, page 20 [2-11]; 1969, page 22 [2-11]; 1970, page 23 [2-11]; 1971, page 23 [2-11]

Rennaissance. Line: 908. Cut: 859. Ice Tea. 10-1/2 oz. 5-5/8 inches tall. **References:** 1967, page 20 [2-17]; 1969, page 22 [2-17]; 1970, page 23 [2-17]; 1971, page 23 [2-17]

Rennaissance. Line: 908. Cut: 859. Juice. 5 oz. 4-3/8 inches tall. **References:** 1967, page 20 [2-16]; 1969, page 22 [2-16]; 1970, page 23 [2-16]; 1971, page 23 [2-16]

Rennaissance. Line: 908. Cut: 859. Plate. 7 inches diam. Actually 7-7/8" Dia. **References:** 1967, page 20 [2-19]; 1969, page 22 [2-19]; 1970, page 23 [2-19]; 1971, page 23 [2-19]

Rennaissance. Line: 908. Cut: 859. Plate. 8 inches diam. Actually 8-3/4" Dia. **References:** 1967, page 20 [2-20]; 1969, page 22 [2-20]; 1970, page 23 [2-20]; 1971, page 23 [2-20]

Rennaissance. Line: 908. Cut: 859. Saucer Champagne. 7 oz. 4-3/4 inches tall. **References:** 1967, page 20 [2-12]; 1969, page 22 [2-12]; 1970, page 23 [2-12]; 1971, page 23 [2-12]

Riviera. Cocktail. **References:** 1964 Advertisement

Riviera. Cordial. **References:** 1964 Advertisement

Riviera. Cordial. 1-1/4 oz. 3-3/4 inches tall. **References:** 1979, page 4 [2-16]; 1982, page 8 [1-5]

Riviera. Footed Ice Tea. **References:** 1964 Advertisement

Riviera. Footed Juice. **References:** 1964 Advertisement

Riviera. Goblet. **References:** 1964 Advertisement

Riviera. Goblet. 12-1/2 oz. 6-5/8 inches tall. **References:** 1979, page 4 [2-12]; 1982, page 8 [1-1]

Riviera. Ice Tea. 13-1/2 oz. 6-1/4 inches tall. **References:** 1979, page 4 [2-17]

Riviera. Red Wine Goblet. **References:** 1964 Advertisement

Riviera. Red Wine Goblet. 9-1/2 oz. 6-3/8 inches tall. **References:** 1979, page 4 [2-14]

Riviera. Saucer Champagne. **References:** 1964 Advertisement

Riviera. Sherbet. 6-1/2 oz. 5 inches tall. **References:** 1979, page 4 [2-13]; 1982, page 8 [1-2]

Riviera. Tulip Champagne. 8 oz. 8-1/2 inches tall. **References:** 1982, page 8 [1-4]

Riviera. White Wine Goblet. **References:** 1964 Advertisement

Riviera. White Wine Goblet. 7 oz. 5-3/4 inches tall. **References:** 1979, page 4 [2-15]; 1982, page 8 [1-3]

Riviera. Line: 1350. Cut: 63. 1305 Dessert-Finger Bowl. 4-1/2" Dia. **References:** 1967, page 13 [2-20]; 1968, page 17 [2-20]; 1969, page 13 [2-20]; 1970, page 14 [2-20]; 1971, page 14 [2-20]; 1972, page 24 [2-20]; 1973, page 29 [2-20]; 1975, page 27 [2-16]; 1977, page 38 [2-16]

Riviera. Line: 1350. Cut: 63. Cocktail. 4-1/2 oz. / 4-3/4" hi. **References:** 1967, page 13 [2-16]; 1968, page 17 [2-16]; 1969, page 13 [2-16]; 1970, page 14 [2-16]; 1971, page 14 [2-16]; 1972, page 24 [2-16]; 1973, page 29 [2-16]

Riviera. Line: 1350. Cut: 63. Cordial. 1-1/4 oz. / 3-3/4" hi. **References:** 1967, page 13 [2-17]; 1968, page 17 [2-17]; 1969, page 13 [2-17]; 1970, page 14 [2-17]; 1971, page 14 [2-17]; 1972, page 24 [2-17]; 1973, page 29 [2-17]; 1975, page 27 [2-14]; 1977, page 38 [2-14]; 1981, page 3 [3-5]

Riviera. Line: 1350. Cut: 63. Goblet. 12-1/2 oz. / 6-5/8" hi. **References:** 1967, page 13 [2-12]; 1968, page 17 [2-12]; 1969, page 13 [2-12]; 1970, page 14 [2-12]; 1971, page 14 [2-12]; 1972, page 24 [2-12]; 1973, page 29 [2-12]; 1975, page 27 [2-10]; 1977, page 38 [2-10]; 1981, page 3 [3-1]

Riviera. Line: 1350. Cut: 63. Ice Tea. 13-1/2 oz. / 6-1/4" hi. **References:** 1967, page 13 [2-19]; 1968, page 17 [2-19]; 1969, page 13 [2-19]; 1970, page 14 [2-19]; 1971, page 14 [2-19]; 1972, page 24 [2-19]; 1973, page 29 [2-19]; 1975, page 27 [2-15]; 1977, page 38 [2-15]

Riviera. Line: 1350. Cut: 63. Juice. 6-1/2 oz. / 5-1/4" hi. **References:** 1967, page 13 [2-18]; 1968, page 17 [2-18]; 1969, page 13 [2-18]; 1970, page 14 [2-18]; 1971, page 14 [2-18]; 1972, page 24 [2-18]; 1973, page 29 [2-18]

Riviera. Line: 1350. Cut: 63. Plate. 7" / Actually 7-7/8" Dia. **References:** 1967, page 13 [2-21]; 1968, page 17 [2-21]; 1969, page 13 [2-21]; 1970, page 14 [2-21]; 1971, page 14 [2-21]; 1972, page 24 [2-21]; 1973, page 29 [2-21]; 1975, page 27 [2-17]; 1977, page 38 [2-17]

Riviera. Line: 1350. Cut: 63. Plate. 8" / Actually 8-3/4" Dia. **References:** 1967, page 13 [2-22]; 1968, page 17 [2-22]; 1969, page 13 [2-22]; 1970, page 14 [2-22]; 1971, page 14 [2-22]; 1972, page 24 [2-22]; 1973, page 29 [2-22]; 1975, page 27 [2-18]; 1977, page 38 [2-18]

Riviera. Line: 1350. Cut: 63. Red Wine Goblet. 9-1/2 oz. / 6-3/8" hi. **References:** 1967, page 13 [2-14]; 1968, page 17 [2-14]; 1969, page 13 [2-14]; 1970, page 14 [2-14]; 1971, page 14 [2-14]; 1972, page 24 [2-14]; 1973, page 29 [2-14]; 1975, page 27 [2-12]; 1977, page 38 [2-12]

Riviera. Line: 1350. Cut: 63. Sherbet. 6-1/2 oz. / 5" hi. **References:** 1967, page 13 [2-13]; 1968, page 17 [2-13]; 1969, page 13 [2-13]; 1970, page 14 [2-13]; 1971, page 14 [2-13]; 1972, page 24 [2-13]; 1973, page 29 [2-13]; 1975, page 27 [2-11]; 1977, page 38 [2-11]; 1981, page 3 [3-2]

Riviera. Line: 1350. Cut: 63. Tulip Champagne. 8 oz. 8-1/2 inches tall. **References:** 1981, page 3 [3-4]

Riviera. Line: 1350. Cut: 63. White Wine. 7 oz. 5-3/4 inches tall. **References:** 1975, page 27 [2-13]; 1967, page 13 [2-15]; 1968, page 17 [2-15]; 1969, page 13 [2-15]; 1970, page 14 [2-15]; 1971, page 14 [2-15]; 1972, page 24 [2-15]; 1973, page 29 [2-15]; 1977, page 38 [2-13]; 1981, page 3 [3-3]

Rosalynn. Beverage. 16 oz. 6 inches tall. Hand Made....Hand Cut. **References:** 1979, page 15 [3-8]

Rosalynn. Champagne Flute. 6 oz. 9-1/4 inches tall. **References:** 1983, page 4 [1-3]

Rosalynn. Cooler. 16 oz. 7-3/8 inches tall. Hand Made....Hand Cut. **References:** 1979, page 15 [3-7]

Rosalynn. Cordial. 2-1/2 oz. 5-1/8 inches tall. **References:** 1979, page 1 [1-4]; 1983, page 4 [1-5]

Rosalynn. Goblet. 13 oz. 7-3/4 inches tall. **References:** 1979, page 1 [1-1]; 1983, page 4 [1-1]

Rosalynn. Hi Ball. 11 oz. 5 inches tall. Hand Made....Hand Cut. **References:** 1979, page 15 [3-9]

Rosalynn. Ice Tea. 14 oz. 6-1/2 inches tall. **References:** 1983, page 4 [1-6]

Rosalynn. Old Fashion. 9-1/2 oz. 3-1/2 inches tall. Hand Made....Hand Cut. **References:** 1979, page 15 [3-11]

Rosalynn. On The Rocks. 14 oz. 4-1/2 inches tall. Hand Made, Hand Cut. **References:** 1979, page 15 [3-10]

Rosalynn. Pony. 3 oz. 3 inches tall. Hand Made....Hand Cut. $30-35. **References:** 1979, page 15 [3-12]

Rosalynn. Sherbet. 9 oz. 5-3/8 inches tall. **References:** 1979, page 1 [1-2]; 1983, page 4 [1-2]

Rosalynn. Wine. 8 oz. 6-3/4 inches tall. **References:** 1979, page 1 [1-3]; 1983, page 4 [1-4]

Rosalynn. Cut: 1452. Bell. 4-1/2 inches tall. **References:** 1979, page 12 [2-4]

Rosalynn. Cut: 1452. Bell. **References:** 1981, page 11 [2-3]; 1983, page 6 [1-2R]

Rosalynn. Line: 3. Cut: 1452. Bell. 4-3/8 inches tall. **References:** 1977, page 22 [3-2]

Rosalynn. Line: 981. Cut: 1452. Cordial. 2-1/2 oz. 5-1/8 inches tall. **References:** 1977, page 26 [1-4]; 1981, page 2 [2-12]

Rosalynn. Line: 981. Cut: 1452. Goblet. 13-1/2 oz. 7-3/4 inches tall. **References:** 1977, page 26 [1-1]; 1981, page 2 [2-9]

Rosalynn. Line: 981. Cut: 1452. Sherbet. 9 oz. 5-3/8 inches tall. **References:** 1977, page 26 [1-2]; 1981, page 2 [2-10]

Rosalynn. Line: 981. Cut: 1452. Wine. 8 oz. 6-3/4 inches tall. **References:** 1977, page 26 [1-3]; 1981, page 2 [2-11]

Rosalynn. Line: 1978. Cut: 1452S. On The Rocks. **References:** 1977, page 25 [3-2]

Rose Design. Etching: 609. Nappy. 4-1/2 inch. **References:** 3, page 11 [2-3]

Rose Design. Etching: 609. Plate. 6-1/4 inch. **References:** 3, page 13 [3-3]

Rose Design. Line: 1. Etching: 609. Decanter. 2 Pint. Cut Neck, Optic. **References:** 3, page 13 [3-1]

Rose Design. Line: 1. Etching: 609. Nappy. 9 inch. **References:** 3, page 12 [1-1]

Rose Design. Line: 1. Etching: 609. Oil. Cut Neck and Star Bottom. **References:** 3, page 13 [2-2]

Rose Design. Line: 1. Etching: 609. Vase. 4 inch. **References:** 3, page 14 [3-1]

Rose Design. Line: 1. Etching: 609. Vase. 7 inch. **References:** 3, page 14 [3-2]

Rose Design. Line: 1. Etching: 609. Vase. 9 inch. **References:** 3, page 14 [3-3]

Rose Design. Line: 1. Etching: 609. Vase. 11 inch. **References:** 3, page 14 [3-4]

Rose Design. Line: 3. Etching: 609. Comport. **References:** 3, page 11 [2-6]

Rose Design. Line: 4. Etching: 608. Oil. Cut Neck. **References:** 3, page 13 [2-1]

Rose Design. Line: 5. Etching: 609. Vase. 12 inch. **References:** 3, page 14 [1-1]

Rose Design. Line: 5. Etching: 609. Vase. 10 inch. **References:** 3, page 14 [1-2]

Rose Design. Line: 5. Etching: 609. Vase. 7 inch. **References:** 3, page 14 [1-3]

Rose Design. Line: 5. Etching: 609. Vase. 5 inch. **References:** 3, page 14 [1-4]

Rose Design. Line: 10. Etching: 609. Jug. 54 oz. **References:** 3, page 12 [2-1]

Rose Design. Line: 34. Etching: 609. Fruit. **References:** 3, page 11 [2-1]

Rose Design. Line: 40. Etching: 609. Cream. **References:** 3, page 12 [1-3]

Rose Design. Line: 40. Etching: 609. Jug. 54 oz. Optic. **References:** 3, page 12 [2-2]

Rose Design. Line: 40. Etching: 609. Sugar Bowl. **References:** 3, page 12 [1-2]

Rose Design. Line: 50. Etching: 609. Water Bottle. Cut Neck. **References:** 3, page 13 [3-2]

Rose Design. Line: 300. Etching: 609. Individual Almond. **References:** 3, page 11 [2-2]

Rose Design. Line: 922. Etching: 609. Vase. 6-1/2 inch. **References:** 3, page 14 [2-1]

Rose Design. Line: 922. Etching: 609. Vase. 7-1/2 inch. **References:** 3, page 14 [2-2]

Rose Design. Line: 8000. Etching: 609. Ale. **References:** 3, page 10 [1-5]

Rose Design. Line: 8000. Etching: 609. Brandy. **References:** 3, page 10 [1-9]

Rose Design. Line: 8000. Etching: 609. Claret. **References:** 3, page 11 [1-3]

Rose Design. Line: 8000. Etching: 609. Cocktail. **References:** 3, page 11 [1-4]

Rose Design. Line: 8000. Etching: 609. Cordial. **References:** 3, page 10 [1-8]

Rose Design. Line: 8000. Etching: 609. Custard. **References:** 3, page 13 [1-1]

Rose Design. Line: 8000. Etching: 609. Deminth. **References:** 3, page 11 [1-5]

Rose Design. Line: 8000. Etching: 609. Finger Bowl. **References:** 3, page 13 [1-2]

Rose Design. Line: 8000. Etching: 609. Goblet. 10 oz. **References:** 3, page 10 [1-3]

Rose Design. Line: 8000. Etching: 609. Goblet. 9 oz. **References:** 3, page 10 [1-4]

Rose Design. Line: 8000. Etching: 609. Goblet. 6 oz. Optic. **References:** 3, page 11 [2-5]

Rose Design. Line: 8000. Etching: 609. Grape Fruit. **References:** 3, page 11 [2-4]

Rose Design. Line: 8000. Etching: 609. Large Saucer Champagne. Optic. **References:** 3, page 11 [1-1]

Rose Design. Line: 8000. Etching: 609. Large Sherbert. **References:** 3, page 11 [1-7]

Rose Design. Line: 8000. Etching: 609. Sherbert. **References:** 3, page 11 [1-6]

Rose Design. Line: 8000. Etching: 609. Sherry. **References:** 3, page 10 [1-7]

Rose Design. Line: 8000. Etching: 609. Small Saucer Champagne. **References:** 3, page 11 [1-2]

Rose Design. Line: 8000. Etching: 609. Taper Tumbler. 5 oz. **References:** 3, page 10 [3-9]

Rose Design. Line: 8000. Etching: 609. Tumbler. 14 oz. **References:** 3, page 10 [3-1]

Rose Design. Line: 8000. Etching: 609. Tumbler. 10 oz. **References:** 3, page 10 [3-2]

Rose Design. Line: 8000. Etching: 609. Tumbler. 12 oz. **References:** 3, page 10 [3-3]

Rose Design. Line: 8000. Etching: 609. Tumbler. 8 oz. **References:** 3, page 10 [3-4]

Rose Design. Line: 8000. Etching: 609. Tumbler. 9 oz. **References:** 3, page 10 [3-5]

Rose Design. Line: 8000. Etching: 609. Tumbler. 6-1/2 oz. **References:** 3, page 10 [3-6]

Rose Design. Line: 8000. Etching: 609. Tumbler. 5 oz. **References:** 3, page 10 [3-7]

Rose Design. Line: 8000. Etching: 609. Tumbler. 3-1/2 oz. **References:** 3, page 10 [3-8]

Rose Design. Line: 8000. Etching: 609. Wine. **References:** 3, page 10 [1-6]

Rose Design. Line: 8000. Cut: 43. Etching: 609. Champagne. Hollow Stem. **References:** 3, page 10 [1-2]

Rose Design. Line: 8000. Cut: 43. Etching: 609. Saucer Champ. Hollow Stem. **References:** 3, page 10 [1-1]

Rose Design. Line: 8127. Cut: 39. Etching: 609. Tumbler. 2-1/2 oz. **References:** 3, page 10 [2-1]

Rose Design. Line: 9001. Etching: 609. Tumbler. 8 oz. **References:** 3, page 10 [2-3]

Royalty. Line: 5321. Cut: 1443. 1305 Dessert-Finger Bowl. 4-1/2 inches diam. **References:** 1972, page 22 [2-5]; 1973, page 26 [2-5]

Royalty. Line: 5321. Cut: 1443. Brandy and Liqueur. 2-1/2 oz. 4-1/2 inches tall. **References:** 1972, page 22 [2-4]; 1973, page 26 [2-4]

Royalty. Line: 5321. Cut: 1443. Dessert-Champagne. 11 oz. 4-7/8 inches tall. **References:** 1972, page 22 [2-2]; 1973, page 26 [2-2]

Royalty. Line: 5321. Cut: 1443. Plate. 7 inches diam. Actually 7-7/8" Dia. **References:** 1972, page 22 [2-6]; 1973, page 26 [2-6]

Royalty. Line: 5321. Cut: 1443. Plate. 8 inches diam. Actually 8-3/4" Dia. **References:** 1972, page 22 [2-7]; 1973, page 26 [2-7]

Royalty. Line: 5321. Cut: 1443. Vintage Wine Goblet. 14 oz. 7 inches tall. **References:** 1972, page 22 [2-1]; 1973, page 26 [2-1]

Royalty. Line: 5321. Cut: 1443. White Wine Goblet. 8-1/2 oz. 6-5/8 inches tall. Crystal Foot. Colors Available: Blue/Crystal Foot, Pink/Crystal Foot, Crystal Cut 1443, Blue/Crystal Foot Cut 1443, Pink/Crystal Foot Cut 1443. **References:** 1971, page 41 [2-2]; 1972, page 22 [2-3]; 1973, page 26 [2-3]

Scroll. Line: 3214. Cut: 1309. 1305 Dessert-Finger Bowl. 4-1/2 inches diam. **References:** 1968, page 26 [2-8]

Scroll. Line: 3214. Cut: 1309. Cocktail. 4-1/4 oz. 4 inches tall. **References:** 1968, page 26 [2-4]

Scroll. Line: 3214. Cut: 1309. Cordial. 1-1/2 oz. 3-3/4 inches tall. **References:** 1968, page 26 [2-5]

Scroll. Line: 3214. Cut: 1309. Goblet. 10-1/4 oz. 6-1/8 inches tall. **References:** 1968, page 26 [2-1]

Scroll. Line: 3214. Cut: 1309. Ice Tea. 12 oz. 6-3/4 inches tall. **References:** 1968, page 26 [2-7]

Scroll. Line: 3214. Cut: 1309. Juice. 5-1/4 oz. 4-7/8 inches tall. **References:** 1968, page 26 [2-6]

Scroll. Line: 3214. Cut: 1309. Plate. 7 inches diam. Actually 7-7/8" Dia. **References:** 1968, page 26 [2-9]

Scroll. Line: 3214. Cut: 1309. Plate. 8 inches diam. Actually 8-3/4" Dia. **References:** 1968, page 26 [2-10]

Scroll. Line: 3214. Cut: 1309. Sherbet. 6-1/2 oz. 4-1/2 inches tall. **References:** 1968, page 26 [2-2]

Scroll. Line: 3214. Cut: 1309. Wine. 3-3/4 oz. 5 inches tall. **References:** 1968, page 26 [2-3]

Scroll Design. Etching: 600. Nappy. 8 inch. **References:** 3, page 4 [1-1]

Scroll Design. Etching: 600. Nappy. 4-1/2 inch. **References:** 3, page 4 [1-2]

Scroll Design. Etching: 600. Plate. 6-1/4 inch. **References:** 3, page 5 [2-4]

Scroll Design. Line: 1. Etching: 600. Decanter. 2 Pint. Cut Neck and Star. **References:** 3, page 5 [2-1]

Scroll Design. Line: 1. Etching: 600. Handled Decanter. 2 Pint. Cut Neck and Star. **References:** 3, page 5 [2-3]

Scroll Design. Line: 3. Etching: 600. Comport. **References:** 3, page 5 [2-2]

Scroll Design. Line: 4. Etching: 600. Oil. Cut Neck and Star. **References:** 3, page 6 [1-3]

Scroll Design. Line: 5. Etching: 600. Sherry. Optic. **References:** 3, page 3 [1-5]

Scroll Design. Line: 10. Etching: 600. Jug. 15 oz. **References:** 3, page 6 [1-2]

Scroll Design. Line: 10. Etching: 600. Jug. 54 oz. **References:** 3, page 6 [2-1]

Scroll Design. Line: 40. Etching: 600. Cream. **References:** 3, page 5 [1-1]

Scroll Design. Line: 40. Etching: 600. Jug. 54 oz. **References:** 3, page 6 [2-2]

Scroll Design. Line: 40. Etching: 600. Sugar Bowl. **References:** 3, page 5 [1-2]

Scroll Design. Line: 75. Etching: 600. Water Bottle. **References:** 3, page 6 [2-3]

Scroll Design. Line: 630. Etching: 600. Tumbler. **References:** 3, page 4 [3-1]

Scroll Design. Line: 8000. Etching: 600. Ale. Optic. **References:** 3, page 3 [1-1]

Scroll Design. Line: 8000. Etching: 600. Brandy. Optic. **References:** 3, page 3 [2-4]

Scroll Design. Line: 8000. Etching: 600. Champagne. Hollow and Cut Stem, Optic. **References:** 3, page 3 [2-1]

Scroll Design. Line: 8000. Etching: 600. Claret. Optic. **References:** 3, page 3 [2-5]

Scroll Design. Line: 8000. Etching: 600. Cocktail. Optic. **References:** 3, page 3 [2-6]

Scroll Design. Line: 8000. Etching: 600. Cordial. Optic. **References:** 3, page 3 [1-4]

Scroll Design. Line: 8000. Etching: 600. Custard. Optic. **References:** 3, page 6 [1-4]

Scroll Design. Line: 8000. Etching: 600. Deminth. Optic. **References:** 3, page 3 [2-7]

Scroll Design. Line: 8000. Etching: 600. Finger Bowl. Optic. **References:** 3, page 6 [1-1]

Scroll Design. Line: 8000. Etching: 600. Goblet. 10 oz. Optic. **References:** 3, page 3 [1-8]

Scroll Design. Line: 8000. Etching: 600. Grape Fruit. Optic. **References:** 3, page 4 [3-3]

Scroll Design. Line: 8000. Etching: 600. Large Sherbet. Optic. **References:** 3, page 3 [1-7]

Scroll Design. Line: 8000. Etching: 600. Port. Optic. **References:** 3, page 3 [1-2]

Scroll Design. Line: 8000. Etching: 600. Saucer Champagne. Hollow Stem, Cut Stem, Optic. **References:** 3, page 3 [2-2]

Scroll Design. Line: 8000. Etching: 600. Saucer Champagne. Optic. **References:** 3, page 3 [2-3]

Scroll Design. Line: 8000. Etching: 600. Sherbet. **References:** 3, page 3 [1-6]

Scroll Design. Line: 8000. Etching: 600. Taper Tumbler. 5 oz. Optic. **References:** 3, page 4 [2-8]

Scroll Design. Line: 8000. Etching: 600. Taper Tumbler. 3-1/2 oz. Optic. **References:** 3, page 4 [2-9]

Scroll Design. Line: 8000. Etching: 600. Tumbler. 14 oz. Optic. **References:** 3, page 4 [2-1]

Scroll Design. Line: 8000. Etching: 600. Tumbler. 12 oz. Optic. **References:** 3, page 4 [2-2]

Scroll Design. Line: 8000. Etching: 600. Tumbler. 10 oz. Optic. **References:** 3, page 4 [2-3]

Scroll Design. Line: 8000. Etching: 600. Tumbler. 9 oz. Optic. **References:** 3, page 4 [2-4]

Scroll Design. Line: 8000. Etching: 600. Tumbler. 8 oz. Optic. **References:** 3, page 4 [2-5]

Scroll Design. Line: 8000. Etching: 600. Tumbler. 6-1/2 oz. Optic. **References:** 3, page 4 [2-6]

Scroll Design. Line: 8000. Etching: 600. Tumbler. 5 oz. Optic. **References:** 3, page 4 [2-7]

Scroll Design. Line: 8000. Etching: 600. Wine. Optic. **References:** 3, page 3 [1-3]

Scroll Design. Line: 8701. Etching: 600. Handled Tumbler. 7 oz. **References:** 3, page 4 [3-2]

Sculpture. Line: 975. Bowl. 13 oz. 4-1/2 inches diam. **References:** 1976, page 12 [1-6]

Sculpture. Line: 975. Double Old Fashion. 12 oz. 3-7/8 inches tall. **References:** 1976, page 12 [1-3]

Sculpture. Line: 975. Footed Goblet. 14 oz. 5-1/2 inches tall. **References:** 1976, page 12 [1-5]

Sculpture. Line: 975. Goblet. 17 oz. 5-3/4 inches tall. **References:** 1976, page 12 [1-1]

Sculpture. Line: 975. Hi Ball. 12-1/2 oz. 5-1/4 inches tall. **References:** 1976, page 12 [1-2]

Sculpture. Line: 975. Juice. 6 oz. 4-1/8 inches tall. **References:** 1976, page 12 [1-4]

Seville. Line: 1971. 1311 Dessert-Finger Bowl. 4-3/4 inches diam. Plain Crystal. **References:** 1970, page 11 [2-6]; 1971, page 19 [2-6]; 1971, page 19 [2-6]; 1972, page 27 [2-6]; 1973, page 32 [2-6]

Seville. Line: 1971. Cordial. 1-1/2 oz. 4 inches tall. **References:** 1970, page 2 [1-4]; 1970, page 11 [2-4]; 1971, page 19 [2-4]; 1971, page 19 [2-4]

Seville. Line: 1971. Cordial. 1-1/2 oz. 4 inches tall. Colors Available; Brown, Delphine Blue, Green, Grey, Yellow. **References:** 1971, page 42 [2-3]; 1972, page 10 [2-3]

Seville. Line: 1971. Cordial. 1-1/2 oz. 4 inches tall. Plain Crystal. **References:** 1972, page 27 [2-4]; 1973, page 32 [2-4]

Seville. Line: 1971. Cordial. 1-1/2 oz. 4 inches tall. Colors: Brown, Delphine Blue, Green, Grey, Yellow. **References:** 1973, page 18 [2-3]

Seville. Line: 1971. Goblet. 11-1/2 oz. 7 inches tall. Yellow. **References:** 1970, page 2 [1-1]

Seville. Line: 1971. Goblet. 11-1/2 oz. 7 inches tall. Plain Crystal. $5/10. **References:** 1970, page 11 [2-1]; 1971, page 19 [2-1]; 1971, page 19 [2-1]

Seville. Line: 1971. Goblet. 11-1/2 oz. 7 inches tall. Colors: Brown, Delphine Blue, Green, Grey, Yellow. **References:** 1971, page 42 [2-2]; 1972, page 10 [2-2]

Seville. Line: 1971. Goblet. 11-1/2 oz. 7 inches tall. Plain Crystal. **References:** 1972, page 27 [2-1]; 1973, page 32 [2-1]

Seville. Line: 1971. Goblet. 11-1/2 oz. 7 inches tall. Colors: Brown, Delphine Blue, Green, Grey, Yellow. **References:** 1973, page 18 [2-2]

Seville. Line: 1971. Ice Tea. 14-1/2 oz. 7-1/8 inches tall. Green. **References:** 1970, page 2 [1-5]

Seville. Line: 1971. Ice Tea. 14-1/2 oz. 7-1/8 inches tall. Plain Crystal. **References:** 1970, page 11 [2-5]; 1971, page 19 [2-5]; 1971, page 19 [2-5]; 1972, page 27 [2-5]; 1973, page 32 [2-5]

Seville. Line: 1971. Ice Tea. 14-1/2 oz. 7-1/8 inches tall. Colors: Brown, Delphine Blue, Green, Grey, Yellow. **References:** 1971, page 42 [1-1]; 1972, page 10 [1-1]

Seville. Line: 1971. Ice Tea. 14-1/2 oz. 7-1/8 inches tall. Colors: Brown, Delphine Blue, Green, Grey, Yellow. **References:** 1973, page 18 [1-1]

Seville. Line: 1971. Plate. 7 inches diam. Plain Crystal, Actually 7-7/8" Dia. **References:** 1970, page 11 [2-7]; 1971, page 19 [2-7]; 1971, page 19 [2-7]; 1972, page 27 [2-7]; 1973, page 32 [2-7]

Seville. Line: 1971. Plate. 8 inches diam. Plain Crystal, Actually 8-3/4"Dia. **References:** 1970, page 11 [2-8]; 1971, page 19 [2-8]; 1971, page 19 [2-8]; 1972, page 27 [2-8]; 1973, page 32 [2-8]

Seville. Line: 1971. Sherbet. 7-1/2 oz. 5 inches tall. Grey. **References:** 1970, page 2 [1-2]

Seville. Line: 1971. Sherbet. 7-1/2 oz. 5 inches tall. Plain Crystal. **References:** 1970, page 11 [2-2]; 1971, page 19 [2-2]; 1971, page 19 [2-2]; 1972, page 27 [2-2]; 1973, page 32 [2-2]

Seville. Line: 1971. Sherbet. 7-1/2 oz. 5 inches tall. Colors: Brown, Delphine Blue, Green, Grey, Yellow. **References:** 1971, page 42 [2-1]; 1972, page 10 [2-1]; 1973, page 18 [2-1]

Seville. Line: 1971. Wine. 7 oz. 5-7/8 inches tall. Delphine Blue. **References:** 1970, page 2 [1-3]; 1971, page 42 [1-2]; 1972, page 10 [1-2]

Seville. Line: 1971. Wine. 7 oz. 5-7/8 inches tall. Plain Crystal. **References:** 1970, page 11 [2-3]; 1971, page 19 [2-3]; 1971, page 19 [2-3]; 1972, page 27 [2-3]; 1973, page 32 [2-3]

Seville. Line: 1971. Wine. 7 oz. 5-7/8 inches tall. Colors: Brown, Delphine Blue, Green, Grey, Yellow. **References:** 1973, page 18 [1-2]

Sherwood. Cordial. 1-1/4 oz. 3-3/4 inches tall. **References:** 1979, page 3 [2-4]

Sherwood. Goblet. 12 oz. 6-3/4 inches tall. **References:** 1979, page 3 [2-1]

Sherwood. Ice Tea. 14 oz. 6-3/8 inches tall. **References:** 1979, page 3 [2-5]

Sherwood. Sherbet. 7-1/2 oz. 5 inches tall. **References:** 1979, page 3 [2-2]

Sherwood. Wine. 7-1/2 oz. 6 inches tall. **References:** 1979, page 3 [2-3]

Sherwood. Line: 1967. Cut: 1428. 1305 Dessert-Finger Bowl. 4-1/2" Dia. **References:** 1967, page 6 [2-6]; 1968, page 9 [2-6]; 1969, page 10 [2-14]; 1970, page 10 [2-14]; 1971, page 10 [2-14]; 1972, page 17 [2-14]; 1973, page 22 [2-14]; 1975, page 22 [2-14]; 1977, page 33 [2-14]

Sherwood. Line: 1967. Cut: 1428. Cordial. 1-1/4 oz. / 3-3/4" hi. **References:** 1967, page 6 [2-4]; 1968, page 9 [2-4]; 1969, page 10 [2-12]; 1970, page 10 [2-12]; 1971, page 10 [2-12]; 1972, page 17 [2-12]; 1973, page 22 [2-12]; 1975, page 22 [2-12]; 1977, page 33 [2-12]

Sherwood. Line: 1967. Cut: 1428. Goblet. 12 oz. / 6-3/4" hi. **References:** 1967, page 6 [2-1]; 1968, page 9 [2-1]; 1969, page 10 [2-9]; 1970, page 10 [2-9]; 1971, page 10 [2-9]; 1972, page 17 [2-9]; 1973, page 22 [2-9]; 1975, page 22 [2-9]; 1977, page 33 [2-9]

Sherwood. Line: 1967. Cut: 1428. Ice Tea. 14 oz. / 6-3/8" hi. **References:** 1967, page 6 [2-5]; 1968, page 9 [2-5]; 1969, page 10 [2-13]; 1970, page 10 [2-13]; 1971, page 10 [2-13]; 1972, page 17 [2-13]; 1973, page 22 [2-13]; 1975, page 22 [2-13]; 1977, page 33 [2-13]

Sherwood. Line: 1967. Cut: 1428. Plate. 7" / Actually 7-7/8" Dia. **References:** 1967, page 6 [2-7]; 1968, page 9 [2-7]; 1969, page 10 [2-15]; 1970, page 10 [2-15]; 1971, page 10 [2-15]; 1972, page 17 [2-15]; 1973, page 22 [2-15]; 1975, page 22 [2-15]; 1977, page 33 [2-15]

Sherwood. Line: 1967. Cut: 1428. Plate. 8" / Actually 8-3/4" Dia. **References:** 1967, page 6 [2-8]; 1968, page 9 [2-8]; 1969, page 10 [2-16]; 1970, page 10 [2-16]; 1971, page 10 [2-16]; 1972, page 17 [2-16]; 1973, page 22 [2-16]; 1975, page 22 [2-16]; 1977, page 33 [2-16]

Sherwood. Line: 1967. Cut: 1428. Sherbet. 7-1/2 oz. / 5" hi. **References:** 1967, page 6 [2-2]; 1968, page 9 [2-2]; 1969, page 10 [2-10]; 1970, page 10 [2-10]; 1971, page 10 [2-10]; 1972, page 17 [2-10]; 1973, page 22 [2-10]; 1975, page 22 [2-10]; 1977, page 33 [2-10]

Sherwood. Line: 1967. Cut: 1428. Wine. 7-1/2 oz. / 6" hi. **References:** 1967, page 6 [2-3]; 1968, page 9 [2-3]; 1969, page 10 [2-11]; 1970, page 10 [2-11]; 1971, page 10 [2-11]; 1972, page 17 [2-11]; 1973, page 22 [2-11]; 1975, page 22 [2-11]; 1977, page 33 [2-11]

Silver Leaf. Line: 355. Cut: 1320. 1305 Dessert-Finger Bowl. 4-1/2 inches diam. **References:** 1967, page 15 [2-9]; 1968, page 19 [2-9]

Silver Leaf. Line: 355. Cut: 1320. Cocktail. 4-3/4 oz. 4-1/2 inches tall. **References:** 1967, page 15 [2-4]; 1968, page 19 [2-4]

Silver Leaf. Line: 355. Cut: 1320. Cordial. 1-1/2 oz. 3-1/2 inches tall. **References:** 1967, page 15 [2-5]; 1968, page 19 [2-5]

Silver Leaf. Line: 355. Cut: 1320. Goblet. 10-1/2 oz. 6-1/2 inches tall. **References:** 1967, page 15 [2-1]; 1968, page 19 [2-1]

Silver Leaf. Line: 355. Cut: 1320. Ice Tea. 12 oz. 5-3/4 inches tall. **References:** 1967, page 15 [2-8]; 1968, page 19 [2-8]

Silver Leaf. Line: 355. Cut: 1320. Juice. 5 oz. 4-1/2 inches tall. **References:** 1967, page 15 [2-7]; 1968, page 19 [2-7]

Silver Leaf. Line: 355. Cut: 1320. Parfait. 6-1/2 oz. 7-1/2 inches tall. **References:** 1967, page 15 [2-6]; 1968, page 19 [2-6]

Silver Leaf. Line: 355. Cut: 1320. Plate. 7 inches diam. Actually 7-7/8" Dia. **References:** 1967, page 15 [2-10]; 1968, page 19 [2-10]

Silver Leaf. Line: 355. Cut: 1320. Plate. 8 inches diam. Actually 8-3/4" Dia. **References:** 1967, page 15 [2-11]; 1968, page 19 [2-11]

Silver Leaf. Line: 355. Cut: 1320. Sherbet. 6-3/4 oz. 5 inches tall. **References:** 1967, page 15 [2-2]; 1968, page 19 [2-2]

Silver Leaf. Line: 355. Cut: 1320. Wine. 5 oz. 5-1/2 inches tall. **References:** 1967, page 15 [2-3]; 1968, page 19 [2-3]

Silver Rhapsody. Line: 4. Bell. 5-1/2 inches tall. All Bells Individually Gift Boxed. **References:** 1979, page 13 [4-1]

Sociables. Line: 3875. Beverage. 16 oz. 5-1/8 inches tall. Colors: Crystal, Delphine Blue, Green, Grey, Plum. **References:** 1972, page 6 [1-1]; 1972, page 6 [2-3]; 1973, page 15 [1-1]; 1973, page 15 [2-3]

Sociables. Line: 3875. Dessert. 11-1/2 oz. 2-3/4 inches tall. Colors: Crystal, Delphine Blue, Green, Grey, Plum. **References:** 1972, page 6 [2-2]; 1973, page 15 [2-2]

Sociables. Line: 3875. Goblet. 12-1/2 oz. 3-7/8 inches tall. Colors: Crystal, Delphine Blue, Green, Grey, Plum. **References:** 1972, page 6 [1-2]; 1973, page 15 [1-2]

Sociables. Line: 3875. Juice/Cocktail. 9 oz. 3-1/4 inches tall. Crystal. Colors: Crystal, Delphine Blue, Green, Grey, Plum. **References:** 1972, page 6 [2-1]; 1973, page 15 [2-1]

Solitaire. Bell. 3-3/4 inches tall. **References:** 1979, page 12 [1-4]

Solitaire. Line: 1965. Cut: 1419. 1305 Dessert-Finger Bowl. 4-1/2 inches diam. **References:** 1968, page 11 [2-7]

Solitaire. Line: 1965. Cut: 1419. Cordial. 1-1/4 oz. 4 inches tall. **References:** 1968, page 11 [2-4]

Solitaire. Line: 1965. Cut: 1419. Goblet. 11-3/4 oz. 7-1/4 inches tall. **References:** 1968, page 11 [2-1]

Solitaire. Line: 1965. Cut: 1419. Ice Tea. 13-1/2 oz. 6-3/4 inches tall. **References:** 1968, page 11 [2-6]

Solitaire. Line: 1965. Cut: 1419. Juice. 6 oz. 5-1/2 inches tall. **References:** 1968, page 11 [2-5]

Solitaire. Line: 1965. Cut: 1419. Plate. 7 inches diam. Actually 7-7/8" Dia. **References:** 1968, page 11 [2-8]

Solitaire. Line: 1965. Cut: 1419. Plate. 8 inches diam. Actually 8-3/4" Dia. **References:** 1968, page 11 [2-9]

Solitaire. Line: 1965. Cut: 1419. Sherbet. 7-1/2 oz. 5-1/4 inches tall. **References:** 1968, page 11 [2-2]

Solitaire. Line: 1965. Cut: 1419. Wine. 7-1/2 oz. 6-1/4 inches tall. **References:** 1968, page 11 [2-3]

Starburst. Bell. **References:** 1983, page 6 [4-1L]

Starburst. Bud Vase/Candle Holder. 4 inches tall. **References:** 1983, page 7 [3-2R]

Starburst. Bud Vase/Candle Holder. 2 inches tall. **References:** 1983, page 7 [3-3R]

Starburst. Candle Holder. 5-1/2 inches tall. **References:** 1983, page 7 [3-6R]

Starburst. Candle Holder. 6-1/2 inches tall. **References:** 1983, page 7 [3-8R]

Starburst. Line: 70. Vase. 7 inches tall. **References:** 1983, page 7 [1-3R]

Starburst. Line: 80. Ginger Jar. 6-1/4 inches tall. **References:** 1983, page 6 [4-3L]

Starburst. Line: 90. Ginger Jar. 8-1/2 inches tall. **References:** 1983, page 7 [1-1R]

Starburst. Line: 98. Bud Vase. 6 inches tall. **References:** 1983, page 7 [1-6R]

Sterling Mist. Line: 1969. 1305 Dessert-Finger Bowl. 4-1/2 inches diam. 3/16" Genuine Sterling Silver Band. **References:** 1969, page 18 [1-14]; 1970, page 19 [1-14]

Sterling Mist. Line: 1969. Cordial. 2 oz. 4-1/2 inches tall. 3/16" Genuine Sterling Silver Band. **References:** 1969, page 18 [1-12]; 1970, page 19 [1-12]

Sterling Mist. Line: 1969. Goblet. 14 oz. 6-3/4 inches tall. 3/16" Genuine Sterling Silver Band. **References:** 1969, page 18 [1-9]; 1970, page 19 [1-9]

Sterling Mist. Line: 1969. Ice Tea. 14 oz. 6-3/8 inches tall. 3/16" Genuine Sterling Silver Band. **References:** 1969, page 18 [1-13]; 1970, page 19 [1-13]

Sterling Mist. Line: 1969. Plate. 7 inches diam. 3/16" Genuine Sterling Silver Band, Actually 7-7/8" Dia. **References:** 1969, page 18 [1-15]; 1970, page 19 [1-15]

Sterling Mist. Line: 1969. Plate. 8 inches diam. 3/16" Genuine Sterling Silver Band, Actually 8-3/4" Dia. 1970, page 19 [1-16]

Sterling Mist. Line: 1969. Sherbet. 7-1/2 oz. 5-3/8 inches tall. 3/16" Genuine Sterling Silver Band. **References:** 1969, page 18 [1-10]; 1970, page 19 [1-10]

Sterling Mist. Line: 1969. White Wine Goblet. 7-1/2 oz. 5-1/2 inches tall. 3/16" Genuine Sterling Silver Band. **References:** 1969, page 18 [1-11]; 1970, page 19 [1-11]

Stratford. Line: 3. Cut: 636. Bell. 4-3/8 inches tall. Handmade and Hand Cut. **References:** 1975, page 12 [2-4]; 1976, page 6 [2-2]; 1977, page 22 [2-2]

Stratford. Line: 4. Cut: 636. Bell. 5-1/2 inches tall. **References:** 1979, page 12 [3-1]

Stratford. Line: 476. Cut: 636. 1311 Dessert-Finger Bowl. 4-3/4 inches diam. **References:** 1967, page 19 [1-9]; 1969, page 23 [2-20]; 1970, page 24 [2-20]; 1971, page 24 [2-20]

Stratford. Line: 476. Cut: 636. Claret. 3-1/2 oz. 6-1/8 inches tall. **References:** 1967, page 19 [1-3]; 1969, page 23 [2-14]; 1970, page 24 [2-14]; 1971, page 24 [2-14]

Stratford. Line: 476. Cut: 636. Cocktail. 3 oz. 5-1/4 inches tall. **References:** 1967, page 19 [1-5]; 1969, page 23 [2-16]; 1970, page 24 [2-16]; 1970, page 24 [2-16]; 1971, page 24 [2-16]; 1971, page 24 [2-16]

Stratford. Line: 476. Cut: 636. Cordial. 1 oz. 4-3/4 inches tall. **References:** 1967, page 19 [1-6]; 1969, page 23 [2-17]

Stratford. Line: 476. Cut: 636. Goblet. 9 oz. 8-3/8

inches tall. **References:** 1967, page 19 [1-1]; 1969, page 23 [2-12]; 1970, page 24 [2-12]; 1971, page 24 [2-12]

Stratford. Line: 476. Cut: 636. Ice Tea. 12 oz. 7-1/4 inches tall. **References:** 1967, page 19 [1-8]; 1969, page 23 [2-19]; 1970, page 24 [2-19]; 1971, page 24 [2-19]

Stratford. Line: 476. Cut: 636. Juice. 5-1/2 oz. 5-3/4 inches tall. **References:** 1967, page 19 [1-7]; 1969, page 23 [2-18]; 1970, page 24 [2-18]; 1971, page 24 [2-18]

Stratford. Line: 476. Cut: 636. Plate. 7 inches diam. Actually 7-7/8" Dia. **References:** 1967, page 19 [1-10]; 1969, page 23 [2-21]; 1970, page 24 [2-21]; 1971, page 24 [2-21]

Stratford. Line: 476. Cut: 636. Plate. 8 inches diam. Actually 8-3/4" Dia. **References:** 1967, page 19 [1-11]; 1969, page 23 [2-22]; 1970, page 24 [2-22]; 1971, page 24 [2-22]

Stratford. Line: 476. Cut: 636. Saucer Champagne. 6 oz. 6-1/2 inches tall. **References:** 1967, page 19 [1-2]; 1969, page 23 [2-13]; 1970, page 24 [2-13]; 1971, page 24 [2-13]

Stratford. Line: 476. Cut: 636. Wine. 3 oz. 6 inches tall. **References:** 1967, page 19 [1-4]; 1969, page 23 [2-15]; 1970, page 24 [2-15]; 1971, page 24 [2-15]

Suburbia. Line: 1974. Beverage. 14 oz. 5 inches tall. Crystal. Colors: Crystal, Delphine Blue, Moss Green, Grey, Plum. **References:** 1972, page 6 [TL-2]; 1973, page 16 [TL-2]

Suburbia. Line: 1974. Old Fashion. 9-1/2 oz. 4 inches tall. Crystal. Colors: Crystal, Delphine Blue, Moss Green, Grey, Plum. **References:** 1972, page 6 [TL-1]; 1973, page 16 [TL-1]

Sunburst. Beverage. 16 oz. 6 inches tall. Hand Made....Hand Cut. **References:** 1979, page 15 [4-2]; 1981, page 4 [3-9]; 1983, page 11 [M-1R]

Sunburst. Cooler. 16 oz. 7-3/8 inches tall. Hand Made....Hand Cut. **References:** 1979, page 15 [4-1]

Sunburst. Cordial. 2 oz. 5-1/4 inches tall. **References:** 1979, page 1 [3-12]

Sunburst. Goblet. 9-1/2 oz. 8-1/2 inches tall. **References:** 1979, page 1 [3-9]

Sunburst. Hi Ball. 11 oz. 5 inches tall. Hand Made....Hand Cut. **References:** 1979, page 15 [4-3]; 1981, page 4 [3-10]

Sunburst. Hi Ball. 11 oz. 4-7/8 inches tall. **References:** 1983, page 11 [M-2R]

Sunburst. Old Fashion. 9-1/2 oz. 3-1/2 inches tall. Hand Made....Hand Cut. **References:** 1979, page 15 [4-5]; 1981, page 4 [3-12]; 1983, page 11 [M-4R]

Sunburst. On The Rocks. 14 oz. 4-1/2 inches tall. Hand Made, Hand Cut. **References:** 1979, page 15 [4-4]; 1981, page 4 [3-11]; 1983, page 11 [M-3R]

Sunburst. Pony. 3 oz. 3 inches tall. Hand Made....Hand Cut. **References:** 1979, page 15 [4-6]

Sunburst. Sherbet. 7-1/2 oz. 6-1/2 inches tall. **References:** 1979, page 1 [3-10]

Sunburst. Wine. 5 oz. 7-1/4 inches tall. **References:** 1979, page 1 [3-11]

Sunburst. Cut: 1447. Pony. 3 oz. 3 inches tall. **References:** 1978, page 6 [1-1]

Sunburst. Line: 4. Cut: 1447. Bell. 5-1/2 inches tall. All Bells Individually Gift Boxed. **References:** 1977, page 23 [3-1]; 1979, page 13 [4-4]

Sunburst. Line: 970. Cut: 1447. Cordial. 2 oz. 5-1/4 inches tall. **References:** 1976, page 3 [1-8]; 1977, page 27 [1-8]

Sunburst. Line: 970. Cut: 1447. Goblet. 9-1/2 oz. 8-1/2 inches tall. **References:** 1976, page 3 [1-5]; 1977, page 27 [1-5]

Sunburst. Line: 970. Cut: 1447. Sherbet. 7-1/2 oz. 6-1/2 inches tall. **References:** 1976, page 3 [1-6]; 1977, page 27 [1-6]

Sunburst. Line: 970. Cut: 1447. Wine. 5 oz. 7-1/4 inches tall. **References:** 1976, page 3 [1-7]; 1977, page 27 [1-7]

Sunburst. Line: 1978. Cut: 1447. Old Fashion. **References:** 1977, page 24 [3-1]

Sunburst. Line: 1978. Cut: 1447. On the Rocks. 15-1/2 oz. 4-1/2 inches tall. **References:** 1976, page 11 [1-2]

Sylvia. Cocktail. **References:** 1964 Advertisement

Sylvia. Cordial. **References:** 1964 Advertisement

Sylvia. Footed Ice Tea. **References:** 1964 Advertisement

Sylvia. Footed Juice. **References:** 1964 Advertisement

Sylvia. Goblet. 13-1/2 oz. 6-3/4 inches tall. Gold Band. **References:** 1979, page 6 [1-26]

Sylvia. Goblet. **References:** 1964 Advertisement

Sylvia. Saucer Champagne. **References:** 1964 Advertisement

Sylvia. Sherbet. 7-1/2 oz. 5-1/8 inches tall. Gold Band. **References:** 1979, page 6 [1-27]

Sylvia. White Wine Goblet. **References:** 1964 Advertisement

Sylvia. Wine. 7-3/4 oz. 5-3/4 inches tall. Gold Band. **References:** 1979, page 6 [1-28]

Sylvia. Line: 1963. Cocktail. 5-1/2 oz. / 4-3/4" hi. Gold Band. **References:** 1967, page 11 [2-13]; 1968, page 15 [2-13]; 1969, page 20 [2-13]; 1970, page 21 [2-13]; 1971, page 21 [2-13]; 1972, page 29 [2-13]; 1973, page 34 [2-13]

Sylvia. Line: 1963. Cordial. 1-1/2 oz. / 4" hi. Gold Band. **References:** 1967, page 11 [2-14]; 1968, page 15 [2-14]; 1969, page 20 [2-14]; 1970, page 21 [2-14]; 1971, page 21 [2-14]; 1972, page 29 [2-14]; 1973, page 34 [2-14]; 1975, page 30 [2-11]; 1977, page 41 [2-11]; 1979, page 6 [1-29]

Sylvia. Line: 1963. Goblet. 13-1/2 oz. / 6-3/4" hi. Gold Band. **References:** 1967, page 11 [2-10]; 1968, page 15 [2-10]; 1969, page 20 [2-10]; 1970, page 21 [2-10]; 1971, page 21 [2-10]; 1972, page 29 [2-10]; 1973, page 34 [2-10]; 1975, page 30 [2-8]; 1977, page 41 [2-8]

Sylvia. Line: 1963. Ice Tea. 14 oz. / 6-1/4" hi.. Gold Band. **References:** 1967, page 11 [2-16]; 1968, page 15 [2-16]; 1969, page 20 [2-16]; 1970, page 21 [2-16]; 1971, page 21 [2-16]; 1972, page 29 [2-16]; 1973, page 34 [2-16]; 1975, page 30 [2-12]; 1977, page 41 [2-12]

Sylvia. Line: 1963. Juice. 7 oz. / 5-1/4" hi. Gold Band. **References:** 1967, page 11 [2-15]; 1968, page 15 [2-15]; 1969, page 20 [2-15]; 1970, page 21 [2-15]; 1971, page 21 [2-15]; 1972, page 29 [2-15]; 1973, page 34 [2-15]

Sylvia. Line: 1963. Plate. 7" / Actually 7-7/8" Dia. Gold Band. **References:** 1967, page 11 [2-17]; 1968, page 15 [2-17]; 1969, page 20 [2-17]; 1970, page 21 [2-17]; 1971, page 21 [2-17]; 1972, page 29 [2-17]; 1973, page 34 [2-17]; 1975, page 30 [2-13]; 1977, page 41 [2-13]

Sylvia. Line: 1963. Plate. 8" / Actually 8-3/4" Dia. Gold Band. **References:** 1967, page 11 [2-18]; 1968, page 15 [2-18]; 1969, page 20 [2-18]; 1970, page 21 [2-18]; 1971, page 21 [2-18]; 1972, page 29 [2-18]; 1973, page 34 [2-18]; 1975, page 30 [2-14]; 1977, page 41 [2-14]

Sylvia. Line: 1963. Sherbet. 7-1/2 oz. - 5-1/8" hi. Gold Band. **References:** 1967, page 11 [2-11]; 1968, page 15 [2-11]; 1969, page 20 [2-11]; 1970, page 21 [2-11]; 1971, page 21 [2-11]; 1972, page 29 [2-11]; 1973, page 34 [2-11]; 1975, page 30 [2-9]; 1977, page 41 [2-9]

Sylvia. Line: 1963. Wine. 7-3/4 oz. / 5-3/4" hi. Gold Band. **References:** 1967, page 11 [2-12]; 1968, page 15 [2-12]; 1969, page 20 [2-12]; 1970, page 21 [2-12]; 1971, page 21 [2-12]; 1972, page 29 [2-12]; 1973, page 34 [2-12]; 1975, page 30 [2-10]; 1977, page 41 [2-10]

Tapestry. Beverage. 16 oz. 6 inches tall. Hand Made....Hand Cut. **References:** 1979, page 15 [4-8]; 1981, page 4 [2-5]; 1983, page 11 [2-5R]

Tapestry. Champagne Flute. 6 oz. 9-1/4 inches tall. **References:** 1983, page 5 [1-4]

Tapestry. Cooler. 16 oz. 7-3/8 inches tall. Hand Made....Hand Cut. **References:** 1979, page 15 [4-7]

Tapestry. Cordial. 3 oz. 5-5/8 inches tall. **References:** 1979, page 1 [1-12]

Tapestry. Cordial. 3 oz. 5-1/2 inches tall. **References:** 1983, page 5 [1-5]

Tapestry. Goblet. 13 oz. 7-1/2 inches tall. $90-100. **References:** 1979, page 1 [1-9]; 1983, page 5 [1-1]

Tapestry. Hi Ball. 11 oz. 5 inches tall. Hand Made....Hand Cut. **References:** 1979, page 15 [4-9]; 1981, page 4 [2-6]

Tapestry. Hi Ball. 11 oz. 4-7/8 inches tall. **References:** 1983, page 11 [2-6R]

Tapestry. Ice Tea. 14 oz. 6-1/2 inches tall. **References:** 1983, page 5 [1-6]

Tapestry. Old Fashion. 9-1/2 oz. 3-1/2 inches tall. Hand Made....Hand Cut. **References:** 1979, page 15 [4-11]; 1981, page 4 [2-8]

Tapestry. Old Fashion. 9-1/2 oz. 3-5/8 inches tall. **References:** 1983, page 11 [2-8R]

Tapestry. On The Rocks. 14 oz. 4-1/2 inches tall. Hand Made, Hand Cut. **References:** 1979, page 15 [4-10]; 1981, page 4 [2-7]

Tapestry. On The Rocks. 14 oz. 4-3/8 inches tall. **References:** 1983, page 11 [2-7R]

Tapestry. Pony. 3 oz. 3 inches tall. Hand Made....Hand Cut. **References:** 1979, page 15 [4-12]

Tapestry. Sherbet. 9 oz. 6 inches tall. **References:** 1979, page 1 [1-10]; 1983, page 5 [1-2]

Tapestry. Wine. 7-1/2 oz. 6-1/2 inches tall. **References:** 1979, page 1 [1-11]; 1983, page 5 [1-3]

Tapestry. Cut: 1449. Bell. **References:** 1981, page 11 [3-2]; 1983, page 7 [1-2L]

Tapestry. Cut: 1449S. Hi Ball. 11 oz. 5 inches tall. **References:** 1978, page 6 [1-3]

Tapestry. Line: 4. Cut: 1449. Bell. 5-1/2 inches tall. All Bells Individually Gift Boxed. **References:** 1977, page 23 [5-3]; 1979, page 13 [1-1]

Tapestry. Line: 972. Cut: 1448. Cordial. 3 oz. 5-5/8 inches tall. **References:** 1981, page 1 [1-8]

Tapestry. Line: 972. Cut: 1448. Goblet. 13 oz. 7-1/2 inches tall. $90-100. **References:** 1981, page 1 [1-5]

Tapestry. Line: 972. Cut: 1448. Sherbet. 9 oz. 6 inches tall. **References:** 1981, page 1 [1-6]

Tapestry. Line: 972. Cut: 1448. Wine. 7-1/2 oz. 6-1/2 inches tall. **References:** 1981, page 1 [1-7]

Tapestry. Line: 972. Cut: 1449. Cordial. 3 oz. 5-5/8 inches tall. **References:** 1976, page 4 [1-8]; 1977, page 29 [1-8]

Tapestry. Line: 972. Cut: 1449. Goblet. 13 oz. 7-1/2 inches tall. $90-100. **References:** 1976, page 4 [1-5]; 1977, page 29 [1-5]

Tapestry. Line: 972. Cut: 1449. Sherbet. 9 oz. 6 inches tall. **References:** 1976, page 4 [1-6]; 1977, page 29 [1-6]

Tapestry. Line: 972. Cut: 1449. Wine. 7-1/2 oz. 6-1/2 inches tall. **References:** 1976, page 4 [1-7]; 1977, page 29 [1-7]

Tapestry. Line: 1978. Cut: 1449S. On The Rocks. **References:** 1977, page 25 [2-1]

Timeless. Line: 352. Cut: 1380. 1311 Dessert-Finger Bowl. 4-3/4 inches diam. **References:** 1967, page 18 [1-18]; 1968, page 22 [1-18]

Timeless. Line: 352. Cut: 1380. Claret. 3-3/4 oz. 5-5/8 inches tall. **References:** 1967, page 18 [1-13]; 1968, page 22 [1-13]

Timeless. Line: 352. Cut: 1380. Cocktail. 3 oz. 4-1/4 inches tall. **References:** 1967, page 18 [1-14]; 1968, page 22 [1-14]

Timeless. Line: 352. Cut: 1380. Cordial. 1 oz. 4 inches tall. **References:** 1967, page 18 [1-15]; 1968, page 22 [1-15]

Timeless. Line: 352. Cut: 1380. Goblet. 9 oz. 7-1/4 inches tall. **References:** 1967, page 18 [1-11]; 1968, page 22 [1-11]

Timeless. Line: 352. Cut: 1380. Ice Tea. 12 oz. 7-1/4 inches tall. **References:** 1967, page 18 [1-17]; 1968, page 22 [1-17]

Timeless. Line: 352. Cut: 1380. Juice. 5-1/2 oz. 5-3/8 inches tall. **References:** 1967, page 18 [1-16]; 1968, page 22 [1-16]

Timeless. Line: 352. Cut: 1380. Plate. 7 inches diam. Actually 7-7/8" Dia. **References:** 1967, page 18 [1-19]; 1968, page 22 [1-19]

Timeless. Line: 352. Cut: 1380. Plate. 8 inches diam. Actually 8-3/4" Dia. **References:** 1967, page 18 [1-20]; 1968, page 22 [1-20]

Timeless. Line: 352. Cut: 1380. Sherbet. 6 oz. 5-3/8 inches tall. **References:** 1967, page 18 [1-12]; 1968, page 22 [1-12]

Today. Line: 1976. Dessert. 10-1/2 oz. 2-5/8 inches tall. Crystal with Black Foot. Colors: Black, Crystal, Crystal with Black Foot. **References:** 1972, page 6 [1-1]

Today. Line: 1976. Dessert. 10-1/2 oz. 2-5/8 inches tall. Colors: Black, Crystal, Crystal with Black Foot. **References:** 1973, page 15 [1-1]

Today. Line: 1976. Goblet. 17-1/2 oz. 4-1/8 inches tall. Black. Colors: Black, Crystal, Crystal with Black Foot. **References:** 1972, page 6 [1-2]

Today. Line: 1976. Goblet. 17-1/2 oz. 4-1/8 inches tall. Colors: Black, Crystal, Crystal with Black Foot. **References:** 1973, page 15 [1-2]

Today. Line: 1976. Juice/Wine. 9-1/2 oz. 3-5/8 inches tall. Crystal. Colors: Black, Crystal, Crystal with Black Foot. **References:** 1972, page 6 [1-3]

Today. Line: 1976. Juice/Wine. 9-1/2 oz. 3-5/8 inches tall. Colors: Black, Crystal, Crystal with Black Foot. **References:** 1973, page 15 [1-3]

Traditional. Cordial. 1-1/4 oz. 3-7/8 inches tall. **References:** 1979, page 4 [1-14]

Traditional. Goblet. 12 oz. 7 inches tall. **References:** 1979, page 4 [1-11]

Traditional. Ice Tea. 14 oz. 6-1/4 inches tall. **References:** 1979, page 4 [1-15]

Traditional. Sherbet. 7-1/2 oz. 5-1/8 inches tall. **References:** 1979, page 4 [1-12]

Traditional. Wine. 7-1/2 oz. 6 inches tall. **References:** 1979, page 4 [1-13]

Traditional. Line: 1966. Cut: 1432. 1305 Dessert-Finger Bowl. 4-1/2" Dia. **References:** 1967, page 5 [2-6]; 1968, page 8 [3-6]; 1969, page 8 [1-6]; 1970, page 8 [1-6]; 1971, page 8 [1-6]; 1972, page 19 [1-6]; 1973, page 24 [1-6]; 1975, page 24 [1-6]; 1977, page 35 [1-6]

Traditional. Line: 1966. Cut: 1432. Cordial. 1-1/4 oz. / 3-7/8" hi. **References:** 1967, page 5 [2-4]; 1968, page 8 [3-4]; 1969, page 8 [1-4]; 1970, page 8 [1-4]; 1971, page 8 [1-4]; 1972, page 19 [1-4]; 1973, page 24 [1-4]; 1975, page 24 [1-4]; 1977, page 35 [1-4]

Traditional. Line: 1966. Cut: 1432. Goblet. 12 oz. / 7" hi. **References:** 1967, page 5 [2-1]; 1968, page 8 [3-1]; 1969, page 8 [1-1]; 1970, page 8 [1-1]; 1971, page 8 [1-1]; 1972, page 19 [1-1]; 1973, page 24 [1-1]; 1975, page 24 [1-1]; 1977, page 35 [1-1]

Traditional. Line: 1966. Cut: 1432. Ice Tea. 14 oz. / 6-1/4" hi. **References:** 1967, page 5 [2-5]; 1968, page 8 [3-5]; 1969, page 8 [1-5]; 1970, page 8 [1-5]; 1971, page 8 [1-5]; 1972, page 19 [1-5]; 1973, page 24 [1-5]; 1975, page 24 [1-5]; 1977, page 35 [1-5]

Traditional. Line: 1966. Cut: 1432. Plate. 7" / 7-7/8" Dia. **References:** 1967, page 5 [2-7]; 1968, page 8 [3-7]; 1969, page 8 [1-7]; 1970, page 8 [1-7]; 1971, page 8 [1-7]; 1972, page 19 [1-7]; 1973, page 24 [1-7]; 1975, page 24 [1-7]; 1977, page 35 [1-7]

Traditional. Line: 1966. Cut: 1432. Plate. 8" / 8-3/4" Dia. **References:** 1967, page 5 [2-8]; 1968, page 8 [3-8]; 1969, page 8 [1-8]; 1970, page 8 [1-8]; 1971, page 8 [1-8]; 1972, page 19 [1-8]; 1973, page 24 [1-8]; 1975, page 24 [1-8]; 1977, page 35 [1-8]

Traditional. Line: 1966. Cut: 1432. Sherbet. 7-1/2 oz. / 5-1/8 hi. **References:** 1967, page 5 [2-2]; 1968, page 8 [3-2]; 1969, page 8 [1-2]; 1970, page 8 [1-2]; 1971, page 8 [1-2]; 1972, page 19 [1-2]; 1973, page 24 [1-2]; 1975, page 24 [1-2]; 1977, page 35 [1-2]

Traditional. Line: 1966. Cut: 1432. Wine. 7-1/2 oz. / 6" hi. **References:** 1967, page 5 [2-3]; 1968, page 8 [3-3]; 1969, page 8 [1-3]; 1970, page 8 [1-3]; 1971, page 8 [1-3]; 1972, page 19 [1-3]; 1973, page 24 [1-3]; 1975, page 24 [1-3]; 1977, page 35 [1-3]

True Love. Line: 1963. Cut: 1409. 1305 Dessert-Finger Bowl. 4-1/2" Dia. **References:** 1967, page 8 [2-8]; 1968, page 12 [2-8]

True Love. Line: 1963. Cut: 1409. Cocktail. 5-1/2 oz. / 4-3/4" hi. **References:** 1967, page 8 [2-4]; 1968, page 12 [2-4]

True Love. Line: 1963. Cut: 1409. Cordial. 1-1/2 oz. / 4" hi. **References:** 1967, page 8 [2-5]; 1968, page 12 [2-5]

True Love. Line: 1963. Cut: 1409. Goblet. 13-1/2 oz. / 6-3/4" hi. **References:** 1967, page 8 [2-1]; 1968, page 12 [2-1]

True Love. Line: 1963. Cut: 1409. Ice Tea. 14 oz. / 6-1/4" hi. **References:** 1967, page 8 [2-7]; 1968, page 12 [2-7]

True Love. Line: 1963. Cut: 1409. Juice. 7 oz. / 5-1/4" hi. **References:** 1967, page 8 [2-6]; 1968, page 12 [2-6]

True Love. Line: 1963. Cut: 1409. Plate. 7" / Actually 7-7/8" Dia. **References:** 1967, page 8 [2-9]; 1968, page 12 [2-9]

True Love. Line: 1963. Cut: 1409. Plate. 8" / Actually 8-3/4" Dia. **References:** 1967, page 8 [2-10]; 1968, page 12 [2-10]

True Love. Line: 1963. Cut: 1409. Sherbet. 7-1/2 oz. / 5-1/8" hi. **References:** 1967, page 8 [2-2]; 1968, page 12 [2-2]

True Love. Line: 1963. Cut: 1409. Wine. 7-3/4 oz. / 5-3/4" hi. **References:** 1967, page 8 [2-3]; 1968, page 12 [2-3]

Ultra. Apertif. 8 oz. 8-3/8 inches tall. **References:** 1979, page 5 [3-3]

Ultra. Beverage. 16 oz. 6 inches tall. Hand Made....Hand Cut. **References:** 1979, page 15 [5-2]; 1981, page 4 [2-1]; 1983, page 11 [2-1L]

Ultra. Compote. 16 oz. 4-3/4 inches tall. **References:** 1979, page 5 [3-5]

Ultra. Cooler. 16 oz. 7-3/8 inches tall. Hand Made....Hand Cut. **References:** 1979, page 15

[5-1]

Ultra. Hi Ball. 11 oz. 5 inches tall. Hand Made....Hand Cut. **References:** 1979, page 15 [5-3]; 1981, page 4 [2-2]

Ultra. Hi Ball. 11 oz. 4-7/8 inches tall. **References:** 1983, page 11 [2-2L]

Ultra. Old Fashion. 9-1/2 oz. 3-1/2 inches tall. Hand Made....Hand Cut. **References:** 1979, page 15 [5-5]; 1981, page 4 [2-4]

Ultra. Old Fashion. 9-1/2 oz. 3-5/8 inches tall. **References:** 1983, page 11 [2-4L]

Ultra. On The Rocks. 14 oz. 4-1/2 inches tall. Hand Made, Hand Cut. **References:** 1979, page 15 [5-4]; 1981, page 4 [2-3]

Ultra. On The Rocks. 14 oz. 4-3/8 inches tall. **References:** 1983, page 11 [2-3L]

Ultra. Pony. 3 oz. 3 inches tall. Hand Made....Hand Cut. **References:** 1979, page 15 [5-6]

Ultra. Red Wine Goblet. 15 oz. 7-3/4 inches tall. **References:** 1979, page 5 [3-4]

Ultra. Sparkling Wine Goblet. 15 oz. 8-3/4 inches tall. **References:** 1979, page 5 [3-2]

Ultra. Wine Goblet. 28 oz. 8-3/4 inches tall. **References:** 1979, page 5 [3-1]

Ultra. Line: 1978. Cut: 43. Apertif. 8 oz. 8-3/8 inches tall. **References:** 1975, page 11 [1-3]; 1977, page 11 [1-3]

Ultra. Line: 1978. Cut: 43. Compote. 16 oz. 4-3/4 inches tall. **References:** 1975, page 11 [1-5]; 1977, page 11 [1-5]

Ultra. Line: 1978. Cut: 43. Old Fashion. **References:** 1977, page 25 [3-1]

Ultra. Line: 1978. Cut: 43. On The Rocks. 14 oz. 4-1/2 inches tall. **References:** 1975, page 11 [1-6]; 1976, page 11 [2-3]; 1977, page 11 [1-6]

Ultra. Line: 1978. Cut: 43. Red Wine Goblet. 15 oz. 7-3/4 inches tall. **References:** 1975, page 11 [1-4]; 1977, page 11 [1-4]

Ultra. Line: 1978. Cut: 43. Sparkling Wine Goblet. 15 oz. 8-3/4 inches tall. **References:** 1975, page 11 [1-2]; 1977, page 11 [1-2]

Ultra. Line: 1978. Cut: 43. Wine Goblet. 28 oz. 8-3/4 inches tall. **References:** 1975, page 11 [1-1]; 1977, page 11 [1-1]

Victoria. Cordial. 5-1/2 oz. 4-5/8 inches tall. Gold Band. **References:** 1979, page 6 [1-19]

Victoria. Goblet. 12 oz. 7 inches tall. Gold Band. **References:** 1979, page 6 [1-16]

Victoria. Ice Tea. 12 oz. 6-1/4 inches tall. Gold Band. **References:** 1979, page 6 [1-20]

Victoria. Sherbet. 7-1/2 oz. 5-1/8 inches tall. Gold Band. **References:** 1979, page 6 [1-17]

Victoria. Wine. 7 oz. 5-7/8 inches tall. Gold Band. **References:** 1979, page 6 [1-18]

Victoria. Line: 1235. Cordial. 2 oz. 4-1/2 inches tall. Gold Band. **References:** 1975, page 29 [1-25]; 1977, page 40 [1-25]

Victoria. Line: 1235. Goblet. 12 oz. 7 inches tall. Gold Band. **References:** 1975, page 29 [1-22]; 1977, page 40 [1-22]

Victoria. Line: 1235. Ice Tea. 12 oz. 6-1/4 inches tall. Gold Band. **References:** 1975, page 29 [1-26]; 1977, page 40 [1-26]

Victoria. Line: 1235. Plate. 7 inches diam. Gold Band, Actually 7-7/8" Dia. **References:** 1975, page 29 [1-27]; 1977, page 40 [1-27]

Victoria. Line: 1235. Plate. 8 inches diam. Gold Band, Actually 8-3/4" Dia. **References:** 1975, page 29 [1-28]; 1977, page 40 [1-28]

Victoria. Line: 1235. Sherbet. 7-1/2 oz. 5-1/8 inches tall. Gold Band. **References:** 1975, page 29 [1-23]; 1977, page 40 [1-23]

Victoria. Line: 1235. Wine. 7 oz. 5-7/8 inches tall. Gold Band. **References:** 1975, page 29 [1-24]; 1977, page 40 [1-24]

Victoria. Line: 1235. Cut: 1406. Cocktail. 5-1/2 oz. / 4-5/8" hi. Gold Band. **References:** 1967, page 10 [1-31]; 1969, page 19 [1-34]; 1970, page 20 [1-34]; 1971, page 20 [1-34]; 1972, page 28 [1-34]; 1973, page 33 [1-34]

Victoria. Line: 1235. Cut: 1406. Cordial. 2 oz. / 4-1/2" hi. Gold Band. **References:** 1967, page 10 [1-32]; 1969, page 19 [1-35]; 1970, page 20 [1-35]; 1971, page 20 [1-35]; 1972, page 28 [1-35]; 1973, page 33 [1-35]

Victoria. Line: 1235. Cut: 1406. Goblet. 12 oz. / 7" hi. Gold Band. **References:** 1967, page 10 [1-28]; 1969, page 19 [1-31]; 1970, page 20 [1-31]

Victoria. Line: 1235. Cut: 1406. Goblet. 12 oz. 7 inches tall. Gold Band. **References:** 1971, page 20 [1-31]; 1972, page 28 [1-31]; 1973, page 33 [1-31]

Victoria. Line: 1235. Cut: 1406. Ice Tea. 12 oz. / 6-1/4" hi. Gold Band. **References:** 1967, page 10 [1-34]; 1969, page 19 [1-38]; 1970, page 20 [1-38]; 1971, page 20 [1-38]; 1972, page 28 [1-38]; 1973, page 33 [1-38]

Victoria. Line: 1235. Cut: 1406. Juice. 5 oz. / 4-1/2" hi. Gold Band. **References:** 1967, page 10 [1-33]; 1969, page 19 [1-37]; 1970, page 20 [1-37]; 1971, page 20 [1-37]; 1972, page 28 [1-37]; 1973, page 33 [1-37]

Victoria. Line: 1235. Cut: 1406. Parfait Whiskey Sour. 7 oz. 6-1/4 inches tall. Gold Band. **References:** 1969, page 19 [1-6]; 1970, page 20 [1-36]; 1971, page 20 [1-36]; 1972, page 28 [1-36]; 1973, page 33 [1-36]

Victoria. Line: 1235. Cut: 1406. Plate. 7" / Actually 7-7/8" Dia. Gold Band. **References:** 1967, page 10 [1-35]; 1969, page 19 [1-39]; 1970, page 20 [1-39]; 1971, page 20 [1-39]; 1972, page 28 [1-39]; 1973, page 33 [1-39]

Victoria. Line: 1235. Cut: 1406. Plate. 8" / Actually 8-3/4" Dia. Gold Band. **References:** 1967, page 10 [1-36]; 1969, page 19 [1-40]; 1970, page 20 [1-40]; 1971, page 20 [1-40]; 1972, page 28 [1-40]; 1973, page 33 [1-40]

Victoria. Line: 1235. Cut: 1406. Sherbet. 7-1/2 oz. / 5-1/8" hi. Gold Band. **References:** 1967, page 10 [1-29]; 1969, page 19 [1-32]; 1970, page 20 [1-32]; 1971, page 20 [1-32]; 1972, page 28 [1-32]; 1973, page 33 [1-32]

Victoria. Line: 1235. Cut: 1406. Wine. 7 oz. / 5-7/8" hi. Gold Band. **References:** 1967, page 10 [1-30]; 1969, page 19 [1-33]; 1970, page 20 [1-33]; 1971, page 20 [1-33]; 1972, page 28 [1-33]; 1973, page 33 [1-33]

Waterford. Line: 908. Cut: 879. 1311 Dessert-Finger Bowl. 4-3/4 inches diam. **References:** 1967, page 20 [2-8]; 1969, page 22 [2-8]; 1970, page 23 [2-8]; 1971, page 23 [2-8]

Waterford. Line: 908. Cut: 879. Claret. 3-1/2 oz. 4-3/8 inches tall. **References:** 1967, page 20 [2-3]; 1969, page 22 [2-3]; 1970, page 23 [2-3]; 1971, page 23 [2-3]

Waterford. Line: 908. Cut: 879. Cocktail. 3 oz. 4-5/8 inches tall. **References:** 1967, page 20 [2-4]; 1969, page 22 [2-4]; 1970, page 23 [2-4]; 1971, page 23 [2-4]

Waterford. Line: 908. Cut: 879. Cordial. 1 oz. 3-1/4 inches tall. **References:** 1967, page 20 [2-5]; 1969, page 22 [2-5]; 1970, page 23 [2-5]; 1971, page 23 [2-5]

Waterford. Line: 908. Cut: 879. Goblet. 9 oz. 6 inches tall. **References:** 1967, page 20 [2-1]; 1969, page 22 [2-1]; 1970, page 23 [2-1]; 1971, page 23 [2-1]

Waterford. Line: 908. Cut: 879. Ice Tea. 10-1/2 oz. 5-5/8 inches tall. **References:** 1967, page 20 [2-7]; 1969, page 22 [2-7]; 1970, page 23 [2-7]; 1971, page 23 [2-7]

Waterford. Line: 908. Cut: 879. Juice. 5 oz. 4-3/8 inches tall. **References:** 1967, page 20 [2-6]; 1969, page 22 [2-6]; 1970, page 23 [2-6]; 1971, page 23 [2-6]

Waterford. Line: 908. Cut: 879. Plate. 7 inches diam. Actually 7-7/8" Dia. **References:** 1967, page 20 [2-9]; 1969, page 22 [2-9]; 1970, page 23 [2-9]; 1971, page 23 [2-9]

Waterford. Line: 908. Cut: 879. Plate. 8 inches diam. Actually 8-3/4" Dia. **References:** 1967, page 20 [2-10]; 1969, page 22 [2-10]; 1970, page 23 [2-10]; 1971, page 23 [2-10]

Waterford. Line: 908. Cut: 879. Saucer Champagne. 7 oz. 4-3/4 inches tall. **References:** 1967, page 20 [2-2]; 1969, page 22 [2-2]; 1970, page 23 [2-2]; 1971, page 23 [2-2]

Weatherly. Cocktail. **References:** 1964 Advertisement

Weatherly. Cordial. **References:** 1964 Advertisement

Weatherly. Footed Ice Tea. **References:** 1964 Advertisement

Weatherly. Footed Juice. **References:** 1964 Advertisement

Weatherly. Goblet. **References:** 1964 Advertisement

Weatherly. Red Wine Goblet. **References:** 1964 Advertisement

Weatherly. Saucer Champagne. **References:** 1964 Advertisement

Weatherly. White Wine Goblet. **References:** 1964 Advertisement

Westwind. Line: 352. Cut: 1263. 1311 Dessert-Finger Bowl. 4-3/4 inches diam. **References:** 1967, page 18 [2-18]; 1968, page 22 [2-18]

Westwind. Line: 352. Cut: 1263. Claret. 3-3/4 oz. 5-5/8 inches tall. **References:** 1967, page 18 [2-13]; 1968, page 22 [2-13]

Westwind. Line: 352. Cut: 1263. Cocktail. 3 oz. 4-1/4 inches tall. **References:** 1967, page 18 [2-14]; 1968, page 22 [2-14]

Westwind. Line: 352. Cut: 1263. Cordial. 1 oz. 4 inches tall. **References:** 1967, page 18 [2-15]; 1968, page 22 [2-15]

Westwind. Line: 352. Cut: 1263. Goblet. 9 oz. 7-1/4 inches tall. **References:** 1967, page 18 [2-11]; 1968, page 22 [2-11]

Westwind. Line: 352. Cut: 1263. Ice Tea. 12 oz. 7-1/4 inches tall. **References:** 1967, page 18 [2-17]; 1968, page 22 [2-17]

Westwind. Line: 352. Cut: 1263. Juice. 5-1/2 oz. 5-3/8 inches tall. **References:** 1967, page 18 [2-16]; 1968, page 22 [2-16]

Westwind. Line: 352. Cut: 1263. Plate. 7 inches diam. Actually 7-7/8" Dia. **References:** 1967, page 18 [2-19]; 1968, page 22 [2-19]

Westwind. Line: 352. Cut: 1263. Plate. 8 inches diam. Actually 8-3/4" Dia. **References:** 1967, page 18 [2-20]; 1968, page 22 [2-20]

Westwind. Line: 352. Cut: 1263. Sherbet. 6 oz. 5-3/8 inches tall. **References:** 1967, page 18 [2-12]; 1968, page 22 [2-12]

Whitebrook. Cordial. 1-1/2 oz. **References:** 1967 Advertisement

Whitebrook. Footed Ice Tea. 14-1/4 oz. **References:** 1967 Advertisement

Whitebrook. Footed Juice. 6-3/4 oz. **References:** 1967 Advertisement

Whitebrook. Goblet. 13-3/4 oz. **References:** 1967 Advertisement

Whitebrook. Sherbet. 7-1/2 oz. **References:** 1967 Advertisement

Whitebrook. Wine. 9 oz. **References:** 1967 Advertisement

Wicker. Beverage. 16 oz. 6 inches tall. Hand Made....Hand Cut. **References:** 1979, page 15 [5-8]; 1981, page 4 [3-13]

Wicker. Beverage. 16 oz. 5-3/4 inches tall. **References:** 1983, page 11 [3-5R]

Wicker. Cooler. 16 oz. 7-3/8 inches tall. Hand Made....Hand Cut. **References:** 1979, page 15 [5-7]

Wicker. Cordial. 2 oz. 5-1/4 inches tall. **References:** 1979, page 1 [3-8]

Wicker. Goblet. 9-1/2 oz. 8-1/2 inches tall. **References:** 1979, page 1 [3-5]

Wicker. Hi Ball. 11 oz. 5 inches tall. Hand Made....Hand Cut. **References:** 1979, page 15 [5-9]; 1981, page 4 [3-14]

Wicker. Hi Ball. 11 oz. 4-7/8 inches tall. **References:** 1983, page 11 [3-6R]

Wicker. Old Fashion. 9-1/2 oz. 3-1/2 inches tall. Hand Made....Hand Cut. **References:** 1979, page 15 [5-11]; 1981, page 4 [3-16]

Wicker. Old Fashion. 9-1/2 oz. 3-5/8 inches tall. **References:** 1983, page 11 [3-8R]

Wicker. On The Rocks. 14 oz. 4-1/2 inches tall. Hand Made, Hand Cut. **References:** 1979, page 15 [5-10]; 1981, page 4 [3-15]

Wicker. On The Rocks. 14 oz. 4-3/8 inches tall. **References:** 1983, page 11 [3-7R]

Wicker. Pony. 3 oz. 3 inches tall. Hand Made....Hand Cut. **References:** 1979, page 15 [5-12]

Wicker. Sherbet. 7-1/2 oz. 6-1/2 inches tall. **References:** 1979, page 1 [3-6]

Wicker. Wine. 5 oz. 7-1/4 inches tall. **References:** 1979, page 1 [3-7]

Wicker. Cut: 1446. Bell. **References:** 1981, page 11 [3-1]; 1983, page 7 [1-1L]

Wicker. Line: 4. Cut: 1446. Bell. 5-1/2 inches tall. All Bells Individually Gift Boxed. **References:** 1976, page 7 [2-3]; 1977, page 23 [3-3]; 1979, page 13 [1-2]

Wicker. Line: 70. Vase. 7 inches tall. All Items Gift Boxed. **References:** 1983, page 6 [1-4L]

Wicker. Line: 70. Cut: 1446. Vase. 7 inches tall. **References:** 1981, page 10 [2-4]

Wicker. Line: 970. Cut: 1446. Cordial. 2 oz. 5-1/4 inches tall. **References:** 1976, page 3 [1-4]; 1977, page 27 [1-4]

Wicker. Line: 970. Cut: 1446. Goblet. 9-1/2 oz. 8-1/2 inches tall. **References:** 1976, page 3 [1-1]; 1977, page 27 [1-1]

Wicker. Line: 970. Cut: 1446. Sherbet. 7-1/2 oz. 6-1/2 inches tall. **References:** 1976, page 3 [1-2]; 1977, page 27 [1-2]

Wicker. Line: 970. Cut: 1446. Wine. 5 oz. 7-1/4 inches tall. **References:** 1976, page 3 [1-3]; 1977, page 27 [1-3]

Wicker. Line: 1978. Cut: 1446. On The Rocks. 15-1/2 oz. 4-1/2 inches tall. $20-30X. **References:** 1976, page 11 [2-1]

Wicker. Line: 1978. Cut: 1446. On The Rocks. **References:** 1977, page 24 [2-1]

Windblown. Line: 476. Cut: 900. 1311 Dessert-Finger Bowl. 4-3/4 inches diam. **References:** 1967, page 19 [2-20]

Windblown. Line: 476. Cut: 900. Claret. 3-1/2 oz. 6-1/8 inches tall. **References:** 1967, page 19 [2-14]

Windblown. Line: 476. Cut: 900. Cocktail. 3 oz. 5-1/4 inches tall. **References:** 1967, page 19 [2-16]

Windblown. Line: 476. Cut: 900. Cordial. 1 oz. 4-3/4 inches tall. **References:** 1967, page 19 [2-17]

Windblown. Line: 476. Cut: 900. Goblet. 9 oz. 8-3/8 inches tall. **References:** 1967, page 19 [2-12]

Windblown. Line: 476. Cut: 900. Ice Tea. 12 oz. 7-1/4 inches tall. **References:** 1967, page 19 [2-19]

Windblown. Line: 476. Cut: 900. Juice. 5-1/2 oz. 5-3/4 inches tall. **References:** 1967, page 19 [2-18]

Windblown. Line: 476. Cut: 900. Plate. 7 inches diam. Actually 7-7/8" Dia. **References:** 1967, page 19 [2-21]

Windblown. Line: 476. Cut: 900. Plate. 8 inches diam. Actually 8-3/4" Dia. **References:** 1967, page 19 [2-22]

Windblown. Line: 476. Cut: 900. Saucer Champagne. 6 oz. 6-1/2 inches tall. **References:** 1967, page 19 [2-13]

Windblown. Line: 476. Cut: 900. Wine. 3 oz. 6 inches tall. **References:** 1967, page 19 [2-15]

Windfall. **References:** Advertisement

Windsor. Line: 1235. Cut: 1406. Cocktail. 5-1/2 oz. / 4-5/8" hi. NOT BANDED. **References:** 1967, page 10 [1-40]

Windsor. Line: 1235. Cut: 1406. Cordial. 2 oz. / 4-1/2" hi. NOT BANDED. **References:** 1967, page 10 [1-41]

Windsor. Line: 1235. Cut: 1406. Goblet. 12 oz. / 7" hi. NOT BANDED. **References:** 1967, page 10 [1-37]

Windsor. Line: 1235. Cut: 1406. Ice Tea. 12 oz. / 6-1/4" hi. NOT BANDED. **References:** 1967, page 10 [1-43]

Windsor. Line: 1235. Cut: 1406. Juice. 5 oz. / 4-1/2" hi. NOT BANDED. **References:** 1967, page 10 [1-42]

Windsor. Line: 1235. Cut: 1406. Plate. 7" / Actually 7-7/8" Dia. NOT BANDED. **References:** 1967, page 10 [1-44]

Windsor. Line: 1235. Cut: 1406. Plate. 8" / Actually 8-3/4" Dia. NOT BANDED. **References:** 1967, page 10 [1-45]

Windsor. Line: 1235. Cut: 1406. Sherbet. 7-1/2 oz. / 5-1/8" hi. NOT BANDED. **References:** 1967, page 10 [1-38]

Windsor. Line: 1235. Cut: 1406. Wine. 7 oz. / 5-7/8" hi. NOT BANDED. **References:** 1967, page 10 [1-39]

Windsor. Line: 3800. Beverage. 13-1/2 oz. 5-3/4 inches tall. Crystal Full Sham. **References:** 1978, page 7 [1-3]; 1979, page 16 [1-3]

Windsor. Line: 3800. Old Fashion. 10 oz. 4 inches tall. Crystal Full Sham. **References:** 1978, page 7 [1-4]; 1979, page 16 [1-4]

Woodstock. Line: 578. Cut: 1370. 1305 Dessert-Finger Bowl. 4-1/2 inches diam. **References:** 1968, page 26 [1-8]

Woodstock. Line: 578. Cut: 1370. Cocktail. 5-3/4 oz. 4-3/8 inches tall. **References:** 1968, page 26 [1-4]

Woodstock. Line: 578. Cut: 1370. Cordial. 1-1/2 oz. 3-3/8 inches tall. **References:** 1968, page 26 [1-5]

Woodstock. Line: 578. Cut: 1370. Goblet. 10-1/2 oz. 6-1/8 inches tall. **References:** 1968, page 26 [1-1]

Woodstock. Line: 578. Cut: 1370. Ice Tea. 12-1/2 oz. 6 inches tall. **References:** 1968, page 26 [1-7]

Woodstock. Line: 578. Cut: 1370. Juice. 5-1/2 oz. 4-3/4 inches tall. **References:** 1968, page 26 [1-6]

Woodstock. Line: 578. Cut: 1370. Plate. 7 inches diam. Actually 7-7/8" Dia. **References:** 1968, page 26 [1-9]

Woodstock. Line: 578. Cut: 1370. Plate. 8 inches diam. Actually 8-3/4" Dia. **References:** 1968,

LINE NUMBER INDEX

This index is organized by Line Numbers, as they were used in the various catalogs. Secondarily it is organized by Etching/Cut Numbers and Series Names, when they were used, in that order. This will help the reader use this index as a cross-reference with the other indexes in the book. Shapes, dimensions and volume, color, and other information are also provided whenever available.

Each entry has References to the catalogs and other illustrations in the book, by number or date. The first number identifies the catalog; the second number is the page of the catalog where the item can be found; and the bracketed number is the position of the item on the catalog page. The first position number is the row, and the second is the placement, counting from the left. If the item appears in multiple catalogs, each appearence will be referenced.

This indexing was dependent upon Seneca's own identification of items. At times there may be multiple entries, because of some slightly different way of identifying a product.

While we recognize some of the shortcomings of these indexes, it is hoped that, in the main, they will be useful to the collector in finding a particular item of interest.

References: 4, page 1 [2-2]

Line: 3. Cut: 35. Footed Tumbler. 6 oz. Optic. **References**: 4, page 1 [2-3]

Line: 3. Cut: 35. Footed Tumbler. 9 oz. Optic. **References**: 4, page 1 [2-4]

Line: 3. Cut: 35. Footed Tumbler. 12 oz. Optic. **References**: 4, page 1 [2-5]

Line: 3. Cut: 43. Hospitality. Bell. 4-3/8 inches tall. **References**: 1976, page 6 [1-3]; 1977, page 22 [3-1]

Line: 3. Cut: 57. Decanter. 2 Pint. Optic. **References**: 4, page 27 [2-3]

Line: 3. Cut: 58. Vase. 10 inch. Optic. **References**: 4, page 27 [1-4]

Line: 3. Cut: 121. Footed Tumbler. 2-3/4 oz. Optic. **References**: 4, page 23 [2-1]

Line: 3. Cut: 121. Footed Tumbler. 4 oz. Optic. **References**: 4, page 23 [2-2]

Line: 3. Cut: 121. Footed Tumbler. 6 oz. Optic. **References**: 4, page 23 [2-3]

Line: 3. Cut: 121. Footed Tumbler. 9 oz. Optic. **References**: 4, page 23 [2-4]

Line: 3. Cut: 121. Footed Tumbler. 12 oz. Optic. **References**: 4, page 23 [2-5]

Line: 3. Cut: 121. Laurel. Bell. 4-3/8 inches tall. Handmade and Hand Cut. **References**: 1975, page 12 [2-3]; 1976, page 6 [2-1]; 1977, page 22 [5-3]; 1977, page 22 [5-3]

Line: 3. Cut: 250. Candlestick. **References**: 4, page 2 [1-4]

Line: 3. Cut: 250. Decanter. 1 Pint. Optic. **References**: 4, page 27 [1-3]

Line: 3. Cut: 250. Footed Tumbler. 2-3/4 oz. Optic. **References**: 4, page 2 [2-1]

Line: 3. Cut: 250. Footed Tumbler. 4 oz. Optic. **References**: 4, page 2 [2-2]

Line: 3. Cut: 250. Footed Tumbler. 6 oz. Optic. **References**: 4, page 2 [2-3]

Line: 3. Cut: 250. Footed Tumbler. 9 oz. Optic. **References**: 4, page 2 [2-4]

Line: 3. Cut: 250. Footed Tumbler. 12 oz. Optic. **References**: 4, page 2 [2-5]

Line: 3. Cut: 262. Footed Tumbler. 2-3/4 oz. Optic. **References**: 4, page 20 [2-1]

Line: 3. Cut: 262. Footed Tumbler. 4 oz. Optic. **References**: 4, page 20 [2-2]

Line: 3. Cut: 262. Footed Tumbler. 6 oz. Optic. **References**: 4, page 20 [2-3]

Line: 3. Cut: 262. Footed Tumbler. 9 oz. Optic. **References**: 4, page 20 [2-4]

Line: 3. Cut: 262. Footed Tumbler. 12 oz. Optic. **References**: 4, page 20 [2-5]

Line: 3. Cut: 632. Candlestick. D.E. **References**: 4, page 34 [3-1]; 4, page 34 [3-3]

Line: 3. Cut: 632. Console Bowl. D.E. **References**: 4, page 34 [3-2]

Line: 3. Cut: 636. Stratford. Bell. 4-3/8 inches tall. Handmade and Hand Cut. Lead Crystal Silver and Gold Plated. Bells individually Gift Boxed. **References**: 1975, page 12 [2-4]; 1976, page 6 [2-2]; 1977, page 22 [2-2]; 1978, page 5 [2-1]

Line: 3. Cut: 1318. Celeste. Bell. 4-3/8 inches tall. Handmade and Hand Cut / Featured in display case. **References**: 1975, page 12 [2-2]; 1976, page 6 [2-3]; 1977, page 22 [5-2]

Line: 3. Cut: 1422. Orleans. Bell. 4-3/8 inches tall. Handmade and Hand Cut. **References**: 1975, page 12 [2-1]; 1976, page 6 [2-4]; 1977, page 22 [5-1]

Line: 3. Cut: 1448. Chalice. Bell. 4-3/8 inches tall. **References**: 1977, page 22 [4-1]

Line: 3. Cut: 1450. Classic. Bell. 4-3/8 inches tall. **References**: 1977, page 22 [2-1]

Line: 3. Cut: 1452. Rosalynn. Bell. 4-3/8 inches tall. **References**: 1977, page 22 [3-2]

Line: 4. Bell. 5-1/2 inches tall. Bell individually Gift Boxed. Colors: Accent Red, Delphine Blue, Brown, Moss Green. **References**: 1978, page 5 [1-1]; 1978, page 5 [1-3]

Line: 4. 1978 Christmas. Bell. 5-1/2 inches tall. Bell Individually Gift Boxed, Hand Made Lead Crystal Silver and Gold Plated. **References**: 1978, page 4 [2-1]

Line: 4. 1979 Christmas-Limited Edition. Bell. 5-1/2 inches tall. All Bells Individually Gift Boxed,Gold Plate. **References**: 1979, page 13 [4-3]

Line: 4. Brittany. Bell. 5-1/2 inches tall. All Bells Individually Gift Boxed. **References**: 1979, page 13 [4-2]

Line: 4. Chantilly. Bell. 5-1/2 inches tall. 1/4" Gold Band. All Bells Individually Gift Boxed, Gold. **References**: 1976, page 7 [1-1]; 1977, page 23 [2-1]; 1979, page 13 [2-3]

Line: 4. Cosmopolitan. Bell. 5-1/2 inches tall. All Bells Individually Gift Boxed. **References**: 1979, page 13 [3-1]

Line: 4. Fascination. Bell. 5-1/2 inches tall. Optic. All Bells Individually Gift Boxed. **References**: 1977, page 23 [1-1]; 1979, page 13 [3-2]

Line: 4. Heritage. Bell. 5-1/2 inches tall. All Bells Individually Gift Boxed. **References**: 1979, page 13 [3-4]

Line: 4. Majestic. Bell. 5-1/2 inches tall. All Bells Individually Gift Boxed. **References**: 1979, page 13 [2-4]

Line: 4. Olympia. Bell. 5-1/2 inches tall. 1/4" Platinum Band. All Bells Individually Gift Boxed, Platinum. **References**: 1976, page 7 [1-2]; 1977, page 23 [2-2]; 1979, page 13 [2-2]

Line: 4. Silver Rhapsody. Bell. 5-1/2 inches tall. All Bells Individually Gift Boxed. **References**: 1979, page 13 [4-1]

Line: 4. Etching: 600. Scroll Design. Oil. Cut Neck and Star. **References**: 3, page 6 [1-3]

Line: 4. Etching: 608. Grape Design. Oil. Cut Neck and Star Bottom. **References**: 3, page 9 [3-4]

Line: 4. Etching: 608. Rose Design. Oil. Cut Neck. **References**: 3, page 6 [2-1]

Line: 4. Cut: 43. Cosmopolitan. Bell. 5-1/2 inches tall. **References**: 1976, page 7 [1-3]; 1977, page 23 [4-2]

Line: 4. Cut: 414. Lace Point. Bell. 5-1/2 inches tall. **References**: 1976, page 7 [2-4]; 1977, page 23 [4-1]

Line: 4. Cut: 414. Lace Point. Bell. 5-1/2 inches tall. All Bells Individually Gift Boxed. **References**: 1979, page 13 [3-3]

Line: 4. Cut: 636. Stratford. Bell. 5-1/2 inches tall. **References**: 1979, page 12 [3-1]

Line: 4. Cut: 848. Bell. 5-1/2 inches tall. Hand Made and Hand Cut Lead Crystal Silver and Gold Plated. **References**: 1978, page 5 [2-2]

Line: 4. Cut: 980. La Belle. Bell. 5-1/2 inches tall. All Bells Individually Gift Boxed. **References**: 1976, page 7 [2-1]; 1977, page 23 [5-1]; 1979, page 13 [2-1]

Line: 4. Cut: 1445. Heritage. Bell. 5-1/2 inches tall. **References**: 1976, page 7 [2-2]; 1977, page 23 [5-2]

Line: 4. Cut: 1446. Wicker. Bell. 5-1/2 inches tall. All Bells Individually Gift Boxed. **References**: 1976, page 7 [2-3]; 1977, page 23 [3-3]; 1979, page 13 [1-2]

Line: 4. Cut: 1447. Sunburst. Bell. 5-1/2 inches tall. All Bells Individually Gift Boxed. **References**: 1977, page 23 [3-1]; 1979, page 13 [4-4]

Line: 4. Cut: 1449. Tapestry. Bell. 5-1/2 inches tall. All Bells Individually Gift Boxed. **References**: 1977, page 23 [5-3]; 1979, page 13 [1-1]

Line: 4. Cut: 1451. Brittany. Bell. 5-1/2 inches tall. **References**: 1977, page 23 [3-2]

Line: 4. Cut: 1453. Bell. 5-1/2 inches tall. **References**: 1977, page 23 [1-2]

Line: 5. Ale. 3 oz. **References**: 5-E, page 11 [2-1]

Line: 5. Wine. 4 oz. 5-3/4 inches tall. **References**: 1975/I-75, page 5 [3-3]

Line: 5. 1978 Christmas. Hanging Bell. 2-1/4 inches tall. Bell Individually Gift Boxed, First in a Series, Limited Edition, Lead Crystal. **References**: 1978, page 4 [1-1]

Line: 5. 1979 Christmas. Hanging Bell. 2-1/4 inches tall. All Bells Individually Gift Boxed, Second Edition-Limited To 7,5000. **References**: 1979, page 13 [1-3]

Line: 5. Etching: 600. Scroll Design. Sherry. Optic. **References**: 3, page 3 [1-5]

Line: 5. Etching: 609. Rose Design. Vase. 12 inch. **References**: 3, page 14 [1-1]

Line: 5. Etching: 609. Rose Design. Vase. 10 inch. **References**: 3, page 14 [1-2]

Line: 5. Etching: 609. Rose Design. Vase. 7 inch. **References**: 3, page 14 [1-3]

Line: 5. Etching: 609. Rose Design. Vase. 5 inch. **References**: 3, page 14 [1-4]

Line: 6. Bottle. 24 oz. **References**: 1980, page 4 [2-1]

Line: 6. Bottle. 30 oz. **References**: 1981, page 4 [1-2]; 1982, page 7 [1-2]; 1982, page 7 [1-2]; 1983, page 11 [1-2]

Line: 6. Cocktail. 3 oz. **References**: 5-E, page 10 [1-3]

Line: 6. Gourmet Collection. Bottle. 30 oz. **References**: 1980, page 6 [1-4]

Line: B6. Cut: B 44. Footed Tumbler. 2-3/4 oz. Optic. **References**: 4, page 4 [2-1]

Line: B6. Cut: B 44. Footed Tumbler. 4 oz. Optic. **References**: 4, page 4 [2-2]

Line: B6. Cut: B 44. Footed Tumbler. 6 oz. Optic. **References**: 4, page 4 [2-3]

Line: B6. Cut: B 44. Footed Tumbler. 9 oz. Optic. **References**: 4, page 4 [2-4]

Line: B6. Cut: B 44. Footed Tumbler. 12 oz. Optic. **References**: 4, page 4 [2-5]

Line: 6. Cut: 273. Footed Tumbler. 2-3/4 oz. Optic. **References**: 4, page 5 [2-1]

Line: 6. Cut: 273. Footed Tumbler. 4 oz. Optic. **References**: 4, page 5 [2-2]

Line: 6. Cut: 273. Footed Tumbler. 6 oz. Optic. **References**: 4, page 5 [2-3]

Line: 6. Cut: 273. Footed Tumbler. 9 oz. Optic. **References**: 4, page 5 [2-4]

Line: 6. Cut: 273. Footed Tumbler. 12 oz. Optic. **References**: 4, page 5 [2-5]

Line: 7. Decanter. 30 oz. **References**: 1983, page 11 [1-3]

Line: 7. Hot Whiskey. 3-1/2 oz. **References**: 5-E, page 11 [2-2]

Line: 7. Rhine Wine Goblet. 3-1/2 oz. **References**: 5-E, page 10 [2-1]

Line: 7. Sherry. 2 oz. **References**: 5-E, page 11 [1-3]

Line: 7. Palm Optic. Sherry. 3 oz. 5-1/8 inches tall. **References**: 1982, page 9 [1-5]; 1975/I-75, page 2 [3-1]

Line: 7. Cut: 43. Bottle. 32 oz. **References**: 1980, page 4 [2-2]

Line: 7. Cut: 43. Decanter. **References**: 1981, page 4 [1-3]; 1982, page 7 [1-3]

Line: 10. 54 oz. Optic. **References**: 4, page 32 [2-3]

Line: 10. Bowl. 3 inches tall. Colors: Delphine Blue. **References**: 1978, page 14 [2-H]

Line: 10. Evergreen Tree. 8-1/4 inches tall. Comes in two parts. Colors: Accent Red, Crystal, Moss Green. **References**: 1979, page 7 [1-1]

Line: 10. Tankard. 8, 10, 15, 21, 31, 42, 54, 65, 80 oz. Made Of The Purest Color Lead Glass. **References**: 5-E, page 12 [2-1]

Line: 10. Etching: 600. Scroll Design. Jug. 15 oz. **References**: 3, page 6 [1-2]

Line: 10. Etching: 600. Scroll Design. Jug. 54 oz. **References**: 3, page 6 [2-1]

Line: 10. Etching: 608. Grape Design. Jug. 54 oz. Optic. **References**: 3, page 9 [3-2]

Line: 10. Etching: 609. Rose Design. Jug. 54 oz. **References**: 3, page 12 [2-1]

Line: 10. Cut: 57. Jug. 54 oz. Optic. **References**: 4, page 26 [3-1]

Line: 11. Cocktail. 2-1/2 oz. **References**: 5-E, page 10 [2-3]

Line: 12. Console Bowl. 1 inch. **References**: 4, page 35 [3-2]

Line: 12. Goblet. 8-1/2 oz. **References**: 5-E, page 5 [2-2]

Line: 15. Jug. 8, 16, 48 oz. Made Of The Purest Color Lead Glass. **References**: 5-E, page 12 [2-3]

Line: 15. Cut: 101, Star. Jug. 45 oz. **References**: 2, fig. 6 (p. 43) [2-3]

Line: 15. Cut: 360. Jug. 45 oz. **References**: 2, fig. 6 (p. 43) [2-4]

Line: 16. Cream. Blue. **References**: 4, page 31 [2-2]

Line: 16. Sugar Bowl. Blue. **References**: 4, page 31 [2-1]

Line: 16. Cut: 287. Cream. Optic. **References**: 4, page 25 [1-5]

Line: 16. Cut: 287. Sugar Bowl. Optic. **References**: 4, page 25 [1-4]

Line: 19. Claret. 5-1/2 oz. **References**: 5-E, page 6 [2-2][Listed]

Line: 19. Cordial. 1-1/2 oz. **References**: 5-E, page 6 [2-3][Listed]

Line: 19. Goblet. 8 oz. **References**: 5-E, page 6 [2-1][Listed]

Line: 19. Goblet. 7 oz. **References**: 5-E, page 6 [Listed]

Line: 19. Goblet. 10 oz. **References**: 5-E, page 6 [Listed]

Line: 19. Port. 3-1/2 oz. **References**: 5-E, page 6 [Listed]

Line: 19. Wine. 2-1/2 oz. **References**: 5-E, page 6 [Listed]

Line: 19. Etching: 283. Claret or Champagne. 5-1/2 oz. **References**: 5-E, page 16 [1-3]

Line: 19. Etching: 283. Cordial. 1-1/2 oz. **References**: 5-E, page 16 [1-1]

Line: 19. Etching: 283. Goblet. 9 oz. **References**: 5-E, page 16 [1-4]

Line: 19. Etching: 283. Goblet. 11 oz. **References**: 5-E, page 16 [Listed]

Line: 19. Etching: 283. Goblet. 10 oz. **References**: 5-E, page 16 [Listed]

Line: 19. Etching: 283. Goblet. 8 oz. **References**: 5-E, page 16 [Listed]

Line: 19. Etching: 283. Goblet. 7 oz. **References**: 5-E, page 16 [Listed]

Line: 19. Etching: 283. Port. 3-1/2 oz. **References**: 5-E, page 16 [Listed]

Line: 19. Etching: 283. Wine. 2-1/2 oz. **References**: 5-E, page 16 [1-2]

Line: 20. Jug. 8, 16, 32, 52 oz. **References**: 5-E, page 13 [1-2]

Line: 20. Etching: 608. Grape Design. Jug. 52 oz. **References**: 3, page 9 [3-1]

Line: 20. Cut: 361. Jug. 52 oz. **References**: 2, fig. 6 (p. 43) [2-2]

Line: 21. Cocktail. 3-1/2 oz. **References**: 5-E, page 10 [2-4]

Line: 25. Goblet. 9 oz. **References**: 5-E, page 8 [2-3]

Line: 25. Water Bottle. One Quart. Cut Neck and Star Bottom. **References**: 2, fig. 3 [2-1]

Line: 25. Etchings: N and 75. Water Bottle. One Quart. Cut Neck and Star Bottom. **References**: 2, fig. 3 [2-5]

Line: 26. Beer Series. Beer Goblet. 14 oz. 7-1/2 inches tall. Plain Crystal. **References**: 1978, page 9 [1-1]

Line: 26. Beer Series. Beer Tumbler. 14 oz. 7-1/2 inches tall. **References**: 1979, page 11 [2-1]

Line: 30. 8 inch. P/D Estes. **References**: 4, page 28 [2-5]

Line: 30. 8 inch. **References**: 4, page 30 [2-1]

Line: 30. 8 inch. Blue. **References**: 4, page 31 [3-2]

Line: 30. 8 inch. **References**: 4, page 32 [2-4]

Line: 30. 8 inch. **References**: 4, page 33 [2-2]

Line: 30.]6 inch. **References**: 4, page 33 [3-1]

Line: 30. 7 inch. **References**: 4, page 33 [3-2]

Line: 30. Candlestick. P/D Estes. **References**: 4, page 28 [3-1]; 4, page 28 [3-3]

Line: 30. Candlestick. **References**: 4, page 30 [3-1]; 4, page 30 [3-3]

Line: 30. Candlestick. Blue. **References**: 4, page 31 [3-3]; 4, page 31 [3-5]

Line: 30. Candlestick. **References**: 4, page 35 [3-1]; 4, page 35 [3-3]

Line: 30. Plate, P/D Silvia. 8 inch. **References**: 4, page 26 [2-3]

Line: 30. Cut: 57. Console Bowl. **References**: 4, page 27 [3-3]

Line: 30. Cut: 57. R.E. Candlestick. Optic. **References**: 4, page 25 [2-6]

Line: 30. Cut: 634. Candlestick. Optic, D.E. **References**: 4, page 36 [4-1]

Line: 30. Cut: 634. Candlestick. D.E. **References**: 4, page 36 [4-3]

Line: 33. Goblet. 9 oz. **References**: 5-E, page 5 [2-1]

Line: 34. Brandy. 1 oz. **References**: 5-E, page 7 [Listed]

Line: 34. Champagne. 5-1/2 oz. **References**: 5-E, page 7 [Listed]

Line: 34. Claret. 4 oz. **References**: 5-E, page 7 [Listed]

Line: 34. Cocktail. 4 oz. **References**: 5-E, page 7 [1-3]

Line: 34. Cordial. 1-1/2 oz. **References**: 5-E, page 7 [1-1]

Line: 34. Creme de Menthe. 3 oz. **References**: 5-E, page 11 [1-2]; page 7 [Listed]

Line: 34. Fruit. 7 oz. **References**: 5-E, page 12 [1-3]; page 7 [Listed]

Line: 34. Fruit. 7 oz. Made Of The Purest Color Lead Glass. **References**: 5-E, page 12 [1-3]

Line: 34. Goblet. 8 oz. **References**: 5-E, page 7 [1-4]

Line: 34. Goblet. 11 oz. **References**: 5-E, page 7 [Listed]

Line: 34. Goblet. 10 oz. **References**: 5-E, page 7

[Listed]

Line: 34. Goblet. 9 oz. **References**: 5-E, page 7 [Listed]

Line: 34. Goblet. 6-1/2 oz. **References**: 5-E, page 7 [Listed]

Line: 34. Goblet, S.S. 10 oz. **References**: 5-E, page 7 [Listed]

Line: 34. H.S. Champ. 5 oz. **References**: 5-E, page 11 [2-1]; page 7 [Listed]

Line: 34. H.S.S. Ch'p. 5 oz. **References**: 5-E, page 7 [Listed]

Line: 34. Hot Whiskey. 4-1/2 oz. **References**: 5-E, page 7 [Listed]

Line: 34. Port. 3 oz. **References**: 5-E, page 7 [Listed]

Line: 34. Red Wine Goblet. 4-1/2 oz. **References**: 5-E, page 7 [Listed]

Line: 34. Saucer Champagne. 6 oz. **References**: 5-E, page 7 [Listed]

Line: 34. Saucer Champagne. 5 oz. Hollow Stem. **References**: 5-E, page 11 [2-4]

Line: 34. Sherbert. 5 oz. **References**: 5-E, page 7 [2-2]

Line: 34. Sherry. 2 oz. **References**: 5-E, page 7 [Listed]

Line: 34. Wine. 2-1/2 oz. **References**: 5-E, page 7 [1-2]

Line: 34. Etching: 608. Grape Design. Fruit. **References**: 3, page 8 [2-4]

Line: 34. Etching: 609. Rose Design. Fruit. **References**: 3, page 11 [2-1]

Line: 40. Jug. 16, 32, 54, 73 oz. Made Of The Purest Color Lead Glass. **References**: 5-E, page 12 [2-2]

Line: 40. Sugar and Cream Set. **References**: 5-E, page 13 [2-1]

Line: 40. Etching: 600. Scroll Design. Cream. **References**: 3, page 5 [1-1]

Line: 40. Etching: 600. Scroll Design. Jug. 54 oz. **References**: 3, page 6 [2-2]

Line: 40. Etching: 600. Scroll Design. Sugar Bowl. **References**: 3, page 5 [1-2]

Line: 40. Etching: 608. Grape Design. Cream. **References**: 3, page 9 [2-1]

Line: 40. Etching: 608. Grape Design. Jug. 54 oz. **References**: 3, page 9 [3-3]

Line: 40. Etching: 608. Grape Design. Sugar Bowl. **References**: 3, page 8 [1-6]

Line: 40. Etching: 609. Rose Design. Cream. **References**: 3, page 12 [1-3]

Line: 40. Etching: 609. Rose Design. Jug. 54 oz. Optic. **References**: 3, page 12 [2-2]

Line: 40. Etching: 609. Rose Design. Sugar Bowl. **References**: 3, page 12 [1-2]

Line: 50A. Bowl. 4 inches tall. Colors: Accent Red. **References**: 1978, page 14 [2-F]

Line: 50. Covered Jug. 65 oz. **References**: 5-E, page 13 [1-1]

Line: 50. The Tree. 10-3/4 inches tall. Accent Red w/ Drape Optic. The 4 piece TREE is individually Boxed. **References**: 1978, page 12 [1-1]

Line: 50. The Tree. 10-3/4 inches tall. Lead Crystal. The 4 piece TREE is individually Boxed. **References**: 1978, page 12 [1-2]

Line: 50. The Tree. 10-3/4 inches tall. Moss Green. The 4 piece TREE is individually Boxed. **References**: 1978, page 12 [1-3]

Line: 50. The Tree. 10-3/4 inches tall. Comes in four parts. Colors: Accent Red, Crystal, Moss Green. **References**: 1979, page 7 [1-2]

Line: 50. Water Bottle. Three Pints. Cut Neck and Star Bottom. **References**: 2, fig. 3 [2-3]

Line: 50. Etching: 8, Cut Neck and Star Bottom. Water Bottle. **References**: 5-E, page 19 [3-1]

Line: 50. Etching: 608. Grape Design. Water Bottle. Cut Neck. **References**: 3, page 8 [2-3]

Line: 50. Etching: 609. Rose Design. Water Bottle. Cut Neck. **References**: 3, page 13 [3-2]

Line: 50. Cut: 250. Covered Jug. 65 oz. Optic. **References**: 4, page 26 [3-4]

Line: 52. Champagne Flute. 6-1/2 oz. 9-1/4 inches tall. Lead Crystal. **References**: 1978, page 8 [1-3]

Line: 52. Champagne Flute. 6-1/2 oz. 9-1/4 inches tall. Plain Stem. **References**: 1979, page 11 [1-1]

Line: 54. Champagne Flute. 8-1/2 oz. 9-1/2 inches tall. Lead Crystal. **References**: 1978, page 8 [1-2]

Line: 54. Champagne Flute. 8-1/2 oz. 9-1/2 inches tall. Plain Stem. **References**: 1979, page 11 [1-2]

Line: 60. Goblet. 6 oz. **References**: 5-E, page 5 [1-2]

Line: 70. Tumbler. 1-1/2 oz. **References**: 5-E, page 1 [4-4]

Line: 70. Floral Garden. Vase. 7 inches tall. **References**: 1983, page 7 [1-4R]

Line: 70. Starburst. Vase. 7 inches tall. **References**: 1983, page 7 [1-3R]

Line: 70. Wicker. Vase. 7 inches tall. All Items Gift Boxed. **References**: 1983, page 6 [1-4L]

Line: 70. Cut: 1446. Vase. 7 inches tall. **References**: 1980, page 3 [1-4]

Line: 70. Cut: 1446. Wicker. Vase. 7 inches tall. **References**: 1981, page 10 [2-4]

Line: 75. Water Bottle. One Quart. Cut Neck and Star Bottom. **References**: 2, fig. 3 [2-2]

Line: 75. Water Bottle. 2-1/2 Pints. Made Of The Purest Color Lead Glass. **References**: 5-E, page 12 [1-1]

Line: 75. Etching: 600. Scroll Design. Water Bottle. **References**: 3, page 5 [2-3]

Line: 75. Cut: 222. Water Bottle. One Quart. **References**: 2, fig. 3 [2-4]

Line: 80. Butterfly. Ginger Jar. 6-1/4 inches tall. All Items Gift Boxed. **References**: 1983, page 6 [1-3L]

Line: 80. Harvest. Ginger Jar. 6-1/4 inches tall. All Items Gift Boxed. **References**: 1983, page 6 [1-1L]

Line: 80. Love Birds. Ginger Jar. 6-1/4 inches tall. All Items Gift Boxed. **References**: 1983, page 6 [1-2L]

Line: 80. Starburst. Ginger Jar. 6-1/4 inches tall. **References**: 1983, page 6 [4-3L]

Line: 80. Cut: 958. Ginger Jar. **References**: 1980, page 4 [1-1]

Line: 80. Cut: 958. Harvest. Ginger Jar. 6-1/4 inches tall. **References**: 1981, page 10 [2-1]

Line: 80. Cut: 960. Ginger Jar. **References**: 1980, page 4 [1-2]

Line: 80. Cut: 960. Butterfly. Ginger Jar. 6-1/4 inches tall. **References**: 1981, page 10 [2-3]

Line: 80. Cut: 1457. Love Birds. Ginger Jar. 6-1/4 inches tall. **References**: 1980, page 3 [1-1]; 1981, page 10 [2-2]

Line: 81. All Purpose Wine Goblet. 10-1/2 oz. 5-3/4 inches tall. **References**: 1975/I-75, page 5 [1-1]

Line: 82. Peacock Optic. Wine Goblet. 11 oz. 5-3/4 inches tall. **References**: 1975/I-75, page 3 [1-2]

Line: 82. Cut: 43. Tumbler. 6 oz. **References**: 4, page 25 [2-1]

Line: 84. Etching: 5. Fruit. **References**: 5-E, page 17 [2-3]

Line: 85. Old Fashion. 8 oz. 3-3/8 inches tall. Straight Optic, Sham Weight. **References**: 1982, page 12 [2-5]

Line: 85. Palm Optic. Old Fashion. 7-3/4 oz. 3-3/8 inches tall. Sham Weight. **References**: 1982, page 10 [2-1]; 1982, page 10 [2-1]

Line: 85. Peacock Optic. Old Fashion. 8 oz. 3-3/8 inches tall. Sham Weight. **References**: 1975/I-75, page 6 [2-1]

Line: 85. Cut: 39. Old Fashion. 7-3/4 oz. 3-3/8 inches tall. Sham Weight. Polished Bottom. The cut 43 indicates the Flutes at the base of the Tumblers are 1-3/4" high and 3/4" wide. Tumblers Cut 43 have a hand cut and hand polished (Punty) base. Items available: 14 oz., 12 oz., and 10 oz. Tumbler, 10 oz. Table Tumbler, 7-3/4 oz., 9 oz., and 12 oz. Old Fashion. **References**: 1972, page 31 [1-5]; 1975, page 32 [1-5]; 1977, page 43 [1-5]; 1975/I-75, page 12 [1-5]; 1972, page 31 [3-5]; 1973, page 36 [3-5]; 1975, page 32 [3-5]; 1977, page 43 [3-5]; 1979, page 14 [2-1]; 1982, page 6 [1-9]; 1975/I-75, page 12 [3-5]

Line: 85. Cut: 43. Tumbler. 7-3/4 oz. **References**: 4, page 25 [2-2]

Line: 85. Cut: 45. Old Fashion. 7-3/4 oz. 3-3/8 inches tall. Sham Weight. The cut 43 indicates the Flutes at the base of the Tumblers are 1-1/2" high and 3/4" wide. Tumblers Cut 45 have a flat unpolished base. Items available: 14 oz., 12 oz., and 10 oz. Tumbler, 10 oz. Table Tumbler, 7-3/4 oz., 9 oz., and 12 oz. Old Fashion. **References**: 1972, page 31 [2-5]; 1973, page 36 [2-5]; 1975, page 32 [2-5]; 1977, page 43 [2-5]; 1979, page 14 [2-4]; 1982, page 7 [1-5]; 1975/I-75, page 12 [2-5]

Line: 88. Cut: 39. Old Fashion. 9 oz. 3-5/8 inches tall. Sham Weight. The cut 39 indicates the Flutes at the base of the Tumblers are 1-1/4" high and 1/2" wide. Tumblers Cut 39 have a flat unpolished base. Items available: 14 oz., 12 oz., and 10 oz. Tumbler, 10 oz. Table Tumbler, 7-3/4 oz., 9 oz. Old Fashion. **References**: 1972, page 31 [1-6]; 1975, page 32 [1-6]; 1977, page 43 [1-6]; 1975/I-75, page 12 [1-6]; 1979, page 14 [2-7]

Line: 88. Cut: 43. Old Fashion. 9 oz. 3-5/8 inches tall. Sham Weight. **References**: 1972, page 31 [3-6]; 1973, page 36 [3-6]; 1975, page 32 [3-6]; 1977, page 43 [3-6]; 1982, page 6 [1-10]; 1975/I-75, page 12 [3-6]

Line: 88. Cut: 43. Tumbler. 9 oz. **References**: 4, page 25 [2-3]

Line: 90. Butterfly. Ginger Jar. 8-1/2 inches tall. **References**: 1983, page 6 [2-3L]

Line: 90. Floral Garden. Ginger Jar. 8-1/2 inches tall. **References**: 1983, page 7 [1-2R]

Line: 90. Harvest. Ginger Jar. 8-1/2 inches tall. **References**: 1983, page 6 [2-1L]

Line: 90. Love Birds. Ginger Jar. 8-1/2 inches tall. **References**: 1983, page 6 [2-2L]

Line: 90. Starburst. Ginger Jar. 8-1/2 inches tall. **References**: 1983, page 7 [1-1R]

Line: 90. Cut: 958. Harvest. Ginger Jar. 8-1/2 inches tall. **References**: 1980, page 3 [2-2]; 1981, page 10 [1-1]

Line: 90. Cut: 960. Butterfly. Ginger Jar. 8-1/2 inches tall. **References**: 1980, page 3 [2-1]; 1981, page 10 [1-3]

Line: 90. Cut: 1457. Love Birds. Ginger Jar. 8-1/2 inches tall. **References**: 1980, page 3 [2-3];1981, page 10 [1-2]

Line: 98. Floral Garden. Bud Vase. 6 inches tall. **References**: 1983, page 7 [1-5R]

Line: 98. Starburst. Bud Vase. 6 inches tall. **References**: 1983, page 7 [1-6R]

Line: 100. Creme de Menthe. 2 oz. **References**: 5-E, page 11 [1-1]

Line: 100. Goblet. 9 oz. **References**: 5-E, page 5 [1-1]

Line: 113. Peacock Optic. Whiskey. 2 oz. 2-1/2 inches tall. Sham Weight, 1/2 oz. 1st Line, 1-1/4 Oz. 2nd Line. **References**: 1975/I-75, page 6 [3-2]

Line: 120. Carafe. 20 oz. **References**: 1973, page 10 [1-1]; 1975, page 10 [1-1]; 1977, page 10 [1-1]; 1981, page 4 [1-6]; 1982, page 7 [1-6]; 1983, page 11 [1-6]

Line: 120. Gourmet Collection. Carafe. 20 oz. **References**: 1980, page 6 [1-3]

Line: 124. Spritzer/Sparkling Water. 12 oz. 6-1/4 inches tall. Plain Crystal. **References**: 1979, page 11 [1-4]

Line: 125. Wodka Glass. 1/34 oz. 6 inches tall. Plain Crystal. **References**: 1979, page 11 [1-5]

Line: 128. Cut: 1274. Martha Washington. 1311 Dessert-Finger Bowl. 4-3/4 inches diam. **References**: 1967, page 20 [1-8];x1969, page 22 [1-9]; 1970, page 23 [1-9]; 1971, page 23 [1-9]

Line: 128. Cut: 1274. Martha Washington. Claret. 4 oz. 4-3/8 inches tall. **References**: 1967, page 20 [1-3]; 1969, page 22 [1-3]; 1970, page 23 [1-3]; 1971, page 23 [1-3]

Line: 128. Cut: 1274. Martha Washington. Cocktail. 3-1/2 oz. 4-1/8 inches tall. **References**: 1967, page 20 [1-4];x1969, page 22 [1-5]; 1970, page 23 [1-5]; 1971, page 23 [1-5]

Line: 128. Cut: 1274. Martha Washington. Cordial. 1-1/4 oz. 3-1/4 inches tall. **References**: 1967, page 20 [1-5]; 1969, page 22 [1-6]; 1970, page 23 [1-6]; 1971, page 23 [1-6]

Line: 128. Cut: 1274. Martha Washington. Goblet. 10-1/2 oz. 6-1/8 inches tall. **References**: 1967, page 20 [1-1]; 1969, page 22 [1-1]; 1970, page 23 [1-1]; 1971, page 23 [1-1]

Line: 128. Cut: 1274. Martha Washington. Ice Tea. 12 oz. 6-3/4 inches tall. **References**: 1967, page 20 [1-7];x1969, page 22 [1-8]; 1970, page 23 [1-8]; 1971, page 23 [1-8]

Line: 128. Cut: 1274. Martha Washington. Juice. 5 oz. 5-1/4 inches tall. **References**: 1967, page 20 [1-6]; 1969, page 22 [1-7];x 1970, page 23 [1-7]; 1971, page 23 [1-7]

Line: 128. Cut: 1274. Martha Washington. Plate. 7 inches diam. Actually 7-7/8" Dia. **References**: 1967, page 20 [1-9]; 1969, page 22 [1-10]; 1970, page 23 [1-10]; 1971, page 23 [1-10]

Line: 128. Cut: 1274. Martha Washington. Plate. 8 inches diam. Actually 8-3/4" Dia. **References**: 1967, page 20 [1-10]; 1969, page 22 [1-11]; 1970, page 23 [1-11]; 1971, page 23 [1-11]

Line: 128. Cut: 1274. Martha Washington. Sherbet. 7-1/2 oz. 4-3/4 inches tall. **References**: 1967, page 20 [1-2]; 1969, page 22 [1-2]; 1970, page 23 [1-2]; 1971, page 23 [1-2]

Line: 128. Cut: 1274. Martha Washington. Table Wine Goblet. 5-3/4 oz. 5-1/8 inches tall. **References**: 1969, page 22 [1-4]; 1970, page 23 [1-4]; 1971, page 23 [1-4]

Line: 132. Carafe. 32 oz. **References**: 1973, page 10 [1-2]; 1975, page 10 [1-2]; 1977, page 10 [1-2]; 1981, page 4 [1-4]; 1982, page 7 [1-4]; 1983, page 11 [1-4]

Line: 132. Gourmet Collection. Carafe. 32 oz. **References**: 1980, page 6 [1-2]

Line: 140. Carafe. 40 oz. **References**: 1980, page 4 [2-3];x1981, page 4 [1-5]; 1982, page 7 [1-5]; 1983, page 11 [1-5]

Line: 140. Gourmet Collection. Carafe. 40 oz. **References**: 1980, page 6 [1-1]

Line: 150. Cut: 35. Cocktail. Optic. **References**: 4, page 1 [1-5]

Line: 150. Cut: 35. Cordial. Optic. **References**: 4, page 1 [1-6]

Line: 150. Cut: 35. Goblet. Optic. **References**: 4, page 1 [1-1]

Line: 150. Cut: 35. Saucer Champagne. Optic. **References**: 4, page 1 [1-2]

Line: 150. Cut: 35. Sherbet. Optic. **References**: 4, page 1 [1-3]

Line: 150. Cut: 35. Wine. Optic. **References**: 4, page 1 [1-4]

Line: 150. Cut: 250. Cocktail. Optic. **References**: 4, page 2 [1-6]

Line: 150. Cut: 250. Cordial. Optic. **References**: 4, page 2 [1-7]

Line: 150. Cut: 250. Goblet. Optic. **References**: 4, page 2 [1-1]

Line: 150. Cut: 250. Saucer Champagne. Optic. **References**: 4, page 2 [1-2]

Line: 150. Cut: 250. Sherbet. Optic. **References**: 4, page 2 [1-3]

Line: 150. Cut: 250. Wine. Optic. **References**: 4, page 2 [1-5]

Line: 152. Martini. 5-3/4 oz. 5-5/8 inches tall. **References**: 1980, page 3 [1-2]

Line: 255. Decanter Set. Colors: Blue. **References**: 4, page 30 [2-2]

Line: 255. Cut: 121. Cocktail Shaker. Optic. **References**: 4, page 27 [3-1]

Line: 258. Cut: 358. Cocktail. **References**: 4, page 3 [2-3]

Line: 258. Cut: 358. Cordial. **References**: 4, page 3 [2-1]

Line: 258. Cut: 358. Goblet. **References**: 4, page 3 [2-6]

Line: 258. Cut: 358. Saucer Champagne. **References**: 4, page 3 [2-5]

Line: 258. Cut: 358. Sherbet. **References**: 4, page 3 [2-4]

Line: 258. Cut: 358. Wine. **References**: 4, page 3 [2-2]

Line: 259. Cut: 367. Cocktail. **References**: 4, page 3 [1-5]

Line: 259. Cut: 367. Cordial. **References**: 4, page 3 [1-6]

Line: 259. Cut: 367. Goblet. **References**: 4, page 3 [1-1]

Line: 259. Cut: 367. Saucer Champagne. **References**: 4, page 3 [1-2]

Line: 259. Cut: 367. Sherbet. **References**: 4, page 3 [1-3]

Line: 259. Cut: 367. Wine. **References**: 4, page 3 [1-4]

Line: 260. Claret. Optic. **References**: 4, page 32 [2-1]

Line: 260. Cocktail. Optic. **References**: 4, page 32 [1-7]

Line: 260. Cordial. Optic. **References**: 4, page 32 [1-6]

Line: 260. Finger Bowl. Optic. **References**: 4, page 32 [1-4]

Line: 260. Goblet. Optic. **References**: 4, page 32 [1-1]

Line: 260. Parfait. Optic. **References**: 4, page 32 [1-8]

Line: 260. Saucer Champagne. Optic. **References**: 4, page 32 [1-3]

Line: 260. Sherbet. Optic. **References**: 4, page 32 [1-5]

Line: 260. Wine. Optic. **References**: 4, page 32 [1-2]

Line: B260. Cut: B 44. Cocktail. Optic. **References**: 4, page 4 [1-5]

Line: B260. Cut: B 44. Cordial. Optic. **References**: 4, page 4 [1-6]

Line: B260. Cut: B 44. Goblet. Optic. **References**: 4, page 4 [1-1]

Line: B260. Cut: B 44. Saucer Champagne. Optic. **References**: 4, page 4 [1-2]

Line: B260. Cut: B 44. Sherbet. Optic. **References**: 4, page 4 [1-3]

Line: B260. Cut: B 44. Wine. Optic. **References**: 4, page 4 [1-4]

Line: 260. Cut: 273. Cocktail. Optic. **References**: 4, page 5 [1-5]

Line: 260. Cut: 273. Cordial. Optic. **References**: 4, page 5 [1-6]

Line: 260. Cut: 273. Goblet. Optic. **References**: 4, page 5 [1-1]

Line: 260. Cut: 273. Saucer Champagne. Optic. **References**: 4, page 5 [1-2]

Line: 260. Cut: 273. Sherbet. Optic. **References**: 4, page 5 [1-3]

Line: 260. Cut: 273. Wine. Optic. **References**: 4, page 5 [1-4]

Line: 265. Finger Bowl. Optic, P/D Silvia. **References**: 4, page 29 [1-1]

Line: 265. Finger Bowl. **References**: 4, page 30 [2-3]

Line: 265. Cut: 632. Finger Bowl. Optic, D.E. **References**: 4, page 34 [1-4]

Line: 300. Brandy. 1-1/4 oz. **References**: 5-E, page 8 [1-1]

Line: 300. Brandy. 1 oz. **References**: 5-E, page 8 [Listed]

Line: 300. Brandy. 3/4 oz. **References**: 5-E, page 8 [Listed]

Line: 300. Claret. 4-1/2 oz. **References**: 5-E, page 8 [Listed]

Line: 300. Cocktail. 3-1/2 oz. **References**: 5-E, page 8 [Listed]

Line: 300. Goblet. 8 oz. **References**: 5-E, page 8 [1-4]

Line: 300. Goblet. 13 oz. **References**: 5-E, page 8 [Listed]

Line: 300. Goblet. 12 oz. **References**: 5-E, page 8 [Listed]

Line: 300. Goblet. 11 oz. **References**: 5-E, page 8 [Listed]

Line: 300. Goblet. 9 oz. **References**: 5-E, page 8 [Listed]

Line: 300. Goblet. 7 oz. **References**: 5-E, page 8 [Listed]

Line: 300. Goblet. 6 oz. **References**: 5-E, page 8 [Listed]

Line: 300. Hot Whiskey. 3-1/4 oz. **References**: 5-E, page 8 [Listed]

Line: 300. L. S. Goblet. 10 oz. **References**: 5-E, page 8 [Listed]

Line: 300. L. S. Goblet. 9 oz. **References**: 5-E, page 8 [Listed]

Line: 300. Port. 3-1/2 oz. **References**: 5-E, page 8 [Listed]

Line: 300. S. S. Goblet. 10 oz. **References**: 5-E, page 8 [Listed]

Line: 300. Sherbert. 4-1/2 oz. **References**: 5-E, page 7 [2-3]

Line: 300. Sherbert. 2-1/2 oz. **References**: 5-E, page 8 [1-2]

Line: 300. Tall Champ. 5-1/2 oz. **References**: 5-E, page 8 [Listed]

Line: 300. Wine. 3 oz. **References**: 5-E, page 8 [1-3]

Line: 300. Peacock Optic. Saucer Champagne. 5 oz. 4-1/2 inches tall. **References**: 1975/I-75, page 4 [2-1]

Line: 300. Etching: 5. Almond. **References**: 5-E, page 17 [2-4]

Line: 300. Etching: 5. Brandy. **References**: 5-E, page 17 [1-2]

Line: 300. Etching: 5. Cordial. **References**: 5-E, page 17 [1-1]

Line: 300. Etching: 5. Goblet. 8 oz. **References**: 5-E, page 17 [1-4]

Line: 300. Etching: 5. Sherbert. **References**: 5-E, page 17 [2-2]

Line: 300. Etching: 5. Wine. **References**: 5-E, page 17 [1-3]

Line: 300. Etching: 608. Grape Design. Ale. **References**: 3, page 7 [2-3]

Line: 300. Etching: 608. Grape Design. Brandy. **References**: 3, page 7 [2-8]

Line: 300. Etching: 608. Grape Design. Claret. **References**: 3, page 7 [2-5]

Line: 300. Etching: 608. Grape Design. Cocktail. **References**: 3, page 7 [1-3]

Line: 300. Etching: 608. Grape Design. Cordial. **References**: 3, page 7 [2-9]

Line: 300. Etching: 608. Grape Design. Deminth. **References**: 3, page 7 [1-4]

Line: 300. Etching: 608. Grape Design. Goblet. 8 oz. **References**: 3, page 7 [1-7]

Line: 300. Etching: 608. Grape Design. Goblet. 10 oz. **References**: 3, page 7 [2-1]

Line: 300. Etching: 608. Grape Design. Goblet. 9 oz. **References**: 3, page 7 [2-2]

Line: 300. Etching: 608. Grape Design. Goblet. 6 oz. **References**: 3, page 7 [2-4]

Line: 300. Etching: 608. Grape Design. Handled Custard. **References**: 3, page 7 [1-2]

Line: 300. Etching: 608. Grape Design. Individual Almond. **References**: 3, page 7 [1-2]

Line: 300. Etching: 608. Grape Design. Port. **References**: 3, page 7 [2-6]

Line: 300. Etching: 608. Grape Design. Rhine Wine Goblet. **References**: 3, page 7 [1-5]

Line: 300. Etching: 608. Grape Design. Saucer Champ. **References**: 3, page 7 [1-6]

Line: 300. Etching: 608. Grape Design. Sherbert. **References**: 3, page 7 [1-1]

Line: 300. Etching: 608. Grape Design. Tall Goblet. 9 oz. **References**: 3, page 7 [1-8]

Line: 300. Etching: 608. Grape Design. Wine. **References**: 3, page 7 [2-7]

Line: 300. Etching: 609. Rose Design. Individual Almond. **References**: 3, page 11 [2-2]

Line: 300. Etching: 610. Pansy Design. Ale. **References**: 3, page 16 [1-1]

Line: 300. Etching: 610. Pansy Design. Brandy. **References**: 3, page 16 [1-2]

Line: 300. Etching: 610. Pansy Design. Claret. **References**: 3, page 16 [2-5]

Line: 300. Etching: 610. Pansy Design. Cocktail. **References**: 3, page 16 [1-4]

Line: 300. Etching: 610. Pansy Design. Cordial. **References**: 3, page 16 [2-1]

Line: 300. Etching: 610. Pansy Design. Custard. **References**: 3, page 15 [1-1]

Line: 300. Etching: 610. Pansy Design. Deminth. **References**: 3, page 16 [1-5]

Line: 300. Etching: 610. Pansy Design. Goblet. 10 oz. **References**: 3, page 15 [2-1]

Line: 300. Etching: 610. Pansy Design. Goblet. 9 oz. **References**: 3, page 15 [2-2] [2-3]

Line: 300. Etching: 610. Pansy Design. Goblet. 8 oz. **References**: 3, page 15 [2-4]

Line: 300. Etching: 610. Pansy Design. Goblet. 7 oz. **References**: 3, page 15 [2-5]

Line: 300. Etching: 610. Pansy Design. Goblet. 6 oz. **References**: 3, page 15 [2-6]

Line: 300. Etching: 610. Pansy Design. Port. **References**: 3, page 16 [2-4]

Line: 300. Etching: 610. Pansy Design. Rhine Wine Goblet. **References**: 3, page 16 [1-3]

Line: 300. Etching: 610. Pansy Design. Saucer Champ. **References**: 3, page 16 [1-6]

Line: 300. Etching: 610. Pansy Design. Sherbert. **References**: 3, page 15 [3-1]

Line: 300. Etching: 610. Pansy Design. Sherry. **References**: 3, page 16 [2-2]

Line: 300. Etching: 610. Pansy Design. Wine. **References**: 3, page 16 [2-3]

Line: 300. Cut: 43. Etching: 608. Grape Design. Champagne. Hollow Stem. **References**: 3, page 8 [1-2]

Line: 300. Cut: 43. Etching: 608. Grape Design. Saucer Champ. Hollow Stem. **References**: 3, page 8 [1-4]

Line: 300. Cut: 43. Etching: 610. Pansy Design. Champagne. Hollow Stem. **References**: 3, page 16 [2-6]

Line: 300. Cut: 43. Etching: 610. Pansy Design. Saucer Champ. Hollow Stem. **References**: 3, page 16 [2-7]

Line: 307. Pirouette. 1305 Dessert-Finger Bowl. 4-1/2 inches diam. Shape Plain Twisted Stem. **References**: 1967, page 16 [1-8]; 1968, page 20 [1-8]; 1969, page 16 [1-8]; 1970, page 17 [1-8]; 1971, page 17 [1-8]; 1972, page 26 [1-8]; 1973, page 29 [1-8]

Line: 307. Pirouette. Claret. 3-3/4 oz. 4-1/2 inches tall. Shape Plain Twisted Stem. **References**: 1967, page 16 [1-3]; 1968, page 20 [1-3]; 1969, page 16 [1-3]; 1970, page 17 [1-3]; 1971, page 17 [1-3]; 1972, page 26 [1-3]; 1973, page 29 [1-3]

Line: 307. Pirouette. Cocktail. 4 oz. 3-7/8 inches tall. Shape Plain Twisted Stem. **References**: 1967, page 16 [1-4]; 1968, page 20 [1-4]; 1969, page 16 [1-4]; 1970, page 17 [1-4]; 1971, page 17 [1-4]; 1972, page 26 [1-4]; 1973, page 29 [1-4]

Line: 307. Pirouette. Cordial. 1-1/4 oz. 3-3/8 inches tall. Shape Plain Twisted Stem. **References**: 1967, page 16 [1-5]; 1968, page 20 [1-5]; 1969, page 16 [1-5]; 1970, page 17 [1-5]; 1971, page 17 [1-5]; 1972, page 26 [1-5]; 1973, page 29 [1-5]

Line: 307. Pirouette. Goblet. 10-1/2 oz. 6 inches tall. Shape Plain Twisted Stem. **References**: 1967, page 16 [1-1]; 1968, page 20 [1-1];x1969, page 16 [1-1]; 1970, page 17 [1-1]; 1971, page 17 [1-1]; 1972, page 26 [1-1];x1973, page 29 [1-1]

Line: 307. Pirouette. Ice Tea. 12 oz. 6-3/4 inches tall. Shape Plain Twisted Stem. **References**: 1967, page 16 [1-7]; 1968, page 20 [1-7];x1969, page 16 [1-7]; 1970, page 17 [1-7]; 1971, page 17 [1-7]; 1972, page 26 [1-7]; 1973, page 29 [1-7]

Line: 307. Pirouette. Juice. 5 oz. 5-1/8 inches tall. Shape Plain Twisted Stem. **References**: 1967, page 16 [1-6]; 1968, page 20 [1-6]; 1969, page 16 [1-6]; 1970, page 17 [1-6]; 1971, page 17 [1-6]; 1972, page 26 [1-6]; 1973, page 29 [1-6]

Line: 307. Pirouette. Plate. 7 inches diam. Shape Plain Twisted Stem, Actually 7-7/8" Dia. **References**: 1967, page 16 [1-9]; 1968, page 20 [1-9]; 1969, page 16 [1-9]; 1970, page 17 [1-9]; 1971, page 17 [1-9]; 1972, page 26 [1-9]; 1973, page 29 [1-9]

Line: 307. Pirouette. Plate. 8 inches diam. Shape Plain Twisted Stem, Actually 8-3/4" Dia. **References**: 1967, page 16 [1-10]; 1968, page 20 [1-10]; 1969, page 16 [1-10]; 1970, page 17 [1-10]; 1971, page 17 [1-10]; 1972, page 26 [1-10]; 1973, page 29 [1-10]

Line: 307. Pirouette. Sherbet. 5-1/2 oz. 4-1/2 inches tall. Shape Plain Twisted Stem. **References**: 1967, page 16 [1-2]; 1968, page 20 [1-2]; 1969, page 16 [1-2]; 1970, page 17 [1-2]; 1971, page 17 [1-2]; 1972, page 26 [1-2]; 1973, page 29 [1-2]

Line: 307. Cut: 1213. Arcadia. 1305 Dessert-Finger Bowl. 4-1/2 inches diam. Twisted Stem. **References**: 1967, page 16 [1-18]; 1968, page 20 [1-18]

Line: 307. Cut: 1213. Arcadia. Claret. 3-3/4 oz. 4-1/2 inches tall. Twisted Stem. **References**: 1967, page 16 [1-13]; 1968, page 20 [1-13]

Line: 307. Cut: 1213. Arcadia. Cocktail. 4 oz. 3-7/8 inches tall. Twisted Stem. **References**: 1967, page 16 [1-14]; 1968, page 20 [1-14]

Line: 307. Cut: 1213. Arcadia. Cordial. 1-1/4 oz. 3-3/8 inches tall. Twisted Stem. **References**: 1967, page 16 [1-15]; 1968, page 20 [1-15]

Line: 307. Cut: 1213. Arcadia. Goblet. 10-1/2 oz. 6 inches tall. Twisted Stem. **References**: 1967, page 16 [1-11]; 1968, page 20 [1-11]

Line: 307. Cut: 1213. Arcadia. Ice Tea. 12 oz. 6-3/4 inches tall. Twisted Stem. **References**: 1967, page 16 [1-17]; 1968, page 20 [1-17]

Line: 307. Cut: 1213. Arcadia. Juice. 5 oz. 5-1/8 inches tall. Twisted Stem. **References**: 1967, page 16 [1-16]; 1968, page 20 [1-16]

Line: 307. Cut: 1213. Arcadia. Plate. 7 inches diam. Twisted Stem, Actually 7-7/8" Dia. **References**: 1967, page 16 [1-19]; 1968, page 20 [1-19]

Line: 307. Cut: 1213. Arcadia. Plate. 8 inches diam. Twisted Stem, Actually 8-3/4" Dia. **References**: 1967, page 16 [1-20]; 1968, page 20 [1-20]

Line: 307. Cut: 1213. Arcadia. Sherbet. 5-1/2 oz. 4-1/2 inches tall. Twisted Stem. **References**: 1967, page 16 [1-12]; 1968, page 20 [1-12]

Line: 309. Parfait Whiskey Sour. 6-1/2 oz. 6-1/4 inches tall. **References**: 1975/I-75, page 5 [2-1]

Line: 309. Peacock Optic. Parfait Whiskey Sour. 6-1/2 oz. 6-1/4 inches tall. **References**: 1975/I-75, page 3 [2-1]

Line: 321. Etching: 75. Tumbler. **References**: 5-E, page 19 [1-1]

Line: 331. Cut: 1300. Corinthian. 1305 Dessert-Finger Bowl. 4-1/2 inches diam. **References**: 1967, page 21 [1-8]; 1968, page 25 [1-8]; 1969, page 24 [1-8]; 1970, page 25 [1-8]; 1971, page 25 [1-8]

Line: 331. Cut: 1300. Corinthian. Claret. 4 oz. 5 inches tall. **References**: 1967, page 21 [1-3]; 1968, page 25 [1-3]; 1969, page 24 [1-3]; 1970, page 25 [1-3]; 1971, page 25 [1-3]

Line: 331. Cut: 1300. Corinthian. Cocktail. 4-1/4 oz. 4-1/8 inches tall. **References**: 1967, page 21 [1-4]; 1968, page 25 [1-4]; 1969, page 24 [1-4]; 1970, page 25 [1-4]; 1971, page 25 [1-4]

Line: 331. Cut: 1300. Corinthian. Cordial. 1-1/4 oz. 4 inches tall. **References**: 1967, page 21 [1-5]; 1968, page 25 [1-5]; 1969, page 24 [1-5]; 1970, page 25 [1-5]; 1971, page 25 [1-5]

Line: 331. Cut: 1300. Corinthian. Goblet. 10 oz. 6-1/2 inches tall. **References**: 1967, page 21 [1-1]; 1968, page 25 [1-1]; 1969, page 24 [1-1]; 1970, page 25 [1-1]; 1971, page 25 [1-1]

Line: 331. Cut: 1300. Corinthian. Ice Tea. 11-3/4 oz. 6-1/2 inches tall. **References**: 1967, page 21 [1-7]; 1968, page 25 [1-7]; 1969, page 24 [1-7]; 1970, page 25 [1-7]; 1971, page 25 [1-7]

Line: 331. Cut: 1300. Corinthian. Juice. 5 oz. 5-3/8 inches tall. **References**: 1967, page 21 [1-6]; 1968, page 25 [1-6]; 1969, page 24 [1-6]; 1970, page 25 [1-6]; 1971, page 25 [1-6]

Line: 331. Cut: 1300. Corinthian. Plate. 7 inches diam. Actually 7-7/8"Dia. **References**: 1967, page 21 [1-9]; 1968, page 25 [1-9]; 1969, page 24 [1-9]; 1970, page 25 [1-9]; 1971, page 25 [1-9]

Line: 331. Cut: 1300. Corinthian. Plate. 8 inches diam. Actually 8-3/4" Dia. **References**: 1967, page 21 [1-10]; 1968, page 25 [1-10]; 1969, page 24 [1-10]; 1970, page 25 [1-10]; 1971, page 25 [1-10]

Line: 331. Cut: 1300. Corinthian. Sherbet. 6-1/4 oz. 5-1/8 inches tall. **References**: 1967, page 21 [1-2]; 1968, page 25 [1-2]; 1969, page 24 [1-2]; 1970, page 25 [1-2]; 1971, page 25 [1-2]

Line: 352. Cut: 1229. Caprice. 1311 Dessert-Finger Bowl. 4-3/4 inches diam. **References**: 1967, page 18 [1-8]; 1968, page 22 [1-8]; 1969, page 23 [1-8]; 1970, page 24 [1-8]; 1971, page 24 [1-8]

Line: 352. Cut: 1229. Caprice. Claret. 3-3/4 oz. 5-5/8 inches tall. **References**: 1967, page 18 [1-3]; 1968, page 22 [1-3]; 1969, page 23 [1-3]; 1970, page 24 [1-3]; 1971, page 24 [1-3]

Line: 352. Cut: 1229. Caprice. Cocktail. 3 oz. 4-1/4 inches tall. **References**: 1967, page 18 [1-4]; 1968, page 22 [1-4]; 1969, page 23 [1-4]; 1970, page 24 [1-4]; 1971, page 24 [1-4]

Line: 352. Cut: 1229. Caprice. Cordial. 1 oz. 4 inches tall. **References**: 1967, page 18 [1-5]; 1968, page 22 [1-5]; 1969, page 23 [1-5]; 1970, page 24 [1-5]; 1971, page 24 [1-5]

Line: 352. Cut: 1229. Caprice. Goblet. 9 oz. 7-1/4 inches tall. **References**: 1967, page 18 [1-1]; 1968, page 22 [1-1]; 1969, page 23 [1-1]; 1970, page 24 [1-1]; 1971, page 24 [1-1]

Line: 352. Cut: 1229. Caprice. Ice Tea. 12 oz. 7-1/4 inches tall. **References**: 1967, page 18 [1-7]; 1968, page 22 [1-7]; 1969, page 23 [1-7]; 1970, page 24 [1-7]; 1971, page 24 [1-7]

Line: 352. Cut: 1229. Caprice. Juice. 5-1/2 oz. 5-3/8 inches tall. **References**: 1967, page 18 [1-6]; 1968, page 22 [1-6]; 1969, page 23 [1-6]; 1970, page 24 [1-6]; 1971, page 24 [1-6]

Line: 352. Cut: 1229. Caprice. Plate. 7 inches diam. Actually 7-7/8" Dia. **References**: 1967, page 18 [1-9]; 1968, page 22 [1-9]; 1969, page 23 [1-9]; 1970, page 24 [1-9]; 1971, page 24 [1-9]

Line: 352. Cut: 1229. Caprice. Plate. 8 inches diam. Actually 8-3/4" Dia. **References**: 1967, page 18 [1-10]; 1968, page 22 [1-10]; 1969, page 23 [1-10]; 1970, page 24 [1-10]; 1971, page 24 [1-10]

Line: 352. Cut: 1229. Caprice. Sherbet. 6 oz. 5-3/8 inches tall. **References**: 1967, page 18 [1-2]; 1968, page 22 [1-2]; 1969, page 23 [1-2]; 1970, page 24 [1-2]; 1971, page 24 [1-2]

Line: 352. Cut: 1262. Ardis. 1311 Dessert-Finger Bowl. 4-3/4 inches diam. **References**: 1967, page 18 [2-8]; 1968, page 22 [2-8]

Line: 352. Cut: 1262. Ardis. Claret. 3-3/4 oz. 5-5/8 inches tall. **References**: 1967, page 18 [2-3]; 1968, page 22 [2-3]

Line: 352. Cut: 1262. Ardis. Cocktail. 3 oz. 4-1/4 inches tall. **References**: 1967, page 18 [2-4]; 1968, page 22 [2-4]

Line: 352. Cut: 1262. Ardis. Cordial. 1 oz. 4 inches tall. **References**: 1967, page 18 [2-5]; 1968, page 22 [2-5]

Line: 352. Cut: 1262. Ardis. Goblet. 9 oz. 7-1/4 inches tall. **References**: 1967, page 18 [2-1]; 1968, page 22 [2-1]

Line: 352. Cut: 1262. Ardis. Ice Tea. 12 oz. 7-1/4 inches tall. **References**: 1967, page 18 [2-7];

1968, page 22 [2-7]

Line: 352. Cut: 1262. Ardis. Juice. 5-1/2 oz. 5-3/8 inches tall. **References**: 1967, page 18 [2-6]; 1968, page 22 [2-6]

Line: 352. Cut: 1262. Ardis. Plate. 7 inches diam. Actually 7-7/8" Dia. **References**: 1967, page 18 [2-9]; 1968, page 22 [2-9]

Line: 352. Cut: 1262. Ardis. Plate. 8 inches diam. Actually 8-3/4" Dia. **References**: 1967, page 18 [2-10]; 1968, page 22 [2-10]

Line: 352. Cut: 1262. Ardis. Sherbet. 6 oz. 5-3/8 inches tall. **References**: 1967, page 18 [2-2]; 1968, page 22 [2-2]

Line: 352. Cut: 1263. Westwind. 1311 Dessert-Finger Bowl. 4-3/4 inches diam. **References**: 1967, page 18 [2-18]; 1968, page 22 [2-18]

Line: 352. Cut: 1263. Westwind. Claret. 3-3/4 oz. 5-5/8 inches tall. **References**: 1967, page 18 [2-13]; 1968, page 22 [2-13]

Line: 352. Cut: 1263. Westwind. Cocktail. 3 oz. 4-1/4 inches tall. **References**: 1967, page 18 [2-14]; 1968, page 22 [2-14]

Line: 352. Cut: 1263. Westwind. Cordial. 1 oz. 4 inches tall. **References**: 1967, page 18 [2-15]; 1968, page 22 [2-15]

Line: 352. Cut: 1263. Westwind. Goblet. 9 oz. 7-1/4 inches tall. **References**: 1967, page 18 [2-11]; 1968, page 22 [2-11]

Line: 352. Cut: 1263. Westwind. Ice Tea. 12 oz. 7-1/4 inches tall. **References**: 1967, page 18 [2-17]; 1968, page 22 [2-17]

Line: 352. Cut: 1263. Westwind. Juice. 5-1/2 oz. 5-3/8 inches tall. **References**: 1967, page 18 [2-16]; 1968, page 22 [2-16]

Line: 352. Cut: 1263. Westwind. Plate. 7 inches diam. Actually 7-7/8" Dia. **References**: 1967, page 18 [2-19]; 1968, page 22 [2-19]

Line: 352. Cut: 1263. Westwind. Plate. 8 inches diam. Actually 8-3/4" Dia. **References**: 1967, page 18 [2-20]; 1968, page 22 [2-20]

Line: 352. Cut: 1263. Westwind. Sherbet. 6 oz. 5-3/8 inches tall. **References**: 1967, page 18 [2-12]; 1968, page 22 [2-12]

Line: 352. Cut: 1380. Timeless. 1311 Dessert-Finger Bowl. 4-3/4 inches diam. **References**: 1967, page 18 [1-18]; 1968, page 22 [1-18]

Line: 352. Cut: 1380. Timeless. Claret. 3-3/4 oz. 5-5/8 inches tall. **References**: 1967, page 18 [1-13]; 1968, page 22 [1-13]

Line: 352. Cut: 1380. Timeless. Cocktail. 3 oz. 4-1/4 inches tall. **References**: 1967, page 18 [1-14]; 1968, page 22 [1-14]

Line: 352. Cut: 1380. Timeless. Cordial. 1 oz. 4 inches tall. **References**: 1967, page 18 [1-15]; 1968, page 22 [1-15]

Line: 352. Cut: 1380. Timeless. Goblet. 9 oz. 7-1/4 inches tall. **References**: 1967, page 18 [1-11]; 1968, page 22 [1-11]

Line: 352. Cut: 1380. Timeless. Ice Tea. 12 oz. 7-1/4 inches tall. **References**: 1967, page 18 [1-17]; 1968, page 22 [1-17]

Line: 352. Cut: 1380. Timeless. Juice. 5-1/2 oz. 5-3/8 inches tall. **References**: 1967, page 18 [1-16]; 1968, page 22 [1-16]

Line: 352. Cut: 1380. Timeless. Plate. 7 inches diam. Actually 7-7/8" Dia. **References**: 1967, page 18 [1-19]; 1968, page 22 [1-19]

Line: 352. Cut: 1380. Timeless. Plate. 8 inches diam. Actually 8-3/4" Dia. **References**: 1967, page 18 [1-20]; 1968, page 22 [1-20]

Line: 352. Cut: 1380. Timeless. Sherbet. 6 oz. 5-3/8 inches tall. **References**: 1967, page 18 [1-12]; 1968, page 22 [1-12]

Line: 355. Cut: 1318. Celeste. 1305 Dessert-Finger Bowl. 4-1/2 inches diam. **References**: 1967, page 15 [1-9]; 1968, page 19 [1-9]; 1969, page 17 [2-9]; 1970, page 18 [2-9]; 1971, page 18 [2-9]

Line: 355. Cut: 1318. Celeste. Cocktail. 4-3/4 oz. 4-1/2 inches tall. **References**: 1967, page 15 [1-4]; 1968, page 19 [1-4]; 1969, page 17 [2-4]; 1970, page 18 [2-4]; 1971, page 18 [2-4]

Line: 355. Cut: 1318. Celeste. Cordial. 1-1/2 oz. 3-1/2 inches tall. **References**: 1967, page 15 [1-5]; 1968, page 19 [1-5]; 1969, page 17 [2-5]; 1970, page 18 [2-5]; 1971, page 18 [2-5]

Line: 355. Cut: 1318. Celeste. Goblet. 10-1/2 oz. 6-1/2 inches tall. **References**: 1967, page 15 [1-1]; 1968, page 19 [1-1]; 1969, page 17 [2-1]; 1970, page 18 [2-1]; 1971, page 18 [2-1]

Line: 355. Cut: 1318. Celeste. Ice Tea. 12 oz. 5-3/4 inches tall. **References**: 1967, page 15 [1-8]; 1968, page 19 [1-8];
1969, page 17 [2-8]; 1970, page 18 [2-8]; 1971, page 18 [2-8]

Line: 355. Cut: 1318. Celeste. Juice. 5 oz. 4-1/4 inches tall. **References**: 1967, page 15 [1-7]; 1968, page 19 [1-7]; 1969, page 17 [2-7]; 1970, page 18 [2-7]; 1971, page 18 [2-7]

Line: 355. Cut: 1318. Celeste. Parfait. 6-1/2 oz. 7-1/2 inches tall. **References**: 1967, page 15 [1-6]; 1968, page 19 [1-6]; 1969, page 17 [2-6]; 1970, page 18 [2-6]; 1971, page 18 [2-6]

Line: 355. Cut: 1318. Celeste. Plate. 7 inches diam. Actually 7-7/8" Dia. **References**: 1967, page 15 [1-10]; 1968, page 19 [1-10]; 1969, page 17 [2-10]; 1970, page 18 [2-10]; 1971, page 18 [2-10]

Line: 355. Cut: 1318. Celeste. Plate. 8 inches diam. Actually 8-3/4" Dia. **References**: 1967, page 15 [1-11]; 1968, page 19 [1-11]; 1969, page 17 [2-11]; 1970, page 18 [2-11]; 1971, page 18 [2-11]

Line: 355. Cut: 1318. Celeste. Sherbet. 6-3/4 oz. 5 inches tall. **References**: 1967, page 15 [1-2]; 1968, page 19 [1-2]; 1969, page 17 [2-2]; 1970, page 18 [2-2]; 1971, page 18 [2-2]

Line: 355. Cut: 1318. Celeste. Wine. 5 oz. 5-1/2 inches tall. **References**: 1967, page 15 [1-3]; 1968, page 19 [1-3]; 1969, page 17 [2-3]; 1970, page 18 [2-3]; 1971, page 18 [2-3]

Line: 355. Cut: 1320. Silver Leaf. 1305 Dessert-Finger Bowl. 4-1/2 inches diam. **References**: 1967, page 15 [2-9]; 1968, page 19 [2-9]

Line: 355. Cut: 1320. Silver Leaf. Cocktail. 4-3/4 oz. 4-1/2 inches tall. **References**: 1967, page 15 [2-4]; 1968, page 19 [2-4]

Line: 355. Cut: 1320. Silver Leaf. Cordial. 1-1/2 oz. 3-1/2 inches tall. **References**: 1967, page 15 [2-5]; 1968, page 19 [2-5]

Line: 355. Cut: 1320. Silver Leaf. Goblet. 10-1/2 oz. 6-1/2 inches tall. **References**: 1967, page 15 [2-1]; 1968, page 19 [2-1]

Line: 355. Cut: 1320. Silver Leaf. Ice Tea. 12 oz. 5-3/4 inches tall. **References**: 1967, page 15 [2-8]; 1968, page 19 [2-8]

Line: 355. Cut: 1320. Silver Leaf. Juice. 5 oz. 4-1/2 inches tall. **References**: 1967, page 15 [2-7]; 1968, page 19 [2-7]

Line: 355. Cut: 1320. Silver Leaf. Parfait. 6-1/2 oz. 7-1/2 inches tall. **References**: 1967, page 15 [2-6]; 1968, page 19 [2-6]

Line: 355. Cut: 1320. Silver Leaf. Plate. 7 inches diam. Actually 7-7/8" Dia. **References**: 1967, page 15 [2-10]; 1968, page 19 [2-10]

Line: 355. Cut: 1320. Silver Leaf. Plate. 8 inches diam. Actually 8-3/4" Dia. 1968, page 19 [2-11]

Line: 355. Cut: 1320. Silver Leaf. Sherbet. 6-3/4 oz. 5 inches tall. **References**: 1967, page 15 [2-2]; 1968, page 19 [2-2]

Line: 355. Cut: 1320. Silver Leaf. Wine. 5 oz. 5-1/2 inches tall. **References**: 1967, page 15 [2-3]; 1968, page 19 [2-3]

Line: 355. Cut: 1325. Coventry. 1305 Dessert-Finger Bowl. 4-1/2 inches diam. **References**: 1967, page 15 [2-20]; 1968, page 19 [2-20]; 1969, page 17 [2-20]; 1970, page 18 [2-20]; 1971, page 18 [2-20]

Line: 355. Cut: 1325. Coventry. Cocktail. 4-3/4 oz. 4-1/2 inches tall. **References**: 1967, page 15 [2-15]; 1968, page 19 [2-15]; 1969, page 17 [2-15]; 1970, page 18 [2-15]; 1971, page 18 [2-15]

Line: 355. Cut: 1325. Coventry. Cordial. 1-1/2 oz. 3-1/2 inches tall. **References**: 1967, page 15 [2-16]; 1968, page 19 [2-16]; 1969, page 17 [2-16]; 1970, page 18 [2-16]; 1971, page 18 [2-16]

Line: 355. Cut: 1325. Coventry. Goblet. 10-1/2 oz. 6-1/2 inches tall. **References**: 1967, page 15 [2-12]; 1968, page 19 [2-12]; 1969, page 17 [2-12]; 1970, page 18 [2-12]; 1971, page 18 [2-12]

Line: 355. Cut: 1325. Coventry. Ice Tea. 12 oz. 5-3/4 inches tall. **References**: 1967, page 15 [2-19]; 1968, page 19 [2-19]; 1969, page 17 [2-19]; 1970, page 18 [2-19]; 1971, page 18 [2-19]

Line: 355. Cut: 1325. Coventry. Juice. 5 oz. 4-1/4 inches tall. **References**: 1967, page 15 [2-18]; 1968, page 19 [2-18]; 1969, page 17 [2-18]; 1970, page 18 [2-18]; 1971, page 18 [2-18]

Line: 355. Cut: 1325. Coventry. Parfait. 6-1/2 oz. 7-1/2 inches tall. **References**: 1967, page 15 [2-17]; 1968, page 19 [2-17]; 1969, page 17 [2-17]; 1970, page 18 [2-17]; 1971, page 18 [2-17]

Line: 355. Cut: 1325. Coventry. Plate. 7 inches diam. Actually 7-7/8" Dia. **References**: 1967, page 15 [2-21]; 1968, page 19 [2-21]; 1969, page 17 [2-21]; 1970, page 18 [2-21]; 1971, page 18 [2-21]

Line: 355. Cut: 1325. Coventry. Plate. 8 inches diam. Actually 8-3/4" Dia. **References**: 1967, page 15 [2-22]; 1968, page 19 [2-22]; 1969, page 17 [2-22]; 1970, page 18 [2-22]; 1971, page 18 [2-22]

Line: 355. Cut: 1325. Coventry. Sherbet. 6-3/4 oz. 5 inches tall. **References**: 1967, page 15 [2-13]; 1968, page 19 [2-13]; 1969, page 17 [2-13]; 1970, page 18 [2-13]; 1971, page 18 [2-13]

Line: 355. Cut: 1325. Coventry. Wine. 5 oz. 5-1/2 inches tall. **References**: 1967, page 15 [2-14]; 1968, page 19 [2-14]; 1969, page 17 [2-14]; 1970, page 18 [2-14]; 1971, page 18 [2-14]

Line: 360. Cut: 43. Cosmopolitan. 1305 Dessert-Finger Bowl. 4-1/2" Dia. **References**: 1967, page 12 [2-9]; 1968, page 16 [2-9]; 1969, page 14 [1-11]; 1970, page 15 [1-11]; 1971, page 15 [1-11]; 1972, page 23 [1-11]

Line: 360. Cut: 43. Cosmopolitan. All Purpose Wine Goblet. 8 oz. 5 inches tall. **References**: 1967, page 12 [2-12]; 1968, page 16 [2-12]; 1969, page 14 [1-6]; 1970, page 15 [1-6]; 1971, page 15 [1-6]; 1972, page 23 [1-6]; 1973, page 9 [1-6]; 1975, page 9 [1-6]; 1977, page 9 [1-6]

Line: 360. Cut: 43. Cosmopolitan. Cocktail. 5-1/2 oz. / 4-5/8" hi. **References**: 1967, page 12 [2-5]; 1968, page 16 [2-5]; 1969, page 14 [1-7]; 1970, page 15 [1-7]; 1971, page 15 [1-7]; 1972, page 23 [1-7]; 1973, page 9 [1-7]; 1975, page 9 [1-7]; 1977, page 9 [1-7]

Line: 360. Cut: 43. Cosmopolitan. Cordial. 2 oz. / 4-1/2" hi. **References**: 1967, page 12 [2-6]; 1968, page 16 [2-6]; 1969, page 14 [1-8]; 1970, page 15 [1-8]; 1971, page 15 [1-8]; 1972, page 23 [1-8]; 1973, page 9 [1-8]; 1975, page 9 [1-8]; 1977, page 9 [1-8]; 1981, page 3 [2-6]

Line: 360. Cut: 43. Cosmopolitan. Goblet. 12 oz. / 7" hi. **References**: 1967, page 12 [2-1]; 1968, page 16 [2-1]; 1969, page 14 [1-1]; 1970, page 15 [1-1]; 1971, page 15 [1-1]; 1972, page 23 [1-1]; 1973, page 9 [1-1]; 1975, page 9 [1-1]; 1977, page 9 [1-1]; 1981, page 3 [2-1]

Line: 360. Cut: 43. Cosmopolitan. Ice Tea. 12 oz. / 6-1/4" hi. **References**: 1967, page 12 [2-8]; 1968, page 16 [2-8]; 1969, page 14 [1-10]; 1970, page 15 [1-10]; 1971, page 15 [1-10]; 1972, page 23 [1-10]; 1973, page 9 [1-10]; 1975, page 9 [1-10]; 1977, page 9 [1-10]

Line: 360. Cut: 43. Cosmopolitan. Juice. 5 oz. / 4-1/2" hi. **References**: 1967, page 12 [2-7]; 1968, page 16 [2-7]; 1969, page 14 [1-9]; 1970, page 15 [1-9]; 1971, page 15 [1-9]; 1972, page 23 [1-9]; 1973, page 9 [1-9]

Line: 360. Cut: 43. Cosmopolitan. Plate. 7" / Acutally 7-7/8" Dia. **References**: 1967, page 12 [2-10]; 1968, page 16 [2-10]; 1969, page 14 [1-12]; 1970, page 15 [1-12]; 1971, page 15 [1-12]; 1972, page 23 [1-12]

Line: 360. Cut: 43. Cosmopolitan. Plate. 8" / Acutally 8-3/4" Dia. **References**: 1967, page 12 [2-11]; 1968, page 16 [2-11]; 1969, page 14 [1-13]; 1970, page 15 [1-13]; 1971, page 15 [1-13]; 1972, page 23 [1-13]

Line: 360. Cut: 43. Cosmopolitan. Red Wine Goblet. 9 oz. / 6-1/2" hi. **References**: 1967, page 12 [2-3]; 1968, page 16 [2-3]; 1969, page 14 [1-3]; 1970, page 15 [1-3]; 1971, page 15 [1-3]; 1972, page 23 [1-3]; 1973, page 9 [1-3]; 1975, page 9 [1-3]; 1977, page 9 [1-3]; 1981, page 3 [2-3]

Line: 360. Cut: 43. Cosmopolitan. Sherbet. 7-1/2 oz. / 5-1/8" hi. **References**: 1967, page 12 [2-2]; 1968, page 16 [2-2]; 1969, page 14 [1-2]; 1970, page 15 [1-2]; 1971, page 15 [1-2]; 1972, page 23 [1-2]; 1973, page 9 [1-2]; 1975, page 9 [1-2]; 1977, page 9 [1-2]; 1981, page 3 [2-2]

Line: 360. Cut: 43. Cosmopolitan. Tulip Champagne. 8 oz. 8-1/2 inches tall. **References**: 1969, page 14 [1-5]; 1970, page 15 [1-5]; 1971, page 15 [1-5]; 1972, page 23 [1-5]; 1973, page 9 [1-5]; 1975, page 9 [1-5]; 1977, page 9 [1-5]; 1981, page 3 [2-5]

Line: 360. Cut: 43. Cosmopolitan. White Wine. 7 oz. 5-7/8 inches tall. **References**: 1975, page 9 [1-4]; 1967, page 12 [2-4]; 1968, page 16 [2-4]; 1969, page 14 [1-4]; 1970, page 15 [1-4]; 1971, page 15 [1-4]; 1972, page 23 [1-4]; 1973, page 9 [1-4]; 1977, page 9 [1-4]; 1981, page 3 [2-4]

Line: 406. Tumbler. 1-1/2 oz. **References**: 5-E, page 1 [4-2]

Line: 455. Covered Candy. 8-5/8 inches tall. Black Cover, Crystal Bowl, Black Foot. **References**: 1978, page 14 [1-A]

Line: 455. Cut: 31. Candy Jar. Optic. **References**: 4, page 27 [2-2]

Line: 455. Cut: 58. Jug. 54 oz. Optic. **References**: 4, page 26 [3-2]

Line: 45-8. Cordial. 1-1/4 oz. 7-1/2 inches tall. **References**: 1975/I-75, page 5 [3-1]

Line: 45-8. Vase. 7-1/2 inches tall. Crystal with Black Foot. **References**: 1978, page 15 [2-4]

Line: 459. Cut: 204. Cocktail. **References**: 4, page 6 [1-4]

Line: 459. Cut: 204. Cordial. **References**: 4, page 6 [1-5]

Line: 459. Cut: 204. Goblet. **References**: 4, page 6 [1-1]

Line: 459. Cut: 204. Sherbet. **References**: 4, page 6 [1-2]

Line: 459. Cut: 204. Wine. **References**: 4, page 6 [1-3]

Line: 459. Cut: 286. Vase. 8-1/2 inch. Optic. **References**: 4, page 27 [1-1]

Line: 460. Handled. 10 oz. Handled Ice Tea or Lemonade Glasses. **References**: 5-E, page 15 [2-2]

Line: 463. Palm Optic. Brandy Inhaler. 23 oz. 5-3/4 inches tall. **References**: 1975/I-75, page 2 [2-1]

Line: 465. Cut: 33. Cocktail. Optic. **References**: 4, page 7 [1-5]

Line: 465. Cut: 33. Cordial. Optic. **References**: 4, page 7 [1-6]

Line: 465. Cut: 33. Footed Tumbler. 2-3/4 oz. Optic. **References**: 4, page 7 [2-1]

Line: 465. Cut: 33. Footed Tumbler. 4 oz. Optic. **References**: 4, page 7 [2-2]

Line: 465. Cut: 33. Footed Tumbler. 6 oz. Optic. **References**: 4, page 7 [2-3]

Line: 465. Cut: 33. Footed Tumbler. 9 oz. Optic. **References**: 4, page 7 [2-4]

Line: 465. Cut: 33. Footed Tumbler. 12 oz. Optic. **References**: 4, page 7 [2-5]

Line: 465. Cut: 33. Goblet. Optic. **References**: 4, page 7 [1-1]

Line: 465. Cut: 33. Saucer Champagne. Optic. **References**: 4, page 7 [1-2]

Line: 465. Cut: 33. Sherbet. Optic. **References**: 4, page 7 [1-3]

Line: 465. Cut: 33. Wine. Optic. **References**: 4, page 7 [1-4]

Line: 465. Cut: 57. Finger Bowl. Optic. **References**: 4, page 25 [3-3]

Line: 475. Cut: 31. Cocktail. Optic. **References**: 4, page 8 [1-5]

Line: 475. Cut: 31. Cordial. Optic. **References**: 4, page 8 [1-6]

Line: 475. Cut: 31. Footed Tumbler. 2-3/4 oz. Optic. **References**: 4, page 8 [2-1]

Line: 475. Cut: 31. Footed Tumbler. 4 oz. Optic. **References**: 4, page 8 [2-2]

Line: 475. Cut: 31. Footed Tumbler. 6 oz. Optic. **References**: 4, page 8 [2-3]

Line: 475. Cut: 31. Footed Tumbler. 9 oz. Optic. **References**: 4, page 8 [2-4]

Line: 475. Cut: 31. Footed Tumbler. 12 oz. Optic. **References**: 4, page 8 [2-5]

Line: 475. Cut: 31. Goblet. Optic. **References**: 4, page 8 [1-1]

Line: 475. Cut: 31. Saucer Champagne. Optic. **References**: 4, page 8 [1-2]

Line: 475. Cut: 31. Sherbet. Optic. **References**: 4, page 8 [1-3]

Line: 475. Cut: 31. Wine. Optic. **References**: 4, page 8 [1-4]

Line: 475. Cut: 258. Goblet. Optic. **References**: 4, page 24 [2-1]

Line: 476. Cut: 636. Stratford. 1311 Dessert-Finger Bowl. 4-3/4 inches diam. **References**: 1967, page 19 [1-9]; 1969, page 23 [2-20]; 1970, page 24 [2-20]; 1971, page 24 [2-20]

Line: 476. Cut: 636. Stratford. Claret. 3-1/2 oz. 6-1/8 inches tall. **References**: 1967, page 19 [1-3]; 1969, page 23 [2-14]; 1970, page 24 [2-14]; 1971, page 24 [2-14]

Line: 476. Cut: 636. Stratford. Cocktail. 3 oz. 5-1/4 inches tall. **References**: 1967, page 19 [1-5]; 1969, page 23 [2-16]; 1970, page 24 [2-16]; 1970, page 24 [2-16]; 1971, page 24 [2-16]; 1971, page 24 [2-16]

Line: 476. Cut: 636. Stratford. Cordial. 1 oz. 4-3/4 inches tall. **References**: 1967, page 19 [1-6]; 1969, page 23 [2-17]

Line: 476. Cut: 636. Stratford. Goblet. 9 oz. 8-3/8 inches tall. **References**: 1967, page 19 [1-1]; 1969, page 23 [2-12]; 1970, page 24 [2-12]; 1971, page 24 [2-12]

Line: 476. Cut: 636. Stratford. Ice Tea. 12 oz. 7-1/4 inches tall. **References**: 1967, page 19 [1-8]; 1969, page 23 [2-19]; 1970, page 24 [2-19]; 1971, page 24 [2-19]

Line: 476. Cut: 636. Stratford. Juice. 5-1/2 oz. 5-3/4 inches tall. **References**: 1967, page 19 [1-7]; 1969, page 23 [2-18]; 1970, page 24 [2-18]; 1971, page 24 [2-18]

Line: 476. Cut: 636. Stratford. Plate. 7 inches diam. Actually 7-7/8" Dia. **References**: 1967, page 19 [1-10]; 1969, page 23 [2-21]; 1970, page 24 [2-21]; 1971, page 24 [2-21]

Line: 476. Cut: 636. Stratford. Plate. 8 inches diam. Actually 8-3/4" Dia. **References**: 1967, page 19 [1-11]; 1969, page 23 [2-22]; 1970, page 24 [2-22]; 1971, page 24 [2-22]

Line: 476. Cut: 636. Stratford. Saucer Champagne. 6 oz. 6-1/2 inches tall. **References**: 1967, page 19 [1-2]; 1969, page 23 [2-13]; 1970, page 24 [2-13]; 1971, page 24 [2-13]

Line: 476. Cut: 636. Stratford. Wine. 3 oz. 6 inches tall. **References**: 1967, page 19 [1-4]; 1969, page 23 [2-15]; 1970, page 24 [2-15]; 1971, page 24 [2-15]

Line: 476. Cut: 900. Windblown. 1311 Dessert-Finger Bowl. 4-3/4 inches diam. **References**: 1967, page 19 [2-20]

Line: 476. Cut: 900. Windblown. Claret. 3-1/2 oz. 6-1/8 inches tall. **References**: 1967, page 19 [2-14]

Line: 476. Cut: 900. Windblown. Cocktail. 3 oz. 5-1/4 inches tall. **References**: 1967, page 19 [2-16]

Line: 476. Cut: 900. Windblown. Cordial. 1 oz. 4-3/4 inches tall. **References**: 1967, page 19 [2-17]

Line: 476. Cut: 900. Windblown. Goblet. 9 oz. 8-3/8 inches tall. **References**: 1967, page 19 [2-12]

Line: 476. Cut: 900. Windblown. Ice Tea. 12 oz. 7-1/4 inches tall. **References**: 1967, page 19 [2-19]

Line: 476. Cut: 900. Windblown. Juice. 5-1/2 oz. 5-3/4 inches tall. **References**: 1967, page 19 [2-18]

Line: 476. Cut: 900. Windblown. Plate. 7 inches diam. Actually 7-7/8" Dia. **References**: 1967, page 19 [2-21]

Line: 476. Cut: 900. Windblown. Plate. 8 inches diam. Actually 8-3/4" Dia. **References**: 1967, page 19 [2-22]

Line: 476. Cut: 900. Windblown. Saucer Champagne. 6 oz. 6-1/2 inches tall. **References**: 1967, page 19 [2-13]

Line: 476. Cut: 900. Windblown. Wine. 3 oz. 6 inches tall. **References**: 1967, page 19 [2-15]

Line: 476. Cut: 967. Elegance. 1311 Dessert-Finger Bowl. 4-3/4 inches diam. **References**: 1967, page 19 [2-9]; 1969, page 23 [2-9]; 1970, page 24 [2-9]; 1971, page 24 [2-9]

Line: 476. Cut: 967. Elegance. Claret. 3-1/2 oz. 6-1/8 inches tall. **References**: 1967, page 19 [2-3]; 1969, page 23 [2-3]; 1970, page 24 [2-3]; 1971, page 24 [2-3]

Line: 476. Cut: 967. Elegance. Cocktail. 3 oz. 5-1/4 inches tall. **References**: 1967, page 19 [2-5]; 1969, page 23 [2-5]; 1970, page 24 [2-5]; 1971, page 24 [2-5]

Line: 476. Cut: 967. Elegance. Cordial. 1 oz. 4-3/4 inches tall. **References**: 1967, page 19 [2-6]; 1969, page 23 [2-6]; 1970, page 24 [2-6]; 1971, page 24 [2-6]

Line: 476. Cut: 967. Elegance. Goblet. 9 oz. 8-3/8 inches tall. **References**: 1967, page 19 [2-1]; 1969, page 23 [2-1]; 1970, page 24 [2-1]; 1971, page 24 [2-1]

Line: 476. Cut: 967. Elegance. Ice Tea. 12 oz. 7-1/4 inches tall. **References**: 1967, page 19 [2-8]; 1969, page 23 [2-8]; 1970, page 24 [2-8]; 1971, page 24 [2-8]

Line: 476. Cut: 967. Elegance. Juice. 5-1/2 oz. 5-3/4 inches tall. **References**: 1967, page 19 [2-7]; 1969, page 23 [2-7]; 1970, page 24 [2-7]; 1971, page 24 [2-7]

Line: 476. Cut: 967. Elegance. Plate. 7 inches diam. Actually 7-7/8" Dia. **References**: 1967, page 19 [2-10]; 1969, page 23 [2-10]; 1970, page 24 [2-10]; 1971, page 24 [2-10]

Line: 476. Cut: 967. Elegance. Plate. 8 inches diam. Actually 8-3/4" Dia. **References**: 1967, page 19 [2-11]; 1969, page 23 [2-11]; 1970, page 24 [2-11]; 1971, page 24 [2-11]

Line: 476. Cut: 967. Elegance. Saucer Champagne. 6 oz. 6-1/2 inches tall. **References**: 1967, page 19 [2-2]; 1969, page 23 [2-2]; 1970, page 24 [2-2]; 1971, page 24 [2-2]

Line: 476. Cut: 967. Elegance. Wine. 3 oz. 6 inches tall. **References**: 1967, page 19 [2-4]; 1969, page 23 [2-4]; 1970, page 24 [2-4]; 1971, page 24 [2-4]

Line: 477. Cut: 219. Cocktail. **References**: 4, page 9 [1-5]

Line: 477. Cut: 219. Cordial. **References**: 4, page 9 [1-6]

Line: 477. Cut: 219. Footed Tumbler. 2-3/4 oz. **References**: 4, page 9 [2-1]

Line: 477. Cut: 219. Footed Tumbler. 4 oz. **References**: 4, page 9 [2-2]

Line: 477. Cut: 219. Footed Tumbler. 6 oz. **References**: 4, page 9 [2-3]

Line: 477. Cut: 219. Footed Tumbler. 9 oz. **References**: 4, page 9 [2-4]

Line: 477. Cut: 219. Footed Tumbler. 12 oz. **References**: 4, page 9 [2-5]

Line: 477. Cut: 219. Goblet. **References**: 4, page 9 [1-1]

Line: 477. Cut: 219. Saucer Champagne. **References**: 4, page 9 [1-2]

Line: 477. Cut: 219. Sherbet. **References**: 4, page 9 [1-3]

Line: 477. Cut: 219. Wine. **References**: 4, page 9 [1-4]

Line: 481. Cut: 370. Cocktail. Optic. **References**: 4, page 10 [1-5]

Line: 481. Cut: 370. Cordial. Optic. **References**: 4, page 10 [1-6]

Line: 481. Cut: 370. Footed Tumbler. 2-3/4 oz. **References**: 4, page 10 [2-1]

Line: 481. Cut: 370. Footed Tumbler. 4 oz. **References**: 4, page 10 [2-2]

Line: 481. Cut: 370. Footed Tumbler. 6 oz. **References**: 4, page 10 [2-3]

Line: 481. Cut: 370. Footed Tumbler. 9 oz. **References**: 4, page 10 [2-4]

Line: 481. Cut: 370. Footed Tumbler. 12 oz. **References**: 4, page 10 [2-5]

Line: 481. Cut: 370. Goblet. Optic. **References**: 4, page 10 [1-1]

Line: 481. Cut: 370. Saucer Champagne. Optic. **References**: 4, page 10 [1-2]

Line: 481. Cut: 370. Sherbet. Optic. **References**: 4, page 10 [1-3]

Line: 481. Cut: 370. Wine. Optic. **References**: 4, page 10 [1-4]

Line: 482. Cut: 57. Cocktail. Optic. **References**: 4, page 11 [1-5]

Line: 482. Cut: 57. Cordial. Optic. **References**: 4, page 11 [1-6]

Line: 482. Cut: 57. Footed Tumbler. 2-3/4 oz. Optic. **References**: 4, page 11 [2-1]

Line: 482. Cut: 57. Footed Tumbler. 4 oz. Optic. **References**: 4, page 11 [2-2]

Line: 482. Cut: 57. Footed Tumbler. 6 oz. Optic. **References**: 4, page 11 [2-3]

Line: 482. Cut: 57. Footed Tumbler. 9 oz. Optic. **References**: 4, page 11 [2-4]

Line: 482. Cut: 57. Footed Tumbler. 12 oz. Optic. **References**: 4, page 11 [2-5]

Line: 482. Cut: 57. Goblet. Optic. **References**: 4, page 11 [1-1]

Line: 482. Cut: 57. Saucer Champagne. Optic. **References**: 4, page 11 [1-2]

Line: 482. Cut: 57. Sherbet. Optic. **References**: 4, page 11 [1-3]

Line: 482. Cut: 57. Wine. Optic. **References**: 4, page 11 [1-4]

Line: 482. Cut: 61. Cocktail. Optic. **References**: 4, page 12 [1-5]

Line: 482. Cut: 61. Cordial. Optic. **References**: 4, page 12 [1-6]

Line: 482. Cut: 61. Footed Tumbler. 2-3/4 oz. Optic. **References**: 4, page 12 [2-1]

Line: 482. Cut: 61. Footed Tumbler. 4 oz. Optic. **References**: 4, page 12 [2-2]

Line: 482. Cut: 61. Footed Tumbler. 6 oz. Optic. **References**: 4, page 12 [2-3]

Line: 482. Cut: 61. Footed Tumbler. 9 oz. Optic. **References**: 4, page 12 [2-4]

Line: 482. Cut: 61. Footed Tumbler. 12 oz. Optic. **References**: 4, page 12 [2-5]

Line: 482. Cut: 61. Goblet. Optic. **References**: 4, page 12 [1-1]

Line: 482. Cut: 61. Saucer Champagne. Optic. **References**: 4, page 12 [1-2]

Line: 482. Cut: 61. Sherbet. Optic. **References**: 4, page 12 [1-3]

Line: 482. Cut: 61. Wine. Optic. **References**: 4, page 12 [1-4]

Line: 482. Cut: 64. Goblet. Optic. **References**: 4, page 24 [2-6]

Line: 482. Cut: 204. Footed Tumbler. 2-3/4 oz. **References**: 4, page 6 [2-1]

Line: 482. Cut: 204. Footed Tumbler. 4 oz. **References**: 4, page 6 [2-2]

Line: 482. Cut: 204. Footed Tumbler. 6 oz. **References**: 4, page 6 [2-3]

Line: 482. Cut: 204. Footed Tumbler. 9 oz. **References**: 4, page 6 [2-4]

Line: 482. Cut: 204. Footed Tumbler. 12 oz. **References**: 4, page 6 [2-5]

Line: 482. Cut: 218. Goblet. Optic. **References**: 4, page 24 [1-4]

Line: 482. Cut: 259. Goblet. Optic. **References**: 4, page 24 [1-2]

Line: 482. Cut: 260. Cocktail. Optic. **References**: 4, page 13 [1-5]

Line: 482. Cut: 260. Cordial. Optic. **References**: 4, page 13 [1-6]

Line: 482. Cut: 260. Footed Tumbler. 2-3/4 oz. Optic. **References**: 4, page 13 [2-1]

Line: 482. Cut: 260. Footed Tumbler. 4 oz. Optic. **References**: 4, page 13 [2-2]

Line: 482. Cut: 260. Footed Tumbler. 6 oz. Optic. **References**: 4, page 13 [2-3]

Line: 482. Cut: 260. Footed Tumbler. 9 oz. Optic. **References**: 4, page 13 [2-4]

Line: 482. Cut: 260. Footed Tumbler. 12 oz. Optic. **References**: 4, page 13 [2-5]

Line: 482. Cut: 260. Goblet. Optic. **References**: 4, page 13 [1-1]

Line: 482. Cut: 260. Saucer Champagne. Optic. **References**: 4, page 13 [1-2]

Line: 482. Cut: 260. Sherbet. Optic. **References**: 4, page 13 [1-3]

Line: 482. Cut: 260. Wine. Optic. **References**: 4, page 13 [1-4]

Line: 484. Claret. Optic, P/D Silvia. **References**: 4, page 29 [1-3]

Line: 484. Cocktail. Optic, P/D Silvia. **References**: 4, page 29 [1-5]

Line: 484. Cocktail. **References**: 4, page 33 [1-5]

Line: 484. Cordial. Optic, P/D Silvia. **References**: 4, page 29 [1-4]

Line: 484. Cordial. **References**: 4, page 33 [2-1]

Line: 484. Finger Bowl. **References**: 4, page 33 [1-4]

Line: 484. Footed Tumbler. 12 oz. Optic, P/D Silvia. **References**: 4, page 29 [2-5]

Line: 484. Footed Tumbler. 12 oz. **References**: 4, page 33 [1-8]

Line: 484. Goblet. Optic, P/D Silvia. **References**: 4, page 29 [2-1]

Line: 484. Goblet. **References**: 4, page 33 [1-1]

Line: 484. Parfait. Optic, P/D Silvia. **References**: 4, page 29 [2-4]

Line: 484. Parfait. **References**: 4, page 33 [1-6]

Line: 484. Saucer Champagne. Optic, P/D Silvia. **References**: 4, page 29 [2-2]

Line: 484. Saucer Champagne. **References**: 4, page 33 [1-2]

Line: 484. Sherbet. Optic, P/D Silvia. **References**: 4, page 29 [2-3]

Line: 484. Sherbet. **References**: 4, page 33 [1-3]

Line: 484. Wine. Optic, P/D Silvia. **References**: 4, page 29 [1-2]

Line: 484. Wine. **References**: 4, page 33 [1-7]

Line: 484. Cut: 57. Compote. Optic. **References**: 4, page 27 [2-1]

Line: 484. Cut: 369. Cocktail. Optic. **References**: 4, page 14 [1-5]

Line: 484. Cut: 369. Cordial. Optic. **References**: 4, page 14 [1-6]

Line: 484. Cut: 369. Footed Tumbler. 2-3/4 oz. Optic. **References**: 4, page 14 [2-1]

Line: 484. Cut: 369. Footed Tumbler. 4 oz. Optic. **References**: 4, page 14 [2-2]

Line: 484. Cut: 369. Footed Tumbler. 6 oz. Optic. **References**: 4, page 14 [2-3]

Line: 484. Cut: 369. Footed Tumbler. 9 oz. Optic. **References**: 4, page 14 [2-4]

Line: 484. Cut: 369. Footed Tumbler. 12 oz. Optic. **References**: 4, page 14 [2-5]

Line: 484. Cut: 369. Goblet. Optic. **References**: 4, page 14 [1-1]

Line: 484. Cut: 369. Saucer Champagne. Optic. **References**: 4, page 14 [1-2]

Line: 484. Cut: 369. Sherbet. Optic. **References**: 4, page 14 [1-3]

Line: 484. Cut: 369. Wine. Optic. **References**: 4, page 14 [1-4]

Line: 484. Cut: 632. Claret. Optic, D.E. **References**: 4, page 34 [2-4]

Line: 484. Cut: 632. Cocktail. Optic, D.E. **References**: 4, page 34 [2-2]

Line: 484. Cut: 632. Cordial. Optic, D.E. **References**: 4, page 34 [1-2]

Line: 484. Cut: 632. Footed Tumbler. 12 oz. Optic, D.E. **References**: 4, page 34 [2-6]

Line: 484. Cut: 632. Goblet. Optic, D.E. **References**: 4, page 34 [1-1]

Line: 484. Cut: 632. Goblet, D.E. Optic. **References**: 4, page 25 [1-1]

Line: 484. Cut: 632. Parfait. Optic, D.E. **References**: 4, page 34 [2-5]

Line: 484. Cut: 632. Saucer Champagne. Optic, D.E. **References**: 4, page 34 [2-1]

Line: 484. Cut: 632. Sherbet. Optic, D.E. **References**: 4, page 34 [1-3]

Line: 484. Cut: 632. Wine. Optic, D.E. **References**: 4, page 34 [2-3]

Line: 485. Cut: 58. Cocktail. Optic. **References**: 4, page 15 [1-5]

Line: 485. Cut: 58. Compote. Optic. **References**: 4, page 15 [2-6]

Line: 485. Cut: 58. Cordial. Optic. **References**: 4, page 15 [1-6]

Line: 485. Cut: 58. Footed Tumbler. 2-3/4 oz. Optic. **References**: 4, page 15 [2-1]

Line: 485. Cut: 58. Footed Tumbler. 4 oz. Optic. **References**: 4, page 15 [2-2]

Line: 485. Cut: 58. Footed Tumbler. 6 oz. Optic. **References**: 4, page 15 [2-3]

Line: 485. Cut: 58. Footed Tumbler. 9 oz. Optic. **References**: 4, page 15 [2-4]

Line: 485. Cut: 58. Footed Tumbler. 12 oz. Optic. **References**: 4, page 15 [2-5]

Line: 485. Cut: 58. Goblet. Optic. **References**: 4, page 15 [1-1]

Line: 485. Cut: 58. Saucer Champagne. Optic. **References**: 4, page 15 [1-2]

Line: 485. Cut: 58. Sherbet. Optic. **References**: 4, page 15 [1-3]

Line: 485. Cut: 58. Wine. Optic. **References**: 4, page 15 [1-4]

Line: 486. Cut: 62. Cocktail. Optic. **References**: 4, page 16 [1-5]

Line: 486. Cut: 62. Cordial. Optic. **References**: 4, page 16 [1-6]

Line: 486. Cut: 62. Footed Tumbler. 2-3/4 oz. Optic. **References**: 4, page 16 [2-1]

Line: 486. Cut: 62. Footed Tumbler. 4 oz. Optic. **References**: 4, page 16 [2-2]

Line: 486. Cut: 62. Footed Tumbler. 6 oz. Optic. **References**: 4, page 16 [2-3]

Line: 486. Cut: 62. Footed Tumbler. 9 oz. Optic. **References**: 4, page 16 [2-4]

Line: 486. Cut: 62. Footed Tumbler. 12 oz. Optic. **References**: 4, page 16 [2-5]

Line: 486. Cut: 62. Goblet. Optic. **References**: 4, page 16 [1-1]

Line: 486. Cut: 62. Saucer Champagne. Optic. **References**: 4, page 16 [1-2]

Line: 486. Cut: 62. Sherbet. Optic. **References**: 4, page 16 [1-3]

Line: 486. Cut: 62. Wine. Optic. **References**: 4, page 16 [1-4]

Line: 492. Claret. **References**: 4, page 30 [1-6]

Line: 492. Cocktail. **References**: 4, page 30 [1-8]

Line: 492. Cordial. **References**: 4, page 30 [1-4]

Line: 492. Footed Tumbler. 12 oz. **References**: 4, page 30 [1-9]

Line: 492. Goblet. **References**: 4, page 30 [1-1]

Line: 492. Parfait. **References**: 4, page 30 [1-7]

Line: 492. Saucer Champagne. **References**: 4, page 30 [1-2]

Line: 492. Sherbet. **References**: 4, page 30 [1-3]

Line: 492. Wine. **References**: 4, page 30 [1-5]

Line: 492. Cut: 261. Goblet. Optic. **References**: 4, page 24 [1-3]

Line: 492. Cut: 286. Goblet. Optic. **References**: 4, page 24 [1-1]

Line: 492. Cut: 287. Candlestick. Optic. **References**: 4, page 17 [2-1]

Line: 492. Cut: 287. Cocktail. Optic. **References**: 4,

Line: 558. Cut: 220, Star Bottom. Tumbler. **References**: 2, fig. 7 [3-5]

Line: 558. Cut: 250, Plain Bottom. Tumbler. **References**: 2, fig. 7 [3-4]

Line: 558. Cut: 412, Plain Bottom. Tumbler. **References**: 2, fig. 7 [1-1]

Line: 559. Cut: 270, Plain Bottom. Tumbler. **References**: 2, fig. 7 [1-4]

Line: 559. Cut: 300, Plain Bottom. Tumbler. **References**: 2, fig. 7 [2-1]

Line: 559. Cut: 375, Star Bottom. Tumbler. **References**: 2, fig. 7 [1-2]

Line: 578. Cut: 1370. Woodstock. 1305 Dessert-Finger Bowl. 4-1/2 inches diam. **References**: 1968, page 26 [1-8]

Line: 578. Cut: 1370. Woodstock. Cocktail. 5-3/4 oz. 4-3/8 inches tall. **References**: 1968, page 26 [1-4]

Line: 578. Cut: 1370. Woodstock. Cordial. 1-1/2 oz. 3-3/8 inches tall. **References**: 1968, page 26 [1-5]

Line: 578. Cut: 1370. Woodstock. Goblet. 10-1/2 oz. 6-1/8 inches tall. **References**: 1968, page 26 [1-1]

Line: 578. Cut: 1370. Woodstock. Ice Tea. 12-1/2 oz. 6 inches tall. **References**: 1968, page 26 [1-7]

Line: 578. Cut: 1370. Woodstock. Juice. 5-1/2 oz. 4-3/4 inches tall. **References**: 1968, page 26 [1-6]

Line: 578. Cut: 1370. Woodstock. Plate. 7 inches diam. Actually 7-7/8" Dia. **References**: 1968, page 26 [1-9]

Line: 578. Cut: 1370. Woodstock. Plate. 8 inches diam. Actually 8-3/4" Dia. **References**: 1968, page 26 [1-10]

Line: 578. Cut: 1370. Woodstock. Sherbet. 6-1/2 oz. 4-1/2 inches tall. **References**: 1968, page 26 [1-2]

Line: 578. Cut: 1370. Woodstock. Wine. 4-3/4 oz. 5-1/8 inches tall. **References**: 1968, page 26 [1-3]

Line: 619. Star Bottom, Water Tumbler. **References**: 2, fig. 15 [3-4]

Line: 619. Etching: 7. Water Tumbler. **References**: 2, fig. 15 [2-2]

Line: 619. Etching: 14. Water Tumbler. **References**: 2, fig. 15 [2-1]

Line: 619. Etching: 25. Water Tumbler. **References**: 2, fig. 15 [1-3]

Line: 619. Etching: 28. Water Tumbler. **References**: 2, fig. 15 [1-2]

Line: 619. Etching: 36. Water Tumbler. **References**: 2, fig. 15 [1-1]

Line: 619. Etching: 47. Water Tumbler. **References**: 2, fig. 15 [3-1]

Line: 619. Etching: 50. Water Tumbler. **References**: 2, fig. 15 [3-3]

Line: 619. Etching: 55. Water Tumbler. **References**: 2, fig. 15 [3-2]

Line: 619. Etching: 61. Water Tumbler. **References**: 2, fig. 15 [3-5]

Line: 619. Etching: 74. Water Tumbler. **References**: 2, fig. 15 [2-3]

Line: 619. Etching: 76. Water Tumbler. **References**: 2, fig. 15 [2-5]

Line: 619. Etching: 83. Water Tumbler. **References**: 2, fig. 15 [2-4]

Line: 619. Etching: 103. Water Tumbler. **References**: 2, fig. 15 [2-6]

Line: 619. Etching: N90. Water Tumbler. **References**: 2, fig. 15 [1-4]

Line: 619. Etching: 440. Water Tumbler. **References**: 2, fig. 15 [3-0 partial]

Line: 619. Cut: 101. Water Tumbler. **References**: 2, fig. 15 [1-5]

Line: 619. Cut: 360. Water Tumbler. **References**: 2, fig. 15 [1-6]

Line: 627. Cut: 54. Tumbler. **References**: 2, fig. 8 [1-1]

Line: 630. Tumbler. 9-1/2 oz. Optic. **References**: 5-E, page 18 [2-3]

Line: 630. Tumbler. 9-1/2 oz. **References**: 5-E, page 18 [2-4]

Line: 630. Etching: 1. Tumbler. **References**: 5-E, page 18 [1-2]

Line: 630. Etching: 1, Initial and Wreath. Tumbler. **References**: 5-E, page 18 [2-2]

Line: 630. Etching: 24. Tumbler. **References**: 5-E, page 19 [1-2]

Line: 630. Etching: 75. Tumbler. **References**: 5-E, page 19 [1-4]

Line: 630. Etching: 112. Tumbler. **References**: 5-E, page 18 [1-1]

Line: 630. Etching: 283. Tumbler. **References**: 5-E, page 18 [1-3]

Line: 630. Etching: 320. Tumbler. **References**: 5-E, page 18 [1-4]

Line: 630. Etching: 408. Tumbler. **References**: 5-E, page 18 [2-1]

Line: 630. Etching: 600. Scroll Design. Tumbler. **References**: 3, page 4 [3-1]

Line: 630. Etching: 608. Grape Design. Tumbler. 9-1/2 oz. **References**: 3, page 9 [2-3]

Line: 630. Etching: 609. Rose Design. Tumbler. 9-1/2 oz. **References**: 3, page 10 [2-2]

Line: 630. Cut: N. Etching: 8. Tumbler. Optic. **References**: 5-E, page 19 [1-3]

Line: 630. Cut: 90. Tumbler. **References**: 2, fig. 8 [2-1]

Line: 630. Cuts: 94 and N. Etching: 8. Tumbler. **References**: 2, fig. 8 [2-4]

Line: 631. Cut: 59. Half Sham, Tumbler. **References**: 2, fig. 8 [1-3]

Line: 631. Cut: 220. Half Sham, Tumbler. **References**: 2, fig. 8 [3-3]

Line: 632. Cut: 58. Full Sham, Tumbler. **References**: 2, fig. 8 [1-2]

Line: 632. Cut: 66. Full Sham, Tumbler. **References**: 2, fig. 8 [1-4]

Line: 632. Cut: 68. Full Sham, Tumbler. **References**: 2, fig. 8 [1-5]

Line: 632. Cut: 92. Full Sham, Tumbler. **References**: 2, fig. 8 [2-2]

Line: 632. Cuts: 94 and N. Etching: 8. Full Sham, Tumbler. **References**: 2, fig. 8 [2-3]

Line: 632. Cut: 218. Full Sham, Tumbler. **References**: 2, fig. 8 [3-1]

Line: 632. Cut: 219. Full Sham, Tumbler. **References**: 2, fig. 8 [3-2]

Line: 632. Cut: 222. Full Sham, Tumbler. **References**: 2, fig. 8 [3-4]

Line: 636. Tumbler. 9 oz. 4 inches tall. Straight 16 Optic, Regular Weight. **References**: 1982, page 12 [1-3]

Line: 636. Tumbler. 9 oz. 4 inches tall. Plain & Straight 16 Optic, Regular Weight. **References**: 1975/I-75, page 7 [1-3]

Line: 636. Cut: 39. Table Tumbler. 10 oz. 3-3/4 inches tall. Regular Weight. The cut 39 indicates the Flutes at the base of the Tumblers are 1-1/4" high and 1/2" wide. Tumblers Cut 39 have a flat unpolished base. Items available: 14 oz., 12 oz., and 10 oz. Tumbler, 10 oz. Table Tumbler, 7-3/4 oz., 9 oz. Old Fashion. **References**: 1972, page 31 [1-4]; 1975, page 32 [1-4]; 1977, page 43 [1-4]; 1975/I-75, page 12 [1-4]; 1979, page 14 [2-8]

Line: 636. Cut: 43. Table Tumbler. 10 oz. 3-3/4 inches tall. Sham Weight. **References**: 1973, page 36 [3-4]; 1975, page 32 [3-4]; 1982, page 6 [1-8]; 1975/I-75, page 12 [3-4]; 1972, page 31 [3-4]; 1977, page 43 [3-4]

Line: 636. Cut: 45. Table Tumbler. 10 oz. 3-3/4 inches tall. Sham Weight. **References**: 1972, page 31 [2-4]; 1973, page 36 [2-4]; 1975, page 32 [2-4]; 1977, page 43 [2-4]; 1982, page 7 [1-4]; 1975/I-75, page 12 [2-4]

Line: 769. Custard. 7 oz. Handled Ice Tea or Lemonade Glasses. **References**: 5-E, page 15 [1-2]

Line: 799. Cut: 350, Star Bottom. Tumbler. **References**: 2, fig. 7 [2-2]

Line: 799. Cut: 385, Star Bottom. Tumbler. **References**: 2, fig. 7 [2-3]

Line: 799. Cut: 390, Star Bottom. Tumbler. **References**: 2, fig. 7 [2-4]

Line: 799. Cut: 400, Star Bottom. Tumbler. **References**: 2, fig. 7 [2-5]

Line: 900. Optic, P/D Estes. **References**: 4, page 28 [2-3]

Line: 900. Optic. **References**: 4, page 30 [2-4]

Line: 900. Covered Jug. Blue. **References**: 4, page 31 [2-4]

Line: 900. Cut: 57. Covered Jug. Optic. **References**: 4, page 26 [3-3]

Line: 903. Blue. **References**: 4, page 31 [2-5]

Line: 903. Bud Vase. 8 inch. Blue. **References**: 4, page 31 [1-11]

Line: 903. Cocktail. Blue. **References**: 4, page 31 [1-4]

Line: 903. Cordial. Blue. **References**: 4, page 31 [1-5]

Line: 903. Finger Bowl. Blue. **References**: 4, page 31 [2-3]

Line: 903. Footed Tumbler. 9 oz. Blue. **References**: 4, page 31 [1-8]

Line: 903. Goblet. Blue. **References**: 4, page 31 [1-1]

Line: 903. Hi Ball. 9 oz. Blue. **References**: 4, page 31 [1-9]

Line: 903. Hi Ball. 12 oz. Blue. **References**: 4, page 31 [1-10]

Line: 903. Parfait. Blue. **References**: 4, page 31 [1-7]

Line: 903. Saucer Champagne. Blue. **References**: 4, page 31 [1-2]

Line: 903. Sherbet. Blue. **References**: 4, page 31 [1-3]

Line: 903. Wine. Blue. **References**: 4, page 31 [1-6]

Line: 903. Cut: 267. Finger Bowl. **References**: 4, page 25 [3-1]

Line: 903. Cut: 338. Goblet. Plain. **References**: 4, page 24 [2-4]

Line: 903. Cut: 342. Cocktail. **References**: 4, page 22 [1-5]

Line: 903. Cut: 342. Cordial. **References**: 4, page 22 [1-6]

Line: 903. Cut: 342. Footed Tumbler. 2-1/2 oz. **References**: 4, page 22 [2-1]

Line: 903. Cut: 342. Footed Tumbler. 3-1/2 oz. **References**: 4, page 22 [2-2]

Line: 903. Cut: 342. Footed Tumbler. 5 oz. **References**: 4, page 22 [2-3]

Line: 903. Cut: 342. Footed Tumbler. 9 oz. **References**: 4, page 22 [2-4]

Line: 903. Cut: 342. Footed Tumbler. 12 oz. **References**: 4, page 22 [2-5]

Line: 903. Cut: 342. Goblet. **References**: 4, page 22 [1-1]

Line: 903. Cut: 342. Saucer Champagne. **References**: 4, page 22 [1-2]

Line: 903. Cut: 342. Sherbet. **References**: 4, page 22 [1-3]

Line: 903. Cut: 342. Wine. **References**: 4, page 22 [1-4]

Line: 908. Cut: 859. Rennaissance. 1311 Dessert-Finger Bowl. 4-3/4 inches diam. **References**: 1967, page 20 [2-18]; 1969, page 22 [2-18]; 1970, page 23 [2-18]; 1971, page 23 [2-18]

Line: 908. Cut: 859. Rennaissance. Claret. 3-1/2 oz. 4-3/8 inches tall. **References**: 1967, page 20 [2-13]; 1969, page 22 [2-13]; 1970, page 23 [2-13]; 1971, page 23 [2-13]

Line: 908. Cut: 859. Rennaissance. Cocktail. 3 oz. 4-5/8 inches tall. **References**: 1967, page 20 [2-14]; 1969, page 22 [2-14]; 1970, page 23 [2-14]; 1971, page 23 [2-14]

Line: 908. Cut: 859. Rennaissance. Cordial. 1 oz. 3-1/4 inches tall. **References**: 1967, page 20 [2-15]; 1969, page 22 [2-15]; 1970, page 23 [2-15]; 1971, page 23 [2-15]

Line: 908. Cut: 859. Rennaissance. Goblet. 9 oz. 6 inches tall. **References**: 1967, page 20 [2-11]; 1969, page 22 [2-11]; 1970, page 23 [2-11]; 1971, page 23 [2-11]

Line: 908. Cut: 859. Rennaissance. Ice Tea. 10-1/2 oz. 5-5/8 inches tall. **References**: 1967, page 20 [2-17]; 1969, page 22 [2-17]; 1970, page 23 [2-17]; 1971, page 23 [2-17]

Line: 908. Cut: 859. Rennaissance. Juice. 5 oz. 4-3/8 inches tall. **References**: 1967, page 20 [2-16]; 1969, page 22 [2-16]; 1970, page 23 [2-16]; 1971, page 23 [2-16]

Line: 908. Cut: 859. Rennaissance. Plate. 7 inches diam. Actually 7-7/8" Dia. **References**: 1967, page 20 [2-19]; 1969, page 22 [2-19]; 1970, page 23 [2-19]; 1971, page 23 [2-19]

Line: 908. Cut: 859. Rennaissance. Plate. 8 inches diam. Actually 8-3/4" Dia. **References**: 1967, page 20 [2-20]; 1969, page 22 [2-20]; 1970, page 23 [2-20]; 1971, page 23 [2-20]

Line: 908. Cut: 859. Rennaissance. Saucer Champagne. 7 oz. 4-3/4 inches tall. **References**: 1967, page 20 [2-12]; 1969, page 22 [2-12]; 1970, page 23 [2-12]; 1971, page 23 [2-12]

Line: 908. Cut: 879. Waterford. 1311 Dessert-Finger Bowl. 4-3/4 inches diam. **References**: 1967, page 20 [2-8]; 1969, page 22 [2-8]; 1970, page 23 [2-8]; 1971, page 23 [2-8]

Line: 908. Cut: 879. Waterford. Claret. 3-1/2 oz. 4-3/8 inches tall. **References**: 1967, page 20 [2-3]; 1969, page 22 [2-3]; 1970, page 23 [2-3]; 1971, page 23 [2-3]

Line: 908. Cut: 879. Waterford. Cocktail. 3 oz. 4-5/8 inches tall. **References**: 1967, page 20 [2-4]; 1969, page 22 [2-4]; 1970, page 23 [2-4]; 1971, page 23 [2-4]

Line: 908. Cut: 879. Waterford. Cordial. 1 oz. 3-1/4 inches tall. **References**: 1967, page 20 [2-5]; 1969, page 22 [2-5]; 1970, page 23 [2-5]; 1971, page 23 [2-5]

Line: 908. Cut: 879. Waterford. Goblet. 9 oz. 6 inches tall. **References**: 1967, page 20 [2-1]; 1969, page 22 [2-1]; 1970, page 23 [2-1]; 1971, page 23 [2-1]

Line: 908. Cut: 879. Waterford. Ice Tea. 10-1/2 oz. 5-5/8 inches tall. **References**: 1967, page 20 [2-7]; 1969, page 22 [2-7]; 1970, page 23 [2-7]; 1971, page 23 [2-7]

Line: 908. Cut: 879. Waterford. Juice. 5 oz. 4-3/8 inches tall. **References**: 1967, page 20 [2-6]; 1969, page 22 [2-6]; 1970, page 23 [2-6]; 1971, page 23 [2-6]

Line: 908. Cut: 879. Waterford. Plate. 7 inches diam. Actually 7-7/8" Dia. **References**: 1967, page 20 [2-9]; 1969, page 22 [2-9]; 1970, page 23 [2-9]; 1971, page 23 [2-9]

Line: 908. Cut: 879. Waterford. Plate. 8 inches diam. Actually 8-3/4" Dia. **References**: 1967, page 20 [2-10]; 1969, page 22 [2-10]; 1970, page 23 [2-10]; 1971, page 23 [2-10]

Line: 908. Cut: 879. Waterford. Saucer Champagne. 7 oz. 4-3/4 inches tall. **References**: 1967, page 20 [2-2]; 1969, page 22 [2-2]; 1970, page 23 [2-2]; 1971, page 23 [2-2]

Line: 912. Cuts: 121 and 39. Laurel. 1311 Dessert-Finger Bowl. 4-3/4 inches diam. **References**: 1967, page 17 [1-8]; 1968, page 21 [1-8]; 1969, page 21 [1-8]; 1970, page 22 [1-8]; 1971, page 22 [1-8]

Line: 912. Cuts: 121 and 39. Laurel. Claret. 4 oz. 4-3/4 inches tall. **References**: 1967, page 17 [1-3]; 1968, page 21 [1-3]; 1969, page 21 [1-3]; 1970, page 22 [1-3]; 1971, page 22 [1-3]

Line: 912. Cuts: 121 and 39. Laurel. Cocktail. 3-1/2 oz. 4-3/8 inches tall. **References**: 1967, page 17 [1-4]; 1968, page 21 [1-4]; 1969, page 21 [1-4]; 1970, page 22 [1-4]; 1971, page 22 [1-4]

Line: 912. Cuts: 121 and 39. Laurel. Cordial. 1 oz. 3-5/8 inches tall. **References**: 1967, page 17 [1-5]

Line: 912. Cuts: 121 and 39. Laurel. Cordial. 1 oz. 3-5/8 inches tall. **References**: 1968, page 21 [1-5]; 1969, page 21 [1-5]; 1970, page 22 [1-5]; 1971, page 22 [1-5]

Line: 912. Cuts: 121 and 39. Laurel. Goblet. 10 oz. 6-1/4 inches tall. **References**: 1967, page 17 [1-1]; 1968, page 21 [1-1]; 1969, page 21 [1-1]; 1970, page 22 [1-1]; 1971, page 22 [1-1]

Line: 912. Cuts: 121 and 39. Laurel. Ice Tea. 12 oz. 6 inches tall. **References**: 1967, page 17 [1-7]; 1968, page 21 [1-7];x1969, page 21 [1-7]; 1970, page 22 [1-7]; 1971, page 22 [1-7]

Line: 912. Cuts: 121 and 39. Laurel. Juice. 6 oz. 4-5/8 inches tall. **References**: 1967, page 17 [1-6]; 1968, page 21 [1-6]; 1969, page 21 [1-6]; 1970, page 22 [1-6]; 1971, page 22 [1-6]

Line: 912. Cuts: 121 and 39. Laurel. Plate. 7 inches diam. Actually 7-7/8" Dia. **References**: 1967, page 17 [1-9]; 1968, page 21 [1-9]; 1969, page 21 [1-9]; 1970, page 22 [1-9]; 1971, page 22 [1-9]

Line: 912. Cuts: 121 and 39. Laurel. Plate. 8 inches diam. Actually 8-3/4" Dia. **References**: 1967, page 17 [1-10]; 1968, page 21 [1-10]; 1969, page 21 [1-10]; 1970, page 22 [1-10]; 1971, page 22 [1-10]

Line: 912. Cuts: 121 and 39. Laurel. Saucer Champagne. 7-1/2 oz. 5-1/8 inches tall. **References**: 1967, page 17 [1-2]; 1968, page 21 [1-2]; 1969, page 21 [1-2]; 1970, page 22 [1-2]; 1971, page 22 [1-2]

Line: 912. Cut: 139. Dolly Madison-Jane Eyre. 1311 Dessert-Finger Bowl. 4-3/4 inches diam. **References**: 1967, page 17 [2-18]; 1968, page 21 [2-18]; 1969, page 21 [2-18]; 1970, page 22 [2-18]; 1971, page 22 [2-18]

Line: 912. Cut: 139. Dolly Madison-Jane Eyre. Claret. 4 oz. 4-3/4 inches tall. **References**: 1967, page 17 [2-13]; 1968, page 21 [2-13]; 1969, page 21 [2-13]; 1970, page 22 [2-13]; 1971, page 22 [2-13]

Line: 912. Cut: 139. Dolly Madison-Jane Eyre. Cocktail. 3-1/2 oz. 4-3/8 inches tall. **References**: 1967, page 17 [2-14]; 1968, page 21 [2-14]; 1969, page 21 [2-14]; 1970, page 22 [2-14]; 1971, page 22 [2-14]

Line: 912. Cut: 139. Dolly Madison-Jane Eyre.

Cordial. 1 oz. 3-5/8 inches tall. **References**: 1967, page 17 [2-15]; 1968, page 21 [2-15]; 1969, page 21 [2-15]; 1970, page 22 [2-15]; 1971, page 22 [2-15]

Line: 912. Cut: 139. Dolly Madison-Jane Eyre. Goblet. 10 oz. 6-1/4 inches tall. **References**: 1967, page 17 [2-11]; 1968, page 21 [2-11]; 1969, page 21 [2-11]; 1970, page 22 [2-11]; 1971, page 22 [2-11]

Line: 912. Cut: 139. Dolly Madison-Jane Eyre. Ice Tea. 12 oz. 6 inches tall. **References**: 1967, page 17 [2-17]; 1968, page 21 [2-17]; 1969, page 21 [2-17]; 1970, page 22 [2-17]; 1971, page 22 [2-17]

Line: 912. Cut: 139. Dolly Madison-Jane Eyre. Juice. 6 oz. 4-5/8 inches tall. **References**: 1967, page 17 [2-16]; 1968, page 21 [2-16]; 1969, page 21 [2-16]; 1970, page 22 [2-16]; 1971, page 22 [2-16]

Line: 912. Cut: 139. Dolly Madison-Jane Eyre. Plate. 7 inches diam. Actually 7-7/8" Dia. **References**: 1967, page 17 [2-19]; 1968, page 21 [2-19]; 1969, page 21 [2-19]; 1970, page 22 [2-19]; 1971, page 22 [2-19]

Line: 912. Cut: 139. Dolly Madison-Jane Eyre. Plate. 8 inches diam. Actually 8-3/4" Dia. **References**: 1967, page 17 [2-20]; 1968, page 21 [2-20]; 1969, page 21 [2-20]; 1970, page 22 [2-20]; 1971, page 22 [2-20]

Line: 912. Cut: 139. Dolly Madison-Jane Eyre. Saucer Champagne. 7-1/2 oz. 5-1/8 inches tall. **References**: 1967, page 17 [2-12]; 1968, page 21 [2-12]; 1969, page 21 [2-12]; 1970, page 22 [2-12]; 1971, page 22 [2-12]

Line: 912. Cut: 1006. Ramona. 1311 Dessert-Finger Bowl. 4-3/4 inches diam. **References**: 1967, page 17 [2-8]; 1968, page 21 [2-8]; 1969, page 21 [2-8]; 1970, page 22 [2-8]; 1971, page 22 [2-8]

Line: 912. Cut: 1006. Ramona. Claret. 4 oz. 4-3/4 inches tall. **References**: 1967, page 17 [2-3]; 1968, page 21 [2-3]; 1969, page 21 [2-3]; 1970, page 22 [2-3]; 1971, page 22 [2-3]

Line: 912. Cut: 1006. Ramona. Cocktail. 3-1/2 oz. 4-3/8 inches tall. **References**: 1967, page 17 [2-4]; 1968, page 21 [2-4]; 1969, page 21 [2-4]; 1970, page 22 [2-4]; 1971, page 22 [2-4]

Line: 912. Cut: 1006. Ramona. Cordial. 1 oz. 3-5/8 inches tall. **References**: 1967, page 17 [2-5]; 1968, page 21 [2-5]; 1969, page 21 [2-5]; 1970, page 22 [2-5]; 1971, page 22 [2-5]

Line: 912. Cut: 1006. Ramona. Goblet. 10 oz. 6-1/4 inches tall. **References**: 1967, page 17 [2-1]; 1968, page 21 [2-1]; 1969, page 21 [2-1]; 1970, page 22 [2-1]; 1971, page 22 [2-1]

Line: 912. Cut: 1006. Ramona. Ice Tea. 12 oz. 6 inches tall. **References**: 1967, page 17 [2-7]; 1968, page 21 [2-7]; 1969, page 21 [2-7]; 1970, page 22 [2-7]; 1971, page 22 [2-7]

Line: 912. Cut: 1006. Ramona. Juice. 6 oz. 4-5/8 inches tall. **References**: 1967, page 17 [2-6]; 1968, page 21 [2-6]; 1969, page 21 [2-6]; 1970, page 22 [2-6]; 1971, page 22 [2-6]

Line: 912. Cut: 1006. Ramona. Plate. 7 inches diam. Actually 7-7/8" Dia. **References**: 1967, page 17 [2-9]; 1968, page 21 [2-9]; 1969, page 21 [2-9]; 1970, page 22 [2-9]; 1971, page 22 [2-9]

Line: 912. Cut: 1006. Ramona. Plate. 8 inches diam. Actually 8-3/4" Dia. **References**: 1967, page 17 [2-10]; 1968, page 21 [2-10]; 1969, page 21 [2-10]; 1970, page 22 [2-10]; 1971, page 22 [2-10]

Line: 912. Cut: 1006. Ramona. Saucer Champagne. 7-1/2 oz. 5-1/8 inches tall. **References**: 1967, page 17 [2-2]; 1968, page 21 [2-2]; 1969, page 21 [2-2]; 1970, page 22 [2-2]; 1971, page 22 [2-2]

Line: 920. Vase. 10 inch. Blue. **References**: 4, page 31 [3-1]

Line: 922. Etching: 609. Rose Design. Vase. 6-1/2 inch. **References**: 3, page 14 [2-1]

Line: 922. Etching: 609. Rose Design. Vase. 7-1/2 inch. **References**: 3, page 14 [2-2]

Line: 925. Vase. 10 inch. Blue. **References**: 4, page 31 [3-6]

Line: 960. Cut: 43. Newport. 1311 Dessert-Finger Bowl. 4-3/4 inches diam. **References**: 1973, page 20 [1-6]; 1975, page 20 [1-6]; 1977, page 31 [1-6]

Line: 960. Cut: 43. Newport. Cordial. 1-1/4 oz. 3-7/8 inches tall. **References**: 1973, page 20 [1-4]; 1975, page 20 [1-4]; 1977, page 31 [1-4]; 1981, page 2 [1-12]

Line: 960. Cut: 43. Newport. Goblet. 11-1/2 oz. 7 inches tall. **References**: 1973, page 20 [1-1]; 1975, page 20 [1-1]; 1977, page 31 [1-1]; 1981, page 2 [1-9]

Line: 960. Cut: 43. Newport. Ice Tea. 14 oz. 6-1/4 inches tall. **References**: 1973, page 20 [1-5]; 1975, page 20 [1-5]; 1977, page 31 [1-5]

Line: 960. Cut: 43. Newport. Plate. 7 inches diam. Actually 7-7/8" Dia. **References**: 1973, page 20 [1-7]; 1975, page 20 [1-7]; 1977, page 31 [1-7]

Line: 960. Cut: 43. Newport. Plate. 8 inches diam. Actually 8-3/4" Dia. **References**: 1973, page 20 [1-8]; 1975, page 20 [1-8]; 1977, page 31 [1-8]

Line: 960. Cut: 43. Newport. Sherbet. 7 oz. 5-1/4 inches tall. **References**: 1973, page 20 [1-2]; 1975, page 20 [1-2]; 1977, page 31 [1-2]; 1981, page 2 [1-10]

Line: 960. Cut: 43. Newport. Wine. 7 oz. 6 inches tall. **References**: 1973, page 20 [1-3]; 1975, page 20 [1-3]; 1977, page 31 [1-3]; 1967, page 4 [1-6]

Line: 960. Cut: 1433. Cambridge. 1311 Dessert-Finger Bowl. 4-3/4 inches diam. **References**: 1969, page 6 [1-6]; 1970, page 6 [1-6]; 1971, page 6 [1-6]; 1972, page 16 [1-6]; 1973, page 21 [1-6]; 1975, page 21 [1-6]; 1977, page 32 [1-6]; 19686, page 4 [1-6]

Line: 960. Cut: 1433. Cambridge. Cordial. 1-1/4 oz. / 3-7/8" hi. **References**: 1967, page 4 [1-4]; 1968, page 6 [1-4]; 1969, page 6 [1-4]; 1970, page 6 [1-4]; 1971, page 6 [1-4]; 1972, page 16 [1-4]; 1973, page 21 [1-4]; 1975, page 21 [1-4]; 1977, page 32 [1-4]

Line: 960. Cut: 1433. Cambridge. Goblet. 11-1/2 oz. / 7" hi. **References**: 1967, page 4 [1-1]; 1968, page 6 [1-1]; 1969, page 6 [1-1]; 1970, page 6 [1-1]; 1971, page 6 [1-1]; 1972, page 16 [1-1]; 1973, page 21 [1-1]; 1975, page 21 [1-1]; 1977, page 32 [1-1]

Line: 960. Cut: 1433. Cambridge. Ice Tea. 14 oz. / 6-1/4" hi. **References**: 1967, page 4 [1-5]; 1968, page 6 [1-5]; 1969, page 6 [1-5]; 1970, page 6 [1-5]; 1971, page 6 [1-5]; 1972, page 16 [1-5]; 1973, page 21 [1-5]; 1975, page 21 [1-5]; 1977, page 32 [1-5]

Line: 960. Cut: 1433. Cambridge. Plate. 7" / Actually 7-7/8 inch. **References**: 1967, page 4 [1-7]; 1968, page 4 [1-7]; 1969, page 6 [1-7]; 1970, page 6 [1-7]; 1971, page 6 [1-7]; 1972, page 16 [1-7]; 1973, page 21 [1-7]; 1975, page 21 [1-7]; 1977, page 32 [1-7]

Line: 960. Cut: 1433. Cambridge. Plate. 8" / Actually 8-3/4 inch. **References**: 1967, page 4 [1-8]; 1968, page 6 [1-8]; 1969, page 6 [1-8]; 1970, page 6 [1-8]; 1971, page 6 [1-8]; 1972, page 16 [1-8]; 1973, page 21 [1-8]; 1975, page 21 [1-8]; 1977, page 32 [1-8]

Line: 960. Cut: 1433. Cambridge. Sherbet. 7 oz. / 5-1/4" hi. **References**: 1967, page 4 [1-2]; 1968, page 46 [1-2]; 1969, page 6 [1-2]; 1970, page 6 [1-2]; 1971, page 6 [1-2]; 1972, page 16 [1-2]; 1973, page 21 [1-2]; 1975, page 21 [1-2]; 1977, page 32 [1-2]

Line: 960. Cut: 1433. Cambridge. Wine. 7 oz. / 6" hi. **References**: 1967, page 4 [1-3]; 1968, page 6 [1-3]; 1969, page 6 [1-3]; 1970, page 6 [1-3]; 1971, page 6 [1-3]; 1972, page 16 [1-3]; 1973, page 21 [1-3]; 1975, page 21 [1-3]; 1977, page 32 [1-3]

Line: 960. Cut: 1434. Heirloom. 1311 Dessert-Finger Bowl. 4-3/4" Dia. **References**: 1967, page 4 [3-6]; 1968, page 6 [3-6]; 1969, page 6 [2-14]; 1970, page 6 [2-14]; 1971, page 6 [2-14]

Line: 960. Cut: 1434. Heirloom. Cordial. 1-1/4" oz. / 3-7/8" hi. **References**: 1967, page 4 [3-4]; 1968, page 6 [3-4]; 1969, page 6 [2-12]; 1970, page 6 [2-12]; 1971, page 6 [2-12]

Line: 960. Cut: 1434. Heirloom. Goblet. 11-1/2 oz. / 7" hi. **References**: 1967, page 4 [3-1]; 1968, page 6 [3-1]; 1969, page 6 [2-9]; 1970, page 6 [2-9]; 1971, page 6 [2-9]

Line: 960. Cut: 1434. Heirloom. Ice Tea. 14 oz. / 6-1/4" hi. **References**: 1967, page 4 [3-5]; 1968, page 6 [3-5]; 1969, page 6 [2-13]; 1970, page 6 [2-13]; 1971, page 6 [2-13]

Line: 960. Cut: 1434. Heirloom. Plate. 7" / Actually 7-7/8 inch. **References**: 1967, page 4 [3-7]; 1968, page 6 [3-7]; 1969, page 6 [2-15]; 1970, page 6 [2-15]; 1971, page 6 [2-15]

Line: 960. Cut: 1434. Heirloom. Plate. 8" / Actually 8-3/4 inch. **References**: 1967, page 4 [3-8]; 1968, page 6 [3-8]; 1969, page 6 [2-16]; 1970, page 6 [2-16]; 1971, page 6 [2-16]

Line: 960. Cut: 1434. Heirloom. Sherbet. 7 oz. / 5-1/4" hi. **References**: 1967, page 4 [3-2]; 1968, page 6 [3-2]; 1969, page 6 [2-10]; 1970, page 6 [2-10]; 1971, page 6 [2-10]

Line: 960. Cut: 1434. Heirloom. Wine. 7 oz. / 6" hi. **References**: 1967, page 4 [3-3]; 1968, page 6 [3-3]; 1969, page 6 [2-11]; 1970, page 6 [2-11]; 1971, page 6 [2-11]

Line: 960. Cut: 1435. Old Master. 1311 Dessert-Finger Bowl. 4-3/4" Dia. **References**: 1967, page 4 [2-6]; 1968, page 6 [2-6]; 1969, page 6 [2-6]; 1970, page 6 [2-6]; 1971, page 6 [2-6]; 1972, page 16 [1-14]; 1973, page 21 [1-14]; 1975, page 21 [1-14]; 1977, page 32 [1-14]

Line: 960. Cut: 1435. Old Master. Cordial. 1-1/4 oz. / 3-7/8" hi. **References**: 1967, page 4 [2-4]; 1968, page 6 [2-4]; 1969, page 6 [2-4]; 1970, page 6 [2-4]; 1971, page 6 [2-4]; 1972, page 16 [1-12]; 1973, page 21 [1-12]; 1975, page 21 [1-12]; 1977, page 32 [1-12]; 1981, page 2 [1-16]

Line: 960. Cut: 1435. Old Master. Goblet. 11-1/2 oz. / 7" hi. **References**: 1967, page 4 [2-1]; 1968, page 6 [2-1]; 1969, page 6 [2-1]; 1970, page 6 [2-1]; 1971, page 6 [2-1]; 1972, page 16 [1-9]; 1973, page 21 [1-9]; 1975, page 21 [1-9]; 1977, page 32 [1-9]; 1981, page 2 [1-13]

Line: 960. Cut: 1435. Old Master. Ice Tea. 14 oz. / 6-1/4" hi. **References**: 1967, page 4 [2-5]; 1968, page 6 [2-5]; 1969, page 6 [2-5]; 1970, page 6 [2-5]; 1971, page 6 [2-5]; 1972, page 16 [1-13]; 1973, page 21 [1-13]; 1975, page 21 [1-13]; 1977, page 32 [1-13]

Line: 960. Cut: 1435. Old Master. Plate. 7 inch / Actually 7-7/8 inch. **References**: 1967, page 4 [2-7]; 1968, page 6 [2-7]; 1969, page 6 [2-7]; 1970, page 6 [2-7]; 1971, page 6 [2-7]; 1972, page 16 [1-15]; 1973, page 21 [1-15]; 1975, page 21 [1-15]; 1977, page 32 [1-15]

Line: 960. Cut: 1435. Old Master. Plate. 8 inch / Actually 8-3/4 inch. **References**: 1967, page 4 [2-8]; 1968, page 6 [2-8]; 1969, page 6 [2-8]; 1970, page 6 [2-8]; 1971, page 6 [2-8]; 1972, page 16 [1-16]; 1973, page 21 [1-16]; 1975, page 21 [1-16]; 1977, page 32 [1-16]

Line: 960. Cut: 1435. Old Master. Sherbet. 7 oz. / 5-1/4" hi. **References**: 1967, page 4 [2-2]; 1968, page 6 [2-2]; 1969, page 6 [2-2]; 1970, page 6 [2-2]; 1971, page 6 [2-2]; 1972, page 16 [1-10]; 1973, page 21 [1-10]; 1975, page 21 [1-10]; 1977, page 32 [1-10]; 1981, page 2 [1-14]

Line: 960. Cut: 1435. Old Master. Wine. 4 oz. / 6" hi. **References**: 1967, page 4 [2-3]; 1968, page 6 [2-3]; 1969, page 6 [2-3]; 1970, page 6 [2-3]; 1971, page 6 [2-3]; 1972, page 16 [1-11]; 1973, page 21 [1-11]; 1975, page 21 [1-11]; 1977, page 32 [1-11]; 1981, page 2 [1-15]

Line: 960. Cut: 1436. Ardmore. 1311 Dessert-Finger Bowl. 4-3/4 inches diam. **References**: 1968, page 7 [1-6]; 1969, page 7 [1-6]; 1970, page 7 [1-6]; 1971, page 7 [1-6]; 1972, page 16 [2-6]; 1973, page 21 [2-6]; 1975, page 21 [2-6]; 1977, page 32 [2-6]

Line: 960. Cut: 1436. Ardmore. Cordial. 1-1/4 oz. 3-7/8 inches tall. **References**: 1968, page 7 [1-4]; 1969, page 7 [1-4]; 1970, page 7 [1-4]; 1971, page 7 [1-4]; 1972, page 16 [2-4]; 1973, page 21 [2-4]; 1975, page 21 [2-4]; 1977, page 32 [2-4]; 1981, page 2 [1-4]

Line: 960. Cut: 1436. Ardmore. Goblet. 11-1/2 oz. 7 inches tall. **References**: 1968, page 7 [1-1]; 1969, page 7 [1-1]; 1970, page 7 [1-1]; 1971, page 7 [1-1]; 1972, page 16 [2-1]; 1973, page 21 [2-1]; 1975, page 21 [2-1]; 1977, page 32 [2-1]; 1981, page 2 [1-1]

Line: 960. Cut: 1436. Ardmore. Ice Tea. 14 oz. 6-1/4 inches tall. **References**: 1968, page 7 [1-5]; 1969, page 7 [1-5]; 1970, page 7 [1-5]; 1971, page 7 [1-5]; 1972, page 16 [2-5]; 1973, page 21 [2-5]; 1975, page 21 [2-5]; 1977, page 32 [2-5]

Line: 960. Cut: 1436. Ardmore. Plate. 7 inches diam. Actually 7-7/8" Dia. **References**: 1968, page 7 [1-7]; 1969, page 7 [1-7]; 1970, page 7 [1-7]; 1971, page 7 [1-7]; 1972, page 16 [2-7]; 1973, page 21 [2-7]; 1975, page 21 [2-7]; 1977, page 32 [2-7]

Line: 960. Cut: 1436. Ardmore. Plate. 8 inches diam. Actually 8-3/4" Dia. **References**: 1968, page 7 [1-8]; 1969, page 7 [1-8]; 1970, page 7 [1-8]; 1971, page 7 [1-8]; 1972, page 16 [2-8]; 1973, page 21 [2-8]; 1975, page 21 [2-8]; 1977, page 32 [2-8]

Line: 960. Cut: 1436. Ardmore. Sherbet. 7 oz. 5-1/4 inches tall. **References**: 1968, page 7 [1-2]; 1969, page 7 [1-2]; 1970, page 7 [1-2]; 1971, page 7 [1-2]; 1972, page 16 [2-2]; 1973, page 21 [2-2]; 1975, page 21 [2-2]; 1977, page 32 [2-2]; 1981, page 2 [1-2]

Line: 960. Cut: 1436. Ardmore. Wine. 7 oz. 6 inches tall. **References**: 1968, page 7 [1-3]; 1969, page 7 [1-3]; 1970, page 7 [1-3]; 1971, page 7 [1-3]; 1972, page 16 [2-3]; 1973, page 21 [2-3]; 1975, page 21 [2-3]; 1977, page 32 [2-3]; 1981, page 2 [1-3]

Line: 960. Cut: 1436. Gold Brocade. Plate. 8 inches diam. Actually 8-3/4" Dia., 2 Gold Bands. **References**: 1975, page 21 [2-16]; 1977, page 32 [2-16]

Line: 960. Cut: 1437. Radiance. 1311 Dessert-Finger Bowl. 4-3/4 inches diam. **References**: 1968, page 7 [2-6]; 1969, page 7 [2-6]; 1970, page 7 [2-6]; 1971, page 7 [2-6]

Line: 960. Cut: 1437. Radiance. Cordial. 1-1/4 oz. 3-7/8 inches tall. **References**: 1968, page 7 [2-4]; 1969, page 7 [2-4]; 1970, page 7 [2-4]; 1971, page 7 [2-4]

Line: 960. Cut: 1437. Radiance. Goblet. 11-1/2 oz. 7 inches tall. **References**: 1968, page 7 [2-1]; 1969, page 7 [2-1]; 1970, page 7 [2-1]; 1971, page 7 [2-1]

Line: 960. Cut: 1437. Radiance. Ice Tea. 14 oz. 6-1/4 inches tall. **References**: 1968, page 7 [2-5]; 1969, page 7 [2-5]; 1970, page 7 [2-5]; 1971, page 7 [2-5]

Line: 960. Cut: 1437. Radiance. Plate. 7 inches diam. Actually 7-7/8" Dia. **References**: 1968, page 7 [2-7]; 1969, page 7 [2-7]; 1970, page 7 [2-7]; 1971, page 7 [2-7]

Line: 960. Cut: 1437. Radiance. Plate. 8 inches diam. Actually 8-3/4" Dia. **References**: 1968, page 7 [2-8]; 1969, page 7 [2-8]; 1970, page 7 [2-8]; 1971, page 7 [2-8]

Line: 960. Cut: 1437. Radiance. Sherbet. 7 oz. 5-1/4 inches tall. **References**: 1968, page 7 [2-2]; 1969, page 7 [2-2]; 1970, page 7 [2-2]; 1971, page 7 [2-2]

Line: 960. Cut: 1437. Radiance. Wine. 7 oz. 6 inches tall. **References**: 1968, page 7 [2-3]; 1969, page 7 [2-3]; 1970, page 7 [2-3]; 1971, page 7 [2-3]

Line: 960. Cut: 1438. Gold Brocade. 1311 Dessert-Finger Bowl. 4-3/4 inches diam. With 2 Gold Bands. **References**: 1970, page 7 [2-14]; 1971, page 7 [2-14]; 1972, page 16 [2-14]; 1973, page 21 [2-14]; 1975, page 21 [2-14]; 1977, page 32 [2-14]

Line: 960. Cut: 1438. Gold Brocade. Cordial. 1-1/4 oz. 3-7/8 inches tall. With 2 Gold Bands. **References**: 1970, page 7 [2-12]; 1971, page 7 [2-12]; 1972, page 16 [2-12]; 1973, page 21 [2-12]; 1975, page 21 [2-12]; 1977, page 32 [2-12]; 1981, page 2 [1-8]

Line: 960. Cut: 1438. Gold Brocade. Goblet. 11-1/2 oz. 7 inches tall. With 2 Gold Bands. **References**: 1970, page 7 [2-9]; 1971, page 7 [2-9]; 1972, page 16 [2-9]; 1973, page 21 [2-9]; 1975, page 21 [2-9]; 1977, page 32 [2-9]; 1981, page 2 [1-5]

Line: 960. Cut: 1438. Gold Brocade. Ice Tea. 14 oz. 6-1/4 inches tall. With 2 Gold Bands. **References**: 1970, page 7 [2-13]; 1971, page 7 [2-13]; 1972, page 16 [2-13]; 1973, page 21 [2-13]; 1975, page 21 [2-13]; 1977, page 32 [2-13]

Line: 960. Cut: 1438. Gold Brocade. Plate. 7 inches diam. With 2 Gold Bands, Actually 7-7/8" Dia. **References**: 1970, page 7 [2-15]; 1971, page 7 [2-15]; 1972, page 16 [2-15]; 1973, page 21 [2-15]; 1975, page 21 [2-15]; 1977, page 32 [2-15]

Line: 960. Cut: 1438. Gold Brocade. Plate. 8 inches diam. With 2 Gold Bands, Actually 8-3/4" Dia. **References**: 1970, page 7 [2-16]; 1971, page 7 [2-16]; 1972, page 16 [2-16]; 1973, page 21 [2-16]

Line: 960. Cut: 1438. Gold Brocade. Sherbet. 7 oz. 5-1/4 inches tall. With 2 Gold Bands. **References**: 1970, page 7 [2-10]; 1971, page 7 [2-10]; 1972, page 16 [2-10]; 1973, page 21 [2-10]; 1975, page 21 [2-10]; 1977, page 32 [2-10]; 1970, page 7 [2-11]

Line: 960. Cut: 1438. Gold Brocade. Wine. 7 oz. 6 inches tall. With 2 Gold Bands. **References**: 1971, page 7 [2-11]; 1972, page 16 [2-11]; 1973, page 21 [2-11]; 1975, page 21 [2-11]; 1977, page 32 [2-11]; 1981, page 2 [1-7]

Line: 960. Cut: 1438. Radiance. 1311 Dessert-Finger Bowl. 4-3/4 inches diam. With 2 Gold Bands. **References**: 1969, page 7 [2-14]

Line: 960. Cut: 1438. Radiance. Cordial. 1-1/4 oz. 3-7/8 inches tall. With 2 Gold Bands. **References**: 1969, page 7 [2-12]

Line: 960. Cut: 1438. Radiance. Goblet. 11-1/2 oz. 7 inches tall. With 2 Gold Bands. **References**: 1969, page 7 [2-9]

Line: 960. Cut: 1438. Radiance. Ice Tea. 14 oz. 6-1/4 inches tall. With 2 Gold Bands. **References**: 1969, page 7 [2-13]

Line: 960. Cut: 1438. Radiance. Plate. 7 inches diam. With 2 Gold Bands, Actually 7-7/8" Dia. **References**: 1969, page 7 [2-15]

Line: 960. Cut: 1438. Radiance. Plate. 8 inches diam. With 2 Gold Bands, Actually 8-3/4" Dia.

References: 1969, page 7 [2-16]

Line: 960. Cut: 1438. Radiance. Sherbet. 7 oz. 5-1/4 inches tall. With 2 Gold Bands. **References**: 1969, page 7 [2-10]

Line: 960. Cut: 1438. Radiance. Wine. 7 oz. 6 inches tall. With 2 Gold Bands. **References**: 1969, page 7 [2-11]

Line: 968. Covered Candy. 7-1/8 inches tall. Black Cover, Crystal Bowl, Black Foot. **References**: 1978, page 14 [1-B]

Line: 970. Cut: 1444. America. Cordial. 2 oz. 5-1/4 inches tall. **References**: 1977, page 27 [1-8]

Line: 970. Cut: 1444. America. Goblet. 9-1/2 oz. 8-1/2 inches tall. **References**: 1977, page 27 [1-5]

Line: 970. Cut: 1444. America. Sherbet. 7-1/2 oz. 6-1/2 inches tall. **References**: 1977, page 27 [1-6]

Line: 970. Cut: 1444. America. Wine. 5 oz. 7-1/4 inches tall. **References**: 1977, page 27 [1-7]

Line: 970. Cut: 1444. Heritage. Cordial. 2 oz. 5-1/4 inches tall. **References**: 1976, page 2 [1-4]

Line: 970. Cut: 1444. Heritage. Goblet. 9-1/2 oz. 8-1/2 inches tall. **References**: 1976, page 2 [1-1]

Line: 970. Cut: 1444. Heritage. Sherbet. 7-1/2 oz. 6-1/2 inches tall. **References**: 1976, page 2 [1-2]

Line: 970. Cut: 1444. Heritage. Wine. 5 oz. 7-1/4 inches tall. **References**: 1976, page 2 [1-3]

Line: 970. Cut: 1445. America. Cordial. 2 oz. 5-1/4 inches tall. **References**: 1976, page 2 [1-8]

Line: 970. Cut: 1445. America. Goblet. 9-1/2 oz. 8-1/2 inches tall. **References**: 1976, page 2 [1-5]

Line: 970. Cut: 1445. America. Sherbet. 7-1/2 oz. 6-1/2 inches tall. **References**: 1976, page 2 [1-6]

Line: 970. Cut: 1445. America. Wine. 5 oz. 7-1/4 inches tall. **References**: 1976, page 2 [1-7]

Line: 970. Cut: 1445. Heritage. Cordial. 2 oz. 5-1/4 inches tall. **References**: 1977, page 27 [1-4]

Line: 970. Cut: 1445. Heritage. Goblet. 9-1/2 oz. 8-1/2 inches tall. **References**: 1977, page 27 [1-1]

Line: 970. Cut: 1445. Heritage. Sherbet. 7-1/2 oz. 6-1/2 inches tall. **References**: 1977, page 27 [1-2]

Line: 970. Cut: 1445. Heritage. Wine. 5 oz. 7-1/4 inches tall. **References**: 1977, page 27 [1-3]

Line: 970. Cut: 1446. Wicker. Cordial. 2 oz. 5-1/4 inches tall. **References**: 1976, page 3 [1-4]; 1977, page 27 [1-4]

Line: 970. Cut: 1446. Wicker. Goblet. 9-1/2 oz. 8-1/2 inches tall. **References**: 1976, page 3 [1-1]; 1977, page 27 [1-1]

Line: 970. Cut: 1446. Wicker. Sherbet. 7-1/2 oz. 6-1/2 inches tall. **References**: 1976, page 3 [1-2]; 1977, page 27 [1-2]

Line: 970. Cut: 1446. Wicker. Wine. 5 oz. 7-1/4 inches tall. **References**: 1976, page 3 [1-3]; 1977, page 27 [1-3]

Line: 970. Cut: 1447. Sunburst. Cordial. 2 oz. 5-1/4 inches tall. **References**: 1976, page 3 [1-8]; 1977, page 27 [1-8]

Line: 970. Cut: 1447. Sunburst. Goblet. 9-1/2 oz. 8-1/2 inches tall. **References**: 1976, page 3 [1-5]; 1977, page 27 [1-5]

Line: 970. Cut: 1447. Sunburst. Sherbet. 7-1/2 oz. 6-1/2 inches tall. **References**: 1976, page 3 [1-6]; 1977, page 27 [1-6]

Line: 970. Cut: 1447. Sunburst. Wine. 5 oz. 7-1/4 inches tall. **References**: 1976, page 3 [1-7]; 1977, page 27 [1-7]

Line: 971. Moderne. Cordial. 2 oz. 5-1/4 inches tall. **References**: 1976, page 9 [1-4]

Line: 971. Moderne. Cordial. 2 oz. 5-1/4 inches tall. Crytal Optic. **References**: 1977, page 19 [1-4]

Line: 971. Moderne. Goblet. 9-1/2 oz. 8-1/2 inches tall. **References**: 1976, page 9 [1-1]

Line: 971. Moderne. Goblet. 9-1/2 oz. 8-1/2 inches tall. Crytal Optic. **References**: 1977, page 19 [1-1]

Line: 971. Moderne. Sherbet. 7-1/2 oz. 6-1/2 inches tall. **References**: 1976, page 9 [1-2]

Line: 971. Moderne. Sherbet. 7-1/2 oz. 6-1/2 inches tall. Crytal Optic. **References**: 1977, page 19 [1-2]

Line: 971. Moderne. Wine. 5 oz. 7-1/4 inches tall. **References**: 1976, page 9 [1-3]

Line: 971. Moderne. Wine. 5 oz. 7-1/4 inches tall. Crytal Optic. **References**: 1977, page 19 [1-3]

Line: 972. Cut: 1448. Chalice. Cordial. 3 oz. 5-5/8 inches tall. **References**: 1976, page 4 [1-4]; 1977, page 29 [1-4]; 1981, page 1 [1-4]

Line: 972. Cut: 1448. Chalice. Goblet. 13 oz. 7-1/2 inches tall. **References**: 1976, page 4 [1-1]; 1977, page 29 [1-1]; 1981, page 1 [1-1]

Line: 972. Cut: 1448. Chalice. Sherbet. 9 oz. 6 inches tall. **References**: 1976, page 4 [1-2]; 1977, page 29 [1-2]; 1981, page 1 [1-2]

Line: 972. Cut: 1448. Chalice. Wine. 7-1/2 oz. 6-1/2 inches tall. **References**: 1976, page 4 [1-3]; 1977, page 29 [1-3]; 1981, page 1 [1-3]

Line: 972. Cut: 1448. Tapestry. Cordial. 3 oz. 5-5/8 inches tall. **References**: 1981, page 1 [1-8]

Line: 972. Cut: 1448. Tapestry. Goblet. 13 oz. 7-1/2 inches tall. **References**: 1981, page 1 [1-5]

Line: 972. Cut: 1448. Tapestry. Sherbet. 9 oz. 6 inches tall. **References**: 1981, page 1 [1-6]

Line: 972. Cut: 1448. Tapestry. Wine. 7-1/2 oz. 6-1/2 inches tall. **References**: 1981, page 1 [1-7]

Line: 972. Cut: 1449. Tapestry. Cordial. 3 oz. 5-5/8 inches tall. **References**: 1976, page 4 [1-8]; 1977, page 29 [1-8]

Line: 972. Cut: 1449. Tapestry. Goblet. 13 oz. 7-1/2 inches tall. **References**: 1976, page 4 [1-5]; 1977, page 29 [1-5]

Line: 972. Cut: 1449. Tapestry. Sherbet. 9 oz. 6 inches tall. **References**: 1976, page 4 [1-6]; 1977, page 29 [1-6]

Line: 972. Cut: 1449. Tapestry. Wine. 7-1/2 oz. 6-1/2 inches tall. **References**: 1976, page 4 [1-7]; 1977, page 29 [1-7]

Line: 972. Cut: 1463. Coronet. Cordial. 3 oz. 5-5/8 inches tall. **References**: 1982, page 2 [1-4]

Line: 972. Cut: 1463. Coronet. Goblet. 13 oz. 7-1/2 inches tall. **References**: 1982, page 2 [1-1]

Line: 972. Cut: 1463. Coronet. Ice Tea. 14 oz. 6-1/2 inches tall. **References**: 1982, page 2 [1-5]

Line: 972. Cut: 1463. Coronet. Sherbet. 9 oz. 6 inches tall. **References**: 1982, page 2 [1-2]

Line: 972. Cut: 1463. Coronet. Wine. 7-1/2 oz. 6-1/2 inches tall. **References**: 1982, page 2 [1-3]

Line: 972. Cut: 1463. Garland. Cordial. 3 oz. 5-5/8 inches tall. **References**: 1982, page 2 [2-4]

Line: 972. Cut: 1463. Garland. Goblet. 13 oz. 7-1/2 inches tall. **References**: 1982, page 2 [2-1]

Line: 972. Cut: 1463. Garland. Ice Tea. 14 oz. 6-1/2 inches tall. **References**: 1982, page 2 [2-5]

Line: 972. Cut: 1463. Garland. Sherbet. 9 oz. 6 inches tall. **References**: 1982, page 2 [2-2]

Line: 972. Cut: 1463. Garland. Wine. 7-1/2 oz. 6-1/2 inches tall. **References**: 1982, page 2 [2-3]

Line: 972. Cut: 1463. Regency. Cordial. 3 oz. 5-5/8 inches tall. **References**: 1982, page 2 [2-9]

Line: 972. Cut: 1463. Regency. Goblet. 13 oz. 7-1/2 inches tall. **References**: 1982, page 2 [2-6]

Line: 972. Cut: 1463. Regency. Ice Tea. 14 oz. 6-1/2 inches tall. **References**: 1982, page 2 [2-10]

Line: 972. Cut: 1463. Regency. Sherbet. 9 oz. 6 inches tall. **References**: 1982, page 2 [2-7]

Line: 972. Cut: 1463. Regency. Wine. 7-1/2 oz. 6-1/2 inches tall. **References**: 1982, page 2 [2-8]

Line: 974. Cut: 1450. Classic. Cordial. 2-1/4 oz. 5-1/4 inches tall. **References**: 1976, page 5 [1-8]; 1977, page 30 [1-8]

Line: 974. Cut: 1450. Classic. Goblet. 10 oz. 7-1/2 inches tall. **References**: 1976, page 5 [1-5]; 1977, page 30 [1-5]

Line: 974. Cut: 1450. Classic. Sherbet. 6-1/2 oz. 5-1/2 inches tall. **References**: 1976, page 5 [1-6]; 1977, page 30 [1-6]

Line: 974. Cut: 1450. Classic. Wine. 6 oz. 6-5/8 inches tall. **References**: 1976, page 5 [1-7]; 1977, page 30 [1-7]

Line: 974. Cut: 1451. Brittany. Cordial. 2-1/4 oz. 5-1/4 inches tall. **References**: 1976, page 5 [1-4]; 1977, page 30 [1-4]

Line: 974. Cut: 1451. Brittany. Goblet. 10 oz. 7-1/2 inches tall. **References**: 1976, page 5 [1-1]; 1977, page 30 [1-1]

Line: 974. Cut: 1451. Brittany. Sherbet. 6-1/2 oz. 5-1/2 inches tall. **References**: 1976, page 5 [1-2]; 1977, page 30 [1-2]

Line: 974. Cut: 1451. Brittany. Wine. 6 oz. 6-5/8 inches tall. **References**: 1976, page 5 [1-3]; 1977, page 30 [1-3]

Line: 975. Sculpture. Bowl. 13 oz. 4-1/2 inches diam. **References**: 1976, page 12 [1-6]

Line: 975. Sculpture. Double Old Fashion. 12 oz. 3-7/8 inches tall. **References**: 1976, page 12 [1-3]

Line: 975. Sculpture. Footed Goblet. 14 oz. 5-1/2 inches tall. **References**: 1976, page 12 [1-5]

Line: 975. Sculpture. Goblet. 17 oz. 5-3/4 inches tall. **References**: 1976, page 12 [1-1]

Line: 975. Sculpture. Hi Ball. 12-1/2 oz. 5-1/4 inches tall. **References**: 1976, page 12 [1-2]

Line: 975. Sculpture. Juice. 6 oz. 4-1/8 inches tall. **References**: 1976, page 12 [1-4]

Line: 976. Reflection. Cordial. 2-1/4 oz. 5-1/4 inches tall. **References**: 1976, page 8 [1-4]

Line: 976. Reflection. Cordial. 2-1/4 oz. 5-1/4 inches tall. Crytal Optic. **References**: 1977, page 18 [1-4]

Line: 976. Reflection. Cordial. Colors: Yellow, Charm Blue, Lime, Crystal, Brown. **References**: 1980, page 5 [1-4]

Line: 976. Reflection. Goblet. 13 oz. 7-3/4 inches tall. **References**: 1976, page 8 [1-1]

Line: 976. Reflection. Goblet. 13 oz. 7-3/4 inches tall. Crytal Optic. **References**: 1977, page 18 [1-1]

Line: 976. Reflection. Goblet. Colors: Yellow, Charm Blue, Lime, Crystal, Brown. **References**: 1980, page 5 [1-1]

Line: 976. Reflection. Sherbet. 9 oz. 5-3/8 inches tall. **References**: 1976, page 8 [1-2]

Line: 976. Reflection. Sherbet. 9 oz. 5-3/8 inches tall. Crytal Optic. **References**: 1977, page 18 [1-2]

Line: 976. Reflection. Sherbet. Colors: Yellow, Charm Blue, Lime, Crystal, Brown. **References**: 1980, page 5 [1-2]

Line: 976. Reflection. Wine. 5-3/4 oz. 6-5/8 inches tall. **References**: 1976, page 8 [1-3]

Line: 976. Reflection. Wine. 7 oz. 6-5/8 inches tall. Crytal Optic. **References**: 1977, page 18 [1-3]

Line: 976. Reflection. Wine. Colors: Yellow, Charm Blue, Lime, Crystal, Brown. **References**: 1980, page 5 [1-3]

Line: 978. Fascination. Cordial. 3 oz. 5-5/8 inches tall. **References**: 1976, page 10 [1-4]

Line: 978. Fascination. Cordial. 3 oz. 5-5/8 inches tall. Crytal Optic. **References**: 1977, page 20 [1-4]

Line: 978. Fascination. Goblet. 14 oz. 7-7/8 inches tall. **References**: 1976, page 10 [1-1]

Line: 978. Fascination. Goblet. 14 oz. 7-7/8 inches tall. Crytal Optic. **References**: 1977, page 20 [1-1]

Line: 978. Fascination. Sherbet. 9 oz. 5-1/2 inches tall. **References**: 1976, page 10 [1-2]

Line: 978. Fascination. Sherbet. 9 oz. 5-1/2 inches tall. Crytal Optic. **References**: 1977, page 20 [1-2]

Line: 978. Fascination. Wine. 5-3/4 oz. 6-1/2 inches tall. **References**: 1976, page 10 [1-3]

Line: 978. Fascination. Wine. 5-3/4 oz. 6-1/2 inches tall. Crytal Optic. **References**: 1977, page 20 [1-3]

Line: 981. Cut: 43. Coronation. Cordial. Gold Encrustation. **References**: 1980, page 5 [2-4]

Line: 981. Cut: 43GB. Coronation. Cordial. 2-1/2 oz. 5-1/8 inches tall. **References**: 1981, page 2 [2-4]

Line: 981. Cut: 43. Coronation. Goblet. Gold Encrustation. **References**: 1980, page 5 [2-1]

Line: 981. Cut: 43GB. Coronation. Goblet. 13-1/2 oz. 7-3/4 inches tall. **References**: 1981, page 2 [2-1]

Line: 981. Cut: 43. Coronation. Sherbet. Gold Encrustation. **References**: 1980, page 5 [2-2]

Line: 981. Cut: 43GB. Coronation. Sherbet. 9 oz. 5-3/8 inches tall. **References**: 1981, page 2 [2-2]

Line: 981. Cut: 43. Coronation. Wine. Gold Encrustation. **References**: 1980, page 5 [2-3]

Line: 981. Cut: 43GB. Coronation. Wine. 8 oz. 6-3/4 inches tall. **References**: 1981, page 2 [2-3]

Line: 981. Cut: 1452. Rosalynn. Cordial. 2-1/2 oz. 5-1/8 inches tall. **References**: 1977, page 26 [1-4]

Line: 981. Cut: 1452. Rosalynn. Cordial. 2-1/2 oz. 5-1/8 inches tall. **References**: 1981, page 2 [2-12]

Line: 981. Cut: 1452. Rosalynn. Goblet. 13-1/2 oz. 7-3/4 inches tall. **References**: 1977, page 26 [1-1]; 1981, page 2 [2-9]

Line: 981. Cut: 1452. Rosalynn. Sherbet. 9 oz. 5-3/8 inches tall. **References**: 1977, page 26 [1-2]; 1981, page 2 [2-10]

Line: 981. Cut: 1452. Rosalynn. Wine. 8 oz. 6-3/4 inches tall. **References**: 1977, page 26 [1-3]; 1981, page 2 [2-11]

Line: 981. Cut: 1453. Majestic. Cordial. 2-1/2 oz. 5-1/8 inches tall. **References**: 1977, page 26 [1-8]; 1981, page 2 [2-8]

Line: 981. Cut: 1453. Majestic. Goblet. 13-1/2 oz. 7-3/4 inches tall. **References**: 1977, page 26 [1-5]; 1981, page 2 [2-5]

Line: 981. Cut: 1453. Majestic. Sherbet. 9 oz. 5-3/8 inches tall. **References**: 1977, page 26 [1-6]; 1981, page 2 [2-6]

Line: 981. Cut: 1453. Majestic. Wine. 8 oz. 6-3/4 inches tall. **References**: 1977, page 26 [1-7]; 1981, page 2 [2-7]

Line: 982. Cut: 1445, Dorchester. Elite Collection. Cordial. 2 oz. 4-3/4 inches tall. **References**: 1978, page 2 [1-4]

Line: 982. Cut: 1445, Dorchester. Elite Collection. Goblet. 13-1/2 oz. 7-1/2 inches tall. **References**: 1978, page 2 [1-1]

Line: 982. Cut: 1445, Dorchester. Elite Collection. Sherbet. 8 oz. 5-3/8 inches tall. **References**: 1978, page 2 [1-2]

Line: 982. Cut: 1445, Dorchester. Elite Collection. Wine. 7 oz. 6-3/8 inches tall. **References**: 1978, page 2 [1-3]

Line: 982. Cut: 1454, Grande Baroque. Elite Collection. Cordial. 2 oz. 4-3/4 inches tall. **References**: 1978, page 2 [1-8]

Line: 982. Cut: 1454, Grande Baroque. Elite Collection. Goblet. 13-1/2 oz. 7-1/2 inches tall. **References**: 1978, page 2 [1-5]

Line: 982. Cut: 1454, Grande Baroque. Elite Collection. Sherbet. 8 oz. 5-3/8 inches tall. **References**: 1978, page 2 [1-6]

Line: 982. Cut: 1454, Grande Baroque. Elite Collection. Wine. 7 oz. 6-3/8 inches tall. **References**: 1978, page 2 [1-7]

Line: 10-10. Vase. 10 inches tall. Lead Crystal. **References**: 1978, page 15 [1-3]

Line: 1102. Custard. 6-1/2 oz. Handled Ice Tea or Lemonade Glasses. **References**: 5-E, page 15 [1-1]

Line: 1107. Custard. 5 oz. Handled Ice Tea or Lemonade Glasses. **References**: 5-E, page 15 [1-3]

Line: 1202. Ale. 6 oz. **References**: 5-E, page 6 [Listed]

Line: 1202. Brandy. 3/4 oz. **References**: 5-E, page 6 [1-2]

Line: 1202. Brandy. 1 oz. **References**: 5-E, page 6 [Listed]

Line: 1202. Champagne. 5 oz. **References**: 5-E, page 6 [Listed]

Line: 1202. Claret. 4 oz. **References**: 5-E, page 6 [Listed]

Line: 1202. Cordial. 1 oz. **References**: 5-E, page 6 [1-1]

Line: 1202. Cordial. 1/2 oz. **References**: 5-E, page 6 [Listed]

Line: 1202. Egg. 4 oz. **References**: 5-E, page 9 [2-1]

Line: 1202. Goblet. 7 oz. **References**: 5-E, page 6 [Listed]

Line: 1202. Goblet. 8-1/2 oz. **References**: 5-E, page 6 [1-4][Listed]

Line: 1202. Goblet. 11 oz. **References**: 5-E, page 6 [Listed]

Line: 1202. Goblet. 10 oz. **References**: 5-E, page 6 [Listed]

Line: 1202. Large Liquor. 1-1/2 oz. **References**: 5-E, page 6 [Listed]

Line: 1202. Port. 3 oz. **References**: 5-E, page 6 [1-3]

Line: 1202. S.S. Goblet. 10 oz. **References**: 5-E, page 6 [Listed]

Line: 1202. Sherbert. 5 oz. Optic. **References**: 5-E, page 7 [2-1]

Line: 1202. Sherry. 1-3/4 oz. **References**: 5-E, page 6 [Listed]

Line: 1202. Wine. 2-1/2 oz. **References**: 5-E, page 6 [Listed]

Line: 1202. Etching: 320. Wine. 2-1/2 oz. **References**: 5-E, page 16 [2-3]

Line: 1202. Etching: 412. Wine. 2-1/2 oz. **References**: 5-E, page 16 [2-1]

Line: 1205. Export Beer. 7 oz. **References**: 5-E, page 8 [2-1]

Line: 1207. Champagne. 7-1/2 oz. **References**: 5-E, page 5 [1-3]

Line: 1208. Brandy. 12 oz. 4-3/8 inches tall. **References**: 1980, page 3 [1-3]

Line: 1208. Beer Series. Beer Goblet. 17-1/2 oz. 5-3/4 inches tall. Plain Crystal. **References**: 1978, page 9 [2-2]

Line: 1208. Beer Series. Beer Goblet. 17-1/2 oz. 5-3/4 inches tall. **References**: 1979, page 11 [2-3]

Line: 1209. Champagne. 5-1/2 oz. **References**: 5-E, page 8 [2-2]

Line: 1211. Peacock Optic. Brandy w/ Capacity Line. 2 oz. 3-3/4 inches tall. 3/4 oz. to line.

References: 1975/I-75, page 3 [3-1]

Line: 1211. Peacock Optic. Cordial. 2 oz. 4 inches tall. **References**: 1975/I-75, page 4 [3-1]

Line: 1219. Sherry Port. 5-1/4 oz. 5-1/8 inches tall. **References**: 1975/I-75, page 5 [1-2]

Line: 1235. Parfait Whiskey Sour. 6-1/2 oz. 6-1/4 inches tall. **References**: 1975/I-75, page 5 [1-3]

Line: 1235. Tulip Champagne. 8-1/2 oz. 8-1/4 inches tall. **References**: 1975/I-75, page 5 [2-3]

Line: 1235. Wine Goblet. 13-1/2 oz. 7 inches tall. **References**: 1975/I-75, page 5 [3-2]

Line: 1235. Dundee. Beverage. 13 oz. 5 inches tall. Crystal Full Sham. **References**: 1978, page 7 [3-3]; 1979, page 16 [3-3]

Line: 1235. Dundee. Old Fashion. 10 oz. 4 inches tall. Crystal Full Sham. **References**: 1978, page 7 [3-4]; 1979, page 16 [3-4]

Line: 1235. Epicure Collection. 1305 Dessert-Finger Bowl. 4-1/2" Dia. Plain Crystal, (No Cutting). **References**: 1967, page 10 [2-7]; 1969, page 17 [1-8]; 1970, page 18 [1-8]; 1971, page 18 [1-8]; 1972, page 27 [1-8]; 1973, page 32 [1-8]

Line: 1235. Epicure Collection. Beverage. 15 oz. 5 inches tall. **References**: 1972, page 13 [L-3]; 1973, page 5 [1-12]; 1975/I-75, page 10 [3-1]

Line: 1235. Epicure Collection. Brandy Inhaler. 22 oz. 6 inches tall. **References**: 1972, page 13 [ML]; 1972, page 13 [ML]; 1973, page 5 [1-11]; 1975, page 5 [1-9]; 1977, page 5 [1-9]

Line: 1235. Epicure Collection. Cocktail. 5-1/2 oz. / 4-5/8" hi. Plain Crystal. **References**: 1967, page 10 [2-3]; 1967, page 23 [L-2]; 1968, page 29 [L-2]; 1969, page 17 [1-3]; 1969, page 27 [L-2]; 1970, page 18 [1-3]; 1970, page 29 [BL]; 1971, page 18 [1-3]; 1971, page 29 [BL]; 1972, page 13 [BL]; 1972, page 27 [1-3]; 1973, page 5 [1-4]; 1973, page 32 [1-3]; 1975, page 5 [1-4]; 1977, page 5 [1-4]; 1975/I-75, page 10 [4-2]

Line: 1235. Epicure Collection. Continental Beer. 14 oz. 8-1/8 inches tall. **References**: 1967, page 23 [R-4]; 1968, page 29 [R-4]; 1969, page 27 [R-4]; 1970, page 29 [L-3]; 1971, page 29 [L-3]; 1972, page 13 [L-2]; 1973, page 5 [1-10]; 1975, page 5 [1-8]; 1977, page 5 [1-8]; 1975/I-75, page 10 [2-1]

Line: 1235. Epicure Collection. Cordial. 2 oz. / 4-1/2" hi. Plain Crystal. **References**: 1967, page 10 [2-4]; 1969, page 17 [1-4]; 1970, page 18 [1-4]; 1971, page 18 [1-4]; 1972, page 27 [1-4]; 1973, page 32 [1-4]

Line: 1235. Epicure Collection. Cordial. 2 oz. 4-1/2 inches tall. **References**: 1967, page 23 [R-2]; 1968, page 29 [R-2]; 1969, page 27 [R-2]; 1970, page 29 [BM]; 1971, page 29 [BR]; 1972, page 13 [BR]; 1975, page 5 [1-5]; 1977, page 5 [1-5]; 1975/I-75, page 10 [4-3]

Line: 1235. Epicure Collection. Cordial. 2 oz. 4-1/2 inches tall. Plain Lead Crystal. **References**: 1973, page 5 [1-5]

Line: 1235. Epicure Collection. Dessert-Champagne. 7-1/2 oz. 5-1/8 inches tall. **References**: 1972, page 13 [M]; 1975, page 5 [1-3]; 1977, page 5 [1-3]; 1975/I-75, page 10 [2-2]

Line: 1235. Epicure Collection. Dessert-Champagne. 7-1/2 oz. 5-1/8 inches tall. Plain Lead Crystal. **References**: 1973, page 5 [1-3]

Line: 1235. Epicure Collection. Goblet. 12 oz. / 7" hi. Plain Crystal. **References**: 1967, page 10 [2-1]; 1969, page 17 [1-1]; 1970, page 18 [1-1]; 1971, page 18 [1-1]; 1972, page 27 [1-1]; 1973, page 5 [1-1]; 1973, page 32 [1-1]

Line: 1235. Epicure Collection. Goblet. 12 oz. 7 inches tall. **References**: 1967, page 23 [L-1]; 1968, page 29 [L-1]; 1969, page 27 [L-1]; 1970, page 29 [L-1]; 1971, page 29 [L-1]; 1972, page 13 [L-1]; 1975, page 5 [1-1]; 1977, page 5 [1-1]; 1975/I-75, page 10 [1-1]

Line: 1235. Epicure Collection. Ice Tea. 12 oz. / 6-1/4" hi. Plain Crystal. **References**: 1967, page 10 [2-6]; 1969, page 17 [1-7]; 1970, page 18 [1-7]; 1971, page 18 [1-7]; 1972, page 27 [1-7]; 1973, page 5 [1-8]; 1973, page 32 [1-7]; 1967, page 10 [2-5]

Line: 1235. Epicure Collection. Ice Tea. 12 oz. 6-1/4 inches tall. **References**: 1967, page 23 [R-3]; 1968, page 29 [R-3]; 1969, page 27 [R-3]; 1970, page 29 [R-2]; 1971, page 29 [R-2]; 1972, page 13 [R-3]; 1975, page 5 [1-6]; 1977, page 5 [1-6]; 1975/I-75, page 10 [3-4]

Line: 1235. Epicure Collection. Juice. 5 oz. 4-5/8 inches tall. **References**: 1967, page 23 [L-3]; 1968, page 29 [L-3]; 1969, page 27 [L-3]; 1970, page 29 [BR]; 1971, page 29 [R-4]; 1972, page 13 [R-4]; 1975/I-75, page 10 [4-4]

Line: 1235. Epicure Collection. Juice. 5 oz. 4-1/2 inches tall. Plain Crystal. **References**: 1969, page 17 [1-6]; 1970, page 18 [1-6]; 1971, page 18 [1-6]; 1972, page 27 [1-6]; 1973, page 5 [1-7]; 1973, page 32 [1-6]

Line: 1235. Epicure Collection. Old Fashion. 11-1/2 oz. 3-3/4 inches tall. **References**: 1972, page 13 [L-4]; 1975/I-75, page 10 [4-1]

Line: 1235. Epicure Collection. Old Fashion. 11-1/2 oz. 3-3/4 inches tall. Plain Lead Crystal. **References**: 1973, page 5 [1-13]

Line: 1235. Epicure Collection. Parfait Whiskey Sour. 7 oz. 6-1/4 inches tall. Plain Crystal. **References**: 1969, page 17 [1-5]; 1970, page 18 [1-5]; 1971, page 18 [1-5]; 1972, page 27 [1-5]; 1973, page 32 [1-5]

Line: 1235. Epicure Collection. Parfait-Whiskey Sour. 7 oz. 6-1/4 inches tall. **References**: 1968, page 29 [L-2]; 1970, page 29 [L-2]; 1970, page 29 [L-2]; 1971, page 29 [L-2]; 1972, page 13 [MR]; 1975/I-75, page 10 [3-3]

Line: 1235. Epicure Collection. Parfait-Whiskey Sour. 7 oz. 6-1/4 inches tall. Plain Lead Crystal. **References**: 1973, page 5 [1-6]

Line: 1235. Epicure Collection. Peach Champagne. 24 oz. 8-1/2 inches tall. **References**: 1967, page 23 [L-4]; 1968, page 29 [L-4]; 1969, page 27 [L-4]; 1970, page 29 [L-3]; 1971, page 29 [R-3]; 1972, page 13 [R-2]; 1975, page 5 [1-7]; 1977, page 5 [1-7]; 1975/I-75, page 10 [2-3]

Line: 1235. Epicure Collection. Peach Champagne. 24 oz. 8-1/2 inches tall. Plain Lead Crystal. **References**: 1973, page 5 [1-9]

Line: 1235. Epicure Collection. Plate. 7" / 7-7/8" Dia. Plain Crystal, (No Cutting). **References**: 1967, page 10 [2-8]; 1969, page 17 [1-9]; 1970, page 18 [1-9]; 1971, page 18 [1-9]; 1972, page 27 [1-9]; 1973, page 32 [1-9]

Line: 1235. Epicure Collection. Plate. 8" / 8-3/4" Dia. Plain Crystal, (No Cutting). **References**: 1967, page 10 [2-9]; 1969, page 17 [1-10]; 1970, page 18 [1-10]; 1971, page 18 [1-10]; 1972, page 27 [1-10]; 1973, page 32 [1-10]

Line: 1235. Epicure Collection. Sherbet. 7-1/2 oz. / 5-1/8" hi. Plain Crystal. **References**: 1967, page 10 [2-2]; 1969, page 17 [1-2]; 1969, page 27 [R-1]; 1970, page 18 [1-2]; 1970, page 29 [R-1]; 1971, page 18 [1-2]; 1972, page 27 [1-2]; 1973, page 32 [1-2]

Line: 1235. Epicure Collection. Sherbet. 7-1/2 oz. 5-1/8 inches tall. **References**: 1967, page 23 [R-1]; 1968, page 29 [R-1]; 1971, page 29 [L-4]

Line: 1235. Epicure Collection. Vintage Wine Goblet. 14 oz. 7 inches tall. **References**: 1971, page 29 [R-1]; 1972, page 13 [R-1]; 1975, page 5 [1-2]; 1977, page 5 [1-2]; 1975/I-75, page 10 [1-2]

Line: 1235. Epicure Collection. Vintage Wine Goblet. 14 oz. 7 inches tall. Plain Lead Crystal. **References**: 1973, page 5 [1-2]

Line: 1235. Juliet. Cocktail. 5-1/2 oz. / 4-5/8" hi. Platinum Band. **References**: 1967, page 10 [1-4]; 1969, page 19 [1-4]; 1970, page 20 [1-4]; 1971, page 20 [1-4]; 1972, page 28 [1-4]; 1973, page 33 [1-4]

Line: 1235. Juliet. Cordial. 2 oz. / 4-1/2" hi. Platinum Band. **References**: 1967, page 10 [1-5]; 1969, page 19 [1-5]; 1970, page 20 [1-5]; 1971, page 20 [1-5]; 1972, page 28 [1-5]; 1973, page 33 [1-5]; 1975, page 29 [1-4]; 1977, page 40 [1-4]

Line: 1235. Juliet. Goblet. 12 oz. / 7" hi. Platinum Band. **References**: 1967, page 10 [1-1]; 1969, page 19 [1-1]; 1970, page 20 [1-1]; 1971, page 20 [1-1]; 1972, page 28 [1-1]; 1973, page 33 [1-1]; 1975, page 29 [1-1]; 1977, page 40 [1-1]

Line: 1235. Juliet. Ice Tea. 12 oz. / 6-1/4" hi. Platinum Band. **References**: 1967, page 10 [1-7]; 1969, page 19 [1-8]; 1970, page 20 [1-8]; 1971, page 20 [1-8]; 1972, page 28 [1-8]; 1973, page 33 [1-8]; 1975, page 29 [1-5]; 1977, page 40 [1-5]

Line: 1235. Juliet. Juice. 5 oz. / 4-1/2" hi. Platinum Band. **References**: 1967, page 10 [1-6]; 1969, page 19 [1-7]; 1970, page 20 [1-7]; 1971, page 20 [1-7]; 1972, page 28 [1-7]; 1973, page 33 [1-7]

Line: 1235. Juliet. Parfait Whiskey Sour. 7 oz. 6-1/4 inches tall. Platinum Band. **References**: 1969, page 19 [1-6]; 1970, page 20 [1-6]; 1971, page 20 [1-6]; 1972, page 28 [1-6]; 1973, page 33 [1-6]

Line: 1235. Juliet. Plate. 7" / Actually 7-7/8" Dia. Platinum Band. **References**: 1967, page 10 [1-8]; 1969, page 19 [1-9]; 1970, page 20 [1-9]; 1971, page 20 [1-9]; 1972, page 28 [1-9]; 1973, page 33 [1-9]; 1975, page 29 [1-6]; 1977, page 40 [1-6];x

Line: 1235. Juliet. Plate. 8" / Actually 8-3/4" Dia. Platinum Band. **References**: 1967, page 10 [1-9]; 1969, page 19 [1-10]; 1970, page 20 [1-10]; 1971, page 20 [1-10]; 1972, page 28 [1-10]; 1973, page 33 [1-10]; 1975, page 29 [1-7]; 1977, page 40 [1-7]

Line: 1235. Juliet. Sherbet. 7-1/2 oz. / 5-1/8" hi. Platinum Band. **References**: 1967, page 10 [1-2]; 1969, page 19 [1-2]; 1970, page 20 [1-2]; 1971, page 20 [1-2]; 1972, page 28 [1-2]; 1973, page 33 [1-2]; 1975, page 29 [1-2]; 1977, page 40 [1-2]

Line: 1235. Juliet. Wine. 7 oz. / 5-7/8" hi. Platinum Band. **References**: 1967, page 10 [1-3]; 1969, page 19 [1-3]; 1970, page 20 [1-3]; 1971, page 20 [1-3]; 1972, page 28 [1-3]; 1973, page 33 [1-3]; 1975, page 29 [1-3]; 1977, page 40 [1-3]

Line: 1235. Musette. Cordial. 2 oz. 4-1/2 inches tall. Platinum Band. **References**: 1975, page 29 [1-18]; 1977, page 40 [1-18]

Line: 1235. Musette. Goblet. 12 oz. 7 inches tall. Platinum Band. **References**: 1975, page 29 [1-15]; 1977, page 40 [1-15]

Line: 1235. Musette. Ice Tea. 12 oz. 6-1/4 inches tall. Platinum Band. **References**: 1975, page 29 [1-19]; 1977, page 40 [1-19]

Line: 1235. Musette. Plate. 7 inches diam. Platinum Band, Actually 7-7/8" Dia. **References**: 1975, page 29 [1-20]; 1977, page 40 [1-20]

Line: 1235. Musette. Plate. 8 inches diam. Platinum Band, Actually 8-3/4" Dia. **References**: 1975, page 29 [1-21]; 1977, page 40 [1-21]

Line: 1235. Musette. Sherbet. 7-1/2 oz. 5-1/8 inches tall. Platinum Band. **References**: 1975, page 29 [1-16]; 1977, page 40 [1-16]

Line: 1235. Musette. Wine. 7 oz. 5-7/8 inches tall. Platinum Band. **References**: 1975, page 29 [1-17]; 1977, page 40 [1-17]

Line: 1235. Palm Optic. Brandy Inhaler. 12 oz. 4-5/8 inches tall. **References**: 1982, page 9 [1-6]

Line: 1235. Palm Optic. Brandy Inhaler. 22 oz. 6 inches tall. **References**: 1982, page 9 [2-7]

Line: 1235. Palm Optic. Cocktail. 5-1/2 oz. 4-3/4 inches tall. **References**: 1982, page 9 [2-5]

Line: 1235. Palm Optic. Continental Beer. 14 oz. 8-1/8 inches tall. **References**: 1982, page 9 [2-10]; 1982, page 9 [2-10]

Line: 1235. Palm Optic. Cordial. 2 oz. 4-1/2 inches tall. **References**: 1982, page 9 [2-6]; 1975/I-75, page 2 [3-2]

Line: 1235. Palm Optic. Dessert-Champagne. 7-1/2 oz. 5-1/8 inches tall. **References**: 1982, page 9 [2-4]

Line: 1235. Palm Optic. Goblet. 12 oz. 7 inches tall. **References**: 1982, page 9 [2-2]

Line: 1235. Palm Optic. Ice Tea. 12 oz. 6-1/4 inches tall. **References**: 1982, page 9 [2-8]

Line: 1235. Palm Optic. Juice. 5 oz. 4-5/8 inches tall. **References**: 1982, page 9 [2-1]

Line: 1235. Palm Optic. Martini. 5-1/2 oz. 6 inches tall. **References**: 1982, page 9 [1-1]

Line: 1235. Palm Optic. Parfait Whiskey Sour. 6-1/2 oz. 6-1/4 inches tall. **References**: 1982, page 9 [1-4]; 1975/I-75, page 2 [2-2]

Line: 1235. Palm Optic. Peach Champagne. 24 oz. 8-1/2 inches tall. **References**: 1982, page 9 [2-9]

Line: 1235. Palm Optic. Vintage Wine Goblet. 14 oz. 7 inches tall. **References**: 1982, page 9 [2-3]

Line: 1235. Peacock Optic. Tulip Champagne. 8-1/2 oz. 8-1/4 inches tall. **References**: 1975/I-75, page 3 [1-2]; 1975/I-75, page 3 [1-1]

Line: 1235. Peacock Optic. Wine Goblet. 10-1/2 oz. 6-5/8 inches tall. **References**: 1975/I-75, page 4 [1-2]

Line: 1235. Puritan. Cocktail. 5-1/2 oz. / 4-5/8" hi. Gold Band. **References**: 1967, page 10 [1-13]; 1969, page 19 [1-14]; 1970, page 20 [1-14]; 1971, page 20 [1-14]; 1972, page 28 [1-14]; 1973, page 33 [1-14]

Line: 1235. Puritan. Cordial. 2 oz. / 4-1/2" hi. Gold Band. **References**: 1967, page 10 [1-14]; 1969, page 19 [1-15]; 1970, page 20 [1-15]; 1971, page 20 [1-15]; 1972, page 28 [1-15]; 1973, page 33 [1-15]; 1975, page 29 [1-11]; 1977, page 40 [1-11]

Line: 1235. Puritan. Goblet. 12 oz. / 7" hi. Gold Band. **References**: 1967, page 10 [1-10]; 1969, page 19 [1-11]; 1970, page 20 [1-11]; 1971, page 20 [1-11]; 1972, page 28 [1-11]; 1973, page 33 [1-11]; 1975, page 29 [1-8]; 1977, page 40 [1-8]

Line: 1235. Puritan. Ice Tea. 12 oz. / 6-1/4" hi. Gold Band. **References**: 1967, page 10 [1-16]; 1969, page 19 [1-18]; 1970, page 20 [1-18]; 1971, page 20 [1-18]; 1972, page 28 [1-18]; 1973, page 33 [1-18]; 1975, page 29 [1-12]; 1977, page 40 [1-12]

Line: 1235. Puritan. Juice. 5 oz. / 4-1/2" hi. Gold Band. **References**: 1967, page 10 [1-15]; 1967, page 10 [1-17]; 1970, page 20 [1-17]; 1971, page 20 [1-17]; 1972, page 28 [1-17]; 1973, page 33 [1-17]

Line: 1235. Puritan. Parfait Whiskey Sour. 7 oz. 6-1/4 inches tall. Gold Band. **References**: 1969, page 19 [1-16]; 1970, page 20 [1-16]; 1971, page 20 [1-16]; 1972, page 28 [1-16]; 1973, page 33 [1-16]

Line: 1235. Puritan. Plate. 7" / Actually 7-7/8" Dia. Gold Band. **References**: 1967, page 10 [1-17]; 1967, page 10 [1-19]; 1970, page 20 [1-19]; 1971, page 20 [1-19]; 1972, page 28 [1-19]; 1973, page 33 [1-19]; 1975, page 29 [1-13]; 1977, page 40 [1-13]

Line: 1235. Puritan. Plate. 8" / Actually 8-3/4" Dia. Gold Band. **References**: 1967, page 10 [1-18]; 1969, page 19 [1-20]; 1970, page 20 [1-20]; 1971, page 20 [1-20]; 1972, page 28 [1-20]; 1973, page 33 [1-20]; 1975, page 29 [1-14]; 1977, page 40 [1-14]

Line: 1235. Puritan. Sherbet. 7-1/2 oz. / 5-1/8" hi. Gold Band. **References**: 1967, page 10 [1-11]; 1969, page 19 [1-12]; 1970, page 20 [1-12]; 1971, page 20 [1-12]; 1972, page 28 [1-12]; 1973, page 33 [1-12]; 1975, page 29 [1-9]; 1977, page 40 [1-9]

Line: 1235. Puritan. Wine. 7 oz. / 5-7/8" hi. Gold Band. **References**: 1967, page 10 [1-12]; 1969, page 19 [1-13]; 1970, page 20 [1-13]; 1971, page 20 [1-13]; 1972, page 28 [1-13]; 1973, page 33 [1-13]; 1975, page 29 [1-10]; 1977, page 40 [1-10]

Line: 1235. Victoria. Cordial. 2 oz. 4-1/2 inches tall. Gold Band. **References**: 1975, page 29 [1-25]; 1977, page 40 [1-25]

Line: 1235. Victoria. Goblet. 12 oz. 7 inches tall. Gold Band. **References**: 1975, page 29 [1-22]; 1977, page 40 [1-22]

Line: 1235. Victoria. Ice Tea. 12 oz. 6-1/4 inches tall. Gold Band. **References**: 1975, page 29 [1-26]; 1977, page 40 [1-26]

Line: 1235. Victoria. Plate. 7 inches diam. Gold Band, Actually 7-7/8" Dia. **References**: 1975, page 29 [1-27]; 1977, page 40 [1-27]

Line: 1235. Victoria. Plate. 8 inches diam. Gold Band, Actually 8-3/4" Dia. **References**: 1975, page 29 [1-28]; 1977, page 40 [1-28]

Line: 1235. Victoria. Sherbet. 7-1/2 oz. 5-1/8 inches tall. Gold Band. **References**: 1975, page 29 [1-23]; 1977, page 40 [1-23]

Line: 1235. Victoria. Wine. 7 oz. 5-7/8 inches tall. Gold Band. **References**: 1975, page 29 [1-24]; 1977, page 40 [1-24]

Line: 1235. Cut: 1406. Musette. Cocktail. 5-1/2 oz. / 4-5/8" hi. Platinum Band. **References**: 1967, page 10 [1-22]; 1969, page 19 [1-24]; 1970, page 20 [1-24]; 1971, page 20 [1-24]; 1972, page 28 [1-24]; 1973, page 33 [1-24]

Line: 1235. Cut: 1406. Musette. Cordial. 2 oz. / 4-1/2" hi. Platinum Band. **References**: 1967, page 10 [1-23]; 1969, page 19 [1-25]; 1970, page 20 [1-25]; 1971, page 20 [1-25]; 1972, page 28 [1-25]; 1973, page 33 [1-25]

Line: 1235. Cut: 1406. Musette. Goblet. 12 oz. / 7" hi. Platinum Band. **References**: 1967, page 10 [1-19]; 1969, page 19 [1-21]; 1970, page 20 [1-21]; 1971, page 20 [1-21]; 1972, page 28 [1-21]; 1973, page 33 [1-21]

Line: 1235. Cut: 1406. Musette. Ice Tea. 12 oz. / 6-1/4" hi. Platinum Band. **References**: 1967, page 10 [1-25]; 1969, page 19 [1-28]; 1970, page 20 [1-28]; 1971, page 20 [1-28]; 1972, page 28 [1-28]; 1973, page 33 [1-28]

Line: 1235. Cut: 1406. Musette. Juice. 5 oz. / 4-1/2" hi. Platinum Band. **References**: 1967, page 10 [1-24]; 1969, page 19 [1-27]; 1970, page 20 [1-27]

Line: 1235. Cut: 1406. Musette. Juice. 5 oz. 4-1/2 inches tall. Platinum Band. **References**: 1971, page 20 [1-27]; 1972, page 28 [1-27]; 1973, page 33 [1-27]

Line: 1235. Cut: 1406. Musette. Parfait Whiskey Sour. 7 oz. 6-1/4 inches tall. Platinum Band. **References**: 1969, page 19 [1-26]; 1970, page 20 [1-26]; 1971, page 20 [1-26]; 1972, page 28 [1-26]; 1973, page 33 [1-26]

Line: 1235. Cut: 1406. Musette. Plate. 7" / Actually 7-7/8" hi. Platinum Band. **References**: 1967,

page 10 [1-26]; 1969, page 19 [1-29]; 1970, page 20 [1-29]; 1971, page 20 [1-29]; 1972, page 28 [1-29]; 1973, page 33 [1-29]

Line: 1235. Cut: 1406. Musette. Plate. 8" / Actually 8-3/4" hi. Platinum Band. **References**: 1967, page 10 [1-27]; 1969, page 19 [1-30]; 1970, page 20 [1-30]; 1971, page 20 [1-30]; 1972, page 28 [1-30]; 1973, page 33 [1-30]

Line: 1235. Cut: 1406. Musette. Sherbet. 7-1/2 oz. / 5-1/8" hi. Platinum Band. **References**: 1967, page 10 [1-20]; 1969, page 19 [1-22]; 1970, page 20 [1-22]; 1971, page 20 [1-22]; 1972, page 28 [1-22]; 1973, page 33 [1-22]

Line: 1235. Cut: 1406. Musette. Wine. 7 oz. / 5-7/8 hi. Platinum Band. **References**: 1967, page 10 [1-21]; 1969, page 19 [1-23]; 1970, page 20 [1-23]; 1971, page 20 [1-23]; 1972, page 28 [1-23]; 1973, page 33 [1-23]

Line: 1235. Cut: 1406. Victoria. Cocktail. 5-1/2 oz. / 4-5/8" hi. Gold Band. **References**: 1967, page 10 [1-31]; 1969, page 19 [1-34]; 1970, page 20 [1-34]; 1971, page 20 [1-34]; 1972, page 28 [1-34]; 1973, page 33 [1-34]

Line: 1235. Cut: 1406. Victoria. Cordial. 2 oz. / 4-1/2" hi. Gold Band. **References**: 1967, page 10 [1-32]; 1969, page 19 [1-35]; 1970, page 20 [1-35]; 1971, page 20 [1-35]; 1972, page 28 [1-35]; 1973, page 33 [1-35]

Line: 1235. Cut: 1406. Victoria. Goblet. 12 oz. / 7" hi. Gold Band. **References**: 1967, page 10 [1-28]; 1969, page 19 [1-31]; 1970, page 20 [1-31]; 1971, page 20 [1-31]; 1972, page 28 [1-31]; 1973, page 33 [1-31]

Line: 1235. Cut: 1406. Victoria. Ice Tea. 12 oz. / 6-1/4" hi. Gold Band. **References**: 1967, page 10 [1-34]; 1969, page 19 [1-38]; 1970, page 20 [1-38]; 1971, page 20 [1-38]; 1972, page 28 [1-38]; 1973, page 33 [1-38]

Line: 1235. Cut: 1406. Victoria. Juice. 5 oz. / 4-1/2" hi. Gold Band. **References**: 1967, page 10 [1-33]; 1969, page 19 [1-37]; 1970, page 20 [1-37]; 1971, page 20 [1-37]; 1972, page 28 [1-37]; 1973, page 33 [1-37]

Line: 1235. Cut: 1406. Victoria. Parfait Whiskey Sour. 7 oz. 6-1/4 inches tall. Gold Band. **References**: 1969, page 19 [1-6]; 1970, page 20 [1-36]; 1971, page 20 [1-36]; 1972, page 28 [1-36]; 1973, page 33 [1-36]

Line: 1235. Cut: 1406. Victoria. Plate. 7" / Actually 7-7/8" Dia. Gold Band. **References**: 1967, page 10 [1-35]; 1969, page 19 [1-39]; 1970, page 20 [1-39]; 1971, page 20 [1-39]; 1972, page 28 [1-39]; 1973, page 33 [1-39]

Line: 1235. Cut: 1406. Victoria. Plate. 8" / Actually 8-3/4" Dia. Gold Band. **References**: 1967, page 10 [1-36]; 1969, page 19 [1-40]; 1970, page 20 [1-40]; 1971, page 20 [1-40]; 1972, page 28 [1-40]; 1973, page 33 [1-40]

Line: 1235. Cut: 1406. Victoria. Sherbet. 7-1/2 oz. / 5-1/8" hi. Gold Band. **References**: 1967, page 10 [1-29]; 1969, page 19 [1-32]; 1970, page 20 [1-32]; 1971, page 20 [1-32]; 1972, page 28 [1-32]; 1973, page 33 [1-32]

Line: 1235. Cut: 1406. Victoria. Wine. 7 oz. / 5-7/8" hi. Gold Band. **References**: 1967, page 10 [1-30]; 1969, page 19 [1-33]; 1970, page 20 [1-33]; 1971, page 20 [1-33]; 1972, page 28 [1-33]; 1973, page 33 [1-33]

Line: 1235. Cut: 1406. Windsor. Cocktail. 5-1/2 oz. / 4-5/8" hi. NOT BANDED. **References**: 1967, page 10 [1-40]

Line: 1235. Cut: 1406. Windsor. Cordial. 2 oz. / 4-1/2" hi. NOT BANDED. **References**: 1967, page 10 [1-41]

Line: 1235. Cut: 1406. Windsor. Goblet. 12 oz. / 7" hi. NOT BANDED. **References**: 1967, page 10 [1-37]

Line: 1235. Cut: 1406. Windsor. Ice Tea. 12 oz. / 6-1/4" hi. NOT BANDED. **References**: 1967, page 10 [1-43]

Line: 1235. Cut: 1406. Windsor. Juice. 5 oz. / 4-1/2" hi. NOT BANDED. **References**: 1967, page 10 [1-42]

Line: 1235. Cut: 1406. Windsor. Plate. 7" / Actually 7-7/8" Dia. NOT BANDED. **References**: 1967, page 10 [1-44]

Line: 1235. Cut: 1406. Windsor. Plate. 8" / Actually 8-3/4" Dia. NOT BANDED. **References**: 1967, page 10 [1-45]

Line: 1235. Cut: 1406. Windsor. Sherbet. 7-1/2 oz. / 5-1/8" hi. NOT BANDED. **References**: 1967, page 10 [1-38]

Line: 1235. Cut: 1406. Windsor. Wine. 7 oz. / 5-7/8" hi. NOT BANDED. **References**: 1967, page 10 [1-39]

Line: 1235 (463). Epicure Collection. Brandy Inhaler. 23 oz. 5-3/4 inches tall. **References**: 1975/I-75, page 10 [3-2]

Line: 1282. Astrid. 1305 Dessert-Finger Bowl. 4-1/2" Dia. **References**: 1967, page 9 [2-11]; 1969, page 15 [2-11]; 1970, page 16 [2-11]; 1971, page 16 [2-11]; 1972, page 25 [2-11]; 1973, page 30 [2-11]; 1975, page 28 [2-7]; 1977, page 39 [2-7]

Line: 1282. Astrid. Claret. 5-1/4 oz. / 5-1/2" hi. **References**: 1967, page 9 [2-5]

Line: 1282. Astrid. Claret. 5-1/4 oz. 5-1/2 inches tall. Plain Twisted Stem. **References**: 1969, page 15 [2-5]; 1970, page 16 [2-5]; 1971, page 16 [2-5]; 1972, page 25 [2-5]; 1973, page 30 [2-5]; 1975, page 28 [2-4]; 1977, page 39 [2-4]

Line: 1282. Astrid. Cocktail. 4-1/4 oz. / 4-5/8" hi. **References**: 1967, page 9 [2-6]

Line: 1282. Astrid. Cocktail. 4-1/4 oz. 4-5/8 inches tall. Plain Twisted Stem. **References**: 1969, page 15 [2-6]; 1970, page 16 [2-6]; 1971, page 16 [2-6]; 1972, page 25 [2-6]; 1973, page 30 [2-6]

Line: 1282. Astrid. Cordial. 1-1/4 oz. / 3-3/4" hi. **References**: 1967, page 9 [2-7]

Line: 1282. Astrid. Cordial. 1-1/4 oz. 3-3/4 inches tall. Plain Twisted Stem. **References**: 1969, page 15 [2-7]; 1970, page 16 [2-7]; 1971, page 16 [2-7]; 1972, page 25 [2-7]; 1973, page 30 [2-7]; 1975, page 28 [2-5]; 1977, page 39 [2-5]

Line: 1282. Astrid. Goblet. 10 oz. / 7" hi. Plain Twisted Stem. **References**: 1967, page 9 [2-1]; 1969, page 15 [2-1]; 1970, page 16 [2-1]; 1971, page 16 [2-1]; 1972, page 25 [2-1]; 1973, page 30 [2-1]; 1975, page 28 [2-1]; 1977, page 39 [2-1]

Line: 1282. Astrid. Ice Tea. 11-1/2 oz. / 6-1/8" hi. **References**: 1967, page 9 [2-10]

Line: 1282. Astrid. Ice Tea. 11-1/2 oz. 6-1/8 inches tall. Plain Twishted Stem. **References**: 1969, page 15 [2-10]; 1970, page 16 [2-10]

Line: 1282. Astrid. Ice Tea. 11-1/2 oz. 6-1/8 inches tall. **References**: 1971, page 16 [2-10]; 1972, page 25 [2-10]; 1973, page 30 [2-10]

Line: 1282. Astrid. Ice Tea. 11-1/2 oz. 6-1/8 inches tall. Plain Twisted Stem. **References**: 1975, page 28 [2-6]; 1977, page 39 [2-6]

Line: 1282. Astrid. Juice. 5 oz. / 4-1/2" hi. **References**: 1967, page 9 [2-9]

Line: 1282. Astrid. Juice. 5 oz. 4-1/2 inches tall. Plain Twisted Stem. **References**: 1969, page 15 [2-9]; 1970, page 16 [2-9]; 1971, page 16 [2-9]; 1972, page 25 [2-9]; 1973, page 30 [2-9]

Line: 1282. Astrid. Parfait. 6-3/4 oz. / 5-7/8" hi. **References**: 1967, page 9 [2-8]

Line: 1282. Astrid. Parfait. 6-3/4 oz. 5-7/8 inches tall. Plain Twisted Stem. **References**: 1969, page 15 [2-8]; 1970, page 16 [2-8]; 1971, page 16 [2-8]; 1972, page 25 [2-8]; 1973, page 30 [2-8]

Line: 1282. Astrid. Plate. 7" / Actually 7-7/8" Dia. **References**: 1967, page 9 [2-12]; 1969, page 15 [2-12]; 1970, page 16 [2-12]; 1971, page 16 [2-12]; 1972, page 25 [2-12]; 1973, page 30 [2-12]; 1975, page 28 [2-8]; 1977, page 39 [2-8]

Line: 1282. Astrid. Plate. 8" / Actually 8-3/4" Dia. **References**: 1967, page 9 [2-13]; 1969, page 15 [2-13]; 1970, page 16 [2-13]; 1971, page 16 [2-13]; 1972, page 25 [2-13]; 1973, page 30 [2-13]; 1975, page 28 [2-9]; 1977, page 39 [2-9]

Line: 1282. Astrid. Saucer Champagne. 7-1/2 oz. / 5-1/4" hi. **References**: 1967, page 9 [2-2]; 1969, page 15 [2-2]; 1970, page 16 [2-2]; 1971, page 16 [2-2]; 1972, page 25 [2-2]; 1973, page 30 [2-2]; 1975, page 28 [2-2]; 1977, page 39 [2-2]

Line: 1282. Astrid. Sherbet. 7-1/2 oz. / 3-5/8" hi. **References**: 1967, page 9 [2-3]

Line: 1282. Astrid. Sherbet. 7-1/2 oz. 3-5/8 inches tall. Plain Twisted Stem. **References**: 1969, page 15 [2-3]; 1970, page 16 [2-3]; 1971, page 16 [2-3]; 1972, page 25 [2-3]; 1973, page 30 [2-3]

Line: 1282. Astrid. Table Wine Goblet. 7-1/2 oz. / 6" hi. **References**: 1967, page 9 [2-4]

Line: 1282. Astrid. Table Wine Goblet. 7-1/2 oz. 6 inches tall. Plain Twisted Stem. **References**: 1969, page 15 [2-4]; 1970, page 16 [2-4]; 1971, page 16 [2-4]; 1972, page 25 [2-4]; 1973, page 30 [2-4]; 1975, page 28 [2-3]; 1977, page 39 [2-3]

Line: 1282. Cut: 43. Hospitality. 1305 Dessert-Finger Bowl. 4-1/2" Dia. **References**: 1967, page 12 [1-11]; 1968, page 16 [1-11]; 1969, page 14 [2-13]; 1970, page 15 [2-13]; 1971, page 15 [2-13]; 1972, page 23 [2-13]; 1973, page 28 [2-13]; 1975, page 26 [2-9]; 1977, page 37 [2-9]

Line: 1282. Cut: 43. Hospitality. All Purpose Wine Goblet. 8 oz. 5 inches tall. **References**: 1969, page 14 [2-7]; 1970, page 15 [2-7]; 1971, page 15 [2-7]; 1972, page 23 [2-7]; 1973, page 28 [2-7]; 1975, page 26 [2-6]; 1977, page 37 [2-6]

Line: 1282. Cut: 43. Hospitality. Claret. 5-1/4 oz. / 5-1/2" hi. **References**: 1967, page 12 [1-5]; 1968, page 16 [1-5]; 1969, page 14 [2-5]; 1970, page 15 [2-5]; 1971, page 15 [2-5]; 1972, page 23 [2-5]; 1973, page 28 [2-5]; 1975, page 26 [2-4]; 1977, page 37 [2-4]

Line: 1282. Cut: 43. Hospitality. Cocktail. 4-1/4 oz. / 4-5/8" hi. **References**: 1967, page 12 [1-6]; 1968, page 16 [1-6]; 1969, page 14 [2-8]; 1970, page 15 [2-8]; 1971, page 15 [2-8]; 1972, page 23 [2-8]; 1973, page 28 [2-8]

Line: 1282. Cut: 43. Hospitality. Cordial. 1-1/4 oz. / 3-3/4" hi. **References**: 1967, page 12 [1-7]; 1968, page 16 [1-7]; 1969, page 14 [2-9]; 1970, page 15 [2-9]; 1971, page 15 [2-9]; 1972, page 23 [2-9]; 1973, page 28 [2-9]; 1975, page 26 [2-7]; 1977, page 37 [2-7]; 1981, page 3 [3-15]

Line: 1282. Cut: 43. Hospitality. Goblet. 10 oz. / 7" hi. **References**: 1967, page 12 [1-1]; 1968, page 16 [1-1]; 1969, page 14 [2-1]; 1970, page 15 [2-1]; 1971, page 15 [2-1]; 1972, page 23 [2-1]; 1973, page 28 [2-1]; 1975, page 26 [2-1]; 1977, page 37 [2-1]; 1981, page 3 [3-11]

Line: 1282. Cut: 43. Hospitality. Ice Tea. 11-1/2 oz. / 6-1/8" hi. **References**: 1967, page 12 [1-10]; 1968, page 16 [1-10]; 1969, page 14 [2-12]; 1970, page 15 [2-12]; 1971, page 15 [2-12]; 1972, page 23 [2-12]; 1973, page 28 [2-12]; 1975, page 26 [2-8]; 1977, page 37 [2-8]

Line: 1282. Cut: 43. Hospitality. Juice. 5 oz. / 4-1/2" hi. **References**: 1967, page 12 [1-9]; 1968, page 16 [1-9]; 1969, page 14 [2-11]; 1970, page 15 [2-11]; 1971, page 15 [2-11]; 1972, page 23 [2-11]; 1973, page 28 [2-11]

Line: 1282. Cut: 43. Hospitality. Parfait. 6-3/4 oz. / 5-7/8" hi. **References**: 1967, page 12 [1-8]; 1968, page 16 [1-8]; 1969, page 14 [2-10]; 1970, page 15 [2-10]; 1971, page 15 [2-10]; 1972, page 23 [2-10]; 1973, page 28 [2-10]

Line: 1282. Cut: 43. Hospitality. Plate. 7" / Actually 7-7/8" Dia. **References**: 1967, page 12 [1-12]; 1968, page 16 [1-12]; 1969, page 14 [2-14]; 1970, page 15 [2-14]; 1971, page 15 [2-14]; 1972, page 23 [2-14]; 1973, page 28 [2-14]; : 1975, page 26 [2-10]; 1977, page 37 [2-10]

Line: 1282. Cut: 43. Hospitality. Plate. 8" / Actually 8-3/4" Dia. **References**: 1967, page 12 [1-13]; 1968, page 16 [1-13]; 1969, page 14 [2-15]; 1970, page 15 [2-15]; 1971, page 15 [2-15]; 1972, page 23 [2-15]; 1973, page 28 [2-15]; 1975, page 26 [2-11]; 1977, page 37 [2-11]

Line: 1282. Cut: 43. Hospitality. Saucer Champagne. 7-1/2 oz. / 5-1/4" hi. **References**: 1967, page 12 [1-2]; 1968, page 16 [1-2]; 1969, page 14 [2-2]; 1970, page 15 [2-2]; 1971, page 15 [2-2]; 1972, page 23 [2-2]; 1973, page 28 [2-2]; 1975, page 26 [2-2]; 1977, page 37 [2-2]; 1981, page 3 [3-12]

Line: 1282. Cut: 43. Hospitality. Sherbet. 7-1/2 oz. / 3-5/8" hi. **References**: 1967, page 12 [1-3]; 1968, page 16 [1-3]; 1969, page 14 [2-3]; 1970, page 15 [2-3]; 1971, page 15 [2-3]; 1972, page 23 [2-3]; 1973, page 28 [2-3]

Line: 1282. Cut: 43. Hospitality. Table Wine Goblet. 7-1/2 oz. / 6" hi. **References**: 1967, page 12 [1-4]; 1968, page 16 [1-4]; 1969, page 14 [2-4]; 1970, page 15 [2-4]; 1971, page 15 [2-4]; 1972, page 23 [2-4]; 1973, page 28 [2-4]; 1975, page 26 [2-3]; 1977, page 37 [2-3]

Line: 1282. Cut: 43. Hospitality. Tulip Champagne. 8 oz. 8-1/2 inches tall. **References**: 1969, page 14 [2-6]; 1970, page 15 [2-6]; 1971, page 15 [2-6]; 1972, page 23 [2-6]; 1973, page 28 [2-6]; 1975, page 26 [2-5]; 1977, page 37 [2-5]; 1981, page 3 [3-14]

Line: 1282. Cut: 43. Hospitality. Wine. 7-1/2 oz. 6 inches tall. **References**: 1981, page 3 [3-13]

Line: 1282. Cut: 1120. Dayton. 1305 Dessert-Finger Bowl. 4-1/2" Dia. **References**: 1967, page 9 [1-16]; 1969, page 15 [1-16]; 1970, page 16 [1-16]; 1971, page 16 [1-16]; 1972, page 25 [1-16]; 1973, page 30 [1-16]; 1975, page 28 [1-14]; 1977, page 39 [1-14]

Line: 1282. Cut: 1120. Dayton. Cordial. 1-1/4 oz. / 3-3/4" hi. **References**: 1967, page 9 [1-13]; 1969, page 15 [1-13]; 1970, page 16 [1-13]; 1971, page 16 [1-13]; 1972, page 25 [1-13]; 1973, page 30 [1-13]; 1975, page 28 [1-12]; 1977, page 39 [1-12]; 1981, page 2 [3-12]

Line: 1282. Cut: 1120. Dayton. Goblet. 10 oz. / 7" hi. **References**: 1967, page 9 [1-10]; 1969, page 15 [1-10]; 1970, page 16 [1-10]; 1971, page 16 [1-10]; 1972, page 25 [1-10]; 1973, page 30 [1-10]; 1975, page 28 [1-9]; 1977, page 39 [1-9]; 1981, page 2 [3-9]

Line: 1282. Cut: 1120. Dayton. Ice Tea. 11-1/2 oz. / 6-1/8" hi. **References**: 1967, page 9 [1-15]; 1969, page 15 [1-15]; 1970, page 16 [1-15]; 1971, page 16 [1-15]; 1972, page 25 [1-15]; 1973, page 30 [1-15]; 1975, page 28 [1-13]; 1977, page 39 [1-13]

Line: 1282. Cut: 1120. Dayton. Juice. 5 oz. / 4-1/2 hi. **References**: 1967, page 9 [1-14]; 1969, page 15 [1-14]; 1970, page 16 [1-14]; 1971, page 16 [1-14]; 1972, page 25 [1-14]; 1973, page 30 [1-14]

Line: 1282. Cut: 1120. Dayton. Plate. 7" / Actually 7-7/8" Dia. **References**: 1967, page 9 [1-17]; 1969, page 15 [1-17]; 1970, page 16 [1-17]; 1971, page 16 [1-17]; 1972, page 25 [1-17]; 1973, page 30 [1-17]; 1975, page 28 [1-15]; 1977, page 39 [1-15]

Line: 1282. Cut: 1120. Dayton. Plate. 8" / Actually 8-3/4" Dia. **References**: 1967, page 9 [1-18]; 1969, page 15 [1-18]; 1970, page 16 [1-18]; 1971, page 16 [1-18]; 1972, page 25 [1-18]; 1973, page 30 [1-18]; 1975, page 28 [1-16]; 1977, page 39 [1-16]

Line: 1282. Cut: 1120. Dayton. Saucer Champagne. 7-1/2 oz. / 5-1/4" hi. **References**: 1967, page 9 [1-11]; 1969, page 15 [1-11]; 1970, page 16 [1-11]; 1971, page 16 [1-11]; 1972, page 25 [1-11]; 1973, page 30 [1-11]; 1975, page 28 [1-10]; 1977, page 39 [1-10]; 1981, page 2 [3-10]

Line: 1282. Cut: 1120. Dayton. Table Wine Goblet. 7-1/2 oz. / 6" hi. **References**: 1967, page 9 [1-12]; 1969, page 15 [1-12]; 1970, page 16 [1-12]; 1971, page 16 [1-12]; 1972, page 25 [1-12]; 1973, page 30 [1-12]; 1975, page 28 [1-11]; 1977, page 39 [1-11]

Line: 1282. Cut: 1120. Dayton. Wine. 7-1/2 oz. 6 inches tall. **References**: 1981, page 2 [3-11]

Line: 1282. Cut: 1426. Buckingham. 1305 Dessert-Finger Bowl. 4-1/2" Dia. **References**: 1967, page 9 [1-7]; 1969, page 15 [1-7]; 1970, page 16 [1-7]; 1971, page 16 [1-7]; 1972, page 25 [1-7]; 1973, page 30 [1-7]; 1975, page 28 [1-6]; 1977, page 39 [1-6]

Line: 1282. Cut: 1426. Buckingham. Cordial. 1-1/4 oz. / 3-3/4" hi. **References**: 1967, page 9 [1-4]; 1969, page 15 [1-4]; 1970, page 16 [1-4]; 1971, page 16 [1-4]; 1972, page 25 [1-4]; 1973, page 30 [1-4]; 1975, page 28 [1-4]; 1977, page 39 [1-4]

Line: 1282. Cut: 1426. Buckingham. Goblet. 10 oz. / 7" hi. **References**: 1967, page 9 [1-1]; 1969, page 15 [1-1]; 1970, page 16 [1-1]; 1971, page 16 [1-1]; 1972, page 25 [1-1]; 1973, page 30 [1-1]; 1975, page 28 [1-1]; 1977, page 39 [1-1]

Line: 1282. Cut: 1426. Buckingham. Ice Tea. 11-1/2 oz. / 6-1/8" hi. **References**: 1967, page 9 [1-6]; 1969, page 15 [1-6]; 1970, page 16 [1-6]; 1971, page 16 [1-6]; 1972, page 25 [1-6]; 1973, page 30 [1-6]; 1975, page 28 [1-5]; 1977, page 39 [1-5]

Line: 1282. Cut: 1426. Buckingham. Juice. 5 oz. / 4-1/2" hi. **References**: 1967, page 9 [1-5]; 1969, page 15 [1-5]; 1970, page 16 [1-5]; 1971, page 16 [1-5]; 1972, page 25 [1-5]; 1973, page 30 [1-5]

Line: 1282. Cut: 1426. Buckingham. Plate. 7" / Actually 7-7/8" Dia. **References**: 1967, page 9 [1-8]; 1969, page 15 [1-8]; 1970, page 16 [1-8]; 1971, page 16 [1-8]; 1972, page 25 [1-8]; 1973, page 30 [1-8]; 1975, page 28 [1-7]; 1977, page 39 [1-7]

Line: 1282. Cut: 1426. Buckingham. Plate. 8" / Actually 8-3/4" Dia. **References**: 1967, page 9 [1-9]; 1969, page 15 [1-9]; 1970, page 16 [1-9]; 1971, page 16 [1-9]; 1972, page 25 [1-9]; 1973, page 30 [1-9]; 1975, page 28 [1-8]; 1977, page 39 [1-8]

Line: 1282. Cut: 1426. Buckingham. Saucer Champagne. 7-1/2 oz. / 5-1/4" hi. **References**: 1967, page 9 [1-2]; 1969, page 15 [1-2]; 1970, page 16 [1-2]; 1971, page 16 [1-2]; 1972, page 25 [1-2]; 1973, page 30 [1-2]; 1975, page 28 [1-2]; 1977, page 39 [1-2]

Line: 1282. Cut: 1426. Buckingham. Table Wine Goblet. 7-1/2 oz. / 6" hi. **References**: 1967, page 9 [1-3]; 1969, page 15 [1-3]; 1970, page 16 [1-3]; 1971, page 16 [1-3]; 1972, page 25 [1-3]; 1973, page 30 [1-3]; 1975, page 28 [1-3]; 1977, page 39 [1-3]

Line: 1300. Finger Bowl. **References**: 5-E, page 9 [2-2]

Line: 1302. Etching: 608. Grape Design. Finger Bowl. **References**: 3, page 8 [1-5]

Line: 1302. Cut: N. Etching: 23, Cut Star Bottom. Finger Bowl. **References**: 5-E, page 19 [3-2]

Line: 1350. Cut: 43. Embassy. 1305 Dessert-Finger Bowl. 4-1/2 inches diam. **References**: 1972, page 24 [1-11]; 1973, page 29 [1-11]; 1967, page 13 [1-9]; 1968, page 17 [1-9]; 1969, page 13 [1-11]; 1970, page 14 [1-11]; 1971, page 14 [1-11]; 1975, page 27 [1-9]; 1977, page 38 [1-9]

Line: 1350. Cut: 43. Embassy. All Purpose Wine Goblet. 8 oz. 5 inches tall. **References**: 1969, page 13 [1-6]; 1970, page 14 [1-6]; 1971, page 14 [1-6]; 1972, page 24 [1-6]; 1973, page 29 [1-6]; 1975, page 27 [1-6]; 1977, page 38 [1-6]

Line: 1350. Cut: 43. Embassy. Cocktail. 4-1/2 oz. / 4-3/4" hi. **References**: 1967, page 13 [1-5]; 1968, page 17 [1-5]; 1969, page 13 [1-7]; 1970, page 14 [1-7]; 1971, page 14 [1-7]; 1972, page 24 [1-7]; 1973, page 29 [1-7]

Line: 1350. Cut: 43. Embassy. Cordial. 1-1/4 oz. / 3-3/4" hi. **References**: 1967, page 13 [1-6]; 1968, page 17 [1-6]; 1969, page 13 [1-8]; 1970, page 14 [1-8]; 1971, page 14 [1-8]; 1972, page 24 [1-8]; 1973, page 29 [1-8]; 1975, page 27 [1-7]; 1977, page 38 [1-7]; 1981, page 3 [3-10]

Line: 1350. Cut: 43. Embassy. Goblet. 12-1/2oz. / 6-5/8" hi. **References**: 1967, page 13 [1-1]; 1968, page 17 [1-1]; 1969, page 13 [1-1]; 1970, page 14 [1-1]; 1971, page 14 [1-1]; 1972, page 24 [1-1]; 1973, page 29 [1-1]; 1975, page 27 [1-1]; 1977, page 38 [1-1]; 1981, page 3 [3-6]

Line: 1350. Cut: 43. Embassy. Ice Tea. 13-1/2 oz. / 6-1/4" hi. **References**: 1967, page 13 [1-8]; 1968, page 17 [1-8]; 1969, page 13 [1-10]; 1970, page 14 [1-10]; 1971, page 14 [1-10]; 1972, page 24 [1-10]; 1973, page 29 [1-10]; 1975, page 27 [1-8]; 1977, page 38 [1-8]

Line: 1350. Cut: 43. Embassy. Juice. 6-1/2 oz. / 5-1/4" hi. **References**: 1967, page 13 [1-7]; 1968, page 17 [1-7]; 1969, page 13 [1-9]; 1970, page 14 [1-9]; 1971, page 14 [1-9]; 1972, page 24 [1-9]; 1973, page 29 [1-9]

Line: 1350. Cut: 43. Embassy. Plate. 7" / Actually 7-7/8" Dia. **References**: 1967, page 13 [1-10]; 1968, page 17 [1-10]; 1969, page 13 [1-11]; 1970, page 14 [1-11]; 1971, page 14 [1-11]; 1972, page 24 [1-12]; 1973, page 29 [1-12]; 1975, page 27 [1-10]; 1977, page 38 [1-10]

Line: 1350. Cut: 43. Embassy. Plate. 8" / Actually 8-3/4" Dia. **References**: 1967, page 13 [1-11]; 1968, page 17 [1-11]; 1969, page 13 [1-13]; 1970, page 14 [1-13]; 1971, page 14 [1-13]; 1972, page 24 [1-13]; 1973, page 29 [1-13]; 1975, page 27 [1-11]; 1977, page 38 [1-11]

Line: 1350. Cut: 43. Embassy. Red Wine Goblet. 9-1/2 oz. / 6-3/8" hi. **References**: 1967, page 13 [1-3]; 1968, page 17 [1-3]; 1969, page 13 [1-3]; 1970, page 14 [1-3]; 1971, page 14 [1-3]; 1972, page 24 [1-3]; 1973, page 29 [1-3]; 1975, page 27 [1-3]; 1977, page 38 [1-3]

Line: 1350. Cut: 43. Embassy. Sherbet. 6-1/2 oz. / 5" hi. **References**: 1967, page 13 [1-2]; 1968, page 17 [1-2]; 1969, page 13 [1-2]; 1970, page 14 [1-2]; 1971, page 14 [1-2]; 1972, page 24 [1-2]; 1973, page 29 [1-2]; 1975, page 27 [1-2]; 1977, page 38 [1-2]; 1981, page 3 [3-7]

Line: 1350. Cut: 43. Embassy. Tulip Champagne. 8 oz. 8-1/2 inches tall. **References**: 1969, page 13 [1-5]; 1970, page 14 [1-5]; 1971, page 14 [1-5]; 1972, page 24 [1-5]; 1973, page 29 [1-5]; 1975, page 27 [1-5]; 1977, page 38 [1-5]; 1981, page 3 [3-9]

Line: 1350. Cut: 43. Embassy. White Wine. 7 oz. 5-3/4 inches tall. **References**: 1975, page 27 [1-4]; 1967, page 13 [1-4]; 1968, page 17 [1-4]; 1969, page 13 [1-4]; 1971, page 14 [1-4]; 1972, page 24 [1-4]; 1973, page 29 [1-4]; 1977, page 38 [1-4]; 1981, page 3 [3-8]

Line: 1350. Cut: 63. Mansfield. Cocktail. 4-1/2 oz. / 4-3/4" hi. Gold Band. **References**: 1967, page 11 [1-22]; 1968, page 15 [1-22]; 1969, page 19 [2-22]; 1970, page 20 [2-22]; 1971, page 20 [2-22]; 1972, page 28 [2-22]; 1973, page 33 [2-22]

Line: 1350. Cut: 63. Mansfield. Cordial. 1-1/4 oz. / 3-3/4" hi. Gold Band. **References**: 1967, page 11 [1-23]; 1968, page 15 [1-23]; 1969, page 19 [2-23]; 1970, page 20 [2-23]; 1971, page 20 [2-23]; 1972, page 28 [2-23]; 1973, page 33 [2-23]; 1975, page 29 [2-18]; 1977, page 40 [2-18]

Line: 1350. Cut: 63. Mansfield. Goblet. 12-1/2 oz. / 6-5/8" hi. Gold Band. **References**: 1967, page 11 [1-19]; 1968, page 15 [1-19]; 1969, page 19 [2-19]; 1970, page 20 [2-19]; 1971, page 20 [2-19]; 1972, page 28 [2-19]; 1973, page 33 [2-19]; 1975, page 29 [2-15]; 1977, page 40 [2-15]

Line: 1350. Cut: 63. Mansfield. Ice Tea. 13-1/2 oz. / 6-1/4" hi. Gold Band. **References**: 1967, page 11 [1-25]; 1968, page 15 [1-25]; 1969, page 19 [2-25]; 1970, page 20 [2-25]; 1971, page 20 [2-25]; 1972, page 28 [2-25]; 1973, page 33 [2-25]; 1975, page 29 [2-19]; 1977, page 40 [2-19]

Line: 1350. Cut: 63. Mansfield. Juice. 6-1/2 oz. / 5-1/4" hi. Gold Band. **References**: 1967, page 11 [1-24]; 1968, page 15 [1-24]; 1969, page 19 [2-24]; 1970, page 20 [2-24]; 1971, page 20 [2-24]; 1972, page 28 [2-24]; 1973, page 33 [2-24]

Line: 1350. Cut: 63. Mansfield. Plate. 7" / Actually 7-7/8" Dia. Gold Band. **References**: 1967, page 11 [1-26]; 1968, page 15 [1-26]; 1975, page 29 [2-20]; 1977, page 40 [2-20]

Line: 1350. Cut: 63. Mansfield. Plate. 8" / Actually 8-3/4" Dia. Gold Band. **References**: 1967, page 11 [1-27]; 1968, page 15 [1-27]; 1975, page 29 [2-21]; 1977, page 40 [2-21]

Line: 1350. Cut: 63. Mansfield. Plate. 7 inches diam. Gold Band, Platinum or Gold Banding (No Cutting), Actually 7-7/8" Dia. **References**: 1969, page 19 [2-26]; 1970, page 20 [2-26]; 1971, page 20 [2-26]; 1972, page 28 [2-26]; 1973, page 33 [2-26]

Line: 1350. Cut: 63. Mansfield. Plate. 8 inches diam. Gold Band, Platinum or Gold Banding (No Cutting), Actually 8-3/4" Dia. **References**: 1969, page 19 [2-27]; 1970, page 20 [2-27]; 1971, page 20 [2-27]; 1972, page 28 [2-27]; 1973, page 33 [2-27]

Line: 1350. Cut: 63. Mansfield. Sherbet. 6-1/2 oz. / 5" hi. Gold Band. **References**: 1967, page 11 [1-20]; 1968, page 15 [1-20]; 1969, page 19 [2-20]; 1970, page 20 [2-20]; 1971, page 20 [2-20]; 1972, page 28 [2-20]; 1973, page 33 [2-20]; 1975, page 29 [2-16]; 1977, page 40 [2-16]

Line: 1350. Cut: 63. Mansfield. White Wine. 7 oz. 5-3/4 inches tall. Gold Band. **References**: 1975, page 29 [2-17]; 1967, page 11 [1-21]; 1968, page 15 [1-21]; 1969, page 19 [2-21]; 1970, page 20 [2-21]; 1971, page 20 [2-21]; 1972, page 28 [2-21]; 1973, page 33 [2-21]; 1977, page 40 [2-17]

Line: 1350. Cut: 63. Montclair. Cocktail. 4-1/2 oz. / 4-3/4" hi. Platinum Band. **References**: 1967, page 11 [1-31]; 1968, page 15 [1-31]; 1969, page 19 [2-31]; 1970, page 20 [2-31]; 1971, page 20 [2-31]; 1972, page 28 [2-31]; 1973, page 33 [2-31]

Line: 1350. Cut: 63. Montclair. Cordial. 1-1/4 oz. / 3-3/4" hi. Platinum Band. **References**: 1967, page 11 [1-32]; 1968, page 15 [1-32]; 1969, page 19 [2-32]; 1970, page 20 [2-32]; 1971, page 20 [2-32]; 1972, page 28 [2-32]; 1973, page 33 [2-32]; 1975, page 29 [2-25]; 1977, page 40 [2-25]

Line: 1350. Cut: 63. Montclair. Goblet. 12-1/2 oz. / 6-5/8" hi. Platinum Band. **References**: 1967, page 11 [1-28]; 1968, page 15 [1-28]; 1969, page 19 [2-28]; 1970, page 20 [2-28]; 1971, page 20 [2-28]; 1972, page 28 [2-28]; 1973, page 33 [2-28]; 1975, page 29 [2-22]; 1977, page 40 [2-22]

Line: 1350. Cut: 63. Montclair. Ice Tea. 13-1/2 oz. / 6-1/4" hi. Platinum Band. **References**: 1967, page 11 [1-34]; 1968, page 15 [1-34]; 1969, page 19 [2-34]; 1970, page 20 [2-34]; 1971, page 20 [2-34]; 1972, page 28 [2-34]; 1973, page 33 [2-34]; 1975, page 29 [2-26]; 1977, page 40 [2-26]

Line: 1350. Cut: 63. Montclair. Juice. 6-1/2 oz. / 5-1/4" hi. Platinum Band. **References**: 1967, page 11 [1-33]; 1968, page 15 [1-33]; 1969, page 19 [2-33]; 1970, page 20 [2-33]; 1971, page 20 [2-33]; 1972, page 28 [2-33]; 1973, page 33 [2-33]

Line: 1350. Cut: 63. Montclair. Plate. 7 oz. / Actually 7-7/8" Dia. Platinum Band. **References**: 1967, page 11 [1 35]; 1968, page 15 [1-35]; 1975, page 29 [2-27]; 1977, page 40 [2-27]

Line: 1350. Cut: 63. Montclair. Plate. 8 oz. / Actually 8-3/4" Dia. Platinum Band. **References**: 1967, page 11 [1-36]; 1968, page 15 [1-36]; 1975, page 29 [2-28]; 1977, page 40 [2-28]

Line: 1350. Cut: 63. Montclair. Plate. 7 inches diam. Platinum Band, Platinum or Gold Banding (No Cutting), Actually 7-7/8" Dia. **References**: 1969, page 19 [2-35]; 1970, page 20 [2-35]; 1971, page 20 [2-35]; 1972, page 28 [2-35]; 1973, page 33 [2-35]

Line: 1350. Cut: 63. Montclair. Plate. 8 inches diam. Platinum Band, Platinum or Gold Banding (No Cutting), Actually 8-3/4" Dia. **References**: 1969, page 19 [2-36]; 1970, page 20 [2-36]; 1971, page 20 [2-36]; 1972, page 28 [2-36]; 1973, page 33 [2-36]

Line: 1350. Cut: 63. Montclair. Sherbet. 6-1/2 oz. / 5" hi. Platinum Band. **References**: 1967, page 11 [1-29]; 1968, page 15 [1-29]; 1969, page 19 [2-29]; 1970, page 20 [2-29]; 1971, page 20 [2-29]; 1972, page 28 [2-29]; 1973, page 33 [2-29]; 1975, page 29 [2-23]; 1977, page 40 [2-23]

Line: 1350. Cut: 63. Montclair. White Wine. 7 oz. 5-3/4 inches tall. Platinum Band. **References**: 1975, page 29 [2-24]; 1977, page 40 [2-24]; 1967, page 11 [1-30]; 1968, page 15 [1-30]; 1969, page 19 [2-30]; 1970, page 20 [2-30]; 1971, page 20 [2-30]; 1972, page 28 [2-30]; 1973, page 33 [2-30]

Line: 1350. Cut: 63. Riviera. 1305 Dessert-Finger Bowl. 4-1/2" Dia. **References**: 1967, page 13 [2-20]; 1968, page 17 [2-20]; 1969, page 13 [2-20]; 1970, page 14 [2-20]; 1971, page 14 [2-20]; 1972, page 24 [2-20]; 1973, page 29 [2-20]; 1975, page 27 [2-16]; 1977, page 38 [2-16]

Line: 1350. Cut: 63. Riviera. Cocktail. 4-1/2 oz. / 4-3/4" hi. **References**: 1967, page 13 [2-16]; 1968, page 17 [2-16]; 1969, page 13 [2-16]; 1970, page 14 [2-16]; 1971, page 14 [2-16]; 1972, page 24 [2-16]; 1973, page 29 [2-16]

Line: 1350. Cut: 63. Riviera. Cordial. 1-1/4 oz. / 3-3/4" hi. **References**: 1967, page 13 [2-17]; 1968, page 17 [2-17]; 1969, page 13 [2-17]; 1970, page 14 [2-17]; 1971, page 14 [2-17]; 1972, page 24 [2-17]; 1973, page 29 [2-17]; 1975, page 27 [2-14]; 1977, page 38 [2-14]; 1981, page 3 [3-5]

Line: 1350. Cut: 63. Riviera. Goblet. 12-1/2 oz. / 6-5/8" hi. **References**: 1967, page 13 [2-12]; 1968, page 17 [2-12]; 1969, page 13 [2-12]; 1970, page 14 [2-12]; 1971, page 14 [2-12]; 1972, page 24 [2-12]; 1973, page 29 [2-12]; 1975, page 27 [2-10]; 1977, page 38 [2-10]; 1981, page 3 [3-1]

Line: 1350. Cut: 63. Riviera. Ice Tea. 13-1/2 oz. / 6-1/4" hi. **References**: 1967, page 13 [2-19]; 1968, page 17 [2-19]; 1969, page 13 [2-19]; 1970, page 14 [2-19]; 1971, page 14 [2-19]; 1972, page 24 [2-19]; 1973, page 29 [2-19]; 1975, page 27 [2-15]; 1977, page 38 [2-15]

Line: 1350. Cut: 63. Riviera. Juice. 6-1/2 oz. / 5-1/4" hi. **References**: 1967, page 13 [2-18]; 1968, page 17 [2-18]; 1969, page 13 [2-18]; 1970, page 14 [2-18]; 1971, page 14 [2-18]; 1972, page 24 [2-18]; 1973, page 29 [2-18]

Line: 1350. Cut: 63. Riviera. Plate. 7" / Actually 7-7/8" Dia. **References**: 1967, page 13 [2-21]; 1968, page 17 [2-21]; 1969, page 13 [2-21]; 1970, page 14 [2-21]; 1971, page 14 [2-21]; 1972, page 24 [2-21]; 1973, page 29 [2-21]; 1975, page 27 [2-17]; 1977, page 38 [2-17]

Line: 1350. Cut: 63. Riviera. Plate. 8" / Actually 8-3/4" Dia. **References**: 1967, page 13 [2-22]; 1968, page 17 [2-22]; 1969, page 13 [2-22]; 1970, page 14 [2-22]; 1971, page 14 [2-22]; 1972, page 24 [2-22]; 1973, page 29 [2-22]; 1975, page 27 [2-18]; 1977, page 38 [2-18]

Line: 1350. Cut: 63. Riviera. Red Wine Goblet. 9-1/2 oz. / 6-3/8" hi. **References**: 1967, page 13 [2-14]; 1968, page 17 [2-14]; 1969, page 13 [2-14]; 1970, page 14 [2-14]; 1971, page 14 [2-14]; 1972, page 24 [2-14]; 1973, page 29 [2-14]; 1975, page 27 [2-12]; 1977, page 38 [2-12]

Line: 1350. Cut: 63. Riviera. Sherbet. 6-1/2 oz. / 5" hi. **References**: 1967, page 13 [2-13]; 1968, page 17 [2-13]; 1969, page 13 [2-13]; 1970, page 14 [2-13]; 1971, page 14 [2-13]; 1972, page 24 [2-13]; 1973, page 29 [2-13]; 1975, page 27 [2-11]; 1977, page 38 [2-11]; 1981, page 3 [3-2]

Line: 1350. Cut: 63. Riviera. Tulip Champagne. 8 oz. 8-1/2 inches tall. **References**: 1981, page 3 [3-4]

Line: 1350. Cut: 63. Riviera. White Wine. 7 oz. 5-3/4 inches tall. **References**: 1975, page 27 [2-13]; 1967, page 13 [2-15]; 1968, page 17 [2-15]; 1969, page 13 [2-15]; 1970, page 14 [2-15]; 1971, page 14 [2-15]; 1972, page 24 [2-15]; 1973, page 29 [2-15]; 1977, page 38 [2-13]; 1981, page 3 [3-3]

Line: 1350. Cut: 1403. Regency. 1305 Dessert-Finger Bowl. 4-1/2" Dia. **References**: 1967, page 13 [2-9]; 1968, page 17 [2-9]; 1969, page 13 [2-9]

Line: 1350. Cut: 1403. Regency. Cocktail. 4-1/2 oz. / 4-3/4" hi. **References**: 1967, page 13 [2-5]; 1968, page 17 [2-5]; 1969, page 13 [2-5]

Line: 1350. Cut: 1403. Regency. Cordial. 1-1/4 oz. / 3-3/4" hi. **References**: 1967, page 13 [2-6]; 1968, page 17 [2-6]; 1969, page 13 [2-6]

Line: 1350. Cut: 1403. Regency. Goblet. 12-1/2 oz. / 6-5/8" hi. **References**: 1967, page 13 [2-1]; 1968, page 17 [2-1]; 1969, page 13 [2-1]

Line: 1350. Cut: 1403. Regency. Ice Tea. 13-1/2 oz. / 6-1/4" hi. **References**: 1967, page 13 [2-8]; 1968, page 17 [2-8]; 1969, page 13 [2-8]

Line: 1350. Cut: 1403. Regency. Juice. 6-1/2 oz. / 5-1/4" hi. **References**: 1967, page 13 [2-7]; 1968, page 17 [2-7]; 1969, page 13 [2-7]

Line: 1350. Cut: 1403. Regency. Plate. 7" / Actually 7-7/8" Dia. **References**: 1967, page 13 [2-10]; 1968, page 17 [2-10]; 1969, page 13 [2-10]

Line: 1350. Cut: 1403. Regency. Plate. 8" / Actually 8-3/4" Dia. **References**: 1967, page 13 [2-11]; 1968, page 17 [2-11]; 1969, page 13 [2-11]

Line: 1350. Cut: 1403. Regency. Red Wine Goblet. 9-1/2 oz. / 6-3/8" hi. **References**: 1967, page 13 [2-3]; 1968, page 17 [2-3]; 1969, page 13 [2-3]

Line: 1350. Cut: 1403. Regency. Sherbet. 6-1/2 oz. / 5" hi. **References**: 1967, page 13 [2-2]; 1968, page 17 [2-2]; 1969, page 13 [2-2]

Line: 1350. Cut: 1403. Regency. White Wine Goblet. 7 oz. / 5-3/4" hi. **References**: 1967, page 13 [2-4]; 1968, page 17 [2-4]; 1969, page 13 [2-4]

Line: 1412. Cut: 45. Old Fashion. 9 oz. 3-1/2 inches tall. Sham Weight. The cut 43 indicates the Flutes at the base of the Tumblers are 1-1/2" high and 3/4" wide. Tumblers Cut 45 have a flat unpolished base. Items available: 14 oz., 12 oz., and 10 oz. Tumbler, 10 oz. Table Tumbler, 7-3/4 oz., 9 oz., and 12 oz. Old Fashion. **References**: 1972, page 31 [2-6]; 1973, page 36 [2-6]; 1975, page 32 [2-6]; 1977, page 43 [2-6]; 1979, page 14 [2-5]; 1982, page 7 [1-6]; 1975/I-75, page 12 [2-6]

Line: 1450. Cut: 43. Old Fashion. 12 oz. 3-7/8 inches tall. Sham Weight, Polished Bottom. The cut 43 indicates the Flutes at the base of the Tumblers are 1-3/4" high and 3/4" wide. Tumblers Cut 43 have a hand cut and hand polished (Punty) base. Items available: 14 oz., 12 oz., and 10 oz. Tumbler, 10 oz. Table Tumbler, 7-3/4 oz., 9 oz., and 12 oz. Old Fashion. **References**: 1972, page 31 [3-7]; 1973, page 36 [3-7]; 1975, page 32 [3-7]; 1977, page 43 [3-7]; 1979, page 14 [2-2]; 1982, page 6 [1-11]; 1975/I-75, page 12 [3-7]; 1972, page 31 [2-7]; 1973, page 36 [2-7]; 1975, page 32 [2-7]; 1977, page 43 [2-7]; 1982, page 7 [1-7]; 1975/I-75, page 12 [2-7]

Line: 1500. Tumbler. 2-1/4 oz. Light Barrel, All Tumblers Made In Sham, Half Sham and Optic. **References**: 5-E, page 19 [3-3]; page 4 & 19 [Listed]

Line: 1500. Tumbler. 5 oz. Light Barrel, All Tumblers Made In Sham, Half Sham and Optic. **References**: 5-E, pages 4 & 19 [Listed]

Line: 1500. Tumbler. 5-1/2 oz. Light Barrel, All Tumblers Made In Sham, Half Sham and Optic. **References**: 5-E, page 4 & 19 [Listed]

Line: 1500. Tumbler. 6-1/2 oz. Light Barrel, All Tumblers Made In Sham, Half Sham and Optic. **References**: 5-E, page 4 [Listed]

Line: 1500. Tumbler. 10 oz. Light Barrel, All Tumblers Made In Sham, Half Sham and Optic. **References**: 5-E, page 4 [Listed]

Line: 1500. Etching: 1. Tumbler/gold Band. 2-1/4 oz. Light Barrel Shape. **References**: 5-E, page 19 [3-3]

Line: 1503. Tumbler. 3 oz. Light Barrel, All Tumblers Made In Sham, Half Sham and Optic. **References**: 5-E, page 19 [Listed]

Line: 1506A. Tumbler. 2-1/2 oz. Light Barrel, All Tumblers Made In Sham, Half Sham and Optic. **References**: 5-E, page 4 [2-1]; **5-E, page 19 [listed]**

Line: 1506. Tumbler. 4-1/2 oz. Light Barrel, All Tumblers Made In Sham, Half Sham and Optic. **References**: 5-E, pages 4 & 19 [Listed]

Line: 1509. Tumbler. 6 oz. Light Barrel, All Tumblers Made In Sham, Half Sham and Optic. **References**: 5-E, pages 4 & 19 [Listed]

Line: 1512. Tumbler. 7 oz. Light Barrel, All Tumblers Made In Sham, Half Sham and Optic. **References**: 55-E, pages 4 & 19 [2-2]

Line: 1515. Tumbler. 8-1/2 oz. Light Barrel, All Tumblers Made In Sham, Half Sham and Optic. **References**: 5-E, pages 4 & 19 [Listed]

Line: 1515. Etching: 2. Tumbler/gold Band. 8-1/2 oz. Light Barrel Shape. **References**: 5-E, page 19 [3-4]

Line: 1518. Tumbler. 9 oz. Light Barrel, All Tumblers Made In Sham, Half Sham and Optic. **References**: 5-E, pages 4 & 19 [Listed]

Line: 1521. Tumbler. 13-1/2 oz. Light Barrel, All Tumblers Made In Sham, Half Sham and Optic. **References**: 5-E, pages 4 & 19 [Listed]

Line: 1524. Tumbler. 14 oz. Light Barrel, All Tumblers Made In Sham, Half Sham and Optic. **References**: 5-E, pages 4 & 19 [Listed]

Line: 1600. Tumbler, Sham. 1-1/2 oz. Light Taper Bar. **References**: 5-E, page 1 [2-3]

Line: 1 / 631. Cut: 220. Squat Water Set / Tumblers. **References**: 2, fig. 6 (p. 43) [1-3]

Line: 1820. Crinkle Glass. Beverage. 14 oz. 5-5/8 inches tall. 5W. Colors: Accent Red. **References**: Advertisement

Line: 1820. Crinkle Glass. Bowl. 5 inches diam. 5B. Colors: Topaz. **References**: Advertisement

Line: 1820. Crinkle Glass. Cooler. 20 oz. 6-3/4 inches tall. 5W/2. Colors: Delphine Blue. **References**: Advertisement

Line: 1820. Crinkle Glass. Double Old Fashion. 12 oz. 3-1/2 inches tall. 5R/2. Colors: Moss Green. **References**: Advertisement

Line: 1820. Crinkle Glass. Footed Goblet. 13 oz. 5-1/4 inches tall. 5T. Colors: Moss Green. **References**: Advertisement

Line: 1820. Crinkle Glass. Footed Sherbet. 6 oz. 2-7/8 inches tall. 5S. Colors: Crystal. **References**: Advertisement

Line: 1820. Crinkle Glass. Juice. 6 oz. 4 inches tall. 5W-1/4. Colors: Lime Green. **References**: Advertisement

Line: 1820. Crinkle Glass. Pitcher. 50 oz. 8 inches tall. 5PT. Colors: Moss Green. **References**: Advertisement

Line: 1960. Marlboro. Beverage. 16-1/2 oz. 5 inches tall. Crystal Full Sham. **References**: 1978, page 7 [3-1]; 1979, page 16 [3-1]

Line: 1960. Marlboro. Old Fashion. 9 oz. 4 inches tall. Crystal Full Sham. **References**: 1978, page 7 [3-2]; 1979, page 16 [3-2]

Line: 1962. Chantilly. Cocktail. 4-1/2 oz. / 4-3/4" hi. Gold Band. **References**: 1967, page 11 [1-4]; 1968, page 15 [1-4]; 1969, page 19 [2-4]; 1970, page 20 [2-4]; 1971, page 20 [2-4]; 1972, page 28 [2-4]; 1973, page 33 [2-4]

Line: 1962. Chantilly. Cordial. 1-1/4 oz. / 3-3/4" hi. Gold Band. **References**: 1967, page 11 [1-5]; 1968, page 15 [1-5]; 1969, page 19 [2-5]; 1970, page 20 [2-5]; 1971, page 20 [2-5]; 1972, page 28 [2-5]; 1973, page 33 [2-5]; 1975, page 29 [2-5]; 1977, page 40 [2-5]

Line: 1962. Chantilly. Goblet. 12-1/2 oz. / 6-5/8" hi. Gold Band. **References**: 1967, page 11 [1-1]; 1968, page 15 [1-1]; 1969, page 19 [2-1]; 1970, page 20 [2-1]; 1971, page 20 [2-1]; 1972, page 28 [2-1]; 1973, page 33 [2-1]; 1975, page 29 [2-1]; 1977, page 40 [2-1]

Line: 1962. Chantilly. Ice Tea. 13-1/2 oz. / 6-1/4" hi. Gold Band. **References**: 1967, page 11 [1-7]; 1968, page 15 [1-7]; 1969, page 19 [2-7]; 1970, page 20 [2-7]; 1971, page 20 [2-7]; 1972, page 28 [2-7]; 1973, page 33 [2-7]; 1975, page 29 [2-7]; 1977, page 40 [2-7]

Line: 1962. Chantilly. Juice. 6-1/2 oz. / 5-1/4" hi. Gold Band. **References**: 1967, page 11 [1-6]; 1968, page 15 [1-6]; 1969, page 19 [2-6]; 1970, page 20 [2-6]; 1971, page 20 [2-6]; 1972, page 28 [2-6]; 1973, page 33 [2-6]

Line: 1962. Chantilly. Plate. 7" / Actually 7-7/8" Dia. Gold Band. **References**: 1967, page 11 [1-8]; 1968, page 15 [1-8]; 1969, page 19 [2-8]; 1970, page 20 [2-8]; 1971, page 20 [2-8]; 1972, page 28 [2-8]; 1973, page 33 [2-8]; 1975, page 29 [2-8]; 1977, page 40 [2-8]

Line: 1962. Chantilly. Plate. 8" / Actually 8-3/4" Dia. Gold Band. **References**: 1967, page 11 [1-9]; 1968, page 15 [1-9]; 1969, page 19 [2-9]; 1970, page 20 [2-9]; 1971, page 20 [2-9]; 1972, page 28 [2-9]; 1973, page 33 [2-9]; 1975, page 29 [2-9]; 1977, page 40 [2-9]

Line: 1962. Chantilly. Sherbet. 6-1/2 oz. / 5" hi. Gold Band. **References**: 1967, page 11 [1-2]; 1969, page 19 [2-2]; 1970, page 20 [2-2]; 1971, page 20 [2-2]; 1972, page 28 [2-2]; 1973, page 33 [2-2]; 1975, page 29 [2-2]; 1977, page 40 [2-2]

Line: 1962. Chantilly. White Wine. 7 oz. 5-3/4 inches tall. Gold Band. **References**: 1975, page 29 [2-3]; 1977, page 40 [2-3]; 1967, page 11 [1-3]; 1968, page 15 [1-3]; 1969, page 19 [2-3]; 1970, page 20 [2-3]; 1971, page 20 [2-3]; 1972, page 28 [2-3]; 1973, page 33 [2-3]

Line: 1962. Continental. 1305 Dessert-Finger Bowl. 4-1/2 inches diam. Plain Crystal. **References**: 1970, page 14 [2-9]; 1971, page 14 [2-9]; 1972, page 24 [2-9]; 1973, page 29 [2-9]; 1975, page 27 [2-7]; 1977, page 38 [2-7]

Line: 1962. Continental. Cocktail. 4-1/2 oz. 4-3/4 inches tall. Plain Crystal. **References**: 1970, page !4 [2-5]; 1971, page 14 [2-5]; 1972, page 24 [2-5]; 1973, page 29 [2-5]

Line: 1962. Continental. Cordial. 1-1/4 oz. 3-3/4 inches tall. Plain Crystal. **References**: 1970, page 14 [2-6]; 1971, page 14 [2-6]; 1972, page 24 [2-6]; 1973, page 29 [2-6]; 1975, page 27 [2-5]; 1977, page 38 [2-5]

Line: 1962. Continental. Goblet. 12-1/2 oz. 6-5/8 inches tall. Plain Crystal. **References**: 1970, page 14 [2-1]; 1971, page 14 [2-1]; 1972, page 24 [2-1]; 1973, page 29 [2-1]; 1975, page 27 [2-1]; 1977, page 38 [2-1]

Line: 1962. Continental. Ice Tea. 13-1/2 oz. 6-1/4 inches tall. Plain Crystal. **References**: 1970, page 14 [2-8]; 1971, page 14 [2-8]; 1972, page 24 [2-8]; 1973, page 29 [2-8]; 1975, page 27 [2-6]; 1977, page 38 [2-6]

Line: 1962. Continental. Juice. 6-1/2 oz. 5-1/4 inches tall. Plain Crystal. **References**: 1970, page 14 [2-7]; 1971, page 14 [2-7]; 1972, page 24 [2-7]; 1973, page 29 [2-7]

Line: 1962. Continental. Plate. 7 inches diam. Plain Crystal, 7-7/8" Dia. **References**: 1970, page 14 [2-10]; 1971, page 14 [2-10]; 1972, page 24 [2-10]; 1973, page 29 [2-10]; 1975, page 27 [2-8]; 1977, page 38 [2-8]

Line: 1962. Continental. Plate. 8 inches diam. Plain Crystal, 8-3/4" Dia. **References**: 1970, page 14 [2-11]; 1971, page 14 [2-11];

1972, page 24 [2-11]; 1973, page 29 [2-11]; 1975, page 27 [2-9];

1977, page 38 [2-9]

Line: 1962. Continental. Red Wine Goblet. 9-1/2 oz. 6-3/8 inches tall. Plain Crystal. **References**: 1970, page 14 [2-3]; 1971, page 14 [2-3]; 1972, page 24 [2-3]; 1973, page 29 [2-3]; 1975, page 27 [2-3]; 1977, page 38 [2-3]

Line: 1962. Continental. Sherbet. 6-1/2 oz. 5 inches tall. Plain Crystal. **References**: 1970, page 14 [2-2]; 1971, page 14 [2-2]; 1972, page 24 [2-2]; 1973, page 29 [2-2]; 1975, page 27 [2-2]; 1977, page 38 [2-2]

Line: 1962. Continental. White Wine. 7 oz. 5-3/4 inches tall. Plain Crystal. **References**: 1975, page 27 [2-4]; 1970, page 14 [2-4]; 1971, page 14 [2-4]; 1972, page 24 [2-4]; 1973, page 29 [2-4]; 1977, page 38 [2-4]

Line: 1962. Olympia. Cocktail. 4-1/2 oz. / 4-3/4" hi. Platinum Band. **References**: 1967, page 11 [1-13]; 1968, page 15 [1-13]; 1969, page 19 [2-13]; 1970, page 20 [2-13]; 1971, page 20 [2-13]; 1972, page 28 [2-13]; 1973, page 33 [2-13]

Line: 1962. Olympia. Cordial. 1-1/4 oz. / 3-3/4" hi. Platinum Band.

Refe 1970, page 20 [2-14]; 1971, page 20 [2-14]; 1972, page 28 [2-14]; 1973, page 33 [2-14]; 1975, page 29 [2-11]; 1977, page 40 [2-11]

Line: 1962. Olympia. Goblet. 12-1/2 oz. 6-5/8" hi. Platinum Band. **References**: 1967, page 11 [1-10]; 1968, page 15 [1-10]; 1969, page 19 [2-10]; 1970, page 20 [2-10]; 1971, page 20 [2-10]; 1972, page 28 [2-10]; 1973, page 33 [2-10]; 1975, page 29 [2-8]; 1977, page 40 [2-8]

Line: 1962. Olympia. Ice Tea. 13-1/2 oz. / 6-1/4" hi. Platinum Band. **References**: 1967, page 11 [1-16]; 1968, page 15 [1-16]; 1969, page 19 [2-16]; 1970, page 20 [2-16]; 1971, page 20 [2-16]; 1972, page 28 [2-16]; 1973, page 33 [2-16]; 1975, page 29 [2-12]; 1977, page 40 [2-12]

Line: 1962. Olympia. Juice. 6-1/2 oz. / 5-1/4" hi. Platinum Band. **References**: 1967, page 11 [1-15]; 1968, page 15 [1-15]; 1969, page 19 [2-15]; 1970, page 20 [2-15]; 1971, page 20 [2-15]; 1972, page 28 [2-15]; 1973, page 33 [2-15]

Line: 1962. Olympia. Plate. 7" / Actually 7-7/8" Dia. Platinum Band. **References**: 1967, page 11 [1-17]; 1968, page 15 [1-17]; 1969, page 19 [2-17]; 1970, page 20 [2-17]; 1971, page 20 [2-17]; 1972, page 28 [2-17]; 1973, page 33 [2-17]; 1975, page 29 [2-13]; 1977, page 40 [2-13]

Line: 1962. Olympia. Plate. 8" / Actually 8-3/4" Dia. Platinum Band. **References**: 1967, page 11 [1-18]; 1968, page 15 [1-18]; 1969, page 19 [2-18]; 1970, page 20 [2-18]; 1971, page 20 [2-18]; 1972, page 28 [2-18]; 1973, page 33 [2-18]; 1975, page 29 [2-14]; 1977, page 40 [2-14]

Line: 1962. Olympia. Sherbet. 6-1/2 oz. / 5" hi. Platinum Band. **References**: 1967, page 11 [1-11]; 1968, page 15 [1-11]; 1969, page 19 [2-11]; 1970, page 20 [2-11]; 1971, page 20 [2-11]; 1972, page 28 [2-11]; 1973, page 33 [2-11]; 1975, page 29 [2-9]; 1977, page 40 [2-9]

Line: 1962. Olympia. White Wine. 7 oz. 5-3/4 inches tall. Platinum Band. **References**: 1975, page 29 [2-10]; 1977, page 40 [2-10]; 1967, page 11 [1-12]; 1968, page 15 [1-12]; 1969, page 19 [2-12]; 1970, page 20 [2-12]; 1971, page 20 [2-12]; 1972, page 28 [2-12]; 1973, page 33 [2-12]

Line: 1963. Pristine. Cocktail. 5-1/2 oz. / 4-3/4" hi. Platinum Band. **References**: 1967, page 11 [2-4]; 1968, page 15 [2-4]; 1969, page 20 [2-4]; 1970, page 21 [2-4]; 1971, page 21 [2-4]; 1972, page 29 [2-4]; 1973, page 34 [2-4]

Line: 1963. Pristine. Cordial. 1-1/2 oz. / 4" hi. Platinum Band. **References**: 1967, page 11 [2-5]; 1968, page 15 [2-5]; 1969, page 20 [2-5]; 1970, page 21 [2-5]; 1971, page 21 [2-5]; 1972, page 29 [2-5]; 1973, page 34 [2-5]; 1975, page 30 [2-4]; 1977, page 41 [2-4]; 1979, page 6 [1-24]

Line: 1963. Pristine. Goblet. 13-1/2 oz. / 6-3/4" hi. Platinum Band. **References**: 1967, page 11 [2-1]; 1968, page 15 [2-1]; 1969, page 20 [2-1]; 1970, page 21 [2-1]; 1971, page 21 [2-1]; 1972, page 29 [2-1]; 1973, page 34 [2-1]; 1975, page 30 [2-1]; 1977, page 41 [2-1]

Line: 1963. Pristine. Ice Tea. 14 oz. / 6-1/4" hi. Platinum Band. **References**: 1967, page 11 [2-7]; 1968, page 15 [2-7]; 1969, page 20 [2-7]; 1970, page 21 [2-7]; 1971, page 21 [2-7]; 1972, page 29 [2-7]; 1973, page 34 [2-7]; 1975, page 30 [2-5]; 1977, page 41 [2-5]

Line: 1963. Pristine. Juice. 7 oz. / 5-1/4" hi. Platinum Band. **References**: 1967, page 11 [2-6]; 1968, page 15 [2-6]; 1969, page 20 [2-6]; 1970, page 21 [2-6]; 1971, page 21 [2-6]; 1972, page 29 [2-6]; 1973, page 34 [2-6]

Line: 1963. Pristine. Plate. 7" / Actually 7-7/8" Dia. Platinum Band. **References**: 1967, page 11 [2-8]; 1968, page 15 [2-8]; 1969, page 20 [2-8]; 1970, page 21 [2-8]; 1971, page 21 [2-8]; 1972, page 29 [2-8]; 1973, page 34 [2-8]; 1975, page 30 [2-6]; 1977, page 41 [2-6]

Line: 1963. Pristine. Plate. 8" / Actually 8-3/4" Dia. Platinum Band. **References**: 1967, page 11 [2-9]; 1968, page 15 [2-9]; 1969, page 20 [2-9]; 1970, page 21 [2-9]; 1971, page 21 [2-9]; 1972, page 29 [2-9]; 1973, page 34 [2-9]; 1975, page 30 [2-7]; 1977, page 41 [2-7]

Line: 1963. Pristine. Sherbet. 7-1/2 oz. / 5-1/8" hi. Platinum Band. **References**: 1967, page 11 [2-2]; 1968, page 15 [2-2]; 1969, page 20 [2-2]; 1970, page 21 [2-2]; 1971, page 21 [2-2]; 1972, page 29 [2-2]; 1973, page 34 [2-2]; 1975, page 30 [2-2]; 1977, page 41 [2-2]

Line: 1963. Pristine. Wine. 7-3/4 oz. / 5-3/4" hi. Platinum Band. **References**: 1967, page 11 [2-3]; 1968, page 15 [2-3]; 1969, page 20 [2-3]; 1970, page 21 [2-3]; 1971, page 21 [2-3]; 1972, page 29 [2-3]; 1973, page 34 [2-3]; 1975, page 30 [2-3]; 1977, page 41 [2-3]

Line: 1963. Sylvia. Cocktail. 5-1/2 oz. / 4-3/4" hi. Gold Band. **References**: 1967, page 11 [2-13]; 1968, page 15 [2-13]; 1969, page 20 [2-13]; 1970, page 21 [2-13]; 1971, page 21 [2-13]; 1972, page 29 [2-13]; 1973, page 34 [2-13]

Line: 1963. Sylvia. Cordial. 1-1/2 oz. / 4" hi. Gold Band. **References**: 1967, page 11 [2-14]; 1968, page 15 [2-14]; 1969, page 20 [2-14]; 1970, page 21 [2-14]; 1971, page 21 [2-14]; 1972, page 29 [2-14]; 1973, page 34 [2-14]; 1975, page 30 [2-11]; 1977, page 41 [2-11]; 1979, page 6 [1-29]

Line: 1963. Sylvia. Goblet. 13-1/2 oz. / 6-3/4" hi. Gold Band. **References**: 1967, page 11 [2-10]; 1968, page 15 [2-10]; 1969, page 20 [2-10]; 1970, page 21 [2-10]; 1971, page 21 [2-10]; 1972, page 29 [2-10]; 1973, page 34 [2-10]; 1975, page 30 [2-8]; 1977, page 41 [2-8]

Line: 1963. Sylvia. Ice Tea. 14 oz. / 6-1/4" hi. Gold Band. **References**: 1967, page 11 [2-16]; 1968, page 15 [2-16]; 1969, page 20 [2-16]; 1970, page 21 [2-16]; 1971, page 21 [2-16]; 1972, page 29 [2-16]; 1973, page 34 [2-16]; 1975, page 30 [2-12]; 1977, page 41 [2-12]

Line: 1963. Sylvia. Juice. 7 oz. / 5-1/4" hi. Gold Band. **References**: 1967, page 11 [2-15]; 1968, page 15 [2-15]; 1969, page 20 [2-15]; 1970, page 21 [2-15]; 1971, page 21 [2-15]; 1972, page 29 [2-15]; 1973, page 34 [2-15]

Line: 1963. Sylvia. Plate. 7" / Actually 7-7/8" Dia. Gold Band. **References**: 1967, page 11 [2-17]; 1968, page 15 [2-17]; 1969, page 20 [2-17]; 1970, page 21 [2-17]; 1971, page 21 [2-17]; 1972, page 29 [2-17]; 1973, page 34 [2-17]; 1975, page 30 [2-13]; 1977, page 41 [2-13]

Line: 1963. Sylvia. Plate. 8" / Actually 8-3/4" Dia. Gold Band. **References**: 1967, page 11 [2-18]; 1968, page 15 [2-18]; 1969, page 20 [2-18]; 1970, page 21 [2-18]; 1971, page 21 [2-18]; 1972, page 29 [2-18]; 1973, page 34 [2-18]; 1975, page 30 [2-14]; 1977, page 41 [2-14]

Line: 1963. Sylvia. Sherbet. 7-1/2 oz. - 5-1/8" hi. Gold Band. **References**: 1967, page 11 [2-11]; 1968, page 15 [2-11]; 1969, page 20 [2-11]; 1970, page 21 [2-11]; 1971, page 21 [2-11]; 1972, page 29 [2-11]; 1973, page 34 [2-11]; 1975, page 30 [2-9]; 1977, page 41 [2-9]

Line: 1963. Sylvia. Wine. 7-3/4 oz. / 5-3/4" hi. Gold Band. **References**: 1967, page 11 [2-12]; 1968, page 15 [2-12]; 1969, page 20 [2-12]; 1970, page 21 [2-12]; 1971, page 21 [2-12]; 1972, page 29 [2-12]; 1973, page 34 [2-12]; 1975, page 30 [2-10]; 1977, page 41 [2-10]

Line: 1963. Cut: 63. Grace. 1305 Dessert-Finger Bowl. 4-1/2" Dia. **References**: 1967, page 8 [2-18]; 1968, page 12 [2-18]; 1969, page 12 [2-8]; 1970, page 13 [2-8]; 1971, page 13 [2-8]; 1972, page 22 [1-18]; 1973, page 26 [1-18]; 1975, page 26 [1-14]; 1977, page 37 [1-14]

Line: 1963. Cut: 63. Grace. Cocktail. 5-1/2 oz. / 4-3/4" hi. **References**: 1967, page 8 [2-14]; 1968, page 12 [2-14]; 1969, page 12 [2-4]; 1970, page 13 [2-4]; 1971, page 13 [2-4]; 1972, page 22 [1-14]; 1973, page 26 [1-14]

Line: 1963. Cut: 63. Grace. Cordial. 1-1/2 oz. / 4" hi. **References**: 1967, page 8 [2-15]; 1968, page 12 [2-15]; 1969, page 12 [2-5]; 1970, page 13 [2-5]; 1971, page 13 [2-5]; 1972, page 22 [1-15]; 1973, page 26 [1-15]; 1975, page 26 [1-12]; 1977, page 37 [1-12]

Line: 1963. Cut: 63. Grace. Goblet. 13-1/2 oz. / 6-3/4" hi. **References**: 1967, page 8 [2-11]; 1968, page 12 [2-11]; 1969, page 12 [2-1]; 1970, page 13 [2-1]; 1971, page 13 [2-1]; 1972, page 22 [1-11]; 1973, page 26 [1-11]; 1975, page 26 [1-9]; 1977, page 37 [1-9]

Line: 1963. Cut: 63. Grace. Ice Tea. 14 oz. / 6-1/4" hi. **References**: 1967, page 8 [2-17]; 1968, page 12 [2-17]; 1969, page 12 [2-7]; 1970, page 13 [2-7]; 1971, page 13 [2-7]; 1972, page 22 [1-17]; 1973, page 26 [1-17]; 1975, page 26 [1-13]; 1977, page 37 [1-13]

Line: 1963. Cut: 63. Grace. Juice. 7 oz. / 5-1/4" hi. **References**: 1967, page 8 [2-16]; 1968, page 12 [2-16]; 1969, page 12 [2-6]; 1970, page 13 [2-6]; 1971, page 13 [2-6]; 1972, page 22 [1-16]; 1973, page 26 [1-16]

Line: 1963. Cut: 63. Grace. Plate. 7" / Actually 7-7/8" Dia. **References**: 1967, page 8 [2-19]; 1968, page 12 [2-19]; 1969, page 12 [2-9]; 1970, page 13 [2-9]; 1971, page 13 [2-9]; 1972, page 22 [1-19]; 1973, page 26 [1-19]; 1975, page 26 [1-15]; 1977, page 37 [1-15]

Line: 1963. Cut: 63. Grace. Plate. 8" / Actually 8-3/4" Dia. **References**: 1967, page 8 [2-20]; 1968, page 12 [2-20]; 1969, page 12 [2-10]; 1970, page 13 [2-10]; 1971, page 13 [2-10]; 1972, page 22 [1-20]; 1973, page 26 [1-20]; 1975, page 26 [1-16]; 1977, page 37 [1-16]

Line: 1963. Cut: 63. Grace. Sherbet. 7-1/2 oz. / 5-1/8" hi. **References**: 1967, page 8 [2-12]; 1968, page 12 [2-12]; 1969, page 12 [2-2]; 1970, page 13 [2-2]; 1971, page 13 [2-2]; 1972, page 22 [1-12]; 1973, page 26 [1-12]; 1975, page 26 [1-10]; 1977, page 37 [1-10]

Line: 1963. Cut: 63. Grace. Wine. 7-3/4 oz. / 5-3/4" hi. **References**: 1967, page 8 [2-13]; 1968, page 12 [2-13]; 1969, page 12 [2-3]; 1970, page 13 [2-3]; 1971, page 13 [2-3]; 1972, page 22 [1-13]; 1973, page 26 [1-13]; 1975, page 26 [1-11]; 1977, page 37 [1-11]

Line: 1963. Cut: 1406. Darlene. Cocktail. 5-1/2 oz. / 4-3/4" hi. Gold Band. **References**: 1967, page 11 [2-22]; 1968, page 15 [2-22]

Line: 1963. Cut: 1406. Darlene. Cordial. 1-1/2 oz. / 4" hi. Gold Band. **References**: 1967, page 11 [2-23]; 1967, page 11 [2-19]

Line: 1963. Cut: 1406. Darlene. Goblet. 13-1/2 oz. / 6-3/4" hi. Gold Band. **References**: 1968, page 15 [2-19]

Line: 1963. Cut: 1406. Darlene. Ice Tea. 14 oz. / 6-1/4" hi. Gold Band. **References**: 1967, page 11 [2-25]; 968, page 15 [2-25]

Line: 1963. Cut: 1406. Darlene. Juice. 7 oz. / 5-1/4" hi. Gold Band. **References**: 1967, page 11 [2-24]; 1968, page 15 [2-24]

Line: 1963. Cut: 1406. Darlene. Plate. 7" / Actually 7-7/8" Dia. Gold Band. **References**: 1967, page 11 [2-26]; 1968, page 15 [2-26]

Line: 1963. Cut: 1406. Darlene. Plate. 8" / Actually 8-3/4" Dia. Gold Band. **References**: 1967, page 11 [2-27]; 1968, page 15 [2-27]

Line: 1963. Cut: 1406. Darlene. Sherbet. 7-1/2 oz. / 5-1/8" hi. Gold Band. **References**: 1967, page 11 [2-20]; 1968, page 15 [2-20]

Line: 1963. Cut: 1406. Darlene. Wine. 7-3/4 oz. / 5-3/4" hi. Gold Band. **References**: 1967, page 11 [2-21]; 1968, page 15 [2-21]

Line: 1963. Cut: 1406. Diane. Cocktail. 5-1/2 oz. / 4-3/4" hi. NOT BANDED. **References**: 1967, page 11 [2-31]; 1968, page 15 [2-31]

Line: 1963. Cut: 1406. Diane. Cordial. 1-1/2 oz. / 4" hi. NOT BANDED. **References**: 1967, page 11 [2-32]; 1968, page 15 [2-32]

Line: 1963. Cut: 1406. Diane. Goblet. 13-1/2 oz. / 6-3/4" hi. NOT BANDED. **References**: 1967, page 11 [2-28]; 1968, page 15 [2-28]

Line: 1963. Cut: 1406. Diane. Ice Tea. 14 oz. / 6-1/4" hi. NOT BANDED. **References**: 1967, page 11 [2-34]; 1968, page 15 [2-34]

Line: 1963. Cut: 1406. Diane. Juice. 7 oz. / 5-1/4" hi. NOT BANDED. **References**: 1967, page 11 [2-33]; 1968, page 15 [2-33]

Line: 1963. Cut: 1406. Diane. Plate. 7" / Actually 7-7/8" Dia. NOT BANDED. **References**: 1967, page 11 [2-35]; 1968, page 15 [2-35]

Line: 1963. Cut: 1406. Diane. Plate. 8" / Actually 8-3/4" Dia. NOT BANDED. **References**: 1967, page 11 [2-36]; 1968, page 15 [2-36]

Line: 1963. Cut: 1406. Diane. Sherbet. 7-1/2 oz. / 5-1/8" hi. NOT BANDED. **References**: 1967, page 11 [2-29]; 1968, page 15 [2-29]

Line: 1963. Cut: 1406. Diane. Wine. 7-3/4 oz. / 5-3/4" hi. NOT BANDED. **References**: 1967, page 11 [2-30]; 1968, page 15 [2-30]

Line: 1963. Cut: 1406. Fantasy. Cocktail. 5-1/2 oz. / 4-3/4" hi. Platinum Band. **References**: 1967, page 11 [2-40]; 1968, page 15 [2-40]

Line: 1963. Cut: 1406. Fantasy. Cordial. 1-1/2 oz. / 4" hi. Platinum Band. **References**: 1967, page 11 [2-41]; 1968, page 15 [2-41]

Line: 1963. Cut: 1406. Fantasy. Goblet. 13-1/2 oz. / 6-3/4" hi. Platinum Band. **References**: 1967, page 11 [2-37]; 1968, page 15 [2-37]

Line: 1963. Cut: 1406. Fantasy. Ice Tea. 14 oz. / 6-1/4" hi. Platinum Band. **References**: 1967, page 11 [2-43]; 1968, page 15 [2-43]

Line: 1963. Cut: 1406. Fantasy. Juice. 7 oz. / 5-1/4" hi. Platinum Band. **References**: 1967, page 11 [2-42]; 1968, page 15 [2-42]

Line: 1963. Cut: 1406. Fantasy. Plate. 7" / Actually 7-7/8" Dia. Platinum Band. **References**: 1967, page 11 [2-44]; 1968, page 15 [2-44]

Line: 1963. Cut: 1406. Fantasy. Plate. 8" / Actually 8-3/4" Dia. Platinum Band. **References**: 1967, page 11 [2-45]; 1968, page 15 [2-45]

Line: 1963. Cut: 1406. Fantasy. Sherbet. 7-1/2 oz. / 5-1/8" hi. Platinum Band. **References**: 1967, page 11 [2-38]; 1968, page 15 [2-38]

Line: 1963. Cut: 1406. Fantasy. Wine. 7-3/4 oz. / 5-3/4" hi. Platinum Band. **References**: 1967, page 11 [2-39]; 1968, page 15 [2-39]

Line: 1963. Cut: 1408. First Lady. 1305 Dessert-Finger Bowl. 4-1/4 inches diam. **References**: 1970, page 13 [1-8]; 1976, page 26 [1-6]; 1977, page 37 [1-6]

Line: 1963. Cut: 1408. First Lady. Cocktail. 5-1/2 oz. 4-3/4 inches tall. **References**: 1970, page 13 [1-4]

Line: 1963. Cut: 1408. First Lady. Cordial. 1-1/2 oz. 4 inches tall. **References**: 1970, page 13 [1-5]; 1975, page 26 [1-4]; 1977, page 37 [1-4]; 1981, page 1 [1-12]

Line: 1963. Cut: 1408. First Lady. Goblet. 13-1/2 oz. 6-3/4 inches tall. **References**: 1970, page 13 [1-1]; 1975, page 26 [1-1]; 1977, page 37 [1-1]; 1981, page 1 [1-9]

Line: 1963. Cut: 1408. First Lady. Ice Tea. 14 oz. 6-1/4 inches tall. **References**: 1970, page 13 [1-7]; 1975, page 26 [1-5]; 1977, page 37 [1-5]

Line: 1963. Cut: 1408. First Lady. Juice. 7 oz. 5-1/4 inches tall. **References**: 1970, page 13 [1-6]

Line: 1963. Cut: 1408. First Lady. Plate. 7 inches diam. Actually 7-7/8" Dia. **References**: 1970, page 13 [1-9]; 1975, page 26 [1-7]; 1977, page 37 [1-7]

Line: 1963. Cut: 1408. First Lady. Plate. 8 inches diam. Actually 8-3/4" Dia. **References**: 1970, page 13 [1-10]; 1975, page 26 [1-8]; 1977, page 37 [1-8]

Line: 1963. Cut: 1408. First Lady. Sherbet. 7-1/2 oz. 5-1/8 inches tall. **References**: 1970, page 13 [1-2]; 1975, page 26 [1-2]; 1977, page 37 [1-2]; 1981, page 1 [1-10]

Line: 1963. Cut: 1408. First Lady. Wine. 7-3/4 oz. 5-3/4 inches tall. **References**: 1970, page 13 [1-3]; 1975, page 26 [1-3]; 1977, page 37 [1-3]; 1981, page 1 [1-11]

Line: 1963. Cut: 1409. First Lady. 1305 Dessert-Finger Bowl. 4-1/4" Dia. **References**: 1967, page 8 [1-8]; 1968, page 12 [1-8]; 1969, page 12 [1-8]; 1971, page 13 [1-8]; 1972, page 22 [1-8]; 1973, page 26 [1-8]

Line: 1963. Cut: 1409. First Lady. Cocktail. 5-1/2 oz. / 4-3/4" hi. **References**: 1967, page 8 [1-4]; 1968, page 12 [1-4]; 1969, page 12 [1-4]; 1971, page 13 [1-4]; 1972, page 22 [1-4]; 1973, page 26 [1-4]

Line: 1963. Cut: 1409. First Lady. Cordial. 1-1/2 oz. / 4" hi. **References**: 1967, page 8 [1-5]; 1968, page 12 [1-5]; 1969, page 12 [1-5]; 1971, page 13 [1-5]; 1972, page 22 [1-5]; 1973, page 26 [1-5]

Line: 1963. Cut: 1409. First Lady. Goblet. 13-1/2 oz. / 6-3/4" hi. **References**: 1967, page 8 [1-1]; 1968, page 12 [1-1]; 1969, page 12 [1-1]; 1971, page 13 [1-1]; 1972, page 22 [1-1]; 1973, page 26 [1-1]

Line: 1963. Cut: 1409. First Lady. Ice Tea. 14 oz. / 6-1/4" hi. **References**: 1967, page 8 [1-7]; 1968, page 12 [1-7]; 1969, page 12 [1-7]; 1971, page 13 [1-7]; 1972, page 22 [1-7]; 1973, page 26 [1-7]

Line: 1963. Cut: 1409. First Lady. Juice. 7 oz. / 5-1/4" hi. **References**: 1967, page 8 [1-6]; 1968, page 12 [1-6]; 1969, page 12 [1-6]; 1971, page 13 [1-6]; 1972, page 22 [1-6]; 1973, page 26 [1-6]

Line: 1963. Cut: 1409. First Lady. Plate. 7" / Actually 7-7/8" Dia. **References**: 1967, page 8 [1-9]; 1968, page 12 [1-9]; 1969, page 12 [1-9]; 1971, page 13 [1-9]; 1972, page 22 [1-9]; 1973, page 26 [1-9]

Line: 1963. Cut: 1409. First Lady. Plate. 8" / Actually 8-3/4" Dia. **References**: 1967, page 8 [1-10]; 1968, page 12 [1-10]; 1969, page 12 [1-10]; 1971, page 13 [1-10]; 1972, page 22 [1-10]; 1973, page 26 [1-10]

Line: 1963. Cut: 1409. First Lady. Sherbet. 7-1/2 oz. / 5-1/8" hi. **References**: 1967, page 8 [1-2]; 1968, page 11 [1-2]; 1969, page 11 [1-2]; 1971, page 13 [1-2]; 1972, page 22 [1-2]; 1973, page 26 [1-2]

Line: 1963. Cut: 1409. First Lady. Wine. 7-3/4 oz. / 5-3/4" hi. **References**: 1967, page 8 [1-3]; 1968, page 12 [1-3]; 1969, page 12 [1-3]; 1971, page 13 [1-3]; 1972, page 22 [1-3]; 1973, page 26 [1-3]

Line: 1963. Cut: 1409. True Love. 1305 Dessert-Finger Bowl. 4-1/2" Dia. **References**: 1967, page 8 [2-8]; 1968, page 12 [2-8]

Line: 1963. Cut: 1409. True Love. Cocktail. 5-1/2 oz. / 4-3/4" hi. **References**: 1967, page 8 [2-4]; 1968, page 12 [2-4]

Line: 1963. Cut: 1409. True Love. Cordial. 1-1/2 oz. / 4" hi. **References**: 1967, page 8 [2-5]; 1968, page 12 [2-5]

Line: 1963. Cut: 1409. True Love. Goblet. 13-1/2 oz. / 6-3/4" hi. **References**: 1967, page 8 [2-1]; 1968, page 12 [2-1]

Line: 1963. Cut: 1409. True Love. Ice Tea. 14 oz. / 6-1/4" hi. **References**: 1967, page 8 [2-7]; 1968, page 12 [2-7]

Line: 1963. Cut: 1409. True Love. Juice. 7 oz. / 5-1/4" hi. **References**: 1967, page 8 [2-6]; 1968, page 12 [2-6]

Line: 1963. Cut: 1409. True Love. Plate. 7" / Actually 7-7/8" Dia. **References**: 1967, page 8 [2-9]; 1968, page 12 [2-9]

Line: 1963. Cut: 1409. True Love. Plate. 8" / Actually 8-3/4" Dia. **References**: 1967, page 8 [2-10]; 1968, page 12 [2-10]

Line: 1963. Cut: 1409. True Love. Sherbet. 7-1/2 oz. / 5-1/8" hi. **References**: 1967, page 8 [2-2]; 1968, page 12 [2-2]

Line: 1963. Cut: 1409. True Love. Wine. 7-3/4 oz. / 5-3/4" hi. **References**: 1967, page 8 [2-3]; 1968, page 12 [2-3]

Line: 1963. Cut: 1458. Bouquet. Cordial. 1-1/2 oz. 4 inches tall. **References**: 1982, page 1 [2-4]

Line: 1963. Cut: 1458. Bouquet. Goblet. 13-1/2 oz. 6-3/4 inches tall. **References**: 1982, page 1 [2-1]

Line: 1963. Cut: 1458. Bouquet. Ice Tea. 14 oz. 6-1/4 inches tall. **References**: 1982, page 1 [2-5]

Line: 1963. Cut: 1458. Bouquet. Sherbet. 7-1/2 oz. 5-1/8 inches tall. **References**: 1982, page 1 [2-2]

Line: 1963. Cut: 1458. Bouquet. Wine. 7-3/4 oz. 5-3/4 inches tall. **References**: 1982, page 1 [2-3]

Line: 1963. Cut: 1459. Harvest. Cordial. 1-1/2 oz. 4 inches tall. **References**: 1982, page 1 [2-9]

Line: 1963. Cut: 1459. Harvest. Goblet. 13-1/2 oz. 6-3/4 inches tall. **References**: 1982, page 1 [2-6]

Line: 1963. Cut: 1459. Harvest. Ice Tea. 14 oz. 6-1/4 inches tall. **References**: 1982, page 1 [2-10]

Line: 1963. Cut: 1459. Harvest. Sherbet. 7-1/2 oz. 5-1/8 inches tall. **References**: 1982, page 1 [2-7]

Line: 1963. Cut: 1459. Harvest. Wine. 7-3/4 oz. 5-3/4 inches tall. **References**: 1982, page 1 [2-8]

Line: 1963. Cut: 1460. Arbor. Cordial. 1-1/2 oz. 4 inches tall. **References**: 1982, page 1 [1-4]

Line: 1963. Cut: 1460. Arbor. Goblet. 13-1/2 oz. 6-3/4 inches tall. **References**: 1982, page 1 [1-1]

Line: 1963. Cut: 1460. Arbor. Ice Tea. 14 oz. 6-1/4 inches tall. **References**: 1982, page 1 [1-5]

Line: 1963. Cut: 1460. Arbor. Sherbet. 7-1/2 oz. 5-1/8 inches tall. **References**: 1982, page 1 [1-2]

Line: 1963. Cut: 1460. Arbor. Wine. 7-3/4 oz. 5-3/4 inches tall. **References**: 1982, page 1 [1-3]

Line: 1964. Andover. 1305 Dessert-Finger Bowl. 4-1/2" Dia. Gold Band. **References**: 1967, page 14 [1-7]; 1968, page 18 [1-7]

Line: 1964. Andover. Cordial. 1-1/2 oz. / 3-3/4" hi. Gold Band. **References**: 1967, page 14 [1-4]; 1968, page 18 [1-4]; 1969, page 20 [1-4]; 1970, page 21 [1-4]; 1971, page 21 [1-4]; 1972, page 29 [1-4]; 1973, page 34 [1-4]; 1975, page 30 [1-4]; 1977, page 40 [1-4]

Line: 1964. Andover. Goblet. 13-3/4 oz. / 6-1/2" hi. Gold Band. **References**: 1967, page 14 [1-1]; 1968, page 18 [1-1]; 1969, page 20 [1-1]; 1970, page 21 [1-1]; 1971, page 21 [1-1]; 1972, page 29 [1-1]; 1973, page 34 [1-1]; 1975, page 30 [1-1]; 1977, page 41 [1-1]

Line: 1964. Andover. Ice Tea. 14-1/4 oz. / 6-3/8" hi. Gold Band. **References**: 1967, page 14 [1-6]; 1968, page 18 [1-6]; 1969, page 20 [1-6]; 1970, page 21 [1-6]; 1971, page 21 [1-6]; 1972, page 29 [1-6]; 1973, page 34 [1-6]; 1975, page 30 [1-5]; 1977, page 40 [1-5]

Line: 1964. Andover. Juice. 6-3/4 oz. / 4-3/4" hi. Gold Band. **References**: 1967, page 14 [1-5]; 1968, page 18 [1-5]; 1969, page 20 [1-5]; 1970, page 21 [1-5]; 1971, page 21 [1-5]; 1972, page 29 [1-5]; 1973, page 34 [1-5]

Line: 1964. Andover. Plate. 7" / Actually 7-7/8" Dia. Gold Band. **References**: 1967, page 14 [1-8]; 1968, page 18 [1-8]; 1969, page 20 [1-7]; 1970, page 21 [1-7]; 1971, page 21 [1-7]; 1972, page 29 [1-7]; 1973, page 34 [1-7]; 1975, page 30 [1-6]; 1977, page 40 [1-6]

Line: 1964. Andover. Plate. 8" / Actually 8-3/4" Dia. Gold Band. **References**: 1967, page 14 [1-9]; 1968, page 18 [1-9]; 1968, page 18 [1-9]; 1969, page 20 [1-8]; 1970, page 21 [1-8]; 1971, page 21 [1-8]; 1972, page 29 [1-8]; 1973, page 34 [1-8]; 1975, page 30 [1-7]; 1977, page 40 [1-7]

Line: 1964. Andover. Sherbet. 7-1/2 oz. / 4-3/8" hi. Gold Band. **References**: 1967, page 14 [1-2]; 1968, page 18 [1-2]; 1969, page 20 [1-2]; 1970, page 21 [1-2]; 1971, page 21 [1-2]; 1972, page 29 [1-2]; 1973, page 34 [1-2]; 1975, page 30 [1-2]; 1977, page 40 [1-2]

Line: 1964. Andover. Wine. 9 oz. / 5-5/8" hi. Gold Band. **References**: 1967, page 14 [1-3]; 1968, page 18 [1-3]; 1969, page 20 [1-3]; 1970, page 21 [1-3]; 1971, page 21 [1-3]; 1972, page 29 [1-3]; 1973, page 34 [1-3]; 1975, page 30 [1-3]; 1977, page 40 [1-3]

Line: 1964. Cabaret. Cordial. 1-1/2 oz. 3-3/4 inches tall. Yellow, Crystal Foot. **References**: 1970, page 3 [1-4]

Line: 1964. Cabaret. Cordial. 1-1/2 oz. 3-3/4 inches tall. Greenbrier, Platinum Band, Crystal Foot. **References**: 1970, page 4 [1-4]

Line: 1964. Cabaret. Cordial. 1-1/2 oz. 3-3/4 inches tall. Plain Crystal. **References**: 1970, page 21 [1-20]; 1971, page 21 [1-20]; 1972, page 29 [1-20]; 1975, page 30 [1-18]; 1973, page 34 [1-20]; 1977, page 41 [1-18]

Line: 1964. Cabaret. Cordial. 1-1/2 oz. 3-3/4 inches tall. Yellow/Crystal Foot. Colors Available: Brown/Crystal Foot, Delphine Blue/Crystal Foot, Green/Crystal Foot, Grey/Crystal Foot, Yellow/Crystal Foot. Items Available: Goblet, Sherbet, Wine, Cordial, Ice Tea. **References**: 1971, page 44 [2-3]

Line: 1964. Cabaret. Goblet. 13-3/4 oz. 6-1/2 inches tall. Delphine Blue, Crystal Foot. **References**: 1970, page 3 [1-1]

Line: 1964. Cabaret. Goblet. 13-3/4 oz. 6-1/2 inches tall. Silver Dawn, Platinum Band, Crystal Foot. **References**: 1970, page 4 [1-1]

Line: 1964. Cabaret. Goblet. 13-3/4 oz. 6-1/2 inches tall. Plain Crystal. **References**: 1970, page 21 [1-17]; 1971, page 21 [1-17]; 1972, page 29 [1-17]; 1973, page 34 [1-17]; 1975, page 30 [1-15]; 1977, page 41 [1-15]

Line: 1964. Cabaret. Goblet. 13-3/4 oz. 6-1/2 inches tall. Delphine Blue/Crystal Foot. Colors Available: Brown/Crystal Foot, Delphine Blue/Crystal Foot, Green/Crystal Foot, Grey/Crystal Foot, Yellow/Crystal Foot. Items Available: Goblet, Sherbet, Wine, Cordial, Ice Tea. **References**: 1971, page 44 [2-2]

Line: 1964. Cabaret. Ice Tea. 14-1/4 oz. 6-3/8 inches tall. Brown, Crystal Foot. **References**: 1970, page 3 [1-5]

Line: 1964. Cabaret. Ice Tea. 14-1/4 oz. 6-3/8 inches tall. Sunset Gold, Gold Band, Crystal Foot. **References**: 1970, page 4 [1-5]

Line: 1964. Cabaret. Ice Tea. 14-1/4 oz. 6-3/8 inches tall. Plain Crystal. **References**: 1970, page 21 [1-22]; 1971, page 21 [1-22]; 1972, page 29 [1-22]; 1973, page 34 [1-22]; 1975, page 30 [1-19]; 1977, page 41 [1-19]

Line: 1964. Cabaret. Ice Tea. 14-1/4 oz. 6-3/8 inches tall. Brown/Crystal Foot. Colors Available: Brown/Crystal Foot, Delphine Blue/Crystal Foot, Green/Crystal Foot, Grey/Crystal Foot, Yellow/Crystal Foot. Items Available: Goblet, Sherbet, Wine, Cordial, Ice Tea. **References**: 1971, page 44 [1-1]

Line: 1964. Cabaret. Juice. 6-3/4 oz. 4-3/4 inches tall. Plain Crystal. **References**: 1970, page 21 [1-21]; 1971, page 21 [1-21]; 1972, page 29 [1-21]; 1973, page 34 [1-21]

Line: 1964. Cabaret. Plate. 7 inches diam. Plain Crystal, Actually 7-7/8" Dia. **References**: 1970, page 21 [1-23]; 1971, page 21 [1-23]; 1972, page 29 [1-23]; 1973, page 34 [1-23]; 1975, page 30 [1-20]; 1977, page 41 [1-20]

Line: 1964. Cabaret. Plate. 8 inches diam. Plain Crystal, Actually 8-3/4" Dia. **References**: 1970, page 21 [1-24]; 1971, page 21 [1-24]; 1972, page 29 [1-24]; 1973, page 34 [1-24]; 1975, page 30 [1-21]; 1977, page 41 [1-21]

Line: 1964. Cabaret. Sherbet. 7-1/2 oz. 4-3/8 inches tall. Grey, Crystal Foot. **References**: 1970, page 3 [1-2]

Line: 1964. Cabaret. Sherbet. 7-1/2 oz. 4-3/8 inches tall. Blue Mist, Delphine Blue, Platinum Band, Crystal Foot. **References**: 1970, page 4 [1-2]

Line: 1964. Cabaret. Sherbet. 7-1/2 oz. 4-3/8 inches tall. Plain Crystal. **References**: 1970, page 21 [1-18]; 1971, page 21 [1-18]

Line: 1964. Cabaret. Sherbet. 7-1/2 oz. 4-3/8 inches tall. Grey/Crystal Foot. Colors Available: Brown/Crystal Foot, Delphine Blue/Crystal Foot, Green/Crystal Foot, Grey/Crystal Foot, Yellow/Crystal Foot. Items Available: Goblet, Sherbet, Wine, Cordial, Ice Tea. **References**: 1971, page 44 [2-1]

Line: 1964. Cabaret. Sherbet. 7-1/2 oz. 4-3/8 inches tall. Plain Crystal. **References**: 1972, page 29 [1-18]; 1973, page 34 [1-18]; 1975, page 30 [1-16]; 1977, page 41 [1-16]

Line: 1964. Cabaret. Wine. 9 oz. 5-5/8 inches tall. Green, Crystal Foot. **References**: 1970, page 3 [1-3]

Line: 1964. Cabaret. Wine. 9 oz. 5-5/8 inches tall. Desert Gold, Gold Band, Crystal Foot. **References**: 1970, page 4 [1-3]

Line: 1964. Cabaret. Wine. 9 oz. 5-5/8 inches tall. Plain Crystal. **References**: 1970, page 21 [1-19]; 1971, page 21 [1-19]

Line: 1964. Cabaret. Wine. 9 oz. 5-5/8 inches tall. Green/Crystal Foot. Colors Available: Brown/Crystal Foot, Delphine Blue/Crystal Foot, Green/Crystal Foot, Grey/Crystal Foot, Yellow/Crystal Foot. Items Available: Goblet, Sherbet, Wine, Cordial, Ice Tea. **References**: 1971, page 44 [1-2]

Line: 1964. Cabaret. Wine. 9 oz. 5-5/8 inches tall. Plain Crystal. **References**: 1972, page 29 [1-19]; 1973, page 34 [1-19]; 1975, page 30 [1-17]; 1977, page 41 [1-17]

Line: 1964. Lexington. 1305 Dessert-Finger Bowl. 4-1/2" Dia. Platinum Band. **References**: 1967, page 14 [1-16]; 1968, page 18 [1-16]

Line: 1964. Lexington. Cordial. 1-1/2 oz. / 3-3/4" hi. Platinum Band. **References**: 1967, page 14 [1-13]; 1968, page 18 [1-13]; 1969, page 20 [1-12]; 1970, page 21 [1-12]; 1971, page 21 [1-12]; 1972, page 29 [1-12]; 1973, page 34 [1-12]; 1975, page 30 [1-11]; 1977, page 41 [1-11]

Line: 1964. Lexington. Goblet. 13-3/4 oz. / 6-1/2" hi. Platinum Band. **References**: 1967, page 14 [1-10]; 1968, page 18 [1-10]; 1969, page 20 [1-9]; 1970, page 21 [1-9]; 1971, page 21 [1-9]; 1972, page 29 [1-9]; 1973, page 34 [1-9]; 1975, page 30 [1-8]; 1977, page 41 [1-8]

Line: 1964. Lexington. Ice Tea. 14-1/4 oz. / 6-3/8" hi. Platinum Band. **References**: 1967, page 14 [1-15]; 1968, page 18 [1-15]; 1969, page 20 [1-14]; 1970, page 21 [1-14]; 1971, page 21 [1-14]; 1972, page 29 [1-14]; 1973, page 34 [1-14]; 1975, page 30 [1-12]; 1977, page 41 [1-12]

Line: 1964. Lexington. Juice. 6-3/4 oz. / 4-3/4" hi. Platinum Band. **References**: 1967, page 14 [1-14]; 1968, page 18 [1-14]; 1969, page 20 [1-13]; 1970, page 21 [1-13]; 1971, page 21 [1-13]; 1972, page 29 [1-13]; 1973, page 34 [1-13]

Line: 1964. Lexington. Plate. 7" / Actually 7-7/8" Dia. Platinum Band. **References**: 1967, page 14 [1-17]; 1968, page 18 [1-17]; 1969, page 20 [1-15]; 1970, page 21 [1-15]; 1971, page 21 [1-15]; 1972, page 29 [1-15]; 1973, page 34 [1-15]; 1975, page 30 [1-13]; 1977, page 41 [1-13]

Line: 1964. Lexington. Plate. 8" / Actually 8-3/4" Dia. Platinum Band. **References**: 1967, page 14 [1-18]; 1968, page 18 [1-18]; 1969, page 20 [1-16];

1970, page 21 [1-16]; 1971, page 21 [1-16]; 1972, page 29 [1-16]; 1973, page 34 [1-16]; 1975, page 30 [1-14]; 1977, page 41 [1-14]

Line: 1964. Lexington. Sherbet. 7-1/2 oz. / 4-3/8" hi. Platinum Band. **References**: 1967, page 14 [1-11]; 1968, page 18 [1-11]; 1969, page 20 [1-10]; 1970, page 21 [1-10]; 1971, page 21 [1-10]; 1972, page 29 [1-10]; 1973, page 34 [1-10]; 1975, page 30 [1-9]; 1977, page 41 [1-9]

Line: 1964. Lexington. Wine. 9 oz. / 5-5/8" hi. Platinum Band. **References**: 1967, page 14 [1-12]; 1968, page 18 [1-12]; 1969, page 20 [1-11]; 1970, page 21 [1-11]; 1971, page 21 [1-11]; 1972, page 29 [1-11]; 1973, page 34 [1-11]; 1975, page 30 [1-10]; 1977, page 41 [1-10]

Line: 1964. Cut: 1412. Carousel. 1305 Dessert-Finger Bowl. 4-1/2 inches diam. **References**: 1967, page 14 [1-25]; 1968, page 18 [1-25]; 1968, page 18 [1-25]

Line: 1964. Cut: 1412. Carousel. Cordial. 1-1/2 oz. 3-3/4 inches tall. **References**: 1967, page 14 [1-22]; 1968, page 18 [1-22]; 1968, page 18 [1-22]

Line: 1964. Cut: 1412. Carousel. Goblet. 13-3/4 oz. / 6-1/2" hi. **References**: 1967, page 14 [1-19]; 1968, page 18 [1-19]; 1968, page 18 [1-19]

Line: 1964. Cut: 1412. Carousel. Ice Tea. 14-1/4 oz. 6-3/8 inches tall. **References**: 1967, page 14 [1-24]; 1968, page 18 [1-24]; 1968, page 18 [1-24]

Line: 1964. Cut: 1412. Carousel. Juice. 6-3/4 oz. 4-3/4 inches tall. **References**: 1967, page 14 [1-23]; 1968, page 18 [1-23]; 1968, page 18 [1-23]

Line: 1964. Cut: 1412. Carousel. Plate. 7 inches diam. Actually 7-7/8" Dia. **References**: 1967, page 14 [1-26]; 1968, page 18 [1-26]; 1968, page 18 [1-26]

Line: 1964. Cut: 1412. Carousel. Plate. 8 inches diam. Actually 8-3/4" Dia. **References**: 1967, page 14 [1-27]; 1968, page 18 [1-27]; 1968, page 18 [1-27]

Line: 1964. Cut: 1412. Carousel. Sherbet. 7-1/2 oz. / 4-3/8" hi. **References**: 1967, page 14 [1-20]; 1968, page 18 [1-20]; 1968, page 18 [1-20]

Line: 1964. Cut: 1412. Carousel. Wine. 9 oz. / 5-5/8" hi. **References**: 1967, page 14 [1-21]; 1968, page 18 [1-21]; 1968, page 18 [1-21]

Line: 1964. Cut: 1413. Monte Carlo. 1305 Dessert-Finger Bowl. 4-1/2 inches diam. **References**: 1967, page 14 [2-16]; 1968, page 18 [2-16]

Line: 1964. Cut: 1413. Monte Carlo. Cordial. 1-1/2 oz. 3-3/4 inches tall. **References**: 1967, page 14 [2-13]; 1968, page 18 [2-13]

Line: 1964. Cut: 1413. Monte Carlo. Goblet. 13-3/4 oz. 6-1/2 inches tall. **References**: 1967, page 14 [2-10]; 1968, page 18 [2-10]

Line: 1964. Cut: 1413. Monte Carlo. Ice Tea. 14-1/4 oz. 6-3/8 inches tall. **References**: 1967, page 14 [2-15]; 1968, page 18 [2-15]

Line: 1964. Cut: 1413. Monte Carlo. Juice. 6-3/4 oz. 4-3/4 inches tall. **References**: 1967, page 14 [2-14]; 1968, page 18 [2-14]

Line: 1964. Cut: 1413. Monte Carlo. Plate. 7 inches diam. Actually 7-7/8" Dia. **References**: 1967, page 14 [2-17]; 1968, page 18 [2-17]

Line: 1964. Cut: 1413. Monte Carlo. Plate. 8 inches diam. Actually 8-3/4" Dia. **References**: 1967, page 14 [2-18]; 1968, page 18 [2-18]

Line: 1964. Cut: 1413. Monte Carlo. Sherbet. 7-1/2 oz. 4-3/8 inches tall. **References**: 1967, page 14 [2-11]; 1968, page 18 [2-11]

Line: 1964. Cut: 1413. Monte Carlo. Wine. 9 oz. 5-5/8 inches tall. **References**: 1967, page 14 [2-12]; 1968, page 18 [2-12]

Line: 1964. Cut: 1414. Copenhagen. 1305 Dessert-Finger Bowl. 4-1/2 inches diam. **References**: 1967, page 14 [2-7]; 1968, page 18 [2-7]

Line: 1964. Cut: 1414. Copenhagen. Cordial. 1-1/2 oz. 3-3/4 inches tall. **References**: 1967, page 14 [2-4]; 1968, page 18 [2-4]

Line: 1964. Cut: 1414. Copenhagen. Goblet. 13-3/4 oz. 6-1/2 inches tall. **References**: 1967, page 14 [2-1]; 1968, page 18 [2-1]

Line: 1964. Cut: 1414. Copenhagen. Ice Tea. 14-1/4 oz. 6-3/8 inches tall. **References**: 1967, page 14 [2-6]; 1968, page 18 [2-6]

Line: 1964. Cut: 1414. Copenhagen. Juice. 6-3/4 oz. 4-3/4 inches tall. **References**: 1967, page 14 [2-5]; 1968, page 18 [2-5]

Line: 1964. Cut: 1414. Copenhagen. Plate. 7 inches diam. Actually 7-7/8" Dia. **References**: 1967, page 14 [2-8]; 1968, page 18 [2-8]

Line: 1964. Cut: 1414. Copenhagen. Plate. 8 inches diam. Actually 8-3/4" Dia. **References**: 1967, page 14 [2-9]; 1968, page 18 [2-9]

Line: 1964. Cut: 1414. Copenhagen. Sherbet. 7-1/2 oz. 4-3/4 inches tall. **References**: 1967, page 14 [2-2]; 1968, page 18 [2-2]

Line: 1964. Cut: 1414. Copenhagen. Wine. 9 oz. 5-5/8 inches tall. **References**: 1967, page 14 [2-3]; 1968, page 18 [2-3]

Line: 1965. Cut: 1416. Lafayette. 1305 Dessert-Finger Bowl. 4-1/2 Dia. **References**: 1967, page 7 [1-16]; 1968, page 10 [1-7]; 1969, page 11 [2-16]; 1970, page 12 [2-16]; 1971, page 12 [2-16]; 1972, page 21 [2-16]; 1973, page 25 [2-16]; 1975, page 25 [2-14]; 1977, page 36 [2-14]

Line: 1965. Cut: 1416. Lafayette. Cordial. 1-1/4 oz. / 4" hi. **References**: 1967, page 7 [1-13]; 1968, page 10 [1-4]; 1969, page 11 [2-13]; 1970, page 12 [2-13]; 1971, page 12 [2-13]; 1972, page 21 [2-13]; 1973, page 25 [2-13]; 1975, page 25 [2-12]; 1977, page 36 [2-12]; 1981, page 1 [2-8]

Line: 1965. Cut: 1416. Lafayette. Goblet. 11-3/4 oz. / 7-1/4" hi. **References**: 1967, page 7 [1-10]; 1968, page 10 [1-1]; 1969, page 11 [2-10]; 1970, page 12 [2-10]; 1971, page 12 [2-10]; 1972, page 21 [2-10]; 1973, page 25 [2-10]; 1975, page 25 [2-9]; 1977, page 36 [2-9]; 1981, page 1 [2-5]

Line: 1965. Cut: 1416. Lafayette. Ice Tea. 13-1/2 oz. / 6-3/4" hi. **References**: 1967, page 7 [1-15]; 1968, page 10 [1-6]; 1969, page 11 [2-15]; 1970, page 12 [2-15]; 1971, page 12 [2-15]; 1972, page 21 [2-15]; 1973, page 25 [2-15]; 1975, page 25 [2-13]; 1977, page 36 [2-13]

Line: 1965. Cut: 1416. Lafayette. Juice. 6 oz. / 5-1/2" hi. **References**: 1967, page 7 [1-14]; 1968, page 10 [1-5]; 1969, page 11 [2-14]; 1970, page 12 [2-14]; 1971, page 12 [2-14]; 1972, page 21 [2-14]; 1973, page 25 [2-14]

Line: 1965. Cut: 1416. Lafayette. Plate. 7" / Actually 7-7/8" Dia. **References**: 1967, page 7 [1-17]; 1968, page 10 [1-8]; 1969, page 11 [2-17]; 1970, page 12 [2-17]; 1971, page 12 [2-17]; 1972, page 21 [2-17]; 1973, page 25 [2-17]; 1975, page 25 [2-15]; 1977, page 36 [2-15]

Line: 1965. Cut: 1416. Lafayette. Plate. 8 inches diam. Actually 8-3/4" Dia. **References**: 1967, page 7 [1-18]; 1968, page 10 [1-9]; 1969, page 11 [2-18]; 1970, page 12 [2-18]; 1971, page 12 [2-18]; 1972, page 21 [2-18]; 1973, page 25 [2-18]; 1975, page 25 [2-16]; 1977, page 36 [2-16]

Line: 1965. Cut: 1416. Lafayette. Sherbet. 7-1/2 oz. / 5-1/4" hi. **References**: 1967, page 7 [1-11]; 1968, page 10 [1-2]; 1969, page 11 [2-11]; 1970, page 12 [2-11]; 1971, page 12 [2-11]; 1972, page 21 [2-11]; 1973, page 25 [2-11]; 1975, page 25 [2-10]; 1977, page 36 [2-10]; 1981, page 1 [2-6]

Line: 1965. Cut: 1416. Lafayette. Wine. 7-1/2 oz. / 6-1/4" hi. **References**: 1967, page 7 [1-12]; 1968, page 10 [1-3]; 1969, page 11 [2-12]; 1970, page 12 [2-12]; 1971, page 12 [2-12]; 1972, page 21 [2-12]; 1973, page 25 [2-12]; 1975, page 25 [2-11]; 1977, page 36 [2-11]; 1981, page 1 [2-7]

Line: 1965. Cut: 1419. Solitaire. 1305 Dessert-Finger Bowl. 4-1/2 inches diam. **References**: 1968, page 11 [2-7]

Line: 1965. Cut: 1419. Solitaire. Cordial. 1-1/4 oz. 4 inches tall. **References**: 1968, page 11 [2-4]

Line: 1965. Cut: 1419. Solitaire. Goblet. 11-3/4 oz. 7-1/4 inches tall. **References**: 1968, page 11 [2-1]

Line: 1965. Cut: 1419. Solitaire. Ice Tea. 13-1/2 oz. 6-3/4 inches tall. **References**: 1968, page 11 [2-6]

Line: 1965. Cut: 1419. Solitaire. Juice. 6 oz. 5-1/2 inches tall. **References**: 1968, page 11 [2-5]

Line: 1965. Cut: 1419. Solitaire. Plate. 7 inches diam. Actually 7-7/8" Dia. **References**: 1968, page 11 [2-8]

Line: 1965. Cut: 1419. Solitaire. Plate. 8 inches diam. Actually 8-3/4" Dia. **References**: 1968, page 11 [2-9]

Line: 1965. Cut: 1419. Solitaire. Sherbet. 7-1/2 oz. 5-1/4 inches tall. **References**: 1968, page 11 [2-2]

Line: 1965. Cut: 1419. Solitaire. Wine. 7-1/2 oz. 6-1/4 inches tall. **References**: 1968, page 11 [2-3]

Line: 1965. Cut: 1420. Princess Anne. 1305 Dessert-Finger Bowl. 4-1/2" Dia. **References**: 1967, page 7 [3-16]; 1968, page 11 [2-16]

Line: 1965. Cut: 1420. Princess Anne. Cordial. 1-1/4 oz. / 4 hi. **References**: 1967, page 7 [3-13]; 1968, page 11 [2-13]

Line: 1965. Cut: 1420. Princess Anne. Goblet. 11-3/4 oz. / 7-1/4" hi. **References**: 1967, page 7 [3-10]; 1968, page 11 [2-10]

Line: 1965. Cut: 1420. Princess Anne. Ice Tea. 13-1/2 oz. / 6-3/4" hi. **References**: 1967, page 7 [3-15]; 1968, page 11 [2-15]

Line: 1965. Cut: 1420. Princess Anne. Juice. 6 oz. / 5-1/2" hi. **References**: 1967, page 7 [3-14]; 1968, page 11 [2-14]

Line: 1965. Cut: 1420. Princess Anne. Plate. 7" / Actually 7-7/8" Dia. **References**: 1967, page 7 [3-17]; 1968, page 11 [2-17]

Line: 1965. Cut: 1420. Princess Anne. Plate. 8" / Actually 8-3/4" Dia. **References**: 1967, page 7 [3-18]; 1968, page 11 [2-18]

Line: 1965. Cut: 1420. Princess Anne. Sherbet. 7-1/2 oz. / 5-1/4" hi. **References**: 1967, page 7 [3-11]; 1968, page 11 [2-11]

Line: 1965. Cut: 1420. Princess Anne. Wine. 7-1/2 oz. / 6-1/4" hi. **References**: 1967, page 7 [3-12]; 1968, page 11 [2-12]

Line: 1965. Cut: 1421. Anniversary. 1305 Dessert-Finger Bowl. 4-1/2" Dia. **References**: 1967, page 7 [2-7]; 1968, page 11 [1-7]; 1969, page 11 [1-7]; 1970, page 12 [1-7]; 1971, page 12 [1-7]; 1972, page 21 [1-7]; 1973, page 25 [1-7]; 1975, page 25 [1-6]; 1977, page 36 [1-6]

Line: 1965. Cut: 1421. Anniversary. Cordial. 1-1/4 oz. / 4" hi. **References**: 1967, page 7 [2-4]; 1968, page 11 [1-4]; 1969, page 11 [1-4]; 1970, page 12 [1-4]; 1971, page 12 [1-4]; 1972, page 21 [1-4]; 1973, page 25 [1-4]; 1975, page 25 [1-4]; 1977, page 36 [1-4]; 1981, page 1 [2-4]

Line: 1965. Cut: 1421. Anniversary. Goblet. 11-3/4 oz. / 7-1/4" hi. **References**: 1967, page 7 [2-1]; 1968, page 11 [1-1]; 1969, page 11 [1-1]; 1970, page 12 [1-1]; 1971, page 12 [1-1]; 1972, page 21 [1-1]; 1973, page 25 [1-1]; 1975, page 25 [1-1]; 1977, page 36 [1-1]; 1981, page 1 [2-1]

Line: 1965. Cut: 1421. Anniversary. Ice Tea. 13-1/2 oz. / 6-3/4" hi. **References**: 1967, page 7 [2-6]; 1968, page 11 [1-6]; 1969, page 11 [1-6]; 1970, page 12 [1-6]; 1971, page 12 [1-6]; 1972, page 21 [1-6]; 1973, page 25 [1-6]; 1975, page 25 [1-5]; 1977, page 36 [1-5]

Line: 1965. Cut: 1421. Anniversary. Juice. 6 oz. / 5-1/2" hi. **References**: 1967, page 7 [2-5]; 1968, page 11 [1-5]; 1969, page 11 [1-5]; 1970, page 12 [1-5]; 1971, page 12 [1-5]; 1972, page 21 [1-5]; 1973, page 25 [1-5]

Line: 1965. Cut: 1421. Anniversary. Plate. 7" / Actually 7-7/8" Dia. **References**: 1967, page 7 [2-8]; 1968, page 11 [1-8]; 1969, page 11 [1-8]; 1970, page 12 [1-8]; 1971, page 12 [1-8]; 1972, page 21 [1-8]; 1973, page 25 [1-8]; 1975, page 25 [1-7]; 1977, page 36 [1-7]

Line: 1965. Cut: 1421. Anniversary. Plate. 8" / Actually 8-3/4" Dia. **References**: 1967, page 7 [2-9]; 1968, page 11 [1-9]; 1969, page 11 [1-9]; 1970, page 12 [1-9]; 1971, page 12 [1-9]; 1972, page 21 [1-9]; 1973, page 25 [1-9]; 1975, page 25 [1-8]; 1977, page 36 [1-8]

Line: 1965. Cut: 1421. Anniversary. Sherbet. 7-1/2 oz. / 5-1/4" hi. **References**: 1967, page 7 [2-2]; 1968, page 11 [1-2]; 1969, page 11 [1-2]; 1970, page 12 [1-2]; 1971, page 12 [1-2]; 1972, page 21 [1-2]; 1973, page 25 [1-2]; 1975, page 25 [1-2]; 1977, page 36 [1-2]; 1981, page 1 [2-2]

Line: 1965. Cut: 1421. Anniversary. Wine. 7-1/2 oz. / 6-1/4" hi. **References**: 1967, page 7 [2-3]; 1968, page 11 [1-3]; 1969, page 11 [1-3]; 1970, page 12 [1-3]; 1971, page 12 [1-3]; 1972, page 21 [1-3]; 1973, page 25 [1-3]; 1975, page 25 [1-3]; 1977, page 36 [1-3]; 1981, page 1 [2-3]

Line: 1965. Cut: 1422. Orleans. 1305 Dessert-Finger Bowl. 4-1/2" Dia. **References**: 1967, page 7 [1-7]; 1968, page 10 [2-7]; 1969, page 10 [2-7]; 1970, page 12 [2-7]; 1971, page 12 [2-7]; 1972, page 21 [2-7]; 1973, page 25 [2-7]; 1975, page 25 [2-6]; 1977, page 36 [2-6]

Line: 1965. Cut: 1422. Orleans. Cordial. 1-1/4 oz. / 4" hi. **References**: 1967, page 7 [1-4]; 1968, page 10 [2-4]; 1969, page 10 [2-4]; 1970, page 12 [2-4]; 1971, page 12 [2-4]; 1972, page 21 [2-4]; 1973, page 25 [2-4]; 1975, page 25 [2-4]; 1977, page 36 [2-4]; 1981, page 1 [2-12]

Line: 1965. Cut: 1422. Orleans. Goblet. 11-3/4 oz. / 7-1/4" hi. **References**: 1967, page 7 [1-1]; 1968, page 10 [2-1]; 1969, page 10 [2-1]; 1970, page 12 [2-1]; 1971, page 12 [2-1]; 1972, page 21 [2-1]; 1973, page 25 [2-1]; 1975, page 25 [2-1]; 1977, page 36 [2-1]; 1981, page 1 [2-9]

Line: 1965. Cut: 1422. Orleans. Ice Tea. 13-1/2 oz. / 6-3/4" hi. **References**: 1967, page 7 [1-6]; 1968, page 10 [2-6]; 1969, page 10 [2-6]; 1970, page 12 [2-6]; 1971, page 12 [2-6]; 1972, page 21 [2-6]; 1973, page 25 [2-6]; 1975, page 25 [2-5]; 1977, page 36 [2-5]

Line: 1965. Cut: 1422. Orleans. Juice. 6 oz. / 5-1/2" hi. **References**: 1967, page 7 [1-5]; 1968, page 10 [2-5]; 1969, page 10 [2-5]; 1970, page 12 [2-5]; 1971, page 12 [2-5]; 1972, page 21 [2-5]; 1973, page 25 [2-5]

Line: 1965. Cut: 1422. Orleans. Plate. 7" / Actually 7-7/8" Dia. **References**: 1967, page 7 [1-8]; 1968, page 10 [2-8]; 1969, page 10 [2-8]; 1970, page 12 [2-8]; 1971, page 12 [2-8]; 1972, page 21 [2-8]; 1973, page 25 [2-8]; 1975, page 25 [2-7]; 1977, page 36 [2-7]

Line: 1965. Cut: 1422. Orleans. Plate. 8" / Actually 8-3/4" Dia. **References**: 1967, page 7 [1-9]; 1968, page 10 [2-9]; 1969, page 10 [2-9]; 1970, page 12 [2-9]; 1971, page 12 [2-9]; 1972, page 21 [2-9]; 1973, page 25 [2-9]; 1975, page 25 [2-8]; 1977, page 36 [2-8]

Line: 1965. Cut: 1422. Orleans. Sherbet. 7-1/2 oz. / 5-1/4" hi. **References**: 1967, page 7 [1-2]; 1968, page 10 [2-2]; 1969, page 10 [2-2]; 1970, page 12 [2-2]; 1971, page 12 [2-2]; 1972, page 21 [2-2]; 1973, page 25 [2-2]; 1975, page 25 [2-2]; 1977, page 36 [2-2]; 1981, page 1 [2-10]

Line: 1965. Cut: 1422. Orleans. Wine. 7-1/2 oz. / 6-1/4" hi. **References**: 1967, page 7 [1-3]; 1968, page 10 [2-3]; 1969, page 10 [2-3]; 1970, page 12 [2-3]; 1971, page 12 [2-3]; 1972, page 21 [2-3]; 1973, page 25 [2-3]

Line: 1965. Cut: 1422. Orleans. Wine. 7-1/2 oz. 6-1/4 inches tall. **References**: 1975, page 25 [2-3]; 1977, page 36 [2-3]; 1981, page 1 [2-11]

Line: 1965. Cut: 1423. Capristrano. 1305 Dessert-Finger Bowl. 4-1/2" Dia. **References**: 1967, page 7 [3-7]; 1968, page 10 [2-16]

Line: 1965. Cut: 1423. Capristrano. Cordial. 1-1/4 oz. - 4" hi. **References**: 1967, page 7 [3-4]; 1968, page 10 [2-13]

Line: 1965. Cut: 1423. Capristrano. Goblet. 11-3/4 oz. / 7-1/4" hi. **References**: 1967, page 7 [3-1]; 1968, page 10 [2-10]

Line: 1965. Cut: 1423. Capristrano. Ice Tea. 13-1/2 oz. / 6-3/4" hi. **References**: 1967, page 7 [3-6]; 1968, page 10 [2-15]

Line: 1965. Cut: 1423. Capristrano. Juice. 6 oz. / 5-1/2" hi. **References**: 1967, page 7 [3-5]; 1968, page 10 [2-14]

Line: 1965. Cut: 1423. Capristrano. Plate. 7" / Actually 7-7/8" Dia. **References**: 1967, page 7 [3-8]; 1968, page 10 [2-17]

Line: 1965. Cut: 1423. Capristrano. Plate. 8" / Actually 8-3/4" Dia. **References**: 1967, page 7 [3-9]; 1968, page 10 [2-18]

Line: 1965. Cut: 1423. Capristrano. Sherbet. 7-1/2 oz. / 5-1/4" hi. **References**: 1967, page 7 [3-2]; 1968, page 10 [2-11]

Line: 1965. Cut: 1423. Capristrano. Wine. 1-1/4 oz. / 4" hi. **References**: 1967, page 7 [3-3]; 1968, page 10 [2-12]

Line: 1966. Cut: 43. Aristocrat. 1305 Dessert-Finger Bowl. 4-1/2 inches diam. **References**: 1972, page 19 [2-8]; 1973, page 24 [2-8]; 1967, page 5 [2-14]; 1968, page 8 [3-14]

Line: 1966. Cut: 43. Aristocrat. 1305 Dessert-Finger Bowl. 4-1/2 inches diam. **References**: 1969, page 9 [2-8]; 1970, page 9 [2-8]; 1971, page 9 [2-8]; 1975, page 24 [2-8]; 1977, page 35 [2-8]

Line: 1966. Cut: 43. Aristocrat. All Purpose Wine Goblet. 8 oz. 5 inches tall. **References**: 1969, page 9 [2-5]; 1970, page 9 [2-5]; 1971, page 9 [2-5]; 1972, page 19 [2-5]; 1973, page 24 [2-5]; 1975, page 24 [2-5]; 1977, page 35 [2-5]

Line: 1966. Cut: 43. Aristocrat. Cordial. 1-1/4 oz. / 3-7/8" hi. **References**: 1967, page 5 [2-12]; 1968, page 8 [3-12]; 1969, page 9 [2-6]; 1970, page 9 [2-6]; 1971, page 9 [2-6]; 1972, page 19 [2-6]; 1973, page 24 [2-6]; 1975, page 24 [2-6]; 1977, page 35 [2-6]

Line: 1966. Cut: 43. Aristocrat. Goblet. 12 oz. / 7" hi. **References**: 1967, 1971, page 9 [2-1]; 1972, page 19 [2-1]; 1973, page 24 [2-1]; 1975, page 24 [2-1]; 1977, page 35 [2-1]

Line: 1966. Cut: 43. Aristocrat. Ice Tea. 14 oz. / 6-1/4" hi. **References**: 1967, page 5 [2-13]; 1968, page 8 [3-13]; 1969, page 9 [2-7]; 1970, page 9 [2-7]; 1971, page 9 [2-7]; 1972, page 19 [2-7]; 1973, page 24 [2-7]; 1975, page 24 [2-7]; 1977, page 35 [2-7]

Line: 1966. Cut: 43. Aristocrat. Plate. 7" / Actually 7-7/8" Dia. **References**: 1967, page 5 [2-15]; 1968, page 8 [3-15]; 1969, page 9 [2-9]; 1970, page 9 [2-9]; 1971, page 9 [2-9]; 1972, page 19 [2-9]; 1973, page 24 [2-9]; 1975, page 24 [2-9]; 1977, page 35 [2-9]

Line: 1966. Cut: 43. Aristocrat. Plate. 8" / Actually 8-3/4" Dia. **References**: 1967, page 5 [2-16]; 1968, page 8 [3-16]; 1969, page 9 [2-10]; 1970, page 9 [2-10]; 1971, page 9 [2-10]; 1972, page 19 [2-10]; 1973, page 24 [2-10]; 1975, page 24 [2-10]; 1977, page 35 [2-10]

Line: 1966. Cut: 43. Aristocrat. Sherbet. 7-1/2 oz. / 5-1/8" hi. **References**: 1967, page 5 [2-10]; 1968, page 8 [3-10]; 1969, page 9 [2-2]; 1970,

page 9 [2-2]; 1971, page 9 [2-2]; 1972, page 19 [2-2]; 1973, page 24 [2-2]; 1975, page 24 [2-2]; 1977, page 35 [2-2]

Line: 1966. Cut: 43. Aristocrat. Tulip Champagne. 8 oz. 8-1/2 inches tall. **References**: 1969, page 9 [2-4]; 1970, page 9 [2-4]; 1971, page 9 [2-4]; 1972, page 19 [2-4]; 1973, page 24 [2-4]; 1975, page 24 [2-4]; 1977, page 35 [2-4]

Line: 1966. Cut: 43. Aristocrat. Wine. 7-1/2 oz. / 6" hi. **References**: 1967, page 5 [2-11]; 1968, page 8 [3-11]; 1969, page 9 [2-3]; 1970, page 9 [2-3]; 1971, page 9 [2-3]; 1972, page 19 [2-3]; 1973, page 24 [2-3]; 1975, page 24 [2-3]; 1977, page 35 [2-3]

Line: 1966. Cut: 1430. Kimberly. 1305 Dessert-Finger Bowl. 4-1/2" Dia. 1968, page 8 [1-6]; 1969, page 8 [1-6]; 1970, page 8 [1-6]; 1971, page 8 [1-6]; 1972, page 18 [1-6]; 1973, page 23 [1-6]; 1975, page 23 [1-6]; 1977, page 34 [1-6]

Line: 1966. Cut: 1430. Kimberly. Cordial. 1-1/4 oz. / 3-7/8" hi. **References**: 1967, page 5 [1-4]; 1968, page 8 [1-4]; 1969, page 8 [1-4]; 1970, page 8 [1-4]; 1971, page 8 [1-4]; 1972, page 18 [1-4]; 1973, page 23 [1-4]; 1975, page 23 [1-4]; 1977, page 34 [1-4]; 1981, page 2 [3-8]; 1975/I-75, page 1 [3-2]

Line: 1966. Cut: 1430. Kimberly. Goblet. 12 oz. / 7" hi. **References**: 1967, page 5 [1-1]; 1968, page 8 [1-1]; 1969, page 8 [1-1]; 1970, page 8 [1-1]; 1971, page 8 [1-1]; 1972, page 18 [1-1]; 1973, page 23 [1-1]; 1975, page 23 [1-1]; 1977, page 34 [1-1]; 1981, page 2 [3-5]; 1975/I-75, page 1 [2-1]

Line: 1966. Cut: 1430. Kimberly. Ice Tea. 14 oz. / 6-1/4" hi. **References**: 1967, page 5 [1-5]; 1968, 1972, page 18 [1-5]; 1973, page 23 [1-5]; 1975, page 23 [1-5]; 1977, page 34 [1-5]; 1975/I-75, page 1 [3-1]

Line: 1966. Cut: 1430. Kimberly. Plate. 7" / Actually 7-7/8" Dia. **References**: 1967, page 5 [1-7]; 1967, page 5 [1-7]; 1968, page 8 [1-7]; 1969, page 8 [1-7]; 1970, page 8 [1-7]; 1971, page 8 [1-7]; 1972, page 18 [1-7]; 1973, page 23 [1-7]; 1975, page 23 [1-7]; 1977, page 34 [1-7]

Line: 1966. Cut: 1430. Kimberly. Plate. 8" / Actually 8-3/4" Dia. **References**: 1967, page 5 [1-8]; 1968, page 8 [1-8]; 1969, page 8 [1-8]; 1970, page 8 [1-8]; 1971, page 8 [1-8]; 1972, page 18 [1-8]; 1973, page 23 [1-8]; 1975, page 23 [1-8]; 1977, page 34 [1-8]

Line: 1966. Cut: 1430. Kimberly. Sherbet. 7-1/2 oz. / 5-1/8" hi. **References**: 1967, page 5 [1-2]; 1968, page 8 [1-2]; 1969, page 8 [1-2]; 1970, page 8 [1-2]; 1971, page 8 [1-2]; 1972, page 18 [1-2]; 1973, page 23 [1-2]; 1975, page 23 [1-2]; 1977, page 34 [1-2]; 1981, page 2 [3-6]; 1975/I-75, page 1 [1-2]

Line: 1966. Cut: 1430. Kimberly. Wine. 7-1/2 oz. / 6" hi. **References**: 1967, page 5 [1-3]; 1968, page 8 [1-3]; 1969, page 8 [1-3]; 1970, page 8 [1-3]; 1971, page 8 [1-3]; 1972, page 18 [1-3]; 1973, page 23 [1-3]; 1975, page 23 [1-3]; 1977, page 34 [1-3]; 1981, page 2 [3-7]; 1975/I-75, page 1 [1-1]

Line: 1966. Cut: 1431. Lavalier. 1305 Dessert-Finger Bowl. 4-1/2" Dia. **References**: 1967, page 5 [1-14]; 1968, page 8 [1-14]; 1969, page 8 [2-14]; 1970, page 8 [2-14]; 1971, page 8 [2-14]; 1972, page 18 [2-14]; 1973, page 23 [2-14]; 1975, page 23 [2-14]; 1977, page 34 [2-14]

Line: 1966. Cut: 1431. Lavalier. Cordial. 1-1/4 oz. / 3-7/8" hi. **References**: 1967, page 5 [1-12]; 1968, page 8 [1-12]; 1969, page 8 [2-12]; 1970, page 8 [2-12]; 1971, page 8 [2-12]; 1972, page 18 [2-12]; 1973, page 23 [2-12]; 1975, page 23 [2-12]; 1977, page 34 [2-12]

Line: 1966. Cut: 1431. Lavalier. Goblet. 12 oz. / 7" hi. **References**: 1967, page 5 [1-9]; 1968, page 8 [1-9]; 1969, page 8 [2-9]; 1970, page 8 [2-9]; 1971, page 8 [2-9]; 1972, page 18 [2-9]; 1973, page 23 [2-9]; 1975, page 23 [2-9]; 1977, page 34 [2-9]

Line: 1966. Cut: 1431. Lavalier. Ice Tea. 14 oz. / 6-1/4" hi. **References**: 1967, page 5 [1-13]; 1968, page 8 [1-13]; 1969, page 8 [2-13]; 1970, page 8 [2-13]; 1971, page 8 [2-13]; 1972, page 18 [2-13]; 1973, page 23 [2-13]; 1975, page 23 [2-13]; 1977, page 34 [2-13]

Line: 1966. Cut: 1431. Lavalier. Plate. 7" / Actually 7-7/8" Dia. **References**: 1967, page 5 [1-15]; 1968, page 8 [1-15]; 1969, page 8 [2-15]; 1970, page 8 [2-15]; 1971, page 8 [2-15]; 1972, page 18 [2-15]; 1973, page 23 [2-15]; 1975, page 23 [2-15]; 1977, page 34 [2-15]

Line: 1966. Cut: 1431. Lavalier. Plate. 8" / Actually 8-3/4" Dia. **References**: 1967, page 5 [1-16]; 1968, page 8 [1-16]; 1969, page 8 [2-16]; 1970, page 8 [2-16]; 1971, page 8 [2-16]; 1972, page 18 [2-16]; 1973, page 23 [2-16]; 1975, page 23 [2-16]; 1977, page 34 [2-16]

Line: 1966. Cut: 1431. Lavalier. Sherbet. 7-1/2 oz. / 5-1/8" hi. **References**: 1967, page 5 [1-10]; 1968, page 8 [1-10]; 1969, page 8 [2-10]; 1970, page 8 [2-10]; 1971, page 8 [2-10]; 1972, page 18 [2-10]; 1973, page 23 [2-10]; 1975, page 23 [2-10]; 1977, page 34 [2-10]

Line: 1966. Cut: 1431. Lavalier. Wine. 7-1/2 oz. / 6" hi. **References**: 1967, page 5 [1-11]; 1968, page 8 [1-11]; 1969, page 8 [2-11]; 1970, page 8 [2-11]; 1971, page 8 [2-11]; 1972, page 18 [2-11]; 1973, page 23 [2-11]; 1975, page 23 [2-11]; 1977, page 34 [2-11]

Line: 1966. Cut: 1432. Traditional. 1305 Dessert-Finger Bowl. 4-1/2" Dia. **References**: 1967, page 5 [2-6]; 1968, page 8 [3-6]; 1969, page 8 [1-6]; 1970, page 8 [1-6]; 1971, page 8 [1-6]; 1972, page 19 [1-6]; 1973, page 24 [1-6]; 1975, page 24 [1-6]; 1977, page 35 [1-6]

Line: 1966. Cut: 1432. Traditional. Cordial. 1-1/4 oz. / 3-7/8" hi. **References**: 1967, page 5 [2-4]; 1968, page 8 [3-4]; 1969, page 8 [1-4]; 1970, page 8 [1-4]; 1971, page 8 [1-4]; 1972, page 19 [1-4]; 1973, page 24 [1-4]; 1975, page 24 [1-4]; 1977, page 35 [1-4]

Line: 1966. Cut: 1432. Traditional. Goblet. 12 oz. / 7" hi. **References**: 1967, page 5 [2-1]; 1968, page 8 [3-1]; 1969, page 8 [1-1]; 1970, page 8 [1-1]; 1971, page 8 [1-1]; 1972, page 19 [1-1]; 1973, page 24 [1-1]; 1975, page 24 [1-1]; 1977, page 35 [1-1]

Line: 1966. Cut: 1432. Traditional. Ice Tea. 14 oz. / 6-1/4" hi. **References**: 1967, page 5 [2-5]; 1968, page 8 [3-5]; 1969, page 8 [1-5]; 1970, page 8 [1-5]; 1971, page 8 [1-5]; 1972, page 19 [1-5]; 1973, page 24 [1-5]; 1975, page 24 [1-5]; 1977, page 35 [1-5]

Line: 1966. Cut: 1432. Traditional. Plate. 7" / 7-7/8" Dia. **References**: 1967, page 5 [2-7]; 1968, page 8 [3-7]; 1969, page 8 [1-7]; 1970, page 8 [1-7]; 1971, page 8 [1-7]; 1972, page 19 [1-7]; 1973, page 24 [1-7]; 1975, page 24 [1-7]; 1977, page 35 [1-7]

Line: 1966. Cut: 1432. Traditional. Plate. 8" / 8-3/4" Dia. **References**: 1967, page 5 [2-8]; 1968, page 8 [3-8]; 1969, page 8 [1-8]; 1970, page 8 [1-8]; 1971, page 8 [1-8]; 1972, page 19 [1-8]; 1973, page 24 [1-8]; 1975, page 24 [1-8]; 1977, page 35 [1-8]

Line: 1966. Cut: 1432. Traditional. Sherbet. 7-1/2 oz. / 5-1/8 hi. **References**: 1967, page 5 [2-2]; 1968, page 8 [3-2]; 1969, page 8 [1-2]; 1970, page 8 [1-2]; 1971, page 8 [1-2]; 1972, page 19 [1-2]; 1973, page 24 [1-2]; 1975, page 24 [1-2]; 1977, page 35 [1-2]

Line: 1966. Cut: 1432. Traditional. Wine. 7-1/2 oz. / 6" hi. **References**: 1967, page 5 [2-3]; 1968, page 8 [3-3]; 1969, page 8 [1-3]; 1970, page 8 [1-3]; 1971, page 8 [1-3]; 1972, page 19 [1-3]; 1973, page 24 [1-3]; 1975, page 24 [1-3]; 1977, page 35 [1-3]

Line: 1966. Cut: 1439. Bridal Tiara. 1305 Dessert-Finger Bowl. 4-1/2 inches diam. **References**: 1968, page 8 [2-6]; 1969, page 8 [2-6]; 1970, page 8 [2-6]; 1971, page 8 [2-6]; 1972, page 18 [2-6]; 1973, page 23 [2-6]; 1975, page 23 [2-6]; 1977, page 34 [2-6]

Line: 1966. Cut: 1439. Bridal Tiara. Cordial. 1-1/4 oz. 3-7/8 inches tall. **References**: 1968, page 8 [2-4]; 1969, page 8 [2-4]; 1970, page 8 [2-4]; 1971, page 8 [2-4]; 1972, page 18 [2-4]; 1973, page 23 [2-4]; 1975, page 23 [2-4]; 1977, page 34 [2-4]; 1981, page 2 [3-4]

Line: 1966. Cut: 1439. Bridal Tiara. Goblet. 12 oz. 7 inches tall. **References**: 1968, page 8 [2-1]; 1969, page 8 [2-1]; 1970, page 8 [2-1]; 1971, page 8 [2-1]; 1972, page 18 [2-1]; 1973, page 23 [2-1]; 1975, page 23 [2-1]; 1977, page 34 [2-1]; 1981, page 2 [3-1]

Line: 1966. Cut: 1439. Bridal Tiara. Ice Tea. 14 oz. 6-/14 inches tall. **References**: 1968, page 8 [2-5]; 1969, page 8 [2-5]; 1970, page 8 [2-5]; 1971, page 8 [2-5]; 1972, page 18 [2-5]; 1973, page 23 [2-5]; 1975, page 23 [2-5]; 1977, page 34 [2-5]

Line: 1966. Cut: 1439. Bridal Tiara. Plate. 7 inches diam. Actually 7-7/8" Dia. **References**: 1968, page 8 [2-7]; 1969, page 8 [2-7]; 1970, page 8 [2-7]; 1971, page 8 [2-7]; 1971, page 8 [2-8]; 1972, page 18 [2-7]; 1973, page 23 [2-7]; 1973, page 23 [2-8]; 1975, page 23 [2-7]; 1975, page 23 [2-8]; 1977, page 34 [2-7]; 1977, page 34 [2-8]

Line: 1966. Cut: 1439. Bridal Tiara. Plate. 8 inches diam. Actually 8-3/4" Dia. **References**: 1968, page 8 [2-8]; 1969, page 8 [2-8]; 1970, page 8 [2-8]; 1972, page 18 [2-8]

Line: 1966. Cut: 1439. Bridal Tiara. Sherbet. 7-1/2 oz. 5-1/8 inches tall. **References**: 1968, page 8 [2-2]; 1969, page 8 [2-2]; 1970, page 8 [2-2]; 1971, page 8 [2-2]; 1972, page 18 [2-2]; 1973, page 23 [2-2]; 1975, page 23 [2-2]; 1977, page 34 [2-2]; 1981, page 2 [3-2]

Line: 1966. Cut: 1439. Bridal Tiara. Wine. 7-1/2 oz. 6 inches tall. **References**: 1968, page 8 [2-3]; 1969, page 8 [2-3]; 1970, page 8 [2-3]; 1971, page 8 [2-3]; 1972, page 18 [2-3]; 1973, page 23 [2-3]; 1975, page 23 [2-3]; 1977, page 34 [2-3]; 1981, page 2 [3-3]

Line: 1967. Cut: 1427. Berkshire. 1305 Dessert-Finger Bowl. 4-1/2" Dia. **References**: 1967, page 6 [1-6]; 1968, page 9 [1-6]; 1969, page 10 [2-6]; 1970, page 10 [2-6]; 1971, page 10 [2-6]; 1972, page 17 [2-6]; 1973, page 22 [2-6]; 1975, page 22 [2-6]; 1977, page 33 [2-6]

Line: 1967. Cut: 1427. Berkshire. Cordial. 1-1/4 oz. / 3-3/4" hi. **References**: 1967, page 6 [1-4]; 1968, page 9 [1-4]; 1969, page 10 [2-4]; 1970, page 10 [2-4]; 1971, page 10 [2-4]; 1972, page 17 [2-4]; 1973, page 22 [2-4]; 1975, page 22 [2-4]; 1977, page 33 [2-4]

Line: 1967. Cut: 1427. Berkshire. Goblet. 12 oz. / 6-3/4" hi. **References**: 1967, page 6 [1-1]; 1968, page 9 [1-1]; 1969, page 10 [2-1]; 1970, page 10 [2-1]; 1971, page 10 [2-1]; 1972, page 17 [2-1];x 1973, page 22 [2-1]; 1975, page 22 [2-1]; 1977, page 33 [2-1]

Line: 1967. Cut: 1427. Berkshire. Ice Tea. 14 oz. / 6-3/8" hi. **References**: 1967, page 6 [1-5]; 1968, page 9 [1-5]; 1969, page 10 [2-5]; 1970, page 10 [2-5]; 1971, page 10 [2-5]; 1972, page 17 [2-5]; 1973, page 22 [2-5]; 1975, page 22 [2-5]; 1977, page 33 [2-5]

Line: 1967. Cut: 1427. Berkshire. Plate. 7" / Actually 7-7/8" Dia. **References**: 1967, page 6 [1-7]; 1968, page 9 [1-7]; 1969, page 10 [2-7]; 1970, page 10 [2-7]; 1971, page 10 [2-7]; 1972, page 17 [2-7]; 1973, page 22 [2-7]; 1975, page 22 [2-7]; 1975, page 22 [2-8]; 1977, page 33 [2-7]

Line: 1967. Cut: 1427. Berkshire. Plate. 8" / Actually 8-3/4" Dia. **References**: 1967, page 6 [1-8]; 1968, page 9 [1-8]; 1969, page 10 [2-8]; 1970, page 10 [2-8]; 1971, page 10 [2-8]; 1972, page 17 [2-8]; 1973, page 22 [2-8]; 1977, page 33 [2-8]

Line: 1967. Cut: 1427. Berkshire. Sherbet. 7-1/2 oz. / 5" hi. **References**: 1967, page 6 [1-2]; 1968, page 9 [1-2]; 1969, page 10 [2-2]; 1970, page 10 [2-2]; 1971, page 10 [2-2]; 1972, page 17 [2-2]; 1973, page 22 [2-2]; 1975, page 22 [2-2]; 1977, page 33 [2-2]

Line: 1967. Cut: 1427. Berkshire. Wine. 7-1/2 oz. / 6" hi. **References**: 1967, page 6 [1-3]; 1968, page 9 [1-3]; 1969, page 10 [2-3]; 1970, page 10 [2-3]; 1971, page 10 [2-3]; 1972, page 17 [2-3]; 1973, page 22 [2-3]; 1975, page 22 [2-3]; 1977, page 33 [2-3]

Line: 1967. Cut: 1428. Sherwood. 1305 Dessert-Finger Bowl. 4-1/2" Dia. **References**: 1967, page 6 [2-6]; 1968, page 9 [2-6]; 1969, page 10 [2-14]; 1970, page 10 [2-14]; 1971, page 10 [2-14]; 1972, page 17 [2-14]; 1973, page 22 [2-14]; 1975, page 22 [2-14]; 1977, page 33 [2-14]

Line: 1967. Cut: 1428. Sherwood. Cordial. 1-1/4 oz. / 3-3/4" hi. **References**: 1967, page 6 [2-4]; 1968, page 9 [2-4]; 1969, page 10 [2-12]; 1970, page 10 [2-12]; 1971, page 10 [2-12]; 1972, page 17 [2-12]; 1973, page 22 [2-12]; 1975, page 22 [2-12]; 1977, page 33 [2-12]

Line: 1967. Cut: 1428. Sherwood. Goblet. 12 oz. / 6-3/4" hi. **References**: 1967, page 6 [2-1]; 1968, page 9 [2-1]; 1969, page 10 [2-9]; 1970, page 10 [2-9]; 1971, page 10 [2-9]; 1972, page 17 [2-9]; 1973, page 22 [2-9]; 1975, page 22 [2-9]; 1977, page 33 [2-9]

Line: 1967. Cut: 1428. Sherwood. Ice Tea. 14 oz. / 6-3/8" hi. **References**: 1967, page 6 [2-5]; 1968, page 9 [2-5]; 1969, page 10 [2-13]; 1970, page 10 [2-13]; 1971, page 10 [2-13]; 1972, page 17 [2-13]; 1973, page 22 [2-13]; 1975, page 22 [2-13]; 1977, page 33 [2-13]

Line: 1967. Cut: 1428. Sherwood. Plate. 7" / Actually 7-7/8" Dia. **References**: 1967, page 6 [2-7]; 1968, page 9 [2-7]; 1970, page 10 [2-15]; 1971, page 10 [2-15]; 1972, page 17 [2-15]; 1973, page 22 [2-15]; 1975, page 22 [2-15]; 1977, page 33 [2-15]

Line: 1967. Cut: 1428. Sherwood. Plate. 8" / Actually 8-3/4" Dia. **References**: 1967, page 6 [2-8]; 1968, page 9 [2-8]; 1969, page 10 [2-15]; 1969, page 10 [2-16]; 1970, page 10 [2-16]; 1971, page 10 [2-16]; 1972, page 17 [2-16]; 1973, page 22 [2-16]; 1975, page 22 [2-16]; 1977, page 33 [2-16]

Line: 1967. Cut: 1428. Sherwood. Sherbet. 7-1/2 oz. / 5" hi. **References**: 1967, page 6 [2-2]; 1968, page 9 [2-2]; 1969, page 10 [2-10]; 1970, page 10 [2-10]; 1971, page 10 [2-10]; 1972, page 17 [2-10]; 1973, page 22 [2-10]; 1975, page 22 [2-10]; 1977, page 33 [2-10]

Line: 1967. Cut: 1428. Sherwood. Wine. 7-1/2 oz. / 6" hi. **References**: 1967, page 6 [2-3]; 1968, page 9 [2-3]; 1969, page 10 [2-11]; 1970, page 10 [2-11]; 1971, page 10 [2-11]; 1972, page 17 [2-11]; 1973, page 22 [2-11]; 1975, page 22 [2-11]; 1977, page 33 [2-11]

Line: 1967. Cut: 1429. Young Love. 1305 Dessert-Finger Bowl. 4-1/2" Dia. **References**: 1967, page 6 [2-14]; 1968, page 9 [2-14]; 1969, page 10 [1-6]; 1970, page 10 [1-6]; 1971, page 10 [1-6]; 1972, page 17 [1-6]; 1973, page 22 [1-6]; 1975, page 22 [1-6]; 1977, page 33 [1-6]

Line: 1967. Cut: 1429. Young Love. Cordial. 1-1/4 oz. / 3-3/4" hi. **References**: 1967, page 6 [2-12]; 1968, page 9 [2-12]; 1969, page 10 [1-4]; 1970, page 10 [1-4]; 1971, page 10 [1-4]; 1972, page 17 [1-4]; 1973, page 22 [1-4]; 1975, page 22 [1-4]; 1977, page 33 [1-4]

Line: 1967. Cut: 1429. Young Love. Goblet. 12 oz. / 6-3/4" hi. **References**: 1967, page 6 [2-9]; 1968, page 9 [2-9]; 1969, page 10 [1-1]; 1970, page 10 [1-1]; 1971, page 10 [1-1]; 1972, page 17 [1-1]; 1973, page 22 [1-1]; 1975, page 22 [1-1]; 1977, page 33 [1-1]

Line: 1967. Cut: 1429. Young Love. Ice Tea. 14 oz. / 6-3/8" hi. **References**: 1967, page 6 [2-13]; 1968, page 9 [2-13]; 1969, page 10 [1-5]; 1970, page 10 [1-5]; 1971, page 10 [1-5]; 1972, page 17 [1-5]; 1973, page 22 [1-5]; 1975, page 22 [1-5]; 1977, page 33 [1-5]

Line: 1967. Cut: 1429. Young Love. Plate. 7" / Actually 7-7/8" Dia. **References**: 1967, page 6 [2-15]; 1968, page 9 [2-15]; 1969, page 10 [1-7]; 1970, page 10 [1-7]; 1971, page 10 [1-7]; 1972, page 17 [1-7]; 1973, page 22 [1-7]; 1975, page 22 [1-7]; 1977, page 33 [1-7]

Line: 1967. Cut: 1429. Young Love. Plate. 8" / Actually 8-/34" Dia. **References**: 1967, page 6 [2-16]; 1968, page 9 [2-16]; 1969, page 10 [1-8]; 1970, page 10 [1-8]; 1971, page 10 [1-8]; 1972, page 17 [1-8]; 1973, page 22 [1-8]; 1975, page 22 [1-8]; 1977, page 33 [1-8]

Line: 1967. Cut: 1429. Young Love. Sherbet. 7-1/2 oz. / 5" hi. **References**: 1967, page 6 [2-10]; 1968, page 9 [2-10]; 1969, page 10 [1-2]; 1970, page 10 [1-2]; 1971, page 10 [1-2]; 1972, page 17 [1-2]; 1973, page 22 [1-2]; 1975, page 22 [1-2]; 1977, page 33 [1-2]

Line: 1967. Cut: 1429. Young Love. Wine. 7-1/2 oz. / 6" hi. **References**: 1967, page 6 [2-11]; 1968, page 9 [2-11]; 1969, page 10 [1-3]; 1970, page 10 [1-3]; 1971, page 10 [1-3]; 1972, page 17 [1-3]; 1973, page 22 [1-3]; 1975, page 22 [1-3]; 1977, page 33 [1-3]

Line: 1967. Cut: 1440. Chapel Belle. 1305 Dessert-Finger Bowl. 4-1/2 inches diam. **References**: 1968, page 9 [1-14]

Line: 1967. Cut: 1440. Chapel Belle. Cordial. 1-1/4 oz. 3-3/4 inches tall. **References**: 1968, page 9 [1-12]

Line: 1967. Cut: 1440. Chapel Belle. Goblet. 12 oz. 6-3/4 inches tall. **References**: 1968, page 9 [1-9]

Line: 1967. Cut: 1440. Chapel Belle. Ice Tea. 14 oz. 6-3/8 inches tall. **References**: 1968, page 9 [1-13]

Line: 1967. Cut: 1440. Chapel Belle. Plate. 7 inches diam. Actually 7-7/8" Dia. **References**: 1968, page 9 [1-15]

Line: 1967. Cut: 1440. Chapel Belle. Plate. 8 inches diam. Actually 8-3/4" Dia. **References**: 1968, page 9 [1-16]

Line: 1967. Cut: 1440. Chapel Belle. Sherbet. 7-1/2 oz. 5 inches tall. **References**: 1968, page 9 [1-10]

Line: 1967. Cut: 1440. Chapel Belle. Wine. 7-1/2 oz. 6 inches tall. **References**: 1968, page 9 [1-11]

Line: 1969. Bouquet. 1305 Dessert-Finger Bowl. 4-1/2 inches diam. Plain Crystal. **References**: 1969, page 18 [2-22]; 1970, page 19 [2-22]

Line: 1969. Bouquet. Cordial. 2 oz. 4-1/2 inches tall. Plain Crystal. **References**: 1969, page 18 [2-20]; 1969, page 28 [1-5]; 1970, page 1 [1-4]; 1970, page 19 [2-20]; 1971, page 30 [1-5]; 1972, page 14 [1-5]; 1973, page 28 [1-5]

Line: 1969. Bouquet. Cordial. 2 oz. 4-1/2 inches tall. Yellow. Colors Available: Brown, Delphine Blue, Green, Grey, Yellow. Items Available: Goblet, Sherbet, Wine, Cordial, Ice Tea. **References**: 1971, page 43 [2-1]; 1972, page 9 [2-1]

Line: 1969. Bouquet. Goblet. 14 oz. 6-3/4 inches tall. Plain Crystal. **References**: 1969, page 18 [2-17]; 1969, page 28 [1-1]; 1970, page 19 [2-17]; 1971, page 30 [1-1]; 1972, page 14 [1-1]; 1973, page 28 [1-1]

Line: 1969. Bouquet. Goblet. 14 oz. 6-3/4 inches tall. Delphine Blue. **References**: 1970, page 1 [1-1]

Line: 1969. Bouquet. Goblet. 14 oz. 6-3/4 inches tall. Delphine Blue. Colors Available: Brown, Delphine Blue, Green, Grey, Yellow. Items Available: Goblet, Sherbet, Wine, Cordial, Ice Tea. **References**: 1971, page 43 [2-2]; 1972, page 9 [2-2]

Line: 1969. Bouquet. Ice Tea. 14 oz. 6-3/8 inches tall. Plain Crystal. **References**: 1969, page 18 [2-21]; 1970, page 19 [2-21]

Line: 1969. Bouquet. Ice Tea. 14 oz. 6-3/8 inches tall. Grey. **References**: 1970, page 1 [1-5]

Line: 1969. Bouquet. Ice Tea. 14 oz. 6-/38 inches tall. Grey. Colors Available: Brown, Delphine Blue, Green, Grey, Yellow. Items Available: Goblet, Sherbet, Wine, Cordial, Ice Tea. **References**: 1971, page 43 [1-2]; 1972, page 9 [1-2]

Line: 1969. Bouquet. Plate. 7 inches diam. Plain Crystal. **References**: 1969, page 18 [2-23]; 1970, page 19 [2-23]

Line: 1969. Bouquet. Plate. 8 inches diam. Plain Crystal. **References**: 1969, page 18 [2-24]; 1970, page 19 [2-24]

Line: 1969. Bouquet. Red Wine Goblet. 9-1/2 oz. 6 inches tall. Plain Crystal. **References**: 1969, page 28 [1-3]; 1971, page 30 [1-3]; 1972, page 14 [1-3]; 1973, page 28 [1-3]

Line: 1969. Bouquet. Sherbet. 7-1/2 oz. 5-3/8 inches tall. Plain Crystal. **References**: 1969, page 18 [2-18]; 1969, page 28 [1-2]; 1970, page 19 [2-18]; 1971, page 30 [1-2]; 1972, page 14 [1-2]; 1973, page 28 [1-2]

Line: 1969. Bouquet. Sherbet. 7-1/2 oz. 5-3/8 inches tall. Green. **References**: 1970, page 1 [1-2]

Line: 1969. Bouquet. Sherbet. 7-1/2 oz. 5-3/8 inches tall. Green. Colors Available: Brown, Delphine Blue, Green, Grey, Yellow. Items Available: Goblet, Sherbet, Wine, Cordial, Ice Tea. **References**: 1971, page 43 [2-3]; 1972, page 9 [2-3]

Line: 1969. Bouquet. Sherry/Port. 5 oz. 5-1/4 inches tall. Plain Crystal. **References**: 1969, page 28 [1-6]; 1971, page 30 [1-6]; 1972, page 14 [1-6]; 1973, page 28 [1-6]

Line: 1969. Bouquet. Tulip Champagne. 8 oz. 8-1/8 inches tall. Plain Crystal. **References**: 1969, page 28 [1-7]; 1971, page 30 [1-7]; 1972, page 14 [1-7]; 1973, page 28 [1-7]

Line: 1969. Bouquet. White Wine Goblet. 7-1/2 oz. 5-1/2 inches tall. Plain Crystal. **References**: 1969, page 18 [2-19]; 1969, page 28 [1-4]; 1970, page 19 [2-19]; 1971, page 30 [1-4]; 1972, page 14 [1-4]; 1973, page 28 [1-4]

Line: 1969. Bouquet. Wine. 7-1/2 oz. 5-1/2 inches tall. Brown. **References**: 1970, page 1 [1-3]

Line: 1969. Bouquet. Wine. 7-1/2 oz. 5-1/2 inches tall. Brown. Colors Available: Brown, Delphine Blue, Green, Grey, Yellow. Items Available: Goblet, Sherbet, Wine, Cordial, Ice Tea. **References**: 1971, page 43 [1-1]; 1972, page 9 [1-1]

Line: 1969. Debonair. 1305 Dessert-Finger Bowl. 4-1/2 inches diam. 3/16" Platinum Band. **References**: 1969, page 18 [2-6]; 1970, page 19 [2-6]

Line: 1969. Debonair. Cordial. 2 oz. 4-1/2 inches tall. 3/16" Platinum Band. **References**: 1969, page 18 [2-4]; 1970, page 19 [2-4]

Line: 1969. Debonair. Goblet. 14 oz. 6-3/4 inches tall. 3/16" Platinum Band. **References**: 1969, page 18 [2-1]; 1970, page 19 [2-1]

Line: 1969. Debonair. Ice Tea. 14 oz. 6-3/8 inches tall. 3/16" Platinum Band. **References**: 1969, page 18 [2-5]; 1970, page 19 [2-5]

Line: 1969. Debonair. Plate. 7 inches diam. 3/16" Platinum Band, Actually 7-7/8" Dia. **References**: 1969, page 18 [2-7]; 1970, page 19 [2-7]

Line: 1969. Debonair. Plate. 8 inches diam. 3/16" Platinum Band, Actually 8-3/4" Dia. **References**: 1969, page 18 [2-8]; 1970, page 19 [2-8]

Line: 1969. Debonair. Sherbet. 7-1/2 oz. 5-3/8 inches tall. 3/16" Platinum Band. **References**: 1969, page 18 [2-2]; 1970, page 19 [2-2]

Line: 1969. Debonair. White Wine Goblet. 7-1/2 oz. 5-1/2 inches tall. 3/16" Platinum Band. **References**: 1969, page 18 [2-3]; 1970, page 19 [2-3]

Line: 1969. Grandeur. 1305 Dessert-Finger Bowl. 4-1/2 inches diam. 3/16" Gold Band on edge of PLATE only. **References**: 1969, page 18 [2-14]; 1970, page 19 [2-14]

Line: 1969. Grandeur. Cordial. 2 oz. 4-1/2 inches tall. 3/16" Gold Band on edge of PLATE only. 1970, page 19 [2-12]

Line: 1969. Grandeur. Goblet. 14 oz. 6-3/4 inches tall. 3/16" Gold Band on edge of PLATE only. **References**: 1969, page 18 [2-9]; 1970, page 19 [2-9]

Line: 1969. Grandeur. Ice Tea. 14 oz. 6-3/8 inches tall. 3/16" Gold Band on edge of PLATE only. **References**: 1969, page 18 [2-13]; 1970, page 19 [2-13]

Line: 1969. Grandeur. Plate. 7 inches diam. 3/16" Gold Band on edge of PLATE only, Actually 7-7/8" Dia. **References**: 1969, page 18 [2-15]; 1970, page 19 [2-15]

Line: 1969. Grandeur. Plate. 8 inches diam. 3/16" Gold Band on edge of PLATE only, Actually 8-3/4" Dia. **References**: 1969, page 18 [2-16]; 1970, page 19 [2-16]

Line: 1969. Grandeur. Sherbet. 7-1/2 oz. 5-3/8 inches tall. 3/16" Gold Band on edge of PLATE only. **References**: 1969, page 18 [2-10]; 1970, page 19 [2-10]

Line: 1969. Grandeur. White Wine Goblet. 7-1/2 oz. 5-1/2 inches tall. 3/16" Gold Band on edge of PLATE only. **References**: 1969, page 18 [2-11]; 1970, page 19 [2-11]

Line: 1969. Reflection. 1305 Dessert-Finger Bowl. 4-1/2 inches diam. Gold Bands, 3/16" on Bowl-1/16" on Foot. **References**: 1969, page 18 [1-6]; 1970, page 19 [1-6]

Line: 1969. Reflection. Cordial. 2 oz. 4-1/2 inches tall. Gold Bands, 3/16" on Bowl-1/16" on Foot. **References**: 1969, page 18 [1-4]; 1970, page 19 [1-4]

Line: 1969. Reflection. Goblet. 14 oz. 6-3/4 inches tall. Gold Bands, 3/16" on Bowl-1/16" on Foot. **References**: 1969, page 18 [1-1]; 1970, page 19 [1-1]

Line: 1969. Reflection. Ice Tea. 14 oz. 6-3/8 inches tall. Gold Bands, 3/16" on Bowl-1/16" on Foot. **References**: 1969, page 18 [1-5]; 1970, page 19 [1-5]

Line: 1969. Reflection. Plate. 7 inches diam. Gold Bands, 3/16" on Bowl-1/16" on Foot, Actually 7-7/8" Dia. **References**: 1969, page 18 [1-7]; 1970, page 19 [1-7]

Line: 1969. Reflection. Plate. 8 inches diam. Gold Bands, 3/16" on Bowl-1/16" on Foot, Actually 8-3/4" Dia. **References**: 1969, page 18 [1-8]; 1970, page 19 [1-8]

Line: 1969. Reflection. Sherbet. 7-1/2 oz. 5-3/8 inches tall. Gold Bands, 3/16" on Bowl-1/16" on Foot. **References**: 1969, page 18 [1-2]; 1970, page 19 [1-2]

Line: 1969. Reflection. White Wine Goblet. 7-1/2 oz. 5-1/2 inches tall. Gold Bands, 3/16" on Bowl-1/16" on Foot. **References**: 1969, page 18 [1-3]; 1970, page 19 [1-3]

Line: 1969. Sterling Mist. 1305 Dessert-Finger Bowl. 4-1/2 inches diam. 3/16" Genuine Sterling Silver Band. **References**: 1969, page 18 [1-14]; 1970, page 19 [1-14]

Line: 1969. Sterling Mist. Cordial. 2 oz. 4-1/2 inches tall. 3/16" Genuine Sterling Silver Band. **References**: 1969, page 18 [1-12]; 1970, page 19 [1-12]

Line: 1969. Sterling Mist. Goblet. 14 oz. 6-3/4 inches tall. 3/16" Genuine Sterling Silver Band. **References**: 1969, page 18 [1-9]; 1970, page 19 [1-9]

Line: 1969. Sterling Mist. Ice Tea. 14 oz. 6-3/8 inches tall. 3/16" Genuine Sterling Silver Band. **References**: 1969, page 18 [1-13]; 1970, page 19 [1-13]

Line: 1969. Sterling Mist. Plate. 7 inches diam. 3/16" Genuine Sterling Silver Band, Actually 7-7/8" Dia. **References**: 1969, page 18 [1-15]; 1970, page 19 [1-15]

Line: 1969. Sterling Mist. Plate. 8 inches diam. 3/16" Genuine Sterling Silver Band, Actually 8-3/4" Dia. **References**: 1969, page 18 [1-16]; 1970, page 19 [1-16]

Line: 1969. Sterling Mist. Sherbet. 7-1/2 oz. 5-3/8 inches tall. 3/16" Genuine Sterling Silver Band. **References**: 1969, page 18 [1-10]; 1970, page 19 [1-10]

Line: 1969. Sterling Mist. White Wine Goblet. 7-1/2 oz. 5-1/2 inches tall. 3/16" Genuine Sterling Silver Band. **References**: 1969, page 18 [1-11]; 1970, page 19 [1-11]

Line: 1970 Footed. Brocado. Beverage. 16 oz. 5-7/8 inches tall. Color: Cristalino (Crystal). **References**: 1969, page 29 [2-1]

Line: 1970. Brocado. Beverage. 16 oz. 5-7/8 inches tall. Toledo. **References**: 1970, page 6 [1-5]

Line: 1970 Footed. Brocado. Goblet. 14 oz. 5-1/2 inches tall. Color: Sahara (Yellow). **References**: 1969, page 29 [1-2]

Line: 1970. Brocado. Goblet. 14 oz. 5-1/2 inches tall. Cristalino. **References**: 1970, page 6 [1-1]

Line: 1970 Footed. Brocado. Juice or Wine Goblet. 7-1/2 oz. 4-3/8 inches tall. Color: Morocco (Brown). **References**: 1969, page 29 [1-3]

Line: 1970. Brocado. Old Fashion. 14 oz. 4 inches tall. Avocado. **References**: 1970, page 6 [1-4]

Line: 1970. Brocado. On The Rocks. 10-1/2 oz. 3-5/8 inches tall. Footed. Colors: Toledo (Grey). **References**: 1969, page 29 [2-2]

Line: 1970. Brocado. Roly Poly. 13 oz. 3-1/4 inches tall. Sahara. **References**: 1970, page 6 [1-3]

Line: 1970 Footed. Brocado. Sherbet. 7-1/2 oz. 3-1/2 inches tall. Avocado (Green). **References**: 1969, page 29 [1-1]

Line: 1970. Brocado. Sherbet. 7-1/2 oz. 3-1/2 inches tall. Morocco. **References**: 1970, page 6 [1-2]

Line: 1971. Claremont. 1311 Dessert-Finger Bowl. 4-3/4 inches diam. Platinum Band and Line. **References**: 1970, page 11 [2-14]; 1971, page 19 [2-14]; 1972, page 27 [2-14]; 1973, page 32 [2-14]

Line: 1971. Claremont. Cordial. 1-1/2 oz. 4 inches tall. Platinum Band and Line. **References**: 1970, page 11 [2-12]; 1971, page 19 [2-12]; 1972, page 27 [2-12]; 1973, page 32 [2-12]

Line: 1971. Claremont. Goblet. 11-1/2 oz. 7 inches tall. Platinum Band and Line. **References**: 1970, page 11 [2-9]; 1971, page 19 [2-9]; 1972, page 27 [2-9]; 1973, page 32 [2-9]

Line: 1971. Claremont. Ice Tea. 14-1/2 oz. 7-1/8 inches tall. Platinum Band and Line. **References**: 1970, page 11 [2-13]; 1971, page 19 [2-13]; 1972, page 27 [2-13]; 1973, page 32 [2-13]

Line: 1971. Claremont. Plate. 7 inches diam. Platinum Band and Line, Actually 7-7/8" Dia. **References**: 1970, page 11 [2-15]; 1971, page 19 [2-15]; 1972, page 27 [2-15]; 1973, page 32 [2-15]

Line: 1971. Claremont. Plate. 8 inches diam. Platinum Band and Line, Actually 8-3/4" Dia. **References**: 1970, page 11 [2-16]; 1971, page 19 [2-16]; 1972, page 27 [2-16]; 1973, page 32 [2-16]

Line: 1971. Claremont. Sherbet. 7-1/2 oz. 5 inches tall. Platinum Band and Line. **References**: 1970, page 11 [2-10]; 1971, page 19 [2-10]; 1972, page 27 [2-10]; 1973, page 32 [2-10]

Line: 1971. Claremont. Wine. 7 oz. 5-7/8 inches tall. Platinum Band and Line. **References**: 1970, page 11 [2-11]; 1971, page 19 [2-11]; 1972, page 27 [2-11]; 1973, page 32 [2-11]

Line: 1971. Remembrance. 1311 Dessert-Finger Bowl. 4-3/4 inches diam. Gold Band and Line. **References**: 1970, page 11 [2-22]; 1971, page 19 [2-22]; 1972, page 27 [2-22]; 1973, page 32 [2-22]

Line: 1971. Remembrance. Cordial. 1-1/2 oz. 4 inches tall. Gold Band and Line. **References**: 1970, page 11 [2-20]; 1971, page 19 [2-20]; 1972, page 27 [2-20]; 1973, page 32 [2-20]

Line: 1971. Remembrance. Goblet. 11-1/2 oz. 7 inches tall. Gold Band and Line. **References**: 1970, page 11 [2-17]; 1971, page 19 [2-17]; 1972, page 27 [2-17]; 1973, page 32 [2-17]

Line: 1971. Remembrance. Ice Tea. 14-1/2 oz. 7-1/8 inches tall. Gold Band and Line. **References**: 1970, page 11 [2-21]; 1971, page 19 [2-21]; 1972, page 27 [2-21]; 1973, page 32 [2-21]

Line: 1971. Remembrance. Plate. 7 inches diam. Gold Band and Line, Actually 7-7/8" Dia. **References**: 1970, page 11 [2-23]; 1971, page 19 [2-23]; 1972, page 27 [2-23]; 1973, page 32 [2-23]

Line: 1971. Remembrance. Plate. 8 inches diam. Gold Band and Line, Actually 8-3/4" Dia. **References**: 1970, page 11 [2-24]; 1971, page 19 [2-24]; 1972, page 27 [2-24]; 1973, page 32 [2-24]

Line: 1971. Remembrance. Sherbet. 7-1/2 oz. 5 inches tall. Gold Band and Line. **References**: 1970, page 11 [2-18]; 1971, page 19 [2-18]; 1972, page 27 [2-18]; 1973, page 32 [2-18]

Line: 1971. Remembrance. Wine. 7 oz. 5-7/8 inches tall. Gold Band and Line. **References**: 1970, page 11 [2-19]; 1971, page 19 [2-19]; 1972, page 27 [2-19]; 1973, page 32 [2-19]

Line: 1971. Seville. 1311 Dessert-Finger Bowl. 4-3/4 inches diam. Plain Crystal. **References**: 1970, page 11 [2-6]; 1971, page 19 [2-6]; 1971, page 19 [2-6]; 1972, page 27 [2-6]; 1973, page 32 [2-6]

Line: 1971. Seville. Cordial. 1-1/2 oz. 4 inches tall. Brown. **References**: 1970, page 2 [1-4]

Line: 1971. Seville. Cordial. 1-1/2 oz. 4 inches tall. Plain Crystal. **References**: 1970, page 11 [2-4]; 1971, page 19 [2-4]; 1971, page 19 [2-4]; 1972, page 27 [2-4]; 1973, page 32 [2-4]

Line: 1971. Seville. Cordial. 1-1/2 oz. 4 inches tall. Brown. Colors Available; Brown, Delphine Blue, Green, Grey, Yellow. Items Available: Goblet, Sherbet, Wine, Cordial, Ice Tea. **References**: 1971, page 42 [2-3]; 1972, page 10 [2-3]

Line: 1971. Seville. Cordial. 1-1/2 oz. 4 inches tall. Colors: Brown, Delphine Blue, Green, Grey, Yellow. **References**: 1973, page 18 [2-3]

Line: 1971. Seville. Goblet. 11-1/2 oz. 7 inches tall. Yellow. **References**: 1970, page 2 [1-1]

Line: 1971. Seville. Goblet. 11-1/2 oz. 7 inches tall. Plain Crystal. **References**: 1970, page 11 [2-1]; 1971, page 19 [2-1]; 1971, page 19 [2-1]; 1972, page 27 [2-1]; 1973, page 32 [2-1]

Line: 1971. Seville. Goblet. 11-1/2 oz. 7 inches tall. Yellow. Colors Available; Brown, Delphine Blue, Green, Grey, Yellow. Items Available: Goblet, Sherbet, Wine, Cordial, Ice Tea. **References**: 1971, page 42 [2-2]; 1972, page 10 [2-2]

Line: 1971. Seville. Goblet. 11-1/2 oz. 7 inches tall. Colors: Brown, Delphine Blue, Green, Grey, Yellow. **References**: 1973, page 18 [2-2]

Line: 1971. Seville. Ice Tea. 14-1/2 oz. 7-1/8 inches tall. Green. **References**: 1970, page 2 [1-5]

Line: 1971. Seville. Ice Tea. 14-1/2 oz. 7-1/8 inches tall. Plain Crystal. **References**: 1970, page 11 [2-5]; 1971, page 19 [2-5]; 1971, page 19 [2-5]; 1972, page 27 [2-5]; 1973, page 32 [2-5]

Line: 1971. Seville. Ice Tea. 14-1/2 oz. 7-1/8 inches tall. Green. Colors Available; Brown, Delphine Blue, Green, Grey, Yellow. Items Available: Goblet, Sherbet, Wine, Cordial, Ice Tea. **References**: 1971, page 42 [1-1]; 1972, page 10 [1-1]

Line: 1971. Seville. Ice Tea. 14-1/2 oz. 7-1/8 inches tall. Colors: Brown, Delphine Blue, Green, Grey, Yellow. **References**: 1973, page 18 [1-1]

Line: 1971. Seville. Plate. 7 inches diam. Plain Crystal, Actually 7-7/8" Dia. **References**: 1970, page 11 [2-7]; 1971, page 19 [2-7]; 1971, page 19 [2-7]; 1972, page 27 [2-7]; 1973, page 32 [2-7]

Line: 1971. Seville. Plate. 8 inches diam. Plain Crystal, Actually 8-3/4"Dia. **References**: 1970, page 11 [2-8]; 1971, page 19 [2-8]; 1971, page 19 [2-8]; 1972, page 27 [2-8]; 1973, page 32 [2-8]

Line: 1971. Seville. Sherbet. 7-1/2 oz. 5 inches tall. Grey. **References**: 1970, page 2 [1-2]

Line: 1971. Seville. Sherbet. 7-1/2 oz. 5 inches tall. Plain Crystal. **References**: 1970, page 11 [2-2]; 1971, page 19 [2-2]; 1971, page 19 [2-2]; 1972, page 27 [2-2]; 1973, page 32 [2-2]

Line: 1971. Seville. Sherbet. 7-1/2 oz. 5 inches tall. Grey. Colors Available; Brown, Delphine Blue, Green, Grey, Yellow. Items Available: Goblet, Sherbet, Wine, Cordial, Ice Tea. **References**: 1971, page 42 [2-1]; 1972, page 10 [2-1]

Line: 1971. Seville. Sherbet. 7-1/2 oz. 5 inches tall. Colors: Brown, Delphine Blue, Green, Grey, Yellow. **References**: 1973, page 18 [2-1]

Line: 1971. Seville. Wine. 7 oz. 5-7/8 inches tall. Delphine Blue. **References**: 1970, page 2 [1-3]

Line: 1971. Seville. Wine. 7 oz. 5-7/8 inches tall. Plain Crystal. **References**: 1970, page 11 [2-3]; 1971, page 19 [2-3]; 1971, page 19 [2-3]; 1972, page 27 [2-3]; 1973, page 32 [2-3]

Line: 1971. Seville. Wine. 7 oz. 5-7/8 inches tall. Delphine Blue. Colors Available; Brown, Delphine Blue, Green, Grey, Yellow. Items Available: Goblet, Sherbet, Wine, Cordial, Ice Tea. **References**: 1971, page 42 [1-2]; 1972, page 10 [1-2]

Line: 1971. Seville. Wine. 7 oz. 5-7/8 inches tall. Colors: Brown, Delphine Blue, Green, Grey, Yellow. **References**: 1973, page 18 [1-2]

Line: 1971. Cut: 1441. Bristol. 1311 Dessert-Finger Bowl. 4-3/4 inches diam. **References**: 1971, page 19 [1-14]

Line: 1971. Cut: 1441. Bristol. Cordial. 1-1/2 oz. 4 inches tall. **References**: 1971, page 19 [1-12]

Line: 1971. Cut: 1441. Bristol. Goblet. 11-1/2 oz. 7 inches tall. **References**: 1971, page 19 [1-9]

Line: 1971. Cut: 1441. Bristol. Ice Tea. 14-1/2 oz. 7-1/8 inches tall. **References**: 1971, page 19 [1-13]

Line: 1971. Cut: 1441. Bristol. Plate. 7 inches diam. Actually 7-7/8" Dia. **References**: 1971, page 19 [1-15]

Line: 1971. Cut: 1441. Bristol. Plate. 8 inches diam. Actually 8-3/4" Dia. **References**: 1971, page 19 [1-16]

Line: 1971. Cut: 1441. Bristol. Sherbet. 7-1/2 oz. 5 inches tall. **References**: 1971, page 19 [1-10]

Line: 1971. Cut: 1441. Bristol. Wine. 7 oz. 5-7/8 inches tall. **References**: 1971, page 19 [1-11]

Line: 1971. Cut: 1441. Kingsley. 1311 Dessert-Finger Bowl. 4-3/4 inches diam. **References**: 1970, page 11 [1-14]

Line: 1971. Cut: 1441. Kingsley. Cordial. 1-1/2 oz. 4 inches tall. **References**: 1970, page 11 [1-12]

Line: 1971. Cut: 1441. Kingsley. Goblet. 11-1/2 oz. 7 inches tall. **References**: 1970, page 11 [1-9]

Line: 1971. Cut: 1441. Kingsley. Ice Tea. 14-1/2 oz. 7-1/8 inches tall. **References**: 1970, page 11 [1-13]

Line: 1971. Cut: 1441. Kingsley. Plate. 7 inches diam. Actually 7-7/8" Dia. **References**: 1970, page 11 [1-15]

Line: 1971. Cut: 1441. Kingsley. Plate. 8 inches diam. Actually 8-3/4" Dia. **References**: 1970, page 11 [1-16]

Line: 1971. Cut: 1441. Kingsley. Sherbet. 7-1/2 oz. 5 inches tall. **References**: 1970, page 11 [1-10]

Line: 1971. Cut: 1441. Kingsley. Wine. 7 oz. 5-7/8 inches tall. **References**: 1970, page 11 [1-11]

Line: 1971. Cut: 1442. Kingsley. 1311 Dessert-Finger Bowl. 4-3/4 inches diam. **References**: 1970, page 11 [1-6]; 1971, page 19 [1-6]

Line: 1971. Cut: 1442. Kingsley. Cordial. 1-1/2 oz. 4 inches tall. **References**: 1970, page 11 [1-4]; 1971, page 19 [1-4]

Line: 1971. Cut: 1442. Kingsley. Goblet. 11-1/2 oz. 7 inches tall. **References**: 1970, page 11 [1-1]; 1971, page 19 [1-1]

Line: 1971. Cut: 1442. Kingsley. Ice Tea. 14-1/2 oz. 7-1/8 inches tall. **References**: 1970, page 11 [1-5]; 1971, page 19 [1-5]

Line: 1971. Cut: 1442. Kingsley. Plate. 7 inches diam. Actually 7-7/8" Dia. **References**: 1970, page 11 [1-7]; 1971, page 19 [1-7]

Line: 1971. Cut: 1442. Kingsley. Plate. 8 inches diam. Actually 8-3/4" Dia. **References**: 1970, page 11 [1-8]; 1971, page 19 [1-8]

Line: 1971. Cut: 1442. Kingsley. Sherbet. 7-1/2 oz. 5 inches tall. **References**: 1970, page 11 [1-2]; 1971, page 19 [1-2]

Line: 1971. Cut: 1442. Kingsley. Wine. 7 oz. 5-7/8 inches tall. **References**: 1970, page 11 [1-3]; 1971, page 19 [1-3]

Line: 1972. Bar Pitcher w/Stir Rod. 40 oz. Crystal. **References**: 1975, page 19 [1-2]

Line: 1972. Bowl. 13 oz. 4-1/2 inches tall. Crystal. **References**: 1975, page 19 [1-1]

Line: 1972. Cocktail/Juice. 7-1/2 oz. 3-1/4 inches tall. Brown. **References**: 1975, page 19 [1-3]

Line: 1972. Cascade. Bar Pitcher w/Stir Rod. 40 oz. Crystal. Colors: Accent Red, Brown, Crystal, Lime Green, Moss Green, Ritz Blue, Yellow. **References**: 1977, page 14-15 [1-6]

Line: 1972. Cascade. Beverage. 15-1/2 oz. 5 inches tall. Yellow, Peacock Blue. Colors Available: Crystal, Green, Grey. Items Available: Beverage, Old Fashion. **References**: 1971, page 39 [1-1 & 3-1]

Line: 1972. Cascade. Beverage. 15-1/2 oz. 5 inches tall. Grey. Items Availble: Beverage, Old Fashion, Cocktail/Juice, 6-pc. Cocktail/Juice Set. Colors: Crystal, Green, Grey, Peacock Blue, Yellow. **References**: 1972, page 5 [2-3]

Line: 1972. Cascade. Beverage. 15-1/2 oz. 5 inches tall. Yellow. Items Availble: Beverage, Old Fashion, Cocktail/Juice, 6-pc. Cocktail/Juice Set. Colors: Crystal, Green, Grey, Peacock Blue, Yellow. **References**: 1972, page 5 [2-4]; 1973, page 14 [2-3]; 1973, page 14 [2-4]

Line: 1972. Cascade. Beverage. 15-1/2 oz. 5 inches tall. Moss Green. Colors: Accent Red, Brown, Crystal, Lime Green, Moss Green, Ritz Blue, Yellow. **References**: 1977, page 14-15 [1-2]

Line: 1972. Cascade. Bowl. 13 oz. 4-1/2 inches diam. Crystal. Colors: Accent Red, Brown, Crystal, Lime Green, Moss Green, Ritz Blue, Yellow. **References**: 1977, page 14-15 [1-5]

Line: 1972. Cascade. Cocktail/Juice. 7-1/2 oz. 3-1/4 inches tall. Crystal. Items Availble: Beverage, Old Fashion, Cocktail/Juice, 6-pc. Cocktail/Juice Set. Colors: Crystal, Green, Grey, Peacock Blue, Yellow. **References**: 1972, page 5 [2-2]; 1973, page 14 [2-2]

Line: 1972. Cascade. Cocktail/Juice. 7-1/2 oz. 3-1/4 inches tall. Brown. Colors: Accent Red, Brown, Crystal, Lime Green, Moss Green, Ritz Blue, Yellow. **References**: 1977, page 14-15 [1-7]

Line: 1972. Cascade. Cocktail/Juice Set. Peacock Blue, Mixer 40 oz., Glasses 7-1/2 oz. Items Availble: Beverage, Old Fashion, Cocktail/Juice, 6-pc. Cocktail/Juice Set. Colors: Crystal, Green, Grey, Peacock Blue, Yellow. **References**: 1972, page 5 [1-1]; 1973, page 14 [1-1]

Line: 1972. Cascade. Cooler. 18-1/2 oz. 6-3/4 inches tall. Colors: Crystal. **References**: 1978, page 16 [1-2]

Line: 1972. Cascade. Footed Goblet. 15-1/2 oz. 6 inches tall. Ritz Blue. Colors: Accent Red, Brown, Crystal, Lime Green, Moss Green, Ritz Blue, Yellow. **References**: 1977, page 14-15 [1-1]

Line: 1972. Cascade. Footed Juice/Wine. 9 oz. 4-3/8 inches tall. Accent Red. Colors: Accent Red, Brown, Crystal, Lime Green, Moss Green, Ritz Blue, Yellow. **References**: 1977, page 14-15 [1-3]

Line: 1972. Cascade. Goblet, Bloody Mary Set. 14-1/2 oz. 5-3/4 inches tall. Lead Crystal. **References**: 1978, page 11 [1-2]

Line: 1972. Cascade. Mixer, Bloody Mary Set. 40 oz. Lead Crystal w/Stir Rod. **References**: 1978, page 11 [1-1]

Line: 1972. Cascade. Old Fashion. 11-1/2 oz. 3-3/4 inches tall. Grey, Green, Crystal, Yellow. Colors Available: Peacock Blue. Items Available: Beverage, Old Fashion. **References**: 1971, page 39 [2-1,2,3 & 3-2]

Line: 1972. Cascade. Old Fashion. 11-1/2 oz. 3-3/4 inches tall. Green. Items Availble: Beverage, Old Fashion, Cocktail/Juice, 6-pc. Cocktail/Juice Set. Colors: Crystal, Green, Grey, Peacock Blue, Yellow. **References**: 1972, page 5 [2-1]; 1973, page 14 [2-1]

Line: 1972. Cascade. Old Fashion. 11-1/2 oz. 3-3/4 inches tall. Yellow. Colors: Accent Red, Brown, Crystal, Lime Green, Moss Green, Ritz Blue, Yellow. **References**: 1977, page 14-15 [1-4]

Line: 1973. Galaxy. 1305 Dessert-Finger Bowl. 4-1/2 inches diam. Plain Crystal. **References**: 1971, page 11 [2-6]; 1972, page 20 [2-6]; 1973, page 27 [2-6]

Line: 1973. Galaxy. Cordial. 1-1/2 oz. 4 inches tall. Plain Crystal. **References**: 1971, page 11 [2-4]; 1972, page 20 [2-4]; 1973, page 27 [2-4]

Line: 1973. Galaxy. Cordial. 1-1/2 oz. 4 inches tall. Pink/Crystal Foot. Colors & Designs Available: Blue/Crystal Foot, Pink/Crystal Foot, Blue/Crystal Foot/Cut 1443, Pink/Crystal Foot/Cut 1443, Black Decal and Gold Band, White Decal and Platinum Band. Items Available: Goblet, Sherbet, Wine, Cordial, Ice Tea. **References**: 1971, page 40 [2-4]

Line: 1973. Galaxy. Goblet. 13 oz. 7 inches tall. Plain Crystal. **References**: 1971, page 11 [2-1]; 1972, page 20 [2-1]; 1973, page 27 [2-1]

Line: 1973. Galaxy. Ice Tea. 17-1/2 oz. 7-1/8 inches tall. Plain Crystal. **References**: 1971, page 11 [2-5]; 1972, page 20 [2-5]; 1973, page 27 [2-5]

Line: 1973. Galaxy. Ice Tea. 17-1/2 oz. 7-1/8 inches tall. Blue/Crystal Foot. Colors & Designs Available: Blue/Crystal Foot, Pink/Crystal Foot, Blue/Crystal Foot/Cut 1443, Pink/Crystal Foot/Cut 1443, Black Decal and Gold Band, White Decal and Platinum Band. Items Available: Goblet, Sherbet, Wine, Cordial, Ice Tea. **References**: 1971, page 40 [1-2]

Line: 1973. Galaxy. Plate. 7 inches diam. Plain Crystal, Actually 7-7/8" Dia. **References**: 1971, page 11 [2-7]; 1972, page 20 [2-7]; 1973, page 27 [2-7]

Line: 1973. Galaxy. Plate. 8 inches diam. Plain Crystal, Actually 8-3/4" Dia. **References**: 1971, page 11 [2-8]; 1972, page 20 [2-8]; 1973, page 27 [2-8]

Line: 1973. Galaxy. Sherbet. 7-1/2 oz. 5-1/8 inches tall. Plain Crystal. **References**: 1971, page 11 [2-2]; 1972, page 20 [2-2]; 1973, page 27 [2-2]

Line: 1973. Galaxy. Wine. 8-1/2 oz. 6-3/8 inches tall. Plain Crystal. **References**: 1971, page 11 [2-3]; 1972, page 20 [2-3]; 1973, page 27 [2-3]

Line: 1973. Gold Florentine. 1305 Dessert-Finger Bowl. 4-1/2 inches diam. Black Decal and Gold Band. **References**: 1971, page 11 [1-14]; 1972, page 20 [1-14]; 1973, page 27 [1-14]

Line: 1973. Gold Florentine. Cordial. 1-1/2 oz. 4 inches tall. Black Decal and Gold Band. **References**: 1971, page 11 [1-12]; 1972, page 20 [1-12]; 1973, page 27 [1-12]

Line: 1973. Gold Florentine. Goblet. 13 oz. 7 inches tall. Black Decal and Gold Band. **References**: 1971, page 11 [1-9]; 1972, page 20 [1-9];

$xxxx. References: 1973, page 27 [1-9]

Line: 1973. Gold Florentine. Goblet. 13 oz. 7 inches tall. Black Decal/ Gold Band. Colors & Designs Available: Blue/Crystal Foot, Pink/Crystal Foot, Blue/Crystal Foot/Cut 1443, Pink/Crystal Foot/ Cut 1443, Black Decal and Gold Band, White Decal and Platinum Band. Items Available: Goblet, Sherbet, Wine, Cordial, Ice Tea. **References**: 1971, page 40 [2-1]

Line: 1973. Gold Florentine. Ice Tea. 17-1/2 oz. 7-1/8 inches tall. Black Decal and Gold Band. **References**: 1971, page 11 [1-13]; 1972, page 20 [1-13]; 1973, page 27 [1-13]

Line: 1973. Gold Florentine. Plate. 7 inches diam. Black Decal and Gold Band, Actually 7-7/8" Dia. **References**: 1971, page 11 [1-15]; 1972, page 20 [1-15]; 1973, page 27 [1-15]; 1973, page 27 [1-16]

Line: 1973. Gold Florentine. Plate. 8 inches diam. Black Decal and Gold Band, Actually 8-3/4" Dia. **References**: 1971, page 11 [1-16]; 1972, page 20 [1-16]

Line: 1973. Gold Florentine. Sherbet. 7-1/2 oz. 5-1/8 inches tall. Black Decal and Gold Band. **References**: 1971, page 11 [1-10]; 1972, page 20 [1-10]; 1973, page 27 [1-10]

Line: 1973. Gold Florentine. Wine. 8-1/2 oz. 6-3/8 inches tall. Black Decal and Gold Band. **References**: 1971, page 11 [1-11]; 1972, page 20 [1-11]; 1973, page 27 [1-11]

Line: 1973. Platinum Lace. 1305 Dessert-Finger Bowl. 4-1/2 inches diam. White Decal and Platinum Band. **References**: 1971, page 11 [1-6]; 1972, page 20 [1-6]; 1973, page 27 [1-6]

Line: 1973. Platinum Lace. Cordial. 1-1/2 oz. 4 inches tall. White Decal and Platinum Band. **References**: 1971, page 11 [1-4]; 1972, page 20 [1-4]; 1973, page 27 [1-4]

Line: 1973. Platinum Lace. Goblet. 13 oz. 7 inches tall. White Decal and Platinum Band. **References**: 1971, page 11 [1-1]; 1972, page 20 [1-1]; 1973, page 27 [1-1]

Line: 1973. Platinum Lace. Goblet. 13 oz. 7 inches tall. White Decal/Platinum Band. Colors & Designs Available: Blue/Crystal Foot, Pink/Crystal Foot, Blue/Crystal Foot/Cut 1443, Pink/Crystal Foot/Cut 1443, Black Decal and Gold Band, White Decal and Platinum Band. Items Available: Goblet, Sherbet, Wine, Cordial, Ice Tea. **References**: 1971, page 40 [2-3]

Line: 1973. Platinum Lace. Ice Tea. 17-1/2 oz. 7-1/8 inches tall. White Decal and Platinum Band. **References**: 1971, page 11 [1-5]; 1972, page 20 [1-5]; 1973, page 27 [1-5]

Line: 1973. Platinum Lace. Plate. 7 inches diam. White Decal and Platinum Band, Actually 7-7/8" Dia. **References**: 1971, page 11 [1-7]; 1972, page 20 [1-7]; 1973, page 27 [1-7]

Line: 1973. Platinum Lace. Plate. 8 inches diam. White Decal and Platinum Band, Actually 8-3/4" Dia. **References**: 1971, page 11 [1-8]; 1972, page 20 [1-8]; 1973, page 27 [1-8]

Line: 1973. Platinum Lace. Sherbet. 7-1/2 oz. 5-1/8 inches tall. White Decal and Platinum Band. **References**: 1971, page 11 [1-2]; 1972, page 20 [1-2]; 1973, page 27 [1-2]

Line: 1973. Platinum Lace. Wine. 8-1/2 oz. 6-3/8 inches tall. White Decal and Platinum Band. **References**: 1971, page 11 [1-3]; 1972, page 20 [1-3]; 1973, page 27 [1-3]

Line: 1973. Cut: 1443. Artistry. 1305 Dessert-Finger Bowl. 4-1/2 inches diam. Crystal. **References**: 1972, page 20 [2-14]; 1973, page 27 [2-14]

Line: 1973. Cut: 1443. Artistry. Cordial. 1-1/2 oz. 4 inches tall. Crystal. **References**: 1972, page 20 [2-12]; 1973, page 27 [2-12]

Line: 1973. Cut: 1443. Artistry. Goblet. 13 oz. 7 inches tall. Crystal. **References**: 1972, page 20 [2-9]; 1973, page 27 [2-9]

Line: 1973. Cut: 1443. Artistry. Ice Tea. 17-1/2 oz. 7-1/8 inches tall. Crystal. **References**: 1972, page 20 [2-13]; 1973, page 27 [2-13]

Line: 1973. Cut: 1443. Artistry. Plate. 7 inches diam. Crystal, Actually 7-7/8" Dia. **References**: 1972, page 20 [2-15]; 1973, page 27 [2-15]

Line: 1973. Cut: 1443. Artistry. Plate. 8 inches diam. Crystal, Actually 8-3/4" Dia. **References**: 1972, page 20 [2-16]; 1973, page 27 [2-16]

Line: 1973. Cut: 1443. Artistry. Sherbet. 7-1/2 oz. 5-1/8 inches tall. Crystal. **References**: 1972, page 20 [2-10]; 1973, page 27 [2-10]

Line: 1973. Cut: 1443. Artistry. Wine. 8-1/2 oz. 6-3/8 inches tall. Crystal. **References**: 1972, page 20 [2-11]; 1973, page 27 [2-11]

Line: 1973. Cut: 1443. Enchantment. Sherbet. 7-1/2 oz. 5-1/8 inches tall. Pink/Crystal Foot. Colors & Designs Available: Blue/Crystal Foot, Pink/Crystal Foot, Blue/Crystal Foot/Cut 1443, Pink/Crystal Foot/Cut 1443, Black Decal and Gold Band, White Decal and Platinum Band. Items Available: Goblet, Sherbet, Wine, Cordial, Ice Tea. **References**: 1971, page 40 [2-2]

Line: 1973. Cut: 1443. Intrigue. Wine. 8-1/2 oz. 6-3/8 inches tall. Blue, Crystal Foot. Colors & Designs Available: Blue/Crystal Foot, Pink/Crystal Foot, Blue/Crystal Foot/Cut 1443, Pink/Crystal Foot/Cut 1443, Black Decal and Gold Band, White Decal and Platinum Band. Items Available: Goblet, Sherbet, Wine, Cordial, Ice Tea. **References**: 1971, page 40 [1-1]

Line: 1974. Beer Series. Large Handled Mug. 13 oz. 5 inches tall. Plain Crystal. **References**: 1978, page 9 [2-4]; 1979, page 11 [2-5]

Line: 1974. Beer Series. Small Handled Mug. 11-1/2 oz. 4 inches tall. Plain Crystal. **References**: 1978, page 9 [2-3]; 1979, page 11 [2-4]

Line: 1974. Bellaire. Beverage. 12-1/2 oz. 5 inches tall. Crystal Full Sham. **References**: 1978, page 7 [2-4]; 1979, page 16 [2-4]

Line: 1974. Bellaire. Old Fashion. 10 oz. 4 inches tall. Crystal Full Sham. **References**: 1978, page 7 [2-5]; 1979, page 16 [2-5]

Line: 1974. Fashionables, The. Beverage. 14 oz. 5 inches tall. Crystal with Black Foot, Mixer 40oz./ Glasses 7-1/2oz. Items Available: Goblet, Dessert, Juice/Wine, Beverage, Old Fashion, 6-piece Cocktail/Juice Set. Colors: Black, Brown, Crystal, Crystal with Black Foot, Delphine blue, Green, Plum. **References**: 1972, page 3 [2-3]

Line: 1974. Fashionables, The. Beverage. 14 oz. 5 inches tall. Colors: Black, Brown, Crystal, Crystal w/Black Foot, Delphine Blue, Green, Plum, Yellow. **References**: 1973, page 12 [1-2]

Line: 1974. Fashionables, The. Beverage. 14 oz. 5 inches tall. Black, Plain Crystal. Colors: Accent Red, Black, Brown, Crystal, Delphine Blue, Moss Green, Ritz Blue, Yellow. **References**: 1975, page 14 [2-5]

Line: 1974. Fashionables, The. Beverage. 14 oz. 5 inches tall. Black. Colors: Accent Red, Black, Brown, Crystal, Delphine Blue, Lime Green, Moss Green, Ritz Blue, Yellow. **References**: 1977, page 16 [2-5]

Line: 1974. Fashionables, The. Cocktail/Juice 6 pc. Set. Mixer 40 oz., Glasses 7-1/2 oz. Colors: Black, Brown, Crystal, Crystal w/Black Foot, Delphine Blue, Green, Plum, Yellow. **References**: 1973, page 13 [1-1]

Line: 1974. Fashionables, The. Cocktail/Juice Set. Crystal with Black Foot, Mixer 40oz./Glasses 7-1/2oz. Items Available: Goblet, Dessert, Juice/ Wine, Beverage, Old Fashion, 6-piece Cocktail/ Juice Set. Colors: Black, Brown, Crystal, Crystal with Black Foot, Delphine blue, Green, Plum. **References**: 1972, page 3 [1-1]

Line: 1974. Fashionables, The. Dessert. 11-1/2 oz. 2-7/8 inches tall. Crystal/Black Foot. Colors Available: Black, Brown, Crystal, Crystal with Black Foot, Delphine Blue, Green. Items Available: Goblet, Dessert, Juice/Wine. **References**: 1971, page 37 [3-2]

Line: 1974. Fashionables, The. Dessert. 11-1/2 oz. 2-7/8 inches tall. Crystal with Black Foot, Mixer 40oz./Glasses 7-1/2oz. Items Available: Goblet, Dessert, Juice/Wine, Beverage, Old Fashion, 6-piece Cocktail/Juice Set. Colors: Black, Brown, Crystal, Crystal with Black Foot, Delphine blue, Green, Plum. **References**: 1972, page 3 [3-1]

Line: 1974L. Fashionables, The. Dessert. 11-1/2 oz. 2-7/8 inches tall. Colors: Black, Crystal, Delphine Blue, Green, Plum, Yellow. **References**: 1973, page 12 [3-1]

Line: 1974H. Fashionables, The. Dessert. 11-1/2 oz. 4-5/8 inches tall. Colors: Black, Crystal, Delphine Blue, Green, Plum, Yellow. **References**: 1973, page 13 [2-1]

Line: 1974. Fashionables, The. Goblet. 12-1/2 oz. 4-1/4 inches tall. Delphine Blue. Colors Available: Black, Brown, Crystal, Crystal with Black Foot, Delphine Blue, Green. Items Available: Goblet, Dessert, Juice/Wine. **References**: 1971, page 37 [1-1]

Line: 1974. Fashionables, The. Goblet. 12-1/2 oz. 4-

1/4 inches tall. Crystal/Black Foot. Colors Available: Black, Brown, Crystal, Crystal with Black Foot, Delphine Blue, Green. Items Available: Goblet, Dessert, Juice/Wine. **References**: 1971, page 37 [2-2]

Line: 1974. Fashionables, The. Goblet. 12-1/2 oz. 4-1/4 inches tall. Crystal with Black Foot, Mixer 40oz./Glasses 7-1/2oz. Items Available: Goblet, Dessert, Juice/Wine, Beverage, Old Fashion, 6-piece Cocktail/Juice Set. Colors: Black, Brown, Crystal, Crystal with Black Foot, Delphine blue, Green, Plum. **References**: 1972, page 3 [2-2]

Line: 1974H. Fashionables, The. Goblet. 12-1/2 oz. 6-1/4 inches tall. Colors: Black, Crystal, Delphine Blue, Green, Plum, Yellow. **References**: 1973, page 12 [2-1]; 1973, page 12 [2-2]

Line: 1974. Fashionables, The. Goblet, Bloody Mary Set. 15-1/2 oz. 6-3/4 inches tall. Lead Crystal w/ Black Foot. **References**: 1978, page 10 [1-2]

Line: 1974. Fashionables, The. High Stem Dessert. 11-1/2 oz. 4-5/8 inches tall. Crystal, Plain Crystal. Colors: Accent Red, Black, Brown, Crystal, Delphine Blue, Moss Green, Ritz Blue, Yellow. **References**: 1975, page 14 [1-2]

Line: 1974. Fashionables, The. High Stem Dessert. 11-1/2 oz. 4-5/8 inches tall. Crystal, Hourglass Optic. Colors: Accent Red, Black, Brown, Crystal, Delphine Blue, Moss Green, Ritz Blue, Yellow. **References**: 1975, page 15 [1-2]

Line: 1974. Fashionables, The. High Stem Dessert. 11-1/2 oz. 4-5/8 inches tall. Crystal. Colors: Accent Red, Black, Brown, Crystal, Delphine Blue, Lime Green, Moss Green, Ritz Blue, Yellow. **References**: 1977, page 16 [1-2]

Line: 1974. Fashionables, The. High Stem Goblet. 12-1/2 oz. 6-1/4 inches tall. Ritz Blue, Plain Crystal. Colors: Accent Red, Black, Brown, Crystal, Delphine Blue, Moss Green, Ritz Blue, Yellow. **References**: 1975, page 14 [1-1]

Line: 1974. Fashionables, The. High Stem Goblet. 12-1/2 oz. 6-1/4 inches tall. Ritz Blue, Hourglass Optic. Colors: Accent Red, Black, Brown, Crystal, Delphine Blue, Moss Green, Ritz Blue, Yellow. **References**: 1975, page 15 [1-1]

Line: 1974. Fashionables, The. High Stem Goblet. 12-1/2 oz. 6-1/4 inches tall. Ritz Blue. Colors: Accent Red, Black, Brown, Crystal, Delphine Blue, Lime Green, Moss Green, Ritz Blue, Yellow. **References**: 1977, page 16 [1-1]

Line: 1974. Fashionables, The. High Stem Ice Tea. 15 oz. 6-5/8 inches tall. Black, Plain Crystal. Colors: Accent Red, Black, Brown, Crystal, Delphine Blue, Moss Green, Ritz Blue, Yellow. **References**: 1975, page 14 [1-4]

Line: 1974. Fashionables, The. High Stem Ice Tea. 15 oz. 6-5/8 inches tall. Black, Hourglass Optic. Colors: Accent Red, Black, Brown, Crystal, Delphine Blue, Moss Green, Ritz Blue, Yellow. **References**: 1975, page 15 [1-4]

Line: 1974. Fashionables, The. High Stem Ice Tea. 15 oz. 6-5/8 inches tall. Black. Colors: Accent Red, Black, Brown, Crystal, Delphine Blue, Lime Green, Moss Green, Ritz Blue, Yellow. **References**: 1977, page 16 [1-4]

Line: 1974. Fashionables, The. High Stem Juice/ Wine. 7-1/2 oz. 5-3/8 inches tall. Yellow, Plain Crystal. Colors: Accent Red, Black, Brown, Crystal, Delphine Blue, Moss Green, Ritz Blue, Yellow. **References**: 1975, page 14 [1-3]

Line: 1974. Fashionables, The. High Stem Juice/ Wine. 7-1/2 oz. 5-3/8 inches tall. Yellow, Hourglass Optic. Colors: Accent Red, Black, Brown, Crystal, Delphine Blue, Moss Green, Ritz Blue, Yellow. **References**: 1975, page 15 [1-3]

Line: 1974. Fashionables, The. High Stem Juice/ Wine. 7-1/2 oz. 5-3/8 inches tall. Yellow. Colors: Accent Red, Black, Brown, Crystal, Delphine Blue, Lime Green, Moss Green, Ritz Blue, Yellow. **References**: 1977, page 16 [1-3]

Line: 1974. Fashionables, The. Juice/Wine. 7-1/2 oz. 3-1/2 inches tall. Brown. Colors Available: Black, Brown, Crystal, Crystal with Black Foot, Delphine Blue, Green. Items Available: Goblet, Dessert, Juice/Wine. **References**: 1971, page 37 [2-1]

Line: 1974. Fashionables, The. Juice/Wine. 7-1/2 oz. 3-1/2 inches tall. Crystal/Black Foot. Colors Available: Black, Brown, Crystal, Crystal with Black Foot, Delphine Blue, Green. Items Available, Goblet, Dessert, Juice/Wine. **References**: 1971, page 37 [3-1]

Line: 1974. Fashionables, The. Juice/Wine. 7-1/2 oz. 3-1/2 inches tall. Crystal with Black Foot, Mixer 40oz./Glasses 7-1/2oz. Items Available: Goblet, Dessert, Juice/Wine, Beverage, Old Fashion, 6-piece Cocktail/Juice Set. Colors: Black, Brown, Crystal, Crystal with Black Foot, Delphine blue, Green, Plum. **References**: 1972, page 3 [3-2]

Line: 1974L. Fashionables, The. Juice/Wine. 7-1/2 oz. 3-1/2 inches tall. Colors: Black, Crystal, Delphine Blue, Green, Plum, Yellow. **References**: 1973, page 12 [3-2]

Line: 1974H. Fashionables, The. Juice/Wine. 7-1/2 oz. 5-3/8 inches tall. Colors: Black, Crystal, Delphine Blue, Green, Plum, Yellow. **References**: 1973, page 13 [1-2]

Line: 1974. Fashionables, The. Low Stem Dessert. 11-1/2 oz. 2-7/8 inches tall. Delphine Blue, Plain Crystal. Colors: Accent Red, Black, Brown, Crystal, Delphine Blue, Moss Green, Ritz Blue, Yellow. **References**: 1975, page 14 [2-2]

Line: 1974. Fashionables, The. Low Stem Dessert. 11-1/2 oz. 2-7/8 inches tall. Delphine Blue, Hourglass Optic. Colors: Accent Red, Black, Brown, Crystal, Delphine Blue, Moss Green, Ritz Blue, Yellow. **References**: 1975, page 15 [2-2]

Line: 1974. Fashionables, The. Low Stem Dessert. 11-1/2 oz. 2-7/8 inches tall. Delphine Blue. Colors: Accent Red, Black, Brown, Crystal, Delphine Blue, Lime Green, Moss Green, Ritz Blue, Yellow. **References**: 1977, page 16 [2-2]

Line: 1974. Fashionables, The. Low Stem Goblet. 12-1/2 oz. 4-1/4 inches tall. Accent Red, Plain Crystal. Colors: Accent Red, Black, Brown, Crystal, Delphine Blue, Moss Green, Ritz Blue, Yellow. **References**: 1975, page 14 [2-1]

Line: 1974. Fashionables, The. Low Stem Goblet. 12-1/2 oz. 4-1/4 inches tall. Accent Red, Hourglass Optic. Colors: Accent Red, Black, Brown, Crystal, Delphine Blue, Moss Green, Ritz Blue, Yellow. **References**: 1975, page 15 [2-1]

Line: 1974. Fashionables, The. Low Stem Goblet. 12-1/2 oz. 4-1/4 inches tall. Accent Red. Colors: Accent Red, Black, Brown, Crystal, Delphine Blue, Lime Green, Moss Green, Ritz Blue, Yellow. **References**: 1977, page 16 [2-1]

Line: 1974. Fashionables, The. Low Stem Juice/ Wine. 7-1/2 oz. 3-1/2 inches tall. Moss Green, Plain Crystal. Colors: Accent Red, Black, Brown, Crystal, Delphine Blue, Moss Green, Ritz Blue, Yellow. **References**: 1975, page 14 [2-3]

Line: 1974. Fashionables, The. Low Stem Juice/ Wine. 7-1/2 oz. 3-1/2 inches tall. Moss Green, Hourglass Optic. Colors: Accent Red, Black, Brown, Crystal, Delphine Blue, Moss Green, Ritz Blue, Yellow. **References**: 1975, page 15 [2-3]

Line: 1974. Fashionables, The. Low Stem Juice/ Wine. 7-1/2 oz. 3-1/2 inches tall. Moss Green. Colors: Accent Red, Black, Brown, Crystal, Delphine Blue, Lime Green, Moss Green, Ritz Blue, Yellow. **References**: 1977, page 16 [2-3]

Line: 1974. Fashionables, The. Mixer, Bloody Mary Set. 40 oz. Lead Crystal w/Black Foot With Stir Rod. **References**: 1978, page 10 [1-1]

Line: 1974. Fashionables, The. Old Fashion. 9-1/2 oz. 4 inches tall. Crystal with Black Foot, Mixer 40oz./Glasses 7-1/2oz. Items Available: Goblet, Dessert, Juice/Wine, Beverage, Old Fashion, 6-piece Cocktail/Juice Set. Colors: Black, Brown, Crystal, Crystal with Black Foot, Delphine blue, Green, Plum. **References**: 1972, page 3 [2-1]

Line: 1974. Fashionables, The. Old Fashion. 9-1/2 oz. 4 inches tall. Colors: Black, Brown, Crystal, Crystal w/Black Foot, Delphine Blue, Green, Plum, Yellow. **References**: 1973, page 12 [1-1]

Line: 1974. Fashionables, The. Old Fashion. 9-1/2 oz. 4 inches tall. Brown, Plain Crystal. Colors: Accent Red, Black, Brown, Crystal, Delphine Blue, Moss Green, Ritz Blue, Yellow. **References**: 1975, page 14 [2-4]

Line: 1974. Fashionables, The. Old Fashion. 9-1/2 oz. 4 inches tall. Brown. Colors: Accent Red, Black, Brown, Crystal, Delphine Blue, Lime Green, Moss Green, Ritz Blue, Yellow. **References**: 1977, page 16 [2-4]

Line: 1974. Suburbia. Beverage. 14 oz. 5 inches tall. Crystal. Colors: Crystal, Delphine Blue, Moss Green, Grey, Plum. **References**: 1972, page 6 [TL-2]; 1973, page 16 [TL-2]

Line: 1974. Suburbia. Old Fashion. 9-1/2 oz. 4 inches tall. Crystal. Colors: Crystal, Delphine Blue, Moss Green, Grey, Plum. **References**: 1972, page 6 [TL-1]; 1973, page 16 [TL-1]

Line: 1975. Elsinore. Beverage. 16 oz. 5-3/4 inches tall. Grey. Colors: Crystal, Delphine Blue, Moss Green, Grey, Plum. **References**: 1972, page 7 [BR-1]

Line: 1975. Elsinore. Old Fashion. 12-1/2 oz. 3-3/4 inches tall. Grey. Colors: Crystal, Delphine Blue, Moss Green, Grey, Plum. **References**: 1972, page 7 [BR-2]

Line: 1975. Empire. Beverage. 13 oz. 5-3/4 inches tall. Crystal Full Sham. **References**: 1978, page 7 [2-2]; 1979, page 16 [2-2]

Line: 1975. Empire. Cooler. 16 oz. 7-3/8 inches tall. Crystal Full Sham. **References**: 1979, page 16 [2-1]

Line: 1975. Empire. Old Fashion. 10 oz. 4 inches tall. Crystal Full Sham. **References**: 1978, page 7 [2-3]; 1979, page 16 [2-3]

Line: 1975. Empire. Zombie Tumbler. 16 oz. 7-3/8 inches tall. Crystal Full Sham. **References**: 1978, page 7 [2-1]

Line: 1975. Mardi Gras Optic. Beverage. 16 oz. 5-3/4 inches tall. Grey. Colors: Crystal, Delphine Blue, Moss Green, Grey, Plum. **References**: 1973, page 16 [BR-1]

Line: 1975. Mardi Gras Optic. Old Fashion. 12-1/2 oz. 3-3/4 inches tall. Colors: Crystal, Delphine Blue, Moss Green, Grey, Plum. **References**: 1973, page 16 [BR-2]

Line: 1975. Nocturne. Beverage. 16 oz. 5-3/4 inches tall. Brown. Colors: Black, Brown, Crystal, Lime Green, Plum. **References**: 1972, page 8 [2-4]; 1973, page 17 [2-4]

Line: 1975. Nocturne. Cordial. 1-1/2 oz. 4-5/8 inches tall. Crystal. Colors: Black, Brown, Crystal, Lime Green, Plum. **References**: 1972, page 8 [2-3]; 1973, page 17 [2-3]

Line: 1975. Nocturne. Cordial. 1-1/2 oz. 4-5/8 inches tall. Colors: Black. **References**: 1975, page 17 [4-1]; 1977, page 17 [4-1]

Line: 1975. Nocturne. Goblet. 11 oz. 7-1/2 inches tall. Plum. Colors: Black, Brown, Crystal, Lime Green, Plum. **References**: 1972, page 8 [2-5]; 1973, page 17 [2-5]

Line: 1975. Nocturne. Goblet. 11 oz. 7-1/2 inches tall. Colors: Black. **References**: 1975, page 17 [3-2]; 1977, page 17 [3-2]

Line: 1975. Nocturne. Ice Tea. 15-1/2 oz. 7-1/2 inches tall. Lime Green. Colors: Black, Brown, Crystal, Lime Green, Plum. **References**: 1972, page 8 [1-2]; 1973, page 17 [1-2]

Line: 1975. Nocturne. Ice Tea. 15-1/2 oz. 7-1/2 inches tall. Colors: Black. **References**: 1975, page 13 [1-1]; 1977, page 17 [1-1]

Line: 1975. Nocturne. Old Fashion. 12-1/2 oz. 3-3/4 inches tall. Black. Colors: Black, Brown, Crystal, Lime Green, Plum. **References**: 1972, page 8 [1-1]; 1973, page 17 [1-1]

Line: 1975. Nocturne. Sherbet. 7 oz. 4-5/8 inches tall. Plum. Colors: Black, Brown, Crystal, Lime Green, Plum. **References**: 1972, page 8 [2-2]; 1973, page 17 [2-2]

Line: 1975. Nocturne. Sherbet. 7 oz. 4-5/8 inches tall. Colors: Black. **References**: 1975, page 13 [3-1]; 1977, page 17 [3-1]

Line: 1975. Nocturne. Wine. 8-1/2 oz. 6-1/2 inches tall. Brown. Colors: Black, Brown, Crystal, Lime Green, Plum. **References**: 1972, page 8 [2-1]; 1973, page 17 [2-1]

Line: 1975. Nocturne. Wine. 8-1/2 oz. 6-1/2 inches tall. Colors: Black. **References**: 1975, page 13 [2-1]; 1977, page 17 [2-1]

Line: 1976. Today. Dessert. 10-1/2 oz. 2-5/8 inches tall. Crystal with Black Foot. Colors: Black, Crystal, Crystal with Black Foot. **References**: 1972, page 6 [1-1]

Line: 1976. Today. Dessert. 10-1/2 oz. 2-5/8 inches tall. Colors: Black, Crystal, Crystal with Black Foot. **References**: 1973, page 15 [1-1]

Line: 1976. Today. Goblet. 17-1/2 oz. 4-1/8 inches tall. Black. Colors: Black, Crystal, Crystal with Black Foot. **References**: 1972, page 6 [1-2]

Line: 1976. Today. Goblet. 17-1/2 oz. 4-1/8 inches tall. Colors: Black, Crystal, Crystal with Black Foot. **References**: 1973, page 15 [1-2]

Line: 1976. Today. Juice/Wine. 9-1/2 oz. 3-5/8 inches tall. Crystal. Colors: Black, Crystal, Crystal with Black Foot. **References**: 1972, page 6 [1-3]

Line: 1976. Today. Juice/Wine. 9-1/2 oz. 3-5/8 inches tall. Colors: Black, Crystal, Crystal with Black Foot. **References**: 1973, page 15 [1-3]

Line: 1977. La Chateau. Brandy and Liqueur. 2-1/2 oz. 6 inches tall. Plain Lead Crystal. **References**: 1973, page 6 [1-7]

Line: 1977. La Chateau. Cabinet Wine Goblet. 15-1/2 oz. 9-1/8 inches tall. Plain Lead Crystal. **References**: 1973, page 6 [1-1]

Line: 1977. La Chateau. Dessert-Champagne. 7-1/2 oz. 6-1/8 inches tall. Plain Lead Crystal. **References**: 1973, page 6 [1-6]

Line: 1977. La Chateau. Red Wine Goblet. 12-1/2 oz. 8-5/8 inches tall. Plain Lead Crystal. **References**: 1973, page 6 [1-2]

Line: 1977. La Chateau. Sherry and Port. 5 oz. 7 inches tall. Plain Lead Crystal. **References**: 1973, page 6 [1-5]

Line: 1977. La Chateau. Sparkling Wine Goblet. 9 oz. 8 inches tall. Plain Lead Crystal. **References**: 1973, page 6 [1-3]

Line: 1977. La Chateau. White Wine Goblet. 7 oz. 7-5/8 inches tall. Plain Lead Crystal. **References**: 1973, page 6 [1-4]

Line: 1977. Le Chateau. Brandy and Liqueur. 2-1/2 oz. 6 inches tall. **References**: 1975, page 6 [1-7]

Line: 1977. Le Chateau. Cabinet Wine Goblet. 15-1/2 oz. 9-1/8 inches tall. **References**: 1975, page 6 [1-1]

Line: 1977. Le Chateau. Dessert-Champagne. 7-1/2 oz. 6-1/8 inches tall. **References**: 1975, page 6 [1-6]

Line: 1977. Le Chateau. Red Wine Goblet. 12-1/2 oz. 8-5/8 inches tall. **References**: 1975, page 6 [1-2]

Line: 1977. Le Chateau. Sherry and Port. 5 oz. 7 inches tall. **References**: 1975, page 6 [1-5]

Line: 1977. Le Chateau. Sparkling Wine Goblet. 9 oz. 8 inches tall. **References**: 1975, page 6 [1-3]

Line: 1977. Le Chateau. White Wine. 7 oz. 7-5/8 inches tall. **References**: 1975, page 6 [1-4]

Line: 1977. Cut: 43. Falerno. Brandy and Liqueur. 2-1/2 oz. 6 inches tall. **References**: 1973, page 7 [1-7]; 1975, page 7 [1-7]; 1977, page 7 [1-7]

Line: 1977. Cut: 43. Falerno. Cabinet Wine Goblet. 15-1/2 oz. 9-1/8 inches tall. **References**: 1973, page 7 [1-1]; 1975, page 7 [1-1]; 1977, page 7 [1-1]

Line: 1977. Cut: 43. Falerno. Dessert-Champagne. 7-1/2 oz. 6-1/8 inches tall. **References**: 1973, page 7 [1-6]; 1975, page 7 [1-6]; 1977, page 7 [1-6]

Line: 1977. Cut: 43. Falerno. Red Wine Goblet. 12-1/2 oz. 8-5/8 inches tall. **References**: 1973, page 7 [1-2]; 1975, page 7 [1-2]; 1977, page 7 [1-2]

Line: 1977. Cut: 43. Falerno. Sherry and Port. 5 oz. 7 inches tall. **References**: 1973, page 7 [1-5]; 1975, page 7 [1-5]; 1977, page 7 [1-5]

Line: 1977. Cut: 43. Falerno. Sparkling Wine Goblet. 9 oz. 8 inches tall. **References**: 1973, page 7 [1-3]; 1975, page 7 [1-3]; 1977, page 7 [1-3]

Line: 1977. Cut: 43. Falerno. White Wine. 7 oz. 7-5/8 inches tall. **References**: 1975, page 7 [1-4]; 1973, page 7 [1-4]; 1977, page 7 [1-4]

Line: 1978. Madison. Beverage. 16 oz. 6 inches tall. Crystal Full Sham. **References**: 1978, page 7 [1-1]; 1979, page 16 [1-1]

Line: 1978. Madison. Old Fashion. 14 oz. 4-1/2 inches tall. Crystal Full Sham. **References**: 1978, page 7 [1-2]; 1979, page 16 [1-2]

Line: 1978. Cut: 43. Beverage. 16 oz. 6 inches tall. Sham Weight. **References**: 1982, page 6 [1-1]

Line: 1978. Cut: 43. Hi Ball. 11 oz. 5 inches tall. Sham Weight. **References**: 1982, page 6 [1-2]

Line: 1978. Cut: 43. Old Fashion. 9-1/2 oz. 3-1/2 inches tall. Sham Weight. **References**: 1982, page 6 [1-4]

Line: 1978. Cut: 43. On The Rocks. 14 oz. 4-1/2 inches tall. Sham Weight. **References**: 1982, page 6 [1-3]

Line: 1978. Cut: 43. Beer Series. Beer Goblet. 14 oz. 8-3/4 inches tall. Plain. **References**: 1978, page 9 [1-3]

Line: 1978. Cut: 43. Beer Series. Pony Goblet. 7 oz. 8-1/4 inches tall. Plain. **References**: 1978, page 9 [1-2]

Line: 1978. Cut: 43. Ultra. Apertif. 8 oz. 8-3/8 inches tall. **References**: 1975, page 11 [1-3]; 1977, page 11 [1-3]

Line: 1978. Cut: 43. Ultra. Compote. 16 oz. 4-3/4 inches tall. **References**: 1975, page 11 [1-5]; 1977, page 11 [1-5]

Line: 1978. Cut: 43. Ultra. Old Fashion. **References**: 1977, page 25 [3-1]

Line: 1978. Cut: 43. Ultra. On The Rocks. 14 oz. 4-1/2 inches tall. **References**: 1975, page 11 [1-6]; 1976, page 11 [2-3]; 1977, page 11 [1-6]

Line: 1978. Cut: 43. Ultra. Red Wine Goblet. 15 oz. 7-3/4 inches tall. **References**: 1975, page 11 [1-4]; 1977, page 11 [1-4]; 1975, page 11 [1-2]; 1977, page 11 [1-2]

Line: 1978. Cut: 43. Ultra. Wine Goblet. 28 oz. 8-3/4 inches tall. **References**: 1975, page 11 [1-1]; 1977, page 11 [1-1]

Line: 1978. Cut: 1444. America. Beverage. **References**: 1977, page 24 [1-1]

Line: 1978. Cut: 1444. America. On the Rocks. 15-1/2 oz. 4-1/2 inches tall. **References**: 1976, page 11 [2-2]

Line: 1978. Cut: 1446. Wicker. On The Rocks. 15-1/2 oz. 4-1/2 inches tall. **References**: 1976, page 11 [2-1]

Line: 1978. Cut: 1446. Wicker. On The Rocks. **References**: 1977, page 24 [2-1]

Line: 1978. Cut: 1447. Sunburst. Old Fashion. **References**: 1977, page 24 [3-1]

Line: 1978. Cut: 1447. Sunburst. On the Rocks. 15-1/2 oz. 4-1/2 inches tall. **References**: 1976, page 11 [1-2]

Line: 1978. Cut: 1448. Chalice. Beverage. **References**: 1977, page 24 [1-2]

Line: 1978. Cut: 1448. Chalice. On the Rocks. 15-1/2 oz. 4-1/2 inches tall. **References**: 1976, page 11 [1-3]

Line: 1978. Cut: 1449S. Tapestry. On The Rocks. **References**: 1977, page 25 [2-1]

Line: 1978. Cut: 1450S. Classic. On The Rocks. **References**: 1977, page 24 [2-2]

Line: 1978. Cut: 1451. Brittany. Beverage. 16-1/2 oz. 5-7/8 inches tall. **References**: 1977, page 25 [1-1]

Line: 1978. Cut: 1451. Brittany. Old Fashion. 9-1/2 oz. 3-1/2 inches tall. **References**: 1977, page 25 [1-3]

Line: 1978. Cut: 1451. Brittany. On the Rocks. 15-1/2 oz. 4-1/2 inches tall. **References**: 1976, page 11 [1-1]; 1977, page 25 [1-2]

Line: 1978. Cut: 1452S. Rosalynn. On The Rocks. **References**: 1977, page 25 [3-2]

Line: 1978. Cut: 1453S. Majestic. On The Rocks. **References**: 1977, page 25 [2-2]

Line: 1980. Footed Covered Candy. 6 inches tall. Colors: Moss Green. **References**: 1978, page 14 [2-E]

Line: 1980. No Foot Covered Box. 4-3/4 inches tall. Colors: Delphine Blue. **References**: 1978, page 14 [2-G]

Line: 1980. Vase. 7-1/2 inches tall. Colors: Amber. **References**: 1978, page 15 [2-2]

Line: 1980. Driftwood Casual. Cooler. 22 oz. 6-3/4 inches tall. Colors: Moss Green. **References**: 1978, page 16 [1-1]

Line: 1980. Driftwood Casual. Cooler (Not Featured). Colors: Accent Red, Amber, Brown, Crystal, Delphine Blue, Lime Green, Moss Green, Ritz Blue, Yellow. **References**: 1977, page 12-13 [2-7]

Line: 1980. Driftwood Casual. Dessert-Cereal Bowl. 13-1/2 oz. 5-1/4 inches diam. Yellow. Colors: Accent Red, Amber, Brown, Crystal, Delphine Blue, Lime Green, Moss Green, Ritz Blue, Yellow. **References**: 1975, page 16-17 [2-3]; 1977, page 12-13 [2-3]

Line: 1980. Driftwood Casual. Double Old Fashion. 14 oz. 3-7/8 inches tall. Ritz Blue. Colors: Accent Red, Amber, Brown, Crystal, Delphine Blue, Lime Green, Moss Green, Ritz Blue, Yellow. **References**: 1975, page 16-17 [1-5]; 1977, page 12-13 [1-5]

Line: 1980. Driftwood Casual. Footed Compote. 13 oz. 4-3/4 inches tall. Accent Red. Colors: Accent Red, Amber, Brown, Crystal, Delphine Blue, Lime Green, Moss Green, Ritz Blue, Yellow. **References**: 1975, page 16-17 [2-5]; 1977, page 12-13 [2-5]

Line: 1980. Driftwood Casual. Footed Goblet. 13 oz. 5-3/8 inches tall. Accent Red. Colors: Accent Red, Amber, Brown, Crystal, Delphine Blue, Lime Green, Moss Green, Ritz Blue, Yellow. **References**: 1975, page 16-17 [1-6]; 1977, page 12-13 [1-6]

Line: 1980. Driftwood Casual. Footed Juice/Wine. 10 oz. 3-7/8 inches tall. Crystal. Colors: Accent Red, Amber, Brown, Crystal, Delphine Blue, Lime Green, Moss Green, Ritz Blue, Yellow. **References**: 1975, page 16-17 [2-2]; 1977, page 12-13 [2-2]

Line: 1980. Driftwood Casual. Goblet. 13 oz. 5-1/2 inches tall. Buttercup. **References**: 1970, page 5 [1-1]

Line: 1980. Driftwood Casual. Goblet. 13 oz. 5-1/2 inches tall. Buttercup (Yellow). Colors Available: Amber, Cinnamon (Brown), Crystal, Delphine Blue, Grey, Moss Green, Peacock Blue, Accent Red. Items Available: Ice Tea, Hi Ball, Old Fashion, Roly Poly, Juice, Cocktail, Sherbet, Dessert-Cereal Bowl, Plate, Pitcher 32oz., Pitcher 65oz., Flowerlite, Bud Vase, Covered Dish. **References**: 1971, page 38 [2-3]

Line: 1980. Driftwood Casual. Goblet. 13 oz. 5-1/2 inches tall. Buttercup (Yellow). Items Available: Ice Tea, Hi Ball, Old Fashion, roly Poly, Juice, Cocktail, Goblet, Sherbet, Dessert-Cereal Bowl, Plate, Pitcher 32oz., Pitcher 65oz., Flowerlite, Bud Vase, Covered Dish. Colors: Amber, Buttercup (Yellow), Cinnamon (Brown), Crystal, Delphine Blue, Grey, Moss Green, Peacock Blue, Accent Red. **References**: 1972, page 4 [2-3]

Line: 1980. Driftwood Casual. Goblet. 13 oz. 5-1/2 inches tall. Items Available: Ice Tea, Hi Ball, Old Fashion, Roly Poly, Juice, Cocktail, Goblet, Sherbet, Dessert-Cereal Bowl, Plate, Pitcher 32oz., Pitcher 65oz., Flowerlite, Bud Vase, Covered Dish. Colors: Amber, Buttercup (Yellow), Cinnamon (Brown), Crystal, Delphine Blue, Grey, Moss Green, Peacock Blue, Accent Red, Plum. **References**: 1973, page 11 [1-1]

Line: 1980. Driftwood Casual. Hi Ball. 12 oz. 5-1/8 inches tall. Brown. Colors: Accent Red, Amber, Brown, Crystal, Delphine Blue, Lime Green, Moss Green, Ritz Blue, Yellow. **References**: 1975, page 16-17 [1-2]; 1977, page 12-13 [1-2]

Line: 1980. Driftwood Casual. Ice Tea. 16 oz. 5-3/4 inches tall. Delphine Blue. **References**: 1970, page 5 [1-5]

Line: 1980. Driftwood Casual. Ice Tea. 16 oz. 5-3/4 inches tall. Delphine Blue. Colors Available: Amber, Buttercup (Yellow), Cinnamon (Brown), Crystal, Delphine Blue, Grey, Moss Green, Peacock Blue, Accent Red. Items Available: Hi Ball, Old Fashion, Roly Poly, Juice, Cocktail, Goblet, Sherbet, Dessert-Cereal Bowl, Plate, Pitcher 32oz., Pitcher 65oz., Flowerlite, Bud Vase, Covered Dish. **References**: 1971, page 38 [2-1]; 1972, page 4 [2-1]

Line: 1980. Driftwood Casual. Ice Tea. 16 oz. 5-3/4 inches tall. Items Available: Ice Tea, Hi Ball, Old Fashion, Roly Poly, Juice, Cocktail, Goblet, Sherbet, Dessert-Cereal Bowl, Plate, Pitcher 32oz., Pitcher 65oz., Flowerlite, Bud Vase, Covered Dish. Colors: Amber, Buttercup (Yellow), Cinnamon (Brown), Crystal, Delphine Blue, Grey, Moss Green, Peacock Blue, Accent Red, Plum. **References**: 1973, page 11 [2-1]

Line: 1980. Driftwood Casual. Ice Tea. 16 oz. 5-3/4 inches tall. Moss Green. Colors: Accent Red, Amber, Brown, Crystal, Delphine Blue, Lime Green, Moss Green, Ritz Blue, Yellow. **References**: 1975, page 16-17 [1-1]; 1977, page 12-13 [1-1]

Line: 1980. Driftwood Casual. Juice. 6 oz. 4-1/8 inches tall. Delphine Blue. Colors: Accent Red, Amber, Brown, Crystal, Delphine Blue, Lime Green, Moss Green, Ritz Blue, Yellow. **References**: 1975, page 16-17 [2-6]; 1977, page 12-13 [2-6]

Line: 1980. Driftwood Casual. Old Fashion. 14 oz. 3-3/4 inches tall. Amber. **References**: 1970, page 5 [1-4]

Line: 1980. Driftwood Casual. Old Fashion. 14 oz. 3-3/4 inches tall. Amber. Colors Available: Buttercup (Yellow), Cinnamon (Brown), Crystal, Delphine Blue, Grey, Moss Green, Peacock Blue, Accent Red. Items Available: Ice Tea, Hi Ball, Roly Poly, Juice, Cocktail, Goblet, Sherbet, Dessert-Cereal Bowl, Plate, Pitcher 32oz., Pitcher 65oz., Flowerlite, Bud Vase, Covered Dish. **References**: 1971, page 38 [3-1]; 1972, page 4 [3-1]

Line: 1980. Driftwood Casual. Old Fashion. 14 oz. 3-3/4 inches tall. Items Available: Ice Tea, Hi Ball, Old Fashion, roly Poly, Juice, Cocktail, Goblet, Sherbet, Dessert-Cereal Bowl, Plate, Pitcher 32oz., Pitcher 65oz., Flowerlite, Bud Vase, Covered Dish. Colors: Amber, Buttercup (Yellow), Cinnamon (Brown), Crystal, Delphine Blue, Grey, Moss Green, Peacock Blue, Accent Red, Plum. **References**: 1973, page 11 [2-2]

Line: 1980. Driftwood Casual. On The Rocks. 9-3/4 oz. 3-7/8 inches tall. Yellow. Colors: Accent Red, Amber, Brown, Crystal, Delphine Blue, Lime Green, Moss Green, Ritz Blue, Yellow. **References**: 1975, page 16-17 [2-1]; 1977, page 12-13 [2-1]

Line: 1980. Driftwood Casual. Pitcher. 65 oz. 9-1/2 inches tall. Accent Red. Colors Available: Amber, Buttercup (Yellow), Cinnamon (Brown), Crystal, Delphine Blue, Grey, Moss Green, Peacock Blue, Accent Red. Items Available: Ice Tea, Hi Ball, Old Fashion, Roly Poly, Jice, Cocktial, Boglet, Sherbet, Dessert-Cereal Bowl, Plate, Pitcher 32oz., Flowerlite, Bud Vase, Covered Dish. **References**: 1971, page 38 [1-1]; 1972, page 4 [1-1]

Line: 1980. Driftwood Casual. Pitcher. 65 oz. Accent Red. Colors: Accent Red, Amber, Brown, Crystal, Delphine Blue, Lime Green, Moss Green, Ritz Blue, Yellow. **References**: 1975, page 16-17 [1-7]; 1977, page 12-13 [1-7]

Line: 1980. Driftwood Casual. Pitcher. 32 oz. Ritz Blue. Colors: Accent Red, Amber, Brown, Crystal, Delphine Blue, Lime Green, Moss Green, Ritz Blue, Yellow. **References**: 1975, page 16-17 [1-3]; 1977, page 12-13 [1-3]

Line: 1980. Driftwood Casual. Roly Poly. 12 oz. 3-3/8 inches tall. Moss Green. **References**: 1970, page 5 [1-3]

Line: 1980. Driftwood Casual. Roly Poly. 12 oz. 3-3/8 inches tall. Moss Green. Colors Available: Amber, Buttercup (Yellow), Cinnamon (Brown), Crystal, Delphine Blue, Grey, Peacock Blue, Accent Red. Items Available: Ice Tea, Hi Ball, Old Fashion, Juice, Cocktail, Goblet, Sherbet, Dessert-Cereal Bowl, Plate, Pitcher 32oz., Pitcher 65oz., Flowerlite, Bud Vase, Covered Dish. **References**: 1971, page 38 [2-2]; 1972, page 4 [2-2]

Line: 1980. Driftwood Casual. Roly Poly. 12 oz. 3-1/2 inches tall. Amber. Colors: Accent Red, Amber, Brown, Crystal, Delphine Blue, Lime Green, Moss Green, Ritz Blue, Yellow. **References**: 1975, page 16-17 [1-4]; 1977, page 12-13 [1-4]

Line: 1980. Driftwood Casual. Salad Plate. 8-1/2 inches diam. Crystal. Colors: Accent Red, Amber, Brown, Crystal, Delphine Blue, Lime Green, Moss Green, Ritz Blue, Yellow. **References**: 1975, page 16-17 [2-4]; 1977, page 12-13 [2-4]

Line: 1980. Driftwood Casual. Sherbet. 6 oz. 3 inches tall. Cinnamon. **References**: 1970, page 5 [1-2]

Line: 1980. Driftwood Casual. Sherbet. 6 oz. 3 inches tall. Cinnamon (Brown). Colors Available: Amber, Buttercup (Yellow), Crystal, Delphine Blue, Grey, Moss Green, Peacock Blue, Accent Red. Items Available: Ice Tea, Hi Ball, Old Fashion, Roly Poly, Juice, Cocktail, Goblet, Dessert-Cereal Bowl, Plate, Pitcher 32oz., Pitcher 65oz., Flowerlite, Bud Vase, Covered Dish. **References**: 1971, page 38 [3-2]; 1972, page 4 [3-2]

Line: 1980. Driftwood Casual. Sherbet. 6 oz. 3 inches tall. Items Available: Ice Tea, Hi Ball, Old Fashion, roly Poly, Juice, Cocktail, Goblet, Sherbet, Dessert-Cereal Bowl, Plate, Pitcher 32oz., Pitcher 65oz., Flowerlite, Bud Vase, Covered Dish. Colors: Amber, Buttercup (Yellow), Cinnamon (Brown), Crystal, Delphine Blue, Grey, Moss Green, Peacock Blue, Accent Red, Plum. **References**: 1973, page 11 [2-3]

Line: 1985. Artichoke. Beverage. Mouth blown, hand made and hand finished. Colors: Brown, Crystal, Crystal w/Black Foot, Delphine Blue, Moss Green, Yellow. **References**: 1978, page 3 [1-3]

Line: 1985. Artichoke. Goblet. 6-3/8 inches tall. Mouth blown, hand made and hand finished. Colors: Brown, Crystal, Crystal w/Black Foot, Delphine Blue, Moss Green, Yellow. **References**: 1978, page 3 [1-1]

Line: 1985. Artichoke. Hi Ball. Mouth blown, hand made and hand finished. Colors: Brown, Crystal, Crystal w/Black Foot, Delphine Blue, Moss Green, Yellow. **References**: 1978, page 3 [1-4]

Line: 1985. Artichoke. Juice/Wine. Mouth blown, hand made and hand finished. Colors: Brown, Crystal, Crystal w/Black Foot, Delphine Blue, Moss Green, Yellow. **References**: 1978, page 3 [1-2]

Line: 1985. Artichoke. On The Rocks. Mouth blown, hand made and hand finished. Colors: Brown, Crystal, Crystal w/Black Foot, Delphine Blue, Moss Green, Yellow. **References**: 1978, page 3 [1-5]

Line: 1985. Artichoke. Plate. Mouth blown, hand made and hand finished. Colors: Brown, Crystal, Crystal w/Black Foot, Delphine Blue, Moss Green, Yellow. **References**: 1978, page 3 [1-6]

Line: 2000A. Tumbler. 2 oz. Light Touraine, All Tumblers Made In Sham, Half Sham and Optic. **References**: 5-E, page 4 [2-3]

Line: 2000. Tumbler. 6 oz. Light Touraine, All Tumblers Made In Sham, Half Sham and Optic. **References**: 5-E, page 4 [2-4]

Line: 2000. Tumbler. 2-1/2 oz. Light Touraine, All Tumblers Made In Sham, Half Sham and Optic. **References**: 5-E, page 4 [Listed]

Line: 2000. Cut: 561. Tumbler. 2-1/2 oz. **References**: 2, fig. 1 [2-5]

Line: 2003. Tumbler. 3-1/2 oz. Light Touraine, All Tumblers Made In Sham, Half Sham and Optic. **References**: 5-E, page 4 [Listed]

Line: 2003. Cut: 463. Etching: 22. Tumbler. 3-1/4 oz. **References**: 2, fig. 1 [1-1]

Line: 2003. Cut: 561. Tumbler. 3-1/4 oz. **References**: 2, fig. 1 [2-4]

Line: 2006. Tumbler. 5-1/2 oz. Light Touraine, All Tumblers Made In Sham, Half Sham and Optic. **References**: 5-E, page 4[Listed]

Line: 2006. Cut: 463. Etching: 22. Tumbler. 5-1/2 oz. **References**: 2, fig. 1 [1-2]

Line: 2006. Cut: 561. Tumbler. 5-1/2 oz. **References**: 2, fig. 1 [2-3]

Line: 2009. Tumbler. 6-1/2 oz. Light Touraine, All Tumblers Made In Sham, Half Sham and Optic. **References**: 5-E, page 4 [Listed]

Line: 2009. Cut: 463. Etching: 22. Tumbler. 6-1/2 oz. **References**: 2, fig. 1 [1-3]

Line: 2009. Cut: 561. Tumbler. 6-1/2 oz. **References**: 2, fig. 1 [2-2]

Line: 2012. Tumbler. 8 oz. Light Touraine, All Tumblers Made In Sham, Half Sham and Optic. **References**: 5-E, page 4 [Listed]

Line: 2012. Cut: 463. Etching: 22. Tumbler. 8 oz. **References**: 2, fig. 1 [1-4]

Line: 2012. Cut: 561. Tumbler. 8 oz. **References**: 2, fig. 1 [2-1]

Line: 2015. Tumbler. 9 oz. Light Touraine, All Tumblers Made In Sham, Half Sham and Optic. **References**: 5-E, page 4 [Listed]

Line: 2018. Tumbler. 10 oz. Light Touraine, All Tumblers Made In Sham, Half Sham and Optic. **References**: 5-E, page 4 [Listed]

Line: 2018. Cut: 463. Etching: 22. Tumbler. 10 oz. **References**: 2, fig. 1 [1-5]

Line: 2021. Tumbler. 12 oz. Light Touraine, All Tumblers Made In Sham, Half Sham and Optic. **References**: 5-E, page 4 [Listed]

Line: 2050. Tumbler. 8 oz. Light Touraine, All Tumblers Made In Sham, Half Sham and Optic. **References**: 5-E, page 4 [Listed]

Line: 2050. Tumbler. 10 oz. Light Touraine, All Tumblers Made In Sham, Half Sham and Optic. **References**: 5-E, page 4 [Listed]

Line: 2050. Tumbler. 12 oz. Light Touraine, All Tumblers Made In Sham, Half Sham and Optic. **References**: 5-E, page 4 [Listed]

Line: 2100. Tumbler. 5 oz. Light Touraine, All Tumblers Made In Sham, Half Sham and Optic. **References**: 5-E, page 4 [Listed]

Line: 2100. Tumbler. 8 oz. Light Touraine, All Tumblers Made In Sham, Half Sham and Optic. **References**: 5-E, page 4 [Listed]

Line: 2103. Tumbler. 7-1/2 oz. Light Touraine, All Tumblers Made In Sham, Half Sham and Optic. **References**: 5-E, page 4 [Listed]

Line: 2106. Tumbler. 9 oz. Light Touraine, All Tumblers Made In Sham, Half Sham and Optic. **References**: 5-E, page 4 [Listed]

Line: 2828. Tumbler. 9-1/2 oz. 4-7/8 inches tall. Straight Optic, Regular Weight. **References**: 1982, page 12 [1-5]

Line: 2828. Palm Optic. Tumbler. 9-1/2 oz. 4-7/8 inches tall. Regular Weight. **References**: 1982, page 10 [1-2]

Line: 2828. Peacock Optic. Tumbler. 9-1/2 oz. 4-7/8 inches tall. Regular Weight. **References**: 1982, page 10 [1-2]; 1975/I-75, page 6 [1-2]

Line: 2850. Old Fashion. 9 oz. 3-1/2 inches tall. Plain & Optic, Sham Weight. **References**: 1975/I-75, page 7 [2-1]

Line: 3000. Peacock Optic. Whiskey Sour. 5 oz. 5-5/8 inches tall. **References**: 1975/I-75, page 3 [2-2]

Line: 3214. Cut: 1308. Regal. 1305 Dessert-Finger Bowl. 4-1/2 inches diam. **References**: 1968, page 26 [2-18]

Line: 3214. Cut: 1308. Regal. Cocktail. 4-1/4 oz. 4 inches tall. **References**: 1968, page 26 [2-14]

Line: 3214. Cut: 1308. Regal. Cordial. 1-1/2 oz. 3-3/4 inches tall. **References**: 1968, page 26 [2-15]

Line: 3214. Cut: 1308. Regal. Goblet. 10-1/4 oz. 6-1/8 inches tall. **References**: 1968, page 26 [2-11]

Line: 3214. Cut: 1308. Regal. Ice Tea. 12 oz. 6-3/4 inches tall. **References**: 1968, page 26 [2-17]

Line: 3214. Cut: 1308. Regal. Juice. 5-1/4 oz. 4-7/8 inches tall. **References**: 1968, page 26 [2-16]

Line: 3214. Cut: 1308. Regal. Plate. 7 inches diam. Actually 7-7/8" Dia. **References**: 1968, page 26 [2-19]

Line: 3214. Cut: 1308. Regal. Plate. 8 inches diam. Actually 8-3/4" Dia. **References**: 1968, page 26 [2-20]

Line: 3214. Cut: 1308. Regal. Sherbet. 6-1/2 oz. 4-1/

2 inches tall. **References**: 1968, page 26 [2-12]

Line: 3214. Cut: 1308. Regal. Wine. 3-3/4 oz. 5 inches tall. **References**: 1968, page 26 [2-13]

Line: 3214. Cut: 1309. Scroll. 1305 Dessert-Finger Bowl. 4-1/2 inches diam. **References**: 1968, page 26 [2-8]

Line: 3214. Cut: 1309. Scroll. Cocktail. 4-1/4 oz. 4 inches tall. **References**: 1968, page 26 [2-4]

Line: 3214. Cut: 1309. Scroll. Cordial. 1-1/2 oz. 3-3/4 inches tall. **References**: 1968, page 26 [2-5]

Line: 3214. Cut: 1309. Scroll. Goblet. 10-1/4 oz. 6-1/8 inches tall. **References**: 1968, page 26 [2-1]

Line: 3214. Cut: 1309. Scroll. Ice Tea. 12 oz. 6-3/4 inches tall. **References**: 1968, page 26 [2-7]

Line: 3214. Cut: 1309. Scroll. Juice. 5-1/4 oz. 4-7/8 inches tall. **References**: 1968, page 26 [2-6]

Line: 3214. Cut: 1309. Scroll. Plate. 7 inches diam. Actually 7-7/8" Dia. **References**: 1968, page 26 [2-9]

Line: 3214. Cut: 1309. Scroll. Plate. 8 inches diam. Actually 8-3/4" Dia. **References**: 1968, page 26 [2-10]

Line: 3214. Cut: 1309. Scroll. Sherbet. 6-1/2 oz. 4-1/2 inches tall. **References**: 1968, page 26 [2-2]

Line: 3214. Cut: 1309. Scroll. Wine. 3-3/4 oz. 5 inches tall. **References**: 1968, page 26 [2-3]

Line: 3800. Old Fashion. 11 oz. 3-7/8 inches tall. Plain, Sham Weight. **References**: 1972, page 30 [3-1]; 1973, page 35 [3-1]; 1975, page 31 [3-1]; 1977, page 42 [3-1]; 1975/I-75, page 11 [3-1]

Line: 3800. Old Fashion. 7-1/2 oz. 3-3/8 inches tall. Plain, Sham Weight. **References**: 1972, page 30 [3-2]; 1973, page 35 [3-2]; 1975, page 31 [3-2]; 1977, page 42 [3-2]; 1975/I-75, page 11 [3-2]

Line: 3800. Tumbler. 14 oz. 5-1/2 inches tall. Plain, Sham Weight. **References**: 1972, page 30 [1-1]; 1973, page 35 [1-1]; 1975, page 31 [1-1]; 1977, page 42 [1-1]; 1975/I-75, page 11 [1-1]; 1979, page 14 [3-1]

Line: 3800. Tumbler. 12 oz. 4-7/8 inches tall. Plain, Sham Weight. **References**: 1972, page 30 [1-2]; 1973, page 35 [1-2]; 1975, page 31 [1-2]; 1977, page 42 [1-2]; 1975/I-75, page 11 [1-2]; 1979, page 14 [3-2]

Line: 3800. Tumbler. 5 oz. 2-7/8 inches tall. Plain, Sham Weight. **References**: 1972, page 30 [2-1]; 1973, page 35 [2-1]; 1975, page 31 [2-1]; 1977, page 42 [2-1]; 1975/I-75, page 11 [2-1]; 1979, page 14 [3-5]

Line: 3800. Old Fashion. 11 oz. 3-7/8 inches tall. Plain Sham Weight. **References**: 1979, page 14 [3-3]

Line: 3800. Old Fashion. 7-1/2 oz. 3-3/8 inches tall. Plain Sham Weight. **References**: 1979, page 14 [3-4]

Line: 3800. Windsor. Beverage. 13-1/2 oz. 5-3/4 inches tall. Crystal Full Sham. **References**: 1978, page 7 [1-3]; 979, page 16 [1-3]

Line: 3800. Windsor. Old Fashion. 10 oz. 4 inches tall. Crystal Full Sham. **References**: 1978, page 7 [1-4]; 1979, page 16 [1-4]

Line: 3825. Elsinore. Beverage. 17-1/2 oz. 5-1/2 inches tall. Moss Green. Colors: Crystal, Delphine Blue, Moss Green, Grey, Plum. **References**: 1972, page 7 [MR-1]; 1973, page 16 [MR-1]

Line: 3825. Elsinore. Old Fashion. 13 oz. 4 inches tall. Moss Green. Colors: Crystal, Delphine Blue, Moss Green, Grey, Plum. **References**: 1972, page 7 [MR-2]; 1973, page 16 [MR-2]

Line: 3875. Antique Optic. Beverage. 16 oz. 5-1/8 inches tall. Plum. Colors: Crystal, Delphine Blue, Moss Green, Grey, Plum. **References**: 1972, page 7 [TR-1]; 1973, page 16 [TR-1]

Line: 3875. Antique Optic. Old Fashion. 12-1/2 oz. 3-7/8 inches tall. Plum. Colors: Crystal, Delphine Blue, Moss Green, Grey, Plum. **References**: 1972, page 7 [TR-2]; 1973, page 16 [TR-2]

Line: 3875. Sociables. Beverage. 16 oz. 5-1/8 inches tall. Plum. Colors: Crystal, Delphine Blue, Green, Grey, Plum. **References**: 1972, page 6 [1-1]; 1972, page 6 [2-3]; 1973, page 15 [1-1]; 1973, page 15 [2-3]

Line: 3875. Sociables. Dessert. 11-1/2 oz. 2-3/4 inches tall. Grey. Colors: Crystal, Delphine Blue, Green, Grey, Plum. **References**: 1972, page 6 [2-2]; 1973, page 15 [2-2]

Line: 3875. Sociables. Goblet. 12-1/2 oz. 3-7/8 inches tall. Delphine Blue. Colors: Crystal, Delphine Blue, Green, Grey, Plum. **References**: 1972, page 6 [1-2]; 1973, page 15 [1-2]

Line: 3875. Sociables. Juice/Cocktail. 9 oz. 3-1/4 inches tall. Crystal. Colors: Crystal, Delphine Blue, Green, Grey, Plum. **References**: 1972, page 6 [2-1]; 1973, page 15 [2-1]

Line: 4000. Mark IV. Beverage. 15-1/2 oz. 5-3/8 inches tall. Plum. Colors: Crystal, Delphine Blue, Moss Green, Grey, Plum. **References**: 1972, page 7 [BL-2]; 1973, page 16 [BL-2]

Line: 4000. Mark IV. Old Fashion. 3-7/8 inches tall. Plum. Colors: Crystal, Delphine Blue, Moss Green, Grey, Plum. **References**: 1972, page 7 [BL-1]; 1973, page 16 [BL-1]

Line: 4025. Gentry. Beverage. 17 oz. 5-1/4 inches tall. Delphine Blue. Colors: Crystal, Delphine Blue, Moss Green, Grey, Plum. **References**: 1972, page 7 [ML-2]; 1973, page 16 [ML-2]

Line: 4025. Gentry. Old Fashion. 11-1/2 oz. 3-3/4 inches tall. Delphine Blue. Colors: Crystal, Delphine Blue, Moss Green, Grey, Plum. **References**: 1972, page 7 [ML-1]; 1973, page 16 [ML-1]

Line: 50-10. Vase. 10 inches tall. Crystal with Black Foot. **References**: 1978, page 15 [1-1]

Line: 50-12. Vase. 12 inches tall. Crystal with Black Foot. **References**: 1978, page 15 [2-1]

Line: 5321. Chalet. Dessert-Champagne. 11 oz. 4-7/8 inches tall. Pink/Crystal Foot. Colors Available: Blue/Crystal Foot, Pink/Crystal Foot, Crystal Cut 1443, Blue/Crystal Foot Cut 1443, Pink/Crystal Foot Cut 1443. Item Available: Goblet, Dessert-Champagne, White Wine. **References**: 1971, page 41 [3-2]

Line: 5321. Chalet. Goblet. 14 oz. 7 inches tall. Pink/Crystal Foot. Colors Available: Blue/Crystal Foot, Pink/Crystal Foot, Crystal Cut 1443, Blue/Crystal Foot Cut 1443, Pink/Crystal Foot Cut 1443. Item Available: Goblet, Dessert-Champagne, White Wine. **References**: 1971, page 41 [3-1]

Line: 5321. Chalet. White Wine Goblet. 8-1/2 oz. 6-5/8 inches tall. Pink/Crystal Foot. Colors Available: Blue/Crystal Foot, Pink/Crystal Foot, Crystal Cut 1443, Blue/Crystal Foot Cut 1443, Pink/Crystal Foot Cut 1443. Item Available: Goblet, Dessert-Champagne, White Wine. **References**: 1971, page 41 [3-3]

Line: 5321. Gourmet Collection. Brandy and Liqueur. 2-1/2 oz. 4-1/2 inches tall. Plain Crystal. **References**: 1971, page 27 [1-8]; 1972, page 11 [1-8]; 1973, page 3 [1-9]; 1977, page 2-3 [1-9]

Line: 5321. Gourmet Collection. Brandy and Liqueur. 2-1/2 oz. 4-1/2 inches tall. Plain Lead. **References**: 1975, page 2-3 [1-9]

Line: 5321. Gourmet Collection. Champagne. 9-1/2 oz. 8 inches tall. Plain Crystal. **References**: 1971, page 27 [1-5]; 1972, page 11 [1-5]; 1973, page 3 [1-6]; 1977, page 2-3 [1-6]

Line: 5321. Gourmet Collection. Champagne. 9-1/2 oz. 8 inches tall. Plain Lead. **References**: 1975, page 2-3 [1-6]

Line: 5321. Gourmet Collection. Dessert-Champagne. 11 oz. 4-7/8 inches tall. Plain Crystal. **References**: 1971, page 27 [1-7]; 1972, page 11 [1-7]; 1973, page 3 [1-8]; 1977, page 2-3 [1-8]

Line: 5321. Gourmet Collection. Dessert-Champagne. 11 oz. 4-7/8 inches tall. Plain Lead. **References**: 1975, page 2-3 [1-8]

Line: 5321. Gourmet Collection. Grande Bordeaux. 24 oz. 7-5/8 inches tall. Plain Crystal. **References**: 1973, page 2 [1-1]; 1977, page 2-3 [1-1]

Line: 5321. Gourmet Collection. Grande Bordeaux. 24 oz. 7-5/8 inches tall. Plain Lead. **References**: 1975, page 2-3 [1-1]

Line: 5321. Gourmet Collection. Magnum Wine Goblet. 18 oz. 7-3/8 inches tall. Plain Crystal. **References**: 1971, page 27 [1-1]; 1972, page 11 [1-1]; 1973, page 2 [1-2]; 1977, page 2-3 [1-2]

Line: 5321. Gourmet Collection. Magnum Wine Goblet. 18 oz. 7-3/8 inches tall. Plain Lead. **References**: 1975, page 2-3 [1-2]

Line: 5321. Gourmet Collection. Red Wine Goblet. 10-1/2 oz. 6-7/8 inches tall. Plain Crystal. **References**: 1971, page 27 [1-3]; 1972, page 11 [1-3]; 1973, page 2 [1-4]; 1977, page 2-3 [1-4]

Line: 5321. Gourmet Collection. Red Wine Goblet. 10-1/2 oz. 6-7/8 inches tall. Plain Lead. **References**: 1975, page 2-3 [1-4]

Line: 5321. Gourmet Collection. Sherry and Port. 5 oz. 6 inches tall. Plain Crystal. **References**: 1971, page 27 [1-6]; 1972, page 11 [1-6]; 1973, page 3 [1-7]; 1977, page 2-3 [1-7]

Line: 5321. Gourmet Collection. Sherry and Port. 5 oz. 6 inches tall. Plain Lead. **References**: 1975, page 2-3 [1-7]

Line: 5321. Gourmet Collection. Vintage Wine Goblet. 14 oz. 7 inches tall. Plain Crystal. **References**: 1971, page 27 [1-2]; 1972, page 11 [1-2]; 1973, page 2 [1-3]; 1977, page 2-3 [1-3]

Line: 5321. Gourmet Collection. Vintage Wine Goblet. 14 oz. 7 inches tall. Plain Lead. **References**: 1975, page 2-3 [1-3]

Line: 5321. Gourmet Collection. White Wine. 8-1/2 oz. 6-5/8 inches tall. Plain Lead. **References**: 1975, page 2-3 [1-5]

Line: 5321. Gourmet Collection. White Wine Goblet. 8-1/2 oz. 6-5/8 inches tall. Plain Crystal. **References**: 1971, page 27 [1-4]; 1972, page 11 [1-4]; 1973, page 2 [1-5]; 1977, page 2-3 [1-5]

Line: 5321. Cut: 43. Connoisseur Collection. Brandy and Liqueur. 2-1/2 oz. 4-1/2 inches tall. **References**: 1973, page 8 [1-8]; 1975, page 8 [1-8]; 1977, page 8 [1-8]; 1981, page 3 [2-13]

Line: 5321. Cut: 43. Connoisseur Collection. Champagne. 9-1/2 oz. 8 inches tall. **References**: 1973, page 8 [1-5]; 1975, page 8 [1-5]; 1977, page 8 [1-5]; 1981, page 3 [2-15]; 1981, page 3 [2-14]

Line: 5321. Cut: 43. Connoisseur Collection. Dessert-Champagne. 11 oz. 4-7/8 inches tall. **References**: 1973, page 8 [1-7]; 1975, page 8 [1-7]; 1977, page 8 [1-7]; 1981, page 3 [2-12]

Line: 5321. Cut: 43. Connoisseur Collection. Magnum Wine Goblet. 18 oz. 7-3/8 inches tall. **References**: 1973, page 8 [1-1]; 1975, page 8 [1-1]; 1977, page 8 [1-1]; 1981, page 3 [2-7]

Line: 5321. Cut: 43. Connoisseur Collection. Red Wine Goblet. 10-1/2 oz. 6-7/8 inches tall. **References**: 1973, page 8 [1-3]; 1975, page 8 [1-3]; 1977, page 8 [1-3]; 1981, page 3 [2-9]

Line: 5321. Cut: 43. Connoisseur Collection. Sherry and Port. 5 oz. 6 inches tall. **References**: 1973, page 8 [1-6]; 1975, page 8 [1-6]; 1977, page 8 [1-6]; 1981, page 3 [2-11]

Line: 5321. Cut: 43. Connoisseur Collection. Vintage Wine Goblet. 14 oz. 7 inches tall. **References**: 1973, page 8 [1-2]; 1975, page 8 [1-2]; 1977, page 8 [1-2]; 1981, page 3 [2-8]

Line: 5321. Cut: 43. Connoisseur Collection. White Wine. 8-1/2 oz. 6-5/8 inches tall. **References**: 1975, page 8 [1-4]; 1973, page 8 [1-4]; 1977, page 8 [1-4]; 1981, page 3 [2-10]

Line: 5321. Cut: 1443. Classic. Dessert-Champagne. 11 oz. 4-7/8 inches tall. Blue/Crystal Foot. Colors Available: Blue/Crystal Foot, Pink/Crystal Foot, Crystal Cut 1443, Blue/Crystal Foot Cut 1443, Pink/Crystal Foot Cut 1443. Item Available: Goblet, Dessert-Champagne, White Wine. **References**: 1971, page 41 [3-4]

Line: 5321. Cut: 1443. Illusion. Goblet. 14 oz. 7 inches tall. Pink/Crystal Foot. Colors Available: Blue/Crystal Foot, Pink/Crystal Foot, Crystal Cut 1443, Blue/Crystal Foot Cut 1443, Pink/Crystal Foot Cut 1443. Item Available: Goblet, Dessert-Champagne, White Wine. **References**: 1971, page 41 [1-1]

Line: 5321. Cut: 1443. Illusion. White Wine Goblet. 8-1/2 oz. 6-5/8 inches tall. Pink/Crystal Foot. Colors Available: Blue/Crystal Foot, Pink/Crystal Foot, Crystal Cut 1443, Blue/Crystal Foot Cut 1443, Pink/Crystal Foot Cut 1443. Item Available: Goblet, Dessert-Champagne, White Wine. **References**: 1971, page 41 [2-1]

Line: 5321. Cut: 1443. Royalty. 1305 Dessert-Finger Bowl. 4-1/2 inches diam. **References**: 1972, page 22 [2-5]; 1973, page 26 [2-5]

Line: 5321. Cut: 1443. Royalty. Brandy and Liqueur. 2-1/2 oz. 4-1/2 inches tall. **References**: 1972, page 22 [2-4]; 1973, page 26 [2-4]

Line: 5321. Cut: 1443. Royalty. Dessert-Champagne. 11 oz. 4-7/8 inches tall. **References**: 1972, page 22 [2-2]; 1973, page 26 [2-2]

Line: 5321. Cut: 1443. Royalty. Plate. 7 inches diam. Actually 7-7/8" Dia. **References**: 1972, page 22 [2-6]; 1973, page 26 [2-6]

Line: 5321. Cut: 1443. Royalty. Plate. 8 inches diam. Actually 8-3/4" Dia. **References**: 1972, page 22 [2-7]; 1973, page 26 [2-7]

Line: 5321. Cut: 1443. Royalty. Vintage Wine Goblet. 14 oz. 7 inches tall. **References**: 1972, page 22 [2-1]; 1973, page 26 [2-1]

Line: 5321. Cut: 1443. Royalty. White Wine Goblet. 8-1/2 oz. 6-5/8 inches tall. Crystal Foot. Colors Available: Blue/Crystal Foot, Pink/Crystal Foot, Crystal Cut 1443, Blue/Crystal Foot Cut 1443, Pink/Crystal Foot Cut 1443. Item Available: Goblet, Dessert-Champagne, White Wine. **References**: 1971, page 41 [2-2]

Line: 5321. Cut: 1443. Royalty. White Wine Goblet. 8-1/2 oz. 6-5/8 inches tall. **References**: 1972, page 22 [2-3]; 1973, page 26 [2-3]

Line: 6000. Peacock Optic. Wine Goblet. 10-1/2 oz. 6 inches tall. Short Stem. **References**: 1975/I-75, page 4 [1-1]

Line: 7000. Champagne. 5 oz. **References**: 5-E, page 5 [1-4]

Line: 7000. Wine. 8-1/2 oz. 5-3/4 inches tall. **References**: 1975/I-75, page 5 [2-2]

Line: 7101. Peacock Optic. All Purpose Wine Goblet. 11 oz. 6 inches tall. **References**: 1975/I-75, page 4 [2-2]

Line: 7197. Palm Optic. Wine Goblet. 8 oz. 5-1/4 inches tall. **References**: 1982, page 9 [1-3]; 1975/I-75, page 2 [1-2]

Line: 7199 (1962). Peacock Optic. Brandy. 7 oz. 4-1/8 inches tall. **References**: 1975/I-75, page 3 [3-2]

Line: 7780. Palm Optic. Wine Goblet. 9-1/2 oz. 6-3/8 inches tall. **References**: 1982, page 9 [1-2]; 1975/I-75, page 2 [1-1]

Line: 7856. Beer Series. Pilsner. 14-1/2 oz. 9 inches tall. Straight Optic. **References**: 1978, page 9 [2-1]; 1979, page 11 [2-2]

Line: 8000. Brandy. 1 oz. **References**: 5-E, page 9 [Listed]

Line: 8000. Brandy. 7/8 oz. **References**: 5-E, page 9 [Listed]

Line: 8000. Claret. 4 oz. **References**: 5-E, page 9 [Listed]

Line: 8000. Cocktail. 4 oz. **References**: 5-E, page 9 [Listed]

Line: 8000. Cordial. 7/8 oz. Optic. **References**: 5-E, page 9 [1-1]

Line: 8000. Cordial. 1-1/4 oz. **References**: 5-E, page 9 [Listed]

Line: 8000. Creme de Menthe. 2-1/2 oz. **References**: 5-E, page 9 [Listed]

Line: 8000. Goblet. 9 oz. Optic. **References**: 5-E, page 9 [1-4]

Line: 8000. Goblet. 11 oz. **References**: 5-E, page 9 [Listed]

Line: 8000. Goblet. 10 oz. **References**: 5-E, page 9 [Listed]

Line: 8000. Goblet. 6 oz. **References**: 5-E, page 9 [Listed]

Line: 8000. H.S. Champ. 5-1/4 oz. **References**: 5-E, page 9 [Listed]

Line: 8000. H.S.S. Champ. 6 oz. Optic. **References**: 5-E, page 9 [Listed]

Line: 8000. Large Saucer Champagne. 7 oz. **References**: 5-E, page 9 [Listed]

Line: 8000. Port. 3 oz. Optic. **References**: 5-E, page 9 [1-2]

Line: 8000. Rhine Wine Goblet. 4 oz. Optic. **References**: 5-E, page 9 [1-3]

Line: 8000. Small Saucer Champagne. 6-1/2 oz. **References**: 5-E, page 9 [Listed]

Line: 8000. Tall Champagne. 5-1/2 oz. **References**: 5-E, page 9 [Listed]

Line: 8000. Tall Claret. 6 oz. **References**: 5-E, page 9 [Listed]

Line: 8000. Tumbler. 3-1/2 oz. Light Bell Top, All Tumblers Made In Sham, Half Sham and Optic. **References**: 5-E, page 2 [2-1]

Line: 8000. Tumbler. 5 oz. Light Bell Top, All Tumblers Made In Sham, Half Sham and Optic. **References**: 5-E, page 2 [2-2]

Line: 8000. Tumbler. 6-1/2 oz. Light Bell Top, All Tumblers Made In Sham, Half Sham and Optic. **References**: 5-E, page 2 [2-3]

Line: 8000. Tumbler. 8 oz. Light Bell Top, All Tumblers Made In Sham, Half Sham and Optic. **References**: 5-E, page 2 [2-4]

Line: 8000. Tumbler. 2-3/4 oz. Light Bell Top, All Tumblers Made In Sham, Half Sham and Optic. **References**: 5-E, page 2 [Listed]

Line: 8000. Tumbler. 4-1/2 oz. Light Bell Top, All Tumblers Made In Sham, Half Sham and Optic. **References**: 5-E, page 2 [Listed]

Line: 8000. Tumbler. 7 oz. Light Bell Top, All Tumblers Made In Sham, Half Sham and Optic. **References**: 5-E, page 2 [Listed]

Line: 8000. Tumbler. 9 oz. Light Bell Top, All Tumblers Made In Sham, Half Sham and Optic. **References**: 5-E, page 2 [Listed]

Line: 8000. Tumbler. 10 oz. Light Bell Top, All Tumblers Made In Sham, Half Sham and Optic. **References**: 5-E, page 2 [Listed]

Line: 8000. Tumbler. 12 oz. Light Bell Top, All Tumblers Made In Sham, Half Sham and Optic. **References**: 5-E, page 2 [Listed]

Line: 8000. Tumbler. 14 oz. Light Bell Top, All

Tumblers Made In Sham, Half Sham and Optic. **References**: 5-E, page 2 [Listed]

Line: 8000. Tumbler. 16 oz. Light Bell Top, All Tumblers Made In Sham, Half Sham and Optic. **References**: 5-E, page 2 [Listed]

Line: 8000. Tumbler. 18 oz. Light Bell Top, All Tumblers Made In Sham, Half Sham and Optic. **References**: 5-E, page 2 [Listed]

Line: 8000. Tumbler. 4-1/2 oz. **References**: 5-E, page 2 [Listed]

Line: 8000. Wine. 2 oz. **References**: 5-E, page 9 [Listed]

Line: 8000. Helga. 1305 Dessert-Finger Bowl. 4-1/2 inches diam. Plain Twisted Stem. **References**: 1967, page 16 [2-10]; 1968, page 20 [2-10]; 1969, page 16 [2-10]; 1970, page 17 [2-10]; 1971, page 17 [2-10]; 1972, page 26 [2-10]; 1973, page 31 [2-10]

Line: 8000. Helga. Claret. 5 oz. 5-5/8 inches tall. Plain Twisted Stem. **References**: 1967, page 16 [2-4]; 1968, page 20 [2-4]; 1969, page 16 [2-4]; 1970, page 17 [2-4]; 1971, page 17 [2-4]; 1972, page 26 [2-4]; 1973, page 31 [2-4]

Line: 8000. Helga. Cocktail. 4 oz. 4-5/8 inches tall. Plain Twisted Stem. **References**: 1967, page 16 [2-5]; 1968, page 20 [2-5]; 1969, page 16 [2-5]; 1970, page 17 [2-5]; 1971, page 17 [2-5]; 1972, page 26 [2-5]; 1973, page 31 [2-5]

Line: 8000. Helga. Cordial. 1-1/4 oz. 3-3/4 inches tall. Plain Twisted Stem. **References**: 1967, page 16 [2-6]; 1968, page 20 [2-6]; 1969, page 16 [2-6]; 1970, page 17 [2-6]; 1971, page 17 [2-6]; 1972, page 26 [2-6]; 1973, page 31 [2-6]

Line: 8000. Helga. Goblet. 10-1/2 oz. 6-1/2 inches tall. Plain Twisted Stem. **References**: 1967, page 16 [2-1]; 1968, page 20 [2-1]; 1969, page 16 [2-1]; 1970, page 17 [2-1]; 1971, page 17 [2-1]; 1972, page 26 [2-1]; 1973, page 31 [2-1]

Line: 8000. Helga. Ice Tea. 12-1/4 oz. 6-1/2 inches tall. Plain Twisted Stem. **References**: 1967, page 16 [2-9]; 1968, page 20 [2-9]; 1969, page 16 [2-9]; 1970, page 17 [2-9]; 1971, page 17 [2-9]; 1972, page 26 [2-9]; 1973, page 31 [2-9]

Line: 8000. Helga. Juice. 5 oz. 4-3/4 inches tall. Plain Twisted Stem. **References**: 1967, page 16 [2-8]; 1968, page 20 [2-8]; 1969, page 16 [2-8]; 1970, page 17 [2-8]; 1971, page 17 [2-8]; 1972, page 26 [2-8]; 1973, page 31 [2-8]

Line: 8000. Helga. Parfait. 5-1/2 oz. 6-3/8 inches tall. Plain Twisted Stem. **References**: 1967, page 16 [2-7]; 1968, page 20 [2-7]; 1969, page 16 [2-7]; 1970, page 17 [2-7]; 1971, page 17 [2-7]; 1972, page 26 [2-7]; 1973, page 31 [2-7]

Line: 8000. Helga. Plate. 7 inches diam. Plain Twisted Stem, Actually 7-7/8" Dia. **References**: 1967, page 16 [2-11]; 1968, page 20 [2-11]; 1969, page 16 [2-11]; 1970, page 17 [2-11]; 1971, page 17 [2-11]; 1972, page 26 [2-11]; 1973, page 31 [2-11]

Line: 8000. Helga. Plate. 8 inches diam. Plain Twisted Stem, Actually 8-3/4" Dia. **References**: 1967, page 16 [2-12]; 1968, page 20 [2-12]; 1969, page 16 [2-12]; 1970, page 17 [2-12]; 1971, page 17 [2-12]; 1972, page 26 [2-12]; 1973, page 31 [2-12]

Line: 8000. Helga. Saucer Champagne. 6-1/2 oz. 4-3/4 inches tall. Plain Twisted Stem. **References**: 1967, page 16 [2-2]; 1968, page 20 [2-2]; 1969, page 16 [2-2]; 1970, page 17 [2-2]; 1971, page 17 [2-2]; 1972, page 26 [2-2]; 1973, page 31 [2-2]

Line: 8000. Helga. Sherbet. 6-1/2 oz. 3-1/2 inches tall. Plain Twisted Stem. **References**: 1967, page 16 [2-3]; 1968, page 20 [2-3]; 1969, page 16 [2-3]; 1970, page 17 [2-3]; 1971, page 17 [2-3]; 1972, page 26 [2-3]; 1973, page 31 [2-3]

Line: 8000. Etching: 600. Scroll Design. Ale. Optic. **References**: 3, page 3 [1-1]

Line: 8000. Etching: 600. Scroll Design. Brandy. Optic. **References**: 3, page 3 [2-4]

Line: 8000. Etching: 600. Scroll Design. Champagne. Hollow and Cut Stem, Optic. **References**: 3, page 3 [2-1]

Line: 8000. Etching: 600. Scroll Design. Claret. Optic. **References**: 3, page 3 [2-5]

Line: 8000. Etching: 600. Scroll Design. Cocktail. Optic. **References**: 3, page 3 [2-6]

Line: 8000. Etching: 600. Scroll Design. Cordial. Optic. **References**: 3, page 3 [1-4]

Line: 8000. Etching: 600. Scroll Design. Custard. Optic. **References**: 3, page 6 [1-4]

Line: 8000. Etching: 600. Scroll Design. Deminth. Optic. **References**: 3, page 3 [2-7]

Line: 8000. Etching: 600. Scroll Design. Finger Bowl. Optic. **References**: 3, page 6 [1-1]

Line: 8000. Etching: 600. Scroll Design. Goblet. 10 oz. Optic. **References**: 3, page 3 [1-8]

Line: 8000. Etching: 600. Scroll Design. Grape Fruit. Optic. **References**: 3, page 4 [3-3]

Line: 8000. Etching: 600. Scroll Design. Large Sherbet. Optic. **References**: 3, page 3 [1-7]

Line: 8000. Etching: 600. Scroll Design. Port. Optic. **References**: 3, page 3 [1-2]

Line: 8000. Etching: 600. Scroll Design. Saucer Champagne. Hollow Stem, Cut Stem, Optic. **References**: 3, page 3 [2-2]

Line: 8000. Etching: 600. Scroll Design. Saucer Champagne. Optic. **References**: 3, page 3 [2-3]

Line: 8000. Etching: 600. Scroll Design. Sherbet. **References**: 3, page 3 [1-6]

Line: 8000. Etching: 600. Scroll Design. Taper Tumbler. 5 oz. Optic. **References**: 3, page 4 [2-8]

Line: 8000. Etching: 600. Scroll Design. Taper Tumbler. 3-1/2 oz. Optic. **References**: 3, page 4 [2-9]

Line: 8000. Etching: 600. Scroll Design. Tumbler. 14 oz. Optic. **References**: 3, page 4 [2-1]

Line: 8000. Etching: 600. Scroll Design. Tumbler. 12 oz. Optic. **References**: 3, page 4 [2-2]

Line: 8000. Etching: 600. Scroll Design. Tumbler. 10 oz. Optic. **References**: 3, page 4 [2-3]

Line: 8000. Etching: 600. Scroll Design. Tumbler. 9 oz. Optic. **References**: 3, page 4 [2-4]

Line: 8000. Etching: 600. Scroll Design. Tumbler. 8 oz. Optic. **References**: 3, page 4 [2-5]

Line: 8000. Etching: 600. Scroll Design. Tumbler. 6-1/2 oz. Optic. **References**: 3, page 4 [2-6]

Line: 8000. Etching: 600. Scroll Design. Tumbler. 5 oz. Optic. **References**: 3, page 4 [2-7]

Line: 8000. Etching: 600. Scroll Design. Wine. Optic. **References**: 3, page 3 [1-3]

Line: 8000. Etching: 609. Rose Design. Ale. **References**: 3, page 10 [1-5]

Line: 8000. Etching: 609. Rose Design. Brandy. **References**: 3, page 10 [1-9]

Line: 8000. Etching: 609. Rose Design. Claret. **References**: 3, page 11 [1-3]

Line: 8000. Etching: 609. Rose Design. Cocktail. **References**: 3, page 11 [1-4]

Line: 8000. Etching: 609. Rose Design. Cordial. **References**: 3, page 10 [1-8]

Line: 8000. Etching: 609. Rose Design. Custard. **References**: 3, page 13 [1-1]

Line: 8000. Etching: 609. Rose Design. Deminth. **References**: 3, page 11 [1-5]

Line: 8000. Etching: 609. Rose Design. Finger Bowl. **References**: 3, page 13 [1-2]

Line: 8000. Etching: 609. Rose Design. Goblet. 10 oz. **References**: 3, page 10 [1-3]

Line: 8000. Etching: 609. Rose Design. Goblet. 9 oz. **References**: 3, page 10 [1-4]

Line: 8000. Etching: 609. Rose Design. Goblet. 6 oz. Optic. **References**: 3, page 11 [2-5]

Line: 8000. Etching: 609. Rose Design. Grape Fruit. **References**: 3, page 11 [2-4]

Line: 8000. Etching: 609. Rose Design. Large Saucer Champagne. Optic. **References**: 3, page 11 [1-1]

Line: 8000. Etching: 609. Rose Design. Large Sherbert. **References**: 3, page 11 [1-7]

Line: 8000. Etching: 609. Rose Design. Sherbert. **References**: 3, page 11 [1-6]

Line: 8000. Etching: 609. Rose Design. Sherry. **References**: 3, page 10 [1-7]

Line: 8000. Etching: 609. Rose Design. Small Saucer Champagne. **References**: 3, page 11 [1-2]

Line: 8000. Etching: 609. Rose Design. Taper Tumbler. 5 oz. **References**: 3, page 10 [3-9]

Line: 8000. Etching: 609. Rose Design. Tumbler. 14 oz. **References**: 3, page 10 [3-1]

Line: 8000. Etching: 609. Rose Design. Tumbler. 10 oz. **References**: 3, page 10 [3-2]

Line: 8000. Etching: 609. Rose Design. Tumbler. 12 oz. **References**: 3, page 10 [3-3]

Line: 8000. Etching: 609. Rose Design. Tumbler. 8 oz. **References**: 3, page 10 [3-4]

Line: 8000. Etching: 609. Rose Design. Tumbler. 9 oz. **References**: 3, page 10 [3-5]

Line: 8000. Etching: 609. Rose Design. Tumbler. 6-1/2 oz. **References**: 3, page 10 [3-6]

Line: 8000. Etching: 609. Rose Design. Tumbler. 5 oz. **References**: 3, page 10 [3-7]

Line: 8000. Etching: 609. Rose Design. Tumbler. 3-1/2 oz. **References**: 3, page 10 [3-8]

Line: 8000. Etching: 609. Rose Design. Wine. **References**: 3, page 10 [1-6]

Line: 8000. Cut: 43. Etching: 609. Rose Design. Champagne. Hollow Stem. **References**: 3, page 10 [1-2]

Line: 8000. Cut: 43. Etching: 609. Rose Design. Saucer Champ. Hollow Stem. **References**: 3, page 10 [1-1]

Line: 8000. Cut: 57. Cocktail. Optic. **References**: 4, page 23 [1-5]

Line: 8000. Cut: 57. H.S. Champ. Optic. **References**: 4, page 25 [1-2]

Line: 8000. Cut: 57. H.S.S. Champ. Optic. **References**: 4, page 25 [1-3]

Line: 8000. Cut: 121. Cordial. Optic. **References**: 4, page 23 [1-6]

Line: 8000. Cut: 121. Goblet. Optic. **References**: 4, page 23 [1-1]

Line: 8000. Cut: 121. Saucer Champagne. Optic. **References**: 4, page 23 [1-2]

Line: 8000. Cut: 121. Sherbet. Optic. **References**: 4, page 23 [1-3]

Line: 8000. Cut: 121. Wine. Optic. **References**: 4, page 23 [1-4]

Line: 8000. Cut: 121. Laurel Wreath. 1305 Dessert-Finger Bowl. 4-1/2 inches diam. Optic. **References**: 1967, page 21 [2-10]; 1968, page 25 [2-10]; 1969, page 24 [2-10]; 1970, page 25 [2-10]; 1971, page 25 [2-10]

Line: 8000. Cut: 121. Laurel Wreath. Claret. 5 oz. 5-5/8 inches tall. Optic. **References**: 1967, page 21 [2-4]; 1968, page 25 [2-4]; 1969, page 24 [2-4]; 1970, page 25 [2-4]; 1971, page 25 [2-4]

Line: 8000. Cut: 121. Laurel Wreath. Cocktail. 4 oz. 4-5/8 inches tall. Optic. **References**: 1967, page 21 [2-5]; 1968, page 25 [2-5]; 1969, page 24 [2-5]; 1970, page 25 [2-5]; 1971, page 25 [2-5]

Line: 8000. Cut: 121. Laurel Wreath. Cordial. 1-1/4 oz. 3-3/4 inches tall. Optic. **References**: 1967, page 21 [2-6]; 1968, page 25 [2-6]; 1969, page 24 [2-6]; 1970, page 25 [2-6]; 1971, page 25 [2-6]

Line: 8000. Cut: 121. Laurel Wreath. Goblet. 10-1/2 oz. 6-1/2 inches tall. Optic. **References**: 1967, page 21 [2-1]; 1968, page 25 [2-1]; 1969, page 24 [2-1]; 1970, page 25 [2-1]; 1971, page 25 [2-1]

Line: 8000. Cut: 121. Laurel Wreath. Ice Tea. 13-1/2 oz. 5-3/8 inches tall. Optic. **References**: 1967, page 21 [2-9]; 1968, page 25 [2-9]; 1969, page 24 [2-9]; 1970, page 25 [2-9]; 1971, page 25 [2-9]

Line: 8000. Cut: 121. Laurel Wreath. Juice. 6-1/4 oz. 4 inches tall. Optic. **References**: 1967, page 21 [2-8]; 1968, page 25 [2-8]; 1969, page 24 [2-8]; 1970, page 25 [2-8]; 1971, page 25 [2-8]

Line: 8000. Cut: 121. Laurel Wreath. Parfait. 5-1/4 oz. 6-3/8 inches tall. Optic. **References**: 1967, page 21 [2-7]; 1968, page 25 [2-7]; 1969, page 24 [2-7]; 1970, page 25 [2-7]; 1971, page 25 [2-7]

Line: 8000. Cut: 121. Laurel Wreath. Plate. 7 inches diam. Optic, Actually 7-7/8" Dia. **References**: 1967, page 21 [2-11]; 1968, page 25 [2-11]; 1969, page 24 [2-11]; 1970, page 25 [2-11]; 1971, page 25 [2-11]

Line: 8000. Cut: 121. Laurel Wreath. Plate. 8 inches diam. Optic, Actually 8-3/8" Dia. **References**: 1967, page 21 [2-12]; 1968, page 25 [2-12]; 1969, page 24 [2-12]; 1970, page 25 [2-12]; 1971, page 25 [2-12]

Line: 8000. Cut: 121. Laurel Wreath. Saucer Champagne. 6-1/2 oz. 4-3/4 inches tall. Optic. **References**: 1967, page 21 [2-2]; 1968, page 25 [2-2]; 1969, page 24 [2-2]; 1970, page 25 [2-2]; 1971, page 25 [2-2]

Line: 8000. Cut: 121. Laurel Wreath. Sherbet. 6-1/2 oz. 3-1/2 inches tall. Optic. **References**: 1967, page 21 [2-3]; 1968, page 25 [2-3]; 1969, page 24 [2-3]; 1970, page 25 [2-3]; 1971, page 25 [2-3]

Line: 8000. Cut: 308. Finger Bowl. Optic. **References**: 4, page 25 [3-2]

Line: 8101. Tumbler. 2 oz. Optic, Light Taper Bar. **References**: 5-E, page 1 [1-2]

Line: 8101. Tumbler. 1-1/4 oz. Light Taper Bar. **References**: 5-E, page 1 [4-3]

Line: 8101. Tumbler. 1-1/2 oz. Light Taper Bar. **References**: 5-E, page 1 [Listed]

Line: 8101. Tumbler. 1-3/4 oz. Light Taper Bar. **References**: 5-E, page 1 [Listed]

Line: 8101. Tumbler. 2-1/4 oz. Light Taper Bar. **References**: 5-E, page 1 [Listed]

Line: 8101. Tumbler. 2-1/2 oz. Light Taper Bar. **References**: 5-E, page 1 [Listed]

Line: 8101. Tumbler. 2-3/4 oz. Light Taper Bar. **References**: 5-E, page 1 [Listed]

Line: 8101. Tumbler. 3-1/4 oz. Light Taper Bar. **References**: 5-E, page 1 [Listed]

Line: 8101. Tumbler. 3-1/2 oz. Light Taper Bar. **References**: 5-E, page 1 [Listed]

Line: 8101. Tumbler. 3-3/4 oz. Light Taper Bar. **References**: 5-E, page 1 [Listed]

Line: 8101. Tumbler. 4 oz. Light Taper Bar. **References**: 5-E, page 1 [Listed]

Line: 8101. Tumbler. 4 1/2 oz. Light Taper Bar. **References**: 5-E, page 1 [Listed]

Line: 8101. Tumbler. 5 oz. Light Taper Bar. **References**: 5-E, page 1 [Listed]

Line: 8101. Tumbler. 5 1/2 oz. Light Taper Bar. **References**: 5-E, page 1 [Listed]

Line: 8101. Tumbler. 6 oz. Light Taper Bar. **References**: 5-E, page 1 [Listed]

Line: 8101. Tumbler. 6-1/2 oz. Light Taper Bar. **References**: 5-E, page 1 [Listed]

Line: 8101. Tumbler. 7 oz. Light Taper Bar. **References**: 5-E, page 1 [Listed]

Line: 8101. Cut: 39. Tumbler. 3 oz. Light Taper Bar. **References**: 5-E, page 1 [1-3]

Line: 8101. Cut: 39. Tumbler. 2 oz. Light Taper Bar. **References**: 5-E, page 1 [1-4]

Line: 8102. Tumbler. 2-1/4 oz. Optic, Light Taper Bar. **References**: 5-E, page 1 [1-1]

Line: 8102. Tumbler. 1-1/2 oz. Light Taper Bar. **References**: 5-E, page 1 [2-2]

Line: 8102. Tumbler. 1-3/4 oz. Light Taper Bar. **References**: 5-E, page 1 [2-4]

Line: 8102. Tumbler. 3-1/2 oz. Light Taper Bar. **References**: 5-E, page 1 [2-5]

Line: 8102. Tumbler. 1-1/2 oz. Light Taper Bar. **References**: 5-E, page 1 [3-1]

Line: 8102. Tumbler. 1 oz. Light Taper Bar. **References**: 5-E, page 1 [3-2]

Line: 8102. Tumbler. 1-1/4 oz. Light Taper Bar. **References**: 5-E, page 1 [Listed]

Line: 8102. Tumbler. 2 oz. Light Taper Bar. **References**: 5-E, page 1 [Listed]

Line: 8102. Tumbler. 2-1/2 oz. Light Taper Bar. **References**: 5-E, page 1 [Listed]

Line: 8102. Tumbler. 2-3/4 oz. Light Taper Bar. **References**: 5-E, page 1 [Listed]

Line: 8102. Tumbler. 3 oz. Light Taper Bar. **References**: 5-E, page 1 [Listed]

Line: 8102. Tumbler. 4 oz. Light Taper Bar. **References**: 5-E, page 1 [Listed]

Line: 8102. Tumbler. 4-1/4 oz. Light Taper Bar. **References**: 5-E, page 1 [Listed]

Line: 8102. Tumbler. 4-1/2 oz. Light Taper Bar. **References**: 5-E, page 1 [Listed]

Line: 8102. Tumbler. 5 oz. Light Taper Bar. **References**: 5-E, page 1 [Listed]

Line: 8102. Tumbler. 6 oz. Light Taper Bar. **References**: 5-E, page 1 [Listed]

Line: 8112. Tumbler. 2 oz. **References**: 5-E, page 1 [3-4]

Line: 8127. Old Fashion. 5-1/2 oz. 3 inches tall. Straight Optic, Sham Weight. **References**: 1982, page 12 [2-6]

Line: 8127. Tumbler. 1-1/2 oz. **References**: 5-E, page 1 [2-1]

Line: 8127. Palm Optic. Old Fashion. 5-1/2 oz. 3 inches tall. Sham Weight. **References**: 1982, page 10 [2-2]

Line: 8127. Peacock Optic. Old Fashion. 5-1/2 oz. 3 inches tall. Sham Weight. **References**: 1982, page 10 [2-2]; 1975/I-75, page 6 [3-1]

Line: 8127. Cut: 39. Etching: 608. Grape Design. Tumbler. 2-1/2 oz. **References**: 3, page 9 [2-2]

Line: 8127. Cut: 39. Etching: 609. Rose Design. Tumbler. 2-1/2 oz. **References**: 3, page 10 [2-1]

Line: 8128. Tumbler. 2-3/4 oz. **References**: 5-E, page 1 [3-3]

Line: 8401. Handled. 10 oz. Handled Ice Tea or Lemonade Glasses. **References**: 5-E, page 15 [2-1]

Line: 8401. Tumbler. 2 oz. Light Taper. **References**: 5-E, page 3 [1-1]

Line: 8401. Tumbler. 3 oz. Light Taper. **References**: 5-E, page 3 [1-2]

Line: 8401. Tumbler. 7 oz. Light Taper. **References**: 5-E, page 3 [1-3]

Line: 8401. Tumbler. 9 oz. Light Taper. **References**: 5-E, page 3 [1-4]

Line: 8401. Tumbler. 1-1/2 oz. Light Taper. **References**: 5-E, page 3 [Listed]

Line: 8401. Tumbler. 1-3/4 oz. Light Taper. **References**: 5-E, page 3 [Listed]

Line: 8401. Tumbler. 2-1/2 oz. Light Taper. **References**: 5-E, page 3 [Listed]

Line: 8401. Tumbler. 4 oz. Light Taper. **References**: 5-E, page 3 [Listed]

Line: 8401. Tumbler. 4-1/2 oz. Light Taper. **References**: 5-E, page 3 [Listed]

Line: 8401. Tumbler. 4-3/4 oz. Light Taper. **References**: 5-E, page 3 [Listed]

Line: 8401. Tumbler. 5 oz. Light Taper. **References**: 5-E, page 3 [Listed]

Line: 8401. Tumbler. 5-1/2 oz. Light Taper. **References**: 5-E, page 3 [Listed]

Line: 8401. Tumbler. 6 oz. Light Taper. **References**: 5-E, page 3 [Listed]

Line: 8401. Tumbler. 8 oz. Light Taper. **References**: 5-E, page 3 [Listed]

Line: 8401. Tumbler. 10 oz. Light Taper. **References**: 5-E, page 3 [Listed]

Line: 8401. Tumbler. 11 oz. Light Taper. **References**: 5-E, page 3 [Listed]

Line: 8401. Tumbler. 12 oz. Light Taper. **References**: 5-E, page 3 [Listed]

Line: 8401. Tumbler. 13 oz. Light Taper. **References**: 5-E, page 3 [Listed]

Line: 8401. Tumbler. 14 oz. Light Taper. **References**: 5-E, page 3 [Listed]

Line: 8401. Tumbler. 15 oz. Light Taper. **References**: 5-E, page 3 [Listed]

Line: 8401. Tumbler. 16 oz. Light Taper. **References**: 5-E, page 3 [Listed]

Line: 8401. Tumbler. 18 oz. Light Taper. **References**: 5-E, page 3 [Listed]

Line: 8401. Tumbler. 21 oz. Light Taper. **References**: 5-E, page 3 [Listed]

Line: 8401. Tumbler. 8 oz. 4-3/4 inches tall. Plain & Optic, Sham Weight. **References**: 1975/I-75, page 7 [2-2]

Line: 8402. Tumbler. 4 oz. Light Taper. **References**: 5-E, page 3 [2-1]

Line: 8402. Tumbler. 5 oz. Light Taper. **References**: 5-E, page 3 [2-2]

Line: 8402. Tumbler. 6 oz. Light Taper. **References**: 5-E, page 3 [2-3]

Line: 8402. Tumbler. 8-1/2 oz. Light Taper. **References**: 5-E, page 3 [2-4]

Line: 8402. Tumbler. 3-1/2 oz. Light Taper. **References**: 5-E, page 3 [Listed]

Line: 8402. Tumbler. 4-1/2 oz. Light Taper. **References**: 5-E, page 3 [Listed]

Line: 8402. Tumbler. 7 oz. Light Taper. **References**: 5-E, page 3 [Listed]

Line: 8402. Tumbler. 9 oz. Light Taper. **References**: 5-E, page 3 [Listed]

Line: 8402. Tumbler. 10 oz. Light Taper. **References**: 5-E, page 3 [Listed]

Line: 8402. Tumbler. 11 oz. Light Taper. **References**: 5-E, page 3 [Listed]

Line: 8402. Tumbler. 12 oz. Light Taper. **References**: 5-E, page 3 [Listed]

Line: 8402. Tumbler. 12-1/2 oz. Light Taper. **References**: 5-E, page 3 [Listed]

Line: 8402. Tumbler. 13 oz. Light Taper. **References**: 5-E, page 3 [Listed]

Line: 8402. Tumbler. 14 oz. Light Taper. **References**: 5-E, page 3 [Listed]

Line: 8402. Tumbler. 15 oz. Light Taper. **References**: 5-E, page 3 [Listed]

Line: 8402. Tumbler. 16 oz. Light Taper. **References**: 5-E, page 3 [Listed]

Line: 8402. Tumbler. 18 oz. Light Taper. **References**: 5-E, page 3 [Listed]

Line: 8402. Tumbler. 19 oz. Light Taper. **References**: 5-E, page 3 [Listed]

Line: 8402. Tumbler. 21 oz. Light Taper. **References**: 5-E, page 3 [Listed]

Line: 8701. Tumbler. 4 oz. Light Straight, All Tumblers Made In Sham, Half Sham and Optic. **References**: 5-E, page 4 [1-1]

Line: 8701. Tumbler. 6 oz. Light Straight, All Tumblers Made In Sham, Half Sham and Optic. **References**: 5-E, page 4 [1-2]

Line: 8701. Tumbler. 8 oz. Light Straight, All Tumblers Made In Sham, Half Sham and Optic. **References**: 5-E, page 4 [1-3]

Line: 8701. Tumbler. 10 oz. Light Straight, All Tumblers Made In Sham, Half Sham and Optic. **References**: 5-E, page 4 [1-4]

Line: 8701. Tumbler. 3 oz. Light Straight, All Tumblers Made In Sham, Half Sham and Optic. **References**: 5-E, page 4 [Listed]

Line: 8701. Tumbler. 4-1/2 oz. Light Straight, All Tumblers Made In Sham, Half Sham and Optic. **References**: 5-E, page 4 [Listed]

Line: 8701. Tumbler. 5 oz. Light Straight, All Tumblers Made In Sham, Half Sham and Optic. **References**: 5-E, page 4 [Listed]

Line: 8701. Tumbler. 5-1/2 oz. Light Straight, All Tumblers Made In Sham, Half Sham and Optic. **References**: 5-E, page 4 [Listed]

Line: 8701. Tumbler. 6-1/2 oz. Light Straight, All Tumblers Made In Sham, Half Sham and Optic. **References**: 5-E, page 4 [Listed]

Line: 8701. Tumbler. 7 oz. Light Straight, All Tumblers Made In Sham, Half Sham and Optic. **References**: 5-E, page 4 [Listed]

Line: 8701. Tumbler. 7-1/2 oz. Light Straight, All Tumblers Made In Sham, Half Sham and Optic. **References**: 5-E, page 4 [Listed]

Line: 8701. Tumbler. 9 oz. Light Straight, All Tumblers Made In Sham, Half Sham and Optic. **References**: 5-E, page 4 [Listed]

Line: 8701. Tumbler. 11 oz. Light Straight, All Tumblers Made In Sham, Half Sham and Optic. **References**: 5-E, page 4 [Listed]

Line: 8701. Tumbler. 11-1/2 oz. Light Straight, All Tumblers Made In Sham, Half Sham and Optic. **References**: 5-E, page 4 [Listed]

Line: 8701. Tumbler. 12 oz. Light Straight, All Tumblers Made In Sham, Half Sham and Optic. **References**: 5-E, page 4 [Listed]

Line: 8701. Tumbler. 13 oz. Light Straight, All Tumblers Made In Sham, Half Sham and Optic. **References**: 5-E, page 4 [Listed]

Line: 8701. Tumbler. 14 oz. Light Straight, All Tumblers Made In Sham, Half Sham and Optic. **References**: 5-E, page 4 [Listed]

Line: 8701. Tumbler. 15 oz. Light Straight, All Tumblers Made In Sham, Half Sham and Optic. **References**: 5-E, page 4 [Listed]

Line: 8701. Tumbler. 16 oz. Light Straight, All Tumblers Made In Sham, Half Sham and Optic. **References**: 5-E, page 4 [Listed]

Line: 8701. Tumbler. 17 oz. Light Straight, All Tumblers Made In Sham, Half Sham and Optic. **References**: 5-E, page 4 [Listed]

Line: 8701. Tumbler. 18 oz. Light Straight, All Tumblers Made In Sham, Half Sham and Optic. **References**: 5-E, page 4 [Listed]

Line: 8701. Tumbler. 20 oz. Light Straight, All Tumblers Made In Sham, Half Sham and Optic. **References**: 5-E, page 4 [Listed]

Line: 8701. Tumbler. 14 oz. 5-1/2 inches tall. Straight Optic, Sham Weight. **References**: 1982, page 12 [2-1]

Line: 8701. Tumbler. 10 oz. 5-1/8 inches tall. Straight Optic, Sham Weight. **References**: 1982, page 12 [2-2]

Line: 8701. Tumbler. 9 oz. 5 inches tall. Straight Optic, Sham Weight. **References**: 1982, page 12 [2-3]

Line: 8701. Tumbler. 9 oz. 4-3/4 inches tall. Straight Optic, Sham Weight. **References**: 1982, page 12 [2-4]

Line: 8701. Palm Optic. Tumbler. 14 oz. 5-1/2 inches tall. Sham Weight. **References**: 1982, page 10 [2-3]

Line: 8701. Palm Optic. Tumbler. 10 oz. 5-1/8 inches tall. Sham Weight. **References**: 1982, page 10 [2-4]

Line: 8701. Palm Optic. Tumbler. 12 oz. 5 inches tall. Sham Weight. **References**: 1982, page 10 [2-5]

Line: 8701. Palm Optic. Tumbler. 9 oz. 4-3/4 inches tall. Sham Weight. **References**: 1982, page 10 [2-6]; 1975/I-75, page 7 [3-2]

Line: 8701. Palm Optic. Tumbler. 10 oz. 5-1/8 inches tall. Plain & Palm Optic, Sham Weight. **References**: 1975/I-75, page 7 [3-3]

Line: 8701. Peacock Optic. Tumbler. 14 oz. 5-1/2 inches tall. Sham Weight. **References**: 1982, page 10 [2-3]

Line: 8701. Peacock Optic. Tumbler. 10 oz. 5-1/8 inches tall. Sham Weight. **References**: 1982, page 10 [2-4]

Line: 8701. Peacock Optic. Tumbler. 12 oz. 5 inches tall. Sham Weight. **References**: 1982, page 10 [2-5]

Line: 8701. Peacock Optic. Tumbler. 9 oz. 4-3/4 inches tall. Sham Weight. **References**: 1982, page 10 [2-6]

Line: 8701. Etching: 5. Tumbler. 8 oz. **References**: 5-E, page 17 [2-1]

Line: 8701. Etching: 600. Scroll Design. Handled Tumbler. 7 oz. **References**: 3, page 4 [3-2]

Line: 8701. Cut: 39. Old Fashion. 7-3/4 oz. 3-3/8 inches tall. Sham Weight. **References**: 1973, page 36 [1-5]

Line: 8701. Cut: 39. Old Fashion. 9 oz. 3-5/8 inches tall. Sham Weight. **References**: 1973, page 36 [1-6]

Line: 8701. Cut: 39. Table Tumbler. 10 oz. 3-3/4 inches tall. Regular Weight. **References**: 1973, page 36 [1-4]

Line: 8701. Cut: 39. Tumbler. 14 oz. 5-1/2 inches tall. Regular Weight. **References**: 1972, page 31 [1-1]; 1973, page 36 [1-1]; 1975, page 32 [1-1]; 1977, page 43 [1-1]; 1975/I-75, page 12 [1-1]

Line: 8701. Cut: 39. Tumbler. 12 oz. 5 inches tall. Regular Weight. **References**: 1972, page 31 [1-2]; 1973, page 36 [1-2]; 1975, page 32 [1-2]; 1977, page 43 [1-2]; 1975/I-75, page 12 [1-2]

Line: 8701. Cut: 39. Tumbler. 10 oz. 4-3/4 inches tall. Regular Weight. The cut 39 indicates the Flutes at the base of the Tumblers are 1-1/4" high and 1/2" wide. Tumblers Cut 39 have a flat unpolished base. Items available: 14 oz., 12 oz., and 10 oz. Tumbler, 10 oz. Table Tumbler, 7-3/4 oz., 9 oz. Old Fashion. **References**: 1972, page 31 [1-3]; 1973, page 36 [1-3]; 1975, page 32 [1-3]; 1977, page 43 [1-3]; 1979, page 14 [2-9];1975/I-75, page 12 [1-3]

Line: 8701. Cut: 43. Tumbler. 14 oz. 5-1/2 inches tall. Sham Weight. **References**: 1972, page 31 [3-1]; 1973, page 36 [3-1]; 1975, page 32 [3-1]; 1977, page 43 [3-1]; 1982, page 6 [1-5]; 1975/I-75, page 12 [3-1]

Line: 8701. Cut: 43. Tumbler. 12 oz. 5 inches tall. Sham Weight. **References**: 1972, page 31 [3-2]; 1973, page 36 [3-2]; 1975, page 32 [3-2]; 1977, page 43 [3-2]; 1982, page 6 [1-6]; 1975/I-75, page 12 [3-2]

Line: 8701. Cut: 43. Tumbler. 10 oz. 4-3/4 inches tall. Sham Weight. **References**: 1972, page 31 [3-3]; 1973, page 36 [3-3]; 1975, page 32 [3-3]; 1977, page 43 [3-3]; 1975/I-75, page 12 [3-3]

Line: 8701. Cut: 43. Tumbler. 14 oz. 5-1/2 inches tall. Sham Weight, Polished Bottom. The cut 43 indicates the Flutes at the base of the Tumblers are 1-3/4" high and 3/4" wide. Tumblers Cut 43 have a hand cut and hand polished (Punty) base. Items available: 14 oz., 12 oz., and 10 oz. Tumbler, 10 oz. Table Tumbler, 7-3/4 oz., 9 oz., and 12 oz. Old Fashion. **References**: 1979, page 14 [2-3]

Line: 8701. Cut: 43. Tumbler. 9 oz. 4 inches tall. Sham Weight. **References**: 1982, page 6 [1-7]

Line: 8701. Cut: 45. Tumbler. 14 oz. 5-1/2 inches tall. Sham Weight. **References**: 1972, page 31 [2-1]; 1973, page 36 [2-1]; 1975, page 32 [2-1]; 1977, page 43 [2-1]; 1982, page 7 [1-1]; 1975/I-75, page 12 [2-1]

Line: 8701. Cut: 45. Tumbler. 12 oz. 5 inches tall. Sham Weight. **References**: 1972, page 31 [2-2]; 1973, page 36 [2-2]; 1975, page 32 [2-2]; 1977, page 43 [2-2]; 1982, page 7 [1-2]; 1975/I-75, page 12 [2-2]

Line: 8701. Cut: 45. Tumbler. 10 oz. 4-3/4 inches tall. Sham Weight. **References**: 1972, page 31 [2-3]; 1973, page 36 [2-3]; 1975, page 32 [2-3]; 1977, page 43 [2-3]; 1975/I-75, page 12 [2-3]

Line: 8701. Cut: 45. Tumbler. 12 oz. 5 inches tall. Sham Weight. The cut 43 indicates the Flutes at the base of the Tumblers are 1-1/2" high and 3/4" wide. Tumblers Cut 45 have a flat unpolished base. Items available: 14 oz., 12 oz., and 10 oz. Tumbler, 10 oz. Table Tumbler, 7-3/4 oz., 9 oz., and 12 oz. Old Fashion. **References**: 1979, page 14 [2-6]

Line: 8701. Cut: 45. Tumbler. 9 oz. 4-3/4 inches tall. Sham Weight. **References**: 1982, page 7 [1-3]

Line: 8701-11-1/2. Peacock Optic. Tumbler. 9 oz. 5 inches tall. Sham Weight. **References**: 1975/I-75, page 6 [1-1]

Line: 9001. Tumbler. 1/2 oz. **References**: 5-E, page 1 [4-1]

Line; 9001. Etching: 608. Grape Design. Tumbler. 8 oz. **References**: 3, page 9 [2-4]

Line: 9001. Etching: 609. Rose Design. Tumbler. 8 oz. **References**: 3, page 10 [2-3]

Line: 9002. Tumbler. 1/2 oz. Light Bell Top, All Tumblers Made In Sham, Half Sham and Optic. **References**: 5-E, page 2 [1-1]

Line: 9002. Tumbler. 2 oz. Light Bell Top, All Tumblers Made In Sham, Half Sham and Optic. **References**: 5-E, page 2 [1-2]

Line: 9002. Tumbler. 3 oz. Light Bell Top, All Tumblers Made In Sham, Half Sham and Optic. **References**: 5-E, page 2 [1-3]

Line: 9002. Tumbler. 4 oz. Light Bell Top, All Tumblers Made In Sham, Half Sham and Optic. **References**: 5-E, page 2 [1-4]

Line: 9002. Tumbler. 8 oz. Light Bell Top, All Tumblers Made In Sham, Half Sham and Optic. **References**: 5-E, page 2 [1-5]

Line: 9002. Tumbler. 1 oz. Light Bell Top, All Tumblers Made In Sham, Half Sham and Optic. **References**: 5-E, page 2 [Listed]

Line: 9002. Tumbler. 1-1/2 oz. Light Bell Top, All Tumblers Made In Sham, Half Sham and Optic. **References**: 5-E, page 2 [Listed]

Line: 9002. Tumbler. 2-1/2 oz. Light Bell Top, All Tumblers Made In Sham, Half Sham and Optic. **References**: 5-E, page 2 [Listed]

Line: 9002. Tumbler. 5 oz. Light Bell Top, All Tumblers Made In Sham, Half Sham and Optic. **References**: 5-E, page 2 [Listed]

Line: 9002. Tumbler. 6 oz. Light Bell Top, All Tumblers Made In Sham, Half Sham and Optic. **References**: 5-E, page 2 [Listed]

Line: 9002. Tumbler. 7 oz. Light Bell Top, All Tumblers Made In Sham, Half Sham and Optic. **References**: 5-E, page 2 [Listed]

Line: 9002. Tumbler. 9 oz. Light Bell Top, All Tumblers Made In Sham, Half Sham and Optic. **References**: 5-E, page 2 [Listed]

Line: 9002. Tumbler. 10 oz. Light Bell Top, All Tumblers Made In Sham, Half Sham and Optic. **References**: 5-E, page 2 [Listed]

Line: 9002. Tumbler. 11 oz. Light Bell Top, All Tumblers Made In Sham, Half Sham and Optic. **References**: 5-E, page 2 [Listed]

Line: 9002. Tumbler. 12 oz. Light Bell Top, All Tumblers Made In Sham, Half Sham and Optic. **References**: 5-E, page 2 [Listed]

Line: 9002. Tumbler. 14 oz. Light Bell Top, All Tumblers Made In Sham, Half Sham and Optic. **References**: 5-E, page 2 [Listed]

Line: 9002. Tumbler. 15 oz. Light Bell Top, All Tumblers Made In Sham, Half Sham and Optic. **References**: 5-E, page 2 [Listed]

Line: 9002. Tumbler. 16 oz. Light Bell Top, All Tumblers Made In Sham, Half Sham and Optic. **References**: 5-E, page 2 [Listed]

Line: 9002. Tumbler. 18 oz. Light Bell Top, All Tumblers Made In Sham, Half Sham and Optic. **References**: 5-E, page 2 [Listed]

Line: 9002. Tumbler. 20 oz. Light Bell Top, All Tumblers Made In Sham, Half Sham and Optic. **References**: 5-E, page 2 [Listed]

Line: 90-10. Vase. 10 inches tall. Crystal with Black Foot. **References**: 1978, page 15 [2-5]

Line: 9491. Tumbler. 12 oz. 7 inches tall. Straight 16 Optic, Sham Weight. **References**: 1982, page 12 [1-4]

Line: 9491. Tumbler. 12 oz. 6 inches tall. Plain & Optic, Regular Weight. **References**: 1975/I-75, page 7 [2-3]

Line: 9491. Palm Optic. Tumbler. 12 oz. 6 inches tall. Regular Weight. **References**: 1982, page 10 [1-1]

Line: 9491. Palm Optic. Tumbler. 12 oz. 7 inches tall. Plain & Palm Optic, Sham Weight. **References**: 1975/I-75, page 7 [3-1]

Line: 9491. Peacock Optic. Tumbler. 12 oz. 6 inches tall. Regular Weight. **References**: 1982, page 10 [1-1]

Line: 9491. Peacock Optic. Tumbler. 12 oz. 6-3/8 inches tall. Regular Weight. **References**: 1975/I-75, page 6 [2-2]

Line: 9823. Tumbler. 11 oz. 5-1/8 inches tall. Straight 10 Optic, Regular Weight. **References**: 1982, page 12 [1-1]

Line: 9823. Tumbler. 11 oz. 5-1/8 inches tall. Plain & Straight 10 Optic, Regular Weight. **References**: 1975/I-75, page 7 [1-1]

Line: 9823 (2825). Tumbler. 9 oz. 4-3/4 inches tall. Straight 12 Optic, Sham Weight. **References**: 1982, page 12 [1-2]

Line: 9823 (2825). Tumbler. 9 oz. 3-1/2 inches tall. Plain & Straight 12 Optic, Sham Weight. **References**: 1975/I-75, page 7 [1-2]

ETCHING/CUT NUMBER INDEX

This index is organized by Etching/Cut Numbers, as they were used in the various catalogs. Secondarily it is organized by Line Numbers and Series Names, when they were used, in that order. This will help the reader use this index as a cross-reference with the other indexes in the book. Shapes, dimensions and volume, color, and other information are also provided whenever available.

Each entry has References to the catalogs and other illustrations in the book, by number or date. The first number identifies the catalog; the second number is the page of the catalog where the item can be found; and the bracketed number is the position of the item on the catalog page. The first position

number is the row, and the second is the placement, counting from the left. If the item appears in multiple catalogs, each appearence will be referenced.

This indexing was dependent upon Seneca's own identification of items. At times there may be multiple entries, because of some slightly different way of identifying a product.

While we recognize some of the shortcomings of these indexes, it is hoped that, in the main, they will be useful to the collector in finding a particular item of interest.

Etching: A. Line: 1. Water Set. **References:** 2, fig. 5 [1-2]

Etching: B. Line: 1. Jug. **References:** 2, fig. 3 [1-1]

Etching: B. Line: 1. Water Set. **References:** 2, fig. 5 [2-2]

Etching: C. Line: 1. Jug. **References:** 2, fig. 3 [1-2]

Etching: C. Line: 557. Tumbler. **References:** 2, fig. 9 [1-2]

Etching: D. Line: 1. Jug. **References:** 2, fig. 3 [1-3]

Etching: G. Line: 557. Tumbler. **References:** 2, fig. 9 [2-1]

Etching: H. Line: 557. Tumbler. **References:** 2, fig. 9 [2-2]

Etching: J. Line: 1. Jug. **References:** 2, fig. 3 [1-4]

Etching: J. Line: 557. Tumbler. **References:** 2, fig. 9 [1-4]

Etching: K. Line: 557. Tumbler. **References:** 2, fig. 9 [2-3]

Etching: L. Line: 557. Tumbler. **References:** 2, fig. 9 [2-4]

Etching: M. Line: 557. Tumbler. **References:** 2, fig. 9 [2-5]

Etchings: N and 75. Line: 25. Water Bottle. One Quart. Cut Neck and Star Bottom. **References:** 2, fig. 3 [2-5]

Etching: N. Line: 557. Tumbler. **References:** 2, fig. 9 [2-6]

Etching: O. Line: 557. Tumbler. **References:** 2, fig. 9 [1-3]

Etching: P. Line: 557. Tumbler. **References:** 2, fig. 9 [1-5]

Etching: R. Line: 557. Tumbler. **References:** 2, fig. 9 [3-1]

Etching: S. Line: 1. Jug. **References:** 2, fig. 3 [3-1]

Etching: S. Line: 557. Tumbler. **References:** 2, fig. 9 [3-2]

Etching: T. Line: 1. Jug. **References:** 2, fig. 3 [3-2]

Etching: T. Line: 557. Tumbler. **References:** 2, fig. 9 [3-3]

Etching: U. Line: 1. Jug. **References:** 2, fig. 3 [3-3]

Etching: U. Line: 557. Tumbler. **References:** 2, fig. 9 [3-4]

Etching: V. Line: 1. Jug. **References:** 2, fig. 3 [1-5]

Etching: V. Line: 557. Tumbler. **References:** 2, fig. 9 [3-5]

Etching: X. Line: 1. Jug. **References:** 2, fig. 3 [3-4];

Etching: Y. Line: 1. Jug. **References:** 2, fig. 3 [3-5]

Etching: Y. Line: 557. Tumbler. **References:** 2, fig. 9 [1-1]

Etching: 1. Line: 1. Water Set. **References:** 2, fig. 5 [3-2]

Etching: 1. Line: 630. Tumbler. **References:** 5-E, page 18 [1-2]

Etching: 1, Initial and Wreath. Line: 630. Tumbler. **References:** 5-E, page 18 [2-2]

Etching: 1. Line: 1500. Tumbler/gold Band. 2-1/4 oz. Light Barrel Shape. **References:** 5-E, page 19 [3-3]

Etching: 2. Line: 1515. Tumbler/gold Band. 8-1/2 oz. Light Barrel Shape. **References:** 5-E, page 19 [3-4]

Etching: 3. Line: 557. Tumbler. **References:** 2, fig. 10 [1-2]

Etching: 5. Line: 84. Fruit. **References:** 5-E, page 17 [2-3]

Etching: 5. Line: 300. Almond. **References:** 5-E, page 17 [2-4]

Etching: 5. Line: 300. Brandy. **References:** 5-E, page 17 [1-2]

Etching: 5. Line: 300. Cordial. **References:** 5-E,

page 17 [1-1]

Etching: 5. Line: 300. Goblet. 8 oz. **References:** 5-E, page 17 [1-4]

Etching: 5. Line: 300. Sherbert. **References:** 5-E, page 17 [2-2]

Etching: 5. Line: 300. Wine. **References:** 5-E, page 17 [1-3]

Etching: 5. Line: 8701. Tumbler. 8 oz. **References:** 5-E, page 17 [2-1]

Etching: 7. Line: 557. Tumbler. **References:** 2, fig. 12 [3-4]

Etching: 7. Line: 619. Water Tumbler. **References:** 2, fig. 15 [2-2]

Etching: 8, Cut Neck and Star Bottom. Line: 50. Water Bottle. **References:** 5-E, page 19 [3-1]

Etching: 12. Line: 557. Tumbler. **References:** 2, fig. 12 [3-1]

Etching: 14. Line: 619. Water Tumbler. **References:** 2, fig. 15 [2-1]

Etching: 18. Line: 557. Tumbler. **References:** 2, fig. 10 [2-1]

Etching: 20. Line: 557. Tumbler. **References:** 2, fig. 12 [2-1]

Etching: 24. Line: 557. Tumbler. **References:** 2, fig. 10 [2-2]

Etching: 24. Line: 630. Tumbler. **References:** 5-E, page 19 [1-2]

Etching: 25. Line: 557. Tumbler. **References:** 2, fig. 11 [1-1]

Etching: 25. Line: 619. Water Tumbler. **References:** 2, fig. 15 [1-3]

Etching: 28. Line: 619. Water Tumbler. **References:** 2, fig. 15 [1-2]

Etching: 36. Line: 619. Water Tumbler. **References:** 2, fig. 15 [1-1]

Etching: 45. Line: 557. Tumbler. **References:** 2, fig. 12 [3-3]

Etching: 45N. Line: 557. Tumbler. **References:** 2, fig. 11 [1-2]

Etching: 47. Line: 619. Water Tumbler. **References:** 2, fig. 15 [3-1]

Etching: 47. Line: 557. Tumbler. **References:** 2, fig. 10 [1-0 partial]

Etching: 50. Line: 619. Water Tumbler. **References:** 2, fig. 15 [3-3]

Etching: 54. Line: 557. Tumbler. **References:** 2, fig. 12 [2-4]

Etching: 55. Line: 619. Water Tumbler. **References:** 2, fig. 15 [3-2]

Etching: 60. Line: 557. Tumbler. **References:** 2, fig. 11 [1-3]

Etching: 61. Line: 557. Tumbler. **References:** 2, fig. 12 [3-2]

Etching: 61. Line: 619. Water Tumbler. **References:** 2, fig. 15 [3-5]

Etching: 70. Line: 557. Tumbler. **References:** 2, fig. 12 [2-2]

Etching: 72. Line: 557. Tumbler. **References:** 2, fig. 12 [3-3]

Etching: 74. Line: 557. Tumbler. **References:** 2, fig. 10 [3-3]

Etching: 74. Line: 619. Water Tumbler. **References:** 2, fig. 15 [2-3]

Etching: 75. Line: 321. Tumbler. **References:** 5-E, page 19 [1-1]

Etching: 75. Line: 557. Tumbler. **References:** 2, fig. 11 [1-4]

Etching: 75N. Line: 619. Tumbler. **References:** 2, fig. 15 [1-3]

Etching: 75. Line: 630. Tumbler. **References:** 5-E, page 19 [1-4]

Etching: 76. Line: 619. Water Tumbler. **References:** 2, fig. 15 [2-5]

Etching: 78. Line: 557. Tumbler. **References:** 2, fig. 12 [1-0 partial]

Etching: 79. Line: 557. Tumbler. **References:** 2, fig. 10 [2-3]

Etching: 80. Line: 557. Tumbler. **References:** 2, fig. 11 [1-5]

Etching: 83. Line: 557. Tumbler. **References:** 2, fig. 10 [1-3]

Etching: 83. Line: 619. Water Tumbler. **References:** 2, fig. 15 [2-4]

Etching: 93. Line: 557. Tumbler. **References:** 2, fig. 10 [2-4]

Etching: 95. Line: 557. Tumbler. **References:** 2, fig. 10 [1-1]

Etching: 101. Line: 557. Tumbler. **References:** 2, fig. 10 [1-4]

Etching: 103. Line: 619. Water Tumbler. **References:** 2, fig. 15 [2-6]

Etching: 104. Line: 557. Tumbler. **References:** 2, fig. 10 [3-4]

Etching: 105. Line: 557. Tumbler. **References:** 2, fig. 12 [2-5]

Etching: 106. Line: 557. Tumbler. **References:** 2, fig. 12 [3-5]

Etching: 107. Line: 557. Tumbler. **References:** 2, fig. 10 [2-5]

Etching: 108. Line: 557. Tumbler. **References:** 2, fig. 10 [3-5]

Etching: 110. Line: 557. Tumbler. **References:** 2, fig. 12 [1-1]

Etching: 112. Line: 557. Tumbler. **References:** 2, fig. 12 [1-2]

Etching: 112. Line: 630. Tumbler. **References:** 5-E, page 18 [1-1]

Etching: 114. Line: 557. Tumbler. **References:** 2, fig. 12 [1-3]

Etching: 115. Line: 557. Tumbler. **References:** 2, fig. 12 [1-4]

Etching: 116. Line: 557. Tumbler. **References:** 2, fig. 12 [1-5]

Etching: 117. Line: 557. Tumbler. References: 2, fig. 11 [3-1 partial]

Etching: 117 1/2. Line 557. Tumbler. References: 2, fig. 11 [3-2]

Etching: 118 1/2. Line 557. Tumbler. References: 2, fig. 11 [3-3]

Etching: 121. Line: 557. Tumbler. **References:** 2, fig. 13 [1-4]

Etching: 283. Line: 19. Claret or Champagne. 5-1/2 oz. **References:** 5-E, page 16 [1-3]

Etching: 283. Line: 19. Cordial. 1-1/2 oz. **References:** 5-E, page 16 [1-1]

Etching: 283. Line: 19. Goblet. 11 oz. **References:** 5-E, page 16 [Listed]

Etching: 283. Line: 19. Goblet. 10 oz. **References:** 5-E, page 16 [Listed]

Etching: 283. Line: 19. Goblet. 9 oz. **References:** 5-E, page 16 [1-4]

Etching: 283. Line: 19. Goblet. 8 oz. **References:** 5-E, page 16 [Listed]

Etching: 283. Line: 19. Goblet. 7 oz. **References:** 5-E, page 16 [Listed]

Etching: 283. Line: 19. Port. 3-1/2 oz. **References:** 5-E, page 16 [Listed]

Etching: 283. Line: 19. Wine. 2-1/2 oz. **References:** 5-E, page 16 [1-2]

Etching: 283. Line: 630. Tumbler. **References:** 5-E, page 18 [1-3]

Etching: 302. Line: 557. Tumbler. **References:** 2, fig.

13 [1-1]

Etching: 304. Line: 557. Tumbler. **References:** 2, fig. 13 [2-2]

Etching: 307. Line: 557. Tumbler. **References:** 2, fig. 13 [2-4]

Etching: 308. Line: 1. Water Set. **References:** 2, fig. 5 [3-3]

Etching: 308. Line: 557. Tumbler. **References:** 2, fig. 13 [2-1]

Etching: 310. Line: 557. Tumbler. **References:** 2, fig. 13 [2-3]

Etching: 311. Line: 557. Tumbler. **References:** 2, fig. 13 [1-2]

Etching: 312. Line: 557. Tumbler. **References:** 2, fig. 13 [2-5]

Etching: 313. Line: 557. Tumbler. **References:** 2, fig. 10 [3-2]

Etching: 314. Line: 557. Tumbler. **References:** 2, fig. 13 [3-2]

Etching: 315. Line: 557. Tumbler. **References:** 2, fig. 13 [1-5]

Etching: 316. Line: 557. Tumbler. **References:** 2, fig. 13 [3-4]

Etching: 317, Initial. Line: 557. Tumbler. **References:** 2, fig. 11 [2-3]

Etching: 318, Monogram in any two letters. Line: 557. Tumbler. **References:** 2, fig. 11 [2-4]

Etching: 320. Line: 557. Tumbler. **References:** 2, fig. 10 [3-1]

Etching: 320. Line: 630. Tumbler. **References:** 5-E, page 18 [1-4]

Etching: 320. Line: 1202. Wine. 2-1/2 oz. **References:** 5-E, page 16 [2-3]

Etching: 324. Line: 557. Tumbler. **References:** 2, fig. 13 [3-5]

Etching: 325. Line: 557. Tumbler. **References:** 2, fig. 13 [1-3]

Etching: 326. Line: 1. Water Set. **References:** 2, fig. 5 [1-3]

Etching: 326. Line: 557. Tumbler. **References:** 2, fig. 13 [3-3]

Etching: 335. Line: 557. Tumbler. **References:** 2, fig. 11 [3-4]

Etching: 336. Line: 557. Tumbler. **References:** 2, fig. 11 [3-5]

Etching: 337. Line: 557. Tumbler. **References:** 2, fig. 11 [3-6]

Etching: 343. Line: 1. Water Set. **References:** 2, fig. 5 [2-3]

Etching: 408. Line: 630. Tumbler. **References:** 5-E, page 18 [2-1]

Etching: 412. Line: 1202. Wine. 2-1/2 oz. **References:** 5-E, page 16 [2-1]

Etching: 437. Line: 557. Tumbler. **References:** 2, fig. 14 [2-5]

Etching: 438. Line: 557. Tumbler. **References:** 2, fig. 14 [2-4]

Etching: 439. Line: 557. Tumbler. **References:** 2, fig. 14 [1-2]

Etching: 441. Line: 557. Tumbler. **References:** 2, fig. 14 [2-3]

Etching: 443. Line: 557. Tumbler. **References:** 2, fig. 13 [3-1]

Etching: 444. Line: 1. Tankard Water Set. **References:** 5-E, page 16 [2-2]

Etching: 445. Line: 557. Tumbler. **References:** 2, fig. 14 [3-3]

Etching: 446. Line: 557. Tumbler. **References:** 2, fig. 14 [2-1]

Etching: 447. Line: 1. Water Set. **References:** 2, fig. 5 [2-1]

Etching: 448. Line: 1. Water Set. **References:** 2, fig. 5 [3-1]

Etching: 450. Line: 557. Tumbler. **References:** 2, fig. 14 [3-1]

Etching: 451. Line: 557. Tumbler. **References:** 2, fig. 14 [1-3]

Etching: 452. Line: 557. Tumbler. **References:** 2, fig. 14 [3-2]

Etching: 453. Line: 1. Water Set. **References:** 2, fig. 5 [1-1]

Etching: 453. Line: 557. Tumbler. **References:** 2, fig. 14 [2-2]

Etching: 459. Line: 557. Tumbler. **References:** 2, fig. 14 [1-4]

Etching: 462. Line: 557. Tumbler. **References:** 2, fig. 14 [1-5]

Etching: 600. Scroll Design. Nappy. 8 inch. **References:** 3, page 4 [1-1]

Etching: 600. Scroll Design. Nappy. 4-1/2 inch. **References:** 3, page 4 [1-2]

Etching: 600. Scroll Design. Plate. 6-1/4 inch. **References:** 3, page 5 [2-4]

Etching: 600. Line: 1. Scroll Design. Decanter. 2 Pint. Cut Neck and Star. **References:** 3, page 5 [2-1]

Etching: 600. Line: 1. Scroll Design. Handled Decanter. 2 Pint. Cut Neck and Star. **References:** 3, page 5 [2-3]

Etching: 600. Line: 3. Scroll Design. Comport. **References:** 3, page 5 [2-2]

Etching: 600. Line: 4. Scroll Design. Oil. Cut Neck and Star. **References:** 3, page 6 [1-3]

Etching: 600. Line: 5. Scroll Design. Sherry. Optic. **References:** 3, page 3 [1-5]

Etching: 600. Line: 10. Scroll Design. Jug. 54 oz. **References:** 3, page 6 [2-1]

Etching: 600. Line: 10. Scroll Design. Jug. 15 oz. **References:** 3, page 6 [1-2]

Etching: 600. Line: 40. Scroll Design. Cream. **References:** 3, page 5 [1-1]

Etching: 600. Line: 40. Scroll Design. Jug. 54 oz. **References:** 3, page 6 [2-2]

Etching: 600. Line: 40. Scroll Design. Sugar Bowl. **References:** 3, page 5 [1-2]

Etching: 600. Line: 75. Scroll Design. Water Bottle. **References:** 3, page 6 [2-3]

Etching: 600. Line: 630. Scroll Design. Tumbler. **References:** 3, page 4 [3-1]

Etching: 600. Line: 8000. Scroll Design. Ale. Optic. **References:** 3, page 3 [1-1]

Etching: 600. Line: 8000. Scroll Design. Brandy. Optic. **References:** 3, page 3 [2-4]

Etching: 600. Line: 8000. Scroll Design. Champagne. Hollow and Cut Stem, Optic. **References:** 3, page 3 [2-1]

Etching: 600. Line: 8000. Scroll Design. Claret. Optic. **References:** 3, page 3 [2-5]

Etching: 600. Line: 8000. Scroll Design. Cocktail. Optic. **References:** 3, page 3 [2-6]

Etching: 600. Line: 8000. Scroll Design. Cordial. Optic. **References:** 3, page 3 [1-4]

Etching: 600. Line: 8000. Scroll Design. Custard. Optic. **References:** 3, page 6 [1-4]

Etching: 600. Line: 8000. Scroll Design. Deminth. Optic. **References:** 3, page 3 [2-7]

Etching: 600. Line: 8000. Scroll Design. Finger Bowl. Optic. **References:** 3, page 6 [1-1]

Etching: 600. Line: 8000. Scroll Design. Goblet. 10 oz. Optic. **References:** 3, page 3 [1-8]

Etching: 600. Line: 8000. Scroll Design. Grape Fruit. Optic. **References:** 3, page 4 [3-3]

Etching: 600. Line: 8000. Scroll Design. Large Sherbet. Optic. **References:** 3, page 3 [1-7]

Etching: 600. Line: 8000. Scroll Design. Port. Optic. **References:** 3, page 3 [1-2]

Etching: 600. Line: 8000. Scroll Design. Saucer Champagne. Hollow Stem, Cut Stem, Optic. **References:** 3, page 3 [2-2]

Etching: 600. Line: 8000. Scroll Design. Saucer Champagne. Optic. **References:** 3, page 3 [2-3]

Etching: 600. Line: 8000. Scroll Design. Sherbet. **References:** 3, page 3 [1-6]

Etching: 600. Line: 8000. Scroll Design. Taper Tumbler. 5 oz. Optic. **References:** 3, page 4 [2-8]

Etching: 600. Line: 8000. Scroll Design. Taper Tumbler. 3-1/2 oz. Optic. **References:** 3, page 4 [2-9]

Etching: 600. Line: 8000. Scroll Design. Tumbler. 14 oz. Optic. **References:** 3, page 4 [2-1]

Etching: 600. Line: 8000. Scroll Design. Tumbler. 12 oz. Optic. **References:** 3, page 4 [2-2]

Etching: 600. Line: 8000. Scroll Design. Tumbler. 10 oz. Optic. **References:** 3, page 4 [2-3]

Etching: 600. Line: 8000. Scroll Design. Tumbler. 9 oz. Optic. **References:** 3, page 4 [2-4]

Etching: 600. Line: 8000. Scroll Design. Tumbler. 8 oz. Optic. **References:** 3, page 4 [2-5]

Etching: 600. Line: 8000. Scroll Design. Tumbler. 6-1/2 oz. Optic. **References:** 3, page 4 [2-6]

Etching: 600. Line: 8000. Scroll Design. Tumbler. 5 oz. Optic. **References:** 3, page 4 [2-7]

Etching: 600. Line: 8000. Scroll Design. Wine. Optic. **References:** 3, page 3 [1-3]

Etching: 600. Line: 8701. Scroll Design. Handled Tumbler. 7 oz. **References:** 3, page 4 [3-2]

Etching: 608. Grape Design. Plate. 6-1/2 inch. **References:** 3, page 8 [2-1]

Etching: 608. Line: 1. Grape Design. Decanter. 2 Pint. Cut Neck and Star. **References:** 3, page 8 [2-2]

Etching: 608. Line: 1. Grape Design. Grape Fruit. **References:** 3, page 8 [1-1]

Etching: 608. Line: 1. Grape Design. Nappy. 8 inch. **References:** 3, page 9 [1-1]

Etching: 608. Line: 1. Grape Design. Nappy. 4-1/2 inch. **References:** 3, page 9 [1-3]

Etching: 608. Line: 1. Grape Design. Oil. Cut Neck. **References:** 3, page 8 [2-5]

Etching: 608. Line: 3. Grape Design. Comport. **References:** 3, page 8 [1-3]

Etching: 608. Line: 4. Grape Design. Oil. Cut Neck and Star Bottom. **References:** 3, page 9 [3-4]

Etching: 608. Line: 4. Rose Design. Oil. Cut Neck. **References:** 3, page 13 [2-1]

Etching: 608. Line: 10. Grape Design. Jug. 54 oz. Optic. **References:** 3, page 9 [3-2]

Etching: 608. Line: 20. Grape Design. Jug. 52 oz. **References:** 3, page 9 [3-1]

Etching: 608. Line: 34. Grape Design. Fruit. **References:** 3, page 8 [2-4]

Etching: 608. Line: 40. Grape Design. Cream. **References:** 3, page 9 [2-1]

Etching: 608. Line: 40. Grape Design. Jug. 54 oz. **References:** 3, page 9 [3-3]

Etching: 608. Line: 40. Grape Design. Sugar Bowl. **References:** 3, page 8 [1-6]

Etching: 608. Line: 50. Grape Design. Water Bottle. Cut Neck. **References:** 3, page 8 [2-3]

Etching: 608. Line: 300. Grape Design. Ale. **References:** 3, page 7 [2-3]

Etching: 608. Line: 300. Grape Design. Brandy. **References:** 3, page 7 [2-8]

Etching: 608. Line: 300. Grape Design. Claret. **References:** 3, page 7 [2-5]

Etching: 608. Line: 300. Grape Design. Cocktail. **References:** 3, page 7 [1-3]

Etching: 608. Line: 300. Grape Design. Cordial. **References:** 3, page 7 [2-9]

Etching: 608. Line: 300. Grape Design. Deminth. **References:** 3, page 7 [1-4]

Etching: 608. Line: 300. Grape Design. Goblet. 8 oz. **References:** 3, page 7 [1-7]

Etching: 608. Line: 300. Grape Design. Goblet. 10 oz. **References:** 3, page 7 [2-1]

Etching: 608. Line: 300. Grape Design. Goblet. 9 oz. **References:** 3, page 7 [2-2]

Etching: 608. Line: 300. Grape Design. Goblet. 6 oz. **References:** 3, page 7 [2-4]

Etching: 608. Line: 300. Grape Design. Handled Custard. **References:** 3, page 9 [1-2]

Etching: 608. Line: 300. Grape Design. Individual Almond. **References:** 3, page 7 [1-2]

Etching: 608. Line: 300. Grape Design. Port. **References:** 3, page 7 [2-6]

Etching: 608. Line: 300. Grape Design. Rhine Wine Goblet. **References:** 3, page 7 [1-5]

Etching: 608. Line: 300. Grape Design. Saucer Champ. **References:** 3, page 7 [1-6]

Etching: 608. Line: 300. Grape Design. Sherbert. **References:** 3, page 7 [1-1]

Etching: 608. Line: 300. Grape Design. Tall Goblet. 9 oz. **References:** 3, page 7 [1-8]

Etching: 608. Line: 300. Grape Design. Wine. **References:** 3, page 7 [2-7]

Etching: 608. Line: 630. Grape Design. Tumbler. 9-1/2 oz. **References:** 3, page 9 [2-3]

Etching: 608. Line: 1302. Grape Design. Finger Bowl. **References:** 3, page 8 [1-5]

Etching: 608. Line: 9001. Grape Design. Tumbler. 8 oz. **References:** 3, page 9 [2-4]

Etching: 609. Rose Design. Nappy. 4-1/2 inch. **References:** 3, page 11 [2-3]

Etching: 609. Rose Design. Plate. 6-1/4 inch. **References:** 3, page 13 [3-3]

Etching: 609. Line: 1. Rose Design. Decanter. 2 Pint. Cut Neck, Optic. **References:** 3, page 13 [3-1]

Etching: 609. Line: 1. Rose Design. Nappy. 9 inch. **References:** 3, page 12 [1-1]

Etching: 609. Line: 1. Rose Design. Oil. Cut Neck and Star Bottom. **References:** 3, page 13 [2-2]

Etching: 609. Line: 1. Rose Design. Vase. 4 inch. **References:** 3, page 14 [3-1]

Etching: 609. Line: 1. Rose Design. Vase. 7 inch. **References:** 3, page 14 [3-2]

Etching: 609. Line: 1. Rose Design. Vase. 9 inch. **References:** 3, page 14 [3-3]

Etching: 609. Line: 1. Rose Design. Vase. 11 inch. **References:** 3, page 14 [3-4]

Etching: 609. Line: 3. Rose Design. Comport. **References:** 3, page 11 [2-6]

Etching: 609. Line: 5. Rose Design. Vase. 12 inch. **References:** 3, page 14 [1-1]

Etching: 609. Line: 5. Rose Design. Vase. 10 inch. **References:** 3, page 14 [1-2]

Etching: 609. Line: 5. Rose Design. Vase. 7 inch. **References:** 3, page 14 [1-3]

Etching: 609. Line: 5. Rose Design. Vase. 5 inch. **References:** 3, page 14 [1-4]

Etching: 609. Line: 10. Rose Design. Jug. 54 oz. **References:** 3, page 12 [2-1]

Etching: 609. Line: 34. Rose Design. Fruit. **References:** 3, page 11 [2-1]

Etching: 609. Line: 40. Rose Design. Cream. **References:** 3, page 12 [1-3]

Etching: 609. Line: 40. Rose Design. Jug. 54 oz. Optic. **References:** 3, page 12 [2-2]

Etching: 609. Line: 40. Rose Design. Sugar Bowl. **References:** 3, page 12 [1-2]

Etching: 609. Line: 50. Rose Design. Water Bottle. Cut Neck. **References:** 3, page 13 [3-2]

Etching: 609. Line: 300. Rose Design. Individual Almond. **References:** 3, page 11 [2-2]

Etching: 609. Line: 630. Rose Design. Tumbler. 9-1/2 oz. **References:** 3, page 10 [2-2]

Etching: 609. Line: 922. Rose Design. Vase. 6-1/2 inch. **References:** 3, page 14 [2-1]

Etching: 609. Line: 922. Rose Design. Vase. 7-1/2 inch. **References:** 3, page 14 [2-2]

Etching: 609. Line: 8000. Rose Design. Ale. **References:** 3, page 10 [1-5]

Etching: 609. Line: 8000. Rose Design. Brandy. **References:** 3, page 10 [1-9]

Etching: 609. Line: 8000. Rose Design. Claret. **References:** 3, page 10 [1-3]

Etching: 609. Line: 8000. Rose Design. Cocktail. **References:** 3, page 10 [1-4]

Etching: 609. Line: 8000. Rose Design. Cordial. **References:** 3, page 10 [1-8]

Etching: 609. Line: 8000. Rose Design. Custard. **References:** 3, page 13 [1-1]

Etching: 609. Line: 8000. Rose Design. Deminth. **References:** 3, page 10 [1-5]

Etching: 609. Line: 8000. Rose Design. Finger Bowl. **References:** 3, page 13 [1-2]

Etching: 609. Line: 8000. Rose Design. Goblet. 10 oz. **References:** 3, page 10 [1-3]

Etching: 609. Line: 8000. Rose Design. Goblet. 9 oz. **References:** 3, page 10 [1-4]

Etching: 609. Line: 8000. Rose Design. Goblet. 6 oz. Optic. **References:** 3, page 10 [2-5]

Etching: 609. Line: 8000. Rose Design. Grape Fruit. **References:** 3, page 11 [2-4]

Etching: 609. Line: 8000. Rose Design. Large Saucer Champagne. Optic. **References:** 3, page 11 [1-1]

Etching: 609. Line: 8000. Rose Design. Large Sherbert. **References:** 3, page 11 [1-7]

Etching: 609. Line: 8000. Rose Design. Sherbert. **References:** 3, page 11 [1-6]

Etching: 609. Line: 8000. Rose Design. Sherry. **References:** 3, page 10 [1-7]

Etching: 609. Line: 8000. Rose Design. Small Saucer Champagne. **References:** 3, page 11 [1-2]

Etching: 609. Line: 8000. Rose Design. Taper Tumbler. 5 oz. **References:** 3, page 10 [3-9]

Etching: 609. Line: 8000. Rose Design. Tumbler. 14 oz. **References:** 3, page 10 [3-1]

Etching: 609. Line: 8000. Rose Design. Tumbler. 10 oz. **References:** 3, page 10 [3-2]

Etching: 609. Line: 8000. Rose Design. Tumbler. 12 oz. **References:** 3, page 10 [3-3]

Etching: 609. Line: 8000. Rose Design. Tumbler. 8 oz. **References:** 3, page 10 [3-4]

Etching: 609. Line: 8000. Rose Design. Tumbler. 9 oz. **References:** 3, page 10 [3-5]

Etching: 609. Line: 8000. Rose Design. Tumbler. 6-1/2 oz. **References:** 3, page 10 [3-6]

Etching: 609. Line: 8000. Rose Design. Tumbler. 5 oz. **References:** 3, page 10 [3-7]

Etching: 609. Line: 8000. Rose Design. Tumbler. 3-1/2 oz. **References:** 3, page 10 [3-8]

Etching: 609. Line: 8000. Rose Design. Wine. **References:** 3, page 10 [1-6]

Etching: 609. Line: 9001. Rose Design. Tumbler. 8 oz. **References:** 3, page 10 [2-3]

Etching: 610. Line: 300. Pansy Design. Ale. **References:** 3, page 16 [1-1]

Etching: 610. Line: 300. Pansy Design. Brandy. **References:** 3, page 16 [1-2]

Etching: 610. Line: 300. Pansy Design. Claret. **References:** 3, page 16 [2-5]

Etching: 610. Line: 300. Pansy Design. Cocktail. **References:** 3, page 16 [1-4]

Etching: 610. Line: 300. Pansy Design. Cordial. **References:** 3, page 16 [2-1]

Etching: 610. Line: 300. Pansy Design. Custard. **References:** 3, page 15 [1-1]

Etching: 610. Line: 300. Pansy Design. Deminth. **References:** 3, page 16 [1-5]

Etching: 610. Line: 300. Pansy Design. Goblet. 10 oz. **References:** 3, page 15 [2-1]

Etching: 610. Line: 300. Pansy Design. Goblet. 9 oz. **References:** 3, page 15 [2-2] [2-3]

Etching: 610. Line: 300. Pansy Design. Goblet. 8 oz. **References:** 3, page 15 [2-4]

Etching: 610. Line: 300. Pansy Design. Goblet. 7 oz. **References:** 3, page 15 [2-5]

Etching: 610. Line: 300. Pansy Design. Goblet. 6 oz. **References:** 3, page 15 [2-6]

Etching: 610. Line: 300. Pansy Design. Port. **References:** 3, page 16 [2-4]

Etching: 610. Line: 300. Pansy Design. Rhine Wine Goblet. **References:** 3, page 16 [1-3]

Etching: 610. Line: 300. Pansy Design. Saucer Champ. **References:** 3, page 16 [1-6]

Etching: 610. Line: 300. Pansy Design. Sherbert. **References:** 3, page 15 [3-1]

Etching: 610. Line: 300. Pansy Design. Sherry. **References:** 3, page 16 [2-2]

Etching: 610. Line: 300. Pansy Design. Wine. **References:** 3, page 16 [2-3]

Etching: 117-1/8. Line: 557. Tumbler. **References:** 2, fig. 11 [3-1]

Etching: 118-1/2. Line: 557. Tumbler. **References:** 2, fig. 11 [3-2]

Cut: N. Etching: T, Cut Star Bottom. Line: 1. Nappy. 4 inch. **References:** 5-E, page 19 [2-1]

Cut: N. Etching: 8. Line: 630. Tumbler. Optic. **References:** 5-E, page 19 [1-3]

Cut: N. Etching: 23, Cut Star Bottom. Line: 502. Custard. **References:** 5-E, page 19 [2-2]

Cut: N. Etching: 23, Cut Star Bottom. Line: 1302. Finger Bowl. **References:** 5-E, page 19 [3-2]

Cut: N. Etching: 90. Line: 619. Water Tumbler. **References:** 2, fig. 15 [1-4]

Cut: 2, Initial and Wreath. Line: 557. Tumbler. **References:** 2, fig. 15 [2-1]

Cut: 3, Initial and Wreath. Line: 557. Tumbler. **References:** 2, fig. 15 [2-2]

Cut: 31. Line: 455. Candy Jar. Optic. **References:** 4, page 27 [2-2]

Cut: 31. Line: 475. Cocktail. Optic. **References:** 4, page 8 [1-5]

Cut: 31. Line: 475. Cordial. Optic. **References:** 4, page 8 [1-6]

Cut: 31. Line: 475. Footed Tumbler. 2-3/4 oz. Optic. **References:** 4, page 8 [2-1]

Cut: 31. Line: 475. Footed Tumbler. 4 oz. Optic. **References:** 4, page 8 [2-2]

Cut: 31. Line: 475. Footed Tumbler. 6 oz. Optic. **References:** 4, page 8 [2-3]

Cut: 31. Line: 475. Footed Tumbler. 9 oz. Optic. **References:** 4, page 8 [2-4]

Cut: 31. Line: 475. Footed Tumbler. 12 oz. Optic. **References:** 4, page 8 [2-5]

Cut: 31. Line: 475. Goblet. Optic. **References:** 4,

228

page 15 [2-10]; 1971, page 15 [2-10]; 1972, page 23 [2-10]; 1973, page 28 [2-10]

Cut: 43. Line: 1282. Hospitality. Plate. 7" / Actually 7-7/8" Dia. **References:** 1967, page 12 [1-12]; 1968, page 16 [1-12]; 1969, page 14 [2-14]; 1970, page 15 [2-14]; 1971, page 15 [2-14]; 1972, page 23 [2-14]; 1973, page 28 [2-14]; 1975, page 26 [2-10]; 1977, page 37 [2-10]

Cut: 43. Line: 1282. Hospitality. Plate. 8" / Actually 8-3/4" Dia. **References:** 1967, page 12 [1-13]; 1968, page 16 [1-13]; 1969, page 14 [2-15]; 1970, page 15 [2-15]; 1971, page 15 [2-15]; 1972, page 23 [2-15]; 1973, page 28 [2-15]; 1975, page 26 [2-11]; 1977, page 37 [2-11]

Cut: 43. Line: 1282. Hospitality. Saucer Champagne. 7-1/2 oz. / 5-1/4" hi. **References:** 1967, page 12 [1-2]; 1968, page 16 [1-2]; 1969, page 14 [2-2]; 1970, page 15 [2-2]; 1971, page 15 [2-2]; 1972, page 23 [2-2]; 1973, page 28 [2-2]; 1975, page 26 [2-2]; 1977, page 37 [2-2]; 1981, page 3 [3-12]

Cut: 43. Line: 1282. Hospitality. Sherbet. 7-1/2 oz. / 3-5/8" hi. **References:** 1967, page 12 [1-3]; 1968, page 16 [1-3]; 1969, page 14 [2-3]; 1970, page 15 [2-3]; 1971, page 15 [2-3]; 1972, page 23 [2-3]; 1973, page 28 [2-3]

Cut: 43. Line: 1282. Hospitality. Table Wine Goblet. 7-1/2 oz. / 6" hi. **References:** 1967, page 12 [1-4]; 1968, page 16 [1-4]; 1969, page 14 [2-4]; 1970, page 15 [2-4]; 1971, page 15 [2-4]; 1972, page 23 [2-4]; 1973, page 28 [2-4]; 1975, page 26 [2-3]; 1977, page 37 [2-3]

Cut: 43. Line: 1282. Hospitality. Tulip Champagne. 8 oz. 8-1/2 inches tall. **References:** 1969, page 14 [2-6]; 1970, page 15 [2-6]; 1971, page 15 [2-6]; 1972, page 23 [2-6]; 1973, page 28 [2-6]; 1975, page 26 [2-5]; 1977, page 37 [2-5]; 1981, page 3 [3-14]

Cut: 43. Line: 1282. Hospitality. Wine. 7-1/2 oz. 6 inches tall. **References:** 1981, page 3 [3-13]

Cut: 43. Line: 1350. Embassy. 1305 Dessert-Finge Bowl. 4-1/2 inches diam. **References:** 1972, page 24 [1-11]; 1973, page 29 [1-11]; 1967, page 13 [1-9]; 1968, page 17 [1-9]; 1969, page 13 [1-11]; 1970, page 14 [1-11]; 1971, page 14 [1-11]; 1975, page 27 [1-9]; 1977, page 38 [1-9]

Cut: 43. Line: 1350. Embassy. All Purpose Wine Goblet. 8 oz. 5 inches tall. **References:** 1969, page 13 [1-6]; 1970, page 14 [1-6]; 1971, page 14 [1-6]; 1972, page 24 [1-6]; 1973, page 29 [1-6]; 1975, page 27 [1-6]; 1977, page 38 [1-6]

Cut: 43. Line: 1350. Embassy. Cocktail. 4-1/2 oz. / 4-3/4" hi. **References:** 1967, page 13 [1-5]; 1968, page 17 [1-5]; 1969, page 13 [1-7]; 1970, page 14 [1-7]; 1971, page 14 [1-7]; 1972, page 24 [1-7]; 1973, page 29 [1-7]

Cut: 43. Line: 1350. Embassy. Cordial. 1-1/4 oz. / 3-3/4" hi. **References:** 1967, page 13 [1-6]; 1968, page 17 [1-6]; 1969, page 13 [1-8]; 1970, page 14 [1-8]; 1971, page 14 [1-8]; 1972, page 24 [1-8]; 1973, page 29 [1-8]; 1975, page 27 [1-7]; 1977, page 38 [1-7]; 1981, page 3 [3-10]

Cut: 43. Line: 1350. Embassy. Goblet. 12-1/2oz. / 6-5/8" hi. **References:** 1967, page 13 [1-1]; 1968, page 17 [1-1]; 1969, page 13 [1-1]; 1970, page 14 [1-1]; 1971, page 14 [1-1]; 1972, page 24 [1-1]; 1973, page 29 [1-1]; 1975, page 27 [1-1]; 1977, page 38 [1-1]; 1981, page 3 [3-6]

Cut: 43. Line: 1350. Embassy. Ice Tea. 13-1/2 oz. / 6-1/4" hi. **References:** 1967, page 13 [1-8]; 1968, page 17 [1-8]; 1969, page 13 [1-10]; 1970, page 14 [1-10]; 1971, page 14 [1-10]; 1972, page 24 [1-10]; 1973, page 29 [1-10]; 1975, page 27 [1-8]; 1977, page 38 [1-8]

Cut: 43. Line: 1350. Embassy. Juice. 6-1/2 oz. / 5-1/4" hi. **References:** 1967, page 13 [1-7]; 1968, page 17 [1-7]; 1969, page 13 [1-9]; 1970, page 14 [1-9]; 1971, page 14 [1-9]; 1972, page 24 [1-9]; 1973, page 29 [1-9]

Cut: 43. Line: 1350. Embassy. Plate. 7" / Actually 7-7/8" Dia. **References:** 1967, page 13 [1-10]; 1968, page 17 [1-10]; 1969, page 13 [1-11]; 1970, page 14 [1-11]; 1971, page 14 [1-11]; 1972, page 24 [1-12]; 1973, page 29 [1-12]; 1975, page 27 [1-10]; 1977, page 38 [1-10]

Cut: 43. Line: 1350. Embassy. Plate. 8" / Actually 8-3/4" Dia. **References:** 1967, page 13 [1-11]; 1968, page 17 [1-11]; 1969, page 13 [1-13]; 1970, page 14 [1-13]; 1971, page 14 [1-13]; 1972, page 24 [1-13]; 1973, page 29 [1-13]; 1975, page 27 [1-11]; 1977, page 38 [1-11]

Cut: 43. Line: 1350. Embassy. Red Wine Goblet. 9-1/2 oz. / 6-3/8" hi. **References:** 1967, page 13 [1-3]; 1968, page 17 [1-3]; 1969, page 13 [1-3]; 1970, page 14 [1-3]; 1971, page 14 [1-3]; 1972, page 24 [1-3]; 1973, page 29 [1-3]; 1975, page 27 [1-3]; 1977, page 38 [1-3]

Cut: 43. Line: 1350. Embassy. Sherbet. 6-1/2 oz. / 5" hi. **References:** 1967, page 13 [1-2]; 1968, page 17 [1-2]; 1969, page 13 [1-2]; 1970, page 14 [1-2]; 1971, page 14 [1-2]; 1972, page 24 [1-2]; 1973, page 29 [1-2]; 1975, page 27 [1-2]; 1977, page 38 [1-2]; 1981, page 3 [3-7]

Cut: 43. Line: 1350. Embassy. Tulip Champagne. 8 oz. 8-1/2 inches tall. **References:** 1969, page 13 [1-5]; 1970, page 14 [1-5]; 1971, page 14 [1-5]; 1972, page 24 [1-5]; 1973, page 29 [1-5]; 1975, page 27 [1-5]; 1977, page 38 [1-5]; 1981, page 3 [3-9]

Cut: 43. Line: 1350. Embassy. White Wine. 7 oz. 5-3/4 inches tall. **References:** 1975, page 27 [1-4]; 1967, page 13 [1-4]; 1968, page 17 [1-4]; 1969, page 13 [1-4]; 1970, page 14 [1-4]; 1971, page 14 [1-4]; 1972, page 24 [1-4]; 1973, page 29 [1-4]; 1977, page 38 [1-4]; 1981, page 3 [3-8]

Cut: 43. Line: 1450. Old Fashion. 12 oz. 3-7/8 inches tall. Sham Weight. **References:** 1972, page 31 [3-7]; 1973, page 36 [3-7]; 1975, page 32 [3-7]; 1977, page 43 [3-7]; 1982, page 6 [1-11]; **References:** 1975/I-75, page 12 [3-7]

Cut: 43. Line: 1450. Old Fashion. 12 oz. 3-7/8 inches tall. Sham Weight, Polished Bottom. The cut 43 indicates the Flutes at the base of the Tumblers are 1-3/4" high and 3/4" wide. Tumblers Cut 43 have a hand cut and hand polished (Punty) base. **References:** 1979, page 14 [2-2]

Cut: 43. Line: 1966. Aristocrat. 1305 Dessert-Finger Bowl. 4-1/2 inches diam. **References:** 1972, page 19 [2-8]; 1973, page 24 [2-8]; 1967, page 5 [2-14]; 1968, page 8 [3-14]; 1969, page 9 [2-8]; 1970, page 9 [2-8]; 1971, page 9 [2-8]; 1975, page 24 [2-8]; 1977, page 35 [2-8]

Cut: 43. Line: 1966. Aristocrat. All Purpose Wine Goblet. 8 oz. 5 inches tall. **References:** 1969, page 9 [2-5]; 1970, page 9 [2-5]; 1971, page 9 [2-5]; 1972, page 19 [2-5]; 1973, page 24 [2-5]; 1975, page 24 [2-5]; 1977, page 35 [2-5]

Cut: 43. Line: 1966. Aristocrat. Cordial. 1-1/4 oz. / 3-7/8" hi. **References:** 1967, page 5 [2-12]; 1968, page 8 [3-12]; 1969, page 9 [2-6]; 1970, page 9 [2-6]; 1971, page 9 [2-6]; 1972, page 19 [2-6]; 1973, page 24 [2-6]; 1975, page 24 [2-6]; 1977, page 35 [2-6]

Cut: 43. Line: 1966. Aristocrat. Goblet. 12 oz. / 7" hi. **References:** 1967, page 5 [2-9]; 1968, page 8 [3-9]; 1969, page 9 [2-1]; 1970, page 9 [2-1]; 1971, page 9 [2-1]; 1972, page 19 [2-1]; 1973, page 24 [2-1]; 1975, page 24 [2-1]; 1977, page 35 [2-1]

Cut: 43. Line: 1966. Aristocrat. Ice Tea. 14 oz. / 6-1/4" hi. **References:** 1967, page 5 [2-13]; 1968, page 8 [3-13]; 1969, page 9 [2-7]; 1970, page 9 [2-7]; 1971, page 9 [2-7]; 1972, page 19 [2-7]; 1973, page 24 [2-7]; 1975, page 24 [2-7]; 1977, page 35 [2-7]

Cut: 43. Line: 1966. Aristocrat. Plate. 7" / Actually 7-7/8" Dia. **References:** 1967, page 5 [2-15]; 1968, page 8 [3-15]; 1969, page 9 [2-9]; 1970, page 9 [2-9]; 1971, page 9 [2-9]; 1972, page 19 [2-9]; 1973, page 24 [2-9]; 1975, page 24 [2-9]; 1977, page 35 [2-9]

Cut: 43. Line: 1966. Aristocrat. Plate. 8" / Actually 8-3/4" Dia. **References:** 1967, page 5 [2-16]; 1968, page 8 [3-16]; 1969, page 9 [2-10]; 1970, page 9 [2-10]; 1971, page 9 [2-10]; 1972, page 19 [2-10]; 1973, page 24 [2-10]; 1975, page 24 [2-10]; 1977, page 35 [2-10]

Cut: 43. Line: 1966. Aristocrat. Sherbet. 7-1/2 oz. / 5-1/8" hi. **References:** 1967, page 5 [2-10]; 1968, page 8 [3-10]; 1969, page 9 [2-2]; 1970, page 9 [2-2]; 1971, page 9 [2-2]; 1972, page 19 [2-2]; 1973, page 24 [2-2]; 1975, page 24 [2-2]; 1977, page 35 [2-2]

Cut: 43. Line: 1966. Aristocrat. Tulip Champagne. 8 oz. 8-1/2 inches tall. **References:** 1969, page 9 [2-4]; 1970, page 9 [2-4]; 1971, page 9 [2-4]; 1972, page 19 [2-4]; 1973, page 24 [2-4]; 1975, page 24 [2-4]; 1977, page 35 [2-4]

Cut: 43. Line: 1966. Aristocrat. Wine. 7-1/2 oz. / 6" hi. **References:** 1967, page 5 [2-11]; 1968, page 8 [3-11]; 1969, page 9 [2-3]; 1970, page 9 [2-3]; 1971, page 9 [2-3]; 1972, page 19 [2-3]; 1973, page 24 [2-3]; 1975, page 24 [2-3]; 1977, page 35 [2-3]

Cut: 43. Line: 1977. Falerno. Brandy and Liqueur. 2-1/2 oz. 6 inches tall. **References:** 1973, page 7 [1-7]; 1975, page 7 [1-7]; 1977, page 7 [1-7]

Cut: 43. Line: 1977. Falerno. Cabinet Wine Goblet. 15-1/2 oz. 9-1/8 inches tall. **References:** 1973, page 7 [1-1]; 1975, page 7 [1-1]; 1977, page 7 [1-1]

Cut: 43. Line: 1977. Falerno. Dessert-Champagne. 7-1/2 oz. 6-1/8 inches tall. **References:** 1973, page 7 [1-6]; 1975, page 7 [1-6]; 1977, page 7 [1-6]

Cut: 43. Line: 1977. Falerno. Red Wine Goblet. 12-1/2 oz. 8-5/8 inches tall. **References:** 1973, page 7 [1-2]; 1975, page 7 [1-2]; 1977, page 7 [1-2]

Cut: 43. Line: 1977. Falerno. Sherry and Port. 5 oz. 7 inches tall. **References:** 1973, page 7 [1-5]; 1975, page 7 [1-5]; 1977, page 7 [1-5]

Cut: 43. Line: 1977. Falerno. Sparkling Wine Goblet. 9 oz. 8 inches tall. **References:** 1973, page 7 [1-3]

Cut: 43. Line: 1977. Falerno. Sparkling Wine Goblet. 9 oz. 8 inches tall. **References:** 1975, page 7 [1-3]

Cut: 43. Line: 1977. Falerno. Sparkling Wine Goblet. 9 oz. 8 inches tall. **References:** 1977, page 7 [1-3]

Cut: 43. Line: 1977. Falerno. White Wine. 7 oz. 7-5/8 inches tall. **References:** 1975, page 7 [1-4]

Cut: 43. Line: 1977. Falerno. White Wine Goblet. 7 oz. 7-5/8 inches tall. **References:** 1973, page 7 [1-4]

Cut: 43. Line: 1977. Falerno. White Wine Goblet. 7 oz. 7-5/8 inches tall. **References:** 1977, page 7 [1-4]

Cut: 43. Line: 1978. Beverage. 16 oz. 6 inches tall. Sham Weight. **References:** 1982, page 6 [1-1]

Cut: 43. Line: 1978. Hi Ball. 11 oz. 5 inches tall. Sham Weight. **References:** 1982, page 6 [1-2]

Cut: 43. Line: 1978. Old Fashion. 9-1/2 oz. 3-1/2 inches tall. Sham Weight. **References:** 1982, page 6 [1-4]

Cut: 43. Line: 1978. On The Rocks. 14 oz. 4-1/2 inches tall. Sham Weight. **References:** 1982, page 6 [1-3]

Cut: 43. Line: 1978. Beer Series. Beer Goblet. 14 oz. 8-3/4 inches tall. Plain. **References:** 1978, page 9 [1-3]

Cut: 43. Line: 1978. Beer Series. Pony Goblet. 7 oz. 8-1/4 inches tall. Plain. **References:** 1978, page 9 [1-2]

Cut: 43. Line: 1978. Ultra. Apertif. 8 oz. 8-3/8 inches tall. **References:** 1975, page 11 [1-3]

Cut: 43. Line: 1978. Ultra. Apertif. 8 oz. 8-3/8 inches tall. **References:** 1977, page 11 [1-3]

Cut: 43. Line: 1978. Ultra. Compote. 16 oz. 4-3/4 inches tall. **References:** 1975, page 11 [1-5]

Cut: 43. Line: 1978. Ultra. Compote. 16 oz. 4-3/4 inches tall. **References:** 1977, page 11 [1-5]

Cut: 43. Line: 1978. Ultra. Old Fashion. **References:** 1977, page 25 [3-1]

Cut: 43. Line: 1978. Ultra. On The Rocks. 14 oz. 4-1/2 inches tall. **References:** 1975, page 11 [1-6]

Cut: 43. Line: 1978. Ultra. On the Rocks. 15-1/2 oz. 4-1/2 inches tall. **References:** 1976, page 11 [2-3]

Cut: 43. Line: 1978. Ultra. On The Rocks. 14 oz. 4-1/2 inches tall. **References:** 1977, page 11 [1-6]

Cut: 43. Line: 1978. Ultra. Red Wine Goblet. 15 oz. 7-3/4 inches tall. **References:** 1975, page 11 [1-4]

Cut: 43. Line: 1978. Ultra. Red Wine Goblet. 15 oz. 7-3/4 inches tall. **References:** 1977, page 11 [1-4]

Cut: 43. Line: 1978. Ultra. Sparkling Wine Goblet. 15 oz. 8-3/4 inches tall. **References:** 1975, page 11 [1-2]

Cut: 43. Line: 1978. Ultra. Sparkling Wine Goblet. 15 oz. 8-3/4 inches tall. **References:** 1977, page 11 [1-2]

Cut: 43. Line: 1978. Ultra. Wine Goblet. 28 oz. 8-3/4 inches tall. **References:** 1975, page 11 [1-1]

Cut: 43. Line: 1978. Ultra. Wine Goblet. 28 oz. 8-3/4 inches tall. **References:** 1977, page 11 [1-1]

Cut: 43. Line: 5321. Connoisseur Collection. Brandy and Liqueur. 2-1/2 oz. 4-1/2 inches tall. **References:** 1973, page 8 [1-8]

Cut: 43. Line: 5321. Connoisseur Collection. Brandy and Liqueur. 2-1/2 oz. 4-1/2 inches tall. **References:** 1975, page 8 [1-8]

Cut: 43. Line: 5321. Connoisseur Collection. Brandy and Liqueur. 2-1/2 oz. 4-1/2 inches tall. **References:** 1977, page 8 [1-8]

Cut: 43. Line: 5321. Connoisseur Collection. Brandy and Liqueur. 2-1/2 oz. 4-1/2 inches tall. **References:** 1981, page 3 [2-13]

Cut: 43. Line: 5321. Connoisseur Collection. Champagne. 9-1/2 oz. 8 inches tall. **References:** 1973, page 8 [1-5]

Cut: 43. Line: 5321. Connoisseur Collection. Champagne. 9-1/2 oz. 8 inches tall. **References:** 1975, page 8 [1-5]

Cut: 43. Line: 5321. Connoisseur Collection. Champagne. 9-1/2 oz. 8 inches tall. **References:** 1977, page 8 [1-5]

Cut: 43. Line: 5321. Connoisseur Collection. Champagne. 8 oz. 8-1/2 inches tall. **References:** 1981, page 3 [2-15]

Cut: 43. Line: 5321. Connoisseur Collection. Champagne Flute. 6 oz. 9-1/4 inches tall. **References:** 1981, page 3 [2-14]

Cut: 43. Line: 5321. Connoisseur Collection. Dessert-Champagne. 11 oz. 4-7/8 inches tall. **References:** 1973, page 8 [1-7]

Cut: 43. Line: 5321. Connoisseur Collection. Dessert-Champagne. 11 oz. 4-7/8 inches tall. **References:** 1975, page 8 [1-7]

Cut: 43. Line: 5321. Connoisseur Collection. Dessert-Champagne. 11 oz. 4-7/8 inches tall. **References:** 1977, page 8 [1-7]

Cut: 43. Line: 5321. Connoisseur Collection. Dessert-Champagne. 11 oz. 4-7/8 inches tall. **References:** 1981, page 3 [2-12]

Cut: 43. Line: 5321. Connoisseur Collection. Magnum Wine Goblet. 18 oz. 7-3/8 inches tall. **References:** 1973, page 8 [1-1]

Cut: 43. Line: 5321. Connoisseur Collection. Magnum Wine Goblet. 18 oz. 7-3/8 inches tall. **References:** 1975, page 8 [1-1]

Cut: 43. Line: 5321. Connoisseur Collection. Magnum Wine Goblet. 18 oz. 7-3/8 inches tall. **References:** 1977, page 8 [1-1]

Cut: 43. Line: 5321. Connoisseur Collection. Magnum Wine Goblet. 18 oz. 7-3/8 inches tall. **References:** 1981, page 3 [2-7]

Cut: 43. Line: 5321. Connoisseur Collection. Red Wine Goblet. 10-1/2 oz. 6-7/8 inches tall. **References:** 1973, page 8 [1-3]

Cut: 43. Line: 5321. Connoisseur Collection. Red Wine Goblet. 10-1/2 oz. 6-7/8 inches tall. **References:** 1975, page 8 [1-3]

Cut: 43. Line: 5321. Connoisseur Collection. Red Wine Goblet. 10-1/2 oz. 6-7/8 inches tall. **References:** 1977, page 8 [1-3]

Cut: 43. Line: 5321. Connoisseur Collection. Red Wine Goblet. 10-1/2 oz. 6-7/8 inches tall. **References:** 1981, page 3 [2-9]

Cut: 43. Line: 5321. Connoisseur Collection. Sherry and Port. 5 oz. 6 inches tall. **References:** 1973, page 8 [1-6]

Cut: 43. Line: 5321. Connoisseur Collection. Sherry and Port. 5 oz. 6 inches tall. **References:** 1975, page 8 [1-6]

Cut: 43. Line: 5321. Connoisseur Collection. Sherry and Port. 5 oz. 6 inches tall. **References:** 1977, page 8 [1-6]

Cut: 43. Line: 5321. Connoisseur Collection. Sherry and Port. 5 oz. 6 inches tall. **References:** 1981, page 3 [2-11]

Cut: 43. Line: 5321. Connoisseur Collection. Vintage Wine Goblet. 14 oz. 7 inches tall. **References:** 1973, page 8 [1-2]

Cut: 43. Line: 5321. Connoisseur Collection. Vintage Wine Goblet. 14 oz. 7 inches tall. **References:** 1975, page 8 [1-2]

Cut: 43. Line: 5321. Connoisseur Collection. Vintage Wine Goblet. 14 oz. 7 inches tall. **References:** 1977, page 8 [1-2]

Cut: 43. Line: 5321. Connoisseur Collection. Vintage Wine Goblet. 14 oz. 7 inches tall. **References:** 1981, page 3 [2-8]

Cut: 43. Line: 5321. Connoisseur Collection. White Wine. 8-1/2 oz. 6-5/8 inches tall. **References:** 1975, page 8 [1-4]

Cut: 43. Line: 5321. Connoisseur Collection. White Wine Goblet. 8-1/2 oz. 6-5/8 inches tall. **References:** 1973, page 8 [1-4]

Cut: 43. Line: 5321. Connoisseur Collection. White Wine Goblet. 8-1/2 oz. 6-5/8 inches tall. **References:** 1977, page 8 [1-4]

Cut: 43. Line: 5321. Connoisseur Collection. White Wine Goblet. 8-1/2 oz. 6-5/8 inches tall. **References:** 1981, page 3 [2-10]

Cut: 43. Line: 8701. Tumbler. 14 oz. 5-1/2 inches tall. Sham Weight. **References:** 1972, page 31 [3-1]

Cut: 43. Line: 8701. Tumbler. 12 oz. 5 inches tall. Sham Weight. **References:** 1972, page 31 [3-2]

Cut: 43. Line: 8701. Tumbler. 10 oz. 4-3/4 inches tall. Sham Weight. **References:** 1972, page 31 [3-3]

Cut: 43. Line: 8701. Tumbler. 14 oz. 5-1/2 inches tall. Sham Weight. **References:** 1973, page 36 [3-1]

Cut: 43. Line: 8701. Tumbler. 12 oz. 5 inches tall. Sham Weight. **References:** 1973, page 36 [3-2]

Cut: 43. Line: 8701. Tumbler. 10 oz. 4-3/4 inches tall. Sham Weight. **References:** 1973, page 36 [3-3]

Cut: 43. Line: 8701. Tumbler. 14 oz. 5-1/2 inches tall. Sham Weight. **References:** 1975, page 32 [3-1]

Cut: 43. Line: 8701. Tumbler. 12 oz. 5 inches tall. Sham Weight. **References:** 1975, page 32 [3-2]

Cut: 43. Line: 8701. Tumbler. 10 oz. 4-3/4 inches tall. Sham Weight. **References:** 1975, page 32 [3-3]

Cut: 43. Line: 8701. Tumbler. 14 oz. 5-1/2 inches tall. Sham Weight. **References:** 1977, page 43 [3-1]

Cut: 43. Line: 8701. Tumbler. 12 oz. 5 inches tall. Sham Weight. **References:** 1977, page 43 [3-2]

Cut: 43. Line: 8701. Tumbler. 10 oz. 4-3/4 inches tall. Sham Weight. **References:** 1977, page 43 [3-3]

Cut: 43. Line: 8701. Tumbler. 14 oz. 5-1/2 inches tall. Sham Weight, Polished Bottom. The cut 43 indicates the Flutes at the base of the Tumblers are 1-3/4" high and 3/4" wide. Tumblers Cut 43 have a hand cut and hand polished (Punty) base. Items available: 14 oz., 12 oz., and 10 oz. Tumbler, 10 oz. Table Tumbler, 7-3/4 oz., 9 oz., and 12 oz. Old Fashion. **References:** 1979, page 14 [2-3]

Cut: 43. Line: 8701. Tumbler. 14 oz. 5-1/2 inches tall. Sham Weight. **References:** 1982, page 6 [1-5]

Cut: 43. Line: 8701. Tumbler. 12 oz. 5 inches tall. Sham Weight. **References:** 1982, page 6 [1-6]

Cut: 43. Line: 8701. Tumbler. 9 oz. 4 inches tall. Sham Weight. **References:** 1982, page 6 [1-7]

Cut: 43. Line: 8701. Tumbler. 14 oz. 5-1/2 inches tall. Sham Weight. **References:** 1975/I-75, page 12 [3-1]

Cut: 43. Line: 8701. Tumbler. 12 oz. 5 inches tall. Sham Weight. **References:** 1975/I-75, page 12 [3-2]

Cut: 43. Line: 8701. Tumbler. 10 oz. 4-3/4 inches tall. Sham Weight. **References:** 1975/I-75, page 12 [3-3]

Cut: 43. Etching: 608. Line: 300. Grape Design. Champagne. Hollow Stem. **References:** 3, page 8 [1-2]

Cut: 43. Etching: 608. Line: 300. Grape Design. Saucer Champ. Hollow Stem. **References:** 3, page 8 [1-4]

Cut: 43. Etching: 609. Line: 8000. Rose Design. Champagne. Hollow Stem. **References:** 3, page 10 [1-2]

Cut: 43. Etching: 609. Line: 8000. Rose Design. Saucer Champ. Hollow Stem. **References:** 3, page 10 [1-1]

Cut: 43. Etching: 610. Line: 300. Pansy Design. Champagne. Hollow Stem. **References:** 3, page 16 [2-6]

Cut: 43. Etching: 610. Line: 300. Pansy Design. Saucer Champ. Hollow Stem. **References:** 3, page 16 [2-7]

Cut: B 44. Line: B6. Footed Tumbler. 2-3/4 oz. Optic. **References:** 4, page 4 [2-1]

Cut: B 44. Line: B6. Footed Tumbler. 4 oz. Optic. **References:** 4, page 4 [2-2]

Cut: B 44. Line: B6. Footed Tumbler. 6 oz. Optic. **References:** 4, page 4 [2-3]

Cut: B 44. Line: B6. Footed Tumbler. 9 oz. Optic. **References:** 4, page 4 [2-4]

Cut: B 44. Line: B6. Footed Tumbler. 12 oz. Optic. **References:** 4, page 4 [2-5]

Cut: B 44. Line: B260. Cocktail. Optic. **References:** 4, page 4 [1-5]

Cut: B 44. Line: B260. Cordial. Optic. **References:** 4, page 4 [1-6]

Cut: B 44. Line: B260. Goblet. Optic. **References:** 4, page 4 [1-1]

Cut: B 44. Line: B260. Saucer Champagne. Optic. **References:** 4, page 4 [1-2]

Cut: B 44. Line: B260. Sherbet. Optic. **References:** 4, page 4 [1-3]

Cut: B 44. Line: B260. Wine. Optic. **References:** 4, page 4 [1-4]

Cut: 45. Line: 85. Old Fashion. 7-3/4 oz. 3-3/8 inches tall. Sham Weight. **References:** 1972, page 31 [2-5]

Cut: 45. Line: 85. Old Fashion. 7-3/4 oz. 3-3/8 inches tall. Sham Weight. **References:** 1973, page 36 [2-5]

Cut: 45. Line: 85. Old Fashion. 7-3/4 oz. 3-3/8 inches tall. Sham Weight. **References:** 1975, page 32 [2-5]

Cut: 45. Line: 85. Old Fashion. 7-3/4 oz. 3-3/8 inches tall. Sham Weight. **References:** 1977, page 43 [2-5]

Cut: 45. Line: 85. Old Fashion. 7-3/4 oz. 3-3/8 inches tall. Sham Weight. The cut 43 indicates the Flutes at the base of the Tumblers are 1-1/2" high and 3/4" wide. Tumblers Cut 45 have a flat unpolished base. Items available: 14 oz., 12 oz., and 10 oz. Tumbler, 10 oz. Table Tumbler, 7-3/4 oz., 9 oz., and 12 oz. Old Fashion. **References:** 1979, page 14 [2-4]

Cut: 45. Line: 85. Old Fashion. 8 oz. 3-3/8 inches tall. Sham Weight. **References:** 1982, page 7 [1-5]

Cut: 45. Line: 85. Old Fashion. 7-3/4 oz. 3-3/8 inches tall. Sham Weight. **References:** 1975/I-75, page 12 [2-5]

Cut: 45. Line: 636. Table Tumbler. 10 oz. 3-3/4 inches tall. Sham Weight. **References:** 1972, page 31 [2-4]

Cut: 45. Line: 636. Table Tumbler. 10 oz. 3-3/4 inches tall. Sham Weight. **References:** 1973, page 36 [2-4]

Cut: 45. Line: 636. Table Tumbler. 10 oz. 3-3/4 inches tall. Sham Weight. **References:** 1975, page 32 [2-4]

Cut: 45. Line: 636. Table Tumbler. 10 oz. 3-3/4 inches tall. Sham Weight. **References:** 1977, page 43 [2-4]

Cut: 45. Line: 636. Table Tumbler. 9 oz. 4 inches tall. Sham Weight. **References:** 1982, page 7 [1-4]

Cut: 45. Line: 636. Table Tumbler. 10 oz. 3-3/4 inches tall. Sham Weight. **References:** 1975/I-75, page 12 [2-4]

Cut: 45. Line: 1412. Old Fashion. 9 oz. 3-1/2 inches tall. Sham Weight. **References:** 1972, page 31 [2-6]

Cut: 45. Line: 1412. Old Fashion. 9 oz. 3-1/2 inches tall. Sham Weight. **References:** 1973, page 36 [2-6]

Cut: 45. Line: 1412. Old Fashion. 9 oz. 3-1/2 inches tall. Sham Weight. **References:** 1975, page 32 [2-6]

Cut: 45. Line: 1412. Old Fashion. 9 oz. 3-1/2 inches tall. Sham Weight. **References:** 1977, page 43 [2-6]

Cut: 45. Line: 1412. Old Fashion. 9 oz. 3-1/2 inches tall. Sham Weight. The cut 43 indicates the Flutes at the base of the Tumblers are 1-1/2" high and 3/4" wide. Tumblers Cut 45 have a flat unpolished base. Items available: 14 oz., 12 oz., and 10 oz. Tumbler, 10 oz. Table Tumbler, 7-3/4 oz., 9 oz., and 12 oz. Old Fashion. **References:** 1979, page 14 [2-5]

Cut: 45. Line: 1412. Old Fashion. 9 oz. 3-5/8 inches tall. Sham Weight. **References:** 1982, page 7 [1-6]

Cut: 45. Line: 1412. Old Fashion. 9 oz. 3-1/2 inches tall. Sham Weight. **References:** 1975/I-75, page 12 [2-6]

Cut: 45. Line: 1450. Old Fashion. 12 oz. 3-7/8 inches tall. Sham Weight. **References:** 1972, page 31 [2-7]; 1973, page 36 [2-7]; 1975, page 32 [2-7]; 1977, page 43 [2-7]; 1982, page 7 [1-7]; 1975/I-75, page 12 [2-7]

Cut: 45. Line: 8701. Tumbler. 14 oz. 5-1/2 inches tall. Sham Weight. **References:** 1972, page 31 [2-1]; 1973, page 36 [2-1]; 1975, page 32 [2-1]; 1977, page 43 [2-1]

Cut: 45. Line: 8701. Tumbler. 12 oz. 5 inches tall. Sham Weight. **References:** 1972, page 31 [2-2]; 1973, page 36 [2-2]; 1975, page 32 [2-2]; 1977, page 43 [2-2]

Cut: 45. Line: 8701. Tumbler. 10 oz. 4-3/4 inches tall. Sham Weight. **References:** 1972, page 31 [2-3]; 1973, page 36 [2-3]; 1975, page 32 [2-3]; 1977, page 43 [2-3]

Cut: 45. Line: 8701. Tumbler. 12 oz. 5 inches tall. Sham Weight. The cut 43 indicates the Flutes at the base of the Tumblers are 1-1/2" high and 3/4" wide. Tumblers Cut 45 have a flat unpolished base. Items available: 14 oz., 12 oz., and 10 oz. Tumbler, 10 oz. Table Tumbler, 7-3/4 oz., 9 oz., and 12 oz. Old Fashion. **References:** 1979, page 14 [2-6]

Cut: 45. Line: 8701. Tumbler. 14 oz. 5-1/2 inches tall. Sham Weight. **References:** 1982, page 7 [1-1]; 1975/I-75, page 12 [2-1]

Cut: 45. Line: 8701. Tumbler. 12 oz. 5 inches tall. Sham Weight. **References:** 1982, page 7 [1-2]; 1975/I-75, page 12 [2-2]

Cut: 45. Line: 8701. Tumbler. 10 oz. 4-3/4 inches tall. Sham Weight. **References:** 1975/I-75, page 12 [2-3]

Cut: 45. Line: 8701. Tumbler. 9 oz. 4-3/4 inches tall. Sham Weight. **References:** 1982, page 7 [1-3]

Cut: 54. Line: 627. Tumbler. **References:** 2, fig. 8 [1-1]

Cut: 57. Marmalade. Optic. **References:** 4, page 25 [2-5]

Cut: 57. Mustard. Optic. **References:** 4, page 25 [2-4]

Cut: 57. Plate. 7 inch. **References:** 4, page 26 [2-2]

Cut: 57. Line: 1. Rose Bowl. Optic. **References:** 4, page 25 [3-5]

Cut: 57. Line: 3. Decanter. 2 Pint. Optic. **References:** 4, page 27 [2-3]

Cut: 57. Line: 10. Jug. 54 oz. Optic. **References:** 4, page 26 [3-1]

Cut: 57. Line: 30. Console Bowl. **References:** 4, page 27 [3-3]

Cut: 57. Line: 30. R.E. Candlestick. Optic. **References:** 4, page 25 [2-6]

Cut: 57. Line: 465. Finger Bowl. Optic. **References:** 4, page 25 [3-3]

Cut: 57. Line: 482. Cocktail. Optic. **References:** 4, page 11 [1-5]

Cut: 57. Line: 482. Cordial. Optic. **References:** 4, page 11 [1-6]

Cut: 57. Line: 482. Footed Tumbler. 2-3/4 oz. Optic. **References:** 4, page 11 [2-1]

Cut: 57. Line: 482. Footed Tumbler. 4 oz. Optic. **References:** 4, page 11 [2-2]

Cut: 57. Line: 482. Footed Tumbler. 6 oz. Optic. **References:** 4, page 11 [2-3]

Cut: 57. Line: 482. Footed Tumbler. 9 oz. Optic. **References:** 4, page 11 [2-4]

Cut: 57. Line: 482. Footed Tumbler. 12 oz. Optic. **References:** 4, page 11 [2-5]

Cut: 57. Line: 482. Goblet. Optic. **References:** 4, page 11 [1-1]

Cut: 57. Line: 482. Saucer Champagne. Optic. **References:** 4, page 11 [1-2]

Cut: 57. Line: 482. Sherbet. Optic. **References:** 4, page 11 [1-3]

Cut: 57. Line: 482. Wine. Optic. **References:** 4, page 11 [1-4]

Cut: 57. Line: 484. Compote. Optic. **References:** 4, page 27 [2-1]

Cut: 57. Line: 900. Covered Jug. Optic. **References:** 4, page 26 [3-3]

Cut: 57. Line: 8000. Cocktail. Optic. **References:** 4, page 23 [1-5]

Cut: 57. Line: 8000. H.S. Champ. Optic. **References:** 4, page 25 [1-2]

Cut: 57. Line: 8000. H.S.S. Champ. Optic. **References:** 4, page 25 [1-3]

Cut: 58. Line: 1. Grape Fruit. Optic. **References:** 4, page 25 [3-4]

Cut: 58. Line: 3. Vase. 10 inch. Optic. **References:** 4, page 27 [1-4]

Cut: 58. Line: 455. Jug. 54 oz. Optic. **References:** 4, page 26 [3-2]

Cut: 58. Line: 485. Cocktail. Optic. **References:** 4, page 15 [1-5]

Cut: 58. Line: 485. Compote. Optic. **References:** 4, page 15 [2-6]

Cut: 58. Line: 485. Cordial. Optic. **References:** 4, page 15 [1-6]

Cut: 58. Line: 485. Footed Tumbler. 2-3/4 oz. Optic. **References:** 4, page 15 [2-1]

Cut: 58. Line: 485. Footed Tumbler. 4 oz. Optic. **References:** 4, page 15 [2-2]

Cut: 58. Line: 485. Footed Tumbler. 6 oz. Optic. **References:** 4, page 15 [2-3]

Cut: 58. Line: 485. Footed Tumbler. 9 oz. Optic. **References:** 4, page 15 [2-4]

Cut: 58. Line: 485. Footed Tumbler. 12 oz. Optic. **References:** 4, page 15 [2-5]

Cut: 58. Line: 485. Goblet. Optic. **References:** 4, page 15 [1-1]

Cut: 58. Line: 485. Saucer Champagne. Optic. **References:** 4, page 15 [1-2]

Cut: 58. Line: 485. Sherbet. Optic. **References:** 4, page 15 [1-3]

Cut: 58. Line: 485. Wine. Optic. **References:** 4, page 15 [1-4]

Cut: 58. Line: 632. Full Sham, Tumbler. **References:** 2, fig. 8 [1-2]

Cut: 59, Plain Bottom. Line: 558. Tumbler. **References:** 2, fig. 7 [3-1]

Cut: 59. Line: 631. Half Sham, Tumbler. **References:** 2, fig. 8 [1-3]

Cut: 61. Plate. 5-1/4 inch. **References:** 4, page 26 [1-2]

Cut: 61. Line: 482. Cocktail. Optic. **References:** 4, page 12 [1-5]

Cut: 61. Line: 482. Cordial. Optic. **References:** 4, page 12 [1-6]

Cut: 61. Line: 482. Footed Tumbler. 2-3/4 oz. Optic. **References:** 4, page 12 [2-1]

Cut: 61. Line: 482. Footed Tumbler. 4 oz. Optic. **References:** 4, page 12 [2-2]

Cut: 61. Line: 482. Footed Tumbler. 6 oz. Optic. **References:** 4, page 12 [2-3]

Cut: 61. Line: 482. Footed Tumbler. 9 oz. Optic. **References:** 4, page 12 [2-4]

Cut: 61. Line: 482. Footed Tumbler. 12 oz. Optic. **References:** 4, page 12 [2-5]

Cut: 61. Line: 482. Goblet. Optic. **References:** 4, page 12 [1-1]

Cut: 61. Line: 482. Saucer Champagne. Optic. **References:** 4, page 12 [1-2]

Cut: 61. Line: 482. Sherbet. Optic. **References:** 4, page 12 [1-3]

Cut: 61. Line: 482. Wine. Optic. **References:** 4, page 12 [1-4]

Cut: 62. Line: 486. Cocktail. Optic. **References:** 4, page 16 [1-5]

Cut: 62. Line: 486. Cordial. Optic. **References:** 4, page 16 [1-6]

Cut: 62. Line: 486. Footed Tumbler. 2-3/4 oz. Optic. **References:** 4, page 16 [2-1]

Cut: 62. Line: 486. Footed Tumbler. 4 oz. Optic. **References:** 4, page 16 [2-2]

Cut: 62. Line: 486. Footed Tumbler. 6 oz. Optic. **References:** 4, page 16 [2-3]

Cut: 62. Line: 486. Footed Tumbler. 9 oz. Optic. **References:** 4, page 16 [2-4]

Cut: 62. Line: 486. Footed Tumbler. 12 oz. Optic. **References:** 4, page 16 [2-5]

Cut: 62. Line: 486. Goblet. Optic. **References:** 4, page 16 [1-1]

Cut: 62. Line: 486. Saucer Champagne. Optic. **References:** 4, page 16 [1-2]

Cut: 62. Line: 486. Sherbet. Optic. **References:** 4, page 16 [1-3]

Cut: 62. Line: 486. Wine. Optic. **References:** 4, page 16 [1-4]

Cut: 63. Line: 1350. Mansfield. Cocktail. 4-1/2 oz. / 4-3/4" hi. Gold Band. **References:** 1967, page 11 [1-22]; 1968, page 15 [1-22]; 1969, page 19 [2-22]; 1970, page 20 [2-22]; 1971, page 20 [2-22]; 1972, page 28 [2-22]; 1973, page 33 [2-22]

Cut: 63. Line: 1350. Mansfield. Cordial. 1-1/4 oz. / 3-3/4" hi. Gold Band. **References:** 1967, page 11 [1-23]; 1968, page 15 [1-23]; 1969, page 19 [2-23]; 1970, page 20 [2-23]; 1971, page 20 [2-23]; 1972, page 28 [2-23]; 1973, page 33 [2-23]; 1975, page 29 [2-18]; 1977, page 40 [2-18]

Cut: 63. Line: 1350. Mansfield. Goblet. 12-1/2 oz. / 6-5/8" hi. Gold Band. **References:** 1967, page 11 [1-19]; 1968, page 15 [1-19]; 1969, page 19 [2-19]; 1970, page 20 [2-19]; 1971, page 20 [2-19]; 1972, page 28 [2-19]; 1973, page 33 [2-19]; 1975, page 29 [2-15]; 1977, page 40 [2-15]

Cut: 63. Line: 1350. Mansfield. Ice Tea. 13-1/2 oz. / 6-1/4" hi. Gold Band. **References:** 1967, page 11 [1-25]; 1968, page 15 [1-25]; 1969, page 19 [2-25]; 1970, page 20 [2-25]; 1971, page 20 [2-25]; 1972, page 28 [2-25]; 1973, page 33 [2-25]; 1975, page 29 [2-19]; 1977, page 40 [2-19]

Cut: 63. Line: 1350. Mansfield. Juice. 6-1/2 oz. / 5-1/4" hi. Gold Band. **References:** 1967, page 11 [1-24]; 1968, page 15 [1-24]; 1969, page 19 [2-24]; 1970, page 20 [2-24]; 1971, page 20 [2-24]; 1972, page 28 [2-24]; 1973, page 33 [2-24]

Cut: 63. Line: 1350. Mansfield. Plate. 7" / Actually 7-7/8" Dia. Gold Band. **References:** 1967, page 11 [1-26]; 1968, page 15 [1-26]; 1975, page 29 [2-20]; 1977, page 40 [2-20]

Cut: 63. Line: 1350. Mansfield. Plate. 8" / Actually 8-3/4" Dia. Gold Band. **References:** 1967, page 11 [1-27]; 1968, page 15 [1-27]; 1975, page 29 [2-21]; 1977, page 40 [2-21]

Cut: 63. Line: 1350. Mansfield. Plate. 7 inches diam. Gold Band, Platinum or Gold Banding (No Cutting), Actually 7-7/8" Dia. **References:** 1969, page 19 [2-26]; 1970, page 20 [2-26]; 1971, page 20 [2-26]; 1972, page 28 [2-26]; 1973, page 33 [2-26]

Cut: 63. Line: 1350. Mansfield. Plate. 8 inches diam. Gold Band, Platinum or Gold Banding (No Cutting), Actually 8-3/4" Dia. **References:** 1969, page 19 [2-27]; 1970, page 20 [2-27]; 1971, page 20 [2-27]; 1972, page 28 [2-27]; 1973, page 33 [2-27]

Cut: 63. Line: 1350. Mansfield. Sherbet. 6-1/2 oz. / 5" hi. Gold Band. **References:** 1967, page 11 [1-20]; 1968, page 15 [1-20]; 1969, page 19 [2-20]; 1970, page 20 [2-20]; 1971, page 20 [2-20]; 1972, page 28 [2-20]; 1973, page 33 [2-20]; 1975, page 29 [2-16]; 1977, page 40 [2-16]

Cut: 63. Line: 1350. Mansfield. White Wine. 7 oz. 5-3/4 inches tall. Gold Band. **References:** 1975, page 29 [2-17]; 1967, page 11 [1-21]; 1968, page 15 [1-21]; 1969, page 19 [2-21]; 1970, page 20 [2-21]; 1971, page 20 [2-21]; 1972, page 28 [2-21]; 1973, page 33 [2-21]; 1977, page 40 [2-17]

Cut: 63. Line: 1350. Montclair. Cocktail. 4-1/2 oz. / 4-3/4" hi. Platinum Band. **References:** 1967, page 11 [1-31]; 1968, page 15 [1-31]; 1969, page 19 [2-31]; 1970, page 20 [2-31]; 1971, page 20 [2-31]; 1972, page 28 [2-31]; 1973, page 33 [2-31]

Cut: 63. Line: 1350. Montclair. Cordial. 1-1/4 oz. / 3-3/4" hi. Platinum Band. **References:** 1967, page 11 [1-32]; 1968, page 15 [1-32]; 1969, page 19 [2-32]; 1970, page 20 [2-32]; 1971, page 20 [2-32]; 1972, page 28 [2-32]; 1973, page 33 [2-32]; 1975, page 29 [2-25]; 1977, page 40 [2-25]

Cut: 63. Line: 1350. Montclair. Goblet. 12-1/2 oz. / 6-5/8" hi. Platinum Band. **References:** 1967, page 11 [1-28]; 1968, page 15 [1-28]; 1969, page 19 [2-28]; 1970, page 20 [2-28]; 1971, page 20 [2-28]; 1972, page 28 [2-28]; 1973, page 33 [2-28]; 1975, page 29 [2-22]; 1977, page 40 [2-22]

Cut: 63. Line: 1350. Montclair. Ice Tea. 13-1/2 oz. / 6-1/4" hi. Platinum Band. **References:** 1967, page 11 [1-34]; 1968, page 15 [1-34]; 1969, page 19 [2-34]; 1970, page 20 [2-34]; 1971, page 20 [2-34]; 1972, page 28 [2-34]; 1973, page 33 [2-34]; 1975, page 29 [2-26]; 1977, page 40 [2-26]

Cut: 63. Line: 1350. Montclair. Juice. 6-1/2 oz. / 5-1/4" hi. Platinum Band. **References:** 1967, page 11 [1-33]; 1968, page 15 [1-33]; 1969, page 19 [2-33]; 1970, page 20 [2-33]; 1971, page 20 [2-33]; 1972, page 28 [2-33]; 1973, page 33 [2-33]

Cut: 63. Line: 1350. Montclair. Plate. 7 oz. / Actually 7-7/8" Dia. Platinum Band. **References:** 1967, page 11 [1-35]; 1968, page 15 [1-35]; 1975, page 29 [2-27]; 1977, page 40 [2-27]

Cut: 63. Line: 1350. Montclair. Plate. 8 oz. / Actually 8-3/4" Dia. Platinum Band. **References:** 1967, page 11 [1-36]; 1968, page 15 [1-36]; 1975, page 29 [2-28]; 1977, page 40 [2-28]

Cut: 63. Line: 1350. Montclair. Plate. 7 inches diam. Platinum Band, Platinum or Gold Banding (No Cutting), Actually 7-7/8" Dia. **References:** 1969, page 19 [2-35]; 1970, page 20 [2-35]; 1971, page 20 [2-35]; 1972, page 28 [2-35]; 1973, page 33 [2-35]

Cut: 63. Line: 1350. Montclair. Plate. 8 inches diam. Platinum Band, Platinum or Gold Banding (No Cutting), Actually 8-3/4" Dia. **References:** 1969, page 19 [2-36]; 1970, page 20 [2-36]; 1971, page 20 [2-36]; 1972, page 28 [2-36]; 1973, page 33 [2-36]

Cut: 63. Line: 1350. Montclair. Sherbet. 6-1/2 oz. / 5" hi. Platinum Band. **References:** 1967, page 11 [1-29]; 1968, page 15 [1-29]; 1969, page 19 [2-29]; 1970, page 20 [2-29]; 1971, page 20 [2-29]; 1972, page 28 [2-29]; 1973, page 33 [2-29]; 1975, page 29 [2-23]; 1977, page 40 [2-23]

Cut: 63. Line: 1350. Montclair. White Wine. 7 oz. 5-3/4 inches tall. Platinum Band. **References:** 1975, page 29 [2-24]; 1977, page 40 [2-24]; 1967, page 11 [1-30]; 1968, page 15 [1-30]; 1969, page 19 [2-30]; 1970, page 20 [2-30]; 1971, page 20 [2-30]; 1972, page 28 [2-30]; 1973, page 33 [2-30]

Cut: 63. Line: 1350. Riviera. 1305 Dessert-Finger Bowl. 4-1/2" Dia. **References:** 1967, page 13 [2-20]; 1968, page 17 [2-20]; 1969, page 13 [2-20]; 1970, page 14 [2-20]; 1971, page 14 [2-20]; 1972, page 24 [2-20]; 1973, page 29 [2-20]; 1975, page 27 [2-16]; 1977, page 38 [2-16]

Cut: 63. Line: 1350. Riviera. Cocktail. 4-1/2 oz. / 4-3/4" hi. **References:** 1967, page 13 [2-16]; 1968, page 17 [2-16]; 1969, page 13 [2-16]; 1970, page 14 [2-16]; 1971, page 14 [2-16]; 1972, page 24 [2-16]; 1973, page 29 [2-16]

Cut: 63. Line: 1350. Riviera. Cordial. 1-1/4 oz. / 3-3/4" hi. **References:** 1967, page 13 [2-17]; 1968, page 17 [2-17]; 1969, page 13 [2-17]; 1970, page 14 [2-17]; 1971, page 14 [2-17]; 1972, page 24 [2-17]; 1973, page 29 [2-17]; 1975, page 27 [2-14]; 1977, page 38 [2-14]; 1981, page 3 [3-5]

Cut: 63. Line: 1350. Riviera. Goblet. 12-1/2 oz. / 6-5/8" hi. **References:** 1967, page 13 [2-12]; 1968, page 17 [2-12]; 1969, page 13 [2 12]; 1970, page 14 [2-12]; 1971, page 14 [2-12]; 1972, page 24 [2-12]; 1973, page 29 [2-12]; 1975, page 27 [2-10]; 1977, page 38 [2-10]; 1981, page 3 [3-1]

Cut: 63. Line: 1350. Riviera. Ice Tea. 13-1/2 oz. / 6-1/4" hi. **References:** 1967, page 13 [2-19]; 1968, page 17 [2-19]; 1969, page 13 [2-19]; 1970, page 14 [2-19]; 1971, page 14 [2-19]; 1972, page 24 [2-19]; 1973, page 29 [2-19]; 1975, page 27 [2-15]; 1977, page 38 [2-15]

Cut: 63. Line: 1350. Riviera. Juice. 6-1/2 oz. / 5-1/4" hi. **References:** 1967, page 13 [2-18]; 1968, page 17 [2-18]; 1969, page 13 [2-18]; 1970, page 14 [2-18]; 1971, page 14 [2-18]; 1972, page 24 [2-18]; 1973, page 29 [2-18]

Cut: 63. Line: 1350. Riviera. Plate. 7" / Actually 7-7/8" Dia. **References:** 1967, page 13 [2-21]; 1968, page 17 [2-21]; 1969, page 13 [2-21]; 1970, page 14 [2-21]; 1971, page 14 [2-21]; 1972, page 24 [2-21]; 1975, page 27 [2-17]; 1977, page 38 [2-17]

Cut: 63. Line: 1350. Riviera. Plate. 8" / Actually 8-3/4" Dia. **References:** 1967, page 13 [2-22]; 1968, page 17 [2-22]; 1969, page 13 [2-22]; 1970, page 14 [2-22]; 1971, page 14 [2-22]; 1972, page 24 [2-22]; 1973, page 29 [2-22]; 1975, page 27 [2-18]; 1977, page 38 [2-18]

Cut: 63. Line: 1350. Riviera. Red Wine Goblet. 9-1/2 oz. / 6-3/8" hi. **References:** 1967, page 13 [2-14]; 1968, page 17 [2-14]; 1969, page 13 [2-14]; 1970, page 14 [2-14]; 1971, page 14 [2-14]; 1972, page 24 [2-14]; 1973, page 29 [2-14]; 1975, page 27 [2-12]; 1977, page 38 [2-12]

Cut: 63. Line: 1350. Riviera. Sherbet. 6-1/2 oz. / 5" hi. **References:** 1967, page 13 [2-13]; 1968, page 17 [2-13]; 1969, page 13 [2-13]; 1970, page 14 [2-13]; 1971, page 14 [2-13]; 1972, page 24 [2-13]; 1973, page 29 [2-13]; 1975, page 27 [2-11]; 1977, page 38 [2-11]; 1981, page 3 [3-2]

Cut: 63. Line: 1350. Riviera. Tulip Champagne. 8 oz. 8-1/2 inches tall. **References:** 1981, page 3 [3-4]

Cut: 63. Line: 1350. Riviera. White Wine. 7 oz. 5-3/4 inches tall. **References:** 1975, page 27 [2-13]; 1967, page 13 [2-15]; 1968, page 17 [2-15]; 1969, page 13 [2-15]; 1970, page 14 [2-15]; 1971, page 14 [2-15]; 1972, page 24 [2-15]; 1973, page 29 [2-15]; 1977, page 38 [2-13]; 1981, page 3 [3-3]

Cut: 63. Line: 1963. Grace. 1305 Dessert-Finger Bowl. 4-1/2" Dia. **References:** 1967, page 8 [2-18]; 1968, page 12 [2-18]; 1969, page 12 [2-8]; 1970, page 13 [2-8]; 1971, page 13 [2-8]; 1972, page 22 [1-18]; 1973, page 26 [1-18]; 1975, page 26 [1-14]; 1977, page 37 [1-14]

Cut: 63. Line: 1963. Grace. Cocktail. 5-1/2 oz. / 4-3/4" hi. **References:** 1967, page 8 [2-14]; 1968, page 12 [2-14]; 1969, page 12 [2-4]; 1970, page 13 [2-4]; 1971, page 13 [2-4]; 1972, page 22 [1-14]; 1973, page 26 [1-14]

Cut: 63. Line: 1963. Grace. Cordial. 1-1/2 oz. / 4" hi. **References:** 1967, page 8 [2-15]; 1968, page 12 [2-15]; 1969, page 12 [2-5]; 1970, page 13 [2-5]; 1971, page 13 [2-5]; 1972, page 22 [1-15]; 1973, page 26 [1-15]; 1975, page 26 [1-12]; 1977, page 37 [1-12]

Cut: 63. Line: 1963. Grace. Goblet. 13-1/2 oz. / 6-3/4" hi. **References:** 1967, page 8 [2-11]; 1968, page 12 [2-11]; 1969, page 12 [2-1]; 1970, page 13 [2-1]; 1971, page 13 [2-1]; 1972, page 22 [1-11]; 1973, page 26 [1-11]; 1975, page 26 [1-9]; 1977, page 37 [1-9]

Cut: 63. Line: 1963. Grace. Ice Tea. 14 oz. / 6-1/4" hi. **References:** 1967, page 8 [2-17]; 1968, page 12 [2-17]; 1969, page 12 [2-7]; 1970, page 13 [2-7]; 1971, page 13 [2-7]; 1972, page 22 [1-17]; 1973, page 26 [1-17]; 1975, page 26 [1-13]; 1977, page 37 [1-13]

Cut: 63. Line: 1963. Grace. Juice. 7 oz. / 5-1/4" hi. **References:** 1967, page 8 [2-16]; 1968, page 12 [2-16]; 1969, page 12 [2-6]; 1970, page 13 [2-6]; 1971, page 13 [2-6]; 1972, page 22 [1-16]; 1973, page 26 [1-16]

Cut: 63. Line: 1963. Grace. Plate. 7" / Actually 7-7/8" Dia. **References:** 1967, page 8 [2-19]; 1968, page 12 [2-19]; 1969, page 12 [2-9]; 1970, page 13 [2-9]; 1971, page 13 [2-9]; 1972, page 22 [1-19]; 1973, page 26 [1-19]; 1975, page 26 [1-15]; 1977, page 37 [1-15]

Cut: 63. Line: 1963. Grace. Plate. 8" / Actually 8-3/4" Dia. **References:** 1967, page 8 [2-20]; 1968, page 12 [2-20]; 1969, page 12 [2-10]; 1970, page 13 [2-10]; 1971, page 13 [2-10]; 1972, page 22 [1-20]; 1973, page 26 [1-20]; 1975, page 26 [1-16]; 1977, page 37 [1-16]

Cut: 63. Line: 1963. Grace. Sherbet. 7-1/2 oz. / 5-1/8" hi. **References:** 1967, page 8 [2-12]; 1968, page 12 [2-12]; 1969, page 12 [2-2]; 1970, page 13 [2-2]; 1971, page 13 [2-2]; 1972, page 22 [1-12]; 1973, page 26 [1-12]; 1975, page 26 [1-10]; 1977, page 37 [1-10]

Cut: 63. Line: 1963. Grace. Wine. 7-3/4 oz. / 5-3/4" hi. **References:** 1967, page 8 [2-13]; 1968, page 12 [2-13]; 1969, page 12 [2-3]; 1970, page 13 [2-3]; 1971, page 13 [2-3]; 1972, page 22 [1-13]; 1973, page 26 [1-13]; 1975, page 26 [1-11]; 1977, page 37 [1-11]

Cut: 64. Line: 482. Goblet. Optic. **References:** 4, page 24 [2-6]

Cut: 66. Line: 632. Full Sham, Tumbler. **References:** 2, fig. 8 [1-4]

Cut: 68. Line: 632. Full Sham, Tumbler. **References:** 2, fig. 8 [1-5]

Cut: 73. Line: 1. Tankard. 3 Pint. **References:** 2, fig. 4 [2-1]

Cut: 90. Line: 630. Tumbler. **References:** 2, fig. 8 [2-1]

Cut: 92. Line: 632. Full Sham, Tumbler. **References:** 2, fig. 8 [2-2]

Cuts: 94 and N. Etching: 8. Line: 630. Tumbler. **References:** 2, fig. 8 [2-4]

Cuts: 94 and N. Etching: 8. Line: 632. Full Sham, Tumbler. **References:** 2, fig. 8 [2-3]

Cut: 100. Line: 630. Tumbler. **References:** 2, fig. 8 [2-4]

Cut: 101, Star. Line: 1. Tankard. 3 Pint. **References:** 2, fig. 4 [2-2]

Cut: 101, Star. Line: 15. Jug. 45 oz. **References:** 2, fig. 6 (p. 43) [2-3]

Cut: 101, Plain Bottom. Line: 557. Tumbler. **References:** 2, fig. 7 [3-3]

Cut: 101. Line: 619. Water Tumbler. **References:** 2, fig. 15 [1-5]

Cut: 121. Laurel. Bell. 4-1/2 inches tall. **References:** 1979, page 12 [3-4]

Cut: 121. Line: 1. Oil. Cut Neck, Optic. **References:** 4, page 25 [1-6]

Cut: 121. Line: 3. Footed Tumbler. 2-3/4 oz. Optic. **References:** 4, page 23 [2-1]

Cut: 121. Line: 3. Footed Tumbler. 4 oz. Optic. **References:** 4, page 23 [2-2]

Cut: 121. Line: 3. Footed Tumbler. 6 oz. Optic. **References:** 4, page 23 [2-3]

Cut: 121. Line: 3. Footed Tumbler. 9 oz. Optic. **References:** 4, page 23 [2-4]

Cut: 121. Line: 3. Footed Tumbler. 12 oz. Optic. **References:** 4, page 23 [2-5]

Cut: 121. Line: 3. Laurel. Bell. 4-3/8 inches tall. Handmade and Hand Cut. 1977, page 22 [5-3]

Cut: 121. Line: 3. Laurel. Bell. 4-3/8 inches tall. **References:** 1977, page 22 [5-3]

Cut: 121. Line: 255. Cocktail Shaker. Optic. **References:** 4, page 27 [3-1]

Cut: 121. Line: 8000. Cordial. Optic. **References:** 4, page 23 [1-6]

Cut: 121. Line: 8000. Goblet. Optic. **References:** 4, page 23 [1-1]

Cut: 121. Line: 8000. Saucer Champagne. Optic. **References:** 4, page 23 [1-2]

Cut: 121. Line: 8000. Sherbet. Optic. **References:** 4, page 23 [1-3]

Cut: 121. Line: 8000. Wine. Optic. **References:** 4, page 23 [1-4]

Cut: 121. Line: 8000. Laurel Wreath. 1305 Dessert-Finger Bowl. 4-1/2 inches diam. Optic. **References:** 1967, page 21 [2-10]; 1968, page 25 [2-10]; 1969, page 24 [2-10]; 1970, page 25 [2-10]; 1971, page 25 [2-10]

Cut: 121. Line: 8000. Laurel Wreath. Claret. 5 oz. 5-5/8 inches tall. Optic. **References:** 1967, page 21 [2-4]; 1968, page 25 [2-4]; 1969, page 24 [2-4]; 1970, page 25 [2-4]; 1971, page 25 [2-4]

Cut: 121. Line: 8000. Laurel Wreath. Cocktail. 4 oz. 4-5/8 inches tall. Optic. **References:** 1967, page 21 [2-5]; 1968, page 25 [2-5]; 1969, page 24 [2-5]; 1970, page 25 [2-5]; 1971, page 25 [2-5]

Cut: 121. Line: 8000. Laurel Wreath. Cordial. 1-1/4 oz. 3-3/4 inches tall. Optic. **References:** 1967, page 21 [2-6]; 1968, page 25 [2-6]; 1969, page 24 [2-6]; 1970, page 25 [2-6]; 1971, page 25 [2-6]

Cut: 121. Line: 8000. Laurel Wreath. Goblet. 10-1/2 oz. 6-1/2 inches tall. Optic. **References:** 1967, page 21 [2-1]; 1968, page 25 [2-1]; 1969, page 24 [2-1]; 1970, page 25 [2-1]; 1971, page 25 [2-1]

Cut: 121. Line: 8000. Laurel Wreath. Ice Tea. 13-1/2 oz. 5-3/8 inches tall. Optic. **References:** 1967, page 21 [2-9]; 1968, page 25 [2-9]; 1969, page 24 [2-9]; 1970, page 25 [2-9]; 1971, page 25 [2-9]

Cut: 121. Line: 8000. Laurel Wreath. Juice. 6-1/4 oz. 4 inches tall. Optic. **References:** 1967, page 21 [2-8]; 1968, page 25 [2-8]; 1969, page 24 [2-8]; 1970, page 25 [2-8]; 1971, page 25 [2-8]

Cut: 121. Line: 8000. Laurel Wreath. Parfait. 5-1/4 oz. 6-3/8 inches tall. Optic. **References:** 1967, page 21 [2-7]; 1968, page 25 [2-7]; 1969, page 24 [2-7]; 1970, page 25 [2-7]; 1971, page 25 [2-7]

Cut: 121. Line: 8000. Laurel Wreath. Plate. 7 inches diam. Optic, Actually 7-7/8" Dia. **References:** 1967, page 21 [2-11]; 1968, page 25 [2-11]; 1969, page 24 [2-11]; 1970, page 25 [2-11]; 1971, page 25 [2-11]

Cut: 121. Line: 8000. Laurel Wreath. Plate. 8 inches diam. Optic, Actually 8-3/8" Dia. **References:** 1967, page 21 [2-12]; 1968, page 25 [2-12]; 1969, page 24 [2-12]; 1970, page 25 [2-12]; 1971, page 25 [2-12]

Cut: 121. Line: 8000. Laurel Wreath. Saucer Champagne. 6-1/2 oz. 4-3/4 inches tall. Optic. **References:** 1967, page 21 [2-2]; 1968, page 25 [2-2]; 1969, page 24 [2-2]; 1970, page 25 [2-2]; 1971, page 25 [2-2]

Cut: 121. Line: 8000. Laurel Wreath. Sherbet. 6-1/2 oz. 3-1/2 inches tall. Optic. **References:** 1967, page 21 [2-3]; 1968, page 25 [2-3]; 1969, page 24 [2-3]; 1970, page 25 [2-3]; 1971, page 25 [2-3]

Cuts: 121 and 39. Line: 912. Laurel. 1311 Dessert-Finger Bowl. 4-3/4 inches diam. **References:** 1967, page 17 [1-8]; 1968, page 21 [1-8]; 1969, page 21 [1-8]; 1970, page 22 [1-8]; 1971, page 22 [1-8]

Cuts: 121 and 39. Line: 912. Laurel. Claret. 4 oz. 4-3/4 inches tall. **References:** 1967, page 17 [1-3]; 1968, page 21 [1-3]; 1969, page 21 [1-3]; 1970, page 22 [1-3]; 1971, page 22 [1-3]

Cuts: 121 and 39. Line: 912. Laurel. Cocktail. 3-1/2 oz. 4-3/8 inches tall. **References:** 1967, page 17 [1-4]; 1968, page 21 [1-4]; 1969, page 21 [1-4]; 1970, page 22 [1-4]; 1971, page 22 [1-4]

Cuts: 121 and 39. Line: 912. Laurel. Cordial. 1 oz. 3-5/8 inches tall. **References:** 1967, page 17 [1-5]; 1968, page 21 [1-5]; 1969, page 21 [1-5]; 1970, page 22 [1-5]; 1971, page 22 [1-5]

Cuts: 121 and 39. Line: 912. Laurel. Goblet. 10 oz. 6-1/4 inches tall. **References:** 1967, page 17 [1-1]; 1968, page 21 [1-1]; 1969, page 21 [1-1]; 1970, page 22 [1-1]; 1971, page 22 [1-1]

Cuts: 121 and 39. Line: 912. Laurel. Ice Tea. 12 oz. 6 inches tall. **References:** 1967, page 17 [1-7]; 1968, page 21 [1-7]; 1969, page 21 [1-7]; 1970, page 22 [1-7]; 1971, page 22 [1-7]

Cuts: 121 and 39. Line: 912. Laurel. Juice. 6 oz. 4-5/8 inches tall. **References:** 1967, page 17 [1-6]; 1968, page 21 [1-6]; 1969, page 21 [1-6]; 1970, page 22 [1-6]; 1971, page 22 [1-6]

Cuts: 121 and 39. Line: 912. Laurel. Plate. 7 inches diam. Actually 7-7/8" Dia. **References:** 1967, page 17 [1-9]; 1968, page 21 [1-9]; 1969, page 21 [1-9]; 1970, page 22 [1-9]; 1971, page 22 [1-9]

Cuts: 121 and 39. Line: 912. Laurel. Plate. 8 inches diam. Actually 8-3/4" Dia. **References:** 1967, page 17 [1-10]; 1968, page 21 [1-10]; 1969, page 21 [1-10]; 1970, page 22 [1-10]; 1971, page 22 [1-10]

Cuts: 121 and 39. Line: 912. Laurel. Saucer Champagne. 7-1/2 oz. 5-1/8 inches tall. **References:** 1967, page 17 [1-2]; 1968, page 21 [1-2]; 1969, page 21 [1-2]; 1970, page 22 [1-2]; 1971, page 22 [1-2]

Cut: 139. Line: 912. Dolly Madison-Jane Eyre. 1311 Dessert-Finger Bowl. 4-3/4 inches diam. **References:** 1967, page 17 [2-18]; 1968, page 21 [2-18]; 1969, page 21 [2-18]; 1970, page 22 [2-18]; 1971, page 22 [2-18]

Cut: 139. Line: 912. Dolly Madison-Jane Eyre. Claret. 4 oz. 4-3/4 inches tall. **References:** 1967, page 17 [2-13]; 1968, page 21 [2-13]; 1969, page 21 [2-13]; 1970, page 22 [2-13]; 1971, page 22 [2-13]

Cut: 139. Line: 912. Dolly Madison-Jane Eyre. Cocktail. 3-1/2 oz. 4-3/8 inches tall. **References:** 1967, page 17 [2-14]; 1968, page 21 [2-14]; 1969, page 21 [2-14]; 1970, page 22 [2-14]; 1971, page 22 [2-14]

Cut: 139. Line: 912. Dolly Madison-Jane Eyre. Cordial. 1 oz. 3-5/8 inches tall. **References:** 1967, page 17 [2-15]; 1968, page 21 [2-15]; 1969, page 21 [2-15]; 1970, page 22 [2-15]; 1971, page 22 [2-15]

Cut: 139. Line: 912. Dolly Madison-Jane Eyre.

Goblet. 10 oz. 6-1/4 inches tall. **References:** 1967, page 17 [2-11]; 1968, page 21 [2-11]; 1969, page 21 [2-11]; 1970, page 22 [2-11]; 1971, page 22 [2-11]

Cut: 139. Line: 912. Dolly Madison-Jane Eyre. Ice Tea. 12 oz. 6 inches tall. **References:** 1967, page 17 [2-17]; 1968, page 21 [2-17]; 1969, page 21 [2-17]; 1970, page 22 [2-17]; 1971, page 22 [2-17]

Cut: 139. Line: 912. Dolly Madison-Jane Eyre. Juice. 6 oz. 4-5/8 inches tall. **References:** 1967, page 17 [2-16]; 1968, page 21 [2-16]; 1969, page 21 [2-16]; 1970, page 22 [2-16]; 1971, page 22 [2-16]

Cut: 139. Line: 912. Dolly Madison-Jane Eyre. Plate. 7 inches diam. Actually 7-7/8" Dia. **References:** 1967, page 17 [2-19]; 1968, page 21 [2-19]; 1969, page 21 [2-19]; 1970, page 22 [2-19]; 1971, page 22 [2-19]

Cut: 139. Line: 912. Dolly Madison-Jane Eyre. Plate. 8 inches diam. Actually 8-3/4" Dia. **References:** 1967, page 17 [2-20]; 1968, page 21 [2-20]; 1969, page 21 [2-20]; 1970, page 22 [2-20]; 1971, page 22 [2-20]

Cut: 139. Line: 912. Dolly Madison-Jane Eyre. Saucer Champagne. 7-1/2 oz. 5-1/8 inches tall. **References:** 1967, page 17 [2-12]; 1968, page 21 [2-12]; 1969, page 21 [2-12]; 1970, page 22 [2-12]; 1971, page 22 [2-12]

Cut: 204. Line: 459. Cocktail. **References:** 4, page 6 [1-4]

Cut: 204. Line: 459. Cordial. **References:** 4, page 6 [1-5]

Cut: 204. Line: 459. Goblet. **References:** 4, page 6 [1-1]

Cut: 204. Line: 459. Sherbet. **References:** 4, page 6 [1-2]

Cut: 204. Line: 459. Wine. **References:** 4, page 6 [1-3]

Cut: 204. Line: 482. Footed Tumbler. 2-3/4 oz. **References:** 4, page 6 [2-1]

Cut: 204. Line: 482. Footed Tumbler. 4 oz. **References:** 4, page 6 [2-2]

Cut: 204. Line: 482. Footed Tumbler. 6 oz. **References:** 4, page 6 [2-3]

Cut: 204. Line: 482. Footed Tumbler. 9 oz. **References:** 4, page 6 [2-4]

Cut: 204. Line: 482. Footed Tumbler. 12 oz. **References:** 4, page 6 [2-5]

Cut: 218. Line: 482. Goblet. Optic. **References:** 4, page 24 [1-4]

Cut: 218, Star Bottom. Line: 558. Tumbler. **References:** 2, fig. 7 [1-3]

Cut: 218. Line: 632. Full Sham, Tumbler. **References:** 2, fig. 8 [3-1]

Cut: 219. Line: 477. Cocktail. **References:** 4, page 9 [1-5]

Cut: 219. Line: 477. Cordial. **References:** 4, page 9 [1-6]

Cut: 219. Line: 477. Footed Tumbler. 2-3/4 oz. **References:** 4, page 9 [2-1]

Cut: 219. Line: 477. Footed Tumbler. 4 oz. **References:** 4, page 9 [2-2]

Cut: 219. Line: 477. Footed Tumbler. 6 oz. **References:** 4, page 9 [2-3]

Cut: 219. Line: 477. Footed Tumbler. 9 oz. **References:** 4, page 9 [2-4]

Cut: 219. Line: 477. Footed Tumbler. 12 oz. **References:** 4, page 9 [2-5]

Cut: 219. Line: 477. Goblet. **References:** 4, page 9 [1-1]

Cut: 219. Line: 477. Saucer Champagne. **References:** 4, page 9 [1-2]

Cut: 219. Line: 477. Sherbet. **References:** 4, page 9 [1-3]

Cut: 219. Line: 477. Wine. **References:** 4, page 9 [1-4]

Cut: 219, Star Bottom. Line: 550. Tumbler. **References:** 2, fig. 7 [1-5]

Cut: 219. Line: 632. Full Sham, Tumbler. **References:** 2, fig. 8 [3-2]

Cut: 220, Star Bottom. Line: 558. Tumbler. **References:** 2, fig. 7 [3-5]

Cut: 220. Line: 631. Half Sham, Tumbler. **References:** 2, fig. 8 [3-3]

Cut: 220. Line: 1 / 631. Squat Water Set / Tumblers. **References:** 2, fig. 6 (p. 43) [1-3]

Cut: 222. Line: 75. Water Bottle. One Quart. **References:** 2, fig. 3 [2-4]

Cut: 222. Line: 632. Full Sham, Tumbler. **References:** 2, fig. 8 [3-4]

Cut: 250. Line: 3. Candlestick. **References:** 4, page 2 [1-4]

Cut: 250. Line: 3. Decanter. 1 Pint. Optic. **References:** 4, page 27 [1-3]

Cut: 250. Line: 3. Footed Tumbler. 2-3/4 oz. Optic. **References:** 4, page 2 [2-1]

Cut: 250. Line: 3. Footed Tumbler. 4 oz. Optic. **References:** 4, page 2 [2-2]

Cut: 250. Line: 3. Footed Tumbler. 6 oz. Optic. **References:** 4, page 2 [2-3]

Cut: 250. Line: 3. Footed Tumbler. 9 oz. Optic. **References:** 4, page 2 [2-4]

Cut: 250. Line: 3. Footed Tumbler. 12 oz. Optic. **References:** 4, page 2 [2-5]

Cut: 250. Line: 50. Covered Jug. 65 oz. Optic. **References:** 4, page 26 [3-4]

Cut: 250. Line: 150. Cocktail. Optic. **References:** 4, page 2 [1-6]

Cut: 250. Line: 150. Cordial. Optic. **References:** 4, page 2 [1-7]

Cut: 250. Line: 150. Goblet. Optic. **References:** 4, page 2 [1-1]

Cut: 250. Line: 150. Saucer Champagne. Optic. **References:** 4, page 2 [1-2]

Cut: 250. Line: 150. Sherbet. Optic. **References:** 4, page 2 [1-3]

Cut: 250. Line: 150. Wine. Optic. **References:** 4, page 2 [1-5]

Cut: 250, Plain Bottom. Line: 558. Tumbler. **References:** 2, fig. 7 [3-4]

Cut: 258. Line: 475. Goblet. Optic. **References:** 4, page 24 [2-1]

Cut: 259. Line: 482. Goblet. Optic. **References:** 4, page 24 [1-2]

Cut: 260. Line: 2. Rose Bowl. Optic. **References:** 4, page 27 [1-2]

Cut: 260. Line: 482. Cocktail. Optic. **References:** 4, page 13 [1-5]

Cut: 260. Line: 482. Cordial. Optic. **References:** 4, page 13 [1-6]

Cut: 260. Line: 482. Footed Tumbler. 2-3/4 oz. Optic. **References:** 4, page 13 [2-1]

Cut: 260. Line: 482. Footed Tumbler. 4 oz. Optic. **References:** 4, page 13 [2-2]

Cut: 260. Line: 482. Footed Tumbler. 6 oz. Optic. **References:** 4, page 13 [2-3]

Cut: 260. Line: 482. Footed Tumbler. 9 oz. Optic. **References:** 4, page 13 [2-4]

Cut: 260. Line: 482. Footed Tumbler. 12 oz. Optic. **References:** 4, page 13 [2-5]

Cut: 260. Line: 482. Goblet. Optic. **References:** 4, page 13 [1-1]

Cut: 260. Line: 482. Saucer Champagne. Optic. **References:** 4, page 13 [1-2]

Cut: 260. Line: 482. Sherbet. Optic. **References:** 4, page 13 [1-3]

Cut: 260. Line: 482. Wine. Optic. **References:** 4, page 13 [1-4]

Cut: 261. Line: 492. Goblet. Optic. **References:** 4, page 24 [1-3]

Cut: 262. Line: 3. Footed Tumbler. 2-3/4 oz. Optic. **References:** 4, page 20 [2-1]

Cut: 262. Line: 3. Footed Tumbler. 4 oz. Optic. **References:** 4, page 20 [2-2]

Cut: 262. Line: 3. Footed Tumbler. 6 oz. Optic. **References:** 4, page 20 [2-3]

Cut: 262. Line: 3. Footed Tumbler. 9 oz. Optic. **References:** 4, page 20 [2-4]

Cut: 262. Line: 3. Footed Tumbler. 12 oz. Optic. **References:** 4, page 20 [2-5]

Cut: 262. Line: 493. Cocktail. Optic. **References:** 4, page 20 [1-5]

Cut: 262. Line: 493. Cordial. Optic. **References:** 4, page 20 [1-6]

Cut: 262. Line: 493. Goblet. Optic. **References:** 4, page 20 [1-1]

Cut: 262. Line: 493. Saucer Champagne. Optic. **References:** 4, page 20 [1-2]

Cut: 262. Line: 493. Sherbet. Optic. **References:** 4, page 20 [1-3]

Cut: 262. Line: 493. Wine. Optic. **References:** 4, page 20 [1-4]

Cut: 267. Line: 903. Finger Bowl. **References:** 4, page 25 [3-1]

Cut: 270, Plain Bottom. Line: 559. Tumbler. **References:** 2, fig. 7 [1-4]

Cut: 273. Line: 6. Footed Tumbler. 2-3/4 oz. Optic. **References:** 4, page 5 [2-1]

Cut: 273. Line: 6. Footed Tumbler. 4 oz. Optic. **References:** 4, page 5 [2-2]

Cut: 273. Line: 6. Footed Tumbler. 6 oz. Optic. **References:** 4, page 5 [2-3]

Cut: 273. Line: 6. Footed Tumbler. 9 oz. Optic. **References:** 4, page 5 [2-4]

Cut: 273. Line: 6. Footed Tumbler. 12 oz. Optic. **References:** 4, page 5 [2-5]

Cut: 273. Line: 260. Cocktail. Optic. **References:** 4, page 5 [1-5]

Cut: 273. Line: 260. Cordial. Optic. **References:** 4, page 5 [1-6]

Cut: 273. Line: 260. Goblet. Optic. **References:** 4, page 5 [1-1]

Cut: 273. Line: 260. Saucer Champagne. Optic. **References:** 4, page 5 [1-2]

Cut: 273. Line: 260. Sherbet. Optic. **References:** 4, page 5 [1-3]

Cut: 273. Line: 260. Wine. Optic. **References:** 4, page 5 [1-4]

Cut: 286. Line: 459. Vase. 8-1/2 inch. Optic. **References:** 4, page 27 [1-1]

Cut: 286. Line: 492. Goblet. Optic. **References:** 4, page 24 [1-1]

Cut: 287. Line: 16. Cream. Optic. **References:** 4, page 25 [1-5]

Cut: 287. Line: 16. Sugar Bowl. Optic. **References:** 4, page 25 [1-4]

Cut: 287. Line: 492. Candlestick. Optic. **References:** 4, page 17 [2-1]

Cut: 287. Line: 492. Cocktail. Optic. **References:** 4, page 17 [1-5]

Cut: 287. Line: 492. Cordial. Optic. **References:** 4, page 17 [1-6]

Cut: 287. Line: 492. Footed Tumbler. 2-3/4 oz. Optic. **References:** 4, page 17 [2-2]

Cut: 287. Line: 492. Footed Tumbler. 4 oz. Optic. **References:** 4, page 17 [2-3]

Cut: 287. Line: 492. Footed Tumbler. 6 oz. Optic. **References:** 4, page 17 [2-4]

Cut: 287. Line: 492. Footed Tumbler. 9 oz. Optic. **References:** 4, page 17 [2-5]

Cut: 287. Line: 492. Footed Tumbler. 12 oz. Optic. **References:** 4, page 17 [2-6]

Cut: 287. Line: 492. Footed Tumbler. 4 oz. Optic. **References:** 4, page 18 [2-2]

Cut: 287. Line: 492. Footed Tumbler. 9 oz. Optic. **References:** 4, page 18 [2-4]

Cut: 287. Line: 492. Goblet. Optic. **References:** 4, page 17 [1-1]

Cut: 287. Line: 492. Saucer Champagne. Optic. **References:** 4, page 17 [1-2]

Cut: 287. Line: 492. Sherbet. Optic. **References:** 4, page 17 [1-3]

Cut: 287. Line: 492. Wine. Optic. **References:** 4, page 17 [1-4]

Cut: 293. Line: 492. Cocktail. Optic. **References:** 4, page 18 [1-5]

Cut: 293. Line: 492. Cordial. Optic. **References:** 4, page 18 [1-6]

Cut: 293. Line: 492. Footed Tumbler. 2-3/4 oz. **References:** 4, page 18 [2-1]

Cut: 293. Line: 492. Footed Tumbler. 6 oz. **References:** 4, page 18 [2-3]

Cut: 293. Line: 492. Footed Tumbler. 12 oz. **References:** 4, page 18 [2-5]

Cut: 293. Line: 492. Goblet. Optic. **References:** 4, page 18 [1-1]

Cut: 293. Line: 492. Saucer Champagne. Optic. **References:** 4, page 18 [1-2]

Cut: 293. Line: 492. Sherbet. Optic. **References:** 4, page 18 [1-3]

Cut: 293. Line: 492. Wine. Optic. **References:** 4, page 18 [1-4]

Cut: 299. Plate. 6-1/4 inch. **References:** 4, page 26 [1-1]

Cut: 299. Line: 492. Cocktail. Optic. **References:** 4, page 19 [1-5]

Cut: 299. Line: 492. Cordial. Optic. **References:** 4, page 19 [1-6]

Cut: 299. Line: 492. Footed Tumbler. 2-3/4 oz. Optic. **References:** 4, page 19 [2-1]

Cut: 299. Line: 492. Footed Tumbler. 4 oz. Optic. **References:** 4, page 19 [2-2]

Cut: 299. Line: 492. Footed Tumbler. 6 oz. Optic. **References:** 4, page 19 [2-3]

Cut: 299. Line: 492. Footed Tumbler. 9 oz. Optic. **References:** 4, page 19 [2-4]

Cut: 299. Line: 492. Footed Tumbler. 12 oz. Optic. **References:** 4, page 19 [2-5]

Cut: 299. Line: 492. Goblet. Optic. **References:** 4, page 19 [1-1]

Cut: 299. Line: 492. Saucer Champagne. Optic. **References:** 4, page 19 [1-2]

Cut: 299. Line: 492. Sherbet. Optic. **References:** 4, page 19 [1-3]

Cut: 299. Line: 492. Wine. Optic. **References:** 4, page 19 [1-4]

Cut: 300. Line: 492. Goblet. Optic. **References:** 4, page 24 [2-3]

Cut: 300, Plain Bottom. Line: 559. Tumbler. **References:** 2, fig. 7 [2-1]

Cut: 308. Line: 492. Goblet. Optic. **References:** 4, page 24 [2-5]

Cut: 308. Line: 8000. Finger Bowl. Optic. **References:** 4, page 25 [3-2]

Cut: 326. Line: 1. Console Bowl. **References:** 4, page 27 [3-2]

Cut: 338. Line: 903. Goblet. Plain. **References:** 4, page 24 [2-4]

Cut: 342. Line: 903. Cocktail. **References:** 4, page 22 [1-5]

Cut: 342. Line: 903. Cordial. **References:** 4, page 22 [1-6]

Cut: 342. Line: 903. Footed Tumbler. 2-1/2 oz. **References:** 4, page 22 [2-1]

Cut: 342. Line: 903. Footed Tumbler. 3-1/2 oz. **References:** 4, page 22 [2-2]

Cut: 342. Line: 903. Footed Tumbler. 5 oz. **References:** 4, page 22 [2-3]

Cut: 342. Line: 903. Footed Tumbler. 9 oz. **References:** 4, page 22 [2-4]

Cut: 342. Line: 903. Footed Tumbler. 12 oz. **References:** 4, page 22 [2-5]

Cut: 342. Line: 903. Goblet. **References:** 4, page 22 [1-1]

Cut: 342. Line: 903. Saucer Champagne. **References:** 4, page 22 [1-2]

Cut: 342. Line: 903. Sherbet. **References:** 4, page 22 [1-3]

Cut: 342. Line: 903. Wine. **References:** 4, page 22 [1-4]

Cut: 350, Star Bottom. Line: 799. Tumbler. **References:** 2, fig. 7 [2-2]

Cut: 358. Line: 258. Cocktail. **References:** 4, page 3 [2-3]

Cut: 358. Line: 258. Cordial. **References:** 4, page 3 [2-1]

Cut: 358. Line: 258. Goblet. **References:** 4, page 3 [2-6]

Cut: 358. Line: 258. Saucer Champagne. **References:** 4, page 3 [2-5]

Cut: 358. Line: 258. Sherbet. **References:** 4, page 3 [2-4]

Cut: 358. Line: 258. Wine. **References:** 4, page 3 [2-2]

Cut: 360. Line: 1. Tankard. 3 Pint. **References:** 2, fig. 4 [2-3]

Cut: 360. Line: 15. Jug. 45 oz. **References:** 2, fig. 6 (p. 43) [2-4]

Cut: 360, Plain Bottom. Line: 557. Tumbler. **References:** 2, fig. 7 [3-2]

Cut: 360. Line: 619. Water Tumbler. **References:** 2, fig. 15 [1-6]

Cut: 360, Star. Line: 1 / 1819. Squat Water Set / Tumblers. **References:** 2, fig. 6 (p. 43) [1-4]

Cut: 361. Line: 20. Jug. 52 oz. **References:** 2, fig. 6 (p. 43) [2-2]

Cut: 367. Square Plate. 9 inch. **References:** 4, page 26 [2-1]

Cut: 367. Line: 259. Cocktail. **References:** 4, page 3 [1-5]

Cut: 367. Line: 259. Cordial. **References:** 4, page 3 [1-6]

Cut: 367. Line: 259. Goblet. **References:** 4, page 3 [1-1]

Cut: 367. Line: 259. Saucer Champagne. **References:** 4, page 3 [1-2]

Cut: 367. Line: 259. Sherbet. **References:** 4, page 3 [1-3]

Cut: 367. Line: 259. Wine. **References:** 4, page 3 [1-4]

Cut: 369. Plate. 8 inch. **References:** 4, page 26 [2-4]

Cut: 369. Line: 484. Cocktail. Optic. **References:** 4, page 14 [1-5]

Cut: 369. Line: 484. Cordial. Optic. **References:** 4, page 14 [1-6]

Cut: 369. Line: 484. Footed Tumbler. 2-3/4 oz. Optic. **References:** 4, page 14 [2-1]

Cut: 369. Line: 484. Footed Tumbler. 4 oz. Optic. **References:** 4, page 14 [2-2]

Cut: 369. Line: 484. Footed Tumbler. 6 oz. Optic. **References:** 4, page 14 [2-3]

Cut: 369. Line: 484. Footed Tumbler. 9 oz. Optic. **References:** 4, page 14 [2-4]

Cut: 369. Line: 484. Footed Tumbler. 12 oz. Optic. **References:** 4, page 14 [2-5]

Cut: 369. Line: 484. Goblet. Optic. **References:** 4, page 14 [1-1]

Cut: 369. Line: 484. Saucer Champagne. Optic. **References:** 4, page 14 [1-2]

Cut: 369. Line: 484. Sherbet. Optic. **References:** 4, page 14 [1-3]

Cut: 369. Line: 484. Wine. Optic. **References:** 4, page 14 [1-4]

Cut: 370. Line: 1. Squat Jug. Half Gallon. **References:** 2, fig. 6 (p. 43) [1-1]

Cut: 370. Line: 481. Cocktail. Optic. **References:** 4, page 10 [1-5]

Cut: 370. Line: 481. Cordial. Optic. **References:** 4, page 10 [1-6]

Cut: 370. Line: 481. Footed Tumbler. 2-3/4 oz. **References:** 4, page 10 [2-1]

Cut: 370. Line: 481. Footed Tumbler. 4 oz. **References:** 4, page 10 [2-2]

Cut: 370. Line: 481. Footed Tumbler. 6 oz. **References:** 4, page 10 [2-3]

Cut: 370. Line: 481. Footed Tumbler. 9 oz. **References:** 4, page 10 [2-4]

Cut: 370. Line: 481. Footed Tumbler. 12 oz. **References:** 4, page 10 [2-5]

Cut: 370. Line: 481. Goblet. Optic. **References:** 4, page 10 [1-1]

Cut: 370. Line: 481. Saucer Champagne. Optic. **References:** 4, page 10 [1-2]

Cut: 370. Line: 481. Sherbet. Optic. **References:** 4, page 10 [1-3]

Cut: 370. Line: 481. Wine. Optic. **References:** 4, page 10 [1-4]

Cut: 370. Line 550? Star bottom tumbler. Rerences: 2, fig. 7 [2-0 partial]

Cut: 371. Line: 499. Goblet. Optic. **References:** 4, page 24 [2-2]

Cut: 373. Line: 499. Cocktail. Optic. **References:** 4, page 21 [1-5]

Cut: 373. Line: 499. Cordial. Optic. **References:** 4, page 21 [1-6]

Cut: 373. Line: 499. Footed Tumbler. 2-3/4 oz. Optic. **References:** 4, page 21 [2-1]

Cut: 373. Line: 499. Footed Tumbler. 4 oz. Optic. **References:** 4, page 21 [2-2]

Cut: 373. Line: 499. Footed Tumbler. 6 oz. Optic. **References:** 4, page 21 [2-3]

Cut: 373. Line: 499. Footed Tumbler. 9 oz. Optic. **References:** 4, page 21 [2-4]

Cut: 373. Line: 499. Footed Tumbler. 12 oz. Optic. **References:** 4, page 21 [2-5]

Cut: 373. Line: 499. Goblet. Optic. **References:** 4, page 21 [1-1]

Cut: 373. Line: 499. Saucer Champagne. Optic. **References:** 4, page 21 [1-2]

Cut: 373. Line: 499. Sherbet. Optic. **References:** 4, page 21 [1-3]

Cut: 373. Line: 499. Wine. Optic. **References:** 4, page 21 [1-4]

Cut: 374. Line: 515. Goblet. Optic. **References:** 4, page 24 [1-5]

Cut: 375, Star Bottom. Line: 559. Tumbler. **References:** 2, fig. 7? [1-2]

Cut: 385, Star Bottom. Line: 799. Tumbler. **References:** 2, fig. 7 [2-3]

Cut: 390, Star Bottom. Line: 799. Tumbler. **References:** 2, fig. 7 [2-4]

Cut: 400, Star Bottom. Line: 799. Tumbler. **References:** 2, fig. 7 [2-5]

Cut: 412, Plain Bottom. Line: 558. Tumbler. **References:** 2, fig. 7 [1-1]

Cut: 414. Line: 4. Lace Point. Bell. 5-1/2 inches tall. All Bells Individually Gift Boxed. **References:** 1976, page 7 [2-4]; 1977, page 23 [4-1]; 1979, page 13 [3-3]

Cut: 420, Star Bottom. Line: 558. Tumbler. **References:** 2, fig. 7 [1-0 partial]

Cut: 463. Etching: 22. Line: 2003. Tumbler. 3-1/4 oz. **References:** 2, fig. 1 [1-1]

Cut: 463. Etching: 22. Line: 2006. Tumbler. 5-1/2 oz. **References:** 2, fig. 1 [1-2]

Cut: 463. Etching: 22. Line: 2009. Tumbler. 6-1/2 oz. **References:** 2, fig. 1 [1-3]

Cut: 463. Etching: 22. Line: 2012. Tumbler. 8 oz. **References:** 2, fig. 1 [1-4]

Cut: 463. Etching: 22. Line: 2018. Tumbler. 10 oz. **References:** 2, fig. 1 [1-5]

Cut: 468. Line: 2. Holland Jug. 3 Pint. **References:** 2, fig. 6 (p. 43) [3-3]

Cut: 503. Line: 1. Tankard. 3 Pint. **References:** 2, fig. 4 [3-1]

Cut: 509. Line: 1. Tankard. 3 Pint. **References:** 2, fig. 4 [1-1]

Cut: 514. Line: 1. Tankard. 3 Pint. **References:** 2, fig. 4 [1-2]

Cut: 533-1/2. Line: 2. Holland Jug. 3 Pint. **References:** 2, fig. 6 (p. 43) [3-2]

Cut: 541. Line: 1. Squat Jug. Half Gallon. **References:** 2, fig. 6 (p. 43) [1-2]

Cut: 541. Line: 1. Tankard. 4 Pint. **References:** 2, fig. 4 [1-3]

Cut: 541-1/2. Line: 1. Tankard. 3 Pint. **References:** 2, fig. 4 [3-2]

Cut: 546. Line: 1. Squat Jug. Half Gallon. **References:** 2, fig. 6 (p. 43) [2-1]

Cut: 553. Line: 1. Tankard. 2 Pint. **References:** 2, fig. 4 [1-4]

Cut: 554. Line: 1. Tankard. 4 Pint. **References:** 2, fig. 4 [1-5]

Cut: 560. Line: 1. Tankard. 3 Pint. **References:** 2, fig. 4 [3-3]

Cut: 561. Line: 1. Tankard. 3 Pint. **References:** 2, fig. 6 (p. 43) [3-1]

Cut: 561. Line: 2000. Tumbler. 2-1/2 oz. **References:** 2, fig. 1 [2-5]

Cut: 561. Line: 2003. Tumbler. 3-1/4 oz. **References:** 2, fig. 1 [2-4]

Cut: 561. Line: 2006. Tumbler. 5-1/2 oz. **References:** 2, fig. 1 [2-3]

Cut: 561. Line: 2009. Tumbler. 6-1/2 oz. **References:** 2, fig. 1 [2-2]

Cut: 561. Line: 2012. Tumbler. 8 oz. **References:** 2, fig. 1 [2-1]

Cut: 632. Line: 3. Candlestick. D.E. **References:** 4, page 34 [3-1]; 4, page 34 [3-3]

Cut: 632. Line: 3. Console Bowl. D.E. **References:** 4, page 34 [3-2]

Cut: 632. Line: 265. Finger Bowl. Optic, D.E. **References:** 4, page 34 [1-4]

Cut: 632. Line: 484. Claret. Optic, D.E. **References:** 4, page 34 [2-4]

Cut: 632. Line: 484. Cocktail. Optic, D.E. **References:** 4, page 34 [2-2]

Cut: 632. Line: 484. Cordial. Optic, D.E. **References:** 4, page 34 [1-2]

Cut: 632. Line: 484. Footed Tumbler. 12 oz. Optic, D.E. **References:** 4, page 34 [2-6]

Cut: 632. Line: 484. Goblet. Optic, D.E. **References:** 4, page 25 [1-1]; 4, page 34 [1-1]

Cut: 632. Line: 484. Parfait. Optic, D.E. **References:** 4, page 34 [2-5]

Cut: 632. Line: 484. Saucer Champagne. Optic, D.E. **References:** 4, page 34 [2-1]

Cut: 632. Line: 484. Sherbet. Optic, D.E. **References:** 4, page 34 [1-3]

Cut: 632. Line: 484. Wine. Optic, D.E. **References:** 4, page 34 [2-3]

Cut: 634. Line: 1. Console Bowl. 12 inch. D.E. **References:** 4, page 36 [4-2]

Cut: 634. Line: 30. Candlestick. Optic, D.E. **References:** 4, page 36 [4-1]

Cut: 634. Line: 30. Candlestick. D.E. **References:** 4, page 36 [4-3]

Cut: 634. Line: 499. Cocktail. Optic, D.E. **References:** 4, page 36 [3-4]

Cut: 634. Line: 499. Cordial. Optic, D.E. **References:** 4, page 36 [1-3]; 4, page 36 [2-2]

Cut: 634. Line: 499. Finger Bowl. Optic, D.E. **References:** 4, page 36 [1-1]

Cut: 634. Line: 499. Footed Tumbler. 12 oz. Optic, D.E. **References:** 4, page 36 [2-4]

Cut: 634. Line: 499. Goblet. Optic, D.E. **References:** 4, page 36 [2-1]

Cut: 634. Line: 499. Parfait. Optic, D.E. **References:** 4, page 36 [3-3]

Cut: 634. Line: 499. Saucer Champagne. Optic, D.E. **References:** 4, page 36 [3-1]

Cut: 634. Line: 499. Sherbet. Optic, D.E. **References:** 4, page 36 [3-2]

Cut: 634. Line: 499. Wine. Optic, D.E. **References:** 4, page 36 [2-3]

Cut: 636. Line: 3. Stratford. Bell. 4-3/8 inches tall. Handmade and Hand Cut. **References:** 1975, page 12 [2-4]; 1976, page 6 [2-2]; 1977, page 22 [2-2]

Cut: 636. Line: 4. Stratford. Bell. 5-1/2 inches tall. **References:** 1979, page 12 [3-1]

Cut: 636. Line: 476. Stratford. 1311 Dessert-Finger Bowl. 4-3/4 inches diam. **References:** 1967, page 19 [1-9]; 1969, page 23 [2-20]; 1970, page 24 [2-20]; 1971, page 24 [2-20]

Cut: 636. Line: 476. Stratford. Claret. 3-1/2 oz. 6-1/8 inches tall. **References:** 1967, page 19 [1-3]; 1969, page 23 [2-14]; 1970, page 24 [2-14]; 1971, page 24 [2-14]

Cut: 636. Line: 476. Stratford. Cocktail. 3 oz. 5-1/4 inches tall. **References:** 1967, page 19 [1-5]; 1969, page 23 [2-16]; 1970, page 24 [2-16]; 1970, page 24 [2-16]; 1971, page 24 [2-16]; 1971, page 24 [2-16]

Cut: 636. Line: 476. Stratford. Cordial. 1 oz. 4-3/4 inches tall. **References:** 1967, page 19 [1-6]; 1969, page 23 [2-17]

Cut: 636. Line: 476. Stratford. Goblet. 9 oz. 8-3/8 inches tall. **References:** 1967, page 19 [1-1]; 1969, page 23 [2-12]; 1970, page 24 [2-12]; 1971, page 24 [2-12]

Cut: 636. Line: 476. Stratford. Ice Tea. 12 oz. 7-1/4 inches tall. **References:** 1967, page 19 [1-8]; 1969, page 23 [2-19]; 1970, page 24 [2-19]; 1971, page 24 [2-19]

Cut: 636. Line: 476. Stratford. Juice. 5-1/2 oz. 5-3/4 inches tall. **References:** 1967, page 19 [1-7]; 1969, page 23 [2-18]; 1970, page 24 [2-18]; 1971, page 24 [2-18]

Cut: 636. Line: 476. Stratford. Plate. 7 inches diam. Actually 7-7/8" Dia. **References:** 1967, page 19 [1-10]; 1969, page 23 [2-21]; 1970, page 24 [2-21]; 1971, page 24 [2-21]

Cut: 636. Line: 476. Stratford. Plate. 8 inches diam. Actually 8-3/4" Dia. **References:** 1967, page 19 [1-11]; 1969, page 23 [2-22]; 1970, page 24 [2-22]; 1971, page 24 [2-22]

Cut: 636. Line: 476. Stratford. Saucer Champagne. 6 oz. 6-1/2 inches tall. **References:** 1967, page 19 [1-2]; 1969, page 23 [2-13]; 1970, page 24 [2-13]; 1971, page 24 [2-13]

Cut: 636. Line: 476. Stratford. Wine. 3 oz. 6 inches tall. **References:** 1967, page 19 [1-4]; 1969, page 23 [2-15]; 1970, page 24 [2-15]; 1971, page 24 [2-15]

Cut: 654. Line: 1. Tankard. 3 Pint. **References:** 2, fig. 4 [3-4]

Cut: 848. Line: 3. Bell. 4-3/8 inches tall. Hand Made and Hand Cut Lead Crystal Silver and Gold Plated. Bells individually Gift Boxed. **References:** 1978, page 5 [2-1]

Cut: 848. Line: 4. Bell. 5-1/2 inches tall. Hand Made and Hand Cut Lead Crystal Silver and Gold Plated. **References:** 1978, page 5 [2-2]

Cut: 859. Line: 908. Rennaissance. 1311 Dessert-Finger Bowl. 4-3/4 inches diam. **References:** 1967, page 20 [2-18]; 1969, page 22 [2-18]; 1970, page 23 [2-18]; 1971, page 23 [2-18]

Cut: 859. Line: 908. Rennaissance. Claret. 3-1/2 oz. 4-3/8 inches tall. **References:** 1967, page 20 [2-13]; 1969, page 22 [2-13]; 1970, page 23 [2-13]; 1971, page 23 [2-13]

Cut: 859. Line: 908. Rennaissance. Cocktail. 3 oz. 4-5/8 inches tall. **References:** 1967, page 20 [2-14]; 1969, page 22 [2-14]; 1970, page 23 [2-14]; 1971, page 23 [2-14]

Cut: 859. Line: 908. Rennaissance. Cordial. 1 oz. 3-1/4 inches tall. **References:** 1967, page 20 [2-15]; 1969, page 22 [2-15]; 1970, page 23 [2-15]; 1971, page 23 [2-15]

Cut: 859. Line: 908. Rennaissance. Goblet. 9 oz. 6 inches tall. **References:** 1967, page 20 [2-11]; 1969, page 22 [2-11]; 1970, page 23 [2-11]; 1971, page 23 [2-11]

Cut: 859. Line: 908. Rennaissance. Ice Tea. 10-1/2 oz. 5-5/8 inches tall. **References:** 1967, page 20 [2-17]; 1969, page 22 [2-17]; 1970, page 23 [2-17]; 1971, page 23 [2-17]

Cut: 859. Line: 908. Rennaissance. Juice. 5 oz. 4-3/8 inches tall. **References:** 1967, page 20 [2-16]; 1969, page 22 [2-16]; 1970, page 23 [2-16]; 1971, page 23 [2-16]

Cut: 859. Line: 908. Rennaissance. Plate. 7 inches diam. Actually 7-7/8" Dia. **References:** 1967, page 20 [2-19]; 1969, page 22 [2-19]; 1970, page 23 [2-19]; 1971, page 23 [2-19]

Cut: 859. Line: 908. Rennaissance. Plate. 8 inches diam. Actually 8-3/4" Dia. **References:** 1967, page 20 [2-20]; 1969, page 22 [2-20]; 1970, page 23 [2-20]; 1971, page 23 [2-20]

Cut: 859. Line: 908. Rennaissance. Saucer Champagne. 7 oz. 4-3/4 inches tall. **References:** 1967, page 20 [2-12]; 1969, page 22 [2-12]; 1970, page 23 [2-12]; 1971, page 23 [2-12]

Cut: 879. Line: 908. Waterford. 1311 Dessert-Finger Bowl. 4-3/4 inches diam. **References:** 1967, page 20 [2-8]; 1969, page 22 [2-8]; 1970, page 23 [2-8]; 1971, page 23 [2-8]

Cut: 879. Line: 908. Waterford. Claret. 3-1/2 oz. 4-3/8 inches tall. **References:** 1967, page 20 [2-3]; 1969, page 22 [2-3]; 1970, page 23 [2-3]; 1971, page 23 [2-3]

Cut: 879. Line: 908. Waterford. Cocktail. 3 oz. 4-5/8 inches tall. **References:** 1967, page 20 [2-4]; 1969, page 22 [2-4]; 1970, page 23 [2-4]; 1971, page 23 [2-4]

Cut: 879. Line: 908. Waterford. Cordial. 1 oz. 3-1/4 inches tall. **References:** 1967, page 20 [2-5]; 1969, page 22 [2-5]; 1970, page 23 [2-5]; 1971, page 23 [2-5]

Cut: 879. Line: 908. Waterford. Goblet. 9 oz. 6 inches tall. **References:** 1967, page 20 [2-1]; 1969, page 22 [2-1]; 1970, page 23 [2-1]; 1971, page 23 [2-1]

Cut: 879. Line: 908. Waterford. Ice Tea. 10-1/2 oz. 5-5/8 inches tall. **References:** 1967, page 20 [2-7]; 1969, page 22 [2-7]; 1970, page 23 [2-7]; 1971, page 23 [2-7]

Cut: 879. Line: 908. Waterford. Juice. 5 oz. 4-3/8 inches tall. **References:** 1967, page 20 [2-6]; 1969, page 22 [2-6]; 1970, page 23 [2-6]; 1971, page 23 [2-6]

Cut: 879. Line: 908. Waterford. Plate. 7 inches diam. Actually 7-7/8" Dia. **References:** 1967, page 20 [2-9]; 1969, page 22 [2-9]; 1970, page 23 [2-9]

Cut: 879. Line: 908. Waterford. Plate. 8 inches diam. Actually 8-3/4" Dia. **References:** 1967, page 20 [2-10]; 1969, page 22 [2-10]; 1970, page 23 [2-10]; 1971, page 23 [2-9]; 1971, page 23 [2-10]

Cut: 879. Line: 908. Waterford. Saucer Champagne. 7 oz. 4-3/4 inches tall. **References:** 1967, page 20 [2-2]; 1969, page 22 [2-2]; 1970, page 23 [2-2]; 1971, page 23 [2-2]

Cut: 900. Line: 476. Windblown. 1311 Dessert-Finger Bowl. 4-3/4 inches diam. **References:** 1967, page 19 [2-20]

Cut: 900. Line: 476. Windblown. Claret. 3-1/2 oz. 6-1/8 inches tall. **References:** 1967, page 19 [2-14]

Cut: 900. Line: 476. Windblown. Cocktail. 3 oz. 5-1/4 inches tall. **References:** 1967, page 19 [2-16]

Cut: 900. Line: 476. Windblown. Cordial. 1 oz. 4-3/4 inches tall. **References:** 1967, page 19 [2-17]

Cut: 900. Line: 476. Windblown. Goblet. 9 oz. 8-3/8 inches tall. **References:** 1967, page 19 [2-12]

Cut: 900. Line: 476. Windblown. Ice Tea. 12 oz. 7-1/4 inches tall. **References:** 1967, page 19 [2-19]

Cut: 900. Line: 476. Windblown. Juice. 5-1/2 oz. 5-3/4 inches tall. **References:** 1967, page 19 [2-18]

Cut: 900. Line: 476. Windblown. Plate. 7 inches diam. Actually 7-7/8" Dia. **References:** 1967, page 19 [2-21]

Cut: 900. Line: 476. Windblown. Plate. 8 inches diam. Actually 8-3/4" Dia. **References:** 1967, page 19 [2-22]

Cut: 900. Line: 476. Windblown. Saucer Champagne. 6 oz. 6-1/2 inches tall. **References:** 1967, page 19 [2-13]

Cut: 900. Line: 476. Windblown. Wine. 3 oz. 6 inches tall. **References:** 1967, page 19 [2-15]

Cut: 958. Line: 80. Ginger Jar. **References:** 1980, page 4 [1-1]

Cut: 958. Line: 80. Harvest. Ginger Jar. 6-1/4 inches tall. **References:** 1981, page 10 [2-1]

Cut: 958. Line: 90. Harvest. Ginger Jar. 8-1/2 inches tall. **References:** 1980, page 3 [2-2]; 1981, page 10 [1-1]

Cut: 960. Line: 80. Ginger Jar. **References:** 1980, page 4 [1-2]

Cut: 960. Line: 80. Butterfly. Ginger Jar. 6-1/4 inches tall. **References:** 1981, page 10 [2-3]

Cut: 960. Line: 90. Butterfly. Ginger Jar. 8-1/2 inches tall. **References:** 1980, page 3 [2-1]; 1981, page 10 [1-3]

Cut: 967. Line: 476. Elegance. 1311 Dessert-Finger Bowl. 4-3/4 inches diam. **References:** 1967, page 19 [2-9]; 1969, page 23 [2-9]; 1970, page 24 [2-9]; 1971, page 24 [2-9]

Cut: 967. Line: 476. Elegance. Claret. 3-1/2 oz. 6-1/

8 inches tall. **References:** 1967, page 19 [2-3]; 1969, page 23 [2-3]; 1970, page 24 [2-3]; 1971, page 24 [2-3]

Cut: 967. Line: 476. Elegance. Cocktail. 3 oz. 5-1/4 inches tall. **References:** 1967, page 19 [2-5]; 1969, page 23 [2-5]; 1970, page 24 [2-5]; 1971, page 24 [2-5]

Cut: 967. Line: 476. Elegance. Cordial. 1 oz. 4-3/4 inches tall. **References:** 1967, page 19 [2-6]; 1969, page 23 [2-6]; 1970, page 24 [2-6]; 1971, page 24 [2-6]

Cut: 967. Line: 476. Elegance. Goblet. 9 oz. 8-3/8 inches tall. **References:** 1967, page 19 [2-1]; 1969, page 23 [2-1]; 1970, page 24 [2-1]; 1971, page 24 [2-1]

Cut: 967. Line: 476. Elegance. Ice Tea. 12 oz. 7-1/4 inches tall. **References:** 1967, page 19 [2-8]; 1969, page 23 [2-8]; 1970, page 24 [2-8]; 1971, page 24 [2-8]

Cut: 967. Line: 476. Elegance. Juice. 5-1/2 oz. 5-3/4 inches tall. **References:** 1967, page 19 [2-7]; 1969, page 23 [2-7]; 1970, page 24 [2-7]; 1971, page 24 [2-7]

Cut: 967. Line: 476. Elegance. Plate. 7 inches diam. Actually 7-7/8" Dia. **References:** 1967, page 19 [2-10]; 1969, page 23 [2-10]; 1970, page 24 [2-10]; 1971, page 24 [2-10]

Cut: 967. Line: 476. Elegance. Plate. 8 inches diam. Actually 8-3/4" Dia. **References:** 1967, page 19 [2-11]; 1969, page 23 [2-11]; 1970, page 24 [2-11]; 1971, page 24 [2-11]

Cut: 967. Line: 476. Elegance. Saucer Champagne. 6 oz. 6-1/2 inches tall. **References:** 1967, page 19 [2-2]; 1969, page 23 [2-2]; 1970, page 24 [2-2]; 1971, page 24 [2-2]

Cut: 967. Line: 476. Elegance. Wine. 3 oz. 6 inches tall. **References:** 1967, page 19 [2-4]; 1969, page 23 [2-4]; 1970, page 24 [2-4]; 1971, page 24 [2-4]

Cut: 980. Line: 4. La Belle. Bell. 5-1/2 inches tall. All Bells Individually Gift Boxed. **References:** 1976, page 7 [2-1]; 1977, page 23 [5-1]; 1979, page 13 [2-1]

Cut: 1006. Line: 912. Ramona. 1311 Dessert-Finger Bowl. 4-3/4 inches diam. **References:** 1967, page 17 [2-8]; 1968, page 21 [2-8]; 1969, page 21 [2-8]; 1970, page 22 [2-8]; 1971, page 22 [2-8]

Cut: 1006. Line: 912. Ramona. Claret. 4 oz. 4-3/4 inches tall. **References:** 1967, page 17 [2-3]; 1968, page 21 [2-3]; 1969, page 21 [2-3]; 1970, page 22 [2-3]; 1971, page 22 [2-3]

Cut: 1006. Line: 912. Ramona. Cocktail. 3-1/2 oz. 4-3/8 inches tall. **References:** 1967, page 17 [2-4]; 1968, page 21 [2-4]; 1969, page 21 [2-4]; 1970, page 22 [2-4]; 1971, page 22 [2-4]

Cut: 1006. Line: 912. Ramona. Cordial. 1 oz. 3-5/8 inches tall. **References:** 1967, page 17 [2-5]; 1968, page 21 [2-5]; 1969, page 21 [2-5]; 1970, page 22 [2-5]; 1971, page 22 [2-5]

Cut: 1006. Line: 912. Ramona. Goblet. 10 oz. 6-1/4 inches tall. **References:** 1967, page 17 [2-1]; 1968, page 21 [2-1]; 1969, page 21 [2-1]; 1970, page 22 [2-1]; 1971, page 22 [2-1]

Cut: 1006. Line: 912. Ramona. Ice Tea. 12 oz. 6 inches tall. **References:** 1967, page 17 [2-7]; 1968, page 21 [2-7]; 1969, page 21 [2-7]; 1970, page 22 [2-7]; 1971, page 22 [2-7]

Cut: 1006. Line: 912. Ramona. Juice. 6 oz. 4-5/8 inches tall. **References:** 1967, page 17 [2-6]; 1968, page 21 [2-6]; 1969, page 21 [2-6]; 1970, page 22 [2-6]; 1971, page 22 [2-6]

Cut: 1006. Line: 912. Ramona. Plate. 7 inches diam. Actually 7-7/8" Dia. **References:** 1967, page 17 [2-9]; 1968, page 21 [2-9]; 1969, page 21 [2-9]; 1971, page 22 [2-9]

Cut: 1006. Line: 912. Ramona. Plate. 8 inches diam. Actually 8-3/4" Dia. **References:** 1967, page 17 [2-10]; 1968, page 21 [2-10]; 1969, page 21 [2-10]; 1970, page 22 [2-10]; 1971, page 22 [2-10]

Cut: 1006. Line: 912. Ramona. Saucer Champagne. 7-1/2 oz. 5-1/8 inches tall. **References:** 1967, page 17 [2-2]; 1968, page 21 [2-2]; 1969, page 21 [2-2]; 1970, page 22 [2-2]; 1971, page 22 [2-2]

Cut: 1120. Line: 1282. Dayton. 1305 Dessert-Finger Bowl. 4-1/2" Dia. **References:** 1967, page 9 [1-16]; 1969, page 15 [1-16]; 1970, page 16 [1-16]; 1971, page 16 [1-16]; 1972, page 25 [1-16]; 1973, page 30 [1-16]; 1975, page 28 [1-14]; 1977, page 39 [1-14]

Cut: 1120. Line: 1282. Dayton. Cordial. 1-1/4 oz. / 3-3/4" hi. **References:** 1967, page 9 [1-13]; 1969, page 15 [1-13]; 1970, page 16 [1-13]; 1971, page 16 [1-13]; 1972, page 25 [1-13];

1973, page 30 [1-13]; 1975, page 28 [1-12]; 1977, page 39 [1-12]; 1981, page 2 [3-12]

Cut: 1120. Line: 1282. Dayton. Goblet. 10 oz. / 7" hi. **References:** 1967, page 9 [1-10]; 1969, page 15 [1-10]; 1970, page 16 [1-10]; 1971, page 16 [1-10]; 1972, page 25 [1-10]; 1973, page 30 [1-10]; 1975, page 28 [1-9]; 1977, page 39 [1-9]; 1981, page 2 [3-9]

Cut: 1120. Line: 1282. Dayton. Ice Tea. 11-1/2 oz. / 6-1/8" hi. **References:** 1967, page 9 [1-15]; 1969, page 15 [1-15]; 1970, page 16 [1-15]; 1971, page 16 [1-15]; 1972, page 25 [1-15]; 1973, page 30 [1-15]; 1975, page 28 [1-13]; 1977, page 39 [1-13]

Cut: 1120. Line: 1282. Dayton. Juice. 5 oz. / 4-1/2 hi. **References:** 1967, page 9 [1-14]; 1969, page 15 [1-14]; 1970, page 16 [1-14]; 1971, page 16 [1-14]; 1972, page 25 [1-14]; 1973, page 30 [1-14]

Cut: 1120. Line: 1282. Dayton. Plate. 7" / Actually 7-7/8" Dia. **References:** 1967, page 9 [1-17]; 1969, page 15 [1-17]; 1970, page 16 [1-17]; 1971, page 16 [1-17]; 1972, page 25 [1-17]; 1973, page 30 [1-17]; 1975, page 28 [1-15]; 1977, page 39 [1-15]

Cut: 1120. Line: 1282. Dayton. Plate. 8" / Actually 8-3/4" Dia. **References:** 1967, page 9 [1-18]; 1969, page 15 [1-18]; 1970, page 16 [1-18]; 1975, page 28 [1-16]; 1977, page 39 [1-16]

Cut: 1120. Line: 1282. Dayton. Saucer Champagne. 7-1/2 oz. / 5-1/4" hi. **References:** 1967, page 9 [1-11]; 1969, page 15 [1-11]; 1970, page 16 [1-11]; 1971, page 16 [1-11]; 1972, page 25 [1-11]; 1973, page 30 [1-11]; 1975, page 28 [1-10]; 1977, page 39 [1-10]; 1981, page 2 [3-10]

Cut: 1120. Line: 1282. Dayton. Table Wine Goblet. 7-1/2 oz. / 6" hi. **References:** 1967, page 9 [1-12]; 1969, page 15 [1-12]; 1970, page 16 [1-12]; 1971, page 16 [1-12]; 1972, page 25 [1-12]; 1973, page 30 [1-12]; 1975, page 28 [1-11]; 1977, page 39 [1-11]

Cut: 1120. Line: 1282. Dayton. Wine. 7-1/2 oz. 6 inches tall. **References:** 1981, page 2 [3-11]

Cut: 1213. Line: 307. Arcadia. 1305 Dessert-Finger Bowl. 4-1/2 inches diam. Twisted Stem. **References:** 1967, page 16 [1-18]; 1968, page 20 [1-18]

Cut: 1213. Line: 307. Arcadia. Claret. 3-3/4 oz. 4-1/2 inches tall. Twisted Stem. **References:** 1967, page 16 [1-13]; 1968, page 20 [1-13]

Cut: 1213. Line: 307. Arcadia. Cocktail. 4 oz. 3-7/8 inches tall. Twisted Stem. **References:** 1967, page 16 [1-14]; 1968, page 20 [1-14]

Cut: 1213. Line: 307. Arcadia. Cordial. 1-1/4 oz. 3-3/8 inches tall. Twisted Stem. 1968, page 20 [1-15]

Cut: 1213. Line: 307. Arcadia. Goblet. 10-1/2 oz. 6 inches tall. Twisted Stem. **References:** 1967, page 16 [1-11]; 1968, page 20 [1-11]

Cut: 1213. Line: 307. Arcadia. Ice Tea. 12 oz. 6-3/4 inches tall. Twisted Stem. **References:** 1967, page 16 [1-17]; 1968, page 20 [1-17]

Cut: 1213. Line: 307. Arcadia. Juice. 5 oz. 5-1/8 inches tall. Twisted Stem. **References:** 1967, page 16 [1-16]; 1968, page 20 [1-16]

Cut: 1213. Line: 307. Arcadia. Plate. 7 inches diam. Twisted Stem, Actually 7-7/8" Dia. **References:** 1967, page 16 [1-19]; 1968, page 20 [1-19]

Cut: 1213. Line: 307. Arcadia. Plate. 8 inches diam. Twisted Stem, Actually 8-3/4" Dia. **References:** 1967, page 16 [1-20]; 1968, page 20 [1-20]

Cut: 1213. Line: 307. Arcadia. Sherbet. 5-1/2 oz. 4-1/2 inches tall. Twisted Stem. **References:** 1967, page 16 [1-12]; 1968, page 20 [1-12]

Cut: 1229. Line: 352. Caprice. 1311 Dessert-Finger Bowl. 4-3/4 inches diam. **References:** 1967, page 18 [1-8]; 1968, page 22 [1-8]; 1969, page 23 [1-8]; 1970, page 24 [1-8]; 1971, page 24 [1-8]

Cut: 1229. Line: 352. Caprice. Claret. 3-3/4 oz. 5-5/8 inches tall. **References:** 1967, page 18 [1-3]; 1968, page 22 [1-3]; 1969, page 23 [1-3]; 1970, page 24 [1-3]; 1971, page 24 [1-3]

Cut: 1229. Line: 352. Caprice. Cocktail. 3 oz. 4-1/4 inches tall. **References:** 1967, page 18 [1-4]; 1968, page 22 [1-4]; 1969, page 23 [1-4]; 1970, page 24 [1-4]; 1971, page 24 [1-4]

Cut: 1229. Line: 352. Caprice. Cordial. 1 oz. 4 inches tall. **References:** 1967, page 18 [1-5]; 1968, page 22 [1-5]; 1969, page 23 [1-5]; 1970, page 24 [1-5]; 1971, page 24 [1-5]

Cut: 1229. Line: 352. Caprice. Goblet. 9 oz. 7-1/4 inches tall. **References:** 1967, page 18 [1-1]; 1968, page 22 [1-1]; 1969, page 23 [1-1]; 1970, page 24 [1-1]; 1971, page 24 [1-1]

Cut: 1229. Line: 352. Caprice. Ice Tea. 12 oz. 7-1/4 inches tall. **References:** 1967, page 18 [1-7]; 1968, page 22 [1-7]; 1969, page 23 [1-7]; 1970, page 24 [1-7]; 1971, page 24 [1-7]

Cut: 1229. Line: 352. Caprice. Juice. 5-1/2 oz. 5-3/8 inches tall. **References:** 1967, page 18 [1-6]; 1968, page 22 [1-6]; 1969, page 23 [1-6]; 1970, page 24 [1-6]; 1971, page 24 [1-6]

Cut: 1229. Line: 352. Caprice. Plate. 7 inches diam. Actually 7-7/8" Dia. **References:** 1967, page 18 [1-9]; 1968, page 22 [1-9]; 1969, page 23 [1-9]; 1970, page 24 [1-9]; 1971, page 24 [1-9]

Cut: 1229. Line: 352. Caprice. Plate. 8 inches diam. Actually 8-3/4" Dia. **References:** 1967, page 18 [1-10]; 1968, page 22 [1-10]; 1969, page 23 [1-10]; 1970, page 24 [1-10]; 1971, page 24 [1-10]

Cut: 1229. Line: 352. Caprice. Sherbet. 6 oz. 5-3/8 inches tall. **References:** 1967, page 18 [1-2]; 1968, page 22 [1-2]; 1969, page 23 [1-2]; 1970, page 24 [1-2]; 1971, page 24 [1-2]

Cut: 1262. Line: 352. Ardis. 1311 Dessert-Finger Bowl. 4-3/4 inches diam. **References:** 1967, page 18 [2-8]; 1968, page 22 [2-8]

Cut: 1262. Line: 352. Ardis. Claret. 3-3/4 oz. 5-5/8 inches tall. **References:** 1967, page 18 [2-3]; 1968, page 22 [2-3]

Cut: 1262. Line: 352. Ardis. Cocktail. 3 oz. 4-1/4 inches tall. **References:** 1967, page 18 [2-4]; 1968, page 22 [2-4]

Cut: 1262. Line: 352. Ardis. Cordial. 1 oz. 4 inches tall. **References:** 1967, page 18 [2-5]; 1968, page 22 [2-5]

Cut: 1262. Line: 352. Ardis. Goblet. 9 oz. 7-1/4 inches tall. **References:** 1967, page 18 [2-1]; 1968, page 22 [2-1]

Cut: 1262. Line: 352. Ardis. Ice Tea. 12 oz. 7-1/4 inches tall. **References:** 1967, page 18 [2-7]; 1968, page 22 [2-7]

Cut: 1262. Line: 352. Ardis. Juice. 5-1/2 oz. 5-3/8 inches tall. **References:** 1967, page 18 [2-6]; 1968, page 22 [2-6]

Cut: 1262. Line: 352. Ardis. Plate. 7 inches diam. Actually 7-7/8" Dia. **References:** 1967, page 18 [2-9]; 1968, page 22 [2-9]

Cut: 1262. Line: 352. Ardis. Plate. 8 inches diam. Actually 8-3/4" Dia. **References:** 1967, page 18 [2-10]; 1968, page 22 [2-10]

Cut: 1262. Line: 352. Ardis. Sherbet. 6 oz. 5-3/8 inches tall. **References:** 1967, page 18 [2-2]; 1968, page 22 [2-2]

Cut: 1263. Line: 352. Westwind. 1311 Dessert-Finger Bowl. 4-3/4 inches diam. **References:** 1967, page 18 [2-18]; 1968, page 22 [2-18]

Cut: 1263. Line: 352. Westwind. Claret. 3-3/4 oz. 5-5/8 inches tall. **References:** 1967, page 18 [2-13]; 1968, page 22 [2-13]

Cut: 1263. Line: 352. Westwind. Cocktail. 3 oz. 4-1/4 inches tall. **References:** 1967, page 18 [2-14]; 1968, page 22 [2-14]

Cut: 1263. Line: 352. Westwind. Cordial. 1 oz. 4 inches tall. **References:** 1967, page 18 [2-15]; 1968, page 22 [2-15]

Cut: 1263. Line: 352. Westwind. Goblet. 9 oz. 7-1/4 inches tall. **References:** 1967, page 18 [2-11]; 1968, page 22 [2-11]

Cut: 1263. Line: 352. Westwind. Ice Tea. 12 oz. 7-1/4 inches tall. **References:** 1967, page 18 [2-17]; 1968, page 22 [2-17]

Cut: 1263. Line: 352. Westwind. Juice. 5-1/2 oz. 5-3/8 inches tall. **References:** 1967, page 18 [2-16]; 1968, page 22 [2-16]

Cut: 1263. Line: 352. Westwind. Plate. 7 inches diam. Actually 7-7/8" Dia. **References:** 1967, page 18 [2-19]; 1968, page 22 [2-19]

Cut: 1263. Line: 352. Westwind. Plate. 8 inches diam. Actually 8-3/4" Dia. **References:** 1967, page 18 [2-20]; 1968, page 22 [2-20]

Cut: 1263. Line: 352. Westwind. Sherbet. 6 oz. 5-3/8 inches tall. **References:** 1967, page 18 [2-12]; 1968, page 22 [2-12]

Cut: 1274. Line: 128. Martha Washington. 1311 Dessert-Finger Bowl. 4-3/4 inches diam. **References:** 1967, page 20 [1-8]; 1969, page 22 [1-9]; 1970, page 23 [1-9]; 1971, page 23 [1-9]; 1967, page 20 [1-3]

Cut: 1274. Line: 128. Martha Washington. Claret. 4 oz. 4-3/8 inches tall. **References:** 1969, page 22 [1-3]; 1970, page 23 [1-3]; 1971, page 23 [1-3]

Cut: 1274. Line: 128. Martha Washington. Cocktail. 3-1/2 oz. 4-1/8 inches tall. **References:** 1967, page 20 [1-4]; 1969, page 22 [1-5]; 1970, page 23 [1-5]; 1971, page 23 [1-5]

Cut: 1274. Line: 128. Martha Washington. Cordial. 1-1/4 oz. 3-1/4 inches tall. **References:** 1967,

page 20 [1-5]; 1969, page 22 [1-6]; 1970, page 23 [1-6]; 1971, page 23 [1-6]

Cut: 1274. Line: 128. Martha Washington. Goblet. 10-1/2 oz. 6-1/8 inches tall. **References:** 1967, page 20 [1-1]; 1969, page 22 [1-1]; 1970, page 23 [1-1]; 1971, page 23 [1-1]

Cut: 1274. Line: 128. Martha Washington. Ice Tea. 12 oz. 6-3/4 inches tall. **References:** 1967, page 20 [1-7]; 1969, page 22 [1-8]; 1970, page 23 [1-8]; 1971, page 23 [1-8]

Cut: 1274. Line: 128. Martha Washington. Juice. 5 oz. 5-1/4 inches tall. **References:** 1967, page 20 [1-6]; 1969, page 22 [1-7]; 1970, page 23 [1-7]; 1971, page 23 [1-7]

Cut: 1274. Line: 128. Martha Washington. Plate. 7 inches diam. Actually 7-7/8" Dia. **References:** 1967, page 20 [1-9]; 1969, page 22 [1-10]; 1970, page 23 [1-10]; 1971, page 23 [1-10]

Cut: 1274. Line: 128. Martha Washington. Plate. 8 inches diam. Actually 8-3/4" Dia. **References:** 1967, page 20 [1-10]; 1969, page 22 [1-11]; 1970, page 23 [1-11]; 1971, page 23 [1-11]

Cut: 1274. Line: 128. Martha Washington. Sherbet. 7-1/2 oz. 4-3/4 inches tall. **References:** 1967, page 20 [1-2]; 1969, page 22 [1-2]; 1970, page 23 [1-2]; 1971, page 23 [1-2]

Cut: 1274. Line: 128. Martha Washington. Table Wine Goblet. 5-3/4 oz. 5-1/8 inches tall. **References:** 1969, page 22 [1-4]; 1970, page 23 [1-4]; 1971, page 23 [1-4]

Cut: 1300. Line: 331. Corinthian. 1305 Dessert-Finger Bowl. 4-1/2 inches diam. **References:** 1967, page 21 [1-8]; 1968, page 25 [1-8]; 1969, page 24 [1-8]; 1970, page 25 [1-8]; 1971, page 25 [1-8]

Cut: 1300. Line: 331. Corinthian. Claret. 4 oz. 5 inches tall. **References:** 1967, page 21 [1-3]; 1968, page 25 [1-3]; 1969, page 24 [1-3]; 1970, page 25 [1-3]; 1971, page 25 [1-3]

Cut: 1300. Line: 331. Corinthian. Cocktail. 4-1/4 oz. 4-1/8 inches tall. **References:** 1967, page 21 [1-4]; 1968, page 25 [1-4]; 1969, page 24 [1-4]; 1970, page 25 [1-4]; 1971, page 25 [1-4]

Cut: 1300. Line: 331. Corinthian. Cordial. 1-1/4 oz. 4 inches tall. **References:** 1967, page 21 [1-5]; 1968, page 25 [1-5]; 1969, page 24 [1-5]; 1970, page 25 [1-5]; 1971, page 25 [1-5]

Cut: 1300. Line: 331. Corinthian. Goblet. 10 oz. 6-1/2 inches tall. **References:** 1967, page 21 [1-1]; 1968, page 25 [1-1]; 1969, page 24 [1-1]; 1970, page 25 [1-1]; 1971, page 25 [1-1]

Cut: 1300. Line: 331. Corinthian. Ice Tea. 11-3/4 oz. 6-1/2 inches tall. **References:** 1967, page 21 [1-7]; 1968, page 25 [1-7]; 1969, page 24 [1-7]; 1970, page 25 [1-7]; 1971, page 25 [1-7]

Cut: 1300. Line: 331. Corinthian. Juice. 5 oz. 5-3/8 inches tall. **References:** 1967, page 21 [1-6]; 1968, page 25 [1-6]; 1969, page 24 [1-6]; 1970, page 25 [1-6]; 1971, page 25 [1-6]

Cut: 1300. Line: 331. Corinthian. Plate. 7 inches diam. Actually 7-7/8"Dia. **References:** 1967, page 21 [1-9]; 1968, page 25 [1-9]; 1969, page 24 [1-9]; 1970, page 25 [1-9]; 1971, page 25 [1-9]

Cut: 1300. Line: 331. Corinthian. Plate. 8 inches diam. Actually 8-3/4" Dia. **References:** 1967, page 21 [1-10]; 1968, page 25 [1-10]; 1969, page 24 [1-10]; 1970, page 25 [1-10]; 1971, page 25 [1-10]

Cut: 1300. Line: 331. Corinthian. Sherbet. 6-1/4 oz. 5-1/8 inches tall. **References:** 1967, page 21 [1-2]; 1968, page 25 [1-2]; 1969, page 24 [1-2]; 1970, page 25 [1-2]; 1971, page 25 [1-2]

Cut: 1308. Line: 3214. Regal. 1305 Dessert-Finger Bowl. 4-1/2 inches diam. **References:** 1968, page 26 [2-18]

Cut: 1308. Line: 3214. Regal. Cocktail. 4-1/4 oz. 4 inches tall. **References:** 1968, page 26 [2-14]

Cut: 1308. Line: 3214. Regal. Cordial. 1-1/2 oz. 3-3/4 inches tall. **References:** 1968, page 26 [2-15]

Cut: 1308. Line: 3214. Regal. Goblet. 10-1/4 oz. 6-1/8 inches tall. **References:** 1968, page 26 [2-11]

Cut: 1308. Line: 3214. Regal. Ice Tea. 12 oz. 6-3/4 inches tall. **References:** 1968, page 26 [2-17]

Cut: 1308. Line: 3214. Regal. Juice. 5-1/4 oz. 4-7/8 inches tall. **References:** 1968, page 26 [2-16]

Cut: 1308. Line: 3214. Regal. Plate. 7 inches diam. Actually 7-7/8" Dia. **References:** 1968, page 26 [2-19]

Cut: 1308. Line: 3214. Regal. Plate. 8 inches diam. Actually 8-3/4" Dia. **References:** 1968, page 26 [2-20]

Cut: 1308. Line: 3214. Regal. Sherbet. 6-1/2 oz. 4-1/2 inches tall. **References:** 1968, page 26 [2-12]

Cut: 1308. Line: 3214. Regal. Wine. 3-3/4 oz. 5 inches tall. **References:** 1968, page 26 [2-13]

Cut: 1309. Line: 3214. Scroll. 1305 Dessert-Finger Bowl. 4-1/2 inches diam. **References:** 1968, page 26 [2-8]

Cut: 1309. Line: 3214. Scroll. Cocktail. 4-1/4 oz. 4 inches tall. **References:** 1968, page 26 [2-4]

Cut: 1309. Line: 3214. Scroll. Cordial. 1-1/2 oz. 3-3/4 inches tall. **References:** 1968, page 26 [2-5]

Cut: 1309. Line: 3214. Scroll. Goblet. 10-1/4 oz. 6-1/8 inches tall. **References:** 1968, page 26 [2-1]

Cut: 1309. Line: 3214. Scroll. Ice Tea. 12 oz. 6-3/4 inches tall. **References:** 1968, page 26 [2-7]

Cut: 1309. Line: 3214. Scroll. Juice. 5-1/4 oz. 4-7/8 inches tall. **References:** 1968, page 26 [2-6]

Cut: 1309. Line: 3214. Scroll. Plate. 7 inches diam. Actually 7-7/8" Dia. **References:** 1968, page 26 [2-9]

Cut: 1309. Line: 3214. Scroll. Plate. 8 inches diam. Actually 8-3/4" Dia. **References:** 1968, page 26 [2-10]

Cut: 1309. Line: 3214. Scroll. Sherbet. 6-1/2 oz. 4-1/2 inches tall. **References:** 1968, page 26 [2-2]

Cut: 1309. Line: 3214. Scroll. Wine. 3-3/4 oz. 5 inches tall. **References:** 1968, page 26 [2-3]

Cut: 1318. Line: 3. Celeste. Bell. 4-3/8 inches tall. Handmade and Hand Cut / Featured in display case. **References:** 1975, page 12 [2-2]; 1976, page 6 [2-3]; 1977, page 22 [5-2]

Cut: 1318. Line: 355. Celeste. 1305 Dessert-Finger Bowl. 4-1/2 inches diam. **References:** 1967, page 15 [1-9]; 1968, page 19 [1-9]; 1969, page 17 [2-9]; 1970, page 18 [2-9]; 1971, page 18 [2-9]

Cut: 1318. Line: 355. Celeste. Cocktail. 4-3/4 oz. 4-1/2 inches tall. **References:** 1967, page 15 [1-4]; 1968, page 19 [1-4]; 1969, page 17 [2-4]; 1970, page 18 [2-4]; 1971, page 18 [2-4]

Cut: 1318. Line: 355. Celeste. Cordial. 1-1/2 oz. 3-1/2 inches tall. **References:** 1967, page 15 [1-5]; 1968, page 19 [1-5]; 1969, page 17 [2-5]; 1970, page 18 [2-5]; 1971, page 18 [2-5]

Cut: 1318. Line: 355. Celeste. Goblet. 10-1/2 oz. 6-1/2 inches tall. **References:** 1967, page 15 [1-1]; 1968, page 19 [1-1]; 1969, page 17 [2-1]; 1970, page 18 [2-1]; 1971, page 18 [2-1]

Cut: 1318. Line: 355. Celeste. Ice Tea. 12 oz. 5-3/4 inches tall. **References:** 1967, page 15 [1-8]; 1968, page 19 [1-8]; 1969, page 17 [2-8]; 1970, page 18 [2-8]; 1971, page 18 [2-8]

Cut: 1318. Line: 355. Celeste. Juice. 5 oz. 4-1/4 inches tall. **References:** 1967, page 15 [1-7]; 1968, page 19 [1-7]; 1969, page 17 [2-7]; 1970, page 18 [2-7]; 1971, page 18 [2-7]

Cut: 1318. Line: 355. Celeste. Parfait. 6-1/2 oz. 7-1/2 inches tall. **References:** 1967, page 15 [1-6]; 1968, page 19 [1-6]; 1969, page 17 [2-6]; 1970, page 18 [2-6]; 1971, page 18 [2-6]

Cut: 1318. Line: 355. Celeste. Plate. 7 inches diam. Actually 7-7/8" Dia. **References:** 1967, page 15 [1-10]; 1968, page 19 [1-10]; 1969, page 17 [2-10]; 1970, page 18 [2-10]; 1971, page 18 [2-10]

Cut: 1318. Line: 355. Celeste. Plate. 8 inches diam. Actually 8-3/4" Dia. **References:** 1967, page 15 [1-11]; 1968, page 19 [1-11]; 1969, page 17 [2-11]; 1970, page 18 [2-11]; 1971, page 18 [2-11]

Cut: 1318. Line: 355. Celeste. Sherbet. 6-3/4 oz. 5 inches tall. **References:** 1967, page 15 [1-2]; 1968, page 19 [1-2]; 1969, page 17 [2-2]; 1970, page 18 [2-2]; 1971, page 18 [2-2]

Cut: 1318. Line: 355. Celeste. Wine. 5 oz. 5-1/2 inches tall. **References:** 1967, page 15 [1-3]; 1968, page 19 [1-3]; 1969, page 17 [2-3]; 1970, page 18 [2-3]; 1971, page 18 [2-3]

Cut: 1320. Line: 355. Silver Leaf. 1305 Dessert-Finger Bowl. 4-1/2 inches diam. **References:** 1967, page 15 [2-9]; 1968, page 19 [2-9]

Cut: 1320. Line: 355. Silver Leaf. Cocktail. 4-3/4 oz. 4-1/2 inches tall. 1968, page 19 [2-4]

Cut: 1320. Line: 355. Silver Leaf. Cordial. 1-1/2 oz. 3-1/2 inches tall. **References:** 1967, page 15 [2-5]; 1968, page 19 [2-5]

Cut: 1320. Line: 355. Silver Leaf. Goblet. 10-1/2 oz. 6-1/2 inches tall. **References:** 1967, page 15 [2-1]; 1968, page 19 [2-1]

Cut: 1320. Line: 355. Silver Leaf. Ice Tea. 12 oz. 5-3/4 inches tall. **References:** 1967, page 15 [2-8]; 1968, page 19 [2-8]

Cut: 1320. Line: 355. Silver Leaf. Juice. 5 oz. 4-1/2 inches tall. **References:** 1967, page 15 [2-7]; 1968, page 19 [2-7]

Cut: 1320. Line: 355. Silver Leaf. Parfait. 6-1/2 oz. 7-1/2 inches tall. **References:** 1967, page 15 [2-6]; 1968, page 19 [2-6]

Cut: 1320. Line: 355. Silver Leaf. Plate. 7 inches diam. Actually 7-7/8" Dia. **References:** 1967, page 15 [2-10]; 1968, page 19 [2-10]

Cut: 1320. Line: 355. Silver Leaf. Plate. 8 inches diam. Actually 8-3/4" Dia. **References:** 1967, page 15 [2-11]; 1968, page 19 [2-11]

Cut: 1320. Line: 355. Silver Leaf. Sherbet. 6-3/4 oz. 5 inches tall. **References:** 1967, page 15 [2-2]; 1968, page 19 [2-2]

Cut: 1320. Line: 355. Silver Leaf. Wine. 5 oz. 5-1/2 inches tall. **References:** 1967, page 15 [2-3]; 1968, page 19 [2-3]

Cut: 1325. Line: 355. Coventry. 1305 Dessert-Finger Bowl. 4-1/2 inches diam. **References:** 1967, page 15 [2-20]; 1968, page 19 [2-20]; 1969, page 17 [2-20]; 1970, page 18 [2-20]; 1971, page 18 [2-20]

Cut: 1325. Line: 355. Coventry. Cocktail. 4-3/4 oz. 4-1/2 inches tall. **References:** 1967, page 15 [2-15]; 1968, page 19 [2-15]; 1969, page 17 [2-15]; 1970, page 18 [2-15]; 1971, page 18 [2-15]

Cut: 1325. Line: 355. Coventry. Cordial. 1-1/2 oz. 3-1/2 inches tall. **References:** 1967, page 15 [2-16]; 1968, page 19 [2-16]; 1969, page 17 [2-16]; 1970, page 18 [2-16]; 1971, page 18 [2-16]

Cut: 1325. Line: 355. Coventry. Goblet. 10-1/2 oz. 6-1/2 inches tall. **References:** 1967, page 15 [2-12]; 1968, page 19 [2-12]; 1969, page 17 [2-12]; 1970, page 18 [2-12]; 1971, page 18 [2-12]

Cut: 1325. Line: 355. Coventry. Ice Tea. 12 oz. 5-3/4 inches tall. **References:** 1967, page 15 [2-19]; 1968, page 19 [2-19]; 1969, page 17 [2-19]; 1970, page 18 [2-19]; 1971, page 18 [2-19]

Cut: 1325. Line: 355. Coventry. Juice. 5 oz. 4-1/4 inches tall. **References:** 1967, page 15 [2-18]; 1968, page 19 [2-18]; 1969, page 17 [2-18]; 1970, page 18 [2-18]; 1971, page 18 [2-18]

Cut: 1325. Line: 355. Coventry. Parfait. 6-1/2 oz. 7-1/2 inches tall. **References:** 1967, page 15 [2-17]; 1968, page 19 [2-17]; 1969, page 17 [2-17]; 1970, page 18 [2-17]; 1971, page 18 [2-17]

Cut: 1325. Line: 355. Coventry. Plate. 7 inches diam. Actually 7-7/8" Dia. **References:** 1967, page 15 [2-21]; 1968, page 19 [2-21]; 1969, page 17 [2-21]; 1970, page 18 [2-21]; 1971, page 18 [2-21]

Cut: 1325. Line: 355. Coventry. Plate. 8 inches diam. Actually 8-3/4" Dia. **References:** 1967, page 15 [2-22]; 1968, page 19 [2-22]; 1969, page 17 [2-22]; 1970, page 18 [2-22]; 1971, page 18 [2-22]

Cut: 1325. Line: 355. Coventry. Sherbet. 6-3/4 oz. 5 inches tall. **References:** 1967, page 15 [2-13]; 1968, page 19 [2-13]; 1969, page 17 [2-13]; 1970, page 18 [2-13]; 1971, page 18 [2-13]

Cut: 1325. Line: 355. Coventry. Wine. 5 oz. 5-1/2 inches tall. **References:** 1967, page 15 [2-14]; 1968, page 19 [2-14]; 1969, page 17 [2-14]; 1970, page 18 [2-14]; 1971, page 18 [2-14]

Cut: 1370. Line: 578. Woodstock. 1305 Dessert-Finger Bowl. 4-1/2 inches diam. **References:** 1968, page 26 [1-8]

Cut: 1370. Line: 578. Woodstock. Cocktail. 5-3/4 oz. 4-3/8 inches tall. **References:** 1968, page 26 [1-4]

Cut: 1370. Line: 578. Woodstock. Cordial. 1-1/2 oz. 3-3/8 inches tall. **References:** 1968, page 26 [1-5]

Cut: 1370. Line: 578. Woodstock. Goblet. 10-1/2 oz. 6-1/8 inches tall. **References:** 1968, page 26 [1-1]

Cut: 1370. Line: 578. Woodstock. Ice Tea. 12-1/2 oz. 6 inches tall. **References:** 1968, page 26 [1-7]

Cut: 1370. Line: 578. Woodstock. Juice. 5-1/2 oz. 4-3/4 inches tall. **References:** 1968, page 26 [1-6]

Cut: 1370. Line: 578. Woodstock. Plate. 7 inches diam. Actually 7-7/8" Dia. **References:** 1968, page 26 [1-9]

Cut: 1370. Line: 578. Woodstock. Plate. 8 inches diam. Actually 8-3/4" Dia. **References:** 1968, page 26 [1-10]

Cut: 1370. Line: 578. Woodstock. Sherbet. 6-1/2 oz. 4-1/2 inches tall. **References:** 1968, page 26 [1-2]

Cut: 1370. Line: 578. Woodstock. Wine. 4-3/4 oz. 5-1/8 inches tall. **References:** 1968, page 26 [1-3]

Cut: 1380. Line: 352. Timeless. 1311 Dessert-Finger Bowl. 4-3/4 inches diam. **References:** 1967, page 18 [1-18]; 1968, page 22 [1-18]

Cut: 1380. Line: 352. Timeless. Claret. 3-3/4 oz. 5-5/8 inches tall. **References:** 1967, page 18 [1-13]; 1968, page 22 [1-13]

Cut: 1380. Line: 352. Timeless. Cocktail. 3 oz. 4-1/4 inches tall. **References:** 1967, page 18 [1-14]; 1968, page 22 [1-14]

Cut: 1380. Line: 352. Timeless. Cordial. 1 oz. 4 inches tall. **References:** 1967, page 18 [1-15]; 1968, page 22 [1-15]

Cut: 1380. Line: 352. Timeless. Goblet. 9 oz. 7-1/4 inches tall. **References:** 1967, page 18 [1-11]; 1968, page 22 [1-11]

Cut: 1380. Line: 352. Timeless. Ice Tea. 12 oz. 7-1/4 inches tall. **References:** 1967, page 18 [1-17]; 1968, page 22 [1-17]

Cut: 1380. Line: 352. Timeless. Juice. 5-1/2 oz. 5-3/8 inches tall. **References:** 1967, page 18 [1-16]; 1968, page 22 [1-16]

Cut: 1380. Line: 352. Timeless. Plate. 7 inches diam. Actually 7-7/8" Dia. **References:** 1967, page 18 [1-19]; 1968, page 22 [1-19]

Cut: 1380. Line: 352. Timeless. Plate. 8 inches diam. Actually 8-3/4" Dia. **References:** 1967, page 18 [1-20]; 1968, page 22 [1-20]

Cut: 1380. Line: 352. Timeless. Sherbet. 6 oz. 5-3/8 inches tall. **References:** 1967, page 18 [1-12]; 1968, page 22 [1-12]

Cut: 1403. Line: 1350. Regency. 1305 Dessert-Finger Bowl. 4-1/2" Dia. **References:** 1967, page 13 [2-9]; 1968, page 17 [2-9]; 1969, page 13 [2-9]

Cut: 1403. Line: 1350. Regency. Cocktail. 4-1/2 oz. / 4-3/4" hi. **References:** 1967, page 13 [2-5]; 1969, page 13 [2-5]

Cut: 1403. Line: 1350. Regency. Cordial. 1-1/4 oz. / 3-3/4" hi. **References:** 1967, page 13 [2-6]; 1968, page 17 [2-6]; 1969, page 13 [2-6]

Cut: 1403. Line: 1350. Regency. Goblet. 12-1/2 oz. / 6-5/8" hi. **References:** 1967, page 13 [2-1]; 1968, page 17 [2-1]; 1969, page 13 [2-1]

Cut: 1403. Line: 1350. Regency. Ice Tea. 13-1/2 oz. / 6-1/4" hi. **References:** 1967, page 13 [2-8]; 1968, page 17 [2-8]; 1969, page 13 [2-8]

Cut: 1403. Line: 1350. Regency. Juice. 6-1/2 oz. / 5-1/4" hi. **References:** 1967, page 13 [2-7]; 1968, page 17 [2-7]; 1969, page 13 [2-7]

Cut: 1403. Line: 1350. Regency. Plate. 7" / Actually 7-7/8" Dia. **References:** 1967, page 13 [2-10]; 1968, page 17 [2-10]; 1969, page 13 [2-10]

Cut: 1403. Line: 1350. Regency. Plate. 8" / Actually 8-3/4" Dia. **References:** 1967, page 13 [2-11]; 1968, page 17 [2-11]; 1969, page 13 [2-11]

Cut: 1403. Line: 1350. Regency. Red Wine Goblet. 9-1/2 oz. / 6-3/8" hi. **References:** 1967, page 13 [2-3]; 1968, page 17 [2-3]; 1969, page 13 [2-3]

Cut: 1403. Line: 1350. Regency. Sherbet. 6-1/2 oz. / 5" hi. **References:** 1967, page 13 [2-2]; 1968, page 17 [2-2]; 1969, page 13 [2-2]

Cut: 1403. Line: 1350. Regency. White Wine Goblet. 7 oz. / 5-3/4" hi. **References:** 1967, page 13 [2-4]; 1968, page 17 [2-4]; 1969, page 13 [2-4]

Cut: 1406. Line: 1235. Musette. Cocktail. 5-1/2 oz. / 4-5/8" hi. Platinum Band. **References:** 1967, page 10 [1-22]; 1969, page 19 [1-24]; 1970, page 20 [1-24]; 1971, page 20 [1-24]; 1972, page 28 [1-24]; 1973, page 33 [1-24]

Cut: 1406. Line: 1235. Musette. Cordial. 2 oz. / 4-1/2" hi. Platinum Band. **References:** 1967, page 10 [1-23]; 1969, page 19 [1-25]; 1970, page 20 [1-25]; 1971, page 20 [1-25]; 1972, page 28 [1-25]; 1973, page 33 [1-25]

Cut: 1406. Line: 1235. Musette. Goblet. 12 oz. / 7" hi. Platinum Band. **References:** 1967, page 10 [1-19]; 1969, page 19 [1-21]; 1970, page 20 [1-21]; 1971, page 20 [1-21]; 1972, page 28 [1-21]; 1973, page 33 [1-21]

Cut: 1406. Line: 1235. Musette. Ice Tea. 12 oz. / 6-1/4" hi. Platinum Band. **References:** 1967, page 10 [1-25]; 1969, page 19 [1-28]; 1970, page 20 [1-28]; 1971, page 20 [1-28]; 1972, page 28 [1-28]; 1973, page 33 [1-28]

Cut: 1406. Line: 1235. Musette. Juice. 5 oz. / 4-1/2" hi. Platinum Band. **References:** 1967, page 10 [1-24]; 1969, page 19 [1-27]; 1970, page 20 [1-27]; 1971, page 20 [1-27]; 1972, page 28 [1-27]; 1973, page 33 [1-27]

Cut: 1406. Line: 1235. Musette. Parfait Whiskey Sour. 7 oz. 6-1/4 inches tall. Platinum Band. **References:** 1969, page 19 [1-26]; 1970, page 20 [1-26]; 1971, page 20 [1-26]; 1972, page 28 [1-26]; 1973, page 33 [1-26]

Cut: 1406. Line: 1235. Musette. Plate. 7" / Actually 7-7/8" hi. Platinum Band. **References:** 1967, page 10 [1-26]; 1969, page 19 [1-29]; 1970, page 20 [1-29]; 1971, page 20 [1-29]; 1972, page 28 [1-29]; 1973, page 33 [1-29]

Cut: 1406. Line: 1235. Musette. Plate. 8" / Actually 8-3/4" hi. Platinum Band. **References:** 1967, page 10 [1-27]; 1969, page 19 [1-30]; 1970, page 20 [1-30]; 1971, page 20 [1-30]; 1972, page 28 [1-30]; 1973, page 33 [1-30]

Cut: 1406. Line: 1235. Musette. Sherbet. 7-1/2 oz. / 5-1/8" hi. Platinum Band. **References:** 1967, page 10 [1-20]; 1969, page 19 [1-22]; 1970, page 20 [1-22]; 1971, page 20 [1-22]; 1972, page 28 [1-22]; 1973, page 33 [1-22]

Cut: 1406. Line: 1235. Musette. Wine. 7 oz. / 5-7/8 hi. Platinum Band. **References:** 1967, page 10 [1-21]; 1969, page 19 [1-23]; 1970, page 20 [1-23]; 1971, page 20 [1-23]; 1972, page 28 [1-23]; 1973, page 33 [1-23]

Cut: 1406. Line: 1235. Victoria. Cocktail. 5-1/2 oz. / 4-5/8" hi. Gold Band. **References:** 1967, page 10 [1-31]; 1969, page 19 [1-34]; 1970, page 20 [1-34]; 1971, page 20 [1-34]; 1972, page 28 [1-34]; 1973, page 33 [1-34]

Cut: 1406. Line: 1235. Victoria. Cordial. 2 oz. / 4-1/2" hi. Gold Band. **References:** 1967, page 10 [1-32]; 1969, page 19 [1-35]; 1970, page 20 [1-35]; 1971, page 20 [1-35]; 1972, page 28 [1-35]; 1973, page 33 [1-35]

Cut: 1406. Line: 1235. Victoria. Goblet. 12 oz. / 7" hi. Gold Band. **References:** 1967, page 10 [1-28]; 1969, page 19 [1-31]; 1970, page 20 [1-31]; 1971, page 20 [1-31]; 1972, page 28 [1-31]; 1973, page 33 [1-31]

Cut: 1406. Line: 1235. Victoria. Ice Tea. 12 oz. / 6-1/4" hi. Gold Band. **References:** 1967, page 10 [1-34]; 1969, page 19 [1-38]; 1970, page 20 [1-38]; 1971, page 20 [1-38]; 1972, page 28 [1-38]; 1973, page 33 [1-38]

Cut: 1406. Line: 1235. Victoria. Juice. 5 oz. / 4-1/2" hi. Gold Band. **References:** 1967, page 10 [1-33]; 1969, page 19 [1-37]; 1970, page 20 [1-37]; 1971, page 20 [1-37]; 1972, page 28 [1-37]; 1973, page 33 [1-37]

Cut: 1406. Line: 1235. Victoria. Parfait Whiskey Sour. 7 oz. 6-1/4 inches tall. Gold Band. **References:** 1969, page 19 [1-6]; 1970, page 20 [1-36]; 1971, page 20 [1-36]; 1972, page 28 [1-36]; 1973, page 33 [1-36]

Cut: 1406. Line: 1235. Victoria. Plate. 7" / Actually 7-7/8" Dia. Gold Band. **References:** 1967, page 10 [1-35]; 1969, page 19 [1-39]; 1970, page 20 [1-39]; 1971, page 20 [1-39]; 1972, page 28 [1-39]; 1973, page 33 [1-39]

Cut: 1406. Line: 1235. Victoria. Plate. 8" / Actually 8-3/4" Dia. Gold Band. **References:** 1967, page 10 [1-36]; 1969, page 19 [1-40]; 1970, page 20 [1-40]; 1971, page 20 [1-40]; 1972, page 28 [1-40]; 1973, page 33 [1-40]

Cut: 1406. Line: 1235. Victoria. Sherbet. 7-1/2 oz. / 5-1/8" hi. Gold Band. **References:** 1967, page 10 [1-29]; 1969, page 19 [1-32]; 1970, page 20 [1-32]; 1971, page 20 [1-32]; 1972, page 28 [1-32]; 1973, page 33 [1-32]

Cut: 1406. Line: 1235. Victoria. Wine. 7 oz. / 5-7/8" hi. Gold Band. **References:** 1967, page 10 [1-30]; 1969, page 19 [1-33]; 1970, page 20 [1-33]; 1971, page 20 [1-33]; 1972, page 28 [1-33]; 1973, page 33 [1-33]

Cut: 1406. Line: 1235. Windsor. Cocktail. 5-1/2 oz. / 4-5/8" hi. NOT BANDED. **References:** 1967, page 10 [1-40]

Cut: 1406. Line: 1235. Windsor. Cordial. 2 oz. / 4-1/2" hi. NOT BANDED. **References:** 1967, page 10 [1-41]

Cut: 1406. Line: 1235. Windsor. Goblet. 12 oz. / 7" hi. NOT BANDED. **References:** 1967, page 10 [1-37]

Cut: 1406. Line: 1235. Windsor. Ice Tea. 12 oz. / 6-1/4" hi. NOT BANDED. **References:** 1967, page 10 [1-43]

Cut: 1406. Line: 1235. Windsor. Juice. 5 oz. / 4-1/2" hi. NOT BANDED. **References:** 1967, page 10 [1-42]

Cut: 1406. Line: 1235. Windsor. Plate. 7" / Actually 7-7/8" Dia. NOT BANDED. **References:** 1967, page 10 [1-44]

Cut: 1406. Line: 1235. Windsor. Plate. 8" / Actually 8-3/4" Dia. NOT BANDED. **References:** 1967, page 10 [1-45]

Cut: 1406. Line: 1235. Windsor. Sherbet. 7-1/2 oz. / 5-1/8" hi. NOT BANDED. **References:** 1967, page 10 [1-38]

Cut: 1406. Line: 1235. Windsor. Wine. 7 oz. / 5-7/8" hi. NOT BANDED. **References:** 1967, page 10 [1-39]

Cut: 1406. Line: 1963. Darlene. Cocktail. 5-1/2 oz. / 4-3/4" hi. Gold Band. **References:** 1967, page 11 [2-22]; 1968, page 15 [2-22]

Cut: 1406. Line: 1963. Darlene. Cordial. 1-1/2 oz. / 4" hi. Gold Band. **References:** 1967, page 11 [2-

23]; 1968, page 15 [2-23]

Cut: 1406. Line: 1963. Darlene. Goblet. 13-1/2 oz. / 6-3/4" hi. Gold Band. **References:** 1967, page 11 [2-19]; 1968, page 15 [2-19]

Cut: 1406. Line: 1963. Darlene. Ice Tea. 14 oz. / 6-1/4" hi. Gold Band. **References:** 1967, page 11 [2-25]; 1968, page 15 [2-25]

Cut: 1406. Line: 1963. Darlene. Juice. 7 oz. / 5-1/4" hi. Gold Band. **References:** 1967, page 11 [2-24]; 1968, page 15 [2-24]

Cut: 1406. Line: 1963. Darlene. Plate. 7" / Actually 7-7/8" Dia. Gold Band. **References:** 1967, page 11 [2-26]; 1968, page 15 [2-26]

Cut: 1406. Line: 1963. Darlene. Plate. 8" / Actually 8-3/4" Dia. Gold Band. **References:** 1967, page 11 [2-27]; 1968, page 15 [2-27]

Cut: 1406. Line: 1963. Darlene. Sherbet. 7-1/2 oz. / 5-1/8" hi. Gold Band. **References:** 1967, page 11 [2-20]; 1968, page 15 [2-20]

Cut: 1406. Line: 1963. Darlene. Wine. 7-3/4 oz. / 5-3/4" hi. Gold Band. **References:** 1967, page 11 [2-21]; 1968, page 15 [2-21]

Cut: 1406. Line: 1963. Diane. Cocktail. 5-1/2 oz. / 4-3/4" hi. NOT BANDED. **References:** 1967, page 11 [2-31]; 1968, page 15 [2-31]

Cut: 1406. Line: 1963. Diane. Cordial. 1-1/2 oz. / 4" hi. NOT BANDED. **References:** 1967, page 11 [2-32]; 1968, page 15 [2-32]

Cut: 1406. Line: 1963. Diane. Goblet. 13-1/2 oz. / 6-3/4" hi. NOT BANDED. **References:** 1967, page 11 [2-28]; 1968, page 15 [2-28]

Cut: 1406. Line: 1963. Diane. Ice Tea. 14 oz. / 6-1/4" hi. NOT BANDED. **References:** 1967, page 11 [2-34]; 1968, page 15 [2-34]

Cut: 1406. Line: 1963. Diane. Juice. 7 oz. / 5-1/4" hi. NOT BANDED. **References:** 1967, page 11 [2-33]; 1968, page 15 [2-33]

Cut: 1406. Line: 1963. Diane. Plate. 7" / Actually 7-7/8" Dia. NOT BANDED. **References:** 1967, page 11 [2-35]; 1968, page 15 [2-35]

Cut: 1406. Line: 1963. Diane. Plate. 8" / Actually 8-3/4" Dia. NOT BANDED. **References:** 1967, page 11 [2-36]; 1968, page 15 [2-36]

Cut: 1406. Line: 1963. Diane. Sherbet. 7-1/2 oz. / 5-1/8" hi. NOT BANDED. **References:** 1967, page 11 [2-29]; 1968, page 15 [2-29]

Cut: 1406. Line: 1963. Diane. Wine. 7-3/4 oz. / 5-3/4" hi. NOT BANDED. **References:** 1967, page 11 [2-30]; 1968, page 15 [2-30]

Cut: 1406. Line: 1963. Fantasy. Cocktail. 5-1/2 oz. / 4-3/4" hi. Platinum Band. **References:** 1967, page 11 [2-40]; 1968, page 15 [2-40]

Cut: 1406. Line: 1963. Fantasy. Cordial. 1-1/2 oz. / 4" hi. Platinum Band. **References:** 1967, page 11 [2-41]; 1968, page 15 [2-41]

Cut: 1406. Line: 1963. Fantasy. Goblet. 13-1/2 oz. / 6-3/4" hi. Platinum Band. **References:** 1967, page 11 [2-37]; 1968, page 15 [2-37]

Cut: 1406. Line: 1963. Fantasy. Ice Tea. 14 oz. / 6-1/4" hi. Platinum Band. **References:** 1967, page 11 [2-43]; 1968, page 15 [2-43]

Cut: 1406. Line: 1963. Fantasy. Juice. 7 oz. / 5-1/4" hi. Platinum Band. **References:** 1967, page 11 [2-42]; 1968, page 15 [2-42]

Cut: 1406. Line: 1963. Fantasy. Plate. 7" / Actually 7-7/8" Dia. Platinum Band. **References:** 1967, page 11 [2-44]; 1968, page 15 [2-44]

Cut: 1406. Line: 1963. Fantasy. Plate. 8" / Actually 8-3/4" Dia. Platinum Band. **References:** 1967, page 11 [2-45]; 1968, page 15 [2-45]

Cut: 1406. Line: 1963. Fantasy. Sherbet. 7-1/2 oz. / 5-1/8" hi. Platinum Band. **References:** 1967, page 11 [2-38]; 1968, page 15 [2-38]

Cut: 1406. Line: 1963. Fantasy. Wine. 7-3/4 oz. / 5-3/4" hi. Platinum Band. **References:** 1967, page 11 [2-39]; 1968, page 15 [2-39]

Cut: 1408. Line: 1963. First Lady. 1305 Dessert-Finger Bowl. 4-1/4 inches diam. **References:** 1970, page 13 [1-8]; 1976, page 26 [1-6]; 1977, page 37 [1-6]

Cut: 1408. Line: 1963. First Lady. Cocktail. 5-1/2 oz. 4-3/4 inches tall. **References:** 1970, page 13 [1-4]

Cut: 1408. Line: 1963. First Lady. Cordial. 1-1/2 oz. 4 inches tall. **References:** 1970, page 13 [1-5]; 1975, page 26 [1-4]; 1977, page 37 [1-4]; 1981, page 1 [1-12]

Cut: 1408. Line: 1963. First Lady. Goblet. 13-1/2 oz. 6-3/4 inches tall. **References:** 1970, page 13 [1-1]; 1975, page 26 [1-1]; 1977, page 37 [1-1]; 1981, page 1 [1-9]

Cut: 1408. Line: 1963. First Lady. Ice Tea. 14 oz. 6-1/4 inches tall. **References:** 1970, page 13 [1-7]; 1975, page 26 [1-5]; 1977, page 37 [1-5]

Cut: 1408. Line: 1963. First Lady. Juice. 7 oz. 5-1/4 inches tall. **References:** 1970, page 13 [1-6]

Cut: 1408. Line: 1963. First Lady. Plate. 7 inches diam. Actually 7-7/8" Dia. **References:** 1970, page 13 [1-9]; 1975, page 26 [1-7]; 1977, page 37 [1-7]

Cut: 1408. Line: 1963. First Lady. Plate. 8 inches diam. Actually 8-3/4" Dia. **References:** 1970, page 13 [1-10]; 1975, page 26 [1-8]; 1977, page 37 [1-8]

Cut: 1408. Line: 1963. First Lady. Sherbet. 7-1/2 oz. 5-1/8 inches tall. **References:** 1970, page 13 [1-2]; 1975, page 26 [1-2]; 1977, page 37 [1-2]; 1981, page 1 [1-10]

Cut: 1408. Line: 1963. First Lady. Wine. 7-3/4 oz. 5-3/4 inches tall. **References:** 1970, page 13 [1-3]; 1975, page 26 [1-3]; 1977, page 37 [1-3]; 1981, page 1 [1-11]

Cut: 1409. Line: 1963. First Lady. 1305 Dessert-Finger Bowl. 4-1/4" Dia. **References:** 1967, page 8 [1-8]; 1968, page 12 [1-8]; 1969, page 12 [1-8]; 1971, page 13 [1-8]; 1972, page 22 [1-8]; 1973, page 26 [1-8]

Cut: 1409. Line: 1963. First Lady. Cocktail. 5-1/2 oz. / 4-3/4" hi. **References:** 1967, page 8 [1-4]; 1968, page 12 [1-4]; 1969, page 12 [1-4]; 1971, page 13 [1-4]; 1972, page 22 [1-4]; 1973, page 26 [1-4]

Cut: 1409. Line: 1963. First Lady. Cordial. 1-1/2 oz. / 4" hi. **References:** 1967, page 8 [1-5]; 1968, page 12 [1-5]; 1969, page 12 [1-5]; 1971, page 13 [1-5]; 1972, page 22 [1-5]; 1973, page 26 [1-5]

Cut: 1409. Line: 1963. First Lady. Goblet. 13-1/2 oz. / 6-3/4" hi. **References:** 1967, page 8 [1-1]; 1968, page 12 [1-1]; 1969, page 12 [1-1]; 1971, page 13 [1-1]; 1972, page 22 [1-1]; 1973, page 26 [1-1]

Cut: 1409. Line: 1963. First Lady. Ice Tea. 14 oz. / 6-1/4" hi. **References:** 1967, page 8 [1-7]; 1968, page 12 [1-7]; 1969, page 12 [1-7]; 1971, page 13 [1-7]; 1972, page 22 [1-7]; 1973, page 26 [1-7]

Cut: 1409. Line: 1963. First Lady. Juice. 7 oz. / 5-1/4" hi. **References:** 1967, page 8 [1-6]; 1968, page 12 [1-6]; 1969, page 12 [1-6]; 1971, page 13 [1-6]; 1972, page 22 [1-6]; 1973, page 26 [1-6]

Cut: 1409. Line: 1963. First Lady. Plate. 7" / Actually 7-7/8" Dia. **References:** 1967, page 8 [1-9]; 1968, page 12 [1-9]; 1969, page 12 [1-9]; 1971, page 13 [1-9]; 1972, page 22 [1-9]; 1973, page 26 [1-9]

Cut: 1409. Line: 1963. First Lady. Plate. 8" / Actually 8-3/4" Dia. **References:** 1967, page 8 [1-10]; 1968, page 12 [1-10]; 1969, page 12 [1-10]; 1971, page 13 [1-10]; 1972, page 22 [1-10]; 1973, page 26 [1-10]

Cut: 1409. Line: 1963. First Lady. Sherbet. 7-1/2 oz. / 5-1/8" hi. **References:** 1967, page 8 [1-2]; 1968, page 11 [1-2]; 1969, page 11 [1-2]; 1971, page 13 [1-2]; 1972, page 22 [1-2]; 1973, page 26 [1-2]

Cut: 1409. Line: 1963. First Lady. Wine. 7-3/4 oz. / 5-3/4" hi. **References:** 1967, page 8 [1-3]; 1968, page 12 [1-3]; 1969, page 12 [1-3]; 1971, page 13 [1-3]; 1972, page 22 [1-3]; 1973, page 26 [1-3]

Cut: 1409. Line: 1963. True Love. 1305 Dessert-Finger Bowl. 4-1/2" Dia. **References:** 1967, page 8 [2-8]; 1968, page 12 [2-8]

Cut: 1409. Line: 1963. True Love. Cocktail. 5-1/2 oz. / 4-3/4" hi. **References:** 1967, page 8 [2-4]; 1968, page 12 [2-4]

Cut: 1409. Line: 1963. True Love. Cordial. 1-1/2 oz. / 4" hi. **References:** 1967, page 8 [2-5]; 1968, page 12 [2-5]

Cut: 1409. Line: 1963. True Love. Goblet. 13-1/2 oz. / 6-3/4" hi. **References:** 1967, page 8 [2-1]; 1968, page 12 [2-1]

Cut: 1409. Line: 1963. True Love. Ice Tea. 14 oz. / 6-1/4" hi. **References:** 1967, page 8 [2-7]; 1968, page 12 [2-7]

Cut: 1409. Line: 1963. True Love. Juice. 7 oz. / 5-1/4" hi. **References:** 1967, page 8 [2-6]; 1968, page 12 [2-6]

Cut: 1409. Line: 1963. True Love. Plate. 7" / Actually 7-7/8" Dia. **References:** 1967, page 8 [2-9]; 1968, page 12 [2-9]

Cut: 1409. Line: 1963. True Love. Plate. 8" / Actually 8-3/4" Dia. **References:** 1967, page 8 [2-10]; 1968, page 12 [2-10]

Cut: 1409. Line: 1963. True Love. Sherbet. 7-1/2 oz. / 5-1/8" hi. **References:** 1967, page 8 [2-2]; 1968, page 12 [2-2]

Cut: 1409. Line: 1963. True Love. Wine. 7-3/4 oz. / 5-3/4" hi. **References:** 1967, page 8 [2-3]; 1968, page 12 [2-3]

Cut: 1412. Line: 1964. Carousel. 1305 Dessert-Finger Bowl. 4-1/2 inches diam. **References:** 1967, page 14 [1-25]; 1968, page 18 [1-25]; 1968, page 18 [1-25]

Cut: 1412. Line: 1964. Carousel. Cordial. 1-1/2 oz. 3-3/4 inches tall. **References:** 1967, page 14 [1-22]; 1968, page 18 [1-22]; 1968, page 18 [1-22]

Cut: 1412. Line: 1964. Carousel. Goblet. 13-3/4 oz. / 6-1/2" hi. **References:** 1967, page 14 [1-19]; 1968, page 18 [1-19]; 1968, page 18 [1-19]

Cut: 1412. Line: 1964. Carousel. Ice Tea. 14-1/4 oz. 6-3/8 inches tall. **References:** 1967, page 14 [1-24]; 1968, page 18 [1-24]; 1968, page 18 [1-24]

Cut: 1412. Line: 1964. Carousel. Juice. 6-3/4 oz. 4-3/4 inches tall. **References:** 1967, page 14 [1-23]; 1968, page 18 [1-23]; 1968, page 18 [1-23]

Cut: 1412. Line: 1964. Carousel. Plate. 7 inches diam. Actually 7-7/8" Dia. **References:** 1967, page 14 [1-26]; 1968, page 18 [1-26]; 1968, page 18 [1-26]

Cut: 1412. Line: 1964. Carousel. Plate. 8 inches diam. Actually 8-3/4" Dia. **References:** 1967, page 14 [1-27]; 1968, page 18 [1-27]; 1968, page 18 [1-27]

Cut: 1412. Line: 1964. Carousel. Sherbet. 7-1/2 oz. / 4-3/8" hi. **References:** 1967, page 14 [1-20]; 1968, page 18 [1-20]; 1968, page 18 [1-20]

Cut: 1412. Line: 1964. Carousel. Wine. 9 oz. / 5-5/8" hi. **References:** 1967, page 14 [1-21]; 1968, page 18 [1-21]; 1968, page 18 [1-21]

Cut: 1413. Line: 1964. Monte Carlo. 1305 Dessert-Finger Bowl. 4-1/2 inches diam. **References:** 1967, page 14 [2-16]; 1968, page 18 [2-16]

Cut: 1413. Line: 1964. Monte Carlo. Cordial. 1-1/2 oz. 3-3/4 inches tall. **References:** 1967, page 14 [2-13]; 1968, page 18 [2-13]

Cut: 1413. Line: 1964. Monte Carlo. Goblet. 13-3/4 oz. 6-1/2 inches tall. **References:** 1967, page 14 [2-10]; 1968, page 18 [2-10]

Cut: 1413. Line: 1964. Monte Carlo. Ice Tea. 14-1/4 oz. 6-3/8 inches tall. **References:** 1967, page 14 [2-15]; 1968, page 18 [2-15]

Cut: 1413. Line: 1964. Monte Carlo. Juice. 6-3/4 oz. 4-3/4 inches tall. **References:** 1967, page 14 [2-14]; 1968, page 18 [2-14]

Cut: 1413. Line: 1964. Monte Carlo. Plate. 7 inches diam. Actually 7-7/8" Dia. **References:** 1967, page 14 [2-17]; 1968, page 18 [2-17]

Cut: 1413. Line: 1964. Monte Carlo. Plate. 8 inches diam. Actually 8-3/4" Dia. **References:** 1967, page 14 [2-18]; 1968, page 18 [2-18]

Cut: 1413. Line: 1964. Monte Carlo. Sherbet. 7-1/2 oz. 4-3/8 inches tall. **References:** 1967, page 14 [2-11]; 1968, page 18 [2-11]

Cut: 1413. Line: 1964. Monte Carlo. Wine. 9 oz. 5-5/8 inches tall. **References:** 1967, page 14 [2-12]; 1968, page 18 [2-12]

Cut: 1414. Line: 1964. Copenhagen. 1305 Dessert-Finger Bowl. 4-1/2 inches diam. **References:** 1967, page 14 [2-7]; 1968, page 18 [2-7]

Cut: 1414. Line: 1964. Copenhagen. Cordial. 1-1/2 oz. 3-3/4 inches tall. **References:** 1967, page 14 [2-4]; 1968, page 18 [2-4]

Cut: 1414. Line: 1964. Copenhagen. Goblet. 13-3/4 oz. 6-1/2 inches tall. **References:** 1967, page 14 [2-1]; 1968, page 18 [2-1]

Cut: 1414. Line: 1964. Copenhagen. Ice Tea. 14-1/4 oz. 6-3/8 inches tall. **References:** 1967, page 14 [2-6]; 1968, page 18 [2-6]

Cut: 1414. Line: 1964. Copenhagen. Juice. 6-3/4 oz. 4-3/4 inches tall. **References:** 1967, page 14 [2-5]; 1968, page 18 [2-5]

Cut: 1414. Line: 1964. Copenhagen. Plate. 7 inches diam. Actually 7-7/8" Dia. **References:** 1967, page 14 [2-8]; 1968, page 18 [2-8]

Cut: 1414. Line: 1964. Copenhagen. Plate. 8 inches diam. Actually 8-3/4" Dia. **References:** 1967, page 14 [2-9]; 1968, page 18 [2-9]

Cut: 1414. Line: 1964. Copenhagen. Sherbet. 7-1/2 oz. 4-3/4 inches tall. **References:** 1967, page 14 [2-2]; 1968, page 18 [2-2]

Cut: 1414. Line: 1964. Copenhagen. Wine. 9 oz. 5-5/8 inches tall. **References:** 1967, page 14 [2-3]; 1968, page 18 [2-3]

Cut: 1416. Line: 1965. Lafayette. 1305 Dessert-Finger Bowl. 4-1/2 Dia. **References:** 1967, page 7 [1-16]; 1968, page 10 [1-7]; 1969, page 11 [2-16]; 1970, page 12 [2-16]; 1971, page 12 [2-16]; 1972, page 21 [2-16]; 1973, page 25 [2-16]; 1975, page 25 [2-14]; 1977, page 36 [2-14]

Cut: 1416. Line: 1965. Lafayette. Cordial. 1-1/4 oz. / 4" hi. **References:** 1967, page 7 [1-13]; 1968, page 10 [1-4]; 1969, page 11 [2-13]; 1970, page 12 [2-13]; 1971, page 12 [2-13]; 1972, page 21 [2-13]; 1973, page 25 [2-13]; 1975, page 25 [2-12]; 1977, page 36 [2-12]; 1981, page 1 [2-8]

Cut: 1416. Line: 1965. Lafayette. Goblet. 11-3/4 oz. / 7-1/4" hi. **References:** 1967, page 7 [1-10]; 1968, page 10 [1-1]; 1969, page 11 [2-10]; 1970, page 12 [2-10]; 1971, page 12 [2-10]; 1972, page 21 [2-10]; 1973, page 25 [2-10]; 1975, page 25 [2-9]; 1977, page 36 [2-9]; 1981, page 1 [2-5]

Cut: 1416. Line: 1965. Lafayette. Ice Tea. 13-1/2 oz. / 6-3/4" hi. **References:** 1967, page 7 [1-15]; 1968, page 10 [1-6]; 1969, page 11 [2-15]; 1970, page 12 [2-15]; 1971, page 12 [2-15]; 1972, page 21 [2-15]; 1973, page 25 [2-15]; 1975, page 25 [2-13]; 1977, page 36 [2-13]

Cut: 1416. Line: 1965. Lafayette. Juice. 6 oz. / 5-1/2" hi. **References:** 1967, page 7 [1-14]; 1968, page 10 [1-5]; 1969, page 11 [2-14]; 1970, page 12 [2-14]; 1971, page 12 [2-14]; 1972, page 21 [2-14]; 1973, page 25 [2-14]

Cut: 1416. Line: 1965. Lafayette. Plate. 7" / Actually 7-7/8" Dia. **References:** 1967, page 7 [1-17]; 1968, page 10 [1-8]; 1969, page 11 [2-17]; 1970, page 12 [2-17]; 1971, page 12 [2-17]; 1972, page 21 [2-17]; 1973, page 25 [2-17]; 1975, page 25 [2-15]; 1977, page 36 [2-15]

Cut: 1416. Line: 1965. Lafayette. Plate. 8 inches diam. Actually 8-3/4" Dia. **References:** 1967, page 7 [1-18]; 1968, page 10 [1-9]; 1969, page 11 [2-18]; 1970, page 12 [2-18]; 1971, page 12 [2-18]; 1972, page 21 [2-18]; 1973, page 25 [2-18]; 1975, page 25 [2-16];
1977, page 36 [2-16]

Cut: 1416. Line: 1965. Lafayette. Sherbet. 7-1/2 oz. / 5-1/4" hi. **References:** 1967, page 7 [1-11]; 1968, page 10 [1-2]; 1969, page 11 [2-11]; 1970, page 12 [2-11]; 1971, page 12 [2-11]; 1972, page 21 [2-11]; 1973, page 25 [2-11]; 1975, page 25 [2-10]; 1977, page 36 [2-10]; 1981, page 1 [2-6]

Cut: 1416. Line: 1965. Lafayette. Wine. 7-1/2 oz. / 6-1/4" hi. **References:** 1967, page 7 [1-12]; 1968, page 10 [1-3]; 1969, page 11 [2-12]; 1970, page 12 [2-12]; 1971, page 12 [2-12]; 1972, page 21 [2-12]; 1973, page 25 [2-12]; 1975, page 25 [2-11]; 1977, page 36 [2-11]; 1981, page 1 [2-7]

Cut: 1419. Line: 1965. Solitaire. 1305 Dessert-Finger Bowl. 4-1/2 inches diam. **References:** 1968, page 11 [2-7]

Cut: 1419. Line: 1965. Solitaire. Cordial. 1-1/4 oz. 4 inches tall. **References:** 1968, page 11 [2-4]

Cut: 1419. Line: 1965. Solitaire. Goblet. 11-3/4 oz. 7-1/4 inches tall. **References:** 1968, page 11 [2-1]

Cut: 1419. Line: 1965. Solitaire. Ice Tea. 13-1/2 oz. 6-3/4 inches tall. **References:** 1968, page 11 [2-6]

Cut: 1419. Line: 1965. Solitaire. Juice. 6 oz. 5-1/2 inches tall. **References:** 1968, page 11 [2-5]

Cut: 1419. Line: 1965. Solitaire. Plate. 7 inches diam. Actually 7-7/8" Dia. **References:** 1968, page 11 [2-8]

Cut: 1419. Line: 1965. Solitaire. Plate. 8 inches diam. Actually 8-3/4" Dia. **References:** 1968, page 11 [2-9]

Cut: 1419. Line: 1965. Solitaire. Sherbet. 7-1/2 oz. 5-1/4 inches tall. **References:** 1968, page 11 [2-2]

Cut: 1419. Line: 1965. Solitaire. Wine. 7-1/2 oz. 6-1/4 inches tall. **References:** 1968, page 11 [2-3]

Cut: 1420. Line: 1965. Princess Anne. 1305 Dessert-Finger Bowl. 4-1/2" Dia. **References:** 1967, page 7 [3-16]; 1968, page 11 [2-16]

Cut: 1420. Line: 1965. Princess Anne. Cordial. 1-1/4 oz. / 4 hi. **References:** 1967, page 7 [3-13]; 1968, page 11 [2-13]

Cut: 1420. Line: 1965. Princess Anne. Goblet. 11-3/4 oz. / 7-1/4" hi. **References:** 1967, page 7 [3-10]; 1968, page 11 [2-10]

Cut: 1420. Line: 1965. Princess Anne. Ice Tea. 13-1/2 oz. / 6-3/4" hi. **References:** 1967, page 7 [3-15]; 1968, page 11 [2-15]

Cut: 1420. Line: 1965. Princess Anne. Juice. 6 oz. / 5-1/2" hi. **References:** 1967, page 7 [3-14]; 1968, page 11 [2-14]

Cut: 1420. Line: 1965. Princess Anne. Plate. 7" / Actually 7-7/8" Dia. **References:** 1967, page 7 [3-17]; 1968, page 11 [2-17]

Cut: 1420. Line: 1965. Princess Anne. Plate. 8" / Actually 8-3/4" Dia. **References:** 1967, page 7 [3-18]; 1968, page 11 [2-18]

Cut: 1420. Line: 1965. Princess Anne. Sherbet. 7-1/

2 oz. / 5-1/4" hi. **References:** 1967, page 7 [3-11]; 1968, page 11 [2-11]

Cut: 1420. Line: 1965. Princess Anne. Wine. 7-1/2 oz. / 6-1/4" hi. **References:** 1967, page 7 [3-12]; 1968, page 11 [2-12]

Cut: 1421. Line: 1965. Anniversary. 1305 Dessert-Finger Bowl. 4-1/2" Dia. **References:** 1967, page 7 [2-7]; 1968, page 11 [1-7]; 1969, page 11 [1-7]; 1970, page 12 [1-7]; 1971, page 12 [1-7]; 1972, page 21 [1-7]; 1973, page 25 [1-7]; 1975, page 25 [1-6]; 1977, page 36 [1-6]

Cut: 1421. Line: 1965. Anniversary. Cordial. 1-1/4 oz. / 4" hi. **References:** 1967, page 7 [2-4]; 1968, page 11 [1-4]; 1969, page 11 [1-4]; 1970, page 12 [1-4]; 1971, page 12 [1-4]; 1972, page 21 [1-4]; 1973, page 25 [1-4]; 1975, page 25 [1-4]; 1977, page 36 [1-4]; 1981, page 1 [2-4]

Cut: 1421. Line: 1965. Anniversary. Goblet. 11-3/4 oz. / 7-1/4" hi. **References:** 1967, page 7 [2-1]; 1968, page 11 [1-1]; 1969, page 11 [1-1]; 1970, page 12 [1-1]; 1971, page 12 [1-1]; 1972, page 21 [1-1]; 1973, page 25 [1-1]; 1975, page 25 [1-1]; 1977, page 36 [1-1]; 1981, page 1 [2-1]

Cut: 1421. Line: 1965. Anniversary. Ice Tea. 13-1/2 oz. / 6-3/4" hi. **References:** 1967, page 7 [2-6]; 1968, page 11 [1-6]; 1969, page 11 [1-6]; 1970, page 12 [1-6]; 1971, page 12 [1-6]; 1972, page 21 [1-6]; 1973, page 25 [1-6]; 1975, page 25 [1-5]; 1977, page 36 [1-5]

Cut: 1421. Line: 1965. Anniversary. Juice. 6 oz. / 5-1/2" hi. **References:** 1967, page 7 [2-5]; 1968, page 11 [1-5]; 1969, page 11 [1-5]; 1970, page 12 [1-5]; 1971, page 12 [1-5]; 1972, page 21 [1-5]; 1973, page 25 [1-5]

Cut: 1421. Line: 1965. Anniversary. Plate. 7" / Actually 7-7/8" Dia. **References:** 1967, page 7 [2-8]; 1968, page 11 [1-8]; 1969, page 11 [1-8]; 1970, page 12 [1-8]; 1971, page 12 [1-8]; 1972, page 21 [1-8]; 1973, page 25 [1-8]; 1975, page 25 [1-7]; 1977, page 36 [1-7]

Cut: 1421. Line: 1965. Anniversary. Plate. 8" / Actually 8-3/4" Dia. **References:** 1967, page 7 [2-9]; 1968, page 11 [1-9]; 1969, page 11 [1-9]; 1970, page 12 [1-9]; 1971, page 12 [1-9]; 1972, page 21 [1-9]; 1973, page 25 [1-9]; 1975, page 25 [1-8]; 1977, page 36 [1-8]

Cut: 1421. Line: 1965. Anniversary. Sherbet. 7-1/2 oz. / 5-1/4" hi. **References:** 1967, page 7 [2-2]; 1968, page 11 [1-2]; 1969, page 11 [1-2]; 1970, page 12 [1-2]; 1971, page 12 [1-2]; 1972, page 21 [1-2]; 1973, page 25 [1-2]; 1975, page 25 [1-2]; 1977, page 36 [1-2]; 1981, page 1 [2-2]

Cut: 1421. Line: 1965. Anniversary. Wine. 7-1/2 oz. / 6-1/4" hi. **References:** 1967, page 7 [2-3]; 1968, page 11 [1-3]; 1969, page 11 [1-3]; 1970, page 12 [1-3]; 1971, page 12 [1-3]; 1972, page 21 [1-3]; 1973, page 25 [1-3]; 1975, page 25 [1-3]; 1977, page 36 [1-3]; 1981, page 1 [2-3]

Cut: 1422. Orleans. Bell. 4-1/2 inches tall. **References:** 1979, page 12 [2-1]

Cut: 1422. Orleans. Bell. **References:** 1981, page 11 [2-2]; 1983, page 6 [1-3R]

Cut: 1422. Line: 3. Orleans. Bell. 4-3/8 inches tall. Handmade and Hand Cut. **References:** 1975, page 12 [2-1]; 1976, page 6 [2-4]; 1977, page 22 [5-1]

Cut: 1422. Line: 1965. Orleans. 1305 Dessert-Finger Bowl. 4-1/2" Dia. **References:** 1967, page 7 [1-7]; 1968, page 10 [2-7]; 1969, page 10 [2-7]; 1970, page 12 [2-7]; 1971, page 12 [2-7]; 1972, page 21 [2-7]; 1973, page 25 [2-7]; 1975, page 25 [2-6]; 1977, page 36 [2-6]

Cut: 1422. Line: 1965. Orleans. Cordial. 1-1/4 oz. / 4" hi. **References:** 1967, page 7 [1-4]; 1968, page 10 [2-4]; 1969, page 10 [2-4]; 1970, page 12 [2-4]; 1971, page 12 [2-4]; 1972, page 21 [2-4]; 1973, page 25 [2-4]; 1975, page 25 [2-4]; 1977, page 36 [2-4]; 1981, page 1 [2-12]

Cut: 1422. Line: 1965. Orleans. Goblet. 11-3/4 oz. / 7-1/4" hi. **References:** 1967, page 7 [1-1]; 1968, page 10 [2-1]; 1969, page 10 [2-1]; 1970, page 12 [2-1]; 1971, page 12 [2-1]; 1972, page 21 [2-1]; 1973, page 25 [2-1]; 1975, page 25 [2-1]; 1977, page 36 [2-1]; 1981, page 1 [2-9]

Cut: 1422. Line: 1965. Orleans. Ice Tea. 13-1/2 oz. / 6-3/4" hi. **References:** 1967, page 7 [1-6]; 1968, page 10 [2-6]; 1969, page 10 [2-6]; 1970, page 12 [2-6]; 1971, page 12 [2-6]; 1972, page 21 [2-6]; 1973, page 25 [2-6]; 1975, page 25 [2-5]; 1977, page 36 [2-5]

Cut: 1422. Line: 1965. Orleans. Juice. 6 oz. / 5-1/2" hi. **References:** 1967, page 7 [1-5]; 1968, page 10 [2-5]; 1969, page 10 [2-5]; 1970, page 12 [2-5]; 1971, page 12 [2-5]; 1972, page 21 [2-5]; 1973, page 25 [2-5]

Cut: 1422. Line: 1965. Orleans. Plate. 7" / Actually 7-7/8" Dia. **References:** 1967, page 7 [1-8]; 1968, page 10 [2-8]; 1969, page 10 [2-8]; 1970, page 12 [2-8]; 1971, page 12 [2-8]; 1972, page 21 [2-8]; 1973, page 25 [2-8]; 1975, page 25 [2-7]; 1977, page 36 [2-7]

Cut: 1422. Line: 1965. Orleans. Plate. 8" / Actually 8-3/4" Dia. **References:** 1967, page 7 [1-9]; 1968, page 10 [2-9]; 1969, page 10 [2-9]; 1970, page 12 [2-9]; 1971, page 12 [2-9]; 1972, page 21 [2-9]; 1973, page 25 [2-9]; 1975, page 25 [2-8]; 1977, page 36 [2-8]

Cut: 1422. Line: 1965. Orleans. Sherbet. 7-1/2 oz. / 5-1/4" hi. **References:** 1967, page 7 [1-2]; 1968, page 10 [2-2]; 1969, page 10 [2-2]; 1970, page 12 [2-2]; 1971, page 12 [2-2]; 1972, page 21 [2-2];
1973, page 25 [2-2]; 1975, page 25 [2-2]; 1977, page 36 [2-2]; 1981, page 1 [2-10]

Cut: 1422. Line: 1965. Orleans. Wine. 7-1/2 oz. / 6-1/4" hi. **References:** 1967, page 7 [1-3]; 1968, page 10 [2-3]; 1969, page 10 [2-3]; 1970, page 12 [2-3]; 1971, page 12 [2-3]; 1972, page 21 [2-3]; 1973, page 25 [2-3]; 1975, page 25 [2-3]; 1977, page 36 [2-3]; 1981, page 1 [2-11]

Cut: 1423. Line: 1965. Capristrano. 1305 Dessert-Finger Bowl. 4-1/2" Dia. **References:** 1967, page 7 [3-7]; 1968, page 10 [2-16]

Cut: 1423. Line: 1965. Capristrano. Cordial. 1-1/4 oz. - 4" hi. **References:** 1967, page 7 [3-4]; 1968, page 10 [2-13]

Cut: 1423. Line: 1965. Capristrano. Goblet. 11-3/4 oz. / 7-1/4" hi. **References:** 1967, page 7 [3-1]; 1968, page 10 [2-10]

Cut: 1423. Line: 1965. Capristrano. Ice Tea. 13-1/2 oz. / 6-3/4" hi. **References:** 1967, page 7 [3-6]; 1968, page 10 [2-15]

Cut: 1423. Line: 1965. Capristrano. Juice. 6 oz. / 5-1/2" hi. **References:** 1967, page 7 [3-5]; 1968, page 10 [2-14]

Cut: 1423. Line: 1965. Capristrano. Plate. 7" / Actually 7-7/8" Dia. **References:** 1967, page 7 [3-8]; 1968, page 10 [2-17]

Cut: 1423. Line: 1965. Capristrano. Plate. 8" / Actually 8-3/4" Dia. **References:** 1967, page 7 [3-9]; 1968, page 10 [2-18]

Cut: 1423. Line: 1965. Capristrano. Sherbet. 7-1/2 oz. / 5-1/4" hi. **References:** 1967, page 7 [3-2]; 1968, page 10 [2-11]

Cut: 1423. Line: 1965. Capristrano. Wine. 1-1/4 oz. / 4" hi. **References:** 1967, page 7 [3-3]; 1968, page 10 [2-12]

Cut: 1426. Line: 1282. Buckingham. 1305 Dessert-Finger Bowl. 4-1/2" Dia. **References:** 1967, page 9 [1-7]; 1969, page 15 [1-7]; 1970, page 16 [1-7]; 1971, page 16 [1-7]; 1972, page 25 [1-7]; 1973, page 30 [1-7]; 1975, page 28 [1-6]; 1977, page 39 [1-6]

Cut: 1426. Line: 1282. Buckingham. Cordial. 1-1/4 oz. / 3-3/4" hi. **References:** 1967, page 9 [1-4]; 1969, page 15 [1-4]; 1970, page 16 [1-4]; 1971, page 16 [1-4]; 1972, page 25 [1-4]; 1973, page 30 [1-4]; 1975, page 28 [1-4]; 1977, page 39 [1-4]

Cut: 1426. Line: 1282. Buckingham. Goblet. 10 oz. / 7" hi. **References:** 1967, page 9 [1-1]; 1969, page 15 [1-1]; 1970, page 16 [1-1]; 1971, page 16 [1-1]; 1972, page 25 [1-1]; 1973, page 30 [1-1]; 1975, page 28 [1-1]; 1977, page 39 [1-1]

Cut: 1426. Line: 1282. Buckingham. Ice Tea. 11-1/2 oz. / 6-1/8" hi. **References:** 1967, page 9 [1-6]; 1969, page 15 [1-6]; 1970, page 16 [1-6]; 1971, page 16 [1-6]; 1972, page 25 [1-6]; 1973, page 30 [1-6]; 1975, page 28 [1-5]; 1977, page 39 [1-5]

Cut: 1426. Line: 1282. Buckingham. Juice. 5 oz. / 4-1/2" hi. **References:** 1967, page 9 [1-5]; 1969, page 15 [1-5]; 1970, page 16 [1-5]; 1971, page 16 [1-5]; 1972, page 25 [1-5]; 1973, page 30 [1-5]

Cut: 1426. Line: 1282. Buckingham. Plate. 7" / Actually 7-7/8" Dia. **References:** 1967, page 9 [1-8]; 1969, page 15 [1-8]; 1970, page 16 [1-8]; 1971, page 16 [1-8]; 1972, page 25 [1-8]; 1973, page 30 [1-8]; 1975, page 28 [1-7]; 1977, page 39 [1-7]

Cut: 1426. Line: 1282. Buckingham. Plate. 8" / Actually 8-3/4" Dia. **References:** 1967, page 9 [1-9]; 1969, page 15 [1-9]; 1970, page 16 [1-9]; 1971, page 16 [1-9]; 1972, page 25 [1-9]; 1973, page 30 [1-9]; 1975, page 28 [1-8]; 1977, page 39 [1-8]

Cut: 1426. Line: 1282. Buckingham. Saucer Champagne. 7-1/2 oz. / 5-1/4" hi. **References:** 1967, page 9 [1-2]; 1969, page 15 [1-2]; 1970, page 16 [1-2]; 1971, page 16 [1-2]; 1972, page 25 [1-2]; 1973, page 30 [1-2]; 1975, page 28 [1-2]; 1977, page 39 [1-2]

Cut: 1426. Line: 1282. Buckingham. Table Wine Goblet. 7-1/2 oz. / 6" hi. **References:** 1967, page 9 [1-3]; 1969, page 15 [1-3]; 1970, page 16 [1-3]; 1971, page 16 [1-3]; 1972, page 25 [1-3]; 1973, page 30 [1-3]; 1975, page 28 [1-3]; 1977, page 39 [1-3]

Cut: 1427. Line: 1967. Berkshire. 1305 Dessert-Finger Bowl. 4-1/2" Dia. **References:** 1967, page 6 [1-6]; 1968, page 9 [1-6]; 1969, page 10 [2-6]; 1970, page 10 [2-6]; 1971, page 10 [2-6]; 1972, page 17 [2-6]; 1973, page 22 [2-6]; 1975, page 22 [2-6]; 1977, page 33 [2-6]

Cut: 1427. Line: 1967. Berkshire. Cordial. 1-1/4 oz. / 3-3/4" hi. **References:** 1967, page 6 [1-4]; 1968, page 9 [1-4]; 1969, page 10 [2-4]; 1970, page 10 [2-4]; 1971, page 10 [2-4]; 1972, page 17 [2-4]; 1973, page 22 [2-4]; 1975, page 22 [2-4]; 1977, page 33 [2-4]

Cut: 1427. Line: 1967. Berkshire. Goblet. 12 oz. / 6-3/4" hi. **References:** 1967, page 6 [1-1]; 1968, page 9 [1-1]; 1969, page 10 [2-1]; 1970, page 10 [2-1]; 1971, page 10 [2-1]; 1972, page 17 [2-1]; 1973, page 22 [2-1]; 1975, page 22 [2-1]; 1977, page 33 [2-1]

Cut: 1427. Line: 1967. Berkshire. Ice Tea. 14 oz. / 6-3/8" hi. **References:** 1967, page 6 [1-5]; 1968, page 9 [1-5]; 1969, page 10 [2-5]; 1970, page 10 [2-5]; 1971, page 10 [2-5]; 1972, page 17 [2-5]; 1973, page 22 [2-5]; 1975, page 22 [2-5]; 1977, page 33 [2-5]

Cut: 1427. Line: 1967. Berkshire. Plate. 7" / Actually 7-7/8" Dia. **References:** 1967, page 6 [1-7]; 1968, page 9 [1-7]; 1969, page 10 [2-7]; 1970, page 10 [2-7]; 1971, page 10 [2-7]; 1972, page 17 [2-7]; 1973, page 22 [2-7]; 1975, page 22 [2-7]; 1977, page 33 [2-7]

Cut: 1427. Line: 1967. Berkshire. Plate. 8" / Actually 8-3/4" Dia. **References:** 1967, page 6 [1-8]; 1968, page 9 [1-8]; 1969, page 10 [2-8]; 1970, page 10 [2-8]; 1971, page 10 [2-8]; 1972, page 17 [2-8]; 1973, page 22 [2-8]; 1975, page 22 [2-8]; 1977, page 33 [2-8]

Cut: 1427. Line: 1967. Berkshire. Sherbet. 7-1/2 oz. / 5" hi. **References:** 1967, page 6 [1-2]; 1968, page 9 [1-2]; 1969, page 10 [2-2]; 1970, page 10 [2-2]; 1971, page 10 [2-2]; 1972, page 17 [2-2]; 1973, page 22 [2-2]; 1975, page 22 [2-2]; 1977, page 33 [2-2]

Cut: 1427. Line: 1967. Berkshire. Wine. 7-1/2 oz. / 6" hi. **References:** 1967, page 6 [1-3]; 1968, page 9 [1-3]; 1969, page 10 [2-3]; 1970, page 10 [2-3]; 1971, page 10 [2-3]; 1972, page 17 [2-3]; 1973, page 22 [2-3]; 1975, page 22 [2-3]; 1977, page 33 [2-3]

Cut: 1428. Line: 1967. Sherwood. 1305 Dessert-Finger Bowl. 4-1/2" Dia. **References:** 1967, page 6 [2-6]; 1968, page 9 [2-6]; 1969, page 10 [2-14]; 1970, page 10 [2-14]; 1971, page 10 [2-14]; 1972, page 17 [2-14]; 1973, page 22 [2-14]; 1975, page 22 [2-14]; 1977, page 33 [2-14]

Cut: 1428. Line: 1967. Sherwood. Cordial. 1-1/4 oz. / 3-3/4" hi. **References:** 1967, page 6 [2-4]; 1968, page 9 [2-4]; 1969, page 10 [2-12]; 1970, page 10 [2-12]; 1971, page 10 [2-12]; 1972, page 17 [2-12]; 1973, page 22 [2-12]; 1975, page 22 [2-12]; 1977, page 33 [2-12]

Cut: 1428. Line: 1967. Sherwood. Goblet. 12 oz. / 6-3/4" hi. **References:** 1967, page 6 [2-1]; 1968, page 9 [2-1]; 1969, page 10 [2-9]; 1970, page 10 [2-9]; 1971, page 10 [2-9]; 1972, page 17 [2-9]; 1973, page 22 [2-9]; 1975, page 22 [2-9]; 1977, page 33 [2-9]; 1967, page 6 [2-5]

Cut: 1428. Line: 1967. Sherwood. Ice Tea. 14 oz. / 6-3/8" hi. **References:** 1968, page 9 [2-5]; 1969, page 10 [2-13]; 1970, page 10 [2-13]; 1971, page 10 [2-13]; 1972, page 17 [2-13]; 1973, page 22 [2-13]; 1975, page 22 [2-13]; 1977, page 33 [2-13]

Cut: 1428. Line: 1967. Sherwood. Plate. 7" / Actually 7-7/8" Dia. **References:** 1967, page 6 [2-7]; 1968, page 9 [2-7]; 1969, page 10 [2-15]; 1970, page 10 [2-15]; 1971, page 10 [2-15]; 1972, page 17 [2-15]; 1973, page 22 [2-15]; 1975, page 22 [2-15]; 1977, page 33 [2-15]

Cut: 1428. Line: 1967. Sherwood. Plate. 8" / Actually 8-3/4" Dia. **References:** 1967, page 6 [2-8]; 1968, page 9 [2-8]; 1969, page 10 [2-16]; 1970, page 10 [2-16]; 1971, page 10 [2-16]; 1972, page 17 [2-16]; 1973, page 22 [2-16]; 1975, page 22 [2-16]; 1977, page 33 [2-16]

Cut: 1428. Line: 1967. Sherwood. Sherbet. 7-1/2 oz. / 5" hi. **References:** 1967, page 6 [2-2]; 1968, page 9 [2-2]; 1969, page 10 [2-10]; 1970, page 10 [2-10]; 1971, page 10 [2-10]; 1972, page 17 [2-10]; 1973, page 22 [2-10]; 1975, page 22 [2-10]; 1977, page 33 [2-10]

Cut: 1428. Line: 1967. Sherwood. Wine. 7-1/2 oz. / 6" hi. **References:** 1967, page 6 [2-3]; 1968, page 9 [2-3]; 1969, page 10 [2-11]; 1970, page 10 [2-11]; 1971, page 10 [2-11]; 1972, page 17 [2-11]; 1973, page 22 [2-11]; 1975, page 22 [2-11]; 1977, page 33 [2-11]

Cut: 1429. Line: 1967. Young Love. 1305 Dessert-Finger Bowl. 4-1/2" Dia. **References:** 1967, page 6 [2-14]; 1968, page 9 [2-14]; 1969, page 10 [1-6]; 1970, page 10 [1-6]; 1971, page 10 [1-6]; 1972, page 17 [1-6]; 1973, page 22 [1-6]; 1975, page 22 [1-6]; 1977, page 33 [1-6]

Cut: 1429. Line: 1967. Young Love. Cordial. 1-1/4 oz. / 3-3/4" hi. **References:** 1967, page 6 [2-12]; 1968, page 9 [2-12]; 1969, page 10 [1-4]; 1970, page 10 [1-4]; 1971, page 10 [1-4]; 1972, page 17 [1-4]; 1973, page 22 [1-4]; 1975, page 22 [1-4]; 1977, page 33 [1-4]

Cut: 1429. Line: 1967. Young Love. Goblet. 12 oz. / 6-3/4" hi. **References:** 1967, page 6 [2-9]; 1968, page 9 [2-9]; 1969, page 10 [1-1]; 1970, page 10 [1-1]; 1971, page 10 [1-1]; 1972, page 17 [1-1]; 1973, page 22 [1-1]; 1975, page 22 [1-1]; 1977, page 33 [1-1]

Cut: 1429. Line: 1967. Young Love. Ice Tea. 14 oz. / 6-3/8" hi. **References:** 1967, page 6 [2-13]; 1968, page 9 [2-13]; 1969, page 10 [1-5]; 1970, page 10 [1-5]; 1971, page 10 [1-5]; 1972, page 17 [1-5]; 1973, page 22 [1-5]; 1975, page 22 [1-5]; 1977, page 33 [1-5]

Cut: 1429. Line: 1967. Young Love. Plate. 7" / Actually 7-7/8" Dia. **References:** 1967, page 6 [2-15]; 1968, page 9 [2-15]; 1969, page 10 [1-7]; 1970, page 10 [1-7]; 1971, page 10 [1-7]; 1972, page 17 [1-7]; 1973, page 22 [1-7]; 1975, page 22 [1-7]; 1977, page 33 [1-7]

Cut: 1429. Line: 1967. Young Love. Plate. 8" / Actually 8-/34" Dia. **References:** 1967, page 6 [2-16]; 1968, page 9 [2-16]; 1969, page 10 [1-8]; 1970, page 10 [1-8]; 1971, page 10 [1-8]; 1972, page 17 [1-8]; 1973, page 22 [1-8]; 1975, page 22 [1-8]; 1977, page 33 [1-8]

Cut: 1429. Line: 1967. Young Love. Sherbet. 7-1/2 oz. / 5" hi. **References:** 1967, page 6 [2-10]; 1968, page 9 [2-10]; 1969, page 10 [1-2]; 1970, page 10 [1-2]; 1971, page 10 [1-2]; 1972, page 17 [1-2]; 1973, page 22 [1-2]; 1975, page 22 [1-2]; 1977, page 33 [1-2]

Cut: 1429. Line: 1967. Young Love. Wine. 7-1/2 oz. / 6" hi. **References:** 1967, page 6 [2-11]; 1968, page 9 [2-11]; 1969, page 10 [1-3]; 1970, page 10 [1-3]; 1971, page 10 [1-3]; 1972, page 17 [1-3]; 1973, page 22 [1-3]; 1975, page 22 [1-3]; 1977, page 33 [1-3]

Cut: 1430. Line: 1966. Kimberly. 1305 Dessert-Finger Bowl. 4-1/2" Dia. **References:** 1967, page 5 [1-6]; 1968, page 8 [1-6]; 1969, page 8 [1-6]; 1970, page 8 [1-6]; 1971, page 8 [1-6]; 1972, page 18 [1-6]; 1973, page 23 [1-6]; 1975, page 23 [1-6]; 1977, page 34 [1-6]

Cut: 1430. Line: 1966. Kimberly. Cordial. 1-1/4 oz. / 3-7/8" hi. **References:** 1967, page 5 [1-4]; 1968, page 8 [1-4]; 1969, page 8 [1-4]; 1970, page 8 [1-4]; 1971, page 8 [1-4]; 1972, page 18 [1-4]; 1973, page 23 [1-4]; 1975, page 23 [1-4]; 1977, page 34 [1-4]; 1981, page 2 [3-8]; 1975/I-75, page 1 [3-2]

Cut: 1430. Line: 1966. Kimberly. Goblet. 12 oz. / 7" hi. **References:** 1967, page 5 [1-1]; 1968, page 8 [1-1]; 1969, page 8 [1-1]; 1970, page 8 [1-1]; 1971, page 8 [1-1]; 1972, page 18 [1-1]; 1973, page 23 [1-1]; 1975, page 23 [1-1]; 1977, page 34 [1-1]; 1981, page 2 [3-5]; 1975/I-75, page 1 [2-1]

Cut: 1430. Line: 1966. Kimberly. Ice Tea. 14 oz. / 6-1/4" hi. **References:** 1967, page 5 [1-5]; 1968, page 8 [1-5]; 1969, page 8 [1-5]; 1970, page 8 [1-5]; 1971, page 8 [1-5]; 1972, page 18 [1-5]; 1973, page 23 [1-5]; 1975, page 23 [1-5]; 1977, page 34 [1-5]; 1975/I-75, page 1 [3-1]

Cut: 1430. Line: 1966. Kimberly. Plate. 7" / Actually 7-7/8" Dia. **References:** 1967, page 5 [1-7]; 1967, page 5 [1-7]; 1968, page 8 [1-7]; 1969, page 8 [1-7]; 1970, page 8 [1-7]; 1971, page 8 [1-7]; 1972, page 18 [1-7]; 1973, page 23 [1-7]; 1975, page 23 [1-7]; 1977, page 34 [1-7]

Cut: 1430. Line: 1966. Kimberly. Plate. 8" / Actually 8-3/4" Dia. **References:** 1967, page 5 [1-8]; 1968, page 8 [1-8]; 1969, page 8 [1-8]; 1970, page 8 [1-8]; 1971, page 8 [1-8]; 1972, page 18 [1-8]; 1973, page 23 [1-8]; 1975, page 23 [1-8]; 1977, page 34 [1-8]

Cut: 1430. Line: 1966. Kimberly. Sherbet. 7-1/2 oz. / 5-1/8" hi. **References:** 1967, page 5 [1-2]; 1968, page 8 [1-2]; 1969, page 8 [1-2]; 1970, page 8 [1-2]; 1971, page 8 [1-2]; 1972, page 18 [1-2]; 1973, page 23 [1-2]; 1975, page 23 [1-2]; 1977, page 34 [1-2]; 1981, page 2 [3-6]; 1975/I-75, page 1 [1-2]

Cut: 1430. Line: 1966. Kimberly. Wine. 7-1/2 oz. / 6" hi. **References:** 1967, page 5 [1-3]; 1968, page 8 [1-3]; 1969, page 8 [1-3]; 1970, page 8 [1-3]; 1971, page 8 [1-3]; 1972, page 18 [1-3]; 1973, page 23 [1-3]; 1975, page 23 [1-3]; 1977, page 34 [1-3]; 1981, page 2 [3-7]; 1975/1-75, page 1 [1-1]

Cut: 1431. Line: 1966. Lavalier. 1305 Dessert-Finger Bowl. 4-1/2" Dia. **References:** 1967, page 5 [1-14]; 1968, page 8 [1-14]; 1969, page 8 [2-14]; 1970, page 8 [2-14]; 1971, page 8 [2-14]; 1972, page 18 [2-14]; 1973, page 23 [2-14]; 1975, page 23 [2-14]; 1977, page 34 [2-14]

Cut: 1431. Line: 1966. Lavalier. Cordial. 1-1/4 oz. / 3-7/8" hi. **References:** 1967, page 5 [1-12]; 1968, page 8 [1-12]; 1969, page 8 [2-12]; 1970, page 8 [2-12]; 1971, page 8 [2-12]; 1972, page 18 [2-12]; 1973, page 23 [2-12]; 1975, page 23 [2-12]; 1977, page 34 [2-12]

Cut: 1431. Line: 1966. Lavalier. Goblet. 12 oz. / 7" hi. **References:** 1967, page 5 [1-9]; 1968, page 8 [1-9]; 1969, page 8 [2-9]; 1970, page 8 [2-9]; 1971, page 8 [2-9]; 1972, page 18 [2-9]; 1973, page 23 [2-9]; 1975, page 23 [2-9]; 1977, page 34 [2-9]

Cut: 1431. Line: 1966. Lavalier. Ice Tea. 14 oz. / 6-1/4" hi. **References:** 1967, page 5 [1-13]; 1968, page 8 [1-13]; 1969, page 8 [2-13]; 1970, page 8 [2-13]; 1971, page 8 [2-13]; 1972, page 18 [2-13]; 1973, page 23 [2-13]; 1975, page 23 [2-13]; 1977, page 34 [2-13]

Cut: 1431. Line: 1966. Lavalier. Plate. 7" / Actually 7-7/8" Dia. **References:** 1967, page 5 [1-15]; 1968, page 8 [1-15]; 1969, page 8 [2-15]; 1970, page 8 [2-15]; 1971, page 8 [2-15]; 1972, page 18 [2-15]; 1973, page 23 [2-15]; 1975, page 23 [2-15]; 1977, page 34 [2-15]

Cut: 1431. Line: 1966. Lavalier. Plate. 8" / Actually 8-3/4" Dia. **References:** 1967, page 5 [1-16]; 1968, page 8 [1-16]; 1969, page 8 [2-16]; 1970, page 8 [2-16]; 1971, page 8 [2-16]; 1972, page 18 [2-16]; 1973, page 23 [2-16]; 1975, page 23 [2-16]; 1977, page 34 [2-16]

Cut: 1431. Line: 1966. Lavalier. Sherbet. 7-1/2 oz. / 5-1/8" hi. **References:** 1967, page 5 [1-10]; 1968, page 8 [1-10]; 1969, page 8 [2-10]; 1970, page 8 [2-10]; 1971, page 8 [2-10]; 1972, page 18 [2-10]; 1973, page 23 [2-10]; 1975, page 23 [2-10]; 1977, page 34 [2-10]

Cut: 1431. Line: 1966. Lavalier. Wine. 7-1/2 oz. / 6" hi. **References:** 1967, page 5 [1-11]; 1968, page 8 [1-11]; 1969, page 8 [2-11]; 1970, page 8 [2-11]; 1971, page 8 [2-11]; 1972, page 18 [2-11]; 1973, page 23 [2-11]; 1975, page 23 [2-11]; 1977, page 34 [2-11]

Cut: 1432. Line: 1966. Traditional. 1305 Dessert-Finger Bowl. 4-1/2" Dia. **References:** 1967, page 5 [2-6]; 1968, page 8 [3-6]; 1969, page 8 [1-6]; 1970, page 8 [1-6]; 1971, page 8 [1-6]; 1972, page 19 [1-6]; 1973, page 24 [1-6]; 1975, page 24 [1-6]; 1977, page 35 [1-6]

Cut: 1432. Line: 1966. Traditional. Cordial. 1-1/4 oz. / 3-7/8" hi. **References:** 1967, page 5 [2-4]; 1968, page 8 [3-4]; 1969, page 8 [1-4]; 1970, page 8 [1-4]; 1971, page 8 [1-4]; 1972, page 19 [1-4]; 1973, page 24 [1-4]; 1975, page 24 [1-4]; 1977, page 35 [1-4]

Cut: 1432. Line: 1966. Traditional. Goblet. 12 oz. / 7" hi. **References:** 1967, page 5 [2-1]; 1968, page 8 [3-1]; 1969, page 8 [1-1]; 1970, page 8 [1-1]; 1971, page 8 [1-1]; 1972, page 19 [1-1]; 1973, page 24 [1-1]; 1975, page 24 [1-1]; 1977, page 35 [1-1]

Cut: 1432. Line: 1966. Traditional. Ice Tea. 14 oz. / 6-1/4" hi. **References:** 1967, page 5 [2-5]; 1968, page 8 [3-5]; 1969, page 8 [1-5]; 1970, page 8 [1-5]; 1971, page 8 [1-5]; 1972, page 19 [1-5]; 1973, page 24 [1-5]; 1975, page 24 [1-5]; 1977, page 35 [1-5]

Cut: 1432. Line: 1966. Traditional. Plate. 7" / 7-7/8" Dia. **References:** 1967, page 5 [2-7]; 1968, page 8 [3-7]; 1969, page 8 [1-7]; 1970, page 8 [1-7]; 1971, page 8 [1-7]; 1972, page 19 [1-7]; 1973, page 24 [1-7]; 1975, page 24 [1-7]; 1977, page 35 [1-7]

Cut: 1432. Line: 1966. Traditional. Plate. 8" / 8-3/4" Dia. **References:** 1967, page 5 [2-8]; 1968, page 8 [3-8];
1969, page 8 [1-8]; 1970, page 8 [1-8]; 1971, page 8 [1-8]; 1972, page 19 [1-8]; 1973, page 24 [1-8]; 1975, page 24 [1-8]; 1977, page 35 [1-8]

Cut: 1432. Line: 1966. Traditional. Sherbet. 7-1/2 oz. / 5-1/8 hi. **References:** 1967, page 5 [2-2]; 1968, page 8 [3-2]; 1969, page 8 [1-2]; 1970, page 8 [1-2]; 1971, page 8 [1-2]; 1972, page 19 [1-2]; 1973, page 24 [1-2]; 1975, page 24 [1-2]; 1977, page 35 [1-2]

Cut: 1432. Line: 1966. Traditional. Wine. 7-1/2 oz. / 6" hi. **References:** 1967, page 5 [2-3]; 1968, page 8 [3-3]; 1969, page 8 [1-3]; 1970, page 8 [1-3]; 1971, page 8 [1-3]; 1972, page 19 [1-3]; 1973, page 24 [1-3]; 1975, page 24 [1-3]; 1977, page 35 [1-3]

Cut: 1433. Line: 960. Cambridge. 1311 Dessert-Finger Bowl. 4-3/4" Dia. **References:** 1967, page 4 [1-6]; 1969, page 6 [1-6]; 1970, page 6 [1-6]; 1971, page 6 [1-6]; 1972, page 16 [1-6]; 1973, page 21 [1-6]; 1975, page 21 [1-6]; 1977, page 32 [1-6]; 19686, page 4 [1-6]

Cut: 1433. Line: 960. Cambridge. Cordial. 1-1/4 oz. / 3-7/8" hi. **References:** 1967, page 4 [1-4]; 1968, page 6 [1-4]; 1969, page 6 [1-4]; 1970, page 6 [1-4]; 1971, page 6 [1-4]; 1972, page 16 [1-4]; 1973, page 21 [1-4]; 1975, page 21 [1-4]; 1977, page 32 [1-4]

Cut: 1433. Line: 960. Cambridge. Goblet. 11-1/2 oz. / 7" hi. **References:** 1967, page 4 [1-1]; 1968, page 6 [1-1]; 1969, page 6 [1-1]; 1970, page 6 [1-1]; 1971, page 6 [1-1]; 1972, page 16 [1-1]; 1973, page 21 [1-1]; 1975, page 21 [1-1]; 1977, page 32 [1-1]

Cut: 1433. Line: 960. Cambridge. Ice Tea. 14 oz. / 6-1/4" hi. **References:** 1967, page 4 [1-5]; 1968, page 6 [1-5]; 1969, page 6 [1-5]; 1970, page 6 [1-5]; 1971, page 6 [1-5]; 1972, page 16 [1-5]; 1973, page 21 [1-5]; 1975, page 21 [1-5]; 1977, page 32 [1-5]

Cut: 1433. Line: 960. Cambridge. Plate. 7" / Actually 7-7/8 inch. **References:** 1967, page 4 [1-7]; 1968, page 4 [1-7]; 1969, page 6 [1-7]; 1970, page 6 [1-7]; 1971, page 6 [1-7]; 1972, page 16 [1-7]; 1973, page 21 [1-7]; 1975, page 21 [1-7]; 1977, page 32 [1-7]

Cut: 1433. Line: 960. Cambridge. Plate. 8" / Actually 8-3/4 inch. **References:** 1967, page 4 [1-8]; 1968, page 6 [1-8]; 1969, page 6 [1-8]; 1970, page 6 [1-8]; 1971, page 6 [1-8]; 1972, page 16 [1-8]; 1973, page 21 [1-8]; 1975, page 21 [1-8]; 1977, page 32 [1-8]

Cut: 1433. Line: 960. Cambridge. Sherbet. 7 oz. / 5-1/4" hi. **References:** 1967, page 4 [1-2]; 1968, page 46 [1-2]; 1969, page 6 [1-2]; 1970, page 6 [1-2]; 1971, page 6 [1-2]; 1972, page 16 [1-2]; 1973, page 21 [1-2]; 1975, page 21 [1-2]; 1977, page 32 [1-2]

Cut: 1433. Line: 960. Cambridge. Wine. 7 oz. / 6" hi. **References:** 1967, page 4 [1-3]; 1968, page 6 [1-3]; 1969, page 6 [1-3]; 1970, page 6 [1-3]; 1971, page 6 [1-3]; 1972, page 16 [1-3]; 1973, page 21 [1-3]; 1975, page 21 [1-3]; 1977, page 32 [1-3]

Cut: 1434. Line: 960. Heirloom. 1311 Dessert-Finger Bowl. 4-3/4" Dia. **References:** 1967, page 4 [3-6]; 1968, page 6 [3-6]; 1969, page 6 [2-14]; 1970, page 6 [2-14]; 1971, page 6 [2-14]

Cut: 1434. Line: 960. Heirloom. Cordial. 1-1/4" oz. / 3-7/8" hi. **References:** 1967, page 4 [3-4]; 1968, page 6 [3-4]; 1969, page 6 [2-12]; 1970, page 6 [2-12]; 1971, page 6 [2-12]

Cut: 1434. Line: 960. Heirloom. Goblet. 11-1/2 oz. / 7" hi. **References:** 1967, page 4 [3-1]; 1968, page 6 [3-1]; 1969, page 6 [2-9]; 1970, page 6 [2-9]; 1971, page 6 [2-9]

Cut: 1434. Line: 960. Heirloom. Ice Tea. 14 oz. / 6-1/4" hi. **References:** 1967, page 4 [3-5]; 1968, page 6 [3-5]; 1969, page 6 [2-13]; 1970, page 6 [2-13]; 1971, page 6 [2-13]

Cut: 1434. Line: 960. Heirloom. Plate. 7" / Actually 7-7/8 inch. **References:** 1967, page 4 [3-7]; 1968, page 6 [3-7]; 1969, page 6 [2-15]; 1970, page 6 [2-15]; 1971, page 6 [2-15]

Cut: 1434. Line: 960. Heirloom. Plate. 8" / Actually 8-3/4 inch. **References:** 1967, page 4 [3-8]; 1968, page 6 [3-8]; 1969, page 6 [2-16]; 1970, page 6 [2-16]; 1971, page 6 [2-16]

Cut: 1434. Line: 960. Heirloom. Sherbet. 7 oz. / 5-1/4" hi. **References:** 1967, page 4 [3-2]; 1968, page 6 [3-2]; 1969, page 6 [2-10]; 1970, page 6 [2-10]; 1971, page 6 [2-10]

Cut: 1434. Line: 960. Heirloom. Wine. 7 oz. / 6" hi. **References:** 1967, page 4 [3-3]; 1968, page 6 [3-3]; 1969, page 6 [2-11]; 1970, page 6 [2-11]; 1971, page 6 [2-11]

Cut: 1435. Line: 960. Old Master. 1311 Dessert-Finger Bowl. 4-3/4" Dia. **References:** 1967, page 4 [2-6]; 1968, page 6 [2-6]; 1969, page 6 [2-6]; 1970, page 6 [2-6]; 1971, page 6 [2-6]; 1972, page 16 [1-14]; 1973, page 21 [1-14]; 1975, page 21 [1-14]; 1977, page 32 [1-14]

Cut: 1435. Line: 960. Old Master. Cordial. 1-1/4 oz. / 3-7/8" hi. **References:** 1967, page 4 [2-4]; 1968, page 6 [2-4]; 1969, page 6 [2-4]; 1970, page 6 [2-4]; 1971, page 6 [2-4]; 1972, page 16 [1-12]; 1973, page 21 [1-12]; 1975, page 21 [1-12]; 1977, page 32 [1-12]; 1981, page 2 [1-16]

Cut: 1435. Line: 960. Old Master. Goblet. 11-1/2 oz. / 7" hi. **References:** 1967, page 4 [2-1]; 1968, page 6 [2-1]; 1969, page 6 [2-1]; 1970, page 6 [2-1]; 1971, page 6 [2-1]; 1972, page 16 [1-9]; 1973, page 21 [1-9]; 1975, page 21 [1-9]; 1977, page 32 [1-9]; 1981, page 2 [1-13]

Cut: 1435. Line: 960. Old Master. Ice Tea. 14 oz. / 6-1/4" hi. **References:** 1967, page 4 [2-5]; 1968, page 6 [2-5]; 1969, page 6 [2-5]; 1970, page 6 [2-5]; 1971, page 6 [2-5]; 1972, page 16 [1-13]; 1973, page 21 [1-13]; 1975, page 21 [1-13]; 1977, page 32 [1-13]

Cut: 1435. Line: 960. Old Master. Plate. 7 inch / Actually 7-7/8 inch. **References:** 1967, page 4 [2-7]; 1968, page 6 [2-7]; 1969, page 6 [2-7]; 1970, page 6 [2-7]; 1971, page 6 [2-7]; 1972, page 16 [1-15]; 1973, page 21 [1-15]; 1975, page 21 [1-15]; 1977, page 32 [1-15]

Cut: 1435. Line: 960. Old Master. Plate. 8 inch / Actually 8-3/4 inch. **References:** 1967, page 4 [2-8]; 1968, page 6 [2-8]; 1969, page 6 [2-8]; 1970, page 6 [2-8]; 1971, page 6 [2-8]; 1972, page 16 [1-16]; 1973, page 21 [1-16]; 1975, page 21 [1-16]; 1977, page 32 [1-16]

Cut: 1435. Line: 960. Old Master. Sherbet. 7 oz. / 5-1/4" hi. **References:** 1967, page 4 [2-2]; 1968, page 6 [2-2]; 1969, page 6 [2-2]; 1970, page 6 [2-2]; 1971, page 6 [2-2]; 1972, page 16 [1-10]; 1973, page 21 [1-10]; 1975, page 21 [1-10]; 1977, page 32 [1-10]; 1981, page 2 [1-14]

Cut: 1435. Line: 960. Old Master. Wine. 4 oz. / 6" hi. **References:** 1967, page 4 [2-3]; 1968, page 6 [2-3]; 1969, page 6 [2-3]; 1970, page 6 [2-3]; 1971, page 6 [2-3]; 1972, page 16 [1-11]; 1973, page 21 [1-11]; 1975, page 21 [1-11]; 1977, page 32 [1-11]; 1981, page 2 [1-15]

Cut: 1436. Line: 960. Ardmore. 1311 Dessert-Finger Bowl. 4-3/4 inches diam. **References:** 1968, page 7 [1-6]; 1969, page 7 [1-6]; 1970, page 7 [1-6]; 1971, page 7 [1-6]; 1972, page 16 [2-6]; 1973, page 21 [2-6]; 1975, page 21 [2-6]; 1977, page 32 [2-6]

Cut: 1436. Line: 960. Ardmore. Cordial. 1-1/4 oz. 3-7/8 inches tall. **References:** 1968, page 7 [1-4]; 1969, page 7 [1-4]; 1970, page 7 [1-4]; 1971, page 7 [1-4]; 1972, page 16 [2-4]; 1973, page 21 [2-4]; 1975, page 21 [2-4]; 1977, page 32 [2-4]; 1981, page 2 [1-4]

Cut: 1436. Line: 960. Ardmore. Goblet. 11-1/2 oz. 7 inches tall. **References:** 1968, page 7 [1-1]; 1969, page 7 [1-1]; 1970, page 7 [1-1]; 1971, page 7 [1-1]; 1972, page 16 [2-1]; 1973, page 21 [2-1]; 1975, page 21 [2-1]; 1977, page 32 [2-1]; 1981, page 2 [1-1]

Cut: 1436. Line: 960. Ardmore. Ice Tea. 14 oz. 6-1/4 inches tall. **References:** 1968, page 7 [1-5]; 1969, page 7 [1-5]; 1970, page 7 [1-5]; 1971, page 7 [1-5]; 1972, page 16 [2-5]; 1973, page 21 [2-5]; 1975, page 21 [2-5]; 1977, page 32 [2-5]

Cut: 1436. Line: 960. Ardmore. Plate. 7 inches diam. Actually 7-7/8" Dia. **References:** 1968, page 7 [1-7]; 1969, page 7 [1-7]; 1970, page 7 [1-7]; 1971, page 7 [1-7]; 1972, page 16 [2-7]; 1973, page 21 [2-7]; 1975, page 21 [2-7]; 1977, page 32 [2-7]

Cut: 1436. Line: 960. Ardmore. Plate. 8 inches diam. Actually 8-3/4" Dia. **References:** 1968, page 7 [1-8]; 1969, page 7 [1-8]; 1970, page 7 [1-8]; 1971, page 7 [1-8]; 1972, page 16 [2-8]; 1973, page 21 [2-8]; 1975, page 21 [2-8]; 1977, page 32 [2-8]

Cut: 1436. Line: 960. Ardmore. Sherbet. 7 oz. 5-1/4 inches tall. **References:** 1968, page 7 [1-2]; 1969, page 7 [1-2]; 1970, page 7 [1-2]; 1971, page 7 [1-2]; 1972, page 16 [2-2]; 1973, page 21 [2-2]; 1975, page 21 [2-2]; 1977, page 32 [2-2]; 1981, page 2 [1-2]

Cut: 1436. Line: 960. Ardmore. Wine. 7 oz. 6 inches tall. **References:** 1968, page 7 [1-3]; 1969, page 7 [1-3]; 1970, page 7 [1-3]; 1971, page 7 [1-3]; 1972, page 16 [2-3]; 1973, page 21 [2-3]; 1975, page 21 [2-3]; 1977, page 32 [2-3]; 1981, page 2 [1-3]

Cut: 1436. Line: 960. Gold Brocade. Plate. 8 inches diam. Actually 8-3/4" Dia., 2 Gold Bands. **References:** 1975, page 21 [2-16]; 1977, page 32 [2-16]

Cut: 1437. Line: 960. Radiance. 1311 Dessert-Finger Bowl. 4-3/4 inches diam. **References:** 1968, page 7 [2-6]; 1969, page 7 [2-6]; 1970, page 7 [2-6]; 1971, page 7 [2-6]

Cut: 1437. Line: 960. Radiance. Cordial. 1-1/4 oz. 3-7/8 inches tall. **References:** 1968, page 7 [2-4]; 1969, page 7 [2-4]; 1970, page 7 [2-4]; 1971, page 7 [2-4]

Cut: 1437. Line: 960. Radiance. Goblet. 11-1/2 oz. 7 inches tall. **References:** 1968, page 7 [2-1]; 1969, page 7 [2-1]; 1970, page 7 [2-1]; 1971, page 7 [2-1]

Cut: 1437. Line: 960. Radiance. Ice Tea. 14 oz. 6-1/4 inches tall. **References:** 1968, page 7 [2-5]; 1969, page 7 [2-5]; 1970, page 7 [2-5]; 1971, page 7 [2-5]

Cut: 1437. Line: 960. Radiance. Plate. 7 inches diam. Actually 7-7/8" Dia. **References:** 1968, page 7 [2-7]; 1969, page 7 [2-7]; 1970, page 7 [2-7]; 1971, page 7 [2-7]

Cut: 1437. Line: 960. Radiance. Plate. 8 inches diam. Actually 8-3/4" Dia. **References:** 1968, page 7 [2-8]; 1969, page 7 [2-8]; 1970, page 7 [2-8]; 1971, page 7 [2-8]

Cut: 1437. Line: 960. Radiance. Sherbet. 7 oz. 5-1/4 inches tall. **References:** 1968, page 7 [2-2]; 1969, page 7 [2-2]; 1970, page 7 [2-2]; 1971, page 7 [2-2]

Cut: 1437. Line: 960. Radiance. Wine. 7 oz. 6 inches tall. **References:** 1968, page 7 [2-3]; 1969, page 7 [2-3]; 1970, page 7 [2-3]; 1971, page 7 [2-3]

Cut: 1438. Line: 960. Gold Brocade. 1311 Dessert-Finger Bowl. 4-3/4 inches diam. With 2 Gold Bands. **References:** 1970, page 7 [2-14]; 1971, page 7 [2-14]; 1972, page 16 [2-14]; 1973, page 21 [2-14]; 1975, page 21 [2-14]; 1977, page 32 [2-14]

Cut: 1438. Line: 960. Gold Brocade. Cordial. 1-1/4 oz. 3-7/8 inches tall. With 2 Gold Bands. **References:** 1970, page 7 [2-12]; 1971, page 7 [2-12]; 1972, page 16 [2-12]; 1973, page 21 [2-12]; 1975, page 21 [2-12]; 1977, page 32 [2-12]; 1981, page 2 [1-8]

Cut: 1438. Line: 960. Gold Brocade. Goblet. 11-1/2 oz. 7 inches tall. With 2 Gold Bands. **References:** 1970, page 7 [2-9]; 1971, page 7 [2-9]; 1972, page 16 [2-9]; 1973, page 21 [2-9]; 1975, page 21 [2-9]; 1977, page 32 [2-9]; 1981, page 2 [1-5]

Cut: 1438. Line: 960. Gold Brocade. Ice Tea. 14 oz. 6-1/4 inches tall. With 2 Gold Bands. **References:** 1970, page 7 [2-13]; 1971, page 7 [2-13]; 1972, page 16 [2-13]; 1973, page 21 [2-13]; 1975, page 21 [2-13]; 1977, page 32 [2-13]

Cut: 1438. Line: 960. Gold Brocade. Plate. 7 inches diam. With 2 Gold Bands, Actually 7-7/8" Dia. **References:** 1970, page 7 [2-15]; 1971, page 7 [2-15]; 1972, page 16 [2-15]; 1973, page 21 [2-15]; 1975, page 21 [2-15]; 1977, page 32 [2-15]

Cut: 1438. Line: 960. Gold Brocade. Plate. 8 inches diam. With 2 Gold Bands, Actually 8-3/4" Dia. **References:** 1970, page 7 [2-16]; 1971, page 7 [2-16]; 1972, page 16 [2-16]; 1973, page 21 [2-16]

Cut: 1438. Line: 960. Gold Brocade. Sherbet. 7 oz. 5-1/4 inches tall. With 2 Gold Bands. **References:** 1970, page 7 [2-10]; 1971, page 7 [2-10]; 1972, page 16 [2-10]; 1973, page 21 [2-10]; 1975, page 21 [2-10]; 1977, page 32 [2-10]; 1981, page 2 [1-6]

Cut: 1438. Line: 960. Gold Brocade. Wine. 7 oz. 6 inches tall. With 2 Gold Bands. **References:** 1970, page 7 [2-11]; 1971, page 7 [2-11]; 1972, page 16 [2-11]; 1973, page 21 [2-11]; 1975, page 21 [2-11]; 1977, page 32 [2-11]; 1981, page 2 [1-7]

Cut: 1438. Line: 960. Radiance. 1311 Dessert-Finger Bowl. 4-3/4 inches diam. With 2 Gold Bands. **References:** 1969, page 7 [2-14]

Cut: 1438. Line: 960. Radiance. Cordial. 1-1/4 oz. 3-7/8 inches tall. With 2 Gold Bands. **References:** 1969, page 7 [2-12]

Cut: 1438. Line: 960. Radiance. Goblet. 11-1/2 oz. 7 inches tall. With 2 Gold Bands. **References:** 1969, page 7 [2-9]

Cut: 1438. Line: 960. Radiance. Ice Tea. 14 oz. 6-1/4 inches tall. With 2 Gold Bands. **References:** 1969, page 7 [2-13]

Cut: 1438. Line: 960. Radiance. Plate. 7 inches diam. With 2 Gold Bands, Actually 7-7/8" Dia. **References:** 1969, page 7 [2-15]

Cut: 1438. Line: 960. Radiance. Plate. 8 inches diam. With 2 Gold Bands, Actually 8-3/4" Dia. **References:** 1969, page 7 [2-16]

Cut: 1438. Line: 960. Radiance. Sherbet. 7 oz. 5-1/4 inches tall. With 2 Gold Bands. **References:** 1969, page 7 [2-10]

Cut: 1438. Line: 960. Radiance. Wine. 7 oz. 6 inches tall. With 2 Gold Bands. **References:** 1969, page 7 [2-11]

Cut: 1439. Line: 1966. Bridal Tiara. 1305 Dessert-Finger Bowl. 4-1/2 inches diam. **References:** 1968, page 8 [2-6]; 1969, page 8 [2-6]; 1970, page 8 [2-6]; 1971, page 8 [2-6]; 1972, page 18 [2-6]; 1973, page 23 [2-6]; 1975, page 23 [2-6];

1977, page 34 [2-6]

Cut: 1439. Line: 1966. Bridal Tiara. Cordial. 1-1/4 oz. 3-7/8 inches tall. **References:** 1968, page 8 [2-4]; 1969, page 8 [2-4]; 1970, page 8 [2-4]; 1971, page 8 [2-4]; 1972, page 18 [2-4]; 1973, page 23 [2-4]; 1975, page 23 [2-4]; 1977, page 34 [2-4]; 1981, page 2 [3-4]

Cut: 1439. Line: 1966. Bridal Tiara. Goblet. 12 oz. 7 inches tall. **References:** 1968, page 8 [2-1]; 1969, page 8 [2-1]; 1970, page 8 [2-1]; 1971, page 8 [2-1]; 1972, page 18 [2-1]; 1973, page 23 [2-1]; 1975, page 23 [2-1]; 1977, page 34 [2-1]; 1981, page 2 [3-1]

Cut: 1439. Line: 1966. Bridal Tiara. Ice Tea. 14 oz. 6-/14 inches tall. **References:** 1968, page 8 [2-5]; 1969, page 8 [2-5]; 1970, page 8 [2-5]; 1971, page 8 [2-5]; 1972, page 18 [2-5]; 1973, page 23 [2-5]; 1975, page 23 [2-5]; 1977, page 34 [2-5]

Cut: 1439. Line: 1966. Bridal Tiara. Plate. 7 inches diam. Actually 7-7/8" Dia. **References:** 1968, page 8 [2-7]; 1969, page 8 [2-7]; 1970, page 8 [2-7]; 1971, page 8 [2-7]; 1972, page 18 [2-7]; 1973, page 23 [2-7]; 1975, page 23 [2-7]; 1977, page 34 [2-7]

Cut: 1439. Line: 1966. Bridal Tiara. Plate. 8 inches diam. Actually 8-3/4" Dia. **References:** 1968, page 8 [2-8]; 1969, page 8 [2-8]; 1970, page 8 [2-8]; 1971, page 8 [2-8]; 1972, page 18 [2-8]; 1973, page 23 [2-8]; 1975, page 23 [2-8]; 1977, page 34 [2-8]

Cut: 1439. Line: 1966. Bridal Tiara. Sherbet. 7-1/2 oz. 5-1/8 inches tall. **References:** 1968, page 8 [2-2]; 1969, page 8 [2-2]; 1970, page 8 [2-2]; 1971, page 8 [2-2]; 1972, page 18 [2-2]; 1973, page 23 [2-2]; 1975, page 23 [2-2]; 1977, page 34 [2-2]; 1981, page 2 [3-2]

Cut: 1439. Line: 1966. Bridal Tiara. Wine. 7-1/2 oz. 6 inches tall. **References:** 1968, page 8 [2-3]; 1969, page 8 [2-3]; 1970, page 8 [2-3]; 1971, page 8 [2-3]; 1972, page 18 [2-3]; 1973, page 23 [2-3]; 1975, page 23 [2-3]; 1977, page 34 [2-3]; 1981, page 2 [3-3]

Cut: 1440. Line: 1967. Chapel Belle. 1305 Dessert-Finger Bowl. 4-1/2 inches diam. **References:** 1968, page 9 [1-14]

Cut: 1440. Line: 1967. Chapel Belle. Cordial. 1-1/4 oz. 3-3/4 inches tall. **References:** 1968, page 9 [1-12]

Cut: 1440. Line: 1967. Chapel Belle. Goblet. 12 oz. 6-3/4 inches tall. **References:** 1968, page 9 [1-9]

Cut: 1440. Line: 1967. Chapel Belle. Ice Tea. 14 oz. 6-3/8 inches tall. **References:** 1968, page 9 [1-13]

Cut: 1440. Line: 1967. Chapel Belle. Plate. 7 inches diam. Actually 7-7/8" Dia. **References:** 1968, page 9 [1-15]

Cut: 1440. Line: 1967. Chapel Belle. Plate. 8 inches diam. Actually 8-3/4" Dia. **References:** 1968, page 9 [1-16]

Cut: 1440. Line: 1967. Chapel Belle. Sherbet. 7-1/2 oz. 5 inches tall. **References:** 1968, page 9 [1-10]

Cut: 1440. Line: 1967. Chapel Belle. Wine. 7-1/2 oz. 6 inches tall. **References:** 1968, page 9 [1-11]

Cut: 1441. Line: 1971. Bristol. 1311 Dessert-Finger Bowl. 4-3/4 inches diam. **References:** 1971, page 19 [1-14]

Cut: 1441. Line: 1971. Bristol. Cordial. 1-1/2 oz. 4 inches tall. **References:** 1971, page 19 [1-12]

Cut: 1441. Line: 1971. Bristol. Goblet. 11-1/2 oz. 7 inches tall. **References:** 1971, page 19 [1-9]

Cut: 1441. Line: 1971. Bristol. Ice Tea. 14-1/2 oz. 7-1/8 inches tall. **References:** 1971, page 19 [1-13]

Cut: 1441. Line: 1971. Bristol. Plate. 7 inches diam. Actually 7-7/8" Dia. **References:** 1971, page 19 [1-15]

Cut: 1441. Line: 1971. Bristol. Plate. 8 inches diam. Actually 8-3/4" Dia. **References:** 1971, page 19 [1-16]

Cut: 1441. Line: 1971. Bristol. Sherbet. 7-1/2 oz. 5 inches tall. **References:** 1971, page 19 [1-10]

Cut: 1441. Line: 1971. Bristol. Wine. 7 oz. 5-7/8 inches tall. **References:** 1971, page 19 [1-11]

Cut: 1441. Line: 1971. Kingsley. 1311 Dessert-Finger Bowl. 4-3/4 inches diam. **References:** 1970, page 11 [1-14]

Cut: 1441. Line: 1971. Kingsley. Cordial. 1-1/2 oz. 4 inches tall. **References:** 1970, page 11 [1-12]

Cut: 1441. Line: 1971. Kingsley. Goblet. 11-1/2 oz. 7 inches tall. **References:** 1970, page 11 [1-9]

Cut: 1441. Line: 1971. Kingsley. Ice Tea. 14-1/2 oz. 7-1/8 inches tall. **References:** 1970, page 11 [1-13]

Cut: 1441. Line: 1971. Kingsley. Plate. 7 inches diam. Actually 7-7/8" Dia. **References:** 1970, page 11 [1-15]

Cut: 1441. Line: 1971. Kingsley. Plate. 8 inches diam. Actually 8-3/4" Dia. **References:** 1970, page 11 [1-16]

Cut: 1441. Line: 1971. Kingsley. Sherbet. 7-1/2 oz. 5 inches tall. **References:** 1970, page 11 [1-10]

Cut: 1441. Line: 1971. Kingsley. Wine. 7 oz. 5-7/8 inches tall. **References:** 1970, page 11 [1-11]

Cut: 1442. Line: 1971. Kingsley. 1311 Dessert-Finger Bowl. 4-3/4 inches diam. **References:** 1970, page 11 [1-6]; 1971, page 19 [1-6]

Cut: 1442. Line: 1971. Kingsley. Cordial. 1-1/2 oz. 4 inches tall. **References:** 1970, page 11 [1-4]; 1971, page 19 [1-4]

Cut: 1442. Line: 1971. Kingsley. Goblet. 11-1/2 oz. 7 inches tall. **References:** 1970, page 11 [1-1]; 1971, page 19 [1-1]

Cut: 1442. Line: 1971. Kingsley. Ice Tea. 14-1/2 oz. 7-1/8 inches tall. **References:** 1970, page 11 [1-5]; 1971, page 19 [1-5]

Cut: 1442. Line: 1971. Kingsley. Plate. 7 inches diam. Actually 7-7/8" Dia. **References:** 1970, page 11 [1-7]; 1971, page 19 [1-7]

Cut: 1442. Line: 1971. Kingsley. Plate. 8 inches diam. Actually 8-3/4" Dia. **References:** 1970, page 11 [1-8]; 1971, page 19 [1-8]

Cut: 1442. Line: 1971. Kingsley. Sherbet. 7-1/2 oz. 5 inches tall. **References:** 1970, page 11 [1-2]; 1971, page 19 [1-2]

Cut: 1442. Line: 1971. Kingsley. Wine. 7 oz. 5-7/8 inches tall. **References:** 1970, page 11 [1-3]; 1971, page 19 [1-3]

Cut: 1443. Line: 1973. Artistry. 1305 Dessert-Finger Bowl. 4-1/2 inches diam. Crystal. **References:** 1972, page 20 [2-14]; 1973, page 27 [2-14]

Cut: 1443. Line: 1973. Artistry. Cordial. 1-1/2 oz. 4 inches tall. Crystal. **References:** 1972, page 20 [2-12]; 1973, page 27 [2-12]

Cut: 1443. Line: 1973. Artistry. Goblet. 13 oz. 7 inches tall. Crystal. **References:** 1972, page 20 [2-9]; 1973, page 27 [2-9]

Cut: 1443. Line: 1973. Artistry. Ice Tea. 17-1/2 oz. 7-1/8 inches tall. Crystal. **References:** 1972, page 20 [2-13]; 1973, page 27 [2-13]

Cut: 1443. Line: 1973. Artistry. Plate. 7 inches diam. Crystal, Actually 7-7/8" Dia. **References:** 1972, page 20 [2-15]; 1973, page 27 [2-15]

Cut: 1443. Line: 1973. Artistry. Plate. 8 inches diam. Crystal, Actually 8-3/4" Dia. **References:** 1972, page 20 [2-16]; 1973, page 27 [2-16]

Cut: 1443. Line: 1973. Artistry. Sherbet. 7-1/2 oz. 5-1/8 inches tall. Crystal. **References:** 1972, page 20 [2-10]; 1973, page 27 [2-10]

Cut: 1443. Line: 1973. Artistry. Wine. 8-1/2 oz. 6-3/8 inches tall. Crystal. **References:** 1972, page 20 [2-11]; 1973, page 27 [2-11]

Cut: 1443. Line: 1973. Enchantment. Sherbet. 7-1/2 oz. 5-1/8 inches tall. Pink/Crystal Foot. Colors & Designs Available: Blue/Crystal Foot, Pink/Crystal Foot, Blue/Crystal Foot/Cut 1443, Pink/Crystal Foot/Cut 1443, Black Decal and Gold Band, White Decal and Platinum Band. Items Available: Goblet, Sherbet, Wine, Cordial, Ice Tea. **References:** 1971, page 40 [2-2]

Cut: 1443. Line: 1973. Intrigue. Wine. 8-1/2 oz. 6-3/8 inches tall. Blue, Crystal Foot. Colors & Designs Available: Blue/Crystal Foot, Pink/Crystal Foot, Blue/Crystal Foot/Cut 1443, Pink/Crystal Foot/Cut 1443, Black Decal and Gold Band, White Decal and Platinum Band. Items Available: Goblet, Sherbet, Wine, Cordial, Ice Tea. **References:** 1971, page 40 [1-1]

Cut: 1443. Line: 5321. Classic. Dessert-Champagne. 11 oz. 4-7/8 inches tall. Blue/Crystal Foot. Colors Available: Blue/Crystal Foot, Pink/Crystal Foot, Crystal Cut 1443, Blue/Crystal Foot Cut 1443, Pink/Crystal Foot Cut 1443. Item Available: Goblet, Dessert-Champagne, White Wine. **References:** 1971, page 41 [3-4]

Cut: 1443. Line: 5321. Illusion. Goblet. 14 oz. 7 inches tall. Pink/Crystal Foot. Colors Available: Blue/Crystal Foot, Pink/Crystal Foot, Crystal Cut 1443, Blue/Crystal Foot Cut 1443, Pink/Crystal Foot Cut 1443. Item Available: Goblet, Dessert-Champagne, White Wine. **References:** 1971, page 41 [1-1]

Cut: 1443. Line: 5321. Illusion. White Wine Goblet. 8-1/2 oz. 6-5/8 inches tall. Pink/Crystal Foot. Colors Available: Blue/Crystal Foot, Pink/Crystal Foot, Crystal Cut 1443, Blue/Crystal Foot Cut 1443, Pink/Crystal Foot Cut 1443. Item Available: Goblet, Dessert-Champagne, White Wine. **References:** 1971, page 41 [2-1]

Cut: 1443. Line: 5321. Royalty. 1305 Dessert-Finger Bowl. 4-1/2 inches diam. **References:** 1972, page 22 [2-5]; 1973, page 26 [2-5]

Cut: 1443. Line: 5321. Royalty. Brandy and Liqueur. 2-1/2 oz. 4-1/2 inches tall. **References:** 1972, page 22 [2-4]; 1973, page 26 [2-4]

Cut: 1443. Line: 5321. Royalty. Dessert-Champagne. 11 oz. 4-7/8 inches tall. **References:** 1972, page 22 [2-2]; 1973, page 26 [2-2]

Cut: 1443. Line: 5321. Royalty. Plate. 7 inches diam. Actually 7-7/8" Dia. **References:** 1972, page 22 [2-6]; 1973, page 26 [2-6]

Cut: 1443. Line: 5321. Royalty. Plate. 8 inches diam. Actually 8-3/4" Dia. **References:** 1972, page 22 [2-7]; 1973, page 26 [2-7]

Cut: 1443. Line: 5321. Royalty. Vintage Wine Goblet. 14 oz. 7 inches tall. **References:** 1972, page 22 [2-1]; 1973, page 26 [2-1]

Cut: 1443. Line: 5321. Royalty. White Wine Goblet. 8-1/2 oz. 6-5/8 inches tall. Crystal Foot. Colors Available: Blue/Crystal Foot, Pink/Crystal Foot, Crystal Cut 1443, Blue/Crystal Foot Cut 1443, Pink/Crystal Foot Cut 1443. Item Available: Goblet, Dessert-Champagne, White Wine. **References:** 1971, page 41 [2-2]; 1972, page 22 [2-3]; 1973, page 26 [2-3]

Cut: 1444. Line: 970. America. Cordial. 2 oz. 5-1/4 inches tall. **References:** 1977, page 27 [1-8]

Cut: 1444. Line: 970. America. Goblet. 9-1/2 oz. 8-1/2 inches tall. **References:** 1977, page 27 [1-5]

Cut: 1444. Line: 970. America. Sherbet. 7-1/2 oz. 6-1/2 inches tall. **References:** 1977, page 27 [1-6]

Cut: 1444. Line: 970. America. Wine. 5 oz. 7-1/4 inches tall. **References:** 1977, page 27 [1-7]

Cut: 1444. Line: 970. Heritage. Cordial. 2 oz. 5-1/4 inches tall. **References:** 1976, page 2 [1-4]

Cut: 1444. Line: 970. Heritage. Goblet. 9-1/2 oz. 8-1/2 inches tall. **References:** 1976, page 2 [1-1]

Cut: 1444. Line: 970. Heritage. Sherbet. 7-1/2 oz. 6-1/2 inches tall. **References:** 1976, page 2 [1-2]

Cut: 1444. Line: 970. Heritage. Wine. 5 oz. 7-1/4 inches tall. **References:** 1976, page 2 [1-3]

Cut: 1444. Line: 1978. America. Beverage. **References:** 1977, page 24 [1-1]

Cut: 1444. Line: 1978. America. On the Rocks. 15-1/2 oz. 4-1/2 inches tall. **References:** 1976, page 11 [2-2]

Cut: 1445. Line: 4. Heritage. Bell. 5-1/2 inches tall. **References:** 1976, page 7 [2-2]; 1977, page 23 [5-2]

Cut: 1445. Line: 970. America. Cordial. 2 oz. 5-1/4 inches tall. **References:** 1976, page 2 [1-8]

Cut: 1445. Line: 970. America. Goblet. 9-1/2 oz. 8-1/2 inches tall. **References:** 1976, page 2 [1-5]

Cut: 1445. Line: 970. America. Sherbet. 7-1/2 oz. 6-1/2 inches tall. **References:** 1976, page 2 [1-6]

Cut: 1445. Line: 970. America. Wine. 5 oz. 7-1/4 inches tall. **References:** 1976, page 2 [1-7]

Cut: 1445. Line: 970. Heritage. Cordial. 2 oz. 5-1/4 inches tall. **References:** 1977, page 27 [1-4]

Cut: 1445. Line: 970. Heritage. Goblet. 9-1/2 oz. 8-1/2 inches tall. **References:** 1977, page 27 [1-1]

Cut: 1445. Line: 970. Heritage. Sherbet. 7-1/2 oz. 6-1/2 inches tall. **References:** 1977, page 27 [1-2]

Cut: 1445. Line: 970. Heritage. Wine. 5 oz. 7-1/4 inches tall. **References:** 1977, page 27 [1-3]

Cut: 1445, Dorchester. Line: 982. Elite Collection. Cordial. 2 oz. 4-3/4 inches tall. **References:** 1978, page 2 [1-4]

Cut: 1445, Dorchester. Line: 982. Elite Collection. Goblet. 13-1/2 oz. 7-1/2 inches tall. **References:** 1978, page 2 [1-1]

Cut: 1445, Dorchester. Line: 982. Elite Collection. Sherbet. 8 oz. 5-3/8 inches tall. **References:** 1978, page 2 [1-2]

Cut: 1445, Dorchester. Line: 982. Elite Collection. Wine. 7 oz. 6-3/8 inches tall. **References:** 1978, page 2 [1-3]

Cut: 1446. Wicker. Bell. **References:** 1981, page 11 [3-1]; 1983, page 7 [1-1L]

Cut: 1446. Line: 4. Wicker. Bell. 5-1/2 inches tall. All Bells Individually Gift Boxed. **References:** 1976, page 7 [2-3]; 1977, page 23 [3-3]; 1979, page 13 [1-2]

Cut: 1446. Line: 70. Vase. 7 inches tall. **References:** 1980, page 3 [1-4]

Cut: 1446. Line: 70. Wicker. Vase. 7 inches tall. **References:** 1981, page 10 [2-4]

Cut: 1446. Line: 970. Wicker. Cordial. 2 oz. 5-1/4 inches tall. **References:** 1976, page 3 [1-4]; 1977, page 27 [1-4]

Cut: 1446. Line: 970. Wicker. Goblet. 9-1/2 oz. 8-1/2 inches tall. **References:** 1976, page 3 [1-1]; 1977, page 27 [1-1]

Cut: 1446. Line: 970. Wicker. Sherbet. 7-1/2 oz. 6-1/2 inches tall. **References:** 1976, page 3 [1-2]; 1977, page 27 [1-2]

Cut: 1446. Line: 970. Wicker. Wine. 5 oz. 7-1/4 inches tall. **References:** 1976, page 3 [1-3]; 1977, page 27 [1-3]

Cut: 1446. Line: 1978. Wicker. On The Rocks. 15-1/2 oz. 4-1/2 inches tall. **References:** 1976, page 11 [2-1]; 1977, page 24 [2-1]

Cut: 1447. Sunburst. Pony. 3 oz. 3 inches tall. **References:** 1978, page 6 [1-1]

Cut: 1447. Line: 4. Sunburst. Bell. 5-1/2 inches tall. All Bells Individually Gift Boxed. **References:** 1977, page 23 [3-1]; 1979, page 13 [4-4]

Cut: 1447. Line: 970. Sunburst. Cordial. 2 oz. 5-1/4 inches tall. **References:** 1976, page 3 [1-8]; 1977, page 27 [1-8]

Cut: 1447. Line: 970. Sunburst. Goblet. 9-1/2 oz. 8-1/2 inches tall. **References:** 1976, page 3 [1-5]; 1977, page 27 [1-5]

Cut: 1447. Line: 970. Sunburst. Sherbet. 7-1/2 oz. 6-1/2 inches tall. **References:** 1976, page 3 [1-6]; 1977, page 27 [1-6]

Cut: 1447. Line: 970. Sunburst. Wine. 5 oz. 7-1/4 inches tall. **References:** 1976, page 3 [1-7]; 1977, page 27 [1-7]

Cut: 1447. Line: 1978. Sunburst. Old Fashion. **References:** 1977, page 24 [3-1]

Cut: 1447. Line: 1978. Sunburst. On the Rocks. 15-1/2 oz. 4-1/2 inches tall. **References:** 1976, page 11 [1-2]

Cut: 1448. Line: 3. Chalice. Bell. 4-3/8 inches tall. **References:** 1977, page 22 [4-1]

Cut: 1448. Line: 972. Chalice. Cordial. 3 oz. 5-5/8 inches tall. **References:** 1976, page 4 [1-4]; 1977, page 29 [1-4]; 1981, page 1 [1-4]

Cut: 1448. Line: 972. Chalice. Goblet. 13 oz. 7-1/2 inches tall. **References:** 1976, page 4 [1-1]; 1977, page 29 [1-1]; 1981, page 1 [1-1]

Cut: 1448. Line: 972. Chalice. Sherbet. 9 oz. 6 inches tall. **References:** 1976, page 4 [1-2]; 1977, page 29 [1-2]; 1981, page 1 [1-2]

Cut: 1448. Line: 972. Chalice. Wine. 7-1/2 oz. 6-1/2 inches tall. **References:** 1976, page 4 [1-3]; 1977, page 29 [1-3]; 1981, page 1 [1-3]

Cut: 1448. Line: 972. Tapestry. Cordial. 3 oz. 5-5/8 inches tall. **References:** 1981, page 1 [1-8]

Cut: 1448. Line: 972. Tapestry. Goblet. 13 oz. 7-1/2 inches tall. **References:** 1981, page 1 [1-5]

Cut: 1448. Line: 972. Tapestry. Sherbet. 9 oz. 6 inches tall. **References:** 1981, page 1 [1-6]

Cut: 1448. Line: 972. Tapestry. Wine. 7-1/2 oz. 6-1/2 inches tall. **References:** 1981, page 1 [1-7]

Cut: 1448. Line: 1978. Chalice. Beverage. **References:** 1977, page 24 [1-2]

Cut: 1448. Line: 1978. Chalice. On the Rocks. 15-1/2 oz. 4-1/2 inches tall. **References:** 1976, page 11 [1-3]

Cut: 1449. Tapestry. Bell. **References:** 1981, page 11 [3-2]; 1983, page 7 [1-2L]

Cut: 1449S. Tapestry. Hi Ball. 11 oz. 5 inches tall. **References:** 1978, page 6 [1-3]

Cut: 1449. Line: 4. Tapestry. Bell. 5-1/2 inches tall. All Bells Individually Gift Boxed. **References:** 1977, page 23 [5-3]; 1979, page 13 [1-1]

Cut: 1449. Line: 972. Tapestry. Cordial. 3 oz. 5-5/8 inches tall. **References:** 1976, page 4 [1-8]; 1977, page 29 [1-8]

Cut: 1449. Line: 972. Tapestry. Goblet. 13 oz. 7-1/2 inches tall. **References:** 1976, page 4 [1-5]; 1977, page 29 [1-5]

Cut: 1449. Line: 972. Tapestry. Sherbet. 9 oz. 6 inches tall. **References:** 1976, page 4 [1-6]; 1977, page 29 [1-6]

Cut: 1449. Line: 972. Tapestry. Wine. 7-1/2 oz. 6-1/2 inches tall. **References:** 1976, page 4 [1-7]; 1977, page 29 [1-7]

Cut: 1449S. Line: 1978. Tapestry. On The Rocks. **References:** 1977, page 25 [2-1]

Cut: 1450. Line: 3. Classic. Bell. 4-3/8 inches tall. **References:** 1977, page 22 [2-1]

Cut: 1450. Line: 974. Classic. Cordial. 2-1/4 oz. 5-1/4 inches tall. **References:** 1976, page 5 [1-8]; 1977, page 30 [1-8]

Cut: 1450. Line: 974. Classic. Goblet. 10 oz. 7-1/2 inches tall. **References:** 1976, page 5 [1-5]; 1977, page 30 [1-5]

Cut: 1450. Line: 974. Classic. Sherbet. 6-1/2 oz. 5-

1/2 inches tall. **References:** 1976, page 5 [1-6]; 1977, page 30 [1-6]

Cut: 1450. Line: 974. Classic. Wine. 6 oz. 6-5/8 inches tall. **References:** 1976, page 5 [1-7]; 1977, page 30 [1-7]

Cut: 1450S. Line: 1978. Classic. On The Rocks. **References:** 1977, page 24 [2-2]

Cut: 1451. Brittany. Ice Server. 7-3/4 inches tall. **References:** 1978, page 6 [1-2]

Cut: 1451. Line: 4. Brittany. Bell. 5-1/2 inches tall. **References:** 1977, page 23 [3-2]

Cut: 1451. Line: 974. Brittany. Cordial. 2-1/4 oz. 5-1/4 inches tall. **References:** 1976, page 5 [1-4]; 1977, page 30 [1-4]

Cut: 1451. Line: 974. Brittany. Goblet. 10 oz. 7-1/2 inches tall. **References:** 1976, page 5 [1-1]; 1977, page 30 [1-1]

Cut: 1451. Line: 974. Brittany. Sherbet. 6-1/2 oz. 5-1/2 inches tall. **References:** 1976, page 5 [1-2]; 1977, page 30 [1-2]

Cut: 1451. Line: 974. Brittany. Wine. 6 oz. 6-5/8 inches tall. **References:** 1976, page 5 [1-3]; 1977, page 30 [1-3]

Cut: 1451. Line: 1978. Brittany. Beverage. 16-1/2 oz. 5-7/8 inches tall. **References:** 1977, page 25 [1-1]

Cut: 1451. Line: 1978. Brittany. Old Fashion. 9-1/2 oz. 3-1/2 inches tall. **References:** 1977, page 25 [1-3]

Cut: 1451. Line: 1978. Brittany. On the Rocks. 15-1/2 oz. 4-1/2 inches tall. **References:** 1976, page 11 [1-1]; 1977, page 25 [1-2]

Cut: 1452. Rosalynn. Bell. 4-1/2 inches tall. **References:** 1979, page 12 [2-4]

Cut: 1452. Rosalynn. Bell. **References:** 1981, page 11 [2-3]; 1983, page 6 [1-2R]

Cut: 1452. Line: 3. Rosalynn. Bell. 4-3/8 inches tall. **References:** 1977, page 22 [3-2]

Cut: 1452. Line: 981. Rosalynn. Cordial. 2-1/2 oz. 5-1/8 inches tall. **References:** 1977, page 26 [1-4]; 1981, page 2 [2-12]

Cut: 1452. Line: 981. Rosalynn. Goblet. 13-1/2 oz. 7-3/4 inches tall. **References:** 1977, page 26 [1-1]; 1981, page 2 [2-9]

Cut: 1452. Line: 981. Rosalynn. Sherbet. 9 oz. 5-3/8 inches tall. **References:** 1977, page 26 [1-2]; 1981, page 2 [2-10]

Cut: 1452. Line: 981. Rosalynn. Wine. 8 oz. 6-3/4 inches tall. **References:** 1977, page 26 [1-3]; 1981, page 2 [2-11]

Cut: 1452S. Line: 1978. Rosalynn. On The Rocks. **References:** 1977, page 25 [3-2]

Cut: 1453. Line: 4. Bell. 5-1/2 inches tall. **References:** 1977, page 23 [1-2]

Cut: 1453. Line: 981. Majestic. Cordial. 2-1/2 oz. 5-1/8 inches tall. **References:** 1977, page 26 [1-8]; 1981, page 2 [2-8]

Cut: 1453. Line: 981. Majestic. Goblet. 13-1/2 oz. 7-3/4 inches tall. **References:** 1977, page 26 [1-5]; 1981, page 2 [2-5]

Cut: 1453. Line: 981. Majestic. Sherbet. 9 oz. 5-3/8 inches tall. **References:** 1977, page 26 [1-6]; 1981, page 2 [2-6]

Cut: 1453. Line: 981. Majestic. Wine. 8 oz. 6-3/4 inches tall. **References:** 1977, page 26 [1-7]; 1981, page 2 [2-7]

Cut: 1453S. Line: 1978. Majestic. On The Rocks. **References:** 1977, page 25 [2-2]

Cut: 1454, Grande Baroque. Line: 982. Elite Collection. Cordial. 2 oz. 4-3/4 inches tall. **References:** 1978, page 2 [1-8]

Cut: 1454, Grande Baroque. Line: 982. Elite Collection. Goblet. 13-1/2 oz. 7-1/2 inches tall. **References:** 1978, page 2 [1-5]

Cut: 1454, Grande Baroque. Line: 982. Elite Collection. Sherbet. 8 oz. 5-3/8 inches tall. **References:** 1978, page 2 [1-6]

Cut: 1454, Grande Baroque. Line: 982. Elite Collection. Wine. 7 oz. 6-3/8 inches tall. **References:** 1978, page 2 [1-7]

Cut: 1457. Line: 80. Love Birds. Ginger Jar. 6-1/4 inches tall. **References:** 1980, page 3 [1-1]; 1981, page 10 [2-2]

Cut: 1457. Line: 90. Love Birds. Ginger Jar. 8-1/2

inches tall. **References:** 1980, page 3 [2-3]; 1981, page 10 [1-2]

Cut: 1458. Line: 1963. Bouquet. Cordial. 1-1/2 oz. 4 inches tall. **References:** 1982, page 1 [2-4]

Cut: 1458. Line: 1963. Bouquet. Goblet. 13-1/2 oz. 6-3/4 inches tall. **References:** 1982, page 1 [2-1]

Cut: 1458. Line: 1963. Bouquet. Ice Tea. 14 oz. 6-1/4 inches tall. **References:** 1982, page 1 [2-5]

Cut: 1458. Line: 1963. Bouquet. Sherbet. 7-1/2 oz. 5-1/8 inches tall. **References:** 1982, page 1 [2-2]

Cut: 1458. Line: 1963. Bouquet. Wine. 7-3/4 oz. 5-3/4 inches tall. **References:** 1982, page 1 [2-3]

Cut: 1459. Line: 1963. Harvest. Cordial. 1-1/2 oz. 4 inches tall. **References:** 1982, page 1 [2-9]

Cut: 1459. Line: 1963. Harvest. Goblet. 13-1/2 oz. 6-3/4 inches tall. **References:** 1982, page 1 [2-6]

Cut: 1459. Line: 1963. Harvest. Ice Tea. 14 oz. 6-1/4 inches tall. **References:** 1982, page 1 [2-10]

Cut: 1459. Line: 1963. Harvest. Sherbet. 7-1/2 oz. 5-1/8 inches tall. **References:** 1982, page 1 [2-7]

Cut: 1459. Line: 1963. Harvest. Wine. 7-3/4 oz. 5-3/4 inches tall. **References:** 1982, page 1 [2-8]

Cut: 1460. Line: 1963. Arbor. Cordial. 1-1/2 oz. 4 inches tall. **References:** 1982, page 1 [1-4]

Cut: 1460. Line: 1963. Arbor. Goblet. 13-1/2 oz. 6-3/4 inches tall. **References:** 1982, page 1 [1-1]

Cut: 1460. Line: 1963. Arbor. Ice Tea. 14 oz. 6-1/4 inches tall. **References:** 1982, page 1 [1-5]

Cut: 1460. Line: 1963. Arbor. Sherbet. 7-1/2 oz. 5-1/8 inches tall. **References:** 1982, page 1 [1-2]

Cut: 1460. Line: 1963. Arbor. Wine. 7-3/4 oz. 5-3/4 inches tall. **References:** 1982, page 1 [1-3]

Cut: 1463. Line: 972. Coronet. Cordial. 3 oz. 5-5/8 inches tall. **References:** 1982, page 2 [1-4]

Cut: 1463. Line: 972. Coronet. Goblet. 13 oz. 7-1/2 inches tall. **References:** 1982, page 2 [1-1]

Cut: 1463. Line: 972. Coronet. Ice Tea. 14 oz. 6-1/2

inches tall. **References:** 1982, page 2 [1-5]

Cut: 1463. Line: 972. Coronet. Sherbet. 9 oz. 6 inches tall. **References:** 1982, page 2 [1-2]

Cut: 1463. Line: 972. Coronet. Wine. 7-1/2 oz. 6-1/2 inches tall. **References:** 1982, page 2 [1-3]

Cut: 1463. Line: 972. Garland. Cordial. 3 oz. 5-5/8 inches tall. **References:** 1982, page 2 [2-4]

Cut: 1463. Line: 972. Garland. Goblet. 13 oz. 7-1/2 inches tall. **References:** 1982, page 2 [2-1]

Cut: 1463. Line: 972. Garland. Ice Tea. 14 oz. 6-1/2 inches tall. **References:** 1982, page 2 [2-5]

Cut: 1463. Line: 972. Garland. Sherbet. 9 oz. 6 inches tall. **References:** 1982, page 2 [2-2]

Cut: 1463. Line: 972. Garland. Wine. 7-1/2 oz. 6-1/2 inches tall. **References:** 1982, page 2 [2-3]

Cut: 1463. Line: 972. Regency. Cordial. 3 oz. 5-5/8 inches tall. **References:** 1982, page 2 [2-9]

Cut: 1463. Line: 972. Regency. Goblet. 13 oz. 7-1/2 inches tall. **References:** 1982, page 2 [2-6]

Cut: 1463. Line: 972. Regency. Ice Tea. 14 oz. 6-1/2 inches tall. **References:** 1982, page 2 [2-10]

Cut: 1463. Line: 972. Regency. Sherbet. 9 oz. 6 inches tall. **References:** 1982, page 2 [2-7]

Cut: 1463. Line: 972. Regency. Wine. 7-1/2 oz. 6-1/2 inches tall. **References:** 1982, page 2 [2-8]